ISBN 978-1-5281-9990-2
PIBN 10964852

1 MONTH OF
FREE
READING

at

www.ForgottenBooks.com

By purchasing this book you are eligible for one month membership to ForgottenBooks.com, giving you unlimited access to our entire collection of over 1,000,000 titles via our web site and mobile apps.

To claim your free month visit:
www.forgottenbooks.com/free964852

THE

LITERARY NEWS

A Monthly Journal of Current Literature.

[NEW SERIES.]

Vol. XVI.

1895.

NEW YORK
PUBLICATION OFFICE, 59 DUANE STREET,
1895.

THE LITERARY NEWS.

INDEX TO VOL. XVI. (NEW SERIES) 1895.

BOOKS FOR YOUNG PEOPLE.

INDEX TO ADVERTISERS.

i

LITERARY NEWS

AN ECLECTIC REVIEW OF
CURRENT LITERATURE
~ILLUSTRATED~

CONTENTS.

VOL·XVI·№ 1   JANUARY ~ 1895 $ 1.00 YEARLY
10 cts. PER NO.

~ PUBLICATION OFFICE ~
· 28 ELM STREET NEW YORK ·

ENTERED AT THE POST OFFICE AT NEW YORK AS SECOND CLASS MATTER

The Literary News

In winter you may reade them, ad ignem, by the fireside; and in summer, ad umbram, under some shadie tree; and therewith pass away the tedious howres.

| VOL. XVI. | JANUARY, 1895. | No. 1 |

Travels in Three Continents—Europe, Asia, Africa.

DR. J. M. BUCKLEY has travelled for years and has always made use of the new things he saw and heard among the strange inhabitants of strange countries, for the cheer and enlightenment of the less fortunate, kept at home by the iron chains of circumstance. In these protracted tours, Dr. Buckley learned by experience that a certain amount of information is necessary to the interpretation of what is taken work that is the result of his journeys, brought out in very handsome shape by Messrs. Hunt & Eaton, must be warmly welcomed by all, as it will aid those who contemplate such a journey to prepare for it, will refresh the recollection of those who preceded Dr. Buckley, and will enable such as do not expect to cross the ocean to see, while looking through his eyes, almost as well as with their own.

CHARACTERISTIC VIEW OF LOURDES.

in by eye and ear, and in preparing his narratives for the stay-at-homes he has always endeavored to interweave such knowledge with the natural flow of his eloquent description. In his travels through Europe, Asia, and Africa, Dr. Buckley naturally has traversed much ground often travelled over, and almost as often described by travellers. But as he truly says, "Every traveller sees what he takes with him, and because of this I hope there will be a place for another record of travel in many of the most interesting parts of the world." The

The great journey begins in New York, from which city Dr. Buckley sailed on November 21, 1888. He was accompanied by a member of the senior class in Amherst, who evidently proved that necessary ideal for a journey—a congenial companion. The itinerary was from New York to London, across to Paris, through France to Spain, where the travellers first began to loiter, giving much attention to the buildings and the people of Madrid, Toledo, Cordova, Seville, and Granada. A general view is given of the bull-fights of Spain before crossing to "Afric's

From "Travels in Three Continents."   Copyright, 1894, by Hunt & Eaton.
ISLE OF PATMOS.

and Bethany, Nazareth and modern Palestine, which give Dr. Buckley a starting-point for some very stimulating reflections on the Christian religion and its progressive work in the world. Again Europe is reached by way of Damascus, Beirut, the Ægean Islands, Smyrna, and Ephesus, until on the classic soil of Athens and Corinth, Dr. Buckley explains the Greek mind and the history of thought with which the Grecian lands are synonymous. A rapid course through Constantinople, Roumelia, Bulgaria, Servia, Hungary, Vienna, and Paris brings the travellers to Havre, where they finally shipped for New York on the 10th of May, 1889. Not quite six months of travel, and what a vast amount of new and old knowledge is made fascinating by Dr. Buckley's fine literary methods. And made of enduring service also by a remarkably well-made index, which keeps the delightful contents get-at-able at a moment's notice. A cursory reading of this index gives a better idea of the book than pages of description. There is no padding. Dr. Buckley offers solid information in enduring shape.

sunny fountains." Roaming around the north coast of Africa, they gaze upon the wondrous scenery of Morocco, Tangiers, Algiers, and their neighboring islands, and then again make for European land, and journey to the heart of civilization, and the sights history and associations have made familiar from generation to generation. Marseilles, the French Riviera, Genoa, Milan, Venice, Florence, Rome, Naples, Vesuvius and Pompeii are all commented upon, by a mind full of thoughts born of the thoughts of the greatest thinkers of all time, and a pen made sure by long years of cultured writing. Once more Africa is reached, and Egypt, Cairo, Memphis, the pyramids, the Sphinx, Thebes, and the Nile come under consideration. A very clear and fair idea is given of Mohammedanism while journeying towards the Holy Land. Asia is then presented in the sacred places of Jerusalem, Bethlehem, Jordan, Jericho

Nearly one hundred illustrations beautify the large, clearly printed pages. The work is substantially bound with typical oriental decoration, and makes a specially sumptuous book, which there is no doubt will take rank among the very most reliable of works of travel. The well-travelled paths are set in new light in this fine book. (Hunt & Eaton. $3.50.)

From "Travels in Three Continents."   Copyright, 1894, by Hunt & Eaton.
SCENE IN ORAN.

Life and Adventures of John Gladwyn Jebb.

THE life of John Gladwyn Jebb reads like an invention from the fertile brain of Jules Verne, or Rudyard Kipling, or H. Rider Haggard. The latter has written a fitting introduction to this strange and varied life, which, in hairbreadth escapes, ups and downs of fortune, meetings with noted men, connection with Utopian schemes, and remarkable influence of personality, far transcends the limits of plausible imagination. Mr. Haggard had a personal acquaintance with the hero of these startling adventures which began in 1889, and ended with Mr. Jebb's death in 1893. During that time they were much thrown together, travelled extensively in Mexico, and became warm friends. Mr. Haggard speaks with emotion of his friend's warm heart, loyal nature, truth, self-forgetfulness, "complete colossal unselfishness," and always brave and generous instincts.

John Gladwyn Jebb was an only child, born of well-to-do English parents in 1841. In 1850 he entered school at Bonn, and in 1852 was for several years put under the care of an English rector. He learned readily and showed many and most varied gifts. His talent for drawing amounted almost to genius, and he had a voice for singing of remarkable beauty. From earliest youth he showed the desire for freedom and change that formed the spirit of his life. He longed to enter the navy, but his family favored the army. As soon as his age permitted he was sent on active service in India. On the voyage to India he first became interested in hypnotism, secondsight, and spiritualism, being much thrown with those with whom the occult was business or pastime. Jebb soon left the army and went to Oxford, devoting himself to civil engineering and practical sciences of various kinds. He had an independent income, but lost half of it in an investment in a steel gun-barrel factory at Glasgow, and invested the rest in bad investments and insolvent banks. Penniless at twenty-six, he next tried sheep-farming in the Highlands, then shipbuilding and drumming up trade in America for the White Star Steamship Company, then first

From "Life and Adventures of John Gladwyn Jebb." Copyright, 1895, by Roberts Brothers.

starting its successful career. While on these American trips Mr. Jebb fell in with General Fremont, fresh from California gold-fields, and his roving mind and restless body turned eagerly to mining and big-game shooting. Coffee-planting in Brazil, treasure-hunting in Mexico, starting an Omlette Company in New York City to manufacture an article of food to take the place of eggs, studying spiritualism in Boston, and esoteric Buddhism in London with Madame Blavatsky, bull-fights, the reconstruction of Mexico under General Diaz, all succeed each other in bewildering rush in this exciting life history. The story of Maximilian and Carlotta and the Mexican troubles is interwoven skilfully. It is a book delightful to read and full of interesting facts regarding the last fifty years throughout the world. (Roberts. $1.25.)

Story of the Crusades.

THE latest addition to the *Story of the Nation* series is a scholarly history of "The Crusades," by F. A. Archer and Charles L. Kingsford. This volume limits its survey of that vast and strange expression of the religious sentiment in the Latin Kingdom of Jerusalem. The authors have not embraced within the limits of their work an account of the Fourth Crusade, the Latin Empire of Constantinople, or those developments and perversions of the crusading idea which led to the so-called crusades against the Albigensians and the Emperor Frederick. It cannot be denied that the glamour and romance of crusading expeditions has often caused the practical achievements of crusaders in the East to be overlooked and underrated. Yet it is through the history of the Kingdom of Jerusalem that the true character and importance of the crusades can alone be discerned. The story of that religious struggle, rich in its romance and its influence upon the history of the world, is related most instructively and elaborately in the valuable study before us. (Putnam. $1.50.)—*Philadelphia Press.*

Glimpses of Unfamiliar Japan.

THE author of these volumes is well known as the acute and sympathetic student of the varied races of the countries bordering the Mexican Gulf. His collection of "Gumbo," or mixed-dialect proverbs and descriptive sketches of the people of Louisiana and the West Indies, showed him to be the possessor of an exuberant, almost rank, vocabulary, and a literary style that suggested rather what burst forth from the wine-press than wine mellowed by time. His excursions into distant regions of thought resulted in interesting, but, on the whole, unsatisfactory booklets, such as "Stray Leaves from Strange Literature," "Some Chinese Ghosts," etc. Fascinated by the comparatively new field of what may be called Shinto-Japan, he entered the country about four years ago, resolved to see those phases of Japanese life which are fast vanishing away. Living among a people so simple in their tastes and habits as the rural Japanese, Mr. Hearn, who suggests the literary chameleon, has absorbed the form and color of his environment. One who has read his former writings cannot but be struck at once with the subdued coloring, the refined simplicity, which have now become his habit. The former rankness is no more.

In one respect these volumes, by their contribution of knowledge and philosophy, mark a distinct point of progress in our acquaintance through books, with the Japanese. While the Americans — Brown and Hepburn — first, by grammar and lexicon, blazed the way through the Japanese language, and that splendid trio of English students—Satow, Aston, and Chamberlain—with the helpful reinforcement of

WALLS OF ANTIOCH.

SMUGGLERS ON THE FRONTIER.

Lowder, McClatchie, Mounsey. Hawes, Gubbins, and Bramson—opened Japanese chronology, history, archæology and literature to our view, and Miss Bird—a typical name amid a host of travellers—spied out the land and brought back reports, it may be said that the psychological study of the Japanese has been chiefly the work of the Americans Lyman and Lowell, and, last and best of all, Mr. Hearn.

One will find in these volumes descriptions of travel, wonderful accounts of famous temples and neighborhoods, charming stories of personal experience, and not a few pictures which, by their marvellous accuracy and sympathetic touch, recall the natural wonders of the sea-girt Islands of the Sun ; but, beyond and above those things which the skilled traveller and literary artist transfers to his pages, Mr. Hearn has succeeded in photographing, as it were, the Japanese soul. There seems to be something in his own physical and intellectual make-up that renders him sensitive on all sides to what is peculiar in the Japanese character. In studying the paintings of Wirgman, La Farge, Wores, Parsons, and other artists who have seen or dreamed in Japan, one sees faithful transcripts or ideal conceptions of Japanese life. But no other artist, paint he in words or in pigments, has so thoroughly succeeded in catching and fixing those Japanese traits which are so elusive, yet so ingrained and innate. (Houghton, Mifflin & Co. 2 v., $4.)—*New York Tribune.*

The Borderland of Czar and Kaiser.

THE chapters which compose this volume have already won their way to public recognition in the pages of *Harper's Monthly,* where they have brought a new and different indictment against Russia and her methods of government. The work was intended to be a happy combination of Poultney Bigelow's pen and Frederic Remington's pencil, genial and graphic, which might leave a lasting impression of the more attractive and picturesque side of Russia. Russia, however, gave them a reception which put all this quite out of the question, and left on this written and pictured record the stamp of her decision that the world shall neither see nor know her as she is. The book is no such probing of the deep sores that afflict the State as we had from Mr. Kennan. It is a simpler chronicle of events, but no less impressive in its way, and always given in bright, lively, and rather merry style, which relieves the book of the wear and drone of solemn complaint. Russian impenetrability proved too much for the carrying out of our American explorers' plans on the lines marked out by them in advance ; but the lines they were forced into furnished matter in abundance for a highly entertaining book. In the Prussian borderlands their experiences were, of course, very different. There Mr. Bigelow was quite at home, especially among military people. The volume abounds in military sketches. In fact, the impression it gives rather confirms the impression which has gotten abroad, that all Prussia, like Berlin, is getting militarized. Remington's illustrations are copious, good and spirited. The publishers have given the book a very attractive cover, printed and manufactured in the best manner. (Harper. $2.)—*The Independent.*

The Golden House.

MR. WARNER'S new novel bears a close relationship to the studies of New York social life in fiction that other contemporary writers, including Mr. Howells, Mr. Crawford, Mr. Brander Matthews, Mrs. Burton Harrison, and the lady who reserves, but does not conceal, her identity under the pseudonym of Julien Gordon, have given us. The same society, the same clubs and clubmen, the same odorous and forlorn "east side," the same general tone is observed in all these works. Mr. Warner even harks back to the dance of the variety hall "artist," called Carmencita, in John Sargent's studio, which was supposed to have set "society" agog, and to have given it a new kind of thrill, some years ago. Mr. Matthews has already celebrated this event in a story.

The body of fiction which Mr. Warner has thus enriched derives a large measure of dignity, quite apart from its merit, which

From "The Golden House."   Copyright, 1894, by Harper & Brothers.
CARMEN.

is not to be lightly dismissed, from its uniformity of tone and thought and the likeness of its scenes and characters. This is not the result of collaboration, or, in any case, so far as we may judge, of deliberate imitation. And each New York novel of the authors named may, therefore, be taken as corroborative proof of the essential truth to the subject of all the others. Therefore, we have already at hand a body of fictitious literature that will be of priceless value to the future historian for the pictures it provides of social customs, and the idea it gives of social spirit and commercial ways, in the metropolis of this republic in the last years of the nineteenth century.

The value of "The Golden House," as a "document" thus having been disposed of, it remains only to briefly consider it as a work of literary art. As such it is more than respectable. Mr. Warner is an able writer, with a command of wit and the power of graphic description. His plot is slight, but serviceable, and his personages are many and of varied traits. His scene encompasses all of New York that comes under the eye of fashionable folks, and some of it that is not often mentioned at dinner-tables. We refer, of course, to the crowded tenement districts of the east side, a portion of this town which one small set of writers for the periodicals is constantly holding up as its most picturesque part, and that most neglected in fiction, while another set is diligently at work all the time translating all its grimy facts and all its odors into an endless supply of reading-matter for the polite.

Mr. Warner treats of the misery of the New York poor with gentle sympathy and no trace of mock sentimentality. Of the poetic charm of his episodic romance among the helpers of the poor, in which an ascetic Anglican priest and a female physician are involved, we cannot speak too highly, though we should not care to commit ourselves to an opinion of its truth to nature, because of a lack of familiarity with the sentimental qualities of ascetic Anglicans and ladies who practice medicine.

But the main drift of the story is all in familiar channels, and no one can doubt its truth. The "swell" husband, who is forced to battle along with a cold and heartless world on a beggarly yearly income of $20,000 ; the sweet, patient, charitable wife whom he neglects ; the questionable wife of the great financier, who uses this couple to get into "society," and in return opens a way to profitable speculation for the "swell," which leaves him penniless in the *dénouement ;* the financier, himself, who is a wonderfully impressive figure, and no more to be understood than financiers usually are ; the beautiful, discontented spinster, and all the other personages at the afternoon teas and evening "functions," that Mr. Warner describes, are interesting and recognizable.

Mr. Smedley's pictures add much to the interest of the story. They are charming pictures and apt illustrations, and each provides an excellent object lesson in deportment for people about to go into New York "society." (Harper. $2.) —*N. Y. Times.*

The People of the Mist.

THE best possible criticism on Mr. Rider Haggard's last story is in the dedication. He says: "I dedicate this effort of 'primeval and troglodyte imagination,' this record of barefaced and flagrant adventure, to my godsons, in the hope that therein they may find some store of healthy amusement." Not one of his previous novels, not even "She," is so fraught with "troglodyte imagination" and "flagrant adventure" as "The People of the Mist." Miraculous escapes, wonderful snake-worshipping tribes, and rubies and sapphires by the eight-pound sack are the "store of healthy amusement" provided. Nothing but the unexpected happens in Mr. Haggard's stories, but we cannot harden our hearts to carp at this book on the score of unreality, in gratitude for the thrilling hours of suspense caused us by the endless perils of the hero and the heroine. Whether this is really "healthy amusement" for boys we cannot decide, but all rules are relaxed in the holiday season. So writes the Boston *Literary World.* Rider Haggard's charm is hard to define, but very real to the vast army of readers who hail his every word as a personal treat. Straight-laced pedagogues may reason about the dangers of his fascinations, but no amount of reasoning impairs the fascination. All healthy, natural spirits are refreshed by Rider Haggard's absurdities. It is good to keep an interest in just such startling adventures as he furnishes at all times. (Longmans, Green & Co. $1.25.)

My Lady.

"MY LADY" is a delightful story for adults, by Miss Marguerite Bouvet, who has already charmed the thousands who have read her

From "My Lady." Copyright, 1894, by A. C. McClurg & Co.
CONSULTING MÈRE TOINETTE.

favorite children's stories, "Sweet William," "Prince Tip Top," etc. It is a fine example of the power to tell a tale of tender love in *pure Saxon English.* Recounting the fortunes of French refugees to England in the days of the Revolution of '93 and of Bonaparte, it affords glimpses of life both in England and France. The English nurse, who devotes her whole heart and life to the young heroine, and the young French marquis, whose love for the latter is so great and unselfish that he hides it on discovering that she loves his friend, are finely portrayed. The book is sure to increase its author's fame, both by its fascination as a story and by its simple, unaffected style. The illustrations, by Miss Helen M. Armstrong, are very dainty and appropriate, and admirably preserve the spirit of the story. Miss Marguerite Bouvet has shown talent that is an earnest of better things to come. (A. C. McClurg & Co. $1.25.)

Philip and His Wife.

THE story of Philip and his wife Cecil and their sprite-like child has been so much discussed during its appearance in the *Atlantic Monthly* that it has become difficult to say anything that has not been said and thought by many. And still the ever-recurring questions remain unanswered owing to the consummate art of the author of "John Ward, Preacher" and "The Story of a Child." What does Mrs. Deland herself think would have been the right thing for Philip and his wife to do? Does she approve of Philip? Does she think all matrimonial unhappiness should be borne without murmuring? What did happen? What does she intend her readers to think of her latest work? Did she work successfully from her premises to an intended end, or did she herself become conscious of the ramification of her subject and finish abruptly because she had no helpful solution to offer to the problem which is as old as man? The history of Philip and his wife is primarily a study of the marriage relation. A morbidly conscientious, somewhat narrow-minded man and a superficial, selfish, pleasure- and excitement-craving woman are married in their first youth. They have one child, beloved by both. By the father with an outlook for the child's future good, with plans of education, systematic training, pride of fatherhood and realization of responsibility ; by the mother with the brute affection of the dam, the unreasonableness of exhausted or excited nerves, the vanity of motherhood, the desire for a plaything. This child becomes the constant source of disunion—the only link of union. Superficial readers will readily think that the ethical significance of Mrs. Deland's book lies in the study of divorce and the attitude towards this question of Philip Shore, his wife and their friend Roger Carey. Philip asks after estrangement from his wife : "Is not marriage without love as spiritually illegal as love without marriage is civilly illegal ?" Philip's wife asserts to Philip's friend Carey : "I believe the world would be much better off if divorce were easier. In fact, I think it's a pity people have to wait until they actually come to blows before they can separate."

But read more carefully the large purpose of Mrs. Deland's story is not a question of divorce or separation. It is a study in human selfishness, shown as tellingly in the uncompromising, conventional virtues of the husband as in the littleness, indulgence, lack of sympathy, unrest and indifference of the wife. Philip Shore holds the most selfish opinion of the duty he owes himself to develop his high-est self according to his highest ideal ; Cecil Shore is a beautiful animal, keenly alive to sensuous impressions, longing for ease and repose. While pondering separation, after a terrible scene with his wife, Philip sends for his friend, Roger Carey, a brilliant lawyer whom he wishes to consult. Then comes Mrs. Deland's cleverest work. The end is unsatisfactory from a reader's standpoint. It does not seem natural that Cecil should let Philip have his child, it does not seem a finished piece of work that Mrs. Deland has left with us. But experienced thought, knowledge of life, of love, of marriage and its duties, temptations, responsibilities and quicksands, of man's and woman's natures and special points of view, fail to suggest an ending that will solve the many problems suggested. The minor characters are very well drawn. Mrs. Deland's work is original, strong, and full of suggestions. (Houghton, Mifflin & Co. $1.25.)

Children of Circumstance.

A NOVEL of totally different kind from the average is "Children of Circumstance." Although the writer cannot resist the feminine temptation to introduce as the principal male figure a rather invertebrate specimen of the sex, though the book ends without settling the final fortunes of the principal characters, and though the only important love-scene that occurs in its pages is conducted on both sides with the easy pleasantry of a dispassionate flirtation, there is plenty of powerful writing throughout. The story is mainly connected with some of the darker sides of London life, and the quixotic efforts of Margaret Dering, a girl of twenty, to reclaim the fallen women of the West End. The fact that neither the methods nor the results of her process could, under any circumstances, be capable of realization in actual life, need not be counted as any disparagement of the author's sincere and spirited effort to inspire a tenderer feeling towards the erring humanity whose lot she describes. The theme is, of course, by no means a new one, and Wilkie Collins' "New Magdalene" will at once occur as a novel written with similar purpose ; but it may be doubted whether the trenchant satire of the latter work is to be compared for real effectiveness with the dignified pathos of "Iota's" handiwork. A word must be said for the characters of the story : they are drawn with a masterly hand, and the analysis of motives and actions is conducted with an appreciative humor which stamps the book as a worthy successor to "A Yellow Aster," the novel which first brought this author into notice. (Appleton. 50 c.; $1.)—*London Academy.*

Tales of Adventure.

EVERY adventure-loving youth will hug this volume to himself and hie to a corner where he can feast undisturbed upon its contents, and a rare old feast he will have. In these days of adventures of the sickly-sentimental order, a volume with the right whiff and odor of excitement about it cannot be too highly praised, especially if it is written with the purpose of emphasizing virtue instead of painting vice so alluringly that evil ways have a subtle attraction. The author of these "Stirring Tales of Colonial Adventure" signs himself "Skipp Borlase," and under this signature will appeal to the hearts of those boys who have already read his numerous volumes of well-told adventures. The first tale in this collection is a fair sample of those that follow. It shows how a father misjudged his two sons, one of whom was only the son of his adoption. His own son is a strong, honest, but physically ugly lad, while the other is deceitful and treacherous in the same proportion that he is straight of limb and beautiful. The author introduces the two lads with a telling incident, and continues his story to prove his estimation of their various characters, and to give his readers a taste of the fruits of right and wrong, together with a genuine adventure. Each of the tales supplies fuel for the readers' imaginations, and strengthens their impressions of the essential characteristics of heroism. (Warne. $1.50.)—*Boston Herald.*

From " Stirring Tales of Adventure."   Copyright, 1894, by F. Warne & Co

A MISSILE GRAZED MY SHOULDER.

Round the Red Lamp.

IN "Round the Red Lamp : being facts and fancies of medical life," Dr. Conan Doyle gives his fertile imagination free play once more. His stories on medical life run on parallel lines with his popular adventures of a private detective. For a reader condemned to an unbroken regimen of Conan Doyle they might be considered just a little oppressive in flavor, especially as they add to plot and incidental interest the elements of physical suffering and ghastly detail. It is unnecessary to say that they will not have so many readers as the livelier and less pessimistic "Sherlock Holmes" series. They are almost invariably morbid ; and, indeed, when the author is resolutely optimistic, as in "A Question of Diplomacy," he does not thereby raise the level of excitement, though he pleasantly varies the entertainment. These tales are skilful, attractive, and eminently suited to give relief to the mind of a reader in quest of distraction. (Appleton. $1.50.)— *Athenæum.*

Vernon's Aunt.

SARA JEANNETTE DUNCAN (Mrs. Everard Cotes) has once more enjoyed herself on her native literary heath, and produced a story pure and simple, without moral or purpose, that cannot fail to delight her constantly growing circle of appreciative readers. Vernon's aunt is a straight-laced, conventional English lady of uncertain age, who is seized with a desire to see her nephew, who has for years been in India. She sails away upon a ship, which becomes to her a most enjoyable resting-place before the voyage is ended. On her arrival she is met by her nephew, and there follows a delicious story of absurd misadventures, which often throw the sedate spinster into consternation. The author's former strong and absorbing novel, "A Daughter of To-Day," did not offer her the same chance to show the exuberant humor, the happy facility in telling description which her new extravaganza again brings into play. Humor and good-natured sparkling satire are the special gifts of Mrs. Cotes, and she has again reached the inimitable charm of "A Social Departure" and "The Simple Adventures of a Memsahib." (Appleton. $1 : pap., 50 c.)

From "Vernon's Aunt." Copyright, 1895, by D Appleton & Co.

I SALUTE YOU.

Life and Letters of John G. Whittier.

THE opening chapters in this memoir of Whittier are made especially interesting by the pictures given of New England life in the earlier part of the present century. Whittier was born in 1807, the family homestead being the East Parish of Haverhill, Mass. The characteristic features of home life in rural districts of New England had then not very much changed from what the original settlers of the country had made them. For those old enough to recall these as they may have still more or less been in their own childhood, the descriptions here found of the Whittier home will be full of interest, renewing and brightening memories which, under conditions so greatly changed as the present ones are may have much faded away. There is also much in this earlier narrative to illustrate the career which the author in subsequent pages details. Much of what was characteristic of the poet, in his fidelity to conviction, his horror of oppression, his simple yet noble and stalwart manhood were matters of heredity with him. The reader recognizes at this point of view his indebtedness to the author for the full account given of the Whittier ancestry, with descriptions of that simple and wholesome New England life which, fostered in the boy, fully developed in the man those qualities which made him, with all his Quaker gentleness and kindliness, so much a champion in the great moral battles of the period. Many details of Whittier's early life, as here given, will be new to most readers ; the difficulties overcome in securing such education as he had, the early date in his life at which attention was drawn to his superior gifts as a poet, his adventures in journalism, characteristic even there, his consecration in the cause of liberty and of reform while as yet a mere youth. Much of what belongs to the later life is made to appear in Whittier's own letters, which make up a considerable portion of the two volumes. The biographer, however, renders important service in the details given in connection with mention of notable poems and other writings as from time to time they appear, as also of Whittier's association with notable men of the period, especially leaders in the great anti-slavery struggle. Much added interest is given to the narrative by insertion of poems which, although published in Whittier's own lifetime, were not included by him in his books, as from time to time appearing. These "estrays" are often of very peculiar biographical as well as poetical interest. (Houghton, Mifflin & Co. 2 v., $4.)—*Chicago Standard.*

Maelcho.

THERE is no gainsaying the fact that "Maelcho" is anything but cheerful reading. The scene and time chosen—Ireland *circa* 1580—preclude the possibility of all hilarity in an author who has made such extensive use of State papers and contemporary documents as Miss Lawless. All the same, "Maelcho" is not lugubrious‚ though deeply tragic, and, so far from being unendurable, is usually interesting and occasionally fascinating. Although the story is admittedly an historical romance, we have no hesitation in saying that more may be learnt as to the relations between England and Ireland, and more information gained as to the mode of life and actual aspect of the country three hundred years ago than in any regular history with which we are acquainted. But the amount of mere information that the book contains is, after all, only one of its minor merits. Lovers of incident will find that it abounds in thrilling—even blood-curdling—incidents. Lovers of the picturesque will find no lack of those vivid descriptions which bring the sounds and scents and colors of the Irish landscape into our ears and nostrils and before our eyes. Miss Lawless has the intimate knowledge of a naturalist as well as the vision of an artist, and thus the settings of the various episodes of which her book is made up invariably add to their effectiveness. But above and beyond all, the book charms by reason of the breadth of view, the magnanimity and the tenderness which animate the author in dealing with a theme which is always dreary and often gruesome. There is no attempt to extenuate the inherent weaknesses of the Celtic character any more than to palliate the brutal savagery of the English soldiery. "Maelcho," in this respect, is a standing rebuke to those critics who deny to women the attribute of impartiality. Finally, it may be noted that although the narrative, as the author very accurately describes her work, is devoid of love interest, it is full of excellent characterization. The portraits of Maelcho, a truly noble savage ; of Hugh Gaynor, the sturdy and dogged English youth ; and of Fenwick, the accomplished, ambitious, and relentless officer of fortune, are all good in their different ways. Here, in short is a moving romance in which, by means entirely legitimate, and with a wholesome avoidance of partisanship, fine writing, or sensationalism, Miss Lawless has set before us, in all its shame and agony, one of the most painful chapters in

the history of Ireland. The pathos of "Grania" by this author will not soon be forgotten. The same rare power is shown in this record of people suffering from strifes extending over two centuries. (Appleton. $1.50.) — *London Athenæum.*

From "Vernon's Aunt." Copyright, 1895, by D. Appleton & Co.

THE SURPRISED AUNT.

Maria Edgeworth's Life and Letters.

THESE volumes contain the first satisfactory story of the life of a woman concerning whom decidedly erroneous notions have been entertained. From them it is possible to learn just what sort of woman Miss Edgeworth was, and to understand how she came to occupy her unique position in literature. A collection of her letters was printed a short time after her death, in 1849, but its circulation was confined rigorously to those who were noted as intimate friends of the authoress. This is the first publication of her correspondence for general circulation, and through it the public will get a view of Miss Edgeworth which heretofore only her personal acquaintances have been permitted to enjoy.

The one thing which stands out in boldest relief in the story of her life is that she was her father's child—he dominated her life and gave direction to her literary propensities. While he lived he governed her pen, and he lived so long that by the time he died she had acquired a literary habit which had become a second nature to her. If her father had died while she was a young girl, Miss Edgeworth would have become an authoress, and undoubtedly would have become famous, for she was a bright girl, much given to story-telling and story-writing.

What sort of work she would have done it is of course impossible to say, but it is clear enough that, left to herself, she would not have taken lines parallel to those along which her father led her. She might have turned out some extremely interesting love-stories, which would have been read eagerly to-day by those who call her "Belinda" and other highly moral stories "bread-and-buttery" books. At the time when her father assumed censorship Miss Edgeworth had it in her to achieve success in almost any line of light literature.

Most of the letters are addressed to relatives. Few are written to the literary men and women with whom Miss Edgeworth was on familiar terms. At the same time there are many pleasing references to celebrities. (Houghton, Mifflin & Co. 2 v., $4.)—*Mail and Express.*

Sea and Land.

PROF. N. S. SHALER, who holds the chair of geology in Harvard University, has written for students of nature who are not scientists a very entertaining book on the features of coasts and oceans, with special reference to the life of man. His object is to introduce to unprofessional readers certain interesting phenomena of the sea-shore and of the depths of the ocean. In no other fields are large and important truths which are distinctly related to human interests so readily to be traced, yet the treatises which deal with these matters are few in number and generally of a recondite character. The aim has been to separate from the great body of technical knowledge concerning shores and seas those features which have value for the reason that they may serve to enlarge the reader's conception as to the methods of nature. As commonly observed, or as learned from text-books, these truths appear to be fragmentary, and lead to no extended notions as to the workings of the earth's machinery ; thus the student is not led to form those conceptions which it is most important that he should gain. In part the matter pre-

sented has appeared in the pages of *Scribner's Magazine.* The volume is very handsomely brought out, and many illustrations are scattered through the interesting text. (Scribner. $2.50.)

Beside the Bonnie Brier Bush.

THE title of this book gives little hint of the significance of the stories which make it up, but the wonder and admiration with which one closes the book testify to its fitness as an emblem of Scottish sturdiness and beauty. Unlike many short stories, which are best enjoyed when read separately, this series demands a consecutive reading for each tale, which deepens the impression of unity created by the pictures of simplicity, piety, humor, and caution in the people of Drumtochty. It is no wonder that this new writer, "Ian Maclaren" (who is Rev. John Watson of Liverpool), has leaped into sudden fame, for the gift of the Holy Spirit is his—to transmute homely deeds into shining marvels. One weary alike of characterless sermons and the well-conned Bible may take up this volume, attracted by the brisk opening lines ; while repelled by the dialect, he is soon

From "Sea and Land."   Copyright, 1894, by Charles Scribner's Sons.
FISHES OF PECULIAR FORM.

reading new meanings into Bible texts through these stories.

It would be hard to speak critically of a book so full of trust and grace, but fortunately the enjoyment of it is not marred by any lack of literary finish. It is a faithful transcript of characteristics which are fading away and which are here presented with a rare quaintness of style. The book is well gotten up, with wide margined pages and attractive drab and green binding. (Dodd, Mead & Co. $1.25.)—*Boston Literary World.*

Catherine de Medici.

BALZAC'S method in writing the historical novel was most precise. In the introduction to the novel now under notice his method can be followed. It is the philosophy of history, colored, perhaps, by that period of unrest which influenced the writer. France, when this work was composed, had just gone through internal strife, and was on the eve of beginning it over again, and Honoré de Balzac was immensely conservative. He dreaded the time which was to come.

If an author has to throw himself into the times about which he writes, Balzac possessed that power. It was not necessary for him to excite his romantic potentiality. That was always forthcoming. What he did was to make himself the statesman, the noble, the man of commerce, of the sixteenth or seventeenth century. He steered very clear of religious enthusiasms. As a good Catholic, upholding the religion he believed in, Balzac cared less for it in describing Huguenot times. He hardly brings creeds into prominence. He studies the situation, and, with that prodigious acumen he possessed—an acumen far above that of any romance-writer who ever lived—he understands many of the underlying motives.

In this book the portraits of Catherine de Medici, of Mary, Queen of Scots, and of Mary Touchet are wonderfully drawn. In contrast with the bluster of the chiefs of the many civil factions is shown the stern devotion of some of the leading Huguenots. We may care for the torrential force of a Victor Hugo in his historical novel, but more for the exact lights of Balzac. You get from the modern Frenchman the truer historical picture.

It is needless to say how well done is Miss Wormeley's translation, or how thoroughly she understands her text and the conception of the master romancist, and once again an American public has to thank the lady for a fuller appreciation of Balzac. (Roberts. $1.50.)—*The New York Times.*

"HOW'S THE WATER THIS MORNING?"

The Royal Marine.

WHAT is a young man to do, who is not sure whether he has proposed to the girl of his heart and been accepted by her, or whether he has simply dreamed both proposal and acceptance? This is the unpleasant predicament in which Brander Matthews places his hero in this bright little idyl of Narragansett Pier. The "Royal Marine"—so called from her *chic* yachting suit, ornamented with stripes and the crowned V. R. of the English navy—is a lovely Kentucky girl, who promptly captures the heart of young Warren Payn, on his vacation trip to Narragansett. Their acquaintance advances auspiciously, and at last one evening, while comfortably settled with a cigar, for a doze on the bridge of the Casino, Payn meets the charming Miss Carroll returning from the Casino dance, pleads his suit, is accepted, and while meditating on his happiness dozes off, awaking to face the fateful question—"Was it all a dream?" The miserable uncertainty in which he lingers, his efforts to discover indirectly whether he is an accepted suitor or not, and the way in which he is at last released from his predicament, furnish material for an amusing romance of a summer's week. It is gotten up in the neat shape and dainty costume of the *Harper's Little Novel Series* which prove tempting at first sight. (Harper. $1.)

From "Henry of Navarre."   Copyright, 1894, by J. B. Lippincott Co.

JEANNE PRESENTING THE PRINCES.

Henry of Navarre.

THE value of Mr. Blair's book lies not in the original study of documents, but in the graphic view it gives of a character unique in the history of France. Henry IV. for freedom of speech and for the liveliness and eccentricity of his humor comes nearer to President Lincoln than any European potentate. He was a man of genius whose manners the polished world could not change. Few kings were ever better known to their subjects than Henry of Navarre. In fact, they knew him so well and became so familiar with him that they underrated his abilities, and had to correct their estimate in the light of his achievements. A great many things contributed to make of this king an exception in the line of extremely polished and artificial personages to whom it fell to rule and gradually to ruin France. In the first place his grandfather was possessed by the fear that he could not outlive his boyhood. He was therefore sent to live in the open air, to mingle with all classes of people, to hunt and become familiar with the life of field and forest. He became an adept in the rude and ready wit that delighted the people. His answers were always quick and always to the purpose, but they were not expressed with the euphuistic delicacy usual at court. Long afterward his knowledge of the forests enabled him to handle troops in a way that astonished his opponents.

As a possible heir to the French throne, he fell in early youth into the care of Catharine de Medici. While he imbibed some learning in Paris, the most important lesson taught him there seems to have been the almost vulpine skill with which he foiled the plots of a Court reckoned, after the massacre of St. Bartholomew, to be the bloodiest and most unscrupulous in Europe. In the midst of an environment so perilous he seems to have put on an antic disposition. His real powers were deftly concealed under an air of folly and indifference. Here his unpolished manners stood him in good stead and he was under no temptation to become a courtier.

When he escaped from Paris and from the dangerous machinations of Catharine, it was only to become a partisan leader in a series of wars that were embittered by all the hatreds of religion, as well as the entanglements of politics. His reputation for folly had preceded him, and it took more than one victory to convince the men of Navarre and the Protestants of France that they had one of the most resourceful leaders known to the military annals of France or of Europe. The same inventiveness and organizing skill which made him, with the single exception of the Duke of Parma, the first soldier of his age, also led him as King of France to systematize the government in a way hitherto unknown. He might almost be said to have originated the modern plan of bureaus and departments. But without the patient Sully he never would have had the persistence to carry out his designs. He fought battles, he did not carry on campaigns. That was his defect as a soldier and as a statesman. No man of his time handled troops as well on the field as he ; but no man was less tolerant than he of the strategy which defeats an enemy without fighting, and wears him out by disappointment.

The wide pages of Mr. Blair's book are profusely illustrated with portraits, and the volume is a worthy tribute to a man who was magnificently great in spite of oddities astonishing in one born in the purple. (Lippincott. $4.)— *N. Y. Tribune.*

The Story of Babette.

RUTH McENERY STUART has written a charming romance in " The Story of Babette." It is the story of a lovely young Creole girl, stolen from her family in the confusion incident upon the Mardi-Gras carnival, and figuring afterwards, first in a gypsy camp, then as the adopted niece of a childless and wealthy old couple, in both of which conditions her beauty, combined with her gentle and lovable character, win for her devoted friends. The author has availed herself to the full of the novelist's license, and ingeniously constructed her plot to form those happy coincidences necessary to bring out triumphant over all difficulties her charming heroine, and harbor her safely at last beneath the roof of her afflicted parents. There is a simplicity of method in the narrative which makes it appear so honest as to bear the semblance of absolute truth in spite of such improbable happenings as the old gypsy woman's flight at night with the almost dying Babette, closely followed by the feeble-minded Noute, by whom she is pushed, most opportunely, into an open door and almost into the arms of the benevolent doctor, who saves the child's life and adopts her. The incidental descriptions of the Mardi-Gras, of the gypsy children and Babette playing on the beach, and some of the minor characters are very good. (Harper. $1.50.)—*The Beacon.*

The Story of Lawrence Garthe.

ANY one who has read Maurus Jókai's " Eyes Like the Sea," with its six-times married heroine, will be amused to compare Bessy with Bella, the heroine of Mrs. Ellen Olney Kirk's latest novel. " Bella" has only been married four times, but for absolute absence of any moral sense she will compare favorably with Bessy. Each of these heroines is endowed with the same charm of nature which manages to preserve an appearance of innocence and youthfulness in spite of very doubtful experiences. Bella is very cleverly contrasted with Constance. Constance is the most highly developed modern instance of the Puritan type. The situation into which Lawrence Garthe is thrown between Constance, whom he wishes to marry, and Bella, the divorced mother of his child, are powerfully handled. Of course, the story ends well, a little too well for life, but on the whole the book is worth reading, and will sustain its author's high reputation for ability and careful work. (Houghton, Mifflin & Co. $1.25.) —*The Literary World.*

From " The Story of Babette."　　　　　Copyright, 1894, by Harper & Brothers.

BABETTE AND HER PLAYMATES.

The Literary News.

An Eclectic Monthly Review of Current Literature.

EDITED BY A. H. LEYPOLDT.

JANUARY, 1895.

ROBERT LOUIS STEVENSON.

To every one of the strangely differing characters who together have been "the reading public," for whom Robert Louis Stevenson has labored, the announcement of his death came as a personal message, bringing a keen sense of personal loss. For days hope lingered that the telegraph had blundered. But now it is known beyond doubt or hope, that on December 3, '94, Robert Louis Stevenson was suddenly stricken with apoplexy, and scarcely twenty-four hours after lay buried on the summit of Pala Mountain, amid his dearly loved South Sea Island surroundings.

For fifteen years Stevenson's writings have been sure of readers, but "the reading public" has commonly but a vague idea of what his diligence as a whole has reached, either in number of volumes or in literary significance. His published works number close upon thirty volumes, all written in twenty years by a man who is dead at forty-four.

Stevenson himself has told us in "Memories and Portraits" how he became a writer, and by unremitting labor developed his at first limited capacities. The facts are few and known to all. The son of Thomas Stevenson, the light-house builder, and the grandson of Robert Stevenson, the inventor of the revolving light, he was born at Edinburgh, November 15, 1850.

ROBERT LOUIS STEVENSON.

He was a delicate, impulsive boy, revelling in books, but without inclination for study. He was graduated at the University of Edinburgh. " No one," said Stevenson, " had more certificates and less education." From his earliest years he aspired to write, and strongly objected to his father's plans to make of him a civil engineer. To be "merely a writer" seemed a lazy, profitless existence to his father's Scotch thrift and mechanical mind, and finally Stevenson consented to compromise and study law. This, however, he found equally distasteful. At the age of twenty-three it was found necessary that the young invalid should seek a kinder climate, and then began those wanderings in search of health which finally led him to his last resting-place.

By the sands of the sea, in the forests and on the mountains the young writer now began his life-work. He taught himself to write the purest English that has been written since Charles Lamb laid down his pen. He played the "sedulous ape," he has told us, to Ruskin, Hazlitt, Sir Thomas Browne and to all the great ones of the past. He saw everything about him with an eye that absorbed every touch of beauty and noted every incongruity and oddity, and then he described what he saw with brevity, clearness, vivacity, vividness, inimitable humor and originality always controlled by all-pervading grace. By hard work Stevenson made for himself a style all his own, and then used this subtle instrument to give to the world the proof that the human thought, the imagination, the love of mankind, the intense pleasure in existence which by it he brought home to his readers, are his truest, surest claims to a lasting place in literature.

His style was the first call to recognition, but year by year his fertility and versatility, his hoard of varied gifts of marvellous number have made his "calling and election sure," and his very last work of art, "The Ebb Tide," gave promise in directions as yet unworked in all his masterpieces.

Stevenson's private and literary life have been closely connected. For ten years "the reading public" has known at almost every moment the corners of the earth in which the suffering man sought relief, and in quick succession has received book after book bearing the impress of new sights and sounds and changing human and natural surroundings. Shortly after his wanderings began he met Sidney Colvin, always generously disposed towards young talent and with a genius at discovering it. This successful author, to whom later Stevenson dedicated his " Travels with a Donkey in the Cevennes," first introduced his work to the public.

His first published paper appeared in the *Portfolio* when he was twenty-three years old, under the pen-name of L. S. Stoneven. It was called " Roads." His second, written the same winter at Mentone, whither he had been sent for his health, was entitled "Ordered South."

William Ernest Henley also very early paid tribute to the great gifts of Stevenson, and helped him in many ways towards a hearing. "Will o' the Mill" was his first published story, and that was written in France. The next was "A Lodging for the Night," written at the same time with the delightful " Study on Villon," afterward republished in " Familiar Studies." " The New Arabian Nights" was begun at the Burford Bridge Inn, where Mr. Stevenson had gone in order to be near George Meredith. The Arabian Nights stories were continued in London, Edinburgh, Paris, Barbazon, and finished at Le Monastier—all within about five months. That same year he had brought out his first volume, "An Inland Voyage." " The Pavilion on the Links " was begun in London and finished by its wandering author in Monterey, Cal. " Treasure Island " was begun at Braemar, in the Scotch highlands, and finished at Davos, in Switzerland — the whole acomplished in two " bursts " of fifteen days each—Mr. Stevenson's quickest piece of work.

With " Treasure Island " Mr. Stevenson became famous. It was translated into many languages, and since 1883 every reader has been eager to read all that could be got at bearing the magic name of Robert Louis Stevenson. In 1879 Stevenson travelled in the United States and took to himself an American wife, whom he had met in Paris some time before. Mrs. Stevenson had been married to Samuel C. Osborne, a rich man of San Francisco, and the circumstances of separation and remarriage with Stevenson were highly romantic. The two children remained under her care and have always been tenderly loved by their stepfather, who, in collaboration with his stepson, Lloyd Osborne, has accomplished much of his later work.

Mr. Stevenson had made his trip to America in the steerage and had gone across country in an emigrant train. The adventures of this trip were recorded in articles written for *Longmans' Magazine* and the *Saturday Review*. The " Dynamiters " and " The Silverado Squatters " were the fruits of this visit among us. In 1887 he visited America and found relief for a time in the beautiful Adirondacks. In 1886 appeared the book by which Stevenson is perhaps best known among the many, the gruesome psychological story of " Dr. Jekyll and Mr. Hyde." It was with a view to protecting his rights in the dramatization of this work, which in Richard Mansfield's hands has been one of the greatest stage successes of the last half dozen years, that Stevenson once more came among us. Mr. George Iles, who was fortunate enough to meet the author and his delightful family during this stay at Lake Saranac, describes his appearance at that time with felicitous words:

Robert Louis Stevenson was a Norseman. As I first saw him in the Adirondacks seven winters ago, my first impression was that a Scandinavian stood before me. He was tall and very thin, with the extreme pallor of a life-long invalid. In his abundant light brown hair thrown behind his ears; his forehead—both high and wide—lighted by large eyes set far apart, as always in men of the first power of imagination; the curve of feature, the expression that indescribably heightened effect of his stories as he told them with all the fire of a born actor, there was testimony to the Norse blood that has so much enriched the Scottish race.

It was Mrs. Stevenson who planned a yachting cruise to the South Seas in search of a place where the suffering invalid could breathe and move about without pain. Almost every island was visited, and finally Stevenson found an ideal home at Apia, Samoa. The descriptions of this home, brought from time to time by travellers who have made a pilgrimage to the shrine of the greatest romancer since Walter Scott, read like Stevenson's own word-pictures of the beautiful places he saw in dreams. Here at last his homelessness found a home, and he felt for the first time that all nature and friends could do to ease the pain he had borne all his life could be attained among the beauties of the South Sea, surrounded by the natives who, one and all, became his worshippers. With his ever ready sympathy he threw himself heart and soul into the study of the political conditions of his new home, and in 1892, in his "A Foot-note to History: Eight Years of Trouble in Samoa," arraigned Germany for injustice and misrule, and pointed out the strength and weakness of its position in Samoa. Since 1888 Stevenson has inhabited Vailina, his beautiful residence built in Scotland and put up by loving hands in Apia. His health had seemed somewhat better, hemorrhages had been less frequent, and some even hoped that his later years might be free from constant pain. On Thanksgiving Day, November 29, he entertained some American friends, and on December 3 was feeling brighter, had done a long morning's work, and was enjoying his dinner, when the summons came. The press has told over and over how the natives hewed a path through the jungle and bush to the top of the mountain, how his step son and daughter accompanied the body to its resting-place 1200 feet above the sea, how the natives mourned, and how all the world mourns the premature death of Robert Louis Stevenson.

We cannot but ask : "Had he more to write, or had he done his best?" Many there are who think, as Stevenson did himself, that in "Kidnapped" he reached his height, and yet "The Ebb-Tide" held a note that might have become the keynote to an entirely new order of writing. His published works are: "An Inland Voyage " (1878) ; "Edinburgh : Picturesque Notes " (1879); "Travels with a Donkey in the Cevennes " (1879); "Virginibus Puerisque, and Other Papers " (1881) ; "Familiar Studies of Men and Books " (1882); "New Arabian Nights " (1882); "The Dynamiter: More New Arabian Nights " (1885, with his wife); "Treasure Island " (1883); "The Silverado Squatters " (1883) ; "A Child's Garden of Verse " (1885); "Prince Otto" (1885); "The Strange Case of Dr. Jekyll and Mr. Hyde " (1886); "Kidnapped: Memoirs and the Adventures of David Balfour, etc. " (1886); "Underwoods " (1887); "The Merry Men, and Other Tales " (1887); "Memoirs and Portraits " (1887); "The Black Arrow " (1888); "The Master of Ballantrae " (1889); "Ballads " (1891); "The Wrecker" (with Lloyd Osborne, 1891–92); "A Foot-note to History: Eight Years of Trouble in Samoa" (1892); "David Balfour" (1893); "Island Nights' Entertainments " (1893); "The Ebb-Tide " (1894).

Besides all this, says Mr. Iles, much else was written — poems, short stories, articles for magazines and newspapers, and three romances which remain unfinished. If the reader of this rare spirit finds a dull chapter here and there in his books, let him remember how good Stevenson is at his best, and further let him bear in mind that death was always imminent over him; that often when worn and weary he spurred himself to exertion that he might provide for those whom he would leave behind as he wished for.

A memorial tribute to Stevenson was offered in a gathering of literary people under the auspices of "The Uncut Leaves," on the evening of Friday, January 4, at Carnegie Hall, in New York City. Clarence C. Stedman was chosen chairman, and every lover of Stevenson should make sure of a copy of a paper giving his complete address on that occasion. It was a notable gathering, and many writers spoke with deep feeling of their comrade-at-letters. At this writing the note of all comment is chiefly personal. Stevenson was beloved personally and all judgment is hushed for the moment in the presence of death. Whether Stevenson's romances, almost all without heroines, will live and make him a place for all time ; or whether time will show that in his essays and desultory moralizing and philosophizing lies his enduring reputation, must remain for others to determine.

The memory of the man will never fade from those who met him. As one of his friends has said :

"Stevenson had all that deep fascination which attends upon a man of genius who is truly approachable. There was about him not a trace of affectation. He was easy and hearty in his greetings, and the strong fund of humor of which he was possessed made him a most delightful companion. No one ever came to know him who did not come to love him. He made every one his friend."

The first volume has appeared of a final edition of his works, to be known as the *Edinburgh* edition, to be complete in thirty volumes. The Scribners will handle it in this country. His faithful friend Sidney Colville, is the editor.

———

IN the February issue of THE LITERARY NEWS will appear a review of the general aspect of the publications of 1894, and also a list of the most important publications of the year just ended. About 5000 books were turned out by the publishers, many of course new editions of old favorites. It shall be the endeavor of THE LITERARY NEWS to direct attention to the very best among them—those it would be well to read if one lays claim to keeping up with the best among the latest, and those it would be wise to buy if circumstances favor such self-culture and enduring enjoyment. The survey of the books of the year will be undertaken in a spirit of fair criticism, regardless of generally received opinions or prejudices. The only aim will be to bring to mind the books that have the first claim to permanent life, of those published in 1894.

The Aftermath of 1894.

Curb, Snaffle, and Spur.—Mr. Anderson's manual will be a useful one to those for whom it is designed. His advice seems to be sensible, at least from a civilian point of view, and the illustrations, which are taken from photographs, add immensely to the value of the little book. Riders who do not belong to the cavalry will find his advice worth remembering. (Little, Brown & Co. $1.50.)

Crowell's New Sets of Standards. — In the preparation of *Crowell's New Illustrated Library*, it has been the aim of the publishers to produce a series of books that would meet the wants of those desiring inexpensive editions in attractive bindings, carefully edited, illustrated by the best artists, printed on good paper from clear type, and especially appropriate for holiday gifts or library use. In the pursuance of this plan no pains or expense have been spared to make this series the finest that has ever been produced at so low a price. (*Per volume*, $1.50.)

Quiet Stories from an Old Woman's Garden.—This book, by Alison McLean, is well named. It is made up of half a dozen stories of rural life, far from the noise and activities of trade. They have the odors of the garden and the meadow and forests, and touch the heart and make the reader wiser and better. One seldom finds rural English life more charmingly sketched. It enlarges the human soul, and enlarges its capacities to love the pure and the good and beautiful to read the chapters. What better could be said of a book? (Warne. $1.25.)

The Old Brick Churches of Maryland.—A six months' tour among the old brick churches of Maryland has furnished material for a delightful book, full of historic memories and reminiscences of colonial and revolutionary days. The narrative is by Helen West Ridgely, the many full-page and text illustrations are by Miss Sofie de Butts Stewart, and both author and artist have brought out to the utmost the charms and pleasures of this "pleasure-trip in quest of the old brick churches." The book is a small quarto, beautifully printed and daintily bound. (Randolph. $2.50.)

International Sunday-School Lessons.— "The Illustrative Notes for 1895," by Jesse Lyman Hurlbut and Robert Remington Doherty, is Mr. Hurlbut's Sunday-School Guide for the coming year, done, says *The Independent*, on substantially the same plan which has brought his previous volumes into such widely extended use, with original selected comments, illustrations literary and graphic, notes on Eastern life, and copious maps. The illustrative features of the guide are more striking than ever. The hints to teachers, and the arrangement of the material for presentation and use in the school, indicate everywhere the work of an editor who is himself a good teacher. (Hunt & Eaton. $1.25.)

Lorenzo Lotto.—In his earlier volume, "The Venetian Painters of the Renaissance," Mr. Berenson won for himself a name as a scholarly and appreciative art critic. In his new work he makes an exhaustive study of Lotto, claiming for this painter the interest of having represented that considerable Italian minority, which at the height of the Renaissance was less in sympathy with the dominant Paganism, and therefore more inclined toward the Reformation. The book contains thirty full-page heliotype reproductions of the most representative works of Lotto and his precursor, Alvise Vivarini. In addition to its value to the art student, the volume is so attractively illustrated that it is admirably suited for use as a gift-book. (Putnam. $3.50.)

Twelve Bad Men.—It is probably true that some people would be more interested in the "Lives of the Saints" than in the "Newgate Calendar," but the proportion would be very small. Wickedness is generally attractive, and every one knows that there is something fascinating about a very bad man. Therefore it is unnecessary to dwell upon the interest of these "original studies of prominent scoundrels"—the title of the book is its own recommendation. The studies are by different writers, and cover a wide range of unworthies, from "Black Bothwell," to Thomas Wainewright, the poisoner. They are edited by Thomas Seccombe, sub-editor of the "Dictionary of National Biography," and have numerous portraits. (Putnam. $3.50.)

L'Abbé Daniel.—The little story of "The Abbé Daniel," by André Theuriet, which has been exquisitely and sympathetically translated by Mrs. Nathan Haskell Dole, is one of the most delightful things in its way that has of late years been added to prose fiction. It is a very simple tale, very simply told, but it has the indescribable quality called charm, and its pathos is so tender and genuine, and its humor so spontaneous and natural, that to find its parellel one is almost obliged to go back to Goldsmith and "The Vicar." Theuriet is a poet, as Goldsmith was, and he has appreciation of human nature on its lovable side. "The Abbé Daniel" is got up in a style that makes it doubly attractive. There are a score or more of dainty illustrations after French originals, and the binding, though delicate, is very pretty. (Crowell. $1.)

Brentano's Publications.—Brentano's cater to the leisure classes. Lovers of the stage, of music, and of games may be gratified from their list. On it may be found Eric Mackay's "Love-Letters of a Violinist," illustrated by thirty-five designs in charcoal by James Fagan; "Princesses in Love," by Henri Pène Du Bois, also illustrated by James Fagan; and "French Folly in Maxims," in four bewitching little volumes. *A Library of Masks and Faces* is the general title of a series prepared by William T. Price, which will contain biographical and critical essays on the great European and American actors and actresses. "Charles Macready" and "Charlotte Cushman" are discussed in the two volumes now ready. Foster's "Whist Manual" and, "Baby's Biography" may also be turned to account as Christmas gifts.

Two Dainty Volumes. — Mrs. Huntington Smith's admirable compilation, "Golden Words for Daily Counsel," is full of comforting and helpful extracts, and has met with a success which will surely be increased by the new edition illustrated with portraits of sixteen of the best known of the authors, and whose words are enshrined in its pages. Another tasteful gift-book is the illustrated edition of "Faber's Hymns." The author of "Hark! Hark! My Soul! Angelic Songs are Swelling," and of "O Paradise!" needs no introduction to religious readers. Many of Faber's hymns were specially composed for the London Oratory, which he founded, and of which he was so long the head; but they have an interest and beauty quite apart from the narrower use to which he put them, and the majority of them have been accepted by the whole Christian world without distinction of creed. The collection, which Mr. Bridgman has so sympathetically illustrated, will be found acceptable to all classes of readers. (Crowell. *8a.*, $1.25.)

The Yellow Fairy Book.—First in our rapidly lengthening list of books of fairy and other stories published especially to meet the claims of our young people, says the London *Literary World*, we must certainly rank Mr. Andrew Lang's "Yellow Fairy Book," an addition to the series which is becoming as tinted as the famous coat of many colors. The continual drain on his resources has sent Mr. Lang further afield for the materials with which to build the present volume, and, in consequence, there is a greater sense of originality about the contents, which have been levied from Russian, German, French, Icelandic, and Red Indian folk and fairy stories, and are, if not entirely new to us, at least comparatively so. Mr. Lang explains that he has published this book entirely for children, and so that they are pleased he does not very much care for what other people may say. "The Yellow Fairy Book" is well and copiously illustrated, and tastefully presented—in a yellow binding, of course, as the title necessitates. (Longmans, Green & Co. $2.)

D. Appleton & Co.'s Miscellaneous Publications.—Not strictly to be classed as holiday publications, but most suitable as gift-books, are "Woman's Share in Primitive Culture," by Otis Tufton Mason, the first volume of the *Anthropoligical Series*, edited by Frederick Starr, of the University of Chicago, which traces the interesting period when with fire-making began the first division of labor—a division of labor based upon sex—the man going to the field or forest for game, while the woman at the fireside became the burden-bearer, basketmaker, weaver, potter, agriculturist, and domesticator of animals ($1.50); "In the Track of the Sun," readings from the diary of a globe-trotter, by Frederick Diodati Thompson, profusely illustrated with engravings from photographs and from drawings by Harry Fenn, of which *The Outlook* says: "We know of no equally convenient and handsome publication illustrating a journey round the world" ($6); and Professor Maspero's "The Dawn of Civilization," edited by Rev. Professor Sayce, with map and nearly 500 illustrations.

American Foot-Ball for Schools and Colleges.—This is one of the books that fill "long-felt wants," A. A. Stagg and Henry L. Williams know the game of football as it is played to-day. "Now here is a book," says the N. Y. *Times*, "which will make it all clear. It tells the duties and dodges of centres, guards, tackles, ends, and backs. It describes the manner in which each ought to play his position individually, and it gives in plain language the theory of team plays, signals, and general football tactics. But it goes further. It describes with the aid of intelligible and easily understood diagrams, sixty-nine different methods of attack, including all the long passes and 'criss-cross' plays, which are likely to come into use again under the new rules. Any spectator at a football game, after a study of this book, ought to know where to look for clever work and to appreciate it as thoroughly as the college boys do. Football has become the national fall game of the country, and every American naturally desires to understand it. This book will give him the required aid." (Appleton. $1.25.)

Flammarion's Popular Astronomy.—"M. Camille Flammarion is the most popular scientific writer in France. Of the present work no fewer than one hundred thousand copies were sold in a few years. It was considered of such merit that the Montyon Prize of the French Academy was awarded to it ; it has also been selected by the Minister of Education for use in the public libraries—a distinction which proves that it is well suited to the general reader. The subject is treated in a very popular style, and the work is at the same time interesting and reliable. It should be found very useful by those who wish to acquire a good general knowledge of astronomy without going too deeply into the science. In translating this work I have endeavored to make as close a translation as possible, with, of course, due regard to the English idiom. I have reduced the figures given by the author to English measures. Many new illustrations have been added, and I have also given some notes with reference to recent researches and discoveries, so as to bring the work up to date." Thus writes J. Ellard Gore, who has made the translation of this edition of Flammarion's work, which the publishers have provided with three plates and 288 illustrations. (Appleton. $4.50.)

Historical Characters of the Reign of Queen Anne.—It is always pleasant and profitable, says *The Nation*, to study the treatment by an intelligent woman of matters that have been handled chiefly by men ; and especially is this the case when the characters and actions of women are the subjects of discussion. Even where there is no lack of sympathy and good-will, men can hardly avoid judging women by masculine standards, and pronouncing an action wrong or weak because it would have been wrong or weak in a man. So, as a study of a woman by a woman, we have read with especial pleasure the vivid and sympathetic sketch of Queen Anne which Mrs. Oliphant here gives us. Certainly that royal lady has had rather hard measure dealt to her by writers of this century, among whom, as the greatest sinner against knowledge, Macaulay is most to blame. The extreme partisanship which so seriously vitiates his history, saw in Anne a Tory, a High-Churchwoman, and a dislike not without cause of his glorified William ; and the least of these crimes deserved no mercy, and even justified a little wresting of the truth "in the cause of the right," as Mr. Wegg puts it. Much space in the volume is devoted to Swift, Defoe, and Addison. The external appearance of this very attractive volume, with all the furtherances of the printer's, engraver's, and binder's arts, is worthy of the Century Company. ($6.)

Survey of Current Literature.

☞ *Order through your bookseller.—"There is no worthier or surer pledge of the intelligence and the purity of any community than their general purchase of books; nor is there any one who does more to further the attainment and possession of these qualities than a good bookseller."*—Prof. Dunn.

ART, MUSIC, DRAMA.

APTHORP, W. FOSTER. Musicians and music lovers, and other essays. Scribner. 12°, $1.50.
Contents: Musicians and music lovers; Johann Sebastian Bach; Additional accompaniments to Bach's and Handel's scores; Giacomo Meyerbeer; Jacques Offenbach; Two modern classicists; John Sullivan Dwight; Some thoughts on musical criticism; Music and science.

FREYTAG, GUSTAV. Freytag's technique of the drama: an exposition of dramatic composition and art; an authorized tr. from the 6th German ed., by Elias J. MacEwan. Griggs. 12°, $1.50.
An historical and philosophical exposition of dramatic composition and art, stating the general principles governing the structures of plays, the creation of characters, and the rules of acting. The qualifications of actors are clearly set forth, and attention is given to stage arrangement. An important feature of the work is its critical examination of the plan, motive, color, characters, etc. of the principal dramas of Sophocles, Shakespeare, Lessing, Goethe, and Schiller, thus making it of special value to dramatic authors, critics, and students of literature. Dr. Freytag ranks among the first of living playwrights and novelists, and play-goers will find in the work that which must be helpful to a better appreciation of the nature and value of the drama.

HEALY, G. P. A. Reminiscences of a portrait painter. McClurg. 12°, $1.50.

MARGARET, (*pseud.*) Theatrical sketches here and there with prominent actors. Merriam Co. nar. 16°, 75 c.

BIOGRAPHY, CORRESPONDENCE, ETC.

BRACE, C. LORING. The life of Charles Loring Brace chiefly told in his own letters; ed. by his daughter, [Emma Brace.] Scribner. pors. 8°, $2.50.
The story of Mr. Brace's life may almost be said to be the history of philanthropic effort in the United States. Thirty-five years ago he first turned his attention to the youthful criminals and outcasts of the city of New York—the result being the establishment of the grand and useful organization of the 'Children's Aid Society, which now comprises industrial schools, night schools, lodging-houses like the News-Boys' Lodgings and the Girls' Lodging-House—farm school for boys, summer and health homes, dressmaking and typewriting schools, a printing shop, etc. Through these, thousands of waifs and strays have been rescued, taught to earn a living, and placed in comfortable homes. The organization has furnished to many cities in this country and Europe an inspiration and a model. He was the author of "Gesta Christi," "The unknown God," "The dangerous classes

of New York," etc. His daughter tells his life from his earliest years, through his correspondence, which is held together by her comments and exposition.

BROOKS, NOAH. Abraham Lincoln and the downfall of American slavery. Putnam. il. 12°, (Heroes of the nations ser., no. 14.) $1.50.
Now added to The heroes of the nations series. First published in 1888.

CARY, E. George William Curtis. Houghton, Mifflin & Co. 12°, (American men of letters.) $1.25.

DUMAS, ALEX. Napoleon; from the French, by J. B. Larner. Putnam. 12°, $1.50.
A brief and interesting biography of Napoleon. This is the first time it appears in the English language.

GROSSMANN, *Mrs.* EDWINA BOOTH. Edwin Booth: recollections by his daughter, Edwina Booth Grossmann, and letters to her and his friends. The Century Co. pors. 8°, $3. *Edition de luxe*, on Holland paper, $12.50; on Whatman paper, $25.
Mrs. Grossmann's recollections cover twenty-eight pages, and describe Edwin Booth as a loving father, most tender in all his family relations. The rest of the handsome volume is occupied with letters from Booth to his daughter and to others of his friends. They are simple and unaffected, and convey a more intimate knowledge of the character of the man than could be gained from any memoir. The regular edition and the *edition de luxe* are illustrated with twenty artotype reproductions of portraits, trophies, etc., of the great actor, and are printed and bound in a most artistic form.

HARE, A. J. C., *ed.* Life and letters of Maria Edgeworth. Houghton, Mifflin & Co. 2 v., 8°, $4.

LINTON, W. J. Threescore and ten years; 1820 to 1890; recollections. Scribner. por. 8°, $2.

MASSON, FRÉDÉRIC. Napoleon and the women of his court; from the French. Lippincott. pors. 8°, $5.

MASSON, FRÉDÉRIC. Napoleon at home: the daily life of the emperor at the Tuileries; tr. by Ja. E. Matthew. Lippincott. 2 v., 12 pl. 8°, $7.50.

PICKARD, S. T. Life and letters of John Greenleaf Whittier. Houghton, Mifflin & Co. 2 v., pors. il. 12°, $4.

RITCHIE, *Mrs.* ANNE THACKERAY. Chapters from some unwritten memoirs. Harper. 8°, $2.
Reminiscences of Jasmin, Chopin, Louis Philippe, Mrs. Kemble, Madame Martin, and of Mrs. Ritchie's early home, and the many noted people that visited her father are contained in

chapters entitled : My poet ; My musician ;
My triumphal arch ; My professor of history ;
My witch's caldron ; In Kensington ; To Wei-
mar and back ; *Via* Willis' rooms to Chelsea ;
In Villeggiatura ; Tout chemin ; Mrs. Kemble.

SMILES, S. Josiah Wedgwood, F.R.S.; his per-
.sonal history. Harper. por. 12°, $1.50.
The subject of this biography came from a
distinguished family of English potters in Staf-
fordshire ; it was he, individually, however,
that made the name of Wedgwood famous.
He was born in 1730, and died 1795. In 1769
he opened new potteries at Etruria, in Stafford-
shire, on a large scale, and assisted by the
artist Flaxman, and other artists of equal merit,
turned out the celebrated Wedgwood and Bentley pottery. His chief artistic feat was the production of an accurate copy, in clay, of the
celebrated glass Portland vase. This work relates all these incidents, with facts of his early
life, etc., in Smiles' popular style.

STEARNS, FRANK PRESTON. Life and genius of
Jacopo Robusti, called Tintoretto. Putnam.
12°, $2.25.
Jacopo Robusti, commonly called " Tintoretto," was born in Venice in 1518 and died 1594.
He was one of the greatest painters of the
Venetian or of any school ; his works, mostly
frescoes, were made in Venice, many of them
still remaining to view in the churches and
palaces. A thorough life of Tintoretto in English has long been needed—one that should
understandingly set forth his work and his genius—we have it here. A list of his paintings
and where they are is given.

ROBBINS, ALFRED F. The early public life of
William Ewart Gladstone, four times prime
minister. Dodd, Mead & Co. 12°, $1.50.
Covers the first thirty years of Gladstone's
life, from his birth in 1809, until 1840. There
are chapters on : His father as merchant ; His
father as politician ; His Eton education ; At
Oxford ; The young parliamentary hand ; His
relation to slavery ; His ecclesiastical development ; In Peel's first ministry ; Progress in
and out of Parliament ; Church and State ; Mr.
Gladstone and his critics ; Educational and
philanthropic endeavor ; Continued parliamentary success ; Once more a minister.

WALKER, FRANCIS A. General Hancock. Appleton. 12°, (Great commanders ser., no. 10.)
$1.50.
Contents : Birth and education ; Down to the
great Rebellion ; Williamsburg to Antietam ;
Fredericksburg ; Chancellorsville ; Gettysburg
—the first, second, and third day ; After Gettysburg ; The Wilderness—first and second
day ; Spottsylvania ; The salient ; The North
Anna and the Totopotomy ; Cold Harbor ; Petersburg ; Deep Bottom ; Reams' Station ; The
Boydton Road ; After the war.

WRIGHT, T. The life of Daniel Defoe. ¹ Randolph. il. 8°, $3.75.

DESCRIPTION, GEOGRAPHY, TRAVEL, ETC.

BAKER, *Mrs.* WOODS. Pictures of Swedish life;
or, Svea and her children. Randolph. 8°,
$3.75.

CARPENTER, MARY THORN. In Cairo and Jeru-

salem: an Easter note-book. Randolph. 12°,
$1.50.

CHAMBERS' concise gazetteer of the world; topographical, statistical, historical. Lippincott. 8°, hf. leath., $2.50.

MONTBARD, G. The land of the sphinx ; il. by
the author. Dodd, Mead & Co. 4°, $4.

DOMESTIC AND SOCIAL.

MILLER, J. R., *D.D.* Secrets of happy home
life: what have you to do with it? Crowell. 12°, leatherette, 35 c.

BURDETTE, ROB. J., BURNETT, *Mrs.* FRANCES
HODGSON, BOK, E. W., [*and others.*] Before he
is twenty: five perplexing phases of the boy
question considered. Revell. 12°, 75 c.
Contents : The father and his boy, by Robert
J. Burdette; When he decides, by Frances
Hodgson Burnett; The boy in the office, by Edward W. Bok; His evenings and amusements,
by Mrs. Burton Harrison; Looking toward a
wife, by Mrs. Lyman Abbott. These articles
were originally written for *The Ladies' Home
Journal.*

EDUCATION, LANGUAGE, ETC.

DAVIDSON, T. The education of the Greek
people and its influence on civilization. Appleton. 12°, (International education ser.,
no. 28.) $1.50.
" In my recent book, ' Aristotle and the ancient educational ideals,' I endeavored to set
forth the facts of Greek education in historical
order. The present brief work has an entirely
different purpose—which is, to show how the
Greek people were gradually educated up to
that stage of culture which made them the teachers of the whole world, and what the effect
of that teaching has been. Hence, education, in
its narrow, pedagogic sense, is presented, but
in the barest outline, while prominence is given
to the different stages in the growth of the
Greek polit'cal, ethical, and religious consciousness, and the effect of this upon Greek history
and institutions, as well as upon the after-
world."—*Preface.*

PANCOAST, H. S. An introduction to English
literature. Holt. 16°, $1.25.
Based upon the author's " Representative
English literature." He has taken the historical and critical of that book, omitting all the
selections and notes, and has added some two
hundred pages of entirely new matter. The
text has thus been nearly doubled in length,
and the book, as a whole, brought within slightly smaller limits. Teachers who do not wish to
be restricted to prescribed selections will probably prefer this to the first-named book in teaching English literature.

PHYFE, W. H. P. Five thousand words often
misspelled. Putnam. 16°, 75 c.
A carefully selected list of words difficult to
spell, with directions for spelling and for the
division of words into syllables ; with an appendix containing the rules and list of amended
spellings recommended by the Philological Society of London and the American Philological
Society. A special feature of this list is the insertion of proper names difficult to spell, also of
words and phrases from foreign languages.

While Webster's International Dictionary has been adopted as the standard authority, all important variations in spelling given in Worcester, Stormonth, the Century, and Standard dictionaries are quoted.

VAN DYKE, J. C. A text-book of the history of painting. Longmans, Green & Co. 12°, (College histories of art.) $1.50.
The object of this series of text-books is to provide concise, teachable histories of art for class-room use in schools and colleges. The main facts of history as settled by the best authorities are given. The bibliography cited at the head of each chapter will be found helpful to the reader who wishes to enter into particulars. At the end of each chapter are enumerated the principal extant works of an artist, school, or period, and where they may be found. This volume on painting, the first of the series, omits mention of such works in Arabic, Indian, Chinese, and Persian art as may come properly under the head of ornament—a subject proposed for separate treatment.

FICTION.

ALLEN, J. LANE. A Kentucky cardinal: a story. Harper. il. 16°, (Harper's little novels.) $1.
The natural beauties of Kentucky in the year 1850 are described month by month with the art of the writer of "The blue grass region of Kentucky." The Kentucky cardinal is a beautiful red-breasted bird, whose nesting and family life the author has watched with loving eye. A little love idyl is sketched with lightest touch among the rhapsody the author offers to nature and her songsters.

BARING-GOULD, SABINE. Kitty Alone: a story of three fires. Dodd, Mead & Co. 12°, $1.25.
Coombe Cellars, the pretty scene of a prettier love-story, lies in the southern part of Devonshire. Kitty Alone is the daughter of a man full of schemes for making money, visionary and unpractical, who keeps his friends in continual mental unrest. Her name has been given her because she seems to live within herself among her uncongenial, rough surroundings. After suffering accusation and trial through circumstantial evidence, Kitty Alone finds happiness with her faithful, joyous lover.

BARRETT, FRANK. The justification of Andrew Lebrun: a novel. Appleton. 12°, (Appleton's town and country lib., no. 157.) $1; pap., 50 c.
An old clockmaker whose leisure hours have been spent in deep scientific experiments in chemistry, buys an old house in the slums of London, to which is attached a chemical laboratory unused for one hundred years. The former owner has imposed certain conditions upon a buyer, all of which the old chemist fulfils. The consequences are strange and weird, and the story works up to a most exciting climax. Suspended animation and chemical resuscitation are the secrets carefully guarded by the old deserted laboratory.

BIKÉLAS, DEMETRIOS. Tale from the Ægean ; tr. by Leonard Eckstein Opdycke; with an introd. by H. Alonzo Huntington. McClurg. 16°, $1.
Eight little stories, originally written in modern Greek and now translated into English,

make up this attractive little volume. M. Bikélas is, perhaps, the most popular living author in his own land; his historic tale, "Loukis Laras," made so great a sensation when published at Athens about fifteen years ago that it was translated into nearly every language of Europe. Of these tales some are sad, some imbued with a gentle humor—cheerful rather than merry—and all are pure and refined in sentiment. But their especial value lies in the realistic pictures they paint of Greek life in our own times—the social customs, dress, courtship, and marriage.

BLACK, CLEMENTINA. An agitator: a novel. Harper. 16°, (Harper's little novels.) $1.
Kit Brand, the agitator, is secretary of a labor union which has been directing a strike of English wire-workers. Kit is a single-minded man who has lost his wife and child and gives up all personal pleasures, his whole intelligence and strength to help his fellow-workman. Circumstantial evidence makes it appear that Kit is unfaithful to his trust, and he is imprisoned and prosecuted. Some wise thoughts regarding capital and labor are interwoven.

BOUVET, MARGUERITE. My lady: a story of long ago; il. by Helen Maitland Armstrong. McClurg. 16°, $2.50.
The heart-history of a young girl, related by her old nurse. "My Lady's" girlhood is passed, and her wooing takes place in the old family château in Provence. The story is set in the days of the French Empire, but the historical interest is slight, and it is mainly a love-tale, pure and simple.

CABLE, G. W. John March, southerner. Scribner. 12°, $1.50.

CATHERWOOD, MARY HARTWELL. The lady of Fort St. John: an historical novel. Houghton, Mifflin & Co. 16°, (Riverside pap. ser.) pap., 50 c.

CROCKETT, S. R. The lilac sunbonnet: a love-story. Appleton. 12°, $1.50.

CROCKETT, S. R. The play-actress. Putnam. 24°, $1.
In a Scotch parish, a great preacher had ended a stirring mission sermon, when a young woman approached him, leading a little child, which she convinced him was his dead son's baby-girl. She explained that she and her sister, the child's mother, were "play-actresses," and on this account unfit to bring up a daughter. The aunt had carefully taught the little girl. The great preacher goes to London to look up the mother, and the pathetic tale gives glimpses of the perfect self-sacrifice of sisterly love, sacrifice in a wholly hopeless cause. The great preacher hears a sermon from the heart of a "play-actress."

DELAND, *Mrs.* MARGARET. Philip and his wife. Houghton, Mifflin & Co. 12°, $1.25.

DILLINGHAM, LUCY. The missing chord: a novel. G. W. Dillingham. 12°, $1.25.
Juliet Lea, the daughter of a mother devoted to social pleasure, decides to study music in Berlin before making her *début* in New York society. The story tells of her life with an aunt and cousin who are surrounded by German

students and artists. Love comes to Juliet and changes the artistic bent of her life. She marries an American professor devoted to the improvement of his fellowmen. After a short year her life is once more wholly changed, and the unselfishness of her husband seems almost visionary.

DOYLE, A. CONAN. Round the red lamp: being facts and fancies of medical life. 2d ed. Appleton. 12°, $1.50.
Fifteen short stories, most of which emphasize the graver side of life. The red lamp is the usual sign of the general practitioner in England. Many of these tales have medical interest. The separate titles are: Behind the times; The first operation; A straggler of '15;' The third generation; A false start; the curse of Eve; Sweethearts; A physiologist's wife; The case of Lady Lennox; A question of diplomacy; A medical document; Lot No. 249; The Los Amigos fiasco; The doctors of Hoyland; The surgeon talks.

FORD, PAUL LEICESTER. The honorable Peter Stirling and what people thought of him. Holt. 12°, $1.50.

GORDON, JULIEN, [pseud. for Mrs. Julia Van Rensselaer Cruger.] Poppæa. Lippincott. 12°, $1.

HARRIS, FRANK. Elder Conklin, and other stories. Macmillan & Co. 12°, $1.25.

HARRISON, Mrs. CONSTANCE CARY, [Mrs. Burton Harrison.] A bachelor maid ; il. by Irving. R. Wiles. The Century Co. 12°, $1.25.

HARTE, BRET. The bell-ringer of Angel's, and other stories. Bost., Houghton, Mifflin & Co. 12°, $1.25.
Eight of the most recent stories of the author of "The luck of Roaring Camp," entitled: The bell-ringer of Angel's ; Johnnyboy ; Young Robin Gray ; The sheriff of Siskyon; A rose of Glenbogie; The mystery of the Hacienda ; Chu Chu; My first book.

HOPE, ANTHONY, [pseud. for Anthony Hope Hawkins.] The god in the car. Appleton. (Appleton's town and country lib., no. 154.) 12°, $1; pap., 50 c.

HOPE, ANTHONY, [pseud. for Anthony Hope Hawkins.] The indiscretion of the duchess: being a story concerning two ladies, a nobleman, and a necklace. 1 il., 16°, 75 c.

HOSMER, JA. K. How Thankful was bewitched. Putnam. 12°, (The Hudson lib., no. 3.) pap., 50 c.
The novel is founded on an event in the history of Meadowboro, supposed to have occurred in the days of Cotton Mather. An old record, dating from the time the town was a Puritan outpost, and purporting to be written by Thankful Pumry, is authority for a singular story, which presents the remarkable incidents in the life of Thankful before and after she was taken into captivity by the French and Indians; in brief, effort is made to show that a bell formerly cast for the Jesuits is endowed with supernatural power, and that the said bell is the cause of the strange experience chronicled.

IOTA, [pseud. for Mrs. Mannington Caffyn.]

Children of circumstance: a novel. Appleton. 12°, (Appleton's town and country lib., no. 155.) $1; pap., 50 c.

JOHNSTONE, EDITH. A sunless heart. [Anon.] Ward, Lock & Bowden, Ltd. 12°, $1.25.

KING, C. Under fire; il. by C. B. Cox. Lippincott. 12°, $1.25.

KIRK, Mrs. ELLEN OLNEY, ["Henry Hayes," pseud.] The story of Lawrence Garthe. Houghton, Mifflin & Co. 12°, 1.25.

LAWLESS, EMILY. Maelcho: a sixteenth century narrative. Appleton. 12°, $1.50.

LINTON, Mrs. E. LYNN. The one too many. F. Tennyson Neely. 12°, (Neely's international lib.) $1.25.
The "one too many," the delicate, pretty daughter of an ambitious widow, is given in marriage to an unmitigated prig, who spends his life educating and cramming his wife with facts in which she takes no interest As a foil to the young wife's submissive suffering, four "advanced" girls are introduced, who hold a B. A. degree and are full of plans for the regeneration of mankind. The story is chiefly laid in rural England, where the rich man lives who has bought his fair young bride. The end is tragic.

LOCKE, W. J. At the gate of Samaria: a novel. Appleton. 12°, (Appleton's town and country lib., no. 156.) $1; pap., 50 c.

McGLASSON, EVA WILDER. Ministers of grace: a novelette. Harper. il. 16°, (Harper's little novels.) $1.
An old clergyman who has been asked to resign by his congregation is prostrated by the shock, and comes to an eastern seaside resort with his daughter to recruit his shattered nerves. The hotel is full of worldly guests, and the old man suffers from their hilarity and ungodly pursuits. A successful young actress, on vacation, betrays to the old preacher how his daughter has earned the money needed to supply his many invalid needs. The old man's prejudices lead him to harshness, but in the end all is well.

MACLAREN, IAN, [pseud. for Rev. John Maclaren Watson.] Beside the bonnie brier bush. Dodd, Mead & Co. 12°, $1.25.

MATTHEWS, JA. BRANDER. The royal marine: an idyl of Narragansett Pier. Harper. 16°, (Harper's little novels.) $1.

MORRISON, ARTHUR. Martin Hewitt : investigator. Harper. 12°, (Harper's Franklin sq. lib., new ser., no. 755.) pap., 50 c.
Seven short stories describing cases in which Martin Hewitt played the part of an astute and ingenious detective. The separate titles are : The Lenton Croft robberies ; The loss of Sammy Crockett ; The case of Mr. Faggatt ; The case of the Dixon torpedo; The Quinton jewel affair ; The Stanway cameo mystery; The affair of the tortoise.

NORRIS, W. E. The despotic lady. Lippincott. 12°, $1.
The despotic lady is a religious reformer, the mother of a young girl with whom an incipient

poet has fallen madly in love. This friend, a confirmed bachelor, heir to the old Hexham title, undertakes to tame the preaching dragon, but is almost captured himself in his friendly devotion. A secret in the past of the righteous exhorter, held by the poet's father, is worked to bring about happiness for all.

OLIPHANT, *Mrs.* MARG. O. W. Who was lost and is found : a novel. Harper. 12°, $1.50.

PASTON, G. A bread-and-butter miss : a sketch in outline. Harper. 12°, $1.

RAYMOND, WALTER, ["Tom Cobbleigh," *pseud.*] Love and quiet life : Somerset idylls. Dodd, Mead & Co. 12°, $1.25.
The author of "Gentleman Upcott's daughter" has written another idyll of Somersetshire in the years immediately preceding the Oxford Tractarian movement. Love comes to Marian Burt in early girlhood, and with it disillusionment and sorrow—then a long quiet life of upwards of three score years and ten. The father, the old, retired nonconformist minister, is a fine character study. Rustic life and religious prejudices are the motives.

SACHER-MASOCH, LEOPOLD V. Jewish tales ; from the French, by Harriet Lieber Cohen. McClurg. 12°, $1.

SHELDON, C. M. The crucifixion of Phillip Strong. McClurg. 12°, $1.
Philip Strong accepted a call to become the pastor of a fashionable church in a town of 80,000 inhabitants, the richest among them being millowners, employing 20,000 people. Fearlessly the minister preached the duties of professing church-members to their God, their fellow-men, and themselves. His earnest purpose was to show the appointed work of a modern church professing to follow the teachings of Christ. He was morally crucified.

SMITH, *Mrs.* ELIZ. T. T.,[*formerly* L. T. Meade,] *and* Halifax, Clifford, *M.D.* Stories from the diary of a doctor ; il. by A. Pearse. Lippincott. il. 12°, $1.25.
Twelve stories, presenting some cases supposed to have come under the direct attention of a young London physician. It is claimed by their collaborating authors that several of the tales included are founded on actual experience, and that all have been written with a close observance to medical facts, and in accordance with the advances made in surgery during the last decade. Among the subjects are : Hypnotism and catalepsy ; My first patient ; My hypnotic patient ; Very far west ; The heir of Chartelpool ; A death certificate ; The wrong prescription ; The Horror of Studley Grange ; Ten years' oblivion ; An oak coffin ; Without witnesses ; Trapped, and the Ponsonby diamonds.

SWAN, ANNIE S., [*Mrs.* Burnett Smith.] A lost ideal. Ward, Lock & Bowden, Ltd. 12°, $1.25.

VALENTINE, OSWALD. Helen. Putnam. nar. 16°, (Incognito lib., no. 5.) 50 c.

WARNER, C. DUDLEY. The golden house : a novel ; il. by W. T. Smedley. Harper. 12°, hf. leath., $2.

HISTORY.

ANDREWS, E. B. History of the United States. Scribner, 2 v., 12°, $4.

BLAIR, E. T. Henry of Navarre and the religious wars. Lippincott. 4°, $4.

CESARESCO, EVELYN MARTINENGO (*Countess*). The liberation of Italy, 1815–1870. Scribner, 8°, (Events of our own time series.) $1.75.
A retrospect in which are traced the principal factors that worked toward Italian unity. "Italy from the Battle of Lodi to the Congress of Vienna" is the subject of the first chapter. After is related the history of the Carbonari and the Society of Young Italy, Mazzini's propaganda, the accession of Charles Albert, and events leading to the election of Pius IX.; the insurrection in Sicily, and the expelling of the Austrians from Milan and Venice; the arrival of Garibaldi and abdication of Charles Albert; the history of the House of Savoy; "The war for Lombardy," "What unity cost," "The march of the thousand," "The meeting of the waters," "Beginnings of the Italian Kingdom," "Rome or death," "The war for Venice," "The last crusade," and "Rome the capital," are the topics of the concluding chapters. Contains portraits of Garibaldi, Mazzini, Victor Emmanuel, and Cavour.

GARDINER, S. RAWSON. History of the Commonwealth and Protectorate, 1649–1660. V. 1, 1649–1651. Longmans, Green & Co. 8°, $7.

GONTAUT, *Duchesse de.* Memoirs of the Duchesse de Gontaut, Gouvernante to the children of France during the Restoration, 1773–1836 ; from the French by Mrs. J. W. Davis. Dodd, Mead & Co. 2 v., 226 ; 252 p. pors. 8°, $5 ; *large-pap. ed.*, 2 v., full leath., *net*, $12.

GOODWIN, MAUD WILDER. The colonial cavalier ; or, southern life before the Revolution ; il. by Harry Edwards. Lovell, Coryell & Co. 12°.

HARRISON, F. The meaning of history, and other historical pieces. Macmillan. 8°, $2.25.

LATIMER, *Mrs.* ELIZ. WORMELEY. England in the nineteenth century. McClurg. pors. 8°, $2.50.
A popularly and attractively written résumé of English history fresh from the reign of George the Third to Queen Victoria's Jubilee year. Mrs. Latimer has made use of many family and personal reminiscences, thus giving many new and unpublished details and anecdotes—the work being therefore less of a compilation than some of her previous books in the same line—though "France in the nineteenth century," also contained personal reminiscences. Her father, though American born, became an admiral in the English navy—hence her opportunity for learning the inside history of the English court. Queen Victoria's reign, her domestic life to the present, with her marriage, the death of the Prince Consort, and the marriages of her children and grandchildren, are told in a pleasant, gossipy way.

LUCKOCK, HERBERT MORTIMER (*Dean*). The history of marriage, Jewish and Christian, in relation to divorce and certain forbidden degrees. Longmans, Green & Co. 12°, $1.75.

MACLAY, EDGAR STANTON. A history of the United States navy from 1775 to 1894; with technical revision by Roy C. Smith. In 2 v. Appleton. il. maps, diagrams, 8°, $7.

MASPERO, G. The dawn of civilization, (Egypt and Chaldæa;) ed. by the Rev. A. H. Sayce; tr. by M. L. McClure. Appleton. 4°, $7.50.
This volume is an attempt to put together in a lucid and interesting manner all that the

monuments have revealed to us concerning the earliest civilization of Egypt and Chaldæa. The results of archæological discovery, accumulated during the last thirty years or so, are of such a vast and comprehensive character that none but a master mind could marshall them in true historical perspective. Prof. Maspero is perhaps the only man in Europe fitted by his laborious researches and great scholarship to undertake such a task, and the result of his effort will be found herein. The period dealt with covers the history of Egypt from the earliest date to the fourteenth dynasty, and that of Chaldæa during its first empire. The book is brought up to the present year, and deals with the recent discoveries of Koptos and Dahabur.

WARNER, BEVERLEY E. English history in Shakespeare's plays. Longmans, Green & Co. 12°, $1.75.

LITERATURE, ESSAYS, MISCELLANEOUS AND COLLECTED WORKS.

BESANT, WALTER, PAYN, JA., RUSSELL, W. CLARK, [*and others.*] My first book ; the experiences of Walter Besant, James Payn, W. Clark Russell, Grant Allen, Hall Caine, G. R. Sims, [*and others ;*] with an introd. by Jerome K. Jerome. 8°, $2.50.

CURTIS, G. W. Literary and social essays. Harper. 12°, $2.50.
Contents: Emerson (1854); Hawthorne (1854); The works of Nathaniel Hawthorne (1864); Rachel (1855); Thackeray in America (1853); Sir Philip Sidney (1857); Longfellow (1882); Oliver Wendell Holmes (1891); Washington Irving (1889).

DICKINSON, EMILY. Letters of Emily Dickinson ; ed. by Mabel Loomis Todd. Roberts. por. il. 16°, $2.

HUXLEY, T. H. Evolution and ethics, and other essays. [V. 9 of "Collected essays."] Appleton. 12°, $1.25.
Contents : Evolution and ethics. Prolegomena [1894] ; Evolution and ethics [1893] ; Science and morals [1886] ; Capital—the mother of labor [1886] ; Social diseases and worse remedies [1891].

JOHNSON, LIONEL. The art of Thomas Hardy, with a por. etched from life by W. Strang, and a bibliography by J. Lane. Dodd, Mead & Co. por. 12°, *net*, $2.

MORTON, W. F., *comp.* Women in epigram : flashes of wit, wisdom, and satire from the world's literature. McClurg. 16°, $1.

POE, EDGAR ALLAN. Works; with an introd. and a memoir, by R. H. Stoddard. *Fordham ed.* A. C. Armstrong & Son. 6 v., pors. pl. fac-similes, 12°, $7.50.

REPPLIER, AGNES. In the dozy hours, and other papers. Houghton, Mifflin & Co. 12°, $1.25.
Contents : In the dozy hours ; A kitten ; At the novelist's table ; In behalf of parents ; Aut Cæsar, aut nihil ; A note on mirrors ; Gifts ; Humor, English and American ; The discomforts of luxury—a speculation ; Lectures ; Reviewers and reviewed ; Pastels — a query ; Guests ; Sympathy ; Opinions ; The children's age ; A forgotten poet ; Dialogues ; A curious contention ; The passing of the essay.

SHAKESPEARE, W. Glossary and index of characters to Shakespeare's works ; comp. from the best authorities. Putnam. por. 24°, 40 c. ; flex. mor., 75 c.

SIMONDS, W. E. An introduction to the study of English fiction. Heath. 12°, $1.
The English novel, as a specific form of art, arose with Richardson and Fielding between the years 1740 and 1750 ; but English fiction dates back to the Jutes, Angles, and Saxons, and their narrative romances in verse and prose. A general résumé is given of these old romances; those of Elizabeth's reign are grouped on a two-page schedule made by date and subject. A list of one hundred novels "which for one reason or another are worth reading " is given, including twenty continental novels. Half of the book is devoted to selections from early fiction, including Beowulf, King Horn, Arcadia, Forbonius, and Prisceria (unabridged), Moll Flanders, Tom Jones, Pamela, Tristram Shandy, etc.

STRACHEY, *Sir* E. Talk at a country house: fact and fiction. Houghton, Mifflin & Co. 12°, $1.25.

MENTAL AND MORAL PHILOSOPHY.

ADAMS, FRANCIS. A child of the age. Roberts. 16°, $1.
A study of the psychological development of a brilliant mind, left wholly uncontrolled by a guiding faith or the slightest regard for the feelings of others. Bertram Leicester tells his own story from his first vague recollections of a neglected childhood through his school and college life, and his final practical fight for a living. Highly intellectual, passionately emotional, dreamily introspective, wholly impulsive, his career works happiness neither for himself nor others.

MORE, PAUL ELMER, *ed.* The great refusal: being letters of a dreamer in Gotham. Houghton, Mifflin & Co. 16°, $1.

SHARMAN, H. RISBOROUGH. The power of the will; or, success. Roberts. 16°, 50 c.
Demonstrates that by cultivating the will, strengthening it by constant and careful exercise, a man may attain the highest success in life that is possible to his natural ability, while with an uncontrolled will no quantity of talents can bring forth desired success. Self-conquest is the law of Christian religion and the root of all lasting success.

NATURE AND SCIENCE.

SHALER, N. S. Sea and land features of coasts and oceans, with special reference to the life of man. Scribner. il. 8°, $2.50.

POETRY.

BROWNING, ROB. Poetical works; *new and complete ed.*, cont. "Asolando ;" with historical notes, to the poems. *Complete definitive ed.* Macmillan. 9 v., 8°, $20.

DE VERE, AUBREY. Selections from the poems of Aubrey De Vere ; ed., with a preface, by G. E. Woodberry. Macmillan. 12°, $1.25.

HAZARD, CAROLINE. Narragansett ballads, with songs and lyrics. Houghton, Mifflin & Co. 16°, $1.

HOSMER, F. L., *and* GANNETT, W. C. The thought of God in hymns and poems. *2d ser.* Roberts Bros. 16°, $1.
The first series was entered in "Weekly Record," P. W., Dec. 17, '85, [726.] The authors are Unitarians. full of the highest poetical conception of the fatherhood of God. There are fifty-seven short poems on every variety of

subjects, thirty-two by F. L. Hosmer, and twenty-five by William C. Gannett.

KENDALL, MAY. Songs from Dreamland. Longmans, Green & Co. 16°, $1.75.

LONGFELLOW, S. Hymns and verses. Houghton, Mifflin & Co. 12°, $1.

MAETERLINCK, MAURICE. Pélléas and Mélisande : a drama in five acts ; tr. by Erving Winslow. Crowell. 16°, $1.

PETERSON, ARTHUR. Penrhyn's pilgrimage. Putnam. 16°, $1.
A journey through Japan and China described in verse.

ROGERS, ROB. CAMERON. The wind in the clearing, and other poems. Putnam. 8°, $1.25.
A collection of short poems, variously entitled " The dancing faun," " The death of Argas," " Destiny," " Barset Wood," " To Violet," " Thackeray's birthday," etc.

SIMONDS, ARTHUR B. American song : a collection of representative American poems ; with analytical and critical studies of the writers ; with introds. and notes. Putnam. 12°, $1.50.

WILLIAMS, ALFRED M. Studies in folk-song and popular poetry : essays. Houghton, Mifflin & Co. 12°, $1.50.

WILSON, ROB. BURNS. Chant of a woodland spirit. Putnam. sq. 12°, pap., $1.
A poem, portions of which originally appeared in *Harper's Monthly* and *The Century Magazine.*

POLITICAL AND SOCIAL.

CURRY, J. L. M. The southern states of the American Union considered in their relations to the constitution of the United States and to the resulting union. Putnam. 12°, $1.25.

McCLUNG, D. W. Money talks: some of the things it says when it speaks. The Rob. Clarke Co. il. 12°, $1.
Discusses the necessity for definitions; notes are not money; money per head; supply and demand; outcry in time of panic; labor neither a credit nor a fiction, but hard cash; the great fall in silver; early attempts to establish a mint, etc., etc.

MARDEN, ORISON SWETT. Pushing to the front; or, success under difficulties: a book of inspiration and encouragement to all who are struggling for self-elevation along the paths of knowledge and of duty. Houghton, Mifflin & Co. pors. 12°, $1.50.
Falls in the same general class with Smiles' " Self-Help " and Dr. Mathews' " Getting on in the world." Such chapter heads as " The man and the opportunity," " Boys and girls with no chance," " An iron will," " Possibilities in spare moments," " Round boys in square holes," " Concentrated energy," " Manners," " Enthusiasm," " The victory in defeat," etc,, give a hint of the practical and helpful nature of the book. Apt and telling anecdotes, which illustrate or enforce the author's statements, are given with marvellous profusion, and serve at once to emphasize the excellent points of the book, and to make it wonderfully readable. Illustrated with twenty-four portraits of eminent persons.

TOWNSEND, C. Forty witnesses to success: talks to young men. A. D. F. Randolph & Co. 12°, 75 c.
Based upon six hundred answers in evidence obtained from forty statesmen, lawyers, merchants, bankers, manufacturers, judges, scientists, and instructors as to the cause of success or failure in life.

SPORTS AND AMUSEMENTS.

BELLAMY, W. A century of charades. Houghton, Mifflin & Co. 16°, $1.
Contains a hundred original charades, the construction of which is exceedingly ingenious.

PORTLAND (*pseud.*) *ed.* The whist table: a treasury of notes on the royal game, by " Cavendish," C. Mossop, A. C. Ewald, and C. Hervey; to which is added solo whist and its rules, by Abraham S. Wilks. Imported by Scribner. pors. 12°, $3.

THEOLOGY, RELIGION AND SPECULATION.

ALLEN, ALEX. V. G. Religious progress. Houghton, Mifflin & Co. 12°, $1.
The author is professor in the Episcopal Theological School in Cambridge, Mass. Contains two lectures. The first deals with religious progress in the experience of the individual ; the second with religious progress in the organic life of the church. As a whole, the book is an eloquent and liberal plea for church unity.

BROOKS, PHILLIPS, (*Bp.*) Essays and addresses: religious, literary, and social; ed. by the Rev. J. Cotton Brooks. Dutton. por. 12°, $2.
The collection of essays and addresses here presented comprises all of which any record at all satisfactory has been preserved of Bishop Brooks' public utterances outside of the pulpit. The chronological sequence has been observed as far as possible as illustrating in an interesting manner the development of his thought.

CLARKE, *Rev.* H. W. A history of tithes. 2d *ed.* Imported by Scribner. 12°, (Social science ser.) $1.
Contents: Introduction ; Before the Christian era ; From the Christian era to the council of Masçon ; The Roman mission to England ; The first documentary statement of tithes in England; Archbishop Egbert's works ; The first public lay-law for the payment of tithes ; King Ethelwulf's alleged grant of tithes ; Tithe laws made by Anglo-Saxon kings ; Origin of our modern parish churches and boundaries ; The laws of Ethelred II.; The first poor law act ; Canons for payment of tithes; Appropriation of tithes to monasteries; Infeudations—exemptions from payment of tithes; Monasteries; Dissolution of monasteries ; Tithes in the city and liberties of London ; The Commutation Act of 1836; Tithes of church in Wales ; Tithe Act—remarks upon the act.

FOUARD, CONSTANT (*Abbé*). Saint Paul and his mission; tr. with the author's sanction and co-operation, by G. F. X. Griffith. Longmans, Green & Co. map, 12°, $2.

HEPWORTH, G. H. Herald sermons. Dutton. por. 12°, $1.
The brief and timely sermons that have been appearing lately upon the editorial page of the Sunday New York *Herald* are here collected in u volume.

LOWELL, PERCIVAL. Occult Japan; or, the way of the gods: an esoteric study of Japanese personality and possession. Houghton, Mifflin & Co. il. 12°, $1.75.
A careful study of the Shinto faith of Japan in its more unfamiliar forms and mysterious usages. It adds not a little to a philosophical explanation of hypnotism, and, indeed, of human consciousness.

Books for the Young.

CHANDLER, *Mrs.* IZORA C. Three of us: Barney, Cossack, Rex; il. by the author. Hunt & Eaton. il. 12°, $2

CHURCH, *Rev.* ALFRED J. Stories from English history from Julius Cæsar to the Black Prince. Macmillan. il. 12°, $1.
Contains the stories of the first and second coming of Julius Cæsar, King Caractacus, Boadicea, Vortigern, King Arthur, King Alfred, How England became Christian, How King Athelstan fought at Brunanburg, The story of King Canute, Harold the Earl, Harold the King, William, Duke of Normandy, William, King of England, Thomas à Becket, King Richard's crusade, Magna Charta, Battle of Bannockburn, The battle of Crécy, How Calais was taken, The great battle of Poitiers.

FENN, G. MANVILLE. First in the field: a story of New South Wales; il. by W. Rainey. Dodd, Mead & Co. 12°, $1.50.
Dominic Braydon was the son of an English doctor, who had immigrated to Australia on account of his health, leaving Dominic in Kent,at school; just as the latter was becoming very much dissatisfied, his father sends for him. Misadventures, including a perilous journey, and the incident which led his brother-in-law to refer to him as " First in the field," are faithfully described in a story of constant action.

FIELD, EUGENE. Love-songs of childhood. Scribner. 16°, $1.
Forty-two poems for children, by the author of " A little book of western verse," etc. Bound in blue with graceful decorations in white on front cover.

MARSHALL, EMMA. Kensington Palace in the days of Queen Mary II.: a story. Macmillan. por. il. 12°, $1.50.
The story opens in 1690, about the time of the battle of the Boyne. Queen Mary II., while awaiting the return of William III. from Ireland, is prevailed upon to accord an audience to Sir Redvers Brooke, who induces her majesty to look upon his daughter Margery as a prospective lady-in-waiting. Besides the interesting incidents of Margery's career at Court, at Kensington Palace, many events of historic interest are given, notably those in which the queen is the central figure. It is claimed that attempt is made to represent this queen in a different light from that in which she is generally seen. The d'Angleterre memories is one of the sources of historic information on which the tale is founded.

MOLESWORTH, *Mrs.* MARY LOUISE, [" Ennis Graham," *pseud.*] My new home ; il. by L. Leslie Brooke. Macmillan. 12°, $1.
The scene opens in the Middlemore Hills ; Helena Wingfield, an orphan, tells in a quaint and irresistible way the story of her life at Windy Gap Cottage, introducing in her narration the incidents that led her grandmother to leave Windy Gap for a finer London residence, and also tells why she ran away from her new home.

STEVENSON, ROB. L. Will o' the mill. Joseph Knight Co. 12°, (Cosy corner ser.) 50 c.
An allegorical story which pictures the life of a lonely boy who lived at an old mill, situated in a remote valley between two high mountains; this lad was fated for years to watch from a distance the passing of many travellers, and finally the mill where he lives is, on account of his adopted father's greed, transformed into an inn ; then the wayfarers are brought into direct touch with him, and his opinions of life are confirmed. His views of death are realized and described in the last chapter.

STUART, RUTH McENERY. The story of Babette, a little Creole girl. Harper. il. 12°, $1.50.

WINCHESTER, M. E., [*pseud.* for M. E. Whatman.] A double cherry : a story. Macmillan. il. 12°, $1.25.
Claude and Roy, " the double cherry," are the sons of a proud aristocrat who has met with reverses and is earning a miserable living as a violinist in London. Claude has talent for drawing and painting, but his father insists on his spending hours learning the violin. After the father's death the boys have a very hard time, but the end is happy.

RECENT FRENCH AND GERMAN BOOKS.

FRENCH.

Arene, P. Domnine............................. $1 00
Babeau, Alb. Le Louvre et son histoire. $3.60 ; pap.. 3 00
Bonnefont. Les chants nationaux de France ... 1 80
Dellesalle. Dictionnaire d'argot............. 2 25
France, Anatole. Le jardin d'épicure............ 1 00
Gaulot, Paul. Henriette Bussenil............... 1 00
Job. Les epics de France....................... 3 00
Le Bon, G. L'équitation actuelle et ses principes. 3 00
Le Faure. Les exploits de Calveloche. ....
Lepelletier. Une femme de cinquante ans...... 1 00
Le Roux. Notes sur la Norvège................. 1 00
Parigot, H. Genie et métier..................... 1 00
Seailles, G. Ernest Renan....:............... 1 00
Uzanne. Contes pour les bibliophiles............ 7 50
— Profils perdus.............................. 4 80
Verne, J. Mirifiques aventures de Mastro Antifer. 3 60

GERMAN.

Bernhardt, M. Die Perle....................... 1 85
Beyrich, K. Stoff und Weltäther.............. 1 00
Buchmann. Geflügelte Worte. *Jubileeed.* 100th thousand. 4 00

Byr, R. Ein Reiterschwert....................... $1 70
Dietrichsen *and* Munthe. Wood architecture of Norway. 220 illus. German text......... 15 00
Ebers. Im Schmiedefeuer. Roman aus dem alten Nürnberg. 2 v........................... 4 00
Eschstruth, N. v. Die Haidehexe.............. 2 00
— Von Gottes gnaden. 2 v................... 4 00
Falb. Ueber Erdbeben, Kintische Tage, Sündfluth, und Eiszeit........................... 2 00
Haensel, Dr. E. Ein Ausflug nach Brasilien und den Pldatastaaten. $1.80 ; pap.............. 1 35
Hesse-Wartegg, E. v. Korea, Land und leute.. 2 50
Jokai, M. Das Affenmädchen............. .... 1 00
Ohnda, Dr. A. Freund Allert. Ein künstlerleben. 400 illus ....:............... 6 70
Schobert, H. Moderne'ehen. Roman. 3 v..... 4 00
Schubin, O. Woher tönt dieser Missklang durch die Welt. Roman. 3 v..................... 4 00
Spielhagen, Fr. Stimme des himmels. 2 v..... 2 65
Stern. Studien zur Literatur der Gegenwart..... 4 20
Sudermann, H. Es war....................... 2 00
Volkelt. Æsthetische Zeitfragen................ 1 85
Wolff, Julius. Das schwarze Weib.............. 2 35

ARTICLES IN DECEMBER AND JANUARY MAGAZINES.

Articles marked with an asterisk are illustrated.

ARTISTIC, MUSICAL AND DRAMATIC.—*Atlantic* (Dec.), Suggestions on Architecture of Schoolhouses, C. H. Walker ; (Jan.), Symphony Illustrated by Beethoven's Fifth in C Minor, Goepp; Meaning of an Eisteddfod, Edith Brower.—*Cath. World* (Jan.), Fra Angelico,* Sarah C. Flint.—*Century* (Dec.), The Holy Family, Picture by Guipon; Adoration of the Shepherds, Picture by Dagnan-Bouveret; Appearance to the Shepherds, Picture by Von Uhde ; (Jan.), Mother and Sleeping Child, Picture by F. H. Tompkins; Govaert Flinck, Cole.—*Chautauquan,* Painters' Art in England, Townsend.—*Cosmopolitan* (Dec.), Relations of Photography to Art,* Breese ; Musical Instruments of the World,* Isaac H. Hall; (Jan.), Theatrical Season in New York,* Metcalfe.—*Lippincott's* (Dec.), Living Pictures at the Louvre, A. N. Sanborn ; (Jan.), Herbert Beerbohm Tree, Gilbert Parker.—*Nine. Century* (Dec.), Music of Japan, Laura A. Smith.—*Outing* (Dec.), The Japanese Theatre,* E. B. Rogers.—*Scribner's* (Dec.), Cast Shadows,* P. G. Hamerton ; George F. Watts,* C. Monkhouse; (Jan.), American Wood-Engravers —Henry Wolf.*—*West. Review* (Nov.), Musical Criticism and Critics, Jacob Bradford; The Stage as an Educator, J. P. Walton.

BIOGRAPHY, CORRESPONDENCE, ETC.—*Century* (Dec.), Francesco Crispi, (Por.), W. J. Stillman. —*Chautauquan* (Jan.), Famous Revivalists of the U. S.—*Lippincott's* (Dec.), Some Notable Women of the Past, Esmè Stuart.—*Popular Science* (Dec.), Zadoc Thompson; (Jan.), Denison Olmsted (Por.).

DESCRIPTION, TRAVEL. — *Atlantic* (Dec.), Venice, S. V. Cole.—*Century* (Jan.), Scenes in Canton,* O'Driscoll ; Armor of old Japan,* M. S. Hunter.—*Chautauquan* (Jan.), Some Historic Landmarks of London, Gennings.— *Harper's* (Dec.), An Arabian Day and Night,* Bigelow ; Time of the Lotus,* Parsons; Show-places of Paris,* Davis ; (Jan.), With the Hounds in France,* Sears; Fujisan,* Parsons.—*Nine. Century* (Nov.). Fruit Ranching (California), Twist. —*Outing* (Jan.), Sledging Picnic in North China,* Alethe L. Craig.—*Scribner's* (Jan.), A Tuscan Shrine,* Edith Wharton.

DOMESTIC AND SOCIAL.—*Chautauquan* (Jan.), Aspects of Social Life in the East End of London, S. Moody.—*Fort. Review* (Nov.), Burning Questions of Japan, Savage-Landor.— *Lippincott's* (Jan.), New Year's Days in Old New York, Fawcett.—*Pop. Science* (Dec.), Economic Theory of Woman's Dress, Dr. T. Veblen.—*Scribner's* (Jan.), Art of Living—Income,* Robert Grant.

EDUCATIONAL.—*Atlantic* (Jan.), Gallia Rediviva, Cohn ; Want of Economy in the Lecture System, Trowbridge.—*Century* (Jan.), Festivals in Amer. Colleges for Women,* Susan G. Walker ; Henrietta E. Hooker; Eliz. E. Boyd, *and others.*—*Fort. Review* (Nov.), True University for London, Crackanthorpe.—*Forum* (Jan.), New Aid to Education; Travelling Libraries, Eastman ; Increasing Cost of Collegiate Education, Thwing.—*North Am. Review* (Dec.), Catholic School System in Rome, Monsignor Satolli.—*Pop. Science* (Dec.), The University as a Scientific Workshop, Paulsen.

FICTION.—*Arena* (Dec.), A Woman in the Camp, Garland ; (Jan.), Drama in Tatters, Harte.—*Atlantic* (Dec.), Christmas Eve and Christmas Day at an Eng. Country House, Strachey ; In Jackson's Administration, Lucy L. Pleasants; Christmas Angel, Harriet L. Bradley;(Jan.), A Singular Life, I., Eliz. S. Phelps; Joint Owners in Spain, Alice Brown; A Village Stradivarius, I., Kate D. Wiggin.—*Cath. World* (Dec.), The Hillwood Christmas Ball, Mrs. M. E. Henry-Ruffin ; A Christmas in Cloudland,* J. J. O'Shea *and others* ; (Jan.), Three Lives Lease, Jane Smiley.—*Century* (Dec.), Christmas Guest, Ruth McE. Stuart ; A Neighbor's Landmark, Sarah O. Jewett ; One Woman's Way, Hibbard; A Walking Delegate, Kipling ; (Jan.), Wanted—A Situation, Harriet Allen ; A Lady of New York,* R. Stewart ; Their Cousin Lethy, R. M. Johnston.—*Chautauquan* (Dec.), Evelyn Moore's Poet. I., Grant Allen ; (Jan.), Story of an Ugly Girl, Miss E. F. Andrews.— *Cosmopolitan* (Dec.), A Parting and a Meeting,* Howells ; On Frenchman's Bay,* Mrs. Burton Harrison; (Jan.), A Three-Stranded Yarn, W. C. Russell.—*Harper's* (Dec.), Paola in Italy,* Gertrude Hall ; The Simpletons, I., Hardy ; People We Pass,* Ralph; The Colonel's Christmas,* Harriet P. Spofford ; Richard and Robin, Grant ; (Jan.), Hearts Insurgent,* II., Hardy ; A War Debt. Jewett ; Princess Aline,* Davis.— *Lippincott's* (Dec.), Mrs. Hallam's Companion, Mrs. M. J. Holmes ; Creed of Manners, E. F. Benson ; (Jan.), Waifs of Fighting Rocks, McIlvaine ; "Mrs. Santa Claus," Marjorie Richardson; Question of Responsibility, Imogen Clark.—*Outing* (Dec.), A Jamestown Romance,* Sara B. Kennedy ; The Captain's Bet,* T. S. Blackwell ; (Jan.), Winning a Christmas Bride,* A. C. Vance ; Bas' Therese,* Jean P. Rudd.— *Overland* (Jan.), Tim Slather's Ride, G. P. Hurst; Relapses of Pap, L. B. Bridgman.— *Scribner's* (Dec.), Matrimonial Tontine Benefit Association,* Grant ; Mantle of Osiris, W. L. Palmer ; Primer of Imaginary Geography,* Brander Matthews ; (Jan.), The Amazing Marriage,I.,George Meredith; Sawney's Deer-Lick,* C. D. Lanier.

HISTORY.—*Cath. World* (Jan.), Gregory the Great and the Barbarian World,* T. J. Shahan. — *Century* (Dec.), Old Maryland Homes and Ways,* J. W. Palmer ; (Jan.), Glimpses of Lincoln in War Time, Brooks.—*Harper's* (Jan.), Fortunes of the Bourbons * Kate M. Rowlands; New York Slave-Traders,* Janvier.—*Lippincott's* (Jan.), Christmas Customs and Superstitions, Eliz. F. Seat.

HYGIENIC AND SANITARY.—*Pop. Science* (Dec.), Athletics for City Girls, Mary T. Bissell ; (Jan.), Twenty - five Years of Preventive Medicine, Mrs. H. M. Plunkett; School-Room Ventilation as an Investment, Knight.

LITERARY.—*Arena* (Dec.), Guy de Maupassant, Tolstoi; (Jan.), Religion of Longfellow's Poetry, Savage.—*Atlantic* (Dec.), Ghosts, Agnes Repplier; New Criticism of Genius, Aline Gorren; Some Personal Reminiscences of Walter Pater, Wm. Sharp; Dr. Holmes, Scudder; (Jan.), The Author of "Quabbin" (Francis H. Underwood), Trowbridge.— *Cath. World* (Jan.), Consecrated Mission of the Printed Word,* Marg. E. Jordan ; Tennyson and Holmes,* S. M. Miller.—*Chautauquan* (Dec.),

Some Contemporary Eng. Novelists, Jeannette L. Gilder. — *Fort. Review* (Nov.), Women's Newspapers, Evelyn March-Phillipps; (Dec.), Robert Louis Stevenson—A Critical Study, Gwynn.—*Forum* (Dec.), Chief Influences on My Career, Philip G. Hamerton; Reading Habits of the English People, Collier; New Story-Tellers and the Doom of Realism, W. R. Thayer; (Jan.), Dickens' Place in Literature, F. Harrison. — *Harper's* (Dec.), Taming of the Shrew,* Comment by Lang; (Jan.), Shakespeare's Americanisms, Lodge. — *Lippincott's* (Jan.), With the Autocrat, F. M. B. ; Socialist Novels, Kaufmann.—*Nine. Century* (Dec.), Decay of Bookselling, Stott.—*North Am. Review* (Dec.), Two Great Authors—Holmes, H. C. Lodge; Froude, Goldwin Smith; (Jan.), What Paul Bourget Thinks of Us, "Mark Twain."—*Overland* (Jan.), Stedman and Some of His British Contemporaries,* Mary J. Reid.—*West. Review* (Nov.), Meredith's Nature Poetry, Revell; A Dominant Note of Some Recent Fiction, Bradfield; (Dec.), Religion and Popular Literature, Hannan.

MEDICAL SCIENCE.—*Cosmopolitan* (Jan.), Pasteur,* Charcot. — *Fort. Review* (Dec.), The Spread of Diphtheria, Robson Roose.—*Pop. Science* (Jan.), Two Lung-Tests, F. L. Oswald.

MENTAL AND MORAL. —*North Am. Review* (Jan.), Concerning Nagging Women, Edson.—*Scribner's* (Jan.), Mental Characteristics of the Japanese, Ladd.

NATURE AND SCIENCE.—*Chautauquan* (Dec.), The World's Debt to Astronomy, Newcomb.—*Pop. Science* (Jan.), Ethics in Natural Law, Janes.

POETRY. — *Arena* (Dec.), Oliver Wendell Holmes, B. W. James; If Christ Should Come To-Day, J. G. Clark.—*Atlantic* (Jan.), Alcyone, Lampman.—*Cath. World* (Dec.), Venite Adoremus, O'Shea.—*Century* (Dec.), The First Word, G. P. Lathrop; How to the Singer Comes the Song, Gilder; (Jan.), To France, Florence E. Coates. — *Harper's* (Dec.), Stops of Various Quills,* Howells ; The Coronal, Annie Fields ; Love and Death, Tadema; (Jan.), The Moth, Z. D. Underhill.—*Lippincott's*, Yule Charm, M. S. Paden; On Christes Day, Susie M. Best.—*Outing* (Jan.), King Skate,* Turner.—*Overland*, Song of the Balboa Sea, Joaquin Miller.—*Scribner's* (Dec.), McAndrew's Hymn,* Kipling; A Modern Sir Galahad, Hannah P. Kimball; An Old Sorrow, Dorothea Lummis; (Jan.), A Forgotten Tale,* Doyle ; The Wanderers, H. P. Spofford.

POLITICAL AND SOCIAL.—*Arena* (Dec.), Wellsprings and Feeders of Immorality, Flower ; Abolition of War, Vrooman; (Jan.), Lust Fostered by Legislation, Flower; America's Shame, Symposium on the Age of Consent Laws, by Powell, Gardener, Willard, *and others*; Sweating System in Philadelphia, Adeline Knapp.—*Atlantic* (Jan.), Survival of the American Type, Denison. — *Chautauquan* (Dec.), Social Life in Eng. in the Nineteenth Century, Ashton ; (Jan.), Triumph of Japan, Arnold. — *Fort. Review* (Nov.), China, Japan, and Corea, Gundry.—*Forum* (Dec.), Death of the Czar and the Peace of Europe, Dodge ; Status and Future of the Woman-Suffrage Movement, Mary P. Jacobi ; Charity that Helps and Other Charity, Jane E. Robbins ; (Jan.), Are Our Moral Standards Shifting ?, Hart; Report of the Strike Commis-

sion, H. P. Robinson ; Dangers in Our Presidential Election System, Schouler; Anatomy of a Tenement Street, Sanborn.—*Harper's* (Dec.), Evolution of the Country Club,* Whitney.—*Nine. Century* (Nov.), People's Kitchens in Vienna, Edith Sellers. — *North Am. Review* (Dec.), Brigandage on Our Railroads, Hampton; How the Czar's Death Affects Europe, Stepniak; Meaning of the Elections, Babcock, Faulkner ; (Jan.), Problems Before the Western Farmer, Gov. of Kansas; Young Czar and His Advisers, C. Emory Smith; Our Trade with China, W. C. Ford.—*Outing* (Dec.), National Guard of N. Y. State,* Hardin ; *Overland* (Jan.), Evolution in Shipping and Ship-Building on the Pacific Coast,* I. M. Scott *and others*; Naval Control of Pacific Ocean,* Manson.—*Scribner's* (Jan.), Beginnings of Amer. Parties,* Noah Brooks.

SPORTS AND AMUSEMENTS.—*Lippincott's* (Jan.), Ducks of the Chesapeake, C. D. Wilson.—*Outing* (Dec.), Football in the South,* Miles; (Jan.), Two Tries for Turkey,* Sandys.

THEOLOGY, RELIGION, AND SPECULATION.—*Arena* (Dec.), Real Significance of the World's Parliament of Religions, Müller.—*Cath. World* (Jan.), Humanism of Peter, Mullaney.—*Chautauquan* (Dec.), A Christmas Meditation, Vincent.—*Cosmopolitan* (Jan.), The Young Man and the Church, E. W. Bok.—*Forum* (Jan.), The Labor Church, J. Trevor.—*Nine. Century* (Dec.), Why I Am Not an Agnostic, Müller.—*North Am. Review* (Dec.), The Salvation Army, Briggs. —*Scribner's* (Jan.), Salvation Army Work in the Slums, Maud B. Booth.

Freshest News.

HOUGHTON, MIFFLIN & Co. have books of great interest and literary importance in Horace Scudder's "Childhood in Literature and Art ;" Sir Edward Strachey's "Talk at a Country House ;" Rev. Dr. W. B. Wright's "Master and Men," a thoughtful book, contrasting current Christianity with that of Christ ; "Life and Letters of John Greenleaf Whittier ;" "Life, Letters, and Diary of Lucy Larcom ;" "Autobiography of Frances Power Cobbe ;" "Life and Letters of Maria Edgeworth ;" "Familiar Letters of Thoreau ;" "Familiar Letters of Walter Scott ;" and "Pushing to the Front," by Orison Swett Marden, with portraits of famous persons. Few styles of reading are of greater educational value than good biographies of epoch-making people.

LONGMANS, GREEN & Co. have just issued some very important books. "Memorials of St. James' Palace," by Edgar Sheppard, is in two volumes, with eight copper plates, thirty-three full-page plates, and thirty-four illustrations in the text ; "History of the Commonwealth and Protectorate, 1649–1660," by Samuel Rawson Gardiner, of which volume I is now ready, shows all the learning and accuracy of its author, and is made valuable by fourteen fine maps ; "English History in Shakespeare's Plays," by Beverley E. Warren, has remarkable chronologies, and a fine bibliography and well-made index ; and "From Edinburgh to the Antarctic," by W. G. Burn Murdoch, introduces readers to places known only to few travellers, and makes its varied information valuable with many illustrations and maps.

ROBERTS BROTHERS have just issued "Life and Adventures of John Gladwyn Jebb," by his widow, with an introduction by Rider Haggard, which is fully noticed elsewhere; volume IV. of the "History of the People of Israel," by Ernest Renan, is ready, and "The Woman Who Did," by Grant Allen, and "Prince Zaleski," by M. P. Shiel, have just been added to the *Key-Note Series.* "Discords," by George Egerton, also in that series, is a book it needs experience and knowledge of life to rightly understand, but a book full of vitality, thought and rare feeling. Among the more recent books of Roberts Brothers are: "As a Matter of Course," by Anna Payson Call; a third edition of "The World Beautiful," by Lilian Whiting; "Ballads in Prose," by Nora Hopper; and "The Great God Pan and the Inmost Light," by Arthur Machen.

D. APPLETON & CO. have just ready "The Land of the Sun," by Christian Reid, a picturesque travel romance, in which the author takes her characters from New Orleans to fascinating Mexican cities like Guanajuato, Zacatecas, Aguas Calientes, Guadalajara, and of course the City of Mexico. "The Presidents of the United States," made up of contributions by John Fiske, Carl Schurz, William E. Russell, Daniel C. Gilman, Robert C. Winthrop, George Bancroft, John Hay, and others, edited by James Grant Wilson, with twenty-three steel portraits, fac-simile letters, and other illustrations; "Appleton's Handbook of Winter Resorts" is again revised up to date, and there are several new novels whose authors and titles

promise great things. "Vernon's Aunt," by Sara Jeannette Duncan (now Mrs. Everard Cotes), is an East Indian romance, full of irresistible fun; "Dust and Laurels," by Mary L. Pendered, is a fine study in nineteenth century womanhood; and "The Justification of Andrew Lebrun," by Frank Barrett, and "At the Gate of Samaria," by William J. Locke, may be highly recommended.

G. P. PUTNAM'S SONS have in preparation a valuable and representative work by J. J. Jusserand, entitled "A Literary History of the English People," from the earliest times to the present date. The work will be completed in three volumes, of which the first volume, covering from the "Earliest Times to the Renaissance," is now ready. The author of "Piers Plowman, 1363-1399," of "English Wayfaring Life in the 14th Century," and many other erudite studies in literary subjects is eminently fitted for his new undertaking. "The Story of Vedic India," by Z. A. Ragozin, is the new volume in *The Story of the Nation Series;* and "Prince Henry (the navigator) of Portugal" is the latest addition to *The Heroes of the Nations Series.* Volume III. of H. D. Traill's great work on "Social Life in England" is nearly ready, and the Putnams are also bringing out an edition of Le Gallienne's "The Book-Bills of Narcissus." The new forthcoming novels are: "The Doctor, His Wife and the Clock," by Anna Katharine Green, to be issued in the *Autonym Library;* and "A Woman of Impulse," by Justin Huntly McCarthy, the new volume in the *Hudson Library.*

NEW BOOKS.

A Literary History of the English People,

From the Earliest Times to the Present Date. By J. J. JUSSERAND, author of "English Wayfaring Life in the 14th Century," etc. To be complete in 3 vols. Part I. From the Origins to the Renaissance. 8vo, $3.50.

The Story of Vedic India.

By Z. A. RAGOZIN, author of "The Story of Chaldea," etc., etc. Being No. XLIV. in the "Story of the Nations" Series. Fully illustrated. 12mo, cloth, $1.50; half leather, gilt tops, $1.75.

The Doctor, His Wife and the Clock.

By ANNA KATHARINE GREEN, author of "The Leavenworth Case." Being No. 3 in the Autonym Library. Oblong 24mo, cloth, 50 c.

A Woman of Impulse.

By JUSTIN HUNTLY McCARTHY. Being No. 4 of the Hudson Library. 12mo, cloth, $1.00; paper, 50 cents.

Prince Henry (the navigator)

Of Portugal, and the Age of Discovery in Europe. By C. R. BEAZLEY, M.A., Fellow of Merton College, Oxford. Being No. 12 in the "Heroes of the Nations" Series. 12mo, cloth, $1.50; half leather, gilt tops, $1.75.

Very fully illustrated with reproductions of contemporary prints, and of many maps, coast charts, and mappemondes, illustrating the progress of geographical discovery in Europe.

The Book-Bills of Narcissus.

By RICHARD LE GALLIENNE, author of "The Religion of a Literary Man," etc. 12mo, cloth, $1.00.

Social Life in England.

A Record of the Progress of the People in Religion, Laws, Learning, Arts, Science, Literature, Industry, Commerce, and Manners, from the Earliest Times to the Present Day. By Various Writers. Edited by H. D. TRAILL, D.C.L., Sometime Fellow of St. John's College, Oxford. To be completed in six volumes. Per vol., $3.50. (Vol. III. *nearly ready.*)

Descriptive prospectuses of the "Story of the Nations" and the "Heroes of the Nations," and quarterly "Notes," giving full descriptions of the season's publications, sent on application.

G. P. PUTNAM'S SONS, New York and London.

LITERARY NEWS

AN ECLECTIC REVIEW OF
CURRENT LITERATURE
~ILLUSTRATED~

CONTENTS.

VOL-XVI-N°2   FEBRUARY~1895 $1.00 YEARLY   10 cts. PER NO.

~PUBLICATION OFFICE~
· 28 ELM STREET NEW YORK·
ENTERED AT THE POST OFFICE AT NEW YORK AS SECOND CLASS MATTER

The Literary News

In winter you may reade them, ad ignem, by the fireside; and in summer, ad umbram, under some shadie tree; and therewith pass away the tedious howres.

VOL. XVI.   FEBRUARY, 1895.   No. 2

The Land of the Sun.

WE close this book uncertain whether to review it as fiction or as a record of travel. Suppose we try it first as a novel. In that case we cannot say that it is an unmixed success.

descend to the level of figures to justify herself in the eyes of Philistines, but she writes lovingly and as one thoroughly saturated with an admiration for all things Mexican. Did we

From "Land of the Sun."   Copyright, 1894, by D. Appleton & Co.

LA VIGA CANAL.

The plot is of the simplest, and of the unexpected there is not a trace. . . .

But there is another and a far more successful side. As a record of what is to be seen in Mexico it is not only very interesting, but it is told in a charmingly picturesque way. The author sets out with the determination to admire everything she sees, and to write lovingly of the people, and she carries out her determination unflinchingly. She say that she sees everything through rose-colored glasses, but imperfectly expresses her unmeasured admiration. We can recall no such undiscriminating enthusiasm in late books of travel, and Mrs. Tiernan's statements—pleasant reading though they make—would have greater weight if they showed a more judicial spirit. There is nothing statistical in her fervor and she does not

say all things? We must make a single exception—her dislike of the government occasionally shows itself and in bitter words, but it is not too much to say that her views of Mexican politics are unlikely to meet with the assent of the majority of her American readers. The defeat of Maximilian has passed into history as an example of retributive justice, and no mere sentimental regret for his fate and that of Carlotta is likely to reverse the judgment which the world has passed upon his attempt to found a throne in an American republic. But the book is a delightful one if we decline to look upon it as a novel and exclude the few political allusions, for she describes Mexico in such glowing colors that it makes one long to see it—as she saw it. The illustrations are a score of good half-tones. (Appleton. $1.75.)—*Public Opinion.*

Harvard College by an Oxonian.

HARVARD men will be interested to hear what so distinguished an Oxonian as Dr. Hill has to say of the University by the Charles, although his book is meant, of course, primarily for the instruction of those who have never seen Harvard. Dr. Hill spent several months in Cambridge, and he writes, not from the confused impressions of a chance traveller, but out of an ample fund of knowledge. Indeed, his comprehension of the peculiar merits, as well as the peculiar faults of Harvard, is remarkably subtile and acute. He gives a brief but entertaining account of its origin, history, and growth, from which his English readers will be able to correct some of the false impressions which have gained ground about our institutions of learning. He compares it most intelligently with Oxford, and points out, with scrupulous fairness, where it is superior to the older university as well as where it is inferior. The praise he bestows will make the hearts of Harvard men glow with pride ; and they will have to acknowledge, with regret, that the unfavorable criticisms are equally well deserved. In fact, Dr. Hill's book is an unconscious witness to the desirability of the changes proposed by the late Frank Bolles, secretary to the University—changes which, we understand, President Eliot in his infinite wisdom does not altogether approve. One or two small errors of fact in the volume might be cited were it worth while. For example, it is hard to believe that the function of " afternoon tea " is unknown in Cambridge. (Macmillan. $2.25.)—*Providence Sunday Journal.*

At the Gate of Samaria.

ANOTHER of the army of emancipated women, a hater of conventional formulas, a restless seeker after the mysteries of life, appears in the heroine of "At the Gate of Samaria," by W. J. Locke. While still young, Clytie Davenant wearied of her English country home, " Durdleham, with its soullessness, its stagnation, its prim formulas." She had artistic tastes, and yielded to the temptation to smuggle condemned books into the house and to read them surreptitiously. It was not unnatural that such a type of the young, fearless womanhood of the day should acquire the habit of holding her head back, with the chin pointing upward, free of the throat, for the attitude emphasizes the girl's determination to solve the " riddle of life " in her own way. It was just as natural, too, that at last she should break the chains which bound her to Durdleham and seek freedom from its stiff conventionalities in the art life of London. Her fate was the usual one which men seem prone to inflict upon the emancipated woman in fiction. If she had not met Hammerdike, who appealed to the romantic and imaginative side of her nature, but who was at heart an utterly worthless fellow, of abundant physical prowess, but devoid alike of moral courage and of character. a less dramatic, not to say tragic, result might have attended the girl's attempt to solve the mystery of life. Her experience was indeed sad and bitter, both as a wife and as a mother. The story is told with ease and fluency. The name on the title cannot conceal the sex of the author. (Appleton. $1; pap., 50 c.)—*The Tribune.*

THE CAMPUS.

Henry the Navigator.

THIS volume, by C. Raymond Beazley, aims at giving an account, based throughout upon original sources, of the progress of geographical knowledge and enterprise in Christendom throughout the Middle Ages, down to the middle or even the end of the fifteenth century, as well as a life of Prince Henry the Navigator, who brought this movement of European Expansion within sight of its greatest successes. That is, as explained in Chapter I., it has been attempted to treat exploration as one continuous thread in the story of Christian Europe from the time of the conversion of the Empire ; and to treat the life of Prince Henry as the turning-point, the central epoch in a development of many centuries : this life, accordingly, has been linked as closely as possible with what went before and prepared for it ; one-third of the text, at least, has been occupied with the history of the preparation of the earlier time, and the difference between our account of the eleventh and fifteenth century discovery, for instance, will be found to be chiefly one of less and greater detail. This difference depends, of course, on the prominence in the later time of a figure of extraordinary interest and force, who is the true hero in the drama of the geographical conquest of the outer world that starts from Western Christendom. The interest that centres round Henry is somewhat clouded by the dearth of complete knowledge of his life ; but enough remains to make something of the picture of a hero, both of science and of action.

Our subject, then, has been strictly historical, but a history in which a certain life, a certain biographical centre, becomes more and more important, till from its completed achievement we get our best outlook upon the past progress of a thousand years, on this side, and upon the future progress of those generation, which realized the next great victories of the geographical advance.

From "Henry the Navigator."   Copyright, 1894, by G. P. Putnam's Sons.

GATEWAY AT BELEM.

The series of maps which illustrate this account give the same continuous view of the geographical development of Europe and Christendom down to the end of Prince Henry's age. These are, it is believed, the first English reproductions in any accessible form of several of the great charts of the Middle Ages, and taken together they will give, it is hoped, the best view of Western or Christian map-making before the time of Columbus that is to be found in any English book, outside the great historical atlases. Covers from Middle Ages to the Modern World. (Putnam. $1.50.)—*Extract from Preface.*

American Charities.

WE have been reading an intensely interesting book, entitled "American Charities ; a Study in Philanthropy and Economics." Its author, Amos G. Warner, Ph.D., is a professor in the Leland Stanford University, California. Mr. Warner has done his work with great pains and caution. He is not to be reckoned a radical, and he seems to have no special hobby. On the contrary, he treats his subject in a quiet and scientific manner, and gives us the impression that he is an entirely safe man to follow. He begins his essay by a few general statements as to the way in which poverty has been regarded in times past, and shows that among most of the enlightened heathen nations the subject was seriously discussed and measures taken to prevent or to remedy the evil. He then proceeds to a consideration of the causes which produce poverty, and in this part of his subject he is specially interesting. His theory is not single headed, but Hydra headed, so to speak. That is to say, he doesn't tell us that over production or low wages are the sole cause of poverty, but furnishes us with a long catalogue of the causes that have combined to create a very deplorable condition of affairs, such as heredity, environment, intoxicants, sickness, accidents which maim and disable. Best of all, he is rather optimistic, and gives us hope that in the course of a few thousand years we may reach such a social development that extreme poverty at least will be done away with, and the sufferings of the poor be reduced to a minimum.

Here, for instance, is a tabulated statement which is very suggestive. The author says that it is a very interesting puzzle to find out how many, or what proportion of those people who seek for relief are really worthy of it, and this estimate, made by sifting about thirty thousand cases, is certainly very encouraging. Of these thirty thousand persons, such as we would find in the average city, a little over ten per cent. are regarded as worthy of continuous relief. Something over twenty-six per cent. are worthy of temporary relief—a little help now and then to bridge over the expense of a sickness or a funeral. The most encouraging statement is that more than forty per cent. need work rather than relief, and would not ask for help if they could get steady labor. That percentage will, we believe, hold good throughout the country. Give the people plenty to do, at even decent wages, and, barring accidents or any unexpected emergencies, they have self-respect enough to live within their incomes, and too much pride to ask for assistance from any charitable organization.

This may seem to some of our readers too optimistic a view to take of the situation, but we think not. Professor Warner's volume will bear out the statement. Last of all, we come to those who are regarded as wholly unworthy of relief, the creatures who make a profession of begging and take their chances on the sidewalk or at the basement door. Unfortunately, the number of these is quite large, and we are furnished with a warning that indiscriminate giving does not accomplish much good. Twenty-three per cent. nearly of our thirty thousand, or considerably over six thousand, are accounted unworthy after careful investigation. These figures will probably represent the general average of good and bad cases in all the large cities of America.

Professor Warner's chapter on the causes of degeneration, or the reasons why poverty is a necessity under our present social regime, is a calm, judicial and eminently satisfactory discussion of the subject. He believes, as does every one who has paid any attention to this serious matter, that greed and selfishness, or, in a word, that society is itself responsible for a tremendous amount of the crime which we are compelled to punish, and the poverty which we must needs relieve.

There are also chapters on the almshouse, on the homeless poor, on dependent children, on the destitute sick, on the insane and the feeble minded, who are the wards of the community, and these are very grave chapters, suggestive, and with an element of tragedy running through them which will appeal to every thoughtful man. The book is thoroughly practical, and it ought to be read carefully, even studied, by every one who has a home of his own to maintain and who feels a certain degree of responsibility for the condition of the unfortunate who are in his neighborhood. (Crowell. $1.75)—*N. Y. Herald.*

Wealth Against Commonwealth.

THIS is a history, by Henry Demarest Lloyd, of the origin and growth of the richest monopoly in the world, the combination known as the Standard Oil Trust.

More than sixty years ago it was known that illuminating oil of an excellent quality could be extracted from bituminous coal; and in 1860 there were more than threescore manufactories of it in this country. In that year it was first discovered that vast deposits of rock-oil lie under the soil of Pennsylvania and adjoining States. Throughout wide districts, wherein wells were driven, the oil flowed like water. The cost was almost nothing, and in ten years the native product could be bought in any quantity for ten cents a barrel. Thousands of men at once learned the simple business of distilling it for use, and refineries sprang up everywhere.

It seemed that no department of human activity offered less encouragement to the spirit of monopoly than the production, refinement, and distribution of this natural oil. Yet hardly five years passed, after the value of the great discovery became known, before a mysterious power was felt to interfere with the business in every branch, from the sinking of new wells to the final distribution of oil among consumers. The refiners were the first to suffer. Those who paid the standard prices announced by the railroads for transportation found themselves undersold. Their business became unprofitable. Many were compelled either to close their works or to sell them at nominal prices to a combination, the only purchaser. This little group of refiners, whose home was Cleveland, were masters of every important line of railway by which oil could be carried from the wells to the refineries, and thence to the several great markets. They had secret contracts with these roads, entitling them to enormous preferences in rates, and even to a large bonus out of the higher rates charged to other shippers. Courts and legislatures, the men and committees of Congress, were appealed to, investigations were held, every engine which public opinion or the business interests of the independent refiner could command was tried in attacking these discriminations. But the result was everywhere the same. The business of refining oil became and remains practically a complete monopoly in the hands of the Standard Oil Company.

Some of the men who conceived the combination in question are now, by virtue of this monopoly which they have organized, princes among the millionaires of the world, with estates

From "England in the Nineteenth Century."　Copyright, 1894, by A. C. McClurg & Co.

ALBERT EDWARD, THE PRINCE CONSORT.

already equal to the proudest dukedom of England, and with incomes larger than those of many kings. It is the magnificence of this success which impresses the imagination of him who reads their exploits. The robber knights of Europe took their lives in their hands when they sallied forth in pursuit of plunder, and deeds of strength and daring, inspiring, the novelist and the poet, divert the thoughts of readers from the outrageous wrongs they perpetuated and the frightful misery they inflicted. In a somewhat similar manner readers of the story of the great monopoly may for a time forget the injustice and oppression, the defiance of law, and the contempt for the rights which the law is designed to protect, which have marked its whole career. They may even, for a time, be stirred to admiration of the ingenious devices, the persistent and vigorous pursuit of a fixed policy, the unremitting devotion of a number of conspirators to the interests of all, which have overcome the obstacles of law, morality, and public opinion, as well as those of ordinary competition, and secured to a handful of men the enjoyment and profit of one of nature's greatest gifts to mankind, almost as conclusively as if it were their creation. With this in view, it may be said that no more wonderful romance of real life has ever been written than Mr. Lloyd's book. (Harper. $2.50.)

Napoleon.

THE origin of the present sketch is not clear. Dumas seems to have written first a drama, and then a life in the more technical sense. The translator is right in putting the date of the latter at an earlier year than 1868, where it is placed by Mr. Percy Fitzgerald.

The sketch itself has no special importance, save as all writings about Napoleon have importance when his life and character are taken up for fresh study and delineation. It is not certain that we are getting out of the present interest much that is truly philosophical and comprehensive in regard to this man, judgments upon whom differ so widely. The details of his life will be much better known, but it is doubtful whether the man will be. There is here a chance for some clear mind to do a great work. Perhaps the present interest will hasten the day.

We are grateful to Mr. Larner for yielding to the solicitations of his friends and giving us this translation, also for the close adherence to the original. It is a highly descriptive, nervous, brisk narrative. The translator has done his work well. (Putnam. $1.50.)—*Public Opinion.*

In the Heart of the Bitter-Root Mountains.

HIGH on the western slope of the Bitter-Root Mountains of eastern Idaho, hundreds of miniature streams dash their foaming waters fresh from fields of perpetual snow into four main forks which form the headwaters of the Clearwater River. Skirting the bases of lofty mountains, surging against the naked faces of projecting cliffs, leaping over precipices, and ever and anon struggling with innumerable boulders planted firmly in their beds, the roaring forks of the Clearwater River follow their sinuous courses westward. Scores of creeks and branches, draining a territory thousands of square miles in area, add constantly to their volume. These tributaries have for ages been eroding the solid granite. Deep gulches and cañons have been formed, many miles in extent, converting the whole region into a wild, tangled mass of irregular mountain ranges and spurs, whose ragged crests and peaks tower to altitudes of four to eight thousand feet above the sea. The less precipitous slopes are cov-

From Green's "Illustrated Short History of the English People"　　Harper & Bros.

THE "BELLEROPHON" (SHIP WHICH CARRIED NAPOLEON TO ST. HELENA).

ered with a dense growth of pine, fir, cedar and tamarack, while many steep hillsides with northern exposures have impenetrable thickets of pine and fir saplings. Occasionally, large rockbound areas are found, covered with moose-brush, and here and there, sometimes clinging to almost vertical hillsides and often occupying the tiny flats nestling by the sides of the tortuous water-courses, are dense patches of brush, yielding in their season a profusion of berries.

Iola, the Senator's Daughter.

MANNERS change, men do not, or, as Thackeray expressed it, "human nature is pretty much the same in Regent Street as in the Via Sacra." In "Iola" the author, Mansfield Lovell Hillhouse, presents a picture of business classes in Rome some nineteen centuries ago, and Publius Neuvanus is the successful merchant. Neuvanus has been first a soldier under Julius Cæsar, but has known how to unite

From " In the Heart of the Bitter-Root Mountains."   Copyright, 1895, by G. P. Putnam's Sons.
FROM THE RIDGE NORTH OF CAMP.

This veritable wilderness, whose forests abound in game, and whose streams teem with trout, covers an area equal to that of the State of West Virginia. It can boast of not having a single permanent habitation of man, not even a wagon road. The story of the "Carlin Hunting Party" who sought their pleasure in these regions from September to December, 1893, is told by an enthusiast who hides under the name of Heclawa. All the illustrations in this work will be found to be accurate and reliable, having been reproduced directly from photographs. The Indians were, of course, the original explorers of this wild region, and there are, in the more accessible localities, unmistakable evidences of their early presence. They may have had permanent villages, but the rigorous climate and the excessive snowfall to which the district is subject during the winter months probably drove them out of the mountains at that season. (Putnam. $1.50.)

fighting and trading. While his comrade Brusco has been subjected to all the buffets of fortune, Neuvanus has been the lucky man.

Iola is the daughter of Neuvanus and has been bred in luxury. Mr. Hillhouse describes in an elaborate manner Roman interiors, and in the course of his study we have Virgil and Horace in the Forum, a banquet, the baths, the chariot race, and many other episodes. Iola is loved by the gentle youth Horus Marcius, and Horus represents a literary Roman. After many vicissitudes of fortune, Iola and Horus are happy.

The current of the story runs smoothly, and the writer of this classical romance has good descriptive powers. There is, however, this misfortune about the classical antiquarian romance. It is a ground which has been almost exhausted by the prolific Ebers. The ways and manners of the Roman, minutely described by the indefatigable Mommsen, have little that is novel to-day. If, however, you incline too much to the romantic incidents in a novel of 1900 years ago you lose the classical feeling ; or if, on the contrary, you go in too strongly for Roman or Greek antiquities, you are not in touch with human passion. Notwithstanding these drawbacks, "Iola" is a well-written book, replete with erudition and of decided interest. (Putnam. $1.25.)—*N. Y. Times.*

The Presidents of the United States.

WE have Macaulay's authority for the presumption that a biographer is usually a literary vassal, bound by the immemorial law of his tenure to render homage and to allow the customary services to his lord, but while the estimates made by the different biographers in the book before us may in some instances be open to criticism as being founded on excessive admiration of the subject to the exclusion of carefully exercised judgment, as a rule there is a gratifying absence of undiscriminating panegyric. Such writers as Bancroft, Fiske, Schurz, Gilman, and Winthrop—so well equipped by nature and education for their tasks—are unlikely to commit gross errors in this direction. The purpose for which much of the matter was prepared—for Appleton's Cyclopædia of American Biography—necessarily imposed economy of space, condensation of details of action and entire absence of anecdote. Consequently that sort of interest which is aroused by minute personal description and picturesque elaboration will not be excited by a perusal of this volume

But the instruction to be derived from twenty-three papers, the work of nineteen writers, whose names are familiar from connection with historical researches, is invaluable. If no history can give us the whole truth, surely the lives of the twenty-three Presidents of the United States by so many hands, approaches very nearly to an accurate, connected and complete narrative of the events of the past hundred

LINCOLN'S FIRST HOME.

years, for of these they were a part. A few instances of apparent partisan inaccuracy occur to us, but usually a disposition to weigh evidence carefully and to set down conclusions fairly is obvious. The biographers of General Harrison and Mr. Cleveland—well as they have done their work—are unavoidably weighed down by the consciousness that they are writing of men who are still with us. It seems to be—it must of necessity be—that no biography of a living person can have proper weight, for there is a certain degree of dispassion which is supposed to be unattainable by the author if he is on familiar terms with him of whom he writes, an over-estimation is usually apparent in the result of his labors. On the other hand; if it be the work of one who has no personal acquaintance with the subject of his story, he commonly errs through lack of proper material.

From what we have said as to the necessary exercise of the art of compression, it may be inferred that the book is a mere mass of dates, figures and facts put together as compactly as possible. On the contrary, it makes most interesting reading, not to the historical student alone, but to the intelligent non-specialist reader also, and if narrative is sometimes manipulated into conformity with a purely partisan point of view, these are but spots upon the sun. If the worse is sometimes made to appear the better cause, we must place it to the account of poor, weak human nature and be grateful that we at least are above the passions and weaknesses that flesh and spirit are heir to.

The volume is a handsome one of 526 pages, neatly printed and bound tastefully. The illustrations are numerous and good—the twenty-three steel portraits are unexceptionable. (Appleton. $3.50.)—*Public Opinion.*

The Flower of Gala Water.

"THE Flower of Gala Water" is one of Mrs. Barr's most delightful novels of Scottish life and scenery. In her portrayal of Scotch character and manners she has no superior among contemporary writers. Her heroines are vital with love and feminine qualities, and possess an individuality which is charming. They have the freshness of youth and health, and impart to her pages their own attractiveness. Mrs. Barr's fine sentiment and vigor of conviction have ample expression in her latest novel. No one can read it without having every noble feeling vitalized and exalted. It is this moral quality which renders "The Flower of Gala Water" a book to be placed in the hands of every boy and every girl. (Bonner. $1.25 ; pap., 50 c.)

Love in Idleness.

MR. MARION CRAWFORD is one of the most versatile of living novelists. One is never sure what to expect from him, and that alone conduces to his wide popularity. The American in him is becoming more pronounced than the Roman-American ; and there are fewer excursions to lonely English parishes, Munich byways, and mysterious Bohemian castles. "Love in Idleness" is a pretty little love-story : pretty in its setting, in its sentiment, in its style, and, I

finds his highest achievement in " To Leeward " and " A Roman Singer." (Macmillan. $2.) *The Beacon.*

The Colonial Cavalier.

A DELIGHTFUL sketch of the Colonial Cavalier in his home, church, state, and social relations. We are made acquainted with the whole man ; we go with him through his love-story and we see him as a husband ; his trade, his friends,

From "The Flower of Gala Water."　　　Copyright, 1894, by Robert Bonner's Sons.

IN THE CONSERVATORY.

may add, in its "get-up." Its *format*, indeed, is delightful : in size, shape, flexibility, as well as in its type and binding, no better pocket volume is on the market. The scene of the story is a much-frequented seaside resort, not far from New York ; the chief *dramatis personæ* are Fanny Trehearne and Louis Lawrence. There is also a dangerous but unsuccessful rival ; and three ladies rather relentlessly depicted as ludicrous old maids, whereas they are simply thwarted in their true vocation. The narrative is occupied with the peculiar form of flirtatiousness affected by the heroine. Those who think "A Cigarette Maker's Romance" one of his best books, will rank "Love in Idleness" even higher than do those who, like the present writer,

his foes, his amusements, his dress, are vividly brought into view. This little book of three hundred pages has condensed into most charming and interesting form a whole library of historical information. The reader feels that he is looking at a picture whose values are preserved, and into which nothing has been worked to produce effects, nor omitted for the sake of prettiness. The historical student will perhaps object that Mrs. Goodwin has not by some method identified her authorities, but the general reader will thank her for giving him a book which reveals in all his charm, with his vices and his virtues that too little known gentleman, "The Colonial Cavalier." (Lovell, Coryell & Co. $1.)—*The Outlook.*

HALL CAINE.

Talk at a Country House.

SIR EDWARD S. STRACHEY, Bart., who dedicates this book to his children, is represented in the frontispiece, taken from a painting by one Henry Strachey, as a benignant-looking old gentleman, with a pointed white beard, standing in a wainscoted hall. Portraits of his ancestors, by Lely, perhaps, look down upon him, and a sagacious cat watches him from a respectful distance. He wears spectacles, and leans on a stout walking-stick ; on his head is a soft felt hat with a narrow brim and high crown, and his black frock-coat is loose and ancient. He holds in one hand a copy of a periodical, which we take to be the London *Athenæum*, as its page is too large for *Notes and Queries.*

Sir Edward's talks in a country house consist of conversations in Somersetshire between a country squire and one Foster, whose vague personality, the reader at first infers, thinly veils the identity of Sir Edward, until he presently discerns that the venerable author is also the squire. Both halves of Sir Edward's ego are great readers and prodigious talkers, and their range of subjects is large and varied.

Ancient England and the literary quality of "Love's Labour's Lost ;" the comparative merit of the two forms of Berowne and Biron ; Ben Jonson and Persian poetry ; the Strachey family, and its old portraits ; English politics, love, and marriage ; Tennyson's poetry and his friendship with Maurice ; Camelot and the Round Table, and the arrowheaded inscriptions are only a few of the main topics, the discussion of which suggests many others. It seems that one of the chapters, the first, appeared as a magazine article in Fraser's about half a century ago ; and Sir Edward has been a contributor to the *Atlantic Monthly* in recent years. His little book belongs to the same order of literature as the pleasant ramblings on beaten tracks and in the by-ways of Isaac Disraeli. Such books are hardly in fashion nowadays, but they are more congenial companions for the leisure moments of cultivated folks than many that are popular. (Houghton, Mifflin & Co. $1.25.)—*N. Y. Times.*

Dawn of Civilization.

IN a quarto volume of nearly 800 pages appears an English version of the great work by Prof. G. Maspero, entitled "The Dawn of Civilization ; Egypt and Chaldea." The book has been translated by Mr. M. L. McClure, a member of the committee of the Egyptian Exploration Fund, and is edited by Mr. A. H. Sayce, the well-known Professor of Assyriology at Oxford. The reader scarcely needs to be reminded that Prof. Maspero's intimate acquaintance with Egypt and its literature, and the opportunities of discovery afforded him by his position for several years as the director of the Bulak Museum, give him a unique claim to speak with authority on the history of the Nile

Valley. In the case of Babylonia and Assyria, on the other hand, he no longer speaks at first hand, but he has thoroughly studied the latest and best authorities on the subject, and has weighed their statements with the judgment which comes from an exhaustive acquaintance with a similar department of knowledge. Mr. Sayce, however, dissents from his views regarding two points, which are of considerable importance. These are the geographical situation of the land of Magan, which most Assyriologists concur in placing in the immediate vicinity of Egypt, and the historical character of the annals of Sargon of Accad, which Prof. Maspero seems inclined to regard as legendary. (Appleton. $7 50.)—*The Sun.*

History of Art in Primitive Greece—Mycenæan Art.

WE find on our table a very delightful work, entitled "History of Art in Primitive Greece—Mycenæan Art." It is from the French of Georges Parrot and Charles Chipiez, and is profusely illustrated.

Although we have here two volumes of more than five hundred pages each, or a work of more than one thousand pages in all, the book is still an abridgment, as the translator says in his preface. The expense of publication was certainly very great, but we cannot help regretting, from the point of view which a student

naturally takes, that any eliminations of the original text were found necessary. It is explained, however, in these words : "The conditions of the book market are not the same in Paris as they are in this country. Generally the expenses of publication of educational and scientific works are in part, if not wholly, defrayed by government. Here they fall entirely on private enterprise, so that it has been deemed advisable to slightly abridge the text in those portion s that are somewhat tumid with ' padding.'" We hardly see the opportunity for using the words "tumid" and "padding" in a work which is remarkably lucid and thoroughly interesting in all its details, and in which the authors have for their sole object the ambition to make their book complete in all its parts.

Perhaps the sale will be confined to the literary class, but it is a book which every man of leisure and every thoughtful business man can read with int rest and profit. There are thousands of college graduates who are engaged in what the English despise as "trade," and who have not lost their taste for just such matters as these, and there are other thousands of men who have never been to college, but, nevertheless, love art in all its forms, and would be glad to know something of its origin. These, if they have the money to spare, will invest a few dollars in this work, and find plenty of food for thought in its pages during the long winter

AT CLOSE QUARTERS.

evenings that are upon us. Take such prolific subjects as these, for example : the stone age in Greece, the characteristics of Mycenæan architecture, gates, mouldings, decorations, religious architecture, civil architecture, the architecture of house and palace, painting, pottery, glass, wood, ivory, and stone, all so well illustrated that the author's meaning is caught at a glance, What better reading can any one find than is here afforded, and about a period which seems to be almost miraculous?

It is a noble work, and great credit is due to the publishers for their costly undertaking. (Armstrong. $15; $22; $50.)—*N. Y. Herald.*

The Great God Pan.

MESSRS. ROBERTS BROTHERS have lately published here, in conjunction with Mr. John Lane, London, "The Great God Pan," and "The Inmost Light," two comparatively short tales by Mr. Arthur Machen, whose name is new to us, though he figures on his title page as the author of "The Chronicle of Clemendy," and the translator of "The Heptameron" and "Le Mozen de Parvenir." It is not easy to say what these tales are, for though they deal, or profess to deal, with men and women of our own day, and with events of real life,it is in such a fantastic way, and with such extraordinary results, that the impression they leave on the mind is rather that of troubled dreams than of actual or possible occurrences in any country, or condition of society, of which we have knowledge. The scenes of both are apparently laid in London, but they are really laid in a populous *terra incognita* similar to that which Poe imagined as the home of his Waldemars and Lenores, and the haunt of his Conqueror Worms. The intellectual quality which the production of such things demands is imagination, the activity of which should not be regulated, but encouraged, without regard to consequences, and their most potent motive should be the elucidation of some scientific or psychological problem, no matter what one, provided it be sufficiently profound and recondite. The transference of the soul of one person to the body of another by hypnotism is not a bad subject, when properly and plausibly handled; and the creation of a new soul from the ashes of an old body affords a large scope for the ingenuities of pseudo chemistry and mysticism. His heroine is a beautiful woman, who ruins the souls and bodies of those over whom she casts her spells, being as good as a Suicide Club, if we may say so, to those who love her; and to whom she is Death. Something like this is, we take it, the interpretation of Mr. Machen's uncanny parable, which is too morbid to be the production of a healthy mind. (Roberts. $1.)—*Mail and Express.*

The Use of Life.

WHEN Sir John Lubbock writes on science he writes for students ; when he writes on other things he has a special but a wider audience in view. It might be difficult to define for whom exactly "The Pleasure of Life" and "The Beauties of Nature" were intended, but there is no such doubt about the present volume. It is a gift-book, and a good one too, for the very young, for those to whom the difficulties and problems of life are mere names. Sir John Lubbock speaks of life in the most cheerful tones, and inculcates the thrifty, prudent virtues in a wholesome fashion. It is very proper that youth should be so addressed, and that they should read from an elementary text-book first, till life puts such questions to them that no such text-book will answer. To those who have had such questions put to them the complacent sententiousness of this guide will sound a little flippant and irreverent, but it cannot be meant for them. Sir John quotes from surely all the authors dead and living in support of his downright cocksure maxims, but it is mostly by the vague generalities of his authorities he is reinforced, by such sentiments as may delight the literary or the symmetrical sense but could never be of service to a thinking mind. It is only the record of special individual experiences that can help where help is needed, and biographies of sinners contain better counsel than books of the most faultless maxims. (Macmillan. $1.25.)—*The Bookman.*

The History of the United States.

THE excuse needed for adding to the long list another history of the United States is given by the author, E. Benjamin Andrews, in his claim to utilize recent researches, to make the narrative continuous, to note both the political evolution of the country and its social life, to observe due proportion in the space given to the different phases of the nation's career, to present the matter in natural periods, to separate the fore-history from the history proper, and to secure such accuracy as will make these volumes a work of reference. These are large claims, but an examination of President Andrews' work shows that the claims are well founded, if they be confined to the general outlines of the whole history; and even then the marvel is that there is so much of detail in the narrative and so much of color in the style, when it is considered that the whole story is confined to seven hundred pages, though it begins with America before Columbus and comes down to 1888; indeed, to 1894 on some themes. On the whole it is heartily to be commended as sure to find and to keep a place in the world of readers, and sure also to delight and instruct them. (Scribner. 2 v., $4.)—*N. Y. Observer.*

Studies in Folk-Song and Popular Poetry.

MR. ALFRED M. WILLIAMS has put together eleven essays (several of which are republished from magazines) analyzing and illustrating various phases of folk-song. The subjects are well worth the time and care they have demanded. Mr. Williams' style is clear and direct, and the result is a delightful volume which makes no claim to exhaustive treatment, but manages to say a great deal in a short space and inclines the reader to wish for more. The chapter on American sea songs is probably the best known of these essays. In considering the ballads and popular rhymes of our Civil War, Mr. Williams notes the fact that they are not to be compared in quality with those which have been produced by much lighter struggles, for instance by the Jacobite Rebellion in Scotland. No great song embodies and interprets the spirit of the nation as does Die Wacht am Rhein or the Marseillaise despite the success of such poems as Mrs. Howe's "Battle Hymn" and General Pike's lines to Dixie. Mr. Williams accounts for this by saying that the Americans are not a singing people in the bent of their genius nor are the conditions of civilization favorable to this form of expression. "The newspaper has taken the place of the ballad as a means of influencing the popular mind, and poetry has passed from the people to the literary artists." Nevertheless the essayist has succeeded in finding plenty of material for an interesting and instructive paper. The many readers—we trust there are many—who have been fascinated by the revelations of Roumanian poetry given by The Bard of the Dimbovitza will read with pleasure Mr. Williams' comments thereon. Here, as in discussing the folk-songs of lower Brittany, Poitou, and Hungary, he gives more examples than when writing of the Scotch or English ballads, with which we are more familiar. (Houghton, Mifflin & Co. $1.50.)—*Boston Literary World.*

The Literary Shop.

THE prejudices, eccentricities, and autocratic rule of the magazine editor supply James L. Ford with abundant material for satirical treatment in "The Literary Shop." Mr. Ford has a theory that American literature is practically regulated in its development by the men in

From "Edwin Booth."   Copyright, 1894, by The Century Co.
EDWIN BOOTH AND HIS FATHER.

charge of the popular illustrated periodicals, and as these men seek primarily to gratify the tastes of the great mass of readers, the result is a literary trend that makes for mediocrity, superficiality and untruth in essence and technique. Fortunately, even Mr. Ford recognizes in later manifestations of magazine literature indications of a more liberal and wholesome tendency. He pays his respects to a number of the great editors, from Robert Bonner, of the old *Ledger* days, down to Mr. Bok, of the *Ladies' Home Journal*, whom he designates as "the crown prince of American letters," and he describes some of the literary fads of the past and present with a wit that can hardly fail to amuse even his victims. A number of short sketches bound up in the volume deal with the same theme in different ways. The reporter who falls from bohemianism, succumbs to the fascinations of afternoon tea, gets into "society" and acquires the Swelled Head seems to be the particular object of Mr. Ford's satire. He also deals effective thrusts at current ideas of culture via "reading classes" and clubs. (Richmond. $1.25.)—*The Beacon.*

LOUISE IMOGEN GUINEY.

A Little English Gallery.

THIS is one of the most delightful collections of essays published for years. While Miss Guiney is destitute of that delicious wit and humor which make Miss Agnes Repplier's essays so unusual, Miss Guiney far surpasses Miss Repplier in the delicate discrimination of her criticism. Where Miss Repplier loves to keep in the highroads of literature, saying keen words about the books and characters dear to us all, Miss Guiney has a knack of discovering delightful byways in the book world, and introducing new friends to us, whose names we already knew, but whose characters were quite unknown to us before.

"A Little English Gallery" gives us a delightful picture of George Herbert's mother, afterward Lady Danvers; a careful and sympathetic criticism of Henry Vaughan's life and poetry; and a very entertaining sketch of Samuel Johnson's friends, Topham Beauclerk and Bennet Langton. The other two essays in the volume, on Farquhar and Hazlitt, are much less interesting; the one on Hazlitt is especially lacking in clearness and precision.

The best essay is the one on Vaughan, which is fine and really masterly in its way. Miss Guiney's taste in quotation is very happy, and we cannot forbear requoting one of the characteristic verses which she chooses from Vaughan's beautiful but too little known work:

> Follow the cry no more. There is
> An ancient way,
> All strewed with flowers and happiness,
> And fresh as May.

One could wish that Miss Guiney had a more flowing style; there is a certain congestion of ideas in her sentences which sometimes makes them difficult to follow. She is unfortunately not gifted with the limpid clearness which is one of the greatest charms in Miss Repplier's essays. Miss Guiney has a genius, however, for descriptive adjectives, and since Matthew Arnold we remember no one whose adjectives are more vividly and precisely used than Miss Guiney's. Altogether "A Little English Gallery" deserves to occupy an honored place among American essays. (Harper. $1.)—*Literary World.*

Nonsense Songs and Stories.

EDWARD LEAR'S "Nonsense Songs and Stories" have just been issued in a ninth and revised edition, with additional songs and an introduction by so genial a critic and so able a *littérateur* as Sir E. Strachey. Sir Strachey begins with a dissertation on sense and nonsense which will be a treat to the cultured reader; and then follows up his explanations by personal anecdotes and descriptions of Lear, of his many talents, his high aims and ambitions, his many disappointments and never-failing "humanness," which are touching and wholly delightful.

Lear was born in 1812 and began to draw for daily bread about 1827, coloring prints, screens and fans, and also making drawings of morbid diseases for hospitals and certain physicians. In 1831 he obtained employment at the Zoölogical Society, and the following year completed a volume of colored drawings of birds on a large scale. From that time work crowded upon him, and he travelled much to make the studies for his many illustrations to now noted works of natural history. In 1846 he was called to give drawing lessons to Queen Victoria. In that year he published his first "Book of Nonsense," a collection of rhymes without sense or reason but wholly funny by reason of incongruities, contrasts and utter nonsense.

These rhymes and their successors have been given over to children chiefly, but no child can understand the perfection of the characters drawn by a consummate artist, or truly appreciate the brain rest and stimulus of the idiotic rhymes. "Alice in Wonderland" is the only thing that has touched on Mr. Lear's nonsense with real success. This new edition of "Nonsense Songs and Stories" is sumptuously gotten up. To any one who does not know Mr. Lear's books a great treat is in store. (Warne. $1.25)

Three of Us.

BARNEY, Cossack, and Rex, three dogs of varied gifts, flourishing under varied conditions, are the heroes of three stories, all of decided interest. All these dogs are loved by the little and big human animals with whom they spend their ups and downs of canine life, and the genial story-teller who brings their talents and defects before her eager readers proves herself possessed of the great gift of talking to children in a manner to reach their loyal, impulsive little hearts. She has the further gift of appealing to their observant, wondering, appreciative eyes, and has pictured all the dogs her pen teaches them to love and pity in all their various joys and vicissitudes with a pencil equally practical and equally appealing to the very best in children. The publishers have made a very pretty book, designed especially for the holiday season, but good throughout the year for every boy and girl who has a birthday coming, and a dog who is just one shade less dear than the dearest human being in the child's world. Mrs. Izora C. Chandler has accomplished a work of which she may be justly proud. (Hunt & Eaton. $2.)

The Ralstons.

MARION CRAWFORD'S new novel, "The Ralstons," is in some ways an even more fascinating depiction of New York life than was "Katherine Lauderdale," of which the later story is a direct and natural sequel.

In "The Ralstons," Mr. Crawford's dramatic sense is permitted full play. The surroundings having already been sufficiently elaborated, interest is concentrated on the men and women who figure in the tale. Of New York as a city of magnificent and terrible contrasts—New York in the purely material aspect—one gets but slight glimpses. What one does get is a vital, vivid, wonderfully picturesque and memorable impression of New York as the scene of human passions, fears and hopes. The characters all have a definite part to perform, each contributes to the general advancement of the plot, and in their relations with each other they have the independence and the mutuality of influence which are always to be found where men and women mingle in formal association or close companionship. Katherine Ralston, still known to her world as Katherine Lauderdale, is the central figure, and upon her portrait the author lavishes exquisite sympathy and delicacy of feeling. It is no ideal portrait that he draws, for Katherine is not perfect; but Mr. Crawford makes no apologies for her faults, as he does not seek to glorify her virtues. His is the artistic attitude.

The best thing that can be said for "The Ralstons," in the estimation of the average reader, is that it is immensely entertaining; once in the full swing of the narrative, one is carried on quite irresistibly to the end. The

From "Three of Us."

SHE COULD WEAR GOLDEN SLIPPERS.

style is throughout easy and graceful and the text abounds in wise and witty reflections on the realities of existence. As for Mr. Crawford's humor it is charmingly indirect, spontaneous and alluring. He winds up by saying that his only object in writing "The Ralstons" was to please ; he has, however, done more ; he has made his story, consciously or not, a source of agreeable edification. It is pleasant to learn that the further fortunes of Katherine in the rôle of millionaire and matron are to supply the theme of another tale yet to come. (Macmillan. 2 v., $2.)—*The Beacon.*

A Child of the Age.

ENGLISH or foreign, there is no work among those now before me which is so original as that of the late Francis Adams. "A Child of the Age" was intended as a prelude to a series of books, which should cohere on one broad, general motive. Masterpieces, Adams hoped and believed, they were to be. "A Child of the Age" is certainly not a masterpiece ; it has not even just escaped that rank. Only the most ill-balanced judgment could claim such pre-eminence for it. At most, it is original, moving, often fascinating ; a great deal, no doubt, but not all that is needful. It is also written in a disconnected, sometimes slovenly, and often grotesque fashion ; and the "blind hysterics" of this particular Child of the Age are as tiresome and unconvincing as those of the much abused Tennysonian Celt. The method of Francis Adams in this strange book is that of a realist, who has reached the extreme of impressionism. If the story had been written with more reserve—that is, if the author had more firmly held the reins of his emotion—the result would have been much more impressive. In Francis Adams we have a belated member of the Spasmodic school, ready at any page to go one better than Dobell or Alexander Smith. At times he tells, in gasps and sobs and pantings, what restrained prose would convey with far keener and more profound effect. But there are passages, episodes, one or two whole chapters, which prove that Francis Adams was a writer of remarkable achievement as well as of altogether exceptional promise. The drawback to the book is its author's evident belief in the fineness of his hero's nature. But in actual life Leicester would be an intolerable person— insanely arrogant, exquisitely sentimental, and selfish almost to the extreme of brutality. If this is the new wine of the age, it leaves a bad flavor on the palate. Perhaps, however, Francis Adams did consciously imagine Leicester not merely as a brooding phantasist, but also as an ill-bred and selfish youth, redeemed by several

brilliant qualities, and once or twice a noble trait. No one who reads this latest addition to the *Keynotes* series will fail to appreciate the truth and delicacy of the portraiture of Rosy, the young girl who gives all to Bertram Leicester in exchange for his fugitive passion. The chapter in which is described the *finale* of their drama is a strongly realized and moving piece of writing. (Roberts. $1.) — *London Academy.*

In the Dozy Hours.

MISS REPPLIER has added another volume of essays to her list. There are a score of them, with subjects ranging from kittens to pastels, and all marked by the sprightly touch which has become a marked characteristic of her literary productions. With the essayist, style is of pre-eminent importance, more so than even choice of subject, and Miss Repplier early made the humanities her elected form of literature and the light essay her special medium. We cannot recall that she has deviated from the line she has chosen, and year by year she has perfected her style until she has earned an enviable place among the essayists of America. She has a sense of humor which is almost masculine (*pace* Miss Repplier), and a sense of the ridiculous which is probably a feminine trait, and a fluency of expression, which is also presumably attributed to her sex. Comparisons are odious, but Mr. Augustine Birrell sometimes comes to one's mind when reading Miss Repplier's work, and not to her disadvantage either. She has also a vein of good common sense which makes her papers more than mere vehicles of entertainment.

"Aut Cæsar aut Nihil" is an earnest plea for her position on the much vexed woman question. She pleads for that true dignity of womanhood which compels her to disavow any movement which sets up another standard than that established for man. Where all is so excellent it is difficult to select, but we may allude to the paper on "Lectures," which is a capital hit at that desire to be considered cultured which finds its expression in attendance at lectures which are but as dust and ashes to the ambitious listener. For, as she says, "the necessity of knowing a little about a great many things is the most grievous burden of the day." Her illustrations and quotations are apt at all times, and particularly so in this paper.

While her essays show the marks of care they cannot be said to smell of the lamp ; they betray the result of thoughtful reading and clever application, and as novels constitute so large a proportion of light literature, her line of work calls for especial attention. (Houghton, Mifflin & Co. $1.25.)—*Public Opinion.*

Che Literary News.

An Eclectic Monthly Review of Current Literature.

EDITED BY A. H. LEYPOLDT.

FEBRUARY, 1895.

THE BOOKS OF 1894.

To GIVE the "reading public" a concise view of the literary output in the English language of an entire year, that shall be fairly representative of its general tendency, of its distinctive specialties and of its average quality, is an undertaking beset with difficulties.

AMERICAN BOOKS.

CLASSIFICATIONS.	1893 New Books.	1893 New Editions.	1894 New Books.	1894 New Editions.
Fiction	772	360	573	156
Law	400	30	440	45
Theology and Religion	597	45	442	26
Education and Language	387	10	426	16
Juvenile	436	38	315	29
Poetry and the Drama	166	78	133	133
Political and Social Science	199	13	233	21
Literary History and Miscellany	183	141	208	29
History	122	30	163	24
Physical and Mathematical Science	113	10	141	24
Biography, Memoirs	204	15	140	21
Medical Science, Hygiene	129	21	118	42
Description, Travel	170	21	116	28
Fine Art and Illustrated Books	120	15	127	11
Useful Arts	117	9	118	20
Sports and Amusements	55	5	50	6
Domestic and Rural	60	4	42	9
Mental and Moral Philosophy	24	5	42	7
Humor and Satire	27	3	10	
Totals	4281	853	3837	647
	4281		3837	
	5134		4484	

ENGLISH BOOKS.

CLASSIFICATIONS.	Books by American authors, incl. new eds. in U. S.	Books by English and other foreign authors, incl. new eds manuf. in U.S.	Books by English authors imported, bound or in sheets, into U. S.
Fiction	370	997	62
Law	474	1	10
Theology and Religion	184	22	262
Education and Language	330	22	90
Juvenile	261	22	61
Poetry and the Drama	107	82	77
Political and Social Science	174	8	72
Literary History and Miscellany	132	35	50
History	125	14	48
Physical and Mathematical Science	76	11	78
Biography, Memoirs	50	32	79
Medical Science Hygiene	145	1	14
Description, Travel	83	17	44
Fine Art and Illustrated Books	93	7	38
Useful Arts	92	....	46
Sports and Amusements	33	....	23
Domestic and Rural	31	2	14
Mental and Moral Philosophy	28	4	17
Humor and Satire	9	....	1
	2681	577	1086

These lists duplicate each other inextricably, and we shall make no effort to separate the American and English books of 1894 by any national chemistry. Together they represent the contributions of a year by authors who write the English language for the inspiration, the encouragement, the instruction and the entertainment of the "reading public."

Fiction, always demanded and supplied in larger quantities than any other form of literature, received this year several notable additions, distinguished however more for literary workmanship than for lasting interest or ethical truth. Many authors seem to have worked by contract system this year, and the work can necessarily only be classed with the more or less expert labor of the writer-tradesmen, whom practice has made perfect in the "tricks of the trade." Political and social problems, particularly the vexed questions arising from the present unnatural antagonism between men and women, have formed the keynote of the great bulk of this year's fiction. Stories appealing to trained, cultivated minds and written wholly to afford recreation after the real labor of life, would need no second figure in their enumeration. Woman's unrest and its cause in sex, circumscribed education and political inequality, was pointed out in hundreds of novels, which did neither their authors nor their readers justice or credit. On the whole, when we have mentioned one dozen novels we must think hard to remember the next one that was anything more than the popular attraction of a few weeks.

Things look more hopeful when we turn to work depending upon realities and authenticated facts. Several works of rare merit in subject and method were added to the literature of biography. In this field there have been many volumes during the past few years that also bore traces of the hurry, skurry, pitchfork method of contract compilation. It seems as though the writers feared the interest in their subjects would die before they could throw together the material collected by steam and telegraph and sifted almost by sleight of hand. Some really good works appeared in the department of history. The average of merit was high and the titles on the next page show the periods and subjects covered in the most notable books. An epidemic of Napoleonic memoirs, histories and collections of gossip marked the year.

Literary criticism and books about books appeared in several works of great merit. Good critics are needed more than all else to make the literature of England and America what it should be. A critic who knows the subject better than the author he dissects, who knows at a glance what is in the volume before him that no other volume has covered, who judges fearlessly but kindly and helpfully, who, regardless of the author's former achievement or present fame, pronounces upon his work as though it were the first contribution of a new writer, and who signs and stands by his decisions, is the literary need of the hour.

The great financial depression of the past two years and the questions asked more and more persistently day by day regarding the rights of capital, the duties and responsibilities and privileges of labor, the future political, social and domestic sphere of woman, the possibilities and dangers of large cities, and the hundred other problems which are the outcome of natural growth or are brought about by greed, steam and the inherent selfishness of men and women, called out an unusually large number of works dealing with social and political science. No department of writing this year contains more honest work, undertaken from the purest motives.

The general tone of the religious writings showed the spirit of research far more than the spirit of controversy. Authors of every denomination seemed to lean more towards pointing out man's need of faith and aspiration than towards claiming to describe and explain the objects and forms of such needed faith.

Some very valuable works of reference bear the date of 1894. Only those who know the special difficulties of such compilations can appreciate the vast amount of knowledge. labor, and money that produced such invaluable works as Bartlett's "Concordance to Shakespeare;" Strong's "Concordance to the Bible;" Walker's "Concordance to the Bible;" "The Century Encyclopædia of Names and Places;" Funk & Wagnalls' "Standard Dictionary;" Lippincott's "Gazetteer of the World;" and Larned's "History for Ready Reference."

Two or three publications deserve a word owing to oddness or beauty of manufacture. Of such are "The Documents in Evidence," a book made up of fac-simile letters; "The Art of Writing Fiction," purporting to be an author's type-written copy of his work bound in covers representing a common file for manuscript ; the new "Prayer-Book of the Protestant Episcopal Church," printed by De Vinne ; and "Liber Scriptorum," the first book of the Authors' Club, containing one hundred contributions with autograph signatures in all the 250 copies printed.

During the year we have been visited by Dean Hole, A. Conan Doyle, David Christie Murray and Paul Bourget. Their visits have led to much journalistic writing, little of which seems worthy of future booksetting.

We sorrow to realize that the year just ended has placed upon the long roll of the honored dead the names of Oliver Wendell Holmes, Christina Rossetti, Robert Louis Stevenson, Constance Fenimore Woolson, Edmund Yates, Philip Gilbert Hamerton, Walter Pater, Prof. W. D. Whitney, James Anthony Froude, Prof. Henry Morley, Prof. G. J. Romanes, Susan Fenimore Cooper, and Jane G. Austin.

Who is now doing the work these names stand for? Who is training for it in the spirit they put into their work? True literature would seem to have been robbed rather than enriched in 1894 !

The Best Books of 1894.

BIOGRAPHY, CORRESPONDENCE, ETC.

Cary, E. George William Curtis. $1.25..*Houghton, M*
Church, S. H. Oliver Cromwell. $3.........*Putnam*
Cobbe, Frances Power, Life of. 2 v. $4.*Houghton, M*
Dickinson, Emily. Letters of Emily Dickinson. 2. v. $2.................... ....*Roberts*
Dickson, W. K. L., *and* Antonia. Life and adventures of Thomas A. Edison. $4.50.................*Crowell*
Edgeworth, Maria. Life and letters. 2 v.
                                                    Houghton, M
Fiske, John. Edward Livingston Youmans. $2..*Appleton*
Froude, J. A. Life and letters of Erasmus. $2.50.
                                                    Scribner
Gray, Asa. Letters. 2 v. $4..............*Houghton, M*
Grossmann, E. Edwin Booth. $3-$25........*Century*
Hare, A. J. C. Story of two noble lives. 3 v. $8.
                                                    Randolph
Lee, Fitzhugh. General Lee. $1.50...........*Appleton*
Liddon, H. Parry (*Canon*) and others. Life of Edward Bouverie Pusey. In 4 v. V. 3. $4.50..*Longmans, G*
Linton, W. J. Threescore and ten years, 1820 to 1890; recollections. $2...........................*Scribner*
Longfellow, S. Memoir and letters. $1.50.
                                                    Houghton, M
Martin, T. Commerford. The inventions, researches, and writings of Nikola Tesla. $4.
                                                    The Electrical Engineer
Pasquier memoirs. 3 v. $7.50.............*Scribner*
Pickard. Life and letters of John G. Whittier. 2 v. $4...................... .. ..*Houghton, M*
Prothero, R. E., *and* Bradley, G. G. Life and correspondence of Arthur Penrhyn Stanley. 2 v. $8.
                                                    Scribner
Robbins, A. F. Early public life of William Ewart Gladstone. $1.50 ....*Dodd, M*
Robertson, Rev. Alex. Fra Paolo Sarpi, the greatest of the Venetians. $1.50................*Whittaker*
Sabatier, Paul. Life of St. Francis of Assisi. $2.50.
                                                    Scribner
Salt, Richard Jeffries. 90c....................*Macmillan*
Seccombe, T. Lives of twelve bad men. $3.50.
                                                    Putnam
Sherman, W. T., *and* J. The Sherman letters. $3.
                                                    Scribner
Straus, Oscar S. Roger Williams, the pioneer of religious liberty. $1.25..........................*Century*
Thoreau, H. D. Familiar letters. $4 ....*Houghton, M*
Wright, T. Life of Daniel Defoe. $3.75....*Randolph*
Wright, W. Life of the Brontës in Ireland. $1.50..*Appleton*

FICTION.

Baring-Gould S. Kitty alone. $1.25........*Dodd, M*
Barlow, *Miss* Jane. Kerrigan's quality. $1.25.*Dodd, M*
Black, W. The handsome Humes. $1.50... ..*Harper*
— Highland cousins. $1.75.....................*Harper*
Blackmore, R. D. Perlycross. $1.75.........*Harper*
Bouvet, Margerite. My lady. $2.50....... ..*McClurg*
Cable, G. W. John March, southerner. $1.50..*Scribner*
Caine, Hall. The Manxman. $1.50...........*Appleton*

Chamberlain, H. R.　6,000 tons of gold.　$1.25.
Flood & V
Christian, Sydney.　Sarah, a survival.　pap. 50c.　*Harper*
Craddock, Charles Egbert.　His vanished star.　$1.25.
Houghton, M
Crawford, Katharine Lauderdale.　2 v., $2..*Macmillan*
Crockett, S. R.　The lilac sunbonnet　$1.50..*Appleton*
— The play actress.　$1...........................*Putnam*
— The raiders.　$1.50...........................*Macmillan*
Dean, *Mrs.* Andrew.　Lesser's daughter.　50c..*Putnam*
Deland, *Mrs.* Margaret.　Philip and his wife.　$1.25.
Houghton, M
Dostoyevsky, F.　Poor folk.　$1...............*Roberts*
Du Maurier, G.　Trilby.　$1.75...............*Harper*
Egerton, George.　Discords.　$1...............*Roberts*
Ferguson, V. Munro.　Music hath charms.　$1.25.
Harper
Ford, Paul Leicester.　The Hon. Peter Stirling.　$1.50.
Holt
Frederic, Harold.　The copperhead.　$1.......*Scribner*
Gardner, Sarah M. H.　Quaker idyls.　75c........*Holt*
Goodwin, Maud W.　The colonial cavalier.　$1.
Lovell, C
Hardy, Thomas.　Life's little ironies.　$1.25...*Harper*
Harraden, Beatrice.　Ships that pass in the night.　$1.
Putnam
Harris, F.　Elder Conklin.　$1.25...........*Macmillan*
Hope, Anthony.　Prisoner of Zenda.　75c.......*Holt*
— The god in the car.　$1 ; pap., 50c........1....*Appleton*
Howells, W. D.　A traveller from Altruria.　$1.50.
Harper
Jerome, J. K.　John Ingerfield.　75c...............*Holt*
Kenealy, Arabella.　Dr. Janet of Harley Street.　pap.,
50c..*Appleton*
Kipling, Rudyard.　The jungle book.　$1.50..*Century*
Kirk.　The story of Lawrence Garthe.　$1.25.*Houghton, M*
La Rame, Louise de.　The silver Christ and the lemon
tree.　$1.25...................................*Macmillan*
Lawless, Maelcho.　$1.50.......................*Appleton*
Locke, W. J.　(*pseud.*)　At the gate of Samaria.　$1 ;
pap., 50c.....................................*Appleton*
Lyall, Edna.　Doreen, the story of a singer.　$1.25.
Longmans, G
Maartens, Maarten.　The greater glory.　$1.50.*Appleton*
Maclaren, Ian.　Beside the bonnie brier bush.　$1.25.
Dodd, M
Meredith, G.　Lord Ormont and his Aminta.　$1.50.
Scribner
Mitchell, W.　Two strings to his bow.　$1.25.
Houghton, M
Moore, G.　Esther Waters.　25c.................*Weeks*
Morgan, Emily M.　The flight of the swallow.　75c.
Randolph
O'Grady.　The bog of stars.　pap., 50c.........*Kenedy*
Parker, Gilbert.　Trail of the sword.　$1 ; pap., 50c.
Appleton
Pool, Maria Louise.　Out of step.　$1.25........*Harper*
Praed, *Mrs.* Campbell.　Christina Chard.　$1 ; pap.,50c.
Appleton
Steel, Flora Annie.　The flower of forgiveness.　$1.
Macmillan
— The potter's thumb.　$1.50...................*Harper*
Stevenson, R. L.　Will o' the mill.　50c.......*Knight*
— and Osborne, Lloyd.　The ebb tide.　$1.25.
Stone & Kimball
Stockton.　Pomona's travels.　$1.50........*Scribner*
Story of Margrédel.　$1.......................*Putnam*
Stretton, Hesba.　The highway of sorrow.　$1.25.
Dodd, M
Ward, Mary A.　Marcella.　2 v.　$2.......*Macmillan*
Warner, C. Dudley.　The golden house.　$1..*Harper*
Weyman, Stanley J.　My Lady Rotha.　$1.25.
Longmans, G
— Under the red robe.　$1.25..............*Longmans, G*
White, Percy.　Mr. Bailey-Martin.　$1........*Lovell, C*
Wilkins, Mary E.　Pembroke.　$1.50..........*Harper*
Wilkins, W. H.　The green bay tree.　50c........*Tait*
Wood, Joanna E.　The untempered wind.　50c...*Tait*
Woolson, Constance Fenimore.　Horace Chase.　$1.25.
Harper

HISTORY.

Adams, C. Francis.　Massachusetts, its historians and
its history.　$1........................ . *Houghton, M*
Alger, J. G.　Glimpses of the French Revolution.　$1.75.
Dodd, M
Andrews, E. B.　History of the United States.　2 v.
$4...*Scribner*

Griffis, W. E.　Brave little Holland.　75c..*Houghton, M*
Harrison, F.　The meaning of history.　$2.25.
Macmillan
Holst, H. v.　The French Revolution.　2 v.　$3.50.
Callaghan
Lee, Fitzhugh.　General Lee.　$1.50...........*Appleton*
Lockyer, J. N.　The dawn of astronomy.　$5.
Macmillan
Maclay, Edgar Stanton.　A history of the United States
Navy, 1775–1894.　2 v.　$7...............*Appleton*
Maspero, G.　Dawn of civilization (Egypt and Chal-
dæa.)　$7.50..................................*Appleton*
Oliphant, *Mrs.* Marg. O. W.　Hist. characters of the
reign of Queen Anne.　$6...............*Century*
Philipson, D.　Old European Jewries.　$1.25.
Jewish Pub. Soc. of America
Ropes, J. Codman.　The story of the Civil War.　Pt. 1.
$1.50...*Putnam*
Taylor, J. M.　Maximilian and Carlotta.　$1.50.*Putnam*
Winsor, Justin.　Cartier to Frontenac.　$4.
Houghton, M
Walissewski, K.　Around a throne.　2 v.　$7.50.
Lippincott
— The romance of an empress.　$1............*Appleton*

LITERARY MISCELLANY.

Boyesen.　Commentary on the writings of Ibsen.　$2.
Macmillan
Brooke, S. A.　Tennyson ; his art and relation to mod-
ern life.　$1.75................................*Macmillan*
Curtin, Jeremiah, *comp.*　Hero-tales of Ireland.　$2.
Little, B
Johnson, L.　The art of Thomas Hardy.　$2..*Dodd, M*
Strachey, *Sir* E.　Talk at a country house.　$1.25.
Houghton, M
Traubel, H. L.　*In re* Walt Whitman.　$2...　...*McKay*
Usanne, Octave.　Book-hunter in Paris.　$5..*McClurg*
Warner, B. E.　English history in Shakespeare's plays.
$1.75...*Longmans*
Wendell, Barrett.　William Shakespeare : a study in
Elizabethan literature.　$1.75...............*Scribner*
Williams, A. M.　Studies in folk-song and popular
poetry.　$1.50..............................*Houghton, M*

POLITICAL AND SOCIAL ECONOMICS.

Clarke, H. W.　A history of tithes.　$1.......*Scribner*
Conkling, A. R.　City government in the United
States.　$1...................................*Appleton*
Ely, R. T.　Socialism and social reform.　$1.50..*Crowell*
Hobson, J. A.　The evolution of modern capitalism.
$1.25...*Scribner*
Hoffman, Frank Sargent.　The sphere of the state.
$1.50...*Putnam*
Kidd, B.　Social evolution.　$2.50.........*Macmillan*
Leavitt, S.　Our money wars.　pap., 50c..*Arena Pub. Co*
Lloyd, H. D.　Wealth against commonwealth.　$2.50.
Harper
McClung, D. W.　Money talks.　$1...*R. Clarke & Co*
Mason, Otis Tufton.　Woman's share in primitive cul-
ture.　$1.50..................................*Appleton*
Ostrogaraki, M.　Rights of women.　$1......*Scribner*
Traill, Henry Duff.　Social England.　$3.50....*Putnam*
Ward, C. Osborne.　The equilibration of human apti-
tudes.　$1.25.......................... *Nat. Watchman Co*
Warner, A. G.　American charities.　$1.75.... *Crowell*

MISCELLANEOUS BOOKS.

Davidson, T.　Education of the Greek people and its
influence on civilization.　$1.50...............*Appleton*
Drummond, H.　Ascent of man.　$2..............*Pott*
Ellis, Havelock.　Man and woman : a study of human
secondary sexual character.　$1.25...........*Scribner*
Flint, Rob.　Historical Philosophy in France, Belgium,
and Switzerland.　V. 1.　$4.................*Scribner*
Hearn, Lafcadio.　Unfamiliar Japan.　2 v.　$4.
Houghton, M
Hittell, J. S.　History of the mental growth of mankind
in ancient times.　4 v.　$6...................*Holt*
Horne, Herbert P.　The binding of books.　$2.
Scribner
Lubbock, *Sir* J.　The use of life.　$1.25....*Macmillan*
Newbolt, W. C. E.　Speculum sacerdotum.　$2.
Notovitch, N.　The unknown life of Jesus Christ.
$1.50...*Dillingham*
Winslow, Anna Green, Diary of.　$1.25..*Houghton, M*
Wright, J.　Early Bibles of America, revised and en-
larged.　$3...................................*Whittaker*

ARTICLES IN FEBRUARY MAGAZINES.

Articles marked with an asterisk are illustrated.

ARTISTIC, MUSICAL AND DRAMATIC.—*Arena*, Italy of the Renaissance, Flower.—*Atlantic*, New Figures in Literature and Art, I., Daniel Chester French, Cortissoz.—*Century* Characteristics of George Inness, Sheldon.—*Forum*, Outlook for Decorative Art in America, Fowler.—*Godey's* Private Picture Galleries of the United States—Munger collection,* Cooper.—*Harper's*, Art in Glasgow,* Eliz. R. Pennell ; Music in America (with portrait), Weeks.—*Nine. Century* (Jan.), Paintings at Pompeii, Kennedy.—*Scribner's*, Recent work of Elihu Vedder,* Brownell ; American Wood-Engravers—Gustav Kruell.*

BIOGRAPHY, CORRESPONDENCE, ETC.—*North Am. Review*, Recollections of Robert Louis Stevenson, Andrew Lang. — *Scribner's*, Some Old Letters, ed. by Jas. F. Dwight.—*West. Review* (Jan.), In Memoriam—Dr. John Chapman.

DESCRIPTION, TRAVEL.—*Atlantic*, Voyage in the Dark, Robinson.—*Century*, Death of Emin Pasha,* Mohun.—*Chautauquan*, Famous Bridges of the World, Jamison.—*Harper's*, Down the West Coast,* Lummis ; The H'yakushos' Summer Pleasures,* Sen Katayama ; Oudeypore, the City of the Sunrise, Weeks.—*Scribner's*, End of the Continent* (Patagonia), Spears.

DOMESTIC AND SOCIAL.—*Century*, People in New York,* M. G. Van Rensselaer ; In the Gray Cabins of New England, Rebecca Harding Davis.—*Chautauquan*, Sensible View of Marriage, Lucy B. Cope.—*Fort. Review*, Ethics of Shopping, Lady Jeune.—*Nine. Century* (Jan.), Women under Islam, Lucy M. J. Garnett.—*North Am. Review*, The Matrimonial Puzzle, Boyesen.—*Scribner's*, Art of Living—the Dwelling,* Grant. *West. Review*, Defence of the Modern Girl, By One of them.

EDUCATIONAL.—*Atlantic*, Subtle Art of Speech-Reading, Mrs. A. G. Bell.—*Forum*, Student-Honor and College Examinations, Stevens.—*Godey's*, Vassar College,* Eliz. E. Boyd.—*North Am. Review*, Why We Need a National University, Newcomb.

FICTION. — *Atlantic*, Life of Nancy, Sarah Orne Jewett ; "Come Down," A. M. Ewell.—*Century*, End of the Game, Alice Brown ; He Would A-Wooing Go, Humphrey ; The Boy, Ruth Mc.E. Stuart.—*Chautauquan*, The Blue Bonnet, Barnard; "For the Dearest," Emily Huntington.—*Godey's*, Bentley's " Beat,"* Lida R. McCabe ; Smoke Rings,* Frank Chaffee; In De Vorsean,* F. M. Livingston.—*Harper's*, John Sanders, Laborer,* F. Hopkinson Smith; Merry Maid of Arcady,* Mrs. Burton Harrison; A Domestic Interior, Grace King ; Love in the Big Barracks, * Ralph.—*Lippincott's*, The Chapel of Ease, Harriet Riddle Davis; Quong Lee, Lynde ; A Precedent, Alice M. Whitlock. — *Scribner's*, Bisnaga's Madeline, Beard ; A Moral Obliquity, Lynde.

HISTORY.—*Century*, Lincoln, Chase, and Grant, Noah Brooks. — *Harper's*, New York Colonial Privateers,* Janvier.

HYGIENIC AND SANITARY.—*Atlantic*, Physical Training in the Public Schools, O'Shea.—*West. Review* (Jan.), Struggle for Healthy Schools, Davies.

LITERARY.—*Atlantic*, Champion of the Middle Ground, Edith M. Thomas ; Celia Thaxter, Annie Fields.—*Century*, Oliver Wendell Holmes, Annie Fields.—*Chautauquan*, Journalism in the Congregational and Presbyterian churches, Foster.—*Forum*, The Great Realists and the Empty Story-Tellers, Boyesen.—*Godey's*, Sappho —The Woman and the Time,* S. M. Miller.—*Lippincott's*, Lingo in Literature, Elam.—*Nine. Century* (Jan.), Defoe's "Apparition of Mrs. Veal," Aitken.—*North Am. Review*, Literature and the Eng. Book Trade, Ouida.—*Scribner's*, James A. Froude, Birrell.— *West. Review* (Jan.), Towards the Appreciation of Emile Zola, Townshend ; William Cullen Bryant, Bradfield.

MEDICAL SCIENCE.—The Serum Treatment of Diphtheria, Armstrong.

MENTAL AND MORAL.—*Arena*, Dynamics of Mind, I., Henry Wood.—*North Am. Review*, The Psychical Comedy, Minot.

NATURE AND SCIENCE.—*Atlantic*, The Frosted Pane, Roberts. — *Chautauquan*, The World's Debt to Electricity, Trowbridge.—*Lippincott's*, The Diamond-Back Terrapin, Fitzgerald ; A Walk in Winter, C. C. Abbott.—*Pop. Science*, Nature's Triumph, Rodway.

POETRY.—*Atlantic*, The Dancer, Ednah P. Clarke. — *Century*, The Passing of Muhammed, Edwin Arnold.—*Godey's*, A Valentine,* Suckling.—*Harper's*, " Vox Clamantis," Tabb. —*Lippincott's*, With Weyman in Old France, Powell.—*Scribner's*, A Question of Privilege, Bret Harte ; The City of Dream Rosamund Marriott-Watson.

POLITICAL AND SOCIAL.—*Arena*, The President's Currency Plan, W. J. Bryan ; Penology in Europe and America, S. J. Barrows ; The New Woman of the South, Josephine K. Henry; Sexual Purity and the Double Standard, Bellangee ; Gambling, C. H. Hamlin.—*Atlantic*, A Study of the Mob, Boris Sidis ; Russia as a Civilizing Force in Asia, J. M. Hubbard; Present Status of Civil Service Reform; T. Roosevelt.—*Century*, New Weapons of the United States Army, Victor L. Mason.—*Chautauquan*, Dr. Parkhurst and His Work, A. C. Wheeler.—*Fort. Review* (Jan.), The Collapse of China at Sea, S. Eardley-Wilmot.—*Forum*, Should the Government Retire from Banking? W. C. Cornwell; Why Gold is Exported, A. S. Heidelbach ; The Social Discontent, I., Its Causes, Henry Holt ; Steps towards Government Control of Railroads, C. D. Wright.—*Godey's*, Nihilism Up to Date, Gribayedoff.—*Harper's*, French Fighters in Africa,* P. Bigelow ; What is Gambling? John Bigelow.—*Lippincott's*, Fate of the Farmer, Powers.—*Nine. Century* (Jan.) Triumph of Japan, Douglas.—*North Am. Review*, The Financial Muddle, J. S. Morton ; W. M. Springer ; H. W. Cannon ; Politics and the Farmer.—*Pop. Science*, Symbols. Helen Zimmern.—*Scribner's*, Passing of the Whigs,* Noah Brooks.— *West. Review* (Jan.), Wanted: a Newer Trade Unionism,* Stobart.

THEOLOGY, RELIGION AND SPECULATION.—*Arena*, True Occultism, Margaret B. Peeke.—*Forum*, Religious Study of a Baptist Town (Westerly, R. I.), W. B. Hale.—*Nine. Century* (Jan.), Auricular Confession and the English Church, Canon Shore.—*North Am. Review*, The New Pulpit, H. R. Haweis.

Survey of Current Literature.

☞ *Order through your bookseller.*—"*There is no worthier or surer pledge of the intelligence and the purity of any community than their general purchase of books; nor is there any one who does more to further the attainment and possession of these qualities than a good bookseller.*"—PROF. DUNN.

ART, MUSIC, DRAMA.

ÆSOP. The fables of Æsop: selected, told anew, and their history traced, by Jos. Jacobs; done into pictures by R. Heighway. *Edition de luxe.* Macmillan. 12°, (Cranford ser.) buckram, *net*, $14.

BALDRY, A. LYS. Albert Moore, his life and works; il. with 10 photogravures and about 70 other il. Macmillan 4°, $22.50.

BARLOW, JANE. The end of Elfintown; il. by Laurence Housman. *Edition de luxe.* Macmillan. 8°, silk, *net*, $9.

CORIDON'S song, and other verses; with il., by Hugh Thomson, and an introd. by Austin Dobson. *Edition de luxe.* Macmillan. 8°, (Cranford ser.) buckram, *net*, $14.

CROCKETT, S. R. The stickit minister and some common men. *8th and il. ed.* [*Edition de luxe.*] With a prefatory poem now first printed, by Rob. L: Stevenson, in fac-simile, glossary of Scottish words, etc. Macmillan. 12°, *net*, $7.

PRICE, W. T. A life of Charlotte Cushman, Brentano's, por. 24°, (Library of masks and faces.) 75 c.

PRICE, W. T. A life of William Charles Macready. Brentano's, por. 24°, (Library of masks and faces.) 75c.
With these little books a new series of handy volumes is begun, devoted to biographical and critical essays of the great American and European actors and actresses. Aimed " to be an adjustment of the records which, in many particulars, are in danger of being obscured by errors and by friendly and unfriendly misapprehensions."

STEARNS, FRANK PRESTON. Life and genius of Jacopo Robusti, called Tintoretto. 12°, $2.25.
Jacopo Robusti, commonly called " Tintoretto," was born in Venice in 1518 and died 1594. He was one of the greatest painters of the Venetian or of any school; his works, mostly frescoes, were made in Venice, many of them still remaining to view in the churches and palaces. A thorough life of Tintoretto in English has long been needed—one that should understandingly set forth his work and his genius—we have it here, A list of his paintings and where they are is given.

SWIFT, JONATHAN. Travels into several remote nations of the world, by Lemuel Gulliver; with a preface by H. Craik; il. by C. E. Brock. *Edition de luxe.* Macmillan. 8°, (Cranford ser.) buckram, *net*, $14.

WINTER, W. Life and art of Joseph Jefferson; with some account of his ancestry and of the Jefferson family of actors. Macmillan. 12°, $2.25.

BIOGRAPHY, CORRESPONDENCE, ETC.

BELLOC, M. A., *and* Shedlock, M., *eds.* Edmond and Jules de Goncourt, with letters and leaves from their journals; comp, and tr. by M. A. Belloc and M. Shedlock. Dodd, Mead & Co. 2 v., 8°, $7.50.

CHURCH, R. W. (*Dean*). Life and letters of Dean Church; ed. by his daughter, Mary C. Church, with a preface by the Dean of Christ Church. Macmillan. 12°, $1.50.

DAILEY, ABRAM H. Mollie Fancher, the Brooklyn enigma: an authentic statement of facts in the life of Mary J. Fancher, the psychological marvel of the nineteenth century. The G. F. Sargent Co. pors. 12°, $1.50.
Mary J. Fancher has for years been a puzzle to her friends and to skilled experts in mental and physical science. She was born in Massachusetts in 1848. At sixteen years of age ill-health forced her to leave school. Shortly after she was thrown from her horse. She is supposed to have received spinal injuries. In 1866 she suffered from acute lung trouble and her case was deemed hopeless. She since has been subject to spasms and trances, has lost the sense of sight, hearing, and touch, but seems to have received a power of second sight and double and even sextuple consciousness. The book is made up of the testimony of many who have studied her case. She is still alive and her condition remains about the same.

GODWIN, PARKE. Commemorative addresses: George William Curtis, Edwin Booth, Louis Kossuth, John James Audubon, William Cullen Bryant. Harper. 12°, $1.75.
" It is no slight thing for the youth of the country to have heard Mr. Godwin speak of such men as he has clasped hands with. He is the last of the little group of orators to whom the public turns naturally for commemorative addresses. His memory reaches back of the middle years of the century and holds with singular tenacity the details of his intimate knowledge of the fine minds which have given to the century its value as a historic and literary period. Already the names and events that are familiar to his lips have a certain significance to us as belonging to a past order. Already the lives that are to him pulsing with vital associations have become to us landmarks of a time that has taken on a semblance of antiquity in comparison with the immediate and very different present.
" Mr. Godwin is an artist of the old school, and his portraits have that which portraits do not always have, an indisputable likeness to the sitter. Posterity may yield its admiration to very different art, but when it desires to find out how the chief people of Mr. Godwin's generation looked to their companions, they may go with assurance to this gallery of portraits."— *N. Y. Times.*

HERMANN, PAUL. Das leben des Fürsten Bismarck : eine geschichte der wieder geburt der deutschen nation. Fred. Klein Co., [Julius Salomon & Co.] il. 12°, $1 ; pap., 50 c.
Notwithstanding the numberless volumes devoted to Bismarck the author claims there is still room for a cheap biography, well printed on good paper, which, written on free soil, can tell the story of the making of the German empire without any political coercion. He ranks Bismarck with Frederick the Great, and makes a telling comparison of the work accomplished by these heroes of two centuries. The many Germans who came to America in the midst of the events with which the author deals in excellent German will appreciate the immense work he has put into these gleanings from the Bismarck literature which covers half a century.

JEBB, *Mrs.* J. GLADWYN. A strange career: life and adventures of John Gladwyn Jebb, by his widow ; with an introd. by H. Rider Haggard. Roberts. por., 12°, $1.25,

JOINVILLE, FRANÇOIS FERDINAND PHILIPPE L. Marie D'Orleans (*Prince de*) Memoirs (*vieux souvenirs*) of the Prince de Joinville ; from the French by Lady Mary Loyd ; il. from drawings by the author. Macmillan. 8°, $2.25.
The Prince de Joinville was the third son of Louis Philippe and was born in 1818. He was for many years in the French navy, becoming a rear-admiral in 1844. On the breaking out of our late war in 1861, he came to this country with his young son, and his nephews, the Comte de Paris and the Duc de Chartres, the two latter becoming members of McClellan's staff. The present volume ends with the year 1848, the year of the revolution which deprived his father of his throne. The volume is rich in anecdote and personal reminiscences.

VEDDER, H. C. American writers of to-day. Silver, Burdett & Co. 12°, $1.50.
Literary and biographical papers on Edmund Clarence Stedman, Francis Parkman, W. D. Howells, H. James, C. Dudley Warner, T. Bailey Aldrich, Mark Twain, Francis Marion Crawford, Frances Hodgson Burnett, C. Egbert Craddock, Elizabeth Stuart Phelps, Adeline D. T. Whitney, Bret Harte, E. E. Hale, E. Eggleston, G. Washington Cable, R. H. Stoddard, Francis R. Stockton, and Joaquin Miller.

DESCRIPTION, GEOGRAPHY, TRAVEL, ETC.

APPLETON'S handbook of winter resorts : for tourists and invalids, giving complete information as to winter sanitariums and places of resort in the United States, the West Indies, the Bermudas, the Sandwich Islands, and Mexico. *New ed.*, December, 1894, *rev. to date ;* with maps, table of railroad fares, etc. Appleton. 12°, pap., 50 c.

BIGELOW, POULTNEY. The borderland of Czar and Kaiser : notes from both sides of the Russian frontier; il. by F. Remington. Harper. 12°, $2.

BUCKLEY, J. M. Travels in three continents : Europe, Asia, Africa. Hunt & Eaton. il. 8°, $3.50.

BUTLER, W., *D.D.* The land of the Veda : being personal reminiscences of India, its people, castes, thugs, and fakirs, its religions, mythology, principal monuments, palaces, and mausoleums ; with the incidents of the great Sepoy Rebellion. *New ed.* Hunt & Eaton. il. 8°, $2.

DENNIS, JA. TEACKLE. On the shores of an inland sea. Lippincott. il. 12°, 75 c.
Describes a voyage to Alaska from San Francisco, and a visit to some of the chief ports of Alaska from a missionary standpoint.

DOMESTIC AND SOCIAL.

LITTLE EPICURE (THE) : 700 choice receipts. The Baker & Taylor Co. 16°, $1.
The price of the materials accompany each receipt, the aim being to enable housekeepers to know the cost of each dish at average market prices, and to provide in each recipe a quantity sufficient for six persons. The book is not designed to instruct beginners in minute details pertaining to the proper preparation of dishes in daily use—that department having already been ably treated by other writers. The author simply wishes to show that one can be both economical and hospitable. In the index the price of each dish is also given.

EDUCATION, LANGUAGE, ETC.

BURSTALL, SARA A. The education of girls in the United States. Macmillan. 12°, *net,* $1.

DE GARMO, C. Herbart and the Herbartians. Scribner. 12°, (Great educators ser.) *net,* $1.
The founder and disciples of a school noted chiefly for work in psychology.

FICTION.

BARLOW, JANE. The end of Elfintown ; il. by Laurence Housman. Macmillan. 16°, $1.50.

BARR, *Mrs.* AMELIA E. The flower of Gala Water : a novel ; il. by C. Kendrick. Bonner. 12°, (The Ledger lib., no. 119.) $1.25; pap., 50 c.

CHAMBERLAIN, H..R. 6000 tons of gold. Flood & Vincent. 12°, $1.25.
" Mr. H. R. Chamberlain has written a story of remarkable ingenuity in ' 6000 tons of gold.' This is a consideration, in highly picturesque and interesting form, of what would happen in case a large amount of gold should suddenly be added to the currency of a nation, or of the world. It is probable that not many have thought how astounding and how disastrous the effects of such an addition would be ; certainly nobody has followed out the consequences, in the shape of a readable and vivid story, with such an application of logic and supply of illuminative detail. The instruction that is contained in such a story is particularly valuable at this time, in view of the discussions that have been maintained regarding the free coinage of silver and the possibility of employing silver as a standard of value. ' 6000 tons of gold ' first appeared in serial form in the *Chautauquan,* and was afterwards published anonymously in England, where it excited an unusual interest."—*The Sun.*

DOYLE, A. CONAN. The parasite : a story ; il. by Howard Pyle. Harper. 12°, $1.
"' The parasite ' is another of Dr. A. Conan Doyle's capital stories having for a background the profession of which he is a member. It is a study of mesmeric and hypnotic phenomena. A

scholarly physician, skeptical of all save material things, is compelled to acknowledge the subtle and elusive influence of a female medium. Notwithstanding her physical deformity and facial homeliness, the medium who falls in love with the doctor exerts her influence so powerfully that he is drawn to her at most unconscionable hours of the day and night. But the doctor does not yield without struggling valiantly against such despotism, and although he is a severe sufferer he is happily released in the end. The story is admirably told, and there is present in the volume that indefinable grace of style characteristic of Dr. Doyle's best work. From the same house is sent a new edition of Dr. Doyle's 'White Company.' Many competent critics believe that no novel of recent years is more praiseworthy than this. Dr. Doyle is obviously a close student of Sir Walter Scott, and in this romance he has succeeded in reproducing the heroic spirit and energy of the great Wizard of the North. At least two characters in the 'White Company' are drawn with the masterly strength of genius."—*Philadelphia Press.*

DOYLE, A. CONAN. The white company : a novel ; il. by G. Willis Bardwell. (*New lib. ed.*) Harper. il. 12°, $1.75.

EGERTON, G., (*pseud.* for *Mrs.* Clairmonte.) Discords. Roberts Bros. 16°, $1.

ESCHSTRUTH, NATALY V. (*Baroness*). The opposite house : a novel ; from the German, by Mary J. Safford ; il. by H. M. Eaton. Bonner. 16°, (Ledger lib., no. 118.) $1 ; pap., 50 c.
The handsome young hero is from the merchant class of Germans ; his father had made an immense fortune in a mill, which the son had largely squandered at the gaming-table and upon a beautiful dancer. His life breaks his mother's heart, her sudden death bringing his reckless career to a standstill. He determines to reform, and is upheld in his intentions by the young Baroness who lives in the "opposite house." These young people love each other, but are for a long time separated by class prejudices, and the bitter enmity of a discarded mistress and her equally unscrupulous partner in vice.

MACHEN, ARTHUR. The great god Pan and The inmost light. Roberts . 16°, $1..

PENDERED, MARY L. Dust and laurels: a study in nineteenth century womanhood. Appleton. 16°, (Appleton's town and country lib., no. 158.) $1; pap., 50 c.

REID, CHRISTIAN, [*pseud.* for *Mrs.* Frances C. Fisher.] The land of the sun (*vistas Mexicanas*). Appleton. il. 12°, $1.75.

STEVENSON, ROB. L. Will o' the mill. Joseph Knight Co. 12°, (Cosy corner ser.) 50 c.
An allegorical story which pictures the life of a lonely boy who lived at an old mill, situated in a remote valley between two high mountains; this lad was fated for years to watch from a distance the passing of many travellers, and finally the mill where he lives is, on account of his adopted father's greed transformed into an inn; then the wayfarers are brought into direct touch with him, and his opinions of life are confirmed. His views of death are realized and described in the last chapter.

HISTORY.

ALGER, J. G. Glimpses of the French Revolution . myths, ideals, and realities. Dodd, Mead & Co. 12°, $1.75.
Papers on general incidents or phases of the French Revolution. Under the title of "Myths" Mr. Alger disproves many sensational stories regarding the Reign of Terror, which have gained general credence—such as leather being made out of human skins, the last supper of the Girondins, etc. "Utopias" deals with the many impracticable and visionary schemes of the time. Other chapters tell their own tale through their titles, which are : "Adoration of the Magi," "Prophetesses and Viragoes," "Children," "The revolutionary tribunal," "Women as victims," and "The prisons."

ARCHER, T. A., *and* KINGSFORD, C. L. The crusades: the story of the Latin Kingdom of Jerusalem. Putnam. il. map. 12°, (The story of the nations ser., no. 43.) $1.50 ; hf. leath., $1.75.

FERGUSON, H. Essays in American history. Pott. 12°, $1.25.
The four essays are entitled "The Quaker in New England," "The witches," "Sir Edmund Andros," and "The loyalists."

GRAETZ, H. History of the Jews. V. 4, From the rise of Kabbala (1270 C.E.) to the permanent settlement of the Marranos in Holland (1618 C.E.) Jewish Pub. Soc. of America, 1894. 8°, $3.
Contents : Cultivation of the Kabbala, and proscription of science ; The first expulsion of the Jews from France, and its consequences ; The age of the Asherides and of Gersorides ; The black death ; The age of Chasdäi Crescas and Isaac Ben Shesbet ; Jewish apostates and the disputation at Tortosa ; The Hussites—progress of Jewish literature ; Capistiano and his persecution of the Jews ; The Jews in Italy and Germany before the expulsion from Spain ; The Inquisition in Spain ; Expulsion of the Jews from Spain ; Expulsion of the Jews from Navarre and Portugal ; Results of the expulsion of the Jews from Spain and Portugal—general view ; Reuchlin and the Talmud ; The Kabbala and Messianic fanaticism—the Marranos and the Inquisition : Strivings of eastern Jews for unity ; The Jews in Turkey ; The Jews in Poland ; Settlement of Jews in Holland : The Dutch Jerusalem and the Thirty Years' war.

HOLM, ADOLF. The history of Greece, from its commencement to the close of the independence of the Greek people ; authorized tr. from the German. In 4 v. V. 1, Up to the end of the sixth century B.C. Macmillan. 12°, $2.50.
"The first volume of Dr. Holm's History, now presented (the first of four), embraces the period from beginning of Greek life to the end of the sixth century B.C. The material is well digested (the chapters being short and homogeneous in contents), the style is compact and lucid, the notes are rich and cover a wide range of citation, and the temper of the discussion is dignified and confidence-inspiring. As a compendious and thorough presentation of the latest and best conclusions of archæological, critical and

logical inquiry after the realties that lie veiled in the early twilight of Greek story, this work promises to be of the highest value, and to become a standard authority."—*The Watchman.*

HOLST, H. v. The French Revolution: tested by Mirabeau's career: twelve lectures on the history of the French Revolution, delivered at the Lowell Institute, Boston, Mass. Callaghan. 2 v., 12°, $3.50.
Readers and critics are asked in a prefatory note to take this work for what it purports to be : not a book on the history of the French Revolution, but merely some lectures on it, composed principally with a view to illustrating and criticising some of its main features by the opinions and career of the foremost political genius of its first phase. V. 1 contains : The heritage of Louis XIV. and Louis XV.; Paris and Versailles ; Mending the old garments with new cloth ; The Revolution *before* the Revolution ; A typical family tragedy of portentous historical import; The states general ; A rudderless craft in a storm-tossed sea. V. 2 contains : The party of one man; The 5th and 6th of October, 1789, and the memoir of the 15th ; The decisive defeat of the 7th of November ; Other defeats and mischievous victories ; Mirabeau and the court; The end of a unique tragedy.

SCHARF, J. T. History of the Confederate states navy from its organization to the surrender of its last vessel ; its stupendous struggle with the great navy of the United States, the engagements fought in the rivers and harbors of the south, and upon the high seas, blockade-running, first use of ironclads and torpedoes, and privateer history. *2d ed.* Jos. McDonough. por. il. 4°, $3.50.

WHARTON, ANNE HOLLINGSWORTH. Colonial days and dames; with il. by E. S. Holloway. Lippincott. il. 12°, $1.25.
Interesting glimpses of social and domestic life, north and south, in colonial days, gathered from many sources, are embraced in seven chapters, entitled : Colonial days ; Women in the early settlement; A group of early poetesses; Colonial dames; Old landmarks ; Wedding and merry-making; Legend and romance. By the author of " Through colonial doorways."

WILSON, JA. GRANT, *ed.* The presidents of the United States, 1789-1894 ; by J. Fiske, C. Schurz, W. E. Russell, (*and others.*) Appleton. por. 8°, $3.50.

HUMOR AND SATIRE.

FORD, JA. L. The literary shop, and other tales. G. H. Richmond & Co. 12°, $1.25.

LITERATURE, COLLECTED WORKS.

BOOK-LOVER'S almanac for the year 1895 ; *3d year.* Duprat & Co. il. 12°, pap., $3; $6.
Contents : Of the extra illustration of books, by W. L. Andrews ; Balzac as publisher—his bitter experience, 1825-1830, by G. Ferry ; Dr. Rabelais—poem, by Eugene Field ; A poet's publisher—Humphrey Moseley, 1640-1659, by Beverly Chew; The decline of wood-engraving, by W. J. Linton; Ballade of rare books, by M. A. B. Evans; Recent ex-libris ; A book from the library of St. Helena; Suggestions how to bind our books, by W. Matthews. Prognostications gathered from the writings and sayings of eminent men and women during the past year

accompany calendars for the twelve months. Printed on linen paper, each page encircled with a border printed in pale-green ink.

CLOUSTON, W. A. Hieroglyphic Bibles, their origin and history : a hitherto unwritten chapter of bibliography ; with fac-similes of old wood-cut il., and a new hieroglyphic Bible told in stories by F. A. Lang, with hundreds of tiny colored pictures. F. A. Stokes Co. 4°, bds., $9.

COLUMBIAN lunar annual for the third year of the fifth American century, [by D. G. Porter,] [1895.] The Poet Lore Co. 8°, pap., 25 c.

CURTIN, JEREMIAH, *comp.* Hero-tales of Ireland ; collected by Jeremiah Curtin. Little, Brown & Co. 12°, $2.
" The people of this country ought to be grateful to that accomplished American scholar, Jeremiah Curtin, for the translations from varied and quite dissimilar foreign languages, which he has added to our literature. His version of the wonderful novels of Sienkiewicz opens up to us a most interesting department of history, of which English-speaking people have hitherto been profoundly ignorant ; and his latest publication, ' Hero-tales of Ireland,' is perhaps quite as valuable, with the added charm of a wild, delightful, primeval, Celtic imagination. Possibly we appreciate these stories more thoroughly from the circumstance that by an agreement with this journal, they were personally collected by Mr. Curtin in the least known parts of Ireland, where the peasantry still use the ancient Celtic tongue, and accordingly first made their appearance in English in our columns. But we are sure that our readers will thank us for the information that they can now be procured in a very handsome yet convenient volume. A present more welcome than a copy of this volume could not be made to a student of folk lore."—*The Sun.*

HOPPER, NORA. Ballads in prose, (Irish legends ;) with a title-page and cover by Walter West. Roberts. sq. 12°, $1.50.

LEWES, L. The women of Shakespeare ; from the German, by Helen Zimmern. Putnam. 8°, $2.50.

MORTON, F. W., *comp.* Woman in epigram : flashes of wit, wisdom, and satire from the world's literature. McClurg. 16°, $1.
" ' Woman in epigram' is the title of a little volume compiled by Frederick W. Morton, who sets out by declaring that ' woman is an enigma of the ages—the world's sphinx. To one she has seemed divine; to another satanic,' and he proceeds to set forth the opinions of a multitude of poets, novelists, historians, painters, and statesmen to show the diversity of opinion on the subject. After all he leaves the subject as he finds it. The compiler draws very freely from himself, and we are bound to say his opinions are much worthier a place in the collection than those of some other authors much better known."—*The Sun.*

PHELPS, AUSTIN, *D.D.*, *and* FRINK, H. A. Rhetoric, its theory and practice : " English style in public discourse." Scribner. 12°, *net,* $1.25.

SALA, G. A. Things I have seen and people I have known. Cassell. 2 v., por. 12°, $3.
A collection of essays and sketches. These

subjects are : The real Thackeray ; Charles Dickens as I knew him ; Charles Dickens in Paris ; Paris fifty years ago ; Parisian streets in days of yore ; A most famous funeral ; On the rail ; Under the stars and stripes ; In a Mexican sombreio ; Usurers of the past ; " Fi Fa " and " Ca Sa " ; The fast life of the past ; Pantomimes past and present ; Operas remembered ; Songs that come back to me ; Pictures that haunt me ; Taverns that have vanished ; Dinners departed and discussed ; Cooks of my acquaintance ; Costumes of my infancy ; Handwriting of my friends.

MENTAL AND MORAL PHILOSOPHY.

CALL, ANNIE PAYSON. As a matter of course. Roberts. 16°, $1.
"Mrs. Call announces that the aim of this book is to 'assist towards the removal' of nervous irritants, which are not only the cause of much physical disease, but materially interfere with the best possibilities of usefulness and pleasure in everyday life. She holds that 'this sham civilization, this selfish refinement of barbarous propensities, this clashing of nervous systems instead of the clashing of weapons is largely, if not entirely, the cause of the variety and extent of nervous trouble throughout the world. It is not confined to nervous prostration ; if there is a defective spot organically the nervous irritation is almost certain to concentrate upon it. No such superficial remedies as rest and food will effect a cure.' In other words, Mrs. Call believes that the mental and nervous disorders of the age are due to the imperfection—the barbarousness—of modern civilization. She has a great many things to say in the line of this thought."— *Chicago Inter-Ocean.*

HYSLOP, JA. H. The elements of ethics. Scribner. 8°, $2.50.

LADD, G. T. Philosophy of mind : an essay in the metaphysics of psychology. Scribner. 8°, $3.

NATURE AND SCIENCE.

BARING-GOULD, SABINE. The deserts of Southern France : an introduction to the limestone and chalk plateaux of ancient Aquitaine ; il. by S. Hutton and F. D. Bedford. Dodd, Mead & Co. 2 v., 8°, *net,* $8.
The south-centre of France has its own history which is little known, this interesting bit of country being practically unexplored. Baring-Gould has written a history for the unlearned of a land he carefully studied and learned to love. The geologic formations, the deposits and the rude stone monuments, relics of prehistoric ages, are explained for the "general reader," and the beautiful scenery, the picturesque castles, and the quaint churches find adequate and charming description with pen and pencil. The land also abounds in historic reminiscences. In an appendix there is a list of authorities to be consulted for further information, covering 10 pages.

CHEIRO, (*pseud.*) Cheiro's language of the hand : a complete practical work on the sciences of cheirognomy and cheiromancy, containing the system, rules, and experience of Cheiro the palmist ; il. by Theo. Doré ; re-

productions of famous hands taken from life. Brentano's. por. 8°, $2.
The anonymous author of this work claims to be both a seer and a palmist ; he reads the character from the hand, and looks into the future at the same time, for those who make him personal visits ; in the present work he writes of palmistry as a science, and offers many facts, both medical and scientific, to demonstrate that " as the hands are the servants of the system, so also all that affects the system affects them." The book is interestingly illustrated with pictures of typical hands, abnormal hands, and hands of famous people.

MELLIAR, *Rev.* A. FOSTER. The book of the rose. Macmillan. 12°, $2.75.

POETRY.

BRIDGES, ROB. The growth of love. T. B. Mosher. 8°, (English reprint ser., no. 3.) 400 small copies, *net,* $1.50 ; 40 *large-pap.* copies, *net,* $5 ; 10 Japan vellum, *net,* $10.

LYTLE, W. HAINES. Poems. Ed. with memoir, by W. H. Venable. Robert Clarke Co. 12°, $1.25.

PARTRIDGE, W. ORDWAY. The song-life of a sculptor. Roberts. 16°, $1.

SWINBURNE,. ALGERNON C. Félise : a book of lyrics chosen from the works of Algernon Charles Swinburne. T. B. Mosher. nar. 8°, (Bibelot ser., no. 4.) flex. vellum, 725 copies, *net,* $1 ; 25 copies on Japan vellum, *net,* $2.50.

POLITICAL AND SOCIAL.

BEMIS, E. W. Relation of labor organizations to the American boy and to trade instruction. Phil. Amer. Acad. of Pol. and Soc. Sci. 8°, (Publications of the society.) pap., 25 c.
An answer to an article published in the *Century Magazine* for May, 1893, inspired by the late Col. Auchmuty, which among other things said : "the American boy has no rights which organized labor is bound to respect"— "he is refused admission to nearly all trade-unions, and is boycotted if he attempts to work as a non-union man." The many interesting facts and statistics offered by the writer show that this is not an exact presentation of the case.

BEVAN, WILSON LLOYD. Sir William Petty : a study in English economic literature. Amer. Economic Assoc. 8°, (Publications of the society, v. 9, no. 4.) pap., 75 c.
Sir William Petty was a celebrated English statistician and political economist, born in 1623 and died 1687. His chief works are : " Treatise of taxes and contributions," " Political arithmetic," " Essay concerning the multiplication of mankind," " Down survey of Irish lands," etc. This monograph was prepared because the writer believed Petty deserved more attention than he had hitherto received. It gives a very full account of its subject's life, his writings, etc. A list of works used or referred to covers a page. Bibliography of the printed works of Sir William Petty (3 pages).

BÖHM-BAWERK, EUGEN V. The ultimate standard of value. Amer. Acad. of Pol. and Soc. Sci. 8°, (Publications of the society, no. 128.) pap., 50 c.

DEVINE, E. T. The economic function of woman. Amer. Acad. of Poll. and Soc. Sci. 8°, (Publications of the society, no. 133.) pap., 15 c.

Man is largely the producer, woman the contsumer. The author says—"to woman has fallen he task of directing how the wealth brought into the house shall be used, whether much or little shall be made of it, and what kind of wealth shall be brought. In the current theories, the importance of this latter function has been absurdly underestimated. With a clearer recognition of its true relation to the whole subject of wealth, there must result an increased respect on the part of economists for the industrial functions which woman performs."

GLADSTONE, W. EWART. Thoughts from the writings and speeches of W. E. Gladstone; comp. by special permission, and edited by G. Barnett Smith. Stokes. 12°, $2.50.

GÖHRE, PAUL. Three months in a workshop: a practical study; from the German, by A. B. Carr: with a prefatory note by R. T. Ely. Scribner. 12°, (Social science ser.) $1.

Prof. Ely in his prefatory note tells the story of this volume: "The author, a theological student, perplexed by conflicting theories and reports touching the lot of the wage-earners, their habits of thought, their struggles and their aspirations, determines to become a wage-earner himself, and, donning the garb of a workman, finds employment in a large manufacturing establishment in industrial Saxony. He mingles for three months with his fellows, who never suppose him to be anything else than 'a wage earner; he shares their life, participates in their amusements, attends their political meetings, and then tells what he has seen and heard with that simplicity which is in itself literary art of a high order." The book was greeted by the wealth and culture of Germany like a revelation, and has had many excellent practical results.

GOULD, J. M., and TUCKER, G. F. The federal income tax. Little, Brown & Co. 12°, net, $1.

OSTRANDER, D. Social growth and stability: a consideration of the factors of modern society and their relation to the character of the coming state. Griggs. 12°, $1.

A few of the subjects considered are as follows: Foreign and native labor; Railroads and machinery; Over-production and commercial stagnation; Not charity but statesmanship wanted; The brotherhood of man; The eight-hour day; The American people composite; Restricted immigration; Free-trade injuries; Protection beneficial; Competition the root of all evil; The government as a common carrier; Strikes; Trusts; Christianity as a social factor; The ultimate destruction of evil; The reading of books; Hard work essential to success.

PRICHARD, MARIA FRANCES. Parliamentary usage for women's clubs and for deliberative bodies other than legislative. Robert Clarke Co. 24°, leatherette, 30 c.

A treatise on parliamentary practice, which fully sustains itself as a guide and book of reference for the club member. It is thoroughly practical—its statements being so direct, concise, and clear as to be fully understood by those just initiated into club relationships; and yet the advanced sections of the book being sufficiently

comprehensive to class it as a manual for the experienced and efficient officer of any deliberative body.

SHAW, ALBERT. Municipal government in Great Britain. The Century Co. 8°, $2.

WARD, C. OSBORNE. The equilibration of human aptitudes and powers of adaptation. National Watchman Co. 12°, $1.25.

The Translator to the United States Department of Labor received his conceptions of the economic adjustment of differing human aptitudes from Charles Darwin, whose keen, analytical judgment in the physical world first gave him the key to the height on which the student of conditions must stand in order to perceive society as a panorama and reason intelligently upon cause and effect. The volume contains chapters on the mechanism of society, the discord of faculties, the plagiaries of genius, the piracy of aptitudes, the concord of faculties, comparative claims, etc. The author claims that a pure political government must absorb both the isolated individual and the segregated society into a great business-like universality of mutual help and progress. He looks for all progress to a conscientious use of the only weapon for reasoning beings—the ballot.

WARNER, AMOS G. American charities: a study in philanthropy and economics. Crowell. 12°, (Library of economics and politics, no. 4.) $1.75.

SPORTS AND AMUSEMENTS.

YOUNG, FRANKLIN K., and HOWELL, EDWIN C. The minor tactics of chess: a treatise on the deployment of the forces in obedience to strategic principle. Roberts. 16°, $1.

THEOLOGY, RELIGION AND SPECULATION.

BIBLE. New Testament. A translation of the four Gospels from the Syriac of the Sinaitic palimpsest, by Agnes Smith Lewis. Macmillan. 12°, net, $1.90.

BRIGGS, C. A. D.D. The Messiah of the gospels. Scribner. 8°, $2.

In the autumn of 1886 "Messianic prophecy" was published as the first of a series of volumes upon the Messianic ideal. (*See* notice, P. W., "Weekly Record." Nov. 13. '86, [772.] Dr. Briggs' share in the Revision Movement of the Presbyterian Church has delayed the second volume of the series which is now offered and treats of the Messianic ideas of pre-Christian Judaism and of the Messiah of the Gospels. Dr. Briggs thinks the Christian Church has looked too much upon a cross with a dead Saviour upon it. He wishes the cross to be held more as a symbol of the resurrection as well as the death, and aims to inspire all Christians with a living faith that will make them do away with all that is sad, gloomy, and sour in religion and cling to its brightness and hope.

CARUS, PAUL. The gospel of Buddha: according to old records. Westermann. 12°, $1.50.

The contents are chiefly derived from the old Buddhist canon. Many passages are copied literally from the translations of the original texts. For those who want to trace the Buddhism of this book to its fountain-head a table of reference has been added, which indicates the main sources of various chapters and points out the parallelisms with western thought, especially in the Christian Gospels. The book aims to impress readers with the poetic grandeur of Buddha's personality and to set them thinking on the religious problems of to-day. A comparison of the agreements and differences between the two greatest religions of the world is made in a fair philosophic spirit.

CHURCH CLUB OF NEW YORK. The rights and pretensions of the Roman see : lectures delivered in 1894 under the auspices of the Church Club of New York. E. & J. B. Young & Co. 12°, *net*, 50 c.

The lectures gathered in this volume are the natural sequel of the course in 1893 on "The Six Œcumenical Councils of the undivided Catholic Church." Their subjects are: "St. Peter and the primacy of the Roman see," "Sardica and appeals to Rome," "Rome, Constantinople, and the rise of Papal supremacy," "The growth of the Papal supremacy and feudalism," "The Babylonian exile and the Papal schism," and "The syllabus and Papal infallibility."

FERGUSON, H. Four periods in the life of the church. Pott. 12°, $1.25.

Four lectures delivered in Christ Church, Hartford, Ct., in the Lent of 1892. Their titles are: The church of the first three centuries; The church of the Christian Empire ; The church of western Europe ; The Reformation in western Europe.

GRIFFIS, W. ELLIOT, *D.D.* The religions of Japan from the dawn of history to the era of of Meiji. Scribner. 12°, $2.

LAGRANGE, C. The great pyramid, by modern science: an independent witness to the literal chronology of the Hebrew Bible and British Israel identity, in accordance with Brück's law of the life of nations: with a new interpretation of the time-prophecies of Daniel and St. John from the French ; recently rev., with five new appendices by the author, and a short note by C. Piazzi Smyth. A. D. F. Randolph & Co. 12°, $3.

PROTESTANT Episcopal church, Congress of the. Papers, addresses and discussions at the Sixteenth Church Congress of the United States held in Boston, November 13, 14, 15 and 16. Whittaker. 8°, pap., $1.

PROTESTANT Episcopal church hymnal ; *rev. and enl.* in accordance with the action of the general convention of the Protestant Episcopal Church in the United States of America in the year 1892; ed. by Rev. C. L. Hutchins. D. B. Updike. 4°, flex. leath., $5.

SUBHADRA, BHIKSHU, *comp.* Buddhist catechism : an introd. to the teachings of the Buddha Gótamo ; comp. from the holy writings of the Southern Buddhists ; with explanatory notes for the use of Europeans ; from the 4th German ed. Putnam. 12°, $1.

A concise representation by question and answer of Buddhism according to the Ceylonese Pali manuscripts of the Tipitakum. Contains only fundamental outlines of Buddha's doctrine, all legendary, mystic, and occult additions of his teachings being omitted. Compiled for those who are seeking neither lifeless dogmas nor results of science, but a doctrine free from all dogmas and forms, in accordance with nature and her laws, embracing the highest truths, equally satisfying to mind and heart. The answers to 174 questions embody this doctrine. A running commentary of footnotes explains the accurate meanings of the terms employed.

WALKER, CORNELIUS, *D.D.* Outlines of Christian theology. Whittaker. 12°, $1.50.

Presents in brief outline the leading topics in a course of theological study which is substantially that which the writer has pursued with his classes successively during the last eighteen or twenty years in the Theological Seminary of Virginia.

Books for the Young.

BAMFORD, MARY E. In Editha's days : a tale of religious liberty. Amer. Baptist Pub. Soc. 12°, (The crown ser., no. 3.) $1.25.

The story is placed in England in the reign of Henry VIII., and in the low countries when they were under the rule of Charles V. and his son, Philip II. The story deals mostly with the persecutions of the "Anabaptists."

BRABOURNE (*Lord*), Knatchbull-Hugessen, E. H. (*Lord* Brabourne). The magic oak tree, and Prince Filderkin. Macmillan. 16°, (Children's lib.) 75 c.

HENDERSON, W. J. Sea-yarns for boys, spun by an old salt. Harper. il. 12°, $1.25.

About nineteen humorous stories of the sea of marvellous detail and adventure. Originally published in *The Young People*.

JÓKAI, MAURICE, SAND, GEORGE, [*pseud.* for Mme. A. L. A. D. Dudevant,] *and* Laboulaye, E. [*and others.*] The golden fairy-book ; il. by H. A. Millar. Appleton. 8°, $2.

Carefully selected stories from Russian, Servian, Hungarian, French, Portuguese, and other sources. Beautifully illustrated.

PRICE, ELEANOR C. In the lion's mouth: the story of two English children in France, 1789-1793. Macmillan. 12°, $1.50.

The two children who are thrown in the "lion's mouth" of the French Revolution are English orphans, a brother and sister, sent to France in 1789 by a wicked uncle anxious to steal their inheritance. The little village in Anjou, where they are lodged in the major's household, is soon wild with revolutionary tumult. The brother and sister cast in their lots with the "aristocrats" of the château, and pass bravely through imprisonment, suffering and danger to rescue at the hands of the loyal Vendéans, and ultimate safety in their English home.

SWAN, ANNIE S., [*Mrs.* Burnett Smith.] Airlie's mission ; il. by Lilian Russell. Hunt & Eaton. 12°, 50 c.

Airlie Keith was the daughter of a Scotchman who had labored for years in the African mission field. Although Airlie's sympathies were in Tahai, at the time of her father's death, she decided on account of her own ill-health to go to the home of Scotch relatives. The story tells of some of the changes in the Keith household, which were wrought by the presence and influence of Airlie, and dwells especially on the girl's return to her father's African work.

YECHTON, BARBARA. The "gentle-heart" stories ; il. by Mary Fairman Clark. Pott. 12°, $1.

Binds together the children's stories of Roland Gentleheart ; By forgiving, win forgiveness; Dorothy's temptations ; Hope Beresford's lesson; Teddy's experience; Bonnie Prince Charlie.

Freshest News.

ALL lovers of literature will be gratified to learn that Mrs. Thackeray Ritchie intends to bring out a new edition of her father's works, with biographical and explanatory notes.

R. F. FENNO & Co. have just issued "A Son of Hagar," by Hall Caine, illustrated by Albert Hencke, which is full of the old fire and subtile knowledge of human nature that make his books so delightful to the weary novel-reader.

"SILK-WARP TRILBY" is the name of a pretty material to be used for next season's street and travelling costumes. It is in Jacquard effects, and in evening colors the tints are as delicate and handsome as silks costing nearly double the price.

THE MERRIAM COMPANY announce as the hit of the year a parody of "Trilby" which bears the inverted name of "Billtry." Mary Kyle Dallas has cleverly taken off the characteristic features of Du Maurier's literary style, the artist has done the same for the drawings.

THE HOME PUBLISHING CO. will bring out early in February a new novel by A. C. Gunter, called "The First of the English"—a title that seems to indicate an historical romance, if any title can be taken as an index to any book, now-adays. At all events, it is said to abound in incident and "go."

ROBERT M. LINDSAY, Philadelphia, has published the interesting etching by William Hole, A.R.S.A., entitled "A Canterbury Pilgrimage." The procession as described by Chaucer is led by the knight and the monk, followed by the three priests, the prioress, the chapelaine, squire, and the rest of the pilgrims. The last to issue from the gate is Chaucer himself. The group is well drawn, each figure being easily distinguished. The etching is copyrighted and makes an appropriate ornament to the walls of the parlor or the study of a literary man or to a library.

FREDERICK WARNE & Co. have some books of very pleasing contents which they offer in nice volumes. The "Quiet Stories from an Old Woman's Garden," by Allison McLean, now in the second edition, are most suitable for reading aloud; and the ninth edition of Edward Lear's "Nonsense Songs and Stories" has been greatly enlarged and has an introduction by Sir E. Strachey, whose exquisite literary taste is acknowledged by his peers in the art of writing criticisms. Books full of practical hints are "The Duties of Servants" and "Waiting at Table," a practical guide by a "member of the aristocracy."

ROBERT BONNER'S SONS have just issued a new novel by Mrs. A. E. Barr, called "The Flower of Gala Water." Like most of her books it is a story of Scottish life and scenery, telling of the homely household duties and not untroubled love stories of a "sonsie" Scotch lass. Mrs. Barr is always pleasant and interesting in her portrayal of girl life, and she is at her best among Scottish surroundings. A new German translation recently issued by the Bonners, which still holds its own, is "The Opposite House," from the German of Nataly von Esch-struth—a romantic love-story of a *bourgeois* hero, who loves a lady of high degree.

PAUL BOURGET's new book "Outre Mer" is shortly to be issued here, in the original French. It is a brilliant description and analysis of his impressions of America, obtained chiefly at the time of the World's Fair. Interesting glimpses of M. Bourget's ideas were afforded through newspaper interviews at the time; and his mature exposition of what he saw and thought of the United States should be not only intrinsically interesting, but a valuable addition to that fascinating and salutary—if not always pleasant—class of books in which "ithers see us." Alphonse Daudet's long-expected novel "La Petite Paroisse" is also in preparation by Meyer Bros., the publishers of "Outre Mer," and will be issued almost simultaneously.

"CHIMMIE FADDEN, whose artless narratives of his experiences among the "four hundred" and out of it have brightened the columns of the New York *Sun* during the past year or so, has attempted to reach a wider audience. These lively tales, in which Edward Townsend so graphically pictures the characteristics and dialect of a decidedly "tough" New York City gamin, are just issued in book form by Lovell, Coryell & Co. Besides the stories relating to the inimitable "Chimmie," the "Duchess," "Miss Fannie," and his other associates, the volume will contain Mr. Townsend's "Major Max Stories," also well known to readers of the *Sun.*

G. W. DILLINGHAM has just ready some half-dozen new books. "Drilby Re-versed" is a travesty of Du Maurier's famous novel, by Leopold Jordan, with 60 comic illustrations by Philip and Earl Ackerman. The novels include "Lore and Law," by Esther Jacobs, called "the story of a singer's life," and presumably based on Miss Jacobs' own history, as revealed a year or so since in a breach-of-promise suit in the New York courts; "Celeste," by Elizabeth M. Sutton; "The Strange Disappearance of Eugene Comstock," by Mrs. Mary R. P. Hatch; "Caught: a Romance of Three Days," by George Douglas Tallman; and "Astor," a novel by Paul Randall. Besides these there are: "Rob Rockafellow," a story told in the form of a diary —the diary being that of a Boston society man; and "The Banker and the Typewriter," a contribution to the "comic" literature of the subject.

HUNT & EATON have four books which, originally published for the holiday season, bid fair to hold their own among the good books of the new year. These are Prof. Buckley's "Travels in Three Continents," a delightful chronicle of intelligent and appreciative journeying in Europe, southern and central France, Spain, Gibraltar, Italy, Greece, and other famous corners of the earth; "The Land of the Vedas," personal reminiscences of India, by Rev. William Butler, who tells also the thrilling details of the great Sepoy rebellion; "Up the Susquehanna," a series of pleasant letters written while travelling from the Chesapeake Bay to Otsego Lake and the Alleghanies, by H. C. Pardoe; and "Three of Us: Barney, Cossack, Rex," a delightful "dog story" by Mrs. Izora C. Chandler, whose pictures of canine life and sentiments are appreciated by grown people as well as by little folks.

CHOICE ILLUSTRATED NOVELS.

LITERARY NEWS

AN ECLECTIC REVIEW OF
CURRENT LITERATURE
~ILLUSTRATED~

CONTENTS.

VOL-XVI-No3   MARCH ~ 1895 $1.00 YEARLY
10 CTS. PER NO.

~ PUBLICATION OFFICE ~
· 28 ELM STREET NEW YORK·

ENTERED AT THE POST OFFICE AT NEW YORK AS SECOND CLASS MATTER

The Literary News

In winter you may reade them, ad ignem, by the fireside; and in summer, ad umbram, under some shadie tree; and therewith pass away the tedious howres.

| VOL. XVI. | MARCH, 1895. | No. 3 |

Life of Mr. George Augustus Sala.

WE have read Mr. Sala's "Life and Adventures" with the liveliest interest. Here at last is an autobiographer who is not only frank, but who even appears at times, in the exuberance of his candor, to bear himself a grudge. It may be meanly urged that Mr. Sala, as an Old Journalistic Hand, is unable from long habit to abstain from "racy" personalities and revelations, even at his own expense; and that his frankness as to the follies and escapades of his youth rings more of an unrepentant Master Shallow than of a broken and a contrite heart. But the great fact of frankness remains; and with it goes hand-in-hand the twin autobiographical virtue of modesty—for Mr. Sala, so far from being with monotonous regularity the hero of his own "Adventures," not seldom emerges conspicuously at "the smaller end of the horn."

Mr. Sala was born in 1828, at London, where his mother, widowed shortly after his birth, was a teacher of singing, and, later, an actress. Madam Sala had a distinguished *clientèle*, and played at the leading theatres; but, with five young children on her hands, she had no little trouble bringing the proverbial ends together.

From "Life of George Augustus Sala." Copyright, 1895, by Charles Scribner's Sons.

GEORGE AUGUSTUS SALA.

Mr. Sala's formal entry into journalism was not auspicious. About 1850 he became editor and co-proprietor of *Chat*, a half-penny weekly, in the theoretical "profits" of which he was kindly allowed to participate. But there were, in practice, no profits; and, the chief owner of *Chat* judiciously absconding, Mr. Sala and his associates found themselves "under the unpleasant necessity of fighting for the small change in the till."

Mr. Sala's lane, like all others, had its turning. The decisive turn came with the close of the Crimean war, when he was commissioned by Dickens to go to Russia in order to write a series of descriptive articles for *Household Words*. His forte soon became apparent. From that date on, Mr. Sala's autobiography lapses largely into a perhaps unavoidably jumbled record of his adventures in one country or another as a press correspondent—the reader of it being whisked about geographically in a way suggesting that at times the writer must have been, like the Irishman's bird, "in two places at once." From 1856 downwards, wherever matters of an exciting nature were stirring—wars or rumors of wars, coronations, political murders, revolutions, exhibitions, and the like journalistically exploitable doings—there was Mr. Sala in the thick of it with his pencil and notebook.

Mr. Sala's book amply fulfils its author's intent to "give the general public a definite idea of the character and the career of a working journalist in the second, third and fourth decades of the Victorian era." (Scribner. 2 v., $5.)—*The Dial.*

The Devil's Playground.

QUITE one of the best of the batch of books sent to us this month is "The Devil's Playground." There is a spontaneity of utterance, a freshness of style, and a wealth of vivid local coloring which leaves the reader, at the close of the book, with the conviction that the author is not only writing about people, places, and things with whose characteristics he is perfectly familiar, but that the events and adventures of his own life must have been his inspiration and inducement to put pen to paper to describe them. We have seen it stated that John Mackie has led the same kind of roving life that his hero Dick Travers went through. We cannot vouch for this as a fact, but it may well be so. The title of the book is derived from the name of a weird district called "The Devil's Playground," where "great unseemly scarred and jagged sides of chocolate-colored clay, intersected by jet-black seams and yellow and

From " The Devil's Playground." Copyright, 1894, by F. A. Stokes Co.

HIS SATANIC MAJESTY MAKES A MOVE.

pink, with here and there patches of alkali showing dazzling white," enclosed a valley from whose bed rose up "huge pillar-like masses of clay, like gigantic mushrooms, some perfectly round and tapered towards their summits, resembling sugar-loaves, so sprinkled were they by a gleaming and mica-like substance ; others, again, bulbous-shaped and ungainly." It is here that the culminating scene of the story is laid. Of Mr. Mackie's sense of humor we cannot say much. The buffoonery of Cousin Ned is doubtless intended to serve as a relief and a foil to the sombre thoughts and reflections of the two chief characters, but it is of a feeble sort and jars horribly. The action of the story chiefly takes place in a blizzard, where Dick and the girl of his heart, now another man's wife, get lost. Dick finally rescues her, and the story ends satisfactorily with the hero's getting himself engaged to a rich and eminently satisfactory English girl. But where there is so much to praise in the book as a whole we are loath to pick holes in regard to the minor parts, and we look forward with interest to further contributions from Mr. Mackie's pen. (Stokes. 75 c.)—*Westminster Review.*

The Pygmies.

THE treatise on "The Pygmies," by the late A. de Quatrefages, which in the translation by Frederick Starr forms the second volume in the *Anthropological Series,* is the first systematic attempt to determine the ethnography of the "little blacks" to show how far they confirm the beliefs and traditions of antiquity, and to determine their relation to the white and yellow races. It is to the second object that Professor de Quatrefages devoted himself chiefly in the present work, and consequently the book appeals to other than strictly student of natural science. The preliminary chapter is concerned with an examination of the ancient beliefs regarding the pygmies as viewed in the light of modern science, and the chapters that follow deal respectively with the general history and physical characters of the Eastern pygmies ; the intellectual, moral and religious characters of the Mincopies ; the Negritos other than Mincopies ; the Negrillos or African pygmies ; and the religious beliefs of the Hottentots and Bushmen. To sum up the main conclusions to be derived from the volume, it may be said that Professor de Quatrefages succeeded in proving the real importance of the pygmies as a factor in the problem of racial development, while his comparison of their manners, customs, and mythologies is full of decided interest. The book has thirty-one illustrations after photographs and drawings of skulls. There is an index. (Appleton. $1.75.)—*The Beacon.*

From "Trans-Caspia."   Copyright, 1895, by R. Clarke Company.

THE MARKET AT BOKARA.

Travels in Turkestan.

TRANS-CASPIA is the journal of a man who started from St. Petersburg with the intention of travelling across the Trans-Caspian territory of Russia, and eventually exploring the Vale of Cashmere. He got as far as the Chinese border, and then turned back. It seems that the poor man is a dyspeptic, or at least that his doctor classes him as such. He came to such a pass that, as he viewed it, there were only two things for him to do: He could go on, and die ; or he could go home, and get well. He decided that it would be better to go home.

As it is, we get the story of a tour in Turkestan, over which Mr. Shoemaker and a friend travelled sufficiently to see its points of interest. It would not be worth while to go from here to Turkestan just for the sake of journeying through the country and writing a book about it, but as Mr. Shoemaker had been there and had made some entries in his journal about the people, the scenery, the cities, and the hardships of his journey, it was a proper thing to publish what he had "written on the spot," and to illustrate the text with some photographs taken by the author. We have heard a good deal about Turkestan, but not so much that we may not welcome Mr. Shoemaker's sprightly descriptions and his photographic illustrations.

Mr. Shoemaker made the trip from Usin-Ada to Samarkand over the Trans-Caspian Railway, and, after reading his story of the journey, the wonder grows that such a railroad should have been built. Trains run three times a week, and cover the distance of about nine hundred miles in sixty hours. A good part of the way there is nothing to look at but a most abominable desert, across which clouds of sand are swept by winds so hot that they would be hard to bear even without their accompaniment of sand. Every now and then the trains stop while the section hands shovel the sandbanks off the track. The trains make unconscionable halts at the regular stations for no apparent cause, but the inference is drawn that the train hands postpone as long as they dare setting forth again into the hot, sultry plains. Certainly they do not stay in order to give travellers opportunity to get their meals, for the meals are furnished in dining cars. These dining cars are ordinary freight cars painted white.

Benches run down the centre of the cars, and chairs are placed on either side. "The messes" are described as "something terrible." Mr. Shoemaker says he was puzzled for a time trying to determine from what sort of animal the meat he ate came. His conclusion was that it was part of an oil tank. "What does Russia make out of a land like this?" queries the author. Answering for himself, he says : "Simply, I fancy, the building of a watchtower in the direction of India and the

English, with perhaps an eye to China. There is not a bit of cultivation in all the distance traversed ; no green save in patches, on which the few miserable natives cower shudderingly."

After leaving Samarkand Mr. Shoemaker travelled in a wagon, visiting Tashkend, Kokand, Marghilan, and Osh. From Osh he made his start for the Vale of Cashmere. His travelling companion went north into the mountains to hunt. Whether he came back alive is more than Mr. Shoemaker knows—he would be very glad to know that he still is living. (The Robert Clarke Co. $1.50.)— N. Y. Times.

Occult Japan.

THIS work describes a distinct "find" by its brilliant author, Percival Lowell, during a recent sojourn in Japan, viz., of an elaborate system of possession-trance practised by one of the sects of Shinto, the ethnic faith of Japan. Introductory or sequent to this main theme are accounts of Shinto miracles, pilgrimages, "gohei," and the Ise shrines. Much care was rightly bestowed upon tracing this curious cult to its real source, the primitive Shinto faith as distinguished from the imported Buddhism, and thus a distinct contribution has been made to what is at last receiving deserved attention, the ethnic faith of Japan.

The treatise stands a model of keen observation, deep insight, and scientific analysis, while over all this rigidly scientific material and method is thrown the charm of a style that implies the blending of scientist and poet. The abounding satire, epigram, alliteration, and metaphor would as much repay a perusal with purpose of entertainment, as its soberer merits would for instruction in an absolutely new field. (Houghton, Mifflin & Co. $1.75.)—The Nation.

Pelleas and Melisande.

THIS is a prettily gotten out drama of the Belgian poet and dramatist, whose weird, symbolical, but fascinating and powerful plays have excited the literary world to wonder and admiration in the last two years. The works of this author, though always given the dramatic form, are impractical to stage representation, and, indeed, half their force and curious charm would be lost in action behind the footlights. The characters and ideas of Maeterlinck must move in the vision of the reader's strangely excited imagination to have their real significance and deep, potential value. This play, which is in three acts, is probably the greatest work of its author, and though there is in it a symbolism that each reader must attempt to interpret for himself, perhaps not always succeeding to entire satisfaction, the story has an intense, vivid, empathic vitality, veritism that is seen through the romance of the poet's fancy like a giant truth overwhelming in its awful impressiveness. It is the story of Francesca da Rimini in other form ; but the skeleton is nothing ; it is the mysterious manner in which the author leads its personages through the maze of destiny that distinguishes Maeterlinck pre-eminently and gives him a unique place among writers. There is an infinity of pathos in this play, angry passion, consuming love, unutterable despair, yet there is not a passage of studied writing that the reader can detect, and we must infer that which most moves us. It is a wonderful work, of which much might be written with interest, but it is one of those creations that may not be described and gain no value from critical comment. The book must be read, and each one must judge of it for himself. Its interest may not be pointed out in a critique, however carefully or elaborately written, but we commend it heartily to the intelligent and poetic reader as a thing that cannot fail to delight him. (Crowell. $1.)—Chicago Inter-Ocean.

On India's Frontier.

NEPAL, the subject of these pages, the mountainous home of a recklessly brave and hardy race known as Gurkhas, ranks as the most powerful and favored of India's frontier tribe.

Outside of a small, select British official class, who have been posted there at different times by the India Government to watch after its interests, the number of other foreigners permitted to visit Nepal can be counted on one's fingers, and these, during their short-licensed sojourn in that territory, are under constant espionage. No wonder, then, that Nepal is a terra incognita—an unknown as well as a mysterious land—to the outside world. Though nominally subservient to China, paying its tribute quintennially to the Celestial Empire, it virtually recognizes the direct supremacy of Great Britain, to which power first and foremost, in the personnel of its foreign office, application must be made for any permission to enter this country's borders, declaring in detail the plan and object of the applicant's projected trip, with all particulars concerning himself ; and, even then, his request is likely to be denied. Hence the title of the little book "On India's Frontier ; or, Nepal, the Gurkhas' Mysterious Land." (Tait. $2.50.)—Preface.

The Book-Bills of Narcissus.

WITH all its digressions and appeals to the gentle reader, says *The Saturday Review*, "Mr. Le Gallienne's book is a study of character, a study of the spiritual growth and evolution of a poetic young gentleman whose many charms proved irresistible with certain booksellers and other young persons. The portraiture is delicately wrought. The pleasant touches of humor or pathos, the little strokes of irony, are so blended that you cannot detect any positive evidence of moral judgment, even when censure may seemed to be implied. The whole record, in short, is harmonious, and artist and work are as one. The deliberate quaintness of style, as of a new Euphaes, or a Euphaes with something of the poetic grace of the old, and a manner that is his own, is in perfect agreement with the theme." The conclusion of the reviewer is that "Mr. Le Gallienne has achieved the end he had in view. He has made the 'rose of Narcissus to bloom anew.'"

"The Book-Bills of Narcissus" appeared in England three or four years ago and were at once appreciated by literary people, who

From "The Book-Bills of Narcissus."   Copyright, 1895, by
G. P. Putnam's Sons.

A POET.

soon exhausted a first edition. A second has followed, and now we have the third, to which the author has added a new chapter, introducing a little element of humorous romance into his descriptions of the mind of a young poetic *litterateur*, who following out his wholly unpractical idiosyncrasies, is forced to sell many of the books he has collected in days of prosperity and self-indulgence. These books furnish the text for dissertations on life and literature. Many of the critics have been severe with the author, but it is hard to think any critic can be so hardened that he cannot get some delightful moments in skimming through "The Book-Bills of Narcissus" (Putnam. $1.)

Degeneration.

A COPYRIGHTED English translation of Max Nordau's great work, "Entartung," has been published under the title "Degeneration." "Briefly stated," says Richard Burton in *The Critic*, "Nordau's theme is the degeneracy of modern art, literature and philosophy, exampled in such men as Ibsen and Maeterlinck, Whitman and Wagner, Verlaine and Mallarmé, Tolstoï and Zola. These marked personalities he regards, in his own phrase, as types of 'a degenerative psychosis of the epileptoid order.' This gives a hint at once of the author's originative impulse ; he is a disciple of Lombroso, who in his "Man of Genius" sought to 'show that from the point of view of the biological and psychological laboratory, genius and insanity if not coterminous and interchangeable, were at least first-cousins. Nordau's book is a more direct and a far wider application of this idea, because he is himself a literary producer and judge, and in large degree adduces specific examples and analyzes them. He regards such catchwords as *fin de siècle*, decadent, and the like, as significant of the unwholesome, diseased nature and work of the popular makers of literature, and of the age that hails them.' The German thinker's zeal for his theory carries him, at times, to absurd extremes, and almost always he is one-sided, unfair, and coldly unsympathetic with the real aim and spirit of the writer he traduces. Nordau's mood is scientific, not æsthetic. . . .

But while we may lay finger on the intemperance, the harshness and the illogic of "Degeneration" we should miss not to recognize that Nordau has some ground for his robust deliverances. It is significant that such a book could have been written nowadays by so able a thinker. . . . That the maker of contemporary literature and art should be handled thus roughly, studied as pathological material instead of æsthetic phenomena, will perhaps help to create an audience for wholesomer literature, and if once the demand become imperative, we shall see less and less of this deification of the lawless, the obscene and the sensual in our latest writing. . . . Degenerates may be geniuses, but this is vastly other than to say that geniuses are degenerates. In the meantime let it not be forgotten that the healthy demand of society for wholesome art and letters will be a tremendous therapeutic agency in correcting all excess which threatens to throw those 'small insanities' out of balance." (Appleton.)

A Modern "Anatomy of Melancholy."

IT is nearly three centuries since Robert Burton wrote his "Anatomy of Melancholy "— a work the more remarkable because it was the production of an age of hope and action rather than an age of introspection and depression. This standard text-book has now received a kind of companion in a volume which sets forth at great length, with the utmost particularity, and evidently from the standpoint of a very ample scholarship in philosophy, literature, and art, the sources, the moods, and the temper of melancholy at the end of the nineteenth century. Never before in the history of the world has melancholy received so many artistic expressions as during the present century. The sadness which left its permanent impress in the fugitive lines of the Greek anthology was largely the expression of a decadent civilization—of men who were aware of the decline of civic, religious, and personal life. This century, on the other hand, has been marked by strenuous activities, by high hopes, and by immense forward impulses. Side by side, however, with the strain and stir of the century, there has been a morbid vein of thought and feeling which has shown itself again and again in men of sensitive temper like Leopardi, Leconte de Lisle, Heine, Alfred de Musset, Guy de Maupassant, Amiel, and in the work of a great number of novelists of more or less power and insight.

The most complete expression of this temper and attitude which has recently been given the English-speaking world is to be found in "The Melancholy of Stephen Allard "—a book remarkable for its breadth of knowledge, for its power of following all the sinuosities which the melancholy mood pursues, and for its skill in conveying the general impression of futility in which the melancholy mood delights. The un-

known author of this book makes the complete tour of the world of purely human resource, and finds that all things are dust and ashes. He seeks by turns every source of consolation, and finds them all inadequate. He goes to science, to the philosophers, to the poets, the artists, the moralists, and the mystics, and none of them satisfy him. The book is a study in melancholy. It is a document of human nature at the end of a century which has seen so many high hopes disappointed. Nothing will ever really satisfy man but God ; and neither science, art, democracy, nor human progress in any of its features can slake the undying thirst of the human race. Yet the writer of this book has his moods of hope, and is able to quote, as expressive of his own aspiration, the noble sentence of Plato: "The true philosopher . . . is content if only he may live his earthly life pure of injustice or unrighteousness, and quit the present scene in peace and kindliness, with bright hopes." "The Melancholy of Stephen Allard " is not a book to be read for inspiration or guidance, but it possesses deep interest for those who want to know the disease of their own time. (Macmillan. $1.75.)—*The Outlook.*

Greek Studies.

A MELANCHOLY interest attaches to the volume of " Greek Studies" by the late Walter Pater, prepared for the press by his friend, Charles L. Shadwell, of Oriel College, and published by Macmillan. Posthumous work always makes a special appeal, and this series of essays is thoroughly representative of the culture, the finished and beautiful style and the classic bias of the distinguished critic. But these are but specks in the ointment. The book contains nine papers, mostly dealing with Greek art and sculpture ; especially fine are the first four, in which dominant classic myths are studied, the titles, " A Study of Dionysius ; the Spiritual Form of Fire and Dew," " The Bacchanals of Euripides" (showing one phase of the Bacchus cult as used in the Greek drama), and two studies on the myth of Demeter and Persephone. The fifth, " Hippolytus Veiled," treats of the earlier, purer form of that legend, before it appears veiled in another country than Attica and in the handling of Ovid. " The Beginnings of Greek Sculpture" furnish food for papers on the heroic age and the age of graven images, full of suggestive points ; there is one on the " Marbles of Ægina " and a final one on " The Age of Athletic Prize-Men ; A Chapter in Greek Art "—as good a statement of the excellencies and limitations of the Greek genius working in plastic forms and with chief regard to the superficies as we have ever seen. The characteristics of these mellow, charming essays are, their complex music of diction, at times the sentences becoming too involved not to tax the reader's eye and mind ; subtlety and refinement of thought and feeling and a searching out of the underlying ideal concept in these productions of the Greeks which to the more careless attention seem coarse or meaningless. The last tract makes Pater's work dignified and noble. This, presumably his last book, is a welcome addition to classical studies. (Macmillan. $1.75.)—*Hartford Daily Courant.*

A Literary History of the English People.

"MANY histories have preceded this one," says Mr. Jusserand in his preface to "A Literary History of the English People," and many others will follow. Such is the charm of the subject that volunteers will never be lacking to undertake this journey, so hard, so delightful, too. The portion of the great work now published covers from the Origins to the Renaissance. More has been done during the last fifty years to shed light on the Origins than in all the rest of modern times. The task is an immense one ; its charm can scarcely be expressed. The dead of Westminster have left behind them a posterity, youthful in its turn, and life-giving. Bacon, Hobbes, and Locke are the ancestors of many poets who have never read their works, but who have breathed an air impregnated with their thought. It is proposed to divide this work into three volumes, but each volume will

make a complete whole in itself, the first telling the literary story of the English up to the Renaissance; the second up to the accession of King Pope, the last up to our own day. The ages during which the national thought expressed itself in languages which were not the national one will not be allowed to remain blank, as if, for complete periods, the inhabitants of the island had ceased to think at all. The growing into shape of the people's genius will be studied with particular attention. Jusserand's delightful style is well known, and he is at his best in this work, which he tells us in the happiest way is wholly "a labor of love." (Putnam. 3 pts.)

The Aims of Literary Study.

THROUGH the Macmillans, Prof. Hiram Corson, of Cornell, has just published a delightful little plea for the direct study of literature as literature instead of wandering all around it in studies of the times, the grammar and everything but the literature itself. We refer to "The Aims of Literary Study," a prettily printed booklet

From "Literary History of the English People."   Copyright 1895, by G. P. Putnam's Sons.
MEDIÆVAL LONDON.

whose value is in the inverse ratio of its size. Professor Corson is not impressed with the results produced by college training as it now is. He says that the men are not trained to read or speak. He says that on Commencement days and grand occasions the Faculties bring out the men who have the most *natural* genius for writing or speaking with some such flourish as this, "Behold, ladies and gentlemen, what we have done for these dear young men." When what they should say is: "Ladies and gentlemen, these speakers are the best we have to show. They are selected not as having profited most by the training we give them (*for we have no training worth mention*) but for their natural *aptitude.*" His own ideal of an elocutionary training could hardly be improved. It is based on a golden passage in Gilbert Austin's "Chironomia":

"Words are to be delivered from the lips as beautiful coins newly issued from the mint, deeply and accurately impressed, perfectly finished, neatly struck by the proper organs, distinct, in due succession, and of due weight."

Right, in every letter of it. No good elocution can come from a half-formed, semi-masticated speech that issues in crushed or toneless fragments from the mouth and sounds to the ear as a page of broken type looks to the eye. Professor Corson is one of our best Shakespearian critics. He writes with sense, and grows more pithy and pointed as he advances. (Macmillan. $1.)—*The Independent.*

Municipal Government in Great Britain.

It is difficult to overestimate the importance of the problems discussed in this volume, and while Dr. Shaw disclaims any intention of prescribing European remedies for American diseases, or of suggesting any degree of imitation, or of constructing an argument, the facts presented cannot fail to open the eyes of those who have fancied that progress was foreign to English town government. Many of us have overlooked the fact that there are a number of manufacturing towns in Great Britain which have been growing almost as fast as some of our most enterprising cities, and that although large towns may be alike the world over, improved methods have obtained with them to a much greater extent than with us. The structure of English municipal government, as Dr. Shaw says, possesses principles of a permanent nature, and indeed there are not nearly so many important variations in the whole range of municipal institutions from Great Britain to Southeastern Europe as in the United States. It is probably true, as he says, that one of the

reasons why municipal reform proceeds so haltingly with us is that many citizens who desire sincerely to aid in the regeneration of their town life, have formed no definite municipal ideas. To such citizens the knowledge of what has been done abroad in the last thirty years must have a marked value, even if the application of some of the theories may seem inadvisable and impracticable here.

The sewage problem is dealt with at length, as well as schools, libraries, parks, markets, police, baths, and other matters. The feature of taxation is but lightly touched upon with the explanation that as it is the tenant in England who pays the taxes and upon yearly assessed rental values, comparisons with American tax rates would be difficult ; but assuming that the difference is not very great, the Englishman gets more for his money than the American. The question of municipal debt has not been gone into as fully as we should have liked—there are but few figures given on this important point. The value of the book is enhanced by the clear, well-digested manner in which the facts are set forth. (Century Co. $2.)—*Public Opinion.*

Our Fight with Tammany.

It was natural that the successive moves in the recent campaign for good government in New York City should be reviewed by the prime mover in it, the Rev. Charles H. Parkhurst, D.D., and in "Our Fight with Tammany" the pastor of the Madison Square Presbyterian Church gives a concise and pointed history of the whole movement, from the reorganization of the Society for the Prevention of Crime, in 1891, to the election of last November, and the conclusion of the Lexow inquiry. It is a history that should interest every patriotic American, and it is related in that terse, forcible manner of expression for which the author is famous.

Dr. Parkhurst relates the circumstances that led him to accept the presidency of the Society for the Prevention of Crime, and then gives in full the memorable discourse delivered from his pulpit on February 14, 1892, which he rightly calls "the first gun of the campaign," and in which he made the most scathing analysis of Tammany's corruption that had ever before been uttered.

Dr. Parkhurst arraigns fiercely the political influences that threaten to undo the results of the triumph so arduously secured, and calls on honest citizens to see to it that the fight so valiantly fought shall not prove to be an empty victory. (Scribner. $1.25.)—*The Beacon.*

Vincent's "Actual Africa."

THIS volume is a most comprehensive and entertaining one, giving, in a popular manner, accurate general information concerning the Africa of the present day. Mr. Vincent not only completely circled the continent, but made many expeditions into its vast and mysterious interior. Nearly all the capitals and important towns (native and foreign) of the seaboard territories were inspected ; the great island of Madagascar was traversed ; several of the western archipelagoes w e r e visited ; the peak of Teneriffe was scaled in midwinter ; a long excursion was made through the centre of the Boer republics and British colonies ; t h e N i l e , Quanza, Congo, Kassai, Sankuru and Kuilu rivers were ascended—the latter for the first time by a white man ; and in the very core of Africa's heart a most interesting spot was reached— the curious capital of the famous Basongo chieftain, Pania Mutembo.

Everywhere that Mr. Vincent went he used his camera, and hence has been able to illuminate his text by upwards of one hundred h a n d s o m e engravings, showing many interesting and novel sights and scenes exactly as he saw them in the strange countries traversed. The story of Mr. Vincent's arduous and often dangerous journey is told in an enthusiastic, yet unaffected manner, which rivets the eager attention of the reader from beginning to end. It is more elaborately illustrated than any book upon the subject, and contains a large map carefully corrected to date.

" A new volume from Mr. Frank Vincent," says the *N. Y. Tribune,* " is always welcome, for the reading public have learned to regard him as one of the most intelligent and observing of travellers." (Appleton.)

A MOORISH SOLDIER.

The Honorable Peter Stirling.

PROBABLY the complications and corruptions of political life in New York City were never before made the theme of a protracted love-story, pervaded with such pure sentiment as this one by Mr. Paul Leicester Ford. Of the mismanagement and villany practised in the wards, of bossism, obstructions to reform, delays in justice, factions, wranglings and riots, we have had more or less in fiction, but nothing

From "Jack O'Doon."   Copyright, 1894, by Henry Holt & Co.
MERCY AND JACK.

like this. Here are over four hundred pages
which read like actual history of certain political movements and persistent and successful
work for reform, with a fine, tender love-story
running pure and sweet, an undercurrent in a
life openly pledged to rough partisan work and
rude companionship in squalid places. Fortunately, Peter Stirling is a man's hero. If a
woman writer had created him, she would
have been laughed at for placing her ideal so
high. Mr. Ford is responsible for a very
unusual but, let us believe, a possible character, and having started him on his eventful
career he has stood bravely by him and helped
him through. In these days of disappointing
novels, when it is so much the custom to leave
the hero and heroine in unsatisfactory circumstances, it is pleasing to meet an author who
has regard for them and sees to it that all ends
happily. Many readers will care nothing for
the politics, but they will enjoy the love-story.
It is a good one. Peter is the kind of lover
dear to the heart of the novel-reader. He was
worthy the sweet singleness of devotion he received, and the book, even with the tiresome
politics, is very readable and very enjoyable.
Mr. Ford is well known as an expert collector
and editor of Americana, but his many literary
friends received the announcement of a novel
from his pen with liveliest curiosity. He has
succeeded. (Holt. $1.50.)—*The Literary World.*

The Doctor, His Wife and the Clock.

ANNA KATHARINE GREEN, well known as the
author of "The Leavenworth Case," is the
third writer for the *Autonym Library.* "The
Doctor, His Wife and the Clock" is a detective story concerned with a murder, which is
not too prominent, having for its principal
characters a beautiful wife devoted to a blind
husband, and unwittingly concerned in the
murder, and a tender-hearted but astute detective. The story is not forced, is simply
related, and has a very good and original plot
for its basis. The style of the books coming
out in this *Autonym Library* is very attractive,
with its limp cloth covers, clear type and wide
margins. Any one of them makes a convenient
and pleasing volume for a travelling companion.
(Putnam. 50 c.)—*The Beacon.*

Jack O'Doon.

MARIA BEALE has written a story of devotion.
On the Virginia coast lives Capt. Blessington,
who is a kind-hearted, ignorant man, and given
to much profanity. Miss Mercy is the Captain's
daughter, and her aunt Polly, a narrow-minded
personage devoted to tracts, scarcely knows
how to manage Mercy. The girl has a foster-
brother, Jack O'Doon, the mate of a vessel. An
artist, Abercrombie, rather fascinates Mercy. It
is believed that Jack has been lost at sea, but
he turns up. Mercy's heart is somewhat divided between Abercrombie and Jack. Finally,
both Jack and Abercrombie get into a quick-
sand, and the sailor sacrifices his life in rescuing Abercrombie. Then Mercy ponders over
this question : "Has Algie Abercrombie one
quality as noble as Jack's love for me or his
devotion to his fellow-men ?" Having been
satisfied in her own mind that Algie Abercrombie has not these qualities, but being quite decided that the painter wants somebody to take
care of him, she agrees to console him. (Holt.
75 c.)—*N. Y. Times.*

Illustrated Standard Novels.

"CASTLE RACKRENT" and "The Absentee"
form the first volume of a promised series of great
interest, of *Illustrated Standard Novels.* Just
what entitles a novel to rank as a "standard"
is not always easy to say, and the term needs
definition. We have no difficulty to recognize
the really great works, which live through all
time, but there are novels "without which no
gentleman's library is complete" that not only
have ceased to be generally read, but that are no
longer very attractive even to the professed
novel-reader. Yet some of these were immensely significant in their day and have a place
not to be overlooked in the development of

modern fiction. We should say that a judicious selection of these, in chronological order, would form a series of great value, for some of the most famous novels are not now easily accessible. We do not recognize any such systematic project in the Messrs. Macmillans' prospectus, which has, however, an interest of its own. It apparently aims at the reproduction of various individual novels of note, presented separately, but each with a critical introduction and with illustrations by modern artists that will help to commend it anew to modern readers.

The two of Miss Edgeworth's Irish stories chosen for the first issue of this series are of the class whose celebrity is, in some measure at least, historical. Some of Miss Edgeworth's stories are perennial, though it cannot be said that the recent revival of critical interest in her work has induced a great popular following. But "Castle Rackrent," which was one of her earliest publications, was a story with a purpose, that while it produced a prodigious effect in its time, had the element of transitoriness that the political novel always has. "The Absentee," though it belongs to the same class, displays a firmer and maturer art. Without the freshness of the earlier tale, it has wider observation and a larger grasp of human nature, and the reader will find that, while in some respects old-fashioned, it still retains a great deal of the interest with which it was read in youth.

It is a good thing to be thus tempted to read some of the old stories again, and the succeeding volumes of the series will furnish some instructive experiments in this line. We are next to have some of Captain Marryat—"Japhet in search of a Father," illustrated by H. M. Brock, with an introduction by David Hannay—and then Michael Scott's "Tom Cringle's Log," which used to be immensely esteemed. Others on the list are "Maid Marian" and "Crotchet Castle," for which Mr. Saintsbury will furnish the introduction; the "Annals of the Parish" of Thomas Galt; George Borrow's "Lavengro," introduced by Mr. Birrell; the "Adventures of Hajji Baba," Miss Edgeworth's "Ormond," Miss Ferrier's "Marriage," illustrated by

Hennessy, and, best of all, "Sense and Sensibility," illustrated by Hugh Thomson, with an introduction by Austin Dobson. These are not all really "standard" novels, but they are all novels that have had a vogue and have left some kind of literary impression that has endured. Their republication, in a form that is attractive and convenient, and at the same time inexpensive, is a distinct service that will be appreciated by many readers, and especially by those who like to own the novels that are worth reading. (Macmillan. *Ea.*, $1.25.)—*Philadelphia Times.*

Messire.

WHOEVER has read either Mrs. Crompton's charming story, "The Gentle Heritage," or "Master Bartelmy," both of which are gems amongst the literature written for children, will be eager to secure anything new from the same writer. "Messire" contains three stories.

From "Messire."

"IT IS LETTY'S OWN IDEA."

The first tells how a beautiful boy is entrusted by his dying father in Australia to an old soldier, who is to carry him home to England and confide him to two maiden aunts, whose only heir he is. The old ladies' dismay when he appears with his strange nurse ; their attempt to separate them and find a situation for "Brown" ; the child's love for his queer nurse and attendant, and Brown's devotion to the child, and how the separation finally came about, are all told in the author's inimitable way. The second story is a brief but exquisite sketch of how Glück, a little German boy, started out to find the edge of the world, and travelled through fields and vineyards and pine woodlands, enjoying the wild flowers, the orchards, the nut-trees, the springs running down the hillsides, and beds of wild strawberries, until he reached the mountain-top, where he seemed to see spread out in the evening light the whole of the world and the plains of heaven beyond. Then Uncle Peter came along and carried him home, tired but happy. The third story, "Pippo, Letty and I," is told in innocent child language by one of the little girls, Bet, and reveals brother Pippo's selfishness and disobedience, the patient endurance of his tyranny by his two little sisters because it was just Pippo, and Pippo was their brother, and finally the righteous judgment that fell upon Pippo. They are all three charming stories, sweet and wholesome in tone, written in pure English, and pleasing to young or old. (Dutton., 75 c.)—*The Beacon.*

Sir Richard Owen.

THE Messrs. Appleton have published a book which has been looked for since the death of the subject two years ago, "The Life of Richard Owen," by his grandson. There seems to have been an exceptionally large supply of materials for these volumes owing to the subject's habit of preserving every paper or letter that came to his hand. Of his own letters no less than 1200 remain, while more than 15,000 letters received from others have been placed at the disposal of the biographer. Moreover, both Owen and his wife were in the habit of keeping diaries, and, although his own journal was somewhat disconnected, that of his wife is a full record from 1834 to 1873, not only of the important facts, but even of the trivial details of their joint lives. The biographer's main duty, therefore, has been that of compressing the ample information attainable regarding his subject's private life. Not being himself a scientist, he has wisely caused the scientific portions of this volume to be revised by Mr. C. Davies Sherborn, and he has secured from Prof. Huxley an essay on Owen's position in ana-

tomical science, which is the most valuable feature of the book.

The subject of this biography was more than 88 years old when he died on Dec. 18, 1892, having been born at Lancaster on July 20, 1804. He was the son of a West India merchant, and received his early education at the grammar school of his native town, where one of his school-fellows was William Whewell, afterwards the well-known master of Trinity College, Cambridge. At the age of 20 he matriculated at the University of Edinburgh, and two years later he became a member of the Royal College of Surgeons in London, after which he began life as a general practitioner. His appointment on the recommendation of Dr. Abernethy to the post of assistant curator of the Hunterian Museum led him to give his attention exclusively to the study of comparative anatomy. It was to comparative anatomy and paleontology that he devoted almost the whole of his scientific career, which may be said to have begun even before the publication of the "Memoir on the Pearly Nautilus" in 1832, and which did not end until 1889. For the actual scope and precise worth of his work we shall refer presently to Prof. Huxley's essay, but there is no doubt that, so far as public and official recognition is concerned, no English man of science in this century has been more highly honored at home and abroad. Mr. Owen received the cross of the Legion of Honor as early as 1855, and was subsequently made a Chevalier of the Prussian Order of Merit, and a Knight of the Bath. (Appleton. 2 v. $7.50.)—*N. Y. Sun.*

Noemi.

MR. BARING-GOULD writes the mediæval story, with its savagery. He selects that period when parts of France, as Guyenne, were English, and the people uncertain as to their allegiance. Sometimes they were for Henry of England, at other times for the Crown of France. The nobility were given to acts of violence, and the country was a scene of murder and rapine. Freebooters harried the land, and merchants and peasants were robbed. It was the paradise of the free companies, made up of the idle and vicious, and so no man's life was safe.

Mr. Baring-Gould's principal character and heroine is Noemi. She performs some wonderful feats, as jumping down the sides of a precipitous cliff, after knocking away the wooden steps. In doing that she nearly upsets Jean del Peyra, a handsome young lad, who is engaged in whittling an arrow stock.

The story is replete with action. There are many fights with burnings and stormings. (Appleton. $1; pap., 50c.)—*N. Y. Times.*

La Fayette in the American Revolution.

IN these beautifully printed volumes Mr. Tower gives us a delightful picture of the youngest officer who ever held the commission of major-general in the Army of the United States, and the background of the picture is the no less interesting subject, the participation of France in our War of Independence. How imperfect one of these subjects would be if treated apart from the other the reader of these volumes will appreciate, as he learns from unquestionable evidence how active La Fayette was in shaping the course of France after she had declared war against England, and the confidence which the French cabinet placed in him and its willingness to follow his advice.

It is fully time that a work treating of La Fayette in the American Revolution should have been written; and, while we cannot regret the delay which has made it possible for it to be prepared with all the advantages modern research affords, it is unquestionably true that La Fayette's reputation has suffered for the want of such a work; and, besides this, it has not been creditable to this country that services so eminent as those he rendered should not have received signal recognition in the historical literature of our country.

It has remained for Mr. Tower to correct this omission, and he has performed the self-imposed task in a way not only creditable to himself, but in one that will prove gratifying to others.

His volumes show that he has spared no pains to make a thorough investigation of his subject, and that he has brought to his work a well-trained mind and a knowledge of modern languages that has enabled him to pursue his studies in original documents gathered from the archives of France and elsewhere. He has weighed the evidence he has collected with great fairness, and has drawn his conclusions with true historic instinct, stating them with an earnestness that carries conviction with it. He has made for himself a place in the field of letters. (Lippincott. 2 v., $8.)—*The American.*

Vedic India.

MADAME Z. A. RAGOZIN, who has made a life-long study of India, has again two books on that most interesting of lands, both designed for the *Story of the Nations Series.* "The Story of Brahmanic India" has not yet left the press, but "The Story of Vedic India" is just ready for distribution. Madame Ragozin has already instructed her fascinated readers in "The Story of Chaldea," "The Story of Assyria," "The

From "Vedic India."   Copyright, 1895, by G. P. Putnam's Sons.
FIRST INCARNATION OF VISHNU.

Story of Media, Babylon, and Persia." The story of Vedic India rests upon the Vedas, the oldest writings in the world with the exception of the Pentateuch. These writings are supposed to have been compiled in the sixteenth century before Christ. The Hindoos hold that their Vedas are coeval with creation.

The illustration shows the first incarnation of Vishnu, when he took the form of a fish in order to recover the Sacred Scriptures supposed to have been lost in the Deluge. (Putnam. $1.50.)

"Billtry."

MRS. MARY KYLE DALLAS has had the wisdom to assure her readers that she is making fun in a kindly spirit of a book of which she is an ardent and sincere admirer. She says :

" Though without the great, beautiful 'Trilby' this absurd little 'Billtry' would

From "Billtry."   Copyright, 1895, by The Merriam Co.

"BILLTRY."

never have been. It is simply the reverse of the question—'the other side of the shield'—the '*what might have been*'—had the bachelor artists of the Parisian studios been bachelor girls of Gotham, and their model masculine, instead of feminine—Billtry, in fact, instead of Trilby—and even of this I did not take thought until the morsel was written."

In this little squib "Billtry" has the beautiful feet, and they are reproduced in candy and soap for various purposes to help the girl artists make money. One of these draws pigs, the other angels, and one speaks something that stands for Spanish, in imitation of

the generous doses of French scattered through Mr. Du Maurier's inimitable, critic-disarming story.

Pictures, also "parodies," of the artist-author's drawings are used to illustrate the extravagant text. One of these is of Billtry, who loves a bottle in the possession of his wife, takes doses from the same, then stands upon his head and plays the accordion with his "beautiful toes." In it all Mrs. Kyle Dallas has only had "the simple and innocent object of making you laugh." (Merriam Co. $1; pap., 50 c.)

Chimmie Fadden.

MR. EDWARD W. TOWNSEND'S newly published book, "Chimmie Fadden, Major Max, and Other Stories," is something that is well calculated to touch the popular liking, and I predict for it a success much greater than is commonly won by publications of the same general kind. Both the "Chimmie Fadden" and the "Major Max" tales originally appeared in the *Sun*, and are to be reckoned among the best of the dialect and character sketches that have ever been printed in that distinguished newspaper ; which is saying a good deal for them, for the *Sun* has published some famously able stories in this line. In the "Chimmie Fadden" tales there is, I suppose, a more popular element than the "Major Max' conversations can boast. It is to be said that "Chimmie" is a character who will deserve his success, no matter how great it may prove to be; he is gifted in imagination and in speech, and is powerful to amuse and delight any sort of reader. At the same time the "Major Max" conversations will be found to contain for a smaller circle of readers a still greater charm. These sketches, in surprising contrast to the "Chimmie Fadden" tales, so far as their literary treatment is concerned, are models of light and amusing fancy and graceful and deft expression. Mr. Townsend, with equal facility and effectiveness, can be broad in his humor, or he can be delicate; and he can tell a story that would win approbation in the Fourth ward, or pursue a question of nice philosophy in a manner to delight the fastidious. The other tales and sketches in this volume are concerned with San Francisco and the West, and are admirable in various ways. I recommend the book with a clear conscience, and with something more than that, I have liked it myself, and I believe that others will like it. May it bring to its very able author the success that he deserves. If it succeeds according to its merits he will have no reason to complain. (Lovell, Coryell & Co. $1; pap., 50 c.)—*Town Topics.*

The Women of Shakespeare.

THE translator, who has done her work excellently, reminds us in her preface that we have two books on Shakespeare's women—and of course both Mrs. Jameson and Lady Martin are delightful writers—but points out with much reason that there is ample room for Dr. Lewes' work. One is instantly prepossessed by the author's two principles, which are first of all to take Shakespeare's women in the chronological order from Venus of "Venus and Adonis" to Queen Catherine, and next to allow each character to grow out of her play. The details of the play are only used to develop and interpret the subjects of study, and the reader's mind therefore is not distracted, but is always kept in focus. This plan Dr. Lewes works out after the most laborious and conscientious fashion, omitting no one and doing injustice to none. No words can exaggerate the thoroughness or sanity of the book, which satisfies you on every page that the author has done his work, and there are occasional passages of genuine feeling, as in the tribute to Desdemona's saintliness. One naturally tests such studies at critical points, and it is saying much for Dr. Lewes that his Portia is all that her admirers could desire, for surely she is the queen of Shakespeare's women, and his Lady Macbeth is a powerful and convincing reading that shows both insight and charity. Among many instances of minute and sensible criticism is the remark that Juliet, and some of the other maidens, knew more than was good for them, and that in consequence some of the noblest passages in her speech are stained. It is not possible in this brief review to enter into intricate critical questions, but the Shakespeare student will notice that while Dr. Lewes adopts the three periods of division, he does not apportion the plays as has been most commonly done, but throws "Two Gentlemen of Verona" and "Love's Labour's Lost" into the second period. This book supplies a distinct want, and is a valuable addition to Shakespearian literature. (Macmillan. $2.50.)—*"Ian Maclaren" in The Bookman.*

The Growth of the Idylls of the King.

THIS scholarly monograph is another of the many indications that meet one on every side of how far the Germanization of our intellectual pursuits has gone, passing beyond the sphere of classical philology and pure science, and invading the domain of literature. The present volume investigates the *Quellen* in the genuine spirit of the Herr Professor, but with a certain deftness and grace of touch and an underlying æsthetic sympathy with Tennyson's noblest work that are quite foreign to the "one, two, three" methods of his models.

The design of the study is to show that Tennyson's obligations to Malory have been exaggerated by the critics; that the poem shows a gradual but steady evolution; and that the work itself in its final form embodies the poet's matured view of life—a somewhat pessimistic view, and one far removed from the hopeful optimism of his youth, that found expression in the earlier idylls. In the working out of this plan Dr. Jones has gathered and arranged a mass of information as to texts, variants, revisions in manuscript, and other matters that are extremely instructive to the critical student of Tennyson; and has shown a keen literary sense that will commend cer-

IN THE FIELDS.

tain chapters of his little volume to that larger host who never think of texts, or variants, or sources, but merely accept with delight the noble creation of a great master, and thank God for it. (Lippincott. $1.50.)—*The Bookman.*

Lucy Larcom.

A SWEET and noble soul passed out of this life when Lucy Larcom died. The graciousness of her nature, her well-balanced character, her aspirations for all that was uplifting to herself and helpful to others, her tenderness and modesty and self-sacrifice could not have been understood by most of those familiar with her writings but for this revelation in her life, letters, and diary. The history as told in these pages, much of it in her own words, was comparatively uneventful, but it has unusual charm. All along from her childhood in a home of Puritan simplicity in Beverly to the closing scene in Boston at nearly threescore and ten it is a record of absorbing interest, showing the growth of a true, lovely, and lovable womanhood.

Of the New England womanhood of the last generation, nurtured in a well-ordered household, subjected to privations, stuggling against obstacles, always handicapped, but borne on by a resistless determination to learn and know and possess all that was best, Lucy Larcom was a striking and admirable example. Nothing is more apparent in these pages than that she made the utmost of her life. Her judgment was excellent, her intuitions were keen, her nature was sound and healthy. She was able to give calm and wise consideration to the perplexing questions which came up in her life. She was never the sport of impulse, but there was the staying and reliable quality in her make-up which must be defined in one word as principle. The question most difficult to settle concerned her spiritual experiences, convictions, and duties.

This volume has been carefully, and reverently loyally prepared by Daniel Dulany Addison, who appreciated her rare qualities. The sweet, benignant face of Miss Larcom fronts the title-page. (Houghton, Mifflin & Co. $1.25.)—*Boston Literary World.*

Stories by Charles Egbert Craddock.

A NEW volume of stories by Charles Egbert Craddock will be hailed with acclamation by those who read any bright stories with pleasure, and with quiet delight by those who know how specially fine is the art of the writer of "In the Stranger People's Country." There are five stories, entitled "The Phantoms of the Foot-Bridge," "His Day in Court," "'Way Down in Lonesome Cove," "The Moonshiners at Hoho-Hehee Falls," and "The Riddle of the Rocks." The illustrations are specially well done. Miss Craddock is so true a word painter that an artist has little to do but to make a copy from her poetic realistic text. It is always good to see the work of Miss Craddock, scattered so lavishly in the magazines, "brought to cover" in an attractive volume. (Harper. $1.50.)

From "The Phantoms of the Foot-Bridge."   Copyright, 1895, by Harper & Brothers.

THE BLACKSMITH'S SHOP.

Ropes' Story of the Civil War.

It is well known that, for upward of thirty years, Mr. John Codman Ropes of Boston has made a study of the records of the war between the States, and the first outcome of his studies, "The Army Under Pope," was generally accepted as proof of his qualifications for the composition of an impartial and accurate history of the whole contest. This work has now been undertaken, and we have now before us the first volume of "The Story of the Civil War." We may say at once that the expectations based on the author's former narrative will be found here fulfilled. Entirely impartial it is perhaps impossible for any contemporary observer to be; that not Thucydides himself could claim. Mr. Ropes, for his part, is convinced that the assertion made by the Southern States of a right to secede from the Union was not well grounded, and he makes no secret of his conviction on this point. But while, holding this conviction, he cannot entirely veil his satisfaction at the triumph of the Union cause, he is at great pains to point out, both in the preface and incidentally throughout the volume, that the great mass of the Southern people believed themselves to have a right to secede, and that to this belief should be largely ascribed the unanimity, persistency, and amazing vigor of their efforts. In his judgment, he tells us, the war should not be so depicted as to imply that the North and the South differed and quarrelled about the same things. As a matter of fact, the questions presented to men of the North were not the same as those with which their Southern contemporaries had to deal. The two parties may justly be compared to the knights of the fable who fought over the shield which had on one side a golden and on the other a silvern face.

At the very outset of this volume, the reader acquires confidence in the writer's purpose and ability to evince the largest measure of impartiality attainable, owing to the stress which he lays on the radical differences regarding the object of political allegiance, which actually existed among the representative statesmen of the country in the year 1860. Mr. Ropes says truly that "it is not possible to exaggerate the importance of these conceptions of political duty ; for they directly affected the attitude of every man toward the questions of the day. If a man held that his State was his country, it was his duty, if he proposed to be a patriotic citizen, to serve under the flag of his State."

In the four volumes within which this narrative will be comprised, no one will look to see collected all the details of the Civil War, recourse for which must be had to more comprehensive histories or to that most capacious receptacle of nearly all that can be known regarding the incidents of the contest, the war records which have been published by the Federal Government. The author's design is limited to enabling the reader to obtain a general view of the struggle, and to see its events in their proper order and perspective. (Putnam. $1.50.)—*N. Y. Sun.*

History of the People of the United States.

The long-awaited fourth volume of McMaster's great work is now ready. It opens with the war on the frontier and along the Lakes at the beginning of 1812 and ends with the inauguration of Jackson. It deals with the blockade of the coast by Great Britain, the war along the Gulf Coast, Jackson's Indian Wars, the New Orleans Campaign, the general condition of the country during the war, the Presidential election, the return of peace and its effects, the disorders of the currency after 1814, the rise of manufacturing industries, the development of municipal and State governments, the growth of inter-State communication and the introduction of steamboats, the periodical literature of the time and the growth of religious, trade and comic papers and magazines, the movement of population westward, the admission of Missouri, the reasons for the pro-slavery sentiment, and its effects, down to 1824; the Adams Administration, and the opening of the Erie Canal and other internal improvements.

Much space is given to Socialistic movements like that of Owen, and the beginning of Mormonism, with a general account of the effects of the development of new ideas. Professor McMaster has devoted a great deal of attention to the study of early periodical literature, and also to the mental fermentation which found expression in various Socialistic and other eccentric ways. (Appleton. vol. 4, $2.50.)—*N. Y. Tribune.*

The Great Ice Age.

It is incorrect to suppose of a book entitled "The Great Ice Age, and Its Relation to the Antiquity of Man," by James Geikie, which now lies before us in its third edition, that the ordinary layman, the man of affairs, finds nothing in it to interest him, and that its value is confined to experts. There is a large class, consisting not only of those who have had the advantages of an academic education, but also of those who, without ever having enjoyed that privilege, are studious and thoughtful, whose libraries are filled with just such solid literature as this volume represents ; and to all of them this work of Professor Geikie will appeal with singular force. He is not merely an authority on the topic in hand, and an authority whose opinions must receive great weight, but he writes in a style that is thoroughly popular and alluring. You might think that any writer must needs be dull when talking of the glacial aspect of Greenland, or of the rock striations and groovings of Scotland, or of the glacial and post glacial deposits of England, but Professor Geikie has a peculiar charm for even the ordinary reader, and to begin a chapter on any one of these subjects is to feel the spell of his magnetic style and to become irresistibly drawn to the author until through actual weariness the work must be laid down.

The part of the book which has most interested us happens to be that in which he discusses the glacial phenomena of Northern Europe and the wonderful relics of by-gone eons which have given us a clue to the convulsions through which the earth passed in its adolescence. Here is an extract which is full of suggestion :

"Before the commencement of the glacial period Europe was in the enjoyment of a delightful climate, certainly more genial and equable than the present. This is clearly evinced by the character of the pliocene flora, which appears to have been transitorial between that of the preceding sub-tropical miocene and the present. . . . Considerable areas which are now dry land were then under water. Then the low grounds of Italy were still submerged, the valley of the Po forming a great arm of the sea, which likewise penetrated into the mountain valleys of the Alps. The valley of the Arno, and Sicily, to some extent, were similarly under water, and the like was the case with the lower reaches of the Rhone and wide tracts in the maritime districts of Southwestern France. The sea also covered the south and southeast of England, and overflowed at the same time a broad area in Belgium and a small part of Northern France. . . .

"England was visited by elephants, rhinoceroses and hippopotamuses and great herds of various kinds of deer, as well as by bears, wolves, and other carnivora."

This quotation is made at random, and, interesting as it is, it is no more so than any other paragraphs that might be chosen by chance. Professor Geikie is a wonderfully attractive writer, and not even a boy in one of our high-schools could fail to get a comparatively clear idea of that strange and weird epoch in our earth history when there was no Gulf Stream, and when snow and ice held undisputed sway. (Appleton $7.50.)—*N. Y. Herald.*

The Great Refusal.

THE introduction tells us that it is edited by Paul Elmer More, and that it is part of the literary remains of a scholarly young man, the identity of whom is carefully concealed, whose learning was wasted in the vapors of mysticism. Whether we are to take this literally, or whether the book was really written by the putative editor, we do not know. It is in a nebulous, epistolary form, and addressed to a lady whom he calls Lady Esther. The sub-title—"Letters of a Dreamer"—gives an idea of the scheme. While not characterized by marked originality of conception and thought, it bears the stamp of delicacy of touch and refinement of sentiment. There are many passages having a tender beauty, not only captivating the eye and ear, but leaving impressions as of aphorisms on the mind of the reader. There are a number of short poems, and one of several pages, which are in good taste and show considerable poetical ability. The writer has or had a good ear for rhythm and his measures flow smoothly. He has followed the currents of his thoughts wherever they led him, and while the form is epistolary, there is much that is impersonal and not especially applicable to Lady Esther. It is a book which will bear a reading and a picking up again at odd times. (Houghton, Mifflin & Co. $1.)

Three Score and Ten Years.

WHAT Mr. W. J. Linton would care to say of the art he loves, and in which he is so distinguished, he probably said in "The Masters of Wood-Engraving;' it does not, at any rate, claim the lion's share in these recollections of "Three Score and Ten Years." And neither in the text, nor yet in the strong, genial old face that is the book's frontispiece, does one find quite the fanatically fierce radical that perhaps one chiefly remembers him to have been portrayed. Possessed of a passion of protest and revolt against what he considered the wrongs of a country, a race, a class, or individuals, undoubtedly he shows himself to have been ; but justice, tenderness, pity, and sense of humor are as inevitably betrayed as radicalism, and the capacity of bitter resentment and acrimony. Sir Charles Gavan Duffy says of him in "Conversations with Carlyle," referring to Carlyle's calling Linton "a well-meaning, but extremely windy creature of the Louis Blanc, George Sand, etc., species," that he was "less a French Republican of the school of George Sand and Louis Blanc than an English Republican of the school of Milton and Cromwell."

The book is not an autobiography, nor do the recollections define very exactly the sequence of the years, but they are interesting in their crowded desultoriness. Some of them, it is true, concern people unknown to, or perhaps displeasing to the reader ; but more are occupied with personages in all walks of life, but especially in art and literature, famous, or deserving to be so for their qualities. They are told in language simple, graphic, with a little flavor of antiquity harmonizing with the author's portrait, and with some of the people and events he recalls. Austin Dobson dedicated to Mr. Linton his "Thomas Bewick and his Pupils" as "Engraver and Poet, the steadfast apostle of Bewick's white line ; " and wrote on the fly-leaf of the complimentary copy sent :

> "Not white thy graver's path alone ;
> May the sweet Muse with whitest stone
> Mark all the days to come, and still
> Delay thee on Parnassus Hill."

(Scribner. $2.)—*Providence Sunday Journal.*

A Manual of the Study of Documents.

THIS handy volume, by Persifor Frazer, will be found of great use to all persons interested in the study of penmanship and of the individual character of handwriting. It is a "counterfeit detector," for it will enable one, after some study of its pages, to detect fraud and forgery. In addition to the old methods of research there are several new suggestions for the detection of counterfeit writing. Dr. Frazer suggests that the term Bibliotics is broad enough to apply to any object which it may be desired to investigate—such as parchment, wax tablets, papyrus, printing paper, stone, or any other substance capable of receiving and retaining characters. Under the head of "Grammapheny" he would include all that relates to the discovery of fraud, and under that of "Plassopheny" all that relates to forgery. In the development of his subject he goes into valuable *minutiæ* under the head of physical examination, studying all that belongs to the manner of writing, the instrument, the fluid used, evidences of tampering, scanning under various lights, the use of magnifying instruments, the substances written upon, the composite photography of signatures, the tremor of feebleness, illiteracy, or fraud, and the writing done by guided hands. In part second he enters into the detail of inks and their testing, the reagents used by forgers, and the method of reaction, winding up with a digest of the laws relating to the testimony of experts on handwriting. The book is very interesting, and gives the result of a lifetime of study of this important specialty. Apart from its curious interest as a flower growing in one nook of the garden of literature, it is an exceedingly useful manual for all persons to whom the detection of fraud and the establishment of truth is a question of supreme practical interest. The book is very well printed and illustrated and has a good index. (Lippincott. $2.)—*Boston Literary World.*

The Woman Who Did.

IT is a pity that so remarkable a book should bear a title which savors a little of the cheap catchiness of posters, advertisements and parodies. Grant Allen has done much excellent work since he began to write some twenty years ago. He combines scientific accuracy and imagination and poetry in rare degree. His special field is natural science, and evolution has been the branch to which he has devoted many volumes. His logical powers are trained and he reasons clearly, proving all statements step by step from any premises he accepts or invents as the bases of his treatises and stories.

He tells us that this little volume has been written wholly to please himself, and every line shows how exacting has been his demand upon himself to produce a work that should remain a pleasure to him.

The story is slight. A girl born in the conventional atmosphere that surrounds the high dignitaries of the Established Church has graduated from Girton, and enters life full of the noblest enthusiasm to help her sister women free themselves from conventional bonds and live a pure, self-sacrificing life, using all their highest powers and capacities to advance the true cause of woman and make her the true, inspiring helpmate of man, kept up to his highest ideal by her strength and purity. She believes that the present laws and customs of marriage are degrading to the woman and irksome and unnatural to the man. Almost immediately upon leaving college she meets a man who understands the purity of motive and the self-sacrificing purpose that underlie her startling plans and theories. Many conversations present the man's, the woman's and the conventional views of the institution of marriage.

After long deliberation the young people agree to live their lives according to the girl's theories. The consequences of this decision, leading to the tragic climax, are told with rare insight into the eternal opposition of the unchanging forces of nature and the constantly changing forces of social conditions. The woman leads a martyr's life, and from her nearest and dearest meets only with condemnation. (Roberts. $1.)

Che Literary News.

An Eclectic Monthly Review of Current Literature.

EDITED BY A. H. LEYPOLDT.

MARCH, 1895.

W. E. FOSTER'S REFERENCE LISTS.

THE librarian of the Providence Public Library, Mr. William E. Foster, is among the few that are "called" as well as "chosen" to their profession. He recognizes the true educational purpose of a library for which the people pay, and the responsibility which rests upon its librarian to instruct his townsmen what treasures they may procure with their tax-money, and how far-reaching may be the mental and moral, the political and social results of an intelligent and systematic use of the literary property on which they have a claim as good citizens.

Mr. Foster is a man of broad interests, fully abreast with his day, and he knows the value of exact information in dealing with the questions of the hour, as presented to large masses of men from day to day in a press nominally free, but influenced consciously or unconsciously, or controlled autocratically by party, power or money. To make aimless readers thinkers, and to give vitality and purpose to undirected ambitions and idiosyncrasies, or vague desires, has been this earnest librarian's ideal for many years—an ideal to which he has sacrificed all personal ambition, and for which he has done work requiring gifts and training that no money can buy.

Filled with youthful enthusiasm, Mr. Foster fifteen years ago began to make up "Reference Lists" for the use of the readers of the Providence Public Library, calling attention to the works and periodicals contained in the library bearing upon the important questions of the day, or the heroes of the hour in war, politics, or literature. Some kindred spirits hailed Mr. Foster's plan with delight, and he was encouraged to print his lists (which had until then only been written and put up within the walls of the library) so that they might prove of use in other libraries, and also guide and remind readers privileged to buy books. After four years of struggle, from 1880 to 1884, Mr. Foster found it impossible to get his great undertaking upon a basis warranting the expense of proper help, and still more impossible to do all the work himself added to the onerous duties of superintending a growing library; and the "Reference Lists" could not any more be made public.

But Mr. Foster's enthusiasm still lives, and he sees more and more the great need of such a work as he offers. Perhaps, too, he hopes that in a decade readers may have become conscious of such need, and he once more offers his "Reference Lists," at the trifling cost of 50 cents a year. Every month he covers three subjects. The January issue gave information on Oliver Wendell Holmes, the Corean War, and Buddhism; February's lists referred to Robert Louis Stevenson, Municipal government, and German literature.

No one who has not seen these lists can understand their great importance. A better guide to bookbuying it would be hard to find.

———

READERS would do well to ponder some thoughts condensed from a lecture given many years ago by Mr. W. E. Foster upon the right selection of books and the right methods of reading:

A. *The right selection of books.* (1) Personal adaptation should guide us. (2) Our reading should have a tendency towards symmetrical development ; it should not be exclusively technical, nor exclusively general. (3) We should begin where we are interested. An investigation of a subject will lead from that into other fields. It may be objected that this requires a suggestive habit of mind. But a suggestive habit of mind is not born in any man[?], and it may be acquired by any man. Let once a beginning be made, and the further we go the surer we are of recognizing some familiar event or topic ; the dread of unfamiliarity vanishes after we have taken the first few steps. (4) There must be discrimination in our reading ; aimlessness is one of the worst evils.

B. *Right methods of reading.* (1) Definiteness of purpose is as necessary here as in the selection. We must have a clear idea of just what we wish to get out of each book. (2) System, a scientific adjustment of means to ends. (3) We must read in a comparative way. It is not safe to judge any question apart from its relations. The reader must take a survey of the whole field before beginning at any one point. (4) In using reference lists it is not necessary to read every book and every chapter referred to. We must select what on the whole would best serve our purpose. We are not to ignore our interest, however some one book might particularly attract the attention of some one reader. The plan of reading by a reference list does not apply to all books. Imagine a man going through Milton or Shakespeare in this ruthless manner ! The plan applies to the works of "the literature of knowledge." "The literature of power" needs a different treatment. Books which have an organic unity, following out a central subject or thought, must be read as a whole. (5) We should review our reading at times.

ARTICLES IN MARCH MAGAZINES.

Articles marked with an asterisk are illustrated.

ARTISTIC, MUSICAL AND DRAMATIC.—*Century,* Eugène Ysaye;* Jean Carriès, Sculptor and Potter.*—*Fort. Review* (Feb.), Note on Ibsen's "Little Eyolf," The Editor.—*Forum,* A Week in New York Theatres, Speed.—*Harper's,* The American Academy at Rome,* Cortissoz.—*Scribner's,* American Wood-Engravers—F. S. King;* Orchestral Conducting and Conductors, Apthorp.

BIOGRAPHY, CORRESPONDENCE, ETC.—*Atlantic,* William Dwight Whitney, Lanman.—*Cath. World,* Sir John Thompson, McKenna.—*Chautauquan,* Chauncey M. Depew, Morris.—*Nine. Century* (Feb.), Reminiscences of Christina Rossetti. Watts.—*Popular Science,* Thomas Nuttall (Por.).

DESCRIPTION, TRAVEL.—*Cath. World,* Pictures on the Galway Coast,* Marguerite Moore.—*Century,* Beyond the Adriatic,* Harriet W. Preston.—*Chautauquan,* Underground Railway in London, Daniell—*Harper's,* The Literary Landmarks of Jerusalem,* Hutton ; Industrial Region of Northern Alabama, Tennessee, and Georgia,* Ralph.—*Lippincott's,* Glimpse of Cuba, Reeve.—*McClure's,* An Ocean Flyer ;* An Alpine Pass on Ski,* Doyle.

DOMESTIC AND SOCIAL.—*Lippincott's,* Furs in Russia, Isabel F. Hapgood ; A Question of Costume, W. D. McCrackan.—*North Am. Review,* Nagging Women, Lady Somerset, Marion Harland, Harriet P. Spofford.—*Pop. Science,* The Mother in Woman's Advancement, Mrs. Burton Smith.—*Scribner's,* Art of Living—House-Furnishing and the Commissariat,* Grant.

EDUCATIONAL.—*Atlantic,* Direction of Education, Shaler.—*Cath. World,* Scope of Public School Education, Spalding.—*Harper's,* New York Common Schools, Olin.—*Nine. Century* (Feb.), Language *vs.* Literature at Oxford, Collins.—*Pop. Science,* Scientific Method in Board Schools, Armstrong; Biological Work in Secondary Schools, McClatchie.

FICTION.—*Atlantic,* The Seats of the Mighty, I., Gilbert Parker; Gridou's Pity, I., Grace H. Peirce.—*Cath. World,* A Modern Iconoclast, Spellissy.—*Century,* A Vital Question, Hibbard; The Hard Trigger,* Edwards.—*Harper's,* A Californian, Geraldine Bonner; The Second Missouri Compromise,* Wister; Fame's Little Day,* Sarah O. Jewett; An Every-Day Affair, Olga Flinch.—*Lippincott's,* A Tame Surrender, Charles King; Luck of the Atkinses, Margaret B. Yeates; Fulfilment, Eliz. K. Carter.—*McClure's,* Lord of Chateau Noir, Doyle; La Toussaint,* Weyman; A Blizzard,* Mrs. E. V. Wilson.—*Scribner's,* Circle in the Water, I., Howells; Hughey, Macknight ; Revenge,* Abbe C. Goodloe.

HISTORY.—*Century,* Two War-Times Conventions, Noah Brooks.—*Scribner's,* History of the Last Quarter-Century in the United States,* I., E. B. Andrews; When Slavery Went Out of Politics,* Noah Brooks.—*West. Review* (Feb.), Historical Lessons from American Archæology, Hewitt.

INDUSTRIAL.—*Pop. Science,* Copper, Steel, and Bank Note Engraving,* Dickinson; An Old Industry (Indigo-Making), Mary H. Leonard; Bookbinding, Sanderson.

LITERARY.—*Atlantic,* Secret of the Roman Oracles, Lanciani ; Some Confessions of a Novel-Writer, Trowbridge ; A Pupil of Hypatia, Harriet W. Preston and Louise Dodge.—*Cath. World,* A Prince of Scribblers (Horace Walpole), Rossman.—*Century,* Cheating at Letters, Bunner.—*Fort. Review* (Feb.), Novels of Hall Caine, Saintsbury.—*Forum,* Charlotte Brontë's Place in Literature, Harrison ; The Two Eternal Types in Fiction, Mabie.—*Lippincott's,* The Artist's Compensations, Lawton.—*McClure's,* F. M. Crawford—A Conversation,* Bridges.—*North Am. Review,* Mark Twain and Paul Bourget, Max O'Rell.—*Scribner's,* Thoreau's Poems of Nature, Sanborn.

MEDICAL SCIENCE.—*Chautauquan,* The World's Debt to Medicine, J. S. Billings.—*Forum,* Anti-Toxine Treatment of Diphtheria, L. Emmett Holt.—*McClure's,* Diphtheria Anti-Toxine—Its Production,* W. H. Park; New Treatment of Diphtheria,* H. M. Biggs.

MENTAL AND MORAL.—*Cath. World,* Hypnotism (Charcot), Seton.—*Nine. Century* (Feb.), Social Evolution, Kidd.—*North Am. Review,* What Psychical Research has Accomplished, Podmore.

NATURE AND SCIENCE.—*Century,* Hermann von Helmholtz (Por.), Martin; Horse Market,* Merwin.—*Harper's,* Heredity, Mivart.—*Lippincott's,* Story of the Gravels, Bashore.—*Pop. Science,* Scientific Work of Tyndall, Lord Rayleigh; Beginnings of Agriculture, Bourdeau.—*Scribner's,* Bedding-Plants,* Parsons.

POETRY.—*Atlantic,* Evening in Salisbury Close, Scollard; At the Granite Gate, Carman.—*Century,* Summers, Josephine H. Nicholls.—*Harper's,* The Ascending Magdalen,* Minna C. Smith; A Singer Awaiting an Answer, Marguerite Merington; Like the Good God, Marrion Wilcox; Society, Howells.—*Lippincott's,* Robert Louis Stevenson, Richard Burton.—*Nine. Century* (Feb.), A New Year's Eve (Christina Rossetti), Swinburne.—*Scribner's,* Three Sonnets, Fullerton; Land-Locked, Going; The Last Prayer, Campbell.

POLITICAL AND SOCIAL.—*Atlantic,* Immigration and Naturalization, Everett; Some Words on the Ethics of Co-operative Production, Ludlow.—*Banker's,* Credit of the U. S. Government; How Much has the Country Lost by Low Prices of Products ?; World's Wool Situation, North; History of Bank Currency, Gilman.—*Century,* Blackmail as a Heritage, Buel.—*Chautauquan,* New Reign in Russia, Yarros.—*Forum,* Business World *vs.* the Politicians, Eckels; Our Blundering Policy, Lodge; What Would I Do with the Tariff ?, Carnegie; Is the Income Tax Constitutional ?, Seligman; The Social Discontent, Holt.—*Harper's,* Trial Trip of a Cruiser,* Sicard.—*Nine. Century* (Feb.), Is Bimetalism a Delusion ?, Tuck.—*North Am. Review,* Is an Extra Session Needed ?, Tracey, Storer, Patterson and Cousins; Two Years of Democratic Diplomacy, Davis; Must We Have the Cat-o-Nine Tails ?, Gerry; Future of Silver, Bland.—*West. Review* (Feb.), Betting and Gambling.

THEOLOGY, RELIGION, AND SPECULATION.—*Fort. Review* (Feb.), Ancestor Worship in China, Gundry.—*McClure's,* The Lord's Day, Gladstone.—*Nine. Century* (Feb.), Auricular Confession and the Church of England, Canon Carter.—*North Am. Review,* The Old Pulpit and the New, Bhp. Foss.—*West. Review,* (Feb.), Free Thought, Agnosticism, Skepticism, Dewey.

Survey of Current Literature.

☞ *Order through your bookseller.*—"*There is no worthier or surer pledge of the intelligence and the purity of any community than their general purchase of books; nor is there any one who does more to further the attainment and possession of these qualities than a good bookseller.*"—PROF. DUNN.

ART, MUSIC, DRAMA.

RAYMOND, G. LANSING. Rhythm and harmony in poetry and music ; together with music as a representative art : two essays in comparative æsthetics. Putnam. 8°, $1.75.

REINTZEL, MARG., *comp.* The musician's yearbook. Dutton. 16°, $1.
Appropriate readings for every day in the year selected from the sayings of celebrated musicians and renowned authors. Mozart, Mendelssohn, Beethoven, Weber, and Schumann are some of the musicians represented. Among the authors are Shakespeare, Francis Bacon, George Eliot, Goethe, Thompson, and many others.

FLETCHER, ROB., *M.D.* Anatomy and art : the annual address read before the Philosophical Society of Washington, December 12, 1894. Judd & Detweiler. 8°, pap., *n. p.*

BIOGRAPHY, CORRESPONDENCE, ETC.

MASSON, D. Life of John Milton, narrated in connection with the political, ecclesiastical, and literary history of his time. Macmillan. 8°, $4.50.

SALA, G. A. The life and adventures of George Augustus Sala, written by himself. Scribner. 2 v., por. 8°, $5.

DESCRIPTION, GEOGRAPHY, TRAVEL, ETC.

BALLANTINE, H. On India's frontier ; or, Nepal, the Gurkhas' mysterious land. J. Selwin Tait & Sons. map, il. 12°, $2.50.

SHOEMAKER, M. M. Trans-Caspia: the sealed provinces of the czar. The Robert Clarke Co. por. il. 12°, $1.50.
"Mr. Shoemaker has before written some very interesting volumes of travel and 'Trans-Caspia' is still another. He sees well and describes admirably. The journey led through the ordinarily sealed provinces of the Czar and about which little has been known from American tourists. Starting from St. Petersburg, the journey led over the Dariel Pass, to Tiflis, to Baku, and the oil regions of the Caspian. From there to the plains of Turkistan, and the Desert of the Black Sands ; Bokhara, Samarcand, over the steppes to Tashkend. ancient Kokand, Ash, through Paradise to the deserts of China, through the deserted cities of the Turkoman, to Trebizond and Stamboul. The story is admirably told, and the beautifully clear print and striking illustrations add to the enjoyment of the book."—*Chicago Inter-Ocean.*

VINCENT, FRANK. Actual Africa ; or, the coming continent. A tour of exploration. With map and 105 full-page illustrations. 8°.

DOMESTIC AND SOCIAL.

MOTHER HUBBARD'S cupboard: recipes collected by the Young Ladies' Society, First Baptist Church, Rochester. *5th ed.* Scranton, Wetmore & Co. 8°, pap., 50 c.
Recipes for soups, fish, vegetables, bread, pies, plain and fancy desserts, cake, pickles, salads, beverages, sweets, etc.

EDUCATION, LANGUAGE, ETC.

DE GARMO, C. Herbart and the Herbartians. Scribner. 12°, (Great educators ser.) *net,* $1.

EATON, *Rev.* ARTHUR WENTWORTH. College requirements in English entrance examinations (Examination papers for 1893 and 1894). *2d ser.* Ginn. 12°, *net,* $1.20.

MARTIN, G. H. The evolution of the Massachusetts public school system: a historical sketch. Appleton. 12°, (International education ser., no. 29.) $1.50.
This is only a sketch—a study, not a history of education in Massachusetts. It aims to show the evolutionary character of the public-school history of the state, and to point out the lines along which the development has run, and the relation throughout to the social environment. Incidentally, it serves to illustrate the slow, wavering, irregular way by which the people under popular governments work out their own social progress. The material was originally given as lectures with the titles: The early legislation—its principles and precedents; Schools before the Revolution; The district school and the academy; Horace Mann and the revival of education; The modern school system; The modern school. Author is Supervisor of Public Schools, Boston, Mass.

PAULSEN, F. The German universities: their character and historical development; authorized tr. by E: Delevan Perry, with an introd. by Nicholas Murray Butler. Macmillan. 12°, $2.
"The work, which originally appeared as a part of the elaborate report sent by the German government with its educational exhibit to the World's Fair at Chicago, is of the very first importance to promoters of the higher education here in America, where the disposition to assimilate the best features of German university methods is noteworthy. Professor Paulsen shows clearly how the unified atmosphere of the German universities has promoted solidarity of interests, made possible a free interchange of advantages; and by giving members of different faculties frequent opportunities for pursuing their work under the most favorable auspices, has tended to form a veritable 'aristocracy of intellect' as a counterbalancing force in the social organism against the domination of hereditary influences and the materialism of wealth. A thoughtful and suggestive introduction on the relation of German universities to the problems of higher education in the United States, by Professor N. M. Butler, is a noteworthy feature of the volume. The

translator has added a few serviceable foot-notes for the benefit of readers not acquainted with German university customs. Appendices contain useful statistics and a bibliography."— *The Beacon.*

FICTION.

ALLEN, GRANT. The woman who did. Roberts. 16°, $1.

BARING-GOULD, SABINE. Noémi. Appleton. 12°, (Appleton's town and country lib., no. 160.) $1; pap., 50 c.

Aquitaine, in France, in the stormy days of the raids of the Free Companies in the fifteenth century, is the scene of a dramatic historical romance. Noémi is the supposed daughter of the robber chief Le Gros Guillem and has a noble nature, which her environment of crime and bloodshed has not destroyed; her father's horrible reprisals of the poor and oppressed are witnessed by her with deep indignation. She endeavors to prevent them, and is aided in her efforts by Jean Del Peyra, whom she loves.

BEALE, MARIA. Jack O'Doon: a novel. Holt. 1 il. nar. 16°, buckram, 75 c.

CAINE, HALL. A son of Hagar; il. by Albert Hencke. R. F. Fenno & Co., 112 5th Avenue. por. 12°, $1.

The same scene is used here—Cumberland, England—as in "The shadow of a crime." The hero is the opposite of the hero of that story. Hall Caine says in his preface: "In this novel the aim has been to penetrate into the soul of a bad man, and to lay bare the processes by which he is tempted to fall." The temptation is a woman whom two brothers love—to win her from his brother Paul, Hugh Ritson does not hesitate at a crime. He finds his opportunity in the misfortunes and sins of his mother, who has brought an illegitimate child into the world. The manners and customs of the Cumbrian peasants are realistically presented.

COBB, SYLVANUS, *jr.* The king's mark: a novel. Bonner. 12°, (Popular ser., no. 57.) pap., 25 c.

The story is founded on an episode of history. Frederick the Great, for diplomatic and humane reasons, is supposed to play the part of a student, and marks the arm of a newly born infant with a Latin cross; this infant, Feodor Von Allendorf, the hero of the story, later wins the heart of his sovereign by frustrating the plot of some Saxon rebels, and by outwitting a diplomat of rank. The policy of Frederick the Great in regard to his proposed invasion of Saxony is seen, as is also Saxony's position in regard to the crown. The character caste is mostly composed of famous historic personages who lived about 1756.

COTES. *Mrs.* EVERARD. [Sara Jeanette Duncan.] Vernon's aunt: being the Oriental experiences of Miss Lavinia Moffat; il. by Hal Hurst. Appleton. 12°, $1.25.

COUPERUS, LOUIS. Majesty. A novel. Translated by A. Teixeira de Mattos and Ernest Dowson. Appleton. 12°.

CRAWFORD, F. MARION. The Ralstons. Macmillan. buckram, 16°, $2.

DEMENT, R. S. Ronbar: a counterfeit presentiment. G. W. Dillingham. 12°, $1.50.

Richard Ronbar, who is pictured in the opening chapters as a well-known figure in New York literary and social circles, conceiving a desire to go west, settles in Colorado, where he unfolds to two trusted associates a prospectus of what he calls independent free silver coinage. They agreeing to help him carry out his plan, have a remarkable experience, which is given in a story that introduces some facts in the history of silver coin countries, notably the United States, and which refers to the repeal of the Sherman act, deals with the question of relative values, and finally states individual theories about unlimited coinage.

DOYLE, A. CONAN. Beyond the city. E. A. Weeks & Co. 12°. (Enterprise ser., no. 8.) pap., 25 c.

Two maiden ladies living "beyond the city" of London rent some of their land to a builder, who puts up three villas. The novel tells the story of the people who become tenants of these cottages, the most important of whom is a handsome widow who works for the emancipation of women and teaches her young girl.

EDGEWORTH, MARIA. Castle Rackrent and The absentee; with introd. by Anne Thackeray Ritchie. Macmillan. 12°, (Illustrated standard novels. no. 1.) $1.25.

GREEN, ANNA KATHARINE, [*Now Mrs.* C. Rohlfs.] The doctor, his wife, and the clock. Putnam. nar. 12°, (Autonym lib., no. 3.) 50 c.

HARLEY, (*pseud.*) In the veldt. Longmans, Green & Co. 12°, pap., 50 c.

Stories and sporting sketches with the scene in South Africa.

HARRADEN, BEATRICE. Things will take a turn, and other stories. Rand, McNally. 12°, (Globe lib., v. 1, no. 159.) pap., 25 c.

Contains also "The umbrella-mender" and "An idyll of London."

HECLAWA, [*pseud.* for A. L. Artman Himmelwright.] In the heart of the Bitter-Root Mountains: the story of the Carlin hunting party, September-December, 1893. Putnam. map, il. 12°, $1.50.

HOPPIN, EMILY HOWLAND. Under the Corsican. J. Selwin Tait & Sons. 12°, $1.

LUDLUM, JEAN KATE. Under oath: an Adirondack story. Bonner. 12°, (Popular ser., no. 58.) pap., 25 c.

While Allan Mansfield is riding along a lonely mountain pass, he is mysteriously kidnapped, and as unexpectedly and mysteriously released, through the intercession of a strange woman, who first imposes on Allan the solemn oath of secrecy as to this incident in his life. Her reasons are evident later, when all the characters in the novel are seen in a striking and sensational situation, when she is induced to reveal her own tragic history.

McCARTHY, JUSTIN HUNTLEY. A woman of impulse. Putnam. 12°, (Hudson lib., no. 4,) $1; pap., 50 c.

The hero is a literary man and a Liberal; he had set forth his creed in the "Cry for liberty," that a few critics considered a great book. His whole career is changed by a chance meeting with a beautiful girl in the British Museum, with whom he is permitted to become acquainted, and to whom he loses his heart. To tell the story of this "woman of impulse" would be to give away the secret of the author's plot, which is fresh and novel, and full of surprises.

MACKIE, J. The Devil's playground: a story of the wild northwest. F. A. Stokes Co. il. 16°, buckram, 75 c.

MACQUOID, *Mrs.* KATHARINE S. BERRIS. United States Book Co. 12°, (Lakewood ser., no. 2.) pap., 50 c.

NEVINSON, H. W. Neighbors of ours: slum stories of London. Holt. 1 il. nar. 16°, (Buckram ser.) buckram, 75 c.

Contents : Old Parky; An aristocrat of labor; The "St. George" of Rochester; Mrs. Simon's baby; Sissero's return; Litty Scotty; A man of genius; In the spring; Father Cris'mas; Only an accident.

"There is no close connection between the stories, but the people are all of the same class and the same manner of living. The frankness and rude wit with wh'ch the women bandy opinions is one of the amusing features of a book which runs the gamut of human emotions. A reading is well repaid, whether the object be diversion or a desire for information, and the dialect is easily mastered. Didacticism is entirely absent, yet a moral or two crops out, not the less impressive for being couched in the vernacular of the Tower Hamlets."—*Public Opinion.*

PAYN, JA. In Market Overt: a novel. Lippincott Co. 12°, (Lippincott's select novels, no. 165.) $1; pap., 50 c.

"'In Market Overt' is James Payn's most recent novel. The story of the book is, briefly, as follows: John Barton, an Oxford undergraduate, saves young Lord Trevor from drowning. The nobleman's gratitude not only helps his preserver out of the financial difficulties which compass a young man when trying to pay his own way through a university, but follows him later when Barton undertakes to act as a tutor to the nobleman's sons. Barton marries, has two handsome daughters and opens a school at Leadon. In time a favorite pupil ruins the village belle, and John Barton's downfall follows. Of course his fortunes mend, but the book should be read to discover just how."—*Kate Field's Washington.*

RUSSELL, W. CLARK. The good ship *Mohock.* Appleton. 12°, (Appleton's town and country lib., no. 159.) $1; pap., 50 c.

"Mr. Clark Russell's ability to discover new situations at sea is equalled only by the remarkable appearance of verisimilitude which he contrives to impart to incidents wholly improbable. Nothing could be more unlikely than this story of 'The Good Ship *Mohock*,' but that is a conclusion which comes to one some time after reading the book. It never suggests itself while the stirring pages are before the reader. Perhaps it would not be easy to find anything which would be a greater tribute to Mr. Russell's art than this; but it is inevitable that a reviewer should again express the familiar surprise that this author succeeds so well in bringing before the mental vision of the reader such vivid pictures of ships and their handling with so small a parade of technicalities. It would be a very easy matter to give an outline of the plot of this book and show how the well-laid plan came to grief through an unfortunate meeting w'th a suspicious cruiser, but

that would be unfair to the author, to the publishers, and to the reader, who, if he loves sea pictures and forecastle stories, cannot do better than to read this yarn."—*N. Y. Times.*

WILKES, CLEMENT. Sidney Forrester. H. W. Hagemann. 12°, (Castleton's ser., no. 1.) pap., 50 c.

Sidney Forrester was the son of a New York girl and a sea captain; soon after his birth, his father went away on a cruise, during which his vessel was reputed lost. Sidney's mother finally dying of grief, he is adopted by a wealthy, but penurious grandmother. The story deals with his life in her house, the interest centring in a plot of his Uncle Ambrose to defraud him of his birthright.

YEATS, S. LEVETT. The honour of Savelli: a romance. Appleton. 12°, (Appleton's town and country lib., no. 16.) $1; pap., 50 c.

HISTORY.

HINDS, ALLEN B. The making of the England of Elizabeth. Macmillan. 12°, *net*, 90 c.

LARNED, JOSEPHUS NELSON. History for ready reference from the best historians, biographers and specialists; their own words in a complete system of history; for all uses, extending to all countries and subjects and representing for both readers and students the better and newer literature of history in the English language; with historical maps by Alan C. Reiley. In 5 v. V. 4, Nicæa to Tunis. C. A. Nichols Co. maps, 4°, $5; buckram, $6; shp., $6; hf. mor., $7.50.

The subjects to which the largest space is given in this volume are: North Carolina, 5 p.; Ohio, 5 p.; Papacy, 64 p.; Pennsylvania, 7 p.; Printing and the press, 20 p.; Rome, 96 p.; Russia, 32 p.; Scandinavian states, 19 p.; Scotland, 42 p.; Slavery, 20 p.; Social movements, 26 p.; Spain, 44 p.; Tariff legislation, 25 p. Contains maps of Central Europe (1556), Eastern Europe (1768), Roman Empire (A.D. 116), Europe (A.D 565), Eastern Europe and Central Europe in 1715; four development maps of Spain, 9th, 11th, 12th, and 13th centuries; also a logical outline in colors of Roman history and chronological tables ninth and tenth centuries.

RENAN, ERNEST. History of the people of Israel from the rule of the Persians to that of the Greeks. [In 5 v. V. 4.] Roberts Bros. 8°, $2.50.

Books 7 and 8 are contained in this volume relating to "Judea under Persian rule" and "The Jews under Greek Dominion." Some of the subjects of the chapters are as follows : Re-establishment of divine worship at Jerusalem—new laws of ritual; The end of the house of David; The triumph of the high-priest over the Nasi; Levitical additions to the Torah; Legendary story of Ezra; The final consolidation of the Torah; The last gleams of prophecy; The Samaritans; What the Jews borrowed from Persia; The decadence of Jewish literature; The Greek translation of the Pentateuch; Literature of the Alexandrine Jews; Jesus, son of Sorach; The persecution of Antiochus; The evident necessity of rewards in a future life; The Book of Daniel; Princely rule of Judas Maccabeus.

TOWER, CHARLEMAGNE, *jr.* The Marquis de La Fayette in the American Revolution; with some account of the attitude of France toward the War of Independence. Lippincott. 2 v., $8.

HUMOR AND SATIRE.

DALLAS, MARY KYLE. Billtry. The Merriam Co. il. 12°, (Waldorf ser., no. 21.) pap., 50 c.
A parody of Du Maurier's "Trilby."

JORDAN, LEOPOLD. Drilby reversed; il. by Philip and Earle Ackerman. G. W. Dillingham. unp. 12°, pap., 50 c.
A burlesque of Du Maurier's "Trilby" in rhyme.

TOWNSEND, E. W. Chimmie Fadden, Major Max, and other stories. Lovell, Coryell & Co. 12°, (Illustrated ser., no. 24.) $1; pap., 50 c.
"Chimmie Fadden" is a New York newsboy, who enters the employment of a rich family as footman, as a reward for a service rendered the young lady of the house; he tells his experience, which is unique and amusing, in the "slang" of the Bowery in a succession of chapters, entitled: Chimmie Fadden makes friends; Chimmie enters polite society; Meets the Duchess; Observes club life; Mr. Fadden's political experience; Chimmie Fadden in court, etc. The "Major Max" stories take the reader into a higher stratum of society. Both series appeared in the New York *Sun*.

LITERATURE, MISCELLANEOUS AND COLLECTED WORKS.

BOOKWORM (The): *7th series:* an illustrated treasury of old-time literature. A. C. Armstrong & Son. il. 8°, $3.

BOOK-PLATE annual and armorial year book, 1895. Macmillan. 4°, (Ex-libris ser.), *net*, $1.75.

CORSON, HIRAM. The aims of literary study. Macmillan. 18°, 75 c.

FUNK, I. K., *D.D.*, MARCH, FRANCIS A., GREGORY, DAN. S., *D.D. eds.* A standard dictionary of the English language upon original plans, designed to give, in complete and accurate statement, in the light of the most recent advances in knowledge and in the readiest form for popular use, the meaning, orthography, pronunciation, and etymology of all the words and the idiomatic phrases in the speech and literature of the English-speaking peoples, prepared by more than two hundred specialists and other scholars under the supervision of I. K. Funk. *Two-volume ed.* V. 2. Funk & Wagnalls Co. 48°, (for two volumes,) rus. *subs.*, $15; or complete in 1 v., *subs.*, $12.
See notice, "Weekly Record," P. W., Dec. 30, '93 [1144] of whole work.

JONES, R. The growth of the Idylls of the king. Lippincott. 12°, $1.50.

LE GALLIENNE, R. The book-bills of Narcissus; an account rendered by R. Le Gallienne; with a frontispiece by Rob. Fowler. Putnam. 1 il. 12°, $1.

PATER, WALTER H. Greek studies; a series of essays: prepared for the press by C. L. Shadwell. Macmillan. 12°, $1.75.

SAINTSBURY, G. E. BATEMAN. Corrected impressions: essays on Victorian writers. Dodd, Mead & Co. por. 16°; $1.25.

SMITH, GARNET. The melancholy of Stephen Allard: a private diary; ed. by Garnet Smith. Macmillan. 12°, $1.75.

TEN BRINK, BERNHARD. Five lectures on Shakespeare; tr. by Julia Franklin. Holt. 12°, $1.25.
They are entitled: The poet and the man; The chronology of Shakespeare's works; Shakespeare as dramatist; Shakespeare as a comic poet; Shakespeare as tragic writer.

TYLER, MOSES COIT. Three men of letters. Putnam. 12°, $1.25.
Three monographs: "George Berkeley and his American visit" refers to the eminent Anglican clergyman who came to this country in 1729; "A great college president and what he wrote" has for its subject Timothy Dwight, one of the first presidents of Yale College; the third paper is called "The literary strivings of Mr. Joel Barlow" —discusses another writer of revolutionary days. Contains a list of books and other printed documents, cited in these papers, with places and dates of publication.

WARNER, BEVERLEY E. English history in Shakespeare's plays. Longmans, Green & Co. 12°, $1.75.

NATURE AND SCIENCE.

MACH, ERNST. Popular scientific lectures; tr. by T. J. McCormack. The Open Court Pub. Co. il. 12°, $1.
Titles of the lectures: The forms of liquids; The fibres of corti; On the causes of harmony; On the velocity of light; Why has man two eyes? On symmetry; On the fundamental concepts of static electricity; On the principle of the conservation of energy; On the economical nature of physical inquiry; On transformation and adaptation in scientific thought; On the principle of comparison in physics; On the relative educational value of the classics and the mathematico-physical sciences.

MELLIAR, *Rev.* A. FOSTER. The book of the rose. Macmillan. 12°, $2.75.

WILD flowers of America: flowers of every state in the American Union, by a corps of special artists and botanists. G. H. Buek & Co. col. pl. obl. 12°, $3.50; $5.

POETRY.

LANIER, SIDNEY. Select poems; ed. with an introd., notes and bibliography, by Morgan Calloway, jr. Scribner. por. 16°, *net*, $1.

LARNED, *Miss* AUGUSTA. In woods and fields. Putnam. 16°, $1.
A collection of poems.

TABB JOHN B. Poems. *2d edition.* Copeland & Day. 18°, $1.
"Father Tabb writes sonnets in which compression, lucidity, correctness of form and melody of phrasing are all well attained. It is seldom that one meets in contemporary verse with a volume in which the artistic qualities and refinement of idea are so definitely manifest as they are in Father Tabb's ' Poems.'"
—*The Beacon.*
"It should be added that the publishers have made a very tasteful volume of Father Tabb's poems, the wide margins giving a most attractive appearance to the clearly printed pages."—*N. Y. Times.*

TRASK, *Mrs.* KATRINA, [*Mrs.* Spencer Trask.] Sonnets and lyrics. A. D. F. Randólph & Co. 12°, $1.

VEEDER, EMILY ELIZ. In the garden, and other poems. Lippincott. 16°, $1.

POLITICAL AND SOCIAL.

CORNWALL, W. C. The currency and the banking law of the Dominion of Canada, considered with reference to currency reform in the United States. Putnam. sq.,S°, pap., 75 c.

The first part of this pamphlet, entitled "Canadian banking system—its growth and present operation," embraces the substance of an address delivered at the American Bankers' Convention, New Orleans, Nov. 12, 1891. It caused American bankers to examine the Canadian currency system, and so favorably have they been impressed with it, that at their convention at Baltimore in September of '94, its main features were reproduced in what is called the "Baltimore plan" of currency reform. The Banking Act of Canada is given entire in the second part of the book.

FONDA, ARTHUR I. Honest money. Macmillan. diagram, 12°, $1.

Points out the faults of our present currency system, as well as the merits and defects of the various changes that have been proposed for its betterment, and outlines a system which, the author thinks, seems to meet the requirements and to correct existing faults. Chapters on: Value and the standard of value; Money; Existing monetary systems; Stability of gold and silver values; Criticism of some gold standard arguments; Foreign commerce; Money in the United States; A new monetary system; Merits and objections considered.

GUYOT, YVES. The tyranny of socialism ; ed., with an introd., by I. H. Levy. Scribner. 12°, (Social sci. ser.) $1.

J., W. The rights of labor: an inquiry as to the relation of employer and employed. C. H. Kerr & Co. 12°, 25 c.

An anonymous work by a young lawyer of Chicago, whose name is for the present withheld. He explains the present status of employer and employee before the law, with clearness and precision, and then goes on to advocate a specific reform in the law that would secure to the workmen a share in the product.

HAMMOND, BASIL E. The political institutions of the ancient Greeks. Macmillan. 8°, net, $1.25.

LEASE, *Mrs.* MARY ELIZ. The problem of civilization solved. Laird & Lee. por. 12°, (Library of choice fiction, no. 2.) pap., 50 c.

Mrs. Lease, of Kansas City, is a populist leader and lecturer; she points out in this volume the great evils that menace our civilization in chapters called, "The riddle of the sphinx," "The foes and evils of civilization," "Anarchy the offspring of monopoly," "Over-population," "Militarism," "The nationalization of the races," etc. Her remedies are set forth in chapters entitled "Colonization of the tropics," "Government ownership of railroads and telegraphs," "Resources and transportation to the tropics," etc.

MOFFETT, S. E. Suggestions on government. Rand, McNally & Co. 12°, $1; pap., 50 c.

The writer points out that our executive administration—local, state, and national—is in-

efficient. "It is in the hands of political professionals, who are necessarily administrative amateurs. Devoting their chief attention to the science of politics, they are naturally unable to go deeply into the science of government." The first requisite of reform he holds to be the close contact between the individual citizen and the agents his vote has summoned to conduct public affairs. The "boss" system must be abolished.

OSTRANDER, D. Social growth and stability: a consideration of the factors of modern society and their relation to the character of the coming state. S. C. Griggs & Co. 12°, $1.

A few of the subjects considered are as follows: Foreign and native labor; Railroads and stagnation; Not charity but statermanship wanted; The brotherhood of man; The eight-hour day; The American people composite; Restricted immigration; Free-trade injuries; Protection bereficial; Competition the root of all evil; The government as a common carrier; Strikes; Trusts; Christianity as a social factor; The ultimate destruction of evil; The reading of books; Hard work essential to success.

PALMER, FRANK LOOMIS. The wealth of labor. The Baker & Taylor Co. 12°, $1.

Contents : The necessity of a new statement; Exchange in primitive communities; The experimental exchanges of a student of Bastiat in these primitive communities; Maintaining the profit of exchange ; Various systems that distribute and equalize the profits of labor ; The consideration of capital and capitalization before a final deduction can be made ; Exchange able value in a community determined by the cost of labor to obtain in preduction ; Deductions; Opinion.

PARKHURST, C. H., *D.D.* Our fight with Tammany. Scribner. 12°, $1.25.

RICARDO, D. The first six chapters of "The Principles of political economy," etc. Macmillan. 12°, (Economic classics.) flex. cl., 75 c.

SMITH, ADAM. Select chapters and passages from "The wealth of nations." Macmillan. 12°, (Economic classics, ed. by W. J. Ashley) 75 c.

THEOLOGY. RELIGION AND SPECULATION.

COWAN, H., *D.D.* Landmarks of church history to the Reformation. A. D. F. Randolph & Co. 24°, (Guild text-books.) pap., 30 c.

Author is Professor of Church History in the University of Aberdeen. His method is chronological and he combines severe accuracy with a concise, but readable and untechnical text. He singles out the chief events in ecclesiastical history during sixteen hundred years and makes clear their causes and effects. An excellent arrangement of type brings out the important and less important facts, and a series of foot-notes point out and explain difficulties. Short bibliography, "Some books on church history" (2 pages).

GERHART, EMANUEL V., *D.D.* Institutes of the Christian religion ; with an introd. by Philip Schaff, D.D. In 2 v. V. 2. Funk & Wagnalls Co. 8°, $3.

The first volume was published in 1891, by A. C. Armstrong & Son. The present volume contains five books dealing with: Anthropology, or, doctrine on the Adamic race ; Christology, or, doctrine on Jesus Christ; Pneumatology, or, doctrine on the Holy Spirit; Soteriology, or, the doctrine on personal salvation; Eschatology, or, doctrine on the last things. The author is professor of systematic and practical theology in Theological Seminary of the Reformed Church, Lancaster, Pa.

GRANT, G. M., *D.D.* Religions of the world in relation to Christianity. A. D. F. Randolph & Co. 24°, (Guild text-books.) pap., 30 c.
The author is the principal of Queen's University, Canada. He believes "that Jesus is 'the way, the truth, and the life,' and that his religion is the absolute religion. Therefore he believes it to be right and wise to call attention to the excellent features of Confucianism, Hindooism, Buddhism, and Mohammedanism rather than to their defects.

HALL, *Rev.* FRANCIS J. The historical position of the Episcopal church; published under the auspices of the Chicago Clericus. Young Churchman Co. 12°, *net*, 50 c.; pap., 20 c.
A paper read before the Church History Club of the Divinity School (Baptist), of the University of Chicago, Dec. 11, 1894. and before the Chicago Clericus (Episcopal), Dec. 17, 1894.

HILEY, R. W., *D.D.* A year's sermons; based upon some of the scriptures appointed for each Sunday morning. In 2 v. V. 1, January to June. V. 2, July to December. Longmans, Green & Co. 12°, *ea.*, $2. (*Corr. price.*)

LILIENTHAL, HERMANN. Lent past and present: a study of the primitive origin of Lent, its purpose and usages; with an introd. by J. Williams, D.D. Whittaker. 12°, 75 c.
The lectures here printed were delivered as sermons on the Sunday mornings of last Lent to the author's congregation in Wethersfield, Ct. Their titles are: The primitive origin of Lent; the primitive purpose of Lent; Lenten observances; Fasting; Holy Week.

MACCOLL, MALCOLM, (*Canon*.) Life here and hereafter: sermons preached in Ripon Cathedral and elsewhere. Longmans, Green & Co. 12°, $2.25.

MAMREOV, PETER V. F., ANNA F., *and* B. A. F. Iesät Nassar: the story of the life of Jesus the Nazarene. Sunrise Pub. Co. sq.12°, $2.
This story of the life of Jesus the Nazarene is given in an altogether novel form. While founded on strictly Christian and Jewish secular and ecclesiastical histories, as also on traditions and legends of oriental and occidental nations, the personages who figure in the tale are presented as every-day mortals. The authors are Russians who were born in Jerusalem and lived many years in Syria, Palestine, and Egypt, and had exceptional advantages for research. There is, strictly speaking, no fiction in the story—the persons introduced being either historical or legendary. Quotations are given in an appendix from the historical and other works on which each chapter of the story is founded. There is also a description of the religious, social, and political condition of the Jews, Romans, Egyptians, and Parthians, and their relations to each other.

MURRAY, *Rev.* ANDREW. The holiest of all: an exposition of the epistle to the Hebrews. A. D. F. Randolph & Co. 8°, *net*, $2.
"When first I undertook the preparation of this exposition in Dutch for the Christian people among whom I labor," Dr. Murray says in his preface, "it was under a deep conviction that the epistle just contained the instruction they needed. In reproducing it in English this impression has been confirmed, and it is as if nothing could be written more exactly suited to the state of the whole church of Christ in the present day. . . . In every possible way it sets before us the truth that it is only the full and perfect knowledge of what Christ is and does for us that can bring us to a full and perfect Christian life."

PERKINS, MARY H., ["Dorcas Hicks," *pseud.*] From my corner; looking at life in sunshine and shadow. A. D. F. Randolph & Co. nar. 16°, 50 c.
Helpful papers; a few of the titles are: Wrong at the start; From the back seat; Those few sweet words; A paradox of Saint Peter; Secret things; Are your windows washed? Tired eyes; Infirmities; Suffer them to come unto Me; etc.

VINCENT, MARVIN R., *D.D.* Biblical inspiration and Christ. A. D. F. Randolph & Co. 12°, pap., 25 c.
A large part of this pamphlet was published in the *New World* of March, 1893. The author dwells in detail upon the distinction between Revelation and Scripture: giving the Bible its place as "a record, a medium, a revelation of divine revelation interpenetrated with human elements." He warns that scholastic descriptions and definitions of inspiration lead nowhere, but "if we begin with the spirit of Jesus we do not need there." "If the personal Christ can be appre henced, so also can the inspiration of cripture as an expression of his divine and human personality."

VINCENT, MARVIN R., *D.D.* That monster, the higher critic. A. D. F. Randolph & Co sq. 12°, pap., 25 c.
A plea for the "Higher critic" to supplement the "Textual critic." The writer thinks ignorant piety and intelligent criticism are opposed on utterly false premises and to false issues. He explains what the learned critic should do as an interpreter of Scripture, and disapproves strongly of deferring matters involving scholarship to the vote of church dignitaries whose only claim is piety and position in a special church. He speaks fearlessly and is evidently against those who condemned Dr. Briggs and Dr. Smith. He thinks the idea is being fostered that the higher criticism is a dangerous monster.

WACE, H., *D.D.* Christianity and Agnosticism: reviews of some recent attacks on the Christian faith. Whittaker. 8°, $2.50.
Contents: On agnosticism: a paper read at the Manchester Church Congress, 1888; Agnosticism, a reply to Professor Huxley (from the *Nineteenth Century*, March, 1889); Christianity and agnosticism, a further reply to Professor Huxley (from the *Nineteenth Century*, May, 1889); The historical criticism of the New Testament (from the *Quarterly Review*, Oct., 1886); The latest attack on Christianity (from the *Quarterly Review*, July, 1887). Appendix contains: Robert Elsmere and Christianity and The speaker's commentary on the New Testament, vs. 1 and 2, two essays published in the *Quarterly Review*, Oct., 1888, and April, 1881.

WATKINS, OSCAR D. Holy matrimony: a treatise on the divine laws of marriage. Macmillan. 8°, $5.

RECENT FRENCH AND GERMAN BOOKS.

FRENCH.

Adeline, J. Les Arts de production vulgarisés. 8°, cloth............................ $3 60
Alexandre, A. Hist. populaire de la peinture. Vol. II. Ecoles Flamande et Hollandaise. 8°, il. 3 00
Almanach de Gotha, 1895. Cloth................ 2 70
Berenger. L'Aristocratie intellectuelle.......... 1 00
Bourges, E. Sous la hache (1793)................ 1 00
Brada. Notes Sur Londres..... .. ..se.1 00
Calmettes. Simplette......... .. .. 1 00
Daudet. Petite Paroisse......................... 1 00
D'Annunzio, G. Episcopo & Cie............... 1 00
Dugas, L. L'Amitié Antique, d'après les moeurs populaires et les théories des philosophes........ 2 25
Dunan. Théorie psychologique de l'Espace. (Bibl. de Phil. Contemp.) 12°.......................... 75
Funck-Brentano. L'Homme et sa Destinée... 2 25
Gonse. La Sculpture Française, du 14ieme au 19ieme Siècle. 4°, il., bound.................... 18 00
Goyau, Paraté, Fabre. Le Vatican. 4°, il., hf. mor.. 12 00
Greef, G. de. Le Transformisme Social. (Bibl. de Phil. Contemp.) 8°............................ 2 25
Gyp. Leurs Ames................................ 1 00
Labiche, E. Théatre Choisi. 8°, il., cloth...... 6 00
Lariviere, Chas. de. Catherine II. et la Revolution Française................................ 1 00
Lavisse et Rambaud. Hist. Générale du 19me siècle à nos jours. Vol. v. Les guerres de la religion. 8°.................................... 3 60
Loti, P. Le Désert.............................. 1 00
Maspero. Hist. Ancienne des Peuples de l'Orient Classique. Vol. I. Les Origines : Egypt & Chaldée. 8°, il., bound............................ 12 40
Munts, E. Hist. de l'Art pendant la Renaissance.

Vol. III. Italic : La fin de la renaissance. 8°, il., bound............. ... . $12 90
Rod, Ed. Les Roches Blanches.................. 1 00
Sainte-Aulaire, A. de. Carlistes et Christinos.. 1 00
Thomas, P. Felix. La Suggestion, son rôle dans l'education. (Bibl. de Phil. Contemp.) 12°..... 75
Wyzewa, T. de. Chez les Allemands : L'Art et les Moeurs.................................... 1 00

GERMAN.

Elster, O. Venus Imperatrix 1 35
Essen, M. v. Vergangenes aus dem Leben eines Diplomaten.................. 70
Gerhardt, M. Leben um Leben. 2 vols........ 2 65
Gotthelf, H. Marcelle...................... 1 35
Hartmann, Ed. v. Die sozialen Kernfragen..... 3 35
Hermann, H. Flammen im Herzen............. 1 70
Hoffmann, H. Wider den Kurfürsten. 3 vls. . 4 65
Jensen, Wm Die Erbin von Helmstede........ 2 00
Lauff, J. Die Hauptmannsfrau................. 2 00
Menga. Vollendung u. Zerstörung............... 1 00
Panzer, F. Lohengrinstudien.................. 55
Petersdorff. Briefe von Ferd. Gregorovius an H. von Thile............................ 2 00
Sturokow. Der Herr von Zalaur...... .... 1 35
Suttner, B. v. Ein Manuscript................. 1 00
Suttner, A. G. v. Eine Moderne Ehe.......... 1 70
Wald-Zedtwitz. Wie's doch so anders kam. 2 vols..................................... 3 00
Weissenfels, R. Goethe im Sturm und Drang. I..................................... 3 35
Wolters, W. Geliebt Werden................. 1 70
Zapp. Der neue Don Quixote................. 1 35
Zobeltitz, F. v. Die Johanniter................. 2 00

Freshest News.

TOWN TOPICS have just issued the fifteenth volume of the popular series of *Tales from Town Topics*, containing David Christie Murray's story entitled "Why? Says Gladys," and selections from the tid-bits of their snappy weekly. They also call attention to Amélie Rives' bright story entitled "The Sang-Digger," which still sells steadily.

F. TENNYSON NEELY has just published in *Neely's Prismatic Library*, "Father Stafford," by Anthony Hope ; also "The King in Yellow," by Robert E. Chambers, author of "In the Quarter," bound in buckram with gilt tops, in the neat style of this attractive series. Emile Zola's "Lourdes" is now ready in *Neely's International Library*, and in the paper-covered *Neely's Library of Choice Fiction*.

E. P. DUTTON & Co. have this year prepared an unusually large and attractive line of Easter booklets and tokens, the text for which has been taken from the works of Bishop Phillips Brooks, Rev. J. R. Macduff, Frances Ridley Havergal, Charlotte Murray, and others, all of which have been appropriately illustrated and exquisitely printed. They have also prepared a great variety of smaller cards in colors and monotone.

ROBERTS BROTHERS have just ready a new volume in the *Keynotes Series*, entitled "The Woman Who Did," a strong story by Grant Allen; the fourth volume of Renan's "History of the People of Israel," of which the fifth vol-

ume will follow shortly; also, a new edition of the five volumes of Robert Louis Stevenson which bear their imprint: "Travels with a Donkey in the Cevennes"; "An Inland Voyage"; "The Silverado Squatters"; "Treasure Island"; and "Prince Otto." "The Sons of Ham," a tale of the New South by Louis Pendleton; and "Prince Zaleski," by M. P. Shiel, will also very shortly be added to the American copyright edition of the *Keynotes Series*.

THE SUNRISE PUBLISHING CO., N. Y., have just published "Iesût Nassar," the story of the life of Jesus the Nazarene, by Peter F., Anna F., and B. A. F. v. Mamreov. These authors have enjoyed exceptional advantages and opportunities for research on matters social and religious in the lands of Syria, Palestine and Egypt. They were born in Jerusalem of Russian parents who went to the Holy Land for the express purpose of acquiring light upon the conflicting dogmas of the Christian, Jewish and Mohammedan creeds. The authors treat of Jesus as a human being and give the history of his ancestors as it is given in the secular historical Jewish literature. The appendix, devoted to notes, citations and explanations, occupies nearly one-third of the book.

FREDERICK A. STOKES COMPANY have published a series of "Famous Queens and Martha Washington Paper Dolls," by Elizabeth S. Tucker, artist of "A Year of Paper Dolls." The set represents Queen Isabella of Spain, 1492; Queen Elizabeth of England, 1558; Queen Marie Antoinette of France, 1789; Martha Washington, 1775; Queen Louise of Prussia, 1797 ; Queen Victoria of England, 1837; and

Queen Margherita of Italy, 1868. Miss Tucker has given the features of the different historical characters, as well as accurate representation of different costumes worn by them, adapting them especially for kindergartens and schools for children. The water-color sketches have been admirably reproduced in colors, and in a high grade of work rarely used in publications of this kind.

G. P. PUTNAM'S SONS have in preparation an illustrated edition of Captain Marryat's famous story, "Mr. Midshipman Easy." The designs for the book will be prepared by representative American artists. In their *Famous Novels* series they will include the Baroness Tautphœus' story, "At Odds," which will be issued uniform with their editions of "The Initials" and "Quits." They also have in preparation for the same series, editions of "Richelieu" and "Agincourt," by G. P. R. James. It is planned to follow these with other of the more noteworthy of James' historical novels. They have also in preparation a practical handbook in the elocutionary art, by Hugh Campbell, R. F. Brewer, Henry Neville, and Clifford Harrison, entitled "Voice, Speech, and Gesture." It will have over 100 illustrations by Dargravel, Ramsey, and others.

THOS. Y. CROWELL & COMPANY announce for immediate publication "The Christian State a Political Vision of Christ," by the Rev. George D. Herron, Professor of Applied Christianity at Grinnell College. Professor Herron has aroused extraordinary interest during the past year by his outspoken criticism upon our modern society and particularly upon the "dormant oblivious Church." Multitudes of newspaper editorials have been written attacking and defending him for his advanced notions. They have in preparation a new book on domestic architecture, by Louis H. Gibson, of Indianapolis, author of a work on "Convenient Houses," to be entitled "Beautiful Houses." Prof. Richard T. Ely's "Socialism and Social Reform," which Thos. Y. Crowell & Co. have in its fourth edition, has been officially adopted at Chautauqua in a special course of readings in sociology.

HENRY HOLT & Co. have just issued Ten Brink's "Five Lectures on Shakespeare," translated by Julia Franklin; "Jack O'Doon," a romantic tale, in the *Buckram Series*, of the North Carolina coast, by Maria Beale; Johnson's "Rasselas," edited by C. F. Emerson, Professor at Cornell; "German Prose and Poetry for Early Reading," edited, with introduction, notes and vocabulary, by T. B. Bronson, Master in the Lawrenceville School; "Stories from Grimm, Andersen, and Hauff, and poems by various authors," edited, with introduction, notes and vocabulary, by T. B. Bronson; Hauff's "Karavane," with poems by various authors, vocabulary and portrait, edited by T. B. Bronson; "Three Classic German Tales" (Kleist's "Verlobung in San Domingo," Goethe's "Neue Melusine," and Zschokke's "Der Todte Gast"), edited by A. B. Nichols, Instructor in Harvard; and Benedix's comedy "Der Dritte," edited by Miss Marion P. Whitney, of the Hillhouse High School, New Haven.

HOUGHTON, MIFFLIN & Co. have just ready "Louisiana Folk-Tales," collected and arranged by Alcée Fortier, Professor of the Romance Languages in Tulane University, Louisiana, being a companion volume to the "Folk-Tales of Angola," and containing fifteen animal tales, twelve märchen, and in the appendix fourteen stories only known in English; volume VII. of Sargent's "Silva of North America"; a new edition of Rev. A. V. G. Allen's "Continuity of Christian Thought"; an edition of Bret Harte's "Susy" in the *Riverside Paper Series;* and in the *Riverside Literature Series* "A Selection From Child Life in Poetry"; and "A Selection From Child Life in Prose," edited by John G. Whittier. Among their very latest books are "Stories of the Foot-Hills," by Margaret C. Graham; "Half a Century with Judges and Lawyers," by Joseph A. Willard; "Commentaries on Insurance," by Charles F. Beach, Jr.; "The Fast and Thanksgiving Days of New England," by Rev. William de Loss Love, Jr., containing three proclamations in *fac-simile;* and a new edition of "The First Napoleon," by John C. Ropes.

D. APPLETON & Co. have in preparation the fourth volume of McMaster's "History of the People of the United States"; "Degeneracy," a brilliant if somewhat distorted analysis, by Max Nordau, of the literary, æsthetic and social phases of the end of the century; "Evolution and Effort," by Edmond Kelly, who discusses evolution in its application to the religious and political life of the day, with illustrations drawn from recent events in New York; "The Wish," a novel, by Hermann Sudermann (the author of "Die Ehre," a realistic play that may be familiar to Americans), with a biographical introduction by Elizabeth Lee; "Majesty," a novel, by Louis Couperus, translated by A. Teixeira de Mattos and Ernest Dowson; and two new novels in the *Town and Country Library*—"The Honour of Savelli," by T. Levett Yeats, a romance of an adventurer in Italy in the turbulent days of the Borgias, and "Kitty's Engagement," by Florence Warden. A series of little books dealing with various branches of knowledge, and treating each subject in clear, concise language, as free as possible from technical words and phrases, though written by writers of authority, is also announced. The series will be entitled *The Library of Useful Stories,* the first of which will be "The Story of the Stars," by G. F. Chambers, with 24 illustrations. Other volumes in preparation are: "The Story of the Earth," by Prof. H. G. Seeley; "The Story of Primitive Man," by Edward Clodd; and "The Story of the Solar System," by G. F. Chambers. They also have ready the second volume in the *Anthropological Series,* a work by A. de Quatrefarges, entitled "The Pygmies." The peculiar intellectual, moral, and religious characteristics of the small, black races of Africa have been carefully noted by the late French Professor of Natural History. His work has been translated by Professor Frederick Starr. The new volume in the *Town and Country Library* is "Noémi," a new volume by S. Baring-Gould; and there is also just issued the third edition, largely rewritten, of James Geikie's "The Great Ice Age."

LITERARY NEWS

AN ECLECTIC REVIEW OF
CURRENT LITERATURE
~ILLUSTRATED~

CONTENTS.

VOL. XVI-No. I APRIL ~ 1895 $1.00 YEARLY
10 CTS. PER NO.

~ PUBLICATION OFFICE ~
· 28 ELM STREET NEW YORK ·

ENTERED AT THE POST OFFICE AT NEW YORK AS SECOND CLASS MATTER

The Literary News

In winter you may reade them, ab ignem, by the fireside; and in summer, ab umbram, under some shadie tree; and therewith pass away the tedious howres.

VOL. XVI.   APRIL, 1895.   No. 4

A New Biography of Gladstone.

HENRY W. LUCY, who has written "The Right Honorable W. E. Gladstone—a Study from Life," has off and on for twenty years taken notes of Gladstone's speeches from the gallery of the House of Commons. He says in his [7] preface : "The obvious difficulty of writing within the limits of this volume a sketch of the career of Mr. Gladstone is the superabundance of material. The task is akin to that of a builder having had placed at his disposal materials for a palace, with instructions to erect a cottage residence, leaving out nothing essential to the larger plan. I have been content, rapidly to sketch, in chronologi-

From "The Right Hon. W. E. Gladstone."   Copyright, 1886, by Roberts Bros.

W. E. GLADSTONE.

had unusual opportunities of studying the subject." Mr. Lucy wrote a sketch of Gladstone in 1880, which was brought out in this country in *Harper's Half-Hour Series;* and in his large work, entitled "The Diary of Two Parliaments," published in London in 1886, the second volume treated of the "Gladstone Parliament, 1880–1885." Mr. Lucy will also be remembered as the author of "Gideon Fleyce," an epoch-making political novel published in 1882. His style is delightful and his subject—the great scholar-statesman of Europe, four times Premier of the leading nation of the world—is of inexhausti-

cal order, the main course of a phenomenally busy life, enriching the narrative wherever possible with autobiographical scraps to be found in the library of Mr. Gladstone's public speeches, supplementing it by personal notes made over a period of twenty years, during which I have ble interest. The book deals wholly with the public career of Gladstone, but is full of little personal touches, giving a fair and vivid picture of his individuality. An excellent digest of one of the most important periods of European and world history. (Roberts. $1.25.)

The Literature of the Georgian Era

AN essay in literary history which has been recently published by the Harpers may be cordially commended as a text book to American high schools and colleges. We refer to " The Literature of the Georgian Era," by the late William Minto, Professor of English Literature and Logic in the University of Aberdeen. In a treatise on logic, inductive and deductive, which the author contributed some years ago to the series of university manuals, he laid great stress upon the superiority of inductive over deductive reasoning, and he has faithfully practised what he preached in the lectures which make up the book before us. His studies differ from much work of the kind in being historical before they are critical ; he has not begun by saturating his mind with what others have said upon the subject, but has gone straight to the authors themselves about whom he intended to discourse, and has read their writings thoroughly before expressing an opinion on them. By the simple expedient of refraining from speaking of any book until he had read it, he has succeeded in imparting a refreshing originality to his own composition. The general effect of his lectures is, first, to stimulate the reader to follow the lecturer's example and verify assertions for himself, and, secondly, to give him the assurance that, should he do this, he is likely to find that many current conceptions are unfounded. Thus, as regards the poetry of the Georgian era, Mr. Minto undertakes to refute a number of prevailing misconceptions; for instance, the supposed tyranny of Pope, the revolutionizing of poetry attributed to Cowper, and the alleged lack of artistic education on the part of Burns. Almost equally striking and suggestive are the lecturer's references to the various masters of English prose fiction, from Richardson and Fielding to Scott and Bulwer. (Harper. $1.50.) —*The Sun.*

John Addington Symonds.

EVERY one remembers Carlyle's saying that, if the life of any man were recounted with absolute veracity, it would be of surpassing interest from the light it would throw upon the human soul. There has been many an attempt, not counting Rousseau's, to answer the hard condition of unflinching truth-telling. The latest, and one of the most striking, is made in a biography of John Addington Symonds, compiled from his papers and correspondence by Horatio F. Brown. This book is constructed on a plan which, so far as we know, is new. It is biographical in form, but autobiographical in substance. The subject, in-

deed, left an autobiography and a diary as well as a great quantity of letters addressed to intimate friends. These materials are woven into a consecutive narrative, the source of each particular paragraph being indicated in a footnote, and without any break in the text. By this arrangement the readableness of the volume is singularly enhanced. To the question why the autobiography was not printed separately, the compiler answers by quoting a remark made by Symonds himself, that " autobiographies, written with a purpose, are likely to want atmosphere. A man, when he sits down to give an account of his own life from the point of view of art, or passion, or of a particular action, is apt to make it appear as though he were nothing but an artist, nothing but a lover, or that the action he seeks to explain was the principal event in his existence. The report has to be supplemented in order that a true portrait may be painted." Mr. Brown adds on his own account that autobiographies being written at one period of life inevitably convey the tone of that period; they are not contemporaneous evidence, and are, therefore, of inferior value to diaries and letters. The latter portray the man more truly at each moment, and progressively from moment to moment. Especial stress is properly laid upon the choice of materials and method of arrangement in the case of the biography of such a man as Symonds, which depends for its interest upon psychological development. He was a man of means, and travelled for the sake of his health, or for the accumulation of knowledge; but his journeys were not of the kind which led to external adventures. On the other hand, for a biography of the psychological order, the material is as rich and varied as the temperament of the man who created it. This is, in truth, an extraordinary book as regards the rigor of self-scrutiny, and the frankness of self-disclosure. (Scribner. 2 v., $12.50.) —*The Sun.*

PROEM TO A VICTORIAN ANTHOLOGY.

ENGLAND ! since Shakspere died no loftier day
   For thee than lights herewith a century's goal—
   Nor statelier exit of heroic soul
   Conjoined with soul heroic—nor a lay
Excelling theirs who made renowned thy sway
   Even as they heard the billows which outroll
   Thine ancient sea, and left their joy and do e
   In song, and on the strand their mantles gray.
Star-rayed with fame thine Abbey windows loom
   Above his dust, whom the Venetian barge
   Bore to the main ; who passed the twofold marge
To slumber in thy keeping: yet make room
   For the great Laurifer, whose chanting large
   And sweet shall last until our tongue's far doom.
EDMUND CLARENCE STEDMAN, in the *Century* (March).

America's Celebrities.

PHOTOGRAPHS of well-known people have a peculiar attraction to most of us; we have, or think we have, a. better notion of the personality of a speaker, writer or statesman if we know whether he is tall or short, dark or light, bearded or smooth-shaven—if we can, in fact, form an idea of his personal as well as his mental individuality. Some two hundred and fifty of the best-known men and women of America are thus brought before us in the handsome folio volume of portraits and biographical sketches, entitled "America's Greatest Men and Women." It is essentially a picture gallery of the present, including, with but two or three exceptions—among them Frederick Douglass—only persons now living. The portraits are not restricted to a single field, as literature or science. They include men of public affairs statesmen, lawyers, writers, sculptors, soldiers, poets, clergymen, inventors, and men who have won "celebrity" by wealth or business activity. Among the writers, especially, whose "counterfeit presentments" are here set forth, are W. D. Howells, Julia Ward Howe, Edward Everett Hale, Charles A. Dana, Ella Wheeler Wilcox, Capt. King, T. W. Higginson, Mrs. Southworth, Kate Field, "Gath," G. W. Cable, Lew Wallace, "Octave Thanet," Richard Harding Davis, Elizabeth Stuart Phelps, James Whitcomb Riley and E. C. Stedman. The portraits are "process" cuts, printed on smooth, heavy paper, each portrait taking a page and being set in a broad, cream-colored border. Appended to every portrait is a short biographical sketch, summarizing the chief events in the life of its subject. The book is tastefully bound in heavy dull blue canvas, simply stamped in gilt. It is a book newspaper readers will find useful in verifying points occurring in discussions of the news of the hour. (Conkey. $4.)

THE DESTINY-MAKER.

SHE came; and I
  who lingered there,
I saw that she
    was very fair;
And. with my sighs
  that pride suppress'd,
There rose a trembling
    wish for rest.
  But I, who had resolv'd to be
  The maker of my destiny,
  I turned me to my task and wrought,
  And so forgot the passing thought.

She paused, and I who question'd there,
I heard she was as good as fair;
And in my soul a still small voice
Enjoin'd me not to check my choice.
  But I, who had resolved to be
  The maker of my destiny,
  I bade the gentle guardian down
  And tried to think about renown.

She left; and I who wander, fear
There's nothing more to see or hear;
Those walls that ward my paradise
Are very high, nor open twice.
  And I, who had
    resolved to be
  The maker of
    my destiny,
  Can only wait
    without the gate
  And sit
    and sigh—
      " Too late !
        too late ! "

From Raymond's "Pictures in Verse." (Putnam. 75 c.)

From " Pictures in Verse."

THE DESTINY-MAKER.

Opium Eating and Its Effects.

BECAUSE Samuel Coleridge wrote "Kubla Khan" in an opium trance, and because Thomas De Quincey has told us in a classic of English literature of the delights of visiting Covent Garden under the sublime intoxication of the poppy plant, we may, perhaps, have lost sight of the baneful influence of the drug which caused these masterpieces to come into being. If we have we may certainly be restored to more perfect sight if we look through the eyes of Mr. William Rosse Cobbe, who, in a volume entitled "Dr. Judas, a Portrayal of the Opium Habit," gives with great frankness of confession and considerable purity of diction a record of his own experiences with the drug.

Indeed, one entire chapter of Mr. Cobbe's book, and many parts of other chapters, are devoted to showing that De Quincey was not only wrong in some of his statements, but distinctly unjustified in what he wrote, because he threw around the opium habit a halo of literary beauty, which has tempted many to destruction.

Born under hereditary conditions which made him a nervous and easily irritated lad ; being in constant peril through the war ; harassed by religious doubts, and finally entering the ministry (foolishly, he says) and then taking up the profession of journalism, Mr. Cobbe easily drifted into a state where some stimulant seemed to be necessary. Suffice it to say that opium became that stimulant and that for years he was its slave. His deliverance from its thralldom caused this book to be written, and the recentness of the deliverance is what makes the book so interesting.

That which will probably attract to it the attention of the unscientific reader more than anything else are the chapters devoted to the effect of the drug, especially those describing the hallucinations that follow a long-continued indulgence in it. And here it must be noticed as peculiarly interesting that Mr. Cobbe, notwithstanding his criticism of De Quincey, seems to have experienced the same adventures in his dreams. That he describes them in much the same language does not mean that he is guilty of plagiarism, but that the poppy blooms red wherever it grows, and that after all De Quincey knew what opium did even if he seemed to woo or do.

It would take too long to tell of the things that can be seen and heard by the opium victim, which are too often of this book, but it is certainly surprising to learn that there are in the United States, according to Mr. Cobbe as many who use it or use it as those of drugs and a very easy use of alcohol. Several instances are given where De Quincey's enormous doses have been surpassed. The English man's

largest daily dose was 320 grains of opium in the form of laudanum. The author mentions a resident of Southern Illinois, who consumed 1072 grains a day ; another in the same State who contented himself with 1685 grains, and, finally, another whose daily consumption amounted to 2345 grains.

Scarcely touching upon the scientific features of the habit, this book is still full of such an intimate knowledge of what can be called a disease that it should be a valuable addition to medical literature. At the same time it is general enough in its scope, and brilliant enough in its language, to make it entertaining to the ordinary reader. (Griggs. $1.50.)—*Chicago Times.*

Maeterlinck's Plays.

MAETERLINCK cannot claim greater fame on this side of the Atlantic than has been given him by allusion in newspapers or the books of other authors. As one of that school which is styled the Decadent, and which appears to include nearly all who write what may shock Mrs. Grundy, his foreign reputation has been made. "Symbolical" is the self-chosen title by which it prefers to be known, and its claim is that it concerns itself chiefly with people, and that in many cases it conceives even inanimate things as having a fictitious kind of personality. If this does not convey a clear idea of the character of the works it produces, its admirers must be blamed who have chosen so to describe it. If they had gone farther, and said that their school evinced a marked preference for the morbid and dismal, it would have more clearly defined its trend.

Maeterlinck may be selected as a type of the cult. Just why he should have been called the Flemish Shakespeare, as he has been by some of his adulators, is not clear, as there appears to be absolutely nothing on which to base a resemblance, however faint, and it is time wasted to seek for similitudes. . . . There is a certain charm to his work which it would be difficult to define. It lies more in his subject —extended beyond reasonable bounds though his situations often are—and in that attraction which allusions to the unseen and the tread of invisible feet have for all readers of drama. This feature is beloved of Maeterlinck and is ever present even when it is not entirely intelligible. M. Maeterlinck discriminates very delicately. The King in "The Princess Maleine" is very different from the King in "The Seven Sisters," and both differ from the King in "Pelleas and Melisande." As to the value of the characters, opinions may differ ; but the power of conceiving and drawing is conspicuous. Published in the *Irving Free Library.* Stone & Kimball. $1.50.—*Paris Review.*

From "The White Tsar."

The White Tsar, and Other Poems.

UNDER this title J. Selwin Tait & Sons have brought out a very handsome volume of poems, of which the one that gives the title sings of the joys and sorrows that come into the life of a white bear in the frozen North. Henry Bedlow has written the graphic words and J. Steeple Davis has made the pictures. The paper is thick and printed only on one side, with limitless margins, and the first appearance of the book is distinctly of holiday nature.

The poem which accompanies the illustration we have chosen gives an idea of the author's enthusiastic style:

Morn's frankincense etherially faint ;
   The sweet contention of the birds in song,
The Oriole's anthem and the Swallow's plaint,
   The Thrush, the Laureate of the Choral throng.
The Constellations' glory and the Moon's,
   Studding the sapphire vastness of the skies ;
The salt-sea freshness of the sandy dunes,
   The thrill and pathos of Immensities.

(Tait. $3.50.)

Iesät Nassar.

WE happen to have on our table at the present moment a bulky volume of over seven hundred pages, which we have carefully examined, and which seems to us to contain a great deal which will both interest and instruct the reader. It is entitled "Iesät Nassar; the Story of the Life of Jesus, the Nazarene." Its authors are two brothers and a sister—Peter V. F. Mamreov, Anna F. Mamreov, and B. A. F. Mamreov, and it is from the press of the Sunrise Publishing Company, of New York.

The treatment of the subject in hand is from a very novel standpoint. While it is radical in many parts, in other parts it is exceedingly conservative. The authors regard Jesus as a pure-minded, unselfish Hebrew, and they admit but little of the supernatural into their narrative. Still, the general tone of the book is wholly reverent, and they repeat the story of the resurrection, for example, with faith in all its details, accompanying it with a recital of the many legends which have naturally gathered about the career of so singular a being as Jesus.

These authors were born in Jerusalem, of Russian parents, and were brought up in the strictest faith. While pursuing their studies they enjoyed exceptional advantages, because they were in possession of a firman from the Sultan of Turkey. The prestige thus afforded gave them opportunities not usually accorded. One of them held some relation to the United States Consulate at Jerusalem, and another was with the Palestine Exploration Society, whose headquarters were in that city.

We suspect that the book must be taken with a large grain of salt, and yet we readily admit that we have read it with a considerable degree of pleasure. The motives which prompted the authors to write this biography were of the highest, and there is no attempt in any part of it to discredit the main facts as they have been generally accepted. On the contrary, these facts are surrounded with such a cloud of legends and quotations from a thousand and one ancient writers that the reader becomes fascinated, even though he is also somewhat confused.

The biography opens with an account of the direct ancestors of Jesus, and this leads to a long, possibly an unnecessarily long, description of the manners and customs prevailing at the time of Jesus' birth, all of which is certainly valuable.

The whole story is in some respects novel and will appeal to a certain large class of readers. At any rate, it will certainly interest them, and there is no reason why it should have any influence to lessen their faith in the historic Jesus.

As we have before intimated, we do not accept the volume without a large number of doubts, but, at the same time, it is a contribution to the literature of an important subject, and as such it has a place in every well-furnished library. (Sunrise Pub. Co. $2.)—*N. Y. Herald.*

Majesty.

THERE have been many workers among novelists in the field of royal portraiture, but it may be safely stated that few of those who have essayed this dubious path have achieved more striking results than M. Couperus. "Majesty" is an extraordinarily vivid romance of autocratic imperialism, and the main aim of the book is so legitimate, and its treatment so sympathetic and artistic, that it is to be regretted that the author should have adopted the portrait form at all. The striking but superficial resemblance between the leading characters of the story and those of more than one reigning imperial house, will, no doubt, prove a bait to readers hungry for personalities ; but the real merits of the book—its dramatic intensity and powerful characterization—are entirely independent of this factitious interest. Foremost amongst the *dramatis personæ* is the Crown Prince Othomar, a truly tragic figure, with noble instincts hampered by a delicate constitution, a Hamlet-like irresoluteness of purpose, and hedged round on every side by Procrustean etiquette. The contrast between him and his bluff sailor cousin, Prince Herman of Gothland, and his devotion for his mother, the empress (a woman whose natural warmth of heart has been numbed and paralyzed by the atmosphere of terror and melancholy which girds the throne), are drawn with great skill, and in the latter case with exquisite tenderness. M. Couperus does not merely turn the search-light of his analysis on the domestic life of the Cæsars of to-day : he paints them also in their relations with courtiers and advisers ; in their rare moments of contact with the masses ; hurrying feverishly from function to function ; strange, frozen, lonely figures, oppressed, in the words of the empress, with "the immeasurable melancholy of being rulers." The effect of the whole book is greatly heightened by M. Couperus' artistic use of contrast and his sense of humor. The letter of the little ten-year-old Prince Berengar, describing to his brother the ceremony of his appointment as a Knight of St. Ladislas, is not only charming in itself, but it forms a most admirable anticlimax to the passionate love scene which has gone before. It only remains to be added that the translation has been executed creditably rather than brilliantly. (Appleton. $1.50.)—*The Academy.*

La Petite Paroisse.

THE new novel by Alphonse Daudet, "La Petite Paroisse," shows the same exquisite feeling and touch as the earlier works of the master, with little diminution of strength. The artist still enjoys his powers of vision and expression; the analyst retains his skill and precision; the story-teller still has the charm and attraction of old. What is perhaps more marked is the profound sympathy of Daudet for all suffering, and the intense desire he feels to raise and brighten. He is an optimist in "La Petite Paroisse," and his kindly touch gives even Charlexis and the old duke redeeming features here and there. The book recalls "Mme. Bovary" in some respects. The two heroines have much in common at first; Daudet's does not sink as low, and is finally restored and pardoned. The story is a simple one, the fall and redemption of a married woman, tyrannized over by a despotic, narrow-minded mother-in-law. It is told with all the wondrous grace and poetry which are Daudet's special gifts, in that sunny French of which he possesses the secret, full of delicate suggestiveness of tint and color. No more than "Mme. Bovary" does it make sin alluring, but it lacks, happily, the cruel impassibility and bitter vividness of Flaubert's famous book. (Meyer. $1.)—*The Nation.*

The Tale of Chloe.

POSSIBLY Mr. Meredith would long ere this have contrived to republish "The Tale of Chloe" had he thought very highly of its two companions that help to swell it into a volume. The first story is a gem, as perfect in its kind as anything he has written. To read it is to feel at once aggrieved it was not ours long ago, and delighted it has been kept back for our present enjoyment. It is not easy to be grateful for the two others. "The House on the Beach" is dull and improbable. "The Case of General Ople" is rather funny, but it is a hobbledehoy farce. Both are extreme instances of Mr. Meredith's habit, in which only Carlyle surpassed him, of riding a joke to death.

The first story begins in a tone of gentle satire, with quaint reflections on amorous dukes in general, and a particular description, from his own lips, of the early matrimonial delights of the elderly duke who married the milkmaid, and who, loving her to distraction, has been persuaded to expose her to the perils of the Wells that she may have the amusement she craves and the experience she lacks. The story never loses the tone of high-bred comedy save when it takes you behind the scenes with Chloe, Chloe who had given fortune and family and all for love, and missed it. She is one of Mr. Meredith's chosen

From "The Tale of Chloe."   Copyright, 1895, by Ward, Lock & Bowden, Ltd.

GEORGE MEREDITH.

ladies, very loving, much-enduring, smiling for all her wounds, gentle, decorous, distinguished.

The milkmaid duchess, too, so healthy, so vain, so selfish, so good-natured and blunt, is a triumph, especially in the scene where she returns, reckless and excited, after losing her money at the tables.

The whole story delights and stimulates, but the best it does is to give us Chloe, the gentle, the generous, the trusting, and the far-seeing, for a friend. (Ward, Lock & Bowden. $1.50.)— *The Bookman.*

Thoughts on Religion.

THE Open Court Publishing Company of Chicago have put forth a small volume entitled "Thoughts on Religion," by the late George John Romanes, edited by Charles Gore, Canon of Westminster. It is well known that Mr. Romanes was one of the most zealous and conspicuous among the English disciples of Darwin. This fact of itself would attract readers. What renders the book before us even more interesting is the additional fact that, in 1878, Mr. Romanes published an anonymous work with a wholly skeptical conclusion, entitled "A Candid Examination of Theism," by *Physicus.* In that volume he expressed the conviction that we have no alternative but to conclude that the hypothesis of mind in nature is now logically proved to be as certainly superfluous as the very basis of all science is certainly true. "There can," he said, "no longer be any more doubt that the existence of a God is wholly unnecessary to explain any of the phenomena of the universe, than there is that if I leave go of my pen it will fall upon the table." At what date the intellect of this scientist began to react from the conclusion of the " Candid Examination" the editor is unable to say; but, after a period of ten years, in his Rede lecture of 1885, his attitude towards religion was observed to be much changed. This lecture on Mind and Motion consisted of a severe criticism of the materialistic account of mind. During the remaining years of his life his intellect was continuously and increasingly active on the problems of metaphysics and theology. At his death, in the early summer of 1894, he left among his papers a collection of notes for a work which he was intending to write on the fundamental questions of religion. It is these notes, together with two unpublished essays on the influence of science upon religion, which have been placed before us in this volume. The main position which he aimed to establish was this: Scientific ratiocination cannot find adequate grounds for belief in God; but the pure agnostic—that is to say, the agnostic whose mind is open and unwarped by prejudice or antecedent assumption—must recognize that God may have revealed Himself by other means than that of scientific ratiocination. As religion is for the whole man, so all human faculties may be required to seek after God and find Him through emotions and experiences of an extra-rational kind. The pure agnostic must be prepared to welcome evidence of all sorts. Such is the position which Mr. Romanes aimed to show was tenable. (Open Court Publishing Co. $1.25.)— *The Sun.*

The Uses and Dangers of Hypnotism.

A POPULAR exposition of the methods of hypnotism may not be without its disadvantages, but popular interest in the subject is so intense and so general that attempts to bring its details within the range of the average reader were sure to be made. On the whole, it is a matter for congratulation that the self-elected task of preparing the first popular manual on the subject in this country should have fallen upon a person so competent and discreet as Dr. James R. Cocke shows himself to be in his volume on "Hypnotism: How it is done; Its uses and dangers." Dr. Cocke is moderately successful in avoiding technicalities, and he succeeds very well in fulfilling the conditions indicated by his title. He gives at the outset little or no space to the historical side of his subject, but enters at once upon a discussion of the phenomena of hypnotism, its effect upon the special senses, the possibilities of auto-hypnosis, the detection of attempted simulation of the hypnotic state, the dangers attending the practice of hypnotism, its effects upon the lower animals, and its curative power. It is to this last-mentioned phase of the subject that Dr. Cocke devotes most space. He describes the method of applying hypnotism in disease, indicates its possible usefulness and limitations in surgery, and has instructive chapters on the value of therapeutic suggestion in the treatment of dipsomania, the drug habits, illusions, functional and organic disease in general, and that protean malady known as neurasthenia, or nervous exhaustion. The French experiments in the transference of sensation are briefly outlined, the relation of hypnotism to normal sleep is examined, and a chapter is given to the allied topics of telepathy, thought transference and mind reading. An account of the various theories of hypnotism, a sketch of its history, and a bibliography containing something over two hundred and fifty titles, with an excellent index, complete the volume. (Arena Pub. Co. $1.50.)— *The Beacon.*

Napoleon's Military Career.

THIS is a handsomely printed book, and more than usually spirited in illustration. Few artists succeed so well in war pictures that emphasize the text so pointedly as the artist in these pages. The volume makes up 514 pages. It can scarcely be spoken of as a military history of Napoleon, but a rare collection of historical, personal and anecdotal collection of the great soldier, presented in picturesque style. The world loves a hero, and it never seems to tire in recounting and listening to the story of the life of the man who held all Europe at his saddle-bow and dictated and shaped the

this son of a poor Corsican gentleman, who, as his greatest biographer has said of him, 'played in the world the parts of Alexander, Hannibal, Cæsar and Charlemagne.'"

This is undoubtedly a truth. Bonaparte was the military genius which the world studies to-day with as profound an interest as it did a lifetime ago. Military men still look with wonder and admiration upon the tactics of Napoleon, and study his evolutions. War has been greatly changed by modern inventions, but " the tactics" of war are the same to-day as then. It takes genius in a commander to win battles, even when aided by Gatling guns

From "Napoleon's Military Career."　　　

NAPOLEON ON THE HEIGHTS AT LIGNY.

policies of the very islands of the seas. Speaking of the present revival of Napoleonic literature—for there is such just now—Mr. Montgomery B. Gibbs says :

" The revival of interest in the career of the man who for fifteen years had been the glory of France has in no way caused the hasty writing, or publication, of this anecdotal military history. It is the result of years of study, and represents not only a careful reading of those authorities which all must have access to who would write intelligently of the subject, but also of the more recent volumes which have appeared from time to time, each having something new to reveal concerning the seemingly inexhaustible fund of information pertaining to

and all improvements in fire-arms. Mr. Gibbs, in his book, seeks to introduce the man to his readers by his pen pictures, and succeeds admirably. The anecdotes and incidents of a life when not in the presence of a great emergency are the best criterion to judge of men correctly. Napoleon was great in his minutiæ as well as in the larger events in which great results were reached. It is neither overdone in praise and adulation nor rugged with unnecessary criticism. The time has passed when any admirer can make of Napoleon a faultless hero, and our author makes no attempt to do so. The lover of military literature will find the chapters of this new Napoleon book charming. (Werner. $1.25.)—*Chicago Inter-Ocean.*

Ballads and Songs.

JOHN DAVIDSON is prodigal of every divine gift, pouring out untold treasures from his celestial cornucopia. Fancy and imagination, wit and humor, fun and epigram, characterization and creation and observation, insight and philosophy, passion and emotion and sincerity—all are his. Nothing is lacking from that long catalogue by which Imlac convinced Rasselas that it was impossible to be a poet. He will turn you a metaphor as deftly as any Elizabethan dramatist, and wields as rich a vocabulary. Nature he loves, and next to nature, man, if one may adapt Landor. And all these glorious gifts have found vent in the most diverse artistic or inartistic shapes—novels, dramas, eclogues, ballads, Reisebilder—some written for the market, but the bulk in defiance of it. Of these products of a somewhat riotous genius, only a few have the hall-mark of perfection—some pieces about music-halls, a sheaf of ballads, a bundle of songs, a set of eclogues; but they are already quite enough baggage to go down to posterity with. And it is significant that all Mr. Davidson's chief successes are won when he surrenders himself to the inspiration of the modern. . . . This is the work that we need. (Copeland & Day. $1.50.)—*I. Zangwill, in the Cosmopolitan.*

A Priestess Unveiled.

THERE are Theosophists who venerate the memory of Madame Blavatsky with unimpaired devotion, although the fraud of her pretensions to be regarded as a performer or exhibitor of miracles has been proved to the satisfaction of all reasonable men and women. The Psychical Society, after careful investigation, condemned her as an arch impostor; and now this book, a translation from a Russian original, tells us how Mr. Solovyoff, a countryman of the High Priestess of Theosophy, arrived at a similar conclusion by carrying out an independent inquiry of his own. He played a part which few men would find congenial, for he watched and waited, acting as a spy on a woman who regarded him as a friend. But though we may not unreservedly admire Mr. Solovyoff as revealed in his own book, it is impossible to refuse admiration to the skill with which he tells his story.

The most important chapters of the book, so far as relates to the question of Madame Blavatsky's good faith, are those which record the oral and written admissions she made to Mr. Solovyoff and the letters she wrote to Mr. Aksakoff, a Russian editor. These prove conclusively that Madame Blavatsky was a spiritualist in America (a fact she latterly denied) before she became a Prophetess of Theosophy in Europe and Asia, and that she invented her "Mahatmas" at a comparatively late period in her career.

The traffic of Madame Blavatsky and her fellow-spiritualists in America with the Unseen World does not appear to have been at all times a paying business.

We may conclude by heartily recommending "A Modern Priestess of Isis" to all who have a taste for biography or are fond of a story. They will find in Mr. Solovyoff's pages a vivid picture of an extraordinary woman who, stained though her life's record was by systematic fraud and deception, was endowed with many attractive qualities and possessed a wonderfully magnetic power of fascination. And they will be carried away by a narrative which, while substantially true, has all the charm of fiction. (Longmans, Green & Co.)—*Alec McMillan, in the London Literary World.*

From " Four American Universities."   Copyright, 1895, by Harper & Brothers.

HAMILTON HALL, COLUMBIA UNIVERSITY.

NEW LIBRARY OF COLUMBIA COLLEGE.

Four American Universities.

HARVARD, Yale, Princeton, and Columbia are the four American universities that are described and illustrated in this handsome volume. They form, indeed, a noble group, representative of the highest development of American education, and emphasizing the intimate relation between the growth of national character and that of individual character. Each of these universities is the subject of a separate essay, and each is brought still more clearly before the reader by excellent illustrations. Prof. Charles Eliot Norton finds in Harvard a theme on which he can discourse *con amore ;* the chronicler of Yale is Arthur T. Hadley ; Prof. W. M. Sloane writes of Princeton; and Columbia is described by Brander Matthews. The articles, while affording sufficiently comprehensive views of the historical development of the universities, aim especially to present an idea of the more intangible "atmosphere" of each—the personality of the college, so to speak. So well has this aim been carried out that the reader, while realizing the unity of purpose common to all, is at the same time impressed with the intrinsic individuality of each. The illustrations are good and abundant. There are folding "birds-eye views" of each university, and views of representative interiors, of individual buildings, and surrounding grounds are scattered lavishly through the text. Here is Harvard College in 1739—three gaunt and barn-like structures set about an open square—strange contrast to the noble colony of to-day, embowered in its park-like grounds. The seals of the various universities are shown; there is the "old fence" of Yale; the silver medal of King's College (now Columbia); and plans of the fine new buildings with which Columbia proposes to crown Riverside Heights. Artistically the volume is attractive and interesting. As an exposition of the highest educational standards of America it is of still deeper interest. Such a view as is here afforded of the part the American university plays in American life make the words of George William Curtis seem truly prophetic, when he said: "When I say that the American college is now required to train American citizens, I do not mean that it is to abdicate its highest possible function, which is not to impart knowledge, but to stimulate that intellectual and moral power of which I speak. It is a poor education, believe me, that gives accuracy in grammar instead of a love of letters; that leaves us master of the integral calculus and slaves of sordid spirit and mean ambition. When I say that it is to train Americans, I mean not only that it is to be a gnome of the earth, but also a good genius of the higher sphere. With one hand it shall lead the young American to the secrets of material skill; it shall equip him to enter into the fullest trade with all the world ; but with the other it shall lead him to lofty thought. The college shall teach him the secret and methods of material success ; but above it all, it shall admonish him that man does not live by bread alone, and that the things which are eternal are unseen." (Harper. $3.50.)

"ARE YOU INJURED?"

Prince Zaleski.

PRINCE ZALESKI, whose remarkable exploits are chronicled by M. P. Shiel in the three stories put together under that title, is a sort of sublimated Sherlock Holmes. The prince is a Russian, dwells in solitude in a lonely, half-ruined palace, and there, surrounded by miscellaneous relics of antiquity and occult literature, gives himself up to study and meditation. He refuses to contaminate his mind by reading the newspapers, but keeps the run of what is going on in the world by the very convenient faculty of intuition. To him comes in perplexity one of the ordinary race of man and begs for light on certain criminal mysteries. The circumstances attending the death of an English nobleman, the theft of a marvellous Persian jewel, and the work of the secret society which has doomed a large portion of humanity to death, are the three special problems to which Prince Zaleski is invited to give his attention, and each of these problems he solves with an attendant exuberance of philosophic speculation which cannot fail to impress profoundly the conventional non-metaphysical mind. Mr. Shiel has certainly produced three stories of quite unusual merit, as far as the use of the element of mystery is concerned. . . . The theory advanced by Prince Zaleski in the tale of the Society of Sparta is one that has some little sociological significance. The prince contends that in times gone by, war has been the destroyer of the greatest and most prosperous states, because, through this agency, the very flower of their manhood has been prematurely annihilated; but in modern times, he urges, an effect far more destructive and sure is involved in the progress of medical science, because now nature is cheated on the other side, and the weak and sickly are kept alive. Whatever one may think of the scientific value of such literature as "Prince Zaleski," one cannot deny that Mr. Shiel has succeeded in giving a new flavor to the romance of mystery and terror. (Roberts. $1.)—*The Beacon.*

The Face and the Mask.

TWENTY-FOUR short stories by Robert Barr are collected in the pretty volume entitled "The Face and the Mask." It is a little difficult at first to understand just why this title should have been chosen. Facing the table of contents of the book is a statue with two faces standing on a pedestal, and at the side of it appears the following explanatory dialogue:

The Personal Conductor: "It is a statue of no importance whatever."

The Personally Conducted: "Yes, but what does it mean?"

The Personal Conductor: "I don't suppose it means anything in particular. It is not by any well-known artist, and the guide-books say nothing about it."

The Personally Conducted: "Perhaps the sculptor intended to typify life; the tragic face representing one side of existence and the comic mask another."

The Personal Conductor: "Very likely. This way to the Louvre, if you please."

All is action in the stories written by the author of "In the Midst of Alarms," "The Steamer Chair," and other bright tales that come to mind, which have charmed his readers during the past few years. The publishers have brought out the book in their pretty *Twentieth Century Series*. The illustrations are by A. Hencke. The one we have chosen illustrates "The Predicament of De Plonville," a specially characteristic tale showing the author's dramatic ability and his fund of sparkling humor at their very best. (Stokes. 75 c.)

The Technique of Sculpture.

THE chief object in the publication of this book has been to offer a practical as well as a theoretical knowledge of sculpture. Suggestions have been made that may prove useful even to advanced students, although the author had in mind, mainly, the thought of furnishing a guide to beginners. A brief account has been given of the history of sculpture from prehistoric times, in order that the student might know how sculpture came to be, what the world has produced in this art, and what principles have guided the great masters.

The author has been led to undertake the work because of the many questions asked him regarding the technique of his art. Many still think that a sculptor, when he wishes to produce a statue, obtains a block of marble, and carves directly from the stone. The whole process, from the working of the clay to the final execution in bronze and marble, has been gone over, sketches have been made especially for this book, designed to illustrate the difficult processes which it is next to impossible to describe by word alone. It is believed that these sketches will be of great value to the lay reader as well as to the professional student. The drawings were made with great care and especially for this work by Charles M. Sheldon and Vesper L. George. Much more might have been written, but brevity has been aimed at, so that the book produced might be easily handled. The author has drawn from every source possible. The data and facts contained have been gathered from many men and books and tested by actual experience. It is hoped that the work may not only fulfil its designed mission, and be helpful to the student who has to work alone, but that it may lead to a more definite and sympathetic understanding and appreciation of the great, calm, and enduring art of sculpture. (Ginn. $1.10.)—*From the Preface.*

Vistas.

VISTAS, by William Sharp, comes to us in the oddly designed green binding of the *Green Tree Library*, a book which is quite as lawlessly free from all that savors of the conventional. It is a group of sketches for the most part dramatic in form and wholly dramatic in conception and spirit. What aim there is cannot well be explained. The author says that he cannot, and naturally his readers will have to be satisfied with the poetic imagery and the yearnings after the unseen, without endeavoring to analyze motives very closely. The author has a well-rounded gift of word-painting, and uses it very effectively, especially in environment description. The dialogue is often strong, being untrammelled by any fear of breaking through the laws of usage. But *cui bono?* (Stone & Kimball. $1 25)—*Public Opinion.*

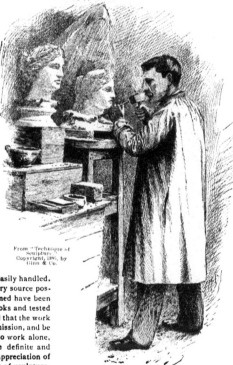

From "Technique of
Sculpture."
Copyright, 1895, by
Ginn & Co.

THE FINISHER AT WORK.

Tryphena in Love.

IT is almost as good as a trip to Somerset-shire to read "Tryphena in Love." The story comes like a breath of fresh air from wooded hills and ripe harvest fields. Somersetshire, indeed, is Mr. Walter Raymond's "native heath," as he proved a year or so ago, when "Gentleman Upcott's Daughter" and "Young Sam and Sabina" first introduced us to that pleasant region of homeliness and rustic shrewd-ness. But "Tryphena in Love" far excels his previous work, though it, too, is a village pasto-ral. The story is set in the little hamlet of Stow, in an old farm-house that was once a lordly manor. Here, in the historic "chamber where the king hid" lies, year after year, John Petti-grew, only child of energetic Aunt Joshua Pettigrew, an invalid, dreamy, full of poetic fancies, with an uncomprehended longing for books and the refinements of life. Here, too, is Tryphena—a very queen of curds and cream —his devoted comrade and slave, whose devo-tion is but the sign of a deeper sentiment of which she herself is hardly conscious. The "chamber where the king hid" is the goal of many curious tourists, and among the visitors is one whose coming changes all the quiet life

And there she stood
in the doorway—

at Manor Farm. She is young, wealthy, im-pulsive, and, touched by the mental loneliness of the invalid lad, opens to him a new world of books, refinement and culture, and awakens a passionate and hopeless love. How it all comes out the reader must discover. There is pathos as well as pleasure in the discovery, but on the whole, the smiles have the best of it throughout the story, which is a very April mixture. It is appropriately issued in a new series, the *Iris*—"that gracious thing made up of tears and light," is daintily bound in pale-gray green, and illustrated with graceful drawings, by I. W. West. (Macmillan. 75 c.)

The Christian State.

THE present era of industrial and political unrest naturally calls out many advocates and prophets of a new dispensation, and among these none seem to be more aggressive and sincere than the expositors of what is known as Christian socialism. Of the latter, Prof. George D. Herron, who holds the chair of ap-plied Christianity at Grinnell College, Iowa, holds a prominent place. His commencement oration at the University of Nebraska, last June, in which he made a scathing arraign-ment of American society and pointed out the necessity of definite and harmonious action on the part of all the Christian sects if the country were to be saved from violence, has attracted not a little attention in the columns of the press, and, as the author claims, has been sadly mis-interpreted and misrepresented. In a course of six lectures on "The Christian State: a politi-cal vision of Christ," lectures originally deliv-ered in churches of various American cities, he has undertaken to set forth his views more at length and in detail. Professor Herron's belief is that the American people are under a nation-al conviction of sin and that they are not only in need, but in search of political redemption, and he holds that the only hope of this is in a revival of both faith and works inspired by the literal teachings of the Sermon on the Mount as a basis not alone of religious work, but of civil and industrial action. In other words, the author looks to co-operation governed by a Christianized state as the only practical way out of our present difficulties. If Professor Herron's book shall result in stirring up the churches to a realization of the fact that their only hope of a continued hold upon the people is in forgetting differences of creed and working together in perfect unanimity for the promotion of the spirit of brotherhood, it will have ac-complished a very desirable task. (Crowell. 75 c.)—*The Beacon.*

A Girl's Life in Virginia.

THIS girl's life was lived before the war, and the author dedicates this memoir of its pleasures to her nieces, "who," she says, "will find in English and American publications such expressions applied to their ancestors as 'cruel slaveowners,' 'inhuman wretches,' 'Southern taskmasters,' 'dealers in human souls,' etc. From these they will naturally recoil with horror. My own life would have been embittered had I believed myself to be descended from such monsters, and that those who come after us may know the truth, I wish to leave a record of plantation life as it was. The truth may thus be preserved among a few, and merited praise may be awarded to noble men and virtuous women who have passed away."

Letitia M. Burwell's reading must have been circumscribed, indeed, if she thinks that it is only in her book of happy reminiscences that a true picture has appeared of that Southern civilization, so full of prose and culture and high thinking, with which so many of us have been so familiar in our younger days. Virginia is dear to all the world, and, as the years grow more since the war, she takes her old place in the right perspective, and her history is studied for its lessons of heroism and its poetry thought by those to whom there should be no North, no South, except as a necessary geographical distinction.

The book is enthusiastically written, and has sixteen full-page illustrations by William A. McCullough and Jules Turcas. (Stokes. $1.50.)

" I DON'T WANT BE FREE NO MORE."

The Sons of Ham.

A BOOK to provoke discussion and criticism is "The Sons of Ham," by Louis Pendleton, the author of "The Wedding Garment," a tale of the life to come, published last year, which showed imagination and originality of plan. His latest volume, however, is more devoted to the subject of several earlier books, namely, Southern life and Southern prejudices and idiosyncrasies." In "Bewitched" Mr. Pendleton told a story of Florida in which there were some excellent studies of colored servants and of a "Voodoo" woman; "In the Wire Grass" was laid in Georgia, some ten or fifteen years after the war and the negro help again was specially studied under the new conditions of freedom; and his thoroughly delightful young people's story of "King Tom and the Runaways" described the dangers and vicissitudes of life in the Georgia swamps. Mr. Pendleton writes of the South as one who knows the little-visited localities and seizes unerringly upon the local weaknesses. He shows earnest study, too, of the social and domestic conditions brought about by the emancipation of an ignorant, superstitious people totally unaccustomed to self-control. A thread of love-story connects a series of events tending toward the solution of the negro problem. The best suggestion offered is to send them all back to Africa. The book is not didactic and the "purpose" is veiled by Mr. Pendleton's practised art as a novel-writer. Many will rise against the gloomy view presented of the colored people, but the author seems to have logic and right in his judgment on the facts imagined to make his dramatic story. (Roberts. $1.)

Beyond the Dreams of Avarice.

MR. BESANT is not the first novelist who has taken for his theme the influence exerted on an average nature by accession, or contemplated accession, to untold wealth. Yet he may be congratulated on the fresh and original way in which he has handled a well-worn motive, and the point and cogency with which he has reinforced the teachings of the anti-plutocratic moralists from Job downwards. "Beyond the Dreams of Avarice" is a romance of intestacy, and possesses the great merit that there is nothing intrinsically improbable in any of the circumstances of the case. It is, in short, a story which might very well come to be reproduced on the stage of real life, and many of the grotesque and pathetic episodes in which it abounds would then inevitably find their counterpart in fact. Nothing is better in the book than the skill with which the author traces the gradual inroads of the *auri sacra fames* on the character of his hero. The heroine is certainly one of the most attractive types of womanhood that Mr. Besant has ever conceived, the various claimants are happily contrasted and cleverly drawn, and the attitude of the press in the matter is described with not a little quiet humor and good-natured satire. In point of style Mr. Besant leaves a good deal to be desired in his present venture; but if his manner lacks distinction, it is at least free from the vices of affectation or extravagance. (Harper. $1.50.)— *The Athenæum.*

The Adventures of Jones.

THE veracious Jones, who never gave a false coloring to anything, here modestly narrates his adventures. Whether Jackson Peters believed him or not has nothing to do with the question, for evidently Jackson Peters was jealous, and had he been given a free flight to his fancy, could have rivalled Jones.

But Jones always insisted on having the floor, and he kept it, and is likely to keep it against all comers. The truthful Munchausen, the ingenious M. de Crac, must withdraw chap-fallen. There is one element these old raconteurs did not possess—and that was scientific knowledge. It was true that the notes of the Baron's bugle were frozen up in the winter and thawed out in the summer, but that is a child-like idea when compared to Jones' comprehension of the use of the Edison phonograph. That instrument gave forth a stentorian "Scat!" when there was observed "a long gray streak of wild-cat reach-ing from the hen-house door to the under-brush about two hundred yards distant." It is Jones' double-header stories which are so effective. Think of the ability of the inventor of the Morning Star Milker, operated "by the motion of the cow's jaw in chewing her cud." Would seedmen this coming spring be good enough to place on their illustrated catalogues a brief mention of "The Jones Ne Plus Ultra Effervescent Watermelon with a faucet in the stem end?" Cold storage houses might do a good business in hibernating bears, sending these fat creatures neatly done up in their original hollow-log packages to England. Mr. Hayden Carruth writes in the sincerest manner the most extraordinary of bounces. (Harper. $1.)—*N. Y. Times.*

MISS WILKINS' CHARACTERS.

No queenly rose she stops to cull,
 Nor lilies richly dight;
But wayside flowers, common, dull,
 That seem to shrink from sight.

No lordly knights nor ladies fair
 Within her world abide;
But homespun women, awkward men,
 Who live in life's aside.

One touch of her consummate art,
 And lo! a romance where
We thought was sordid commonplace
 And trivial round of care:

The drudge a heroine becomes,
 With heart of withered hopes;
The son of toil a hero true,
 As through the dark he gropes.

What scent from old-time gardens blows
 Across our hurried strife!
What pathos here! what humor there!
 Commingled to the life.

ALICE ELIZABETH SAWTELLE in *The Literary World.*

From "The Adventures of Jones."   Copyright, 1895, by Harper & Brothers.

JONES INSPECTS THE IMPROVED WHITED SEPULCHRE.

Out of the East.

MR. HEARN says that five years of intimate association with the Japanese have given him the power to see them unmagnified by the poetic glamour which an almost boundless admiration for the land and the people raised before his eyes during the first half of his life in the Orient. That may be so, but he has certainly lost none of the power evidenced in his "Glimpses of Unfamiliar Japan" to make his readers see through that same early glamour the scenes he describes and the men whose very souls he apparently makes manifest. "Out of the East" is a work of less magnificent proportions than its predecessor, but in it are numberless passages of a beauty quite as great as that which characterized the most notable parts of that remarkable book, while deeper appreciation and keener insight, as regards the great problems Japan is now forcing upon the West for solution, reveal the effect on the writer of added opportunities for observation and study. None of his enthusiasm or of his ability to inspire enthusiasm has departed, but now he shows the meaning of things as well as their picturesque beauty, and corrects not only many of the mistaken judgments that have been formed by others, but a few of his own.

With all his added seriousness of view, however, and notwithstanding the distinctly greater practical value his work now has, it is still upon the marvellous simplicity of his style, at once vigorous and delicate, that most emphasis must be laid. He can clothe an old legend in new words as well as any man living. The phrases he uses have the beauty he finds in tales told at twilight by people who make no distinction between myth and history, for whom ghosts and the gods are as real as the Emperor or his Admirals. With equal perfection, and not less beautifully, does Mr. Hearn describe the happenings of life in the houses and streets around him, the doings of priests and soldiers, the games of children, and the suicide of lovers, the habits of men who dig in the rice-fields, and those of the little white fish that live in wells.

And, really, it is because Mr. Hearn can do so near to infinitely well these things so infinitely difficult, and not because he can explain why Japan will conquer China, that he is a great man and a genius.

The description of scenery, therefore, and the narration of simple stories about the Japanese who lived of old or who live to-day are by far the most precious parts of his books. This "Out of the East" is rich with such treasures.

This volume was not finished until the present war with China was well under way. Kumamoto, the town where Mr. Hearn lived and taught in a Government school, was full of young soldiers making ready for embarkation. He describes them as filled with the very ecstasy of patriotic fervor. To fight for Japan and to die for it in case of slightest need were consuming ambitions in every mind. No thought of personal glory mingled with this devotion to the fatherland and the Emperor.

So far they have been victorious. Mr. Hearn hopes and believes that China will soon be in their power, but he has studied the people of that older realm, and recognizes in them immeasurable potentialities. To tell the end is impossible, and the end will not be reached when Japan and China are again at peace. (Houghton, Mifflin & Co. $1.25.)—*N.Y. Times.*

Half a Century with Judges and Lawyers.

IT is not often that one comes across a volume of reminiscences so thoroughly entertaining as that of Joseph A. Willard, clerk of the Superior Court of this commonwealth, who has gathered up the stories, anecdotes and scenes incident to "Half a Century with Judges and Lawyers." The book partakes to certain extent of the nature of an autobiography, for the first two chapters contain a very interesting sketch of the author's ancestry and early life. Mr. Willard was a pupil of James Freeman Clarke, when the latter was teaching school in Cambridge; he remembers being one of the school children who in 1824 welcomed Lafayette; he sat as a boy under the preaching of the Rev. Abiel Holmes; and he recalls commencements at Harvard that were the occasion of three-day fights between gamblers and roughs which resulted in many black eyes; but as the author says, there were no serious disasters, for even football was played in those days without slugging.

The greater part of his recollections, however, as the title indicates, relate to the Suffolk bar, and on this theme he is delightfully varied and amusing. All the eminent legal lights from the days of Lemuel Shaw down to the present time come within the range of Mr. Willard's memories, and concerning each of them he has some piquant anecdote or incident to relate. Not only the members of the bar, but those who held judicial honors, get many a keen thrust from Mr. Willard, who has a very lively sense of humor, and however effective his satire, is never ill-natured. One or two examples of Mr. Willard's good things may be given.

"I was present (he says) when an attorney used some new recondite word. Judge Wilde said: 'What is that word, what does that mean? I haven't heard it before.' Counsel: 'Please your honor, Mr. Webster has got out a new dictionary with ten thousand new words in it.' Judge Wilde: 'Mercy on us! I hope Choate won't get hold of it.'

"On one occasion after a jury was empanelled

in the Supreme Judicial Court, Judge Shaw cast his eye around and found there were only eleven men. He said : ' Mr. Officer, find the twelfth man.' Some time elapsed, when the officer came in and the judge said, ' Have you found him, Mr. Officer?' 'No, your honor.' ' Where is he?' said the judge. 'I don't know, sir; he's dead.'

"A certain person was nominated for the office of judge of the Court of Common Pleas. A lawyer to whom the fact was mentioned, said : 'I didn't see it in the morning papers.' 'Oh,' was the reply; 'did you look under the head of accidents?'

"When Mr. Barnes was taken ill, it was related that the doctor who felt of his pulse and feet, in response to Mr. Barnes' question as to how he was getting along said : 'Oh, Mr. Barnes, you are doing very well; no person ever died with such warm feet as you have.' 'Oh yes, there was one,' squeaked Barnes. 'Who?' asked the doctor. ' John Rogers,' said Barnes."

Mr. Willard's book abounds in quotable passages, too long for citation here. As a contribution to the literature of the Suffolk bar it will long be read and referred to, and as an example of attractive literature it appeals strongly, not only to the legal fraternity, but to the general public. (Houghton, Mifflin & Co. $1.25.)—*The Beacon.*

The First of the English.

THERE is plenty of " go " in this new story from the ready pen of A. C. Gunter. It is set in the midst of the stormy days when the Netherlands struggled under the tyranny of Philip of Spain, and when Alva and his fierce soldiers made the Low Countries a land of blood and slaughter. The first chapter opens with a sea fight, when a Spanish pleasure galley is captured by the stout little English privateersman *Dover Lass*, commanded by Captain Guy Stanhope Chester, "the first of the English." This *sobriquet* has been bestowed upon Captain Chester by the people of the Netherlands, in recognition of his being the first of his nation sent as a secret agent by Queen Elizabeth to help Holland in her struggle for independence. One of the prisoners in the captured galley is the daughter of Alva. Of course, Chester falls in love with her, and vows to win her, while at the same time he will outwit the plans of the fierce duke. Equally, of course, he is successful both in love and war. The situation, it will be seen, is a very pretty one, affording scope for plenty of fighting, love-making, battle, blood and glory. Mr. Gunter has not neglected his chances, and he conducts the reader through a breathless succession of exciting episodes to the final orthodox conclusion wherein all true novel-readers find exceeding joy. The tone of the book is thoroughly healthy, and the climax satisfactory. (Home Pub. Co. 50 c.)

Latin Poetry.

THE Percy Turnbull Foundation at Johns Hopkins has given to the world another volume which forms a fit companion to Professor Jebb's book on "Greek Poetry." Such books are sure to find a wide welcome ; for they are signs of the coming emancipation of the classics from the thraldom of philology. Professor Tyrrell loves the Latin poets for their own sake, as well as for the opportunities of textual emendation which they afford. He has a very attractive style, and his frank refusal to subscribe to some traditional opinions adds interest to the lectures.

For instance, he is an out-and-out heretic when he discusses Horace. It is delightful to find a distinguished scholar confirming one's own private opinion that Horace is a masterly artist but not a creative poet. Many readers will be surprised to learn how largely the Satires and Epistles are borrowed, both as to form and material, from Lucilius, of whose works only fragments have come down to us. It is well known that the Odes are closely imitated from Greek models. But as a polished versifier and maker of brilliant phrases, Professor Tyrrell gives Horace all the honor that the most ardent admirer could ask. There are many interesting things said about Virgil ; famous lines are discussed, Virgil is compared with Homer, and some very just remarks are offered in criticism of recent translations of the Æneid. Two of the most interesting chapters in the book are those on Lucretius and Catullus, two authors not very generally read by college undergraduates, but among the greatest of the Latin poets.

We shall be surprised if this book does not send many a reader to those dusty upper shelves where his Horace and Virgil have lain since college days, to renew the charm of their immortal syllables. As Professor Tyrrell happily says: "At a verse from the Æneid, the sun goes back for us on the dial ; our boyhood is recreated, and returns to us for a moment like a visitant from a happy dreamland." (Houghton, Mifflin & Co. $1.)—*Public Opinion.*

A New Version of the Sermon on the Mount.

THE title of this admirable book by William Burnett Wright is well suited to the matter of which it treats. Its plan is unique and very ingenious. In the opening chapter the author deals with " Puzzles," which are presented to plain men as they contemplate the most conspicuous characteristics which distinguish Christendom from heathendom. The second chapter deals with " A Fertile Source of Puzzles," namely, the regarding of the Epistles, especially those of Paul, as inspired commentaries upon the Gospels. Then follow chapters devoted to an exposition of each of the Beatitudes — the poor in spirit, the mourners, the meek, those who hunger and thirst after righteousness, the merciful, the pure in heart, the peacemakers. After each exposition a character-sketch of some person who seemed to the author to furnish an illustration of the truth presented is given, to help the reader see the Saviour more nearly as He is, by looking at each of those qualities which He manifested in perfection as it shines obscurely through some one of His disciples. With reference to the expositions of the Beatitudes, it must be said that many of the thoughts are new, fresh, and occasionally even startling. The author states his conception of Christ's thought clearly, concisely and cogently. No one can possibly mistake his meaning. The writer believes thoroughly in the necessity of individual regeneration and personal righteousness as the sole condition of a changed environment. Altogether this volume is a worthy and distinct contribution to current religious thought, and will be welcomed by hosts of readers. (Houghton, Mifflin & Co. $1.25.)— *The Watchman.*

As Others Saw Him.

WHAT did the Scribes and Pharisees know and think of Jesus? For nearly nineteen centuries all Christendom has lamented the bigotry, blindness and cruelty of those who caused or consented to His death. Would it not be exceedingly interesting to know just how He seemed to a learned, thoughtful, patriotic, devout Jew of His day? A writer, whose name is withheld, has attempted to reproduce for us the attitude and views of such a man, in a small book with the above title. It purports to be written by a Scribe at Alexandria, about twenty-five years after the Crucifixion. He was in Jerusalem during the public life of Jesus, and was a member of the Sanhedrim which delivered Him to death. He endeavors to represent how the Jews, of different classes, were impressed when Jesus drove the moneychangers from the Temple, taught in the synagogue at Jerusalem, tested the rich young man, forgave the woman taken in adultery, baffled His questioners, made His triumphal entry into the city, alienated the people by His refusal to lead a revolt against the Roman power, was examined by the Sanhedrim, condemned by Pilate and crucified. The book is profoundly reverent, is written with great clearness and literary charm, and cannot fail to interest very many thoughtful readers. (Houghton, Mifflin & Co. $1.25.)—*Mail and Express.*

Strong's Bible Concordance.

"THE Exhaustive Concordance of the Bible," by James Strong, S.T.D., is a bulky quarto volume of 1809 pages, and is not merely a concordance, but an admirable library of the Bible as well. It shows every word of the text of the common English version of the Canonical books, and every occurrence of each word in regular order, together with a comparative concordance of the authorized and revised versions, including the American variations. There is an appendix giving a complete list of the occurrence of forty-seven unimportant words, such as a, as, in, etc. Following that are a concise dictionary of the words in the Hebrew Bible, with their renderings in the authorized English version, a table showing the places where the Hebrew and the English Bibles differ in the division of chapters and verse, and a concise dictionary of the words in the Greek testament, with their renderings in the authorized English version.

The whole volume is a splendid example of profound scholarship and patient research, and will very much enhance the already great reputation of Dr. Strong. Without making any invidious comparisons, it may be safely said that in completeness, simplicity and accuracy it is excelled by no concordance in the language. (Hunt & Eaton. $6.)—*N. Y. Tribune.*

Lent, Past and Present.

THIS handy little book is a charming combination of fine scholarship, clear literary presentation, and devout and reasonable spirit. The author has made a careful investigation of authorities, and shows with reasonable certainty the origin of this memorial institution at the beginning of the second century. From a number of days, gradually increasing to a fortnight, the term of observance was gradually extended to thirty-six days, and next to forty. It was originally intended as a season of mourning for the death and burial of the Saviour, but gradually the custom was made enriching and influential because of deeper meanings which were read or infused into it. The author, Hermann Lilienthal, M.A., temperately and wisely discusses the subject of fasting, refusing to lay down any definite hard-and-fast rules, while heartily believing that fasting is but a special application of the higher principle of abstinence. He discusses Holy Week with a temper and richness of erudition and withal a simplicity of style that will, we think, win to the observance of Lent many who are not members of the denomination of the author, which is the Protestant Episcopal. (Whittaker. 75 c.)—*Boston Literary World.*

Che Literary News.

An Eclectic Monthly Review of Current Literature.

EDITED BY A. H. LEYPOLDT.

APRIL, 1895.

THE STANDARD DICTIONARY.

THE second volume of "The Standard Dictionary" completes a monumental work of which the publishers may well be proud and for which the whole writing fraternity owes them gratitude. It must be a matter of peculiar gratification to them that so great an undertaking has been brought to completion in five short years. The amount of thought, energy, endurance, and perseverance, condensed into those years can only be faintly imagined by those who have in a small way been through similar trials in the compiling of catalogues, book-lists, indexes, etc. A virtuoso can be truly estimated only by one who has struggled with the same difficulties he sees overcome with such artistic ease.

The editor-in-chief of this compact, model dictionary is the Rev. Dr. I. K. Funk, the consulting editor, Prof. F. A. March, the managing editor, the Rev. D. S. Gregory, and they have been assisted by nearly 200 specialists in various departments. The great difficulty in the courageous enterprise of preparing a dictionary so immediately to follow "The Century Dictionary" has been the deciding what could advantageously be left out of that collection of words in use in the English language, so that the work in preparation should have the great advantage of less bulk, and at the same time should contain new words and terms, that study, comparison and daily use had proved needed in a work, intended to be first and foremost thoroughly adapted for constant daily use. We shall not endeavor to compare "The Standard Dictionary" with its predecessors as regards abstract worth. Every dictionary, conscientiously made by those who have fitted themselves for the work by the study of all the material the work of others has brought together, must add its quota of improvement and of additional usefulness. "All can raise the flower now, for all have got the seed" may truthfully be said of dictionaries. In 1755 Dr. Johnson compiled his great work which brought upon him the greatest adulation, the severest criticism that any dictionary is ever likely to meet with. This monumental work that he hewed from the rough, with implements invented during his slow progress, recorded 2886 words under the letter A. Since then, Worces-

ter's Dictionary has entered 6983 words under the first letter of the alphabet; "Stormonth's Dictionary," 4692; "Webster's International Dictionary," 8358; "The Century Dictionary," 15,621," and "The Standard Dictionary," 19,736. The full number of vocabulary terms in these dictionaries for the entire alphabet is as follows: Johnson, 45,000; Stormonth, 50,000; Worcester, 105,000; Webster (International), 125,000; Century (six volumes, complete), 225,000; Standard (by actual count), 301,865, exclusive of the appendix, which contains 47,468 entries.

Nearly 150 years of discoveries, inventions, enterprises, political upheavals, psychological speculations, religious differences, international commerce, international travel, and the daily widening interests of an increasing population, with a higher average of intelligence and growing advantages of education, have introduced an army of words into the English language.

Another advantage of the latest dictionary lies in the fact that if a word has two or more meanings the most common meaning is given first. That is, preference has been given to the "order of usage" over what is termed the "historical order." The aim has been to remove everything that stands between the vocabulary word and the meaning most generally sought after by the average reader, and in this way enable him to get the information desired with ease and certainty. The obsolescent and obsolete meanings and the etymology are given last.

Another very interesting feature is the table under notable words. Thus under "constellation" Professor Simon Newcomb has given the names and locations of all the constellations; under "man" is Professor D. G. Brinton's classification of the races of mankind based upon ethnological grounds; under "measure" are given the names of upwards of 800 different measures, the country in which they are used, the class (liquid, dry, etc.), national equivalents, United States and British equivalents, and metric equivalents; under "order" are the names of the orders of chivalry, the country, when founded, and the reputed founder.

The amount of learning, quickness of perception and skill in classification displayed in this feature of the dictionary calls for new delight and admiration with every new success in finding so much information made so get-at-able.

All this erudition can be had in one volume at $12, in good binding, or in two volumes at $15, a price which puts the dictionary within the means of a large majority of the writing fraternity.

MAGAZINE ARTICLES.

Articles marked with an asterisk are illustrated.

ARTISTIC, MUSICAL AND DRAMATIC.—*Atlantic*, Macbeth, John F. Kirk.—*Century*, Madame Réjane (Por.), Justin H. M'Carthy; Ferdinand Bol,* Cole; Bernhard Stavenhagen (Por.), Henry T. Finck.—*Fort. Review* (March), Acting, Henry Irving; Venetian Art at the New Gallery, Claude Phillips. — *Lippincott's*, Grand Opera, Mme. Nellie Melba; Hiram Powers in Washington.—*Nine. Century* (March), Rembrandt and Sir Joshua Reynolds, Sir Charles Robinson; Maurice Maeterlinck, Richard Hovey; Chinese drama, George Adams.—*Scribner's*, Four Easter Pictures, Drawn by Smedley, Lynch, Abbey, and Weeks; Amer. Wood-Engravers, William B. Closson.*

BIOGRAPHY, CORRESPONDENCE. — *Atlantic*, Talk Over Autographs, I., George B. Hill.— *Chautauquan*, Florence Nightingale, Harriet E. Banning. — *Forum*, Studies of Notable Men: Lord Rosebery, Justin M'Carthy. — *Popular Science*, Lardner Vanuxem (Por.).

DESCRIPTION, TRAVEL. — *Chautauquan*, Great Tunnels of the World, Robert Jamison; Smallest Republic in the World * (San Marino), John L. Hurst.—*Harper's*, Our National Capital,* Julian Ralph; Paris in Mourning,* R. H. Davis; Venice in Easter,* Arthur Symons; Autumn in Japan,* Alfred Parsons.

DOMESTIC ¡AND SOCIAL.—*Lippincott's*, Cheap Living in Paris, Alvan F. Sanborn; Woman's Lot in Persia, Wolf von Schierbrand; Evolution of Table Manners, Lee J. Vance.

EDUCATIONAL. — *Atlantic*, Expressive Power of English Sounds, Albert H. Tolman ; Basis of Our Educational System, James J. Greenough. — *Century*, Religious Teaching in the Public Schools, Lyman Abbott.—*Forum*, Women in European Universities, Alice Zimmern.— *Harper's*, Recent Progress in the Public Schools, W. T. Harris.—*Scribner's*, Art of Living—Education, Robert Grant.

FICTION.—*Atlantic*, Dumb Foxglove, Annie T. Slosson.—*Century*, Search for an Ancestor, Mrs. R. A. Pryor; A Faithful Failure, G. I. Putnam; An Innocent Offender,* Alice Turner. — *Chautauquan*, Sellin' Ole Master, Martha Young.—*Harper's*, Personal Recollections of Joan of Arc,* I., Louis De Conte; Study Number Three,* Harriet L. Bradley; Cordelia's Night of Romance,* Julian Ralph; Balance of Power, Maurice Thompson. — *Lippincott's*, Alain of Halfdene, Anna Robeson Brown; At the Hop-Pole Inn, Edith E. Bigelow; "The House with the Paint Wore Off," Marjorie Richardson; The Defendant Speaks, Genie H. Rosenfield.— *Scribner's*, In Northern Waters, T. C. Evans; "La Belle Hélène," Abbe C. Goodloe; Question in Art, R. W. Herrick.

HISTORY.—*Century*, Paul Jones,* Molly E. Seawell.—*Nine. Century* (March), The Builder of the Round Towers, Hon. Emily Lawless.— *Scribner's*, Prince Charles Stuart,* Andrew Lang; Who Won the Battle of New Orleans?— *West. Review* (March), Evolution of Modern Society in its Historical Aspects, R. D. Melville; History as Told in the Arabian Nights, J. F. Hewitt.

LITERARY.—*Atlantic*, Louis Stevenson, C. T. Copeland.—*Fort. Review* (March), Two Modern Poets (William Watson and John Davidson), H. D. Traill; Stéphane Mallarmé, Frederic Carrel. —*Forum*, Healthy Tone for Amer. Literature, Richard Burton.—*Lippincott's*, Bucolic Journalism of the West, Mary E. Stickney.—*West. Review* (March), Tyranny of the Modern Novel, D. F. Hannigan.

MEDICAL SCIENCE.—*North Amer. Review*, The Physician and the Social Question, Paul Gibier. — *Popular Science*, Communicated Insanity, Charles W. Pilgrim.

MENTAL AND MORAL.—*Nine. Century* (March), Written Gesture, John Holt Schooling.—*Popular Science*, Some Curiosities of Thinking, M. A. Starr; Personal Equation in Human Truth, R. P. Halleck.

NATURE AND SCIENCE.—*Atlantic*, Flower Lore of New England Children, Alice M. Earle.— *Popular Science*, Some of the "Outliers" Among Birds, R. F. Shufeldt.

POETRY.—*Atlantic*, While the Robins Sang, J. R. Taylor; In Memoriam Stevenson, Owen Wister. — *Century*, Resurrection, Maurice F. Egan; Robert Louis Stevenson; In Tesla's Laboratory, Robert U. Johnson; Love Conquers Death. Florence E. Coates. — *Harper's*, "O Traveller by Unaccustomed Ways," Louise C. Moulton; Romance, Orrin C. Stevens; Awakening, Margaret E, Sangster.—*Lippincott's*, Melba, Champion Bissell; My Tormentor, Robert Beverley Hale. — *Scribner's*, Luke xviii. 11. An Easter Hymn,* Henry McCarter ; To a Greek Victory, Pitts Duffield; The Compass, Edith M. Thomas.

POLITICAL AND SOCIAL.—*Chautauquan*, Methods of Studying Society, Albion W. Small; Labor Bureaus: Conversation with the U. S. Commissioner of Labor, Herbert Johnston.— *Fort. Review* (March), Presidents and Politics in France, A. Filon; The Crisis in Newfoundland, William Greswell. — *Forum*, Real "Quintessence of Socialism," W. H. Mallock; Battle of Standards and the Fall of Prices, Edward Atkinson; Is Sound Finance Possible under Popular Government ?; Study of Beggars and Their Lodgings, Alvan F. Sanborn.—*Harper's*, Club Life Among Outcasts,* Josiah Flynt.—*North Amer. Review*, A Last Tribute, Ex-Speaker Reed; Future of the Torpedo in War, P. H. Colomb; Two Years of American Diplomacy, George Gray; Growing Greatness of the Pacific, by the Hawaiian Minister; Outlook for Parliamentary Government, Hannis Taylor.—*Popular Science*, The Successor of the Railway, Appleton Morgan.

THEOLOGY, RELIGION AND SPECULATION.— *Cath. World*, Musings of a Missionary, Walter Elliott; Inerrancy of Scripture in Light of the Encyclical, P. J. Cormican.—*Century*, Social Problem of Church Unity, F. H. Wines and C. W. Shields (Open Letters). — *Nine. Century* (March), What is Church Authority?, T. Teignmouth Shore ; Mr. Balfour's Attack on Agnosticism, T. H. Huxley.—*North Amer. Review*, Position of Judaism, I. Zangwill; A Word About the "New Pulpit," C. Ernest Smith (Notes and Comments).—*West. Review* (March), The Bible in the Schools, Walter Lloyd.

Survey of Current Literature.

☞ *Order through your bookseller.*—"*There is no worthier or surer pledge of the intelligence and the purity of any community than their general purchase of books; nor is there any one who does more to further the attainment and possession of these qualities than a good bookseller.*"—PROF. DUNN.

ART, MUSIC, DRAMA.

AMERICA'S greatest men and women, photographs and biographies of the most famous living people on the continent, how they look and what they have accomplished ; the faces and the stories of those who are now affecting the history of the country. Conkey. Folio, $4.

CAMPBELL, HUGH, BREWER, R. F., *and* NEVILLE, H. Voice, speech and gesture : a handbook to the elocutionary art ; incl. essays on reciting and recitative, by Clifford Harrison, and on recitation with musical accompaniment, by F. Corder ; ed., with an introd., by Rob. D. Blackman. Putnam. 8°, hf. leath., $3.

FURTWÄNGLER, ADOLF. Masterpieces of Greek sculpture: a series of essays on the history of art ; ed. by Eugénie Sellers. Scribner. il. pl. F. *net*, $15.

IBSEN, H. Little Eyolf: a play. Stone & Kimball,16°, (The green tree lib.) $1.25.

MAETERLINCK, MAURICE. Plays: Princess Maleine, The intruder, The blind, The seven princesses ; tr. by Richard Hovey, with an introd. essay on symbolism. Stone & Kimball. 16°, (The green tree lib.) $1.25.

PARTRIDGE, W. ORDWAY. Technique of sculpture. Ginn. 12°, $1.10.

BIOGRAPHY, CORRESPONDENCE, ETC.

MOULTON, LOUISE CHANDLER. Arthur O'Shaughnessy: his life and his work, with selections from his poems. Stone & Kimball. por. 18°, $1.25.

SYMONDS, J. ADDINGTON. John Addington Symonds: a biography; comp. from his papers and correspondence by Horatio F. Brown. Scribner. 2 v., il. 8°, $12.50.

DESCRIPTION, GEOGRAPHY, TRAVEL, ETC.

BURN, ROBERT. Ancient Rome and its neighborhood: an illustrated handbook to the ruins in the city and Campagna. Macmillan. 12°, (Bohn's illustrated lib.) $2.25.

HEARN, LAFCADIO. Out of the East : reveries and studies in New Japan. Houghton, Mifflin & Co. 12°, $1.25.

LANDOR, A. H. SAVAGE. Corea; or, Cho-sen, the Land of the Morning Calm; il. from drawings by the author. Macmillan. 8°, $4.50.
" In a large octavo volume of three hundred pages the Messrs. Macmillan have published an interesting account of Corea by a recent English visitor Mr. A. Henry Savage-Landor. What we have here is a plain record of observation by a young man who makes no pretensions to literary style, but who has embellished his book with illustrations which are reproductions of sketches make by himself. With the history of the Hermit Kingdom and its age-long relations to China on the one hand and to Japan on the other, the author has, apparently, but little acquaintance. At all events, we learn next to nothing on the subject from this volume. But, about the Coreans as they are, we obtain a great deal of information, and are thereby enabled to comprehend the conditions of the problem which the civilized Japanese have undertaken to solve in the peninsula.
" The truth is that Mr. Savage-Landor went to Corea with the qualifications of an artist rather than with those of an historical student and a scientist. It is the vivid report of his eyes and ears that is chiefly valuable."—*N. Y. Sun.*

LANSDELL, H., *D.D.* Chinese Central Asia: a ride to little Tibet. Scribner. 2 v., map, il. 8°, $5.

VINCENT, FRANK. Actual Africa ; or, the coming continent. Appleton 105 full-page illustrations, 8°, $5.

DOMESTIC AND SOCIAL.

BAILEY, HARRIET P. On the chafing-dish: a word for Sunday night teas. [*New ed.*] G. W. Dillingham. 12°, pap., 50 c.

EDUCATION, LANGUAGE, ETC.

IRVING, WASHINGTON. The Alhambra. *Students' ed.*; for the use of instructors and students of English literature, and of reading classes; ed., with an introduction and notes by Arthur Marvin. Putnam. 12°, $1.

PECK, H. T., *and* ARROWSMITH, R., *comps. ana eds.* Roman life in Latin prose and verse. Am. B'k. Co. il. 12°, $1.50.
A very attractive Latin reading-book, interesting in itself and admirably adapted for use in classes. It contains characteristic extracts from poets and prose writers and a variety of popular songs, inscriptions and fragments that are particularly illustrative of Roman life. The annotations are judicious and the whole make-up of the book is excellent.

FICTION.

AUSTEN, JANE. Pride and prejudice ; with a preface by G. Saintsbury, and il. by Hugh Thomson. *Edition de luxe.* Macmillan. 12°, (Cranford ser.) *net*, $18.

BASSETT, G. Hippolyte and Golden-beak: two stories. Harper. (Harper's American storytellers ser. 12°, $1.25.
The first story deals with a Parisian valet, who plays an interesting part in the adventures

that befell his master and himself at Monte Carlo; a pretty woman makes a real hero of Hippolyte, whose story is told by his master. The second story has as its principal characters an Englishman and a pretty American woman (who are thrown into intimate companionship during a voyage from San Francisco to Japan) and afterwards other people, both Japanese and English. The development of the plot introduces Japanese scenery, and there is an odd Japanese episode, with a tragical ending.

BESANT, WALTER. Beyond the dreams of avarice: a novel. Harper. il. 12°, $1.50.

BULWER-LYTTON, *Sir* E. G. E. L., [*Lord* Lytton.] The last days of Pompeii. Lovell, Coryell & Co. 2 v., il. 8°, $3.50; ¾ levant, $7.

CARRUTH, HAYDEN. The adventures of Jones. Harper. il. 16°, $1.

DAUDET, ALPHONSE. La petite paroisse: mœurs conjugales. Meyer Bros. & Co. 12°, pap., $1.

DOWIE, MÉNIE MURIEL, [*now* Mrs. H. Norman.] Gallia. Lippincott. (Lippincott's select novels, no. 166.). 12°, $1; pap., 50c.

FORTIER, ALCÉE, *comp. and ed.* Louisiana folk-tales in French dialect and English translation. Houghton, Mifflin & Co. 8°, (Memoirs of the American folk-lore society, v. 2.) *net*, $2.

GRAHAM, *Mrs.* MARGARET COLLIER. Stories of the foot-hills. Houghton, Mifflin & Co. 12°, $1.25.
Under this title Mrs. Graham has collected several short stories of Southern California; "The Withrow water-right" and "Alex. Randall's conversion" were first printed in the *Atlantic Monthly;* "Idy" appeared in the *Century.* The others are "The complicity of Enoch Embody," "Em," "Colonel Bob Jarvis," and "Brice."

GLASCOCK, WILL H. Stories of Columbia. Appleton. il. 12°, 75 c.

GUNTER, ARCHIBALD CLAVERING. The first of the English. Home Pub. Co. 12°, $1; pap., 50 c.

HAYNES, EMORY J. A farm-house cobweb: a novel. Harper. 12°, $1.25.
Rural life in Vermont about the time of the late war is the theme of this novel.

HOPE, ANTHONY, [*pseud.* for Anthony Hope Hawkins.] Father Stafford. [*New issue.*] F. Tennyson Neely. 12°, (Neely's prismatic lib.) buckram, 75 c.

HOPE, ANTHONY, [*pseud.* for Anthony Hope Hawkins.] A man of mark. Holt. 16°, buckram. 75 c.
An imaginary South American republic called Aureataland, with its financial difficulties and numerous revolutions, is the theme of this novel. The hero is an Englishman who finds himself there in a responsible position in a bank in 1880.

HUME, FERGUS W. The lone inn: a mystery. Cassell Pub. Co. nar. 12°, (Unknown lib., no. 35.) 50 c.
"The author of 'The mystery of a hansom cab' loves to concoct a mess of muddle, and when he stirs it up, as in 'The lone inn,' his success is distinguished."—*N. Y. Times.*

LEPELLETIER, EDMOND. Madame Sans-Gêne: an historical romance, founded on the play, by Victorien Sardou; from the French, by Louis R. Heller. Home Book Co. 1 il. 16°, 50 c.; pap., 25 c.
"The plot and general outlines of Sardou's Napoleonic play are widely known, but a French writer, M. Edmond Lepelletier, transformed it into a story, some time ago, which has now been translated by L. R. Heller. It is rather difficult to decide whether this substantial novel was written with the view of sharing in the popularity and profit of the play, or of advertising its production, nor is the question one of much importance. But the title is attractive, and the publication of it during the present Napoleonic revival may prove a stoke of business."—*The Critic.*

LINTON, *Mrs.* ELIZA LYNN. The new woman: in haste and at leisure. Merriam Co. 12°, $1.50.

MEREDITH, G. The tale of Chloe. [*Also*] The house on the beach. [*Also*] The case of General Ople and Lady Camper. Ward, Lock & Bowden, 12°, $1.50.

PENDLETON, L. The sons of Ham: a tale of the New South. Roberts. 12°, $1.50.

PHILLPOTTS, EDEN. Some every-day folks. Harper. 12°, (Harper's Franklin square lib., no. 758.) pap., 60 c.
Heatherbridge, a rural hamlet in the beautiful county of Dartmouth, England, is the home of the characters of the quiet story. For the space of one year the author watches the lives of many small people in a very small place. A "high church" priest sets the hearts of his women parishioners in a flurry, and in his efforts for universal popularity gets himself into troublesome conflicts. The doctor of Heatherbridge and his sister are strong characters.

RAYMOND, WALTER, [Tom Cobbleigh, *pseud.*] Tryphena in love. Macmillan. 12°, (Iris. ser.) 75 c.

ROBINSON, HARRY PERRY. Men born equal: a novel. Harper. 12°, $1.25.
"If only we could see that time Macaulay hoped for:

> When none was for a party,
> But all were for the State,
> And the rich man helped the poor,
> And the poor man loved the great.

Then the happy millennium would surely be reached. 'Men born equal' has for its hero Horace Marsh, who is an honest man. Marsh has a liking for politics, and in the Western town he lives in, through his courage and ability, has come to be considered a leader of men. Without distinctly naming the Western city, Mr. Robinson brings into the scene of action traits common to a great many centres of population in the United States. Horace is a lawyer, and his partner is Harter. Harter is a not uncommon political type, and one not to be admired. "Mr. Robinson has a thorough acquaintance with political conditions in the United States, and the lesson he wishes to inculcate is an excellent one."—*N. Y. Times.*

SHIEL, M. P. Prince Zaleski. Roberts Bros. 16°, $1.

STEVENSON, ROB. L. The amateur emigrant from the Clyde to Sandy Hook. Stone & Kimball. 16°, $1.25.

STEVENSON, ROB. L. Popular works. *New ed.* Roberts. 5 v., 16°, $5.
Contents: Travels with a donkey in the Cevennes; An inland voyage; The Silverado squatters; Treasure Island; Prince Otto.

STREET, G. S. Episodes. The Merriam Co. il. nar. 16°, 75 c.
"Is this world so full of social horrors as Mr. G. S. Street would make us believe? Are we all shams and frauds? Are there no happy husbands, no honest wives? Who can deny the specially clever side of this writer's work? There was Mr. Street's 'The autobiography of a boy.' How you hated that worthless creature! You knew it was an exceptional type; but you understood, if critical, the exceeding art of the writer. 'Episodes' is a small volume of short sketches, the briefest of stories. You get some idea of Mr. Street's methods in a story when he writes explaining some four of his characters, 'but a trifle more of description is, unfortunately, unneccessary." Mr. Street's strength lies in his terseness, and that is a high quality, acquired only by long practice."—*N. Y. Times.*

WARDEN, FLORENCE, [*pseud.* for Florence Alice Price, now Mrs. G. E. James.] Kitty's engagement: a novel. Appleton. 12°, (Appleton's town and country lib., no. 162.) $1; pap., 50 c.

HISTORY.

BURKE, ULICK RALPH. A history of Spain from the earliest times to the death of Ferdinand the Catholic. Longmans, Green & Co. 2 v., 8°, $10.50.

GIBBS, MONTGOMERY B. Military career of Napoleon the Great: an account of the remarkable campaigns of the "Man of destiny." The Werner Co. por. il. 12°, hf. mor., $1.25.

GREEN, J. R. History of the English people. *Standard ed.* Lovell, Coryell & Co. il. por. 8°, $5; ¾ cf., $10. *Edition de luxe,* 4 v., il. por. 8°, $7.50; ¾ levant, $15.

HOWELLS, W. COOPER. Recollections of life in Ohio, from 1813-1840; with an introd. by his son, W. Dean Howells. The Robert Clarke Co. por. 8°, $2.
The recollections of Mr. Howells—the father of the novelist—relate to a period very important in the history of Ohio, and form a careful and thorough study of the characteristics of a people destined later to develop among them one of the first American commonwealths. They are primarily the personal memoirs of the author, whose family settled in Eastern Ohio at the close of the pioneer epoch; they were Quakers from the English border of Wales and confronted all the novel hardships of the backwoods. These are graphically narrated; he also deals with a later period showing the growing antislavery feeling in 1840.
"It is as pleasing a book of its kind as we have seen for many a day."—*Chicago Inter-Ocean.*

JACOBS, JOS. An inquiry into the sources of the history of the Jews in Spain. Macmillan. 8°, $1.75.

LOVE, *Rev.* W. DE LOSS, *jr.* The fast and Thanksgiving days of New England; with fac-similes of three proclamations. Houghton, Mifflin & Co. 8°, *net,* $3.

ROPES, J. C. The first Napoleon: a sketch, political and military. *New ed.,* with a new preface and a rare portrait. Houghton, Mifflin & Co. 8°, $2.

SARGENT, H. H., *ed.* Napoleon Bonaparte's first campaign. McClurg. maps, 8°, $1.50.

VILLARI, PASQUALE. The two first centuries of Florentine history ; the republic and parties at the time of Dante ; tr. by Linda Villari. Scribner. pl. 8°, $3.75.

WAGNER, LEOPOLD. Manners, customs and observances ; their origin and signification. Macmillan. 8°, $1.75.

WIRGMAN, A. THEO. The history of the English church and people in South Africa. Longmans, Green & Co. 12°, $1.25.

HUMOR AND SATIRE.

MENTOR, (*pseud.*) Never: a handbook for the uninitiated and inexperienced aspirants to refined society's giddy heights and glittering attainments. G. W. Dillingham. 12°, pap., 50 c.

SCHOOLMASTER (The) in comedy and satire; arranged and ed. for the special use of teachers' Reading circles and Round tables: a companion volume to "The schoolmaster in literature." American Book Co. 8°, $1.40.

LITERATURE, MISCELLANEOUS AND COLLECTED WORKS.

ANNUAL American catalogue, 1894 ; being the full titles, with descriptive notes, of all books recorded in *The Publishers' Weekly,* 1894, with author, title, and subject index, publishers' annual lists, and directory of publishers. [Fifth supplement to the American Catalogue, 1884–90.] Office of *The Publishers' Weekly.* 8°, hf. leath., $3.50.

CHAUCER, GEOFFREY. Complete works ; ed. by Rev. Walter W. Skeat. *Globe ed.* Macmillan. 12°, $1.75.

FLETCHER, W. I., *and* BOWKER, R. R. The annual literary index, 1894 ; including periodicals, American and English ; essays, book-chapters, etc.; with author-index, bibliographies, and necrology ; ed. with the co-operation of members of the American Library Association and of the *Library Journal* staff. Office of *The Publishers' Weekly.* 8°, $3.50.

JUSSERAND, J. J. A literary history of the English people. [In 3 v. V. 1.] From the origins to the Renaissance. Putnam. 8°, $3.50.
Contents: Bk. 1, "The origins," has chapters on: Britannia ; The Germanic invasion ; The national poetry of the Anglo-Saxons ; Christian literature and prose literature of the Anglo-Saxons; Bk. 2, "The French invasion," includes Battle literature in the French language under the Norman and Angevin kings; Latin ; Literature in the English language ; Bk. 3, "England and the English," treats of The new nation ; Chaucer ; The group of poets;

William Langland and his visions ; Prose in the fourteenth century ; The theatre ; The end of the Middle Ages.

MINTO, W. The literature of the Georgian era; ed. with a biographical introd. by W. Knight. Harper. 12°, $1.50.

POE, EDGAR ALLAN. Works ; newly coll. and ed., with memoir, introd., and notes, by Edmund Clarence Stedman and George Edward Woodberry. In 10 v. V. 1, 2 and 3. Stone & Kimball. il. 12°, *ea.*, $1.50.

RUGGLES, H. J. The plays of Shakespeare founded on literary forms. Houghton, Mifflin & Co. 8°, $4.

STRACHEY, *Mrs.* JANE, [*Mrs.* R. Strachey,] *ed.* Poets on poets. Scribner. 16°, (Ideal ser.) $2.

TYRRELL, R. Y. Latin poetry : lectures delivered in 1893 on the Percy Turnbull Memorial Foundation in the Johns Hopkins University. Houghton, Mifflin & Co. 12°, $1.50.

WALLACE, A. Popular sayings dissected. F. A. Stokes Co. 16°, 75 c.
A collection of popular sayings and expressions, with notes explaining their origin and meaning.

MEDICAL.

COBBE, W. ROSSER. Doctor Judas : a portrayal of the opium habit. S. C. Griggs & Co. 12°, $1.50.

MENTAL AND MORAL PHILOSOPHY.

COCKE, JAMES R., *M.D.* Hypnotism: how it is done ; its uses and dangers. Arena Pub. Co. 12°, $1.50.

SPENCER, H. Weismannism once more : reprinted from *The Contemporary Review*, with a postscript. Appleton. 12°, pap., 10 c.

WATSON, J. Comte Mill, and Spencer; an outline of philosophy. Macmillan. 12°, *net*, $1.75.

NATURE AND SCIENCE.

HEYSINGER, I. W., *M.D.* The source and mode of solar energy throughout the universe. Lippincott. il. 12°, $2.
The subject is discussed in chapters entitled: Statements of the problem of solar energy; The constitution and phenomena of the sun; The mode of solar energy ; The source of solar energy; Distribution and conservation of solar energy; Phenomena of the stars ; Temporary stars, meteors, and comets ; Phenomena of comets; Interpretation of cometic phenomena ; The resolvable nebulæ, star clusters and galaxies; The gaseous nebulæ; The nebular hypothesis, its basis and its difficulties; Genesis of solar systems and galaxies; Mosaic cosmogony; Harmony of nature's laws and operations. A good classified index of subject-matter.

JERROLD, WALTER. Electricians and their marvels. Revell. il. 12°, 75 c.

QUATREFAGES, A. DE. The pygmies; tr. by F. Starr. Appleton. il. 12°, (Anthropological ser., no. 2.) $1.75.
The purpose is to make known the scientific truth regarding the fables of antiquity concerning the pygmies and also to show what the pyg-

mies of antiquity really are. *Contents:* The pygmies of the ancients, according to modern science; General history and physical characters of the Eastern pygmies; Intellectual, moral and religious characters of the Mincopies; Nigritos other than the Mincopies; The Negrillos or pygmies of Africa; Religious beliefs of the Hottentots and the Bushmen.

WONDERS of marine life. Appleton. il. 8°, 60 c.

POETRY.

BEDLOW, H. The white tsar, and other poems; il. by J. Steeple Davis. Tait. 4°, $3.50.

DAVIDSON, J. Ballads and songs. Copeland & Day. 16°, $1.50.

GOSSE, EDMUND. In russet and silver. Stone & Kimball. 16°, $1.25.

MASSEY, SUSANNA. God's parable, and other poems. Putnam. 12°, $1.
About sixteen sonnets, some "songs written to be set to music," and forty poems make up this collection. Several of the pieces originally appeared in the *Century* and *Lippincott's*.

RAYMOND, *Rev.* G. LANSING. Pictures in verse; il. by Maud Stumm. Putnam. 12°, 75 c.
Fourteen poems, illustrated with full-page pictures and graceful vignettes; printed on rich paper.

SHARP, W. Vistas. Stone & Kimball. 16°, (The green tree lib.) $1.25.

SOUTHEY, ROB. Poems; chosen and arr. by E. Dowden. Macmillan. 16°, (Golden treasury ser.) $1.

POLITICAL AND SOCIAL.

BALFOUR, ROB. C. Central truths and side issues. Imported by Scribner. 12°, $1.50.

BILLINGS, J. S., *and* HURD, H. M. Suggestions to hospital and asylum visitors. Lippincott. 16°, 50 c.

KNAPP, ADELINE. One thousand dollars a day: studies in practical economics. Arena Pub. Co. 16°, (Beacon ser.) 50 c.; $1.
Contents: One thousand dollars a day, a financial experiment; The sick man, a fable for grown-up boys and girls; The discontented machine, an economic study; Getting ahead, a sketch from life; The earth slept, a vision.

KNIGHT, E. F. Rhodesia of to-day: a description of the present condition and prospects of Matabeleland and Mashonaland. Longmans, Green & Co. 12°, $1.

MCPHERSON, E., *and* RHOADES, H. E., *eds.* Tribune almanac and political register for 1895. The Tribune Assoc. 12°, (Library of Tribune extras, v. 7, no. 1.) pap., 25 c.

PORRITT, E. The break-up of the English party system. American Acad. of Political and Social Science. 8°, (Publications of the society, no. 137.) pap., 25 c.
Since the General Election in England of 1885, there has been an interesting and significant breaking away from the old system of two parties in the House of Commons and in the constituencies. The author in this paper says it is easy to distinguish in the present House of Commons eight groups, namely—the Na-

tionalists, the Liberals, the Radicals, the Conservatives, and Liberal Unionists, etc. The history of each group is traced, with its present make-up, tendencies, and various subdivisions.

SULLIVAN, Sir E. Woman: the predominant partner. Longmans, Green & Co. 12°, 40 c.

TOLMAN, W. HOWE. Municipal reform movements in the United States; with an introductory chapter by C. H. Parkhurst. Revell. 12°, $1.

WHITAKER, JOS., ed. An almanack for 1895: containing an account of astronomical and other phenomena, information respecting the government, finances, population, commerce, and general statistics of the British empire throughout the world; with some notice of other countries. Imported by Scribner. 12°, hf. leath., $1.

WILLIAMS, H. W. Money and bank credits in the United States. American Acad. of Political and Social Science. 8°, (Publications of the society, no. 139.) pap., 25 c.
In the brief space of this paper there has been no attempt to exhaust the subject of currency and banking, but only to outline a development of the present system which would supply some of its deficiencies and remedy some of its defects. The writer's suggestions are in line with the "Baltimore plan."

WOMAN in the business world; or, helps and hints to prosperity. Arena Pub Co. 12°, $1.75; pap., 50 c.

THEOLOGY, RELIGION AND SPECULATION.

ALLEN, Rev. A. V. G. The continuity of Christian thought: a study of modern theology in the light of history. N. ed., with a new preface and a full index. Houghton, Mifflin & Co. 12°, $2.

As others saw him: a retrospect, A.D. 54. Houghton, Mifflin & Co. 12°, $1.25.

BALFOUR, ARTHUR JA. The foundations of belief: being notes introductory to the study of theology. Longmans, Green & Co. 12°, $2.
"It is one of the most notable books of the year, and no one who aims to keep in touch with modern thought can afford to leave it unread."
—Vance Thompson in the Commercial Advertiser.

BETTANY, G. T. A popular history of the Reformation and modern Protestantism. Ward, Lock & Bowden. 8°, $2.

GEIKIE, CUNNINGHAM, D.D. New Testament hours. V. 2, The apostles, their lives and letters. Ja. Pott & Co. maps, il. 8°, $1.50.

HERRON, G. D., D.D. The Christian state: a political vision of Christ; a course of six lectures delivered in churches in various American cities. Crowell. 16°, 75 c.
"Dr. Herron's great purpose is to bring the kingdom of God among men by arousing them to adopt and apply the Christ-life to all human relations, not as religionists, but as Christians—as Christ-men. He adopts the sermon on the mount as civil and industrial law principle, and believes that the teaching of Jesus in its strictest sense is rational and practical, since it is the highest expression of filial affection ever given to men, and that its fulfilment will bring the

Kingdom to earth. Many people fear Dr. Herron's teaching because they suspect him of attempting to establish a new creed or denomination. That is the very antithesis of his purpose. He adopts, instead, the more difficult task of arousing the existing church to a larger living conception of the social Christ. His message is not one of division, but of union; not one of destruction, but of construction. He would not destroy what is, but would pour into it a stimulant and a potency for more intense and unremitting righteousness." — Midland Monthly.

HOWE, REGINALD HEBER, D.D. Quadragesima; or, thoughts for each day in Lent. Whittaker. 12°, net, $1.
Bible texts, prose and poetical selections and reflections by the author, for each day in Lent.

LAWRENCE, E. A., D.D. Modern missions in the East, their methods, successes, and limitations; with an introd. by E. T. Eaton, D.D. Harper. 12°, $1.75.
The substance of this volume was first presented in the form of lectures in Andover Theological Seminary, on the Hyde Foundation, and subsequently in Yale Divinity School and Beloit College. The contents are based upon a twenty months' missionary journey around the world with the express purpose of studying the mission work of various denominations. Dr. Lawrence hopes the work may serve as a text-book for those who wish to look into the science of missions.

McCONNELL, S. D., D.D. Sermon stuff. 2d series. Whittaker. 12°, $1.
Sixty-five outlines of sermons, for the use of preachers, by the rector of St. Stephen's Church, Phila.

MATTER, force, and spirit; or, scientific evidence of a supreme intelligence. Putnam. 12°, $1.

PAGET, FRANCIS, D.D. Studies in the Christian character: sermons with an introductory essay. Longmans, Green & Co., 12°, $1.75.

SATTERLEE, H. Y., D.D. A creedless gospel and the Gospel creed. Scribner. 8°, $2.
"The author set out with the intention of writing a short article on the Apostles' Creed, but the work grew insensibly on his hands as days and months passed by, until it attained the proportions of this volume. It should be added that the book has not been written for unbelievers. Its sole object is to help in conforming the faith of the faithful: to point out and bring back to the memory of nineteenth century Christians the standard of belief and of life which was set before New Testament Christians by Christ himself and the apostles whom he trained."—Preface. Dr. Satterlee is rector of Calvary Church, New York City.

Books for the Young.

BURT, MARY, E., ed. Little nature studies for little people, from the essays of John Burroughs; an introd. to the study of science and nature for primary grades; ed. by Mary E. Burt. Ginn. sq. 12°, bds., 36 c.
Intended as a primary text-book in science

and reading; the motive is to introduce teacher and pupil to a mutual love for the woods and fields, to the study of animals and plants, to the observation of real things in life, and to the methods of a true naturalist. It is adapted from the essays of John Burroughs.

COMMON things and useful information. Nelson. il. 16°, (Royal handbooks of general knowledge.) 50 c.

CRAIK, GEORGIANA M., [*Mrs.* A. W. May.] Bow-wow and mew-mew. Maynard, Merrill & Co. 16°, (Maynard's English classic ser., no. 150.) pap., 12 c.
A story of a little dog and cat.

CROMPTON, FRANCES E. Messire, and other stories. Dutton. il. 12°, 75 c.

DOUGLAS, AMANDA M. In wild rose time. Lee & Shepard. 12°, $1.50.
"The higher and lower life in a great city is the subject of this volume. Through an act of simple kindness, the lives of two children are made happier, and Dilsey Quinn and his sister are the hero and the heroine. Miss Amanda M. Douglas is in perfect sympathy with her characters, and 'In Wild Rose Time' is not alone an entertaining book, but imparts an excellent lesson."—*N. Y. Times.*

DOUGLAS, AMANDA M. Sherburne cousins. Dodd, Mead & Co. 12°, $1.50.
"The 'Sherburne cousins' is the third volume of that readable series of books for the young that delineate the characters making up a bright, intelligent circle of friends in a typical Southern home. The scenes of the history are laid in Europe and this country and the interest deepens as its personages assume the responsibilities of their more mature life. The author, Amanda M. Douglas, tells of the sayings and actions of the various characters in their new relations to one another, with careful regard to actual life, and as a story on sound character building there is no better series of books than these for young people."—*The Outlook.*

FOSTER, ALBEN J. Ampthill Towers. Nelson. 12°, 80 c.

GALL, J. Popular science. Nelson. il. 16°, (Royal handbooks of general knowledge.) 50c.

HALL, BASIL. Voyages and travels of Captain Basil Hall, R. N. Nelson. 8°, $2.

TEMPLE, CORNA. Princess Louise: a tale of the Stuarts. Nelson. 12°, 60 c.

RECENT FRENCH AND GERMAN BOOKS.

FRENCH.

Antoine, C. Marthe Filmer: mœurs néo-Algériennes.	$1 00
Castellane, Marq. de. Les temps nouveaux.	1 00
France, Anatole. Le Puits de Sainte Claire.	1 00
Frehel, J. Tablettes d'Argile.	1 00
Garnier, N. L'Afrique: Anthologie-Géographique.	1 20
Gavard, C. Un diplomate à Londres.	1 00
Gonneville. Souvenirs Militaires.	1 00
Hache, G. Carle et Jacques.	1 00
Hamsun, Kunt. La Faim.	1 00
Hervieu, P. L'Armature.	1 00
Huysmans, I. K. En Route.	1 00
Isoulet, J. La Cité Moderne: Metaphysique de la Sociologie. 8°.	2 25
Jusserand. Le Roman d'un roi d'Ecosse.	75
Lavedan, H. Les Marionnettes.	1 00
Leclercq, J. A travers l'Afrique Australe.	1 20
Letang. Le Lieutenant Philippe.	1 00
Leyret. En plein Faubourg.	1 00
Lorrain. Sensations et Souvenirs.	1 00
Mael, Pierre. Toujours à Toi.	1 00
Mantort, Chev. de. Mémoires. 8°.	2 25
Mary, Jules. Blessée au Cœur.	1 00
Montegut. Le Maréchal Davout.	1 00
Naurouse. Frères d'Armes.	1 00

Pages choisies des Grands Ecrivains. I. M. Guyau.	$1 00
Pavlovsky. Croquis Parisiens.	1 00
Peron, Commandant. Au Niger. 8°.	2 25
Pilo, M. La Psychologie du beau et de l'art.	75
Ram, A. Les petites Sœurs des pauvres.	1 00
Seche. La Morale Janséniste: Educateurs et Moralistes.	1 00
Simond, Capt. La Tour d'Auvergne.	1 00
Strindberg. Le plaidoyer d'un Fou.	1 00
Thoury, Jean Fr. Mémoires. 1789-1830.	1 00
Tinseau, L. de. Dette Oubliée.	1 00

GERMAN.

Lay, Max. Im Geiste Ludwig xiv.	70
Lenbach, E. Wunderliche Leute.	1 00
Meyer, W. A. Wie ich's sah.	1 00
Peters, Dr. Carl. Das Deutsche Ostafrikanische Schutzgebiet.	6 20
Schoenthau, Paul v. Prinzessin Turandot.	70
Schreibershofen, H. v. Im Wechselspiel des Lebens.	70
Schroeder, C. Lady Sibylle. 2 vols.	2 35
Seeck, O. Geschichte des Untergangs der Antiken Welt. Vol. 1 und Anhang.	2 85
Wachsmuth, C. Einleitung in das Studium der Alten Geschichte.	5 35
Zintgraff, Eug. Nord Kamerun.	4 00

Freshest News.

CHARLES SCRIBNER'S SONS will publish in book form Paul Bourget's "Outre-Mer."

A. P. MARSDEN, London, has just issued an historical biography, entitled "Ivan the Terrible: his life and times," by Austen Pember.

GINN & Co. have in preparation "An Introduction to the Study of Literary Criticism," by Charles Mills Gayley, Professor of English Literature in the University of California, and Fred. Newton Scott, Assistant Professor of Rhetoric in the University of Michigan. The two volumes, "Poetics and the Drama" and "Literary Types" (other than the drama), will be ready in the fall.

BLISS, SANDS & FOSTER, London, are about to publish S. R. Crockett's new volume, "Stories Relative to the Ancient Province of Galloway," which will contain some of the author's work produced between 1889 and 1894, and allowed to accumulate. It is to form a special volume of over five hundred pages, and will show the author in every phase of his varied talent as inventor of stories ranging from the idyllic to the grimly tragic.

T. Y. CROWELL & Co. have nearly ready a

book on "Shakespeare's Heroines," by Charles E. L. Wingate, whose design has been to give a sketch of the impersonations of the leading characters in Shakespeare's tragedies and comedies by noted players, from the days of their first production under Shakespeare's personal supervision down to the present time. Numerous anecdotes will illustrate the characteristics of the players and the serious and amusing features of their interpretations.

H. W. HAGEMANN has begun the issue of a pretty series to be known as *The Castleton Series* by the publication of a novel entitled "Sidney Forrester," an unusual story, written by Clement Wilkes. It is a quiet, modest love-story, surely a thing "devoutly to be wished" by those who have absorbed much of the lurid, unwholesome fiction of the present hour. It is to be hoped that this series will be kept pure and clean as is the book with which it starts. Womanly women and chivalrous men are much needed as heroines and heroes of fiction.

DODD, MEAD & CO. will publish shortly a new novel entitled "The Impregnable City," by Max Pemberton, who has been a successful journalist and editor, but has recently severed his connection with *Chums* and other journalistic work to devote himself entirely to literature. He will edit a new series to be issued by Cassell & Co. akin to the *Pseudonym*. Prof. James Schouler has so far revised and rewritten the first two volumes of his "History of the United States under the Constitution," published by Dodd, Mead & Co., as to necessitate the making of new plates. The remaining volumes have also been revised preparatory to printing a new edition of this popular work, which will be issued in April, with the addition of maps. Professor Schouler's final volume on the Civil War, completing his original plan, is now in active preparation.

LOVELL, CORYELL & CO. announce an *Authorized Royalty Edition* of Rudyard Kipling's works, complete in six uniform volumes, and including "Departmental Ditties, Barrack-Room Ballads, and other verses," "Plain Tales from the Hills," "Soldiers Three and In Black and White," "The Phantom 'Rickshaw and Wee Willie Winkie," "The Light that Failed," "Story of the Gadsbys and Under the Deodars," "Mine Own People and The Courtship of Dinah Shadd." These are sold in the set or separately, and in cloth or paper. Kipling's "Indian Tales"—comprising "Plain Tales from thè Hills," "Soldiers Three," and "The Phantom 'Rickshaw"—may also be had in a single large volume. They have in preparation a fine *Easter Edition* of Farrar's "Life of Christ," handsomely bound, printed on light cream-tinted paper," with photogravure frontispiece and illuminated title-page; and have also just ready an *Easter Edition*, in white vellum, of Dr. Cunningham Geikie's "Life and Words of Christ."

G. P. PUTNAM'S SONS have now ready the third volume of their fine edition of "The Works of Thomas Paine," edited by Moncure D. Conway; "The Armenian Crises in Turkey," by Frederick Davis Greene, describing the massacre of 1894 and explaining its antecedents and significance, together with some of the factors that must enter into the solution of this phase of the Eastern question; and an edition of "Historic Doubts Relative to Napoleon Bonaparte," by Richard Whately, Archbishop of Dublin, who endeavored to prove there never existed such a person as Napoleon Bonaparte. *The Heroes of the Nations Series* will have two new volumes, "Louis XIV. and the Zenith of the French Monarchy," by Arthur Hassall, and "Julian, Philosopher and Emperor, and the last struggle of Paganism against Christianity," by Alice Gardner. Special attention is called to the first volume of Jusserand's great work on "The Literary History of English People," which covers the vast subject from the Origins to the Renaissance. It is fascinatingly written and finely illustrated.

HOUGHTON, MIFFLIN & CO. have just ready a new volume by Charles Carleton Coffin, entitled "The Daughters of the Revolution," in which the author sets forth the influence of the women in the struggle of the colonies to attain their independence; "The Story of Christine Rochefort," by Helen Choate Prince, a novel in which the leading motive is anarchism; and "Chocorua's Tenants," by Frank Bolles, a volume of poems that will be particularly welcome to those to whom Chocorua and the region thereabout have become in some pleasant degree enchanted ground through the admirable descriptions of their varied beauty and the charm of their forest inhabitants in the writings of Mr. Frank Bolles. Shortly will be issued a new edition of Minot's "Land Birds and Game Birds of New England"; "St. Augustine of Canterbury," by Rev. E. L. Cutts, a new volume in the series of *English Leaders of Religion*, also, "The United States Internal Revenue Tax System," comprising all internal revenue laws now in force as amended by the act of August 28, 1894, etc., including a history of the development of the internal revenue tax system since the foundation of the Government, by Charles Wesley Eldridge.

D. APPLETON & CO. have some books calculated to make covetousness rule in the heart of every book-lover. The fourth volume of McMaster's "History of the People of the United States" has long been expected, and will be eagerly added to the three already on the shelf. "Degeneration," by Prof. Max Nordau, translated from the second edition of the German work, while presenting a scathing criticism of the decadent art of the day, as shown in the representative arts, in music and in literature, so carefully explains the author's position, by quotation and description, that it offers the reader an all-round-the-world look at the creative genius of the closing century. "Actual Africa," by Frank Vincent, is full from one to the other of its handsome covers of accurately compiled facts gathered on the spot and put forth in convincing language and decorative pictures; "The Story of the Stars," by George F. Chambers ; "Familiar Flowers of Field and Garden," by F. Schuyler Mathews, and "The Handbook of Birds of Eastern North America," by Frank M. Chapman, deal delightfully with natural history; and "Evolution and Effort," by Edmond Kelly, marks the difference between unconscious development and conscious struggle toward special aims, those specially considered being religion and politics. Mrs. Cotes has a new book entitled "The Story of Sonny Sahib"; and Louis Couperus has produced an excellent story in "Majesty."

LITERARY NEWS

AN ECLECTIC REVIEW OF
CURRENT LITERATURE
~ILLUSTRATED~

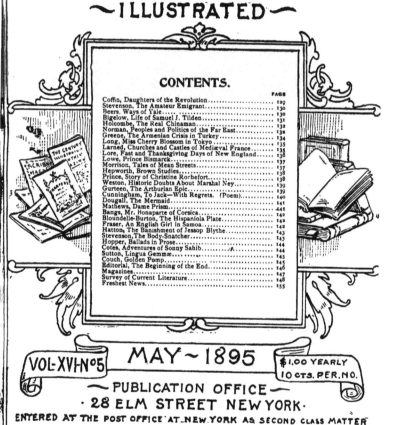

CONTENTS.

VOL·XVI·N°5   MAY~1895 $1.00 YEARLY
10 CTS. PER. NO.

~ PUBLICATION OFFICE ~
· 28 ELM STREET NEW YORK ·
ENTERED AT THE POST OFFICE AT NEW YORK AS SECOND CLASS MATTER

The Literary News

In winter you may reade them, ad ignem, by the fireside; and in summer, ad umbram, under some shadie tree and therewith pass away the tedious howres.

VOL. XVI.   MAY, 1895.   No. 5

Daughters of the Revolution, 1769–1776.

No period in the history of our country surpasses in interest that immediately preceding and including the beginning of the Revolutionary War. Many volumes have set forth the patriotism and heroism of the fathers and sons of the old Colonial days and of the beginnings of the great Republic, but the devotion of the mothers and daughters of that day has received far less tribute. Their influence and part in the struggle of the Colonies for freedom is now set forth by Charles Carleton Coffin in a volume entitled "Daughters of the Revolution and their Times," which, under the form of romance, presents the events, scenes, incidents and spirit of the Colonists at the beginning of the Revolution.

The period was characterized by sublime enthusiasm, self-sacrifice and devotion, not only shown by the American patriots, but by the loyalists, who conscientiously adhered to the English Crown. The sacrifices and sufferings of these loyalists have been generally overlooked, but the author has done them justice in his descriptions of the siege of Boston and the agony of the hour when the adherents of King George found themselves confronted with the appalling fact that they must become aliens, exiles and wanderers, leaving behind all their possessions and estates the hour when there came a sundering of tender ties and the breaking of hearts, a period in which families were divided, parents adhering to the king, sons and daughters giving their allegiance to Liberty.

Many of the characters introduced are imaginary, but they all stand as types of character which really existed, and the events in which they take their part are strictly conformed to historic fact.

The Boston *Gazette* says: "Mr. Charles Carleton Coffin's 'Daughters of the Revolution' will undoubtedly please the children and grandchildren of those who, a generation ago, enjoyed the Carleton war correspondence. It is a story of Boston in the days immediately preceding the Revolution, and describes the condition of the town and marks the contrast be-

From "Daughters of the Revolution."   Copyright, 1895, by Houghton, Mifflin & Co.

ELIZABETH HORTON WARREN.

tween the British soldiery and the Colonists. It is not to be denied that the story is somewhat partisan, but it does not profess to be unadorned history, and young readers are not so competent to judge historical values that it is judicious to paint the shadows of the past too accurately."

The book is bound in buckram and well illustrated. The historic houses are from recent photographs. The portrait of Mrs. Joseph Warren, which we show, forms the frontispiece. It is owned by the proprietors of "The Memorial History of Boston." (Houghton, Mifflin & Co. $1.50.)

The Amateur Emigrant.

A MELANCHOLY interest invests everything that appears with the name of the lamented Stevenson. This little volume, containing his experiences from the time when he embarked on the emigrant ship as second-cabin passenger till his arrival in New York, is vital with the author's individuality. It seems a fit introduction to the man, as well as to the varied jour-

From "Ways of Yale."   Copyright, 1895, by Henry Holt & Co.

IT CROWED REPEATEDLY.

neyings, voyages and adventures with which his name is associated. The Stevenson characteristics, the originality, perception, exquisite fitness of language, piquancy, adaptability, vigor and freshness—all are manifest here. How alert were his senses! How clear his insight! How pervasive his sympathies! And how human he was! How much he made of life, and what treasures in knowledge of character he gained where men less observing would have found nothing!

All these qualities and gifts come into exercise even when the persons Stevenson meets are stowaways or outcasts from civilization, as were some he came in contact with on the voyage. He gathered information from the most unlikely sources, and found good talkers among common kind of men—perhaps he had the faculty to draw out the best they had to give. At any rate, he could avail himself of it and crystallize the thoughts so that his readers cannot resist the attraction. The great literary artist and born story-teller appears in every chapter. The experiences in New York City were unfortunate and perhaps should be taken with a grain of allowance, giving that metropolis the benefit of the doubt. (Stone & Kimball. $1.25.)—*Boston Literary World.*

The Ways of Yale.

CONSULE PLANCO.

In Plancus' days, when life was slow,
We dwelt within the Old Brick Row
    Before Durfee or Welch was built,
    Or gilded youths in Vanderbilt
Looked down upon the mob below.
Then Freshmen did not use to go
'Most every evening to the show;
    Quite inexpensive was *our* gilt
        In Plancus' days.
We had no football then, you know;
All bloodless lay the untrodden snow,
    No gore was shed, no ink was spilt,
    No poet got upon his stilt
To write these frenchified rondeaux,
        In Plancus' days.

HENRY A. BEERS, the clever author of "A Suburban Pastoral," has gathered up a neat little volume of reminiscences which he calls "The Ways of Yale." He lets an undergraduate of the class of '69 make a comparison of student life in the sixties and in the nineties, which is full of humor and also of instructive thought. Poems are scattered through the little book, now pathetic, now irresistibly comic, which add not a little to its charm. Much of the life described is the college life of chums, sports, crammings and studies of any great college, but there are certain characteristics that are peculiar to Yale life, and Yale students and Yale alumni will take special delight in the author's chattings. (Holt. 75 c.)

Life of Samuel J. Tilden.

IT is usually the lot of the biographer to be charged with having written a tribute to the merits of his subject rather than a record of his failings, as well as his virtues. It is not probable that Mr. John Bigelow, whose life of Samuel J. Tilden is to-day published by the Harpers, will escape the fate of his predecessors in this particular field of literature. So large a portion of Mr. Tilden's life was, however, of a public character, and so many of his acts a matter of record, that his biography, of necessity, partakes much of the nature of history, and has to defend its impartiality the prestige of commonly accepted facts. Almost twenty years have softened the asperity of the partisan controversy over the events which gave Mr. Tilden a notoriety unique in the history of this country. Many of the actors in the great political struggle of the winter of 1876–77 have passed away, and to those who remain, its issues are long dead. The bitterness engendered by it has died a natural death, and time's perspective has almost corrected the inaccuracies of mental vision inseparable from party bias.

Partisanship has in a great measure ceased to be the fashion of the hour. Economic and financial questions, along lines not coincident with those of the two great parties, occupy the attention of the people in national affairs, as do municipal problems in the more closely related concerns of self-government. Thus, in many ways, the time is auspicious for a fair, sober and judicious consideration of the character of one of the most notable figures in our political life. Whatever may be the final judgment upon Samuel J. Tilden, it should never be forgotten that he did not plunge the country into civil war at a time when many men feared he would, and excited partisans urged him to go to Washington and take the oath of office, a step which would almost certainly have caused bloodshed. Natural justice, the justice of time and events, demands that analysis of motives should not reach the point of depriving a man of the credit of doing a good action, or failing to do a bad one, because it is assumed that he lacked courage to do otherwise. Whatever may have been the motive, the good and its results remain.

The literary reputation of Mr. Bigelow and the knowledge of his life-long friendship with Mr. Tilden have caused the work he has finished to be looked for with interest and expectation for several years. It had been generally understood that Mr. Tilden confided to him the task of telling the full story of his life and put him in possession of such facts and papers as were necessary. The work could hardly have been placed in better hands. Acquainted with the subject of his labors since he was his fellow law student, and bound to him by ties of affectionate respect and esteem, Mr. Bigelow has

From "The Life of Samuel J. Tilden."   Copyright, 1895, by Harper & Brothers.

SAMUEL JONES TILDEN, *Circa* 1874.

that intimate knowledge of the personality of Mr. Tilden requisite to the correct weighing of motives and the proper and authoritative interpretation of actions. An additional qualification is the judicial turn of mind, the result of a lifetime at the bar, which so greatly aids in the calm, dispassionate statement of a case. Mr. Bigelow has most interestingly displayed this quality throughout his book. The trained lawyer has been constantly invoked to restrain the hot partisanship of the friend. . . .

Mr. Bigelow has included in each of the two octavo volumes of 400 pages, which comprise his work, a voluminous appendix containing full extracts from many of Mr. Tilden's State papers, copies of telegrams, correspondence and addresses relating to the work of the Electoral Commission, the genealogy of the Tilden family, list of the eight hundred books read by Mr. Tilden during the last four years of his life and much other interesting matter. (Harper. 2 v., $6.)—*N. Y. Commercial Adver-tiser.*

The Real Chinaman.

OF course every American who has been privileged to spend some time in China is now more or less anxious to tell about it. There has been quite a flood of literature of this kind.

LI HUNG CHANG.

Some of the books sent forth are the merest trash ; others possess an abiding value. It is facts that are wanted, not theories. The people of the United States are abundantly willing to think well of the Chinese, if they can find just reason for so doing. The national prejudice is chiefly confined to those of limited intelligence. At the same time there is a well-defined determination that America shall not be Orientalized ; in other words, that the customs of China shall not be transplanted to this continent ; and this for good and sufficient reasons. It is all right for intelligent travellers to present a clear account of what they have seen and heard. Chester Holcombe, the author of this book, was for some years interpreter, and later Secretary of the American Legation, and for a time Acting Minister of the United States at Pekin. Therefore, he must have had exceptional opportunities for obtaining correct information. He seems to have his own opinion of Chinese history, as generally presented on this side of the world, and in order that there may be no misunderstanding with his readers, he frankly says :

"This volume is neither a defence, apology, criticism, nor panegyric. It is rather an explanation. It attempts to give a few of the results of many years of residence among the Chinese, in the course of which the author was brought into close and familiar relations with all classes of the people, in nearly every section of the Empire. In it an effort is made to describe and explain some of the more prominent factors in the national life, and to show why some of their ways, so odd to us, are natural to them. Facts are dealt with rather than opinions. The book represents an effort to outline, with a few broad sweeps of the pen, the Chinaman as he is."

The illustrations, from photographs, give a bird's-eye view of Chinese life. The book is without sensationalism. It is a plain and evidently truthful narrative, and its pages are not marred like those of some recent books treating of the people of the East. Still, some of the peculiar ways of the Chinese are subjects of discussion in a manner not altogether agreeable. The average traveller seems to think it incumbent upon him to show the dark side of the picture, no matter what the effect upon his readers. (Dodd, Mead & Co. $2.)—*Philadelphia Telegraph.*

People and Politics of the Far East.

MR. NORMAN's book is on a much larger scale than Mr. Curzon's recent work, "Problems of the Far East" and there is delightful and refreshing contrast between the two. Mr. Curzon represents the traditions of Tory England,

and his suggestions and prophecies hover on the verge of Jingoism. Furthermore, his brilliant work is already, in all probability, antiquated, because the Corea which he described justifies Japan in her course in Corea, for he shows that Japan, besides bringing the peninsular state into the circle of civilized nations, is the creator of her trade and incipient industries.

From "People and Politics of the Far East."　　　　Charles Scribner's Sons.

AT KO-SI-CHANG: THE KING OF SIAM AND THE SECOND QUEEN.

and partly imagined exists no more, while it is evident that there is to be a China, hereafter, very different from that pictured in the old books. Mr. Norman takes what we imagine to be the Liberal or more rational view of British foreign politics, for he actually believes that it is possible for England and Russia to be friends. From first to last he has exposed the inherent weakness of China, even to demonstrating that there is no such thing as China in the sense of a political entity. He exults with delight in the fact that the Japanese war has done what nothing else has been able to do—made known the truth about this colossal sham. His admiration for Japan borders almost on the sentimental. Mr. Norman thinks that he knows well what the terms of the peace settlement between Japan and China will be. China is a morass of abomination that needs to be, in the interests of humanity and civilization, partitioned, drained, filled up, and its malaria destroyed by planting abundantly the eucalyptus trees of British soldiers, forts and custom-houses. Mr. Norman

The five chapters devoted to Siam give what we believe to be the best discussion of the actual situation to-day. The criticism of the action of France is searching and the indictment is tremendous, but we cannot see that Mr. Norman has in the least exaggerated the facts. . . .

In conclusion, he sums up his work in "An Eastern Horoscope," calling attention to the fact "that powerful and jealous nations are plotting for our inheritance." He sees the most hopeful portent in the declaration of a Liberal Prime Minister that "the party of a small England, of a shrunk England, of a degraded England, of a neutral England, of a submissive England, has died."

It is but sheer justice to call attention to the excellent book-making and editing, and to the four maps and the threescore illustrations, the latter excellently selected and reproduced from original photographs. The literary arrangement and proportion and the well-made index commend this book, which is of the first order of literary merit. (Scribner. $4.)—*The Nation.*

The Armenian Crisis in Turkey.

A TIMELY contribution to our knowledge regarding Armenia and the recent massacres there is a book just issued by Mr. Frederick Davis Greene, for several years a resident in that country. The book is entitled "The Armenian Crisis in Turkey." It has an introduction by the Rev. Dr. Josiah Strong; following comes evidence of the atrocities, the genuineness of which is certified by Governor Greenhalge, Miss Willard, Mr. William Lloyd Garrison, Mrs. Liver-

From "Armenian Crisis in Turkey."　　Copyright, 1895, by G. P. Putnam's Sons.

ARMENIAN GIRLS OF VAN.

more, Dr. Edward Everett Hale, Mrs. Julia Ward Howe, President Walker, ex-Governor Russell, and other well-known persons. The book is supplemented by a valuable appendix containing important letters from General Lew Wallace, Dr. Cyrus Hamlin, and others, added

From "Armenian Crisis in Turkey."　Copyright, 1895, by G. P. Putnam's Sons.

"IRREGULAR" TURKISH SOLDIER.

to which is a valuable bibliography of Armenian history, literature, topography, and of Mohammedanism. Mr. Greene was for nearly four years a missionary of the American Board in Van, the centre of Armenia. Having now resigned his connection with the Board, he writes as the representative of no society, and is connected with none. It is easy for any one in casually taking up this volume to say that it is somewhat hysterically written; it is certainly true that the treatment is not only hasty but partial, and is at the expense of literary form. The sympathizer with humanity, however, the civilizer and the Christian, cannot read the book through (any more than he can that equally stirring and also recently published volume, Professor Errera's on the Jews in Russia) without feeling that a race capable of as high achievement as has recently been shown by the Bulgarians, since their emancipation from a like slavery, has been in fact ground in the dust under the heel of the cruel Turk. The part of the book entitled "A Chapter of Horrors" is almost beyond belief The massacre of last September is, of course, the main and burning theme of the writer. The setting, however, which is given to the picture is, first, information about Turkish Armenia, the physical aspects, inhabitants, and administration of the country, and, secondly, a consideration of some of the factors which enter into the solution of this phase of the Eastern question. Of these factors the culminating one is the Treaty of Berlin in general, and the action (or rather inaction) of Great Britain in particular. Mr. Greene's opinion is, naturally enough, that the only treatment for the "sick man" is a surgical one. To make this opinion the stronger he appends a chapter on previous acts of Turkish tragedy—the massacres of the Greeks in 1822, of the Nestorians in 1850, of the Syrians in 1860, of the Cretans in 1867, of the Bulgarians in 1876, of the Yezidis in 1892, and now of the Armenians in 1894. The book has twenty illustrations and an excellent map. A timely publication, fitted to give needed information to general readers. (Putnam. $1; pap., 60c.)—*The Outlook.*

Miss Cherry Blossom of Tokyo.

MR. JOHN LUTHER LONG gives us a capital love-story, taking us out into fresh fields and pastures new. The scene is laid in the Eastern capital on the banks of the Sumida. The lover is a secretary of the United States Legation, and the young lady is Miss Sakura, whose father, with a name which we may translate Ancient Daddy, is lord of the Mikado's kitchen. Miss Cherry Blossom has been educated in America, and has learned just enough of our social life to make her dangerous or unhappy in Japan ; for, despite all the professions of civilization of the New Japanese, the factor of individualism, so prominent in countries we call civilized, was very nearly next to unknown and is only just beginning to emerge in the Japan of Meiji. The story is told by means of conversation, and the clever author has undoubtedly had sufficient experience of the woman's world in Japan to get the Japano-English pronunciation perfectly. The local color is also correct in minute details, and there is not too much gore in the story, though one or two corpses are duly deposited on the soil of the land of the holy gods. After properly evading or judiciously conforming to Japanese procedure, the young American gets on board the outward bound steamer, and to the native detective or Japanese naval officer Mr. Holley gives assurance of the non-existence of the person inquired for, while he introduces "Mr. and Mrs. Holley, citizens of the United States." The story is capitally told ; but evidently the author, who has been so true to the minutest detail of Japanese life, ideals and cus-

toms, did not watch his printer and *confrères* for on the very title-page, right under the author's name, is the unmistakable cheap cast type-cut, which represents a nondescript being, who as to fan and umbrella might possibly pass for a native of Nippon, but who in coat, petticoat, trousers and thick, flat-soled shoes turned up at the end is an unmitigated Chinaman. Alas, too, for *Yamato Damashii* when the American printer gets hold of it ! (Lippincott. $1.25.)—*Boston Literary World.*

Churches and Castles of Mediæval France.

THIS book is a record of a traveller's impressions of the great monuments of France. The author hopes it may bring other travellers to see the wonderful churches and castles he describes. It is easy for the student to gain information about these historic buildings, but, nevertheless, it may be of some use to tell what effect they produce upon one who does not wish

From "Churches and Castles of Mediæval France." Copyright, 1895, by Charles Scribner's Sons.
THE CATHEDRAL OF AMIENS.

to study deeply into all their history and the minute details of the building of them but who does love their beauty and cares about the place they hold in the history of the French people.

To one who loves Gothic architecture there are few cathedrals more interesting than the cathedral of Amiens, of which we show an illustration.

It was built in 1220 to 1288—the sixty-eight years' work of the two bishops Everard, who founded it, and Godfrey, who carried it to completion and consecrated it. The author quotes freely from many writers on art, notably Ruskin, and his own comments show taste, study and enthusiasm, tempered by strong religious feeling. Among the historic monuments pictured are the cathedrals of Tours, Beauvais, Chartres, Bourges, Rheims, the Church of St. Etienne du Mont, Notre Dame de Poitiers, St. Denis, etc. And among the ancient castles are the Châteaux of Henry of Navarre, of Langeais, of Chaumont, of Chinon, etc. No better book can be found to take upon a summer run through France. (Scribner. $1.50.)

The Fast and Thanksgiving Days of New England.

THERE still may be found in the remoter parts of New England a few persons who observe fast days and the Thanksgiving Days as they were observed in the Colonial times and in the early decades of the Republic. These few persons believe, as the Fathers believed, that if the crops are good, the country is prosperous, the public health satisfactory, all these things have been ordered specially to indicate that the Great Ruler of the universe is pleased with the people.

They also believe that sickness, drought, freshets, fires, storms, and everything else that is disagreeable and hard to bear are manifestations of God's displeasure. If a man loses his wife, they say he has been sinful and the Lord has taken away his helpmate in order to remind him of his responsibility to a higher power than any on earth. If a herd of cows, in its ignorance of the laws of nature, assembles beneath a tree in the pasture in order to escape the downpour and falls dead in a heap when the lightning comes, these same good people tell us that the man who owned the cows had "wandered from the sight of the Lord."

As Mr. Love puts it:

They (the Pilgrim Fathers) found no place for the discipline of chastening love. Regarding all dire happenings as punishments and all blessings as approvals, they seem to have thought that their moral status before God was thus written out in events. They connected every calamity or deliverance with their present sin or virtue. As the former had a particular voice of warning and the latter a testimony of forgiveness, every event approached them with its shadow before and its sunshine afterwards, to be recognized by fasting and thanksgiving.

Mr. Love makes no plea for the restoration of the spirit with which the Fathers kept their fasts ; his purpose is to exhibit what that spirit was, and how it weakened with advancing years. He thinks that "pious purpose, preserving courage, and honest faith of these good men" are "as worthy of regard as their oaken chests, spinning-wheels, and warming-pans." (Houghton, Mifflin & Co. $3.)—*N. Y. Times.*

THE THEATRICAL KING.

Prince Bismarck.

THE short life of "Prince Bismarck," by Charles Lowe, M.A., is an excellent piece of literary work. The sketch is based on the "Historical Biography" of the German ex-chancellor, published by the same author ten years ago, but he has made use of much fresh material and has brought the narrative down to the reconciliation between Bismarck and the Emperor in January, 1894. Mr. Lowe tells the whole story in twelve chapters, first outlining concisely Bismarck's life as student and squire, and then going on to relate his services as a parliamentarian, in the German Diet, as ambassador, in the wars with Denmark and Austria, in the formation of the North German Confederation, in the war with France, as peace-maker of Europe, in the struggle with the Vatican, and as "Major-Domo of the Reich," the narrative concluding with a picturesque chapter headed "A Fall Like Lucifer's." Mr. Lowe has the

From "Lowe's Prince Bismarck."   Copyright, 1895, by Roberts Brothers.

PRINCE BISMARCK.

art of narrating events in a natural and logical way, and through this whole history of the development of united Germany he makes the personality of Bismarck the dominant factor. In relating the differences between the German and the ex-chancellor, Mr. Lowe conveys the impression that Wilhelm II. has behaved throughout the whole affair with a great deal of consideration and magnanimity—an impression which those familiar with the public acts and deeds of his youthful majesty will find it hard to accept without some modification. The portrait which forms the frontispiece is indicative of Bismarck's character. (Roberts. $1.25.) —*The Beacon.*

Tales of Mean Streets.

ARTHUR MORRISON'S "Tales of Mean Streets" deals with life and scenes in the East End of London, and in their quiet and assured realism, their firm grasp of character, their unforced dramatic intensity and skilful command of dialect, show literary ability of a very high order ; it is perhaps needless to add that the revelations they give of the depths of the London slums is vivid and poignant. One need only read a page of any of these stories to see that the author is no mere dilettante or random "slummer," but a man who has lived intimately among the people he portrays, and who knows alike their good qualities as well as their weaknesses. Mr. Morrison has not only a sense of pathos and of tragedy, but the sense of humor also (is it possible to have one without the other ?) and his stories unfold themselves in a simple and natural way, starting out with no artificial situations and leading up to no predetermined climax, but making in each instance a complete picture, a cross section, as it were, through strata of human existence which the English writer of fiction has as yet barely touched. Perhaps the strongest of these "Tales of Mean Streets" are those making up the trilogy entitled "Lizerunt." Certainly, the promise held forth in "Tales of Mean Streets" is enough to justify in sympathetic readers an eager anticipation of any other writings that may come from the same pen. (Roberts. $1.) —*The Beacon.*

From "Brown Studies." Copyright, 1895, by E. P. Dutton & Co.

LET ME THINK A MOMENT.

Brown Studies.

No American writer of the day seems to be better qualified than the Rev. George H. Hepworth to touch the minds and hearts of the people on themes connected with the religion of every-day life. To Mr. Hepworth religion is not a metaphysical abstraction or a manifestation of sentiment ; it is a personal state or condition, and implies health of body and sane and wholesome ways of living and thinking. This author's latest volume, "Brown Studies ; or, Camp Fires and Morals," sets forth his views on a background of wild wood experiences, through which a charming thread of romance runs. The first chapter takes the reader straight into the heart of the Adirondacks, and introduces him to the attractions of camp-life and to several delightful woodland characters. Amid the scenes and the surroundings thus brought to view, the author takes up such topics as "Do Flowers have Souls?" "Logs and Love," "Families in Boxes," "Mistakes in Marriage," "A Man's World," "Why do we Marry?" etc. What the author really does in the course of this delightfully unconventional narrative is to discuss that ever new and ever old problem of the relations of men and women, with a sincerity of motive, a reverence and candor, that to young readers especially ought to be very helpful. There is not a word of cant or sentimentality in the whole volume ; the tonic influences of uncontaminated nature are in it, and it is full of the generous impulse to make people better and wiser. (Dutton. $1.25.)— *The Beacon.*

Story of Christine Rochefort.

"THIS is an unusual story," says the *Boston Literary World,* "to be the first attempt of a young writer, for, if we mistake not, Mrs. Helen Choate Prince makes in it her *début* before the reading world. It is a story of Blois in our end of the nineteenth century ; the characters are in part working-people, and the problems dealt with are those vexed and difficult ones which concern manufacturing economics and the socialistic agitation. The story ends happily, and throughout exhibits a sweetness and elevation of tone which is in charming contrast to the generality of modern novels. Its theme is unusual, and the grace and delicacy with which it is worked out are more unusual still."

"Anarchism is treated in its pages," says the *Boston Literary Gazette,* "in a masterful and yet impartial way that commands attention. The sufferings of the poor are not concealed; neither are the trials and tribulations of the rich. Life is painted as it is, with the cares that come to every class, high or low—care which neither revolution nor anarchism can relieve. The enthusiastic, honest, theoretical reformer is shown in these pages, as well as the blatant humbug who lives upon the workingman by describing the imaginary relief for all the woes of humanity that would come from deeds of violence. In contrast to these we have the parish priest who goes about unostentatiously doing good. The heroine is an intellectual but weak, visionary woman, who is led astray by the eloquence of a man whom she admires, and she is not in sympathy with her husband, a worthy manufacturer, until she has been tried in the furnace of keen mental suffering. The French provincial town of Blois is the scene of the

principal incidents of the novel, which introduces an exciting uprising of the working-
people. The story is one of our own time,
which cannot fail to excite discussion and lead
to good results, and it is intensely interesting
from cover to cover."

"'The Story of Christine Rochefort,' by
Helen Choate Prince," says the *Portland Transcript,* "is one of a number of novels appearing at just this time, which deal with the
subject of organized labor and its attitude towards capital. It may also be said at once that
it is one of the best of the romances built about
that theme, for this reason, that it really does
show forth the truth of how little the Socialists
are prepared for the power they clamor after,
how slight is often their sense of responsibility,
how reckless and ungoverned their impulses and
passions. Yet the country is full of true sympathy and understanding, its heart beats for
and with the rank and file of the people, as,
indeed, to what else should a God-given heart
respond?"

"While we think that the author has failed,"
says *Public Opinion,* "to fully interpret her
obviously high conception of the
character of De Martel, there
remains a story of much interest,
excellently planned and well
written, with a moral evolved
which in these troublous times
is of value." (Houghton, Mifflin & Co.)

Marshal Ney and History.

JAMES A. WESTON, Rector of
the Church of the Ascension, at
Hickory, a small town of North
Carolina, has just written a very
interesting book entitled "Historic Doubts as to the Execution
of Marshal Ney." Mr. Weston
divides his work into two parts.
In Part I. he gives the life of
Marshal Ney as we all know it
from the pages of a vast literature in almost every language.
In copious foot-notes Mr. Weston gives his authorities for historical statements and quotes
with discretion from the best
known writers upon that most
fascinating of periods—the day
of Napoleon the General, the
Emperor, the deposed exile.

Marshal Ney was born at Saar-
Louis, about twenty-six miles
from Metz, on the 10th of January, 1769. He was carefully
educated by the monks of St.

Augustine, and at the age of thirteen he began
the study of law at the office of the notary of
his native village. He soon yearned for the
excitement and glories of a military life, and
after braving untold hardships to attain his
ambition he enlisted in the army in his nineteenth year. His career is known to all students of history. It is said Wellington dreaded
him more than any general Napoleon ever
sent to meet him. The point of history on
which Mr. Weston casts doubt is the fact that
Marshal Ney was executed for disloyalty to the
Bourbon King in 1815.

In Part II. Mr. Weston gives his varied reasons for believing that Peter S. Ney, who died
at Hickory, North Carolina, in 1846, was the
hero whom Wellington failed to save from the
wrath of the king whom he could have influenced to spare him. This part begins with
a long array of incidents received as historical
upon which time has thrown doubt. It is full
of interest. Mr. Weston writes with vivid enthusiasm and his style is exhilarating.

The publishers have made a very sumptuous
book of this exceptionally attractive and sug-

From "Marshal Ney."　　Copyright, 1896, by Thomas Whittaker.

MARSHAL NEY.

(Engraved by H. R. Cook, 1817.)

gestive material. It is gotten up with the simplicity and richness of an enduring scientific work. Many portraits, fac-similes of handwriting, edicts and decrees signed by great names of the past add to the value and attractiveness of the pages. It is something new and it is put into the very best shape. (Whittaker. $3.)

From " La Jeunesse Doree." Copyright, 1896, by Cushing & Co.

THE OLD WORLD FOR HER GOES SIGHING.

Poets on Poets.

MR. WILLIAM WATSON is the best contemporary illustration of the skill and insight with which poets sometimes comment on their kinsmen, for nobody has said better things in briefer compass about Wordsworth, Shelley, Byron and some other modern poets, than Mr. Watson. It was a happy thought to collect in one volume the criticisms of poets on poetry, confining the selection, in this case, to the writers of English verse. Mrs. Richard Strachey, who acts as the editor of " Poets on Poets," finds that the instinct for criticism is so widely distributed that she is able to quote from almost every great English poet except Marlowe and Shakespeare. She also discovers that, on the whole, the judgment of the poets agrees substantially with the judgment which readers have pronounced. This volume has an essential and permanent value because it presents the judgment, not of a body of men who look at verse in a critical temper, but the work of men inspired by the creative spirit, whose point of view is therefore essentially different from that of the man of distinctively critical temper. (Scribner. $1.25.) —*The Outlook.*

ON A COPY OF SHAKESPEARE'S SONNETS.

THIS is the holy missal Shakespeare wrote,
    For friends to ponder when they grieve alone ;
Within these collects his great heart would note
    Its joy and fear, its ecstasy and moan ;
Our strength and weakness each was felt by him :
    He yearned and shrank, rejoiced and hoped and bled,
Nor ever will his sacred song be dim
    Though he himself, the Friend of Friends, is dead.
Then, on sad evenings when you think of me,
    Or when the morn seems blithe, yet I not near,
Open this book and read, and I shall be
    The meter murmuring at your bended ear :
I cannot write my love with Shakespeare's art,
But the same burden weighs upon my heart.

(Stone & Kimball. $1.25.)—*From "In Russet and Silver."*

TO JACK—WITH REGRETS.

TO-MORROW you'll hear that I'm married
    —To wealth, a smart title, and gout !
And I try to imagine your feelings,
    And your face, when you first find it out.

Perhaps you will inwardly curse me,
    And wish that all women be hurled
To eternal perdition, and mutter,
    " To be sure it's the way of the world."

Perhaps you may reel and grow dizzy,
    Or only feel weary and numb,
While your eyes will grow dim, cold and stony,
    And your lips become ashen and dumb.

Or do only the heroes of romance,
    Behave in this womanish way ?
While the men of the latter-day century,
    But indifference stolid portray ?

Well, be it one way or the other,
    Repressed or proclaimed "*de haute voix,*"
Try to think of my present position,
    And believe I was left without " *choix.*"

Of course it's a very old story—
    Has happened so often before—
Yet it doesn't quite alter the suffering,
    Or make the wrung heart feel less sore.

Remember, whatever may happen,
    How gross be the lie I must live,
All the past was at least true and blameless
    So you've nothing in that to forgive.

For surely I was not to blame, that
    The future I could not foresee,
Or that life is not just what we will it,
    Or that fate has been stronger than me.

(Cushing. $1.50.)—*From Martha Cunningham's " Jeunesse Doree."*

The Mermaid.

FROM L. Dougall one has come to expect a novel of marked originality in motive and conception and of acute philosophical insight in the depiction of character, and the expectation is not disappointed in this author's latest story, "The Mermaid." The opening scenes are laid on Prince Edward Island and the leading character is Caius Simpson, a farmer's son, who receives a good education and by force of circumstances, rather than by special ambition, adopts the medical profession. He is a youth of unusual mental ability, as far as the assimilation of knowledge is concerned, but the creative faculty has been denied him, and his character at critical moments is apt to show infirmity of will. Into his life comes a strange thread of romance, for as he is walking the shore one day he spies a creature that to all appearance is a mermaid of the traditional type, and in his pursuit of the mystery in which this adventure involves him he meets with many singular experiences. Later on the scene changes to one of the Isles St. Magdalen, where an epidemic of diphtheria has broken out among the fishing population, and Caius, summoned by a message, cannot refuse to give the sufferers much-needed professional aid. The romance begun with the discovery of the mermaid is continued under these new conditions, and the mystery deepens, only to be solved at last in a confession of love that for many a day brings more of sorrow than of joy. The story is throughout strong and harmonious in coloring, though abounding in vivid contrasts, and all the characters, from the bewitching and illusive Josephine to the sardonic O'Shea, are genuine flesh and blood. Miss Dougall in all her novels has displayed a knowledge of masculine character that is really wonderful in range and profundity, and particularly so in a woman writer. "The Mermaid" is a novel so far out of the ordinary run of fiction, and so thoroughly artistic in every line, that it is sure to find a hearty welcome from the select few, if not from the sensation-loving many. And in this, her latest story, the sensational, or rather excitingly romantic, element is made telling use of ; the reader's curiosity is kept on edge—and satisfied. (Appleton. $1; pap., 50 c.)— *The Beacon.*

Dame Prism.

THIS is a new story for young people, by Miss Margaret H. Mathews, the author of "Dr. Gilbert's Daughters." It is a very unusual circumstance for an author who has written a popular work to wait over ten years before bringing out another book. Miss Mathews, however, has published no book since her first one, which had such an astonishing success.

The plot of "Dame Prism" is original and exceedingly interesting. A family of children are suddenly thrown upon their own resources, without friends or money. They get permission to live in a railway car, and the book tells how they make a pretty home there, and fight their way to independence. A delightful and helpful story for children, with sixteen half-tone engravings, after original designs by Miss Elizabeth S. Tucker It has a green linen cover with the title daintily stamped in gold and red ink, and with a figure of one of the little heroines in gold. (Stokes. $1.50.)

From "Dame Prism."   Copyright, 1895, by F. A. Stokes Co.

Mr. Bonaparte of Corsica.

"IT is the testimony of all who knew him in his infancy that Napoleon was a good child. He was obedient and respectful to his mother, and sometimes at night, when, on account of some indigestible quality of his food, or other cause, it was necessary for his father to make a series of forced marches up and down the spacious nursery in the beautiful home at Ajaccio, holding the infant warrior in his arms, certain premonitions of his son's future career dawned upon the parent mind. His anguish was voiced in commanding tones; his wails, like his subsequent addresses to his soldiers, were short, sharp, clear and decisive, nor would he brook the slightest halt in these midnight marches until the difficulties which stood in his path had been overcome."

In these words the world obtains a glimpse of Napoleon's early career which never was brought to view before. And for them an eager public is indebted to Mr. John Kendrick Bangs, who includes them in "Mr. Bonaparte of Corsica."

As may be imagined, the volume is a burlesque history of the "Little Corporal," and while it is not a brilliant bit of humorous literature, still it is pleasantly written. Unfortunately, it abounds in puns, some good, others indifferent, and yet others which were better unused. But there is no question as to the book's selling qualities. Coming, as it does, when all the world and his wife is saturated with serious history regarding Napoleon, "Mr. Bonaparte of Corsica" is timely. Then, Mr. McVickar lavishly has illustrated it with drawings really clever; the Messrs. Harper have provided the volume with costly and elegant dress. (Harper. $1.)—*Mail ana Express.*

From "Mr. Bonaparte of Corsica"   Copyright, 1895, by Harper & Brothers.

NAPOLEON'S HEAD-GEAR.

The Hispaniola Plate.

"THE HISPANIOLA PLATE" suggests "Treasure Island"; and Mr. Bloundelle-Burton would probably not object to be styled a disciple of the late Mr. R. L. Stevenson in style as well as in choice of subject and plot. All the same, he has written a strong and fascinating story; and in making 1893 the sequel to 1693, and giving us a second Crafer, and a second Alderly, has proved that he is by no means lacking in inventive power. But the masterful Phips who figures in the first treasure-hunt is, indeed, a hero after Stevenson's own heart, although without blackguardism. He revels in difficulties; and when it falls to him, as it does twice within this book, to quell a mutiny, he literally rises to the occasion in a manner which shows that he had the making, if not of a Nelson, certainly of a Benbow, in him. It must be admitted, however, that the treasure-hunting "business" in the latter part of the book, when the second Crafer, the descendant of Phips' comrade in arms, appears on the scene, is artificial and melodramatic; that the death by the teeth of sharks of the second Joseph Alderly—though being a murderer and a drunkard he richly deserves such a fate—is lamentably conventional; and that the "In Arcady" passages between the younger Crafer and the sister of Joseph Alderly lack inspiration of the Lucy Desborough sort. Mr. Bloundelle-Burton, however, has created Phips, and that is a sufficient achievement for one book. (Cassell. $1.)—*The Academy.*

An English Girl in Samoa.

A SOJOURN of three months or so "In Stevenson's Samoa" is described in an animated and graceful way by Marie Fraser. The author and her friend took a house on the heights back of Apia and were close neighbors of the Stevensons, of whom they saw a great deal. Robert Louis Stevenson himself, under his Samoan appellation of "Tusitala," figures charmingly in the narrative as the kindly host, the adored protector and friend of the natives, and the industrious, unaffected writer of tales. Miss Fraser writes with discretion and good taste of the happy months in which she was practically an inmate of the Stevenson family, and by those who cherish the them the memory of the great author who has recently gone silent these recollections will be warmly cherished. The book is a record of delightfully unconventional experiences, of amusing trials with native servants, and of frequent festivities in the way of birthday or holiday gatherings, or excursions through the beautiful Samoan scenery. Miss Fraser finds much that is attractive to say of the Samoans, who, when they are not depraved by contact with the villainous South Sea traders, seem to have most fascinating qualities. The picture which the author presents of life in Samoa is charming enough to attract many travellers to that favored country. Her style is easy and unpretentious and not lacking in a certain artlessness. She evidently takes pardonable pride in quoting frequently the title by which her Samoan friends and dependents knew her, "Matalanumoana," or, in English, "The fair young stranger with blue eyes from over the seas." It is fair to suppose that existence in Samoa, even under most favorable conditions, is not an unalloyed dream of bliss, but Miss Fraser very rightly emphasizes its delights, and touches briefly, if at all, upon the shadows in the picture. The book has a roughly engraved frontispiece, in which Mr. Stevenson and Miss Fraser are prominent figures. There is a brief laudatory preface by James Payn. (Macmillan. 80 c.)—*The Beacon.*

The Banishment of Jessop Blythe.

IT is a far cry from Russia to the Peak of Derbyshire, and no greater contrast could be devised, both in character and setting, than that between one of Mr. Joseph Hatton's Nihilist romances and his new story, "The Banishment of Jessop Blythe." The romance is set amongst a community of rope-makers who work in "God's Factory," a cavern in the High Peak, named so reverently rather than profanely, and have been free tenants of the Dukes of Devonshire over two hundred years. They are ruled by seven masters, one of whom is the Jessop Blythe of the title, a ne'er-do-well, who is banished by his companions, as the story opens, for his drinking and shiftless habits. In spite of his prominence in the title, he has only a fitful interest in the story, the real interest being centred in his daughter, Adser, a splendid specimen of Derbyshire young womanhood; the fiery young Welshman who has been nominated to a mastership by Blythe, and Geoffrey Lathkill, a gentleman with an interesting personality and Adser's lover. Above this we are inclined to set the vividly descriptive account of this strange rope-making community and its marvellous factory and surroundings. Occasionally Mr. Hatton allows a suggestion of the guide-book to creep into his descriptions, but more often he is fresh and forcible in his delineations of nature's handiwork. Quibbling is hardly a fair return for so delightful a story,

and we may pass it by, along with the masterly touches with which Mr. Hatton sketches in his characters and their surroundings, to the im-

From "Mr. Bonaparte of Corsica." Copyright, 1895, by Harper & Brothers.

MURAT MADE A FLYING-WEDGE.

pressive scene which banishes Jessop Blythe from the home of his boyhood. . . . "The Banishment of Jessop Blythe" displays some art, more than a little power of observation and delineation, and a breezy freshness that carries the reader by storm. It is, in fact, an excellent story, healthy and well conceived, and worked out in the stirring, vigorous style that characterizes Mr. Hatton's romances, whether they are set in the wilds of Russia or amidst the hills and dales of an English landscape. (Lippincott. $1; pap., 50 c.)—*London Literary World.*

The Body-Snatcher.

THE MERRIAM COMPANY has lately published in its pretty miniature "Violet Series," a collection of short stories by well-known writers, "The Body-Snatcher," by Robert Louis Stevenson. We have no recollection of ever having seen this story among the acknowledged writings of Mr. Stevenson; so we suppose he forgot its existence or did not care to preserve it. Judging from internal evidence, we should say it was one of his earliest productions, his choice of the subject which it handles showing a certain immaturity of judgment on his part, and a wilful determination to offend the susceptibilities of readers by his repulsive realism. It possesses a kind of interest and social value as the depiction of a horrible habit that prevailed in the England of sixty or seventy years ago, and filled the minds of the ignorant with superstitious apprehensions; Burke, Hare and other body-snatchers of the period, real or supposititious, disputing the palm of popularity as bogies with Bony, as they saw him in the shop windows in the caricatures of Gilroy and Hone, and as they miscreated him in their stolid British imagination. There is an element in this story which was native to the genius of De Quincey, over which all monstrous crimes exerted a strange fascination, as most of his readers will remember. There is power, but of a disagreeable, uncanny sort, in "The Body-Snatcher." It is always interesting for critics to get at all the work of an author, but the general reader gains little of such a book. (Merriam Co　40c.)

From "The Story of Sonny Sahib," Copyright, 1895, by D. Appleton & Co.

IN INDIAN GARB.

Ballads in Prose.

Miss Nora Hopper's "Ballads in Prose" is one of the most charming results of the Irish literary revival. The "Ballads" are ghost stories, legends, fairy-tales, all the manifold varieties of popular fiction and superstition filling the very air of Ireland, and they alternate with lovely songs, ripples of poetry that seem to have made themselves so cunning in their workmanship. In prose pieces almost without exception, the note is cruelty, the fanciful, unimaginative cruelty which darkens the dreams of a people which has supped full of horrors. Two of the stories, "Aonan na Righ" and "The Gifts of Aodh and Una," are worthy of Mr. Kipling, and indeed all of Miss Hopper's work is more like his than like that of any living author. The peculiar grace and fluency of her verse suggest his to the memory, and the monstrous formless horror that broods over her heathen stories recalls the atmosphere of those Indian tales in which he brings the dread realities of Eastern life before the happier West. If Miss Hopper continue as she has begun, she need fear no rival, not even the Hon. Emily Lawless. (Roberts. $1.50.)—*Boston Pilot.*

The Story of Sonny Sahib.

Once more Mrs. Everard Cotes, with whom we feel more at ease when we think of her as our amusing, delightful entertainer, Miss Sara Jeannette Duncan, has looked over her collection of Indian reminiscences and put a few of her treasured nuggets into a pretty little volume under the title "The Story of Sonny Sahib." Poor little Sonny was born while his mother was separated from all her people after the horrors of the Indian mutiny at Cawnpore. Her husband, a great English soldier, did not even hear of the birth of the little desolate baby. Kind natives forgot all their hatred of English tyrants at the first look of his baby eyes, and he was as carefully protected as if his parents had lived. Indian life and a baby's place in Indian homes are described with all the author's genial humor and love of her kind. The illustrations are full of life and character and specially good. A charming book for the vacation satchel. (Appleton. $1.)

From " Lingua Gemmæ,"
Copyright, 1894, by
The Merriam Co.

Lingua Gemmæ.

As there is a language of flowers, so there is one of gems. In the pretty volume under notice, Ada L. Sutton has made the effort to give "a clear, concise and comprehensive language of gems, and to illustrate the subjects with appropriate literary selections." There are stones appropriate to the months, and you may learn that if you were born in April you are entitled to such congratulations as only a diamond will confer. January would be a comparatively inexpensive month in case a lover made a gift, for then a garnet would suffice, whereas the necessary accompaniments of a young lady born in May would be an emerald, or if born in July, a ruby. Possibly the superstition about the opal will never pass away, though Mrs. Sutton says that to October belongs this changeable stone.

Precious stones convey, in part, a certain potency irrespective, of course, of their size or quality. To wear a ruby endows you with courage and success in a dangerous crisis. Sport a sapphire and you will be endowed with constancy. We might all be faithful providing we wore the topaz in sufficient quantity, and be wealthy by means of the turquois. No use is there for the fountain of perpetual youth. Carry about with you a beryl, and then everlasting youth will be yours. Beware, however, of the young person who has a predilection for amber. Even the man who smokes a pipe with an amber mouthpiece should be cautious, because this resinous mineral inclines the wearer to disdain. A nagging wife, a cantankerous husband need not call on Dr. Edson or Marion Harland to suggest a cure ; all that would be necessary would be for them to wear onyx, for that enforces conjugal felicity. (Merriam Co. $1.50.)—*N. Y. Times.*

The Golden Pomp.

FLITTING, like the busy bee, over the flowering clover-field of English lyric poetry, Mr. Quiller Couch has gathered rich store of honey. His harvest bears the mysterious label of " The Golden Pomp." The riddle is solved on the title-page by the motto from Ovid, "*Aurea pompa venit.*" In a preface that whets the reader's appetite, the chronicler of the Delectable Duchy defines a lyric as " a short poem—essentially melodious in rhythm and structure —treating summarily of a single thought, feeling, or situation." The selections, 361 in number, are arranged according to kinship of subject rather than chronologically. Shakespeare leads off with " Hark, Hark, the Lark," and other gushes of lyric joy at the advent of spring follow. " The Love Call," an anonymous Theocritan duet between Phyllida and Corydon, is perfect in its artful simplicity. We cannot resist the temptation to quote a stanza:

Phyllida : Here are cherries ripe for my Corydon ;
  Eat them for my sake.

Corydon : Here's my oaten pipe, my lovely one,
  Sport for thee to make.

Phyllida : Here are .hreads, my t ue love, fine as silk,
  To knit thee, to knit thee,
A pair of stockings white as milk.

Corydon : Here are reeds, my true love, fine and neat,
  To make thee, to make thee,
A bonnet to withs'and the heat.

Lately, we believe, Mr. J. M. Barrie has been spending a good deal of time at Fowey with Mr. Couch. Are we right in assuming that the author of "My Lady Nicotine" suggested the inclusion of Robert Wisdome's

A RELIGIOUS USE OF TAKING TOBACCO.

The Indian weed withered quite
Green at morn, cut down at nigh
Shows thy decay ; all flesh is hay;
  Thus think, then drink tobacco.

And when the smoke ascends on high,
Think thou beholds the vanity
Of worldly stuff ; gone with a puff :
  Thus think, then drink tobacco

But when the pipe grows foul within
Think of thy soul defiled with sin,
And that the fire doth it require :
  Thus think, then drink tobacco.

The ashes that are left behind
May serve to put thee still in mind
That unto dust return thou must :
  Thus think, then drink tobacco.

We imagine the modern smoker prefers to ruminate over more cheerful things. Forty pages of notes are models of what notes ought to be —throwing much light on recondite allusions, parallels and sources. (Lippincott. $2.)—*London Literary World.*

The Literary News.

An Eclectic Monthly Review of Current Literature.
EDITED BY A. H. LEYPOLDT.

MAY, 1895.

THE BEGINNING OF THE END.

THE recent exposure and the prompt apprehension of the leader, if not the originator, of a particularly noxious school of moral perversion in literature, art and social conditions awaken the hope that they may result in a healthy reaction against the public exhibition of the intellectual and moral disease which during the past few years has been growing more and more dangerous and shameless.

We fear the subtle moral poison which Mr. Wilde and his followers have helped to inject into our literature and art has taken such hold upon a large part of the public that its effects cannot be suddenly shut off and hidden from sight; but doubtless the malady will now be recognized as disease instead of as "originality," "higher culture," "art for art's sake," "the expanding of individuality," etc., all through the long list, of which even the vocabulary is loathsome to a healthy man, and of which the literature is synonymous with boredom. The symptoms of this disease—idleness, unrest, discontent, selfishness, craving for notoriety—will, we hope, be more carefully watched and their causes treated by those who have kept themselves clear of the pestilence, and who may still be able to direct the misguided emotions of their fellow-beings.

Max Nordau's book on "Degeneration" has been published in English just at a time when its perhaps rather sweeping statements may help to make clear the nature of this degeneracy that seems to be the present curse of people tempted to fads and ego-mania by the leisure that should be a privilege, and an incentive to profitable aspiration. In this book Mr. Nordau devotes several pages to Oscar Wilde, whom he considers as a type of the special kind of degeneration that is a disease recognized by alienists, whose victims should be watched and confined permanently that they may not injure their fellow-mortals. Oscar Wilde himself has stated in his "Intentions," that "even a color sense is more important in the development of the individual than a sense of right and wrong." He has contended that no check of conventionality or fitness or morality should be put upon the imagination of the artist in color, sculpture or letters. Max Nordau comments upon this that "there is a candor which is wholly inadmissible. The artist may be criminal by organic disposition. We do not permit homicidal maniacs, incendiaries, thieves and vagabonds

to expand their individualities in crime, and just as little should we permit the degenerate artist to expand his individuality in immoral works of art and literature."

For the past few years we have been flooded with works of imagination, chiefly novels, that have testified to such lack of control in the author's nature. Some of these books have shown artistic literary technique that seemed to give them a right to exist, but the great mass of these books have had their source in an hysterical craving for notoriety. Sound common sense, natural instincts, healthy men and women, normal social conditions, have been almost wholly lost sight of. There has been a malevolent mania for contradiction, an egomaniacal recklessness, an hysterical longing to make a sensation justified by no exalted aim, serving no apparent purpose whatever. The disciples of this school, setting aside all idea of beauty, have strained after striking subjects and harrowing details. Morbid conditions of mind and body especially have been so popular as to lead the *American Medico-Surgical Journal,* in a recent issue, to remark sarcastically that "as yet there exists no novel of the ear, no drama of the digestive organs, no romance of the kidneys, no pastels of the intestines. Blindness, idiocy, simple mania with delusions, visions and bright lights of hysteria and epilepsy, have each in turn served the modern writer of fiction. Later, it is not unreasonable to expect that several ailments in one book may further the general interest of the twentieth-century romance, when each department of pathology shall have its own special novel." All this is bad enough when well done, but when cheaply imitated it reaches the very lowest form of nastiness.

The public, unfortunately, has been inoculated with the poison of degeneracy, and its demand for more and more of these stories, false to every principle of truth and decency, has brought into the market a host of writers that we should like to see as effectually put out of sight as we hope the notorious English æsthete will be. Publishers should discourage authors who bring these wares to them for publication, and all healthy men and women should be as much ashamed to be in the company of such books as to be in the company of the shameless men and more shameless women they describe. We trust in Mr. Nordau's prediction that time will surely banish this self-limited disease. He has had his book reviewed by many critics, among them W. D. Howells, who disagrees with many of his views. We wish all would read "Degeneracy" for themselves, and form their own conclusions, and do their part towards bringing about reform in this direction.

MAGAZINE ARTICLES.

Articles marked with an asterisk are illustrated.

ARTISTIC, MUSICAL AND DRAMATIC.—*Atlantic*, A Standard Theatre, T. R. Sullivan ; Some Notes on the Art of John La Farge, Cecilia Waern.—*Cath. World*, Genius of Leonardo da Vinci,* O'Shea.—*Century*, Rubinstein, McArthur.—*Chautauquan*. German Drama, Whitman.—*Fort. Review* (Apr.), Landscape at the National Gallery, John Brett.—*Godey's*, Artists in their Studios,* W. A. Cooper ; Music in America — Ethelbert Nevin, Hughes ; The Museum of the Prado,* Cortissoz. — *Nine. Century* (Apr.), Plays of Thomas Heywood, Swinburne. — *Scribner's*, Wood-Engravers — Stéphane Pannemaker;* French Posters and Book Covers,* Arsène Alexandre.— *West. Review* (Apr.), Shakespeare and a Municipal Theatre, Dillon.

BIOGRAPHY, CORRESPONDENCE. — *Chautauquan*, Gen. Zachary Taylor, R. D. St. John.—*Forum*, Prince Bismarck, T. A. Dodge.—*Lippincott's*, A Young Corean Rebel (Soh Kwang Pom), Haddo Gordon.—*Pop. Science*, The Illustrious Boerhaave, W. T. Lusk (Por.).

DESCRIPTION, TRAVEL.—*Atlantic*, Christmas Shopping at Assuân, Agnes Repplier.—*Cath. World*, Corner of Arcadie,* M. A. Taggart ; Bit of the Old World in the New, H. A. Adams; Glimpses of Italy,* E. C. Foster.—*Godey's*, How to Go to Europe for Three Hundred Dollars,* J. A. Locke.—*Harper's*, In Sunny Mississippi, J. Ralph ; Some Wanderings in Japan,* A. Parsons.—*McClure's*, Gaston Tissandier, the Balloonist,* R. H. Sherard.—*Outing*, The Paris of China (Pekin), Annetta J. Halliday-Antona.

DOMESTIC AND SOCIAL.—*Chautauquan*, Fashions of the Nineteenth Century, Alice M. Earle. —*West. Review* (Apr.), Evolution of the Sex, A. G. P. Sykes.

EDUCATIONAL.—*Cath. World*, Centenary of Maynooth College,* G. McDermot.—*Godey's*, Bryn Mawr College,* Madeline V. Abbott.—*McClure's*, A Prairie College* (Knox), Madame Blanc.—*North Am. Review*, Elementary Education, W. T. Harris.

FICTION.—*Atlantic*, A Faithful Failure, Eliza O. White.—*Cath. World*, Le Père Philippe, Mary B. O'Reilly; Sae's Lamp, F. A. Doughty. —*Century*, The Princess Sonia,* I., Julia Magruder ; Lucinda,* L. E. Mitchell ; Two Shadowy Rivals, R. M. Johnston; Regret, Kate Chopin.—*Chautauquan*, Story of Fidelity, Eleanor Lambec.—*Godey's*, Modern Sympathy,* Eleanor Waddle; An Unsettled Account,* M. Orde ; The Sphinx,* F. C. Williams.—*Harper's*, La Tinaja Bonita,* O. Wister ; By Hook or Crook,* R. Grant ; Dutch Kitty's White Slippers,* J. Ralph.—*Lippincott's*, The Lady of Las Cruces, Christian Reid ; Odds on the Gun ; Martha's Headstone, Edith Brower.—*McClure's*, What She Could, Ian Maclaren ; A Game Postponed, Gertrude Smith.—*Outing*, Chestnuts with a History, Margaret B. Rudd ; Old Uncle Vanderveer, E. Fawcett.—*Scribner's*, Story of Bessie Costrell, I., Mrs. H. Ward ; A Short Study in Evolution, Abbe C. Goodloe.

HISTORY.—*Atlantic*, Dr. Rush and Gen. Washington, P. L. Ford.—*Chautauquan*, Queer Customs of the City of London, J. C. Thornley.—*Lippincott's*, Effacing the Frontier, W. T. Larned.—*McClure's*, The Second Funeral of Napoleon,* Ida M. Tarbell.—*Pop. Science*, Archæology in Denmark,* F. Starr.

INDUSTRIAL —*Lippincott's*, On a Shad-Float, D. B. Fitzgerald.—*Pop. Science*, Office of Luxury, P. L. Beaulieu ; Woman as an Inventor and Manufacturer.*

LITERARY.—*Atlantic*, Leconte de Lisle, P. T. Lafleur.—*Chautauquan*, Some Curiosities of Scottish Literature, W. W. Smith ; Journalism in the Protestant Episcopal Church, G. A. Carstensen.—*Fort. Review* (Apr.), Literary Degenerates, Janet E. Hogarth.—*Forum*, The Government as a Great Publisher, A. R. Spofford — *Lippincott's*, An Artist's Habitat, W. T. Linton.—*McClure's*, Journalism, C. A. Dana.— *North Am. Review*, Glimpses of Charles Dickens, C. Dickens, the younger.—*West Review* (Apr.), Arthur Schopenhauer, M. Todhunter ; Poetry of Christina G. Rossetti, Alice Law.

NATURE AND SCIENCE.—*Atlantic*, Mars, I., Atmosphere, P. Lowell ; A Week on Walden's Ridge, I., B. Torrey; Tramps with an Enthusiast, Olive T. Miller.—*Century*, Conquest of Arid America,* W. E. Smythe.—*Godey's*, The Angora Cat,* R. K. James.—*Lippincott's*, High Fliers and Low Fliers, W. Warren Brown ; The Menu of Mankind, C. D. Wilson.—*North Am. Review*, Progress of Meteorology, F. Waldo ; Latest News of Mars, E. S. Holden (Notes and Comments).—*Pop. Science*, An Old Naturalist* (Conrad Gesner), W. K. Brooks ; Work of the Naturalist in the World, C. S. Minot ; Race Mixture and National Character, L. R. Harley. —*Scribner's*, Will the Electric Motor Supersede the Steam Locomotive ? J. Wetzler.

POETRY.—*Cath. World*, Agnes of Dunbar, Lilian A. B. Taylor.—*Century*, Unanswered, C. B. Going ; A Norse Child's Requiem, B. Carman ; Land of Lost Hopes, Edith M. Thomas.— *Harper's*, Grass and Flowers, J. V. Cheney.— *Scribner's*, Fool's Gold, Edith M. Thomas ; The Wind, Munkittrick ; Into the Dark, Winter.

POLITICAL AND SOCIAL.—*Atlantic*, Political Depravity of the Fathers, J. B. McMaster.— *Century*, A Chapter of Municipal Folly, A. C. Bernheim.—*Fort. Review* (Apr.), Historical Aspect of the Monetary Question, A. Del Mar ; China Problem and Its Solution, E. T. C. Werner.—*Forum*, Canadian and American Systems of Government, J. G. Bourinot ; Future of the Great Arid West, E. V. Smalley ; Coming Equality of Opportunity, C. D. Wright.—*Harper's*, Men's Work Among Women, B. Morgan. —*McClure's*, Tammany, E. J. Edwards.—*Nine. Century* (Apr.), Some American Impressions and Comparisons, Elizabeth L. Banks.—*North Am. Review*, Our Situation as Viewed from Without, Goldwin Smith ; Russia and England, A. Vambéry ; Income Tax : Decision of the Supreme Court, G. S. Boutwell ; Future of Japan, Japanese Minister.—*Scribner's*, Art of Living—Occupation,* R. Grant.

SPORTS AND AMUSEMENTS.—*Forum*, Can We Revive the Olympic Games ? P. Shorey.—*Outing*, Fitting Out for a Cruise, A. J. Kenealy ; Oxford in the Eights Week, Evelyn Burnblum. —*Scribner's*, Golf,* H. E. Howland.

THEOLOGY, RELIGION AND SPECULATION. — *Nine. Century* (Apr.), Foundations of Belief, Martineau ; What Is Church Authority? Carter.—*North Am. Review*, The Preacher and His Province, Gibbons ; Judaism and Unitarianism, Harris (Notes and Comments).—*Pop. Science*, Kidd on "Social Evolution," Le Sueur.

Survey of Current Literature.

☞ *Order through your bookseller.*—"*There is no worthier or surer pledge of the intelligence and the purity of any community than their general purchase of books; nor is there any one who does more to further the attainment and possession of these qualities than a good bookseller.*"—PROF. DUNN.

ART, MUSIC, DRAMA.

BOLTON, *Mrs.* ʲHENRIETTA IRVING. The Madonna of St. Luke : the story of a portrait; with an introductory letter by Daniel Huntington. Putnam. 12°, $1.25.

All that is known about the portraits of the Virgin Mary which tradition tells us were painted by the Evangelist St. Luke is included in this little volume. The most venerated of these portraits is that preserved in the Church of Santa Maria Maggiore, Rome, and the book opens with an account of the miraculous circumstances attending the foundation of that basilica. In four sections the author writes of St. Luke as a painter, narrates the history of the Madonna in the Borghese Chapel, shows the influence of the portrait upon art, and describes a score of paintings and sculptures commonly attributed to St. Luke. The illustrations are chiefly from paintings by old masters.

ECHEGARAY, José. The son of Don Juan: an original drama in three acts; tr. by Ja. Graham. Roberts. por. 16°, $1.

" Echegaray is the Spanish Ibsen. He has more fire and more of the old spirit of romance than the Norwegian pessimist, but he can be just as commonplace and cold-blooded when he chooses to be, and he is quite as brilliant an example of ' degeneration,' in Dr. Max Nordau's application of that word. In this unpleasant but powerful study of social and physical disease he is avowedly a follower of Ibsen. The work was suggested by a reading of Ibsen's play we know as 'Ghosts.' The play is neither so simple nor so strong as 'Ghosts,' but Echegaray has a sense of humor which the prophet of Norway seems to lack. A sense of humor in this kind of a work is as incongruous, however, as laughter at the dissecting-table. Mr. Graham provides an informing sketch of the career of Echegaray, who is sixty-three years old, and a native of Madrid; a mathematician, and a linguist; ' commenced dramatist ' at the age of forty-two (the age at which his Don Juan married), and has written fifty savory pieces. In his translation Mr. Graham clings peristently to Spanish idioms."—*N. Y. Times.*

EHRLICH, A. Celebrated pianists of the past and present time: a collection of 116 biographies. Scribner. pors. 8°, $3.

FORD, J. The broken heart ; ed., with notes and introduction, by Clinton Scollard. Holt. 16°, (English readings ser.) bds., 40 c.

" Possibly 1632 or 1633 is the date of John Ford's masterpiece. ' The broken heart.' Born in 1586, Ford died in 1640, and he lived in what Mr. Scollard appropriately terms 'the period of dramatic decline.' On ' The broken heart' Charles Lamb bestowed unstinted praise. It was the catastrophe in the play that Lamb thought was ' so grand, so solemn, and so surprising.' Swinburne, too, of latter-day critics, eulogizes the play. ' Other tragic poems have closed as grandly, with as much or more of moral and poetic force ; none, I think, with such solemn power of spectacular and spiritual effect combined.' The volume, in neat form, with its careful editing, is a valuable addition to that collection the publishers designate as ' English readings.' "—*N. Y. Times.*

MOLIÈRE, J. BAPT. P. DE. Dramatic works; tr. by Katharine Prescott Wormeley. In 6 v. V. 3, Les femmes savantes; Le malade imaginaire. Roberts. 12°, hf. rus., $1.50.

Molière's object in *Les femmes savantes* is to laugh at female pedantry; it is considered one of his best plays, and was first acted at the Théâtre du Palais-Royal, March 11, 1672. *Le malade imaginaire* was the last play Molière wrote; it is a comedy dealing with the love of life and the fear of death. A sketch of the Hôtel de Rambouillet introduces the first play.

WALKER, FRANCIS. Letters of a baritone. Scribner. 12°, $1.25.

These letters, written from ʲFlorence and covering a period of a year and a half, not only give a detailed narrative of the experiences of a young American student of the art of singing, but picture also with sympathy other phases of art life in Italy, and reveal many glimpses, full of charm and color, of the people themselves, their manners, customs, and ways of thought.

BIOGRAPHY, CORRESPONDENCE, ETC.

CLARK, T. M. (*Bp.*) Reminiscences. Whittaker. por. 12°, $1.20.

These reminiscences of the learned and genial Bishop of Rhode Island are brimful of good stories. His review of men and things runs back more than sixty years.

CUTTS, E. L., *D.D.* Augustine of Canterbury. Houghton, Mifflin & Co. 12°, (English leaders of religion ser.) $1.

The career of the first archbishop of Canterbury at the close of the sixth century, when Ethelbert was king of Kent, is narrated in effective style, his sagacious methods and remarkable success are fitly described. Contains a chronological table, a pedigree of the kings of Kent, a pedigree of the Frank kings, and a table of bishops.

FORBES, ARCHIBALD. Colin Campbell, Lord Clyde. Macmillan. 12°, (English men of action ser.) flex. cl., 60 c.; bds., 75 c.

HUBBARD, ELBERT. Little journeys to the homes of good men and great. Putnam. Published monthly, 50 cts. per year. Single copies, 5 cts.

Already issued : George Eliot, Thomas Carlyle, John Ruskin, W. E. Gladstone.

LEE, H. BOYLE. Napoleon Bonaparte: the story of the soldier, the ruler, the prisoner of state: from the history of the past and present centuries. Warne. il.*12°, 75 c.

LOWE, C. Prince Bismarck. Roberts Bros. por. 12°, $1.25.

LUCY, H. W. The Right Honorable W. E. Gladstone: a story from life. Roberts. por. 12°, $1.25.

DESCRIPTION, GEOGRAPHY, TRAVEL, ETC.

BURWELL, LETITIA M. A girl's life in Virginia before the war; il. by W. A. McCullough and Jules Turcas. F. A. Stokes Co. il. 12°, $1.50.
The lady who wrote this sketch belongs to one of the best known and oldest families of the south, and speaks of her subject with authority. She gives a very delightful picture of life on an old-fashioned plantation before the war, where slaves were treated with the greatest care and kindness.

FRASER, MARIE. In Stevenson's Samoa. Macmillan. 1 il. 12°, 80 c.

HOLCOMBE, CHESTER. The real Chinaman. Dodd, Mead & Co. il. 12°, $2.

LARNED, WALTER CRANSTON. Churches and castles of mediæval France. Scribner. il. 8°, $1.50.

NORMAN, H. The peoples and politics of the far East ; travels and studies in the British, French, Spanish, and Portuguese colonies, Siberia, China, Japan, Korea, Siam, and Malaya. Scribner. maps, por. il. 8°, $4.

FICTION.

ARGLES, MRS. MARY, [" The Duchess," *pseud.*, *now* Mrs. Hungerford.] The O'Connors of Ballinahinch. United States Book Co. 12°, (Lakewood ser., no. 6.) pap., 50 c.

BAGBY, ALBERT MORRIS. Miss Träumerei: a Weimar idyl. Albert Morris Bagby. 12°, $1.50.
Weimar, during the closing years of the life of Franz Liszt, is described with sympathy. The classes held by Liszt for the pianists of the world, in which they played before one another and received the criticism of the master, furnish most of the events. Many of the masterpieces of Beethoven, Schumann and Liszt are played by the various artists and described in detail. The hero and heroine are Americans, she a piano virtuosa, he a marvellous tenor.

BARR, ROB. The face and the mask; il. by A. Hencke. F. A. Stokes Co. 16°, buckram, 75 c.
Twenty-four short stories, by the author of ' In the midst of alarms."

BRAINERD, T. H. Go forth and find. Cassell. nar. 12°, (Unknown lib., no. 36.) 50 c.
An old-fashioned love-tale, laid chiefly on the seacoast of Southern California. The characters are few. A married couple, the man's friend, the woman's sister spend a glorious summer full of musical interests. The friend is composing a new musical poem on Tristram and Yseult. That men are made or marred by women is the leading thought.

BURNHAM, CLARA LOUISE, Miss Bagg's secretary: a West Point romance. Houghton, Mifflin & Co. 16°, (Riverside pap. ser., no. 67.) pap., 50 c.

BURTON, J. BLOUNDELLE. The Hispaniola plate (1683–1893). Cassell Pub. Co. 12°, $1.

CHAMBERS, ROB. W. The king in yellow. F. Tennyson Neely. nar. 16°, (Neely's prismatic lib.) 75 c.
" The repairer of reputations," " The mask." " The court of the dragon," and " The yellow sign," the four opening stories, relate chiefly to " The king in yellow," and are fantastic and gruesome. The other stories have their scene in the Quartier Latin, Paris, and are named : " The demoiselle D'Ys," " The prophets' paradise," " The street of the four winds," " The street of the first shell," " The street of our lady of the fields " and " Rue Barrée." By the author of " In the quarter."

COFFIN, C. CARLETON. Daughters of the Revolution and their times, 1769–1776: an historical romance. Houghton, Mifflin & Co. por. map, il. 12°, $1.50.

DAVIS, R. HARDING. The Princess Aline ; il. by C. D. Gibson. Harper. 12°, $1.25.
The hero is a portrait painter strangely susceptible to the charms of the beautiful sex, even when presented in painting or photograph. He succumbs to the fascination of a newspaper portrait of the Princess Aline, the sister of a little German duke of a smaller German Duchy, and immediately leaves America and chases around the cities of Europe in quest of his lady-love. The details of this search and the story of the woman who finally makes a lasting impression make a humorous novelette.
" It is all very bright and pleasing."—*N. Y. Times.*

DEFOE, DAN. Romances and narratives ; ed. by G. A. Aitken; il. by J. B. Yeats. In 16 v. V. 1, The surprising adventures of Robinson Crusoe. V. 2, The farther adventures of Robinson Crusoe. V. 3, The serious reflections of Robinson Crusoe. Macmillan. 3 v., il. por. 8°, $3 ; *limited ed.*, 3 v., $5.

DOUGALL, *Miss* LILY. The mermaid: a lovetale. Appleton. 12°, (Appleton's town and country lib., no. 163.) $1 ; pap., 50 c.

DOYLE, A. CONAN. The mystery of Cloomber. R. F. Fenno & Co. 12°, $1 ; pap., 50 c.
Cloomber Hall was a lonely, uninhabited house, on a Scotch estate within sight of the Irish Sea. All at once an English officer, who has seen service in India, and has a distinguished record, moves into it, with his wife and two children. He erects a high board fence all around the estate, and shows, by many other eccentricities, that he lives in constant terror of a sudden and violent death. The story unravels the mystery. Buddhists and East Indians play a part in a vivid, strange narrative.

GARDNER, G. E. A treasure found—a bride won : a novel ; il. by M. Colin. [*Also*] The swamp secret. Bonner. 12°, (Ledger lib., no. 122.) $1 ; pap., 50 c.
The search for a buried treasure on an uninhabited island of the southern seas, with the dangers and adventures connected with it, is the

subject of the first story. "The swamp secret" is the story of frontier revenge, visited upon a fascinating horse thief.

GERARD, DOROTHEA. An arranged marriage. Appleton. 12°, (Appleton's town and country lib., no. 164.) $1; pap.. 50 c.
The efforts of a self-made Englishman of great wealth to get into society is the leading motive. Finding that his dearly acquired estate and his display of riches fail to catch his country neighbors, he concludes that rank and connections may, and these he determines to obtain through his young daughter. Visiting a health resort in Southern Tyrol near the border of Italy, he meets by accident an impoverished Italian princess, who has an only son, an officer in the Austrian army. The old people plot to marry their young people, exchanging wealth for a title. The unexpected behavior of the principals in the arranged marriage is a fresh and unconventional element.

HATTON, JOS. The banishment of Jessop Blythe: a novel. Lippincott. 12°, (Lippincott select novels, no. 167.) $1; pap., 50 c.

HOPE, ANTHONY, [*pseud.* for Anthony Hope Hawkins.] Sport royal, and other stories. Holt. il. nar. 12°, (Buckram ser.) buckram, 75 c.
Contents: Sport royal; A tragedy in outline; A malapropos parent; How they stopped the run; A little joke; A guardian of morality; Not a bad deal; Middleton's model; My astral body; The Nebraska loadstone; A successful rehearsal.
"Perhaps in 'Sport royal' may be found the germ of that clever romance of Mr. Anthony Hope's 'The prisoner of Zenda.' With maturer powers, in the latter story the author has expanded incidents and accentuated characters. What Mr. Hope has is a Dumas way of conceiving things, given clearly with action, and a snap with a click to his dialogue. It's the 'go' in Anthony Hope which is so taking." — *N. Y. Times.*

LINTON, *Mrs.* ELIZA LYNN. The new woman; In haste and at leisure. The Merriam Co. 12°, $1.50.

LONG, J. LUTHER. Miss Cherry-Blossom of Tôkyô. Lippincott. 12°, $1.25.

MACDONALD, G. Annals of a quiet neighborhood. [*New ed.*] Harper. 12°, (Harper's Franklin sq. lib., new ser., no. 759.) pap.. 50 c.

MOORE, FRANK FRANKFORT. They call it love. Lippincott. 12°, (Lippincott's select novels, no. 168.) $1; pap., 50 c.
Two English girls having spent their lives in acquiring knowledge begin to feel their lives empty of living interests. Miss Cosway is the daughter of a man who has spent his life writing a history of the second century. After writing essays that have ranked her with the third Wrangler at Oxford she feels it her mission to demonstrate to the world that the higher education of woman is responsible for the decay of marriage. Her friend's life is almost wrecked by the lessons she has learned in studying the laws of hered'ty. An American spinster supplies the comic elements. The book is perhaps intended as a parody on the popular novels of the day.

MORRISON, ARTHUR. Tales of mean streets. Roberts. 12°, $1.
An introduction by James MacArthur to the American edition gives some facts relative to Arthur Morrison. His first sketch, "A street," appeared in *Macmillan's Magazine* in Oct. of 1891; it attracted a good deal of attention and was the incentive to this series of short stories and studies describing London East End life with all its miserable sin, poverty and degradation. Mr. Morrison's material was gathered as secretary of an old Charity Trust. "Lizerunt," "Squire Napper," "Without visible means," "Three rounds," "A poor stick," are a few of the titles.

MULHOLLAND, ROSA, Banshee Castle; il. by J. H. Bacon, Scribner. 12°, $1.50.

NODIER, C. Trilby, the fairy of Argyle: tr. [from the French], with introduction, by Nathan Haskell Dole. 1st ed. Estes & Lauriat. sq. 12°, 50 c.

NODIER, C. Trilby, the fairy of Argyle; from the French, by Minna Caroline Smith. Lamson, Wolffe & Co. sq. 16°, bds., 50 c.

PENDERED, MARY L. A pastoral played out. Cassell. 12°, $1.
The author of "Dust and laurels" has here imagined a heroine in strong contrast to the advanced woman of her former story. Gylda Mariold is a beautiful, healthy country girl, who in deference to her lover's theories consents to live with him without a legal or religious ceremony. Driven by debts, this lover marries a Russian princess. Gylda in no manner blames her lover. She leads a wholly noble life and in the end again gives herself to this lover after the princess has become a theosophist and decided that Gylda will make a better wife for her remarkable husband.

PRINCE, HELEN CHOATE. The story of Christine Rochefort. Houghton, Mifflin & Co. 12°, $1.25.

QUEIROS, ECA DE. Dragon's teeth: a novel; from the Portuguese, by Mary J. Serrano. Houghton, Mifflin & Co. 16°, (Riverside pap. ser., extra no. 67.) pap., 50 c.

RHOSCOMYL, OWEN. The jewel of Ynys Galon: being a hitherto unprinted chapter in the history of the sea rovers. Longmans, Green & Co. il. 12°, $1.25.
Seven generations before the story opens, the dying Morgan Dhu, a dreaded pirate whose stronghold was the island of Ynys Galon, off the mainland of Wales, called his twenty-one stalwart sons about him and gave them instructions for the guarding of the Jewel of Ynys Galon. This jewel had been the front-piece in the turban of the Sultan of Algiers and had been brought home with other trophies, among them the favorite slave of the Sultan. The writer is supposed to have deciphered the sensational, blood-thirsty tale from two manuscripts, rescued from the flames and both badly damaged.

RUSSELL, FRANCES E. A quaint spinster. Roberts. 16°, 60 c.

SHELTON, W. H. A man without a memory, and other stories. Scribner. 16°, $1.
Contents: A man without a memory; The

wedding journey of Mrs. Zaintree (born Green-leaf); Uncle Obadiah's Uncle Billy; The missing evidence in "The people *vs.* Dangerking"; "The demented ones"; The horses that responded; "Lights out! 'Liz'beth Rachael"; The widow of the general; The adventures of certain prisoners.

SMOLLETT, TOBIAS G. Novels; il. by G. Cruikshank; with short memoir and bibliography. V. 1, Roderick Random. V. 2 and 3. Peregrine Pickle. Macmillan. 8°, (Bohn's lib.) *net, ea.,* $1.

STEVENSON, ROB. L. The body-snatcher. The Merriam Co. il. sq. 24°, (Merriam's violet ser., no. 2.) 40 c.

TINSEAU, LÉON DE. A forgotten debt, (*Dette oubliée;*) from the French, by Florence Belknap Gilmour. *Authorized ed.* Lippincott. 12°, $1.
    "M. Léon de Tinseau, in depicting Grenoble and the de Bernar family, shows you what is provincial life with its dead monotony. Mlle. Chantal de Monestier is a girl of a noble family, for in Savoy there is an aristocracy dating back from the remotest past. But Mademoiselle had no money, and so she was brought up in a convent. She became an honest, pious young woman, with the most fixed perceptions of what was right or wrong, and with a will of her own.
    "The scene shifts to America, and in his description of Western life, the author shows how vivid must have been his impressions. As Americans, we should feel highly flattered with such views, social or other, as the author takes of us."—*N. Y. Times.*

TRACY, J. P. Shenandoah: a story of Sheridan's great ride. Novelist Pub. Co. 12°, (War ser., v. 1, no. 1.) pap., 25 c.

HISTORY.

DYER, T. F. THISELTON. Strange pages from family papers. Dodd, Mead & Co. il. 12°, $1.50.
    From the histories of the great families of Great Britain are taken the remarkable and romantic incidents and episode gathered together under the following headings: Fatal curses, the screaming skull; eccentric vows; strange banquets; mysterious rooms; indelible blood-stains; curious secrets; the dead hand; devil compacts; family death omens; weird possessions; romance of disguise; extraordinary disappearances; honored hearts; romance of wealth; lucky accidents; fatal passion.

LOVE, W. DE LOSS. *jr.* The fast and thanksgiving days of New England. Houghton, Mifflin & Co. il. fac-simile, 12°, $3.
    An historical study. The author describes the holy seasons of the church, from the time of Gregory the Great; reviews the efforts of Separatists and some Conformists to compromise on the Feasts of Christ; Fasts and Thanksgiving Days in England; and Fasts of the Exiles (in Holland). He gives an account of the Harvest Festival at Plymouth in 1621; of the Fasts and Feasts of New Netherland; the Autumn Thanksgiving Day and the Annual Spring Fast; Fasts occasioned by witchcraft,

Indian and other wars, earthquakes, etc.; the Good Friday Fast in Connecticut, and the Political Fast in Massachusetts, etc., etc.

McMASTER, J. BACH. A history of the people of the United States from the Revolution to the Civil War. In 6 v. V. 4. Appleton. 12°, $2.50.
    The fourth volume opens with the repeal of the British Orders in Council and the close of the armistice concluded just before the surrender of Hull, and takes up the story of the second war for independence. The chapter called "The return of peace" ends the story of the war, and gives with great fulness an account of the treaty-making at Ghent. At this point a new era opens in our history. The war is over, the foreign complications which distracted the country since 1793 no longer trouble it, and the people begin to turn their attention to domestic affairs. The remainder of the volume therefore treats of our economic history. "The disorders of the currency" is a chapter in our annals which has never before been told. Chapters in political reforms, the Missouri Compromise, and the hard times of 1819 and 1820 complete the volume, which is illustrated with many diagrams and maps in outline and in color.

PAINE, T. The writings of Thomas Paine, coll. and ed. by Moncure Daniel Conway. In 4 v. V. 3, 1791-1804. Putnam. 8°, $2.50.
    Contents : Letters to the authors of *Le Républicain*, to the Abbé Sieyes, to Onslow Cranley, to Jefferson, Dantan, George Washington and others ; and essays and other documents. Some of the essays are : On the propriety of bringing Louis XVI. to trial ; Reasons for preserving the life of Louis Capet ; Shall Louis XVI. have respite? Dissertation on first principles of government ; The decline and fall of the English system of finance ; Forgetfulness; Agrarian justice.

RAGOZIN, ZÉNAÏDE A. The story of Vedic India, as embodied principally in the Rig-Veda. Putnam. 12°, (The story of the nations ser., no 44.) il. map, 1.50 ; hf. leath., $1.75.
    The present volume, as originally planned, was to have included the post-Vedic or Brahmanic period, and to have borne the title of "Story of Vedic and Brahmanic India." The overwhelming mass of material made it impossible to keep to the original plan—hence two works in place of one. "The Story of Brahmanic India" will follow this immediately, and will embrace the results attained by the study of the Atharva-Veda, the Brâhmanas, the Upanishads, the Laws, and a synopsis at least of the great epics. Contains a list (4 pages) of works consulted.

RUSSELL, W. HOWARD. The great war with Russia ; the invasion of the Crimea : a personal retrospect of the battles of the Alma, Balaclava, and Inkerman, and of the winter of 1854-55, etc. Routledge. 12°, $2.

WIRGMAN, A. THEO. The history of the English church and people in South Africa. Longmans, Green & Co. 12°, $1.25.

ZIEBER, EUGENE. Heraldry in America. Lippincott. 4°, $10 ; full tky. mor., $15.

HUMOR AND SATIRE.

BANGS, J. KENDRICK. The idiot. Harper. il. 16°. $1.

The young man who enlivened Mrs. Smithers' boarding-house breakfast-table with his sallies of wit and humor in "Coffee and repartee," and called by his friends the "idiot," is again the centre of interest.

He discusses a wide range of topics in the present volume, ranging from the superiority of canal-boats over boarding-houses to the poetry of Swinburne, and from the undesirability of actors as boarders to journalism as a fine art and architecture as a system of charity. Happily, The Idiot has now taken to himself a wife, and hereafter he will not be permitted to do all the talking."—*N. Y. Times.*

LITERATURE, MISCELLANEOUS AND COLLECTED WORKS.

BOYESEN, HJALMAR HJORTH. Essays on Scandinavian literature. Scribner. 12°, $1.50.

Seven essays ; the subjects are : Björnstjerne Björnson, Alexander Kielland. Jonas Lic, Hans Christian And rsen, Contemporary Danish literature, Georg Brandes and Esaias Tegnér.

GURTEEN, S. HUMPHREYS. The Arthurian epic, a comparative study of the Cambrian, Breton, and Anglo-Norman versions of the story, and Tennyson's "Idylls of the king." Putnam. 12°, $2.

HEPWORTH, G. H. Brown studies ; or, campfires and morals. Dutton. Il. 12°, $1.25.

KERSEY, J. A. Ethics of literature. Marion, Ind., published by the author, J. A. Kersey. Bowen-Merrill Co. 8°, $2.

A frank and unconventional estimate of some of the great writers of the world in religion, philosophy, politics, poetry, history, etc. The author believes if there was more independence of thought and judgment, many writers who are now world-famous as great geniuses would sink into obscurity. He applies his searching methods of criticism to such works as Butler's "Analogy," Drummond's "Natural law in the spiritual world," "Paradise lost," Pope's "Essay on man," Carlyle's writings, Emerson's writings, Bryant's poems, "Faust," and many others.

MANLEY, LOUISE. Southern literature, from 1579-1895 ; a comprehensive review, with copious extracts and criticisms, for the use of schools and the general reader ; cont. an appendix with a full list of southern authors. Johnson Pub. Co. il. 12°, $1.50.

Arranged in chronological order, beginning with Captain John Smith, the first writer of Virginia, and ending with Madison Cawein.

NORDAU, MAX. Degeneration; tr. from the 2d ed. of the German work. Appleton. 8°, $3.50.

SYMONDS, J. ADDINGTON. Giovanni Boccaccio as man and author. Scribner. 8°, $2.

POETRY.

BENSON, ARTHUR CHRISTOPHER. Lyrics. Macmillan. 8°, $1.75.

COUCH, ARTHUR T. QUILLER, ["Q," *pseud.*]

comp. The golden pomp: a procession of English lyrics from Surrey to Shirley. Lippincott. 12°, $2.

These 361 lyrics represent Sir Rob. Ayton, T. Champion, W. Drummond of Hawthornden, Herrick, Ben Jonson, Shakespeare, and other less known Elizabethan poets. They are not arranged "in their birthday order," as the compiler's aim has been "not to instruct but merely to please." Following this rule, he has taken first, only the best lyrics of the period, and second arranged this garland, as far as possible, "so that each flower should do its best by its neighbors, either as a foil or by reflection of its color in thought and style." Notes, about 40 pages. Index of first lines. Index of writers.

CUNNINGHAM, MARTHA. The ballad of la jeunesse dorée. and other verses; il. by A. Palmer Cooper. Cushing & Co. sq. 12°, $1.50.

DE TABLEY, J. BYRNE LEICESTER WARREN [*Baron* De Tabley.] Poems, dramatic and lyrical. 2d ser. Macmillan. 8°, $2.

MILLER, CINCINNATUS HINER, ["Joaquin Miller,"] Motherwell, W., *and* Key, Francis Scott. Drei übersetzungen aus dem Englischen von E. Leyh. Cushing & Co. 16°, pap., 25 c.

Translations into German of Joaquin Miller's "Arizonian," W. Motherwell's "Jeanie Morrison," and Francis Scott Key's "Star Spangled Banner."

MILTON, J. L'Allegro, Il Penseroso, and other poems ; with a biographical sketch, introd., an essay on the reading of Milton, and notes; includes "Lycidas" and "Comus"—all of Milton that is required for admission to any American college. Houghton, Mifflin & Co. 16°, (Riverside lit. ser., no. 72.) pap., *net*, 15 c.

TENNYSON, ALFRED (*Lord.*) Enoch Arden, and other poems; with a biographical sketch and notes. Houghton, Mifflin & Co. 16°, (Riverside lit. ser. no. 73.) pap., *net*, 15 c.

POLITICAL AND SOCIAL.

BILLINGS, J. S , *M.D., and* HURD, H. M., *M.D.* Suggestions to hospital and asylum visitors ; with an introd. by S. Weir Mitchell, M.D. Lippincott. 16°, 50 c.

For the use of laymen engaged in managing or inspecting charitable institutions. Meant to train them in observation in questions of cooking, dietetics, ventilation, medical and surgical cleanliness, etc.

BROOKS, NOAH. How the republic is governed. Scribner. 16°, 75 c.

Describes the various branches of the national and state governments in chapters entitled : The federal constitution ; Government of the U. S.; Of the Congress ; The executive department of government ; The judiciary ; National and state rights ; Naturalization ; Presidential electors; The territories ; Treason ; Tariffs and custom-houses ; The Indians ; Public lands ; Sub-treasuries, mints, etc.; Patents and copyrights ; Pensions and the right of suffrage. Contains also the Declaration of Independence and the Constitution of the U. S.

BROOKS, NOAH. Short studies in party politics. Scribner. por. il. 12°, $1.25.

Contents: Some first things in American politics; The passing of the Whigs ; When slavery went out of politics ; The party platforms of sixty years. Illustrated with 27 portraits of the presidents and other American statesmen.

FOOTE, ALLEN RIPLEY. A sound currency and banking system. how it may be secured. Putnam. 12°, (Questions of the day, no. 82.) 75 c.

"A properly appointed monetary commission can devise a sound currency and banking system that will remove the cause of financial panics," says the author in his preface. To assist in securing the appointment of such a commission and as a help to a right understanding of the importance, aim and direction of the work it should do, the papers contained in this book were written. Their titles are : A plea for a sound currency and banking system; How shall a sound currency and banking system be established ? ; Is it a safe time to repeal the national tax on state bank currency? ; The United States Treasury must cease doing a banking business ; Record of the United States Treasury as a bank issue controlled by political exigencies ; Gold redemption by the United States Treasury.

GREENE, F. D. The Armenian crisis in Turkey; the massacre of 1894, its antecedents and significance, with a consideration of some of the factors which enter into the solution of this phase of the Eastern question; with introd. by the Rev. Josiah Strong. Putnam. maps, por. il. 12°, $1 ; pap., 60 c.

HULL-HOUSE maps and papers: a presentation of nationalities and wages in a congested district of Chicago ; with comments and essays on problems growing out of the social conditions, by residents of Hull-House, a social settlement, at 335 South Halsted St., Chicago, Ill. Crowell. maps, diagrams, il. 8°, (Crowell's lib. of economics and politics, v. 5.) $2.50 ; *Special ed.*, with mounted maps, $3.50.

Contents: Prefatory note, by Jane Addams; No. 1, Map notes and comments, by Agnes Sinclair Holbrook; No. 2, The sweating system, by Florence Kelley; No. 3, Wage-earning children. by Florence Kelley and Alzina P. Stevens; No. 4. Receipts and expenditures of cloakmakers in Chicago, by Isabel Eaton; No. 5, The Chicago Ghetto, by C. Zeublin; No. 6, The Bohemian people in Chicago, by Josefa Humpal Zeman; No. 7, Remarks upon the Italian colony in Chicago, by Alessandro Mastro-Valerio; No. 8, The Cook County charities, by Julia C. Lathrop; No. 9, Art and labor, by Ellen Gates Starr; No. 10, The settlement as a factor in the labor movement, by Jane Addams; Appendix, Hull-House, a social settlement.

KELLY, EDMOND. Evolution and efforts, and their relation to religion and politics. Appleton. 12°, $1.25.

The author, who has been prominent in the movement for municipal reform in New York, aims to show in this work that the evolution of to-day is differentiated from the evolution which preceded the advent of man, by the factor of conscious effort; that man, by virtue of his faculty of conscious effort, is no longer the product of evolution but the master of it; that the chief ally of this faculty is religion, and its most fruitful though as yet neglected field is politics; that an alliance between religion and politics is essential to progress in the struggle of humanity with evil and with pain; and that this alliance must practise the gospel of effort and not that of *laissez-faire*.

KIDD, B. Social evolution. *New ed.*, with a new preface. Macmillan. 12°, pap., 25 c.

VARIGNY, C. DE. The women of the United States; from the French by Arabella Ward. Dodd, Mead & Co. 12°, $1.25.

The results of a Frenchman's recent observation of the American woman. Papers that originally appeared in the *Revue des Deux Mondes.* He opens his study with reflections upon woman's part at the beginning of American colonization, the different elements among the colonists, the Puritans and cavaliers, the American women at the commencement of the nineteenth century, etc. Then he notes the "overmastering influence of American women," dilates upon their rights and privileges, flirtations, love and marriage; The legislation for the protection of women and its abuse; Breach of promise cases. American married women and American morals; Marriage and divorce in the United States; Money in American society, etc.

SPORTS AND AMUSEMENTS.

POLE, W. The evolution of whist: a study of the progressive changes which the game has passed through from its origin to the present time. Longmans, Green & Co. 12°, $1.50.

The author, an authority on the subject, divides his book into four parts. Pt. 1, The primitive era, 1500 to 1730, embraces the early history of whist and an account of the primitive game. Pt. 2 is, The era of Hoyle, 1730 to 1860. Pt. 3 discusses The philosophical game, from 1860 onwards. Pt. 4 is devoted to latter-day improvements and includes four pages on "American whist literature." Appendices contain some model whist hands of early date, the Constitution of the American Whist League, the American laws of whist, etc.

WILLARD, FRANCES ELIZ. A wheel within a wheel: how I learned to ride the bicycle; with some reflections by the way. Revell. pors. 16°, 50 c.

THEOLOGY, RELIGION AND SPECULATION.

BEACH, D. NELSON. How we rose. Roberts. 16°, 60 c.

An imaginary picture of life after death; two women who have just died tell of the mysteries that are made plain to them.

BEATTIE, *Rev.* FRANCIS R. Radical criticism: an exposition and examination of the radical critical theory concerning the literature and religious system of the Old Testament scriptures; introd. by W. W. Moore, D.D. Revell. 12°, $1.50.

BRIGGS. C. A., *D.D.* The Messiah of the apostles. Scribner. 8°, $3.

The third of a series of volumes begun with "Messianic prophecy" in 1886, and continued in "The messiah of the gospels" in 1894. It may be considered as the author's interpretation of the New Testament as regards the essential doctrines of Christianity. It considers the messianic idea of the Jews in the first Christian century, the messianic conception of the primitive Jewish Christians, and the evolution of the messianic doctrine of Paul. A fresh study is given of the Book of Revelation, the whole concluding with a summary in systematic presentation of the christology of the apostles.

GOD'S light as it came to me. Roberts. 16°, $1.
The writer narrates her experience in the hope "that it may possibly lead others to some understanding of the reason and necessity of all the suffering and turbulence, both physical and mental, that hold and overpower humanity to-day."

HARNACK, ADOLF, *D.D.* Monasticism : its ideals and its history ; tr. by Rev. C. R. Gillett, with a preface by Arthur C. Giffert, *D.D.* Christian Literature Co. 12°, 50 c.

REED, *Rev.* J. SANDERS. The bishop's blue book. Pott. 12°, $1.

REED, *Rev.* J. SANDERS. The crozier and the keys; a companion book to "The bishop's blue book." Pott. 12°, $1.50.

ROMANES, G. J. Thoughts on religion; ed. by C. Gore. Open Court Pub. Co. 12°, $1.25.
Some unfinished notes on religion and two unpublished essays on "The influence of science upon religion," written by Romanes in 1889. The notes were handed, at the request of the late scientist, to his friend Mr. C. Gore, the Canon of Westminster, a representative of ecclesiastical dogmatism. Mr. Gore decided to publish these notes with his own editorial comments and the unpublished essays in the present form, because they all showed an increasing tendency towards belief, on the part of Prof. Romanes, and a desire to overcome the objections made by science.

SHELDON, H. C. History of the Christian church. Crowell. 5 v., 8°, *per set,* $10.

SHIELDS, C. WOODRUFF. The united church of the United States. Scribner. 8°, $2.50.
A collection of essays. The first, "The united churches of the United States," appeared in the *Century Magazine* of 1885 The others are entitled : Denominational views of church unity; The four articles of church unity; Denominational views of the quadrilateral; The quadrilateral standard among the denominations; The historic episcopate and the three church polities; The historic Presbyterate and the historic Episcopate; The historic liturgy and the historic churches; The sociological question of church unity. The author is a professor in Princeton University.

TALMUD (*The*). Talmudic sayings: selected and arr. under appropriate heads, by Rev. H. Cohen. The Bloch Pub. and Print. Co. 12°, 50 c.; bds., 35 c.
About one hundred maxims, proverbs and sayings from the Talmud, under topical headings.

THOMSON, W. H., *M.D.* The parables and their home: the parables by the lake. Harper. I il. 12°, $1.25,

"In his book on 'The parables by the lake,' recently published by Harper & Brothers, Dr. W. H. Thomson has shown himself not only thoroughly familiar with the geography, manners and customs of the Holy Land, but also a man of deep religious conviction, and clear, logical mind. He holds the degrees of M.D. and LL.D. and is a professor in the University Medical College, New York. His childhood was spent in Palestine, his father, Rev. William McClure Thomson, D.D., having been a missionary there for forty-five years.
"The book includes sections on the parables of the sower, the seed growing secretly, the tares, the draw net, the mustard seed, the leaven, the hid treasure, the pearl and the householder's treasure. The style throughout is concise and pure in diction, and the reader's attention is held from beginning to end."—*Mail and Express.*

Books for the Young.

ALDEN, *Mrs.* ISABELLA M., [" Pansy," *pseud.*] Only ten cents. Lothrop Pub. Co. il. 12°, (Pansy books.) $1.50.
Mrs. Beldon, an extremely poor woman, who wished to gratify her little daughter, expended ten cents in purchasing a cardboard motto, "Blessed are the pure in heart, for they shall see God," which is finally worked in cross-stitch and sent to a Southern mission school for the Christmas tree. This humble gift eventually falls into the hands of a poor child, and becomes a means of effecting the wonderful reforms described.

CASTLEMON, HARRY, [*pseud.* for C. A. Fosdick.] Elam Storm the wolfer; or, the lost nugget. Porter & Coates. il. 12°, (Lucky Tom ser.) $1.25.
An army paymaster and a certain Elam Storm, having started with two equipped government wagons for Grayson, are attacked on the route by highwaymen; when scouts are sent to succor the men of the expedition the only survivor apparently is Elam Storm, junior, a boy of fifteen. This lad insistently maintains that his father had in his possession a nugget of gold which he declares his intention of tracing. The story gives his adventures as a wolfer and other experiences which are the result of his wonderful quest.

GREEN, EVELYN EVERETT. Eustace Marchmont: a friend of the people. A. I. Bradley & Co. il. 12°, $1.25.
Eustace Marchmont, a young Englishman, who had acquired socialistic views through a residence in Germany, comes to Penarvon, Wales, where he soon has a large following among the laboring classes ready for revolt. The story tells of the political revolution which is the result of his advent, and gives the details of his romantic love-story. The time is about 1835.

MATHEWS, MARGARET HARRIET. Dame Prism: a story for girls; il. by Eliz. S. Tucker. F. A. Stokes Co. 12°, $1.50.

RICE, KATHARINE McDOWELL. Stories for all the year, for boys and girls; il. by W. St. John Harper. F. A. Stokes Co. il. pl. 12° $1.50.

RECENT FRENCH AND GERMAN BOOKS.

FRENCH.

Allier, R. La philosophie d'Ernest Renan. Bib. de Phil. contemp $0 75
Art Roë, Sous L'Etendard 1 00
Barante, Baron de. Souvenirs. Vol. 5 .... 2 25
Bergeret et Fragonard. Journal inédit d'un voyage en Italie, 1773-74. 8° 2 25
Bourget, Paul. Outre Mer: Notes sur l'Amerique. 2 vols 2 00
Breton, J. Notes d'un étudiant Français en Allemagne 1 00
Broglie, Duc de. La paix d'Aix-La-Chapelle.... 1 00
Brunet, L. La France à Madagascar, 1815-1895.. 1 00
Chantelauze, R. Louis XVII : son enfance, sa prison, et sa mort............................... 1 00
Clemenceau, G. La Mêlée sociale............... 1 00
D'Avenel. La fortune privee à travers sept siècles... 1 25
De Broc. La vie en France sous le premier empire. 8° 2 25
Delard, Eug. Le Sillon............................ 1 00
Du Barail, Gen. Mes souvenirs. Vol. II 2 25
Encyclopedie des sports: Le sport de l'Aviron. 8°, ll.. 1 80
Eschenbach, M. de Ebner. Ineffaçable.......... 1 00
Franklin, Alf. La vie privée d'autrefois. Les magasins de nouveautés 1 00
— L'Enfant : La naissance, Le baptême 1 00
Helbig W. L'épopée Homerique expliquée par les monuments, translated by Trawinski 3 00
Kovalewsky, Soph. Souvenirs, d'enfance..... 1 00
Lanessan, I. L. de. La colonisation française en Indo-Chine....................................... 1 00
Larue, Chev. de. Hist. du dix huit fructidor: La déportation des députés à la Guyane............ 1 70
Las Casas. Le mémorial de Sainte Hélène. Nouv. ed. 12°. Vol. 1...... .... 1 00
Letang. Le supplice d'un père................... 1 00
Loti, P. Jérusalem 1 00
Marguerite Paul. Fors l'honneur............... 1 00
Mareschal de Bievre. Berthe et Berthine...... 1 00
Martinet, A. Le Prince Imperial, 1856-1879 8°. 2 25
Merouvel, Chas. Rochenoire. 2 vols........... 2 00

Meunier, Mme. S. L'Impossible amitié......... $1 00
Noe, M. Pages d'Orient........................... 1 00
Ohnet, G. La dame en gris....................... 1 00
Pages choisies des grands ecrivains : Rabelais, par E. Huguet..................................... 1 00
Paulin, Gen. Baron. Souvenirs, 1782-1876..... 1 20
Rival, J. Annexés. Scenes de la vie alsacienne... 1 00
Sales, Pierre. La fée du guildo.................. 1 00
Segur, Gen. de. Un aide de camp de Napo'éon. Vol. 3, Du Rhin à Fontainebleau 1 00
Thirria. Napoleon III. avant l'empire. Vol 1... 2 40
Torressani, Chas. de. Le quart d'heure de grâce. 1 00
Vachon. Les Arts et les Industries du Papier en France. 4°. Il. cl 7 50

GERMAN.

Brandes, Georg. William Shakespeare. Erste Lief. (Wird ca. 10 Lief. umfassen) 60
Eden, Carla. Sand in die Augen................. 70
Ego. Liebe.. 1 10
Frits, S. Voran die Liebe......................... 10
Gersdorff, Ada v. Tausend Thaler.............. 1 35
Hacklander, F, W. Madame Lohengrin..... .. 1 00
Heller, O. Unter genialen Menschen........... 40
— Der Weg Zum Frieden 1 70
Kreg, P. E. von. Die rothe Lies. 2 vols......... 1 70
Kuhns. Harte Köpfe............................... 1 35
Marby, A. Der Stern von Mostar................ 70
Mysing, O. Verfolgte Phantasie................. 1 70
Parlow. Uber das Meer. 3 vols................. 2 70
Piening, Th. Der unbekannte Wohlthäter 1 35
Riedel-Ahrens, B. Im grauen Schloss......... 70
Romer, A. Was ist Glück?....................... 1 35
Schellwien. Der Geist der neueren Philosophie. I. Theil...... 80
Schunsin, Tamenaga. Treu bis in den Tod..... 1 00
Stahl, M. Die arme Vornehme................... 70
Weiss, O. Unsere Muttersprache: ihr werden und ihr wesen. Cl.............................. 80
Wilbrandt, A. Die Osterinsel................... 1 35
Zapp, A. Der tolle Schmettwitz............ ... 1 35
Zobeltitz, F. von. Bis in die Wueste........... 70

Freshest News.

CHARLES SCRIBNER'S SONS have in press a new novel by Frank R. Stockton entitled "The Adventures of Captain Horn."

FREDERICK WARNE & Co. will publish shortly an illustrated volume entitled "Angling and How to Angle," by R. B. Marston, editor of the London *Fishing Gazette.*

GEORGE ROUTLEDGE & SONS have made an almost perfect edition of their *Handy Volume* "Shakespeare," in thirteen volumes, gotten up in every beautiful binding imaginable.

T. Y. CROWELL & COMPANY have ready the fifth thousand of Professor Ely's "Socialism and Social Reform," and the second thousand of Professor Warner's "American Charities."

FREDERICK A. STOKES Co. will issue early next month "The Phantom Death, and other stories," in their *Twentieth Century Series.* "The Mite Dictionary" has now been published in England, where it has an immense popularity —80,000 copies having been sold in one year.

LOVELL, CORYELL & Co. will issue May 18, in the *Belgravia Series*, a new volume of Edward W. Townsend's inimitable sketches of Bowery life, entitled "Chimmie Fadden Explains, Major Max Expounds." The 110th thousand of Barrie's "Little Minister" will be

issued in *The Century Series* without illustrations; and also revised and enlarged with ten full-page illustrations.

THOMAS WHITTAKER has just ready "Historic Doubts as to the Execution of Marshal Ney," by James A. Weston, Rector of the Church of the Ascension, Hickory, N. C. Mr. Weston has made a careful study of the times of Marshal Ney and of the voluminous literature devoted to Napoleonic annals. He claims a man who died in North Carolina in 1846 was the celebrated marshal history has taught was shot for treason.

T. F. UNWIN has just issued a dainty little book, entitled "Good Reading about Many Books, mostly by their authors," in which many well-known writers of recent popularity give interesting data concerning themselves and their work. Among the contributors appear the names of S. R. Crockett, Sir Gavan Duffy, Mrs. Craigie ("John Oliver Hobbes"), Henry Norman, W. Martin Conway, Mrs. H. Bradlaugh-Bonner, etc. In many cases portraits of the contributors are given.

J. SELWIN TAIT & SONS have begun a new series of fiction, which will be known as the *Zenda Series*, which owes its name to the fact that "The Prisoner of Zenda," Anthony Hope's great success, marked a distinct change in the style of current fiction. The first volume of the series, now ready, is entitled "A Fiend Incarnate," and is the work of David Malcolm, an English writer; the second volume will be by the same author, and will appear under the title "Fifty Thousand Dollars Ransom," a story which will deal with the exciting events of an American business career.

THE CASSELL PUBLISHING CO. have just issued "The Tiger Lily, a story of a woman," by George Manville Fenn; and "Parson Thring's Secret," by A. W. Marchmont. The additions to *Cassell's Union Square Library* are "Is She Not a Woman? or, Vengeance is Mine," by Daniel Dane; and "The Last Tenant," by B. L. Farjeon. In *Cassell's Sunshine Series* will appear "Out of the Fashion," by L. T. Meade; and "Lisbeth," by Leslie Keith. *Cassell's Unknown Library* has just received new editions of "Mademoiselle Ixe," by Lanoe Falconer; and "The Story of Eleanor Lambert," by Magdalen Brooke.

D. APPLETON & CO. announce another book of "Napoleonic Memoirs," to embody the recollections of General Count de Ségur, an aide-de-camp of Napoleon; and Charles A. Dana's long-announced "The Art of Newspaper Making." "The Marriage of Esther," by Guy Boothby, is the latest addition to the *Town and Country Library;* and other new novels of great interest are "The Gods, the Mortals, and Lord Twickenham," by John Oliver Hobbes; "Bog-Myrtle and Peat," by S. R. Crockett; and "In the Fire of the Forge," by Georg Ebers. New volumes in *The Criminology Series* will be "Our Juvenile Offenders," by D. Morrison; "Criminal Sociology," by Prof. Ferri'; and "Crime, a Social Study," by Prof. Joly.

G. P. PUTNAM'S SONS have now ready "William the Silent," a comprehensive biography of "the moderate man of the XVI. century," by Ruth Putnam, who tells the story of the Prince of Orange as it is found in his own letters, those of his contemporaries, and in the official documents of the period. They have also an interesting batch of "light reading," comprising: "The Countess Bettina," an anonymous addition to the *Hudson Library;* "Yale Yarns," stories of college days, by John Seymour Wood,

issued in the same form as W. K. Post's "Harvard Stories"; "A Gender in Satin," a new novel by "Rita," in the *Incognito Library ;* and "Dr. Izard," a story by Anna Katharine Green, said to be wholly distinct in character from the author's previous books, though possessing marked power and originality.

HOUGHTON, MIFFLIN & CO. will publish during May "Under the Man-Fig," by Mrs. M. E. M. Davis, of New Orleans, of which the scene is laid in Texas during the Civil War; "The Letters of Samuel Taylor Coleridge," edited by Ernest Hartley Coleridge, in two volumes, with sixteen portraits and other illustrations ; a volume of "Mrs. Thaxter's Letters," edited by Mrs. James T. Fields; "The Life of Gen. Thomas Pinckney," of Revolutionary fame, by Rev. Charles Cotesworth Pinckney, of Charleston; and "The Mississippi Basin "by Justin Winsor, to follow his "Cartier to Frontenac," which will cover the struggle in America between England and France from 1697 to 1763, and which will have valuable maps. It is auspicious for the cause of good citizenship that Mr. Cary's "Life of George William Curtis" was one of the six books most in demand during February in twenty representative American cities.

FREDERICK WARNE & CO. will issue immediately the first part of "The Royal Natural History," edited by Professor Lydekker; "The Sheep Doctor," an entirely new work on this important subject, by Prof, Armatage; "Wayside and Woodland Blossoms," a pocket guide to British wildflowers, with colored plates; "The Spirit of Cookery," a popular treatise on the history, science, practice, and ethical and medical import of culinary art, with a dictionary of terms, by Prof. Thudichum; "Dinners Up to Date," with *menus* in French and English; "Paul Heriot's Pictures," by Alison McLean, author of "Quiet Stories from an Old Woman's Garden; "The Legends of King Arthur and His Knights," compiled and arranged by James Knowles (of the *Nineteenth Century Magazine*); "Angling and How to Angle," a practical guide, by R. B. Marston, editor of *The Fishing Gazette;* also, "Eliza Cook's Poems," with additions, will be added to the *Albion Edition* of the poets.

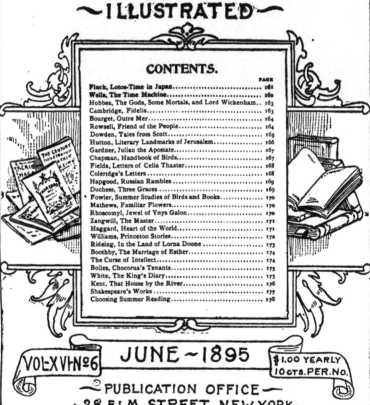

LITERARY NEWS

AN ECLECTIC REVIEW OF
CURRENT LITERATURE
~ILLUSTRATED~

CONTENTS.

VOL. XVI No. 6   JUNE ~ 1895 $1.00 YEARLY   10 CTS. PER. NO.

~ PUBLICATION OFFICE ~
· 28 ELM STREET NEW YORK ·

ENTERED AT THE POST OFFICE AT NEW YORK AS SECOND CLASS MATTER

The Literary News

In winter you may reade them, ad ignem, by the fireside; and in summer, ad umbram, under some shadie tree and therewith pass away the tedious howres.

VOL. XVI.   JUNE, 1895.   No. 6.

Lotos-Time in Japan.

WE have from Charles Scribner's Sons an entertaining addition to the long list of recent books on Japan. This volume, entitled "Lotos- every-day experiences he would probably have in Japan. At the present time interest in the people and civilization of Japan is almost uni-

From Finck's "Lotos-Time in Japan."   Copyright, 1895, by Charles Scribner's Sons.
BEGGARS.

Time in Japan," by Henry T. Finck, the well-known traveller and musical critic, is designed to present a few realistic and unbiased sketches from life and nature, and to exhibit to the reader and possible tourist specimens of the versal, yet the first European who described it lived only two centuries ago, and from that time until about forty years ago it remained hermetically sealed to the rest of the world. Japan still preserves many mediæval customs, the contrast and clash of which with the imported elements of our Occidental civilization produce a multitude of picturesque phenomena that will continue to fascinate and tempt authors and artists for many years to come. This work appears to us a scholarly and brief presentation of the principal points in which Japanese civilization is superior to our own. The author believes that with us there is too marked a tendency to estimate Japanese civilization from a purely material and military point of view. On the other hand, there can be no doubt that this gifted people have as much to teach us in many things as we have to offer them. Japanese civilization, it is claimed, is based on altruism; ours on egotism. Here are some of the elements in their civilization in the possession of which Mr. Finck affirms they manifest their superiority over all the world: In cleanliness and in sincere appreciation of art and nature, in manners and social culture, contempt for the display of wealth, kindness to animals, patriotism, the behavior of crowds and criminals, the attitude of parents and children towards one another and in the rational enjoyment of life, Mr. Finck says that the Japanese are superior to all other nations. The volume is not devoted to philosophical reflections and economic and

From Wells' "Time Machine."   Copyright, 1865, by
                Henry Holt & Co.

THE WHITE SPHINX.

ethical comparisons. The greater portion of it is descriptive of those characteristics of the country with which only the patient and leisurely traveller comes into contact. Most interesting accounts are given of Yokohama, its clubs, young beggars, Oriental Bowery life, its bund and bluff and its women. This delightful chat runs through all the really instructive chapters of the entertaining work, and makes it a body of narrative worthy of wide and careful reading. The book is profusely illustrated with clear and sympathetic drawings. (Scribner. $1.75.)—*Philadelphia Press.*

The Time Machine.

THE latest addition to the *Buckram* series is "The Time Machine, an Invention," a whimsical fantasy, by H. S. Wells. It is a brightly written little book, gruesome at times, flippant now and again, but unflagging in interest. One cannot lay it down unfinished.

The Man who Made the Time Machine was a scientist and inventor. He had a theory, which he argued with much subtlety, that time is a spatial dimension. Clearly, he argued, any real body must have extension in four directions; it must have length, breadth, thickness, and—duration. There is no difference between Time and any of the three dimensions of space, except that one's consciousness moves along it. Acting on this theory, the Time Traveller devised a machine on which he could travel through time as freely as a rifle-ball travels through space. Then he set out on his journey. On his return he told what things had befallen him, and his adventures had been strange beyond belief. He had started at full speed through a twinkling succession of darkness and light; in intermittent darkness he saw the moon spinning swiftly through her quarters from new to full; the jerking sun became a streak of fire as he sped along the "fourth dimension"—Time. He paused in a far future of the Golden Age. It was the year 802701 A.D. He was in a land of brilliant foliage and strange flowers, but a land of huge ruins and unused palaces. Little people out of futurity gathered about him. They were slight creatures, perhaps four feet high, clad in tunics and sandals. They were beautiful, graceful, indescribably frail. Their intelligence was that of five-year-old children. Humanity upon the wane!

A brilliant little book, but no synopsis can give an idea of the graphic and peculiar power of the story. Paradoxical, of course, but the paradox is clever and worked out neatly. You can't afford to miss "The Time Machine." (Holt. 75 c.)—*N. Y. Commercial Advertiser*

The Gods, Some Mortals, and Lord Wickenham.

" THE Gods, Some Mortals, and Lord Wickenham " is the oddly named novel which "John Oliver Hobbes " has put forth, and all the odder because his lordship has very little to do with the story. It may have been the vengeance of the gods which made Warre marry a woman with a history, the horrible reality of which came upon him with stunning force only a few minutes too late, but it looks more like the folly of one of the mortals and the viciousness of another. Anne is a startling conception and Warre is an admirably drawn study. There are but few of the many who produce sketches who are capable of sustained effort, but this strangely powerful story never flags. It has a tragic beauty which never descends to the level of melodrama, it is bright with the incisive touches and cynical wit which the reading public has already learned to attach to this author's work, and it is as far removed from the commonplace as can be desired. (Appleton. $1.50.)—*Public Opinion.*

From "The Gods, Some Mortals, and Lord Wickenham.". ,Copyright, 1895, by
D. Appleton & Co.

JOHN OLIVER HOBBES (MRS. CRAIGIE).

he is behind them in appearance that life begins to be tolerable for him. The period of his early years, in which he is a lonely and ill-used brat, is fully and tellingly described, and forms the most satisfactory portion of the story. For when Caliban has recognized his own genius, one naturally expects him to live up to the discovery. Instead of doing so, his courage fails at a critical moment, and his hesitation costs him the loss of the sweetest joys of life for many a weary year. Out of the school of adversity in which he has been reared the author brings him forth a man of rare tenderness of heart. In the cause of the oppressed and suffering he is chivalrous to the point of Quixotism. The absence of bitterness in his soul against a world that in his early years treated him so churlishly is so remarkable, under the circumstances, that one can only conclude that the author has discovered something analogous to it in some character that has served as Adam's prototype. As a rule the public has not appreciated in the manner deserved the finished work Ada Cambridge has put into her stories. She has written much more than any author should who wishes to remain always upon the highest level of the ability with which he has been gifted, but she has produced nothing that is not worthy to be read. She has a sunny way of looking at life and her books do good. Hidden among the incidents of the plot are many suggestive thoughts upon English rule in foreign lands. (Appleton. pap., 50 c.)—*London Literary World.*

Fidelis.

AN abnormally ugly child forms the centre of interest in Miss Ada Cambridge's striking story of "Fidelis." His monkey face and squat figure make him the butt of his playfellows and the abomination of his mother, and it is not until he has realized that in brain power he is as far in advance of his fellows as

From Rowsell's "A Friend of the People."   Copyright, 18?o,
by F. A. Stokes Co.

CITIZEN ROBESPIERRE.

Outre Mer.

"OUTRE MER" gives the impression of being written too soon, before the "shocks" and "sensations" had resolved themselves into more definite and permanent shape. It is, indeed, a series of notes and sketches with conclusions come to and judgments formed that one cannot always agree with. But it is a singularly interesting work in that it comes from a trained and practised observer, who *sees* and notes things which most of us, with untrained minds, merely glance at and straightway forget. Americans rebel at being pictured as M. Bourget pictures them, but it is well to remember that as they appear, so they are to him—and in a less degree to the average foreigner. It must be allowed, on the other hand, that the French observer is at times under the influence of a theory, formed too easily, and to which, unconsciously, he seeks to adapt some part of what he notes. Yet there is deep truth in Bourget's description of much that marks American life and character, the crudity in certain matters, the love of display, the garishness, the feverishness, the restlessness. These traits it is unpleasant to be reminded of, especially by a master in the art of torturing analysis. Of the translation it can be said that it is above the average and reads easily, only occasionally calling up a smile or causing a knitting of the brows. In these days of misrepresentations of foreign tongues this is much to be thankful for. (Scribner. $1.75.)—*The Nation.*

The Friend of the People.

THIS is a story of mistaken identity. The plot is laid in Paris at the time of the French Revolution, and the author describes many stirring scenes peculiar to the reign and downfall of Louis XVI.

Gervais Bouchard puts on a priest's garb, and, by deceiving his dying mother, receives her confession. Gervais thus learns that his father was not the peasant Bouchard, but the Marquis de Ravignac. Gervais also finds later on that he is the very image of the young Marquis de Ravignac, who has succeeded to the family title and estates.

Gervais, having enjoyed his own way, puts the Marquis out of the way and quietly takes possession of everything that belonged to him. The Marquis, on the day he is married at Versailles to a young ward of Queen Marie Antoinette, is summoned to Soissons to quell a riot. Gervais takes care that the Marquis does not get back to Paris. The Marquis falls a victim to the plots against him, and is carried away and locked up.

Gervais steps into the Marquis's shoes, and every one takes him to be the real Marquis, except the young Marquise. She detects the sham at once, and hides herself away. The Queen, who had been very fond of the real Marquis, receives Gervais at the Court, and though he talks in a very coarse way, she does not discover the imposition.

Gervais, having been given his own way in everything, a large proportion of the story is required to explain how the genuine Marquis de Ravignac regains his name and his wife.

Gervais, besides playing the rôle of Marquis, also writes for one of the papers of the people. He ingratiates himself in the favor of Robespierre by renouncing his stolen title and assuming the name of Citizen Crassus.

The real Marquis de Ravignac escapes in the meanwhile, and returns to Paris, where he is again thrown into prison. Here he meets his wife, who has been imprisoned through the intrigues of Gervais. The Marquis is condemned to die, because he fails to give a satisfactory account of himself. Just as Gervais becomes confident that he is safe from discovery, the story of the fraud reaches Robespierre, who frees the Marquis and his wife. Gervais is saved from the guillotine by his mistress, who stabs him to death. (Stokes. $1.50.)—*N. Y. Times.*

Richard Cœur de Lion and Robin Hood.

THEY had ridden together for some distance when the quick eye of the jester caught sight of some men in armor concealed in a brake not far from where they were.

Almost immediately after three arrows were discharged from the suspected spot, one of which glanced off the visor of the Black Knight.

"Let us close with them said the knight, and he rode straight to the thicket. He was met by six or seven men-at-arms, who ran against him with their lances at full career. Three of the weapons struck against him, and splintered with as little effect as if they had been driven against a tower of steel. The attacking party then drew their swords and assailed him on every side. But many as they were to one they had met their match; and a man reeled and fell at every blow delivered by the Black Knight. His opponents, desperate as they were, now bore back from his deadly blows, and it seemed as if the terror of his single strength was about to gain the battle against such odds when a knight in blue armor, who had kept himself behind the other assailants, spurred forward with his lance, and taking aim, not at the rider but at the steed, wounded the noble animal mortally.

"That was a felon stroke!" exclaimed the Black Knight, as the horse fell to the earth, bearing his rider along with him.

"Shame on ye, false cowards!" exclaimed he in the blue harness; "Do ye fly from the empty blast of a horn blown by a jester?"

Animated by his words, they attacked the Black Knight anew, whose best refuge was now to place his back against an oak, and defend himself with his sword. The felon knight, who had taken another spear, watching the moment when his formidable antagonist was most closely pressed, galloped against him in hopes to nail him with his lance against the tree; but Wamba, springing forward in good time, checked the fatal career of the Blue Knight, by ham-stringing his horse with a stroke of his sword; and horse and man went heavily to the ground.

Almost immediately after, a band of yeomen,

From Dowden's "Tales from Scott."   Roberts Erothers.

THE FLIGHT FROM TORQUILSTONE CASTLE.

GARDEN OF GETHSEMANE.

headed by Locksley, broke forth from the glade, who, joining manfully in the fray, soon disposed of the ruffians, all of whom lay on the spot dead, or mortally wounded.

The visor of the Blue Knight, who lay under his wounded steed, was now opened, and the features of Waldemar Fitzurse were disclosed.

"Stand back, my masters," said the Black Knight to those about him; "I would speak with this man alone. And now, Waldemar Fitzurse, say me the truth; confess who set thee on this traitorous deed."

"Richard," answered the fallen knight, "it was thy father's son."

Richard's eyes sparkled with indignation, but his better nature overcame it. "Take thy life unasked," he said; "but, on this condition, that in three days thou shalt leave England, and that thou wilt never mention the name of John of Anjou as connected with thy felony." Then, turning to where the yeomen stood apart, he said, "Let this knight have a steed, Locksley, and let him depart unharmed. Thou bearest an English heart, and must needs obey me. I am Richard of England!"

At these words the yeomen kneeled down before him, tendering their allegiance, while they implored pardon for their offences.

"Rise, my friends," said Richard. "Your misdemeanors have been atoned by the loyal services you rendered my distressed subjects before the walls of Torquilstone, and the rescue you have this day afforded your sovereign. Arise, my liegemen, and be good subjects in future. And thou, brave Locksley—"

"Call me no longer Locksley, my liege," said the outlaw; "I am Robin Hood, of Sherwood Forest." (Roberts.) — *From Sullivan's " Tales from Scott."*

Literary Landmarks of Jerusa!em.

THE City of Jerusalem will become better understood and more interesting to all who read this carefully written book by Mr. Hutton. He has done for Jerusalem what he had already accomplished for the relatively modern cities of London and Edinburgh in his "Literary Landmarks of London" and "Literary Landmarks of Edinburgh." The present task has met with an unpretentious and reverential treatment.

Mr. Hutton had a definite object in view. He found, he says, when visiting Jerusalem, that there was no book from which visitors could get conveniently such information as they desired to have at hand in going about the city. Mr. Hutton, therefore, decided to prepare a little book that could be carried about in the pocket to meet this need. He has not compiled a guide-book, but he has composed a literary work that gives information in an effective manner.

The book does not contain wearisome discussions as to the correctness of the traditions that ascribe certain events to certain localities. It simply describes the points of interest in and about Jerusalem in a style free from any touch of pedantry.

Mr. Hutton finds Jerusalem a mountain city, around the outside of whose walls one can walk in an hour. Its houses are mean and squalid; its streets are dirty and narrow; commerce is dead; everything is solemn and severe; even the children do not play. Yet these very conditions, in the light of its literature, make the city impressive. At the wailing wall of the Jews, accepted as a part of the actual wall of the temple, Mr. Hutton saw the Jews every day bewailing the desolation that has come on the city, and adding to their lamentations prayers for its restoration to power.

From the wailing wall he follows along the ways that Jesus must have gone, and visits the Mount of Olives, where the olive trees grow as of old, and declares that to him Jerusalem is most fascinating of all cities. He found not far away the sheep pastures, and saw, by chance, a shepherd bearing a lamb in his arms. By many tender touches, Mr. Hutton, in picturing the churches, tombs and streets of Jerusalem, the town of Bethlehem, and other historical places near by, brings constantly before the mind the impressive figure of Jesus Himself. The literary landmarks of the Old Testament also have their fair share of attention.

The fascination of Jerusalem, Mr. Hutton declares, he was unable to dispel by any rationalistic reasoning. In speaking of the Via Dolorosa, he says : " It may be all tradition and all false, but to a man brought up upon the teachings of the New Testament, as accepted by a good father and a good mother, it was awfully real. And I believed it all."

Full-page illustrations made by Frank V. Du Mond, who visited Jerusalem last year to obtain them, add greatly to the value of the book. (Harper. 75 c.)

Julian the Apostate.

ONE of the most admirable of the volumes included in the *Heroes of the Nations* series is entitled " Julian, Philosopher and Emperor," by Alice Gardner, lecturer and associate of Newnham College, Cambridge. To the author was entrusted a most difficult subject, and but few English scholars could have treated it with more thoroughness, skill and discrimination. She has given us in the space at her command a distinct and vivid conception of the complex personality of the imperial reactionist against Christianity, and in some remarkable chapters she has expounded the nature of his philosophical and theological views which seem to have been a compound of neoplatonism and mithraicism. She has, moreover, enabled the reader to reconstruct, in imagination, the environment in which Julian and his contemporaries lived, their personal appearance and dress, the most striking places where they dwelt, and the scenes in which they habitually moved. The book contains many illustrations, largely derived from contemporary art, including especially the ivory diptychs, portraits, and coins of the period. *The Heroes of the Nations* series now number thirteen volumes, covering some of the formative periods of the world's history and proving conclusively that when the time is ripe, the right man will enevitably appear. (Putnam. $1.50; hf. mor., $1.75.)—*The Sun.*

Handbook of Birds.

A POPULAR but authoritative book on birds has been needed for so long that a warm welcome awaits the "Handbook of Birds of Eastern North America," by Frank M. Chapman, of the American Museum of Ornithology. This book, which is most profusely illustrated with pictures from nature, contains keys to the species and descriptions of the plumage, nests, etc., of all birds found east of the Mississippi, and most of those in the extreme West. The author's position has enabled him to learn the special requirements of amateurs and beginners, and the problem of identification, either in the field or study, is reduced to its simplest form. Advance sheets of the book have been read by Prof. Allen, editor of *The Auk*, Olive Thorne Miller, Bradford Torrey, and other ornithologists, who have welcomed and recommended the work to all amateurs and students. The publishers issue a pocket as well as a library edition. (Appleton. $3; $3.50.)—*Brooklyn Times.*

From Gardner's " Julian " Copyright, 1895, by G. P. Putnam's Sons.

Letters of Celia Thaxter.

"LETTERS of Celia Thaxter," edited by her friends Annie Fields and Rose Lamb, is one of the most charming illustrations of character that a reader could wish for. It makes every sympathetic person long to have known the writer of the letters, and that is even more the real art of letter-writing than Sam Weller's dictum that the true art is to excite a wish for more of the same kind. We have that feeling also in reading Mrs. Thaxter's letters, and so delightful are these glimpses of a lovely nature that perhaps in time her editors may give us a second series. The simplicity, earnestness, and wholesome vitality of Celia Thaxter, the very striking presentment she makes of the Isles of Shoal, where she lived so long, her intimate relations with the most distinguished people in New England—these among other considerations make this a really notable book, with a meaning and a flavor all its own. (Houghton, Mifflin & Co. $1.50.)—*Philadelphia Evening Telegraph.*

From "Letters of Celia Thaxter." Copyright, 1895, by Houghton, Mifflin & Co.

MRS. THAXTER AT HER PAINTING-TABLE (1892).

Coleridge's Letters.

EXTERNALLY these two volumes of Coleridge's letters are very attractive, and if, as one naturally supposes, they have been manufactured here in America for the English market as well as our own there is no reason to fear an unfavorable opinion of their mechanical merits. In all respects they do great credit to the Riverside Press. For the series of portraits of the Coleridges and their friends, especially those of the poet himself and that child of genius, Hartley Coleridge, all readers of the "Ancient Mariner" will be grateful.

Mr. Ernest Coleridge has performed his editorial duties with industry and modesty. His introduction notes that no attempt has been previously made to publish a collection of Coleridge's letters, mentions the works in which a few have appeared, and gives particulars as to the abundance of those still unprinted. "A complete edition," he says, "must await the 'coming of the milder day,' a renewed long-suffering on the part of the old enemy, the 'literary public.'" We do not apprehend the early advent of any such infliction, for such it would be if the epistles here given are the best of all. They are not destitute of occasional "profound touches of the human heart," as the editor says, but he also frankly admits that Coleridge as a letter-writer had no style, writing to his friends as if he were talking to them, and letting his periods take care of themselves. . . . For one who seriously studies Coleridge as a character, however, these volumes are a valuable supplement to Mr. James Dykes Campbell's admirable biography. The letters are arranged chronologically (the editor rarely appearing save in footnotes), with the personal reference rather than with a view to showing the development of his literary genius. It is the study of the abnormal that they facilitate, of "a great *tomorrower,*" as Coleridge said of De Quincey and himself —almost incapable of doing anything to-day, his will paralyzed by the opium habit of many years' standing, his mental grasp enfeebled, and the splendid promise of his glorious youth but slightly fulfilled. The "wretched vice" was tempered by the loving care of James Gillman and his wife in the Highgate home, whose "patience must have been inexhaustible, their loyalty unimpeachable, their love indestructible." The volumes will doubtless occupy a secure place on the biographic shelf. (Houghton, Mifflin & Co. 2 v., $6.)—*The Boston Literary World.*

Russian Rambles.

IT is a useful as well as attractive book which Isabelle F. Hapgood has given us under the name of "Russian Rambles." The author's purpose is to describe the common incidents of every-day life in Russia which, in this country, are either not known at all, or grotesquely misunderstood. It is true enough that people frequently go to Russia with the deliberate expectation and intention of seeing queer things. Their general idea seems to be that they will find in the Czar's dominions the Russia of Ivan the Terrible. As the reality is decidedly tame in comparison, they feel bound to supply the missing spice. The author tells us that she was informed that she must abuse Russia if she wished to be popular in the United States. That is a mistake, and we are glad that she did not allow herself to be influenced by this absurd admonition. There is no European people for which intelligent Americans, familiar with the history of their own country, have more sympathy, or to which they recognize so large an indebtment. In three memorable crises Russia has rendered a great service to the American republic.

Among the thirteen chapters of this volume, we have read with especial interest that which describes a visit to the country home of Count Tolstoi. The author is not one of those who are accustomed to call the great Russian writer "crazy" or "not quite right in the head," and so on. She regards him simply as a man with a hobby or controlling idea. His idea happens to be one which, even if we admit that it ought to be generally adopted, must be recognized as difficult of adoption. It is an uncomfortable theory of self-denial, which very few people like to have preached to them in any form. Nor can it be denied that the expositions of his theory lack clearness; this circumstance seems to constitute the sole foundation for the reports of his mental aberrations. The author of this book found him on personal acquaintance to be a remarkably earnest and winning man, although he did not deliberately do or say anything to attract one. (Houghton, Mifflin & Co. $1.50.)—*The Sun.*

The Three Graces.

"THE Duchess" has really outdone herself in "The Three Graces." A breezier, more thoroughly agreeable novel than this is seldom encountered. Indeed, "The Duchess" at her best needs fear no comparison with current fictionists, and "The Three Graces" has everything in it to win popularity—character, humor, plot, and incident. It is an Irish story, with a group of lovely women, and an irascible old squire, conceived on the truest lines of comedy. It may be described as a tale of intrigue, but of intrigue so innocent that no one can take harm from it. "The Duchess" always introduces a thoroughly wholesome, honest, lovable girl, and Janet of this novel is one of the most charming she has given us. (Lippincott.)—*Philadelphia Evening Telegraph.*

From "The Three Graces."   Copyright, 1895, by J. B. Lippincott Co.

JANET.

Summer Studies of Birds and Books.

OVER and over again a reviewer has to repeat about the same phrase : the delight felt when a book of this kind comes across his way. History, politics, economic problems, fiction, may give their momentary zest, but true restfulness and honest enjoyment come when he reads of birds and nature and listens to the singing of the winged vocalists as Mr. Warde Fowler describes them.

Many of these chapters have been read in the United States, and numerous quotations have been made from them, as they appeared originally in *Macmillan's Magazine,* but it is all the better to have them together, and in part rewritten and arranged. One admirable study in this volume has for title "Aristotle on Birds." The old Greek may have blundered at times, but nevertheless he knew much. It does seem probable that Aristotle wrote the greater part of his book on natural history in the beginning of his life, before he had given himself up "to the higher influences of philosophy." Aristotle told about the migration of birds. M. de Quatrefages copied what he said as to the migration of the storks in his history of the pigmies, and Aristotle, as far as the birds were concerned, was correct.

Aristotle said birds hibernated or were torpid in winter, and Gilbert White thought nearly

From Mathews' "Familiar Flowers."
Copyright, 1895, by D.
Appleton & Co.

TALL MEADOW-RUE.

the same thing. Aristotle, as a true Greek, loved music, and so he may be forgiven for exalting the nightingale, the cock bird singing, as he says, "fifteen days and nights without stopping." It is a pretty thing the Greek naturalist tells of the parent bird teaching its little ones how to become songsters, for he believed that birds had a distinct language of their own. "Nothing is to me more astonishing," writes Mr. Fowler, "in the whole history of thought and knowledge, than that the man who wrote the Ethics and Politics should have been capable of putting together such a work. It argues a richness of mind, a variety of interest, a universality of thirst for knowledge, with which we have very little acquaintance in this country."

Some of us have grieved with the author over the loss of his fox-terrier Billy, his faithful and plucky companion for so many years. Billy suddenly disappeared in his old days, held captive, may be, in a drain, where there was perhaps only the scent of his enemy, the fox. Billy's life was a noble one, and he was indeed an honor to Oxford, and the memoir to this old friend is as pretty a chapter on a four-footed friend as you may ever read. (Macmillan. $1.50.)

Familiar Flowers.

"FAMILIAR Flowers of Field and Garden" is the title of a new popular book on flowers, which seems to have profited by the omissions and errors of preceding essays in this direction. It appears that the author, Mr. F. Schuyler Mathews, is a botanist and artist, as well as a writer, and his drawings have a peculiar value. Some special points of his attractive book are the illustrations of the connections between garden and wild flowers, and an elaborate descriptive index showing at a glance the botanical names, seasons, and habitats of the familiar flowers. (Appleton.)—*Brooklyn Times.*

Jewel of Ynys Galon.

TALES of adventure where the slaughter of man is a prominent feature are on the increase. This time it is a Welsh story of pirates, of carnage, of barbarities, which the writer, Owen Rhoscomyl, seems to find enjoyment in narrating. "The Jewel of Ynys Galon" is dedicated to boys who have had intentions of becoming bloodthirsty pirates, to men who have had dreams of becoming fabulously rich by discovering hoarded treasure, and to all who are roused by a "tale of tall fights and reckless adventure." No others will care to read it, and such would do better to let it alone. (Longmans, Green. $1.25.)—*Boston Literary World.*

The Master.

MARK the name of Isaac Zangwill, for it is one which is sure to be high on the roll of English novelists, if it is not already there. Mr. Zangwill is a Jew, and he is at no time more frank and enjoyable than when he is writing about his race, as in such books as " The King of Schnorrers " and in " The Children of the Ghetto." But he is too broad for any single race or sect; and his latest story, which is published in this country by the Harpers, is meant for the world. The volume is a bulky one, which may frighten the dilettante reader ; but he who begins " The Master " will find a charm which will lure him through adventures which are lifelike and full of human interest.

One suspects a large element of autobiography in " The Master "; and this lends it a rare fascination. One praises the novel because (above other reasons) one believes that it has the power of character building—because it holds lofty ideals of character before its readers, particularly young men. This it does by examples, not by preaching—for preaching in a novelist is as unpardonable as romancing in a preacher.

One must confess surprise—a pleasurable surprise, which is largely personal—at finding Mr. Zangwill is familiar with that little corner of Canada which Longfellow made famous in his poem of " Evangeline." Acadia—otherwise known as the basin of Minas—that valley near Annapolis on the Intercolonial railway between Halifax and St. John—is the place selected by Mr. Zangwill for the opening scene of the novel

THE ETERNAL MONOTONE OF THE SEA.

of " The Master." It is easy to see from " Evangeline " that Longfellow never lived in Acadia, but it is impossible to believe that Mr. Zangwill did not at some time walk the dikes and see the " bore " rushing along the thirsty river-bed. Although to-day one of London's foremost *literarians* it is likely that Mr. Zangwill was once as genuine a son of the " bluenose " country as is Bliss Carman, whose "Low Tide on Grand Pré " is precious to all Acadia's English-speaking sons. It is a strong and enduring book. (Harper. $1.75.)—*Chicago Tribune.*

Heart of the World.

" HEART of the World " is a novel of the usual Rider Haggard type. Of course Mr. Haggard's novels do not come within the range of literary criticism. But a great many people read them, watch for them as they do for the postman's visit. Indeed, fiction of this sort—illiterate, inartistic, ludicrous, fatuous—plays a very important part in the lives of many people. They find in it the only form of intellectual excitement which can compete with that aroused by the average melodrama. Here are strange adventures and wonderful heroisms, and they happen, mark you, to every-day folk, who might be walking Broadway instead of scaling the Mountains of the Moon. This is the whole trick of fiction

From Haggard's " Heart of the World."   Longmans, Green & Co.

of the Haggard sort. "Heart of the World " is neither better nor worse than its predecessors. The scene is laid in Mexico. The story rehearses the adventures of an athletic Englishman who loves and weds an Indian princess. There are marvellous descriptions of the "City of the Heart," a mysterious town hemmed in by swamps and unknown mountains; there are priestcraft and brigandage and villainy and love galore; indeed, there are all the usual ingredients of Haggard fiction, dire disaster, dangers untold, hair-breadth escapes, etc. Those who like that sort of thing have a rare pleasure in store. (Longmans, Green & Co.)—*Commercial Advertiser.*

Princeton Stories.

JESSE LYNCH WILLIAMS, the author, is a recent graduate, only three years out. What he has depicted is the Princeton man of to-day—absolutely "up-to-date," as he would say. It is not the man you would *think* you met if you were to spend a few days there, but it is the Princeton man as his fellows know him. When you have read Mr. Williams' stories you will realize that the Princeton man is not of one type, but of a score of types —that, indeed, he is as varied and complex as most other men.

What every Princeton man will feel when he reads these stories is that here is the spirit of the campus-life as he knew it; here is the evanescent charm, the touch of poetry and sentiment that pervades a thousand unpoetic and rather reserved young men. You will find here the good - fellowship depicted without any rant about it. These men have a way of hiding their deepest sentiments under a manner that is often brusque, and clothed in language that is eccentric to say the least. But they have a way of doing the right, the generous thing without any parade. There isn't a prig in these stories, and there are mighty few in Princeton. That type of man can't thrive in a healthy community that enjoys ridicule and is not over-cautious in hurting tender feelings.

The outsider will be impressed with the fact that Princeton, by very reason of being a large college in a small town, has developed its own peculiarly academic life, independent of any city influence. It is a college permeated with traditions, characters and quaint associations; and they are all reflected in these stories that are well written and well constructed, judged from the standard of good American short-story writing. The book ought to find many readers among the sisters, cousins, and aunts of students of Princeton. (Scribner. $1.)— *Droch in Life.*

Coaching Trips Out of London.

LONDON is like a smoky pearl set in a circle of emeralds. Once out of it, though the escape is slow, and patience is needed, we come upon the England we dream of over the drawings of Abbey and Hugh Thomson — the England of "The Quiet Life," of fat meadows, flowing verdure, tiled and thatched cottages, mossy, dripping millwheels, hawthorn hedges, inviting inns, and spacious parks, where the beeches and oak throw out rounded, drooping volumes of foliage, that have the soft density of an exhalation, and where the cuckoo, lark, and nightingale are fearless visitors.

Because London is so environed with beauty, and the roads are good, the coaches thrive; and of the many pleasures of the season, there is nothing to compare with the trips they make, leaving town in the morning, and, with two exceptions, returning in the afternoon.

Let it be said, with due respect to the memory of Mr. Barnum, that "the greatest show on earth" is London, and one of its prettiest "features" is the departure of the coaches from Northumberland Avenue. A smartly dressed crowd is there to see it. Preceded by the musical winding of horns, which rise above the noise of cabs, 'buses and carriages, the coaches turn into the magnificent avenue from the Embankment, or from Trafalgar Square, where the fountains are playing over the flanks and manes of Landseer's lions, and Nelson stands on the foretop of his own monument. They are party-colored, and lettered on the boot and on the panels with the names of the towns and villages they pass through. There is an inside, of course ; but the blinds are down, for nobody ever wants to be inside. Outside there are seats for thirteen, including the box-seat, the privileged position, for which a larger fare is charged.

The coachman, in a long drab jean, or box-cloth, driving-coat reaching to his ankles, overlooks it all, with the eye of the skipper of a double topsail ship when the pilot leaves him and the wind freshens on the bar. A score of details are on his mind ; he must see that the bridles, or headstalls, do not pinch the horses' ears ; that the bits are not too high, or too low, in their mouths ; that bearing-reins, cruppers, pole-chains, and pole-pieces, are adjusted so as to be neither too tight nor too loose ; that the pads are well stuffed, and fitted close to their backs ; that the traces are of the right length, and that the pole-hooks are downward. The old mail-coaches ceased running with the advent of the railways in 1840, and, out of twenty-seven in service up to that year, not one was left. "Few people are aware," says Lord Algernon St. Maur, "of the misery caused by railways to innkeepers, coachmen, guards, post-boys, 'ostlers, and horse-keepers, as it all came to pass so suddenly."

Had profit been the only consideration, the coaches would never have reappeared ; but there had grown up in England many enthusiastic amateurs, who found delight in driving a four-in-hand, and they revived, for their own pleasure, what could no longer be a money-making venture. (T. Y. Crowell.)—*From "In the Land of Lorna Doone."*

From Weed's " Ten New England Blossoms." Copyright, 1895, by Houghton, Mifflin & Co.

A BLOSSOM OF ALL LANDS.

The Marriage of Esther.

"THE Marriage of Esther," by Guy Boothby, is not a common book, although it deals with common, very common people, such as a generation or two ago made the bulk of the population of Australia, New Zealand and other English colonies, to which thousands who left their country for their country's good found their way, some because they were transported thither by the home government, and others because they had exhausted the forbearance and the resources of their relatives and friends, and had nowhere else to go. It is the story of two Englishmen—English gentlemen, let us say, though the fact was not apparent at first—who were down on their luck among the crowd of roughs, convicts, murderers and what not, on Thursday Island, wherever that was, ragged, penniless, friendless and desperate; the story of their curious liking for each other, and what came of it when they obtained employment from the daughter of a pearl fisherman, between whom and one of them love soon grew up, and from this love the adventurous and tragically happy end; for, of course, the heroine, Esther, married the man of her choice, or what would be the sense of the title? It is a vigorous picture of half-barbaric life, with its difficulties and dangers, its criminality and its manliness, and the frank, strong womanhood of Esther, who is as vital and real as one of Charles Reade's women. It is not a story to be analyzed in a few lines, either as a record of reckless colonial life, or as a delineation of character; but to be read at a sitting, which is not difficult, its movement is so rapid and its spirit so human and hearty. (Appleton. pap., 50 c.)—*Mail and Express.*

The Curse of Intellect.

BRIEFLY told, this is the story of a monkey who is taught to think, talk, and write by a man of enormous will-power ; the result is that the monkey is so disgusted with the misery entailed on him by intellect that he kills his teacher and commits suicide himself. The conception does not seem to us altogether novel ; but the monkey's pessimistic view of his position is cleverly exposed, and is perhaps, under the circumstances, natural, for there is a great deal of truth in Renan's remark that " un état qui donnerait le plus grand bonheur possible aux individus serait probablement, au point de vue des nobles poursuites de l'humanité, un état de profond abaissement," and the monkey would be the more qualified to judge from his previous experience of the debased condition. There is a certain amount of cheap satire in the book at the expense of the tame poet, the society woman, and so on ; but there is enough incident to make the story well worth half an hour's reading. (Roberts. $1.) — *The Athenæum.*

From Glascock's "Stories of Columbia."   Copyright, 1894, by D. Appleton & Co.
A MODERN REAPER AND HARVESTER.

From Bolles' " Chocorua's Tenants."   Copyright, 1896, by Houghton, Mifflin & Co.

"TREES WHOSE LEAVES ARE SHED IN AUTUMN."

The Great Crested Flycatcher.

WESTWARD of Chocorua water
Stands an ancient apple orchard,
Overhung by lofty maples,
Bearing scars of many sappings:
Warm and sunny is the orchard,
Plenty are its acid apples.
In its hollows squirrels nestle,
In its branches birds assemble.

Titmice love this orchard's hollows,
Caverns in its trunks and branches
Make them warm and cosey nestings,
Safely hidden from the blue jay.
Here the deer eyed flying-squirrel,
Mice and bluebirds, swallows, adders,
Find in turn their favorite havens;
Here, as well, a harsh voiced tyrant
Makes his home within a cavern.

In this ill-assorted rubbish
Four or five strange eggs are hidden;
They are tinted like the matted
Leaves and grasses, hair and feathers;
From their larger end descending
Countless slender rays or streakings
Seek the point, while in beginning
They are blended in a tangle.

What can be the explanation
Of this bird's persistent fancy?
Why through countless generations
Have they sought for cast-off snake skins
To adorn or guard their nestings
In the hollow of the tree-trunks?
Do the mouse, the snake, and squirrel
Fear a scrap of harmless snake skin?

Wild and wary is this tyrant,
Harsh his screaming, angry whistle,
Strange his comings and his goings,
Strange his likings and his hatings;
Round about Chocorua water
He has found the haunts he fancies,
But in many another valley
None have ever heard his clamor.

He is one that shuns the winter,
Knows no home where snowflakes flutter.
Insect wings proclaim his coming,
Insect death foretells his going,
With the arbutus he enters,
With the goldenrod he passes,
Hither from the south in Maytime,
Thither with the equinoctial.

(Houghton, Mifflin & Co.)—*From Bolles'*
"Chocorua's Tenants."

The King's Diary.

IT appears from the pompous "foreword" of the editor that this little volume is the first of *Cassell's Pocket Library,* and if the series maintains the promise of its first fruits it will be a notable addition to the novel-reader's bookshelves. There is hardly anything but praise to be given to this remarkable story. It is brilliantly written, and is full of the pleasant satire which comes from a genial but penetrating observation of life. It is a study primarily of one of those clever literary men with a twist in their nature which utterly incapacitates them from achieving any successful work. He is thoroughly unpractical and thoroughly lovable, but is a burden to all his worthy and wealthy relatives, and becomes a trial even to his charming and matter-of-fact wife. There is not one of the characters whom one might not have been talking and living with, so admirably are they realized by the author, and it would be difficult to single out any one for especial praise. Perhaps, after the writer of the diary himself, the best is the sleek father-in-law who had the habit of " rubbing the back of his left hand with the palm of his right, as though tickled by an invisible straw," and who had "the air of a man who has not adapted himself to suit his environment, but altered it to suit his own peculiar convenience "; but all are good. The only criticism we would venture on is that the catastrophe at the end is hardly inevitable enough ; the man had the germs of madness in him, but the hansom cab accident is clumsy. (Cassell. 50 c.)—*The Athenæum.*

Watching the New Valet.

"UGH! It looks haunted, that house by the river. I wonder who lives there! It seems the very place for a murder, or one of those dreadful houses where wicked people throw poor, insane relatives to die, unknown and uncared for," she thought, preparing to turn her back upon it, when suddenly she stopped, interested. Surely she knew that figure coming so guardedly and stealthily down the path!

She waited until the man came within a few steps of her, then she stepped from the shadow of the tree where she had been idly leaning, and faced him in her uncompromising, schoolgirl fashion.

"What were you doing in that house? You don't live there, do you?" she asked, sternly.

Yes, Bebé had not been mistaken. She was looking straight into the apologetic, restless eyes of the new valet.

"Oh, mademoiselle, you startle me!" he gasped, removing his hat from his oiled hair, his mustache curving upward in a craven smile.

"What have you been doing down there? Were you not told to wait in the servants' quarters for Mr. Raritan?" she demanded—for Bebé had been accustomed to authority all her spoiled life, and could look as cool and commanding as a young princess upon occasions.

"True, mademoiselle," shrugged the new servant. "But ze maison was ver' hot. I went to take a walk; I remembered zat ol' pless zare. Once a fren' of mine—a poor, sickly young Englishman, leeve zare. I strolled up ze walk for ze remembrance sake of ze time when we used to smoke in zee little garden."

"H'm! You must have lived a long time in this country," sniffed Bébe, suspiciously. "That must have been years and years ago."

"Only two years, mademoiselle—two short years since my fren' live there—poor fellow Zee house ees damp. Eet kill him; I know eet. But advice he would not take."

"Well, you'd better go back! Mr. Raritan won't like to be kept waiting;" and her clear, proud eyes watched him half contemptuously as he minced out of sight.

"There's something uncanny about that little Frenchman. He's like a monkey. I hope Sid will send him about his business," she thought, and then without another look at the house by the river, that was destined to play such a strange part in the fortune of her life, she turned down another road. (Bonner. pap. 50 c.)—*From Kent's "That House by the River."*

"I WANT A WORD WITH YOU."

In Russet and Silver.

WITH his accustomed charm of touch and tender quaintness of thought, Mr. Edmund Gosse wooes our attention to a fresh volume, whose attractive name is suggested and repeated in its binding. There are not many fresh things left to be said in the world, and human emotion repeats and rerepeats itself century by century ; the most that any poet can hope to achieve is to voice the reiterated thought in a new tone and with a fresh cadence, and this Mr. Gosse most happily does.

The Arthurian Epic.

MR. S. HUMPHREYS GURTEEN, graduate of the University of Cambridge, has written '' The Arthurian Epic. A Comparative Study of the Cambrian, Breton and Anglo-Saxon Versions of the Story." This is the second or third book upon the subject that we have read since the death of Lord Tennyson, the supposed eminence of whom, as the Laureate of King Arthur and the Knights of the Round Table, and the delight that he had afforded his thousands of readers in the '' Idyls of the King," was the chief motive of their production. They contained nothing that was not already known to scholars interested in the Arthurian legend in its various forms—in the balladry and romantic prose of Welsh and Breton singers and writers, and in the early English historical narratives, but much that had not come within the knowledge of the average reader of English literature, for whom their materials were recast in a popular form—the belief of the writers being that this admiring but unlearned person might like to know, in reading the '' Idyls of the King," what portions, if any, were due to the invention of Lord Tennyson, and what portions were derived from Malory's '' Morte d'Arthur," Lady Guest's ''Mabinogen," or other and earlier sources. Mr. Gurteen has read, and written enough to supply the reasonable curiosity of Lord Tennyson's readers; and, knowing in advance much that he would be sure to write, and ought to write, in order to elucidate his author, we have read his book with a certain amount of pleasure if not to our entire satisfaction. He has not convinced us that much which is beyond doubt has yet been discovered *in re* the origin, or origins, of the Arthurian legend, which has, we feel sure, no real historical basis to rest upon; and he has not convinced us that the parts of this legend have any, the least Epical significance. For, reading it either as a narrative of the adventures of Merlin and Vivvien, the adventure of Sir Galahad in quest of the Holy Grail, the impassioned, guilty love of Launcelot and Guinevere, or, as an idealization of the personality and mission of King Arthur himself, it is, at least, a collection of episodes which were not meant to be, and which cannot be, gathered into and moulded into an Epic. If anybody could have found, or could have made, an Epic of the Arthurian legend, it was Lord Tennyson, who, ambitious as he was, and great poet as he was, could only use its materials in an idyllic form—in the '' Idyls of the King." Mr. Gurteen's criticisms of Lord Tennyson's use of his matter is temerarious in the extreme. Still, he has written a book which was needed for popular reading, and which Tennysonians ought to place on their shelves beside other commentaries on their favorite author. (Putnam. $2.)—*Mail and Express.*

The Handy Volume Shakespeare.

MORE than a quarter of a century ago the writer decided to give all brides by whom such a gift would be appreciated a set of Shakespeare, and many letters from happy girls are at hand acknowledging the intense satisfaction this one among their few or many wedding gifts had given them. Following the fashion of the hour, sets of Shakespeare are gotten up more and more gorgeously, and no jeweller manufactures more beautiful cases for the gems he sends to please a bride than are now provided for these literary jewels. *The Handy Volume edition* of ''Shakespeare's Works," in thirteen volumes, may be had in cloth, in Venetian, in imitation seal, Alsatian, Persian and in watered silk of every shade, and for every new device in binding there is a box to match. It has been a great wedding season and we hope some of the friends of brides have thought of books when offering gifts. Every one of these books tempts you to touch it, to hold it just a little while, to turn over its clearly printed pages, to handle its thin but opaque

paper, to fit it back once more in the little space it has left among its pretty fellow volumes. And who can ever handle a volume of Shakespeare without reading just a few pages and being lost in surprise that so many dearly loved quotations are found in one man's writings? (Routledge. per set, $7.50; $21.)

The Literary News.

An Eclectic Monthly Review of Current Literature.

EDITED BY A. H. LEYPOLDT.

JUNE, 1895.

CHOOSING SUMMER READING.

WHEN every trunk and closet has been ransacked, and all the momentous questions have been decided as to what will do and not do for another summer; when all the new things have been bought, and changed, and sewed, and fitted, and packed, most women and girls are too tired to care what is put into the very small space generally left for books. We shall wait before giving a list of novels and books of description, until the hard work of getting houses shut up, and resting-places found, and travel accomplished, has been forgotten; then we hope to let the LITERARY NEWS call attention to some of the books "that every one should read," because every one is reading them. But most summer travellers have special interests in connection with which they decide the momentous question of where to go for the summer of 1895. As far as these interests are concerned with sports and pastimes, or with hobbies of gardening, studying astronomy, botanizing, watching or catching birds, etc., we wish to assist their choice, for only a few of these will be needed for every traveller, and every bag and trunk must make room for one or more. Next month we shall give a list of novels for days when outdoor books are only an aggravation.

BOOKS ON NATURE.

Abbott (C. C.), The birds about us, $2.......*Lippincott*
Bolles (Frank), From Blomidon to Smoky, $1.25.
  Houghton, M
Burroughs (J.), Riverby, $1.25..........*Houghton, M*
Chambers (G. F.), The story of the stars, 50c.*Appleton*
Chapman (F. M.), Handbook of birds of eastern
  North America, $3.; $3.50......................*Appleton*
Comstock (J. H. and A. B.), A manual for the study of
  insects, net, $3.75..................*Comstock Pub. Co*
Dana, (*Mrs.* W. S.), According to season, 75c..*Scribner*
— How to know the wild flowers. *New rev. enl. ed.*,
  net, $1.75.................................*Scribner*
Elha (*pseud.*), A naturalist on the prowl, $3....*Scribner*
Emmons (S. F.), Geological guide-book for an excur-
  sion to the Rocky Mountains, $1.50...............*Wiley*
Furneaux (W. S.), Butterflies and moths (British),
  $3.50..*Longmans, G*
Gaye (S.), The great world's farm, *new cheaper ed.*,
  $1.25.......................................*Macmillan*
Grant (J. B.), Our common birds and how to know
  them, net, $1.50............................*Scribner*
Hayward (J. M.), Bird notes, $1.75....... *Longmans, G*
Karr (A.), A tour 'round my garden, $1.50....*Warne*
Kerner *and* Oliver's Natural history of plants, a v.,
  net, $7.50.......................................*Holt*
Keyser (L. S.), In bird land, $1.25.............*McClurg*
Knobel (E.), The beetles, net, 50c..........*Whidden*
— Day butterflies and duskflyers of New England, net,
  50c ....*Whidden*
— Ferns and evergreens of New England, pap., net, 50c.
  Whidden
Knobel (E.), Guide to names of all wild-growing trees
  and shrubs of New England, pap., net, 50c...*Whidden*
Language of flowers, $1.50................. ....*Warne*
McDonald (D), Sweet-scented flowers and fragrant
  leaves, net, $1.50.............................*Scribner*
Mathews (F. S.), Familiar flowers of field and garden.
  $1.75; $2.25. ....*Appleton*
Miller (Olive Thorne), Our home pets, $1.25...*Harper*
Minot (H D.), Land birds and game birds of New Eng-
  land, *new ed.*, $3.50.....................*Houghton, M*
Murray-Aaron (E.), The butterfly-hunters in the
  Caribbees, $2 ....*Scribner*
Parkhurst (H. E.), The birds' calendar, net, $1.50.
  Scribner
Porter (J. H.), Wild beasts, $2...............*Scribner*
Potts (W.), From a New England hillside: notes from
  Underledge, 75c............................*Macmillan*
Prime (W. C.), Among the northern hills, $1....*Harper*
Russell (T.), Meteorology, net, $4..........*Macmillan*
Sargent (C. S.), Notes on the forest flora of Japan, $7.50.
  Houghton, M
— The silva of North America, v. 7, net, $25.
  Houghton, M
Shaler (N. S.), Sea and land features of coasts and
  oceans, $2.50..............................*Scribner*
Sorauer (P.), Treatise on the physiology of plants, $3.
  Longmans, G
Step (E.), Wayside and woodland blossoms..$2.50*Warne*
Torrey (Bradford), A Florida sketch-book, $1.25.
  Houghton, M
Warne's library of natural history, in 36 nos., nos. 1
  and 2, *ea.*, 50c..............................*Warne*
Weed (C. M.), Ten New England blossoms and their
  insect visitors, $1.25. ....*Houghton, M*
Whitcomb (Ida P.), A bunch of wild flowers for the
  children, 50c..............................*Randolph*
Whiting (M. C.) *and* Miller (E.), Wild flowers of the
  northeastern states, net, $1.25.............*Putnam*
Willcox (M. A.), Pocket guide to the common land
  birds of New England, net, 60c..............*Lee & S*
Willis (O. R.), A practical flora, $1.50..*Amer. B'k Co*
Wright (Mabel Osgood), Bird craft: a field-book of two
  hundred song, game, and water birds, $3...*Macmillan*
— The friendship of nature, 75c.; *edition de luxe*, net,
  $3..*Macmillan*
Wonders of marine life, 60c..................*Appleton*

OUTDOOR SPORTS AND EXERCISE.

Allen *and* Sachtleben, Across Asia on a bicycle, $1.50.
  Century
Anderson (E. L.), Curb, snaffle, and spur, $1.50.
  Little, B
Bingham (N. W.), *jr., ed.* Book of athletics and out-
  of-door sports, $1.50........................*Lothrop*
Boardman (S. L.), Handbook of the turf, $1.*O.Judd Co*
Clementson, (G. B.), Road rights and liabilities of
  wheelmen, net, $1.50.......................*Callaghan*
Clyde (H.), Pleasure-cycling, $1............*Little, B*
Flannery (Jerome), American cricket annual for 1895,
  pap., 50c...................................*Flannery*
Galbraith (A. M.), *M.D.*, Hygiene and physical culture
  for women, $1................................*Dodd, M*
Harley (*pseud.*), In the veldt, pap., 50c....*Longmans, G*
Keene (J. H.), The boy's own guide to fishing, $1.
  Lee & S
Lee (Ja. P), Golf in America, $1............*Dodd, M*
Longmans (C. J.) *and* Walrond (H.), Archery, ((Bad-
  minton lib.), $3.50..........................*Little, B*
Macpherson (*Rev.* H. A.) *and others*, The grouse,
  $1.75..*Longmans, G*
Marriott *and* Alcock, The Rugby union game [foot-
  ball], 50c....................................*Routledge*
Oval series of games; ed. by C. W. Alcock: Swimming,
  Cricket, Golfing, Lawn Tennis, 4 v., *ea.*, 50c.*Routledge*
Porter (L. H.), Cycling for health and pleasure, $1.
  Dodd, M
Reynolds (C. B.), The game laws in brief of U. S. and
  Canada, pap., 25c.........*Forest and Stream Pub. Co*
Sampson (C. A.), Strength, $1; pap., 50c...*Rand, McN*
Stagg (A. A.) *and* Williams (H. L.), A scientific and
  practical treatise on American football, *rev.* to date.
  $1.25...*Appleton*
Sullivan (*Sir* E.) *and* Brassey (*Lord*), Yachting, 2 v.
  (Badminton lib.), $7; $10....................*Little, B*
Vaux (C. B.), Canoeing, pap., 10c............*Spalding*
Whitney (C. W.), A sporting pilgrimage, $3.50..*Harper*

MAGAZINE ARTICLES.

Articles marked with an asterisk are illustrated.

ARTISTIC, MUSICAL AND DRAMATIC.—*Century*, Comédie Française at Orange,* Janvier.—*Chautauquan*, Richard Wagner, Mrs. E. W. Hubbard.—*Fort. Review* (May), "King Arthur" on the stage, R. W. Bond; Bach Festival, H. H. Statham.—*Lippincott*, Tyranny of the Pictorial, Fairfield.—*Nine. Century* (May), Mr. Irving on the Art of Acting, "Ouida."—*North Am. Review*, Nordau's Theory of Degeneration—A Painter's View, Kenyon Cox; A Musician's Retort, Anton Seidl.—*Scribner*, American Wood-Engravers—Frank French.*

BIOGRAPHY, CORRESPONDENCE. — *Chautauquan*, Charles A. Dana, Morris.—*Fort. Review* (May), Sophie Kovalevsky, Carter.—*Nine. Century* (May), A Love Episode in Mazzini's Life, Mlle. Melegari.—*Pop. Science*, Timothy Abbott Conrad, C. C. Abbott (Por.). — *West. Review* (May), Charles Bradlaugh, Waterer.

DESCRIPTION, TRAVEL.—*Atlantic*, Pilgrimage to the Great Buddhist Sanctuary of North China, Rockhill; In the Twilight of the Gods, Hearn.—*Century*, Discovery of Glacier Bay,* Muir.—*Harper's*, House Boating in China,* Ralph; The Grand Prix and Other Prizes,* Davis; Rome in Africa,* Sharp.—*Pop. Science*, Two-Ocean Pass,* Evermann; Journeying in Madagascar,* Vincent.—*Scribner's*, Chicago—Before the Fire, After the Fire, and To-Day,* Stone.

DOMESTIC AND SOCIAL.—*New England*, Artistic Domestic Architecture in America,* Ferree.—*North Am. Review*, Modern Woman and Marriage, Eliz. Bisland (Notes and Comments).—*West. Review* (May), Some Modern Ideas about Marriage, E. M. S.

EDUCATIONAL.—*Atlantic*, Vocal Culture in its Relation to Literary Culture, Prof. Corson.—*Forum*, Rational Correction of School Studies, Rice; An American Educational System in Fact, Powell; Why the American Voice is Bad, Osgood.—*New England*, Roxbury Latin School, De Normandie.

FICTION.—*Atlantic*, Rosita, Ellen Mackubin; Through the Windows: Two Glimpses of a Man's Life, F. E. Lester.—*Century*, On a Side Track,* Mary Hallock Foote; The Lady of Lucerne. F. Hopkinson Smith; The Gentleman in the Barrel, C. B. Fernald.—*Chautauquan*, Mademoiselle Clémence, Pouvillon.—*Harper's*, What the Madre Would Not Have,* Meyers; A Miracle, M. E. M. Davis.—*Lippincott's*, Battle of Salamanca, Galdós; "As a Day in June," May D. Hatch; Beset in Aravaipa Cañon, Thomson.—*Scribner's* The Genius of Bowlder Bluff, Abbe C. Goodloe; "The Gentleman from Huron," Hibbard; A Co-operative Courtship, Annie S. Winston.

HISTORY.—*Fort. Review* (May), Prince Bismarck and Prussian Monarchy, Dawson.—*Harper's*, A Frontier Fight,* Gen. Forsyth.—*Nine. Century* (May), Joan of Arc, Mrs. Southwood Hill; The False Pucelle, Lang.—*West. Review* (May), Her Majesty's Treasury, C. E. D. Black.

LITERARY.—*Atlantic*, Some Reminiscences of

Christina Rossetti, Sharp.—*Cath. World*, Wordsworth, His Home and Work, Oléron; Downfall of Zolaism, Lecky.—*Century*, New Public Library in Boston: Its Artistic Aspects, Mrs. S. Van Rensselaer; Its Ideals and Working Conditions, Lindsay Swift—*Forum*, Mr. Kipling's Work, so Far, Bishop; The Great Libraries of the U. S., Putnam.—*Harper's*, First Impressions of Literary New York,* Howells.—*Lippincott's*, Galdós and His Novels, Ogden; Thoreau, Abbott.—*North Am. Review*, As to Age-End Literature, Hazeltine.

MENTAL AND MORAL.—*Pop. Science* Psychology of Woman, Patrick.

NATURE AND SCIENCE.—*Harper's*, A Familiar Guest* (Wasps), Gibson.—*Pop. Science*, Irritability and Movement in Plants,* MacDougal.

POETRY.—*Atlantic*, A Japanese Sword-Song, Mary S. Hunter.—*Cath. World*, The Pentecost, Burke; Dawn, Conway.—*Century*, A Business Transaction,* Roche; The Poet's Day, R. W. Gilder; "Time Brings Roses," Boner.—*Chautauquan*, Ballad of the Eastern Woman, Burton.—*Harper's*, Orisons, Louise I. Guiney; Why Should We Care? J. V. Cheney.—*Scribner's*, Sorrento, Hay; Benevolence, Mrs. J. T. Fields; Edge of Claremont Hill, Van Dyke.

POLITICAL AND SOCIAL. — *Century*, Tribulations of a Cheerful Giver, Howells; Two Tramps in England, Flynt.—*Chautauquan*, How the Poor Live in Paris, Preston.—*Fort. Review* (May), Factory Legislation for Women, Miss March-Phillipps; Mr. Peel and His Predecessors, Traill. — *Forum*, Growth of Am. Nationality, Walker; Free-Silver Argument, Harvey; Grotesque Fallacies of Free Silver, Warner; Studies of Notable Men—Joseph Chamberlain, M'Carthy; Are We Degenerating? Dana.—*Harper's*, The New Czar and What We May Expect from Him, Borges.—*Lippincott's*, Improving the Common Roads, Speed; The Referendum and the Senate; McCrackan.—*North Am. Review*, Power and Wealth of the United States, Mulhall; A Cable Post, Heaton; Military Lessons of the Chino-Japanese War, Sec'y of the Navy; The Silver Question: Germany's Attitude as to a Bi-Metallic Union, Von Mirbach; Silver Standard in Mexico, Mexican Minister.—*Pop. Science*, Decline in Railway Charges, Newcomb.—*West. Review* (May), International Agreements and the Sufferers in War, King; Ought Capital Punishment to be Abolished? Vicars.

SPORTS AND AMUSEMENTS. — *Harper's*, Golf, Old and New, Lang.—*Nine. Century* (May), A May-Queen Festival (with Letters from Ruskin), Faunthorpe.—*Scribner's*, The Bicycle, Wheel of To-Day,* Hubert; Woman and the Bicycle, Marguerite Merington; Social Side of Bicycling,* J. B. Townsend; A Doctor's View of Bicycling,* J. W. Roosevelt.

THEOLOGY, RELIGION AND SPECULATION. — *Cath. World*, Father Hecker and the Establishing of the Poor Clares in the U. S., Hedges; Dr. Heber Newton on the Resurrection, Searle.—*Century*, The New Old Testament, Newman Smyth.—*Nine. Century* (May), True and False Notions of Prayer, Pearson. — *West. Review* (May), Foundations of Belief, Todhunter; Crisis in Free Thought, Dewey.

Survey of Current Literature.

☞ Order through your bookseller.—"There is no worthier or surer pledge of the intelligence and the purity of any community than their general purchase of books; nor is there any one who does more to further the attainment and possession of these qualities than a good bookseller."—Prof. Dunn.

BIOGRAPHY, CORRESPONDENCE, ETC.

BIGELOW, J. The life of Samuel J. Tilden. Harper. pors. il., 8°, $6.

COLERIDGE, S. TAYLOR. Letters of Samuel Taylor Coleridge; ed. by Ernest Hartley Coleridge. Houghton, Mifflin & Co. 2 v., pors. 8°, $6.

DAVIES, H. E. General Sheridan. Appleton. por. maps, 12°, (Great commanders ser., no. 11.) $1.50.
General Davies, the author of this volume, served with distinction under Sheridan in the Army of the Potomac.

ESPINASSE, FRANCIS. Life of Ernest Renan; [with] bibliography of Renan, by J. P. Anderson. Scribner. 8°, (Great writers.) $1.

HUTTON, *Rev.* W. HOLDEN. William Laud. Houghton, Mifflin & Co. 12°, (English leaders of religion ser.) $1.

THAXTER, *Mrs.* CELIA. Letters of Celia Thaxter; ed. by her friends A. F. and R. L. Houghton, Mifflin & Co. por., 12°, $1.50.

DESCRIPTION, GEOGRAPHY, TRAVEL, ETC.

BOURGET, PAUL. Outre-mer; impressions of America. Scribner. 12°, $1.75.

FINCK, H. T. Lotos-time in Japan. Scribner. il. 8°, $1.75.

FRASER, MARIE. In Stevenson's Samoa. Macmillan & Co. il. 16°, 80 c.

HAPGOOD, ISABEL-FLORENCE. Russian rambles. Houghton. Mifflin & Co. 12°, $1.50.

LAMONT, ARCHIBALD. ["John Coming Chinaman," *pseud.*] Bright Celestials; the Chinaman at home and abroad. Putnam. 12°, $2.40.

STANLEY, H. M. My early travels and adventures in America and Asia. Scribner. 2 v. pors., $2.

VINCENT, FRANK. Actual Africa; or, the coming continent: a tour of exploration. Appleton. pors. il. map, 8°, $5.

FICTION.

BALZAC, HONORÉ DE. Lucien de Rubempré; tr. by Katharine Prescott Wormeley. Roberts. 12°, hf. mor., $1.50.

BELL, LILIAN. A little sister to the wilderness. Stone & Kimball. 16°, $1.25.
"Description and characterization are both good, and the spiritual issues of the situation are drawn out with a fine sense of relative values. The dialect is something of a stumbling-block, but the writer has a conscience (as her prefatory note upon this subject shows), and it would hardly be reasonable to expect phonetics of more standard type from her mountaineers. Miss Bell has told a story that deserves atten-

tion, and the sincerity of her workmanship is undoubted."—*The Dial.*

BLAIR, ELIZA NELSON, [*Mrs.* H. W. Blair.] Lisbeth Wilson: a daughter of New Hampshire hills. Lee & Shepard. 12°, $1.50.
The story deals with the New Hampshire of a generation ago, with its homely scenes and plain, sternly conscientious people. The heroine, Lisbeth Wilson, and her lover are separated by her father, onaccount of a difference in religious belief, their troubled courtship making a most interesting story. A very good picture is given of the time, and the habits, customs, manners, opinions, controversies, etc., of the people.

BOOTHBY, GUY. A lost endeavor. Macmillan, (Iris lib.) 75 c.

BOOTHBY, GUY. The marriage of Esther. Appleton. 12°, (Appleton's town and country lib., no. 166) $1; pap., 50 c.
"This story of two friends in Australia has comparatively little of the local coloring which we should expect from a writer like Mr. Guy Boothby, who has published a book of his travels in that far-off country, and there is an atmosphere of unreality about the characters that is even less conducive to the illusion of verity. We meet the friends first at the bar of a hotel, where one is drunk and the other fights for him. They have lost money, friends and reputation, and are at the lowest ebb of respectability. The story tells of their reinstatement to places of trust, of the love-story of one and the self-sacrifice of the other, and this with certain complications that add to the interest of the story."—*Boston Literary World.*

CAMBRIDGE, ADA, [*pseud.* for *Mrs.* Cross.] Fidelis: a novel. Appleton. 12°, (Appleton's town and country lib., no. 167.) $1; pap., 50 c.

COMPTON, HERBERT. A free lance in a far land: being an account of the singular fortunes of Selwyn Fyveways, of Fyveways Hall, in the County of Gloucester, Esquire: for seven years an adventurer in the kingdoms of Hindostan; the same abridged from the original papers and journals of Mr. Fyveways and certain traditions in his family. Cassell. 12°, $1.
An historical romance dealing with the practices of the East India Company some hundred years ago and with the opportunities which Hindostan offered to foreign adventurers in the days between the break-up of the Mogul and the full establishment of the English Empire. The " free lance " is the son of a Roman Catholic baronet and Protestant mother, which fact lies at the bottom of the many adventures which he recounts.

CORELLI, MARIE. The silence of the Maharajah. Merriam Co. 24°, (Merriam's violet ser.) 40 c.

COTES, *Mrs.* EVERARD. [Sara Jeannette Duncan.] The story of Sonny Sahib. Appleton. il. 12°, $1.

CRAWFORD, F. MARION. Sant' Ilario. Macmillan. 12°, (Macmillan's novelists' lib., no. 2.) pap., 50 c.

CROCKETT, S. R. Bog-myrtle and peat: being tales chiefly of Galloway, gathered from the years 1889-1895. Appleton. 12°, $1.50. "These shorter studies in Scotch character and manners have all the charm and humor of Mr. S. R. Crockett's longer tales. They are extremely varied in scene and touch; some are gay and some are grave, but all are delightful in their several ways. 'The back of beyont' has something of the flavor of ' The raiders '; 'Across the March dyke' betrays the hand which wrote 'A lilac sunbonnet'; 'The colleging of Simon Glegg' and ' The minister's loon' are as good as anything in ' The stickit minister'; while ' The glistering beaches' has a fairy quality all its own and altogether charming. Mr. Crockett is surely very high up in the list of modern story writers."—*Boston Literary World.*

CURSE (The) of intellect. Roberts. 16°, $1. A monkey as large as a man, rescued from his forest home by Reuben Power, a Cambridge man, of unusual intelligence, and taught to think and speak and conduct himself like a human being, is the central figure. Power, who is hopelessly sceptical and pessimistic, makes the " beast " his companion. A slight romance is woven around them. The chief point is the "beast's" opinions of men, and the comparisons he makes between his former state of ignorance and his present one of knowledge. He attributes all the vices and weaknesses of mankind to "the curse of intellect."

DANE, DAN. Is she not a woman? or, vengeance is mine. Cassell. 12°, (Union sq. lib., no. 2.) pap., 50 c.

DAVIS, *Mrs.* M. E. M. Under the man-fig. Houghton, Mifflin & Co. 12°, $1.25.

KOVEN, *Mrs.* REGINALD DE. A sawdust doll. Stone & Kimball. 16°, (Peacock lib.) $1.25.

DU BOIS, CONSTANCE GODDARD. A modern pagan : a novel. Merriam Co. 12°, $1.50.

DUVAL, G. The romance of the sword: a Napoleonic novel; tr. by Mary J. Safford. Merriam Co. 12°, $1.50. The sword was given by Catherine II., of Russia, to the Comte d'Artois, brother of Louis XVI., who sold it to a London Jew. It was rescued and given to Napoleon by a dying nobleman. The oft told tale of Napoleon's marriage with Josephine and her sinful extravagance and selfishness is the basis of a story in which this sword influenced many events that brought glory to Napoleon and victory to France.

FENN, G. MANVILLE. The tiger lily: a story of a woman. Cassell. 12°, $1.

FRANCIS, M. E. [*pseud.* for *Mrs.* Francis Blundell, *formerly* Miss M. E. Sweetman.] A daughter of the soil : a novel. Harper. 12°, $1.25.

FULLER, H. B., [" Stanton Page," *pseud.*] With the procession: a novel. Harper. 12°, $1.25.

GISSING, G. Eve's ransom: a novel. Appleton. 12°, (Appleton's town and country lib., no. 165.) $1; pap., 50 c. A sweet girl's face in a photograph album attracts the hero. An old creditor of this hero's father has just given him a sum of money to clear up some old rather " shady" business transactions. Hilliard starts for London, and meets Eve, the original of the picture. She is a superficial girl, leading a careless, even shameful life. Hilliard befriends her in an honorable manner, and after six months sees her marry his friend, to whom she has lied and who knows her character.

HASTINGS, ELIZ. An experiment in altruism. Macmillan. 12°, 75 c. A woman of forty feels she has earned the right to devote herself to mission work in the slums of a great city. Here she meets a woman doctor and an altruist, who is enthusiastically devoted to righting a social system he considered wholly wrong. A young girl of twenty-four and her little orphan godchild, Jean, play leading parts in a sketchy story, showing up the weakness of college settlements and of amateur mission work in the slums.

HOBBES, J. OLIVER, [*pseud.* for *Mrs.* Craigie.] Some good intentions and a blunder. Merriam Co. 24°, (Merriam's violet ser., no. 4.) 40 c.

HOBBES, J. OLIVER, [*pseud.* for *Mrs.* Mary Cra'gie.] The gods, some mortals, and Lord Wickenham. Appleton. por. 12°, $1.50.

HORNE, CALVAN GALE. A Norse idyl. The Robert Clarke Co. il. sq. 8°, $1.50.

KENT, BARBARA. The house by the river: a novel; il. by Warren B. Davis. [*Also*] The children's crusade. Bonner. 12°, (Ledger lib., no. 123.) $1; pap., 50 c.

KINGSLEY, H. The Hillyars and the Burtons: a story of two families. *New ed.*, with a note on old Chelsea church, by Clement Shorter ; il. by Herbert Railton. Ward, Lock & Bowden, Ltd. il. 8°, $1.25.

KINGSLEY, H. Silcote of Silcotes. *New ed.* Ward, Lock & Bowden, Ltd. il. 8°, $1.25.

LEE, MARY CATHERINE. A soulless singer. Houghton, Mifflin & Co. 12°, $1.25. "Victoria Montagu is an exceedingly self-satisfied young lady. Having a good voice, she determines that she will become the great concert singer. She does sing quite correctly, but the audience does not feel ' the magnetic thrill.' Coming home, she consults a distinguished singing master and wants to know why the audience is indifferent. The master says,' Mees Montagu, it is not Elsa, it is not Marguerite who sings. It is Mees Montagu.' In other words, Miss Montagu has no soul, Then the musical young lady in cleaning her gloves burns her hands so fearfully that she has ever afterwards to conceal them. How she finds a musical and other soul is then explained. The musical novel is full of high aspirations, and the author concludes 'A Soulless Singer' by the triumph of Mees Victoria Montagu's ' Ernani Involami.'"—*N. Y Times.*

LOWRY, H. D. Women's tragedies. Roberts. 16°, (keynote ser.) $1. Sixteen short stories: The torque; The great

Ko-ko; The man in the room; The widow's history; The christening; A child's tragedy; Mamie's dream; The good-for-naught; Beauty's lover; The wise women; The sisters; The former age; four stories entitled A Pagan dream; The last Pagan ; The grey wolf ; The coward.

NORRIS, W. E.   St. Ann's.   Cassell.   12°, $1.

PEMBERTON, MAX. The impregnable city : a romance. Dodd, Mead & Co.   12°, $1.25.
The impregnable city is supposed to be under the waters of the Western Pacific. In 1880 an Austrian nobleman made the acquaintance of Count Tolstoï and was seized with the idea of providing a city of refuge for men and women who had come under the ban of courts and governments for their devotion to humanity. A young physician, who is taken to this city from London to relieve the sufferings of a young girl subject to trances, tells the highly romantic story.

PENDLETON, L. Corona of the Nantahalas : a romance. Merriam Co. p. il. nar. 16°, 75 c.
The Nantahalas were inhabitants of the North Carolina mountains in the early seventies. Corona was a little girl rescued from a madman in the woods by a rough farmer who reared her as his own, and for years Corona's only companion was the farmer's deaf and dumb son. A school-teacher happening that way, in two years taught Corona to know and love the Greek classics. To her the characters were real, and the descriptions of her life, her thoughts and actions are poetic and idyllic. Love came to her early and the end clears up the mystery of her parentage and early history.

RAIMOND, C. E. (*pseud.*)   The new moon. Appleton.   12°, $1.
" One of the three important characters that influence the action of this exciting story has an inveterate *penchant* towards auguries, portents, and premonitions. She is plunged into despair when her husband spills the salt, and the first sight of the new moon through glass occasions her a nervous shock that appears to threaten her sanity if not her life. In vivid contrast with this victim of childish terrors is a well-drawn character of the typical healthy girl, courageous and vigorous in mind and body, possessing good practical ability, yet withal tender-hearted and high-principled. The man whose fate is so strangely influenced by these two opposite types of womanhood is a physician, and it is in his person that the story is related. The author relies for success on a certain enthralling quality in the writing that carries his reader along towards a *dénouement* which it is impossible to forecast."— *London Literary World.*

RATHBORNE, ST. GEORGE. The fair maid of Fez : a novel. Home Book Co. il. 16°, 50c.
" Opens and closes in New York, but the burden of the narrative recites the deeds of a young and spirited American who, to recover some family documents of importance in the possession of a renegade countryman, who has become Grand Vizier of the Sultan of Morocco, proceeds to Northern Africa, and with the help of a trusty and resourceful son of the desert makes his way to Fez, leads an attack on the palace of the Moorish Sultan's lieutenant, gains the object of his search and fights his way again out of the country, having meanwhile had a love adventure of romantic interest and won dear experi-

ence of Arab recklessness of life and Moorish knavery."—*Philadelphia Evening Telegraph.*

RICHARDS, *Mrs.* LAURA E. Jim of Hellas; or, in durance vile. [*And*] Bethesda Pool. Estes & Lauriat. 12°, 50 c.
Two little romances of the New England coast. The first tells how " Jim of Hellas," a shipwrecked Greek sailor, won the heart of a middle-aged New England woman; the second story, " The troubling of Bethesda Pool," brings together two elderly lovers and satisfactorily concludes the troubled courtship of two young lovers.

ROWSELL, *Miss* MARY C. The friend of the people : a tale of the reign of terror; il. by A. Hencke and Jos. M. Gleeson. F. A. Stokes Co.   12°, $1.50.

RUSSELL, W. CLARK. The phantom death, and other stories ; il. by F. A. Carter. F. A. Stokes Co.   I il. nar. 16°, 75 c.
Contents : The phantom death; Broker's bay ; The lazarette of the *Huntress*; A memory of the Pacific ; " So unnecessary;" The major's commission ; A nightmare of the doldrums ; " Try for her in fifty;" The "Chiliman's tragedy;" The secret of the dead mate ; The transport *Palestine.*
" Mr. Russell has no rival in the line of marine fiction."—*Mail and Express.*

SCHOERNAICH - CAROLATH (*Prince*). Melting snows; tr. into English by Margaret Symonds. Dodd, Mead & Co.   12°, $1.25.
" One of the prettiest of modern German stories, has been put into an excellent English version by Miss Margaret Symonds, daughter of the talented art writer John Addington Symonds, whose recent death was such a loss to literature. Miss Symonds appears to have inherited the literary gifts of her father in no small measure. The book which she has translated as ' Melting snows' treats of the awakening of the soul in a spirit of the frankest romanticism. While the story is tragic it is not morbid. The catastrophe of the lives of the lovers is completed not in death but in a sentence for life—life which mourns lost love and interrupted friendship, but which rises to the sober fulfilment of everyday duty. ' Melting snows' is a novel of value " —*Philadelphia Evening Telegraph.*

SCOTT, MICHAEL. Tom Cringle's log ; il. by J. A. Symington, with an introd. by Mowbray Morris. Macmillan. 12°, (Illustrated standard novels ser.) $1.25.

STIRLING, A. At daybreak : a novel. Houghton, Mifflin & Co. 16°, (Riverside pap. ser., extra, no. 68.) pap., 50 c.

SUDERMANN, HERMANN. The wish : a novel ; tr. by Lily Henkel ; with a biographical introd. by Eliz. Lee. Appleton.   12°, $1.

SULLIVAN, *Sir* E. Tales from Scott ; with an introd. by E. Dowden. Roberts. il. 12°, $1.

TAYLOR, H. C. CHATFIELD. Two women and a fool : [a novel:] il. by C. D. Gibson. Stone & Kimball. 16°, buckram, $1.50.

TRANSITION : a novel; by the author of "A superfluous woman." Lippincott. 12°, $1.25.
The story of a Girton graduate, who leaves college expecting a life of ease and culture. To her disappointment she discovers that her

father, the rector of an excellent living, has views, which she calls socialistic, against accepting the tithes collected from his parish ; as he has pledged himself to a life of poverty, his daughter seeks and obtains the position of head mistress of a London school. Chance leads her in London among a group of Socialists, cultured, unselfish men, deeply in earnest— one of them being, to her surprise, the man she most admires. The experience she goes through and the change it effects in her opinions is recorded.

VANAMEE, *Mrs.* LIDA OSTROM. Two women ; or, over the hills and far away. Merriam Co. nar. 16°, 75 c.

WELLS, H. S. The time machine : an invention. Holt. I il. nar. 16°, (Buckram ser.) 75 c.

WHITE, ELIZA ORNE. Winterborough. Houghton, Mifflin & Co. 16°, (Riverside pap. ser., no. 68.) pap., 50 c.

WINTER, J. STRANGE, [*pseud.* for *Mrs.* H. E. V. Stannard.] The major's favorite : a novel. J. Selwin Tait & Sons. nar. 16°, 75 c.
"A slight but excellent story, excellently well told."—*London Literary World.*

WRIGHT, *Mrs.* MARY TAPPAN. A truce, and other stories. Scribner. 16°, $1.
Contents : A truce ; "As haggards of the rock ; " "A portion of the tempest ; " From Macedonia ; Deep as first love ; A fragment of a play, with a chorus.

ZANGWILL, I. The master : a novel. Harper. il. 12°, $1.75.

HISTORY.

BARRAS, PAUL FRANÇOIS J. N. *Comte.* Memoirs of Barras, member of the Directorate ; ed. with introduction, prefaces and appendices by George Duruy. In 4 v. V. 1, The ancient régime and the revolution ; V. 2, Directorate up to the 18th Fructidor ; tr. by C. E. Roche. Harper. 8°, per vol., $3.75.

FROUDE, J. ANTHONY. English seamen in the sixteenth century : lectures delivered at Oxford, Easter terms 1893–94. Scribner. 8°, $1.75.
Nine lectures entitled : The sea cradle of the Reformation ; John Hawkins and the African slave trade ; Sir John Hawkins and Philip the Second ; Drake's voyage round the world ; Parties in the state ; The great expedition to the West Indies ; Attack on Cadiz ; Sailing of the Armada ; Defeat of the Armada.
"The book is one which cannot fail to prove delightful reading to every English-speaking man, no matter in what part of the globe he may be found."—*Providence Sunday Journal.*

GARDNER, ALICE. Julian, philosopher and emperor, and the last struggle of Paganism against Christianity. Putnam. il. 12°, (Heroes of the nations ser., no. 13.) $1.50; hf. mor., $1.75.

PETRIE, W. M. FLINDERS. A history of Egypt. V. I, From the earliest times to the XVIth dynasty. Scribner. il. 12°, $2.25.

PUTNAM, RUTH. William the Silent, Prince of Orange, the moderate man of the XVIth century : the story of his life as told in his own letters, in those of his friends and his ene-

mies, and from official sources. Putnam. 400 p. il. 16°, 2 v., $3.75.

SÉGUR, PHILIPPE DE (*Count.*) An aide-de-camp of Napoleon : memoirs of General Count de Ségur of the French Academy, 1800–1812 ; rev. by his grandson, Count L. De Ségur; tr. by H. A. Patchett-Martin. Appleton. por. 12°, $2.

WINSOR, JUSTIN. The Mississippi basin : the struggle in America between England and France, 1697–1763 ; with full cartographical illustrations from contemporary sources. Houghton, Mifflin & Co. 8°, maps, $4.
This volume takes up the story of American exploration where Dr. Winsor left it in his "Cartier to Frontenac." It traces the counter movements of the English and French in adventure, trade and war, for the possession of the Mississippi valley, showing how such movements were directed on geographical lines. The narrative covers the interval from the Treaty of Ryswich (1697) to the Peace of Paris (1763), and is illustrated at every stage by facsimiles of contemporary maps. Full index.

INDUSTRIAL.

DYER, H. The evolution of industry. Macmillan. 12°, $1.50.

MASON, OTIS T. The origins of invention: a study of industry among primitive peoples. Scribner. il. 12°, (Contemporary science ser.) $1.25.
"We are so prone to believe that all the blessings which we now enjoy are the fruit of our modern civilization that it is well for us to be reminded once in a while that our ancestors and other primitive peoples were by no means so obtuse or brutish as many of us ignorantly suppose them to have been. A book which will tend to remove erroneous impressions on this point has just been imported by Charles Scribner's Sons. It is entitled 'The origins of inventions: A study of industry among primitive peoples,' and is the work of Otis T. Mason, A.M., Ph.D. In it the author, with the aid of several curious and interesting illustrations, gives the early history of several inventions, which are now of the first importance. Thus he tells us much about the invention of tools and mechanical devices, of the primitive uses of fire, of early stone working, of the potter's art, of primitive travel and transportation, and of the art of war in days that knew not bullet-proof armor and smokeless powder. His book is, in fact, a storehouse of curious facts concerning primitive peoples, and will, consequently, be found extremely useful by all who are interested in the history of the development of arts and industries."—*N. Y. Herald.*

WALSH, JOS. M. Tea, its history and mystery. [*3d ed.*] Published by the author, Jos. M. Walsh. il. 12°, leatherette, $2.
Contents : Early history and introduction; Geographical distribution; Botanical characteristics and form; Cultivation and preparation; Commercial classification and description; Adulteration and detection; Arts of testing, blending and preparing; Chemical and medicinal properties; World's production and consumption; Tea-culture, a probable American industry.

LITERATURE, MISCELLANEOUS AND COLLECTED WORKS.

DARMESTETER, JA. Selected essays of James

Darmesteter; from the French by Helen B. Jastrow; ed., with an introd. memoir, by J. Morris Jastrow, jr. Houghton, Mifflin & Co. por. 12°, $1.50.

Contents: The religions of the future ; The prophets of Israel; Afghan life in Afghan songs; Race and tradition; Ernest Renan; An essay on the history of the Jews; The Supreme God in the Indo-European Mythology. Darmesteter was one of the foremost scholars of France, especially in the domain of religion and Oriental research.

HALIBURTON, HUGH. Furth in field: a volume of essays on the life, language, and literature of old Scotland. Putnam. 12°, $2.

HUTTON, LAURENCE. Literary landmarks of Jerusalem. Harper. il. 12°, 75 c.

KARPELES, GUSTAV. Jewish literature and other essays. The Jewish Pub. Soc. of America. 12°, $1.25.

Contents: A glance at Jewish literature; The Talmud; The Jew in the history of civilization; Women in Jewish literature; Moses Maimonides; Jewish troubadours and minnesingers; Humor and love in Jewish poetry; The Jewish stage; The Jew's quest in Africa; A Jewish king in Poland; Jewish society in the time of Mendelssohn; Leopold Zunz; Heinrich Heine and Judaism; The music of the synagogue.

LONG, J. D. After-dinner and other speeches. Houghton, Mifflin & Co. 8°, $1.25.

MILES, ALFRED H., *ed.* One thousand and one anecdotes. Whittaker. 12°, $1.50.

"Of Mr. Miles' collection as a whole one may say that it contains little that is not really good and a great deal that is excellent. As a volume for occasional reading in moments of leisure or as an antidote to attacks of the blues, it offers very manifest advantages. A by no means minor attraction of the volume is to be found in the clear and handsome typography which has been given to it by the publishers." — *The Beacon.*

SCUDDER. *Miss* VIDA DUTTON. The life of the spirit in the modern English poets. Houghton, Mifflin & Co. 8°, $1.75.

MENTAL AND MORAL PHILOSOPHY.

MIVART, ST. GEORGE. The helpful science. Harper. 12°, $1.25,

A plea for metaphysics as opposed to sensism and various other fashionable theories, and is one of the many works inevitably destined to appear in the reaction against unbelief. It is characterized by an appearance of simplicity, leading the sceptical reader from admission to admission until he finds himself committed to belief in various things of which he has been loftily contemptuous. Having brought him to this point, the author shows him that he has mistaken self-conceit for real originality, and leaves him with the consoling farewell that the man who depends too much is not only foolish, but dangerous, and that it is through love, the "charity" of the King James version of the New Testament, that we reach the truest analogy possible for us with the ultimate creative purpose of the Divine First Cause.

NATURE AND SCIENCE.

CHAPMAN, FRANK M. Handbook of birds of Eastern North America. Appleton. il. 16°, leath., $3.50.

DANA, *Mrs.* FRANCES THEODORA, [*Mrs.* W. Starr Dana.] How to know the wild flowers: a guide to the names, haunts and habits of our common wild flowers; il. by Marion Satterlee. [*New*] rev. and enl. ed. Scribner. 12°, net, $1 75.

This enlarged edition contains fifty-two new plates—half as many again as can be found in former editions—with the result that in all one hundred and sixty-four American wild flowers are pictured. Sixty or more new flower descriptions are added, raising the number of flowers described to nearly five hundred.

HAYWARD, JANE MARY. Bird notes; ed. by Emma Hubbard; with fifteen il. from drawings by G. E. Lodge. Longmans, Green & Co. 16°, $1.75.

Notes made from personal observation of the habits and appearance of various English birds.

MCDONALD, DONALD. Sweet-scented flowers and fragrant leaves; interesting associations gathered from many sources, with notes on their history and utility; with introd. by W. Robinson. Scribner. 16 pl. 12°, net, $1.50.

PRIME, W. COOPER. Among the northern hills. Harper. 16°, $1.

An out-of-door book rich in sketches of nature, by the author of "Along new England roads." There are twenty chapters on a variety of kindred subjects, as: The primeval forest; A trout stream ; An up-country artist ; Beyond; An old angler; Doughnuts and tobacco ; John Ledyard; An Easter long ago; An old-time Christmas; Along at Thanksgiving; etc.

SCHWARZ, A. The horse: its external and internal organization ; rev. and ed. by G. Fleming. Whittaker. il. obl. 12°, bds., net, 75 c.

An illustrated representation and brief description of the horse, dedicated to lovers and owners of horses, and designed for the instruction of non-commissioned officers and volunteers in cavalry regiments. The drawings are partly from nature and partly from illustrations in Leyh and Frank's" Anatomy."

STEP, E. Wayside and woodland blossoms: a pocket-guide to British wild flowers; for the country rambler; with col. figures of 156 species of flowers, black and white pls. of 22 of the lesser-known trees, and clear descriptions of 400 species of flowers. Warne. 12°, $2.50.

WEED, CLARENCE MOORES. Ten New England blossoms and their insect visitors. Houghton, Mifflin & Co. il. 12°, $1.25.

POETRY.

BEESLY, A. H. Ballads and other verse. Longmans, Green & Co. 16°, $1.75.

BOLLES, FRANK. Chocorua's tenants. Houghton, Mifflin & Co. il. 12°, $1.

ECHEGARAY, JOSÉ. Mariana; an original drama in three acts and an epilogue ; tr. by Ja. Graham. Roberts. por. 16°, $1.

GATES, ELLEN M. H. The treasures of Kurium. Putnam. 12°, $1.

A collection of short poems.

SAWTELLE, MARY ANNA *and* ALICE ELIZ. An olio of verse. Putnam. 16°, 75 c.

Many of these poems appeared in the columns of the Boston *Literary World* and *The Transcript* of Boston.

POLITICAL AND SOCIAL.

DONISTHORPE, WORDSWORTH. Law in a free state. Macmillan. 12°, $2.

Addressed to the large body of English socialists who "inconsistently appeal to socialism for the attainment of certain ends which at first sight seem to be unattainable under a *régime* of freedom." Questions of libel, of cruelty to animals, of copyright, of adulteration, of the relation of the sexes, of rights over land, of nuisance and many others Mr. Donisthorpe considers difficult to solve straight off on the principle of equal liberty. He discusses questions, however, from his point of view quite dispassionately, showing where the socialistic principle must be applied to them.

GILLETTE, KING C. The human drift. The Humboldt Pub. Co. por. il. 8°, (Twentieth Century lib., no. 59.) pap., 50 c.

Outlines the plan of a new civilization and its consummation; the chief factor in its accomplishment is the doing away with competition and the establishment of material equality. This is to be arrived at by a United Stock Company, organized by the people and for the people, with a nominal capital of one thousand million dollars, to gradually absorb and finally control production and distribution, such company having in view the destruction of all tributary industries of the present system which do not contribute or are not necessary to the production and distribution of the necessities of life.

HARVEY, W. H. ["Coin," *pseud.*] A tale of two nations. Coin Publishing Co. 12°, (Coin's financial ser., v. 1, no. 4.) $1 ; pap., 50 c.; *popular ed.,* pap., 25 c.

A love story that gives, the author says, "the history of demonetizaton and depicts the evil spirit and influences that have worked the destruction of American prosperity."

HARVEY, W. H., ["Coin," *pseud.*] Coin's financial school. Coin Publishing Co. por. il. 12°, (Coin's financial ser., v. 1, no. 3.) $1; pap., 50 c.; *popular ed.*, pap., 25 c.

Advocates the free and unlimited coinage of silver by the United States, without international agreement. "Coin" attributes all the recent financial troubles to what he calls the demonetization of silver. The information and statistics given form a history of silver; they are offered in the form of lectures, the speaker often being interrupted by pupils of his school with puzzling questions, which he answers freely.

HARVEY, W. H., ["Coin," *pseud.*] Coin's financial school up to date. Coin Publishing Co. por. il. 12°, (Coin's financial ser., v. 2, no. 6.) $1; pap., 50 c.; *popular ed.*, pap., 25 c.

In this volume "Coin's" acts and utterances since his "school" was taught in Chicago are chronicled, bringing the subject discussed down to date. It is an answer to "Coin's" critics and contains new information. The larger part of the work is in the form of interviews with prominent writers, journalists and public men, who question many of Coin's former statements on the silver question, and receive from him further light on the subject.

HOPKINS, ALPHONSO A. Wealth and waste: the principles of political economy in their application to the present problems of labor, law, and the liquor traffic. Funk & Wagnalls Co. 12°, $1.

The leading topics considered are: Economy and labor; Wealth and its distribution; Consumption and waste; Relation and duty of authority; Harmony of social forces; and Political ways and means. Designed for popular reading and also as a text-book. A list of questions is given with each chapter.

MOORE, JOS. WEST. The American Congress: a history of national legislation and political events, 1774-1895. Harper. 8°, $3.

The history begins with the Continental Congress and its prominent men—narrates very clearly the proceedings in the formation of the nation and the establishment of the government under the Constitution—and then goes on steadily to tell of all the notable legislative and political transactions in the growth and development of the American Republic up to the present time. The book contains many bright sketches of character, has interesting accounts of all the political parties, and abounds in pleasing incidents, anecdotes, and personalities. It also contains important state-papers, famous speeches and debates, and other matter valuable for reference.

MORAN, T. FRANCIS. The rise and development of the bicameral system in America. Johns Hopkins Press. 8°, (Johns Hopkins Univ. studies, 13th ser., no. 5.) pap., 50 c.

WALKER, FRANCIS A. The making of the nation, 1783-1817; with maps and appendices. Scribner. 12°, (American history ser.) $1.25.

The topics relating to this period having special chapters are : The Confederation, 1783-87; The constitutional convention of 1787; The constitution as submitted to the people; Ratification and the inauguration of the government; Washington's first and second terms; The administration of John Adams ; Jefferson's first and second terms; The controversy with England; The war of 1812-15; The civil events of Madison's administration. Appendices contain the electoral vote in detail, 1789-1816; Population of the first four censuses, etc., and the Cabinets of Washington, Adams, Jefferson, and Madison. A bibliography of the period covers 6 pages.

WISNER, E. Cash *vs.* coin: an answer to "Coin's financial school." Kerr & Co. 12°, 25 c.

"Charley Cash," a baggageman on a Southern railroad, happened to be in Chicago when Coin's school was in progress, and accidentally discovered that Coin's success in meeting all his opponents was due to hypnotism. Cash armed himself against this by a charge of electricity, and a debate between the two champions resulted in the complete overthrow of the "16 to 1" argument. Following the short story are other arguments against the free silver theories of "Coin."

SPORTS AND AMUSEMENTS.

CLYDE, HENRY. Pleasure cycling. Little, Brown & Co. 16°, $1.

PORTER, LUTHER H. Cycling for health and pleasure: an indispensable guide to the successful use of the wheel. Dodd, Mead & Co. 16°, $1.

THEOLOGY, RELIGION AND SPECULATION.

WHATELY, R., *D.D.* Historic doubts relative to Napoleon Buonaparte. Putnam. 12°, 75 c.
" This work first appeared in the year 1819 and attracted wide and serious attention. Its purpose is to show that the arguments employed to disprove the historic Christ may be used to disprove the existence of any conspicuous figure in human annals. We are all more or less disturbed by the difficulty in determining what to believe. The distinguished author endeavored to frame some canons which may furnish a standard for determining what evidence is to be received by a sound system of logic."—*Philadelphia Press.*

Books for the Young.

ADAMS, W. T., ["Oliver Optic," *pseud.*] In the saddle. Lee & Shepard. il. 12°, (The blue and the gray—on land ser., no. 2.) $1.50.
Many of the characters prominent in " Brother against brother," the preceding volume of the series, reappear in this volume. The real military operations of the war now begin, and the residents of the section where the scene is laid —the southern part of Kentucky—see and feel the terrors and anxieties of civil war. The operation of a loyal battalion of cavalry raised by the Lyons in protection of railroad bridges, the repressing of partisan onslaughts, and the guarding of towns and villages largely inhabited by citizens loyal to the Union form the basis of the story.

ELLIS, E. S. The path in the ravine. Porter & Coates. 12°, (Forest and prairie ser., no. 2.) $1.25.

FENN, G. MANVILLE. Diamond Dyke; or, the lone farm on the Veldt: a story of South African adventure; with eight il. by W. Boucher. Dutton. 12°, $1.50.
Van Dyke Emson wins his *sobriquet* after an encounter with an ostrich; the bird loses its life in the fight, and the boy dissecting it, finds some valuable diamonds. In addition to this incident, Dyke's unfortunate experiences on an ostrich farm are given, with his adventures with the Kaffirs and two lions.

GLASCOCK, WILL H. Stories of Columbia. Appleton. il. 12°, $1.
The subjects of the stories are: The sea kings; Columbus pleading the cause of America; Columbus in the King and Queen's gardens; Columbus in poverty and in chains; The red man of the forest and plain; The mound builders; Our pilgrim fathers; Our unkind mother; The father of American liberty; The friend of American liberty; The daughters of the Revolution; The pioneers of the Mississippi valley ; Two famous rides; Some naval heroes; Some American boys of genius.

HALL, *Rev.* C. CUTHBERT. The children, the church, and the communion. Houghton, Mifflin & Co. 12°, 75 c.
Two sermons to children by the minister of the First Presbyterian Church of Brooklyn, N. Y. The first deals with the relation of children to the church, and is designed to encourage them to attend church services; the second takes up the relation of children to the communion.

PAULL, *Mrs.* G. A., [Minnie E. Kenney.] Lassie. Whittaker. il. 12°, $1.50.

RECENT FRENCH AND GERMAN BOOKS.

FRENCH.

Alexandre. Jean Carriès; Imagier et Potier, Ill., 4° (Quantin)................................ $6 25
Astor, J. J. Voyage en d'Autres Mondes. 12° (Hachette)................................ 1 00
Bentzon, Th. Jacqueline. 12° (Levy).......... 1 00
Boissier, Gaston. L'Afrique Romaine. 12° (Hachette)................................ 1 00
Brulat, P. La Rédemption. 12° (Charpentier).. 1 00
Brunetiere. La Science et la Religion. 12° (Colin)................................ 15
Castellane, Maréchal de. Journal Vol. I, 1804-23. 8° (Plon)................................ 2 25
Colani, T. Essais de critique. 12° (Chailley).... 1 00
Conte, E. Espagne and Provence. 12° (Levy).. 1 00
Coppee, F. Mon francparler. 3 ieme Serie. 12° (Lemerre)................................ 1 00
Oruppi, J. Linguet : Un Avocat journaliste au 18e Siècle. 12° (Hachette)................ 1 00
Decourcelle, P. Gigolette. Vol. II, amour de Fille. 12°. Librairie Ill.................... 1 00
De Parseval—Deschênes. Graine d'amour. 12° (Dentu)................................ 1 00
Floran, Mary. Carmencita. 12° (Levy)......... 1 00
Gayet, A. L'Art Persan. 8°, cl. (Quantin)...... 1 35
Hermant, A. Le frisson de Paris. 12° (Ollendorf)................................ 1 00
Le Roux, Hugues. Le Festéjadon. 12° (Levy).. 1 00
Massini, Jos. Lettres Intimes. 12° (Perrin)..... 1 00
Merson, O. Les Vitraux. 8°, cl. (Quantin)..... 1 35
Michel, E. Etudes sur l' histoire de l'art. 12° (Hachette)................................ 1 00
Montegut, M. Dernier Cri. 12° (Charpentier). 1 00
Rooh, Godart. Mémoires du Général, 1792-1815. 8° (Flammarion)................................ 1 80
Sales, P. La Maiouine. 12° (Flammarion)....... 1 00

Saxebey, G. Autour d'une dot. 12° (Flammarion) $1 00
Thiebault. Mémoires du général baron. Vol. IV., 1806-13. 8° (Plon)................ 2 25
Tolstoi, L. Plaisirs Cruels. 12° (Charpentier).. 1 00

GERMAN.

Berkow, K. Kinderaugen. 12° (Janke)......... 70
Bernhard. In Treue fest. 12° (Pierson)........ 1 35
Bernhard, M. Buen Retiro. 12° (Keil) 1 50
Borman, G. Bande des Bluts. 12° (Paetel)..... 1 70
Bourget, P. André Cornelis. Aus dem Französischen von Marie Lauer. 12° (Janke)... 70
Dostojewski. Raskolnikow's Schuld und Sühne. 12° (Janke)................................ 70
Eokstein. Nora. 12° (Reissner)................ 1 00
Gersdorff, A. v. Erreichte Wünsche. 12°(Janke). 1 70
Groller, Zehn. Geschichten. 12° (Pierson)...... 1 00
Hansson, O. Vor der Ehe. 12° (Janke)........ 40
Hartwig, G. Schloss Wolkenstein. 12° (Janke). 40
Heimburg, W. Um fremde Schuld. 12° (Keil). 1 70
Lyon, O. Bismarck's Reden und Briefe. 12°, cloth (Teubner)................................ 70
Raimund, G. Zweimal vermählt. 12° (Janke)... 70
Sohobert, H. Ulanenliebe. 12° (Janke)........ 70
Spielhagen, Susi. Eine Hofgeschichte. 12°, cloth (Engelhorn)................................ 50
Stahl, M. Zwei Seelen. 12° (Janke)............ 40
Suttner. Ein Dämon. 12° (Pierson)............ 1 70
Vincenti. Aus goldene Wandertagen. 12° (Pierson)................................ 1 35
Wachenhusen, H. Der Liebe Unverstand. 12° (Janke)................................ 70
Wals-Zedwits, E. v. Drei Paläste. 12° (Janke). 70
Wald, Zedwitz. Die Rose von Cetinge. 12° (Janke)................................ 40

Books for Summer Travellers.

AMERICAN BOOK COMPANY, New York.

Gray's Manual of Botany. Tourists' ed. $2.00.

D. APPLETON & CO., New York.

Appletons' General Guide to the United States. With maps and illustrations. One volume complete, flexible morocco, with tuck, $2.50. Part I., separately, New England and Middle States and Canada, cloth, $1.25. Part II., separately, Southern and Western States, cloth, $1.25.

Appletons' Handbook of Summer Resorts. With maps and illustrations. Small 8vo, paper, 50c.

Appletons' Canadian Guide-Book. One volume complete, Newfoundland to the Pacific Coast. With maps and illustrations. 12mo, $1.25.

Appletons' Guide-Book to Alaska. By Miss E. R. Scidmore. With maps and illustrations. 12mo, $1.25.

Appletons' Dictionary of New York and Its Vicinity. 16mo, paper, 30c.; flex. cloth, 60c.

The White Mountains. By Rev. J. H. Ward. 12mo, cloth, $1.25.

The Land of the Sun. *Vistas Mexicanas.* By Christian Reid. Illustrated. 12mo, cloth, $1.75.

THE CASSELL PUBLISHING CO., New York.

Cassell's Pocket Guide to Europe for 1895. With maps, etc. Bound in leather, $1.50. The model book of its kind for accuracy, fulness, legibility of text and maps, compact beauty and usefulness, and very moderate price.

WATSON GILL, Syracuse, N. Y.

The Adirondacks. Wallace's guide for 1895, now ready. 600 pages, 150 half-tone engravings and large map. The Standard Guide to the Adirondacks. Sold by booksellers, or mailed on receipt of price, $3.50.

HOUGHTON, MIFFLIN & CO., Boston.

Boston Illustrated. Paper, 50c.

Satchel Guide to Europe. Edition for 1894. $1.50.

England Without and Within. By Richard Grant White. $2.00.

Sweetser's New England. $1.50.

Sweetser's White Mountains. $1.50.

Sweetser's Maritime Provinces. $1.50.

Nantucket Scraps. By Jane G. Austin. $1.50.

Mrs. Thaxter's Among the Isles of Shoals. $1.25.

HUNT & EATON, New York.

Travels in Three Continents. By J. M. Buckley, LL.D. Finely illustrated. 614 pages, octavo, cloth, gilt top, $3.50.
A most instructive and fascinating book of travel.

LITTLE, BROWN & CO., Boston.

Pleasure-Cycling. By Henry Clyde. With 34 silhouettes and vignettes. 16mo, cloth, $1.00.

Parkman's Handbook of the Northern Tour. Lakes George and Champlain, Niagara, Montreal, Quebec. 12mo, cloth, $1.50.

JOHN MURPHY & CO., Baltimore, Md.

Mrs. Mary E. Surratt. Her trial, conviction and execution. By David Miller DeWitt. 12mo, cloth, $1.25.

A Marriage of Reason. By Francis Maurice Egan. A story of "society" people of Philadelphia and its suburbs. 12mo, cloth, $1.00.

Army Boys and Girls. By Mrs. Mary G. Bonesteel. A series of brilliant stories of our camps and garrisons. 12mo, cloth, $1.00.

Ada's Trust. By Mrs. A. H. Dorsey. A story of vivid interest. 12mo, cloth, $1.00.

Beth's Promise. By Mrs. A. H. Dorsey. 12mo, cloth, $1.50.

A Washington Winter. By Mrs. M. V. Dahlgren. A vivid delineation of life at the Capital. $1.00.

JOHN MURPHY & CO.—Continued.

Lights and Shadows of a Life. By Mrs. M. V. Dahlgren. A picture of Southern home life. 12mo, cloth, $1.00.

Children of Charles I. of England. By Mrs. C. S. H. Clark. Small quarto, cloth, $1.00.

Down at Caxtons. Brilliant sketches of American authors. By Walter Lecky. Paper, 35 cents.

THOMAS NELSON & SONS, New York.

The Royal Album of Chromo Views. The most exquisite scenery of the British Isles. 253 chromo-views, oblong folio, cloth, extra gilt edges, $7.00.

English Scenery. 120 views. 4to, cloth, $2.50.

Souvenir of Scotland. Its cities, lakes, and mountains. 120 chromo views. 4to, $2.50; and $4.00.

Rambles in Rome. By S. Russell Forbes. With maps, plans, and illustrations. 12mo, cloth extra, $1.50.

Rambles in Naples. By S. Russell Forbes. With maps, plans, and illustrations. 12mo, cloth extra, $1.25.

ROBERTS BROTHERS, Boston.

Jackson (Helen ["H. H."]). Glimpses of Three Coasts. 12mo, $1.50.
These are "Bits of Travel" in California and Oregon, Scotland and England, and Norway, Denmark, and Germany.

— Ramona. A Story. 12mo, $1.50.
Most delightful glimpses of So. California.

— Bits of Travel. Illustrated. Square 18mo, $1.25.

— Bits of Travel at Home. Square 18mo, $1.50.

Drake (Samuel Adams). Old Landmarks and Historic Personages of Boston. With 93 illustrations. 12mo, $2.00.

— Old Landmarks and Historic Fields of Middlesex. With 39 illustrations and maps. 12mo, $2.00.

Aloha. (A Hawaiian Salutation.) By G. L. Chaney. Travels in the Sandwich Islands. With illustrations and map. 16mo, $1.50.

GEORGE ROUTLEDGE & SONS (Ld.), New York.

Hare's (A. J. C.) Literary Traveling Companions.

Edwards's (A. B.) A Thousand Miles up the Nile. Profusely illustrated. 8vo, $2.50.

— Untrodden Peaks and Unfrequented Valleys. A Midsummer Ramble in the Dolomites. Maps and illustrations. 8vo, $2.50.

Caine's (W. S.) A Trip Round the World, 1887–1888. 250 original illustrations. 12mo, cloth, $1.50.

— Picturesque India: an unconventional Guide-Book. 200 illustrations and map. 8vo, cloth, $4.00.

Stow's (John) Survey of London in the Time of Elizabeth. Crown 8vo, $1.00.

E. STEIGER & CO., New York.

Baedeker's and other Guide-Books, in German; also Travellers' Maps, Conversation Books, Grammars, and Dictionaries in all foreign languages.

WARD, LOCK & BOWDEN, Ltd., New York.

On the Cars and Off. Being the Journal of a Pilgrimage along the Queen's Highway to the East, from Halifax, in Nova Scotia, to Victoria, in Vancouver's Island. By Douglas Sladen. Profusely and beautifully illustrated. 8vo, cloth, $6.00.

BRADLEE WHIDDEN, Boston, Mass.

Knobel's Guides in Natural History. Trees and Shrubs. Ferns and Evergreens. Day Butterflies. The Beetles. The Moths. Each 12mo, *net*, 50 cents.

Emerton's Life on the Seashore. Illustrated. 12mo, cloth, $1.50.

Emerton's Spiders. Illustrated. 12mo, cloth, $1.50.

Gould's Modern American Rifle. Illustrated. 12mo, cloth, $2.00.

Gould's Pistols and Revolvers. Illustrated. 12mo, cloth, $1.50.

Freshest News.

FREDERICK WARNE & CO. will publish at once a new humorous story à la Anstey, entitled "A Deal with the Devil," by Eden Phillpotts, author of "Folly and Fresh Air," etc.

D. APPLETON & CO., in commemoration of the issue of the tenth edition of Hall Caine's "Manxman," have published a fine autotype portrait, in a neat oak frame, of the author of that remarkably successful novel.

ROBERTS BROTHERS have just ready in their *Keynotes* series a volume of short stories entitled "Grey Roses," by Henry Harland ("Sidney Luska"), the editor of the *Yellow Book;* also, "Monochromes," by Ella D'Arcy. They have published "The Rise of Wellington," by Gen. Lord Roberts, with illustrations and plans; and "Foam of the Sea," a new volume by Gertrude Hall.

T. Y. CROWELL & CO. have in press for early publication "How Tommy Saved the Barn," by James Otis, a story describing in part the work of the Fresh Air Fund ; also, " In the Land of Lorna Doone, and other pleasurable excursions in England," by William H. Rideing. They will issue next month in an attractive volume the forty-two articles on Abraham Lincoln printed in *The Independent* of April 4, with an introduction by Dr. William Hayes Ward.

R. F. FENNO & CO. have now ready in *Fenno's Buckram Series* the latest books of George Meredith, Mrs. Oliphant, Anthony Hope, and S. Levett-Yeats. They also call attention to their *Lenox Series*, containing some of the most popular books of the most popular authors, every book having the author's portrait upon the cover; and to their *Illustrated Series*, also covering some of the leading books of the hour as well as some of the standard favorites.

GEORGE ROUTLEDGE & SONS have put their *Handy Volume* Shakespeare into several new bindings and casings described elsewhere. A work of lasting usefulness is "Men and Women of the Time," and we are glad to see a four-teenth edition is just ready. Since the last edition appeared death has reaped a rich harvest among celebrated men and women, and the first glance at the new volume makes us realize how few are fit to fill the places in the world left vacant by Prof. Hemholtz, Ernest Renan, Prof. Tyndall, Walter Pater, Froude, Tennyson, Holmes. The editor himself acknowledges his trials in finding new names to put into the places left vacant for them.

LONGMANS, GREEN & CO. have a list of novels that will pass many a rainy day pleasantly and even instructively. "Heart of the World" is a story of Mexican adventure, by Rider Haggard; "Colonel Norton" is by Florence Marryat, and contains some exquisitely written conversations; and among the more important books recently issued are "Nada, the Lily," by C. H. M. Kerr; "The People of the Mist" and "Montezuma's Daughter," by the ever popular Haggard; Stanley J. Weyman's "A Gentleman of France," "The House of the Wolf," "My Lady Rotha," and "Under the Red Robe;" Edna Lyall's "Doreen, the Story of a Singer;" Mrs. Walford's "The Matchmaker," and Owen Rhoscomyl's very strikingly imaginative story, "The Jewel of Ynys Galon."

D. APPLETON & CO. have just ready "The Female Offender," the latest contribution to the literature of criminology, by Prof. Cæsar Lombroso and William Ferrero. In this work Lombroso applies his well-known anthropological methods to women criminals, with the purpose of determining whether and to what extent the female offender differs from the average woman in physical and mental characteristics. They also publish a new volume in the *Great Commanders Series*, being a biography of "General Sheridan," by Gen. Henry E. Davies; a collection of excerpts from Herbert Spencer, setting forth his views on the land question and correcting "current misconceptions of his views"; and two new novels, "The New Moon," by C. E. Raimond, author of "George Mandeville's Husband," and "The Wish," by Hermann Sudermann, who pictures modern life from a distinctly individual standpoint savoring of Ibsen.

NEW PUBLICATIONS.

PUNISHMENT AND REFORMATION,

A Work dealing with Crimes, Prisons and Reformations,

By Dr. F. H. WINES.

Vol. VI. in Crowell's Library of Economics and Politics. 12mo, cloth, with illustrations and index, $1.75.

Dr. Wines, who is well known as a thoroughly practical and trustworthy investigator of the question of the reformation of criminals, has in this volume made a most valuable contribution, which will be indispensable to all who are in any way interested in the subject.

The Narrative of Captain Coignet,

Soldier of the Empire. 1776–1850. An autobiographical account of one of Napoleon's Body Guard. Edited from the original manuscript by LOREDAN LARCHEY. Translated from the French by Mrs. M. Carey. New edition. Fully illustrated. 12mo, cloth, gilt top, $1.50.

(*Third Thousand.*)

In the Land of Lorna Doone

And other Pleasurable Excursions in England. By WM. H. RIDEING. 16mo, gilt top, $1.00. A delightful volume for those who plan to visit England this season.

For sale by all booksellers.

THOMAS Y. CROWELL & CO.,

NEW YORK: 46 East Fourteenth Street.   BOSTON: 100 Purchase Street.

Books that Should be Read.

NEW BOOKS.

HOUGHTON, MIFFLIN & COMPANY,

4 Park Street, Boston ; 11 East 17th Street, New York.

Letters of Celia Thaxter.

Edited by A. F. and R. L. With four portraits. Handsomely printed on the best paper, and carefully bound, cloth, gilt top, uncut front and bottom, each volume bearing a statement that it is a copy of the First Limited Edition. A few copies have been bound entirely uncut, with paper label—making a most desirable volume for collectors or for the purpose of extension. 12mo, $1.50.

A book of singular literary and personal charm, produced in a unique and exceedingly attractive style.

The Mississippi Basin.

The Struggle in America between England and France. 1697-1763. With full cartographical illustrations from contemporary sources. By JUSTIN WINSOR, author of "Cartier to Frontenac," "Christopher Columbus," etc. 8vo, gilt top, $4.00.

This volume takes up the story of American exploration where Dr. Winsor left it in his "Cartier to Frontenac." It traces the counter movements of the English and French, in adventure, trade, and war, for the possession of the Great Valley.

Cartier to Frontenac.

A study of Geographical Discovery in the interior of North America in its Historical Relations, 1534-1700. With full cartographical illustrations from contemporary sources. By JUSTIN WINSOR, editor of "Narrative and Critical History of America." 8vo, gilt top, $4.00.

"The wondrous story has been told by Parkman in half a dozen volumes with a vividness and vivacity not likely to be surpassed, and which have given it a wide popularity. It remained a desideratum to knit together the scattered sketches into one whole body. This Mr. Winsor has done, and that admirably."—*The Nation*, N. Y.

Selected Essays of James Darmesteter.

Translated from the French by HELEN B. JASTROW. Edited, with an introduction, by Prof. MORRIS JASTROW, Jr., of the University of Pennsylvania. With a portrait. 12mo, $1.50.

Contents: The Religions of the Future; The Prophets of Israel; Afghan Life in Afghan Songs; Race and Tradition; Ernest Renan; An Essay on the History of the Jews; The Supreme God in the Indo-European Mythology.

M. Darmesteter was one of the foremost scholars of the French Republic, especially in the domain of religion and Oriental research. To the thoroughness of the German scholar he added the precision and fineness of touch peculiar to the best type of French scholars. This volume contains the ripe fruit of his genius and cannot fail to command the eager attention of thoughtful and cultivated readers.

Daughters of the Revolution.

By CHARLES CARLETON COFFIN, author of "The Drum-Beat of the Nation," etc. With illustrations. *Second edition.* Crown 8vo, $1.50.

"Mr. Coffin's story is one of thrilling interest, and is at the same time an historically accurate presentation of the scenes, events and the spirit of the people of the colonies at the fateful outbreak of the Revolution."—*Boston Advertiser.*

Under the Man-Fig.

By M. E. M. DAVIS. 16mo, $1.25.

"A story of the old South by a writer who knows well how to use the rich material afforded by that picturesque time and people."—*Nashville Banner.*

"An exciting story, and a strong study of character."—*Portland Transcript.*

The Story of Christine Rochefort.

By HELEN CHOATE PRINCE. *Third edition.* 16mo, $1.25.

"Mrs. Prince, granddaughter of Rufus Choate, has written a novel particularly strong in its well-knit style. . . . The personal touches, scenes, and conversations are delightful."—*Chicago Times-Herald.*

"I like everything about it."—HORACE HOWARD FURNESS.

A Soulless Singer.

By MARY CATHERINE LEE, author of "A Quaker Girl of Nantucket" and "In the Cheering-Up Business." 16mo, $1.25.

"The story's motive is the power of human passion to give to a voice which is otherwise noble and well trained the quality of feeling, of soul, which is essential to the really great singer. . . . The story is well written."—*Springfield Republican.*

"A daintier, prettier love-story than this it would be hard to find."—*Chicago Interior.*

Winterborough.

By ELIZA ORNE WHITE, author of "When Molly was Six," etc. Riverside Paper Series. 16mo, 50 cents.

"A most exceptional book. It is a New England tale, but its originality is its strong feature. . . . The humor and the kindly but keen philosophy of 'Winterborough' are admirable."—*Phila. Telegraph.*

Ten New England Blossoms and their Insect Visitors.

By CLARENCE M. WEED, Professor in the New Hampshire Agricultural College. With illustrations. Square 12mo, $1.25.

A book of ten popular and delightful essays on certain blossoms and the visitors they attract.

A Century of Charades.

By WILLIAM BELLAMY. A hundred original charades, ingenious in conception and worked out with remarkable skill. *Fifth thousand.* 18mo, $1.00.

"The cleverest work of its kind known to English literature."—HENRY A. CLAPP, in *Boston Advertiser.*

FOR SALE AT ALL BOOK-STORES.

D. APPLETON & CO.'S NEW BOOKS.

LITERARY NEWS

AN ECLECTIC REVIEW OF
CURRENT LITERATURE
~ILLUSTRATED~

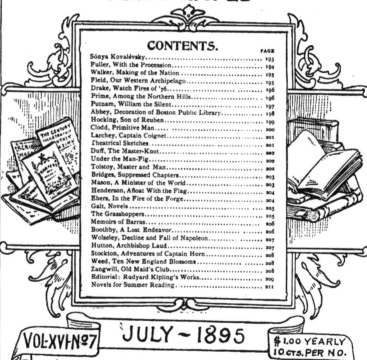

CONTENTS.

VOL. XVI-Nº 7   JULY ~ 1895 $1.00 YEARLY
10 CTS. PER NO.

~ PUBLICATION OFFICE ~
· 28 ELM STREET NEW YORK ·

The Literary News

In winter you may reade them, ab ignem, by the fireside; and in summer, ab umbram, under some shadie tree and therewith passe away the tedious howres.

| VOL. XVI. | JULY, 1895. | NO. 7. |

Sónya Kovalévsky.

ROMANCE and mathematics—how little we connect them in our average minds! Yet they seem to go along, living in the most intimate union all around us.

Of the making of literary fads there is apparently no end. And the latest of these seems likely to be Mme. Kovalévsky, an extraordinary combination of feminine nature with an intellect having somewhat of masculine force, "but yet a woman" to the end; a combination of ambition, of skill and success in exact science and in literature of passion and passing happiness, and the bitterest disappointment with life.

Sónya (or Sophia), with the long wedded name which it takes 48 hours to memorize, was born in 1850 and won almost a European fame in her special field. She became Professor of Mathematics and Lecturer in the University of Stockholm. After a career certainly most romantic, though made grimly and bitterly so through her own disastrous temperament, Sónya died in 1891. Her story now appears in a composite, interesting volume, translated from the Russian and the Swedish, which contains her own "Recollections of Childhood," and a biography by her intimate friend, the the Duchess of Cajanello.

The "Recollections" are bright, but not ex-

From "Sonya Kovalévsky." Copyright, 1895, by The Century Co.
SÓNYA KOVALÉVSKY.

traordinary. They have the same introspectiveness and intense attention to self shown with more mastery and detail in Tolstoi's "Childhood" and "Youth," or, more hysterically, in poor Marie Bashkirtseff's autobiography. The biography by Countess Cajanello is really far more interesting and valuable, because it shows us the developed woman Sónya as she was and as she thought she was. It is a "subjective" and sympathetic, not a critical sketch.

In order to secure independence, Sónya left her father's house and made a "nihilistic" or fictitious marriage with a student named Kovalévsky; a matter of form only, the two not living as man and wife, but each remaining free to study and work separately or together.

This was when she was 18, and she plunged deep into mathematics at St. Petersburg, Heidelberg, and in England. Kovalévsky, although not obliged by their agreement to do so, gave her a quite ideal love, paid her minute attention, and allowed himself to be burdened by her with all sorts of petty cares. She, of course, accepted this readily. Known, from her childish physiognomy, as "the little sparrow," she was small and slender, had a round face, and short, curly chestnut hair, and very mobile features. "Her eyes were sometimes bright and dancing, sometimes dreamy and full of melancholy. Her whole expression was a mixture of childish innocence and deep thought."

But while she also fancied she loved him ideally, she could not learn to respect his individuality or let him alone. "She had a curious liking for ideal and exaggerated friendships. She wanted to have without giving aught in return. · · · She required, too, what she loved, and thought to gain by force what would have been given to her spontaneously had it not been demanded. · · · She also needed to have some one near her who would never leave her and who was interested in all that interested her. self; but she made life unbearable to all who lived with her."

The remark which follows is extremely pertinent and suggestive:

"She was herself too restless, too ill-balanced in temperament, to be satisfied with such loving companionship, although it was her ideal."

The reality of marriage and motherhood and fame brought with them a taste for luxury. To gain money Sónya went into speculations and dragged her husband into them. They turned out badly, but she had implanted the speculative mania in her husband's simple, studious mind, and he continued to follow it when he had been appointed Professor of Paleontology at Moscow. Then Sónya also became jealous of him, without cause, decided to desert him, carrying her little daughter with her, and to resume her studies elsewhere.

A very natural result followed. Her husband, Kovalévsky, who had first given her an ideal protection and practical devotion, without any sort of return on her part, and then had merged all his affections in her and in their child, and had been drawn into the maelstrom of speculation by her, killed himself. Of course, her friends said that this was due to madness, caused by pecuniary troubles. It was one of Kovalévsky's mistakes, perhaps, that, being dead, he was unable to state the truth of the matter.

Though capable of exquisite tenderness, she had an iron will, that did not scruple to wound or crush those whom she loved, and who loved her most, if they stood between her and any aim of hers for an instant. Further, while demanding "illimitable love" from others, she would give only a limited one in return. The Countess Cajanello discovered as much even in friendship with this gifted being. Says the countess: "She wished to have such full possession of the person of whom she was fond that it almost excluded the possibility of individual life in that other person.

"She was continually in want of stimulus. She desired dramatic interests in life, and was ever hungering for high-wrought mental de. lights. She hated with all her heart the gray monotony of every-day life."

Bad training, or lack of genuine training, on the part of her parents, and false ideals of daily life and love in her own mind seem to me the causes of that mingled success and failure which make of Sónya Kovalévsky a luminous wreck. She is a most interesting character study, and a warning to good women of the way they should not follow if they would be wise. All that she achieved in demonstrating woman's intellectual power could have been done without injuring or destroying other lives and blighting her own. Her biographer presents her not as an exception to, but as a proof of, the rule that the life of the heart is the most important, not only for women, but for the whole of the human race. The publication of Sónya Kovalévsky's story, as instilling this truth, ought to have a lasting value. (The Century Co. $1.75.) —*N. Y. Herald.*

With the Procession.

MR. FULLER's muse being urban, it is again of Chicago that he writes. We are taken among the wealthy, but the Marshall family have not attempted to keep up with the procession. It is the old-maid daughter—a nobly planned woman—who unwittingly is the cause of the abandonment of the old homestead, as they name it, although its antiquity is not far-reaching.

Although there are many players on the stage, there are but three which are elaborated to any considerable degree—Jane, her brother Truesdale, and Mrs. Bates, the woman of many millions. An excellent piece of description is Mrs. Bates' humorous exhibition of the splendors of her house. Truesdale's criticisms on the ways of his native Chicago are quite as entertaining when they have a sound foundation as when they are the mere ebullitions of youthful egotism. There is no established promenade to suit his cultivated taste; no cafés, or at least none of the kind that he prefers; and the first nights at the theatres have no value to a person of his discernment and intelligence. He is an adolescent person who has travelled in Europe, much to his mental and moral disadvantage returning with a contempt for the grocery business, in which his father has amassed his millions. Cecilia Ingles hovers around the story, but to no use that we can see. The love story is an undercurrent which is not altogether successful.

Mr. Fuller is not only a close observer but a graphic chronicler, as his "Cliff Dwellers" showed, but his last book is better than his first. Americans in growing cities will be charmed with it. (Harper. $1.25)—*Public Opinion.*

Making of the Nation.

THIS book follows works by Prof. Fisher and Prof. Sloane, in a series of four, which is to be completed in one by Prof. Burgess on the sixty years following 1817. From President Walker's position and known ability something valuable was to be expected; yet his pronounced views on the currency question excited a tremor on first opening his pages. It is eminently satisfactory to be able to say that no such visions intervene to injure the tone of this book, in all of his views, and perhaps with those he most cherishes, we cannot hesitate to commend this book as marked by a pure and lively style, a sound but chastened patriotism, and a recognition at once scholarly and practical of that transcendent idea, the "commonwealth of nations." (Scribner. $1.25.)—*N. Y. Evening Post.*

Our Western Archipelago.

THE summer days are come, and we must go somewhere. Europe is an old story. Why

From Field's " Our Western Archipelago."　　Copyright, 1895, by Charles Scribner's Sons.
BAY OF CHILCAT.

every way worthy of a scholar, a teacher and a publicist.

Of late more space has been given by historians to the first generation after the adoption of the constitution, which their precursors had neglected. This manual, which by its size deprecates comparison with the histories of Adams and McMaster, yields to no book yet published for suggestiveness and penetration.

As is natural in one of President Walker's former occupation, he has much to say of the early censuses of the country, and the significance of the statistics then ascertained; and his book is provided with useful tables, maps, bibliography and index. Without agreeing with not turn to the West and see a little more of our own continent? But one cannot go alone. Even an old traveller does not like to set out on a solitary pilgrimage. But there is a choice in companions and he will have no old fogy but himself. To go to the other extreme he takes the youngest of his household to brighten him up when he is a little dull, and to warm his heart when it is a little cold. So age and youth set out together. And now that he comes to tell the story, he would have all his listeners young in heart, if not in years, loving the sunshine, and looking up to the deep blue sky. (Scribner. $2.)—*Introduction to Dr. Field's " Our Western Archipelago."*

The Watch Fires of '76.

AN historical story that is neither stiff nor hackneyed is furnished by Samuel Adams Drake in "The Watch Fires of '76," in which

From "Watch Fires of '76." Copyright, 1895, by Lee & Shepard.

a group of veterans, by the tavern fire, tell of the events in which they participated in the Revolutionary war. They give free rein to the expression of their opinions regarding those above them. The accuracy of the author in his other books vouches for the correctness of his statements in this volume, and he has certainly, in this story, presented a stirring series of narratives of military adventures, in which important information goes hand in hand with spirited entertainment. (Lee & Shepard. $1 25.)— *Boston Gazette.*

An Old Angler.

AN old man, wading in the shallow edge of the stream, stepping with caution, but firmly, came into view, his eye fixed steadily on the pool, and as full of light and brightness as a boy's eye. He knew what he was about, that was plain enough. He did not look up for some time, but when his glance caught the horses and buckboard, and met mine, he nodded cheerily, but quietly held to his work. It is quite as pleasant to see a fish handsomely taken as to take one yourself. He held his rod in the right hand, well up, and the bend away down to the butt spoke of a weighty fish. The first few rushes had been controlled before the angler came in sight, and now the trout was hanging low down in the water, and swinging slowly from side to side of the pool. Passing his rod to the left hand, he began to use the reel, with judgment, and the fish came nearer. Then he rushed, and the fingers left the reel to run, and the rod bowed a little down to the stream to ease the strain, and I saw his finger press on the line against the rod below the reel to make it drag more heavily. So the fish did not go into the swift water below the pool, but yielding to the persuasion of the rod, turned and gave it up.

In less than five minutes he lay on the green grass, and I weighed him—a plump three pounds; and then I looked up to meet the smiling face of the old angler.

"The boy says he is learning to take trout. I fancy he couldn't have a better teacher."

"Well, I ought to know how to take them here. I've fished this river every spring nigh on to seventy years."

"You began it young."

"Not so very young. I'm eighty-one, and I've caught trout since I was seven years old."

There was a keen pleasure in talking to an experienced angler of this sort, and we talked as cheerily as anglers love to talk. He told me a great many things worth remembering about the habits of the fish in that river. For the habits of trout, like those of men, are different in different localities. Hence it is that books of instruction, and rules about flies for certain seasons, and written ways of fishing are of small account. My experienced friend took no stock in the imitation theory. "Sometimes," he said, "but not often in this water, a trout takes a fly because it looks like a fly of the season; but mostly, I think, they are tempted by the variety which is offered them in something alive and eatable which they haven't tasted before. A trout is a greedy eater. In the freshets he crowds his stomach with sticks and stones and everything which goes along in the thick water."

Surely, it would have gladdened the soul of Izaak to meet this lover of the gentle art. For after I had cast in vain over the pool and wasted my energies for naught, as he sent his flies down under the overhanging bank, where I had been with mine a dozen times, up came that other trout to the golden hackle, and, taking it, was taken.

We passed the day together along the banks of the stream, going for an hour to his home near by for dinner, and coming out afterwards to talk rather than fish by the side of the water. My friend was a very gentle old man. How could one be otherwise who had been for seventy years a lover of the most refining of all arts! (Harper. $1.) *From Prime's "Among the Northern Hills."*

William the Silent, Prince of Orange.

WILLIAM the Silent, Prince of Orange, was a distinctive character, cast in a peculiar period of history. He was in thought and desire centuries ahead of the possibilities of his time, and had to contend with ideas among those he served that were as difficult to overcome as were the forces of the Spanish Crown, with which his life was spent in doing battle.

Had he been able to effect a proper appreciation of his work among those for whom it was done, and obtain a confederation and coalition of the provinces for which he staked his life and his all at any of a number of times during his twenty-five years of faithful endeavor, he would have freed them from Spanish domination. That which he accomplished was of little moment when compared with that which he might have accomplished had he received such support as he was justly entitled to from those who were to reap the benefits of his work.

Many volumes have been written of him and his time, and yet it is doubtful if any have been found to be more readable and accurate than will be those of Ruth Putnam. Her book shows a vast amount of intelligent research among original documents and an unbiased, thoughtful, discriminating study of the histories of her subject. The works of Motley and others that she has drawn upon to a slight extent have been carefully compared with original documents, some of which they had access to, and many of which she has for the first time placed in an intelligible form before English readers. She has reached certain conclusions that do not entirely agree with those reached by former historians of this, the most interesting character of his century, and has made them manifest.

To obtain her material and prepare herself for her work, she visited and made original research at Orange, Dillenburg, Breda, and other places directly connected with his career,

and searched the libraries of the British Museum, the royal libraries of the Hague, and Brussels, and others where trustworthy information could be obtained. In this way she has had access to his correspondence in various languages, in the nature of letters and docu-

From " William the Silent "	Copyright, 1895, by G. P. Putnam's Sons.

THE PRINCE OF ORANGE.

ments, and hundreds of letters and documents written during his time, in connection with affairs in which he was the central figure. She has thus been able to familiarize herself with his motives and follow them through his actions, and also has discovered those of his contemporaries who wrote and spoke eulogistically or with opprobrium. His friendships were not many and his confidences still fewer. The few that are instanced show a loyalty and devotion to him and his cause that are in striking contrast to the many who professed friendship only to sell their influence and knowledge of his affairs to his enemies.

The author's work is confined as nearly as possible to the personality of the Prince of Orange and his individual actions. (Putnam. 2 v., $4.)—*N. Y. Times.*

E. A. Abbey's Work in the Boston Public Library.

E. A. ABBEY's most characteristic work is acknowledged to be the illustration of classic literary subjects. He was chosen as the designer and painter of the prize for the main hall of the great Boston Public Library. He chose the story of the Holy Grail for his theme. Many have wondered why this special subject should have been deemed most fitting for such purpose. Mr. Abbey explains his idea in the following words, taken from a description of his work, with reproductions, just issued by R. H. Russell & Son:

"Thus the Grail story has been the great fountain of Christian romance, and the Arthurian legend, the peculiar gift of the British race to the world's literature, refined and subtilized by the courtly poets of Provence and the German Minnesingers, further Christianized by the monks, who took over for the church the tales they could not bring the people to forget, is the source of all imaginative writing, the most distinctive feature of modern literature. The English language has no romance but leads from it; its stories lie, though unrecognized, in the hearts of the English people, in the nursery tales of our children, in all Christian legend down to the most trivial superstition, like that of thirteen at table. For but two great central stories lie at the root of modern literature, the Nibelungen myth, Teutonic, which is essentially Pagan ; the Arthurian myth, Celtic, which early became Christian ; and, therefore, both from social fact and from historic pride, the Grail story is peculiarly fitted to be the subject of the decoration of a great library, built by a people of British race, and in a room dedicated not to science or the classics alone, but to fiction, poetry, romance—to the reading of the people." (Russell. bds., $1.25.)

Memoirs of General Count de Ségur.

"THE de Ségurs, essentially 'gens de l'épée,' were distinguished as soldiers early in the last century. In addition to their prowess with the sword," says the *N. Y. Times*, "they were diplomatists, and had a strong literary turn. The father of Count Philippe Paul de Ségur, of these memoirs, served under Rochambeau in our Revolutionary struggle, and was ambassador to Russia in 1784. So, by heredity, at least, the aide-de-camp of Napoleon followed the ways of his ancestors. Born in 1780, Philippe Paul lived a long life, dying in 1873. After his death, his 'History, Memoirs, and Miscellania' appeared, and the book is valuable as containing the Count's reminiscences of Napoleon. The latter are separately embodied in this volume which is a most entertaining and interesting work."

This volume forms a natural companion or pendant to the "Memoirs of the Baron de Méneval." The Count de Ségur's military career began in 1800. He was made a general in 1812 and took part in all the wars of the Empire as a member of Napoleon's staff or the commander of a select corps. Hohenlinden, missions to Denmark and Spain, the execution of the Duc d'Enghien, the preparations for the invasion of England, Austerlitz, Ulm, Jena, Berlin, Spain, and the intrigues of Fouché and Bernadotte, are among the subjects of his chapters treated with the advantages of personal knowledge, and, in the earlier pages, of intimate information due to his father's associations and position. The historical value of the memoirs is obvious, and their interest is enhanced by the author's graphic and lucid style. (Appleton. $2.)

From E. A. Abbey's "The Quest of the Holy Grail."
Copyright, by Russell & Son.

A Son of Reuben.

WHEN they got into the lighted street, he said "good-night" very quietly, and turning swiftly on his heel, began to retrace his steps.

She walked on very leisurely, thinking of the pleasant afternoon she had spent. Hugh Sutcliffe had interested her from their first meeting. He was no ordinary operative; a thorough man of the people, and yet standing head and shoulders above his order; faithful to his own kith and kin, and yet having little sympathy with them ; never seeking the society of those in a higher social position than himself, and yet unable to associate with those of his own class. Hence he had been driven to dwell apart and alone. He had found companionship in books, and recreation in study. His hobby had been mechanics; and one of his inventions had been stolen, while he had been saving sufficient money to take out a patent. Such a life-story as his could not fail to interest a woman of such large sympathies as Grace Marsden.

Nor could she keep out of her sympathy a measure of admiration. The man was so patient, so brave, so persevering; so good to his invalid parents and brother; so helpful in every good work; so ready to sacrifice himself for the good of others.

Indeed, from every point of view the man was to be admired. While thousands of young fellows were loafing about waiting for something to turn up, he was trying to turn up something for himself. And in her heart she hoped and prayed that he would succeed.

When she got to her room that night, her thoughts recurred to him again. The portrait of her lover was before her handsome, smiling, and splendidly posed.

But what had he be-

yond his looks? It was as though a voice spoke the question close to her ear. He was handsome, well - educated, respectably connected, with a prospect of sharing his father's wealth when the old man died.

But what had he apart from this? What treasure had he in himself? What could he do if left to shift for himself? Had he ever earned anything in his life? Was he ever likely to do so?

She turned away her eyes at length with a little sigh. "I wish he had a few of Hugh Sutcliffe's excellencies," she said, half aloud ; and then she blushed and sighed again. (Warne. $1.25.)—*From Hocking's " Son of Reuben."*

From Hocking's "Son of Reuben."   Frederick Warne & Co.

SHE MADE AS SWEET A PICTURE OF ENGLISH WOMANHOOD AS ANY ONE COULD DESIRE.

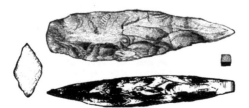

NARROW ADZE, OR PICK. BURWELL, CAMBRIDGE.

Primitive Man.

In the popularization of science no more effective work has been done than that which has been undertaken by the projector of *The Library of Useful Stories*, now in course of publication by the Appletons. This is a series of little books which are to deal with various branches of knowledge, and to treat each subject in clear and concise language, as free as possible from technical words and phrases. Each book will be complete in itself, and will be the work of some writer of authority within

WAR AXE, NOCTKA SOUND.

the province surveyed. The aim of the series is to present the leading facts of science and history in an interesting form, yet without sacrificing accuracy to picturesqueness of treatment. We add that the price will be from

thirty cents to forty cents a volume; that is to say, these little books will be within the reach of all persons who wish to make, at all events a beginning of self-education.

In the example before us, "The Story of Primitive Man," by Edward Clodd, we have in a compendious form the results of the latest investigation into the early history of the human race. The author, who is the president of the Folk-Lore Society, is a well known English anthropologist, and entirely competent to present an up-to-date summary of the extremely interesting subject which he has undertaken to expound. We do not, of course, mean to say that some of his deductions may not be regarded as disputable by some authorities in anthropology, or even that the trustworthiness of his data may not be, in some instances, impeached. In the present state of our knowledge regarding the evolution of man, it is inevitable that differences of opinion should be encountered with relation to the outcome of the researches thus far made. We imagine, however, that no candid person will deny that Mr. Clodd has come as near as any one at the present time is likely to come to an authentic exposition of all the information hitherto gained regarding the earlier stages in the evolution of mankind as distinguished from the anthropoid apes.

The list of books given at the end of this little volume fulfils the twofold purpose of indicating the authorities who have been consulted in its preparation, and of telling the reader where fuller information on the several subjects dealt with is to be found. (Appleton. 40 c.)—*The Sun.*

NARROW ADZE, OR PICK.

Narrative of Captain Coignet.

"THE Narrative of Captain Coignet (Soldier of the Empire), 1776–1850," purports to come from a soldier unknown to fame, who discharged his duty well, and without rising high did rise to a captaincy from the ranks, survived all the chances of war, and lived on into the piping times of peace. This volume is edited from the original manuscript by Lorédan Larchey, who vouches for it as a genuine original, and it is translated by Mrs. M. Carey. We see no reason to question its origin as the personal narrative of a very intelligent soldier who made his way up from the ranks, and being gifted with a firm and vivid memory, afterwards, wrote down his recollections, except that it is a kind of book that might easily be forged. The book has no value for matters of strategy or on the larger questions of diplomacy or campaigning, and the merit of it is that Captain Coignet made no single attempt to write about things that lay out of his range. Inside his range he was a capital observer, and there was much to see and write about. It is not all camp gossip that he gives us, though there may be some. In the main, it is the story of an honest soldier who used his eyes and was a story-teller of the first order. The story is not free from the brutal realism of war, but it has the intense interest of snapshot pictures, true and vivid as far as they go. Inside of these limits he is a first-rate story-teller who has strange luck in seeing the thing which ought to be seen, though it might not amount to much in a history. He was at Waterloo, holding the rank of captain, and has plenty of incidents to report, but nothing important as illustrating the combat. The interesting features of the book are its minor descriptions. These are written by one who knows and by a trained writer. The book is a valuable addition to Napoleana, of which it seems the reading public cannot have enough. (Crowell. $1.50.)—*The Outlook.*

Theatrical Sketches.

THE anonymous author seems thoroughly *au fait* in theatrical gossip, and is an amusing *raconteur.* The little volume contains a medley of bright and characteristic anecdotes of the leading stars of "the profession," as well as of the many lesser luminaries. There are stories of Wallack—to whose memory the book is ded-

From "A Norse Idyll."   Copyright, 1894, by The Robert Clarke Co.
A DAUGHTER OF THE NORTH.

icated—Edwin Booth, Louis James, Henry Irving, Richard Mansfield, "Adonis" Dixey, and many others whose names are household words to playgoers. Nor are these reminiscences and sketches always honeyed. The writer has a sharp pen, and does not hesitate to unveil little foibles, amusing bits of self-esteem, and other lapses of human nature—all of which makes the book piquant and interesting reading. (The Merriam Co. 75 c.)

The Master-Knot.

THE old device of telling a story in letters is resorted to with great effect by Conover Duff. Two men and a woman write these letters, and the characters of the writers are shown forth

From "The Master-Knot.' Copyright 1895, by Henry Holt & Co.
RACING THROUGH THE PARK.

in their different ways of seeing, describing and judging the same objects and circumstances. Both men love the charming heroine, and she, in her whole-hearted way, loves both. At last her higher nature leads her to choose the most unselfish. A note of sadness runs through the little pages, although many are brightened by fine touches of humor. (Holt. 75 c.)

Negotiating for a Second-hand Leg.

MEANWHILE there was quite a little flutter among Liberty's white friends, for his patient and unselfish devotion to his former owner in his misfortunes had won him many. This was no less than a project, originating with Madame de Jolibois, to buy him an artificial leg.

"One in the very latest style, Miss Kizzy explained to Newall, sitting in his office. "I learned from Sarah Hunter, whose uncle-in-law lost his limb at the battle of Shiloh," she went on, "that for a sum which I confess seems large, Peter, these artificial limbs may be procured in the North. I am at present in correspondence with a firm in Philadelphia. In fact, I am negotiating for a second-hand limb "—

"Second-hand!" gasped Newall.

"Second-hand," repeated Miss Kizzy firmly. "The limb which corresponds to Liberty Thornham's proportions, was made, it appears, for a drum-major who lost his limb in a battle during our war. I do not know what battle, for I regret to say that the drum-major was in the Yankee army. I feel that I ought to offer an apology to the people of Thornham for having decided upon buying—if the money can be raised—a limb which has been worn by one of our enemies. But being second-hand (for the drum-major, they inform me, returned it after using it about a year)—*being* second-hand, I get it at half-price."

"How much money have you on hand?" Newall asked, taking out his purse.

"The fund, Peter, amounts as yet to only a few dollars," she returned. "But several people have promised to subscribe, and there will be mite-meetings, in Mrs. Alsbury's yard and elsewhere, for the benefit of the fund. Were it not for the unavoidable expense of Monshur *dee* Jollyboys' trip I could do more myself. Liberty has been informed of this movement. But of course we do not wish Olive to know as yet," she added anxiously.

"You are a good woman, Keziah," Newall said, doubling his subscription, which he could ill afford at the moment, "and if ever a man in this world has done his duty, that man is Lib Thornham."

Madame de Jolibois went away radiant. The fund under her indefatigable generalship grew; but it grew slowly. Sixty dollars was a large sum to raise for such a purpose; and it was a full year before the drum-major's leg came, consigned to Madame de Jolibois.

Long before this Liberty had contrived a pair of crutches strong enough to bear his immense weight. (Houghton, Mifflin & Co. $1.25.)—*From "Under the Man-Fig."*

Master and Man.

TOLSTOY'S "Master and Man" is not much more than a sketch, but it is crowded with those characteristic touches which mark his literary work. His ever-present attention to Russian local customs and minute detail has not become vapid, and he leads up to the sublime sacrifice the master makes for the man in the simple t yet most unexpected fashion. Mr. Howells has an appreciative introduction, and A. Hulme Beaman makes the translation. (Appleton. 75 c.)—*Public Opinion.*

Suppressed Chapters.

THERE are several kinds of cleverness in "Suppressed Chapters and other Bookishness," by Robert Bridges, but they are not so easy to define as to enjoy, for they are not sharply defined, they are occasionally interblended, and they demand for their perfect understanding a more intimate acquaintance with the fiction of to-day than most of their readers are likely to have. They are in a certain sense what the title, "Suppressed Chapters," would suggest to the literary mind, imitations or burlesques of popular authors ; but they are more than that, for this burlesque intention is not only perceived but enforced by the critical spirit in which it is presented, and which exposes the "seamy side" of its originals. The critical suggestions which underlie these "Suppressed Chapters" are of a finer quality than the Chapters themselves, which pale their ineffectual light before Thackeray's "Prize Novelists" or the burlesques in Bayard Taylor's "Echo Club." Mr. Bridges aims his shafts at smaller deer than the victims of the American poet, or the English novelist, the first of the seven being Mr. Anthony Hope, the second Mr. Du Maurier, the third Mr. Richard Le Gallienne, the fourth Heinrich Ibsen, the fifth Mr. George Egerton, the sixth Mr. John Kendrick Bangs, the seventh Mr. Edward S. Martin. If any of these gentlemen have a right to feel aggrieved instead of complimented, it is

Mr. Bangs, whose humor is characterized as the "Idiot Brand." Other authors who are chaffed by Mr. Bridges, in later portions of his volume, are Mr. Kipling, Mme. Sarah Grand, Mrs. W. K. Clifford and Mr. Bridges himself, in his penname of "Droch," and, in brief notices of their novels, Mr. Meredith, Mr. Hall Caine, Mr. Hardy, Mr. Hope, Miss Harraden, Mr. Crawford, Miss Wilkins and Mr. Stevenson. For just what it is, a collection of light trifles, critical, suggestive, humorous, this little volume of Mr. Bridges' is of a kind that is sure to be read, once it is taken in hand, and to be reread, in portions at least, in one's leisure moments. (Scribner. $1.25.)—*Mail and Express.*

A Minister of the World.

STEPHEN CASTLE, installed in the little New England pastorate of Thornton, is perfectly satisfied with his surroundings, until meeting Miss Loring, from New York, he imbibes new ideas. He finally accepts a call to a fashionable New York church, and his action thereafter is interesting chiefly on account of the contrasts which it offers to his former methods. The story first appeared in *The Ladies' Home Jour al,* where it attracted much attention. The author is Caroline Atwater Mason, author of "A Titled Maiden," "A Loyal Heart," etc. The picture shows the first love-making of the young clergyman. (Randolph. 75 c.)

From "A Minister of the World."   Copyright, 1895, by A. D. F. Randolph & Co.

"A KIND OF INVISIBLE AFFINITY BETWEEN US."

"PULL, LADS, PULL!"

Afloat With the Flag.

A GOOD, healthy story, attractively written, full of stirring incident and adventure, Mr. Henderson's book will doubtless find many enthusiastic readers. The difficulty in writing for boys is to keep alive their interest, and at the same time to give them something for a little serious reflection. The author has succeeded admirably in this, for the lad who can read the description of Admiral Benham's manly protection of the American merchantman in the harbor of Rio de Janeiro and not have his patriotism appealed to, must be difficult to move.

Life on a man-of war, with routine, the duties of officers and men, the handling of the ship and its guns, the clearing of the deck for action, and the suspense and anxiety preceding an attack, all these are told very vividly and with an intimate knowledge of naval matters that could only come from much experience. In point of fact, Mr. Henderson himself is an officer in the New York Naval Reserve, and has been a keen student of naval affairs for some years. He has also written a text-book on navigation, and in general is thoroughly equipped to talk on the subject.

The young sailors are fine, manly fellows, in love with their profession, and their life aboard the *Detroit* has a very alluring side. There are pleasant descriptions of midocean, dancing sunlight, fresh salty breezes, and ship bowling over lively seas; or pictures of beautiful harbors with background of smiling tropical vegetation and soft summer skies. Indeed, Mr. Henderson never lets the interest flag all the way through his work. (Harper. $1.25.)— *N. Y. Times.*

In the Fire of the Forge.

PROFESSOR GEORG EBERS works the mine he has dug "for all it is worth." He has shown the shrewdest judgment in this popularizing of the archaic. Having devised a new thing, he has been wise enough, just as Scott and Dickens and the other markedly successful novelists were, to build up and up on that assured foundation, and not to fritter away his force on a dozen modes. Nothing better can happen an author than to be identified with a certain line of work accepted everywhere as his very own, with no one to share or divide it. This is Professor Ebers' good fortune— fortune established, however, by his own labor and discretion. "In the Fire of the Forge," translated from the German by Mary J. Stafford, is a book in the well-known manner, the author's ingenuity being this time exercised in a reproduction of the life and manners of Nuremburg in the thirteenth century. It is, by so much, easier reading than the Romances of Ancient Egypt and Greece, though still, perhaps, too "old-fashioned" to suit the average reader-in-a-hurry. But there is another if smaller class—of leisurely people who read for profit—who will deeply relish this book. (Appleton. 2 v., pap., 80 c.; $1.50.)—*Philadelphia Telegraph.*

Galt's Novels.

It would be amusing to compare the lists of standard English fiction which a dozen or so of well-seasoned novel readers would prepare. By the callow devourers of stories of the present day the wide diversity of taste would be appreciated, but they would be surprised to come across so many titles unknown to them. Standard though they may be styled, editions a-many though they may have passed through, while their merits have saved them from utter oblivion, they nevertheless have been thrust aside in the onward rush.

John Galt is but little more than a name to the present generation. We question whether more than a very few of such lists would contain any of his works. And yet the "Annals of the Parish" is the ancestor in direct line of the Scottish stories which within a few years have taken such a strong hold upon popular favor. His Rev. Micah Balwhidder is a delightful creation; a man without marked eccentricities, without vanity and yet with a certain quality of innocent egotism, true to his calling and yet with a keen eye to the main chance. His three marriages are so comically devoid of all sentiment that when the end comes we are surprised to hear his aspiration to meet on high "the long-departed sheep of his flock, especially the first and second Mrs. Balwhidders." While the Vicar of Wakefield cannot be said to be exactly his prototype, Galt avowedly hoped to achieve in him what Goldsmith had done for England in his Dr. Primrose. But the Scotch parson is in no sense an imitation of the Englishman. Both were simple-minded, well-meaning men, with a slight infusion of egotism, but there the resemblance ended.

Galt's genius is especially adapted to such a work as the "Annals," and he does not suffer by comparison with his latter-day successors. His humor is without travesty, and he never yielded to the temptation to overdo the pathos. Although the "Ayrshire Legatees" is in the epistolary form which is usually so objectionable, there is a thread of narrative connecting the letters which is adroitly managed.

Charles E. Brock's 40 illustrations are capital, and Mr. Ainger's introduction is a good example of blended biography and criticism. We cannot too heartily commend these volumes to the admirers of Mr. Crockett and "Ian Maclaren" Watson. (Macmillan; Roberts. 8 v., *ea.*, $1.25.)—*Public Opinion.*

The Grasshoppers.

The heroine is the daughter of a German mother of domestic old-fashioned notions, who has married an Englishman after a term as governess in English families. This daughter at first insists upon going to college and doing all manner of strange things in the way of dress and breaches of conventionalities. A loss of fortune brings this interesting family to a small German town, and German domestic life and characteristic customs are described with accuracy and humor. Indeed the story will seem inimitably funny to those who have spent any part of their lives among homespun Germans. The heroine with love as teacher gives up her "new woman" fad and settles down to be a charming old-fashioned piece of womanhood of the kind which insists upon the right to share all burdens. (Stokes. $1.)

"HOW DO MEN MAKE A LIVING, DICK?"

Memoirs of Barras.

THE two great volumes of the "Memoirs of Barras," edited by Mr. George Duruff and translated by Mr. C. E. Roche, afford one of the strangest of all the strange revelations conse-

From "A Lost Endeavor."   Copyright, 1895, by Macmillan & Co.
TWO OUTCASTS.

quent upon the publication of the memoirs of his time. Talleyrand never forgot himself throughout his careful pages; Barras simultaneously forgets himself and remembers himself. Dignity he has none, and only a poor semblance of nobility of spirit. No one is too petty and contemptible for his envy; none too high to be spattered by his obloquy. At rare intervals he utters a kind word, but invariably follows it with phrases of contempt. Nevertheless, he impresses the reader as one who tells what he regards as the simple truth. His style, as it appeared in his original manuscript before edited by M. Rousselin de Saint-Albin, was that of Flora Finching, inconsequent, incoherent, but leaving nothing of the writer's feelings and nature unrevealed. The corrections, judging from parallel passages published by the editor, have changed nothing but the rhetoric, and have left the expression of the real Barras entirely intact. The editor's preface professes a deal of virtuous horror for cer-

tain of his revelations, ingenuously indicating in what chapters they may be found, but other writers have forestalled them, and it is not as a chronicle of scandal, but as an historian of civic disturbance, of war, and of revolution that Barras will be most valued. He hated Bonaparte so thoroughly that if he hated him alone, the volume of his malice would be held as conclusive evidence against the Corsican, for it would seem impossible that a structure so huge should not have strong foundations; but he also hated Talleyrand, Robespierre, every one who at any moment thwarted or outshone him. In short, he was one of the worst products of the Revolution. His demerits by no means lessen the value of his work. Making due allowance for his peculiarities, one may learn much from him, for he stood behind the scenes for many a year, he had no scruples as to methods of acquiring knowledge, and reticence is unknown to him. The mirror is a little distorted, but it reflects everything, and these two volumes, ending with the eighteenth Fructidor, will but make readers more eager for the remaining two. They are very handsome books, illustrated with portraits of Robespierre, Danton, Barras and Josephine, and with maps and plans, and knowledge of their contents is essential to the study of France in the years following the downfall of the monarchy. (Harper. $3.75.)— *Boston Gazette.*

A Lost Endeavor.

THREE books from the pen of Guy Boothby have come out within the last few months. The latest, "A Lost Endeavor," appears in the *Iris Series* of Macmillan & Co. It is a delightfully printed little volume, with illustrations by Stanley L. Wood. Very little of the ordinary literary gossip has gone the rounds concerning Mr. Boothby. Perhaps it is only necessary to know that he can write a good novel. The locale of all his stories which one has seen is Thursday Island, "that quaint and but little-known land spot, peering up out of the green seas that separate New Guinea from the most northerly coastline of Australia." There, among pearlers, "beach combers" and the refuse of the old civilizations, the author works out his problems of love and life.

Indeed, Mr. Boothby has a measure of Robert Louis Stevenson's deft skill in telling a story, as you shall see. (Macmillan. 75 c.) —*N. Y. Commercial Advertiser.*

Decline and Fall of Napoleon.

THE various sections into which " The Decline and Fall of Napoleon " is divided are: " The Campaign of 1812." " The Campaign of 1813," "The Campaign of 1814," "The Hundred Days," and " Waterloo." It will thus be seen that the task which Viscount Wolseley set before himself was the treatment of those four years which may be described as the most important of the century. As these chapters are reprints from *The Pall Mall Magazine,* we do not know whether the author had set him bounds which he might not pass, or whether the rather too brief review of the events leading up to the final overthrow of Napoleon is the result of an unimpeded choice. From time to time we have made it clear that those whose hobby is length are no favorites of ours, but, on the other hand, we like to see a notable subject fully discussed, and we are inclined to think that this is one of the books that should be longer. This very mild grumble delivered, we have only admiration left for Viscount Wolseiey's behavior within his limits. His meaning is always plain, and sometimes, roused by his stirring subject, he approaches closely to a really brilliant exposition. His book contains one or two things which are serious blemishes. In one instance a general is represented as engaged in the campaign of 1812 who at that time had been dead for a dozen years. This is clearly a matter for the Psychical Researchers. Again, the discredited story of Wellington's ride to Wavre on the evening before the battle of Waterloo is discussed. We had thought that cock-and-bull story was dead once and for all. These are by no means all the faults which it is possible to advance against " The Decline and Fall of Napoleon," but as the list of vices would be very small when compared with that containing the virtues, there is no need to insist very much upon the author's shortcomings. It is only necessary to add that this is the first volume of " The Pall Mall Library " in which are to appear those articles and short stories from *The Pall Mall Magazine* which are deemed worthy of salvation in book form. This volume promises much for the series. (Roberts. $1.25.) —*London Literary World.*

Archbishop Laud.

ALMOST everybody who has written a biography or a biographical sketch of Archbishop Laud has found it necessary to disapprove of some things he did, and to criticise with more or less severity the spirit he displayed towards those who were disinclined to fall in with his churchly notions. Most of Laud's biographers have said, in substance, that he was altogether too strict in his religion ; that he attached undue importance to small matters ; that he was impolitic in his treatment of the non-conformists, and provoked them so that it was quite certain that, if they should come to hold the upper hand, they would take their revenge. Some of the biographers have said worse than this of Laud, rating him as narrow-minded, cold-blooded, domineering, cruel, and expressing the opinion that, according to the standards of his time, he deserved his punishment—death on the scaffold.

Mr. Hutton takes his stand neither with the extremely adverse critics nor with those who have undertaken to judge Laud fairly—he considers Laud in all essential respects a perfect man. Practically, it is pure panegyric that he has written. The faults he discovers in Laud are inconsequential, and have no reference to the mooted questions relating to the Archbishop's policy and acts as a churchman and a minister of state. He offers his book "as an attempt justly and historically to estimate the character of the great man, to whose pure, conscientious and steadfast soul the Church of England owes so much." It is impossible not

From " Appleton's Canadian Guide-Book "   Copyright, 1895, by D. Appleton & Co.

OLD FIREPLACE AT ENTRY ISLAND.

to recall that the man thus spoken of is the man who had men's ears cropped, their noses slit, and their foreheads branded, to say nothing of fines and imprisonments, simply because they preferred their ways of worshipping God to those of the Archbishop of Canterbury. Mr. Hutton gives us to understand that he approves of everything Laud did as a member of the Star Chamber.

It seems to be a fact that his was the controlling mind in the Star Chamber, and that he was the one in all England most set upon maintaining the supremacy of the English Church. The Puritans knew more about Laud than Mr. Hutton can know, and the bare fact that they hated him because he had persistently persecuted them is an answer to Mr Hutton's assertion, "He sat with other judges," and the argument it carries, that he had no more responsibility for the acts of the chamber than any one of the other Judges. (Houghton, Mifflin & Co. $1.)—*N. Y. Times.*

Adventures of Captain Horn.

MR. STOCKTON'S new volume, "The Adventures of Captain Horn," has been on sale several days, and already the booksellers have greatly reduced their piles thereof. It has made an instantaneous success—a success which has been equalled by no other long story of this fanciful writer, wide as has been his audience in the past. It is unlike anything he has ever produced before, and the sustained

power of the romance is remarkable. Wild and impossible as are the adventures constantly occurring, following one another with unceasing rapidity, leaping from San Francisco to Peru, thence to Maine, and to Paris and Germany and back again, one is impressed with their truth while reading them. It hardly need be said that characters, scenes and incidents are of that peculiar originality which has given Mr. Stockton a position unique among story-tellers. (Scribner. $1.50.)—*Boston Literary World.*

Ten New England Blossoms.

ONE of the prettiest out-of-door books of the season is Clarence Moore Weed's "Ten New England Blossoms and Their Insect Visitors." This volume will be read with special interest in New England, but many of the flowers which it describes are found elsewhere, and the book is so entertaining and so instructive that it will command attention even where the particular flowers which it describes are unknown. The book is unusual in the fact that it not only describes the Mayflower, the spring-beauty, the Jack-in-the-pulpit, and other New England flowers, but also the insects which are particularly drawn to them, and which, in one way or another, are associated with their growth and the dissemination of their seed. The volume is very attractive in its making, and contains a number of well-printed illustrations. (Houghton, Mifflin & Co. $1.25.)—*The Outlook.*

Zangwill's The Old Maid's Club.

THE Old Maid's Club was founded by Lillie Dulcimer at the age of seventeen. According to its conditions of membership, every candidate must be under twenty-five, beautiful, and wealthy, and must have refused at least one offer of marriage. Its by-laws required the members to look upon all men as brothers, not to keep domestic pets, not to have less than one birthday a year, to abjure medicine, art classes, and Catholicism, never to speak to a curate, not to wear curls, caps, etc., and also added a number of general recommendations. The history of this club is facetiously told and brightly illustrated. (Lovell, Coryell. $1.25; pap., 50 c.)

From "The Old Maid's Club."   Copyright, 1895, by Lovell, Coryell & Co.

"IS THAT THE UNIFORM OF THE OLD MAID'S CLUB?"

The Literary News.

An Eclectic Monthly Review of Current Literature.

EDITED BY A. H. LEYPOLDT.

JULY, 1895.

THE ART OF RUDYARD KIPLING.*

SOME six years since, there appeared in India "a sort of book, a long oblong docket, wire stitched, to imitate a D. O. Government envelope, printed on one side only, bound in brown paper, and secured with red tape," in which were gathered a sheaf of verses that had from time to time filled an odd corner in one of the Indian journals. Thus were "Departmental Ditties " born into the world, precursors of the astonishing array of stories and lyrics that are now set before us as the "complete works" of a man who half a dozen years ago was absolutely unknown in literature.

When a writer has attained the dignity of a "new, uniform edition" it may be taken for granted that he is no longer "new"—he has won his spurs and proved himself an accepted knight of the pen. The rapidity with which Mr. Kipling has attained this dignity, the very swiftness and brilliancy of his literary career, have detracted from a just estimate of his work. He has dazzled the eyes of the public, and the public while it enjoys the new sensation, dislikes to take such dazzlement seriously, as something more than a device for its temporary amusement.

Now, the art of Rudyard Kipling, to be judged fairly, must be taken seriously. He is no retailer of marvels and horrors ; no juggler with scenes made to "take"—as some have said. Still less is he bound by the canons and traditions of his art. But he is, in the judgment of those who have followed his work from its beginning, one of the great writers of these our own days ; a writer who, if he never

* New uniform edition of the prose tales of Rudyard Kipling. 6 vols. 1. Plain Tales from the Hills; 2. Life's Handicap, being Stories of Mine Own People ; 3. Soldiers Three, The Story of the Gadsbys, In Black and White ; . Under the Deodars, The Phantom 'Rickshaw, Wee Willie Winkie ; 5. The Light that Failed ; 6. The Naulahka, by Rudyard Kipling and Wolcott Balestier. *Also* Ballads and Barrack-room Ballads. (New York: Macmillan. $1.25 per vol.)

Rudyard Kipling's Works. *Authorized Royalty Edition.* Uniformly bound in 7 vols. 12mo, cloth, gilt top, per vol., $1.25. V. 1, Departmental Ditties, Barrack Room Ballads and other verses.—2, Plain Tales from the Hills.—3, Soldiers Three and In Black and White.—4, The Phantom Rickshaw and Wee Willie Winkie.—5, The Light That Failed.—6, Story of the Gadsbys, and Under the Deodars.—7, Mine Own People, including The Courting of Dinah Shadd, etc. With a critical introduction by Henry James. (Lovell, Coryell.)

produced another line, could rest enduring claims to fame upon these six volumes of his " prose tales," and the three others not included in the "new uniform edition"—the "Ballads," "Many Inventions" and the " Jungle Book."

To know his spell fully the reader must be long to that company of fortunate people who have not lost their faith in romance, and who believe that all things in heaven and earth are not yet known to our philosophy. For Romance is a true goddess, and Rudyard Kipling is one of her anointed. In the face of this statement it seems paradoxical to say that the dominant quality of Kipling's work is its reality. But it is the reality of true romance—not the realism of fiction—the absolute, quiet certainty that these things have happened, and that they must have happened and could have happened in no other way than that set forth by the romancer. Kipling's readers may wonder at his tales ; they cannot doubt. His highest art is the absolute verisimilitude with which he invests the weird and the marvellous. "The Strange Ride of Morrowbie Jukes" to the city of the living dead ; the horrors of the contest with the Silver Man, in "The Mark of the Beast" ; the supernatural mystery of "At the End of the Passage" and "The Phantom 'Rickshaw," these and many more fairly take away one's breath with their daring and their strangeness; yet they bear the unmistakable stamp of verity. We dismiss our reason, and simply say, "I know that these things happened."

Equalling, perhaps surpassing, this faculty of making fiction fact, is the knowledge of human nature that pervades Kipling's books. The secret of this knowledge is not far to seek. He gives it to us when he says:

"I have eaten your bread and salt,
    I have drunk your water and wine,
The deaths ye died I have watched beside,
    And the lives that ye led were mine.

"Was there aught that I did not share,
    In vigil or toil or ease,
One joy or woe that I did not know,
    Dear hearts across the seas ? "

It is just that. He has known them all—the joy and ease, the vigil, toil and woe ; and with that knowledge he can say, " God be thanked—whate'er comes after, I have lived and toiled with Men." And he shows us men indeed. Men neither all good, nor all bad ; but very human. Men strong, yet weak ; fiercely brave, yet subject to wild fears ; capable of sublime self-sacrifice, and of utter failure. Throughout his books there come again and again glimpses of his knowledge of and insight into the springs of human action. Take the awful night when Dick Heldar wrestles with his blindness in "The Light that Failed "; or the scene in "Thrown Away," where the grim deception is evolved that shall screen the memory of The Boy from shame ; or, in a less degree, the scene where Aurelius McGoggin, stricken with aphasia, says blindly: "But I can't understand it. I am quite sane ; but I can't be sure of my own mind, it seems—my *own* memory. I can't understand it—it was my *own* mind and memory !" Perhaps in none of his tales is this knowledge of mankind better shown than in "The Story of the Gadsbys." In the eight short scenes, of less than a dozen pages each, that make up the story, we have love, life, the shadow of death, joy, despair, the sadness of failure, compressed, as it were, into an absolute "human document." "The Story of the Gadsbys" has never won approval in Philistia ; but it is Life, as life is lived.

Woman does not rank with man in Kipling's tales, for the reason, frankly acknowledged, that he knows little of her. The few women that he has given us are perfect of their type ; but the type, though a large one, is by no means the noblest. It is the type of which Mrs. Hauksbee is the representative at one end of the line and Maisie—the shallow, utterly selfish heroine of "The Light that Failed "— at the other. To be sure, we have Minnie Threegan, who might have developed into a woman's woman ; and Ameera, the sweet and truly lovely heroine of "Without Benefit of Clergy,"—one of the most perfect of pathetic histories.

Mr. Kipling gives us not only real tales of real men and women, but he gives them to us in English that is a joy and a revelation. His work is never marred by sloppiness or carelessness of finish. His tales are made up of crystallized sentences that in their turn are composed of words chosen and fitted as are the stones for a mosaics. Yet the whole effect is so simple that it *is* delusive. He does not tell the story; the story tells itself, in lightning-flash phrases that pass from the mind, leaving in their place a picture. Take the brief sentence describing the thunder-storm in "False Dawn":

"The wind seemed to be picking up the earth and pitching it to leeward in great heaps; and the heat beat up from the ground like the heat of the Day of Judgment."

Could anything be more effective, or more simple—at first sight?

Of his humor it is superfluous to speak. It is conceded that the literature of mirth is permanently enriched by such stories as "The Taking of Lungtungpen," "The Incarnation of Krishna Mulvaney" and "My Lord the Elephant "—tales that are unsurpassed for fun,

for *verve* and force ; while there are few of his stories that are not lightened by gleams of dry, quaint humor, sometimes so blended with grim tragedy as to be awesome to a degree.

Pessimism is the fault most frequently charged to Kipling ; and in a measure justly. His cynicism and pessimism are the expression of a strong nature, alive with sympathy for and understanding of suffering, and feeling its impotence to set right a world that is out of joint. He sees too clearly the seamy side of life—the failures, the heartaches, the unfulfilled hopes and the daily struggles—and he finds no remedy. The fatalism of the East has laid its spell upon him. He can but say "Kismet." Life must be lived ; only a craven will shirk its duties and its responsibilities; but the battle must be fought sternly alone, with the blind hope that if there be a Divinity that shapes our ends It will pity and understand. As was to be expected, Kipling is essentially a man's man. Few women care for him or appreciate him. His virility, his pessimism, his lack of any "doxy," his calm disregard of convention, set him without the pale of feminine approval. His men are too profane; his women too fond of admiration, and with him love is but one of the many emotions of life.

It is impossible within the limits of this sketch even to touch upon the distinctive features of Kipling's individual works. They may be roughly grouped into soldier stories, stories of Anglo-Indian society life, stories of native life, novels, ballads, beast stories, and miscellaneous tales. Of these, the soldier stories have won the most immediate fame, as was inevitable from their entire freshness and novelty. "Soldiers Three" accomplished that amazing feat, the opening of a *new* vein in fiction. There is no question that the "Three Musketeers" of "the Widdy" have won immortality as surely as did their forerunners who served in past centuries under His Majesty of France. Learoyd, the impassive ; Ortheris, the irrepressible ; Mulvaney—inimitable, never-to-be-forgotten "Krishna Mulvaney"—to know them is to love them, and to admit them into immediate and intimate friendship. Thomas Atkins is no longer a machine in a red uniform —he is a man and a brother. Let him speak for himself:

"We aren't no thin red 'eroes, nor we aren't no black-
　　guards too,
But single men in barricks, most remarkable like you;
An' if sometimes our conduck isn't all your fancy paints,
Why, single men in barricks don't grow into plaster
　　saints."

If Mr. Kipling had done no more than create "Soldiers Three" he would have earned the gratitude of posterity; for in their company we have heard tales and seen sights to make us laugh, to make us weep, to set our pulses beating and our hearts throbbing, to bring before us in living reality some of the manifold phases of a life of which we knew nothing.

It is as a short-story writer that Kipling is pre-eminent. In this multitude of short stories the uniform degree of excellence is astonishing. All are good; some are better; some are best—as to the latter no two critics agree *in toto*. From the flirtatiousness of "The Rescue of Pluffles" to the tragedy of "Thrown Away," the grim pathos of "The Man Who Was," or the gripping horror of "At the End of the Passage," there is a wide field in which to choose, were choice possible. But it is not; the only thing is to read them all and be duly thankful.

"The Light that Failed," Kipling's first novel, is presented in the Macmillan edition—its final shape—without the orthodox "happy ending" that marred the first edition. It is now, we are told, given as it was originally planned by its writer, and it is immeasurably the gainer thereby, although the bitter sadness of the tale is fairly haunting in its intensity. In "The Light that Failed," as in "The Naulahka," written in conjunction with Wolcott Balestier, Kipling has not reached his highest level; but both books bear his impress and abound in brilliant touches and striking episodes—witness the scenes following Heldar's blindness, his ride to his death across the desert, and Tarvin's night journey to the Gye Mukh, in "The Naulahka."

Of Kipling as a poet it is impossible to speak; for if there are no limits to time there are definite limits to space. Suffice it to say that his verse is as good, if not better, than his prose. He is a born balladist. Whether he gives us light songs of fun and flirtation, rhymes of cynical philosophy, or ballads that stir one's blood, his verse has ever a lilt and a swing that mark it as his own. Let those who doubt his claim to the laurel read "The Song of the Women," "Christmas in India," "Danny Deever," "Mandalay," "The Ballad of East and West," "The King's Jest," and that beautiful conception, "Evarra."

The many phases of the art of Rudyard Kipling cannot be appreciated in a cursory reading of one or two of his tales. Of the many whom they have reached, comparatively few have fully realized the knowledge, the brilliancy, the comprehension of life, the swift sureness of thought that are there revealed. Those who have done so need no critic to set forth his merits or demerits. To those who have never felt his spell we would say that in his company they may, if they will, pass golden hours and learn much that it is good for man to know.—H. E. H.

Novels for Summer Reading.

Allen (J. L.), A Kentucky cardinal, $1..........*Harper*
Balzac, Catharine de Medici, $1.50.. ....*Roberts*
— Lucien de Rubempré, $1.50 ....*Roberts*
Barrett (F.), Justification of Andrew Lebrun, $1 ; pap., 50c...*Appleton*
Bell (L.), A little sister to the wilderness, $1.25.
Stone & K
Besant (W.), Beyond the dreams of avarice, $1.50.
Harper
Bishop (W. H.), A pound of cure, $1...........*Scribner*
Black (C.), An agitator, $1........................*Harper*
Black (W.), Highland cousins, $1.75.......……*Harper*
Blair (E. N.), Lisbeth Wilson, $1.50............*Lee & S*
Boothby (G.), A lost endeavour, 75c..........*Macmillan*
— The marriage of Esther, $1 ; pap., 50c... ...*Appleton*
Brainerd (T. H.), Go forth and find, 50c.......*Cassell*
Burton (J. B.), The Hispaniola plate, $1......*Cassell*
Caine (H.), The deemster, pap., 50c...............*Weeks*
— The Manxman, $1.50............................*Appleton*
Cambridge (A.), Fidelis, $1 ; pap., 50c........*Appleton*
Catherwood (*Mrs.* M. H.), The chase of Saint Castin (short stories), $1.25......................*Houghton*
Chambers (R. W.), The king in yellow, 75c......*Neely*
Clark (F. T.), On Cloud Mountain, $1..........*Harper*
Coffin (C. C.), Daughters of the Revolution, $1.50.
Houghton, M
Colmore (G.), A daughter of music, $1 ; pap., 50c.
Appleton
Cotes (*Mrs. E.*), The story of Sonny Sahib, $1.*Appleton*
— Vernon's aunt, $1.25 ....*Appleton*
Couperus (L.), Majesty, $1.50..................*Appleton*
Craddock (C. E.), The phantoms of the foot-bridge (short stories), $1.50....................... *Harper*
Crawford (F. M.), Love in idleness, $2.....*Macmillan*
— Katharine Lauderdale, 2 v., $2.............*Macmillan*
— The Ralstons, 2 v., $2.......................*Macmillan*
Crockett (S. R.), Bog-myrtle and peat ; tales of Galloway, $1.50................................*Appleton*
— The lilac sunbonnet, $1.50..................*Appleton*
— The play-actress, $1........... ....*Putnam*
Curse (The) of intellect, $1.............. .. ...*Roberts*
Davis (*Mrs.* M. E. M.), Under the man-fig, $1.25.
Houghton, M
D'Arcy (E.), Monochromes (Keynotes ser.), $1..*Roberts*
Dean (*Mrs.* A.), The grasshoppers, $1 ....*Stokes*
— Lesser's daughter, 50c ....*Putnam*
Deland (*Mrs.* M.), Philip and his wife, $1.25.
Houghton, M
Dix (Gertrude), The girl from the farm (Keynotes ser.), $1...*Roberts*
Don, a story by the author of "Miss Toosey's mission," $1...*Roberts*
Dostoievsky, Poor folk, $1.......................*Roberts*
Dougall (L.), The mermaid, $1 ; pap., 50c .....*Appleton*
— The zeit-geist, 75c............................*Appleton*
Doyle (A. C.), Round the red lamp (short stories), $1.50.
Appleton
Du Maurier (G.), Trilby, $1.75...................*Harper*
Ebers (G.), In the fire of the forge, 2 v., $1.50 ; pap., 80c.
Appleton
Egerton (G.), Discords (Keynotes ser.), $1......*Roberts*
Farr (Florence), The dancing faun (Keynotes ser.), $1.
Roberts
Foote (M. H.), Cœur d'Alene, $1.25.......*Houghton, M*
Ford (P. L.), The Honorable Peter Stirling, $1.50..*Holt*
Forster (F.), Major Joshua, $1...... ......*Longmans, G*
Fothergill (J.), Orioles' daughter, $1 ; pap., 50c.
Lovell, C
Francis (M. E.), A daughter of the soil, $1.25...*Harper*
Fuller (H. B.), With the procession, $1.25......*Harper*
Galt (J.), Novels, *new il. ed.*, 8 v., ea., $1.25.....*Roberts*
Gardner (*Mrs.* S. M. H.), Quaker idyls, 75c......*Holt*
Gerard (D.), An arranged marriage, $1 ; pap., 50c.
Appleton
Goodwin (M. W.), The colonial cavalier, $1..*Lovell, C*
— The head of a hundred, $1.25.................*Little, B*
Graham (*Mrs.* M. C.), Stories of the foot-hills, $1.25.
Houghton, M

Green (A. K.), The doctor, his wife and the clock, 50c.
Putnam
Haggard, Heart of the world, $1.25......*Longmans, G*
— The people of the mist, $1.25............*Longmans, G*
Hall (G.), Foam of the sea, $1...................*Roberts*
Harland (H.), Grey roses (Keynotes ser.), $1....*Roberts*
Harris (F.), Elder Conklin (short stories), $1.25.
Macmillan
Harrison (Mrs. C. C.), A bachelor maid, $1.25.*Century*
Hastings (E.), An experiment in altruism, 75c.
Macmillan
Hatton (Jos.) The banishment of Jessop Blythe, $1;
pap., 50c.....................................*Lippincott*
Hobbes (J. O.), The gods, some mortals and Lord
Wickenham, $1.50.........................*Appleton*
Holdsworth (A. E.), Joanna Traill, spinster, pap., 50c.
Cassell
Hope (A.) The god in the car, $1; pap., 50c...*Appleton*
Hornung (E. W.), Tiny Luttrell, $1; pap., 50c..*Cassell*
Hosmer (Ja. K.), How Thankful was bewitched, pap.,
50c..*Putnam*
Iota (*pseud.*), Children of circumstances, $1; pap., 50c.
Appleton
Janvier (T. A.), The women's conquest of New York,
pap., 25c....................................*Harper*
Jokai (M.), Eyes like the sea, $1...............*Putnam*
— Timar's two worlds, $1; pap., 50c.........*Appleton*
Kenealy (A.), Dr. Janet of Harley Street, 75c.; pap.,
50c..*Appleton*
Kingsley (H.), Novels, 5 v., ea., '$1..........*Scribner*
Kirk (Mrs. E. O.), The story of Lawrence Garthe, $1.25.
Houghton, M
Lawless (E.), Maelcho, $1.50..................*Appleton*
Lee (M. C.), A soulless singer, $1.25....*Houghton, M*
Linton (Mrs. E. L.), The new woman, $1.50.*Merriam*
— The one too many, $1.25.......................*Neely*
Locke (W. L.), At the gate of Samaria, $1; pap., 50c.
Appleton
Long (J. L.), Miss Cherry-Blossom of Tōkyō, $1.25.
Lippincott
Lowry (H. D.), Women's tragedies (Keynotes ser.), $1.
Roberts
McClelland (M. G.), The old post-road, $1..*Merriam*
Maclaren (Ian), Beside the bonnie brier bush (short
stories), $1.25..............................*Dodd, M*
Macleod (F.), The mountain lovers (short stories), $1.
Roberts
Machen (A.), The great god Pan, $1...........*Roberts*
Makower (S. V.), The mirror of music (Keynotes ser.),
$1..*Roberts*
Manley (R. M.), The Queen of Ecuador, pap., 50c.
Hagemann
Meredith (G.), Lord Ormont and his Aminta, $1.50.
Scribner
Mitchell (S. W.), When all the woods are green, $1.50.
Century
Montgomery (F.), Colonel Norton, $1.50.*Longmans, G*
Montresor (F. F.), Into the highways and hedges, $1;
pap., 50c....................................*Appleton*
Moore (F. F.), They call it love, $1; pap., 50c.*Lippincott*
Moore (G.), Celibates, $1.50................*Macmillan*
— Esther Waters, pap., 50c......................*Sergel*
Morrison (A.), Tales of mean streets, $1....*Roberts*
Noble (A. L.) and Coann (P. C.), Love and shawl-straps,
pap., 50c......................................*Putnam*
Ohnet (G.), A wife's repentance, pap., 25c....*Weeks*
Oliphant (Mrs. M. O. W.), Two strangers, 75c...*Fenno*
Parker (G.), The trail of the sword, $1; pap., 50c.
Appleton
Pemberton (Max), The impregnable city, $1.25.
Dodd, M
Pendleton (L.), Corona of the Nantahalas, 75c.
Merriam
— The sons of Ham, $1.50....................*Roberts*
Philips (F. C.), A question of color, 50c ... ...*Stokes*
Phillpotts (E.), Some every-day folks, pap., 60c.*Harper*
— A deal with the devil, $1..................*Warne*
Praed (Mrs. C.), Outlaw and lawmaker, $1; pap., 50c.
Appleton
Prevost'(M.), Les demi-vierges (*in French*), pap., $1.
Meyer Bros
Pool (M. L.), Out of step, $1.25................*Harper*
— Two salomes, $1.25............................*Harper*
Prince (H. C.), Story of Christine Rochefort, $1.25.
Houghton, M

Raimond (C. E.), George Mandeville's husband, $1;
pap., 50c....................................*Appleton*
— The new moon, $1............................*Appleton*
Raymond (W.), Love and quiet life, $1.25....*Dodd, M*
— Tryphena in love, 75c....................*Macmillan*
Rhosoomyl (O.), The jewel of Ynys Galon, $1.25.
Longmans, G
Robinson (H. P.), Men born equal, $1.25......*Harper*
Robinson (R. E.), Danvis folks (short stories), $1.25.
Houghton, M
Rollins (C. S.), A Burne-Jones head and other sketches,
$1..*Lovell, C*
Schoenaich-Carolath (*Prince*), Melting snows, $1.25.
Dodd, M
Schulze-Smidt (B.), A madonna of the Alps, $1.25.
Little, B
Sergeant (A.), Dr. Endicott's experiment, 50c....*Cassell*
Sharp (E.), At the Relton Arms (Keynotes ser.), $1.
Roberts
Sheldon (C. M.), The crucifixion of Philip Strong, $1.
McClurg
Shiel (M. P.), Prince Zaleski (Keynotes ser.), $1.*Roberts*
Sienkiewics, Children of the soil, $2.........*Little, B*
Smith (C.), A cumberer of the ground, pap., 60c.
Harper
Steel (F. A.), The potter's thumb, $1.50.......*Harper*
Stevenson (R. L.), Amateur emigrant, $1.25.*Stone & K*
— and Osbourne (L.), The ebb tide, $1.25......*Stone & K*
Stockton (F. R.), Adventures of Captain Horn, $1.50.
Scribner
Tinseau (L. de), A forgotten debt, $1.......*Lippincott*
Tolstoi, Master and man, 75c................*Appleton*
Underwood (F. H.), Doctor Gray's quest, $1.75.
Lee & S
Upward (Allen), The Prince of Balkistan, $1; pap.,
50c..*Lippincott*
Valdes (A. P.), The grandee, $1; pap., 50c.......*Peck*
Vashti and Esther, $1; pap., 50c...............*Appleton*
Warner (C. D.), The golden house, $2.........*Harper*
Watson (A. C.), Off Lynnport light, $1; pap., 50c.
Dutton
Wells (H. S.), The time machine, 75c............*Holt*
Weyman (S. J.), My lady Rotha, $1.25...*Longmans, G*
White (E. O.), Winterborough, pap., 50c.*Houghton, M*
Wood (J. E.), The untempered wind, $1; pap., 50c.*Tait*
Wood (M. L.), The vagabonds, $1.50.........*Macmillan*
Yeats (S. L.), The honour of Savelli, $1; pap., 50c.
Appleton
Zangwill (I.), The master, $1.75.............*Harper*
Zola (E.), Lourdes, $1.25....................*Neely*
Z. Z., A drama in Dutch, $1..................*Macmillan*

EXTRA-ILLUSTRATING.

From " Bookish Ballads," by Harry B. Smith.

AMONG the books I have is one
That teases, tantalizes, taunts me ;
Yea, like a demon or a dun,
That solitary volume haunts me.

It glowers upon me from the shelf,
And on my leisure time encroaches ;
Like some malignant little elf,
It fills my mind with its reproaches.

Wherever I may turn my eyes,
Upon that tome they seem to linger ;
I fancy that it moans and sighs,
And points at me a scornful finger.

It seems to say : " I spoke you fair ;
Yet how, oh ! how have you repaid me ?
You once esteemed me passing rare ;
And yet behold what you have made me !

" Despoiled, I cannot hide my shame ;
'Twill be proclaimed to future ages.
When some book-loving squire or dame
Turns angrily my ravaged pages.

" That book of yours has vast increase
Of plates and prints of your collating ;
Yet you must steal my frontispiece
Because you're 'extra-illustrating.' "

It haunts me like relentless fate ;
Its jeers and sneers I cannot smother—
This book from which I tore a plate
To " extra-illustrate " another.

Survey of Current Literature.

☞ *Order through your bookseller.*—"*There is no worthier or surer pledge of the intelligence and the purity of any community than their general purchase of books; nor is there any one who does more to further the attainment and possession of these qualities than a good bookseller.*"—PROF. DUNN.

BIOGRAPHY, CORRESPONDENCE, ETC.

FAWCETT, MILLICENT GARRETT. Life of her majesty, Queen Victoria. Roberts. 12°, $1.25.

ROBERTS, F. SLEIGH (*Lord*). The rise of Wellington. Roberts. 12°, (Pall Mall Gazette Magazine lib.) $1.
General Lord Roberts' valuable and instructive articles on the "Rise of Wellington" have found especial favor with military readers in all branches of the service, and we have reason to think that the collection of these into a single handy volume will meet with the general approval of military men.

SMALLEY, G. W. Studies of men. Harper. 12°, $2.50.
The greater part of these studies appeared originally in the *New York Tribune.* They relate to the following persons: The German Emperor, Gladstone, Carnot, Bismarck, Oliver Wendell Holmes, Tyndall, Dean Stanley, Sir Samuel Baker, Burne-Jones, Lord Rosebery, Harcourt, Balfour, Huxley, Lord Randolph Churchill, Lord Tennyson, Cardinal Newman, Mrs. Humphry Ward, Froude, George William Curtis, Parnell, William Walter Phelps, and Lord Granville.

STEPHENS, W. R. W. Life and letters of Edward A. Freeman. Macmillan. 2 v., 8°, $7.

FICTION.

AFTER to-morrow. [*Al.o*] The new love; by the author of "The green carnation." The Merriam Co. 24°, (Violet ser., no. 5.) 40 c.

BENSON, E. F. The judgment books: a story. Harper. 16°, (Harper's little novels.) $1.
The story is based upon the odd fancy of a portrait painter, that he loses some of his personality when he paints a portrait or imbibes some of the traits of his subject. His devoted wife ingeniously saves him in a moment when his reason seems deserting him. By the author of "Dodo."

BOOTH, *Mrs.* ELIZA M. J. GOLLAN, ["Rita," *pseud.*, now *Mrs.* Desmond Humphreys.] A gender in satin. Putnam. nar. 12°, (Incognito lib., no. 6,) pap., $1.

CASE, W. SCOVILLE. Forward House: a romance. Scribner. 16°, $1.

D'ARCY, ELLA. Monochromes. Roberts. 16°, (Keynotes series, no. 12.) $1.

DEAN, *Mrs.* ANDREW, [*pseud.* for *Mrs.* Alfred Sidgwick.] The grasshoppers; il. by Walter B. Russell. Stokes. 12°, $1.

DOUGALL, L. The zeit-geist. Appleton. 12°, buckram, 75 c.

EBERS, G. In the fire of the forge: a romance of old Nuremberg; from the German, by Mary J. Safford. Appleton. 2 v., 16°, $1.50; pap., 80 c.

FOTHERGILL, JESSIE. Orioles' daughter. Lovell, Coryell & Co. 12°, $1; pap., 50 c.

FRANCIS, C. E. Every day's news. Putnam. 12°, (Incognito lib., no. 7.) 50 c.

GOODWIN, MAUDE WILDER. The head of a hundred : being the account of certain passages in the life of Humphrey Huntoon, sometyme an officer in the colony of Virginia ; ed. by Maude Wilder Goodwin. Little, Brown & Co. 12°, $1.25

HALL, GERTRUDE. Foam of the sea, and other tales. Roberts. 12°, $1.

HARLAND, HENRY, ["Sidney Luska," *pseud.*] Gray roses. Roberts. 16°, $1. (Keynotes ser., no. 10.)

HOPE, ASCOTT ROB., [*pseud. for* Ascott Robert Hope Moncreiff.] Young traveller's tales. Scribner. 12°, $1.25.

IN tent and bungalow, by An idle exile. Cassell Pub. Co. nar. 12°, (The unknown lib., no. 13.) 25 c.

KINGSLEY, H. Austin Elliot and the Harveys. *New ed.*, with frontispiece by Walter Paget. Ward, Lock & Bowden, Ltd. 8°, $1.25.

MALCOLM, D. A fiend incarnate. Tait. nar. 16°, (The Zenda ser.) 75 c.

MARCHMONT, A. W. Parson Thring's secret. Cassell Pub. Co., 12°, $1.

MASON, CAROLINE ATWATER. A minister of the world. Randolph. 12°, 75 c.

MITCHELL, S. WEIR, *M.D.* Philip Vernon : a tale in prose and verse. The Century Co. 12°, $1.
A dramatic story of the days of Good Queen Bess. It is told mainly in rhyming verse in the form of dialogue, with introductions and brief connecting lines in prose. The time is laid in July, 1588, when the Spanish Armada is hovering off the coast of England. Hugh Langmayde, an English priest, was compelled to flee from his native land during the days of King Henry VIII. On his departure he rescued a young boy, Philip Vernon, from the sea, and carried him with him to Spain. At the opening of the story he has brought Philip back to England. How Philip wins his bride and his estate is the story.

MONTGOMERY, FLORENCE. Colonel Norton : a novel. Longmans, G. 12°, $1.50.

MONTRÉSOR, FRANCES FREDERICA. Into the highways and hedges. Appleton. 12°, (Appleton's town and country lib., no. 168.) $1 ; pap., 50 c.

MOORE, G. Celibates : a novel. Macmillan. 12°, $1.50.
Three stories entitled Mildred Lawson ; John Norton ; and Agnes Lahens.

NEEDELL, *Mrs.* J. Hodder. The vengeance of James Vansittart. Appleton. 12°, (Appleton's town and country lib., no. 169.) $1 ; pap., 50 c.

OLIPHANT, *Mrs.* MARG. O. W. Two strangers. Fenno. 12°, (Autonym lib.) 75 c.

PHILIPS, F. C. A question of color. Stokes. nar. 16°. (Bijou ser.) Buckram, 50 c.
" It is with difficulty that one accepts the principal situation in 'A question of color.' A beautiful young girl who has the world before her, and is engaged to a fine fellow who adores her, is represented as listening to the addresses of a negro. It is true that she did once tell her lover that she was not at all a nice girl, and that he would some day be surprised to find how different she was from what he thought her to be ; but this avowal makes as little impression on the reader as it did on him. The situation once accepted, Mr. Philips has produced a very telling picture. Jan Umgazi, though he ' could still recall dimly the naked savages and mud " kraals " of his youth,' is thoroughly European in every feeling, and his anguish of mind, marvellous resignation, and self-control touch the reader very closely."—*The Academy.*

PHILLPOTTS, EDEN. A deal with the devil. Warne. 12°, $1.

R., (*pseud.*) *ed.* The Countess Bettina : the history of an innocent scandal. Putnam. 12°, 50 c.

SALTUS, EDGAR. When dreams come true : a story of emotional life. The Transatlantic Pub. Co. 12°, pap., 50 c.
" The romance is a delightful one, told by an artist in his best style ; and it is a thing that one may place not only with impunity but with pleasure among the best books on one's library table."—*Phila. Press.*

SCHULZE-SMIDT, B. A madonna of the Alps ; from the German, by Nathan Haskell Dole. Little, Brown & Co. 16°, $1.25.
A young German student earned a scholarship entitling him to three years of art study in Italy, proceeds there by way of the Alps. He makes a companion of his guide who finally invites him to rest a few days in his mountain châlet. The madonna of the Alps is the wife of this guide about whom there hangs a mystery, finally solved by an old priest who is a very original character.

SERGEANT, ADELINE. Dr. Endicott's experiment. Cassell Pub. Co. nar. 12°, (The unknown lib., no. 38.) 50 c.

SIENKIEWICZ, H. Children of the soil ; from the Polish, by Jeremiah Curtin. Little, Brown & Co. 12°, $2.

STOCKTON, FRANK R. The adventures of Captain Horn. Scribner. 12°, $1.50.
" Those readers must be jaded indeed whose nerves do not jump under the excitement of Mr. Stockton's new story. ' The Adventures of Captain Horn' is imaginative in a double sense ; it shows enormous invention, and it quivers with emotional fancy playing about a subject of never-ending interest. That subject is treasure-trove, and many as are the romances of varying kind that have been founded on it, Mr. Stockton has invented a new approach."—*Philadelphia Telegraph.*

SUDERMANN, HERMANN. The wish : a novel ; tr. by Lily Henkel ; with a biographical introd. by Eliz. Lee. Appleton. 12°, $1.
" A study of Sudermann's 'Wish' will be essential for those who are following the tendencies and manifestations of the literature of the day. Simply as a figure in the contemporary literary life of Germany, Sudermann's importance is ranked with that of Kipling or Barrie in England, or Ibsen in the north. All his work may not be relished, but the author is a fact to be reckoned with, and the undeniable power of " The wish " is certain to compel attention."

SULLIVAN, J. W. Tenement tales of New York. Holt. 16°, (Buckram ser.) 75 c.

TOLSTOY, *Count* LYOF N. Master and man ; tr. by A. Hulme Beaman ; with an introd. by W. D. Howells. Appleton. 16°, 75 c.
Another of Tolstoy's elaborations of " Thou shalt love thy neighbor as thyself."

UNDERWOOD, FRANCIS H. Doctor Gray's quest. Lee & Shepard. 12°, $1.75.
" The present novel is one of his best in its reproduction of New England customs and manners more than a generation ago. Some of the old places of resort in Boston are recalled in its pages, and village existence is also truthfully painted. The plot concerns principally the hero's efforts to establish the innocence of a man who has been wrongfully imprisoned in Sing Sing ; but it is never sensational or unnatural. The book is good literature, and deserves to have a permanent place in the library."
—*Boston Gazette.*

UPWARD, ALLEN. The Prince of Balkistan. Lippincott. 12°, (Lippincott's select novels, no. 170.) $1; pap., 50 c.
The terrible rather than the touching is the author's *forte.* Russians, Nihilists, massacres, etc. Prince Bismarck, Gladstone, the Princess of Wales, etc., appear under fictitious names.

WHITE, PERCY, (*pseud.*) A king's diary. Cassell Pub. Co. nar. 12°, (Cassell's unknown lib.) 50 c.

WILLIAMS, JESSE LYNCH. Pinceton stories. Scribner. 16°, $1.
Contents : The winning of the cane; The madness of Poler Stacy ; The hazing of Valliant ; Hero worship; The responsibility of Lawrence; Fixing that freshman ; The scrub quarter-back; When girls come to Princeton; The little tutor; College men ; The man that led the class.

WOOD, J. SEYMOUR. Yale yarns : sketches of life at Yale University. Putnam. 12°, $1.
Contents : One on the governor ; The old fence ; In the political cauldron; " Little Jack " Horner's pie ; With the Dwight Hall heelers ; The " dwarfs " from the last cruise of the " Nancy Brig " ; Old Sleuth's level head ; Nat Hale of '73 ; The dawn tea ; The great Springfield game ; In the toils of the enemy; An hypnotic séance ; A violent enemy ; " Chums over in Old South " ; Commencement, by the author of " Gramercy Park " ; An old beau, etc.

HISTORY.

BARRAS, PAUL FRANÇOIS J. N. (*Comte*) DE. Memoirs of Barras, member of the Directorate ; ed. with a general introd., prefaces and appendices, by G. Duroy. In 4 v. V. 1 and 2 ; tr. by C. E. Roche. Harper. pors., fac-similes, plans, 8°, *ea.*, $3.75.

CLARK, G. H., *D.D.* Oliver Cromwell ; with an introd. by C. Dudley Warner, and il. from old paintings and prints. [*New issue.*] Harper. 12°, $1.25.

CLODD, E. The story of primitive man. Appleton. 16°, (Library of useful stories.) 40 c.

The President of the Folk-Lore Society, a recognized authority, here states in language as free as possible from technical terms the results of the latest investigations into the early history of the human race. A large number of illustrations bring out the distinguishing characteristics of the ancient stone age, the newer stone age and the age of metals. A selected book-list of two pages gives authorities and suggests supplementary reading. Full index.

COIGNET, JEAN-ROCH. The narrative of Captain Coignet (soldier of the empire), 1776–1850; ed., from the original ms., by Loredan Larchey: from the French, by Mrs. M. Carey. [*New popular ed.*] Crowell. 12°, fac-simile, $1.50.

GREGOR, FRANCES. The story of Bohemia. Cranston & Curts. 12°, $1.50.

The historical account of the land of Bohemia reaches back to B.C. 400. From earliest times its people have had a love of freedom that has made them suffer all things in their steady opposition to civil and ecclesiastical oppression. The writer tells in popular style of the battles fought against popes, kings and emperors to the present day. John Huss, one of the great leaders of Reformation, came from Bohemia, and his history occupies many pages.

HASSALL, ARTHUR. Louis XIV. and the zenith of the French monarchy. Putnam. 12°, (Heroes of the nations ser., no. 14.) $1.50; hf. mor., $1.75.

The author's reasons for including Louis XIV. in this series are given in the following paragraph : "As a man he may not have been great, but a great king he certainly was, and the age in which he lived and which bears his name was a great age. Whatever claim he may bear to the title of hero must be based upon the determination and courage shown during the last fourteen years of his reign. . . . Few periods in the reign of any European monarch present more striking examples of real patriotism and heroism than will be found in the history of the great king of France during the years from 1707 to 1713. A list of authorities is given of about a page.

PUTNAM, RUTH. William the Silent, Prince of Orange ; the moderate man of the sixteenth century ; the story of his life as told by his own letters from those of his friends and enemies and from official documents. Putnam. 12°, $3.75.

RIDDLE, ALBERT GALLATIN. Recollections of war times : reminiscences of men and events in Washington, 1860–65. Putnam. 8°, $2.50.

Mr. Riddle was a member of the House of Representatives from the 19th District, Ohio, during the historical 37th Congress, which convened with Lincoln's first administration. He adds from personal observation many new details relative to the men and events of the period. Some of the subjects of his forty-seven chapters are : Washington in 1861 ; Lincoln's inauguration ; The fall of Sumter ; The historical congresses ; Bull Run ; After the battle ; Maryland's efforts to secede ; The war financial measures ; Emancipation ; Democracy in the House, etc., etc.

WOLSELEY, JOS. GARNET (*Viscount.*) The decline and fall of. Napoleon. Roberts. 12°, (Pall Mall Magazine lib.) $1.25.

HUMOR AND SATIRE.

FARMER, LYDIA HOYT. Aunt Belindy's points of view and a modern Mrs. Malaprop : character sketches. Merriam Co. 16°, 75 c.

Aunt Belinda and Mrs. Malaprop discuss women's clubs, summer boarders, dinner parties, balls, receptions, woman's suffrage, the opera, the World's Fair, servants, and many other things. Aunt Belinda and her husband Ebenezer argue the woman question from all sides. Written in Yankee dialect and full of suggestions on the questions of the day, worded with wit and good-natured humor.

TOWNSEND, E. Chimmie Fadden explains, Major Max expounds. Lovell, Coryell. 12°, $1 ; pap., 50 c.

More sketches in the vein of " Chimmie Fadden, Major Max and other stories," which has met with large sale. The present stories have appeared either in the N. Y. *Sun* or the San Francisco *Argonaut*, with the exception of Mr. Fannie Hallowell, a story of 27 pages, which appears in this volume for the first time.

HYGIENIC AND SANITARY.

GALBRAITH, ANNA M., *M.D.* Hygiene and physical culture for women. Dodd, Mead. 12°, $1.

LITERARY MISCELLANY, COLLECTED WORKS, ETC.

BIERSTADT, O. A. The library of Robert Hoe: a contribution to the history of bibliophilism in America; with 110 il. taken from ms. and books in the collection. Duprat. 8°, *net*, $15.

BRIDGES, ROB., [" Droch," *pseud.*] Suppressed chapters and other bookishness. Scribner, 12°, $1.25,

In a perfectly good-natured and irresistibly humorous manner the writer of " Overheard in Arcady " reviews another year of epoch-making writers. The successful books of 1894 are either parodied or criticised with suggestive sarcasm. Du Maurier, Le Gallienne, George Egerton, John Kendrick Bangs, Barrie, Anthony Hope, Meredith, Kipling, Crockett, Crawford, Charles Dana Gibson, and A. B. Frost are among the favorites selected for the witty remarks of " Droch."

DANA, C. A. The art of newspaper making: three lectures. Appleton. 16°, $1.

The separate titles of the lectures are " The modern American newspaper," " The profession of journalism," and " The making of a newspaper man."

"The veteran editor of the *Sun* does more than state the principles on which he has worked out an illustrious career in journalism; he discourses entertainingly on many of the things about which the public knows little and imagines much. He tells how well reporters are paid, and what makes a good managing editor, and how the news is gathered and set up, and what it costs to establish and maintain a daily paper in a city like New York. A survey of the different departments of journalism, in which Mr. Dana drops some judicious observations, is one feature of a book of unusual value."—*N. Y. Mail and Express.*

DITCHFIELD, P. H.   Books fatal to their authors. Armstrong. 16°, (Book lover's lib.), $1.25.

Describes nearly two hundred works which caused their authors to be persecuted for heresy, laxity of morals, rebellion against authority, etc., or caused them so much hard work and so much censure that their health was undermined and their career ruined. The greater number of these books deal with theology and religion, and many of them belong to the stormy period of the Reformation. The author has classified the books by subjects instead of following a chronological plan. An index under names of authors is supplied. A scheme for a building under the auspices of the Royal Literary Fund to be a home for aged authors is sketched with enthusiasm.

ERICHSEN, HUGO, *M.D.*   Methods of authors. The Writer Pub. Co.   12°, $1.

Much of the material for this book was gathered directly from the authors themselves or taken from authentic sources. It is divided into chapters, entitled : Eccentricities in composition ; Care in literary production ; Speed in writing ; Influence upon writers of time and place : Writing under difficulties ; Aids to inspiration ; Favorite habits of work ; Goethe, Dickens, Schiller, and Scott ; Burning midnight oil ; Literary partnership ; Anonymity in authorship ; System in novel-writing ; Traits of musical composers ; The hygiene of writing ; and A humorist's regimen.

GRISWOLD, W. M., *comp.*   A descriptive list of novels and tales dealing with the history of North America. Griswold. 8°, $1.

The second part of " Historical novels," the first being devoted to novels of ancient life. A list, the titles being followed by descriptive extracts taken from the literary columns of leading papers.

GRISWOLD, W. M., *comp.*   A descriptive list of novels and tales dealing with ancient history. Pt. 1, Ancient life. Griswold. pap., 8°, 50 c.

A list of about 125 novels and tales relating to ancient life, followed by full descriptive notices taken from leading literary papers. A useful reference work on the same lines as Mr. Griswold's " Novels of American country life," " American city life," " Romantic novels," " International novels," etc.

MORLEY, H., *and* GRIFFITH, W. HALL.   An attempt towards a history of English literature. Vols. 10, 11, Shakespeare and His Time: under Elizabeth ; under James I. Cassell. 12°, *ea.*, $1.50.

MOULTON, R. G., *ed.*   Four years of novel-reading: an account of an experiment in popularizing the study of fiction ; ed., with an introd., by R. G. Moulton. Heath.   12°, 50 c.

In the introduction the Professor of Literature in English in the Chicago University regards fiction as an art, and claims that taste in fiction needs training. This training has been tried in Backworth, a little mining village of Northumberland (England), for four years. The secretary for the " Classical Novel-Reading Union" there formed gives his report of four years of novel-reading. Then follow articles on " Why is Charles Dickens a more famous novelist than Charles Reade ?" by Miss Ellen Cumpston ; " The character of Clara Middleton ' (Meredith's " The egoist "), by Joseph Fairney ;

" The ideal of asceticism" (Gerard in " The cloister and the hearth "), by Rev. C. G. Hall ; and " Character development in ' Romola,' " by Thomas Dawson.

RIDEING, W. H.   In the land of Lorna Doone and other pleasurable excursions in England. Crowell.   16°, $1.

The author of " Thackeray's London " groups his descriptions of English scenery and English characteristics under the titles " In the land of Lorna Doone" (Exmoor); " In Cornwall with an umbrella"; " Coaching out of London "; " A bit of the Yorkshire coast"; " Amy Robsart, Kenilworth, and Warwick" (Warwick). Mr. Rideing shows judgment in his selection of scenes famous in history and romance.

SMOLLETT, TOBIAS.   Works; ed. by G. Saintsbury.   In 12 v.   V. 1–3, The adventures of Roderick Random. Lippincott.   il. by Frank Richards.   16°, *ea.*, $1.

The principles of editing adopted in this issue of Smollett are the same as those which the editor applied in his presentations of Fielding and Sterne. No annotation is attempted, and the text is reprinted from the standard version. The text has, however, been carefully read throughout to guard against those slips which sometimes hold their ground in frequently reprinted matter. These three volumes are the first of a twelve-volume edition to be completed in six months. Subscriptions received for complete sets only.

SONNENSCHEIN, W. SWAN.   A reader's guide to contemporary literature: being the first supplement to '' The best books"; a reader's guide to the choice of the best available books (about 50,000) in every department of science, art and literature, with the dates of the first and last editions and the price, size, and publisher's name of each book.   Putnam.   4°, $7.50.

Originally designed to form a first supplement to the second edition of '' The best books." The compiler's intention was to furnish five yearly supplements on the original plan of inclusiveness and exclusiveness. He has found it impossible to form a " personal acquaintance " with the more important new books, and has been forced to make " a mere record of practically all new publications in book form which seemed to have lasting value and to present the general consensus of opinion of the most trustworthy scientific reviews." Among these best books are found some " bad " books by well-known authors, but their quality is indicated and warning given. The work supplies the American and English publishers' names and gives the American and English prices; where a series of books deals with the same or kindred subjects, it is inserted collectively as well as separately under author and title; a complete index under authors and subjects guides to entries under classes; and a list of British publishers and learned societies with full addresses makes the work valuable for all booksellers. The first edition appeared in England in 1887.

STARKEY, CYRIL E. F.   Verse translations from classic authors. Longmans, G.   12°, $1.75.

NATURE AND SCIENCE.

FOWLER, W. WARDE.   Summer studies of birds and books. Macmillan.   12°, $1.75.

Contents : Getting ready; To the Engstlen Alp

once more; Among the birds in Wales; The marsh warbler in Oxfordshire and Switzerland; A chapter on wagtails; On the songs of birds; Aristotle on birds; Gilbert White of Selborne; Bindon Hill; Billy, a memoir of an old friend; Departing birds, an epilogue.

HUIDEKOPER, RUSH SHIPPEN, *M.D.* The cat: a guide to the classification and varieties of cats, and a short treatise upon their care, disease, and treatment. Appleton. 16°, $1.
Contains a bibliography (1 p.).
This is a practical book, embodying the results of observation, experience, and intimate knowledge as a veterinary surgeon, and it will be of immediate value to all who are interested in the subject.

LYDEKKER, R., *ed.* The royal natural history. Warne. 8°, (Warne's lib. of natural history, in 36 nos., v. 1, no. 1.) *subs.*, pap., 50 c.
The first number of a new natural history, with two richly colored plates, and a number of text and page illustrations in black and white drawn from life; to be published fortnightly. No.1 contains chapters on the general characteristics of mammals; the man-like apes; Chimpanzees; Gorillas; Orang-Utan; Old-world monkeys, and baboons, their structure and distribution, habits, haunts, etc. Mr. Lydekker has been for some years in the front rank of English naturalists. He is the responsible editor and chief contributor.

MILLER, ELLEN, *and* WHITING, MARGARET CHRISTINE. Wild flowers of the northeastern states; being three hundred and eight individuals common to the northeastern United States, drawn and described from life. Putnam. 4°, $4.50.
Specially designed to make the acquaintance of flowers more easy to non-scientific folk. Numberless traits of race habit and personal traits of growth to which unlearned observers attach significance are given, and life-size pictures of the flowers have been made by the compilers to simplify their recognition. The floral families have been arranged in the order employed in "Gray's manual." There are separate indexes of the scientific and the common names. In every instance the description of the flower faces its pen and ink representation.

POETRY AND DRAMA.

CAWEIN, MADISON. Intimations of the beautiful, and poems. Putnam. 12°, $1.50.

POOLE, FANNY RUNNELLS. A bank of violets: verses. Putnam. 12°, $1.25.
About forty short poems, classified under the headings "Partly fancy," "Among friends," and "Faith." Neatly bound in green with violet border line and bunch of violets on front cover.

TOWNSEND, MARY ASHLEY. Distaff and spindle: sonnets. Lippincott. 12°, $1.50.
Sixty-nine sonnets full of noble, helpful thoughts on inspiring ideals and daily duties, most musically worded. The sonnets are printed on rough paper with uncut edges and the book is bound in smooth cloth with cover design of distaff and spindle.

WINSLOW, *Mrs.* CATHERINE MARY REIGNOLDS, [*Mrs.* Erving Winslow.] Readings from the old English dramatists; with notes. Lee & Shepard. 2 v., 12°, $1.75.
Designed to illustrate the stages in the prog-

ress of English dramatic literature. The first period includes the masques and miracles of the fifteenth and sixteenth centuries. The second period dwells chiefly on Marlowe, with specimens from Lyly, Ben Jonson, Beaumont and Fletcher. The author then passes to the early Stuart drama, including Webster, Massinger, and Ford; and for the Restoration period Farquhar's Inconstant is given. The eighteenth century includes Oliver Goldsmith and Richard Brinsley Sheridan. A large number of carefully selected scenes from the above typical authors are presented, with Mrs. Winslow's comments on the authors, scenes, and characters.

POLITICAL AND SOCIAL.

AMERICAN ECONOMIC ASSOCIATION. Five papers read at the seventh annual meeting, Columbia College, December 27-29, 1894. Macmillan. 8°, (Publications of the society, v. 9, nos. 5-6.) 75 c.
Contents: The modern appeal to legal forces in economic life, by J. B. Clark; The Chicago strike, by Carroll D. Wright; The irregularity of employment, by Davis R. Dewey; The papal encyclical on labor, by J. Graham Brooks; Population and capital, by Arthur T. Hadley.

ASHLEY, W. J. The railroad strike of 1894: the statements of the Pullman Company and the Report of the Commission; with an analysis of the issues, and a brief bibliography. The Church Social Union. 8°, (Publications of the society, ser. B, no. 1.) pap., 10 c.
The main purpose of the Church Social Union is to stimulate and assist careful study of the present industrial situation. This is the first issue of series B. The bibliography of the railroad strike of 1894 (3 p.) is the compilation of Francis Watts Lee, of the Boston Public Library. Mr. Ashley is professor of economic history in Harvard University.

BLANC, *Mme.* THÉRÈSE, ["Theodore Bentzon," *pseud.*] The condition of woman in the United States: a traveller's notes; tr. by Abbey Langdon Alger. Roberts. 12°, $1.25.
"The author sees both the successes and failures of women in their work. The women's clubs and colleges, the value and the dangers of co-education, women's labors among the poor, for the negroes, in industrial schools and in the home all receive her attention. She made her study of the average woman as she is found in the home of modest means, in the workshop, managing charities and teaching school. With a feminine insight superior to race barriers she judges the character of women and the nature of their work in this country. Passing over externals, she analyzes, and she exhibits all that remarkable work of women for the development of one another, and for bettering the moral and physical condition of the race, which is done quietly, which is so much with us a matter of course that we do not often stop to think how remarkable it is or how much good it has done. But for the visitor from abroad it possesses extreme significance."—*N. Y. Tribune.*

BLATCHFORD, ROB., ["Nunquam," *pseud.*] Merrie England: a plain exposition of socialism, what it is and what it is not. Commonwealth Co. 12°, (Commonwealth lib., no. 1.) pap., 10 c.
The author's remedy for the various evils the

working-classes are enduring is socialism—not anarchy—but socialism as now understood and expounded by the best writers. He devotes a series of chapters to commending it and answering the arguments of anti-socialists such as Herbert Spencer, Charles Bradlaugh, and John Morley. He also has much to say on the narrow and unbeautiful and joyless lives of the poor, of the greed of trusts and monopolies, of the growing concentration of wealth in the hands of the few, the rights of the individual, etc., etc. Popularly written.

CORNELISON, I. A. The relation of religion to civil government in the United States of America : a state without a church, but not without a religion. Putnam. 8°, $2.
"Even those who cannot agree with Mr, Cornelison in the views he enunciates will find his book a valuable one, owing to the mass of useful and undoubtedly accurate information which he has taken so much pains to arrange in convenient shape for ready reference. It is certainly a valuable addition to the literature of Church and State."—*N. Y. Commercial Advertiser.*

CROCKER, URIEL H. The cause of hard times. Little, Brown. 16°, 50 c.

KELLEY, JA. P. The law of service : a study in Christian altruism. Putnam. 12°, 75 c.

LOMBROSO, CÆSAR, *and* FERRERO, W. The female offender, with an introduction by W. Douglas Morrison. Appleton. 12°, (Criminology ser.) $1.50.
In "The female offender" we see the manner in which Lombroso applies the anthropological method. He examines whether, and to what extent, the female criminal differs from the average woman in bodily and mental characteristics. As a result of this examination he arrives at many interesting conclusions as to the personal or individual conditions which are calculated to turn women into offenders against criminal law.
"Intended for the scholar and scientist whose interest will vitalize the formidable array of statistics."—*The Examiner.*

MACCOLL, *Rev.* MALCOLM (*Canon.*) England's responsibility towards Armenia. Longmans, G. 8°, pap., 75 c.

MERRILL, J. ERNEST. Ideals and institutions: their parallel development ; a thesis presented at the University of Minnesota for the degree of doctor of philosophy. Hartford, Hartford Seminary Press. 8°, pap., $1.
Contains a list of authorities (2 p.).

NOAILLES, *Duc de.* How to save bimetallism. Amer. Acad. of Pol. and Soc. Sci. 8°, (Publications of the society, no. 140.) pap., 15 c.
A contribution to the silver question. The remedy suggested by the author is to adopt a parallel and independent bimetallism. Let each metal have its own value based on the weight of the coins either in gold or in silver without any proportion or ratio.

POLAND, LAWRENCE. Money : an essay read before the Xavier Lyceum, April 4, 1895. Clarke. 12°, pap., 25 c.
Defines money, and shows what its functions are, etc, ; the larger part of the essay is devoted to bimetallism, and how it may be successfully

established. Points out the evils of free coinage of silver.

SEYMOUR, HORATIO W. Government & Co., Limited : an examination of the tendencies of privilege in the United States. McClurg, 16°, 75 c.

WINES, F. HOWARD. Punishment and reformation : an historical sketch of the rise of the penitentiary system. Crowell. 12°, (Crowell's lib. of economics and politics, no. 6.) $1.75.

SPORTS AND AMUSEMENTS.

STEWART, W. C. Practical angler ; or, the art of trout-fishing, more particularly applied to clear water. Macmillan. 12°, $1.25.

THEOLOGY, RELIGION AND SPECULATION.

TEXT-BOOKS OF RELIGIOUS INSTRUCTION. Cutts, E. L., Hist. of the Church of England, $1; Hervey, A. C., and Hole, C., The Pentateuch, $1; Lyttelton, E, The Gospel of St. Mark, with notes. 75 c. Longmans, Green & Co.

WEIDEMANN, ALFRED. The ancient Egyptian doctrine of the immortality of the soul. Putnam. 12°, $1.
The most important shape which the doctrine of immortality assumed in Egypt centred in the person of Osiris, the most popular of all the gods of Egypt. Wherever his worship spread it carried with it the doctrine of immortality associated with his name. It influenced the systems of Greek philosophy and made itself felt in the teachings of the gnostics. To no close student of the doctrine can it seem strange that Egypt was the first country in which Christianity permeated the whole body of the people. The figures of Christ and of Osiris have much in common. The significance of these facts in the history of the world are set forth by the Professor of Oriental Languages in the University of Bonn.

Books for the Young.

CLARKE, REBECCA SOPHIA, [" Sophia May," *pseud.*] Jimmy Boy. Lee & Shepard. 16° (Little Prudy's children ser.) 75 c.
"Certainly equal in all respects to its predecessors. He is a manly little chap, is Jimmy Boy. He lapses now and then into the naïvete of childishness, which makes him all the more interesting. Children will delight in following him and his fortunes throughout the book, and, as is usual with Miss May, there is a good moral to the book and a healthful atmosphere.—*N. Y. Commercial Advertiser.*

DRAKE, S. ADAMS. The watch-fires of '76. Lee & Shepard. 12°, $1.25.

HENDERSON, W. J. Afloat with the flag. Harper. 12°, $1.25.
The story of four American boys during the Brazilian revolution, two of them attached to the American cruiser *Detriot*, a third in the Brazilian navy, and the fourth in the Brazilian army. The author of "Sea yarns for boys" in this story combines his knowledge of nautical details with his experiences as an officer in the Naval Reserve and gives an inspiring account of the new American navy.

MARSHALL, LUTHER. Thomas Boobig : a complete account of his life and singular disappearance. Lee & Shepard. 12°, $1.50.

MOLESWORTH, *Mrs.* MARY LOUISA, [" Ennis Graham," *pseud.* Sheila's mystery : il. by L. Leslie Brooke. Macmillan. 12°, $1.

Sheila Josselin, a morbid child of ten, prone to misconstrue every act of her parents and little sister, one day overhears a conversation not intended for her ears, and believing herself the heroine of a mystery, and at the same time an ill-used child, runs away from home. Her adventures after this incident are very interesting, and they are followed by an unexpected revelation. The story has an evident moral.

ROUSE, ADELAIDE L. The Deane girls : a home story. A. I. Bradley & Co. 12°, $1 25.

SANGSTER, *Mrs.* MARGARET E. Little knights and ladies : verses for young people. 16°, $1.25.

The charming verses in this collection were nearly all originally written for the various Harper periodicals. A few were first published in the *Congregationalist, Youth's Companion,* and *Christian Intelligencer.* They touch on every subject likely to please young people, and are admirably suited, through their musical rhyme, for committing to memory.

TOMLINSON, EVERETT T. The boy soldiers of 1812. Lee & Shepard. 12°, (War of 1812 ser., no. 2.) $1.50.

VARNEY, G. J. The story of patriots' day, Lexington and Concord, April 19, 1775 ; with poems brought out on the first observation of the anniversary holiday, and the forms in which it was celebrated. Lee & Shepard. 16°, 60 c.

" Every boy and girl will be interested in ' Patriots' day, Concord and Lexington,' by George J. Varney. The author has succeeded admirably in interpolating in his story valuable historical information concerning the early days of the struggle for American independence. The history is at first hand, from documents in possession of the Historical Society of Massachusetts, and is so deftly woven in with the main theme of the story that it becomes not only interesting and of value, but fascinating to the young reader. The account of Paul Revere's famous ride in the hero's own words is perhaps superior to any other part of the book."—*N. Y. Commercial Advertiser.*

RECENT FRENCH AND GERMAN BOOKS.

FRENCH.

Aioard, I. Diamant Noir. 12°. Flammarion.. $1 00
Barras. Mémoires. Vols. I., II. 8°. Hachette. 4 50
Bauer, H. Mémoires d'un jeune homme. 12°. Charpentier.. 1 00
Berkeley, C. de. Instinct du cœur. 12°. Colin. 1 00
Boutry. Choiseul à Rome, 1754-1757. 8°. Lévy. 2 25
Brisson, A. La comédie littéraire. 12°. Colin. 1 00
Broglie, Duc de. L'Alliance Autrichienne. 8°. Lévy.. 2 25
Brunetiere, F. Nouveau Essais de Littérature contemporaine. 12°. Lévy..................... 1 00
Busnach, Wm. Cyprienne Guerard. 12°. Lévy. 1 00
Carette, Mme. Mme. de Motteville. 12°. Ollendorff.. 1 00
Daudet. Mme. Alphonse. 12°. Lemerre....... 90
D'Eiohthal, Eug. Souveraineté du Peuple et du Gouvernement. 12°. Alcan.................... 1 00
De La Sizeranne. "La peinture, anglaise contemporaine." 12°. Hachette.................... 1 00
Des Reaulx. Le roi Stanislaus et Marie Leczinska. 8°. Plon.................................... 2 25
Drux-Brese, Marq. de. Notes et Souvenirs, 1877-1883. 8°. Perrin.............................. 1 00
Duplan, P. Le Capt. Jean Solange. 12°. Lévy. 1 00
Expansion de la France et la diplomatie. 12°. Hachette.. 1 00
Fabregue, A. Crucifix. 12°. Dentu.............. 1 00
Ferry, Jules. Discours. Vol. III. 8°. Colin.. 3 00
Glouvet, Jules de. France, 1418-1499. Roman Hist. 12°. Colin.................................... 1 00
Goncourt. Journal des. Vol. VIII., 1889-1891. 12°. Charpentier................................. 1 00
Grandmaison, G. de. Napoléon et les Cardinaux noirs. 12°. Perrin.............................. 1 00
Ibsen, H. Le petit Eyolf, trad. par Prozor. 12°. Perrin... 1 00
Larroumet, G. Etudes de Littérature et d'art. 12°. Hachette.. 1 00
Lavedan, H. Le Vieux Marcheur. 12°. Lévy. 1 00
Lengle, P. Thérèse, Hist. d'une Alsacienne. 12°. Dentu.. 1 00
Lesueur, D. A force d'aimer. 12°. Lemerre.. 1 00
Longus. Daphnis et Chloë. Ill. de Leroy. 32°. Lemerre... 60
Mael. Amour d'Orient. 12°. Flammarion..... 1 00

Maiseroy, R. Journal d'une rupture. 12°. Ollendorff... $1 00
Maugras, G. Le duc de Lauzun et la cour de Marie Antoinette. 8°. Plon.................... 2 25
Mendes, Catulle. Rue des Filles-Dieu, 56. 12°. Charpentier.. 1 00
Miral, Léon. Les trahisons d'un Amant. 12°. Lévy.. 1 00
Monteil, Col. P. L. De St. Louis à Tripolipar le Lac Tchad. Illustrations de Riou. f°. Alcan. 6 00
Pas, M. Un Amour d'aujourd'hui. 12°. Charpentier... 1 00
Paroy, Comte de. Mémoires, 1789-1797. 8°. Plon.. 2 25
Pillon, L. Année. Philosophique. 8°. Alcan... 1 50
Pouget, Gen. Souvenirs de Guerre. 12°. Plon. 1 00
Pouvillon, E. Pays et Paysages. 12°. Plon.. 1 00
Prevost, Marcel. Notre Compagne. 12°. Lemerre.. 1 00
Saroey, F. Annales du Théâtre, 1894. 12°. Charpentier... 1 00
Verne, Jules. "L'Ile a Hélice," 1re Partie. 12°. Hetzel.. 90
Vigne d'Octon. Petite Amie. 12°. Lemerre... 1 00
Wysewa, T. de. Nos Maitres, Portraits Littéraires. 12°. Perrin................................. 1 00

GERMAN.

Dincklage, F. von. Besiegte Sieger. 12°. Reissner... 35
— In Schwerer Bö. 12°. Reissner................ 70
Golm, R. Der alte Adam und die neue Eva. 12°. Pierson... 1 20
Heiberg, H. Zwischen drei Feuern. 12°. Janke. 2 00
Im Horste des Rothen Adlers. 8°. Kutschbach. 1 00
Jahrbuch der Deutschen. Shakspeare Gesellschaft. 31ster Jahrgang. Cloth, 8°. Weimar... 4 00
Kretzer, M. Im Riesennest. 12°. Pierson...... 50
Loewe, F. Amatus. 12°. Fischer................ 1 00
Meyer, L. "Lehrbuch der Graphologie." 4°. Deutsche Verlags Gesellschaft.................. 1 70
Ortmann, R. Casamicciola. 2 vols. 12°. Reissner... 2 00
Suttner, Bertha V. Eva Siebeck. 12°. Pierson. 1 00
Telmann, K. Ninfa. 12°. Reissner............. 1 00
— Unter den Dolomiten. 12°. Reissner.......... 2 35
Wichert, E. Blinde Liebe. 12°. Reissner..... 1 00

MAGAZINE ARTICLES.

Articles marked with an asterisk are illustrated.

ARTISTIC, MUSICAL AND DRAMATIC.—*Century,* Old Dutch Masters: Gerard Tarburg,* Cole.—*Fort. Review* (Je.), Pictures of the Year, Phillips.—*Forum,* Successful Efforts to Teach Art to the Masses,* Hamlin Garland, A. C. Bernheim, Jane Addams.—*Harper's,* Some Imaginative Types in American Art,* Cortissoz. — *Nine. Century,* The Two Salons, Calonne.—*Scribner,* American Wood-Engravers * (Elbridge Kingsley); Posters and Poster-Designing in England,* Spielmann.

BIOGRAPHY, CORRESPONDENCE. — *Century,* George William Curtis, Wilkinson.—Japanese Life of General Grant;* Personal Memoirs of Robert Louis Stevenson, Gosse; Two Vice-Presidents (John C. Breckinridge and Hannibal Hamlin), Dawes.

DESCRIPTION, TRAVEL.—*Atlantic,* An Architect's Vacation. — *Century,* Bryant and the Berkshire Hills,* Lawrence.—*Harper's,* In the Garden of China,* Julian Ralph.

DOMESTIC AND SOCIAL.—*Century,* American Rural Festivals,* Burton-Harrison; The Tool-House at Home, Putnam (Open Letters).—*Harper's,* Americans in Paris,* Davis.—*Lippincott's,* Whole Duty of Woman, Emily A. Stowe; The New Womanhood, Boyesen.

EDUCATION, LANGUAGE, ETC.—*Fort. Review,* University Degrees for Women, An Oxford B.A.—*Harper s,* University of Pennsylvania,* Thorpe.—*Nine. Century,* After-Careers of University Educated Women, Gordon.

FICTION.—*Atlantic,* Philosopher with an Eye for Beauty, Hale.—*Century,* The Blighting of Mynheer Van Steen: A Kitwyk Story, King; Corinna's Fiammetta, Van Rensselaer; Strike at Mobley's, Matt Crim.—*Harper's,* Annie Tousey's Little Game,* Briscoe; Rosamond's Romance, Hibbard.—*Lippincott's,* A Social Highwayman, Train.—*Scribner's,* The Price of Romance, Herrick; An Assisted Destiny, Lynde; As Told by Her,* Goodloe.

HISTORY.—*Atlantic,* Childhood and Youth of a French " Macon," Ludlow ; The Elizabethan Sea Kings, Fiske.—*Forum,* Proper Perspective of American History, Wilson.

LITERARY.—*Century,* Books in Paper Covers: Notes of a Book-Lover,* Brander Matthews.—*Forum,* Charles Kingsley's Place in Literature, Frederic Harrison.—*Nine. Century* (Je.), Gentle Art of Book Lending, Layard.—*North Am. Review,* Degeneration and Evolution (Reply to Critics, Nordau; Kidd's " Social Evolution," Roosevelt ; Decay of Literary Taste, Gosse); Fenimore Cooper's Literary Offences, Mark Twain.

NATURE AND SCIENCE.—*Atlantic,* Beautiful and Brave was He, Olive Thorne Miller.—*Century,* Picturing the Planets: Portraits of Jupiter, Mars, and Saturn,* Keeler.—*Westminister Review* (Je.), Sex in Fiction, Hannigan; Intimations of a New Poetical Dawn, Bradfield.

POETRY AND DRAMA.—*Atlantic,* Vain Freedom, Moulton ; Song of the Veery, Van Dyke; Mountain-side, Scollard.—*Century,* Abandoned, Cawein ; A Lyric of Joy, Carmen ; To Idleness, Monroe.—*Harper's,* All Soul's Day, Marriott-Watson.—*Scribner's,* To a Maker of Verses, Wilton ; A Moral in Sevres, Mildred Howells; The Smoke, Kimball.

POLITICAL AND SOCIAL.—*Atlantic,* National Transportation department, Fletcher.—*Century,* The Future of War, new weapons. Fitzhugh Lee; Works of Lincoln as Political Classics, Thorpe (Open Letters) ; Religion in Public Schools, Davis (Open Letters).—*Fort. Review* (Je.), Russia and England, French ; Italian Disunion, Crooklands; Hong Cong and the Straits Settlements, Gundry.—*Forum,* Salutary results of the Income-Tax Decision, Edmunds; Political Dangers of the Income-Tax Decision, Whitney; Society's Protection against Degenerates, Nordau ; Sound Currency the Dominant Political Issue, Salomon.—*Harper's,* German Struggle for Liberty,* Bigelow. *Nine. Century,* Bimetalism, MacLeod ; Cross.—*No. Amer. Review,* Contemporary Egypt, Penfield ; Thirty Years in the Grain Trade, Williams; How Free Silver Would Affect Us, Leech; Disposal of a City's Waste, Waring ; " Coin's Financial School" and its censors, Harvey; Industrial Future of the South, Mathew ; Need of Better Roads, Dodge.—*Westminster Review* (Je), Collapse of Socialism, Lloyd; How to Revive Trade; Old and New Finance, Withy; What is the Silver Question ? Irwel; What To Do With Our Habitual Criminals, Strahan.

SPORTS AND AMUSEMENTS.—*Harper's,* Bear-Chasing in the Rocky Mountains,* Remington.—*Scribner's,* Life at the Athletic Clubs,* Edwards. — *Westminster Review* (Je.), Dances, Dancers and Dancing, Beckett.

A SYNDICATE POET.

I ASPIRED to be a poet,
   And resolved that all should know it,
So for noble thoughts long days and nights I racked my
      weary mind,
      Yet each magazine and journal
      With monotony eternal
Returned my great productions, all respectfully declined.

      Every false adjudication
      Drove me nearer desperation,
And unless a change of luck should come I'd meet a
      dreadful fate ;
      So I pondered long and weary
      How to mend my prospects dreary.
Till at last I hit upon the plan to try the syndicate.

      To the factory I started
      And to me they quick imparted
Their shrewd methods of procedure to economize the
      time ;
      By the roll they brought effusions,
      (Vanished all my fond delusions),
And the only things they cared for were the metre and
      the rhyme.

      We began negotiation,
      And without much hesitation
We adjusted slight contentions and agreed upon the pay,
      But there still was one condition
      To secure this proposition :
I must guarantee to turn out a dozen rolls a day.

      Now I'm perfectly contented,
      And my wealth is fast augmented,
For it's wonderful to see how well this enterprise succeeds;
      On the brain it's very lenient,
      For the press it's quite convenient
As the editors can cut verse off in lengths to suit their
      needs.
                        E. J. FLOOD, in the *Boston Pilot.*

BOOKS FOR SUMMER TRAVELLERS.

AMERICAN BOOK COMPANY, New York.
Gray's Manual of Botany. Tourists' ed. $2.00.

D. APPLETON & CO., New York.
Appletons' General Guide to the United States. With maps and illustrations. One volume complete, flexible morocco, with tuck, $2.50. Part I., separately, New England and Middle States and Canada, cloth, $1.25. Part II., separately, Southern and Western States, cloth, $1.25.
Appletons' Handbook of Summer Resorts. With maps and illustrations. Small 8vo, paper, 50c.
Appletons' Canadian Guide-Book. One volume complete. Newfoundland to the Pacific Coast. With maps and illustrations. 12mo, $1.25.
Appletons' Guide-Book to Alaska. By Miss E. R. Scidmore. With maps and illustrations. $1.25.
Appletons' Dictionary of New York and Its Vicinity. 16mo, paper, 30c.; flex. cloth, 60c.
The White Mountains. By Rev. J. H. Ward. 12mo, cloth, $1.25.
The Land of the Sun. *Vistas Mexicanas.* By Christian Reid. Illustrated. 12mo, cloth, $1.75.

THE CASSELL PUBLISHING CO., New York.
Cassell's Pocket Guide to Europe for 1895. With maps, etc. Bound in leather, $1.50.
The model book of its kind for accuracy, fulness, legibility of text and maps, compact beauty and usefulness, and very moderate price.

WATSON GILL, Syracuse, N. Y.
The Adirondacks. Wallace's guide for 1895, now ready. 600 pages, 150 half-tone engravings and large map. The Standard Guide to the Adirondacks. Sold by booksellers, or mailed on receipt of price, $3.50.

HOUGHTON, MIFFLIN & CO., Boston.
Boston Illustrated. Paper, 50c.
Satchel Guide to Europe. Edition for 1894. $1.50.
England Without and Within. By Richard Grant White. $2.00.
Sweetser's New England. $1.50.
Sweetser's White Mountains. $1.50.
Sweetser's Maritime Provinces. $1.50.
Nantucket Scraps. By Jane G. Austin. $1.50.
Mrs. Thaxter's Among the Isles of Shoals. $1.25.

HUNT & EATON, New York.
Travels in Three Continents. By J. M. Buckley, LL.D. Finely illustrated. 614 pages, octavo, cloth, gilt top, $3.50.
A most instructive and fascinating book of travel.

LITTLE, BROWN & CO., Boston.
Pleasure-Cycling. By Henry Clyde. With 34 silhouettes and vignettes. 16mo, cloth, $1.00.
Parkman's Handbook of the Northern Tour. Lakes George and Champlain, Niagara, Montreal, Quebec. 12mo, cloth, $1.50.

JOHN MURPHY & CO., Baltimore, Md.
Mrs. Mary E. Surratt. Her trial, conviction and execution. By David Miller DeWitt. 12mo, cloth, $1.25.
A Marriage of Reason. By Francis Maurice Egan. A story of "society" people of Philadelphia and its suburbs. 12mo, cloth, $1.00.
Army Boys and Girls. By Mrs. Mary G. Bohesteel. A series of brilliant stories of our camps and garrisons. 12mo, cloth, $1.00.
Ada's Trust. By Mrs. A. H. Dorsey. A story of vivid interest. 12mo, cloth, $1.00.
Beth's Promise. By Mrs. A. H. Dorsey. 12mo, cloth, $1.00.
A Washington Winter. By Mrs. M. V. Dahlgren. A vivid delineation of life at the Capital. $1.00.
Lights and Shadows of a Life. By Mrs. M. V. Dahlgren. A picture of Southern home life. 12mo, cloth, $1.00.
Children of Charles I. of England. By Mrs. C. S. H. Clark. Small quarto, cloth, $1.00.
Down at Caxtons. Brilliant sketches of American authors. By Walter Lecky. Paper, 35 cents.

THOMAS NELSON & SONS, New York.
The Royal Album of Chromo Views. The most exquisite scenery of the British Isles. 253 chromo views, oblong folio, cloth, extra gilt edges, $7.00.

THOMAS NELSON & SONS.—Continued.
English Scenery. 120 views. 4to, cloth, $2.50, and mounted, 4to, $4.50; and $4.00.
Souvenir of Scotland. Its cities, lakes, and mountains. 120 chromo views. 4to, $2.50; and $4.00.
Rambles in Rome. By S. Russell Forbes. With maps, plans, and illustrations. 12mo, cloth extra, $1.50.
Rambles in Naples. By S. Russell Forbes. With maps, plans, and illustrations. 12mo, cloth extra, $1.25.

ROBERTS BROTHERS, Boston.
Jackson (Helen ["H. H."]). Glimpses of Three Coasts. 12mo, $1.50.
These are "Bits of Travel" in California and Oregon, Scotland and England, and Norway, Denmark, and Germany.
—— **Ramona.** A Story. 12mo, $1.50.
—— **Bits of Travel.** Illustrated. Square 18mo, $1.25.
—— **Bits of Travel at Home.** Square 18mo, $1.50.
Drake (Samuel Adams). Old Landmarks and Historic Personages of Boston. With 93 illustrations. 12mo, $2.00.
—— **Old Landmarks and Historic Fields of Middlesex.** With 39 illustrations and maps. 12mo, $2.00.
Aloha. (A Hawaiian Salutation.) By G. L. Chaney. Travels in the Sandwich Islands. With illustrations and map. 16mo, $1.50.

GEORGE ROUTLEDGE & SONS (Ld.), New York.
Hare's (A. J. C.) Literary Traveling Companions.
Edwards's (A. B.) A Thousand Miles up the Nile. Profusely illustrated. 8vo, $2.50.
—— **Untrodden Peaks and Unfrequented Valleys.** A Midsummer Ramble in the Dolomites. Maps and illustrations. 8vo, $2.50.
Caine's (W. S.) A Trip Round the World, 1887-1888. 250 original illustrations. 12mo, cloth, $1.50.
—— **Picturesque India:** an unconventional Guide-Book. 200 illustrations and map. 8vo, cloth, $4.00.
Stow's (John) Survey of London in the Time of Elizabeth. Crown 8vo, $1.00.

CHARLES SCRIBNER'S SONS, New York.
The Peoples and Politics of the Far East. Travels and Studies in the British, French, Spanish, and Portuguese colonies, Siberia, China, Japan, Korea, Siam and Malaya. By Henry Norman, author of "The Real Japan." With 60 illustrations and 4 maps. 8vo, $4.00.
New edition for 1895 of
The Index Guide to Travel and Art Study in Europe. By Lafayette C. Loomis. With plans and catalogues of the chief art galleries, maps, tables of routes, and 260 illustrations. *New and revised edition.* 16mo, $3.00.
The Mexican Guide. By T. A. Janvier. *New and revised edition.* With three maps. net, $2.50.
Carlsbad and Its Environments. By John Merrylees. Illustrated. 12mo, $1.50. "The best book on the subject."
A Handbook for Travellers in Japan. Third edition, revised and for the most part rewritten by B. H. Chamberlain and W. B. Mason. With fifteen maps. 12mo, net, $5.00.
The Pacific Coast Scenic Tour. From Southern California to Alaska. By Henry T. Finck. With 24 full-page illustrations. 8vo, $2.00.
Sole Agents for the United States.
Baedeker's Guide-Books. Illustrated with numerous maps, plans, panoramas, and views. 12mo, cloth, viz., all prices net:
The United States. With 17 maps and 22 plans, $3.60. Alps (Eastern), $2.40; Belgium and Holland, $1.80; Egypt (Lower), $3.60; Egypt (Upper) $3.00; France (Northern), $2.10; France (Southern), from the Loire to the Spanish and Italian frontiers, including Corsica, $2.70; Germany (Northern), $2.40; Germany (Southern) and Austria, $2.40; Germany (Rhine from Rotterdam to Constance), $2.10; Great Britain, $3.00; Greece, $2.40; Italy (Northern) $2.40; Italy (Central) and Rome, $1.80; Italy (Southern) and Sicily, etc., $1.80; London and Its Environs, $1.80; Norway, Sweden, and Denmark, $3.00; Paris and Its Environs, $1.80; Palestine and Syria, $3.60; Switzerland, $2.40.

The Literary News

In winter you may reade them, ab ignem, by the fireside; and in summer, ab umbram, under some shadie tree, and therewith pass away the tedious howres.

| VOL. XVI. | AUGUST, 1895. | No. 8. |

The Husband of My Lady Nobody.

YES, though he did not realize it, Otto van Helmont had married his wife for her face—a sweet apparition, bright and fresh among the

From " My Lady Nobody."   Copyright, 1895, by Harper & Brothers.

"FIVE THOUSAND FLORINS, IF A PENNY, MY LADY."

home-flowers, a suggestion of the dear fatherland, a dream of wholesome Dutch girlhood. He had married for that most unsatisfactory of all reasons: "because he had fallen in love." Not even a fortnight—be it remembered—had elapsed between his first sight of Ursula and their engagement. A man must either know his wife before he learns to love her, or else he must never need to love her, or else he will certainly never learn to know her. That last eventuality, the rarest, is surely the most desirable, but only if the love be mutual, and exceedingly great.

Otto, then, had never penetrated into a character whose reserve was so like his own that he could not understand it. He loved his young wife, and kissed her; and he fancied, like so many men, that his consciousness of loving her was sufficient for all her wants. As for her

position in the house, in the family, if it was uncomfortable, could he help that? Was not he himself weighed down by his difficulties, his responsibilities, the worry of universal deepening displeasure? What were the pinpricks she complained of compared to his wounds? Her mamma-in-law was inconsiderate; his mother was unkind. Her dependents were not always courteous, his own people hardened their countenances against him. He could not help thinking that much of her petulant soreness —well, she was young—was provoked by mortification because of the scant dignity or authority her sudden elevation had brought her. Had she not said to him, "I will not be My Lady Nobody; at least, let me not be it to you"?

She was annoyed, then, at being it to him, and to all. The combination vexed her. She had hoped, as My Lady, to be Somebody indeed.

He sighed from irritation. It was not his

fault. Yet he was a little disappointed in Ursula. He had thought hers was an essentially gentle nature, unassuming, unaspiring. Even not desiring to meddle and share in her husband's affairs, because that, for a young girl, is impossible. A thoroughly womanly woman, who cried out in horror at thought of men's work, such as sheep-slaughtering, or of men's play, such as a fox-hunt; a woman who could be tacitly brave, on occasion, able to endure though unable to act. Thus had she revealed herself to him in the week of his swift immersion, his model woman, in a word. That is the worst of tumbling into love. You marry your model woman and have to live with your wife. Now, Ursula was far superior to Otto's ideal. There is nothing more hopeless in human relationships. (Harper. $1.50.)—*From Maarten Maartens' "My Lady Nobody."*

Chiffon's Marriage.*

THE stories of Mme. de Martel de Janville, who calls herself "Gyp," have been very popular, says the *Mail and Express*, with people who can easily read French, but they have thus far either defied the translators altogether, or emerged from their manipulations in a pale and debilitated condition. The present story, which we have from four several translators, through the enterprise of four several publishing houses, is a dainty, fragile tale of a wayward, impetuous, warm-hearted, and, on the whole, rightminded girl—a mere child—whose mother is a purse-proud, cold-hearted termagant. Chiffon, the rag, is a pet name which cannot be exactly translated. Mr. Du Bois chooses as an equivalent "Darling," while the three other translators stick to the French word.

From "Chiffon's Marriage."   Lovell, Coryell & Co.

"GYP."

Corysande is the heroine's baptismal name. She has been petted by her henpecked stepfather and his younger brother, and by an old uncle and aunt, and alternately scolded and neglected by her mother. She is the idol of the servants, and she has for a faithful ally a grotesque bull-dog, Griboulle—Blockhead. She has grown up out of doors, and is graceful in a clumsy, healthy sort of way. She has a sentimental fondness for flowers, but she has also a large share of shrewdness and common-sense. Fear is a stranger to her, and she is no respecter of persons. She is, in fact, a most entertaining little hoyden, and her little romance is as charming as any we have had from France since Halévy wrote "L'Abbé Constantin." But "Gyp's" modern Gallicisms cannot be exactly translated. The book is nearly all conversation, and most of it is Chiffon's frolicsome talk, half-formed sentences, exclamations, expletives, elliptical epigrams.

Ferragus.

THE two stories contained in the new volume of the Roberts edition of Balzac, though separate and distinct, have the same characteristics. In them Balzac, who knew everything, and who had explored every social field, describes the criminal class in France, and for a type he selects Vautrin, and never has such a Napoleonic figure been drawn. For courage, combined with subtlety, for quickness of perception, for ability in changing himself according to his surroundings, Vautrin never had an equal.

As the reviewer, who necessarily has passing before him that endless library of fiction, he cannot help but being conscious how there always are incidents, scenes, and personages which have been appropriated from Balzac, the master. Take the opening chapter of Ferragus—with the nonchalant young man, the mysterious woman, the strange *rencontre*, the sinister physiognomy of the street—those are Bal-

* "Gyp." "Chiffon's Marriage," tr. by M. L. J. Lovell, Coryell. $1; pap., 50 c.
—*Same*, tr. by Mrs. Patchet Martin. Stokes. (*Bijou ser.*) 50 c.
—*Same*, tr. by Mrs. E. Lees Coffee. Hurst. 50 c.
—*Same*. Under title "A Gallic Girl," tr. by Pène Du Bois. Brentano's. $1.25.

zac's ideas, and we have had them repeated since his time over and over again.

Auguste de Maulincour is a meddlesome young man, madly in love with Mme. Desmarets, who is an honest woman. Because De Maulincour is too insistent, and would pry into the woman's action, he comes to his death. His terrible exit from life is due to causes over which Mme. Desmarets has no control. Her destinies are ruled by her father, who is the chief of a band of men who shape fortune to suit themselves, indifferent to any obstacles. Balzac developed this idea in his "History of the Thirteen." Ferragus was grand master of the Devorants, who, as a band, were "more than ordinary kings and judges"—they were executioners. This story is a complete drama, with a sinister conclusion. The famed Ferragus the XXIII. of the dynasty, his vengeance achieved, finds that he has broken his daughter's heart, since her husband suspected her honesty, and the dreaded chief, her father, lapses into senility.

In the "Père Goriot" and in "Lucien de Rubempré," Vautrin, Trompe la Mort, Jacques Collin, the Abbé Herrera, all figured, and it was one and the same criminal who made you hold your breath, so wonderfully did Balzac present him.

We read and ponder over the Italian Professor Lombroso, who catalogues and assorts the criminal classes, and question whether Lombroso is any wiser on the subject than is Balzac. The psychological aspect of crime is, in "The Last Incarnation of Vautrin," wonderfully treated. Why do criminals so suddenly break down, both mentally and physically? Of course, debauch is a destructive element, but that is not all. Balzac explains it. To perpetrate crime demands "the employment of all the forces of life, an agility of mind equal to that of body." Then the vital force in time must be used up. There is "dispersion of energy." The master thief is certain in time to lose his cunning. But why invariably after a successful coup does the criminal plunge at once into vice? Is it because his ill-gotten gains are soon parted with? Balzac doubts that. "After the success of some enterprise they (the criminals) are in such a state of prostration that they rush immediately into all forms of debauchery to recover calmness by exhausting all their forces ; they seek forgetfulness of their crime in the overthrow of their reason.

"The Last Incarnation of Vautrin" is the sequel to "Lucien de Rubempré." Marvellous is the way Vautrin escapes from the toils. Miss Wormeley, in this translation, has had to face many difficulties. Especially troublesome must it have been to turn into English the argot of the French criminal ; but, with her good judgment and many-sided acquaintance, she has been quite equal to the task. "Vautrin" is more than a romance. It is a study in criminology. (Roberts. $1.50.)—*N. Y. Times.*

The Martyred Fool.

"THE Martyred Fool" is a story in Mr. Murray's best style, with much analytical strength, a happy insight into human motive, and a pathetic divination of the struggles and sorrows of a proud heart. As in "Rainbow Gold," there is here a sharp contrast between the sturdy force of a man in humble position and the careless insolence of a "cavalier."

From "Chiffon's Marriage."   F. A. Stokes Co.

"FATHER DE RAGON REMAINED TRANSFIXED."

The conflict between these two natures has a disastrous issue for both. The son of one of the two is the hero of the story, and he inherits the bitterness and the proud struggles of his father. Some readers may regret that Mr. Murray has found a theatre for the manhood of his hero in the plots of Nihilists, anarchists, and dynamiters; but the author's intention is perfectly clear, and his construction is psychologically correct. The strong, rebellious Welsh lad is enthusiastic at first in what he takes to be a resolute fight against the oppressors and bloodsuckers of humanity; but he soon discovers that he has only embraced a fallacy; that instead of liberating captive humanity his desperate comrades are forging new chains for her; and that in place of warring against tyrants he is forced, as an honest man, to come to close grips with assassins. This is how Evan Rhys becomes a fool and a martyr; but at any rate the discipline of his life has made him wise. (Harper. $1.25.)—The *Athenæum.*

The Story of Bessie Costrell.

THE impression produced by this story on its serial publication in *Scribner's Magazine* is intensified when it is read, as it really should be, at one sitting. A novel suffers but little, as a rule, from publication in instalments; but this is one single episode—the story of the catastrophe in the lives of three people, coming up swiftly as a thunderstorm, striking its deathly blow, and passing away as suddenly as it came, to be forgotten by the world, but remembered by its victims. Therefore it is well that this short tale (25,000 words, or thereabouts) has been issued in a volume by itself, to be read and pondered and read again. For the story is full of suggestion and bitter knowledge, and full of the craftsman's finest art as well. Around the three types of poverty that stand out prominently in these pages is grouped a whole village of the lowly, forming the background here, chanting a silent chorus there, contributing of its own temperaments and misery to make the small canvas with its mighty subject complete. To some the swiftness of the story may seem too great, the unity of action too complete, the relativity of details too near perfection for real life; but to them we answer that behind every individual in these pages there stands a class, and that in the rushing life we see about us there is a grandeur of happiness and misery, a unity as of a classic drama, that we miss, each of us, in our individual existences. It is life, not lives, that Mrs. Ward shows us here; poverty itself, rather than one poor woman and two poor men.

Yet the individual has not been sacrificed to the type in "The Story of Bessie Costrell." Bolderfield, the laborer who has scraped together some seventy pounds during a lifetime of roughest toil, and to whom for years this pitiful hoard has been sweetheart, wife and offspring, is as interesting and intelligible as an individual as he is in the author's wider sense. Isaac Costrell is simply a fanatical Dissenter, proud of his reputation, given to melancholia and fits of uncontrollable temper, if we so choose to take him; and Bessie may mean nothing more to us than the woman who was tempted in her narrow, joyless life, and fell. Even then the tale is a work of art; but we prefer to think of it in its broader sense, and, perhaps, to benefit thereby. As the story progressed in *Scribner's,* reference was made in these pages to the literary quality of the work; it is therefore unnecessary to return to that part of the subject here. But we may fitly close with the observation that, while in our opinion Mrs. Ward has in her larger novels shown that the inexorable requirements of the three-volume form at times rested heavily upon her, she has here demonstrated herself superior to the much harder tyranny of the short story, as befits the greatest woman novelist of her day. (Macmillan. 75 c.)—*N. Y. Critic.*

Breaking a Jam.

"HOLD her—hold her now—to the right of the big rock ; then swing to the far shore ; if we go to the right we are gone."

"All right ; let her stern come round," and we drop away.

No talking now, but with every nerve and muscle tense, and your eye on the boil of the water, you rush along. You back water and paddle, the stern swings, she hangs for an instant, she falls in the current, and with a mad rush you take it like a hunting-man a six-bar gate. Now paddle, paddle, paddle. It looks bad—we cannot make it—yes—all right—and we are on the far shore, with the shallows on the other side. This little episode ,was successful, but, as you well know, it cannot last. The next rift, and with a bump she is hung upon a sunken rock, and—jump! jump!—we both flounder overboard in any way possible, so it is well and quickly done. One man loses his hold. the other swings the boat off, and, kicking and splashing for a foothold, the demoralized outfit shoots along. At last one is found, and then at a favorable rock we embark again.

You are now wet, but the tea and sugar are safe, so it's a small matter. A jam of logs and tops is "hung up" on a particularly nasty place, and you have a time getting the boat around it. You walk on rotten tops while the knots stick up beneath you like sabres. " Has " floats calmly out to sea, as it were, on a detached log which he is cutting, and with a hopeless look of despair he totters, while I yell our pipes and tobacco, started off for the settlements—or " drifting to thunder," as Bret Harte said of Chiquita. There was rather a lively and enthusiastic pursuit instituted then, the details of which are forgotten, as my mind was focussed on the grub-pack, but we got her.

From " Pony Tracks."　　　Copyright, 1895, by Harper & Brothers.

BREAKING A JAM.

" Save the axe—you—save the axe ! " and over he goes, only to get wet—and very disgusted, both of which will wear off in time. For a mile the water is so shallow that the boat will not run loaded, and we lead her along as we wade, now falling in over our heads, sliding on slippery stones, hurting our feet, wondering why we had come at all. The boat gets loose, and my heart stands still as the whole boat-load of blankets and grub, with About this time the soles let go on my tennis shoes, and my only pair of trousers gave way. These things, however, become such mere details as to be scarcely noticed when you have travelled since sunrise up to your waist in water, and are tired, footsore, and hungry. It is time to go ashore and camp. Finally the tent is up. You lean against a dead log and swap lies with the guide. (Harper. $3.)— *From Remington's "Pony Tracks."*

Little Knights and Ladies.

ANY one who studies the sweet, womanly face that adorns the leaf opposite the title-page of this little volume will expect to find a large and tender sympathy in the verses. That expectation will not be disappointed. Mrs. Sangster has produced a volume of poems which are wholly suitable for children's reading, and which will be quite as welcome to the children's mothers. It is true that there are no marks of genius in these verses. There is no astonishing revelation of a capacity to put into perfect English the fancies of childhood such as Mr. Stevenson displayed in his "Child's Garden of Verses," but there is a womanly touch which the greater poet's verses lacked and which will win for Mrs. Sangster hundreds of admirers. Children are all fond of pretty stories told in verse, and they will enjoy such charming tales as "Jeanie's Christmas Journey," and the "Maid of the Legion of Honor." Occasionally, however, one meets in this book with poems which will not please the children. One of them is called "Two Wishes," and here it is:

"I wish that the teacher had lessons to learn,"
　Said Molly, the wise little elf;
"She would know they were hard, and be sorry,
　If she had to do them herself."

And the teacher at home, in the gloaming,
　Sighed gently, " I wish that they knew,
The dear little children, how easy
　'Tis just to have lessons to do."

(Harper. $1.25.)—*N. Y. Times.*

From "Little Knights and Ladies." Copyright, 1895, by
　　　　　Harper & Brothers.

The Commodore's Daughters.

"THE Commodore's Daughters " is one of the best of Jonas Lie's novels, and Jonas Lie is far too little known in this country. He is beyond all question the most popular Norwegian novelist. In the admirable introduction which Edmund Gosse has written for this edition you will find a concise and fairly satisfactory account of Lie's life and works. In this review it is only necessary to mention a few salient dates. Born in 1833, it was not until 1870 that his first story appeared. "The Man with Second Sight," as it was called, was a slight affair, but it was the means of procuring for him one of those travelling stipends which in that land of miracles the State awards men of letters. He journeyed through Nordland and Finmark, and in 1871 went to Rome. Since that time novel has followed novel, and to-day Jonas Lie is, as I have said, the most popular novelist writing the Norwegian tongue.

I do not suggest that either you or I will find full satisfaction in these novels; now and again we may yearn for the flesh-pots of De Maupassant; at times we may demand the clash of hardier passions and a fuller measure of high-colored life; but here for a little while is quiet and comely order, and the beauty of sacrifice and gentle lives. On second thought, I shall not take the edge off your pleasure by introducing you in this public place to the two sisters, Cecilia and Martha. You will meet them in the book, and that is better. I trust you will read "The Commodore's Daughters." There are tears and laughter and a healthy human interest in this idyl of land and sea—an idyl which becomes a tragedy as it drifts through the hypocrisies and conventions of its little bourgeois world. (United States Bk. Co. $1; pap., 50 c.)—*N. Y. Commercial Advertiser.*

Trilbyana.

IT is many a year since a book has attained the popularity of Mr. du Maurier's second novel "Trilby" (printed as a serial in *Harper's Monthly*, from January to August, inclusive, and then issued in book form, on Saturday, 8 September, 1894). Several others have sold as well—some even better ; but neither "Looking Backward " nor " Ben Hur " (to name but these two) has captivated the public in the same manner or in the same degree as this romance, this fairy tale of the three British artists, the blanchisseuse who posed for "the altogether," the Parisian masters of painting, and the trans-Rhenish masters of music, in the Latin Quarter of the early fifties. It is a story written out of

From "Trilbyana."   Copyright, 1895, by The Critic Co.

DU MAURIER'S HOUSE.

the author's very heart, and it finds its way straight to the hearts of his readers. This is the secret of its unique success. Its charm is emotional rather than intellectual. With all its art, it impresses one as essentially ingenuous. It is a book to be loved, not merely to be liked or admired.

On 16 June, 1894, *The Critic* printed, with comment, a letter in which Mr. Whistler protested to the editor of an English newspaper against the libellous likeness of himself to be found in the character of Joe Sibley, one of the minor personages in the story of "Trilby." In the fall there were so many sporadic calls for this number of the paper as soon to exhaust the supply carried over from the summer. There seemed to be a general desire on the part of our readers to bind up the Whistler letters, etc., with the text and pictures of "Trilby" as printed in *Harper's Monthly*, the American artist's protest having led to a slight revision of the story before its appearance in book form. The hint was acted upon ; and two pages of "Trilbyana" were printed in *The Critic* of Nov. 17.

Though an extra edition was struck off, the call for this number has at last exhausted the supply ; and the present pamphlet, containing among its many items of interest a majority of those that have found a place in the columns of *The Critic*, may fairly claim to be issued in response to a popular call. (Critic Co. $1; pap., 25 c.)—*From Preface to "Trilbyana."*

Billy Bellew.

IT has probably been said often before, but it is worth repeating, that Mr. Norris eminently possesses the rare gift of representing ladies and gentlemen who behave with perfect good breeding. If his ladies and gentlemen exhibit the defects of their good qualities, and are apt to be a trifle dull, they must be forgiven in an age when unconventionality so often takes the place of excitement, and piquancy is sought in ill-breeding. On the other hand, the adventurers and evil characters of his novels have not the same ring of sincerity about them. Mr. Norris seems to be too fastidious to be able to enter into the feelings of cads and intriguing women, so that the harmless, necessary villain of his stories is frequently a mere puppet. In "Billy Bellew" the hero, though almost incredibly weak, is, partly owing to this very weakness, a gentleman every inch of him, and is as living a character as any well-mannered, honest, and healthy-minded Englishman that you may meet any day. The conventional and respectable family of the Forbeses is also admirable, the correct dulness of their behavior simply oozes out of them, ye they are not boring, as they are so comically admirable in their frigidity; and it is quite in keeping with the rest of them that the pretty girl of the family should be such a brainless and selfish little flirt. The adventuress Mrs. Littlewood and her impossible husband seem rather exaggerated, but not outrageously so, and their vulgarity acts as an excellent foil to Betty Bellew's stupid and chivalrous honesty. May Mr. Norris go on for many more years to come turning out these sound, wholesome novels at the same rapid rate as he has been doing lately! (Harper. $1.50.)—*The Athenæum.*

In Deacon's Orders.

"IN Deacon's Orders and Other Stories" is the title of Walter Besant's latest contribution to the literature of fiction. There are eleven stories in the volume, the initial one of the series being the most elaborate and finished in the book. The disease of what the author aptly calls "religiosity" is treated in the first story, "In Deacon's Orders"; but the author does not wish in this powerful, though morbid, study to confound the semblance of religion with the possession of a genuine religious faith. Paul Leighan, in the tale, is a victim of "religiosity." He possesses a love for things ecclesiastical, but he has no religion, no moral strength, and no comprehension of the meaning of honor. He experiences the exaltation arising from participation in the stately services of the church; he derives pleasure from the hymns that are sung; hears with joy the religious exhortations of others and is himself a powerful pleader. The outward forms of the religious life are carried on with great zeal, while the inner life—the conversation and conduct which are the only true expression of it—is wholly untouched. As truly unconscious as Jonathan Wild or Barry Lyndon seems of his depravity, this young Apollo of the church is of his hypocrisy. He mistakes his emotion for truth, and he experiences immense satisfaction in the contagious enthusiasm resulting from appeals to the sensuous nature. But the author presents Paul Leighan to his readers as a degenerate from his school-days. There are no redeeming phases of character in him to offset the awful meannesses of which he is guilty throughout his life, and of which he seems totally unconscious. Leighan is a liar, cheat, forger, gambler and libertine; nevertheless with all his sordid earnestness, we find him preaching divinely, see him overcome with emotion at the consciousness of the divine life and writhing in agony on the floor of the cathedral. The inevitable end follows and he meets it in America with unctuous hopes and loud professions of faith in God. The story is as powerful as the "Demoniac," but it is a more morbid and unhealthy study, and we feel that it has been unnecessarily overdrawn. The author tells us that it has been his lot to know several victims of "religiosity," and he gives

two examples of men afflicted with such a malady.

The other stories in this volume have appeared in the *Pall Mall Magazine*, *Black and White*, *The Strand*, *The Illustrated London News*, *The Humanitarian* and *The Idler*. Of these, the "Peer and Heiress" and "King David's Friend" are, for freshness, originality, and vivid portrayal of character, superior to the remaining tales, which are somewhat colorless, and, indeed, commonplace. (Harper. $1.25.)—*Phila. Press.*

The Head of a Hundred.

MAUD WILDER GOODWIN, author of "The Colonial Cavalier," has published another story of colonial life, called "The Head of a Hundred." This purports to be some account of his own life, written by one Humphrey Huntoon, a young physician, who came to the Virginia colony in search of fortune, and by his courage and force of character grew to be a person of importance. Of course, there is a woman in the story, the fair daughter of Sir William Romney, who looked with little favor on the poor suitor. This fine gentleman, who wishes his daughter to marry a rich nobleman, intercepts a letter from Humphrey to her, and himself writes a reply in her name that sends her lover to the new country broken-hearted and filled with scorn for this coquette, as he can but think her. He runs across an old friend in James City, and then follow several interesting adventures with the "naturals," as these early settlers called the red men. How he fared in these, the steps that led to his appointment in the service of the colony, and what befell between him and his lady love it would be too bad to tell, when it is such pleasant reading to find out. The book is written in a fresh, charming style, and is not overburdened with "pictures of colonial life," as are so many chronological stories. Indeed, we could well endure more detail as to the daily life of this brave, simple colonial gentleman, who was as calm in the midst of hostile Indians as he would be in the presence of a case requiring his mildest physic. But he was also modest, and probably thought people did not care to hear of himself except as a part of intrinsically interesting events. There is some tragedy in the story, as there must be in all stories of the earliest periods of the colonies, but it ends happily in the main. Anything so wholesome and so old-fashioned in the simplicity of its story-telling is gratifying and refreshing, and if one has not read the author's other story, "The Colonial Cavalier," one would certainly wish to do so after reading this one. (Little, Brown & Co. $1.25.)—*Springfield Republican.*

Guerber's "Legends of the Rhine."

THIS book is intended as a contribution to the study of Folk-lore, and as a Legendary Guide to the Rhine. The Tales have been gathered from many sources, and while *all* the Rhine traditions are not recorded here, the principal ones have been given.

As Teutonic Mythology has been outlined in "Myths of Northern Lands," it has not been included in this volume. The real "Nibelungenlied " and the "Heldensagen" have also been omitted because they form part of the author's work on the " Legends of the Middle Ages."

While countless German authorities have been consulted with great care, the author feels particularly indebted to Mr. Karl Simrock, the German Folk-lorist and Poet of the Rhine, who has versified many of these picturesque tales.

The interest of a Rhine pilgrimage is more of travellers and enable stay-at-homes to glean some idea of the legendary charms of this matchless river. (Barnes. $1.50.)—*From Preface to Guerber's "Legends of the Rhine."*

Meadow Grass.

MISS BROWN's title is purely figurative. All flesh is grass, according to the prophet, and Miss Brown writes about humanity. Her field is a village in New Hampshire, Tiverton by name, and her stories have the fresh charm, the unforced humor, and· convincing clearness that are begot by accurate observation controlled by sympathy, and fostered by a simple and sound literary style.

Only in her first chapter—essay rather than story—devoted to memories of the old district school, and in her last, which is largely devoted to a consideration of the effect on the rustic mind of a two weeks' engagement of a theat-

ENTRANCE TO THE ZUYDER-ZEE.

than doubled by a knowledge, however superficial, of the legends connected with the principal towns, churches, and castles along its banks, so it is hoped that tourists, old and young, will find room in pocket or satchel for this collection.

The book is sent out into the world with a sincere hope that it may enhance the pleasure rical troupe in Tiverton, does her writing seem at all artificial and labored. Her mood in the former is conventionally reminiscent. The essay savors of the writing-desk and the need of making "copy." In the latter she taxes our credulity. The meanest actors could not spend two weeks in a cross-roads village and live, and the matter is all pretty poor stuff, as ancient as Partridge's visit to the Theatre Royal, when Mr. Garrick played in " Hamlet."

But from her second piece, until the next to the last, she holds us in delightful thrall. The simple villagers are pictured with a graphic skill that is not excelled by any contemporary writer of New England tales. In pathos and in humor Miss Brown is equally successful. The story of Heman Blaisdell's persecution and his deliverance, and that of old lady Lamson's holiday, are as good as many of Miss Jewett's. The last is worthy of comparison with " The Passing of Sister Barsett." (Copeland & Day. $1.50.)—*N. Y. Times.*

Selected Essays of James Darmesteter.

WHILE the scope of Darmesteter's studies necessarily made his name familiar to students of Oriental history and literature, his name had become known outside of this comparatively small circle. As Prof. Jastrow well says, he was by general consent, after Renan's death, regarded as the most distinguished scholar of France. His rank among Persian scholars was assured, and on Zoroastrianism he was the undisputed authority. With Renan he had much in common, and it is of Renan that he wrote one of the clearest and most forcible papers in this volume.

Darmesteter was the son of a poor Jewish bookseller and was reared in orthodox tradition, which he abandoned, however, in the course of years. Nevertheless, his essay on "The Prophets of Israel" is thoroughly imbued with the spirit of Hebrew history and is of especial worth. To the student in folk-lore as well as the Orientalist the paper on "Afghan Life in Afghan Songs" is of value. This essay and the one on " The Supreme God in the Indo-European Mythology " were written by Darmesteter in English, which he used with the same ease as French; that on Renan was translated by N. P. Gilman, and the remaining four by Helen B. Jastrow. Prof. Jastrow's preface is in excellent taste and might have been extended to the advantage of his readers. (Houghton, Mifflin & Co. $1.50.) — *Public Opinion.*

My Literary Passions.

" MY Literary Passions," by W. D. Howells, is, within its limitations, one of the most charming personal confessions that we ever read, and if we ever doubted, which we do not remember to have been the case, that he possesses a remarkable talent, not to say a positive genius for autobiographic writing, we doubt no longer. His instinct, while he is following the trail of memory, guides him in

the direction that he ought to take, whether his object is to recover for himself what he was, and what he thought and felt in the past, the very effigies of himself, to revive the phrase of the old painters, or whether it is to enlighten and entertain his readers by satisfying their curiosity with a full and frank revelation of the kind of a man he is. The temptation which attaches to autobiographic writing is so great, especially when the writer has attained eminence, that we generally require a surer endorsement of its veracity than is contained in the words before us, which, professing to disclose what happened, may really depict what might, could, would or should have happened if the writer had ordered his career from the beginning, and had made himself instead of being made by circumstances. With every disposition to tell the truth, there is that in human nature on the imaginative side, or the side of self-love which magnifies or minifies actual occurrences until they lose their true proportion and just value. It is not difficult to believe what we wish to believe, and to persuade ourselves that what might have been really was, invention supplementing memory where it falls short, and supplying it with materials where they do not exist. " I said in my haste all men are liars," said the Scottish dominie, at the beginning of his sermon and added, in a familiar way, no doubt, "Aye, David, mon, and if you belonged in this parish, ye might have said it at your leisure."

We often think of this anecdote in reading the autobiographic writing of men of letters ; never, indeed, of men like Scott, whose veracity was as great as his modesty, but generally of men like Coleridge and Byron and Poe and Pope, who were so little worthy of trust when they wrote about themselves that it is safe to disbelieve them until better evidence than their own is furnished. Mr. Howells belongs to another parish than theirs, we are happy to say, and the gain is ours, as we felt while reading his recent papers in *Harper's Magazine*, on his first visits to Boston and New York, a subject of which we are personally qualified to judge, and have felt a gain in every page of this last book of his, which, charming as it is as a series of outline hints respecting his early years, is still more charming as a simple, modest, unaffected description of the insufficiency of his education, of the immaturity of his tastes, and of the disadvantages under which he labored in his boyhood. If he had wished to magnify himself, as others of the writing craft would, no doubt, have done, given the chance he had, he might easily have made himself more ignorant or more learned than he was; might have divined the path of

From "Water Tramps." Copyright, 1895, by G. P. Putnam's Sons.

THE "SEA BIRD" GOING TO THE RESCUE.

letters in which he was to achieve his success, and so on; but, being right-minded, he wished nothing of the sort, veracity being more to him than fine writing, and the plain portrayal of his personality dearer than any imaginary heroism. (Harper. $1.25.)—*Mail and Express.*

Water Tramps.

THE *Sea Bird* was a little sloop yacht, 30 feet over all, 12 feet beam. Four young men chartered her, and were to pay $20 a week for her. When they started on their cruise after victualling the craft, they had not a penny left, and, besides that, would have to get somehow or other the money to pay for the first week's hire. But among the four young chaps there were an embryo lawyer and a theological student. They were honest, active, good sailors, and capital fishermen, and so they made up their minds to go bluefishing or clamming—berrying if necessary—and so work away and thus defray the expenses of their trip. If the worst came to the worst there were funds obtainable, so as to pay their way. Mr. Bartlett tells of the adventures of these young men in excellent style. Sometimes the treasury, by the sale of fish, was overflowing. At other times there was bankruptcy staring them in the face.

Some swell friends—the Turners—who were steaming around on the *Bianca,* had at times to be evaded. When the money from bluefishing was abundant the lads were dreadfully extravagant. There were cut flowers to deck the yacht with, and when on shore, livery-stable bills

were run up. But somehow luck was on their side, and there was a fair balance generally in their favor. Some of the episodes are neatly put. The whole party came nearly to grief when they had to contribute to a church collection. Sometimes the last cigar was smoked, and there was no money for soap. The "Water Tramps" is a refreshing little volume to be read not alone on the seashore, or on board a yacht, but anywhere. (Putnam. $1.)—*N. Y. Times.*

With the Procession.

"WITH the Procession" is not so impressive a novel in some ways as "The Cliff-Dwellers," with its striking treatment of a vast "sky-scraper" as a kind of pueblo; but it is an uncommonly brilliant and trenchant presentation of phases of Chicago life not brought forward so prominently in the former novel. The family of David Marshall, one of the old settlers, have gradually fallen behind the onward rush of society, living still in their old-fashioned house, and quite strangers to the luxury which his wealth makes possible for them. Jane Marshall, the capable but plain daughter of thirty-three, is given to culture and philanthropy; Rosamund, the youngest, is a beauty and worldly to her finger-tips; Roger, the older son, is a keen lawyer and speculator; Truesdale, the youngest, has travelled long in Europe, while he was supposed to be "getting his education," and he has brought home all the aversion to business of a clever *dilettante* and the moral code of Paris. Jane's social ambition is powerfully awakened by her acquaintance with Mrs. Granger Bates, an old flame of her father's and a truehearted woman, who is at the head of the procession, and the Marshalls fall into line. There is no plot to speak of, and the only tragedy is the peaceful death of David Marshall in his new house. The force of the book is in its telling study of types of Chicago society; its tone is healthy, and its influence must be felt to profit, for without needless exhortation Mr. Fuller makes us feel the supremacy of beauty, goodness, and truth. In a general way "With the Procession" reminds one of Mr.Warner's "Golden House," though it is the less mature work of a younger man. (Harper. $1.25.)—*Boston Literary World.*

Giacinta's Portrait.

THIS street led straight to the opera-house, and suddenly the great building arose before him. It rose up in a massive block against the dark background; feeble jets of gas flickered in the wind on the steps; they threw a sort of half-and-half light on the gigantic boards where the play-bills were posted. Bent's heart beat; he went nearer—yes, it was there! "Undine, romantic operetta in four acts: Fouquè, Albert Lortzing; then Berthalda, daughter of the Emperor Henry; Hugo, Knight of Ringstetten; Kühleborn, a powerful prince of the river; Undine—and instead of her name there were three stars. The three stars were repeated below, and then—Fräulien Giacinta Galieri's first appearance in public." How dead, how cold it looked; how methodically the three stars were printed; how black and stiff the letters of her name! Sadly Bent walked on. It hurt him to see Giacinta's name in print, and open to anybody who chose to look at it. In vain he told himself that this had to be, that it could not be helped, that he himself was a fool to care so much about it; but he could not escape from the bad impression the sight had made upon him.

Thus thinking, he came to the chief bookshop. There was a crowd of people round the window, and cries of wonder and of admiration reached him. As he passed by, he looked mechanically over his shoulder. Then he stopped still—dead still, as though the hand of death had struck him. He saw a lot of books, blue and red, bound with gilt edges and beautiful backs, and there were photographs of celebrated people, of the reigning prince, Schopenhauer, Prince Frederic Charles on horseback riding over the dead bodies of the French, and the crackling shells. But this was not all. In front of everything else, shining in the dazzling light of all the lamps, there was one marvellous

cabinet photograph, and under it, in beautiful Gothic characters. the name of Giacinta Galieri. The portrait was a most extraordinary likeness; but there was a something almost mysterious about it, an expression which it was impossible to define, a look which made one stop to think and wonder. It was a strange mixture of sorrow, of resignation, and of scorn; it was a happy childish face, but there was a look in the eyes which gave one absolute pain. Bent was inside the shop with a bound. An elegant youth, with the sweetest of smiles, came forward to serve him. This engaging young man pranced away to the window, opened it, and, with a gracious movement, swept the picture from under the noses of the people outside, and began to wrap it up in a piece of silver paper.

"Seventeen and a half groschen, if you please," he lisped.

Bent shovelled out his money and paid the youth, then hastily seized his picture and went back into the street. The crowd round the window regarded him angrily. He did not notice them; he hugged his purchase, and ran back home. He wanted to be alone, alone with his picture. His head was raging, he felt half mad. How was it possible for such things to happen? how could Giacinta allow it? Did she know of it? did she approve? No, it could not be. And yet—this was the fashion; it was one of the necessary evils, but it was bitter. What a good thing that he, of all people, should have turned up just at the right minute, and put an end to the thing! How glad he was to be able to bring the picture back into his quiet little room, to have saved it for ever from the curious gaze of the public.

He found a baker's shop, and the sight of the loaves made him realize how hungry he was. He went in and bought two bits of bread and a little fruit and ate them as he went along.

Poor boy! Had he but gone back to the same shop some five minutes later he would have seen a fresh portrait of Giacinta smiling down upon the street. And had he lingered a little longer still he would have seen Herr von Zierow tripping along with a party of friends behind him. Bent would have seen the little man stand by the window, look at Giacinta's picture, pronounce it "delicieuse," and buy it to put in the drawer where he already had a good little hoard of portraits which he termed "conquests," and which had been bought in precisely the same sort of fashion. Von Zierow would open this drawer sometimes after a good dinner and show its contents to his friends. (Dodd, Mead & Co. $1.25.)—*From "Melting Snows."*

The Golden Age.

A PLACE, if you please, ladies and gentlemen; a place, and plenty of room, too, for Kenneth Grahame and his "Golden Age," for it is a precious book, and a sweet and delicate one, for you go back with it to the most delightful of all themes—your own childhood. You might think that all a boy or a girl has ever said has been phonographed over and over again. When it has been attempted, excepting in "Alice in Wonderland," it has been mechanically and monotonously ground out. You heard the creak of the cylinder. How practical at times is Harold, but how at others is he the idealist! And Charlotte! what a whole-souled, perfect little baby woman she is! Then what abundance of fun there is! The children make no attempt to be priggish phenomena. Maybe they are just a trifle cleverer than the usual run of little people.

But it is not all laughing in it, nor is there any crying; only the true poetry of young life, without any exaggerations. The tenderness of it reaches its climax in "The Roman Road." What a glorious happy city the boy chronicles! He tells it all to a wandering artist, who enters *con amore* into the subject. No. The artist does not fool the boy to the top of his bent, for the six-foot painter takes the boy's hand as if he were his equal. The little chap is trotting along the high street of the golden city of his imagination, and the painter strides along with him.

There is pathos, a moral, in the story of Jerry and Rosa, the two dolls Charlotte carries around. Somehow, Kenneth Grahame makes them alive, and there is retribution in the little story, for when Jerry comes to grief—"though the tear of sensibility might moisten the eye, no one who really knew him could deny the justice of his fate." "The Golden Age" is a glorious book—rare of its kind, a discovery, as it were—a little galleon coming back, laden with precious metal, from the El Dorado of your youth. (Stone & Kimball. $1.25.)—*N. Y. Times.*

A LITTLE CITY WAIF.

Lassie.

A PRETTY story of a little city waif, who winds herself around the loving heart of Miss Joy, a single woman, past her youth, whose love-story has had an unexplained interruption. Lassie unconsciously brings the parted lovers together, through their efforts to trace the little one's real history. The book was published some months ago but deserves a wider reading than it has yet enjoyed. It is neatly gotten up and the pictures are pleasing. (Whittaker. 50 c.)

Into the Highways and Hedges.

MISS MONTRÉSOR'S first novel has been long in reaching this side of the Atlantic; but now that it has arrived there can hardly be two opinions as to its remarkable and original power. . . .

Such is a brief outline of the original plot of a novel distinguished in a high degree by noble tone, depth of feeling, and elevation of thought. Miss Montrésor enlists at the outset the interest of the reader who cares for the serious things

SUDERMANN,
Author of "The Wish." D.
Appleton & Co.

of life, and she deepens and retains this interest to the last by her unstrained exposition of the life of men and women whose intellectual errors she sees, but whose central nobility she realizes; as her brief preface says:

"Before and since the days when Socrates found that it was '' impossible to live a quiet life, for that would be to disobey the deity,' there have always been some souls who have counted it worth while to lose all else if haply in the losing they might get nearer to the light from which they came. Their failures, their apparently hopeless mistakes, are often evident enough, yet the mistakes die, and the spirit which animates them lives. It would be dark, indeed, if the torches of those eager runners were to go out."

"Into the Highways and Hedges" has been received with the warmest praise by the English press. We cannot see that a word of their eulogy needs abatement. If Miss Montrésor continues as she has begun she will be a great force in English fiction of the best kind, long remembered when the perverse and morbid sexual school has been forgotten, as it deserves to be.

It is remarkable how high the average of merit continues in the *Town and Country* series. The brown cover with its plain type almost always means a good book and it is always safe to buy almost any one blindfold. (Appleton. $1; pap., 50 c.)—*Boston Litrsery World.*

MISS L. DOUGALL,
Author of "The Zeit-Geist." D.
Appleton & Co.

The Zeit-Geist.

"THE Zeit-Geist" may not have been intended to be a religious book; one would gather that impression from the author's short introduction; and perhaps many dogmatic orthodox readers will not think it is, but it is impossible for one to read it without feeling better for having done so; without having a desire to aid his fellowmen.

The tale of Bart Toyner's struggle with self and sin is a strong, simple one of a most unusual nature. It treats of a struggle that results in a great victory, and the ennobling of a life that learns through God to know of those untold sorrows that creep o'er weary souls that can be alleviated only by closer, warmer heartbeats between man and man.

Heaven, he said, is inside you when you grow to be like God, and through all ages and worlds heaven will be to do as He does; to suffer with those that are suffering and to die with those that are dying. But remember, too, it means to rejoice with those who are rejoicing; and joy is greater than pain and heaviness. And heaven means always to be in peace and strength and delight, because it is along the line of God's will, where His joy flows.

He saw that the whole of the universe goes to develop character, and the one chief heavenly food set within reach of the growing character for its nourishment is the opportunity to embrace malice with love, to gather it in the arms of patience, to convert its shame into glory by willing endurance. (Appleton. 75 c.)—*N. Y. Times.*

Miss Willard on a Bicycle.

"A WHEEL Within a Wheel: How I Learned to Ride the Bicycle, with Some Reflections by the Way," by Frances E. Willard, is ostensibly an account of how the author at "the ripe age of fifty-three" acquired the art of riding a bicycle. If those portions of the narrative immediately concerned with her actual experiences on the wheel had alone been given, the book would have comprised about seven pages, in large type, exclusive of the illustrations; but Miss Willard takes it for granted that we are interested, not only in the technical details of her athletic experiments, but also in all the thoughts called out by her new form of recreation. It will be seen that "A Wheel Within a Wheel" is not exactly a model of construction and style for the literary amateur to follow, but Miss Willard's many friends will undoubtedly prize it, particularly as it contains a lot of portraits of the author, as she appeared both on and off the wheel. (Revell. 50 c.)—*The Beacon.*

Gilbert White of Selborne.

GILBERT WHITE died a hundred years ago, 26th June, 1793; the "Natural History and Antiquities of Selborne" was first published four years earlier. Since then many a book of the same type has appeared and disappeared, but White still keeps his hold upon the English mind. The name of Gilbert White is a household word with every one who loves his own incomparable country, with its thousands of villages as homely and as sheltered at Selborne.

It is strange at first sight that this should be so at a time when we seem passing from a period of poetry and romance into one of stern reality, when the rural population is being drained into the towns, when the squire and the parson are going down in the world, when leisure such as White enjoyed is a rarity and almost a crime, and when the study of economic problems should be driving out of our heads the delights of wild nature or of sport. But the Englishman has always been a strange and self-contradictory creature. With all his commercial instincts and his town-bred vulgarity, his phases of stern Puritanism and political excitement, he has never yet lost that love of the country which is rooted in the life of the manor and the village. Even with the American the same passion still lives; he took it with him to New England in the seventeenth century, and the books of Mr. John Burroughs and Miss Mary Wilkins have lately made us aware how strongly it survives in him in the nineteenth.

What a literature of the fields has sprung up since the "Natural History of Selborne" was first published! Not to mention the poets, from our novelists we seem almost to demand the familiar descriptive background, careless too often whether it be a mere daub, or the work of a master such as Mr. Blackmore or Mr. Hardy. And then again, there is an ever-increasing call for books whose whole intention is to open our wayward eyes to country sights and sounds. Since the days of White we have had Knapp, Howitt, Jesse, Knox, Wood, and others who are still readable and still read; and later, and in a higher region of literature, we have had Kingsley, Jefferies, and Mr. Hamerton. To-day a score of books of the same type are

E. F. BENSON,
Author of "Dodo," D. Appleton & Co.

published every year; and good and bad alike seem to find abundant readers. The Selborne Society has spread all over the land; in most of our public schools there is a Natural History Society, which has taken root in the very citadel of athleticism, and effectually holds its own, issuing its report yearly.

All this literature of the country, all this youthful endeavor, may be traced back not only to the natural instincts of the English country gentleman, like so many other institutions of ours, but to the work of the first country gentleman who could shake himself free from the tyranny of books, and describe what he saw around him in simple and engaging English. White's book has taken possession of the English mind as securely as the "Complete Angler," or even as "Robinson Crusoe." At the distance of a century one may well ask why this is so, and what has given the book its enduring quality. These questions might call forth many answers; I can only state my own. This I will try to do. (Macmillan & Co. $1.75.)—*From Fowler's "Summer Studies of Birds and Book."*

From "On the Point."   Copyright, 1895, by Joseph Knight Co.
MR. MERRITHEW'S SUMMER QUARTERS.

The Literary News.

An Eclectic Monthly Review of Current Literature.

EDITED BY A. H. LEYPOLDT.

AUGUST, 1895.

THOMAS HENRY HUXLEY.

THOMAS HUXLEY was born in 1825. at Ealing, a suburb of London. His father was master in a large semi-public school which at one time had a high reputation. Physically and mentally he was the son of his mother, even in little mannerisms. From his father he inherited only his inborn faculty for drawing, which, unfortunately, was not cultivated, a hot temper, and that amount of tenacity of purpose which unfriendly observers sometimes called obstinacy.

Huxley's mother was a slender brunette, of emotional and energetic temperament.

THOMAS HENRY HUXLEY.
From a photograph by Sarony taken in 1876.

creed, and he commenced the study of medicine under a medical brother-in-law. Later he was horrified to think how very little he ever knew or cared about medicine as the art of healing. The only part of the professional course which really and deeply interested him was physiology, which he has called "the mechanical engineering of living machines." Even when he had made natural science his life-work, he cared chiefly for the architectural and engineering part of the study, "the working out the wonderful unity of plan in the thousands and thousands of diverse living constructions, and the modifications of similar apparatuses to serve diverse ends." All through his student life Huxley acted wholly upon impulse. He worked extremely hard when it pleased him, and when it did not, was extremely idle. He read everything he could lay hands upon, including novels, and took up all kinds of pursuits, to drop them again quite as speedily. The first real and lasting influence towards steadying his mind and practice came to him through Mr. Wharton Jones, who was lecturer on physiology at the Charing Cross School of Medicine. The extent and precision of this man's knowledge impressed the young student greatly, and the severe exactness of his method of lecturing was congenial to Huxley's tastes. It was the only instruction he had received from which he obtained the proper effect of education. Mr. Wharton was extremely kind and helpful, and it was he who suggested the publication of Huxley's first scientific paper in the *Medical Gazette* of 1845.

With no more education than other women of her day, she had great mental capacity. Her most distinguishing characteristic was rapidity of thought. This characteristic she passed on to her son, and to it he traced both his greatest strength and most dangerous weakness.

Huxley's regular school training was of the briefest. The boys he met were average lads with average capacity for good and evil, but he was singularly unfortunate in the men set over him, who, he has told us, "cared about as much for our intellectual and moral welfare as if they were baby-farmers." Very early Huxley became conscious of a great desire to be a mechanical engineer, but it was otherwise de-

Having passed his examinations in 1846, and

being still too young to qualify at the College of Surgeons, Huxley was confronted with the imperative necessity for earning his own bread, and was advised to apply for an appointment for medical service in the navy. The commander of H. M. S. *The Rattlesnake* at this time was looking for an assistant surgeon who knew something of science, and Huxley in due time was appointed to his ship. The opportunities offered for scientific work during the four years' cruise in the South Seas were put to good use by the young surgeon. "To me personally," says Huxley, "the cruise was extremely valuable. It was good for me to live under sharp discipline, to be down on the realities of existence by living on bare necessaries, and more especially to learn to work for the sake of what I got myself out of it, even if it all went to the bottom, and I along with it."

During these four years Huxley sent home communications to the Linnean Society, but they were not published. In 1849 he drew up a more elaborate paper and forwarded it to the Royal Society. On returning to England, in 1850, he found this had been printed and published. For three years after, determining to leave the sea, Huxley applied vainly for a position. During this time he and Professor Tyndall were candidates for chairs in the University of Toronto, Huxley for that of Natural History, and Tyndall for the chair of Physics. At last, in 1854, the Director-General of the Geological Survey offered Huxley the post of Paleontologist and Lecturer on Natural History, an office he held for thirty-one years.

From 1863 to 1869 he was Hunterian Professor at the Royal College of Surgeons. He was twice chosen Fullerian Professor of Physiology at the Royal Institution of Great Britain. In 1869 and 1870 he was president of the Geological Society, having previously served as secretary. During the same period he was president of the Ethnological Society. In 1870 he filled the office of president of the British Association for the Advancement of Science. He was elected a corresponding member of the Academies of Berlin, Munich, St. Petersburg, and other foreign scientific societies. He received honorary degrees from several universities. He was a member of the London School Board from 1870 to 1872. He was elected Lord Rector of the University of Aberdeen in 1872. He became a trustee of the British Museum and a member of the Senate of the University of London. There were no honors in the gift of nations to men of science which did not come naturally to him. He refused recently the decoration of Germany because it was the gift of an Emperor.

This is a brief statement of the facts in the life of Prof. Huxley taken from his own sketch of his life, which appeared in the volume of his collected writings, entitled "Methods and Results" (D. Appleton & Co.). On June 29th the cable announced the death of Thomas Henry Huxley at Eastbourne, England. He succumbed to an attack of bronchitis, followed by a general derangement of the organs of vitality.

With Darwin, Tyndall, and Spencer, Huxley for nearly two generations has stood at the head of science in England; and his has been a directing force in the history of modern progress. He accepted at once the theory of evolution as stated by Darwin in 1858. Tyndall developed this theory on the side of physics, Spencer on the side of social science, Huxley on the side of biology. To the end of his life he maintained that the phenomena of biology were never discordant with the hypothesis of evolution, and were unintelligible where this hypothesis was ignored. As an original investigator Prof. Huxley will not rank with Darwin or Tyndall, and he will be known to future generations less as a great scientist than as one who gave himself successfully to the popularization of science and the development and the organization of scientific education. He was a humanitarian and an enthusiast. All he learned he desired to put within reach of others, and he employed his great gift of expression in written and spoken language to make the educated and uneducated understand, that all the discoveries, theories, and controversies agitating the world were not scientific abstractions, but theories involving truths, which understood, must influence the minds, hearts, and lives of every man, woman, and child who learned to understand them. He was a born teacher, and he had the enthusiasm of a born leader.

In our day when new theories of life are starting up in many minds, when no one is afraid to state the wildest, most untenable hypothesis, when a large public hastens to meet the bearer of any new doctrine, we can hardly understand the spirit in which, in the early sixties, the words uttered by these great English searchers after truth were received. They were called infidels and iconoclasts, and the anathema of the Church was pronounced against them by the most learned and honored of its priesthood. The lectures and papers in which Huxley explained his views denied infidelity and established his position as an agnostic, shook the educated world to its centre. His friend, Herbert Spencer, during Huxley's fierce and bitter combat with the clergy of England, often accused him of having clerical affinities. He had the mind of a theologian and had studied his subject deeply, read widely, was fearlessly courageous, and, after John Bright, the best orator in England, and he delighted in the combat. His intense, bitter, and often irrational prejudice against the representatives of institutional religion was a strange weakness in so well-balanced a mind. A churchman was his *bête noir*. And when in the thick of the fight, he had a dangerous power of sarcasm and a total disregard of the feelings of others, although at heart he was the most lovable of men. He has often explained that he could see no cause for fight between science and religion, but that there must be an undying feud between science and theology. Prof. Huxley's agnosticism was exactly what the word stands for—a state of suspended judgment on matters concerning which he found no basis for positive knowledge or belief. He denied nothing and was always impatient when attempts were made to make him appear as a positive negationist of any faith. He has said himself: "When I reached intellectual maturity I began to ask myself whether I were an atheist, a theist or a pantheist, a materialist or an idealist, a Christian or a free-thinker, and the more I learned and reflected the less ready was the answer, until at last I came to the conclusion that I had neither art nor part with any of these denominations except the last."

And truth and freedom and personal responsibility and perfectibility he preached in season and out of season to the last. His knowledge of scientific facts and of the vastness of knowledge still unattained was such that he found occupation for his whole mind in exploration of the tangible. It has been said that he lacked spiritual insight, but this is hard to maintain of a man who certainly in his day and generation worked unceasingly that the great mass of his fellow-beings might be joint-heirs of all the truth thus far delivered to mankind. He lived during the fifty years when discovery has followed discovery, when every fact has been put to practical use almost before it was verified, when men's intellects were bent to use every new thing for the material improvement of a world they were only beginning to know.

Even before his death a reaction had set in. Material prosperity was established, the world explored, and the men who had borne the burden and heat of the day had begun to feel that all they had acquired did not take away the undefined longing after something no tangible thing can satisfy. Far as science has brought us it can only feed the intellect, and what it is that cries out within us which we call heart and spirit, its scalpel and chemical experiments and agnostic philosophies have not yet brought to light.

It is strange that as Prof. Huxley laid himself down to die he was engaged upon answers to two recent books that have voiced this reaction in philosophies—Kidd's "Social Evolution" and Balfour's "Foundations of belief." It shows how abreast with his generation he was to the very end. Huxley has taught the world to think fearlessly and to despise sham and narrow prejudice.

Let his own words sum up his life-work:

"The objects I have had more or less definitely in view since I began the ascent of my hillock are briefly these: To promote the increase of natural knowledge, and to forward the application of scientific methods of investigation to all the problems of life to the best of my ability, in the conviction that has grown with my growth and strengthened with my strength, that there is no alleviation for the sufferings of mankind except veracity of thought and of actions and the resolute facing of the world as it is when the garment of make-believe, with which pious hands have hidden its uglier features, is stripped off."

George Meredith's Style.

OF course, it may be said that the demands which Mr. Meredith makes of his readers are exorbitant, and that a difficult style is necessarily a bad style. A student of the history of literature, however, knows that the charge of obscurity, which is one of the charges most confidently brought by contemporaries, can be finally adjudicated on only by time. It may be sustained, or it may be refuted. To many of his contemporaries Gray was a tangle of difficulties; for critics of authority in a later period Wordsworth and Shelley and Coleridge wrote unintelligible nonsense; and in our own day we have seen the poetry of Robert Browning slowly but surely expounding itself to a generation. Even caviare, it seems, may become a little fly-blown. Perhaps Mr. Meredith's style is difficult; but difficulty is a relative term, and experience should have taught us that this is a point on which it is wise to reserve an absolute judgment. Sword-practice is difficult to those who have not exercised the muscles of the wrist; and some dancers who foot it merrily in the waltz stand grim against the wall looking condemnation at the lifted leg and pointed toe of the *pas de quatre*. If Mr. Meredith can teach young folk to dance to his music, the most reluctant of us will be forced to admit by-and-by that he has achieved what is the essential thing. Meanwhile it is lawful for any one who pleases to raise a sceptical eyebrow and put the question, "But will he?"

In guessing at the answer to that question

we may find some help from considering another: What has Mr. Meredith to say, be his
manner of saying it good or ill? In a dozen
volumes of prose the eager student of human
nature has told us of his discoveries. Prose is
proved by the achievement of his forty years of
authorship to be the main stream; verse is no
more than a slender affluent. But both are *Dichtung*, and both, it may be added, are *Wahrheit*.
Or, to vary our metaphor, the *Dichtung* written
in prose is the lake, broad-bosomed, with
countless coves and creeks; the *Dichtung* written in verse is a lakelet higher among the
hills, less easy of access, but open to the skies
and to the passage of the stars, though at times
involved in wreathing mists; and a stream runs
down from lakelet to lake, connecting the two
—for Mr. Meredith's prose is at times such prose
as a poet writes, and the thought and feeling
expressed in his novels are fed from the con-
templations of a poet. His subtlety and his
analytic power have in the novels a wider range
of play; his faith and hope are more directly
expressed in his verse. In both prose and
verse his felicities are found in infelicity—or
what for the present seems such; his infelicities
are found amid felicity; he is at once a most alluring and a most provoking writer. (Houghton, Mifflin & Co. $3.)—*From Dowden's " New
Studies in Literature."*

Bartlett's Concordance of Shakespeare.

MR. JOHN BARTLETT's "New and Complete
Concordance of Shakespeare" is the most comprehensive and the most voluminous of the
Shakespearian concordances which have been
compiled in our language or in the German.
It largely exceeds in its citations the familiar
concordance of Mrs. Cowden Clarke, and in its
typography and typographical arrangement it
is distinctly superior to that standard work so
long in use. Its type is larger and clearer,
making reference to it easier. This advantage,
it is true, is offset in part by the greater size of
Bartlett's Concordance, which renders it more
cumbersome. It is a huge quarto of more than
1900 pages, and Mrs. Cowden Clarke's Concordance is a large or royal octavo of only 860
pages; but as a book of reference Bartlett's is
much more convenient, since it gives fuller
quotations of the passages cited. The other
gives merely a clause, usually necessitating a
further reference to Shakespeare himself in
order to obtain a quotable passage. For instance, under Intend, we find in Mrs. Clarke,
" Him first that first intends deceit " (2 Henry
VI.); in Bartlett, " That is good deceit Which
mates him first that first intends deceit." Of
course, there is a great advantage in the fuller

citation in the saving of subsequent consulta-
tions of the passage referred to in the play.
    The number of index words is much larger,
conducing greatly to the assistance of every
one who has occasion to turn to such a concordance. They include examples of the verbs
to be, to do, to have, may, and their tenses, the
auxiliary verb *to let,* and the adjectives *much,
many, more,* and adverbs generally. It is,
therefore, the most complete and serviceable
work of the kind which has yet been prepared,
being both a concordance and a dictionary of
quotations, so that its value practically is un-
approached by any other. Moreover, it is constructed and collated in accordance with the
latest edition of Shakespeare.
    Mr. Bartlett explains modestly in his preface
that the work has been "prepared chiefly in
the leisure taken from active duties, and from
time to time has been delayed by other avocations," but it is a monument to his patient industry, which will become and remain for long
years to come the standard concordance of
Shakespeare. (Macmillan. $14.)—*The Sun.*

The Ameer, Abdur Rahman.

MR. STEPHEN WHEELER, F.R.G.S., and sometime fellow of the Punjab University, gives us
an admirable treatment of the complicated
reigns of Shere Ali and Abdur Rahman during
their defeats and victories, till Abdur finally
triumphed. The straightforward account of
the generally neutral position of England in
regard to the Ameer is supported by quotations
from original state documents and letters.
The biographer presents a very clear idea of
the man, his fortunes and abilities. The
personal incidents are sometimes amusing, as
when he states that the Ameer in holding his
court often kept it in awe, especially the simple
villagers and uncouth hillmen who might chance
to be present, by removing his set of false
teeth, brushing and replacing them. He had
had the advantage of an English dentist, but
to the uninitiated he seemed to be taking himself to pieces. Extracts are given from the
Ameer's publications in regard to his own power
and that of Islam, in which he exhorts his
people to be warriors of God ; even a man of
the lowest rank will receive in paradise seventy-
two houris and eighty-two thousand attend-
ants, and will have seventy couches for his
own repose. An appendix containing the
Ameer's autobiography, given by him during
his exile to the governor-general of Russian
Turkestan, closes this valuable contribution to
the International Series of Public Men of
To-day. (Warne. $1.25.) — *Boston Literary
World.*

Walter Pater's Pleasant Ways.

THOSE who think of Walter Pater as a solemn pundit of æsthetics, says Edmund Gosse in the *Contemporary Review*, may be amazed to know that he delighted in very simple and farcical spectacles and in the broadest of humor. His favorite among modern playwrights was Mr. Pinero, and I shall never forget going with him to see " The Magistrate," when that piece was originally produced. Not a schoolboy in the house was more convulsed with laughter, more enchanted at the romping "business" of the play, than the author of "Marius." He had the gift, when I knew him first, of inventing little farcical dialogues, into which he introduced his contemporaries ; in these the rector of Lincoln generally figured, and Pater had a rare art of imitating Pattison's speech and peevish intonation.

One playful fancy, persisted in so long that even close and old friends were deceived by it, was the figment of a group of relations—Uncle Capsicum and Uncle Guava, Aunt Fancy (who fainted when the word " leg " was mentioned), and Aunt Tart (for whom no acceptable present could ever be found). These shadowy personages had been talked about for so many years that at last, I verily believe, Pater had almost persuaded himself of their existence. Perhaps these little touches will be thought too trifling to be mentioned, but I hold that they were all a part and parcel of his complex and shrouded intellectual life, and therefore not to be forgotten.

MAGAZINE ARTICLES.

Articles marked with an asterisk are illustrated.

ARTISTIC, MUSICAL, DRAMATIC. — *Atlantic,* The New Art Criticism, Mary Logan.—*Century,* Peter Paul Rubens,* Cole.—*Fort. Review* (July.) Pictures of the Year, II.: The French Salons, E. R. Pennell.—*Harper's,* Midsummer Night's Dream,* Lang.—*Lippincott's,* Caricature, Nellie B. McCune.—*Nine. Century* (July.), How to Obtain a School of English Opera, Rowbotham; Colour-Music, Schooling.—*Scribner's,* Pastels of Edwin A. Abbey,* F. Hopkinson Smith; Wood-Engravers, A. Léveillé.

BIOGRAPHY, CORRESPONDENCE. — *Atlantic,* President Polk's Diary, Schouler.—*Century,* Notable Women: Sonya Kovalevsky (Por), Isabel F. Hapgood.

DESCRIPTION, TRAVEL.—*Atlantic,* A Poet's Yorkshire Haunts, Eugenia Skelding.—*Cath. World,* Better than a Trip to Europe,* H. H. Neville.—*Century,* A Bit of Italian Merrymaking: The Lilies of Nola,* Mary Scott-Uda.— *Chautauquan,* Dominion of Canada,* Withrow; Lands of the English Tongue, Cadman.—*Harper's,* Cracker Cowboys of Florida,* Remington; Every-day Scenes in China,* Ralph.—*Lippincott's,* Up Pearson's Lane, Abbott.—*Nine. Century* (July.), My Native Salmon River, Arch. Forbes. — *Scribner's,* All Paris A-wheel,* A. Arsène Alexandre.

DOMESTIC AND SOCIAL.—*Forum,* Appeal to Housekeepers, Christina Goodwin.—*North Am.*

Review, What Men Think of Women's Dress, Crandall (Notes and Comments).

EDUCATIONAL.—*Fort. Review* (July), Against Oxford Degrees for Women, T. Case.—*Forum,* Substitution of Teacher for Text-Book, Rice; Chautauqua: Its Aims and Influence, A. S.Cook.

FICTION.—*Atlantic,* A Woman's Luncheon; Thrift, L. Dougall.—*Century,* Rivalries of Long and Short Codiac, G. W. Edwards; The Cat and the Cherub, C. B. Fernald.—*Chautauquan,* The Senator's Daughters, A. C. Wheeler.—*Harper's,* "Bobbo,"* Wharton; An Evangel in Cyene,Garland; Jimty,* Margaret S. Briscoe; The Little Room, Madelene Y. Wynne.—*Lippincott's,* Little Lady Lee, Mrs. H. L. Cameron; Romance of an Ox-Team, Roberts; A Friend to the Devil, Thompson. — *McClure's,* " Good Hunting,"* Kipling; The Heart of the Princess Osra,* Anthony Hope; The Yellow Dog, Bret Harte; Farming the Taxes,Weyman.—*Scribner's,*" The Wheel of Love,"* Anthony Hope; Our Aromatic Uncle,* H. C. Bunner; Miss Delamar's Understudy,* R. H. Davis; The Rector's Hat,* Noah Brooks; Case of the Guard-House Lawyer,* G. I. Putnam; The "Scab,"* Octave Thanet.

HISTORY. — *Century,* Battle of the Yalu,* P. N. McGiffin; Lessons from the Yalu Fight, A. T. Mahan.—*McClure's,* Moltke in War, Arch. Forbes.

LITERARY.—*Century,* Reminiscences of Literary Berkshire, Sedgwick.—*Chautauquan,* Journalism of the Baptist Church in the U. S.— *Fort. Review* (July.) Leconte de Lisle, Esmé Stuart.—*Forum,* My Literary Recollections, Jókai; The Goethe Archives, Eric Schmidt.— *Harper's,* Roundabout to Boston,* Howells.— *North Am. Review,* "Tendencies " in Fiction, Lang.—*West. Review* (July.) Professor Huxley on Hume and Berkeley, G. C. Greenwood; The Waverley Novels—After Sixty Years, Hannigan.

POETRY.—*Atlantic,* Godfrey's Cove, J. H. Ingham.—*Century,* " Let Me Not Much Complain," T. W. Parsons; " The Green Grass av Owld Ireland," J. W. Riley.—*Harper's,* The Vanished Voice, R. Burton.—*Nine. Century* (July.) Cromwell's Statue, A. C. Swinburne.— *Scribner's,* The Calm, Z. D. Underhill; Summer Song, D. C. Scott; Lights and Shadows, B. P. Blood.

POLITICAL AND SOCIAL.—*Atlantic,* Wrongs of the Juryman, H. N. Shepard; How Judge Hoar Ceased to be Attorney-General, J. D. Cox.—*Chautauquan,* Individual Standard of Living, H. L. Biddle.—*Forum,* Twentieth Century, H. B. Brown; Bond Syndicate, A. B. Hepburn; Drift of Population to Cities, H. J. Fletcher.—*North Am. Review,* Menace of Romanism, President of the A. P. A.; Female Criminals, Griffiths; Solution of War, Mendes; Turning of the Tide, Chief of Bureau of Statistics.—*Scribner's,* Six Years of Civil Service Reform, Roosevelt.

SPORTS AND AMUSEMENTS.—*Century,* Old-Fashioned Fishing, Henry van Dyke; Fox-Hunting in Kentucky,* John Fox, Jr.—*Lippincott's,* The Bicycling Era, J. G. Speed.—*North Am. Review,* What to Avoid in Cycling, Sir B. W. Richardson.

THEOLOGY, RELIGION AND SPECULATION.— *North Am. Review,* Guesses at the Riddle of Existence, Goldwin Smith.—*West. Review* (July.) Sacraments and Rites of the Church, J. Copner.

Survey of Current Literature.

☞ *Order through your bookseller.*—"*There is no worthier or surer pledge of the intelligence and the purity of any community than their general purchase of books; nor is there any one who does more to further the attainment and possession of these qualities than a good bookseller.*"—Prof. Dunn.

ART, MUSIC, DRAMA.

CORBIN, J. The Elizabethan Hamlet: a study of the sources, and of Shakespeare's environment, to show that the mad scenes had a comic aspect now ignored; with a prefatory note by F. Yorke Powell. Scribner. sq. 12°, bds., *net*, $1.25.

DU MAURIER, G. Society pictures. Sergel. unp. il. obl. 24°, $1; pap., 50 c.
One hundred and sixty of Du Maurier's London society pictures, accompanied with a few words of witty dialogue also by Du Maurier.

BIOGRAPHY, CORRESPONDENCE, ETC.

ABBOT, WILLIS J. Carter Henry Harrison: a memoir. Dodd, Mead. por. 8°, $2.50.

BLAIKIE, W. GARDEN, D.D. The personal life of David Livingstone, chiefly from his unpublished journals and correspondence in the possession of his family. Revell. por. 12°, $1.50.
"The purpose of this work is to make the world better acquainted with the character of Livingstone. His discoveries and researches have been given to the public in his own books, but his modesty led him to say little in these of himself, and those who knew him best feel that little is known of the strength of his affections, the depth and purity of his devotion, or the intensity of his aspirations as a Christian missionary. The growth of his character and the providential shaping of his career are also matters of remarkable interest, of which not much has yet been made known."—*Preface.*

DODGE, *Miss* MARY A., ["Gail Hamilton."] Biography of James G. Blaine. The Henry Bill Publishing Co. il. 8°, shp., $3.50; seal rus., $4.25; tky. mor., $7.

HUBBARD, ELBERT. Victor Hugo. Putnam. 16°. (Little journeys to the homes of good men and great.) pap., 5 c.

LECKY, WALTER. Down at Caxton's. Murphy. 12°, pap., 35 c.
Biographical and literary sketches of Richard Malcolm Johnston, F. Marion Crawford, Charles Warren Stoddard, Maurice Francis Egan, John B. Tabb, James Jeffrey Roche, George Parsons Lathrop, Rev. Brother Azarias, Katherine Eleanor Conway, Louise Imogen Guiney, Mrs. Blake, Agnes Repplier. Contains also a paper on Literature and our Catholic poor. Author of "Green graves in Ireland."

LINCOLN, ABRAHAM. Abraham Lincoln: tributes from his associates; reminiscences of soldiers, statesmen and citizens; with introd. by W. Hayes Ward, D.D. Crowell. por. 12°, $1.25; pap., 50 c.
The forty-two articles contained in this volume appeared in the *New York Independent*, April 4, 1895. They were contributed by personal friends and acquaintances of Mr. Lincoln

to commemorate the thirtieth anniversary of his assassination. Their permanent historical value was instantly recognized and numerous requests were made for their publication in book form.

LOYSON, C. HYACINTHE, [*Père* Hyacinthe.] My last will and testament; tr. by Fabian Ware; with an introd. by F. W. Farrar, D.D. Cassell. por. 12°, 50 c.
Three letters explaining the three principal acts of Father Loyson's life—his rejection of the doctrine of Papal Infallibility, his marriage and his belief in the inalienable right of all priests to Christian marriage, and his final formulation of his beliefs. An appendix contains documents relating to his protestation and marriage and to the work of religious reform in France.

RICH, *Mrs.* HELEN HINSDALE. Madame de Stael, the rival of Napoleon. Printed for the author under the direction of Stone & Kimball. 12°, pap., 15 c.
A lecture that the author has often delivered in public. It is a careful analysis of the celebrated French woman's character, influence and works.

ROPES, J. C., DODGE, THEO. A., WALKER, FRANCIS A., *and others.* Critical sketches of some federal and confederate commanders. Houghton, Mifflin & Co. 8°, $2.

WHEELER, STEPHEN. The Ameer Abdur Rahman. Warne. por. il. 12°. (International ser.) $1.25.
Abdur Rahman Khan, born in 1830, was proclaimed Ameer of Afghanistan in 1880. The events of his domestic life and public career are given, and his character as a ruler considered, in chapters entitled: Early endeavors; In banishment; The winning of Cabul; The shaping of a kingdom; The Ameer and his neighbors; The enemy within; The boundaries of Afghanistan; The Durand Mission; A ruler in Islam.

DESCRIPTION, GEOGRAPHY, TRAVEL, ETC.

BARRY, ALFRED (*Canon.*) England's mission to India: some impressions from a recent visit. E. & J. B. Young & Co. 16°, $1.25.

FAGG, *Rev.* J. GERARDUS. Forty years in South China: the life of Rev. John Van Nest Talmage, D.D. A. D. F. Randolph & Co. por. il. 12°, $1.25.
The Rev. John V. N. Talmage was for over forty years identified with the mission at Amoy, China. He was born at Somerville, New Jersey, Aug. 18, 1819, and is a brother of the Rev. T. De Witt Talmage, who furnishes an introduction. By his own wish, he was sent to China in 1847 by the American Board of Foreign Missions of the Reformed Church. His great work there is told by Dr. Fagg, and chapters included on many related subjects.

LUFFMANN, C. BOGUE. A vagabond in Spain. Scribner. fac-simile, 12°, $2.50.

MILN, LOUISE JORDAN. Quaint Korea. Scribner. 12°, $1.75.

MUMMERY, A. F. My climbs in the Alps and Caucasus. Imported by Scribner. il. pl. 4°, net, $7.50.

PARDEE, JEAN. The-Yale-man-up-to-date; with character sketches. 2d ed. The E. P. Judd Co. por. il. 24°, net. $1.
Divided into two parts, "The-Yale-man-up-to-date" and "Character sketches." Under the first heading are papers on : the college widow ; the New Haven flirt ; the out-of-town girl ; the sweet girl at Farmington ; the Yale athlete ; a room in Vanderbilt Hall, etc. The second part embraces pen pictures of Yale celebrities and eccentric characters.

ROBERTS, C. G. D. The Canadian guide-book. Appleton. il. map, 16°, $1.50.
A guide to Eastern Canada and Newfoundland, incl. full descriptions of routes, cities, points of interest, summer resorts, information for sportsmen, etc., and Western Canada to Vancouver's Island. including the Canadian Rocky Mountains and National Park.

SCIDMORE, Miss E. R. Appleton's guide-book to Alaska. New ed. rev. to date. Appleton. maps, il. 12°, flex. cl., $1.25.

WILSON, Mrs. ANNE C. MACLEOD. After five years in India ; or, life and work in a Punjaub district. Imported by Scribner. pls. 8°, $2.

DOMESTIC AND SOCIAL.

BAILEY, HARRIET P. On the chafing-dish : a word for Sunday-night teas. [New ed.] [Also] New things to eat and how to cook them by Mrs. De Salis. G. W. Dillingham. 12°, pap., 50 c.

JEUNE, Lady. Lesser questions. 2d ed. Dodd, Mead & Co. 12°, $1.75.
Contents : A Highland seer and Scotch superstitions; London society; Dinners and diners; Conversation; The revolt of the daughters; The woman of to-day; Extravagance in dress; The crinoline; Helping the fallen; Saving the innocent; Technical education for women; The homes of the poor; The Salvation Army; The domestic servant; The creed of the poor.

LEMCKE, GESINE. European and American cuisine. Appleton. 8°, $2.
A practical and complete guide to household cookery, by the author of " Desserts and salads," who is principal of the Brooklyn Cooking College.

MURREY, T. J. The Murrey collection of cookery books. F. A. Stokes Co. 12°, $1.50.
Contains the following volumes originally published separately : Fifty salads ; Breakfast dainties ; Puddings and dainty desserts ; The book of entrées ; Cookery for invalids ; Practical carving ; Luncheon ; Oysters and fish ; The chafing-dish.

EDUCATION, LANGUAGE, ETC.

DAVIS, NOAH K. Elements of inductive logic. Harper. 12°, $1.
A companion volume to the author's " Elements of deductive logic " ; addressed not only to teachers and academic students, but to graduate and scientific students, and to the general

reader. The matter is in two kinds of type, the larger being for the tyro.

HART, ALBERT BUSHNELL. Studies in American education. Longmans, Green & Co. 12°, $1.25.
Six essays : Has the teacher a profession ? ; Reform in the grammar schools ; University—participation—a substitute for university extension ; How to study history ; How to teach history in secondary schools ; The status of athletics in American colleges. Prof. Hart is of Harvard University and the author of " Introduction to the study of Federal government " and other works.

TAINE, HIPPOLITE ADOLPHE. Les origines de la France contemporaine ; extracts, with English notes, by A. H. Edgren. Holt. por. 16°, bds., 50 c.

FICTION.

BALZAC, HONORÉ DE. Ferragus ; History of the thirteen ; The last incarnation of Vautrin ; from the French, by Katharine P. Wormeley. Roberts. 12°, hf. rus., $1.50.

BALZAC, HONORÉ DE. Novels. V. 1, The wild ass's skin, (La peau de chagrin ;) tr. by Ellen Marriage; with an introd. by G. Saintsbury. Macm'llan. 12°, silk, $1.50.

BARLOW, JANE. Maureen's fairing ; il. by Bertha Newcombe. Macmillan. 12°, (Iris ser.) 75 c.

BARRETT, FRANK. John Ford, his faults and follies, and what came of them ; and His helpmate. United States Book Co. 12°, $1 ; pap., 50 c.
Two stories of every-day English life in which love plays a large part.

BARTLETT, G. HERBERT. Water tramps ; or, the cruise of the Seabird. Putnam. il. 16°, $1.

BEERS, H. A. The ways of Yale in the Consulship of Plaucus. Holt. 1 il. nar. 16°, (Buckram ser.) 75 c.

BESANT, WALTER. In deacon's orders, and other stories. Harper. 12°, $1.25.

BISHOP, W. H. The garden of Eden, U. S. A.: a very possible story. C. H. Kerr & Co. 12°, (Library of progress, no. 15.) $1.
In a story of modern life and love is proposed a common-sense, practical solution of the labor question, not by legislation but by the mutual efforts of individuals. It suggests incidentally a readjustment of domestic economy that will preserve the sacredness of homes, but at the same time release women from their dull round of cooking, dusting, etc., and open up for every woman some useful activity suited to her own taste and capacity. It shows how the isolation and monotony of the farm life of to-day may be obviated, by bringing farm and city together, keeping the best features of each.

BJORNSON, BJORNSTJERNE. The heritage of the Kurts ; from the Norwegian, by Cecil Fairfax. United States Book Co. 12°, $1 ; pap., 50 c.
A study in heredity and systems of education, especially education for girls. The original Kurt was a German skipper of princely family whose ship was brought into a Norwegian habor. The descendants are the characters in

a story of quiet lives. Edmund Gosse has furnished an introduction giving a short characterization of the author's works. The story ends in 1830.

"As fiction 'The heritage of the Kurts' ranks very high among Bjornson's novels. Indeed, I do not know that he has ever excelled the urgent and strenuous vigor of those first few chapters in which he describes the rise and fall of the dark race of the Kurts. Published in 1884 under the title 'Flags are flying in town and over the harbor.'"—*N. Y. Commercial Advertiser.*

CRAIGIE, CHRISTOPHER. An old man's romance: a tale. Copeland & Day. 16°, $1.25.

An old man of seventy is the narrator; he details the causes which interrupted his first love, and relates the consolation he finds in the friendship of the daughter of his early love. The scene is an old New England town.

CURTIN, JEREMIAH, *comp.* Tales of the fairies and of the ghost-world: coll. from oral tradition in southwest Munster. Little, Brown & Co. 12°, $1.25.

D'ARCY, ELLA. Monochromes. Roberts. 16°, (Keynotes series, No. 12.) $1.

A half dozen stories; their names are: The elegie; Irremediable; Poor Cousin Louis; The pleasure pilgrim; White magic; The expiation of David Scott.

DIX, GERTRUDE. The girl from the farm. Roberts. 16°, (Keynotes ser.) $1.

"Distinctly a story with a purpose, that purpose being to demonstrate once more the wrong committed by society in insisting upon a different moral standard for women from that established in the case of men. The story as a whole is a very artistic piece of work because the ethical purpose is not unduly emphasized, but is allowed to work itself out in a perfectly natural way. The Marchants are undoubtedly typical of a class that really exists in American as well as in English life, and rightly considered the book has a lesson which parents everywhere may ponder with profit."—*The Beacon.*

DUFF, CONOVER. The master knot, and "Another story." Holt. 1 il. nar. 16°, Buckram ser. 75 c.

Letters passed between two men friends and a bright intelligent girl tell a love-story with a most pathetic ending. One of the writers settles in Ohio to quarry stone and improve the condition of his laborers; the other, after roaming around the world, becomes partner in a money-making concern. The girl calmly judges both, and chooses for her best development. The tragedy brings her to the home of the other. "Another story" deals with work in university settlements.

ELIOT, GEORGE, [*pseud.* for *Mrs.* J. W. Cross.] Complete works. *New illustrated cabinet ed.* In 24 v. V. 15. Merrill & Baker. il. 12°, *ea.*, $1.50; large-paper, *edition de luxe* (limited to 200 sets), *per set*, $72.

The works issued so far in this edition are as follows: Middlemarch, 3 v.; Felix Holt, 2 v.; Romola, 3 v.; Essays and scenes of clerical life, 2 v.; Theophrastus Such and miscellaneous essays, 1 v.; Daniel Deronda, 3 v.

GALT, J. The annals of the Parish and Ayrshire legatees; il. by C. E. Brock; with an

introd. by Alfred Ainger. Macmillan. 12°, (Macmillan's illustrated standard novels.) $1.25. *Same.* Roberts. 8°, *ea.* $1.25.

"Lovers of Scotch fiction, which is having its day in the reading world, some of it for the second time, will not be sorry to know that the good old house of Blackwood & Sons is about to publish a new illustrated edition of the novels of John Galt, which enjoyed a great vogue in their time, which was the time of the 'Waverley Novels,' and that Mr. S. R. Crockett is to write an introduction to them, a task for which he may be fitted, though we hardly judge so from the character of his own writings."—*Mail and Express.*

GREEN, ANNA KATHARINE [*now Mrs.* C. Rohlfs.] Doctor Izard. Putnam. il. 12°, $1; pap., 50 c.

Dr. Izard, a successful New England physician with a nagging Puritan conscience, endeavors in a roundabout way to settle a modest fortune upon a young girl, so as to in a measure expiate a wrong he has unintentionally done her. He thinks his secret is his own, but his plans have been overheard by a rascal, who personates a man long dead and endeavors to wrest the money from the young heiress. The result is a dramatic confession.

HAEDICKE, PAUL. The 'equalities of Para-Para; written from the dictations of G. Rambler, M.D., by Paul Haedicke. Schuldt-Gathmann Co. il., 12°, (Progressive ser., v. 1, no. 1.) pap., 25 c.

An imaginary African explorer, Dr. Rambler, tells a story of a strange people he claims to have discovered in the heart of the Desert of Sahara, and by whom for nearly a year he was held as a national prisoner. A perfect state of equality exists in Para-Para, every person being reduced artificially, in body and mind, to the normal standard of the equalities. The distinctions of sex have almost disappeared, and the only thinking, self-assertive individuals are the members of a society of outcasts called "Sophs." The social and political problems which brought about the existing condition of the equalities are set forth.

HALL, GERTRUDE. Foam of the sea, and other tales. Roberts. 12°, $1.

Contents: Foam of the sea; In Battlereagh House; Powers of darkness; The late returning; The wanderers; Garden deadly.

"Miss Hall's imagination is largely controlled by her ample knowledge of literature. Its flights do not reveal new fields or develop new ideas. But she has a wonderful gift of language, which she abuses a little sometimes, and fine artistic feeling."—*N. Y. Times.*

HARDY, T. The Mayor of Casterbridge: a story of a man of character. *New ed.*, with etched frontispiece. Harper. 8°, $1.50.

HARLAND, H., ["Sidney Luska," *pseud.*] Gray roses. Roberts. 16°, (Keynotes ser., no. 10.) $1.

Nine stories entitled : The Bohemian girl; Mercedes; A broken looking-glass; The reward of virtue; A reincarnation; Flower o' the quince; When I am king; A responsibility; Castles near Spain.

HARRISON, *Mrs.* CONSTANCE CARY, [*Mrs.* Burton Harrison.] An errant wooing. The Century Co. il. 12°, $1.50.

"In this story Mrs. Burton Harrison has attempted what many before her have essayed to do, namely, to utilize the experiences of a European journey over well-beaten tracks by weaving them in as background and environment in and against which the characters of a novel shall enact their parts. Sooth to say, she has succeeded in her attempt better than many of her precursors. The story of the two young Americans whose grandfather insists upon their marrying each other while their inclinations decide them to marry some one else is entertaining enough to float a great deal of descriptive matter about the Alhambra, Gibraltar, Seville, London, the country lanes of Devonshire, and other localities familiar to other travellers."—*Boston Literary World.*

HOPKINS, SEWARD W. On a false charge: a novel; il. by Hugh M. Eaton. Bonner. 12°, (Ledger lib., no. 121.) $1; pap., 50 c.
A strike in the coal-mines of Pennsylvania, a murder, and an innocent man falsely accused by a bitter enemy are the chief incidents, followed by a trial and the discovery of the real criminal. Love plays a part in the story, and a picture taken from life is given of a miner's hardships and the unjust treatment often accorded him by the "bosses."

HUME, FERGUS. The third volume. Cassell. 12°, $1.
A young English author made a great success with a story in three volumes, entitled "A whim of fate." Its plot told of a murder committed twenty-five years before, and in the "third volume" were given a few details that had not been followed up in the trial. This book, read by different people, about the same time, led to the discovery of some of the actors in the real tragedy, and the novel is a detective story which ingeniously follows and drops some most unexpected clues and finally explains the truth in still more unexpected manner.

IRVING, WASHINGTON. The sketch-book of Geoffrey Crayon, gentn. *Author's rev. ed.* McKay. 8°, $2; $4.

JAMES, H. Terminations. Harper. 12°, $1.25.
"Mr. Henry James has apparently been amusing himself in mystifying the public of late years by producing annually a volume of short stories the plots of which are incomprehensible to the lay mind. This latest volume, although distinguished by even more than his usual subtlety of style, is fortunately quite lucid as to plot. 'The death of the lion' and 'The middle years' might be called studies in hero-worship; the character sketches are simple and sympathetic, the incidents are natural, and the whole point of view of these stories is like a happy return to Mr. James' earlier and pleasanter, if less pyrotechnically clever, literary form. The other two stories are less interesting. 'The Coxon fund' is a most confused tale, and 'The altar of the dead' has a romantic turn quite outside Mr. James' own field."—*Boston Literary World.*

KENNARD, Mrs. E. Wedded to sport. Lovell, Coryell & Co. 12°, (Lakewood ser., no. 13.) pap., 50 c.
Sir Philip Verschoyle, a keen sportsman, being in love with his Cousin Blanche, of like tastes, is foiled in his intention of marrying her on account of his own selfishness. Incited

by pique, he marries a girl of opposite inclinations. The story of this ill-assorted union offers many comparisons and a final tragedy. The scene is in the Midlands, England.

KING, CHARLES. Captain Dreams, and other stories. Lippincott. 12°, $1; pap., 50 c.
"It is Captain King who leads off with his 'Captain Dreams,' and that captain is a singularly absent-minded gentleman, and would have lost his head, but Captain de Remer can fall back on his reserve, Mrs. de Remer, for it is this lady who invariably saves him. There are a number of military gentlemen, a lady and a civilian or two, who follow in Captain King's lead, and there always is a glint of army buttons, and a reminiscence of Benny Havens in the stories. Altogether, 'Captain Dreams' is a highly entertaining collection of yarns."—*N. Y. Times.*

KING, CHARLES. The story of Fort Frayne. Neely. 12°, $1.25.
"The method of its manufacture lends to 'The story of Fort Frayne' a rather choppy quality. It is not as smooth and intelligible as most of Captain King's tales. But it is breezy, spirited, and stirring, and contains some admirable descriptive passages."—*N. Y. Times.*

LONGUS, —. Daphnis and Chloé; traduction d'Amyot revue by P. L. Courier; il. by Paul Leroy. Meyer Bros. 16°, (Collection le-merre illustrée.) pap., 60 c.
A Greek pastoral romance of the fourth or fifth century, attributed to Longus, a Greek sophist. Translated into all European languages. This French translation first appeared in the sixteenth century. The loves of Daphnis and Chloé are said to have furnished the inspiration for Tasso's "Aminta," Allan Ramsay's "Gentle shepherd," St. Pierre's "Paul and Virginia," etc.

MARRYAT, F. Japhet in search of a father; il. by H. M. Brock; with an introd. by D. Hannay. Macmillan. 12°, (Illustrated standard novels.) $1.25.

MARTEL - JANVILLE, (*Countess de*),] ["Gyp," *pseud.*] A Gallic girl (*Le mariage de Chiffon*); tr. by the editor [H. Pène Du Bois]. Brentano's. 8°, (Modern life lib., ed. by H. Pène Du Bois, no. 1.) $1.25.

MARTEL - JANVILLE, (*Countess de*), ["Gyp," *pseud.*] Chiffon's marriage (*Le mariage de Chiffon*); tr. by M. L. J. Lovell, Coryell & Co. 16°, $1; pap., 50 c.

MARTEL - JANVILLE, (*Countess de*), ["Gyp," *pseud.*] Chiffon's marriage; tr. by Mrs. Patchett Martin; il. by H. C. Edwards. Stokes. 16°, (Bijou ser.) 50 c.

MARTEL - JANVILLE, (*Countess de*), ["Gyp," *pseud.*] Chiffon's marriage; from the French, by *Mrs.* E. Lees Coffey. Hurst. 1 il. 16°, 50 c.

MURRAY, D. CHRISTIE. The martyred fool: a novel. Harper. 12°, $1.25.

NEEDELL, Mrs. J. HODDER. The vengeance of James Vansittart. Appleton. 12°, (Appleton's town and country lib., no. 169.) $1; pap., 50 c.
A bright, beautiful girl, to save her family from dire distress, marries the heir of James Vansittart. From low motives of jealousy her

husband is disinherited. He is of a weak nature, and he gives up and lives on a little pittance provided by his wife's grandmother. The life of a woman with a man whom she has never loved and cannot respect is described in detail. A scholarly physician who had great influence in educating Diana Vansittart plays a very important part in her life, and although loving her passionately, teaches her steadily to do her duty to herself and her husband.

NORRIS, W. E.   Billy Bellew : a novel. Harper.   il. 8°, $1.50.

PARKER, GILBERT.   Pierre and his people: tales of the far north. Stone & Kimball.   12°, (Green tree lib.) *net*, $1.25.

PASTON, G.   A study in prejudices.   Appleton. 12°, (Appleton's town and country lib., no. 170.) $1 ; pap., 50 c.
Current prejudices as to innocent and harmful flirtation ; as to art studies for the advancement of art and studies for "pot boilers" ; as to the necessary and superfluous education of women as a means of fitting them to be true and comforting helpmeets to intellectual and artistic husbands; as to the merging of a wife's individuality in her husband's career ; as to the moral law to be meted to men and women—are all discussed in a story in which the narrative, romantic element is still allowed to predominate.

PERRY. BLISS.   The plated city.   Scribner. 12°, $1.25.
The story takes place in a Connecticut town, whose chief industry is silver-plating. The characters around whom the interest centres are Dr. Atwood, the owner of the silver plate works, two young men, a lawyer and an architect, a girl librarian, and a pretty Canadian and her brother, who are suspected of having colored blood in their veins. The story is one of love and intolerance, in which unexpected family secrets are brought to light. The title has a double meaning.

PHILLPOTTS, EDEN.   A deal with the devil. Warne & Co.   il. 12°, $1.
The night before his hundred birthday Mr. Daniel Dolphin has a dream, in which he makes a compost with the devil for ten years more of life. In every year he is to live ten years and to go backwards from his present age to nonexistence. The story is told by his granddaughter. The dream comes true and the incidents of his life as he grows younger hour by hour are described with rare humor.

PUGH, EDWIN W.   A street in Suburbia.   Appleton.   12°, $1.
The "Suburbia" is more a social suburbia than a municipal suburb. A hero of very humble life makes up his mind to marry. He proposes to five girls. Descriptions of these girls are creations in character. The meeting-place for the hero and his special chums is an old school-house. Incidentally the story brings in a treatise on education in rural districts. The stern, biassed judgments of men and things by natural uneducated men who "call a spade a spade" are woven into a very simple plot.

ROOD, H. E.   The company doctor : an American story.   The Merriam Co.   12°, $1.
A story showing the dangers which may result from unrestricted emigration ; the scene is laid in a mining town in the coal regions of Pennsylvania.

SCANLAN, ANNA C.   Dervorgilla; or, the downfall of Ireland; completed and rev., with preface and notes, by C. M. Scanlan.   C. M. Scanlan.   il. map, 12°, *net*, $1.25.
A story of the life and times of Dervorgilla and her husband, Prince O'Rourk, of Breiny, A.D. 1108 to 1193, covering the last years of the Irish monarchy. The customs, dress, games, music, religious councils and wars of the Irish are portrayed, and the causes of Ireland's downfall clearly shown. Each chapter brings out some important fact, custom, or prominent event in the life of Dervorgilla.

SERGEANT, ADELINE.   The mistress of Quest: a novel.   Appleton.   12°,(Appleton's town and country lib., no. 171.) $1; pap., 50 c.
A story of the Cumberland fells sides of England. A selfish artist marries a farmer's daughter ; their child becomes the "Mistress of Quest," the old farmer's property. Later he marries into fashionable circles and dies leaving a daughter of eighteen penniless. The love-story of the two half-sisters, one a tower of strength, the other a pretty, appealing young girl, is worked out with many details, including manslaughter and a domestic tragedy ending in insanity. The climax is reassuring.

WARD, *Mrs.* MARY AUGUSTA. [*Mrs.* T. Humphry Ward.]   The story of Bessie Costrell. Macmillan.   16°, 75 c.

WATSON, AUGUSTA CAMPBELL.   Off Lynnport Light: a novel.   Dutton.   il. 12°, $1; pap., 50 c.
A little New England fishing village, hidden among the rocks where the waters of Long Island Sound empty into the ocean, is the scene. The great-grandfather of the heroine fought side by side with Washington; her grandmother's early love troubles cast their shadows upon Ruth's first romance. An ideal Christian minister makes Ruth his wife and by years of devotion awakens the heart she frankly had told him lay dead in her. The love affairs of an old couple and the part played by a pet dog furnish the contrasting humor for a rather sad story.

HISTORY.

BRUCE, MINER W.   Alaska, its history and resources. gold fields, routes, and scenery. Lowman & Hanford Stationery and Printing Co.   map, il. 8°, $1.25 ; pap., 75 c.
Six years spent in Alaska, first in the interests of journalism and later in connection with the Bureau of Education and the census reports, enable the author to present accurate accounts of the leading industries of the country, its resources, including the great Yukon gold fields, its railroads, the possibilities of a span of communication with the Old World, etc. Great opportunities for investment and for laying the foundations of lucrative business enterprises are foreseen by the writer.

GUERBER, H. A.   Legends of the Rhine. Barnes.   il. 12°, $2.
Intended as a contribution to the study of folklore and as a legendary guide to the Rhine. The tales have been gathered from many sources and include the principal Rhine tradi-

tions. As Teutonic mythology has been outlined in " Myths of northern lands " it is omitted from this volume ; the real " Nibelungenlied" and the " Heldensaagen " also, as they
form part of the author's " Legends of the Middle Ages."

LARNED, JOSEPHUS NELSON. History for ready
reference from the best historians, biographers, and specialists; their own words in a
complete system of history; for all uses, extending to all countries and subjects and representing for both readers and students the
better and newer literature of history in the
English language; with historical maps by
Alan C. Reiley. In 5 v. V. 5. Tunnage to
Zyp and supplement C. A. Nichols Co. maps,
4°, $5; buckram or shp., $6; hf. mor., $7.50.
The supplement contains: 1, Some passages
translated from German and French writings,
touching matters treated in the body of the
work. 2, Some postscripts on recent events,
and some excerpts from recents books. 3.
Treatment of some topics omitted in the body
of the work. 4, Cross-references needed to
complete the subject-indexing of the work
throughout. 5. A complete series of chronological tables, by centuries. 6, A series of dynastic genealogies. 7, Select bibliographies,
partly annotated, of several of the more important fields of history. 8, A list of works,
quoted from in the compilation of this work,
with names of publishers.

PROWSE, D. W. History of Newfoundland;
from the English, Colonial, and foreign records ; with a prefatory note by Edmund
Gosse. Macmillan. maps, il. 8°, $8.
" The 717 pages of the present volume may
deter ordinary readers. But the student and
the statesman will appreciate the value of Judge
Prowse's monumental work, and we shall be
surprised if the diplomatist does not derive
fresh knowledge from its study."—N. Y. Commercial Advertiser.

RHODES, JA. FORD. History of the United
States from the compromise of 1850. V. 3.
1860-1862. Harper. 8°, $2.50.
Volumes 1 and 2 were published in 1892. The
present volume covers nearly three years of
eventful history, ending in the spring of 1892.
The opening chapter is a résumé of our material progress from 1850 to 1860: four other
chapters describe Lincoln's first election, Buchanan's failure, sentiment in the slave States,
the progress of secession, the firing on Sumter,
the outbreak of the Civil War, and the events
which ensued down to the Battle of Shiloh and
the capture of New Orleans.

ROBERTS, F. SLEIGH (Lord.) The rise of Wellington. Roberts Bros. pors. plans, 12°,
(Pall Mall Gazette Magazine lib., no. 2.)
$1.25.
The military career of Wellington naturally
divides itself into three periods—the Indian
period, the Peninsular period, and the period
during which he commanded the allied forces
in the Netherlands, terminating in the battle of
Waterloo. In three chapters, relating in turn
to each of these periods, the principal incidents
of this great soldier's life are briefly described.

HYGIENIC AND SANITARY.

TRACY, ROGER S., M.D. Handbook of sani-

tary information for householders. [New
rev. ed.] Appleton. sq. 16°, 50 c.
Containing facts and suggestions about ventilation, drainage, care of contagious diseases,
disinfection, food and water; with appendices
on disinfectants and plumbers' materials.

LITERARY MISCELLANY, COLLECTED WORKS, ETC.

DANA, J. C., Parsons, J., and Tandy, F. D.
Public Library handbook Denver ; by the
Public Library of Denver [Anon.] The Car-
son-Harper Co. il. 16°, 65 c.; pap., 35 c.;
mor., $1.
J. C. Dana, the librarian of the Denver Public
Library, prepared the following chapters :
Starting a library ; Advertising a library ; Selecting books ; Books suggested for a school
library ; Buying books; Periodicals; Some periodicals suitable for a small library ; Lending
systems for small libraries ; Cataloguing and
classifying a small library. J. Parsons contributed articles on: Lending books, catalogues,
charging books, suggestions to assistants in
issuing cards, sending notices, etc., and other
counter work. F. D. Tandy's chapters are on
accession and routine work, classifying and
cataloguing, binding, taking account of stock,
etc.

GRISWOLD, W. M., comp. A descriptive list of
novels and tales dealing with the history of
North America. W. M. Griswold. 8°, pap.,
$1.
The second part of " Historical novels," the
first being devoted to novels of ancient life.
A chronological list, the titles being followed
by long descriptive extracts taken from the
literary columns of leading papers.

HOWELLS, W. D. My literary passions. 12°,
$1.50.
Essays on : Goldsmith; Cervantes; Irving;
First fiction and drama ; Longfellow's Spanish
student; Scott; Pope; Uncle Tom's cabin; Os-
sian; Shakespeare; Ik Marvel; Dickens; Wordsworth; Lowell; Chaucer; Macaulay; Critics and
reviews; A non-literary episode; Thackeray;
Lazarillo de Tormes; Curtis; Longfellow; Schle-
gel; Tennyson; Heine; De Quincy; Goethe;
George Eliot; Charles Reade; Dante; Goldoni;
Tourguenief; Auerbach; Tolstoy, etc.

MURRAY, ALEX. S. Manual of mythology,
Greek and Roman, Norse and old German,
Hindoo, and Egyptian mythology; rev. and
corr. on the basis of the 20th ed. of Petiscus.
McKay. pls. il. 12°, $1.25.

NATURE AND SCIENCE.

BROOKLYN ETHICAL ASSOCIATION. Life and the
conditions of survival: the physical basis of
ethics, sociology, and religion : popular lectures and discussions before the Brooklyn
Ethical Association. Kerr. 12°, $2.
Contents : Cosmic evolution as related to ethics, by L. G. Janes, M.D.; Solar energy, by A.
Emerson Palmer; The atmosphere and life, by
Rob. G. Ercles, M.D.; Water, by Rossiter W.
Raymond; Food as related to life and survival,
by Prof. W. O. Atwater; The origin of structural variations, by Prof. E. D. Cope; Locomotion and its relation to survival, by Martin L.
Holbrook, M.D.; Labor as a factor in evolution,
by D. Allyn Gorton, M.D.; Protective covering,

by Mrs. Lizzie Cheney Ward; Shelter, as related to the evolution of life, by Z. Sidney Sampson; Habit, by Rev. J. White Chadwick; From natural to Christian selection, by Rev. J. C. Kimball; Sanitation, by Ja. Avery Skilton; Religion as a factor in social evolution, by Rev. E. P. Powell.

COMSTOCK, J. H., *and* BOTSFORD, ANNA. A manual for the study of insects. Comstock Pub. Co. 12°, *net*, $3.75.

HARTMANN, E. v. The sexes compared, and other essays; selected and tr. by A. Kenner. Macmillan. 12°, 90 c.

LYDEKKER, R., *ed.* The royal natural history. Warne. col. pl. il. 8°, (Warne's library of natural history, in 36 nos., v. 1, no. 2.) *subs.*, pap., 50 c.

Treats of American monkeys; White cheeked, white throated, and crested sapajon; Spider monkeys; Squirrel monkeys; Saki monkeys; Howlers and marmosets.

MINOT, H. D. Land birds and game birds of New England. *New ed.*; ed. by W. Brewster. Houghton, Mifflin & Co. il. 8°, $3.50.

SHALER, N. S. Beaches and tidal marches of the Atlantic coast. American Book Co. 8°, (National geographic monographs, v. 1, no. 5.) pap., 20 c.

POETRY AND DRAMA.

AUSTEN, JANE. Duologues and scenes from the novels of Jane Austen; arr. and adapted for drawing-room performance by Rosina Filippi (Mrs. Dawson); il. by Miss Fletcher. Macmillan. 12°, $1.

HERRICK, ROB Selections from the poetry of Robert Herrick; ed. by E. Everett Hale, jr. Ginn. por. 12°, (Athenæum Press ser.) $1.

POLITICAL AND SOCIAL.

BLISS, W. DWIGHT PORTER. A handbook of socialism; a statement of socialism in its various aspects and a history of socialism in all countries, with statistics, biographical notes on prominent socialists, bibliography, calendar, chronological table, and chart. Scribner. 12°, $1.25.

BOUTON, J. BELL. Uncle Sam's church. his creed, Bible, and hymn-book. [*2d ed.*] Lamson, Wolffe & Co. 12°, leatherette, *net*, 50 c.

The cult of patriotism is the author's subject; the following the means by which he would have it spread: by hanging the "Declaration of Independence" and the "Constitution of the United States" entire on the walls of every post-office in the United States; by printing as tracts, Washington's farewell address. his life, a life of John Adams, of Thomas Jefferson and other patriots, and circulating them freely; these pamphlets bound together and illustrated he calls Uncle Sam's Bible; his hymn-book is a collection of patriotic songs. He asks the Government to start a propaganda with these documents for its weapons.

BOYNTON, H. V. The National Military Park, Chickamauga-Chattanooga: an historical guide. The Rob. Clarke Co. maps, il. 8°, $1.50.

A description of the National Military Park and its thirty-six miles of approaches along Missionary Ridge, over Lookout Mountain and about Chickamauga; also contains a history of the campaigns and battles for Chattanooga, with guides to each of the fields; a history of the Chickamauga Memorial Association and of the present park project which took its place; an account of the action of Congress establishing the park; a list of the State Commissioners, with a statement of their work, and a full account of the work completed at the park, that in progress and that contemplated.

DONNELLY, IGNATIUS. The American people's money. Laird & Lee. 1 il. 12°, 50 c.; pap., 25 c.

The scene is a palace sleeping-car on its way from Chicago to the Pacific. The discussion is opened by a bank president and a farmer, others afterwards joining in. Beginning with the currency question and the present condition of finances, the talk wanders to other relative subjects taking in the income tax, trusts, etc., the poverty of the poor, the great wealth now concentrated in a few hands, etc.

GANNETT, H. The building of a nation: the growth, present condition and resources of the United States, with a forecast of the future. The H. T. Thomas Co. col. pl., maps, diagrams, 8°, *subs.*, $2.50.

A statistical summary by the chief geographer of the U. S. Geological Survey and of the Tenth and Eleventh Censuses. It blends in a plain, straightforward account the main physical features of industrial, social and political history which have been factors in the growth of the nation; ingeniously illustrated with many maps and charts in colors.

HARVEY, W. H., ["Coin," *pseud.*] The money of the people. Sergel. 12°, pap., 25 c.

HENSCHEL, ALBERT E. Municipal consolidation: historical sketch of the Greater New York. American News Co. map, sq. 8°, pap., 25 c.

A brief popular account of the progress and meaning of the "Greater New York." The facts and information presented have been culled from a mass of material gathered in the study of municipal affairs. The historical references to the Greater New York are collated here for the first time. The views and suggestions advanced represent the opinions of the author individually, and not in his capacity of Secretary of the Municipal Consolidation Inquiry Commission.

How to govern Chicago, by a practical reformer. C. H. Kerr & Co. 12°, (Library of progress, no. 14.) pap., 25 c.

The author points out the real conditions and requirements of Chicago, reviews its political history for a year or two, exposes the false pretences of reform, and shows, as he says, "in plain, blunt, strong terms, such as may prove valuable to readers in every American city, how to govern Chicago from the standpoint of a practical reformer."

LANDON, MELVILLE D., ["Eli Perkins," *pseud.*] Money, gold, silver, or bimetallism. Kerr. por. il. 12°, pap., 25c.

Against the free coinage of silver and a plea for judicious bimetallism: statistics are furnished throughout by Mr. Preston, Superintendent of the Mint, and Superintendent of the Census Bureau. The book ends with a startling apochrypal story, showing the effect of free coinage on the business and prosperity of the country.

LATANÉ, J. H. The early relations between Maryland and Virginia. [*Also*] Is history past politics? by Herbert B. Adams. The Johns Hopkins Press. 8°, (Johns Hopkins Univ. studies, 13 ser., no. 3–4.) pap., 50 c.

The purpose of this paper is to give an account of the relations between Virginia and Maryland from the settlement of the latter colony to the agreement between Lord Baltimore and the agents of Virginia in November, 1657, when Lord Baltimore was permitted to assume control of the government of his province, which had been taken out of his hands five years before by the commissioners of Parliament, and since that time held by the Puritans.—*Introduction.* Contains a bibliography (1 p.) of books consulted in the preparation of this article.

MONEY, SILAS H., (*pseud.*) Base "Coin" exposed; being the arrest, exposure, and confession of W. H. H. Money, and the dismissal of the so-called "Coin's financial school." Weeks. 1 il. 12°, (Melbourne ser., no. 33.) pap., 25 c.

Under the pseudonym of "Silas Honest Money" an answer is made to "Coin's" free

silver theories. In an appendix Horace White's "Coin's financial fool" is given in full.

RAND, B. A bibliography of economics. Wilson. 8°, $1.25.

SEYMOUR, HORATIO W. Government and Co., limited: an examination of the tendencies of privilege in the United States. McClurg. 16°, 75 c.

The author points out the delirious craze for wealth has laid hold of government in this Republic and has made privilege institutional. He claims privilege has no right to exist in a Republic. The dangers of privilege in lowering the tone of the people are ruthlessly stated. The writer claims the government can never be reformed until the people reform themselves and support the government instead of looking to the government to support the people. A strong plea for a true American spirit and nobler ideals than money and position.

SHAW, W. A. The history of currency, 1252–1894. Putnam. *net*, $8°, 3.75.

WATERLOO, STANLEY. Honest money: "Coin's" fallacies exposed. The Equitable Pub. Co., il. 12°, (Equitable ser., v. 1, no. 1.) pap., 25 c.

RECENT FRENCH AND GERMAN BOOKS.

FRENCH.

Ardel, H. Rêve blanc. 12° (Plon)	$1 00
Barracaud, L. L'Adoration. 12° (Lemerre)	1 00
Baude de Maurceley. Le triomphe du cœur. 12° (Ollendorff)	1 00
Beaume, G. Corbeille d'or. 12° (Plon)	1 00
Bire, E. Journal d'un bourgeois de Paris, pendant la Terreur. I: La Convention. 12° (Levy)	1 00
Bondois, P. Napoléon et la société de son temps. 8° (Alcan)	2 10
Borden, C. de. Le destin d'aimer. 12° (Plon)	1 00
Bourdeau, I. La Rochefoucauld. 12° (Hachette). (Collection des Grands Écrivains Français)	60
Bourienne. Memoires. Nouv. ed. I. 12° (Savine)	1 00
Bovet, M. A. de. Confessions d'une fille de 30 ans. 12° (Lemerre)	1 00
Caro, E. Les lendemains. 12° (Levy)	1 00
Cheneviere, A. Quatre Femmes. 12° (Levy)	1 00
D'Annunzio, G. L'Enfant de Volupté. 12° (Levy)	1 00
Daudet, Léon A. Les Kamtchatka. 12° (Charpentier)	1 00
Delacroix, Eugène. Journal. Vol. III. 8° (Plon)	2 25
Deschamps, G. La vie et les Livres. 12° (Colin)	1 00
Dostoievsky. Le rêve de l'oncle. 12° (Plon)	1 00
Dumas, Fils. Théâtre des Autres. II. 12° (Levy)	1 00
Fouillee, A. Tempérament et caractère. 8° (Alcan)	2 25
Gille, P. Les Mercredis d'un critique. 12° (Levy)	1 00
Greville, H. Le fil d'or. 12° (Plon)	1 00
Gyp. Le cœur d'Ariane. 12° (Levy)	1 00
Gyp. Les Gens Chics. Il. 12° (Charpentier)	1 00
Haussonville, Comte O. de. Lacordaire (Collection des Grands Écrivains Français). 12° (Hachette)	60
Janet, P. Lettres de Mme. de Grignan. 12° (Levy)	1 00
Labruyere, G. de. Chantereine. 12° (Simonis-Empis)	1 00
La Feuillee. Le cahier bleu d'un petit jeune homme. 12° (Levy)	1 00
Legras, J. Au pays Russe. 12° (Colin)	1 00
Livet, G. L'Amour Forcé. Il. 12° (Charpentier)	1 00
Mace, J. Les Soirées de ma tante Rosy. 12° (Hetzel)	90
Moreau-Vauthier, C. Les gamineries de Monsieur Triomphant. 12° (Plon)	1 00
O'Monroy, R. Histoires Tendres. 12° (Levy)	1 00
Paleologue, M. Profil de Femmes. 12° (Levy)	1 00

Psichari, J. Autour de la Grèce. 12° (Levy)	$1 00
Rameau, Jean. L'Amant honoraire. 12° (Ollendorff)	1 00
Renan, E. Ma Sœur Henriette. Il. 8° (Levy)	1 80
Roe, Art. Racheté. 12° (Levy)	1 00
Rosny, I. H. L'autre Femme. 12° (Chailley)	1 00
Saint Amand, Imbert de. Les Exils. 12° (Dentu)	1 00
Saint Elme. Memoires d'une Contemporaine. 8° (Flammarion)	2 10
Saint Maurice, R. Tartufette. 12° (Lemerre)	1 00
Scheffer, Robt. Le chemin nuptial. 12° (Lemerre)	1 00
Segur, Le Maréchal de (1724–1801). Par le Comte de Segur. 8° (Plon)	2 25
Theuriet, A. Flavie. 12° (Charpentier)	1 00
Vanderem, F. Charlie. 12° (Ollendorff)	1 00
Wagner, C. La Vie Simple. 12° (Colin)	1 00

GERMAN.

Berkow, K. Ein Vorurteil. 12° (Janke)	90
Berkow, K. Im Dämmerschein. 12° (Janke)	35
Brachvogel, C. Alltagsmenschen. 12° (Fisher)	1 20
Ebner-Eschenbach, M. von. Margarete. 12° (Cotta)	70
Gayer, O. Esther. 12° (Fisher)	1 35
Hartleben, O. E. Vom Gastfreien Pastor. 12° (Fisher)	70
Junghaus, S. Geschieden. 2 vols. 12° (Deutsche Verlags Anstalt)	2 70
Klinck-Lutelsburg, F. Aus dem Künstlernest. 12° (Deutsche Verlags Anstalt)	1 35
Land, H. Die Tugendhafte. 12° (Fisher)	70
Salinger, E. Bühne des Lebens. 12° (Deutsche Verlags Anstalt)	1 35
Schulze-Smidt, M. "So wachsen deiner Seele Flügel!" 2 vols. 12° (Deutsche Verlags Anstalt)	2 00
Sosnosky, I. von. Aus der Dreiviertelwelt. 12° (Pierson)	1 00
Stahl, M. Manneswert. 12° (Janke)	1 70
Sudermann, H. Schmetterlingsschlacht. 12° (Cotta)	70
Suttner, A. G. von. Nichts Ernsthaftes. 12° (Pierson)	1 00
Telmann, K. Trinacria. 12° (Cotta)	1 35
Thomas, Emil. Erinnerungen aus meinem Leben. 8° (Duncker)	1 00
Tolstoi, L. Iwan, der Narr. 12° (Janke)	90
Wilbrandt, A. Der Meister von Palmyra. 12° (Cotta)	1 00

Literary Miscellany.

SONNET.

I HATE the vast array of modern things,
Gilt, and pale purple, yellow, pink, and white ;
Dull imitations and a thousand light
And weightless books of verse and copyings.
There are so many.　Every season brings
A thousand fashions new, and with delight
Proclaims them beautiful, till I take flight
And turn me to the masters and the kings.
And yet they will not let the masters be ;
I find my Walton in a showy dress ;
Find all the bright, old-age simplicity
Bedecked and botched ; the years of good Queen Bess
Are made the dull Philistine's property ;
And Burns is "popularly" sent to press
—*Philip Henry Savage, in First Poems and Fragments.*

JOHN RAE, the author of several books on economic questions, has written a new biography of Adam Smith.

THE trustees of Johns Hopkins University have invited Prof. Sir Archibald Geikie to be first lecturer on geology on the Williams foundation.

MR. RUDYARD KIPLING's " Jungle Book " has been distinguished by those having in charge the education of the blind.　An edition will soon appear in raised letters.

MADAME DARMESTETER (Mary Robinson) is about publishing the philosophical and moral essays and the impressions of travel which her lamented husband left unfinished.

CHARLES KINGSLEY's daughter, Mrs. Harrison (" Lucas Malet "), has written a new novel with the queer title of " The Power of the Dog."　The hero believes himself haunted by a dog.

MR. W. J. COURTHOPE is a candidate for the chair of poetry at Oxford, shortly to be vacated by Professor Palgrave, and his candidacy is so strongly supported that election seems a foregone conclusion.

THERE is nothing like a great name to conjure with.　" Who is this Dr. Holmes ? " a New England bookseller was recently asked.　He replied : " I've never heard of him, but his wife [Mary J. Holmes] writes lovely books ! "

THE pleasant discovery has just been made at Galashiels, Scotland, of over a hundred letters written by Sir Walter Scott to Mr. Craig, the banker.　The letters were discovered in a box filled with the archives of the old Leith Bank.

A COMMITTEE has been formed in Amsterdam for the erection of a monument to Thomas à Kempis at Zwolle, where he died at the age of ninety-one on July 4, 1471.　The committee invites an international competition for sketches for the proposed monument.

ANNA KATHARINE GREEN (Mrs. Rohlfs) writes that the identity of the plot of her " Doctor Izard " with that of an unnamed recent story is purely accidental.　She adds that the story is all her own, except the incident in the closing chapter, which is the key to the mystery, and is based on a natural occurrence, reported in the press some years ago, and evidently used by the other author in a similar manner.

MR. JAMES PAYN, our readers will be sorry to hear, says *The Bookman*, is almost wholly confined to his bed and chair.　He is only able to write with a pencil, and then with the utmost pain.　All the more credit to him that what he does write has the old high spirits, and is dictated by the old kind heart.　His " Gleams of Memory " is a book most delightful to literary men—a book about themselves and their art, without a single malicious or bitter word between its covers.

THE business aspect of the novel in England is thus reviewed by an article in *Chambers' Journal*.　It seems that the average production there is three every twenty-four hours, and, including reprints, some 200 more.　When there is a novel that has marked life in it, Mudie will take 3000 copies.　If popularity means merit, Mrs. Wood is the great author, for over 1,000,000 of her books have been bought.　During five months 50,000 copies of Hall Caine's " Manxman " have been sold.　Neither publishers nor public always know what is a good book at the start.　For instance, five months elapsed before a few hundred of Barrie's "Auld Licht Idylls" were sold.

IT is said, by those who have seen the MS., that Robert Louis Stevenson's last story, " St. Ives," was left at his death practically completed.　Stevenson had been at work upon this novel for more than a year.　The novel is said to deal with the adventures of a Frenchman captured in the Peninsular War and shut up in Edinburgh Castle.　The posthumous works of Mr. R. L. Stevenson, according to the *Athenæum*, will include a book of " Fables," written in 1888 ; an unfinished romance, " St. Ives," telling of the adventures of a French prisoner who escaped from Edinburgh Castle in 1813 ; " Wier of Hermiston, or, the Lord Justice Clerk," only half written ; " The Northern Light ; or, a family of engineers," a history of the author's family, only brought down by him to the time of the building of the Bell Rock Lighthouse.　To the above must be added, " The Vailima Letters," a selection made by Mr. Sidney Colvin, from the late Mr. Stevenson's correspondence.

THE most interesting figure at the marriage of Miss Violet Maxse to Lord Salisbury's fourth son, says the London *Literary World*, was not that *grand seigneur*, the tall, burly, cynical, but kindly faced Marquis, who had in July, 1888, the pride of being Prime Minister on the 3rd centenary of the repulse of the Spanish Armada by a government of which his great ancestor, Lord Burleigh, was head.　Though the Cecils are " on the top " now as they were in "the spacious times of great Elizabeth," the cynosure of all eyes in the church was the slight figure of an old gentleman who was in such delicate health that he required an aid to help him up the aisle—George Meredith.　George Meredith looks his part.　Genius and distinction are written on his beautiful intellectual head, in his almost inspired expression.　A man of medium height, he has a thin, delicate figure ; a large, noble head, crowned with luxuriant white hair ; a short, crisp, heart-shaped white beard, peaking out like Lord Spencer's ; soft, blue-gray eyes, and a slightly *retroussé* nose.　Though a Home Ruler and a democrat, his manner and voice are decidedly aristocratic.　His is exactly the personality one would have chosen for the writer of such masterpieces as " Richard Feverel " and " Diana of the Crossways."

Freshest News.

--

S. C. Griggs & Co. will publish shortly "Poetry of Literature, English Authors," by Mary Fisher. The work treats of those eminent men in more than one than five hundred years have most influenced the thought of the world. The author attempts to make the reader acquainted not only with the character of their works, but, what is of greater interest, with them as men—what they felt and believed, their way of looking at life, and their experiences.

The Cassell Pub. Co. have just ready "At Heart a Rake," by Florence Marryat; and "Son of Belial," by William Westall, author of "The Phantom City." Their newest additions to the *Union Square Library* are "The Story of a Modern Woman," by Ella Hepworth Dixon; and "A Pastoral Played Out," by Mary L. Pendered, and to the *Unknown Library* they have just added "The Making of Mary," by Jean Forsyth, "A King's Diary," by the author of "Mr. Bailey Martin"; "Gentleman Upcott's Daughter," by Tom Cobleigh, and "A Splendid Cousin," by Mrs Andrew Dean.

Houghton, Mifflin & Co. have just issued Edward Dowden's "New Studies in Literature," chosen from a larger number which appeared during a series of years in *The Fortnightly Review*. It is a book of great interest, especially in the introduction, in which the author reveals his hopes and fears for literature at the present day, especially as those hopes and fears are connected with democratic tendencies and the scientific movement of our century. *The Atlantic Monthly* for August continues Miss Phelps' "A Singular Life"; and contains besides interesting articles on "The Wrongs of a Juryman"; and "A Woman's Luncheon." A very pretty short story by Miss L. Dougall, is entitled "Thitt."

Lovell, Coryell & Co. have just ready in their *Nugget Series* an entertaining collection of stories, from the New York *Sun*, illustrating homely country life, as exemplified in the types to be seen in the smaller towns and villages of the country, and among the gossips congregated in and around the taverns or corner groceries. The volume, which is from the pen of Ed. Mott, author of "Pike County Folk," etc., is entitled "The Old Settler and Squire and Uncle Peleg." They have a few other new copyright summer novels, such as "Her Commodore's Daughters," "Prisoner of the Harem," "Jane" ... the Old Man's Cash, and Ambrose Harte's "French Nan," and Clay's "Love of a Summer Maid."

... [illegible lines] ...

... can do to truly "English" Balzac, but Balzac, although one of the few great world writers, is essentially French in language, and it is impossible to bring out the shades of individual style in translation.

"MONEY AND BANKING," by Horace White, editor of the New York *Evening Post*, will be published by Ginn & Co. towards the end of August. Mr. White illustrates the theme of Money from American history, reviews the various developments of paper and silver currency, and gives the experience of European nations with the gold standard. In treating Banking he explains the functions of a bank, traces the successive phases of American banking, and forecasts its probable future. Eight appendices add much to the value of the work; three of them set forth "The Baltimore Plan," "Secretary Carlisle's Plan," and "Recent Bimetallist Movements in Germany." Mr. White is an uncompromising upholder of the gold standard and an able critic of American currency and banking systems.

G. P. PUTNAM'S SONS have just ready a new instalment of novels to beguile the rainy days in country resorts. Among them is "The Heart of Life," by W. H. Mallock, certainly destined to a prominent place beyond that of summer fiction. It is the novel of contemporary English life on which the author of "The New Republic" has been so long at work, and which is said to be fully up to the standard of his now famous "Romance of the Nineteenth Century." The titles of other novels are: "Elizabeth's Pretenders," by Hamilton Aidé; "Sentimental Studies and a set of village tales," by Hubert Crackanthorpe; "The Honour of the Flag," by William Clark Russell; "Master Wilberforce," by Mrs. Desmond Humphreys ("Rita"); "Her Majesty," by Elizabeth Knight Tompkins; "Cause and Effect," by Ellinor Meirion; "God Forsaken," by Frederick Breton; and "Cherryfield Hall," by Frederick Henry Balfour. They also announce a volume of poems by Howard Chandler Christy, to be entitled "In Camphor."

D. APPLETON & Co. have just ready "An Imaginative Man," by Robert S. Hichens, author of "The Green Carnation," which is a distinct advance upon his former writings, and gives promise of even finer things to come, provided he remains firm in refusing to write as a business speculation for his publishers. Mr. Hichens is a master of epigram, and his new book is ethical, social, and philosophical. The scene is laid in Egypt, chiefly in the immediate vicinity of the Sphinx which takes such strange hold of the imagination of Mr. Hichens' hero. The book requires educated readers, for it is ... of a ... that ... the author wide-read and ... unconventional in methods of thought. Two most excellent stories are ... to be "Stories of Unknown Library." Alderney Sergeant's "A Sense of Quest," and George Gissing's ... the Year of Jubilee," which has already been recognized as the masterwork of a writer of unusual literary ... is a ... name. All who care ... a ... book that should ... not fail to make its way into many standard libraries.

THE NEWEST BOOKS.

Helps for Literary Workers.

Books for Summer Travellers.

AMERICAN BOOK COMPANY, New York.

Gray's Manual of Botany. Tourists' ed. $2.00.

D. APPLETON & CO., New York.

Appletons' General Guide to the United States. With maps and illustrations. One volume complete, flexible morocco, with tuck, $2.50. Part I., separately, New England and Middle States and Canada, cloth, $1.25. Part II., separately, Southern and Western States, cloth, $1.25.

Appletons' Handbook of Summer Resorts. With maps and illustrations. Small 8vo, paper, 50c.

Appletons' Canadian Guide-Book. One volume complete. Newfoundland to the Pacific Coast. With maps and illustrations. 12mo, $1.25.

Appletons' Guide-Book to Alaska. By Miss E. R. Scidmore. With maps and illustrations. 12mo, $1.25.

Appletons' Dictionary of New York and Its Vicinity. 16mo, paper, 30c.; flex. cloth, 60c.

The White Mountains. By Rev. J. H. Ward. 12mo, cloth, $1.25.

The Land of the Sun. *Vistas Mexicanas.* By Christian Reid. Illustrated. 12mo, cloth, $1.75.

THE CASSELL PUBLISHING CO., New York.

Cassell's Pocket Guide to Europe for 1895. With maps, etc. Bound in leather, $1.50. The model book of its kind for accuracy, fulness, legibility of text and maps, compact beauty and usefulness, and very moderate price.

WATSON GILL, Syracuse, N. Y.

The Adirondacks. Wallace's guide for 1895, now ready, 600 pages, 150 half-tone engravings and large map. The Standard Guide to the Adirondacks. Sold by booksellers, or mailed on receipt of price, $3.50.

HOUGHTON, MIFFLIN & CO., Boston.

Boston Illustrated. Paper, 50c.

Satchel Guide to Europe. Edition for 1894. $1.50.

England Without and Within. By Richard Grant White. $2.00.

Sweetser's New England. $1.50.

Sweetser's White Mountains. $1.50.

Sweetser's Maritime Provinces. $1.50.

Nantucket Scraps. By Jane G. Austin. $1.50.

Mrs. Thaxter's Among the Isles of Shoals. $1.25.

HUNT & EATON, New York.

Travels in Three Continents. By J. M. Buckley, LL.D. Finely illustrated. 614 pages, octavo, cloth, gilt top, $3.50. A most instructive and fascinating book of travel.

LITTLE, BROWN & CO., Boston.

Pleasure-Cycling. By Henry Clyde. With 34 silhouettes and vignettes. 16mo, cloth, $1.00.

Parkman's Handbook of the Northern Tour. Lakes George and Champlain, Niagara, Montreal, Quebec. 12mo, cloth, $1.25.

'JOHN MURPHY & CO., Baltimore, Md.

Mrs. Mary E. Surratt. Her trial, conviction and execution. By David Miller DeWitt. 12mo, cloth, $1.25.

A Marriage of Reason. By Francis Maurice Egan. A story of "society" people of Philadelphia and its suburbs. 12mo, cloth, $1.00.

Army Boys and Girls. By Mrs. Mary G. Bonesteel. A series of brilliant stories of our camps and garrisons. 12mo, cloth, $1.00.

Ada's Trust. By Mrs. A. H. Dorsey. A story of vivid interest. 12mo, cloth, $1.00.

Beth's Promise. By Mrs. A. H. Dorsey. 12mo, cloth, $1.50.

A Washington Winter. By Mrs. M. V. Dahlgren. A vivid delineation of life at the Capital. $1.00.

JOHN MURPHY & CO.—Continued.

Lights and Shadows of a Life. By Mrs. M. V. Dahlgren. A picture of Southern home life. 12mo, cloth, $1.00.

Children of Charles I. of England. By Mrs. C. S. H. Clark. Small quarto, cloth, $1.00.

Down at Caxtons. Brilliant sketches of American authors. By Walter Lecky. Paper, 35 cents.

THOMAS NELSON & SONS, New York.

The Royal Album of Chromo Views. The most exquisite scenery of the British Isles. 253 chromo views, oblong folio, cloth, extra gilt edges, $7.00.

English Scenery. 120 views. 4to, cloth, $2.50.

Souvenir of Scotland. Its cities, lakes, and mountains. 120 chromo views. 4to, $2.50; and $4.00.

Rambles in Rome. By S. Russell Forbes. With maps, plans, and illustrations. 12mo, cloth extra, $1.50.

Rambles in Naples. By S. Russell Forbes. With maps, plans, and illustrations. 12mo, cloth extra, $1.25.

ROBERTS BROTHERS, Boston.

Jackson (Helen ["H. H."]). Glimpses of Three Coasts. 12mo, $1.50. These are "Bits of Travel" in California and Oregon, Scotland and England, and Norway, Denmark, and Germany.

— **Ramona.** A Story. 12mo, $1.50. Most delightful glimpses of So. California.

— **Bits of Travel.** Illustrated. Square 18mo, $1.25.

— **Bits of Travel at Home.** Square 18mo, $1.50.

Drake (Samuel Adams). Old Landmarks and Historic Personages of Boston. With 93 illustrations. 12mo, $2.00.

— **Old Landmarks and Historic Fields of Middlesex.** With 39 illustrations and maps. 12mo, $2.00.

Aloha. (A Hawaiian Salutation.) By G. L. Chaney. Travels in the Sandwich Islands. With illustrations and map. 16mo, $1.50.

GEORGE ROUTLEDGE & SONS (Ld.), New York.

Hare's (A. J. C.) Literary Traveling Companions.

Edwards's (A. B.) A Thousand Miles up the Nile. Profusely illustrated. 8vo, $2.50.

— **Untrodden Peaks and Unfrequented Valleys.** A Midsummer Ramble in the Dolomites. Maps and illustrations. 8vo, $2.00.

Caine's (W. S.) A Trip Round the World, 1887-1888. 250 original illustrations. 12mo, cloth, $1.50.

— **Picturesque India!** an unconventional Guide-Book. 200 illustrations and map. 8vo, cloth, $4.00.

Stow's (John) Survey of London in the Time of Elizabeth. Crown 8vo, $1.00.

E. STEIGER & CO., New York.

Baedeker's and other Guide-Books, in German; also Travellers' Maps, Conversation Books, Grammars, and Dictionaries in all foreign languages.

WARD, LOCK & BOWDEN, Ltd., New York.

On the Cars and Off. Being the Journal of a Pilgrimage along the Queen's Highway to the East, from Halifax, in Nova Scotia, to Victoria, in Vancouver's Island. By Douglas Sladen. Profusely and beautifully illustrated. 8vo, cloth, $6.00.

BRADLEE WHIDDEN, Boston, Mass.

Knobel's Guides in Natural History. Trees and Shrubs. Ferns and Evergreens. Day Butterflies. The Beetles. The Moths. Each 12mo, *net*, 50 cents.

Emerton's Life on the Seashore. Illustrated. 12mo, cloth, $1.50.

Emerton's Spiders. Illustrated. 12mo, cloth, $1.50.

Gould's Modern American Rifle. Illustrated. 12mo, cloth, $2.00.

Gould's Pistols and Revolvers. Illustrated. 12mo, cloth, $1.50.

LITERARY NEWS

AN ECLECTIC REVIEW OF
CURRENT LITERATURE
~ILLUSTRATED~

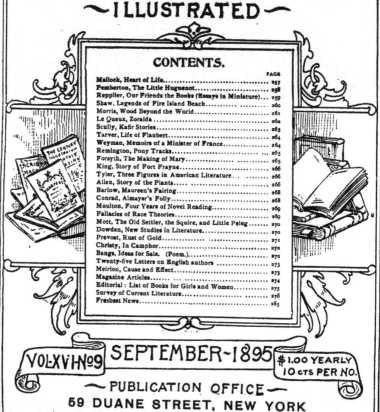

CONTENTS.

VOL. XVI. No 9 SEPTEMBER~1895 $1.00 YEARLY 10 CTS PER NO.

~PUBLICATION OFFICE~
59 DUANE STREET, NEW YORK
ENTERED AT THE POST OFFICE. AT NEW YORK AS SECOND CLASS MATTER

The Literary News

In winter you may reade them, ab ignem, by the fireside; and in summer, ab umbram, under some shadie tree, and therewith pass away the tedious howres.

| VOL. XVI. | SEPTEMBER, 1895. | No. 9. |

The Heart of Life.

THE plot of Mr. Mallock's new novel does not lend itself readily to condensation. It is a problems very closely, and, entering political life, comes rapidly to the front only to discover

W. H. MALLOCK.

chapter in a biography, of which the interest is mainly psychological, the biography of Reginald Pole, a man of great natural gifts and great social advantages, who studies labor that success does not mean happiness. For the love affairs, which might bring him happiness if only they would go right, insist on going so wrong that he is very nearly driven to retire from the House of Commons with nothing to console him for the collapse of his public career. In writing such a chapter in such a biography some ticklish ground has to be crossed. Mr. Mallock does not shrink from crossing it; nor is that the only respect in which "The Heart of Life" may be considered a bold experiment. We should class it as a novel without a hero, but the author dwells so lovingly on the good qualities of his central figure and handles his weaknesses with so much sympathy (ironical sympathy, unless we are much mistaken), that the hasty reader may well be betrayed into supposing that he is offered not only a hero, but a hero he must conscientiously decline to accept as such. A good deal of honest indignation will, we fear, be excited by Master Reginald Pole and his love affairs.

We have said that "The Heart of Life" is subtle This subtlety, in itself neither a fault nor a merit, for there are readers of all sorts, is inevitable considering the nature of some of the problems round which the story plays. The mixture of good and bad in human nature may be more thorough than the conventional Pharisee cares to admit, and real life is not less perplexing than the life Mr. Mallock depicts. Most readers will, however, complain, and in our opinion complain with good reason, that Mr. Mallock does not make things as plain as he might, that some of the characters he draws especially his minor characters, are needlessly eccentric and mysterious.

To sum up our opinion of "The Heart of Life," we must resort to a colloquialism. From first to last the book is "too jolly clever by half," and the biting and incisive epigrams that stud its pages would have gained in effect immensely had they been relieved by a little more genial and homely fun. We have already said quite enough to warn anybody who dislikes peeps at the seamy side of human nature that "The Heart of Life" will in parts not be altogether to his taste. On the other hand,

those who ask for moral problems, and moral problems only, must forgive Mr. Mallock for having introduced some charming descriptive passages, of which the insight and exquisite faithfulness will be recognized by any one who knows the coast scenery of the Bristol Channel. Equally good is the picture of the tranquil dignity of the life led at a country house belonging to the Poles, where Countess Shimna for the first time, she declares, sees what she knew a home would be. (Putnam. $1.25.)—*London Literary World.*

From "The Little Huguenot." Copyright, 1895, by Dodd, Mead & Co.

MAX PEMBERTON.

The Little Huguenot.

UNTIL this time, he had been unable from his place of observation to see anything of the company in the chapel. But now, when the priest had ended the mournful chanting, little acolytes in scarlet cassocks and white cottas kindled the tapers upon the high altar and also those in a chandelier beneath the rood-screen. The new light fell upon a reredos of marble and gold, almost hidden by vases of white flowers. It fell, too, upon the face of an old priest gorgeously robed in a jewelled cope. While taper-bearers and thurifers prostrated themselves before the Host in the monstrance, and a hidden choir began to sing very sweetly the Latin hymn, "O Salutaris Hostia," de Guyon had eyes for none of these, but only for the little group of worshippers who knelt by the chancel gates. Here were some twelve men and women, all seemingly absorbed in their devotions, and all dressed very soberly, and for the most part in plain black. There was not a man amongst them that hid his hair in a wig; not a woman of the company that seemed to know of the coiffure *à boucles badines*, *au berceau d'amour* or *au mirliton*. Simplicity was the note of it all, and de Guyon, when he had shaken off his surprise, admitted that this simplicity was in pretty harmony with the sombre note of the chapel. He might have been watching so many monks and nuns who had clothed themselves in lay dress—but timidly.

In the centre of the little company there knelt a girl whose face was hidden from him, but whose figure and pose were infinitely graceful. He was led to believe by the position she occupied that she must be the countess, and that the men at her side were the poets and philosophers who had come to the château to air their graces and to fill their stomachs. For the time being she was occupied entirely with her devotions, and when she raised the smallest of white hands, it was to bury her face in them while she prostrated herself before the upraised Host. Anon, however, the music died away suddenly ; the last cloud of incense floated to the vaulted roof ; the acolytes extinguished the candles before the altar, and the girl rose and passed down the chapel. De Guyon said to himself that the gossips were right. If a Madonna had come out of one of the pictures above the shrines, and had stood before him, lending flesh and blood to the painter's vision, he could scarce have been more surprised. Such a delicacy of form and feature he had hardly seen in all the six years he had been at Versailles ; had never known eyes in which so much tenderness and emotion seemed to lie. He declared that her mouth was like a rosebud upon which the dew had just fallen. She held herself with the grace of a woman grown gray in practising the courtesies ; yet her limbs had the roundness and suppleness of maturing youth. The black robe, falling from her shoulders prettily yet without panier, and set off only with lace at her neck and wrists. was her best adornment. She wore no jewels ; not so much as a band of gold upon her arm. Her brown hair was simply coiled upon her head. De Guyon said to himself that Legros, with all his art, could not have added to the effect of it. And with this thought he left the chapel to await her in the courtyard. (Dodd, Mead & Co. 75 c)— *From Max Pemberton's " The Little Huguenot."*

Agnes Repplier

Our Friends, the Books.

HAZLITT'S words ring consolingly in these different days, when we have not only ceased reading what is old, but when—a far greater misfortune—we have forgotten how to read " with all the satisfaction in our power," and with a simple surrendering of ourselves to the pleasure which has no peer. There are so many things to be considered now besides pleasure, that we have well-nigh abandoned the effort to be pleased. In the first place, it is necessary to " keep up " with a decent proportion of current literature, and this means perpetual labor and speed, whereas idleness and leisure are requisite for the true enjoyment of books. In the second place, few of us are brave enough to withstand the pressure which friends, mentors and critics bring to bear upon us, and which effectually crushes anything like the weak indulgence of our own tastes. The reading they recommend being generally in the nature of a corrective, it is urged upon us with little regard to personal inclination; in fact, the less we like it, the greater our apparent need. There are people in this world who always insist upon others remodelling their diet on a purely hygienic basis; who entreat us to avoid sweets or acids, or tea or coffee, or whatever we chance to particularly like; who tell us persuasively that cress and dandelions will purify our blood, that celery is an excellent febrifuge ; that shaddocks should be eaten for the sake of their quinine, and fish for its phosphorus; that stewed fruit is more wholesome than raw ; that rice is more nutritious than potatoes — who deprive us, in a word, of that hearty human happiness which should be ours when dining. Like Mr. Woodhouse, they are capable of having the sweetbreads and asparagus carried off before our longing eyes, and baked apples provided as a substitute.

It is in the same benevolent spirit that kindhearted critics are good enough to warn us against the books we love, and to prescribe for us the books we ought to read. With robust assurance they offer to give our tutelage their own personal supervision, and their disinterested zeal carries them occasionally beyond the limits of discretion. I have been both amazed and gratified by the lack of reserve with which these unknown friends have volunteered to guide my own footsteps through the perilous paths of literature. They are so urgent, too, not to say severe, in their manner of proffering assistance: " To Miss Repplier we would particularly recommend "—and then follows a list of books of which I dare say I stand in open need; but which I am naturally indisposed to consider with much kindness, thrust upon me, as they are, like paregoric or a porous plaster. If there be people who can take their pleasures medicinally, let them read by prescription and grow fat! But let me rather keep for my friends those dear and familiar volumes which have given me a large share of my life's happiness. If they are somewhat antiquated and out of date, I have no wish to flout their vigorous age. A book, Hazlitt reminds us, is not, like a woman, the worse for being old. If they are new, I do not scorn them for a fault which is common to all their kind. " Paradise Lost " was once new, and was regarded as a somewhat questionable novelty. If they come from afar, or are compatriots of my own, they are equally well beloved. There can be no aliens in the ranks of literature, no national prejudice in an honest enjoyment of art. The book, after all, and not the date or birthplace of its author, is of material importance. (Houghton, Mifflin & Co. $1.25.) — *From Repplier's "Essays in Miniature."*

Legends of Fire Island Beach and the South Side.

THESE stories embody only a small part of the folk-lore and tradition that pertained to the Great South Bay, Long Island. They were told by a class of men now gone. Fact, imagination and superstition—each contributed its part. In the tavern, among groups of men collected on shore from wind-bound vessels, at gatherings around the cabin fire, and in those small craft that were constantly going from one part of the bay to another, not only these tales, but others, irrevocably lost, were elaborated and made current in days homely and toilsome, yet invested with an atmosphere of romance.

Fire Island Beach is a barrier of sand, stretching for twenty miles along the south coast of Long Island, and separating the Great South Bay from the Atlantic Ocean. To reach it you must make a sail of from three to seven miles, and once upon it, you find it a wild, desolate, solitary spot, wind-searched and surf-pounded.

All along the inner line of the Great South Bay are spots of wondrous beauty which attract summer visitors year after year in spite of the worst railroad service that can well be imagined at this day. All who have seen the places described by Prof. Shaw, of New York University, will read his well-told tales with keen enjoyment. And from the Atlantic to the Pacific can be found people who have summered on the Great South Bay.

The illustrations are from photographs taken by Mr. R Eichemeyer, medallist of the Royal Photographic Society. (Lovell, C. & Co. 75 c.)

TWENTY MILES OF SAND.

The Wood Beyond the World.

THE charm, or one of the charms, of this last book of William Morris is more easily felt than described, and is only felt in the feelings, we which Malory's "Morte d'Arthur" is a fair example. At the age of sixty or thereabouts, William Morris is still pouring out his lovely things, more full of the glory of youth, more

From "The Wood Beyond the World."   Copyright, 1895, by Roberts Bros.

think, by those who are enamored of the invention which underlies all folk-lore, the element of fantasy, with or without a seeming purpose, containing in itself its excuse for being, and are enamored at the same time of the simple, homely, idiomatic diction which characterized the early chroniclers and romancers, and of full of romantic adventure and romantic love, than any of the beautiful poems in his first volumes. By the side of this exhaustless creator of beautiful and lovely things, the youngest of the poets who have just appeared above the horizon seems faded and jaded. (Roberts. $2.50.)—*Mail and Express.*

Zoraida, the One of Wondrous Beauty.

"It grieveth me sorely to think that thou, the woman I adore, art the head of this fierce band of murderous marauders, and wilt lead them to commit merciless massacre and pillage, to"—

"Ah, no!" she cried, raising both her hands as if to arrest my words. "Reproach me not, O Ce-cil! I cannot bear it *from thee!* Thinkest thou that were I not compelled, I would be the cause of this widespread death and desolation; thinkest thou that I would urge onward these wild hordes to deeds horrible and revolting? Thou believest I have a heart of stone, that I have no woman's tenderness, that—that I, a woman of the Desert, am"—and, unable to complete her sentence, she burst into a passionate torrent of tears.

' No, Zoraida, I blame thee not," I tenderly hastened to reassure her. "I know there are circumstances connected with thine hidden past of which I have no knowledge therefore I love thee fondly, awaiting the time when thou art enabled to renounce thy people and become my wife."

"What canst thou think of a woman such as I?" she sobbed bitterly. "Even to thee, so faithful as thou hast been, I am compelled to still preserve my secret, appearing in thine eyes as one to whom the clash of arms is sweeter than the music of the *derbouka,* and the wail of the vanquished the pleasantest sound upon mine ear!"

"But thy position is not of thine own choosing," I said, quietly endeavoring to soothe her.

"No!" she cried wildly,

HADJ ALSALAM.

starting up. "I hate it all! Though each raid enricheth me with gold and jewels of great price, yet there is a curse upon the treasure, obtained, as it is, by the relentless slaughter of the weak. Ah, Ce-cil! if thou couldst only know how acutely I suffer, how these jewels upon me glitter with the fire of deadly hatred as each one telleth its mute but horrible story, a story of rapine and murder for which I—the woman thou lovest, the woman who would willingly give her life for thee—am responsible! Is not my existence one of hollow shams, of feigned daring and wretched duplicity? I loathe myself, and were it not that I look forward to happiness with thee, I would—I would end it all with this!" and she drew from her breast a small keen dagger, with hilt encrusted with turquoises, that she always kept concealed there.

"Speak not of that," I said firmly. "Place thy knife in its sheath. I love thee, Zoraida, I trust in thee, and none shall ever come between us."

"Dost thou place thy faith in me implicitly, notwithstanding that I appear in thine eyes debased, and am unable to give thee explanation?" she asked, half credulously, through her blinding tears.

The jewels upon her flashed with a brilliancy that was dazzling, and the sweet odors of her apartment seemed intoxicating.

"I do," I answered, fervently kissing her with a mad, fierce passion. "Indeed, had it not been for thine exertions, my bones would long ago have been stripped by the vultures."

"Ah! my Amin, thou too art performing for me a mission, the result

"WELL, DO I PLEASE THEE?"

of which will effect stranger things than thou hast ever dreamed," she exclaimed earnestly ; adding, "Our story-tellers relate wondrous things, but none has described such marvels as thou shalt behold. I told thee in Algiers that I was in peril of death, and that thou couldst avert the danger that threatened. These words I now repeat, and trust in thee to save me."

"To save thee I will again face our enemies fearlessly, and strive to reach the *imam* who holdeth the Secret, even though I have been told that the Omen of the Camel's Hoof hath been revealed unto me," I said, entranced by her beauty, and smiling in an endeavor to chase away the gloomy shadow that seemed to have settled upon her. (Stokes.)—*From Le Queux s "Zoraida, a Romance of the Harem and the Great Sahara."*

Kafir Stories.

MR. SCULLY, of whom we had heard nothing at all until his work was announced, writes of South Africa with the sure knowledge, the sympathy, and almost with the vigor that Mr. Kipling bestows upon his Hindu stories The newcomer knows the hills and plains, the bush and the settlements of South Africa well, and he seems to write with a strong moral purpose. While only one of his seven tales treats directly of the missionary and his work, the undertone of them all seems to say, distinctly, that the white man has dealt mistakenly with the Kafir and the Zulu, when he has not purposely or for sordid gain done them harm.

But Mr. Scully is a story teller rather than a moralist. The reader will be particularly grateful for his strongly picturesque tale of adventure and warfare in the days of Zulu glory, when Tschaka was king, "The Quest of the Copper." There is no false sentiment in this or in any of the tales. The faithful, self-sacrificing hero is a naked, murderous savage. His staunch, obedient followers eat raw flesh and slay women and children. But there is something splendid in their courage and fortitude, and the narrative of their long march, their triumphs, their betrayal, and finally their brave death, is thrilling.

There is a ghost story, for no such volume of tales would be complete without one; and there is a yarn about cannibalism powerfully told that will curdle your blood. There are two sad love tales, for the half-naked Kafir girls inspire the genuine love of their fellow-men, and Mr. Scully's two heroines, Martha, with Aryan blood in her veins, and Nomalie, heathen by blood and breeding, are as true to their one passion as any heroine of European poetry or romance.

In short, "Kafir Stories" is worth reading, and the volume merits its place in the popular buckram stories all which are of merit. (Holt. 75 c.)—*N. Y. Times.*

From " Kafir Stories." Copyright, 1895, by Henry Holt & Co.

SAMUEL GOZANI AND MARTHA KAWA.

MY BOOKS.

WHAT are my books ?—my friends, my loves,
  My church, my tavern, and my only wealth ;
My garden ; yea, my flowers, my bees, my doves ;
  My only doctors—and my only health.

FAITH REBORN.

"THE old gods pass," the cry goes round,
" Lo ! how their temples strew the ground ; "
Nor mark we where on new-fledged wings,
Faith, like the phœnix, soars and sings.

ART.

ART is a gypsy
  Fickle as fair,
Good to kiss and flirt with,
  But marry—if you dare !

(Copeland & Day. $1.25.)—*From " Le Gallienne's Poems."*

"SHE GAVE HER MODEST ANSWER."

Life of Flaubert.

THIS is not a complete Life of Flaubert. It is a biography with gaps in it. But it contains a number of very interesting letters. They reveal the real Flaubert in the character of a lover, and as a thinker on ethics and art. He appears to have been a lover of a too strictly literary cast. As a lover, he obviously had limitations and, if one may use a slang expression, was careful not to give himself away.

"Madame Bovary," a sort of Female Rake's Progress, ending in misery and suicide, was the first of Flaubert's published works. It attracted great attention, partly owing to its undeniable merit, and partly because it was made the subject of a criminal prosecution, which, as Flaubert himself says, proved a gigantic advertisement for him. After "Madame Bovary" came "Salammbô," a romance of great power, though not comparable to "Madame Bovary" as a work of art. "Salammbô" was followed by a few minor works which had very limited success. "Madame Bovary" and "Salammbô" may be said to be the two pillars on which Flaubert's literary reputation rests.

Flaubert, though immensely superior in subtlety and style to the writers of the naturalistic school who came after him and invoked his name, set them the example of selecting repulsive and ri-ky subjects as not unsuited for literary treatment. The works produced by him as a votary of "Art for Art's Sake" served as an encouragement to imitators who may be said to have gone very near to turning into worshippers of filth for filth's sake. In this sense Flaubert was a forerunner of Zola. His admirers will find his personality vividly presented in Mr. Tarver's book. (Appleton. $2.) —*London Literary World.*

From the Memoirs of a Minister of France.

A NEW book by Stanley J. Weyman means delight to all readers of fiction of the good old kind, full of events, full of detail, full of spirit in the telling. Introspection and subtile analysis of subtler points of character are foreign to the author of "A Gentleman of France;" "My Lady Rotha," "Under the Red Robe," "The House of the Wolf," etc. He has a story to tell, something that happened, and he possesses the power to interest from the first sentence. His newest offering is a collection of short stories dealing with events supposed to have taken place during the reigns of Henry IV. and Louis XIII. The Minister of France who relates them seems imbued with a contagious sense of humor, and also seems to have had means of getting behind the scenes of the outside pomp of royal functions and whispering to the onlookers some of the hidden reasons for much that was taking place in the high circles of France during the close of the 16th and at the beginning of the 17th centuries. The separate stories bear the titles: Clockmaker of Poissy, The Tennis Balls, Two Mayors of Bothfort, La Toussaint, The Lost Cipher, Governor of Gueret, The Open Shutter, The Maid of Honour, Farming the Taxes, The Cat and the King, The Man of Monceaux, At Fontainebleau.

Thirty-four spirited illustrations, of which fifteen are full-page, enliven the bright text, and Stanley Weyman's admirers will have nothing to complain of on the publishers' part in preparing them this new treat. The same publishers have on their list "A Gentleman of France," "My Lady Rotha," "Under the Red Robe," and "The House of the Wolf." (Longmans, Green & Co. $1.25.)

Pony Tracks.

THIS is a vastly entertaining book, written in nearly every vein of humor, packed with the downright realism of the Plains, in war and sport, and such civil life as the army brings with it and maintains around it. The illustrations are full of spirit—the spirit of the subject. The humor of the book has echo in it of the frontiersman's grave play with a tough problem, as, for example, his account of the camp fare as "a few ounces of bacon, some of those accursed crackers which are made to withstand fire, water and weevil, a quart of coffee blacker than evil," etc.; or this:

"The men have scouted hard for a month and have lost two nights' sleep, so at the halts for the wagons they lop down in the dust of the road, and sleep, while the little ponies stand over them, ears down, head hanging, eyes shut, and one hind foot drawn up on its toe. Nothing can look so dejected as the pony, and doubtless few things have more reason to feel so."

As to army duty in the far West, nothing ever yet put into type, or, we are disposed to add, which can ever be put into type, represents the living reality better. (Harper. $3.)—*Independent.*

The Making of Mary.

THE heroine of Miss Jean Forsyth's story, "The Making of Mary," belongs to the order of young person familiarly described as "a handful." The "Mary" of the title starts in life with nothing except her Christian name that she can call her own, and begs, works, or fights her way among the generous-hearted people of the United States till she reaches the age of seventeen, and gets adopted into the family of a philanthropic lady. But her position as a member of a family of standing, so far from serving as a point of rest in her chequered career, is merely a starting-post for sundry vagaries involving a considerable outlay to her open-handed patron. Alike at home and abroad, Mary proves impossible and impracticable. An ineradicable weakness for flirting mars every new career that her fertile imagination so readily sketches out. At length, when her friends have exhausted their efforts on her behalf, Providence takes her in hand, and "the making of Mary" is achieved in an entirely unlooked-for fashion. The story is told from the point of view of a newspaper man, the husband of Mary's patron, and the record of her aberrations is full of raciness and humor. In the matter of liveliness, as well as in variety of incident, the book recalls the widely popular "Helen's Babies." (Cassell. 50 c.)—*London Literary World.*

FREDERICK REMINGTON.

Fort Frayne.

CAPT. CHARLES KING'S " Fort Frayne" is in the unusual position of a story which was once written in collaboration as a drama, of which the manuscript was subsequently lost. Capt. King then rewrote it as a novel without the assistance of his collaborators. It is, of course, of army life that he tells his tale. He is staunchly loyal to his first love, and having sought the bubble reputation at the cannon's mouth (the metaphor is sufficiently accurate for the purpose), it is with affection that he dwells upon the manifold merits of the regular army, its devotion to duty under obloquy, its self-sacrifices, and its unhesitating bravery. He is not, however, so bigoted a West Pointer that he has not a kind word for the citizen soldier, even though, as in this instance, the zealous member of the Seventh New York has an exaggerated conviction of his duty to his regiment. One of the many sides of the Indian question plays its part, and is set forth with evident truth and fairness. Capt. King has done no better literary work than this, and nothing in his chosen line will be read with greater interest. The portrait here given forms the frontispiece of a very neatly made book. (Neely. $1.25.)—*Public Opinion.*

From." Fort Frayne."   Copyright, 1895, by Tennyson & Neely.

CAPT. CHARLES KING.

Three Figures in American Literature.

THAT part of the public who believe that America, if she has not yet reached her intellectual golden age, has at any rate evolved a written product which should excite the interest of all her loyal sons, will welcome a new book by Professor Moses Coit Tyler, called " Three Men of Letters," and issued between two important epochs in his monumental history of our literature George Berkeley, hitherto greeted mainly as the author of "Westward the course of empire takes its way," here appears as the philanthropic idealist who would have dedicated this nation in its early day to learning and religion, by means of the mammoth university which Walpole's politic but broken promise failed to support with financial aid.   President Dwight, of Yale, is depicted as the ascetic student seeking mental liberation through starvation of body, and as the author of the imitative pastoral poem, "Greenfield Hill." "The Columbiad," one of our early would-be epics, far greater in conception than in execution, is described in connection with the ambition, the self-complacency, and the miscellaneous avocations of its author, Mr. Joel Barlow. It is profitable to see these figures against the background of contemporary Europe—to know that Swift's " Vanessa " left Dean Berkeley a cosey legacy, that the amiable Cowper criticised Dwight's inevitable epic and praised one of his sermons, that Barlow, in the troublous time of the Reign of Terror, was made a French citizen by the National Convention. Such unexpected historical encounters, together with the author's pure style, his lurking humor, his occasional tone of mild satire not preventing full and cordial appreciation, make the little book delightful to read and a charming earnest of greater things to come. (Putnam. $1.25.)—*The Dial*

The Story of the Plants.

THE study of botany has advanced with long strides since Francis Bacon, Lord Chancellor of England, "handled fully" the differences between plants and living things. The change finds expression in Mr. Grant Allen's statement that the plant is a living thing, and the great commandment of modern botanists who are fond of referring to the "dry old bones" of the earlier science is that the study of the vegetable world should resemble that of the animal world, in that it should have to do not so much with the classification of plants and the preservation of specimens as with the observation of the processes of life. The functions of the plant, its relations to the insect world, the long story of its adaptation to its environment—it is with these that the botanist of to-day is deeply concerned, and he finds in them an element of romance that he makes use of in greater or less degree, according to his sensitiveness to it. Mr. Grant Allen has always had a keen sense of the romantic in nature, and it is a quality that gives him no slight advantage as a popularizer. The unscientific reader to whom he brings the general results of recent scientific research will probably have his attention caught and held by the statement that "plants marry and are given in marriage" and "rear families," and the subsequent lively discussion of what is called their "marriage customs" as no amount of bald assertion concerning fertilization and cross-fertilization could catch and hold it. The personal element is brought in until there is no excuse for indifference left to him to

"I FELT A TIMID TOUCH UPON MY SLEEVE."

whom nothing human is foreign, since so much that suggests human nature is found in vegetable nature. If this mode of presentation seems a little cheap and tricky to the ardent scientist who finds in "the fact" enough of wonder to satisfy any one, it should be remembered that there are comparatively few people in the world who prefer their truth, together with their furniture, unvarnished. It amuses them to see in it the reflection of outside things, it seems to them that they get more for their money, and so, for that matter, they do. Those who read Mr. Grant Allen's "useful story" need not be

so very young or so very uneducated to know more than they did before about chlorophyl and protoplasm and the part played by plants in what we glibly call the drama of life, without much conception of what we mean by it. The little book has a considerable scope, carrying the reader rapidly from the earliest "green jelly" stage of vegetation through the simpler forms and variations of the less evolved plant to the complex "labor-saving" development of the more evolved, with a more or less full account of the motive for, or, more strictly speaking, the end attained by, the variations from the earlier forms, and the reader is left impressed by the problems of the struggle for existence in the plant world. The books of this series are intended specially for schools, but they are fascinating for all readers. (Appleton. 40 c.) —*N. Y. Times.*

From "Maureen's Fairing." Copyright, 1895, by Macmillan & Co.
"A THING OF SHREDS AND PATCHES."

Maureen's Fairing.

OF the eight stories by Miss Jane Barlow that make up this volume those that reveal the daily life of the Irish peasant, with his homely philosophy, his quaint humor, and his quick sympathy, are far and away the best. The initial tale, which gives its name to the book, is an exquisite piece of refined and artistic writing. Nothing could be better in its way than the bit of dialogue at the beginning between Mrs. O'Dell and Mrs. Halpine, and the two garrulous old women contrast happily with imaginative Rody O'Dell and his blind sister, Maureen. The latter are accustomed to go in the evening to the old Rath—a circular space of smooth green turf—where Rody weaves romances for his sister's diversion—"quare ould invintions, whin the rabbits come out here of an evenin', lettin' on to her 'twas the fairies were in it." Maureen loses her evening's entertainment and her faith in Rody through the inadvertence of Christy McKenna, but she gains the young sailor for her lover, and soon after they are happily married. "Goodness help you, lad," says Mrs. O'Dell, "and what at all will you be doin' wid only a dark wife to keep house for you?" "Bedad, ma'am, I'll tell you that aisy, if you'll tell me what I'm to do widout her; for me soul to the saints, if I know, be any manner of manes." "Stopped by Signal" is full of delicious drollery, and "A Cream-Coloured Cactus" completes the trio of masterpieces in the volume. With every new book Miss Jane Barlow ratifies the verdict of literary experts that she is a writer of enduring excellence. (Macmillan. 75 c.)—*Boston Literary World.*

Almayer's Folly.

"ALMAYER'S FOLLY" is unmistakably a serious and valuable contribution to literature. The idea is not only original, but the subtle development of the central and ruling motive is splendidly conceived and carried out. The gradual sapping of Almayer's moral and mental powers, the unequal contest going on in his mind between the essential selfishness of a weak moral nature and the affection for his daughter Nina, born of a Malay wife whom he married for the dreams of avarice which she was expected to realize for him; the sudden gust of passionate uprising against fate—which shows the dignity there is even in the ruins of a man—ere his hopes sink in the night of absolute despair are only equalled by the same masterly portrayal of Nina — poor Nina ! — in whose breast there slumbered, despite her education and early training among her father's people, the ineradicable instincts of the Malay mother, which, under favoring circumstances, asserted their racial strength and encompassed the overthrow of the white man. Civilization had not shown its good side to her, and was only the more despised and detested by contrast with the bravery and vigorous manhood of the Malay lover for whom Nina abandoned her loved and loving European father. She is a fine illustration of what may happen to the Malay in the transition which Mr. Swettenham sees is imminent. The phase of character is a revelation to us, and in this whole story of an Eastern river we are impressed with the fact that a new vein has been struck in fiction. It is a work to make one long for more from the same pen. In the novelty of its local color, in the daring originality of its dramatic force, in the fresh disclosure of new scenes and characters, in the noble and imaginative handling of life's greatness and littleness, "Almayer's Folly" has no place in the prevalent fiction of the hour, which, like a flooded stream, sweeps past us into oblivion. It leaps at once to a place of its own—a place which ought to rank its author high among novelists worthy of the name in its best sense. In the scenery and atmosphere of the story the hand of the artist reveals itself. The sombre and languid air of a semi-civilized life is most skilfully conveyed—the dreamy river, its islands and reed banks, the thunder-storms, the thirst for the gains of civilization, and the contempt for its restraints, are vividly impressed on the imagination. Mr. Conrad has not only achieved a great success in realizing for us the fundamental truths underlying existence in a land and among a people almost unknown to the Far West—he deserves it. His book is one to be read and reread. (Macmillan. $1.25.) —*The Bookman.*

Four Years of Novel Reading.

THE editor of this little book introduces himself as Professor of Literature in English in the University of Chicago, which we interpret as a somewhat expansive rendering of the ordinary Professor of English literature. His book belongs in the educational class and is an essay not towards the popularizing of fiction, but of the *study* of fiction, and that fiction of the select and classical variety. Mr. Moulton leads off with an apologetic introduction in which he says the best he can for novel reading. What he says holds for all classical novels and for a good many that fall several degrees lower, provided they are read wisely, but concedes the demoralizing influence of the diet of fiction on which so many people are living nowadays. As a corrective he proposes a scheme of more serious study of classical novels, one which has been in successful operation in an English mining town for four years and which is fully described in this little book. The members agree on a list, read one classical novel a month, noting points that are sent out in connection with each novel. They then prepare and read critical essays. Four representative examples are published by Professor Moulton. (Heath. 50 c.)— *Public Opinion.*

Fallacies of Race Theories.

THE object of these essays is to combat the growing tendency to exaggerate the influence of race alone. Race is now often and inconsiderately set down as a sufficient and final explanation of national characteristics. To counteract such views Mr. Babington has not entered on a systematic and abstract discussion of race theories in general. He has taken the more practical course of testing by results. He reviews the progress and changing phases of the principal nations of whose civilization we have reliable accounts, and shows that their history explains far more than their descent. With this object he traces the social changes in the Roman Empire, and the injurious effects of the Barbaric invasions; he brings forward much that has lain unnoticed as to Gauls and Germans, and deals with many of Herr Mommsen's views with critical severity. He also inquires whether there are really distinct English and Irish races; and finally he analyzes the cause of Chinese stagnation as being due to their philosophical and political systems, not their race—an argument much confirmed by recent events.

He thus shows that the mental and moral characteristics which distinguish groups of men, called nations, are mainly the results of the circumstances in which they have been placed and trained, their "env ronment," and that along with this they grow and change, gradually taking "the form and pressure" of the influences acting on them. He denies the popular "Theory of Race," which makes the present qualities of groups of men almost wholly de-

From "Maureen's Fairing." Copyright, 1895, by Macmillan & Co.
A LOYAL IRISH WOMAN.

pendent on those of their ancestors long centuries before, transmitted by heredity from the remote past.

Mr. Babington's unexpected death in November, 1893. prevented this publication being made under his own superintendence; and hence the essays, so far as completed, have been edited by his friend, Mr. Hercules H. G. MacDonnell. The author's skill has made the really deep subject of interest to all intelligent readers. (Longmans, Green & Co. $2.)

From "The Old Settler, the Squire, and Little Peleg." Copyright, 1895, by United States Book Co.

"THEN FOLKS GOT TO SAYIN' TH'T OL' MISS HAGENCRUFT WERE A WITCH."

The Old Settler, the Squire, and Little Peleg.

THE Old Settler and the Squire who figure in these sketches are characters drawn from life. The originals were in their day typical representatives of the backwoods lounger and gossiper. The Old Settler, with his irascibility and his extravagant imagination, and the Squire always ready to flag him and to lead him on to his grandest flights, are among the pleasant recollections of the author's boyhood. While the tales here told may not be just the ones the Old Settler was wont to be ready to regale his hearers with, they faithfully depict the manner of his telling. Little Peleg, who is made responsible here for the bringing forth of some of the Old Settler's most astounding narratives, is brought into the stories as the veteran's grandson.

These sketches, or a large number of them, appeared originally in the N. Y. *Sun*, to which the author is indebted for their widespread popularity. This is their first appearance in book form. There are twenty-five separate tales, all full of life and knowledge of human nature. (United States Book Co. $1.)

Dowden's New Studies in Literature.

PROF. DOWDEN has added to his reputation by bringing his writings before a more leisurely class of readers than they would be likely to have in a periodical publication, and has afforded these readers the pleasure that results from the opportunity of placing a thoroughly good book on their choicest shelves. Mr. Dowden is one of the not very large number of modern British scholars who have devoted themselves to the study of literature as literature, and to the writing of criticisms as criticisms, and he has proved his proficiency both as a critic and as a scholar. Deficient in the graces of style, for his touch is rather a heavy one, and not solicitous to be thought original or to promulgate novel opinions, his learning is large and exact, his judgment sound and catholic, and his decisions for the most part as satisfactory as instructive. The papers in this volume of his cover a great deal of ground, the exploration of which demanded several kinds of talent, all of which had to be well kept in hand. Four of these papers are poetic studies, one of such an enigmatic early master as John Downe ; the rest of such different masters and pupils as Coleridge, George Meredith, and Robert Bridges. There are five different studies on Goethe, and two on literary criticism in France, the final paper being on "The Teaching of English Literature," the introductory one consisting of an examination of the democratic tendencies of the age and their bearing on literature and art. Large views of literature and acute criticisms give the satisfaction which attaches to all sound, well-considered, scholarly writing. (Houghton, Mifflin & Co. $3.)—*Mail and Express.*

Rust of Gold.

It may be at once said that the author of "Rust of Gold ".is the owner of enviable literary powers, which have enabled him to write a really brilliant book that has the "exotic virtue" of entertainment and suggestiveness. Francis Prevost gives one the rare impression that he has found the medium, in the *conte*, most suited to his talents and temperament, and even when his book has passed its third reading the impression remains—unfaltering. The story entitled "Grass Upon the House-tops" is possibly that one which offers most distinctly the best characteristics of this new and welcome writer. To meet with wit of a high and subtle order, restraint, and, above all, distinction in the telling of a tale, it is usually safest to go straight to, let us say, Henry James, Thomas Hardy, or Marriott Watson among recent writers. But "hereinafter," as lawyers say, the man who can produce for our pleasure sighs, or smiles, a "Rust of Gold" claims place equal with these. For of such is the "elect of Parnassus." In

"Grass Upon the House-tops" the study of the doctor's wife, Madge Guest and her curious cicisbeo, the poet possesses at once the definite value of skilful pencraft and the elusive charm of "style." Mrs. Guest "had married a country doctor for bis wit, and she would do the next best she could for any one who was wittier. Saltoun Pedley, poet and persifleur, *was* wittier, but an accident prevented Madge Guest from doing "the next best" for him. After the accident he went to his rooms, and then committing his inmost soul to a poem, as though to a priest, passed down into the silence. Of the remaining eight tales, "An Exotic Virtue " and "The Skirts of Chance" are, past a doubt, those destined for the most praise. E. W. Hornung's "An Idle Singer" stood recorded as the most charming study of a literary topic until the reading of "The Skirts of Chance." If Francis Prevost is not accorded the "due praise that is the meed of doing well," our shame will be great upon us. (Longmans, Green & Co. $1.25.)—*Books of To-day and To-morrow.*

From " In Camphor."

They are all put away in camphor now,
The soft warm wraps and the furs ;
She wore them in hours of happiest play,
These garments so dear that were hers.

THE KEY TO THE CAMPHOR CHEST.

A FAINT ring at the door-bell.
  " A child," my sad heart said.
" The band is small and trembling,
  Or weak for want of bread."

And when the bell was answered,
  A child scarce ten years old—
Whose clothes were thin and threadbare—
  Stood shivering in the cold.

Two little shoes with toes out,
  Two little hands both red,
Oh, dear sad eyes, how wistful,
  Longing, yet filled with dread.

" If you 've some clothes for children"—
  She seemed quite dumb from fear—
You see I have n't any "—
  And waiting, dropped a tear.

This lowly child I looked at ;
  " The camphor chest "—I said,
" Its soft warm furs and clothing
  Not needed by my dead."

I took her hand—'t was trembling,
  And led her to the chest ;
Must I unlock my heart's grief
  To help this child—God 's guest ?

I took a soft warm bonnet,
  With fresh bow knots of lace,
And tying on I whispered,
  " Let mother keep that face ! "

Her cold thin hands transparent
  These gloves seem just to fit;
Her sweet eyes lost their sadness,
  And smiles began to flit.

Shoes hardly worn and stockings,
  Soft flannels, frocks and furs—
" You, little girl, are welcome ;
  All of them once were hers."

The chest will soon be empty,
  For love has found the key ;
I hear Him gently whisper,
  " Ye did it unto Me."

(Putnam. $1.25.)—*From "In Camphor."*

IDEAS FOR SALE.

I'm in literary culture, and I've opened up a shop,
Where I'd like ye, gents and ladies, if you're passing by
  to stop.
Come and see my rich assortment of fine literary seed
That I'm selling to the writers of full many a modern
  screed.

I have motifs by the thousand, motifs sad and motifs gay.
You can buy 'em by the dozen, or I'll serve 'em every
  day;
I will serve 'em in the morning, as the milkman serves
  his wares;
I will serve 'em by the postman, or I'll leave 'em on your
  stairs.

When you get down to your table with your head a
  vacuum,
You can say unto your helpmeet, " Has that quart of
  ideas come
That we ordered served here daily from that plotman
  down the street ? "
And you'll find that I've been early my engagement to
  complete.

Should you want a book of poems that will bring you
  into fame,
Let me send a sample package that will guarantee the
  same,
Holding " Seeds of thought from Byron, Herrick, Chaucer, Tennyson."
Plant 'em deep, and keep 'em watered, and you'll find the
  deed is done.

I've a hundred comic packets that would make a Twain
  of Job ;
I have " Seeds of Tales Narcotic ; Tales of Surgeons and
  the Probe."
I've a most superb assortment, on the very cheapest
  terms,
Done up carefully in tinfoil, of my A 1 " Trilby Germs."

So perchance if you're ambitious in a literary line,
Be as dull as e'er you can be, you will surely cut a shine,
If you'll only take advantage of this opportunity,
When you're passing by to stop in for a little chat with
  me.

You may ask me, in conclusion, why I do not seek myself
All the laurel and the glory of these seeds I sell for pelf.
I will tell you, though the confidence I can't deny is rash,
I'm a trifle long on laurels, and a little short of cash.
          —*John Kendrick Bangs,*
    In Harper's Magazine for August.

" Under the hawthorne, where the sun is pale,
  The fairies told a marvellous tale."

Twenty-five Letters on English Authors.

As a text-book and guide through the labyrinths of literature, the letters have value, as their author has a clear conception of that of which she has written, enforced and fortified by a clean, healthy mind, that has been influenced only by the best critics. She advises all to eschew poor, weak, anæmic stuff, and that which had its origin in disease. Therein she is unquestionably right. Read nothing but that which will elevate and improve one; adopt a high standard, and cling to it. The young and impressionable reader cannot afford to do otherwise, even if an older reader may, which is doubtful. As one should strive to get only the best in life, so he or she should strive only for the best in literature. Nothing that is detrimental or degrading in literature can be read without having its effect.

Reading "only for recreation" is a poor excuse for wasting time on books that have an evil influence, books that lower the moral tone. "Ah! but I do not remember that which I read; I am merely killing time," such a reader will say, thinking that he is honest in the assertion. But he is not. He is gratifying a desire that will lead him to retain much that he reads, and so blunt his sensibilities to the higher and nobler things of life. Nothing that is ever read is entirely obliterated from the mind. It will be recalled when least expected, and its influence will then be perceived if the person is honest with himself. And so books like this one by Mary Fisher are of inestimable value in starting young readers on the proper paths.

The author says: "One should read as one eats—with appetite only." This is well, but it should be looked to that the appetite be healthy, and does not crave books that produce a mental dyspepsia, but rather seeks those that serve as mental tonics, and so brace us for a purer, a healthier life. In pursuit of her object, after a short chapter on the origin and development of the English language, the author devotes a letter to Chaucer, and from him comes down through the various literary periods to Ruskin and Tennyson. To some of the more prominent authors she devotes entire chapters; others she gives in groups, as their individuality had not so marked an influence on the literature of their time.

She is a stout defender of industrious habits and close application. She does not overlook the fact that geniuses are occasionally born, and to those who would write she gives sage advice, while stating that the saddest history in the world is that of geniuses. What she says of Sir Walter Scott she says more or less positively of others, to whom she directs her pupil's attention. It is sound advice and well worth considering:

"Do you know Scott as a novelist? If you don't, begin to make his acquaintance at once. You are of the right age to enjoy him. If you wait until you are maturer, you may find your interest in old castles and romantic adventures on the wane. You may wish to take your history and fiction separately, and you will miss the pleasure of growing up with some characters you cannot afford not to know. Better far miss anything about 'Trilby,' or 'Katharine Lauderdale,' or 'Marcella,' than miss knowing 'Jeanie Deans,' 'Dominie Sampson,' 'Meg Merrilies,' and a score of others who will still be walking among men, hale and hearty, when 'Trilby's' feet are dust and ashes.

"I sometimes feel very sorry for the children of to-day, for whom children's magazines and countless children's books leave no time or no desire to get acquainted with these immortal classics that as much belong to childhood as their right to dream and love and be happy— 'Pilgrim's Progress,' 'Robinson Crusoe,' 'Don Quixote,' 'Arabian Nights,' 'Gulliver's Travels,' 'Paul and Virginia,' 'The Vicar of Wakefield,' and Walter Scott's novels. I dare say I have omitted as many equally good, but these are the books on which I should base a child's literary taste." (Griggs. $1.50.)—*New York Times.*

Cause and Effect.

THE leading characters in Ellinor Meirion's "Cause and Effect," a story of a season at the Riviera, are of strongly contrasted types. A fascinating but perfidious Russian, and a countrywoman of similar character and attractions, stand out in striking relief by the side of an English girl brought up in a clerical set, and a dogmatic and strait-laced young curate, who has made up his mind to marry her. The fact that she is not particularly anxious for the union only serves to whet his desire to clinch an engagement between them before she is carried off to the perilous distractions of Monte Carlo. She, however, succeeds in preserving her liberty until she falls a ready prey to the Russian rake and Nihilist. The point that the author seems to wish to emphasize is that in the treatment of a girl with feeling and imagination, it is not safe to ignore these dangerous factors in her composition. They have an inconvenient way of asserting themselves, regardless of opposition. The story is well told, and all the characters have been carefully considered. A few of the secondary personages, such as Miss O'Hara, the frivolous but shrewd Irish girl, and Mrs. Percival, the cynical observer of the petty life of a cathedral town, are particularly well sketched. (Putnam. 75 c.)— *London Literary World.*

MAGAZINE ARTICLES FOR SEPTEMBER.

Articles marked with an asterisk are illustrated.

ARTISTIC, MUSICAL AND DRAMATIC.—*Century*, Flemish Old Masters,* Timothy Cole.—*Chautauquan*, Arts and Industries of Venice, Molmenti.—*Fortnightly Review* (Aug.), Eleanora Duse, William Archer.—*Harper's*, Notes on Indian Art,* Lord Weeks.—*Lippincott's*, The Decadent Drama, Edward Fuller.—*Nineteenth Century* (Aug.), Dialogue on the Drama, Kennedy.—*Scribner's*, Wood ·Engravers,* Clément Bellenger; Photography in Fiction, Alex. Black.

BIOGRAPHY, CORRESPONDENCE, ETC.—*Catholic World*, A Great Engineer, John J. O'Shea; What George Canning Owed to an Irish Actor, Patrick Sarsfield Cassidy.—*Century*, Recollections of Henry Clay,* McDowell.—*Chautauquan*, Glimpses of Noble Lives, Grace Dodge.—*Fortnightly Review* (Aug.), Professor Huxley, by several Scientists.—*Forum*, Professor Huxley, Richard H. Hutton.—*North American*, Professor Huxley, Sir William H. Flower.

DESCRIPTION, TRAVEL, ETC.—*Atlantic*, Chickamauga, Torrey.—*Century*, Hunting Customs of the Omahas,* Fletcher ; National Military Park,* Boynton.—*Chautauquan*, Notable Inns Around London, Nettie Louise Beal.—*Cosmopolitan*, The Ancient Capital of Cuba,* Hyatt; House-Party at Abbotsford.—*Harper's*, Three Gringos in Central America,* Richard Harding Davis; Evolution of the Cow-Puncher,* Wister. — *Scribner's*, Au Large (Canada),* Van Dyke.

DOMESTIC AND SOCIAL. — *Chautauquan*, The Ideal Hostess, Emily Huntington Miller.

EDUCATION, LANGUAGE, ETC.—*Forum*, Methods and Difficulties of Child Study, Barus.

FICTION.—*Atlantic*, Mystery of Witch-Face Mountain, Charles Egbert Craddock.—*Catholic World*, Sister Katherine, Mary Boyle O'Reilly; The Master's Cup, "Hildegarde"; A Swiss Legend, T. L. L. Teeling.—*Century*, Cup of Trembling, Mary Hallock Foote; All My Sad Captains,* Sarah Orne Jewett.—*Chautauquan*, A Boy of To-Day, Martha Young.—*Cosmopolitan*, The Nixey Chord, Boyesen; Tempted by the Devil, Conan Doyle.—*Harper's*, Jamie, Ian Maclaren; People We Pass,* Julian Ralph; At the Grand Hotel du Paradis,* Janvier.— *Lippincott's*, A Case in Equity, Lynde; The Literary Woman at the Picnic, Ella Wheeler Wilcox.—*Scribner's*, A Photograph (Girls' College Life),* Goodloe; The Art of Living—The Case of Man,* Robert Grant.

HISTORY.—*Century*, Life in the Tuileries under the Second Empire, Part I.,* Bicknell.— *Harper's*, The German Struggle for Liberty,* Bigelow.

LITERARY.—*Atlantic*, Guides: a Protest, Agnes Repplier.—*Catholic World*, Canadian Poets and Poetry, O'Hagan.—*Century*, On the Writing of History, Wilson.—*Fortnightly Review* (Aug.), Beauty and Saints, Vernon Lee.— *Forum*, George Eliot's Place in Literature,

Frederic Harrison.—*Godey's*, Women, Writers of the Day, Willets.—*Lippincott's*, Molière, Ellen Duval.

MENTAL AND MORAL.—*Harper's*, Mental Telegraphy Again, Mark Twain.

NATURE AND SCIENCE. — *Century*, Aquatic Gardening, Connelly. — *Cosmopolitan*, In the Realm of the Wonderful Hudson. — *North American*, Crop Conditions and Prospects, Assistant Statistician of Agricultural Dept.

POETRY AND DRAMA.—*Atlantic*, A Sailor's Wedding, Bliss Carman; Tiger Lilies, Michael Field.—*Century*, Moon Flower,* Julia Schayer; Ballad of Chickamauga, Maurice Thompson; The Constitution's Last Fight,* Roche, Together Against the Stream, Will H. Thompson.—*Harper's*, The Trilogy, Julian Hawthorne; Pebbles, Howells.

POLITICAL AND SOCIAL.—*Atlantic*, President Polk's Administration, James Schouler.—*Catholic World*, The Trend of Total Abstinence; An Introduction to the Study of Society, McDermot.—*Chautauquan*, Fresh Air Work in New York City, W. H. Tolman.—*Cosmopolitan*, Brigham Young and Modern Utah, Cockerill; A Famous Crime, George C. Holt.—*Fortnightly Review* (Aug.), Ministerial Responsibility, Sidney Low.—*Nineteenth Century* (Aug.), Old Age Homes in Austria, Sellers.— *Westminster Review* (Aug.), Censorship of the Press in Russia, Burton; Old Age Pensions, Williams; Religious Instruction in the Public Schools of the United States, Joseph Henry Crooker.—*North American*, Why Women do Not Want the Ballot, Bishop of Albany; Our Reviving Business, Comptroller of the Currency; The Cuban Situation, Late Mayor of Havana; Country Roads and Trolleys, J. Gilmer Speed.—*Forum*, Municipal Progress and the Living Wage, Means; Enforcement of Law, Roosevelt; Criminal Anthropology, Lombroso; Shall Cuba be Free, Clarence King; Benefits of Hard Times,Edward Atkinson; Civil Service as a Career, Newcomb; Unsanitary Condition of Public Schools and Public Indifference, Douglas H. Stewart.— *Godey's*, The Stage and the Church, Fletcher; Cuban Revolution,Hughes.—*Harper's*,Arabia—Islam and the Eastern Question, Dr. Wm. H. Thomson.

SPORTS AND AMUSEMENTS. — *Chautauquan*, Outdoor Sports in and About New York, Mandigo.—*Godey's*, Pleasures of Yachting,* Locke; Recent Amateur Photography,* Crane.—*Lippincott's*, Crabbing, Wilson.—*Outing*, Cup Champions and Their Crews,* Burchard; Fox Hunting by Moonlight,* Humphreys; Cycling on the Palisades of the Hudson,* Ernest Ingersoll; International Athletics of 1895; Family Camping,* Emily H. Palmer.—*Scribner's*, Country Clubs and Hunt Clubs in America,* Martin; The Bicycle in History and Romance (The Point of View.)

THEOLOGY, RELIGION, AND SPECULATION.— *Catholic World*, Law of Moses and the Higher Criticism, Hewit; Monasticism in Scotland, Austin; The Lustre of the Light of Asia, Ryan. —*Nineteenth Century*, Spencer *versus* Balfour, Mivart; Theological Pessimism, Frederic Harrison.

Che Literary News.

An Eclectic Monthly Review of Current Literature.

EDITED BY A. H. LEYPOLDT.

SEPTEMBER, 1895.

LIST OF BOOKS FOR GIRLS AND WOMEN.

In 1892, at the Lakewood Conference of the American Library Association, Mr. George Iles offered a paper on "The Evaluation of Literature," which was discussed with considerable interest. Mr. Iles contended that libraries should have some system of obtaining reviews of new books in various fields of literature that would give an expert's view of the comparative merits of new works and those already existing, and also fearlessly point out deficiencies and criticise methods. All such criticism was to be signed, and publishers and librarians were called upon to look about them for the right men to do such critical work upon the appearance of the book, untrammelled by any commercial or other considerations but the intrinsic value of the book. The publishing section of the American Library Association decided to publish work of this kind if it could be put into shape. Women and girls were thought to need special direction in the use of libraries, and the first annotated list of books was undertaken to supply their needs. In 1894, at the Lake Placid Conference, this list was put into preparation by collaboration under direction of Miss Ellen M. Coe. Miss Coe married shortly after, and Mr. Iles, who is a member of the Executive Committee of the Publishing Section, undertook the arduous task of taking charge of the work and providing the needed expert labor. It could not have fallen into better hands. Mr. Iles knows what he wants, and is untiring in his efforts to attain it. He has planned this list to appear in five parts, of which the first two, "Fiction" and "Biography," are now issued by the Library Bureau of Boston. The fiction list has been compiled by a "Reviewer for *The Nation*," which means capacity and literary experience. This department represents about 250 authors and their most noted works, ranging from Richardson's epoch-making novels to Du Maurier's "Trilby." In every case a short biographical note is made of the author, and in every case where the novel mentioned deals with any historical, political, social, or ethical subject the ground covered is indicated in a terse note. The publishers and prices of the books are given, and also the shelf number of the Dewey classification, that it may be of use to librarians in finding books asked for. This part of the work has fallen almost wholly upon Mr. Iles. Part 2 entitled Biography, by Assistant Librarians of the New York Free Circulating Library ; History, by Reuben G. Thwaites; Travel, by Miss A. R. Hasse ; Literature : Poetry, Essays, Criticism, by Graeme Mercer Adam; and Folklore, by Stewart Culin, is a great advance on Part 1 for thoroughness and sense of proportion. If the list improves part by part in like ratio, it will be most valuable at "the finish." The other departments to complete this very valuable list will be—Part 3 : Fine Arts, by Russell Sturgis ; Music, by H. E. Krehbiel, musical editor of the N. Y. *Tribune*. Part 4 : Education, Self-culture, Science, by Miss Angeline Brooks, Olive Thorne Miller, Prof. E. R. Shaw and others. Part 5 : Useful Arts, Livelihoods, Country Occupations, Domestic Economy, Recreations and Sports, by various contributors. These parts, together with lists of works of reference and of periodicals, and hints on forming and managing girls' and women's clubs, and a thorough index, will be issued in October as an octavo volume with pages four times the size of those of the parts.

Although gotten up ostensibly for women and girls, the collaborators have had in mind all readers of average culture, and the selection of books makes a valuable reading list for all time and all localities. The little booklets of fiction and general literature are attractive in size, type, paper. Although the criticisms naturally show personal bias, they are in the main trustworthy and generally liberal.

A BALLADE OF POETS.

Where are the poets of the past
    Whose voices rang divinely true ?—
Whose thoughts munificent and vast
    From stars and suns their music drew ?—
    To whom the gods a welcome blew,
And lamps from far Parnassus shone ? . . .
    None dare the heights to which they flew,
Since Alfred Tennyson is gone.

The freshening gale strained spar and mast,
    The billows great and greater grew ;
The vessel forward sped and fast,
    Nor port nor anchorage she knew ;
    Naught recked they of the circling view—
Their only end was to sweep on. . . .
    Vanished are captain, ship, and crew,
Since Alfred Tennyson is gone.

Now lesser men their fortunes cast
    In lesser seas, and zephyrs woo ;
Their lutes are thin, they cannot last—
    We listen but to say adieu.
    The artificial gems they strew
Of specious glitter fade anon. . . .
    Is there no granite left to hew,
Since Alfred Tennyson is gone ?

ENVOY.

Fled are the mighty bards and few ;
    The ways of song are barren, wan. . . .
Fled is the perfect manner, too,
    Since Alfred Tennyson is gone.
        —A. T. Schuman, in *The Dial*.

Survey of Current Literature.

☞ Order through your bookseller.—"There is no worthier or surer pledge of the intelligence and the purity of any community than their general purchase of books; nor is there any one who does more to further the attainment and possession of these qualities than a good bookseller."—PROF. DUNN.

BIOGRAPHY, CORRESPONDENCE, ETC.

HAYGOOD, ATTICUS G., *sr.* The monk and the prince. Foote & Davies Co. 12°, $1.
A study and critical review of the character and career of Savonarola and of Lorenzo de Medici. The writer does not hold Savonarola in high esteem as a reformer.

HUBBARD, ELBERT. W. M. Thackeray. Putnam. 16°, (Little journeys to the homes of good men and great.) pap., 5 c.

HUBBARD, ELBERT. William Wordsworth. Putnam. 16°, (Little journeys to the homes of good men and great.) pap., 5 c.

KOVALÉVSKY, SONIA. Sonia Kovalévsky: biography and autobiography. (1) Memoir by A. C. Leffler (Edgren), Duchessa di Cajanello; (2) Reminiscences of childhood, written by herself; tr. by Louise Von Cossel. Macmillan. por. 12°, $1.25.

REAY, MARTHA, *and* HACKMAN, JA. The love letters of Mr. H. and Miss R., 1775-1779; ed. by Gilbert Burgess. Stone & Kimball. 12°, $1.50.

REID, STUART J. Lord John Russell. Harper. por. 12°. (Prime ministers of Queen Victoria.) $1.

STEPHEN, LESLIE. Life of Sir James Fitzjames Stephen, Bart., K. C. S. I.; by his brother. Putnam. pors. 8°, *net*, $4.50.

TARBELL, IDA M. A short life of Napoleon Bonaparte. S. S. McClure, Limited. pors. 8°, (McClure's magazine library, no. 1.) pap., 50 c.
Profusely illustrated by many pictures never before published from the Hon. Gardiner G. Hubbard's collection of Napoleon engravings, supplemented by pictures from the collections of Prince Victor Napoleon, Prince Roland Bonaparte, Baron Larrey and others.

WATTS, H. Miguel de Cervantes; his life and works. *New ed. rev. and enl.*, with a complete bibliography and index. Macmillan. por. 8°, $2.50.

DESCRIPTION, GEOGRAPHY, TRAVEL, ETC.

KING, MOSES, *ed.* How to see Boston: a trustworthy guide-book. Moses King. il. maps and plans, sq. 16°, (King's handbook.) pap., 25 c.
The edition is entirely a new book. The street maps and plans are all new and record the latest changes. The illustrations are from latest photographs. The p'an contemplates a dozen or more easy half-day routes, on foot or by street-cars, as the book is prepared for the masses. The text was written chiefly by M. F. Sweetser. Full index.

REMINGTON, F. Pony tracks. Harper. il. 8°, $3.
Sketches of pioneer life chiefly in the West,

dedicated to the fellows who made the tracks. Contents: Chasing a major-general; Lieutenant Casey's last scout; Sioux outbreak in South Dakota; An outpost of civilization; Rodes at Los Ojos; In the Sierra Madre with the punchers; Black water and shallows; Coaching in Chihuahua; Stubble and slough in Dakota; Policing in Yellowstone; Model squadron; Affair of the —th of July; Colonel of the First Cycle Infantry; Merry Christmas in Sibley Tepee; Bear-chasing in the Rocky Mountains. 70 illustrations. Cover design covered with pony tracks.

SOMERSET, H. SOMERS. The land of the muskeg; with a preface by A. Hungerford Pollen; il. from sketches by A. H. Pollen and instantaneous photographs. Imported by Lippincott. maps, por. 8°, $4.
Description of a hunting trip for grizzly bears and other large game in Alberta, Athabasca, and British Columbia. The region travelled over is largely unexplored and given over to the Indians, and is controlled by the Hudson's Bay Company. The party consisted of two young Englishmen and two Americans, and suffered many privations in their search for sport and adventure.

WHITE, CAROLINE EARLE. A holiday in Spain and Norway. Lippincott. 12°, pap., 50 c.
Descriptive letters by the author of "Love in the tropics," etc.

DOMESTIC AND SOCIAL.

KAPPELER, G. J. Modern American drinks: how to mix and serve all kinds of cups and drinks. Merriam Co. 16°, $1.
"The book is especially designed for use in hotels, clubs, buffets, and barrooms of the higher class. It tells how to make cups, crustas, cobblers, coolers, egg-nogs, fixes, fizzes, flips, juleps, lemonades, punches, poussé cafés, and other drinks, hot and cold, alcoholic and non-alcoholic. Most of the receipts are very simple, and may be followed easily. As they are grouped and classified systematically, the book will prove very convenient for those whom it was intended to serve."—*N. Y. Times.*

LOWNDES, *Rev.* ARTHUR. The power of woman. Pott. 8°, 25 c.

SALIS, *Mrs.* HARRIET A. DE. Gardening à la mode: fruits. Longmans, Green & Co. 16°, bds., 60 c.

EDUCATION, LANGUAGE, ETC.

GUERBER, H. A. Contes et légendes; première partie. American Book Co. 12°, 60 c.
Intended as an introduction to general French reading. The stories are told as simply as possible, with much repetition of the same words and idiom, to enable pupils to acquire a large vocabulary almost unconsciously. A vocabulary and a few notes are added for the benefit of such pupils as have missed connecting les

sons, but the plan is for oral instruction. Chiefly for blackboard illustration.

LANE, F. H. Elementary Greek education. Bardeen. 16°, leatherette, 50 c.

The aims, methods, and results of education during the "age of heroes," rendered immortal by the epic poets, and the period of "state education" which closed with the Peloponnesian War, 404 B.C., are here outlined.

OAKLEY, ISABELLA G. Simple lessons in the study of nature for the use of pupils. W. Beverley Harison. 16°, 75 c.

A question book with answers withheld until observation and experiment suggest them. Intended to introduce inductively the study of botany, zoölogy, and (to a small extent) natural philosophy. The first book is adapted to children of the average age of nine years, and contains work for one year.

PARMELE *Mrs.* MARY. The evolution of an empire: a brief historical sketch of England. W. Beverley Harison. 12°, 75 c.

"Mainly an attempt to trace to their sources some of the currents which enter into the life of England to-day, and to indicate the startingpoints of some among the various threads—legislative, judicial, social, etc.—which are gathered into the imposing strands of English civilization in this closing 19th century."—*Preface.* An excellent foundation for a more elaborate study of English history.

WEBSTER's Academic dictionary : a dictionary of the English language ; with an appendix cont. various useful tables ; abridged from "Webster's International dictionary." American Book Co. il. 8°, hf. leath., $1.50.

"Webster's Academic dictionary" appeared in 1867 abridged from the old dictionary ; now it is an entirely new book abridged from the "International dictionary." The alterations consist chiefly in the increase of the amount of matter, the improvements in typography, the method of indicating pronunciation, and the use of new and better illustrations (the number has been increased from 350 to over 800). In the appendix much space has been saved by consolidating into one the various pronouncing vocabularies of proper names. The lists of abbreviations, foreign quotations and mythological personages have been enlarged.

FICTION.

BALDWIN, *Mrs.* ALFRED. The story of a marriage. *New rev. ed.* Imported by J. B. Lippincott. 1 il. 12°, $1.50.

The hero is a well-to-do young Englishman of the leisure class, with broad ideas of equality ; his dream is to elevate and reform the working class, by education and intermarriage with a rank above it. He carries his views into effect by making the beautiful but ignorant daughter of a market gardener his wife. The disastrous results of this marriage and the overthrow of his theories are the themes of this novel.

BALZAC, HONORÉ DE. Novels. V. 2, The Chouans (*Les Chouans*); tr. by Ellen Marriage ; with introd. by G. Saintsbury. Macmillan. il. 12°, silk, $1.50.

BATES, *Mrs.* LINDON W. Bunch-grass stories. Lippincott. 12°, $1.25.

Contents: Resurrection on the Umpqua ; The substitute ; The great concern ; Inspiration at the cross-roads ; The black shell ; Taken in at Oarés ; The Mavericks of the trail ; A transferred town.

BELDEN, JESSIE VAN ZILE. Fate at the door. Lippincott. 12°, buckram, $1.

Returning to New York from India after an absence of many years, John Strathmore is thrown into constant companionship with Mr. and Mrs. Courtlandt, rich New Yorkers of the "smart" set—Ernest Courtlandt being an old friend of his schooldays. Between Mrs. Courtlandt and Strathmore an affection grows up, which seriously affects the fate and happiness of each.

BIERCE, AMBROSE. Black beetles in amber. Johnson & Emigh. 12°, (Popular authors' ser., no. 1.) pap., 50 c.

BLOOMFIELD, WALTER. Holdenhurst Hall : a novel ; il. by Warren B. Davis. Bonner. 12°, (Ledger lib., no. 126.) $1 ; pap., 50 c.

BOULGER, *Mrs.* DORA HENRIETTA, ["Theo. Gift," *pseud.*] An island princess : a story of six weeks—and afterwards. Putnam. 12°, (The Hudson lib., no. 7.) $1 ; pap., 50 c.

An imaginary "English island in the Atlantic Ocean many thousand miles away," somewhat barren and little visited except by an occasional English man-of-war, which embraces among its inhabitants only one grown-up "lady-girl," is the scene of a pathetic love-story. Jean Conniston, "the island princess," is wooed and won by Lieut. Keith Fenwick, of H. M. S. *Parnassus*, who sails away at the end of six weeks and forgets her.

BROWN, ALICE. Meadow-grass : tales of New England life. Copeland & Day. 16°, $1.50.

Contents: Number five ; Farmer Eli's vacation ; After all ; Told in the poorhcuse ; Heman's Ma ; Heart'sease ; Mis' Wadleigh's guest ; A righteous bargain ; Joint owners in Spain ; At Sudleigh fair ; Bankrupt ; Nancy Boyd's last sermon ; Strollers in Tiverton.

BUTTERWORTH, HEZEKIAH. In old New England : the romance of a colonial fireside. Appleton. 12°, (Appleton's town and country lib., no. 173.) $1 ; pap., 50 c.

Short stories : Pardon Ponder, pedagogue ; The haunted oven, or, a regular old-fashioned Thanksgiving ; Wych Hazel, the Jew ; Captain Tut-tut-Tuttle and the miracle clock ; The inn of the good woman ; The bewitched clambake ; The miraculous basket ; No room in the inn, or, the old madhouse in the orchard ; Nix's mate ; Old "Bunker Hill" ; Milo Mills's Fourth of July poem ; Husking stories, songs, and fiddlers ; King Philip's last hunt.

"A charming book of stories, as cleverly conceived as they are pleasantly written."—*N. Y. Times.*

COBBLEIGH, TOM, [*pseud.* for Walter Raymond.] Gentleman Upcott's daughter. [*New issue.*] Cassell. nar. 12°, (The "unknown" lib., no. 20.) pap., 25 c.

CRACKANTHORPE, HUBERT. Sentimental studies, and a set of village tales. Putnam. 12°, $1.

Short stories by the author of "Wreckage." The "sentimental studies" are entitled : A commonplace chapter ; Battledore and Shuttlecock ; In Cumberland ; Modern melodrama ;

Yew-trees and Peacocks. The titles of the villages tales are : Lisa-La-Folle ; The white maize ; Saint-Pé ; Etienne Mattou ; The little priest ; Gaston Lalanne's child.

DAVIS, VARINA ANNE JEFFERSON. The veiled doctor : a novel. Harper. 12°, $1.25.
The daughter of Jefferson Davis tells a sad story of which the scene is a sleepy old town quite out of the lines of present travel, and the time almost a century ago. The doctor who had been the strength and comfort of his patients succumbs to abject fear and horror when told that he is the victim of a disease which must end in disfigurement and painful death. He is married and his wife and he live separate lives in the same house. The suffering of mind and heart borne by man and wife are old with dramatic power.

DEAN, Mrs. ANDREW, [pseud. for Mrs. Alfred Sidgwick.] A splendid cousin. [New issue.] Cassell. nar. 12°, (The "unknown" lib., no. 18.) pap., 25 c.

DIX, GERTRUDE. The girl from the farm. Roberts. 16°, (Keynotes ser.) $1.
The daughter of the Dean of an old English cathedral returns home after graduating with high honors at Newnham. She longs for congenial work in the reform movements of the day, but sees her duty calls her to assist her almost blind father in his literary work. Just as she has made her sacrifice of personal ambition a nearer duty still meets her in the person of "the girl from the farm." The compatibility of higher education and true womanhood is strongly shown in a well-told love-story.

DOYLE, A. CONAN, and others. Strange secrets. Fenno. 12°, $1.
"These fourteen stories make up a creepy collection purporting to be from the pen of A. Conan Doyle and others, although no names are given to identify the authorship of any of them. They are of varying degrees of interest and merit, but, as a whole, the quality is quite above the average. Several are very good ghost stories; in others the tantalizing secret has nothing to do with spectral appearances. There is sufficient variety to satisfy the most exacting taste for the marvellous, and there will not be lacking readers who will 'snatch a fearful joy' over even the most gruesome of them."—Boston Literary World.

FORSYTH, JEAN, (pseud.) The making of Mary. Cassell. nar. 12°, (The unknown lib.) 50 c.

GISSING, G. In the year of Jubilee. Appleton. 12°, (Appleton's town and country lib., no. 172.) $1; pap., 50 c.
The incidents of the novel occur in Camberwell, England, in the time of the Jubilee given in honor of the fifty years' reign of Queen Victoria. Nancy Lord having made a secret and hasty marriage just before the death of her father, learns that there is a clause forbidding her marriage under a specified age. The story centres in her action thereafter and in the mystery in her married life.

HABBERTON, J., [and others.] Where were the boys? and other short stories from Outing. Outing Pub. Co. nar. 16°, (Outing lib., v. 2, no. 1.) pap., 25 c.
Contents: Where were the boys? by J. Hab-

berton; In a far countree, by H. Cadle Tenney; George Dale's ambition, by Lorenzo Griswold; The captain's ghost, by Patience Stap'eton; The doctor's yarn, by Francis Trevelyan; The romance of a dead letter, by Frank Dempster Sherman.

HAWLEY, J. G. An appendix to Trilby : translations [of the foreign phrases in Du Maurier's "Trilby."] The Richmond & Backus Co. 16°, pap., 25 c.

HICHENS, ROB. S. An imaginative man. Appleton. 12°, $1.25.

HUME, FERGUS. The white prior : a family mystery. Warne. 16°, pap., 40 c.

KINGSLEY, H. Old Margaret, and other stories. New. ed., with frontispiece by Robert Sauber. Ward, Lock & Bowden, Ltd. 8°, $1.25.

LEAN, Mrs. FRANCIS, [formerly Florence Marryat.] At heart a rake. Cassell. 12°, $1.
Another "new woman" is introduced in Lady Phyllis Macnaughton. Against her husband's wishes she joins a woman's club where the manners and conversations are decidedly vulgar. She is warm-hearted and is led away to do most unconventional things, generally with good motives. Finally she feels trammelled and leaves her husband. She soon repents, however, and decides that the new woman of club and sporting fame is "at heart a rake."

LELAND, C. GODFREY ["Hans Breitmann," pseud.], comp. Legends of Florence collected from the people and retold by C. Godfrey Leland. Macmillan. 12°, $1.75.

MAARTENS, MAARTEN, [pseud. for J. Vander Poorsen Schwartz.] My lady nobody : a novel. Harper. il. 12°, $1.75.

MACMAHON, ELLA. A modern man; il. by Ida Lovering. Macmillan. 16°, (Iris ser.) 75 c.
A modern man is a lawyer of great talent, who has been the protégé of Lord Pomfret, and intends to marry the daughter of this most aristocratic English nobleman. After his engagement other ladies prove fascinating to him, but, when at last married, he confesses that he has become the husband of a wife truly suited to the complex needs of "a modern man."

MALLOCK, W. HURRELL. The heart of life. Putnam. 12°, $1.25.

MARSH, R. Mrs. Musgrave—and her husband. Appleton. 12°, (Appleton's town and country lib., no. 174.) $1; pap., 50 c.
The story of a woman born with a homicidal mania; she marries, concealing from her husband that she is the daughter of a murderer who had been hung. She follows her instincts in killing a man who threatens to betray her story to her husband. The description of her husband's suspicions turned to certainty, their wild flight from England to France, and the final tragedy when run down by the officers of the law, is thrillingly written.

MEIRION, ELLINOR. Cause and effect. Putnam. 16°, buckram, 75 c.

MORIER, JA. The adventures of Hajji Baba, of Ispahan; il. by H. R. Millar; with introd. by G. Curzon. Macmillan. 12°. (Macmillan's illustrated standard novels.) $1.25.

PARKER, GILBERT. When Valmond came to Pontiac: the story of a lost Napoleon. Stone & Kimball. 16°, $1.50.

PEMBERTON, MAX. The little Huguenot: a romance of Fontainebleau. Dodd, Mead & Co. por. nar. 16°, 75 c.

RUSSELL, W. CLARK. The honour of the flag. Putnam. nar. 12°, (Autonym lib., no. 4.) 50 c.
Eight stories of adventures at sea—namely: The honour of the flag; Cornered!; A midnight visitor; Plums from a sailor's duff; The strange adventures of a South seaman; The adventures of three sailors; The strange tragedy of the *White Star;* The ship seen on the ice.

SCULLY, W. C. Kafir stories. Holt. 1 il. nar. 16°, (Buckram ser.) 75 c.
Contents: The Eumenides in Kafirland; The fundamental axiom; Kelison's Nemesis ; The quest of the copper ; Ghamba ; Ukush Wama ; Umtagati. Glossary of Kafir words.

SHARP, EVELYN. At the Relton arms. Roberts. 16°, (Keynotes ser., no. 13.) $1.
An emotional musician, given to the performance of his own compositions, and a spendthrift favorite, are the sons of the squire of Relton, a man devoted to theoretical reform and philanthropy at the expense of his duties as husband and father. The love affairs of these two sons furnish the material for a story which introduces a very strong-minded and beautiful woman.

STUART, ESMÉ. Harum scarum: the story of a wild girl. The International News Co. 12°, (Authors' library.) $1.25; pap., 50 c.
The familiar story of a penniless young relation, who came from the free untrammelled life of Australia into the stiff surroundings of English aristocratic life. In this case this relation is a girl, full of noble impulses and love of her kind, who eats in the kitchen, rides bareback, insists upon the convenience of the companion being considered, and generally incenses her aunt, the duchess, by her fearless truth and total ignorance of class distinctions.

SUPER, *Mrs.* EMMA LEFFERTS. One rich man's son. Cranston & Curts. il. 12°, 90 c.
"How can we save from temporal and eternal ruin the sons and daughters of wealth?" is the question Mrs. Super's story aims to answer. It gives the plan that the mother of one rich man's son conceived for saving her boy, telling how heroically she carried it out.

THOMPSON, E. W. Old man Savarin, and other stories. Crowell. 16°, $1.
Contents: Old man Savarin; The privilege of the limits; McGrath's bad night; Great Godfrey's lament; The red-headed windego; The shining cross of Rigand; Little Baptiste; The ride by night; Drafted; A turkey apiece; Grandpapa's wolf story; The Waterloo veteran; John Bedell; Verbitzsky's stratagem.

WALFORD, *Mrs.* LUCY BETHIA. Ploughed, and other stories. Longmans, Green & Co. 12°, (Longmans' paper lib., no. 9.) pap., 50 c.
The author of "The baby's grandmother" draws in "Ploughed" the picture of a young scion of an ancient house who has been "ploughed"—left behind in the Oxford examinations by his own fault. The remaining stories are entitled "An Eastern cadet," "Only a pocket-handkerchief," and "Until seven times?"

WARD, *Mrs.* MARY AUGUSTA, [*Mrs.* T. Humphry Ward.] History of David Grieve. Macmillan. 12°, (Macmillan's novelists' lib.) pap., 50 c.

WESTALL, W. Sons of Belial. Cassell. 12°, $1.

WILLIAMS, G. F. Bullet and shell: a soldier's romance; il. from sketches among the actual scenes, by Edwin Forbes. [*New cheaper ed.*] Fords, Howard & Hulbert. 8°, $1.50.
It is doubtful if in this generation we can get a story of the civil war of thirty odd years ago that is not a bit one-sided. Twenty years from now some one will write us a novel worth reading of this Titanic struggle, the greatest civil war ever fought. Any book dealing with it in an honest way is, therefore, acceptable. Major Williams fought some, knew Grant, Sheridan, Sherman, the dare-devil Custer, Meade and the rest, and he tells a rollicking series of stories of camp life, in which there is no bravado—only some graphic sketches of things that came under the eye of Major Williams himself. The book is illustrated, but the illustrations are merely incidental. Major Williams' stories are good enough without them.

WINTER, J. STRANGE, [*pseud.* for *Mrs.* H. E. V. Stannard.] A magnificent young man, 12°, (Lippincott's select novels, no. 172.) $1; pap., 50 c.
Bladensbrook of Bladensbrook was a magnificent young man of immense size and great personal beauty. His father had been killed by a kick from a horse when the boy was five years old, and all his life his mother and he had lived as the great people of the neighborhood. His affections settled upon the rector's daughter. At the age of twenty-one he, by imprudent action, got himself into trouble, which for a year brought sorrow to all who held him dear.

ZOLA, ÉMILE. A love episode (*Une page d'amour*); tr. with a preface by Ernest A. Vizetelly; il. by François Thévenot. Lippincott. 8°, $2.

HISTORY.

SEEBOHM, F. Tribal system in Wales: part of an inquiry into the structure and methods of tribal society. Longmans, Green & Co. 8°, $4.

WITHERS, ALEX. SCOTT. Chronicles of border warfare ; or, a history of the settlement by the whites of northwestern Virginia, and of the Indian wars and massacres in that section of the state ; with reflections, anecdotes, etc. *New ed.*, ed. and annot. by Reuben Gold Thwaites ; with an addition of a memoir of the author and several illustrative notes, by Lyman Copeland Draper. The Robert Clarke Co. por. 8°, $2.50.
Originally published at Clarkesburg, in northwestern Virginia, in 1831. For the preparation of this new edition the services of Dr. Draper were engaged some five years ago ; Dr. Draper had spent many years in collecting material in this line, and was eminently fitted to edit Withers' work ; he died, unfortunately, before completing more than a third of the annotations, Mr. Thwaites taking up the work where Dr. Draper left it. Mr. Thwaites completed the annotations, added an analytical index and a selected bibliography, included in the index. As Dr. Draper's literary executor and as secre-

tary of the State Historical Society of Wisconsin, he possessed ample 'means for the proper elucidation of Withers' text.

HUMOR AND SATIRE.

LEAR, E. The book of nonsense. 13*th ed.*, with all the original pictures and verses. Warne. 4°, $2.

LITERATURE, MISCELLANEOUS AND COLLECTED WORKS.

AMERICAN LIBRARY ASSOCIATION, Publishing Section. List of books for girls and women and their clubs ; edited by George Iles. Part 1: Fiction; chosen and annotated by a reviewer for *The Nation.* Bost., Library Bureau, 1895. 160 p. Tt. 10 c.

COLERIDGE, S. TAYLOR. The golden book of Coleridge ; ed., with an introd., by Stopford A. Brooke. Macmillan. 16°, silk, $1.50.

COURTHOPE, W. J. A history of English poetry, V. 1, The middle ages ; Influence of the Roman empire ; The encyclopædic education of the church ; The feudal system. Macmillan. 8°, $2.50.

DOWDEN, E. New studies in literature. Houghton, Mifflin & Co. 12°, $3.
The separate studies are entitled : Mr. Meredith in his poems ; Poetry of Rob. Bridges ; Poetry of John Donne ; Amours de voyage ; Goethe (5 essays), including a document hitherto unpublished ; Coleridge as a poet ; Edmond Scherer ; Literary criticism in France ; Teaching of English literature.

FISHER, MARY. Twenty-five letters on English authors. Griggs & Co. 12°, $1.50.

FRAZER, J. G. Passages of the Bible chosen for their literary beauty and interest. Macmillan. 12°, $2.

GUERBER, H. A. Myths of northern lands, narrated with special reference to literature and art. American Book Co. il. 12°, $1.50.
A companion to "Myths of Greece and Rome" and "The legends of the Rhine." The myths of northern lands formed the basis of the religious belief and of the first attempts at poetry for Danes, Swedes, Icelanders, Germans, English and French people. Intended especially for libraries and schools. Glossary and complete index.
"It may be said that his work throughout is highly creditable, showing that he has mastered his subject and that he knows how to treat it in order to make it both instructive and entertaining."—*N. Y. Times.*

JACK, ADOLPHUS ALFRED. Thackeray: a study. Macmillan. 12°, $1.50.

SMITH, J. E. A. The poet among the hills— Oliver Wendell Holmes in Berkshire. Pittsfield. Blatchford. por. 12°, $1.
The poems relating to Berkshire and vicinity, some of them now first published, with historic and descriptive incidents concerning the poems, the poet and his literary labors; also his poetic personal and ancestral relations to the county.

MENTAL AND MORAL PHILOSOPHY.

BLACK, J. S. The Christian consciousness, its relation to evolution in morals and in doctrine. Lee & Shepard. 12°, $1.25.

SCRIPTURE, E. W. Thinking, feeling, doing. Flood & Vincent, The Chautauqua Century Press. il. 12°, $1.50.
The writer is director of the Psychological Laboratory in Yale University. This is the first book written in the English language on the new, or experimental, psychology. It has been written expressly for the people in untechnical English. 209 illustrations serve to make clear the laboratory work done in testing how fast a dog thinks; what we actually see; why the bicycle girl appears so short; shape of the sky; time of thought in school children, etc., etc. Particularly aims to enforce that observation or watching is the fundamental method of all knowledge.

WILLIAMS, H. G. Outlines of psychology: designed for use in teachers' classes, normal schools and institutes, and as a guide for all students of applied psychology. 3*d ed.* Syracuse. Bardeen. 16°, 75 c.
Definitions and principles are not extensively elucidated, but the facts of the science are plainly stated in their relation to each other, with ample suggestions to the student who desires to make further investigations. It has been the aim to incorporate the cardinal principles that underlie all empirical psychology, and to show the inseparable relationship existing between these principles and the successful practice of the teacher.

NATURE AND SCIENCE.

BABINGTON, W. DALTON. Fallacies of race theories as applied to race characteristics: essays. Longmans, Green & Co. 12°, $2.

VAN DYKE, THEO. S. Game birds at home. Fords, Howard & Hulbert. 12°, $1.50.
"The chief charm of the book for the general reader lies in the exquisite sensitiveness to beauty found in its descriptions of nature, but sportsmen will, on the other hand, get as much, perhaps more, satisfaction from the evidences of a trained eye and skilled hand 'born of forty years of play with the gun and eighteen years of writing for the sportsmen of America.'"— *N. Y. Times.*

POETRY.

ARNOLD, *Sir* EDWIN. The tenth muse, and other poems. Longmans, Green & Co. 12°, $1.50.

IN camphor ; il. by Howard Chandler Christy. Putnam. 8°, $1.25.
A collection of short poems.

PREVOST, FRANCIS. Rust of gold. Ward, Lock & Bowden, Ltd. 12°, $1.

ROSSETTI, CHRISTINA GEORGINA. Verses ; reprinted from "Called to the saints," "Time flies," "The face of the deep." Young. 12°, $1.50.

POLITICAL AND SOCIAL.

BAKER, F. GRENFELL. The model republic: a history of the rise and progress of the Swiss people. Imported by Scribner. 8°, *net*, $5.

HARGER, C. G., *jr.* The true standard of value. Hartman & Cadick. 12°, (The well worth reading ser.) pap., 10 c.

MITCHELL, W. B. Dollars, or, what? a little common sense applied to silver as money. The American News Co. 12°, pap., 25 c.
Argument against the free coinage of silver.

Intended especially for ordinary readers who are not up in the technique of the controversy and need statements worded in general language.

MORGAN, T. J.   Patriotic citizenship.   American Book Co.   por. 12°, $1.

The essential feature is a catechism of about one hundred and forty short, direct questions, with as many concise, comprehensive answers, in which the author states clearly his own views on all the topics discussed.   The text of the answers is followed by brief citations from a wide range of authorities, ancient and modern, but chiefly American.   The topics are patriotism, the flag, the discovery, the colonists, civil liberty, labor, capital, etc.   The object of the book is to stimulate patriotism.   Intended for use in upper grammar grades.

MUHLEMAN, MAURICE L.   Monetary systems of the world; a study of present currency systems and statistical information relative to the volume of the world's money; with complete abstracts of various plans proposed for the solution of the currency problem.   Nicoll.   12°, $2.

The compiler of this book is Deputy Assistant Treasurer United States, New York.   He has enlarged and included the greater part of his "Money of the United States," bringing the statistics down to date and especially enlarging the account of our State banking systems prior to 1863.   The information on the monetary systems of other nations is less exhaustive but is taken from official sources.   Attention is also given to international exchanges, the movement of precious metals, the clearing-house systems, and the recently proposed national and international measures to improve currency systems.

PEABODY, H. W.   Address in opposition to bimetallism before the Commercial Club of Boston at the Parker House, March 16, 1895.   H. W. Peabody.   8°, pap., 10 c.

Mr. Peabody deems the time has come for all who are not professedly bimetallists to array themselves together and to see that their views are expressed to the public for their instruction, and to encourage them if they are in favor of sound money to be known as such in the community.   In this pamphlet he declares his own position.

PEABODY, H. W.   Published letters and address of Henry W. Peabody in favor of sound money, and in opposition to the bimetallic theories for the United States, Boston, March 1, 1895.   H. W. Peabody.   8°, pap., 10 c.

Letters written to the Boston *Advertiser* and Boston *Herald* during 1894 and 1895, and an address delivered before the Massachusetts Reform Club on February 15, 1895.   Mr. Peabody holds that the various silver bills have been put forward primarily in the interests of the silver-producing states and not for the needs of the country.   He thinks the people should be instructed in the true principles of the subject; and he urges that the practical and present-day aspect of the question should not be lost sight of in an endeavor to trace out its theoretical subtleties.

STANTON, S. WARD.   American steam vessels.   Smith & Stanton.   il. obl. 8°, $5.

Over 200 illustrations of celebrated steam vessels of all classes that have been built in the United States since Fulton's "Clermont" in 1807.   They are printed on heavy coated paper, each followed by a description and history of the vessel.   The pictures appear in chronological order.   Illustrations of the earlier steamers are taken from lithographs, drawings, woodcuts or paintings, the later boats from photographs, plans, sketches, etc.   Special attention is given to the Mississippi River boats so famous in their day.

WOOD, STANLEY.   Stanley Wood's answer to "Coin's financial school"; il. by Frank Beard.   A. B. Sherwood Pub. Co.   12°, (Sherwood's educational ser., v. 1, no. 1.), pap., 25 c.

Quotes verbatim from "Coin's financial school," giving the page, and then meets and overthrows Coin's arguments.   Shows the fallacy of the silver arguments in a good-natured way.

THEOLOGY, RELIGION AND SPECULATION.

AMERICAN Institute of Christian Philosophy.   Christ and the church: essays concerning the church and the unification of Christendom ; with an introd. by Amory H. Bradford, D.D.   Revell.   12°, $1.50.

Lectures delivered at Chautauqua, July 5-12, 1894.   They were prepared without consultation between the writers.   The object was to give as great a variety of views as possible as to the essentials of a creed for a United Church.   The reunion of Christendom is formulated as it appears to an Episcopalian, a Congregationalist, a Presbyterian, a Disciple, a missionary to the higher classes of China, etc.   Dedicated to the memory of Dr. Deems, of the Church of the Strangers. New York, whose life-work and life-dream was a union of the Christian bodies.

COLEMAN, LEIGHTON (*Bp.*)   The church in America.   Ja. Pott & Co.   12°, (National church history ser.) $2.50.

CUTTS, E. L., *D.D.*   History of the Church of England.   Longmans, Green & Co.   16°, (Text-book of religious instruction, no. 1.) $1.

DRIVER, S. R., *D.D.*   A critical and exegetical commentary on Deuteronomy.   Scribner.   8°, (International critical commentary on the Holy Scriptures, ed. by Rev. C. A. Briggs, Rev. S. R. Driver, and Rev. Alfred Plummer.)   *net*, $3.

This is the first volume issued of the International Critical Commentary—a series designed chiefly for students and clergymen, and written in a compact style.   The commentary will be international and interconfessional, and will be free from polemical and ecclesiastical bias.   It will be based upon a thorough critical study of the original texts of the Bible, and upon critical methods of interpretation.   Historical and archæological questions, as well as questions of Biblical theology, are included in the plan of the commentary, but not practical or homiletical exegesis.

GIBBES, EMILY OLIVER.   Reflections on Paul according to the Acts in the New Testament.   C. T. Dillingham.   12°, $1.25.

HOPKINS. E. WASHBURN.   The religions of India.   Ginn.   8°, (Handbooks on the history of religions, ed. by Morris Jastrow, jr., v. 1.) $2.20.

The initial volume of a new series for the general reader and the student. The general aim of the series is to bring together the ascertained results of scholarship. A uniform plan of treatment will be followed in the various volumes. After the introduction, which is devoted in each volume to a setting forth of the sources and the method of study, a chapter follows on the land and the people; next the beliefs are presented, including the pantheon, the relation to the gods, views of life and death, the rites—both official ones and the popular customs—the religious literature and architecture, a general estimate of the religion, its history, etc. This narrative is richly annotated. Full bibliography (23 p.). Index.

HUNTINGTON, F. D. (*Bp.*) Social problems and the church. The Church Social Union. 8°, (Publications of the society, ser. A, no. 3.) pap., 10 c.
The Bishop of Central New York wrote this essay for *The Forum* in 1890. He holds the church responsible for many of the problems with which its members are struggling, and arraigns it for not taking a more decided stand in bettering the world.

HUNTINGTON, W. R. The spiritual house: a first lesson in architecture. Ja. Pott & Co. 12°, *net*, 25 c.

KERNAHAN, COULSON. God and the ant. Ward, Lock & Bowden, Ltd. 16°, pap., 25 c.
"In 'God and the ant,' a booklet, Mr. Coulson Kernahan, who has a trenchant way of dealing with certain vital subjects, represents the ant, that is, man, calling God to account. The judgment day is made to have a different meaning from the accepted one. Man demands of his Creator the reason why there should be suffering, sins, and penalties, and makes excuses for his own conduct. It is in the form of a vision, the meaning of which is revealed and the explanation given in the recognition of Christ as the burden-bearer and the sufferer for the sins of the human race."—*Boston Literary World.*

LEONARD, *Rev.* DELAVAN L. A hundred years of missions; or, the story of progress since Carey's beginning; introd. by Arthur T. Pierson, D.D. Funk & Wagnalls Co. 12°, $1.50.
A book full of dates and references especially intended for the Young People's Societies of America. Dr. A. T. Pierson has written the preface. He pronounces the book unique in design and method. All Christian missions receive due mention for work accomplished. A good index directs to various features of special denominational work, and to its geographical distribution.

LYON, WILLARD D. Sketch of the history of Protestant missions in China. Revell. 16°, pap., 15 c.

MURRAY, *Rev.* ANDREW. Let us draw nigh; the way of a life abiding continually in the secret of God's presence: meditations on Hebrews x. 19–25. *Author's ed.* Randolph & Co. sq. 16°, 50 c.

NEEDHAM, *Mrs.* G. C. Woman's ministry: a scriptural exposition of woman's place in the church of God. Revell. 16°, 50 c.

PARKS, LEIGHTON. The theology of Phillips Brooks. Damrell & Upham. 8°, pap., 50 c.

TEACHER, (*The*) and the class: a symposium of Sunday-school teaching. Revell. 16°, 50 c.
Contents: Heart-power in Sunday-school work, by Rev. J. R. Miller; The teacher's qualifications, by the Rev. Ja. Stalker; The teacher out of school, by Bishop Vincent; The teacher's preparation, by Sarah Geraldina Stock; The teacher's ideal, by the Rev. Robert Forman Horton; The teacher shepherding the flock, by Ralph Wells; The teacher at work, by the Rev. H. S. B. Yates; The teacher's responsibility, by the Rev. W. Douglas Mackenzie; The teacher's reward, by Archdeacon Farrar.

TISDALL, *Rev.* W. ST. CLAIR. The religion of the crescent; or Islam: its strength, its weakness, its origin, its influence; being the James Long lectures on Muhamadanism, for the years 1891–1892. Young. 16°, (Non-Christian religious systems.) $1.50.

Books for the Young.

ADAMS, W. T., [Oliver Optic, *pseud.*] In the saddle. Lee & Shepard. 12°, (The blue and the gray—on land ser., No. 2.) $1.50.

FOWLER, HENRIETTA EDITH. The young pretenders; il. by Philip Burne-Jones. Longmans, Green & Co. il. 12°, $1.50.

HAWKINS, EMMA D. KELLEY. Four girls at Cottage City. Continental Printing Co. 12°, $1.
Four cheery New England girls start on a vacation and settle in Cottage City, Maine. Their experience *en route* and after arrival (notably the hunting a boarding-house, and the introduction of the masculine element, in the shape of two next door neighbors, who play important parts in the lives of two of the girls) makes a bright story.

NEHER, BERTHA M. Among the giants: a story introducing six common giants. A. Flanagan. 12°, 50 c.
A story with a lesson; the giants are the faults and failings often belonging to the young—such as selfishness, carelessness, bad temper, little lies, etc.; with the aid of the fairies, Truth, Self-control, Obedience, Honesty, etc., the giants are in time slain. This is all worked into a pleasant story with boy and girl characters who are depicted as being transformed, under the better influence of a gentle young girl, into model young people.

OTIS, JA., [*pseud.* for Ja. Otis Kaler.] How Tommy saved the barn. Crowell. 12°, 50 c.
Tells of the arrival and sojourn at a Maine farm of three little city waifs, a lame boy, a mature, wise little girl, and the lively and lovable Tommy. Will specially appeal to those interested in the work of the Fresh Air Fund.

POTTS, JA. H., *D.D.* Little Arthur; or, the ministry of a child: a tribute to the memory of Arthur Ninde Potts; by his father. Cranston & Curts. 24°, leatherette, 40 c.

WARE, ELLA REEVE. Three little lovers of nature. A. Flanagan. il. 12°, 35 c.; pap., 25 c.
The doings of three happy little children of ten, eight and five, who loved everything in nature—the birds and flowers, the trees and insects—are recorded for a whole year; the record

begins with the finding of the first blossoms of spring, and ends with Christmas festivals. The narrative is very instructive, being full of details of flowers, birds, etc., and the appearance of nature at the different periods of the year.

WHITE, *Mrs.* LUCY CECIL, [*formerly* Lucy C. White.] Alison's adventures; or, the Broderick estate: a story for girls. Porter & Coates. il. 12°, $1.25.

On the death of Mrs. Gildersleeve, on whom Alison Fane believed herself to be dependent,

the girl appeals as a last resource to a Mrs. Broderick, and learns that the latter is her grandmother. Mrs. Broderick ungraciously consents to give the girl a temporary home, and imposes certain conditions upon her; later, these conditions are supplemented by a solemn trust. The story tells how Alison fulfils her trust, and gives in detail her business experiences in Exeford, a small manufacturing town. Some of the incidents occur in New York City and Washington.

RECENT FRENCH AND GERMAN BOOKS.

FRENCH.

Basin, R. Terre d'Espagne. 12°. Lévy........ $1 00
Berr, de Turique. Madame and Monsieur. 12°. Lévy... 1 00
Bertheroy, J. Le roman d'une âme. 18°. Colin. 1 00
Brada. Jeunes Madames. 12°. Lévy............ 1 00
Burdeau, A. Une Evasion, Souvenirs de 1871. 12°. Colin..................................... 40
Darmesteter, J. Critique et Politique. 12°. Lévy.. 1 00
D'Artois, Le Sergent. Balthazar. 12°. Lévy.. 1 00
Daudet, E. La Police et les Chouans sous le Consulat et l'Empire. 12°. Plon.............. 1 00
D'Hesecques, Comte F. Souvenirs d'un page, de la cour de Louis XVI. 12°. Perrin.......... 1 00
Flagy. La reine Nadège. 12°. Lévy............ 1 00
Geruses, P. A pied, A Cheval, en Voiture. Ill. de Crafty. 8°. Lévy......................... 1 80
Lanson, G. Pages Choisies de Balzac. 12°. Colin...................................... 1 00

Lamy, E. Études sur le second empire. 8°. Lévy.. $2 25
Lavedan, H. Une Cour. 12°. Lévy............ 1 00
Pensa. L'Egypte et le Soudan. 12°. Hachette. 1 00
Rosane, J. Maldonne. 12°. Colin............ 1 00
Spuller, E. Royer-Collard (Collection des Grands Ecrivains Français). 12°. Hachette............ 60
Texte, Jos. J. J. Rousseau. 12°. Hachette...... 1 00
Verlaine, P. Confessions. 12°. (Fin de Siècle). 1 00

GERMAN.

Groger, Fannie. Adhimukti. 12°. Fischer.... 50
Hartwig, G. Licht und Schatten. 12°. Janke. 35
Koenig, E. A. Eine Miethkaserne. 12°. Janke. 35
Wachenhusen, H. Der Vampyr. 12°. Janke. 35
Wachenhusen, H. Eine Geborene. 12°. Janke. 35
Wachenhusen, H. My lady. 12°. Janke...... 35
Wald-Zedtwitz. Aus dem Grünen Winkel. 12°. Janke... 35

Literary Miscellany.

The Bookman for August-September contains a bibliography of Björnson, by William H. Carpenter.

W. E. FOSTER's Reference Lists for August are devoted to "Thomas Henry Huxley" and "Marine Life." The September issue will have a list on Yachts and Yachting.

THE SEVEN WONDERS OF THE WORLD.—The seven wonders can be readily committed to memory with this bit of doggerel, on the thirty-days-hath-September plan:

The *Pyramids* first, which in Egypt were laid;
Next *Babylon's garden*, for Amytis made;
Then *Mausolos' tomb*, of affection and guilt;
Fourth, the *Temple of Dian*, in Ephesus built;
The *Colossus of Rhodes*, cast in brass, to the sun;
Sixth *Jupiter's statue*, by Phidias done;
The *Pharos of Egypt*, last wonder of old;
Or the *Palace of Cyprus*, cemented with gold.

NATIONAL MEMORIAL TO HUXLEY.—A representative meeting of friends and admirers of the late Mr. Huxley was held recently in the rooms of the Royal Society, under the chairmanship of Lord Kelvin, to consider what steps should be taken to initiate a national memorial. It was determined to call a general public meeting after the autumn recess, and, in the meantime, to form a general committee. Sir John Lubbock (15 Lombard Street) has consented to act as treasurer, and Prof. G. B. Howes (Royal College of Science, South Kensington) as secretary to the provisional committee.

THE PUBLISHERS WANT IT.—"The price paid to Mrs. Humphry Ward by Messrs. Smith & Elder for 'The Story of Bessie Costrell,'" says *The Athenæum,* "is well over a thousand pounds. The work has been largely subscribed, as it needed to be under such circumstances." "That is," says *The Critic,* "let us say for convenience, $5000 for the English book rights. For the American book rights $5000 was probably paid, and for the English and American serial rights, some $5000 more. I dare say there was something worth while from Canada and Australia; but even if there was not, $15,000 is a 'tidy' sum for a story of not more than 25,000 words. Sixty cents a word beats the record. Where are Mr. Kipling and Mrs. Burton Harrison, now?"

THE AUTHOR OF "THE MASTER."—"Mr. Zangwill," says *The Mail and Express,* "has a lovable personality and is a delightful companion. He is a brilliant talker, for he does not save all his good things for his books: and he likes to listen as well as to talk. His sweetness of disposition remained untouched by the hard grind of his youth, and it is unspoiled by his present success. He possesses the quaintest of humor, the dryest of wit and the keenest appreciation of good qualities in others. He is in his thirty-second year. It is not strange that people often think of him as a much older man. In spite of his enthusiasm in anything in which he is interested and an often childlike enjoyment of little things, the sorrows and the injustice of human lives have sunk deep into his heart Personally he might be described as an ungainly man, awkward and unconventional in his movements and in his dress, with dark, irregular features, a mop of curly black hair and large, pathetic, near-sighted eyes. His American trip has been often postponed, but it is probable the next year will see him there, and that he will deliver some of the lectures that have helped to make him famous in England. Not alone a novelist and a lecturer, he is a playwright and a critic, and is doing noticeable work in the last capacity in several periodicals."

MAYO W. HAZELTINE.—"Comparatively little is known," says *Vanity*, by the myriad readers of the *N. Y. Sun*, as to the personality of that 'M. W. H.,' whose book reviews in that paper have for many years been a feature of international admiration. Having carried everything before him at Harvard, Mr. Hazeltine crossed over to England to do likewise at Oxford, where he occupied the rooms at St. John's College once tenanted by King Charles 'the Martyr.' Then he amused himself for a time by mingling with the great world of London, after which he returned to this country and betook him to literary work with the result that to-day he ranks 'facile princeps' among contemporary critics. Privileged friends speak with enthusiasm of Mr. Hazeltine's fascinating personality. His manners are of the court courtly, and his conversation is noted for its facile and urbane charm, while his knowledge is cyclopædic in its completeness. His memory, too, is something prodigious. He can discourse with cultured fluency on any subject, from a problem in political economics to the shade of the latest debutante's frock. His lithe, over-tall frame, pale, intellectual features, and incipient stoop, tell their own tale, for Mr. Hazeltine is an indefatigable worker, but though he 'scorns delights and lives laborious days,' the dinners and other entertainments given by him and his charming wife, who, by the way, is a cousin of the Duchess of Portland, at their residence in Washington, are such that Cabinet Ministers and Ambassadors owning cooks covet invitations."

THE AUTHOR OF "ALICE IN WONDERLAND."— The Rev. Charles Lutwidge Dodgson (Lewis Carroll), the author of "Alice in Wonderland," says a writer in *The Ladies' Home Journal*, has spent the greater part of his life in college. He was elected a student, *i. e.*, a fellow of Christ Church in 1854, and from 1855 to 1881 he was mathematical tutor. His subject is mathematics, and he has contributed a number of books to its literature. Curiously enough, he hardly realizes that his fame has come to him, not as the advanced mathematician but as the author of the most fascinating nonsense that ever was written. When in the first flush of her success "Alice" was in every hand and her Wonderland adventures were the delight of grown-up people as well as of children, Her Majesty Queen Victoria sent a message to the author begging him to send her his next book. Like all her subjects, she was anxious to hear more of the delightful child, whose prototype was the daughter of the dean of Christ Church. She was much astounded to receive soon after a copy of "An Elementary Treatise on Determinants," by C. L. Dodgson, for in those days he had managed to preserve his incognito, and Her Majesty, like the rest of the world, believed him a mere humorist. Mr. Dodgson is a clergyman in deacon's orders; he was never ordained a priest, owing, it is said, to a slight hesitancy of speech, which prevents his speaking in public. This, however, he has in a measure overcome, and he now not infrequently reads the lessons and prayers at the college services in the Cathedral. He has even occasionally been known to preach at the special services for the college servants. He is a creature of habit and in term time is never absent from his own particular seat in St. Mary's.

ACCORDING to *The Bookman*, the most called-for books in the East during the month just passed were as follows:

"The Story of Bessie Costrell." By Mrs. Humphry Ward. 75 cts. (Macmillan.)

"Beside the Bonnie Brier Bush." By Ian Maclaren. $1.25. (Dodd, Mead.)

"The Prisoner of Zenda." By Anthony Hope. 75 cts. (Holt.)

"The Adventures of Captain Horn." By Frank R. Stockton. $1.50. (Scribner)

"Fort Frayne." By Captain Charles King. $1.25. (Neely.)

"The Princess Aline." By Richard Harding Davis. $1.25. (Harper.)

"The Woman Who Did." By Grant Allen. $1. (Roberts)

"Tryphena in Love." By Walter Raymond. 75 cts. (Macmillan.)

"Chimmie Fadden," "Major Max, and other stories." By E. W. Townsend. Paper, 50 cts.; cloth, $1. (Lovell, Coryell.)

"Handbook to the Birds of Eastern North America." By Frank M. Chapman. $3. (Appleton)

"Familiar Flowers of Field and Garden." By F. Schuyler Mathews. $1.75. (Appleton.)

"How to Know the Wild Flowers." By Mrs. William Starr Dana. Revised edition, net, $1.75. (Scribner.)

"Degeneration." By Max Nordau. $3.50. (Appleton.)

"With the Procession." By H. B. Fuller. $1.25. (Harper.)

"Princeton Stories." By J. L. Williams. $1. (Scribner.)

"Yale Yarns." By J. S. Wood. $1. (Putnam.)

"Social Evolution." By Benjamin Kidd. Paper, 25 cts.; cloth, $1.50. (Macmillan.)

The books which led the sales in the West:

"Trilby." By George Du Maurier. $1.75. (Harper.)

"Beside the Bonnie Brier Bush." By Ian Maclaren. $1.25. (Dodd, Mead.)

"Chiffon's Marriage." By Gyp. 50 cts. (Hurst : Brentano; Lovell, Coryell; Stokes.)

"The Adventures of Captain Horn." By F. R. Stockton. $1.50. (Scribner.)

"The Story of Bessie Costrell." By Mrs. Humphry Ward. 75 cts. (Macmillan.)

"The Manxman." By Hall Caine. $1.50. (Appleton.)

"The Prisoner of Zenda." By Anthony Hope. 75 cts. (Holt)

"Handbook to the Birds of Eastern North America." By Frank M. Chapman. $3. (Appleton)

"The Master." By I. Zangwill. $1.75. (Harper)

"An Errant Wooing." By Mrs. Burton Harrison. $1.50. (Century Co.)

"The Woman Who Did." By Grant Allen. $1. (Roberts.)

"The World Beautiful." By Lilian Whiting. $1 and $1.25. (Roberts.)

"The Princess Aline." By R. H. Davis. $1.25. (Harper.)

"With the Procession." By Henry B. Fuller. $1.25. (Harper.)

"A Little Sister to the Wilderness." By Lilian Bell. $1.25. (Stone & Kimball.)

"Chimmie Fadden." First and Second Series. By E. W. Townsend. Each, paper, 50 cts.; cloth, $1. (Lovell, Coryell.)

"Degeneration." By Max Nordau. $3.50. (Appleton.

Freshest News.

R. F. FENNO & Co. announce "A Galloway Herd," a new novel by S. R. Crockett; "A Soldier of Fortune," by L. T. Meade; "Strange Secrets," by A. Conan Doyle; and "An Infatuation," a new story by "Gyp," said to be in her sprightliest style.

G. P. PUTNAM'S SONS have just issued Mallock's "The Heart of Life," noticed elsewhere in this issue; "Elizabeth's Pretenders," an authorized American edition of Hamilton Aïdé's new novel; "God Forsaken," a novel by Frederic Breton; and "Her Majesty," a romance of to-day, by Elizabeth Knight Tompkins. In more enduring literature they have "The Life of Sir James Fitzjames Stephen," by his brother, Leslie Stephen, destined to take its place among the few biographies of first order which this generation has received; and "Painting, Sculpture and Architecture as Representative Arts," by George L. Raymond.

ROBERTS BROTHERS will publish at once "The Wood Beyond the World," by William Morris, with frontispiece by Burne-Jones, printed on antique English paper with decorative cover; "From Dreamland Sent," a volume of poems by Lilian Whiting; "All Men Are Liars," a novel by James Hocking; "From Jerusalem to Nicæe," the Lowell lectures delivered by Philip Stafford Moxom; a new illustrated edition of John Galt's novels, with introduction by S. R. Crockett and text revised and edited by D. Storrar Meldrum; Balzac's novel "The Start in Life," and several new volumes in the *Keynotes Series.*

LOVELL, CORYELL & Co. have a list of new and forthcoming novels of great average merit. They have just issued translations of "The Heritage of the Kurts," by Björnstjerne Björnson; and "The Commodore's Daughters," by Jonas Lie; also Zangwill's "Old Maid's Club"; "Legends of Fire Island Beach," by Prof. Edward Richard Shaw; and "The Old Settler, the Squire, and Little Peleg," by Edward Mott, of the N. Y. *Sun.* Among the books in preparation are "A Daughter of the Tenements," by Edward W. Townsend, author of "Chimmie Fadden"; "As the Wind Blows," by Eleanor Merron; "Eunice Quince," a New England story of 1800, by Mrs. L. P. M. Curran; and "The Sheik's White Slave," by Raimond Raife.

F. WARNE & Co. have just issued "The Desert Ship," by John Bloundelle Burton, illustrated by Hume Nisbet and W. Buckley; and "Paul Heriot's Pictures," a new volume of short stories by the author of "Quiet Stories from an Old Woman's Garden." They have also ready the eighth edition of "The Legends of King Arthur and His Knights of the Round Table," edited by the editor of the *Nineteenth Century,* a verbatim reprint of the original edition of "The Life and Letters of Edward Gibbon," with his "History of the Crusades," with copious index; and Sir Walter Scott's "Essays on Chivalry, Romance and the Drama." J. L. W.'s "The Spirit of Cookery" is a book that must be studied to appreciate its great store of useful information.

HOUGHTON, MIFFLIN & Co. promise a new volume composed of the last poems of James Russell Lowell, edited by his life-long friend Charles Eliot Norton, and carefully printed with rubricated title-page and initials. The frontispiece is a new portrait of Lowell selected by his family as the best existing likeness of the poet. The whole form and style of the volume harmonize with its literary and memorial character, and at the same time are sufficiently decorative to make it a desirable holiday gift. William E. Griffis has written a book on "Townsend Harris," first American Envoy to Japan; "Christ's Idea of the Supernatural" is a book on which Rev. John H. Dennison has been engaged for several years; and there is a new edition of Agnes Repplier's "Essays in Miniature," with a new essay on ghosts appearing for the first time in book form.

D. APPLETON & Co. call special attention to the fiction of very superior merit they have published during the summer season. "Bog-Myrtle and Peat," and "The Lilac Sunbonnet," by S. R. Crockett, are lively, vigorous stories, displaying an expert knowledge of human nature; "In the Fire of the Forge," by Georg Ebers; "Master and Man," by Leo Tolstoi; "Majesty," by Louis Couperus; and "The Wish," by Hermann Sudermann, are notable foreign novels in excellent translations; of "The Zeit-Geist," by Miss L. Dougall; "The New Moon," by C. E. Raimond; "A Street in Suburbia," by Edwin Pugh; "The Gods, Some Mortals, and Lord Wickenham"; and "The Story of Sonny Sahib," by Mrs. Everard Cotes, we have already expressed most satisfied opinions. The very newest novels published by the house are "Not Counting the Cost," by Tasma; "Mrs. Musgrave and Her Husband," by Richard Marsh; and "In Old New England," by Hezekiah Butterworth. Tarver's "Life of Flaubert" and Grant Allen's "Story of Plant Life" are noticed elsewhere in this issue.

FREDERICK A. STOKES Co. have permitted us to make extracts from advance sheets of William Le Queux's "Zoraida," a romance of the Harem and the Great Sahara, full of stirring incidents, with twenty-four full-page illustrations by Harold Piffard. They have several new works of fiction just ready to appear. In the *West End Series* will be "A Comedy in Spasms," by the author of "The Yellow Aster"; in the *Twentieth Century Series* "Dead Man's Court," by M. J. Hervey; and "The sale of a Soul," by F. Frankfort Moore; and in the *Bijou Series,* "A Bubble," by L. B. Walford; and "Private Tinker and Other Stories," by John Strange Winter. Other books of interest just ready are "Runic Rocks," by William Jensen; "Egyptian Tales," by W. M. Flinders Petrie; "Dilemmas," by Ernest Dowson; "Name this Child," by Wilfred Hugh Cresson; and "Fables and Fabulists," by Thomas Newbigging. A beautiful series of historical paper dolls, by Elizabeth Tucker, can be called for as "Princes and Princesses Paper Dolls." The personages represented are: Mary Queen of Scots as she appeared in 1554; Crown Princess Wilhelmina of Holland, 1887; An American Princess, 1895; Infanta Marguerite of Spain, 1842; Charles Philipe, Dauphin of France, 1774; Crown Prince Wilhelm Friedrich of Germany, 1890; Albert Edward, Prince of Wales, 1855.

LITERARY NEWS

AN ECLECTIC REVIEW OF CURRENT LITERATURE

~ILLUSTRATED~

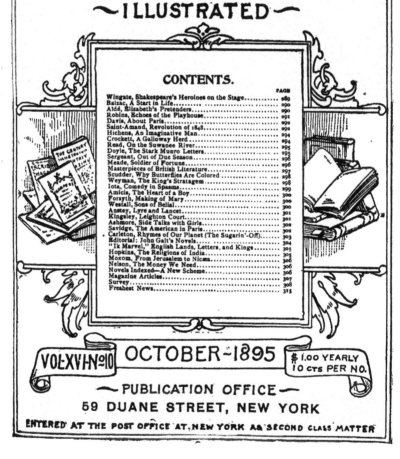

CONTENTS.

VOL XVI-No 10   OCTOBER-1895 $ 1.00 YEARLY
10 CTS PER NO.

~PUBLICATION OFFICE~
59 DUANE STREET, NEW YORK
ENTERED AT THE POST OFFICE AT NEW YORK AS SECOND CLASS MATTER

The Literary News

In winter you may reade them, ab ignem, by the fireside; and in summer, ab umbram, under some shadie tree, and therewith pass away the tedious howres.

| VOL. XVI. | OCTOBER, 1895. | No. 10. |

Shakespeare's Heroines on the Stage.

IN so far as it is a literary sin to attempt the writing of any bit of history in a brief and anecdotical vein, I cry *Peccavi*. But what would you? To obtain simply the foundation for this book required patience-trying researches among rows in mentally struggling through such a ponderous work. For their sakes I have made this book as short as I could; I hope none will wish it were shorter.

In the present volume the "heroines" hold

From "Shakespeare's Heroines on the Stage." Copyright, 1895, by T. Y. Crowell & Co.
ELLEN TERRY AS PORTIA.

dust-covered shelves where rested antique playbills and moth-eaten records. To produce the much-desired, but as yet unexisting, "Complete History of Shakespeare on the Stage," would necessitate the patience of Job and the age of Methuselah. I have not the one, nor can I reasonably expect the other. And even if I had both gifts I should not ask my friends, the gentle readers, to emulate the man of sorthe centre of the stage— to speak in their own language; but within the descriptions, criticisms, and anecdotes regarding their lives and their impersonations will be found sufficient historical record, it is hoped, to serve as a portion of the one missing book in Shakespearian lore. And if, in their mind's eye, admirers of the plays in the library, and admirers of the players on the stage, cannot, through this medium, see the impersonators and impersonations which delighted their fathers and their fathers' fathers before them, while they also catch a glimpse of the Shakespearian acting of to-day, then I have failed to give pleasure to more than one person in the world—myself; for to me the work was a pleasure. My good helpmate, the proof-reader, whispers in my ear that he, too, has read the work thoroughly; but simply the fact that he has endured the book does not prove that it will be enduring. "Time is the old justice that examines all such offenders."

Under any circumstances the pictures must prove attractive. Most of them are copies of rare and interesting prints, a large number of which were kindly loaned, for reproduction, by Mr. John Bouvé Clapp, of Boston. Three of the chapters, I must add (Hermione, Cleopatra, and Imogen), have been enlarged from articles written originally by me for the *Cosmopolitan,* and are now reprinted, with their illustrations, by the permission of the editor of that magazine. (Crowell. $2.) — *Preface by C. E. L. Wingate.*

A Start in Life.

BALZAC, who knew every phase of Parisian life, begins the longest story of the four found in this volume with a description of the different modes of transportation. The word *coucou,* for a vehicle, common in the thirties, is scarcely in use to-day. Once, too, the *grandes messagerie* took under their charge travelling France, but the diligence is even as rare to-day in that country as is the stage-coach in the United States.

Balzac describes the début of Oscar Husson, whose mother had been the Aspasia of the Directory. Oscar, who is a commonplace lad, has been spoiled by his fond mother. Balzac, who was especially fond of the interior of the French lawyer's or notary's office, draws a faithful picture of it. The Count de Serizy has a faithless land agent, who has feathered his nest at the count's expense, and de Serizy, incognito, travels in a coucou to his property, in order to forestall M. Moreau. The steward, with some acquaintances, is trying to buy a big bit of property adjacent to the de Serizy grounds, in order to sell it at an enhanced price to the count. In the coucou are Oscar, a lawyer's clerk, two of the plotters, and two painters. This gives Balzac the chance to show up the *blageur,* George, the notary's clerk, filling completely that character. Oscar chimes in and makes many inpertinent remarks relating to Mme. Serizy. The count himself gleans the secrets of the attempts to be made to play him

false. In the conclusion Balzac shows himself the master. He briefly sketches the future of all the people. The Aspasia becomes a *dévote;* Oscar, who was fast going to the dogs, becomes a soldier, and then a good cavalry officer.

"The Vendetta" has to do with true Corsicans, who really are like our Apaches. Piombo, who has followed Napoleon and his fortunes to France, true to the record, has killed with his own hand all the Portas. Per contra, the Portas had murdered any Piombo they could come across. Piombo had exterminated all of the hated Portas save one child, Luigi. In time Piombo is made a baron. In 1815 Mlle. Genevra Piombo falls in love with an officer, who is hidden away in the painter Servin's atelier. The young man's life would be sacrificed were he discovered. Genevra saves him, and the two wed against the will of the baron, for when he learns that Luigi, his son-in-law, is of that hated race, the Portas, the old Baron sees his daughter starve and her husband die, and at the conclusion coolly remarks, "He has spared me a shot, for he is dead." Once more we have to call attention to the admirable work done by Miss Wormeley in these translations. (Roberts. $1.50)—*N. Y. Times.*

Elizabeth's Pretenders.

THE lightness and dexterity of touch which have marked Mr. Hamilton Aïdé's most successful ventures are conspicuously displayed in his new novel. Elizabeth is a most engaging specimen of the strong-minded heroine. Her sudden disillusionment, her flight, and her sojourn in Paris are treated with unfailing discretion, while nothing could be better than the contrast between her various "pretenders." The lion-hunting, fortune-seeking colonel, the ambitious young politician, the decadent poet, and the American artist are all excellent in their way. Mr. Aïdé's dialogue is full of point, and a humor which is none the less genuine for its gentleness, while the relations between Alaric Baring and his devoted sister a·e drawn with an unforced and convincing pathos. Altogether this is an uncommonly attractive novel, in which the strong situations are handled with notable reticence, and the lighter episodes are carried through with the grace and elegance of an accomplished man of the world. Incidentally some critical remarks are made on the "impressionist" school of painting. The novel shows that rare combination of a self-reliant, strong-minded girl, who at the same time is womanly in all things. (Putnam. $1; pap., 50 c.)—*The Athenæum.*

Echoes of the Playhouse.

THE most brilliant star in this galaxy was the beautiful Mrs. Abington, who had such various claims to celebrity. She was the questionable heroine of several as questionable amours (had not Garrick called her "that worst of women"?) and she came out of the dregs of

> But see—'tis false! in Nature's style
> She comes, by Fancy dress d;
> Again gives Comedy her smile,
> And Fashion all her taste."

This was the Abington who delighted the audience that night, critics and laymen alike,

From "Echoes of the Playhouse."　　Copyright, G. P. Putnam's Sons.

MRS. ABINGTON AS "LADY SADLIFE" IN COLLEY CIBBER'S COMEDY, "THE DOUBLE GALLANT." FROM A DRAWING BY ISAAC TAYLOR.

London life. Yet she triumphed over her surroundings, developed into an actress of rare spirit and humor, set the fashions of society, which even admitted her within its well-guarded precincts, had her portrait painted by the great Sir Joshua Reynolds, and earned the encomiums of Horace Walpole. It was the latter who wrote of her, referring to an unfounded rumor that she had retired from the stage:

> "Sad with the news, Thalia mourned;
> The Graces joined her train;
> And naught but sighs for sighs return'd
> Were heard at Drury Lane.

by her performance of the elegant Lady Teazle. She had been a kitchen wench, a seller of flowers (did not a few persons with inconvenient memories recall her nickname of "Nosegay Fan"?), and an errand-girl to a French milliner; but she could play the country miss turned woman of fashion with a naturalness and sureness of touch that bespoke the duchess rather than the cobbler's daughter.

As the Lady Teazle proved so admirable, likewise did the Sir Peter of Thomas King, the intimate friend of Garrick, and a conservative actor whose epigrammatic, dryly amusing style must have seemed just suited to the part. How could it have been otherwise with a man of whom Charles Lamb wrote so picturesquely: "His acting left a taste on the palate sharp and sweet like a quince ; with an old, hard, rough, withered face, like a john-apple, puckered up into a thousand wrinkles; with shrewd hints and tart replies." (Putnam. $2.)—*From Robins' " Echoes of the Playhouse."*

About Paris.

THE papers dealing with observations and experiences in the French capital, which Richard Harding Davis has contributed during the last year or so to a popular magazine, make a handsome and welcome volume collected under the title of "About Paris," with abundant illustrations by Charles Dana Gibson. Mr. Davis is not an elaborately subtle or aggressively analytical writer. His observations are largely objective and he does not attempt to deal as a rule in the niceties of psychological discrimina-

A FRENCH LOAF.

tion. He has, however, both the ability and the good sense to describe things as he sees them, and his impressions may safely be accepted as those of the average well-educated man of the world. Mr. Davis portrays in an effective way the charcteristics of the streets of Paris and the outward aspect of the people who frequent them. He makes a tour of what he calls "the show places," meaning by that the dance-halls and cafés of questionable resort, with a glance at the slums generally. He has an account of the scene at Carnot's funeral which is worthy of being treasured as an historical document. He sets forth with vivid appreciation the circumstances attending the race for the "Grand Prix," and depicts with no lack of humor the reception of a new member at the French Academy. And he winds up with a discussion of "Americans in Paris," in which humor, satire and sound common sense are suitably intermingled. Mr. Davis is very severe upon the American colony in Paris, but there is reason to believe that he is entirely justified in his animadversions, and his arraignment of our exiled compatriots for their snobbery, vulgarity, and cheap assumption of wickedness will not fail to be keenly relished by those who do not think that residence in a foreign city necessarily implies the adoption of foreign ideals or the vapid striving after illusive cosmopolitanism. Mr. Gibson's illustrations are, of course, a welcome feature of the book, which is handsomely got up in a pretty light-blue binding. (Harper. $1.25.)—*The Beacon.*

The Revolution of 1848.

IN the latest volume of his French historical series, entitled "The Revolution of 1848," M. Imbert de Saint-Amand shows that the close of Louis Philippe's career was quite in keeping with his second-rate reign. He was driven from the throne and from France by a little manifestation of turbulence on the part of the irresponsible gamins of Paris that should have been repressed by the police, only neither the police nor the government, nor the king himself, seems to have known or cared very much about what was going on. The most active and most influential of the revolutionists even had no distinct purpose in view, and up to the last moment evidently had no idea of upsetting the government. The most that any of them expected to accomplish was to force a change of ministry ; and when they found, to their surprise, that the flimsy monarchy was actually destroyed, they were virtually unprepared with any plan for establishing a new government. The great political upheaval was brought about by a lot of riotous boys of the streets, followed by the looting and burning of the Tuileries by a gang of thieves. It did not require much of a demonstration to dethrone the moderate, meek-spirited king, who really did not care very much whether he continued to reign or not. After describing the first indications of disturbance, the author says:

saying, 'Six or seven bad! Oh! there are easily seventeen or eighteen.' Louis Philippe relied on all the others. That is what ruined him."

What ruined him was his lack of pluck and

MARIE AMÉLIE, QUEEN OF THE FRENCH.

tinued to reign or not. After describing the first indications of disturbance, the author says:

"They might have been easily repressed, however, if the government had not conceived the fatal notion of calling out the National Guard. This guard had founded the monarchy of July, and was to destroy it. At bottom, Louis Philippe must have suspected it a little, since he had for several years refrained from passing it in review. Still, he was of the opinion that the majority of this citizen soldiery were still loyal to him. Some one having reported to him that General Jacqueminot had said, 'Out of three hundred and eighty-four companies there are six or seven badly disposed, all the rest are sincerely attached to the monarchy'; the king confined himself to

resolution, not only at the moment but all through his life.

Of all the revolutions to which France has been subjected, this of 1848 appears to have been the most contemptible. There was no reason for breaking up the government at the time, and nobody of any consequence really wanted to break it up. It simply went to pieces for lack of cohesive power before the first breath of hostile agitation. The revolution was as paltry as the government it destroyed—a sort of little revolution for a penny.

M. de Saint-Amand's work is fairly well done, as usual; but, as usual, it is mainly editorial. He has compiled and arranged all the newspaper clippings and other excerpts he has been able to lay hands on in such a way as

From "Little Journeys." Copyright by G. P. Putnam's Sons.

VICTOR HUGO.

to make a connected narration, and has added a copious and well-classified index. The book is well printed on good paper, and the portrait illustrations are satisfactorily reproduced.— (Scribner. $1.25.)—*Philadelphia Telegraph.*

An Imaginative Man.

MR. ROBERT S. HICHENS, author of " The Green Carnation," has written in "An Imaginative Man" a story about which the opinions of novel-readers will differ greatly, for those who take it up in the hope of becoming at once interested in its plot, which simple word means almost anything nowadays, in the shape of incidents that human ingenuity can devise, will be disappointed before they have proceeded far, and if they happen to have a more exciting book at hand will be likely to leave it unfinished, while those who, caring little or nothing for mere plot, begin to read it as a purely literary production, wherein social or moral questions may be discussed, urban or provincial manners depicted, or the customs and passions of men and women analyzed and portrayed, will perceive, first of all, its literary cleverness, its unexpected and clever suggestiveness, keenness of observation and its profound knowledge of the intricate motives that influence human action and the manifestations of temperament that determine character, and will read on and on, with increasing enjoyment and the satisfaction which no common writer ever affords. It is not easy to classify a writer like Mr. Hichens, for to say that his forte is the portrayal of character is to speak in general terms, there are so many ways of portraying character—obvious and recondite, with the heavy brush of the scene-painter and the delicate pencil of the caricatuiist, but, at a venture, we should say that his method or painting portraits was " from within outward "; that he was a student of psychology, who was interested in tracking its secrets to their lurking-places more for the pleasure which the pursuit promised than the acquisition of knowledge thereby, and with no deliberate intention of turning that knowledge to account; and that he rather preferred, on the whole, to investigate the narrow and dark passages of the mind than its broad and sunny places. "An Imaginative Man " will be found a remarkable book for those who care for striking and profound studies of psychological and intellectual portraiture, and a very readable one—at least we have found it such—for those who are interested in the march-travelled Egypt of to-day, where the scenes are laid, in the shadow of the great Sphinx, which exercised such a mysterious influence over the destiny of the Denisons. (Appleton. $1.25)—*Mail and Express.*

A Galloway Herd.

"THE story deals with the happenings to the wife and child of a Scottish minister's prodigal son, whom the reader finds in the opening pages of the book on his death-bed in London, amid squalid surroundings, brightened at the close by the friendly offices of one of the minister's flock, who is on a visit to the metropolis. Deprived by death of their natural protector, and also of the minister, whom death too seizes, the wife and child find a home in the moorland farm of the Galloway Elder, who had made their acquaintance in London. Here is the scene of the chief incidents in the book, and the canvas on which is limned, with great literary art, the homely domestic life and quiet happenings of the story. The idyllic life at Drumquhat is, of course, chequered not only by the arrival of the London waifs but by the intrusion of characters who figured in the early career of the minister's son's widow. The book is good enough to stand on its own merits without any help from the fad for everything Scotch. It has movement and swing and incident quite as if realism had never been heard of, yet when he comes to humorous bits of character Crockett is quite as particular as Howells to preserve the atmosphere of actuality." (Fenno. $1; pap., 50 c.)—*Brooklyn Eagle.*

On the Suwanee River.

"ON the Suwanee River" is the title of Mr. Opie Read's latest novel. The interest, which takes root in a mysterious killing, is well sustained from beginning to end ; but the plot strikes one as attenuated, as if it could be told in a shorter story. It may be, because one became acquainted with Mr. Read's writings when he was a teller of short stories, that all his novels nowadays impress one as sketches which have been flattened out to fill the proportions of a book. The personages of the present story are strongly tinged with sensationalism. The heroine is a mysterious young woman who enters the little Southern village, and, without revealing anything regarding her antecedents, finds employment in a real-estate office and a shelter in the home of the minister. It is afterward developed that on her rests the shadow of a homicide. The minister is an eccentric character, who is as brave as a lion and is addicted in equal parts to strong language and heretical doctrines. His sister is an extremely sentimental young woman, who falls in love with a train-robber— or thinks she does, which amounts to the same thing. A comical character is that of Commodore Adams, a sort of Southern Micawber, whom the author draws with a quiet humor but not with much sympathy. The commodore, however, serves to recall many of those lovable figures of Southern manliness which people other of Mr. Read's books. It strikes one, by the way, that this author has drawn numerous types of Southern manhood, while one cannot remember a single character of a woman to whom he has given charm. The heroine of the present work is cold ; and as to the only other young woman in the book—the clergyman's sister—she is a fool. There are dreamy bits of description of scenery in the story, which are written with more sincerity than is brought to bear on the human studies. (Laird & Lee. 75 c.; pap., 50 c.)—*Chicago Tribune*.

The Stark Munro Letters.

" THE Stark Munro Letters" have not the fascination of the unique Sherlock Holmes, but the book is a bit of real literature. It narrates the struggles of a young medical man to secure a footing, and the courage and energy of this person are not less than admirable. There are some excellent sketches of character apart from that of Dr. Munro himself, the principal one being that of a strange mixture of genius and charlatanism named Cullingworth, who nearly wrecks the manly Munro, but whose influence is happily thrown off in time. The book has a curious life-like quality, almost impelling a conviction that its material has been taken from facts in the author's knowledge, and yet we have so high an opinion of Dr. Doyle's invention that we do not insist upon this theory. Certainly the excellent philosophizing which we take to have been the real

From " Dick and Jack's Adventures on Sable Island." Copyright, 1895, by Laird & Lee.

THE RACE.

reason for the production of this book is all the author's own. In one of the early letters Munro (who is an Englishman writing to an American correspondent) says: "I have often wondered why some of those writing fellows don't try their hands at drawing the inner life of a young man. They are very fond of analyzing the feelings of their heroines, while they have little to say of the inner development of their heroes. I have a vivid recollection of what I went through myself—the shrinking shyness, alternating with absurd fits of audacity; the agonies over imaginary slights; the extraordinary sexual doubts; the deadly fears caused by non-existent diseases; the vague emotion produced by women; the aggressiveness caused by fear of being afraid; the sudden blacknesses and the profound self-distrust—I dare bet you have felt every one of them just as I have and that the first lad of eighteen whom you see out of your window is suffering from them now." Dr. Munro—or shall we say Dr. Doyle?—is concerned principally in these letters with this interesting subject, the main count in it being one not included in the foregoing summary of youth-fears—namely, the strange religious fears which beset the young. These are, of course, not confined to either sex, but Dr. Doyle considers them from the view of the young man. And from our view he gives some very wise, cheery, and wholesome advice looking to the annulment of the bigotry which has crushed and is crushing so many young lives. This is not an idle book, nor one of mere amusement, though it has much that is amusing in it; it has been deeply thought out and has true purpose. Its reading will be an epoch-making event in many a life. (Appleton. $1.50.)—*Philadelphia Telegraph.*

From "Tenement Tales of New York."   Copyright, 1895, by
                Henry Holt & Co.
——
J. W. SULLIVAN.

Out of Due Season.

In "Out of Due Season" Miss Sergeant does herself more justice, and with a theme no more original than the last we dealt with. Adam Bede was a carpenter, and he sorrowed for a girl and conquered self in much the same way that Gideon Blake, the hero of Miss Sergeant's story, who is also a carpenter, does. Here the trouble is due to an erring wife and the loss of a little son who might have supplied her place. Gideon Blake comes through his trial nobly, and if the forgiveness he is depicted as extending to the erring and shallow-hearted woman who has so misunderstood and wronged him is somewhat ideal the teaching is distinctly good. Miss Sergeant is at home with the inhabitants of little country towns and villages, and can draw an effective picture of their every-day life and condition. The characterization here is especially pleasing, from shallow little Emmy Enderby to old Obed Pilcher, the young man's uncle. Gideon Blake is a somewhat inconsistent character. His fits of savage ill-temper hardly accord with the real affection he is represented as having for his wife, and we are not prepared for such a complete recognition of man's chief duty as he eventually displays. The story is well put together and has one or two points of more than passing interest and importance. (Appleton. $1; pap., 50 c.)—*London Literary World.*

A Soldier of Fortune.

Connoisseurs of really good fiction will be attracted by the latest novel from the pen of Mrs. L. T. Meade, author of "The Medicine Lady," entitled "A Soldier of Fortune." Mrs. Meade's greatest charm lies in the simplicity in which she tells her story. There is no effort and strain after-effect revealed in this author's writing, yet her work is fraught with intense interest. The main theme in "A Soldier of Fortune" is the altruism practised by a woman of noble and sterling qualities, set in contrast to the egoism and selfishness of an unrestrained and impulsive lass. The contrast is made the sharper by an exquisitely set love-story. The character-drawing stands out in bold relief and there is a consequentiality about their actions and environment which is striking. The book is bound to awaken more than a passing interest. The problem of altruism, so complex and subtle, is at least clearly and graphically set down, even though a final solution of it cannot frankly be confessed to have been found by Mrs. Meade. This piece of fiction has unrefutably the merit of a moderate tone, which same praise can be but sparingly given to the present productions in the field of fictional writing. (Fenno. $1; 50 c.)—*Commercial Advertiser.*

Masterpieces of British Literature.

THE favorable reception given to "Masterpieces of American Authors" has led the publishers to put forth this companion volume, constructed on similar lines. It will be evident, however, on a moment's consideration that the conditions in this case are less simple. It is very easy to reflect a general agreement in choosing the authors to be represented in a selection from American classic literature, and in the main to determine what choice should be made from their writings. But in any survey of the classic literature of England, Scotland and Ireland, reaching back as it does into remote time, there is opportunity for much divergence of opinion as to the best· selection to be made.

The editor, seeking advice from many experienced teachers of English, has been governed by a few plain considerations The space at his command had to be used frugally. The object to be kept in view was rather the agreeable introduction to great literature than drill in grammar or elocution. Hence it seemed desirable to proceed from the easy to the more difficult, and by a natural course this meant the ascent from the contemporary to the more remote. But it was necessary to stop short of the archaic forms. The plan forbade fragments, and it was not practicable to introduce an entire play of Shakespeare or to give anything from Spenser or Chaucer.

The equipment of the book has been in the way of brief biographical introductions, to enable the reader to apprehend something of the historical relations of each author, and of such footnotes as would explain difficulties in words or passages and occasionally stimulate to further inquiry; but as a rule, whenever a question could be answered by reference to a good dictionary it has been ignored in the footnotes.

As far as possible in accordance with the title of the book the selections have given opportunity for illustrating the scope of the author's genius, but in one or two instances, notably in the case of Wordsworth and Burns emphasis has been laid upon one form, the lyrical, as best suited to the demands of the reader. In brief, the book does not profess to be a comprehensive survey of British literature, but such a compilation from the writings of story-tellers, poets, and essayists, as may give an appreciative reader a generous draught from the well of good English. By the time a young reader has reached this book he ought to be ready for large enjoyment of literature. The extracts are from Ruskin, Macaulay, Dr. John Brown, Tennyson, Dickens, Wordsworth, Burns, Lamb, Coleridge, Byron, Cooper, Gray, Goldsmith, Addison and Steele, Milton, and Bacon. (Houghton, Mifflin & Co. $1.)—*From the Preface.*

Oliver Goldsmith.

From " Masterpiece s of British Literature "   Copyright, 1895, by
Houghton, Mifflin & Co.

Why Butterflies are Colored.

FOR protection during the brief existence of the butterfly life itself, there is a very plain provision on the part of nature in the protective colors of the wings. Especially is this the case with the Oeneis, which, on alighting (which it ordinarily does on the bare gray rocks), invariably closes its wings back to back, and the sign of their early departure ; for, in the many years that I have searched for them with special pains, I have never seen more than a dozen or two specimens in a single day. Yet this is not at all true of Oeneis, and one hardly need to be anxious, in our generation at least, concerning its persistence, for the

OLDEST NEW ENGLAND BUTTERFLIES.

settles upon one side as if reclining, the point of the wings away from the wind, where it clings to the roughnesses of the rocks and is seldom blown from its foothold. In this position the peculiar gray mottling of the under surface of the exposed portions of the wings so closely resembles the gray rocks themselves, flecked with minute brown and yellow-green lichens, that it is almost impossible to discover one in its resting-place unless one has seen it alight. The resemblance is of a very marked character, and is unquestionably a great means of protection.

With regard to the Brenthis, we have here again a case of protective resemblance, though to a less extent ; for in the brilliant red and ashy checkered surface of the under wings, seen when the insect is at complete rest, we have contrasted colors frequently to be met with in the subalpine region in the latter part of the season, when frosts have begun their work. But whether these protective resemblances are very necessary in a district where so few birds are found—hawks and snow-birds being almost the only persistent inhabitants—may perhaps be doubted, and the markings which we find on these insects may be only their ancestral inheritance, useful on the Arctic barrens where birds are more various and plentiful. The Brenthis, indeed, seems really doomed to destruction. In the scanty numbers that one may find upon the mountain-slopes, one sees

butterfly is as abundant in its native haunts in proper season as almost any of the more favored inhabitants of lower levels. (Houghton, Mifflin & Co. $1.50.)—*From Scudder's " Frail Children of the Air."*

The King's Stratagem, and Other Stories.

HALF a dozen short stories by Mr. Weyman are here collected in a little volume that the publishers design to be the first of a series of light modern fiction. The first tale which gives the book its name was probably written to order, as it belongs to the Henry of Navarre period, and, slight as it is, is of the quality the reading public has come to expect from Mr. Weyman. The other five are of a miscellaneous character, and modern, and, as a matter of fact, very much like the short stories of a thousand and one other English writers who make their living, or part of it, writing for the magazines.

" The Body Birds of Court " is a Welsh tale; " In Cupid's Toils " has its scenes partly among the streams and rocks of Norway, partly in London, in the season ; " A Blore Manor Episode " is a rather conventional love-story, while the remaining ones, " The Drift of Fate" and " The Fatal Letter," are clearly studies in the art of romance-building, or rather the art of incident-weaving, that must belong to Mr. Weyman's term of novitiate.

It is likely that all the tales, except the first,

were written some years ago, before Weyman received his first great triumph with "The House of the Wolf." They are as well worth reading, though, as most short stories that live long enough to appear in book form. (Platt & Bruce. 50 c.)—*N. Y. Times.*

A Comedy in Spasms.

"THERE is no question as to the aptness of the title the author of 'The Yellow Aster' has bestowed upon her story in the *Zeitgeist Library.* It deals with spasms of good and evil fortune from the first page to the last, and it is spasmodic even in its manner of construction and narration. The author varies in style between the epigrammatic and the commonplace; she qualifies the language of intense passion with the newest of new slang. Her heroine is described by one of her friends as 'gusty about the moral sense,' and speaks of herself as half disposed to 'magenta sins'—a poor sort of plagiarism on the Hebrew seer, who knew nothing of aniline dyes. But Elizabeth Marrable did herself as much injustice by talking in that way as 'Iota' does herself by forcing her slang and constructing jokes out of Scriptural turns of expression. This indication of feebleness was commented on in these columns when 'Children of Circumstance' was reviewed, and apparently it is the only point in regard to which 'Iota' has declined to profit by the counsel of a well-intentioned critic. Her method of story-telling has unquestionably improved; she is more shapely, more natural, less

SHE WALKED SWIFTLY, A TALL, ERECT FIGURE.

is no lack of color in her temptations; but we should not have called Elizabeth a heroine if she had been steeped to the lips in aniline dyes. Nor should we have called 'Iota' a good novelist, on this and previous occasions, if she had not produced and confirmed the impression that she can read her own sex shrewdly and describe it with pathetic sincerity." "It is not a tract upon the 'woman question' or any

strained. Spasms notwithstanding, intensity granted and allowed for, she has drawn in Elizabeth a type of which nature produces many examples—quick-witted, a clever talker, easily fallen in love with, capable of great sacrifices for relatives who do not appreciate her, and capable of both self-abandonment and splendid renunciation for a man really worthy of her love. 'Gusty' no doubt she is, but an excellent sort of heroine nevertheless. As for 'magenta sins,' she only talks of them. There

other question, it is a work of art, abounding in brilliant and delicate characterization and sparkling with flashes of keen insight into the recesses of the human heart. There is not a badly or even a carelessly drawn character in the book, though as a matter of course some of the portraits are more skilfully executed than others. The dialogue suffers from a surplusage of almost Meredithian cleverness." (Stokes. $1.)—*The Athenæum, and Books of To-day and To-morrow.*

The Heart of a Boy.

How the chimney-sweep lost thirty solid through a hole in his pocket, and how a lot of sympathizing school-girls made the loss good to him, and nearly buried him in flowers besides; how a boy sat for five days in the hospital at the bedside of a patient who he thought was his father, and then discovered that it was not his father at all; how little Carlo Nobis was made by his father to apologize to the charcoal man for saying to the charcoal man's little boy, " Your father is a worthless ragged man." These incidental tales, and a hundred more like them, are contained in " The Heart of a Boy," a story by Edmondo de Amicis, a book that has reached its one hundred and sixty-sixth edition in the original Italian, and that is once more published in a translation by Prof. G. Mantellini. The sentiment is a little more pronounced than our boys are apt to get in their stories, but " The Heart of a Boy " is full of interest and will find plenty of English readers. (Laird & Lee. 75 c.)—*N. Y. Sun.*

From " The Heart of a Boy." Copyright, 1895, by Laird & Lee.

A BOY.

The Making of Mary.

THE little American story which Miss Forsyth has called "The Making of Mary" is sparkling and vivacious ; and there is not a little humor in it which is inseparable from the evolution of the heroine's character. Mary Mason is a child of unknown parents, who has been deserted in an extraordinary fashion, and who gets passed on from one hand to another, until she secures a home in the house of a Michigan journalist. From this home she refuses to be dislodged, and in course of time she causes great commotion in the family. Mrs. Gemmell, the wife of the journalist, is a warm-hearted Theosophist. She endeavors to "mother" the fugitive child, whose humorous eccentricities are supposed to play an important part in her "making." But Mary soon begins to "boss the show "; and as she grows up into an attractive young woman, and flirts outrageously with every eligible and ineligible man she meets, the Gemmell household is eventually plunged into a state of despair. The situation is only relieved when Mary obtains a place in a nursing institution. Here she contracts small-pox and loses her beauty, and we are left to speculate on the future in the light of Nurse Dean's remark: " I shouldn't be at all surprised if the small-pox were just the making of Mary." Gemmell is well drawn ; he is somewhat tried by his wife's Theosophic notions, and we sympathize with him when he says, " It's better to believe too much than too little, but you Theosophists swallow an awful lot." (Cassell. 50 c.)—*Academy.*

Sons of Belial.

THIS story of middle-class Lancashire life is far better than anything Westall has yet written. It relates the fortunes of a father and his sons who from being journeymen moulders become the great manufacturers of the town. The story is full of shrewdness, with just enough sentiment interwoven to unite that side of life to business sagacity. The son Jack is sent away to school, and there comes across a wicked uncle. The fortunes of these two persons constantly recross each other, and the culmination of events, in the recognition of his wife as Mrs. Clinchworthy, married to another man, is worked out in an admirable manner, though it is an old theme. He ceases his demands and disappears forever when he learns that his wife's second husband has brought up his child as if the boy had been Clinchworthy's own child. There is a great deal of rugged nobility in all the characters, and virtue seems of stouter stuff when clad in Lancashire dialect. With little description the atmosphere of the story is yet so thoroughly local that one cannot soon forget the peculiarities it traces, the drunkenness it tries to subdue, and the money closeness of the men and women, but also their sturdy integrity and fidelity to each other. (Cassell. $1.)—*Boston Literary World.*

Lyre and Lancet.

IT is a brilliant little comedy which F. Anstey has set before us in "Lyre and Lancet: a Story in Scenes." The situation upon which the plot turns can be very briefly outlined. An English minor poet of the decadent school is invited to spend a few days at a country-house through the influence of one of the feminine admirers of his writings, and at the same time a veterinary expert is summoned to pronounce judgment on a favorite horse. Through a series of misunderstandings, which seem to be natural enough as the author describes them, the identity of the two men is transposed, and upon their arrival the "vet" is taken into the drawing-room and received as if he were the poet, while the poet is relegated to the servants' quarters. In the scenes that follow the horseman, in spite of his lack of culture, shows himself to be a good deal of a gentleman, while the poet reveals himself as an insufferable cad. The story is given throughout in dramatic form, and about thirty characters are brought upon the boards, each one of them very cleverly individualized. If the situations are now and then a little strained, and if the humor runs a little thin, the reader will easily pardon this out of thankfulness for the incitement to mirth which is to be found in generous measure scattered through these pages. It is good, wholesome fun, too, that "Lyre and Lancet" affords. It is keenly satirical, yet is without a trace of cynicism, and those who take it up in an indulgent mood may be safely promised at least one hearty laugh to every chapter. The author of "Vice Versa" takes time to turn out good work, and has thus far escaped the exhaustion of providing for the insatiable magazine. (Macmillan. $1.25.)—*Beacon.*

From "Lyre and Lancet."   Copyright, 1895, by Macmillan & Co.
"WHAT ON EARTH POSSESSED YOU TO ASK A LITERARY FELLOW DOWN HERE?"

Reginald Hetheridge and Leighton Court.

WHAT a delightfully bantering manner had Henry Kingsley; and he was possessed, too, of that particular and rare talent of buttonholing you peculiar to Thackeray. Then, besides, he could write such pure English. Pray you, read that page 203, where Laura sits at the organ and tries to play on it and cannot, and it concludes: "She sent away the boy who blew the bellows, and began to cry. It is hard to laugh at an utterly lone woman crying over the keys of an organ. I cannot; and I am quite sure that you cannot, either."

There are only two men who can describe a horse, and they are the brothers Kingsley. Mare Swallow and The Elk are the equine heroine and hero. Chirpy are Lady Emily and her mother, Lady Southmolton, who follow the ways of the departed Hannah More, and believe that the human species has deteriorated because the tenets of Hannah are no longer followed. Most neatly worked up are Henry Kingsley's eccentric personages, as Lord Hatterleigh, whose inside is always getting wrong.

Hatterleigh is dull and awkward, but the thorough gentleman. It is Henry Kingsley's exuberance of invention which is so remarkable, but what he wanted was something of the pose, the balance of Charles; and then the heroics of the epics of history did not suit him. In "Leighton Court" the plot is as old as the paleozoic period. There is a lover, Laura's lover, who is believed to be dead, but who comes to view again. He even appears in the opening scene as a paid huntsman, and at the close he is Sir Robert Poyn'z, and a Victoria Cross to boot.

It is by that dash of romantic color which Henry Kingsley throws in his canvas that he carries you away. He just sketches a little picture of a fight in India, and in a dozen words you have a portrait of Napier. Henry Kingsley is literature, and the appreciation of him is enhanced by the publication of his exceedingly brilliant romances. (Ward, Lock & Bowden, Ltd. $1.25.)—*N. Y. Times.*

Side Talks with Girls.

WISDOM and kindliness, now and then a touch of humor, and an all-pervading strain of good, sound common sense, are efficiently combined in the monitions of Ruth Ashmore, as they are expressed in her "Side Talks with Girls." The author does not make the mistake of being too obvious in her didacticism, nor on the other hand does she content herself with the enunciation of general precepts. Her aim is to stimulate a true regard for high ideals of personal conduct, and to this end she takes into consideration the broad principles that make for the development of a strong and noble character, and as supplementary to these expounds the requirements of social life in all the varying phases that come under the head of good manners. One of the most suggestive points made by Ruth Ashmore, and to which she gives significant emphasis, is that politeness is to etiquette as the greater to the less, and that true politeness is founded on goodness of heart. There are chapters explaining the conditions confronting the country girl who comes to the city for employment, and other chapters showing what the country girl may do to make her life richer and fuller and more profitable to herself and others. Other chapters deal with the question of religion, minor faults, choice of books, the use of slang, the responsibilities of friendship, home duties, the relations of hostess and visitor, the art of travelling, care of the health, courtship, betrothal and the first years of marriage. It is a sensible, wholesome little book, and every thoughtful girl will benefit from its reading ; it is also fair to say that serious-minded young men ought not to be ashamed to give attention to such a volume, because it will enable them to understand young women better and thereby to come nearer to a true appreciation of their good qualities. (Scribner. $1.)—*Beacon.*

WHEN BURNS WAS BORN.

WHEN Burns was born,
The winter clouds had gathered with the morn,
The snow and ice were camping through the vale,
The cottage trembled 'neath a savage gale,
That seemed to know the tiny priest of mirth
And strive to sweep his refuge from the earth.
The little city near him slept and thrived,
And did not know its prophet had arrived,
Who soon should make its three short letters known
Wherever Fame a sounding blast has blown,
    With silver horn !

Upon that morn
A hundred songs that now the world adorn
With pictures it will never let depart,
Where lying deep in Nature's yearning heart,
The daisy oft had glittered from the hill,
But waited for her plough-boy lover still ;
The wounded hare had suffered sore and long,
But never yet had heard its funeral song ;
The cunning mouse had plied its petty craft,
But had not sent the world a text that laughed
    Mankind to scorn !

John Barleycorn
Prepared his sweetest rose and sharpest thorn,
The witches set their heads and hoofs to work
To hunt O'Shanter from the ancient kirk ;
The hills began to put themselves in tune
To voice the care that lurked in " Bonnie Doon " ;
The world would soon a world of love enshrine
Within the golden bars of " Auld Lang Syne " ;
The cotter's home produced its greatest grief,
But fame and glory, far beyond belief—
    When Burns was born !

(Harper. $1.)—*From Carleton's " Rhymes of Our Planet."*

The American in Paris.

IN "The American in Paris" Dr. Eugene Coleman Savidge has stretched a bold canvas and painted a signally opportune picture.

Few Americans realize the significant relation of the United States to the Franco-Prussian War. Dr. Savidge shows that it was Louis Napoleon's attempt to "prick the Republican bubble in North America," and its ignominious failure, which gave Bismarck the opportunity to tempt the French to allow Sadowa. Sadowa sealed the unity of Germany, and it was United Germany's menace to humiliated, unready France which led to Sedan and the Republic. The new German Empire put universal suffrage in its Constitution, and insisted upon it in the new French Republic, where Gambetta had already disfranchised the Bonapartists as well as the Orleanists.

All this will not be pleasant reading to imperialists. The American standpoint, and the uncompromising antagonism between American ideas and the theory of the " divine right," are constantly presented. But it will appeal strongly to what Dr. Savidge calls the " strong affirmative Americanism" in the United States.

The novel form has been effectively used. The author presents an impressionable American, an *attaché* of our Paris Legation, to the gaudy Court of the Second Empire. With unwavering stroke he draws the evolution of this would-be cosmopolitan through the byways of an intrigue with one of Napoleon's *cocodettes*, through all the horrors of the siege, the commune, and the Orangerie, into a sturdy American, awakened to the dignity of his country and its influence at home and abroad. The strongest bit in the book is his journey to the army headquarters at Chene, where his inamorata was supposed to be part of the scandalous household of Napoleon, and the account of the night bargaining by telegraph between the emperor and empress, in which a deliberate sacrifice of the army was made for dynastic considerations. Quite as stirring are the French cavalry charge at Sedan, the balloon combat, the burning of Paris and the escape of the communards through the catacombs.

One instantly grasps the biographical feature when reading the good things of "condensed-meat quality " said by Bismarck of Moltke, William, Napoleon, Eugénie, Gladstone, Sheridan, of German unity, of Americans, of the republican movement and democratic demon, of priests and men with rocket powder, etc., or the utterances of Louis Napoleon on Grant, Bismarck, American sympathy with the Republic; or what Sheridan has to say about French and German leaders, and the French, German, and American soldier. There is a distinct thought-provoker in the contrast between the American German and the Imperial German, and Bismarck's claim that his countrymen in the United States are but German colonists with home rule.

The work is a vivid piece of condensation, arrangement, and presentation. The author has presented dramatically the striking events and personages of the world-changing conflict. (Lippincott. $1.)—*Commercial Advertiser.*

THE SUGARIN'-OFF.

"An' when the sap was boilin' there
Till we could taste it in the air,
We woodland boys, with hearts awhirl,
Each took a cupful to his girl,
An' cuddled down with her, and ate,
With just the white snow for a plate.
You see that first-class candy shop
Up yonder where them school-girls stop ?
They've gathered sweetness there that's worth
As much as any now on earth :
But they've got nothin' that's in sight

THE SUGARIN'-OFF.

Of what we ate that starlit night!
An' up on Woodland avenue,
A young-old lady, kind an' true,
With han'some tresses gray enough,
But still on earth, 'an' up to snuff,'
Will tell you, when we go that way
(If she hasn't changed her mind to-day),
That, though the years have brought her nigh
All earthly goods that cash can buy,
She'd give 'em all for that one night
When, from the sap fire's fadin' light,
We wandered homeward side by side,
An' kindled flames that never died,
An' felt confession's sudden charm,
An' slowly walkin' arm in arm,
With no one there to laugh or scoff,
Just had a private sugarin'-off !"

(Harper. $1.25.)—*From Carleton's " Rhymes of Our Planet."*

The Literary News.

An Eclectic Monthly Review of Current Literature.

EDITED BY A. H. LEYPOLDT.

OCTOBER, 1895.

JOHN GALT'S NOVELS.*

IT is cause for rejoicing that so many of the authors our grandsires delighted in are being introduced to the present generation in most attractive form, and introduced by men specially fitted to bring out the characteristics that made these old writers famous and beloved. The success of these undertakings encourages the hope that the readers of the land are turning from the highly sensational fiction which has been the disgrace of the past few years to fiction, in which they meet gentlemen and gentlewomen and learn to know the manners and customs and surroundings of the characters rather than their morbid mental and physical aberrations. We have welcomed with thanks the new editions of Miss Ferrier, Miss Edgeworth, Miss Austen, John Galt, and others who picture life when people took time to be courteous and considerate, in outward manner at least.

"It is a somewhat noticeable circumstance," says *The Literary World*, "that two reprints of any of the novels of forgotten John Galt should

From "Annals of the Parish."   Copyright, 1895, by Roberts Bros.
JOHN GALT.

appear simultaneously. The two tales from his pen which Macmillan brings out in one volume, Roberts Brothers have put into two, with the disadvantage in the latter case of running one novel over into a second volume and beginning a second where the first leaves off. Volumes complete by themselves would be preferable to volumes of uniform size. The Roberts edition is the smaller of the two, and presents a neat page with wide margins, a portrait of the author, and four other pictures. The illustrations in Macmillan's single volume are numerous and striking, and of such artistic value that many of them are separately copyrighted. They are all worthy of careful examination. Macmillan's edition contains a biographical and critical sketch of Galt; Roberts's has the same, with the addition of an 'introduction' by Mr. S. R. Crockett, and Mr. D. Storrar Meldrum has revised and edited the text. Altogether considering the single-volume convenience and the superior illustrations in the one case, and the light weight, wealth of introductory matter, and footnotes in the other, the reader who wishes to own Galt at all in modern dress will find it hard to choose."

In his "introduction" Mr. Crockett says: "The books of John Galt appear so excellent and precious to me that I am anxious that the world of reading-people should not forget them in the press of things new. There was never a more ravelled, hither-and-thither life than that of John Galt. Yet there are no books in our national literature which convey so melodious and continuous an impression of peace. . . . But there is a warning and I will set it in the forefront. There are many things which we have been accustomed to find in great

* JOHN GALT'S NOVELS. With an introduction by S. R. Crockett and portrait and illustrations from drawings by John Wallace. Published in connection with William Blackwood & Sons. The text revised and edited by D. Storrar Meldrum. Roberts. 16mo, cloth, $1.25 each: "The Annals of the Parish and the Ayrshire Legatees," 2 vols.; "Sir Andrew Wylie," 2 vols.; "The Provost and the Last of the Lairds," 2 vols; "The Entail," 2 vols.

fiction, and even in the more clever imitations of great fiction, to which Galt was completely a stranger. Galt's best books do not contain even the rudiments of a plot. One day progresses after another, much like a douce housekeeper's life in the quiet town of Irvine, punctuated only by the yet greater peace of the recurrent Sabbath-day. There is no plot in the lives of such men, no intrigue save that continual one of recurrent self-interest, which Galt treats with a kindliness and an understanding that are unparalleled.

"Galt is a tired man's author, and to such as love him there is no better tonic and restorative. It is better than well to read him on a winter's night by the fireside, tasting every paragraph, too happy and too much at ease to be critical. We read Galt as we go to a but-and-ben in the happily unimproved Isle of Arran, prepared to put up with many things for the sake of the large leisureliness, the rustic air, and the encompassing quiet of heathery mountains and sheltered sea. I can, indeed, understand some people not liking John Galt, but, all the same, I am mortally sorry for them."

John Galt, a Scottish author, was born at Irvine in Ayrshire in 1779. He was the son of a West Indian sea-captain. He began life as clerk in the custom-house at Greenock, but early took up literary work, removed to London in 1803, became a member of Lincoln's Inn, and sought to make literature his profession. The necessities of life took him to the Continent on commercial enterprises, but he returned to England in 1814. In 1820 his "Ayrs. ire Legatees" appeared in *Blackwood's*, but the "Annals of the Parish" was written earlier, with the ambition to do for Scotland what Goldsmith in "The Vicar of Wakefield" had done for England. The two books together made Galt's reputation, and were followed by a multitude of writings, few of which are known to readers of this generation, but many of which will be appreciated when once they have been tasted.

English Lands, Letters, and Kings.

THE third volume in the series of graceful studies by Donald G. Mitchell deals with the varied and extended epoch of Queen Anne and the Georges. Without attempting in any way to make a formal chronicle of the progress of English literature within the limits of the period indicated by the sub-title Mr. Mitchell has sketched out what amounts to a comprehensive and connected review of the leading English authors from Swift to Wordsworth. The sketches are all life-like, although they are nothing more than sketches, for the author has the art of summing up in a single page or

even in a paragraph the essential characteristics of a noteworthy personality and the range and import of the representative writings of a given author. Even to those who are familiar with the main details of English literature during the period referred to Mr. Mitchell's volume will be found an agreeable means of reviving old impressions, while those who take up the subject for the first time in its natural sequence ought to find it as entertaining as a novel and as instructive as a government report. Mr. Mitchell is doing really admirable work in placing the fruits of modern erudition so agreeably before the general reader. It is probable that one more volume will complete the series, and then a conspectus of the entire extent of English history, in its literary aspect, down to the close of the nineteenth century will be accessible in a form not too elementary to be beneath educated notice, and at the same time simple and attractive enough to be to youthful minds a source of very wholesome pleasure. (Scribner. $1.50.)—*The Beacon.*

The Religions of India.

THE initial volume in the new *History of Religions Series* is an account of "The Religions of India," by Edward Washburn Hopkins. The purpose of the editor of this series is to illustrate the modern methods of historical investigation and to set forth the generally accepted results of scholarship in volumes of moderate size dealing with the various religions that shall serve at once as books of reference and as text-books for colleges and schools. The distinguishing features of the series are two, namely, each volume treating of a particular religion is to be intrusted to the hands of a competent specialist, while at the same time, with a view of assuring unity to the series, the treatment of the several subjects will follow, so far as possible, a uniform order. That is to say, each volume will begin with an introductory chapter setting forth the sources of information. This will be followed by a section on the land and people under consideration. The third division, forming, as it were, the kernel of the book, will embody a full exposition of the beliefs and rites, the art and literature of the religion under review. A fourth division will present the history of the religion and set forth its relation to other modes of faith ; and, finally, each volume will be furnished with a substantial bibliography, with indexes and maps, and, where they are needed, with illustrations. We add that polemical discussion will be rigorously excluded, every subject being examined exclusively from the historical side. (Ginn. $2.20.)—*The Sun.*

From Jerusalem to Nicæa.

THE lectures delivered at the Lowell Institute, Boston, by the Rev. P. S. Moxom last winter on the early Christian Church attracted a good deal of deserved attention on account of the graceful way in which they summarized a rich store of erudition on the topic with which they dealt and the tone of discrimination and liberality of judgment exercised by the author in handling debatable themes. These lectures, expanded somewhat by the introduction of illustrative quotations from the ecclesiastical fathers, are now published in book form under the title "From Jerusalem to Nicæa" (Roberts Bros., 12mo, pp. 457, $1.50). Starting out with a review of the rise and spread of Christianity through the missionary efforts of the disciples Dr. Moxom goes on to outline the organization of the early church, and follows this with a concise account of the personal characteristics and devoted labors of the apostolic fathers. In the two chapters that follow, the struggle with heathenism is considered, first in relation to the persecutions and then as manifested in the efforts of the apologists. The heresies that vexed the early church are next carefully analyzed, and the volume concludes with chapters on "The Christian School of Alexandria" and "The First Œcumenical Council." As an outline of early Christian history designed to present the facts clear from all perplexing argument, Dr. Moxom's lectures will be prized by the student both as a guide to research and for handy reference. The serviceableness of the work in this last respect is made possible through an excellent index prepared by Professor William Mathews. (Roberts. $1.50.)—*The Beacon.*

The Money We Need.

ONE of the soundest of books on sound money is "The Money We Need," by Henry Loomis Nelson. It is happily said that the purpose of the book is the exact opposite to that which is sought to be established in that preposterous affair, Coin's "Financial School." This treatise on the character of money shows that it is not quantity but quality that we need in our money ; that the quality must be such as is demanded by the commercial world ; that gold is the only money having that quality ; that all representatives of money, like paper, checks, notes, bills of exchange, etc., must be honest and actually represent what they profess to represent—the gold money of commerce. The treatise also shows that we have now very much more money in this country than is needed by the business of the country, and that there is even gold enough in the country to sustain

paper money largely in excess of all that is now in circulation. It also shows that since what is called the demonetization of silver in 1873 took place the country has greatly prospered, and that it has paid off a large part of its indebtedness ; that all temporary increases of the public debt have been the result of silver legislation, which also has not advanced the price of silver. On the contrary, every law in aid of silver has been followed by a decline in its price. It also shows that prices of general commodities have not depended upon the prices of silver. The chapter on "Bimetallism in History" shows, from an examination of the coinage laws of different nations from 1600 to the present time, that no nation ever succeeded in maintaining the two metals in circulation at the same time. (Harper. 50 c.)—*Brooklyn Times.*

Novels Indexed—a New Scheme.

IN these days of hop-skip-and-jump reading, when a solid page of description is a horror, and literature is judged by the amount of white paper left between the lines of dialogue, says *Tid-Bits* the proposition that indexes be attached to works of fiction—more particularly the summer novel—and not confined to works of law and government reports, will appeal favorably to many.

To show its advantages, we give below extracts from such an index to a brilliant novel soon to be issued, which, if you wish, we will glance down. If Maud likes descriptions and abhors love scenes, she will look for:

"Description—
    Castles at sunset, pp. 3, 13.
    Heroine's dresses, pp. 38, 54, 68, 69, etc.
    Scenery, pp. 1, 4, 56, etc."

And another will turn to "Love":

"Love—
    Definition of, pp. 3, 6, 99.
    Explanation of attributes, pp. 50, 61.
    Lionel falls in, p. 17.
    Lionel falls out, p. 180."

Just see how well that works! No time lost! Why, dear, you could read a hundred novels a day with an index, and thus keep abreast of the times. When you have finished with "love" you might turn to "kissing."

"Kissing; see Kiss.
"Kiss—
    Discretion in employment of, p. 93.
    Lionel's first p. 81.
    The 'Bernhardt,' 'Langtry' styles, pp. 72, 90.
    What is a, pp. 37, 50.
    When to take, and how, p. 192.
    Where actually occurring, pp. 15, 16, 17, 18, 23, 24, 25, 26, 34, 35, 36, etc."

What a saving of time! No slow hunting through vacant pages. Just turn to what you want.—*Mail and Express.*

MAGAZINE ARTICLES.

ARTISTIC, MUSICAL, AND DRAMATIC.—*Cath. World*, Locarno and the Madonna del Sasso,* E. M. Lynch; An Artist Philosopher (Gilbert Stuart), F. H. Sweet.—*Fort. Review* (Sept.), Case of Wagner, Nietzsche.—*Forum*, The Actor, the Manager, and the Public, Malone.—*Nine. Century* (Sept.), Romantic and Contemporary Plays of Thomas Heywood, Swinburne; Romance of Leonardo da Vinci, Count de Calonne; Picture Sales of 1895, Roberts.—*Scribner's*, American Wood-Engravers—William Miller; American Posters, Past and Present,* Bunner.

BIOGRAPHY, CORRESPONDENCE.—*Popular Science*, Thomas Henry Huxley, Foster; David Hosack (Por.).—*Scribner's*, Mr. Huxley (Por.), Smalley.

DESCRIPTION, TRAVEL.—*Atlantic*, The Wordsworth Country on Two Shillings a Day, Sanborn.—*Century*, Cruise on the Norfolk Broads,* Anna B. Dodd; Glave's Career,* R. H. Russell. —*Harper's*, Hindoo and Moslem,* Weeks; At the Sign of the Balsam Bough,* Van Dyke; Queen Victoria's Highland Home,* Hunter.— *North Am. Review*, Atlanta Exposition, Gov. of Georgia.—*Scribner's*, University of Chicago,* Herrick; Mr. Stevenson's Home Life at Vailima, Osbourne. — *West. Review* (Sept.), The Smallest Republic in the World (San Marino), Miller.

DOMESTIC AND SOCIAL.—*Lippincott's*, Domestic Service, Mary C. Hungerford.—*North Am. Review*, Study in Wives, Max O'Rell, Grant Allen, *and others*.—*Scribner's*, Art of Living— Case of Woman,* Robert Grant.

EDUCATIONAL. — *Century*, Marriage Rate of College Women, Millicent W. Shinn.—*Forum*, Higher Pay and a Better Training for Teachers, Speed.

FICTION.—*Atlantic*, The Countess Potocka, Susan Coolidge.— *Cath. World*, Change of Heart, J. H. L.; Pedro: The Tale of a Young Tramp, Anna E. Buchanan. — *Century*, Theodosia Burr,* J. W. Palmer; Rivalries of Long and Short Codiac, G. W. Edwards; An Earlier Manner, G. A. Hibbard; Sonny's Schoolin', Ruth McE. Stuart.—*Chautauquan*, A Prodigal's Welcome, James Buckham.—*Harper's*, Coupons of Fortune, Mary S. Cutting; Alone in China,* Ralph; Jamie the Kid,* Flynt. —*Lippincott's*, My Strange Patient, W. T. Nichols.—*Scribner's*, Lamp of Psyche, Edith Wharton.

HISTORY. — *Harper's*, Ronzano, Bernard O'Reilly. — *Lippincott's*, The King of Rome, Eliz. S Perkins.

HUMOR AND SATIRE.—*Century*.—Fun on the Stump: Humors of Political Campaigning in Kentucky, E. J. McDermott.

LITERARY.—*Century*, Keats in Hampstead,* West; Influence of Keats, Van Dyke; Nordau's "Degeneration": Its Value and Its Errors, Lombroso.—*Chautauquan*, Literature as a Resource, Mabie.—*Fort. Review* (Sept.), Coleridge and His Critics, Nowell C. Smith.—*Forum*, The Renascence in English, Burton.—*Harper's*, Gift of Story-telling, Brander Matthews.

NATURE AND SCIENCE.—*Atlantic*, Weather and Weather Wisdom, Ellen O. Kirk; Lookout Mountain, Torrey.—*Chautauquan*, Relation of Science to Industry, Shaler.—*Fort. Review* (Sept.), Thomas Huxley and Karl Vogt, Haeckel.—*North Am. Review*, Birds in Flight and the Flying Machine, Maxim.—*Popular Science*, Trout Culture,* Mather; Life of Water Plants, Büsgen.—*Scribner's*, Domesticated Birds,* Shaler.

POETRY.—*Atlantic*, The Arctic, Tabb; Second Thoughts, Field.—*Cath. World*, At Moonrise, Waggaman; Mary Mother, Eliz. G. Martin.— *Century*, The Tide of the Past, Edith M. Thomas; Glave, Gilder.—*Chautauquan*, Days and Days, Edith H. Kinney.—*Harper's*, Bookra, Warner.—*Scribner's*, Summer's Will, Martha G. Dickinson.— *West. Review* (Sept.), The Ebb and Flow of the Tide, Parr.

POLITICAL AND SOCIAL.—*Atlantic*, Genius of Japanese Civilization, Hearn.—*Century*, How Men Become Tramps, Flynt. — *Chautauquan*, Hist. of Suffrage in Legislation in the U. S., Blackmar.—*Fort. Review* (Sept.), Awakening of China, Davies.—*Forum*, Present Aspect of the Silver Question, Fairchild; Well-Meant but Futile Benevolence: The Remedy, Thwing; Demand and Supply under Socialism, Mallock; Political Leaders of the Reconstruction Period, Ross.—*Harper's*, The Future in Relation to American Naval Power, Mahan.—*Lippincott's* (Sept.), Permanent Dominion in Asia, Lyall.— *North Am. Review*, Politics and the Insane, Dr. H. S. Williams; Liquor Question: Environment and Drink, Dr. J. F. Waldo *and* Dr. D. Walsh; The Saloon and the Sabbath, F. C. Iglehart; Is Socialism Advancing in England?, W. G. Blackie; Rural Free Mail Delivery, G. M. Stahl (Notes and Comments).—*Popular Science*, War as a Factor in Civilization, C. Morris.— *West. Review* (Sept.), T. H. Huxley and Sunday Observance, Jane A. H. Simpson; Ethical Solution of Our Social Problem, C. Ford.

SPORTS AND AMUSEMENTS.—*North Am. Review*, Hunting Large Game, Gen. Miles.— *Popular Science*, Hunting with Birds of Prey,* M. E. Blanc.

THEOLOGY, RELIGION, AND SPECULATION.— *Cath. World*, History of Philosophy as Applied to the Church, C. M. O'Leary; A New Road from Agnosticism to Christianity, A. F. Hewit. —*Nine. Century*, Islâm and Its Critics, Ameer Ali; The Kutho-Daw, Müller.—*Popular Science*, Recent Recrudescence of Superstition, I., E. P. Evans.

PROFESSOR MINTO.

NATURE, that makes Professors all day long,
And, filling idle songs with idle song,
Turns out small Poets every other minute,
Made earth for men—but seldom puts men in it.

Ah, Minto, thou of that minority
Wert man of men—we had deep need of thee !
Had Heaven a deeper? Did the heavenly chair
Of Earthly Love wait empty for thee there ?

(Copeland & Day)—*From* Le Gallienne's
"*Robert Louis Stevenson: An Elegy and Other Poems.*"

Survey of Current Literature.

Order through your bookseller.—"There is no worthier or surer pledge of the intelligence and the purity of any community than their general purchase of books; nor is there any one who does more to further the attainment and possession of these qualities than a good bookseller."—PROF. DUNN.

ART, MUSIC, DRAMA.

ROBBINS, E., *jr.* Echoes of the playhouse; reminiscences of some past glories of the English stage. Putnam. 12°, $2.

WINGATE, CHARLES E. L. Shakespeare's heroines on the stage, with illustrations from photographs and rare prints. Crowell. 12°, $2.

BIOGRAPHY, CORRESPONDENCE, ETC.

BEAMAN, A. HULME. M. Stambuloff. Warne. pors., 12°, (Public men of to-day ser.) $1.25.
"Political partisanship runs too high in Bulgaria for the truth easily to be made known, and the author of the present book frankly says that he writes from the point of view of the friends of the murdered minister. Nevertheless, he is fair enough, and admits that one of Stambuloff's enemies was tortured to death, and a few other facts of the kind, which are among the charges of Stambuloff's most violent enemies. The author maintains with regard to the Bulgarian revolts in the days of Turkish rule that 'the popular idea that the party was encouraged morally and supported financially by Russia is a mistaken one.' Nevertheless he states a considerable number of facts which show that the support of the Russian consuls was invariably given to the Bulgarian insurgents under circumstances where the agents and servants of any other government would have declined to interfere. It comes out clearly that Prince Alexander was merely a puppet, and that the whole credit for his military successes must be ascribed to Stambuloff."—*Chicago Tribune.*

HORSTMAN, C., *ed.* Yorkshire writers: Richard Rolle, of Hampole; an English father of the church and his followers. Macmillan. 8°, (Lib. of early English writers, v. 1.) *net,* $2.60.

PLARR, VICTOR G. Men and women of the time: a dictionary of contemporaries. *14th ed.,* rev. and brought down to the present time. Routledge. 8°, $6.

TARVER, J. C. Gustave Flaubert as seen in his works and correspondence. Appleton. por., 8°, buckram, $4.

DESCRIPTION, GEOGRAPHY, TRAVEL, ETC.

BATTYE, AUBYN TREVOR. Ice-bound on Kolgnev: a chapter in the exploration of Arctic Europe, to which is added a record of the natural history of the island. Macmillan. 8°, $7.

CONWAY, (*Sir*) W. MARTIN. The Alps from end to end; il. by A. D. McCormick. Macmillan. 8°, $7.

DAVIS, R. HARDING. About Paris; il. by C. Dana Gibson. Harper. 12°, $1.25.

SMITH, GOLDWIN. A trip to England. Macmillan. 32°, (Macmillan's miniature ser., no. 3.) pap., 25 c.

EDUCATION, LANGUAGE, ETC.

FROEBEL, F. The mottoes and commentaries of Friedrich Froebel's "Mother play"; mother communings and mottoes rendered into English verse, by Henrietta R. Eliot; prose commentaries translated and accompanied with an introd., treating of the philosophy of Froebel, by Susan E. Blow. Appleton. il., 12°, (International education ser., no. 31.) $1.50.
"What Froebel saw in the heart of the child he has told us in the 'Mother play.' In this precious volume he 'deciphers all that the child feels in cipher,' and translates for mothers the hieroglyphic of their own instinctive play. As a child's book this little collection of songs and games is unique in literature. As a mother's book, likewise, it has no ancestry and no posterity. It is the greatest book for little children and the greatest book for mothers in the world. When all women shall have laid to heart its lessons, the ideal which hovers before us in the immortal pictures of the Madonna will be realized, for then, at last, each mother will revere and nurture in her child the divine humanity. Am I told that I dream impossible things? I repel the suggestion of doubters, themselves deceived by the 'hypocritic days,' and fortify my soul with the assurance of the prophetess who, sitting serene in the midst of the revolving wheel of time, declares:
"'Den lieb'ich der unmogliches begehrt!'"
—*Introduction by Translator.*

ROARK, RURIC N. Psychology in education; designed as a text-book, and for the use of the general reader. American Book Co. 12°, $1.
"Prof. Roark has written his book in a manner that will cause it to commend itself to all teachers and students, and if it were not for the seeming impossibility of getting parents of young children to realize the important functions that they have to perform, they would read it, commend it, and enable their children to profit by the good advice that it contains. It is not that the professor tells new and startling facts; it is that he states what all thoughtful people know but to which they do not give sufficient weight. As a teacher of teachers, whether standing in the relation of preceptor or parent to the child, the book is of much value. The author should produce upon the same lines as those upon which he has produced this book a book for parents. It would benefit the parents and lead to healthier and stronger minds among the young, and so elevate materially the standard of our youth."—*New York Times.*

WHITE, FRANCIS H. Pupils' outline studies in the history of the United States. American Book Co. sq. 12°, pap., 30 c.
These outlines are adapted to the standard

school histories, which they are intended to supplement. They present a systematic combination of devices, old and new, the whole so arranged as to be easily used. Students are required to locate places, trace routes, follow lines of development, make pictures of objects illustrating civilization, write out opinions, and classify knowledge. Lists of supplementary reading are furnished of histories, poems, and novels (3 p.).

FICTION.

AIDÉ, HAMILTON. Elizabeth's pretenders. Putnam. 12°, (Hudson lib., no. 9) $1; pap., 50 c.

AMICIS, EDMONDO DE. The heart of a boy (*Cuore*): a story from the 166th Italian ed., by G. Mantellini. Laird & Lee. 12°, 75 c.

BALZAC, HONORÉ DE. A start in life; tr. by Katharine Prescott Wormeley. Roberts. 12°, $1.50.

BEAUMONT, MARY. A Ringby lass, and other stories; il. by I. Walter West. Macmillan. 16°, (Iris ser., no. 5.) 75 c.
Contents: A Ringby lass; Jack; The white Christ; Miss Penelope's tale; The revenge of her race.
" These stories, there are five of them, the longest being ' The Ringby lass,' all have distinguishing qualities of cleanness, force, and originality. ' The white Christ ' is particularly pathetic. This volume is charming as to make-up, with its delicate illustrations."— *N. Y. Times.*

BRETON, F. God forsaken: a novel. Putnam. 12°, (Hudson lib., no. 7.) $1.25; pap., 50 c.

CAMPBELL, GERALD. The Joneses and the Asterisks: a story in monologue; il. by F. H. Townsend. The Merriam Co. 12°, $1.25.
" Mr. Gerald Campbell has utilized with very happy effect a somewhat novel structural scheme —the telling of a light, bright society story in a series of monologues spoken by the leading characters in the genially satirical narrative drama. Mrs. Jones, the shallow, worldly, and inexpressibly vulgar mother, who has set her mind upon marrying her daughter to the dissolute young cad, Lord Asterisk, is a most delicious study; and, indeed, there is not one either of the newly arrived Joneses or of the ancient, but equally ill-bred, Asterisks who is not conceived in a spirit of genuine humor. Mr. Campbell's book does not call for a lengthy comment, but the reader who seeks for a laugh in its pages will not find that his search is vain." — *The Academy.*

CRAWFORD, F. MARION. Mr. Isaacs: a tale of modern India. Macmillan. 12°, (Macmillan's novelists' lib., v. 1, no. 5.) pap., 50 c.

CROCKETT, S. RUTHERFORD. A Galloway herd. Ferris. 12°, $1; pap., 50 c.

CROSSE, VICTORIA, [*pseud.* for *Miss* Vivien Cory.] A woman who did not. Roberts. 16°, (Keynotes ser.) $1.

DAWE, W. CARLTON. Yellow and white. Roberts. 16°, (Keynotes ser.) $1.

DOYLE, A. CONAN. The Stark Munro letters: being a series of twelve letters, written by J. Stark Munro, M.B., to his friend and former fellow-student, Herbert Swanborough, of

Lowell, Mass., during the years 1881–1884; ed. and arranged by A. Conan Doyle. Appleton. il. 12°, $1.50.

GALT, J. Novels; ed. by D. Storrar-Meldrum. [*New il. ed.*] In 8 v. V. 1 and 2, Annals of the parish and The Ayrshire legatees; with introd. by S. R. Crockett; por. and ils. by J. Wallace. Roberts. 12°, $2.50.

GISSING, G. The emancipated. Way & Williams. 12°, $1.25.

GOODLOE, ABBE CARTER. College girls; il. by C. Dana Gibson. Scribner. 12°, $1.25.

GOULD, NAT. ["Verax," *pseud.*] Only a commoner. Routledge. 12°, (The Lafayette lib., no. 1.) pap., 50 c.
" This is a ' no nonsense ' story. There is the yeoman father and his good son Tom Wilde. The family has lived on a farm as tenants of the duke for three generations. Then there is the utterly bad agent, Hugh Ralton, who has a grudge against the Wildes. Ralton makes it so uncomfortable for the yeoman that he has to leave England, and father and son go to Tasmania to seek their fortunes. The agent is turned off by the duke because he is found out a rascal, and he, too, goes to Tasmania. Much of the book has to do with the bad behavior of Ralton, and there is a great deal about horses and horse-racing."—*N. Y. Times.*"

HARDY, T. Two on a tower. *New ed.* Harper. 8°, $1.50.
" Contains an etched frontispiece by H. Macbeth Raeburn, and a map of Wessex, showing all localities in Hardy's tales. The preface by the author is well worthy the attention of those who wish to get directly at his views and opinions of a work which was greatly misunderstood by many readers and critics when it was originally printed, thirteen years ago. The subject of a pure woman who is forced into doing wrong is no longer a strange one in the field of fiction." —*Boston Gazette.*

HOLLAND, CLIVE. My Japanese wife. Macmillan. 24°, pap., 50 c.

KING, C. Captain Close and Sergeant Crœsus (two stories). Lippincott. 12°, $1; pap., 50 c.

KINGSLEY, C. Works. *New pocket ed.* In 11 v. V. 1, Hypatia; v. 2, Alton Locke. Macmillan. 8°, *ea.*, 75 c.

KINGSLEY, H. Leighton Court: a country house story. [*New uniform ed.*] Scribner's Sons. 16°, $1.

LAWLESS, EMILY. Grania: a story of an island. Macmillan. 12°, (Macmillan's novelists' lib., v. 1, no. 4.) pap., 50 c.

LE QUEUX, W. Zoraida: a romance of the harem and the Great Sahara; il. by Harold Piffard. Stokes. 12°, $1.50.

MAARTENS, MAARTEN, [*pseud.* for J. Vander Poorten Schwartz.] The black-box murder, by the man who discovered the murderer. Fenno. 12°, (Lenox ser., no. 31.) pap., 25 c.

MACDONALD, GEORGE. Lilith: a romance. Dodd, Mead & Co. 12°. $1.25.

MACLEOD, FIONA. The mountain lovers. Roberts. 16°, (Keynotes ser., no. 17.) $1.

MAKOWER, STANLEY V. The mirror of music. Roberts. 16°, (Keynotes ser., no. 15.) $1.

MARTEL DE JANVILLE, SIBYLL GABRIELLE MARIE ANTOINETTE, (Comtesse) de, [" Gyp," pseud.] An infatuation ; from the French by Elise Paul. Fenno. 16°, 50 c.; pap., 25 c.

MORRIS, W. The wood beyond the world. Roberts. ill., 8°, $3.

MOTT, E. The old settler, the squire, and little Peleg ; il. by D. A. McKellar. United States Book Co. 12°, $1 ; pap., 50 c.

PEACOCK, T. LOVE. Maid Marion and Crotchet Castle ; il. by F. H. Townsend ; with introd. by G. Saintsbury. Macmillan. 12°, (Macmillan's illustrated standard novels, no. 6.) $1.25.

READ, OPIE P., [" Arkansaw traveller," pseud.] On the Suwanee River: a romance. Golden-rod. ed. Laird & Lee. il. 12°, 75 c.; 50 c. Same, (Pastime ser.) pap., 25 c.

SERGEANT, ADELINE. Out of due season : a mezzotint. Appleton. 12°, (Appletons' town and country lib., no. 176.) $1 ; pap., 50c.

SHAW, E. R. Legends of Fire Island beach and the south side. United States Book Co. il. 12°, 75 c.

SMITH, Mrs. ELIZ. THOMAS, [formerly L. T. Meade.] A soldier of fortune. Fenno. 12°, $1 ; pap., 50 c.
" The story is naturally told and has an excellent moral tone to it. It relates the love of an English journalist for an attractive but impulsive girl, whose volatile nature is in sharp contrast with the strong character and high ideals of another girl, who was the school playmate of the journalist, and who suppresses her love for him in favor of her unworthy rival. At a crisis in the story Nelly Brown intervenes and carries the day, though with an abnegation and unselfishness that does her honor. There is a capital plot to the story, which is as admirably wrought out as it is well conceived. The characters are drawn with skill and their several fortunes are followed with a genuine interest."—Philadelphia Press.

STOKER, BRAM. The Watter's Mou. Appleton. 12°, 75 c.
A story of the courageous act of a young girl divided in mind between pride in her lover's sense of duty as a member of the coast guard, and fear for her father's safety, who, she fears, has been working with smugglers. The Watter's Mou is a little cove or harbor on the Scottish coast of the North Sea.

TASMA, [pseud. for Mrs. Jessie Couvreur.] Not counting the cost. Appleton. 12°, (Appleton's town and country lib., no. 175.) $1; pap., 50 c.

TENNYSON, MARY H. A cruel dilemma. Cassell. 12°, (Cassell's Union sq. lib., no. 10,) pap., 50 c.
An English baronet of sixty, a widower with an only daughter, becoming weary of books and study, takes a trip alone to Folkestone. Chance throws him into the hands of a beautiful adventuress with whom he becomes infatuated and eventually marries. This woman, with the aid of accomplices, first drives his daughter from her home and then tries to kill Sir Richard For-

rest with slow poison. The daughter, without friends or money, almost starves to death in London, her lover, from whom she has been separated by misrepresentation, finding her when a moment more would have been too late.

WALLACE, LEW. Ben-Hur : eine geshichte aus der zeit des Herrn Jesu ; ins Deutsche übertragen von H. W. S. [Ben-Hur in German.] Harper. 16°, $1.50.

WARDEN, FLORENCE, [pseud. for Florence Alice Price, now Mrs. G. E. James]. A spoilt girl. Lippincott. (Lippincott's select novels, no. 173.) $1 ; pap., 50 c.

WARDEN, GERTRUDE. The gray wolf's daughter. International News Co. 12°, (Authors' lib., no. 13.) $1.25 ; pap., 50 c.

WELLS, H. G. Select conversations with an uncle (now extinct), and two other reminiscences. The Merriam Co. 12°, $1.25.
The objects are : Of conversations and the anatomy of fashion ; The theory of the perpetual discomfort of humanity ; The use of ideals ; The art of being photographed ; Bagshot's mural decorations ; On social matters ; The joys of being engaged ; La belle dame sans merci ; On a tricycle ; An unsuspected masterpiece; The great change ; The pains of marriage ; A misunderstood artist ; The man with a nose.

WEYMAN, STANLEY J. From the memoirs of a minister of France. Longmans, Green & Co. il. 12°, $1.25.
" Stanley J. Weyman's stories are among the most interesting romantic tales of the day, and are too well known to be in need of recommendation. 'From the memoirs of a minister of France' is full of the qualities that have recommended the romances of Mr. Weyman hitherto, and it will be welcomed and approved by many readers."—N. Y. Sun.

WOOLSON, Miss CONSTANCE FENIMORE. The front yard, and other Italian stories. Harper. il. 12°, $1.25.
Six short stories and sketches, depicting diversified incidents and scenes in Italy. " The front yard " tells of a middle-aged New England woman who married a young Italian and went with him to live in Italy ; her one hope in her sordid life was to have a real New England front yard in place of the dirt of her Italian home. The other stories are: " Neptune shore," " A pink villa," " The street of the Hyacinth," "A Christmas party," and " In Venice."

HISTORY.

BLISS, Rev. W. D. P. Arbitration and conciliation in industrial disputes. The Church Social Union. 8°, (Publications of the society, ser. B, no. 3.) pap., 10 c.
A reprint from advance sheets of an article prepared for "The encyclopædia of social reform." First are presented the facts of the case as developed in different countries, particularly in France, England, and America. After this historical sketch, statements are placed side by side of the chief advantages and difficulties of arbitration, together with the conflicting views of the subject taken by various thinkers.

BOSCAWEN, W. ST. CHAD. The Bible and the monuments; the primitive Hebrew records in the light of modern research. Young. il. 8°, $2.

The Babylonian and Assyrian versions of those traditions which are found in the early chapters of Genesis are placed before readers, and such comparisons instituted as seemed to the author within the range of fair criticism. In what manner the comparison has tended to establish the authenticity and faithfulness of the Hebrew records, the reader is left to form his own opinion. Both the Hebrew records and the inscriptions from the monuments are treated simply as ancient literature.

HOLM, ADOLF. The history of Greece from its commencement to the close of the independence of the Greek nation; authorized tr. from the German. In 4 v. V. 2, The fifth century B.C. Macmillan. 12°, $2.50.

MITCHELL, DONALD G., [" Ik Marvel," *pseud.*] English lands, letters, and kings. V. 3, Queen Anne and the Georges. Scribner. 12°, $1.50.

MOMMSEN, THEODOR. History of Rome; tr. with sanction of the author by W. Purdie Dickson. *New ed. rev.* throughout and embodying recent additions. Scribner. 12°, $10.

An entirely new edition from new plates. The translation conforms to the eighth German edition. " As compared with the first English edition, the more considerable alterations of additions, omissions, or substitution amount, I should think," the translator says, "to wellnigh a hundred pages. I have corrected various errors in renderings, names, and dates; and I have still further broken up the text into paragraphs and added marginal headings." The index is also enlarged. A very neat edition; good paper and type; small page and ample margins.

SAINT-AMAND, IMBERT DE. The revolution of 1848; tr. by Elizabeth Gilbert Martin. Scribner. pors., 12°, (Famous women of the French court.) $1.25.

SALEILLES, R. The development of the present constitution of France. American Acad. of Political and Social Science. 8°, (Publications of the society, no. 151.) pap., 50 c.

HUMOR AND SATIRE.

ANSTEY, F., [*pseud.* for F. Anstey Guthrie.] Lyre and lancet: a story in scenes. Macmillan. il. 16°, $1.25.

BROWN, H. E. Betsey Jane on wheels: a tale of the bicycle craze. W. B. Conkey Co. il. 12°, (White City ser., v. 2, no. 11.) pap., 25 c.

" It is pleasant reading, and can be recommended to dyspeptics and hypochondriacs. While it is not uproariously funny, it has a good deal of fun, the illustrations being particularly clever and comical. In a word, it is a book which is admirable for an idle hour, and which cannot do harm to any one."—*N. Y. Herald.*

LITERARY MISCELLANY, COLLECTED WORKS, ETC.

GLEANINGS, pure, pointed, and practical; gathered especially for the members of the Christian Endeavor and Epworth League as suggestive for half-minute talks; with a thought index. G. W. Jacobs & Co. 16°, 60 c.

A collection of noble sentiments gleaned from the prose-writings of H. Drummond, J. Ruskin, F. W. Robertson, C. Kingsley, Thomas à Kempis, G. MacDonald, F. W. Farrar, Phillips Brooks, and the poems of Alfred Tennyson, Jean Ingelow, J. Keble, W. Cowper, Frances Ridley Havergal, W. Wordsworth, Mrs. Browning, and H. W. Longfellow.

JEFFERIES, R. Thoughts from the writings of Richard Jefferies: selected by H. S. H. Waylen. Longmans, Green & Co. 16°, $1.25.

LAMB, C. Essays of Elia; ed. with introds. and notes by N. L. Hallward and S. C. Hill. Macmillan. 12°, (Macmillan's English classics.) *net,* 50 c.

MASTERPIECES of British literature; with biographical sketches, notes, and portraits. Houghton, Mifflin & Co. 12°, $1.

Selections (prose and poetry) representing some of the finest efforts of Ruskin, Macaulay, Dr. John Brown, Tennyson, Dickens, Wordsworth, Burns, Lamb, Coleridge, Byron, Cowper, Gray, Goldsmith, Addison and Steele, Milton and Bacon.

REPPLIER, AGNES. Essays in miniature. Houghton, Mifflin & Co. 12°, buckram, $1.25.

WELLS, B. W. Modern German literature. Roberts. 12°, $1.50.

" A good account, plain, informing, and not too long. It treats briefly of the origins of German literature, has something like thirty pages upon Klopstock, Wieland, and Herder, gives about the same space to Lessing, devotes one hundred pages to Goethe, seventy to Schiller, and chapters of about thirty pages each to Richter and the romantic school, to Heine, and to imaginative German literature since 1850. It is a book not for the specialist, but for the general student and reader, and, as we say, it seems to serve its purpose very well."—*N. Y. Sun.*

MEDICAL.

KELLOGG, J. H., *M.D.* The art of massage, its physiological effects and therapeutic applications. Modern Medicine Pub. Co. il. 8°, hf. leath., $3.

After a brief sketch of the history of massage, and an outline of the parts especially concerned in massage, the author gives in twenty pages a lucid statement of the physiological effects of massage, in which the subject is brought up to the latest date. The following chapter is devoted to the therapeutic applications of massage, in which the general indications are clearly pointed out. Fifty pages are devoted to the several procedures of massage, which are considered under seven heads. A number of new procedures, especially in connection with abdominal and pelvic massage, are described. The other chapters deal with mechanical massage, scientific physical training, studies of individual and comparative muscular strength in men and women, the rest cure, etc.

MENTAL AND MORAL PHILOSOPHY.

ROMANES, G. J. Mind and motion, and monism. Longmans, Green & Co. 12°, $1.25.

NATURE AND SCIENCE.

HUDSON, W. H. British birds ; with a chapter on structure and classification, by Frank E. Beddard ; with 8 colored pl. from original drawings by A. Thorburn, and figures in black and white from original drawings by G. E. Lodge and from photographs of nature by R. B. Lodge. Longmans, Green & Co. il. 12°, $3.50.

WRIGHT, J. Garden flowers and plants ; a primer for amateurs. Macmillan. il. 16°, *net,* 35 c.

POETRY AND DRAMA.

CARLETON, WILL. Rhymes of our planet. Harper. por., il. 12°, $1.25.

KROEKER, KATE FREILIGRATH, *comp.* A century of German lyrics. Stokes. 16°, $1.

LE GALLIENNE, R. Robert Louis Stevenson, an ˙ elegy, and other poems mainly personal. Copeland & Day. 8°, bds., $1.25.

ROBINSON, C. NEWTON. The viol of love: poems. Lamson, Wolffe & Co. 12°, $1.50.

SCOTT, *Sir* WALTER. Poetical works ; with author's introds. and notes ; ed. by J. Logie Robertson. *Complete [India-pap.] ed.* Nelson. 12°, $3.
 ˙ This edition is believed to contain every known poem and fragment of verse that Scott wrote. Printed on India paper, gilt edges.

SHELLEY, PERCY BYSSHE. Lyric poems ; ed. by Ernest Rhys. Macmillan. 8°, (Lyric poets.) $1.

POLITICAL AND SOCIAL.

BOURINOT, J. G. How Canada is governed : a short account of its executive, legislative, judicial, and municipal institutions, with an historical outline of their origin and development. The Copp, Clarke Co., Ltd. il.[12°, $1. Divided into seven parts, treating of : Growth of the constitution ; The imperial government ; The Dominion government ; The provincial governments ; Municipal government in the provinces ; School government in the provinces ; Government in the Northwest territories. A concluding chapter on the duties and responsibilities of Canadian citizens. Appendix contains the constitution of the Dominion of Canada. Analytical index. Bibliographical notes at the end of each division refer to authorities for further study. The work is free from technical language. Author is clerk of the Canadian House of Commons.

NELSON, H. LOOMIS. The money we need : a short primer on money and currency. Harper. il. 16°, 50 c.

WETZEL, W. A. Benjamin Franklin as an economist. The Johns Hopkins Press. 8°. (Johns Hopkins Univ. studies, 13th ser., no. 9.) pap., 50 c.
 " The purpose of this monograph has been not to weave together fragmentary expressions into an artificial whole, but rather to present such of Franklin's views as seem fairly entitled to the rank of economic theories."—*Preface.* Contains a bibliography (1 p.).

WILLIAMS *Mrs.* TALCOTT, *ed.* The story of a woman's municipal campaign, by the Civic Club for school reform in the Seventh Ward of Phil. American Acad. of Political and

Social Science. 8°, (Publications of the society, no. 150.) pap., 50 c.
 In the Philadelphia municipal election of February, 1895, the Civic Club, a reform organization of women, began its work for school reform by endeavoring to secure the election of women as ward school directors. This pamphlet contains the reports of a special campaign made in the Seventh Ward. They describe "the personal experiences of the candidates, the method, means, and personnel of organization, the character and conditions of ward political life, its vote and political organizations, the cause of failure, and the path to ultimate success."

SPORTS AND AMUSEMENTS.

BICKERDYKE, J. Sea-fishing ; with contributions on Antipodean and foreign fish, by W. Senoir; Tarpon, by A. C. Harmsworth ; Whaling, by *Sir* H. W. Gore-Booth ; il. by C. Napier Hemy, R. T. Pritchett, W. W. May, and others. Little, Brown & Co. il. 12°,(Badminton lib.) $3.50.

MACPHERSON, *Rev.* H. A.; WORTLEY, A. J. STU˙ ART ; *and* SHAND, ALEX. INNES. The pheasant: natural history, by Rev. H. A. Mac˙ pherson ; Shooting, by A. J. Stuart-Wortley˙ Cookery, by Alex. Innes Shand. Longmans˙ Green & Co. il. 12°. (Fur and feather ser.) $1.75.

THEOLOGY, RELIGION AND SPECULATION.

MACARTHUR, *Rev.* ROB. STUART. Quick truths in quaint texts. American Baptist Pub. Soc. 12°, $1.25.
 Twenty sermons preached in the Calvary Baptist Church, N. Y. City, on consecutive summer Sunday evenings.

MILNE, *Rev.* J. R. The doctrine and practice of the eucharist ; as deduced from scripture and the ancient liturgies. Longmans, Green & Co. 12°, $1.25.

MOXOM, PHILIP STAFFORD. From Jerusalem to Nicæa: the church in the first three centuries. Roberts. 12°, (Lowell lectures.) $1.50.
 Contents: The rise and spread of Christianity ; The organization of the early church ; The apostolic fathers; The struggle with heathenism : the persecutions ; The struggle with heathenism: the apologists ; The struggle with the church: heresies ; The Christian school of Alexandria ; The first œcumenical council. Index.
 " A series of lectures delivered under the auspices of the Lowell Institute in Boston. One of the virtues of the book is that the history is entirely unsectarian. It gives the facts as they have been handed down, and while it breathes a Christian spirit, it is content to let the events speak for themselves. The gradual development of Christianity is skilfully shown, and although, as the author says in his preface, scholars will not find anything new, the general reader gets a great deal of information, in concise form, that he could obtain elsewhere only by going through voluminous and sometimes not easily procurable church histories. The book begins with the life and teachings of Jesus, told in a terse and simple way, and it takes the reader through the early and turbulent period of Christianity that preceded the first Ecumenical Council. When that is reached

the lectures end. It is a valuable work for Sunday-school superintendents.' — *Commercial Advertiser*,

REED, *Rev.* J. SANDERS. The crozier and the keys : a companion volume to " The bishop's blue book." Pott. 12°, $1.50.

REED, *Rev.* J. SANDERS. The bishop's blue book. Pott. 12°, $1.

SCHAUFFLER, A. F., *D.D.* Ways of working ; or, helpful hints for Sunday-school officers and teachers. Wilde. 12°, $1.

THOMPSON, HUGH MILLER (*Bp.*) The world and the wrestler's personality and responsibility. Whittaker. 12°, (The Bohlen lectures for 1895.) $1.
Four lectures on : Personality of man ; Personality of God ; Personality of God ; Personality of man.

Books for the Young.

ASHMORE, RUTH. Side talks with girls. Scribner. 12°, $1.
The subjects are varied and the manner is informal. There are twenty-two essays, concerned with such matters as the social life of a girl, girl life in New York City, the country girl, quiet walks for girls, a girl's religious life, the small faults of girls, what a girl should read, the art of travelling easily, the physical life of a girl, the young wife's first year, and the young husband's first year. The style is simple and admirable, and the talks make easy and interesting reading."—*N. Y. Sun.*

BURTON, J. BLOUNDELLE. The desert ship : a story of adventure by sea and land ; il. by Hume Nisbet and W. Buckley. Warne. 12° $1.25.
The scene is the great Colorado Desert, which local traditions says was once a sea opening from the Gulf of California. It is likewise believed that in the middle of the great desert (once the Vermillion Sea) there is stranded a Spanish galleon laden with treasures. Incited by an English sea captain's description of this wonder of the new world, which he claims to have seen, Philip Drage sails from Bristol in quest of "The El Fernando Rey, or, "The desert ship." His adventures *en voyage* are described.

CONANT, CHARA B. Miss Canary. American Baptist Pub. Soc. 1 il., 12°, $1.
A story for young readers. "Miss Canary" is a pet name bestowed upon their young governess by a family of boys and girls. Annie Carey is only sixteen when she goes out into the world to earn a living; her pretty yellow hair and exquisite voice gain her her name. She afterward goes to Dresden to have her voice trained, and finds an admirer.

CONNELL, SARAH G. The little ladies of Ellenwood and their hidden treasure. G. W. Jacobs & Co. 1 il., 12°, $1.
The "hidden treasure" was contentment. The Bailey children only found it after a long series of misfortunes. Their father fails in business, and they have to leave beautiful Ellenwood and reside in a cottage; they learn to earn some money, and in spite of serious troubles are not unhappy.

DRYSDALE, W. The young reporter: a story of Printing House Square; il. by C. Copeland. W. A. Wilde & Co. 12°, (Brain and brawn ser.) $1.50.
Richard Sumner was, in printer's parlance, "printer's devil" in the office of a weekly country newspaper when he made his first hit by a skilful piece of reporting, which secured him a place on the reportorial staff of a well-known New York daily. His adventures thereafter are given, notably how he handled his Sing Sing assignment and the robbery of a well-known millionaire's grave, how he interviewed President Diaz, and what came of his interview, with a final account of his literary venture.

FOSTER, *Rev.* ALBERT J. Ampthill Towers. Nelson. 12°, 80 c.
Ampthill Towers in Bedfordshire was up to the end of the sixteenth century a royal residence. Anne Boleyn visited it with Henry the Eighth while his divorce from Katharine was pending, and it was afterward the refuge for several years of the latter unhappy queen. With this historical background there is a pretty love-story, the chief actors being faithful adherents of Queen Katharine.

HOCKING, SILAS K. Doctor Dick, and other tales. Warne. 12°, $1.

McCOOK, H. CHRISTOPHER. Old farm fairies: a summer campaign in Brownieland against King Cobweaver's pixies: a story for young people. G. W. Jacobs & Co. il. 12°. $1.50.
Mr. McCook is known as the author of an exhaustive work on " American spiders and their spinning work"; the information collected in the making of this book has been made use of in the present work, which is an instructive story on the habits of our spiders and other insect forms. The spiders are assigned the part of pixies or goblins, while the brownies or "household fairies" are made to personify those insect forms, especially useful to man, against which spiders wage continual war; human characters are also introduced. As the book was written twenty years ago, though only just published, the writer disclaims any imitation of Palmer Cox.

OXLEY, J. MACDONALD. My strange rescue, and other stories of sport and adventure in Canada. Nelson. il. 12°, $1.25.
Many of these stories and sketches were first published in *Our Youth, Youth's Companion, Harper's Young People*, and *Golden Days*. They tell of thrilling encounters with bears, expeditions in canoes and on snowshoes, include scenes from Indian life, etc. They have their scene in the Canadian lumbering camp, on Sable Island, and on the coast of Anticosti.

PEMBRIDGE, [*pseud.*] Whist; or, Bumblepuppy: thirteen lectures addressed to children. Warne. 12°, $1.

STORY of Joseph and his brethren, for the young; with col. il. Nelson. 24°, bds., 35 c.

STORY of Queen Esther, for the young, with col. il. Nelson. 24°, bds., 35 c.

STORY of the prophet Daniel, for the young; with col. il. Nelson. 24°, bds., 35 c.

TEMPLE, CERONA. Princess Louise: a tale of the Stuarts. Nelson. 12°, 60 c.
The story begins in France in the year 1697,

at the Chateau of St. Germani, where James the Second of England spent his exile as the guest of Louis XIV. The " Princess Louise " was his young daughter, and it is her pathetic story, and the story of her friend, Mary Plowden, that are the principal themes. The scene all through is in France.

TOMLINSON, EVERETT T. Three colonial boys: a story of the times of '76; il. by C. Copeland. W. A. Wilde & Co.   12°, (War of the revolution ser., no. 1.) $1.50.

The first volume of a new series for young readers; it is introductory to the war of independence, dealing principally with New York City life and the first feeling aroused in the colonies by the action of Great Britain. It shows the feeling between the Whigs and Tories, discusses the London Trading and Whaleboat warfare, the characteristics of the soldiers, and the sending of the powder from New Jersey to Cambridge. The three young heroes are drawn into the events of the times.

TOMPKINS, ELIZ. KNIGHT. An unlessoned girl: a story of school life. Putnam.   12°, $1.25.

WHISHAW, F. Boris, the bear-hunter: a tale of Peter the Great and his times. Nelson. il. 12°, $1.25.

Boris, the great bear-hunter, lived about two hundred years ago, far away in the north of Europe in Archangel. He became a sailor in the service of Peter the Great, and there being an opportune bear, who attacks Peter, Boris saves the czar's life. Various adventures and episodes of Russian history during the seventeenth century follow.

RECENT FRENCH AND GERMAN BOOKS.

FRENCH.

Aicard, J. L'été à l'ombre. 12° (Flammarion).. $1 00
Champsaur, F. Marquisette. 12° (Ollendorff).
Garofalo, R. La superstition socialiste. 8° (Alcan).. 1.50
Gennevraye. Un château ou l'on s'amuse. 12° (Hetzel) 90
Ibsen, H. Empereur et Galiléen. 12° (Lavine).. 1 00
Journal (Le) de la Belle Meunière, Le Genl. Boulanger et son Amie. 12° (Dentu)............... 1 00
Keller, G. Roméo et Juliette au Village. (Collection Chardon Bleu.) 12° (Borel).............. 75
Lemonnier, C. La faute de Mlle. Charvet. 12° (Dentu).. 1 00
Le Roux, Hughes. Je deviens colon Moers Algériennes. 12° (Levy)........................... 1 00
Mael, P. Celles qui savent aimer. 12° (Ollendorff)... 1 00
Rapp. Mémoires du Général, 1772–1821. 12° (Garnier).. 1 00
Ricard. A prix fixe et à la carte. 12° (Levy)... 1 00
Rosny, J. H. Les Origines. (Collection Papyrus.) 12° (Borel)................................... 90
Sarcey, F. Grandeur et Decadence de Minon-Minette. (Collection Illustrée.) 12° (Ollendorff) 60

GERMAN.

Conrad-Ramlo, M. Im Gnadenwald. 12° (Reissner)... 1 00
Haidheim, L. Hilf dir selbst. 12° (Janke)...... 1 70
Herrmann, O. Mein Schutzengel. 12° (Pierson). 50
v. Kahlenberg, H. Ein Narr. 12° (Reissner). 1 00
Wichert, E. Die verlorene Tochter. 12° (Reissner).. 35
Wolff, H. Prinzessin ohne Land und Krone. 12° (Georgi).. 70
Wolters, W. Mädchen am See. 12° (Pierson).. 70
Zapp, A. Martha und Maria. 12° (Georgi)....... 70
— Moderne Frauen. 12° (Georgi)............... 35

Freshest News.

HENRY HOLT & CO. announce three new stories in their *Buckram Series :* Mears' "Emma Lou: Her Book," is the diary of a lively girl; Hopkins' "Lady Bonnie's Experiment" is a clever little pastoral of quaint conceit, satirical, with a decidedly lyrical note on the new woman, leading to a droll and swift *dénouement ;* and Buchan's "Sir Quixote of the Moors" recounts the romantic experiences of le Sieur de Rohan on the Scottish moors when the English were hunting the Covenanters.

T. Y. CROWELL & CO. have just ready "Under the Old Elms," by Mary B. Claflin, containing remembrances of Charles Sumner, Henry Wilson, Henry Ward Beecher, Mrs. Stowe, and others; "Shakespeare's Heroines on the Stage," by C. E. L. Wingate, noticed elsewhere in this issue; and a new illustrated edition of "Cuore," de Amicis' world-renowned story, which in this new dress will appeal strongly to shoppers purchasing books for school-boys during the Christmas season.

FORDS, HOWARD & HULBERT have just issued "Game Birds at Home," by Theodore S. Van Dyke, a volume describing outdoor delights with quail, woodcock, the different grouse, ducks, geese, cranes, plover, snipe, etc., and also their houses and habits; a new edition of "Bullet and Shell," Major George F. Williams' soldier's romance of the Civil War, to which have been added many spirited illustrations; and a new edition up to date of their ever-popular "Library of Poetry and Song," first edited by William Cullen Bryant, to which have now been added forty-eight poems by later authors, illustrated either with portraits of the authors or with half-tone engravings of drawings, etchings, and paintings by well-known artists.

THE CENTURY CO. will publish during October and November "Old Dutch and Flemish Masters," exquisite engravings by Timothy Cole, with text by Prof. John C. Van Dyke and by the engraver; "The Second Jungle Book," by Rudyard Kipling; "Kitwyk Stories," delightful stories of village life in Holland, by Anna Eichberg King; "A Madeira Party," two stories of the days of our fathers, by Dr. S. Weir Mitchell; "Life in the Tuileries under the Second Empire," by Anna L. Bicknell, who for nine years resided in the Tuileries with a family of the court of Napoleon; and "The Illustration of Books," a suggestive handbook by Joseph Pennell, the well-known artist and illustrator. The Century Company are making preparations to bring out some fine juveniles for the holidays, which will receive full notice in a later issue.

ROBERTS BROTHERS have added several new volumes to their *Keynotes Series,* which, however one may argue about the motives for the existence of some of them, are one and all of high literary merit. The latest comers are "The Woman Who Did Not," a story of shipboard flirtation, by Victoria Crosse; "The Mountain Lovers," by Fiona Macleod, dreamy and full of poetic imagery, yet giving the impression of sombre strength; "Yellow and White," by W. Carlton Dawe, a bunch of short stories with Asian background and muscular Englishmen for heroes, whose standards of morality have suffered under an Indian sun; and "The Mirror of Music," by Stanley V. Makower, the diary of an hysterical girl suffering from music mania and morbid introspection. Aubrey Beardsley still furnishes all the title-pages for these weird, suggestive books, in which many of the heroines are as incomprehensible and eccentric as his counterfeit presentments of them.

FREDERICK A. STOKES COMPANY have just issued "Zoraida," by William Le Queux, a romance of the harem and the Great Sahara, full of stirring incidents. In the *West End Series* they have put "A Comedy in Spasms," by the author of "The Yellow Aster"; "Anne of Argyle, or, The Cavalier and the Covenant," by George Eyre Todd, and "Lakewood," by Mary Harriott Norris. The new novels in the *Twentieth Century Series* are "The Sale of a Soul," by F. Frankfort Moore; "Dead Man's Court," by M. H. Hervey; "Sinners Twain," by John Mackie; and "Toxin," by Ouida; to the *Bijou Series* has been added "Bohemia Invaded," by James L. Ford, author of "The Literary Shop"; "A White Baby," by James Welsh; and "The Red Spell," by Francis Gribble, a story of the French Commune. "Rhymes and Roses" is a new book of poems by the most popular of Southern poets, Samuel Minturn Peck; and a collection of poems by Mary Berri Chapman is to appear under the title of "Lyrics of Love and Nature."

WARD, LOCK & BOWDEN, LIMITED, will publish at once "The Boy in Grey, and Other Stories," forming the twelfth and concluding volume in their new uniform edition of "The Novels of Henry Kingsley," edited by Clement K. Shorter, all printed from type specially cast, on good paper, and neatly and handsomely bound in cloth, or, if purchased in sets, to be had in three-quarter morocco with gilt tops. The forthcoming volume will include a biographical sketch of Henry Kingsley, by his nephew, Maurice Kingsley, giving a fair literary estimate of the work of Henry Kingsley, who, by such eminent critics as James Payn, Andrew Lang, Augustus Birrell, and many more is held to have been a far better novelist than his brother Charles. Although written a generation ago these books appeal to the most modern readers. Many of the works have been less popular than others, but in this new uniform shape will again be read equally with his great successes "Geoffry Hamlin," "Ravenshoe," "The Hillyars and Burtons," "The Silcotes of Silcote," etc., and will receive a new estimate as to their relative rank in the appreciation of a newer generation.

D. APPELTON & Co. announce a new and revised edition of "Uncle Remus," by Joel Chandler Harris, with 112 illustrations by A. Frost. They have just ready "Gustave Flaubert," by John Charles Tarver, founded on the works and correspondence of the great French novelist, one of the most interesting literary publications of the season. "The Stark Munro Letters," by A. Conan Doyle, have already reached a second edition; and other novels sure to be popular are "In Old New England," by Hezekiah Butterworth; "Not Counting the Cost," by Tasma; "Out of Due Season," by Adeline Sergeant; "Scylla or

Charybdis?" by Rhoda Broughton; "The Red Badge of Courage," a story of the Civil War, by Stephen Crane; "The Watter's Mou'," by Bram Stoker; and "In Defiance of the King," a romance of the American Revolution, by Chauncey C. Hotchkiss. Other volumes of interest and well-put information are "The Beginnings of Writing," by Walter J. Hoffman; "The Psychology of Number," by James A. McLellan; and "The Mottoes and Commentaries of Froebel's Mother Play," rendered into English verse by Henrietta R. Eliot.

G. P. PUTNAM'S SONS are issuing an edition of James Fenimore Cooper's works in thirty-two volumes, to be known as *The Mohawk edition*. They will be printed from new plates and bound in the general style of the new *Hudson edition* of "Irving's Works." The edition will be sold in sets or separate volumes according to the convenience of the buyer. The new numbers in the *Heroes of the Nations Series* are "Charles XII. and the Collapse of the Swedish Empire, 1682-1719," by R. Nisbet Bain; "Lorenzo de Medici," by Edward Armstrong; and "Joan of Arc," by Mrs. Oliphant. *The Elia Series* will be a selection of famous books offered as specimens of the best literature and of artistic typography and book-making. The selections thus far planned for are from Marcus Aurelius, Epictetus, Charles Lamb, and John Ruskin. "Israel Among the Nations," by Anatole Leroy Beaulieu, translated by Frances Hellmann, is a study of the Jews and anti-semitism: and "Old Diary Leaves," by Henry Steele Olcott, will give the true story of the Theosophical Society. The *Waldering edition* of "At Odds," by the Baroness Tautphœus, and the *Fontainebleau edition* of James' "Richelieu," will be in demand unquestionably for holiday purchase.

HOUGHTON, MIFFLIN & Co. are preparing a beautiful holiday edition, in two volumes, of Mrs. Jane G. Austin's "Standish of Standish," with twenty full-page photogravure illustrations by Frank T. Merrill. The new *Cambridge edition* of "The Complete Poetical and Dramatic Works of Robert Browning" will be a miracle of book-making, compressing all of Browning's wonderful works into a single condensed volume containing a biographical sketch, notes, an appendix containing Browning's essay on Shelley, indexes to titles and first lines, printed on opaque paper and attractively bound. New works of fiction are "The Village Watch-Tower," by Miss Wiggin, several short stories of New England life; "The Wise Woman," by Mrs. Burnham, who aims to do away with conventionalities and promote a more sincere social life; "Clarence," by Bret Harte; and "The Coming of Theodora," by Eliza Orne White, a novel which, it is said, will cause discussion. "John Knox," by Florence A. McCunn. is the new volume in the *British Leaders of Religion* series; Samuel H. Scudder has prepared a delightful book on butterflies, under the title "Frail Children of the Air"; and Rev. Dr. George A. Gordon's "The Christ of To-Day" is a strong, thoughtful book, possessing peculiar attractions for earnest readers. The *Cambridge edition* of "Oliver Wendell Holmes' Poems" and "A Victorian Anthology," edited by E. C. Stedman, will be noticed in a later issue.

ROBERTS' NEW BOOKS.

READY FOR OCTOBER.

THE WOOD BEYOND THE WORLD.

By WILLIAM MORRIS. With frontispiece by E. Burne-Jones. Crown 8vo, printed on antique English paper, with decorative cover, $3.00.

JOHN GALT'S NOVELS.

A new illustrated edition published in connection with Messrs. William Blackwood & Sons. With an introduction by S. R. Crockett, and portrait and illustrations from drawings by John Wallace. The text revised and edited by D. Storrar Meldrum. Each 16mo, cloth, $1.25 per vol.

THE ANNALS OF THE PARISH AND THE AYRSHIRE LEGATEES. 2 vols.

"The shrewder, cannier side of Scottish life, with more worldliness and less romance, is depicted in his pages."—*Bookman.*

FROM JERUSALEM TO NICÆA.

The Church in the First Three Centuries. (Lowell lectures.) By PHILIP STAFFORD MOXOM, author of "The Aim of Life." 12mo, cloth, $1.50.

MODERN GERMAN LITERATURE.

By BENJAMIN W. WELLS, Ph.D. 12mo, cloth, $1.50.
It is an excellent popular account of the rise and progress of German literature, comprehensive, and well adapted to its purpose.

A START IN LIFE.

By HONORÉ DE BALZAC. Translated by Miss K. P. Wormeley. 12mo, half russia, $1.50.

KEYNOTES SERIES.

Cover designs and title-pages by Aubrey Beardsley. Copyrighted under the International Copyright Law. Each 16mo, cloth, $1.00.

A WOMAN WHO DID NOT. By VICTORIA CROSSE.
"Powerful and absorbing."

THE MIRROR OF MUSIC. By STANLEY V. MAKOWER.

YELLOW AND WHITE. By W. CARLTON DAWE.
"Few, if any, of the preceding volumes are better."—*Publishers' Circular.*

THE MOUNTAIN LOVERS. By FIONA MACLEOD.
"A kind of tragic sweetness in the loves and sorrows of these simple folk."—*The Album.*

Previous Volumes.

KEYNOTES. By GEORGE EGERTON.
"Full of strength and feverish with intense life."—*Transcript.*

THE DANCING FAUN. By FLORENCE FARR.
"Full of dramatic power."—*Boston Home Journal.*

POOR FOLK. Translated from the Russian of F. Dostoievsky by Lena Milman. With a preface by George Moore.

A CHILD OF THE AGE. By FRANCIS ADAMS.

THE GREAT GOD PAN AND THE INMOST LIGHT. By ARTHUR MACHEN.

DISCORDS. By GEORGE EGERTON.
"The vitality of the stories is remarkable."—*Baltimore American.*

PRINCE ZALESKI. By M. P. SHIEL.

THE WOMAN WHO DID. By GRANT ALLEN.
"A very remarkable story."—*Boston Home Journal.*

WOMEN'S TRAGEDIES. By H. D. LOWRY.
"The strength and power may not be denied."—*N. Y. Times.*

GREY ROSES. By HENRY HARLAND.
"The writer one of singular power."—*Boston Courier.*

AT THE FIRST CORNER, and Other Stories. By H. B. MARRIOTT WATSON.

MONOCHROMES. By ELLA D'ARCY.
"Decidedly these tales are worth reading."—*Woman's Journal.*

AT THE RELTON ARMS. By EVELYN SHARP.

THE GIRL FROM THE FARM. By GERTRUDE DIX.

Each volume with specially designed title-page by Aubrey Beardsley. 16mo, $1.00.

SOLD BY ALL BOOKSELLERS.

ROBERTS BROTHERS, Publishers,   -   -   Boston.

LITERARY NEWS

AN ECLECTIC REVIEW OF CURRENT LITERATURE

~ILLUSTRATED~

CONTENTS.

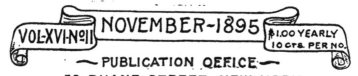

VOL·XVI·Nº11   NOVEMBER–1895 $1.00 YEARLY   10 CTS. PER NO.

~PUBLICATION OFFICE~
59 DUANE STREET, NEW YORK
ENTERED AT THE POST OFFICE AT NEW YORK AS SECOND CLASS MATTER

The Literary News

In winter you may reade them, ad ignem, by the fireside; and in summer, ad umbram, under some shadie tree, and therewith pass away the tedious houres.

VOL. XVI.   NOVEMBER, 1895.   No. 11.

Life in the Tuileries.

"LIFE in the Tuileries Under the Second Empire" is a gorgeous volume, written by Anna L. Bicknell. It is attractive in binding and letterpress, and will feel quite at home among the best books in the scholar's shelf. You understand, to start with, that the volume contains no argument concerning the strength or weakness of the career of Napoleon III., and you must not expect a learned dissertation on the times which the little Napoleon made rather exciting.

But since Miss Bicknell, an intelligent and wide-awake Englishwoman, was a governess and also a personal friend of the daughters of the Duchesse de Tascher de la Pagerie and as she lived at the Tuileries and held almost daily intercourse with the family of Napoleon, the diary which she kept must needs be invaluable. She saw his majesty and Eugénie under a variety of pleasant as well as trying circumstances, both when they were on their dignity and when they threw off all reserve, and what she tells us is therefore piquant, gossipy, instructive, and altogether satisfactory to the curiosity of the public. She wields a facile pen, and her style is conversational and fascinating. There are descriptions of court dresses and manners, and hints at a thousand and one complications and intrigues such as may be found in court circles, which always abound in jealousies and quarrels. There are anecdotes of Napoleon, for whom Miss Bicknell has a very tender place in her heart, and other anecdotes of Eugénie, whom Miss Bicknell seems to have regarded with some suspicion from the first. It is a delightful volume of nearly three hundred pages and abundantly illustrated. I have found in the book more pleasure than I dare speak of in cold and unsympathetic type. (Century Co. $2.25.) —*N. Y. Herald.*

From "Life in the Tuileries."   Copyright, 1895, by The Century Co.

THE PRINCE IMPERIAL.

Great Missionaries of the Church.

THIS is a book of biographies which will perhaps be read with more interest than usual at the present time, when the whole subject of missionary effort is being discussed so widely. No one denies that there have been many earnest Christian workers among the unconverted, and the sacrifices they have made demand respect. But this is only one side of a question which need not be argued here. In this volume the Church is somewhat vaguely used to cover a large number of diverse faiths, and among the heroes selected are some whose labors would not be universally approved. There is also a tone of somewhat too obvious piousness, if the phrase may be pardoned, on the part of the authors. In spite of these defects, however, it is as good a book as could be expected under the circumstances. (Crowell. $1.50.)—*Providence Sunday Journal.*

Clarence.

IT is a pleasant duty to convey our best thanks to Mr. Bret Harte for his capital story "Clarence." Ever since "A Waif of the Plains" was issued we have been absorbingly interested by all the changes of fortune occurring in the lives of Susy, Jim Hooker, and Clarence Brant. To our sorrow, the author makes no remark at the end of this volume with regard to further developments, and we very much fear that we have come upon the end of the adventures of three characters that have been delightful to us for a long time. We must, then, be thankful for present mercies, and proceed to write down a recommendation of this latest arrival from the writer who has contributed so generously to the joy of the reading public. Shortly after the commencement of this story Clarence and his wife, late widow of John Peyton, disagree, the subject of dispute being that *casus belli* which set the North and South of America at loggerheads. Mrs. Brant conspires with some advocates of slavery, and there is a splendid scene at the Robles Ranche, where the angered husband clears the house of the men who have assembled to plot against his sympathies. After the breaking out of the war we find Clarence in command of a division of the Northern army, and a very clever account is given of the way in which his wife managed to play the spy under his nose. Incidents full of interest follow one another so closely that the reader hardly has time to take breath. We shall not disclose the termination of the tale, but shall content ourselves by saying that all who have the pleasure of perusal to come are lucky folks. The occasional glimpses of the fascinating Susy are very welcome, as are the moments when Jim Hooker

JOHN COLERIDGE PATTESON.

comes to the front. (Houghton, Mifflin & Co. $1.25.)—*London Literary World.*

My Sister Henrietta.

THERE are few things in literature to compare in simple and tender eloquence with the tribute which the late eminent French scholar, Ernest Renan, left behind him in the little document called "My Sister Henrietta," which has been so sympathetically and felicitously translated by Abby L. Alger. Henrietta Renan was twelve years older than her famous brother, and from his early boyhood, according to his account of her, manifested for him a loving solicitude almost motherly in its range and intensity. She it was who toiled unremittingly as a teacher to pay off the indebtedness due to her father's misfortunes, who made possible the entrance of Ernest upon his scholastic career, and who, during the fifteen years in which he was pursuing the studies upon which his reputation was based, cared for all his material wants, and, more than that, was to him a constant and inspiring intellectual companion. When, in 1860, he went out to Syria, charged with a scientific commission by the French Government, she went with him, and underwent bravely all the hardships and privations to which they were subjected, but succumbed at the last to an attack of pernicious fever, with which both the explorers were smitten, and from which Ernest himself barely escaped with his life. The story of this gentle, assiduous, aspiring life, given over as it was to the highest ideals, is told by Renan with a candor and depth of appreciation that are most touching. It is clear enough that Henrietta Renan was one of the strivers after perfection, and the lesson of her life, told as it is with so much grace and charm, will remain as one of the precious things in literature. (Roberts Bros. $1.25.)—*The Beacon.*

Life of Margaret Winthrop.

MESSRS. CHARLES SCRIBNER'S SONS have in preparation, under the general title of "Women of Colonial and Revolutionary Times," a series of volumes the plan of which is not only to present carefully studied portraits of the most distinguished women of Colonial and Revolutionary times, but as a background for these portraits, to include therewith pictures and scenes of domestic and social life instead of the more public political and historical life of the people during these periods of national development. Special pains have been taken to select as the subjects of the different volumes representative women, who will at once be accepted as types of the best that their age had to offer, and those whose womanly lives reflect the social customs of their days. Puritan Eng-

land, for example, as it existed in the reign of James I., is depicted in the life of Margaret Winthrop—the daughter of Sir John Tyndal, a gentleman of repute in Essex County, England —who became the wife of John Winthrop, Governor of Massachusetts. In contrast with the hardships that Winthrop and his followers endured in New England, in the second quarter of the seventeenth century, the lavish hospitality of Virginia, as exemplified in the lives of its landed gentry, illuminated the lives of Martha Washington and Dolly Madison. The patriotic life that the women of Massachusetts led is recalled, and with illustrations, in this memoir of Mary Otis Warren, the legends of other good women of the olden time shedding lustre upon the sex which they adorned, and which their descendants are proud to remember. The authors of this series, so far as it has been determined, are Alice Morse Earle, who has undertaken the study of " Margaret Winthrop"; Anne Hollingsworth Wharton, who is to follow with the study of " Martha Washington"; Maud Wilder Goodwin, with the study of " Dorothy Payne Madison," and Alice Brown, with the study of " Mary Otis Warren." That these ladies have been wisely chosen for these tasks, which in their hands will, no

From "College Girls."　　　　　　Copyright, 1895, by Charles Scribner's Sons.

THEY WANTED HIM TO PUT THEM IN HIS STORIES.

doubt, be labors of love, is evident from the lines of literary work in which they have already distinguished themselves. Mrs. Earle in "Customs and Fashions in Old New England," Miss Wharton in "Through Colonial Doorways," Miss Goodwin in "The Colonial Cavalier," and Miss Brown in "Meadow Grass Tales of New England Life." (Scribner. $1.25.)—*Mail and Express.*

The Men of the Moss-Hags.

MR. CROCKETT has broken new ground with an out-and-out historical or political novel on a subject which is much his own. For he has ever declared his hereditary sympathy, as a "West-Country Whig," with the heroes of the Covenant, and certainly the rough actions and stormy scenes of the seventeenth century in Scotland afford a fine field for the author's descriptive powers, whether of wild nature or of wilder men. More, it is impossible for any one with the smallest imagination or sympathy not to feel much respect for the tenacious fidelity of the hillmen, even though he may be most earnestly convinced that Woodrow was a credulous romancer ; that the Whigs after Philiphaugh, and on many another occasion, had set the example of bloodthirstiness ; and that their triumph at any time previous to the arrival of the sane, cool-blooded, and tolerant William of Orange would have resulted in the establishment of a cruel ecclesiastical tyranny to which the rule of the latitudinarian curates, selfish statesmen, and bullying dragoons of King Charles would have been mildness itself. Mr. Crockett has rightly chosen for his hero and narrator one of those Earlstoun Gordons, a branch, we believe, of Kenmure, who are the subjects of the only spirited contemporary ballad produced by the Presbyterian partisans. With a deference always paid by romancers to the modern spirit, he has described William Gordon as a political rather than a religious recusant. The confession which he nobly makes at the dread hour when the shadow of the scaffold is before him is conceived in a wiser spirit than most "testimonies" of the time :

"I die (so they recorded my words) in the faith my father taught me, and for which my father died ; neither for king nor bishop will I change it. Neither for love nor lands will I recreant or swear falsely. I am a Gordon of Earlstoun. I die for the freedom of this land. God do so to me and more also, if ever I gave my back to a foe, or my shoulder to a friend all the days of my life ! That is all my testimony. God have mercy on my sinful soul, for Christ's sake. Amen !"

We can feel more sympathy for such a one than for the thorough-going enthusiasts whom ignorance and oppression, to say nothing of hot Celtic blood, converted into dangerous fanatics. Yet the glimpses we have of Cameron and Peden are well calculated to command respect. Of Claverhouse we have a tolerably just picture, though Mr. Crockett seems to believe the legend of John Brown of Priesthill in the form made famous by Macaulay. *En revanche,* Grierson (here called Grier) of Lag, Johnstone (surely the modern *e* in the Border name is an anachronism), and other local persecutors have the horrid attributes assigned them by tradition. The narrative always touches its best when there is a racy bit of fighting or an unusually close escape in which William Gordon is an actor or a witness. "The Bicker in the Snow" at Holyrood, with the incident of Lochinvar's head, is wonderfully told, as is the strange conversion effected in Wildcat Wat Gordon, Will's Cavalier cousin, on the whole the most life-like portrait in the book. The fight at Ayrsmoss, and the duel between Wat and Peter Inglis are other instances of graphic detail. The women, two—Lady Lochinvar and the brave and pious Maisie, who inspires much of the hero's constancy to his faith—are good and honest flesh and blood. The measure given us is full to a fault ; and we could have spared the Wigton martyrdom, the *réchauffe* and misquotation of the old joke about Clavers and Knox, and the verses on Baldoon, which we fancy Scott used in one of his introductions or notes. But it were unjust to grumble at the generosity of what, to those who can read a Scottish romance of an heroic kind, must prove an intellectual feast. It seems to us better work than Mr. Crockett has done since the days of "The Stickit Minister." (Macmillan. $1.50.) —*The Athenæum.*

Westminster.

THESE papers by Walter Besant in their original form first appeared in the *Pall Mall Magazine.* Additions have been made in some of the chapters, especially in the three chapters entitled "The Abbey."

"As in the book entitled 'London,' of which this is the successor, I do not pretend to offer a History of Westminster. The story of the Abbey Buildings, of the Great Functions held in the Abbey, of the Monuments in the Abbey, may be found in the pages of Stanley, Loftie, Dart, and Widmore. The History of the Houses of Parliament belongs to the history of the country, not that of Westminster. It has been my endeavor, in these pages, (1) to show, contrary to received opinion, that the Isle of Bramble was a busy place of trade long before London existed at all. (2) To restore the vanished Palaces of Westminster and White-

WESTMINSTER ABBEY.

hall. (3) To portray the life of the Abbey, with its Services, its Rule, its Anchorites, and its Sanctuary. (4) To show the connection of Westminster with the first of English printers. And, lastly, to present the place as a town and borough, with its streets and its people."

The publishers have made a fine book, with many most interesting illustrations by William Patten and others.—(Stokes. $3 ; full gilt, $4.)

In Defiance of the King.

I COME very gladly, to two books from D. Appleton & Co. which fit into this list of useful works admirably. They are both founded on facts—the one on facts of the old Revolution of the last century and the other on incidents of the late Civil War. They are not specially for the young, though they are good books to place within reach of your boys' greedy minds, but appeal to all sorts and conditions of men. "In Defiance of the King" is the title of the first, which is from the pen of Chauncey C. Hotchkiss. It is written in dramatic style, and though I dislike to spend much time on mere stories—for li e is short—I found myself profoundly interested. The plot is good, and the incidents follow in quick succession. It is not an elongated story, and you feel that the author has something of value to communicate and is going in a straight line from chapter first to finis. I think you will find pleasure in it; at any rate, I did. (Pap., 50 c.) —N. Y. Herald.

The Red Badge of Courage.

THE next is called "The Red Badge of Courage." It is by Stephen Crane, and is a well-told story. Perhaps it is all the more interesting because it deals with recent events, and while we read a crowd of reminiscences force their way into the mind and demand recognition. I like the book, and very cheerfully commend it. Indeed, this tendency among writers nowadays to get away from mere fiction and roam through the territory of facts is something to be encouraged. There are dramas in every page of our country's history, and Mr. Hotchkiss and Mr. Crane have found two of them and made good use of them. (Pap., 50 c.)—N. Y. Herald.

At Tuxter's.

"AT Tuxter's" is a cheerful tale of lowly life in London, and is written by G. B. Burgin in what is meant to be the small shopkeeper class dialect. It is not the coster language, or any other well-known London tongue. It is very likely a dialect got up for this story in lieu of learning an accurate one. It is the kind of dialect many writers adopt when they want to quote the speech of the uneducated laboring class not of foreign birth. English writers, however, usually put in many "'ows" and "hawfuls." Mr. Burgin seems to forget to do this generally. Perhaps he omitted them purposely. He doubtless knows more about it than most of us.

The Tuxters were a fat old husband who made coffins and a penurious wife who kept a shop on the corner, and they had no children. A little stranger wanders in one day and the old fat husband decides to adopt it, notwithstanding the protests of the loud-talking wife.

From "The Mushroom Cave."

THE DIME HIS SOLE CASH POSSESSION.

In the end it comes out all right, with a discovery of gentle blood and wealth and love and happiness for all.

The book is wholesome and clean and should prove amusing to many readers, which, according to some people, embraces the scope of the novel. (Putnam. $1.)—*Commercial Advertiser.*

The Story of a Governess.

ONE can always be sure of finding a well-told as well as an entertaining story in a novel of Mrs. Oliphant's. It will be difficult in the multitude of works that have come from her industrious pen to indicate the place to be assigned to "The Story of a Governess," just published. This, however, may be said, that there is in it much of the author's best and most characteristic work, with the facile power, for which Mrs. Oliphant is noted, of sketching character and portraying emotion. Janet, the heroine of the story, is a delightful study, and the reader will not fail to be interested in her and in the incidents and play and movement of the book. The plot is ingenious and not improbable, and the characters, which are more or less familiar to the readers of Mrs. Oliphant's Scottish novels, are drawn and contrasted with remarkable cleverness. (Fenno. $1.25.)

Against Human Nature.

IN "Against Human Nature" Maria Louise Poole shows how an emotional and unconventional North Carolina mountain-girl, Temple Crawford, "experiences religion under the preaching of a cultivated minister, Richard Mercer, who falls in love with her, but who hides his real feelings and asks her to marry him for "regard and mutual helpfulness." Thinking that she can "do great good" in this way, she marries him without loving him—"against human nature" Their religious work together breaks down Temple's health. She goes to the New England home of Almina Drowdy, who had formerly lived with her in North Carolina, to recuperate. While there and away from her husband she suddenly discovers that she loves her husband even more passionately than he loves her. Miss Pool has made herself so high a standard that it is great satisfaction to note she never sinks below her highest level. (Harper. $1.25.)—*Providence Sunday Journal.*

From "A Window in Thrums." Copyright, 1885, by R. F. Fenno & Co.

Three New Novels.

HERE are three handy little volumes, attractively bound, from the Frederick A. Stokes Company. It frequently happens that a busy man wants to go away from carking care for an hour or so, for the sake of mental and physical rest. He does this by going to the theatre of an evening, where he laughs at the follies of the farce. He can accomplish the same purpose by means of a book of fiction—a bit of light literature which does not make too large a drain on his attention. He runs through the story with absorbing interest and gets recreation and refreshment from it. These books will serve him admirably. "The Dead Man's Court" (75 c.), by Maurice H. Hervey, illustrated by Frank M. Gregory, is just what he needs. The time is not wasted by reading it, for it is a wholesome, breezy book. ' Private Tinker, and other stories " (50 c.), by John Strange Winter, will do very well to occupy a second evening. It will make the time pass quickly, and some of the stories are fascinating. If he is inclined to continue along this line he will find something to tingle his nerves and make him unwilling to go to bed in "The Sale of a Soul," by F. Frankfort Moore (75 c.). I shouldn't like anything better than a warm day, a hammock under an elm or chestnut, and this bit of a volume. That afternoon would be worth remembering.

The Wise Woman.

"THE Wise Woman" is the excellent title of an excellent story by Clara Louise Burnham, who wrote a romance of the World's Fair a couple of years ago called "Sweet Clover," and who is also the author of "Dr. Latimer" and "Dearly Bought," and several other wholesome American stories.

Miss Burnham — or Mrs. Burnham : woman writers ought to state which they are on the fly-leaf—writes realism. It is not offensive realism. It is pretty much the right sort of realism that deals with the ordinary situations of ordinary life with the sympathetic touch that makes the reader recognize something, not wonder at something. That is what one wants when he goes to realism. If he wants a thrill he should seek elsewhere.

It is woman's realism, and is, perhaps, not quite consistent. It is so hard for a woman to be impartial. Two or three characters that the author became very fond of in the writing she could not help making a little nicer than they really would have been, and one or two that he wanted to satirize she could not help making a little more ridiculous than they really would have seemed. Not that one would like the story or Miss Burnham less on that account, however.

"The Wise Woman" is a story of a New York suburb, probably one of the Oranges, and contains much bright but not cutting satire on the society there. The ambitious mother that did not want her two attractive girls to have anything to do with another attractive girl who happened also to earn her own living, saw what a big mistake she had made when the wealthy young doctor that she had selected for one of her daughters married this very same young woman that designed bonnets. And in addition to this, the bonnet designer's handsome brother, who is an electrician or something mechanical, won the heart of the other daughter of the ambitious mother, which makes interesting reading.

In the bringing about of all this the wise woman, who is a bright little old maid who says clever things, plays a quiet but important part. That wise woman is a good one.

There is much of human interest in this book, and the love-story is very pretty. Or, rather, there are two love-stories. They are both pretty. Mrs. Burnham's books always fulfil what is supposed to be the true function of the novel. The humor is genuine, the situations consistently natural. (Houghton, Mifflin & Co. $1.25.)—*Commercial Advertiser.*

The Beginnings of Writing.

THIS volume is intended to trace the first steps in the development of writing among the North American Indians. Dr. Hoffman is well qualified to do this work. He has been an enthusiastic student of American ethnology, was with Lieutenant Wheeler's expedition into Nevada and Arizona in 1871, post-surgeon in Dakota in 1872, when he was able to study the ethnology of the Sioux, and later, in connection with Professor Haydon's survey and in the Bureau of Ethnology, continued work and study among the American Indians. Linguistics, pictography, and religions have received his prolonged and devoted attention. The volume before us seems to be what was to be expected from such an author. Beginning with a general definition of pictography it proceeds to show what Indian monuments remain of it on stone and other materials, how they are to be interpreted, their interpretation as symbols, as gesture signs and attributes, mnemonic signs, and conventional signs and comparisons. The book is one of great interest as a study in the philosophy of expression, written from a full knowledge and on a broad basis of comparative criticism. (Appleton. $1.75.)—*The Independent.*

A Singular Life.

THIS is a story of remarkable power and significance, dealing with the experience of a young clergyman who, regarded as unsound by the ecclesiastical council called to instal him in a church, takes up with a humble life of service in the seaport town to which he had been called, but in the abandoned quarter of the town. Here he sets up the Church of the Love of Christ, for his own life is an attempt at realizing the life of Christ of reality, and struggles single-handed with the vice, especially the intemperance, in the midst of which he lives. There is no repulsive scene-painting, but the characters of liquor dealers, fishermen, and plain people are sharply drawn. The golden thread of romance which runs through the story is the love which springs up between the hero and the daughter of the old professor of divinity, a picturesque and brilliant girl. The heroic struggles of this single-hearted man in the spirit of absolute devotion and self-forgetfulness, the stormy experiences through which he passed, and the crowning success which the heavens granted—all this, told as only Miss Phelps could tell it, makes "A Singular Life" a story of thrilling interest and of profound suggestion. The woman who marries the devoted preacher is a fine character-study. Her keen sense of humor and true pride are inimitably pictured. (Houghton, Mifflin & Co. $1.25.)

Joan Haste.

MR. H. RIDER HAGGARD is not exactly himself in his latest romance, " Joan Haste." We like him the better for it, since the story, however intense it may be, runs, at least, on the confines of probability, and that with a diminished quantum of death and gore. We followed it with care as it pursued its serial course through the pages of the *Pall Mall Magazine*, and then found it sufficiently baffling and piquant. Yet, the double sacrifice made by Joan is quite superhuman, after the manner of all the virtues of Mr. Haggard's heroes and heroines. This author, however, knows rarely the difficult trick of telling a story, and he has told the story of " Joan Haste " very well, indeed. (Longmans, Green & Co. $1.25.)—*N. Y. Commercial Advertiser.*

A Set of Rogues.

FRANK BARRETT can always be depended upon to produce a novel of incident well worth reading for its plentiful surprises and dramatic forcefulness, but in "A Set of Rogues " he has quite surpassed himself in spontaneity of invention and intensity of romantic contrast. The rogues, whose imaginary experiences he describes with so much unction, consist of a band of strolling players, impoverished by the hard times that followed the great fire and the plague in London during the reign of Charles II., and who in their miserable condition fall a ready prey to the schemes of a sedate Spanish villain and enter upon an elaborate plot, by which one of their number, the vivacious and daring Moll Dawson, is to impersonate a young English woman of wealth, held captive in Barbary, and gain possession of her estates. The scene shifts from England to Spain and back to England, then to Morocco and back to England again ; the situations are many and varied, from encounters with brigands in the Pyrenees to dealings with Moorish pirates ; and in every instance the rogues maintain their picturesque individuality and fulfil their parts with unfaltering zest. Mr. Barrett has woven his romance in varied texture, and while he has never sought to disguise or excuse the wickedness of his principal characters, he has not failed on the other hand to make them decisively and even delightfully human. Jack Dawson and his daughter Moll are as real as any of the people who throng the pages of Defoe and Fielding, and while the chronicle of their experiences may not be regarded as altogether edifying by the conventional mind, hey manifest first and last traits of generosity and self-sacrifice that in the eyes of the sympathetic reader will atone for a multitude of sins. (Macmillan. $1.50.)—*The Beacon.*

" YOUR DAUGHTER ! "

NOCTURNE.

BLUE-GRAY the sea,
Ink blue the sky,
  Above one glimmering star :
And the sullen surge,
In a measured dirge,
  Thunders across the bar.

A sea-gull's cry
From far, from high,
  Falls like a dying wail ;
While the beacon-track
Of the star burns black,
  In the wake of a lurid sail.

What stroke ? What bell ?
No soul can tell,
  For the dread and the horror born
Of the clamorous heart of the throbbing deep :
But its mighty pulses rhythm keep,
  And the ship rides safe at morn !

(Houghton, Mifflin & Co. $1.25.) — *From
"The Tower."*

The Kitwyk Stories.

A ROUND dozen of stories by Anna Eichberg
King have been gathered into a volume with
the above title. The scene of each of the tales
is laid in Holland, and they are full of local
coloring. That the author is thoroughly familiar
with all phases of life in this quaint little kingdom, and is saturated with its spirit, needs no
further proof than these pages. She writes in
full sympathy with the scenes she depicts, and
she has touches of the quiet humor so characteristic of the Netherlands. The life that she depicts is that of the well-ordered households of
the burgomaster, the dominie, and the comfortable burgher. No intrigue or violent passion could lurk beneath such roofs, but Mrs.
King finds romance in plenty. Her character
sketches have the vividness of actual portraits.
George Wharton Edwards is always at home
in drawing Dutch scenes, and his illustrations
fit peculiarly well with the text. The cover of
the book, in white and blue, is an imitation of
old Delft ware. (The Century Co. $1.50.)

The Coming of Theodora.

MRS. ELIZA ORNE WHITE has never written
anything as good as "The Coming of Theodora,"
the story of an intolerably good woman. It is
only a simple family history ; only an account
of one of the thousands of unsuccessful efforts
to give a household two heads ; only one of
those tales by which each reader hopes that all
others will take warning, and then continues his
own life as if it had never been written, but it is
told with such art that it cannot well be forgotten, although its moral may be unheeded. Besides four excellently well-described adult
characters, the story presents a disagreeable
child of a new type, a pleasant relief from the
followers of Budge and Toddie, but quite as
powerful for mischief. (Houghton, Mifflin &
Co. $1.25.)—*Boston Saturday Evening Gazette.*

"I ask not proud philosophy
To teach me what thou art."
—CAMPBELL.

From "The Satires of Cynicus."   Copyright, 1895, by George D. Hurst.

Lilith.

IT is best to be candid. Dr. George Macdonald's "Lilith" is without doubt an extremely beautiful book, but it is also extremely baffling, and we are not ashamed to admit that the proper interpretation of many passages in it eludes us. Perhaps we are more than ordinarily dense ; perhaps Dr. Macdonald is more than ordinarily allegorical upon this occasion. It may be that "Lilith" is one of those books that reveal themselves slowly after being much studied. We only know one fact with regard to it that is beyond all question—we feel bewildered after reading the chapters which it contains. Parts of "Lilith" are obvious enough, but there are portions of the book which are capable of being explained in several ways, and when this happens the student is not unnaturally at a loss. What with magic mirrors ; lands that exist and exist not ; a character that is a compound of a raven, of a librarian, and of no less a personage than Adam ; giants, tiny lovers with laughs like far-away sheepbells, and so on, and so on— we have more often than not been exceedingly perplexed. Much we understand, though much is as yet hidden from us. It is grateful to turn from the translation to the manner of the rendering. This is astonishingly well done, and it is easy to see the handicraft of a man who is the master of both prose and poetry. Some of the descriptions are to be lingered over and loved. Probably many will not be able to survive the first three or four chapters, but if these are passed without vexation supervening it is most likely that the patient reader will persevere to the end. We assure him that he will travel in company with delight, and we hope that he will prove able to provide himself with a satisfactory elucidation of the whole meaning of "Lilith." The book undoubtedly is an example of fine literature. (Dodd, Mead. $1.25.)—*London Literary World.*

Cruising Among the Caribbees.

CHARLES AUGUSTUS STODDARD is an old traveller, though for a long while yet he should not be called an old man. He is known not so

From "Cruising Among the Caribbees."   Copyright, 1895, by Charles Scribner's Sons.

A WEST INDIAN TYPE.

much as the editor of the *Observer*, but as a very easy and comfortable tourist in various quarters of the globe, and an interesting correspondent. He has recently taken a most enviable trip in Southern waters, and this pleasant volume is the result. Think of wandering away from New York in a snow-storm, and after a few days finding yourself in tropical waters and scenery ! Oh, the joy of it, and what a pity we don't all do it ! But those who can do not care to, and those who would like to cannot. That is the way the world wags just at present. There is Barbados, and Antigua, and St. Lucia, and St. Kitts, and St. Vincent, and Trinidad, the haunts of the old buccaneers, the breeding-places of superstition and voudooism, a blue sky, the Southern Cross blazing in the heavens, fields covered with flowers! Mr. Stoddard has seen it all, and tells us about it in a very agreeable and fascinating way. If we were all editors and could take the same trip! (Scribner. $1.50.)—*N. Y. Herald.*

Not Counting the Cost.

THE novels in Appleton's *Town and Country Library* are generally of a character to excite the interest of the lover of good fiction, and "Not Counting the Cost," by Tasma, is one of the best in an excelent series. It abounds in scenes of a mingled romantic and realistic nature that are always entertaining, and the characters are drawn with an intuitive knowledge of human nature and a literary skill that makes them strikingly true to life. The story opens in Tasmania, and the earlier chapters abound in a wealth of local color that is fascinating. The heroine is a young woman whose husband is a religious maniac, but he opportunely dies before the tale ends, and gives her an opportunity to find a more companionable partner. She goes to Paris with her family, and their struggles there, while they lead a Bohemian existence, are very cleverly described, especially where the young woman, in her extremity, poses as a figure in a beauty show. The book steadily holds the attention, and is as clever as it is absorbing. (Appleton. $1 ; pap., 50 c.)—*Saturday Evening Gazette.*

The Village Watch-Tower.

MRS. WIGGIN has that nice balance of mind that distinguishes between the real and the accidental. The latter never overweighs the former in her stories. We are never left oppressed with the sense of uniform dreariness as we sometimes are in Miss Wilkins's remarkable characterizations. Underneath oddities and local customs we feel the individual made of good flesh and blood, like ourselves, with whom we have that something, be it ever so little, that keeps us from being alien one to another. There could hardly be a more wholly pathetic picture than the tenderly drawn outline of Tom, "one of God's fools, a foot-loose pilgrim in this world of ours, a poor, addle-pated, simple-minded, harmless creature—in village parlance, 'a softy,'" rebelling against the "poor farm," retreating from the well-intentioned villagers to the upper story of his shanty, drawing the ladder that served him as a staircase up after him, and politely assuring his visitors that "Tom ain't ter hum. Tom's gone to Bonney Eagle." When, with rude charity, his beloved semblance of a home

is burned to the ground to prevent his obstinate flights from the poor farm, the culmination of the little tragedy is reached, yet even this is touched in with a light hand, left vaguely suggestive and alluring, as the true sketch should be. The gem of the collection is, however, "The Fore-Room Rug." (Houghton, Mifflin & Co. $1.)—*N. Y. Times.*

Townsend Harris.

DR. WILLIAM ELLIOT GRIFFIS, author of "Japan" and "Brave Little Holland," sustains in his life of "Townsend Harris, First American Envoy in Japan," the reputation which he has achieved for notably good work. The author's familiarity with the history, the religions, and the national development of Japan is well known to the readers of the literature of the far East. Dr. Griffis's contribution to this volume is really limited to the introduction, which traces the course of Harris's life until he left the United States for Japan. The greater portion of the book is a transcript of the journal which Mr. Harris faithfully kept during his long residence in the empire of Japan. The story is an inspiring one, revealing to us a man whose consecration to duty and whose large activities challenge our attention and command our respect. After fourteen years in a village in the Empire State thirty-two in the metropolis of the continent, six on the Pacific Ocean and in far Oriental lands, Harris, when fifty-two years of age, became, like the great Goritomo, a lonely dweller in rocky Idzu. Harris, in a large sense, may be called the real overthrower of Tycoonism, of the feudal system and military rule, and the restorer of national unity. Of the powerful influence of his actions upon the development of the representative institutions now established in Japan, there can be no doubt whatever. In the making of that new kind of Asiatic state and man that have surprised Europe, Townsend Harris was a potency acknowledged by none more than the Japanese themselves. He was the greatest of the foreign diplomatists, and he was the recognized teacher of a sensitive people who delighted in calling him "the nation's friend." As Dr. Griffis enjoyed for years the friendship of the subject of this memoir, additional interest attaches to this journal. This book is very timely, since the subject of the revision of the treaties with Japan will necessarily occupy much attention during the present year, and probably it will be continued by the delay in the completion of treaties between Japan and the various governments of Europe for years to come. (Houghton, Mifflin & Co. $2.)—*Philadelphia Press.*

American Steam Vessels.

THIS book is the first of its kind that has ever been published. It presents in chronological order accurate illustrations and descriptions of the various types of American steamers, lake, river, ocean, naval, beginning with the first practical steamboat, Fulton's *Clermont*, and continuing down to those of the present day. In its pages will be found most of the famous and historical steam vessels of the country, numbering nearly three hundred. The descriptions, as well as the illustrations, are all pen drawings, entirely original, and by the same author-artist. Moreover, the smaller illustrations that embellish the descriptive pages, in each case, present in different view from that of the main illustrations of the steamers, the vessels described. Not alone to the thousands of Americans who, as owners, officers, or travellers upon the steam vessels of our country, and who have a love for the craft, will this work particularly appeal, but also to the builders, owners, officers and travellers upon foreign steam vessels. The compiler is Samuel Ward Stanton. (Smith & Stanton. §5.) —*N. Y. Observer.*

The Princess Sonia.

"THE Princess Sonia," which is being read on every hand, has undoubtedly "made a hit," and it will serve to attract a strong interest to its author, Julia Magruder, whose work in fiction has not altogether received the attention which it merits. Miss Magruder, although thousands will know of her for the first time through "The Princess Sonia," is not a novice in literary work. Some eight years ago, if I mistake not, she issued "Across the Chasm," through the Scribners, a novel of the North and South, which attracted considerable attention and was very successful. Then she wrote and published a story called "The Child Amy," which added to her fame. Two years ago came a very strong story, "A Beautiful Alien," published as a serial in one of the popular magazines, and it made a greater success than anything which Miss Magruder had previously done. Now comes "The Princess Sonia," and shortly will issue from the same author's pen a longer novel called "The Violet," which C. D. Gibson is now illustrating, and which is considered by Miss Magruder's friends and editors to be the best thing she has done. Miss Magruder is a Southern girl who makes her home in North Carolina. She comes of an old Virginia family, and has received her education in the South and in Washington, her father having practised law at the capital for many years. Of recent years she has travelled abroad quite extensively, but has now settled down to literary work in her Southern home. Miss Magruder often spends a social fortnight in New York. She is a young woman, and very charming to look upon, quite above medium height, and of slight but gracefully proportioned figure. Her head is small but well shaped, and her hair, worn low, is light brown in color. Her complexion is fair, and her eyes gray and very expressive. She dresses simply, has unaffected manners, and has that delicious soft Southern accent in her speech which is as music to Northern ears. The Latin Quarter of Paris is the scene of the pretty romance. A young American girl and the Princess are the chief characters. (Century Co. $1.25.)—*Commercial Advertiser.*

THE BEAUTIFUL YOUNG WOMAN.

The Literary News.

An Eclectic Monthly Review of Current Literature.

EDITED BY A. H. LEYPOLDT.

NOVEMBER, 1895.

EDWARD WILLIAM THOMSON.

A FEW weeks ago appeared a volume of short stories, entitled "Old Man Savarin, and other stories" (T. Y. Crowell & Co.), which al-

EDWARD WILLIAM THOMSON.

though called modestly "off-hand stories" show to the initiated a practised hand and reliable, guiding taste. "Of the fourteen stories only one," says *The Critic,* "so much as recognizes the existence of the once important Cupid. Yet even the most sentimental maiden will not toss this book aside for lack of vital interest. It is intensely human, vividly true to life. The tales are kaleidoscopic—bright bits of human experience, each rapidly succeeding another, hardly any two alike, yet all blending in a harmonious impression. Mr. Thomson is not a plot-maker. He has no faculty for intricate interlacing of events, the dove-tailing of situations, and the springing of mines of dazzling, unexpected *dénouement.* His genius does not lie in this direction ; but he can take a simple incident, or a single dramatic event, and clothe it with such vividness of color and feeling that one as readily spares plot and complication as a diagram of inflorescence in a rose or a cosmic scaffolding about the evening star. Take, for instance, a story like ' The Shining Cross of Rigaud,' with its idealism, its pathos, its poetical handling, and imagine it blurred and expanded by a conventional plot ! Yet there are tales of intense action in this little volume, thrilling by their rapid movement."

Speaking of the book to a compatriot of Mr. Thomson's, he kindly consented to write to the author and beg a few personal details of his literary career. We shall not touch Mr. Thomson's reply. It speaks for itself.

October 13, 1895.

MY DEAR GEORGE ILES : You tell me that the editor of LITERARY NEWS, well disposed to my story-book, wishes to give it the benefit of an extended "Personal Notice" of me ; but I suspect my old friend of being the instigator to that benevolent editorial disposition. At any rate I am too—shall we say shy ?—to act on your suggestion that it would be discreet for me to write the "personal" and then repose in bland confidence that you would energetically brace up the laudatory parts.

Though I am neither insensible to your kindness in the matter, nor to the power of the LITERARY NEWS to aid the sale of "Old Man Savarin," nor averse from having my publisher's large wallet and my own small one fattened a little by the Editorial Courtesy, I am sure there could be nothing of interest to the public in a "personal" about me. I am not eight feet high, nor a centenarian, nor an infant prodigy, nor a football player, nor a millionaire, nor individually of concern to the intelligent public. Moreover, my opinion is that the intelligent public sneers and yawns and swears a great deal more than editors presume over "personal notices" about people like myself, whose work is the only thing of theirs that the public can care for—or can't, as the case may be. The glory of being a fit subject for "personals" is naturally a perquisite of Messrs. Corbett and Fitzsimmons, the poor Two-Headed Boy, Challengers for the Cup, Headless Roosters, and the Deserving Rich who get their names regularly mentioned in "Society Columns," and sometimes in the instructive pages of *Life.* But the Blush of Shame would mantle the Cheek of Modesty did your humble servant do himself proud (as appears the custom) in a "personal," especially as it occurs to him that his publishers may gain more if he should offer you and the NEWS something probably interesting, and certainly connected with the subject you so amiably propose.

In the reviews and notices of generous literary editors anent my small book, it has been frequently remarked that I have, in certain tales, written the French-Canadian dialect of English in an understandable manner. Now, I have not written French-Canadian dialect of English at all, and for a sufficient reason—there is no such dialect.

There is a Canadian dialect of French—usually called the French-Canadian *patois* by patronizing people who know little or no French—though such authorities as Mr. Frechette and Mr. William Maclennan declare, I believe, that it is much purer French than is spoken by the "common people" in France. But when you reflect on the so-called French-Canadian dialect of English, you will perceive that it is not a dialect, but simply broken English, varying as to correctness according to the acquaintance of the individual with a language which is not his mother-tongue.

A dialect of English, such as the Scotch, or Irish, or Yankee, or that of the Tennessee mountaineers, is, I take it, some well-established form of the language, common to a multitude of people bred similarly and mostly living in one district. It is a local language, varied little in its usage by those nurtured in it.

But French-Canadian English varies with almost every user; its degrees of correctness range between the exquisite literary English, slightly modulated by French tones, that is spoken by such finished orators as Mr. Laurier or Mr. Chapleau, and the scarcely intelligible English of a *habitant* beginning to practise in the foreign tongue. Here is no local fixed form of English; here is no dialect ; here is nothing but a great variety of cases of broken English, in some of which the language is spoken with perfect facility. What the story-writer in, or the reporter of French-Canadian English must do is to choose the case that he will represent or report ; and his choice will, of course, be determined by the literary purpose that he entertains.

If his design is not, as mine was, merely to flavor some stories with French Canadianism, but is to exhibit the interesting philological peculiarities of that broken English, he will choose as Mr. William Maclennan did in those charming stories which appeared some years since in *Harper's Magazine*. It is true that their fine and unusual literary quality, though remarked by the keen appreciation of Mr. W. D. Howells, was hidden from readers too lazy to encounter the trifling difficulty of making out the so-called "dialect." But it is also true that the "dialect" was itself a pleasure to those who knew French well enough to value aright Mr. Maclennan's subtle skill in the medium he employed.

It is surprising that Mr. Howells himself should recently have written, in *Harper's Weekly*, as if there were a French-Canadian "dialect" of English. Incidentally he referred to Mr. Maclennan's work in such sort as to indicate in himself a belief that the Montreal writer was the pioneer in that "dialect" field, a credit which Mr. Maclennan would, I am sure, be quick to disclaim. The pioneer was, so far as I know, Mr. Rowland E. Robinson, a Vermonter, whose French-Canadian Antwine, in "Uncle Lisha's Shop" and "Sam Lovell's Camps," is perfectly represented as to his racial peculiarities, his broken English, and his individuality, which is one of the most lively and amusing, I venture to say, in American literature.

I am the more desirous that justice should be done to the Vermonter in this matter, because I regard him as an American writer who has nothing like the honor he deserves in his own country. His books, published by the Forest and Stream Company and by Houghton, Mifflin & Co., disclose a variety of Yankees so interesting, so amusing, so lovable, and so fond of the open sky and the fairness of Nature in their own land, that one is inclined, for their sake, to love Yankees in general—suspecting them to be truly kin to Mr. Robinson's delightful people. He is a true humorist of rare quality, whose spontaneous work may well be cherished for generations after the books of the *farceurs* of the hour shall have vanished in the limbo of old masks and old moons.

Yours very truly,
EDWARD W. THOMSON.

ST. BOTOLPH CLUB, BOSTON.

FOR YOU.

If you might always have, love,
　The sunshine and the flowers,
And I the co'd and loneliness
　Of bitter and wintry hours—
If any sweetness in my life
　Would answer to your claim,
And I might bear whatever loss,
　Whatever wrong or pain
Would otherwise fall to you, love,
　As falls the autumn rain—
I think I could not ask, love,
　For any happier hours
Than just to know God gives to you
　The sunshine and the flowers.

(Roberts. $1.)—"*From Dreamland Sent.*"

LIVING.

How passionately I will my life away
Which I would give all that I have to stay ;
How wildly I hurry for the change I crave,
To hurl myself into the changeless grave.

(Harper, $2.50.)—*From '*Stops *of* Various Quills.*"

Survey of Current Literature.

☞ *Order through your bookseller.*—"*There is no worthier or surer pledge of the intelligence and the purity of any community than their general purchase of books; nor is there any one who does more to further the attainment and possession of these qualities than a good bookseller.*"—PROF. DUNN.

ART, MUSIC, DRAMA.

BELL, *Mrs.* NANCY R. E. MEUGENS, [*pseud.* N. d'Anvers.] Masterpieces of the great artists, A.D. 1400–1700: a selection of the most celebrated pictures of the old masters, reproduced directly from the original pictures ; with descriptions and introd.; il. by Gleeson White. Macmillan. 43 il. 8°, $7.50.

BELLA, E., *ed.* A collection of posters: the illustrated catalogue of the first exhibition, 1894–95, Royal Aquarium, London. Imported by Brentano's. nar. 8°, pap., *net*, 50 c.
The catalogue is preceded by an interesting article on posters by Joseph Thacher Clarke. The catalogue represents 258 specimens of English and French posters taken from private collections and exhibited at the Royal Aquarium, London. The book is illustrated with twenty page pictures of the most notable of the posters.

FIELD, EUGENE. A little book of profitable tales; with an etched por. by W. H. W. Bicknell. [*Cameo ed.*] Scribner. 16°, $1.25.
Now issued in the attractive binding of the *Cameo ed.*, with a medallion head in relief on front cover. Etched portrait of Field as frontispiece.

FOSTER, BIRKET, (*ill.*) Pictures of rustic landscape, by Birket Foster; with passages in prose and verse selected by J. Davidson; with por. and 30 engravings. Longmans, Green & Co. 8°, $3.50.
Quotations from Richard Jeffries, John Davidson, Robert Louis Stevenson, Izaak Walton, Philip Gilbert Hamerton, Thomas Carlyle, George Eliot, Charles Lamb, William Hazlitt, Wordsworth, James Thomson, Matthew Arnold, Tennyson, and others, illustrated with thirty engravings. Square shape, in simple, strong binding.

BIOGRAPHY, CORRESPONDENCE, ETC.

BAIN, R. NISBET. Hans Christian Andersen: a biography. Imported by Dodd, Mead & Co. por. il. 8°, buckram, $3.50.
Biographical information about Hans Christian Andersen is scarce and scattered and uncollected, and almost all in foreign tongue. The author has gone carefully over all the data existing in letters and memoirs and the autobiography of the great story-teller. He gives us a picture of Andersen as a shrewd, observant man, an excellent linguist, and an unwearied traveller, who was acquainted with all the leading men of his day. Several drawings from original sketches by Andersen are included in the volume. Born in 1805, he lived until 1875 and during this long life took interest in all things.

CREEGAN, C. C., *D.D.*, and GOODNOW, *Mrs.* JOSEPHINE A. B. Great missionaries of the church; with an introd. by Francis E. Clark, D.D. Crowell & Co. por. 12°, $1.50.
Contains biographies of twenty-three men who spent their lives in self-sacrificing efforts for the enlightenment of benighted races. Such heroes as Bishop Patteson, the martyr of Malanesia; Griffith John, missionary to Turkey; Bishop Thoburn, of India; Bishop Crowther, of the Niger; Joseph Hardy, of Neesima; John Williams, the martyr of Polynesia; Adoniram Judson; Bishop Taylor; Robert Moffat; Marcus Whitman, most romantic of all pioneers; Bishop Hannington, of Eastern Africa; and David Livingstone, the great explorer.

DE PEYSTER, J. WATTS, ["Anchor," *pseud.*] The real Napoleon Bonaparte. [Tivoli P. O., Dutchess Co., J. Watts De Peyster. 4°, pap., 75 c.
The author has drawn upon every known source to prove that Napoleon was "the father of lies," an "arch-hypocrite," a "Jonathan Wild the Great," etc. The essay gives evidence of considerable research and strong prejudice. Reprinted from the *College Student*, Lancaster, Pa.

EARLE, *Mrs.* ALICE MORSE. Margaret Winthrop; with fac-simile reproduction. Scribner. 12°. (Women of Colonial and Revolutionary times.) *net*, $1.25.
The heroine of this volume, the introductory one of a new and interesting series, was the third wife of the John Winthrop who played so important a part in the founding of New England. Her letters, of which the book is largely made up, and the occasional extracts from her husband's letters, afford a delightfully gossipy chronicle of the period in which they lived, especially during the time John Winthrop was Governor of Massachusetts. This new series aims "to present not only carefully studied portraits of the most distinguished women of Colonial and Revolutionary times, but to offer as a background for these portraits pictures of the domestic and social instead of the political and more public life of the people."

FITZGERALD, E. The letters of Edward Fitzgerald to Fanny Kemble; collected and ed. by W. Aldis Wright. Macmillan. 12°, (Eversley ser.) $1.50.

HARTMANN, SADAKICHI C. Conversations with Walt Whitman, by Sadakichi; written in 1894. E. P. Coby & Co. 8°, pap., 50 c.

HOLDEN, E. S. The Mogul emperors of Hindustan, A.D. 1398–A.D. 1707, Scribner. por. il. 8°, $2.
Brief accounts of the kings who ruled India for three eventful centuries. The author in an introductory note says the work is " not intended to give the history of the reigns in question, but rather to present such views of the chief personages involved as an intelligent reader of the histories themselves might wish to carry away." The chief authorities consulted have been the memoirs of the emperors themselves, the standard histories of Persia, India, and

Tartary, records of early missions and voyages, etc. Illustrated with authentic portraits.

HUBBARD, ELBERT. Charles Dickens. Putnam. 16°, (Little journeys to the homes of good men and great, no. 10.) pap., 5 c.

HUBBARD, ELBERT. Oliver Goldsmith. Putnam. 16°, (Little journeys to the homes of good men and great, no. 11.) pap., 5 c.

HUBBARD, ELBERT. Jonathan Swift. Putnam. 16°, (Little journeys to the homes of good men and great, no. 6.) pap., 5 c.

MacCUNN, FLORENCE A. John Knox. Houghton, Mifflin. por. 12°, (Leaders of religion ser.) $1.

RENAN, ERNEST. My sister Henrietta; with photogravure il. from paintings by Henri Scheffer and Ary Renan; tr. by Abby L. Alger. Roberts. 12°, $1.25.

THAYER, W. M. Turning-points in successful careers. Crowell. pors. 12°, $1.50.
Contains concise biographies of fifty men and women; in each case the early life is traced in some detail up to that turning-point which, in the case of most men, brings the one chance, and which only successful men make the home port for fortune. The successful conclusion of the life is hereby briefly sketched to show the justification.

WILLARD, ASHTON R. A sketch of the life and work of the painter Domenico Morelli. Houghton, Mifflin. por. il. 8°, $1.25.
A chapter from the history of contemporary Italian art. Morelli was born in Naples in 1826, and ranks among the foremost Italian painters of this century. The story of his early struggles is interestingly told. The book is printed on heavy paper with wide margins and is illustrated with seven heliotypes reproducing his principal pictures and also a portrait of himself. A list of his pictures is given.

WINGATE, C. E. L. Shakespeare's heroines on the stage; with il. from photographs and rare prints. Crowell. pors. 12°, $2.
Information in the shape of anecdote, gossip, criticism, etc., relating to Mrs. Bellamy, Mrs. Cibber, Miss O'Neill, Mrs. Abendon, Elizabeth Farren, Louisa Brunton, Ellen Tree, Mrs. Mary Robinson, Julia Marlowe, Madame Modjeska, Mrs. Langtry, Mrs. Siddons, Ellen Terry, and dozens of other famous actresses who have identified themselves with "Juliet," "Beatrice," "Hermione," "Perdita," "Viola," "Imogen," "Rosalind," "Cleopatra," "Lady Macbeth," "Queen Katharine," "Portia," "Katharine," "Ophelia," and "Desdemona."

DESCRIPTION, GEOGRAPHY, TRAVEL, ETC.

BALDWIN, C. SEARS, *comp. and ed.* Specimens of prose description. Holt. 16°, (English readings.) bds., 50 c.
Includes Ancient Athens (Newman); Paris before the Second Empire (du Maurier); Bees (Burroughs); Byzantium (Gibbon); Geneva (Ruskin); The storming of the Bastille (Carlyle); La Gioconda, etc. (Pater); Blois (Henry James); Spring in a side street (Brander Matthews); Scenes from western life (Hamlin Garland); A night among the pines, etc. (Steven-

son). Suitable for colleges and highest school classes.

CORNISH, C. J. Wild England of to-day and the wild life in it; il. from drawings by Lancelot Speed, and from photographs. Macmillan. 8°, $3.50.

CRAWFORD, F. MARION. Constantinople; il. by Edwin L. Weeks. Scribner. 8°, buckram, $1.50.
F. Marion Crawford has seen Constantinople again and again and under every possible aspect. He describes in detail the location, the surroundings, the habits, customs, daily life, indoor and outdoor life of the many inhabitants of every race that live within its limits. For the original Turk, Crawford has only praise and considers him the victim of his fellow countrymen. He thinks the various "races will strive for ages yet over the world's great bone of contention—Constantinople." Profusely illustrated with full-page pictures. Bound in canvas with elaborate green stamping.

DORR, JULIA C. R. The flower of England's face: sketches of English travel. Macmillan. 24°, 75 c.
Contents: A week in Wales; Banbury cakes and the Isle of Wight; A day of contrasts; In the Forest of Arden; At the Peacock Inn; At Haworth; From the border of Inverness; To Cawdor Castle and Culloden Moor; An enchanted day.

EICKEMEYER, C., *and* WESTCOTT, LILIAN. Among the Pueblo Indians; il. with photographs taken by the authors. The Merriam Co. 8°, $1.75.

MARSH, HERBERT. Two seasons in Switzerland; with il. from photographs by O. Williamson. Dodd, Mead ,& Co. 8°, buckram, $3.50.
The author is a member of the Alpine Club. During the many years spent in the Royal Navy he often looked toward the Alps and desired to explore them. In 1887 and in 1891-92 he carried out his desire, and this volume is based on the notes he took during those expeditions. He had hoped to go once more, but in 1894 was appointed staff-surgeon to the *Northampton*, still in active service. Written with spirit, the book gives a vivid description of the trials and difficulties as well as the beauties of Alpine travel.

NADAL, E. S. Notes of a professional exile. Century Co. 1 il. 24°, (Thumb-nail ser.) leath., $1.
The author was for some time secretary of legation. A number of sketches of life as seen at an imaginary European watering-place. Americans and Europeans are the actors. Contains analysis of the character and foibles of the American woman. Daintily bound in stamped leather.

STODDARD, C. A. Cruising among the Caribbees : summer days in winter months. Scribner. il. 8°, $1.50.

EDUCATION, LANGUAGE, ETC.

ROE, E. T. The modern Webster pronouncing and defining dictionary of the English language. Laird & Lee. por. 16°, 25 c.
Containing all words sanctioned by good au-

thority, excluding only such as are rare, purely technical, or obsolete ; with a collection of words, phrases, maxims, and mottoes from classical and modern foreign languages ; abbreviations in common use and instructions in proof-reading.

TUCKER, GILBERT M. Our common speech. Dodd, Mead & Co. 12°, $1.25.
Six papers on topics connected with the proper use of the English language, the changes which that tongue is undergoing on both sides of the sea, and the labor of lexicographers to explain the meaning of the words of which it is composed. *Contents:* Locutios in fabrica ; Degraded words ; The Revised Version of the New Testament; Old dictionaries: some of their characteristics and curious features ; Modern dictionaries ; American English ; Alphabetical index of English words referred to. Bibliography of American English, 9 p.

FICTION.

BALZAC, HONORÉ DE. The marriage contract. [*Also*] A double life, and The peace of a home; tr. by Katharine Prescott Wormeley. Roberts. 12°, $1.50.

BARRETT, Frank. A set of rogues, to wit: Christopher Sutton, John Dawson, the Señor Don Sanchez del Castello de Castelañe, and Moll Dawson: their wicked conspiracy, and a true account of their travels and adventures ; with many other surprising things now disclosed for the first time, as the faithful confession of Christopher Sutton. Macmillan. 12°, $1.50.

BOULTON, HELEN M. Josephine Crewe: a novel. Longmans, Green & Co. 12°, $1.25.

BROWN, HELEN DAWES. The Petrie estate. Houghton, Mifflin. 16°, (Riverside pap. ser.) pap., 50 c.

BURGIN, G. B. At Tuxter's. Putnam. 12°, (Hudson lib., no. 10.) $1; pap., 50 c.

BURNHAM, *Mrs.* CLARA LOUISE. The wise woman: a novel. Houghton, Mifflin. 12°, $1.25.
The wise woman is a maiden lady of experience who uses her influence to impress upon her younger sister women that there is no true foundation for the generally received conventionalities of society. Especially in a charming story she appeals to Americans to have no standards of social caste but character, education, and good morals. An elderly Long Island couple open their home to the different young couples learning to live true lives.

CÉCILE : a tale of the great native rebellion of 1850–53. Warne. 12°, pap., 40 c.
The scene is Auckland, just before the Kaffir outbreak said to have been incited by Pierre Marais. Andries Marthinus, farmer in the employ of Gerhard de Cilliers, dares to aspire to the hand of his master's daughter, and at the same time to make love to a Kaffir girl, who betrays to her ingrate lover the movements of her people. Acting on his knowledge Marthinus makes a bold stroke to compel Cécile to accept him for her husband. The intervention of Zana, however, brings about an unlooked-for ending of a dramatic story.

CRANE, STEPHEN. The red badge of courage : an episode of the American civil war. Appleton. 12°, $1.
A graphic analysis of the volunteer in battle. The time is the late war, and the chief figure a New England boy who goes to the front with a romantic picture in his "mind's eye" of the picturesqueness and heroism of war. The reality is described in a succession of powerful scenes, which lay bare all the hideousness of war, and also much of its commonplaceness and misery.

CRAWFORD, F. MARION. Katharine Lauderdale. *New ed.* Macmillan. 12°, $1.

CROCKETT, S. RUTHERFORD. The men of the moss-hags : being a history of adventure taken from the papers of William Gordon, of Earlstoun in Galloway, and told over again by S. R. Crockett. Macmillan & Co. 12°, $1.50.
The moss-hags of Scotland are pits or sloughs where peat has been dug. The story is historical, covering the last days and great defeat of the Covenanters by troops led by John Claverhouse of Dundee. Richard Cameron is introduced and the struggles of the Cameronians described with much detail. Two chapters are devoted to the "conventicles" and "conversions." Gives a stirring account of the encounters of the adherents of William III. and James II. with the fanatical but courageous warriors for religious freedom. The love-story is quiet and pathetic.

EDGEWORTH, MARIA. Ormond: a tale; il. by C. Schloesser; with an introd. by Anne Thackeray Ritchie. Macmillan & Co. 12°, (Macmillan's illustrated standard novels.) $1.25.

EDWARDS, G. WHARTON. The rivalries of Long and Short Codlac. Century Co. 1 il., 24°, (Thumb-nail ser.) leath., $1.
The author is chronicler of life among the islands that lie off the coast of Maine. Rude and sturdy fisherfolk are his subject. Ten short stories. Daintily bound in stamped leather.

ELIOT, GEORGE, [*pseud.* for *Mrs.* J. W. Cross.] Silas Marner; with a biographical sketch of George Eliot and notes. Houghton, Mifflin. 16°, (Riverside lit. ser., double no., no. 83.) pap., *net*, 30 c.; linen, *net*, 40 c.

ELIOT, GEORGE, [*pseud.* for *Mrs.* J. W. Cross.] Silas Marner; ed., with notes and an introd., by Rob. Herrick. Longmans, Green & Co. por. 12°, (Longmans' English classics, no. 2.) 75 c.

FLETCHER, J. S. When Charles the First was king: a romance of Osgoldcross, 1632–1649. A. C. McClurg. 12°, $1.50.

GISSING, G. The emancipated: a novel. Way & Williams. 12°, $1.50.

GORDON, JULIEN, [*pseud.* for *Mrs.* Julia Van Rensselaer Cruger.] A wedding, and other stories. Lippincott. 12°, $1.

GOODWIN, MAUD WILDER. The colonial cavalier; or, southern life before the Revolution; il. by Harry Edwards. [*New ed.* with notes.] Little, Brown & Co. 12°, $2.

GRANT, ROB. The bachelor's Christmas, and other stories; il. by C. D. Gibson, I. R. Wiles, A. B. Wenzell, and C. Carleton. Scribner. 12°, $1.50.

The title-story tells of a bachelor who was extensively an uncle, having seven nephews and five nieces and their respective mothers to whom to send bundles on Christmas eve. When he was close on forty a Christmas party brought him a wife. The other stories are entitled: An eye for an eye; In fly-time; Richard and Robin; The matrimonial Tontine Benefit Association; By hook or crook. The illustrations are a feature of the festive-looking red volume.

HAGGARD, H. RIDER. Joan Haste. Longmans, Green & Co. il. 12°, $1.25.

HARTE, FRANCIS BRET. Clarence. Houghton, Mifflin & Co. 12°, $1.25.

HILL, GRACE LIVINGSTON. Katharine's yesterday, and other Christian Endeavor stories. Lothrop Pub. Co. il. 12°, $1.50.

Sixteen stories designed to inculcate the principles that underlie the Christian Endeavor movement are entitled: Katharine's yesterday; Christian Endeavor leaven; Some peculiar people in our society; How Adelaide went to the convention; Why Adelaide stayed home from the convention; John Chamberlain's Easter coat; They might but they didn't; Pledge-makers and pledge-breakers; An old missionary meeting; Some carols for the Lord; Because of the Pharisees; For whom Christ died; Living epistles; The unknown God; Under the window; The minister's bonnet.

HINKSON, *Mrs*. KATHARINE TYNAN. The way of a maid. Dodd, Mead & Co. 12°, $1.25.

The "maid" was a sweet Irish lassie of the Roman Catholic faith, given to exuberant spirits, bright garments, and unaccountable fits of depression. Her bosom friend was the daughter of a Protestant woman who played Lady Bountiful to help the population, and was especially useful in straightening out the hard feelings engendered by different creeds. The picturesqueness of life in Ireland to outsiders and its grind to the natives is worked into a story making for tolerance in all things.

HOCKING, JOS. All men are liars. Roberts. 12mo, $1.50.

HOPKINS, TIGHE. Lady Bonnie's experiment. Holt. 1 il. 16°, (Buckram ser.) 75 c.

HOTCHKISS, CHAUNCEY C. In defiance of the king: a romance of the American Revolution. Appleton. 12°, (Appleton's town and country lib., no. 178.) $1; pap., 50 c.

A tale of patriotic adventure ranging from Lexington, the burning of Norwalk, the British occupation of Long Island, and thrilling experiences on Long Island Sound to Benedict Arnold's descent on New London and the massacre at Fort Griswold. The love-story which is interwoven will be found a charming idyl.

IOTA. [*pseud.* for *Mrs.* Mannington Caffyn.] A comedy in spasms; il. by Izora C. Chandler. Stokes. 12°, $1.

KING, ANNA EICHBERG. Kitwyk stories. Century Co. il. 12°, $1.50.

LEMON, IDA. Matthew Furth. Longmans, Green & Co. 12°, $1.25.

Matthew Furth was a dock-laborer. From his early youth he had promised a poor girl who fetched and carried for the neighborhood to make her his wife. The story tells how she relied upon his words and how his life took him far away from her, also how all things worked together for good and how the giant workman, full of brute strength and courage, became a tender lover and husband.

LE QUEUX, W. Zoraida: a romance of the harem and the Great Sahara; il. by Harold Piffard. Stokes. il. 12°, $1.50.

McMANUS, L. The red star. Putnam. nar. 12°, (Autonym lib., no. 5.) 50 c.

The time was 1806. Basil Pahlen, Count Vassillevitch, captain of the Imperial Russian Guards had betrothed himself to Halka, Countess Mnizek, for political reasons, and for the same reasons was compelled, against his will, to keep his troth. Trusting to his bride's honor he confided to her the secret of his life, and she contrived reasons for them to live apart. Later Count Vassillevitch met his Polish wife masquerading as a soldier in the French army. She told him that she was following "The red star of her destiny." The issues of this meeting are romantic.

MAGRUDER, JULIA. The Princess Sonia; with il. by C. Dana Gibson. Century Co. 12°, $1.25.

MARSHALL, EMMA. The white king's daughter: a story of the Princess Elizabeth. Macmillan. 12°, $1.25.

MITCHELL, S. WEIR, *M.D.* A Madeira party. Century Co. 1 il., 24°, (Thumb-nail ser.) leath., $1.

Two stories: A Madeira party; A little more Burgundy. The title-story is a chapter of quaint lore about Madeira wine, its history and its choice vintages, put into the words of a group of Philadelphia *gourmets*. The second story is a dramatic tale of the French Revolution at the time of the death of Robespierre. Daintily bound in stamped leather.

PLYMPTON, A. G. A bud of promise: a story for ambitious parents. Roberts. 16°, 50 c.

POOL, MARIA LOUISE. Against human nature. Harper. 12°, $1.25.

ROY, NEIL. The horseman's word: a novel. Macmillan. 12°, $1.25.

SAVIDGE, EUGENE COLEMAN. The American in Paris: a biographical novel of the Franco-Prussian War: the siege and commune of Paris; from an American standpoint. Lippincott. 12°, $1.

SHIPTON, HELEN. The Herons. Macmillan. 12°, $1.

STOCKTON, FRANK R. A chosen few; short stories; with an etched por. by W. H. W. Bicknell. [*Cameo ed.*] Scribner. 16°, $1.25.

Contents: A tale of negative gravity; Asaph; "His wife's deceased sister"; The lady, or the tiger?; The remarkable wreck of the *Thomas Hyde*; Old Pipes and the Dryad; The transferred ghost; "The philosophy of relative existences"; A piece of red calico. These stories were selected from several collections of Stockton's short stories, as representative of the author's best-known work in this line.

Bound in green cloth with a medallion head in relief on front cover. Contains an etched portrait of Stockton.

SWAN, ANNIE S., [Mrs. Burnett Smith.] Fettered yet free : a study in heredity. Dodd, Mead & Co. 12°, $1.25.
The scene is Scotch. Although fettered by the hereditary curse of love of drink, by noble efforts its victim frees himself and becomes a useful member of society. The characters are numerous, and the story, though written for a purpose, is full of happenings told with spirit.

TIREBUCK, W. EDWARDS. Miss Grace of All Souls. Dodd, Mead & Co. 12°, $1.25.
A study of two varieties of the modern woman —one Nance Ockleshaw, the homely, dutiful wife of the miner, representative of the old order, and the other Miss Grace Walde, the thoughtful daughter of an easy-going vicar, representative of the new. Grace becomes sympathetically attached to Nance, and by degrees to her son Sam, an advanced democratic young miner, who unconsciously throws light upon the question of labor as between man and man, woman and woman, and as between the church and the state. These two young people become the centre of a social problem which is dramatically worked out.

TOLSTOY, Count LYOF N. Master and man : a story ; rendered from the Russian into English by S. Rapoport and J. C. Kenworthy. Crowell. 12°, leatherette, 35 c.

TOMPKINS, ELIZ. KNIGHT. An unlessoned girl: a story of school life. Putnam. 1 il. 12°, $1.25.

WALFORD, Mrs. LUCY BETHIA. A bubble; with frontispiece by H. C. Edwards. Stokes. 1 il. 16°, (The bijou ser.) 50 c.
Clara, the daughter of a proud English general in command of troops at Edinburgh, grows weary of solitude. She accepts the invitation of a professor's wife and meets Dirom, one of the most talented scholars of the university. To her it is fun, to him the love of his life. She finally marries station and wealth, and then it is reported his fine brain has given way under excessive study. But it had not—"it was the bubble which had burst."

WEYMAN STANLEY J. The snowball. Merriam. il. 24°, (Merriam's violet ser., no. 6.) 40 c.
A story founded on the events attending the trial and execution of M. de Biron in 1602. King Henry of Navarre, his queen and ministers are the actors. One of the most important warnings to the king against his trusted secretary is thrown into the royal carriage in a snowball.

WHITE, ELIZA ORNE. The coming of Theodora. Houghton, Mifflin. 12°, $1.25.

WIGGIN, Mrs. KATE DOUGLAS. The village watch-tower. Houghton, Mifflin & Co. 12°, $1.
Six short stories : The village watch-tower ; Tom o' the bluebb'ry plains ; The nooning tree ; The fore-room rug ; A village Stradivarius ; The midnight cry. They are clever studies of life in a New England village, displaying close observation and delightful flashes of humor.

ZOLA, EMILE. Jacques Damour, [and other stories ;] Englished by W. Foster Apthorp. Authorised ed. Copeland & Day. 12°, $1.25.
The other stories are entitled : Madame Neigeon ; Nautas ; How we die ; The Coqueville spree ; The attack on the mill. Covered in bright yellow cloth, with black lines and lettering.

HISTORY.

BAIRD, H. M. The Huguenots and the revocation of the Edict of Nantes. Scribner. 2 v. maps, il. 8°, $7.50.

BICKNELL, ANNA L. Life in the Tuileries under the Second Empire. The Century Co. pors. il. 8°, $2.25.

BROOKS, NOAH. Washington in Lincoln's time. Century Co. 12°, $1.25.
In 1862 Mr. Noah Brooks went to Washington as correspondent for the *Sacramento Union*, and he remained until the close of the Civil War through the beginning of the stormy administration of Andrew Johnson. He became intimate with President Lincoln, who discussed momentous questions with him. From the scrap-books kept at that time this book has been prepared. Good index.

CLAFLIN, Mrs MARY B. Under the old elms. Crowell. il. 16°, $1.
"The old elms" was the name given by Henry Ward Beecher to Governor Claflin's beautiful estate at Newtonville, Mass., rich in historic association, and at different times the residence of three governors, beginning with Gen. Hull, of Revolutionary fame. Mrs. Claflin has gathered up a sheaf of charming personal recollections of the many famous men and women of our day who have been entertained under its roof, among whom were Charles Sumner, Henry Wilson, James Freeman Clarke, Henry Ward Beecher, Mrs. Stowe, and others.

DEFOE, DAN. Journal of the plague year ; ed., with notes and an introd., by G. Rice Carpenter. Longmans, Green & Co. por. 12°, (Longmans' English classics.) 75 c.
Defoe's original title, "The journal of the plague year," has been restored in this edition. The current title, "The history of the plague," comes from the second edition, published after Defoe's death. An introduction gives a biography of Defoe, an account of his works, especially "The journal of the plague year." Followed by "Suggestions for teachers and students," which includes some lists of books for further reading.

GEORGE, HEREFORD B. Battles of English history. Dodd, Mead & Co. plans, map, 8°, $2.
The author is fellow of New College, Oxford. He has taught history all his life. He here describes the great land-battles of eight centuries, including the battles of Hastings, Bannockburn, Crecy, Flodden, Waterloo, the Crimea, and the battles for supremacy in India. Describes especially the changes of equipment and mode of fighting from the landing of William the Conqueror to the latest troubles in the East Indies. Maps and plans of eighteen battles.

GRIFFIS, W. ELLIOT. Townsend Harris, first American envoy in Japan. Houghton, Mifflin. por. 8°, $2.
In all previous books on Japan, and in all

references to the history of the treaty-making with Japan, there is a gap between Commodore Perry's work and the treaties made almost simultaneously with the United States and European nations, the long work which Mr. Harris did in the education of the Japanese rulers being apparently unknown. In this book Dr. Griffis omits what may be found in other books which treat of various phases of Japanese life, and gives Mr. Harris's journals, which contain matter of unique value.

LANO, PIERRE DE.　The Emperor Napoleon III.; from the French by Helen Hunt Johnson. Dodd, Mead & Co. por. 12°, (The secret of an empire ser., no. 2.) $1.25.
The second volume of this romantic and largely anecdotal history of the Second Empire is chiefly a psychological study of the man, almost unconsciously forced to play a leading part in the history of nations. Many controversies have arisen about the statements made in the author's previous works about the court of Napoleon III., but the author insists upon his claim that he is making a faithful representation of the period so full of romance and of terror. The gloom of Napoleon's character is specially dwelt upon.

RANSOME, CYRIL.　An advanced history of England, from the earliest times to the present day. Macmillan. 12°, *net*, $2.25.

RENAN, ERNEST.　History of the people of Israel. In 5 v. V. 5, Period of Jewish independence and Judea under Roman rule: with full index to the 5 v. Roberts. 8°, *ea.*, $2.50.

SEWELL, ELIZ. M.　Outline history of Italy, from the fall of the Western Empire; with preface by Lucy H. M. Soulsby. Longmans, Green & Co. map, 16°, 90 c.

SMITH, GOLDWIN.　Oxford and her colleges : a view from the Radcliffe; ils. reproduced from photographs. Macmillan. 16°, $1.50.

TRAILL, H. DUFF, *ed.*　Social England : a record of the progress of the people from the earliest times to the present day, by various writers. In 6 v. V. 4. From the accession of James I. to the death of Anne. Putnam. 12°, $3.50.

HUMOR AND SATIRE.

CHAMBLISS, W. H.　Chambliss's diary; or, society as it really is; il. with over 50 copper-pl. half-tones and photo-engs., incl. 25 society pictures by Laura E. Foster. Chambliss & Co., por. 12°, $1.
Mr. Chambliss is a prominent society man of San Francisco ; he spent many years in the navy, has travelled, and had other opportunities for studying his fellow-men; his book is a pointed satire against what the writer calls the " Parvenuocracy "—which includes all that is vulgar and objectionable in American social life. He indulges largely in personalities and gives real names. Contains a list of " American heiresses (up to date) who have married titled paupers."

PEMBRIDGE. (*pseud.*)　Whist, or bumblepuppy: thirteen lectures addressed to children. *Rev. enl. ed.* Warne. 12°, $1.
Satirical advice aimed at careless whist-players. " Bumblepuppy," says the author, " is persisting to play whist, either in utter ignorance of all its known principles, or in defiance of them, or both."

LITERARY MISCELLANY, COLLECTED WORKS, ETC.

ARNOLD, MATTHEW.　The function of criticism at the present time, (reprinted from " Essays in criticism,") and An essay on style, by Walter Pater. Macmillan. ₄24°, 75 c.; pap., 25 c.

BREWSTER, W. T., *ed.*　Specimens of narration; chosen and ed. by W. T. Brewster. Holt. 16°, (English readings.) bds., 50 c.
Includes selections from Scott, Thackeray, Hawthorne, Jane Austen, George Eliot, Stevenson, and Henry James. Pt. 1, Elements of narrative—plot, character, setting, and purpose; pt. 2, Combination of the elements of narration; pt. 3, Various kinds of narrative; pt. 4. Technique of good narrative. An introduction is devoted to a definition of narration, the elements of narrative, principles of composition, kinds of narrative, and directions to the student. Bibliography (3 p.).

DAVIDSON, J.　Sentences and paragraphs. Dodd, Mead & Co. 16°, $1.
Seventy-seven sentences and paragraphs, ranging from the single epigram to the longest essayette, all full of suggestive thoughts. Many of these epigrams are sharp and sarcastic, but they always command respect and invite reflection. The author of " Fleet Street eclogues " and " Ballads and songs " is specially telling in his epigrams on writers and books.

DIXON, THERON S. E.　Francis Bacon and his Shakespeare. The Sargent Pub. Co. 12°, $1.50.
Mr. Dixon presents data in this work, which he says have convinced him, "beyond a reasonable doubt, that Francis Bacon wrote the Shakespearian plays." The parallelisms between the plays and Bacon's acknowledged writings quoted are certainly very striking and difficult to explain merely on the grounds of coincidence. The work will be accepted as an unusually intelligent and valuable contribution to the Bacon-Shakespeare controversy.

MACKAIL, J. W.　Latin literature. Scribner. 12°, (The university ser.) *net*, $1.25.
Divided into three parts—" The republic," " The Augustan age," and " The empire." Pt. 1 deals with origins of Latin literature, early epic and tragedy; Comedy, Plautus and Terence; Early prose, the " Satura," or mixed mode: Lucretius: Lyric poetry; Catullus; Cicero; Prose of the Ciceronian age; Cæsar and Sallust. Pt. 2 is devoted to Virgil, Horace, Propertius, and the elegists; Ovid, Livy, the lesser Augustans. Pt. 3 opens with the writers of the time of Nero, and goes down to the beginnings of the Middle Ages. Index of authors.

WALKER, HUGH.　The greater Victorian poets. Macmillan. 8°, $2.50.

MENTAL AND MORAL PHILOSOPHY.

BOK, E. W.　Successward: a young man's book for young men. Fleming H. Revell Co. 12°, buckram, $1.
Mr. Bok is editor of the *Ladies' Home Journal;* his subjects are : A correct knowledge of

himself; What, really, is success?; The young man in business; His social life and amusements; Sowing his wild oats; In matters of dress; His religious life; His attitude toward women; The question of marriage.

HARDWICKE, HENRY. The art of living long and happily. Putnam. 12°, $1.

THAYER, W. M. Aim high: hints and helps for young men. Whittaker. 12°, 75 c.
Discusses briefly and pointedly a number of practical topics, under the following headings: Character and influence; Thoughts upon thinking; Springs of knowledge; Beacon-lights; Guiding-lights; A bit for boys.

THAYER, W. M. Womanhood: hints and helps for young women. Whittaker. 12°, 75 c.
Chapters on the following topics, illustrated with many anecdotes: Power and possibilities; Discipline and duty; Caution and counsel; Fancies and failings; Themes for thought.

NATURE AND SCIENCE.

ATKINSON, PHILIP. Electricity for everybody; its nature and uses explained. The Century Co. por. il. 12°, $1.50.
Intended to meet the public demand for information in regard to the nature and uses of electricity and the various kinds of apparatus by which it is generated and employed. This information is given in the simplest form consistent with clearness, fulness, and strict scientific accuracy. Matter of merely historical character has been wholly omitted.

SCUDDER, S. HUBBARD. Frail children of the air: excursions into the world of butterflies. Houghton, Mifflin. 12°, $1.50.
These thirty-one papers are a small selection for the general reader of those published in the author's "Butterflies of the Eastern United States and Canada"—a work so costly as to reach relatively few, and one which was mainly addressed to the specialist. As far as possible the papers have been divested of technical details and in many cases revised or extended, to bring them up to date.

POETRY AND DRAMA.

KROEKER, KATE FREILIGRATH, *comp.* A century of German lyrics; selected, arr., and tr. by Kate Freiligrath Kroeker. Stokes. 16°, $1.
From German poets of the 18th and 19th centuries—Von Arnim, Karl Beck, Chamisso, Felix Dahn, Droste-Hülshof, Eichendorff, Freiligrath, Geibel, Goethe, Grillparzer, Hamerling, Hartmann, Heine, Paul Heyse, Keller, Lenau, Müller, Rückert, Scheffel, Uhland, and others.

LOWELL, JA. RUSSELL. Last poems. Houghton, Mifflin. por. 12°, $1.25.
Contains: The oracle of the gold-fishes; Turner's old *Téméraire;* St. Michael the weigher; A valentine; An April birth at sea; Love and thought; The nobler lover; On hearing a sonata of Beethoven's; Verses; On a bust of General Grant. The book is printed only on one side of fine uncut paper, wide margins, top gilt; the title-page and initials are rubricated, and the frontispiece is a new portrait of Mr. Lowell, selected by his family as the best likeness of him.

NASON, *Mrs.* EMMA HUNTINGTON. The tower, with legends and lyrics. Houghton, Mifflin. 12°, $1.25.

SAPPHO. Memoir, text, selected renderings, and a literal tr. by H. Thornton Wharton. *3d ed.* Imported by McClurg. por. il. 12°, *net*, $2.25.
Although no new verses justifiably attributable to Sappho have been discovered of late years, Mr. Wharton has been able to add to his third edition a considerable amount of fresh matter, as well as new metrical versions; the bibliography too of the books and articles in Sapphic literature has been greatly expanded, covering now 19 pages. The book is issued in the same size as the previous editions, bound in blue cloth, ornamented and lettered in gold. The design of the cover has been made by Aubrey Beardsley. There are three photogravure illustrations.

THOMPSON, FRANCIS. Sister songs: an offering to two sisters. Imported by Copeland & Day. 1 il., 4°, $1.50.

POLITICAL AND SOCIAL.

ARMSTRONG, K. L., *ed.* The little statesman: a middle-of-the-road manual for American voters. Schulte Pub. Co. 12°, (Ariel lib. ser., no. 6.) pap., 50 c.
Contents: A short history of American politics; The steps in the growth of American liberty; The constitution of the U. S.; The new declaration of independence—the Omaha platform; A new study of political economy based on the Omaha platform; Sectionalism in American politics; Laws of property; Interest and usury; Debt and slavery; The land question; An exposition of the single tax, by W. F. Cooling; Co-operation; Direct legislation; A bird's-eye view of American financial history, by S. Leavitt; The transportation problem.

CARROLL, E., *jr.* Principles and practice of finance. Putnam. 8°, $1.75.
A practical guide for bankers, merchants, and lawyers; with a summary of the national and state banking laws, and the legal rates of interest, tables of foreign coins, and a glossary of commercial and financial terms. The book is divided into two parts. The first deals only with the principles of finance; the second is confined to the practical application of those principles through the machinery of finance and commerce.

LINCOLN, ABRAHAM, *and* DOUGLAS, STEPHEN A. Political speeches and debates of Abraham Lincoln and Stephen A. Douglas, 1854–1861; ed. by Alonzo T. Jones. International Tract Soc. pors., il. 8°, buckram, $1.75.
In this edition the place and date of the speech and the name of the speaker appear at the top of each page; sub-heads, indicating the leading points discussed, are scattered at short intervals through the speeches, and the most famous passages are printed in black letters.

SPRAGUE, *Rev.* FRANKLIN M. The laws of social evolution: a critique of Benjamin Kidd's "Social evolution" and a statement of the true principles which govern social progress. Lee & Shepard. 12°, $1.
"In this critique we have endeavored to analyze the main theses of 'Social evolution,' and we have found them to be contrary to universally accepted principles and axiomatic truths. Our aim, however, so far from being mere refutation or explanation, has been also constructive. While the work is necessarily

controversial, if we have exposed error, we have substituted what we conceived to be truth, thus seeking positive rather than merely negative results."—*Preface.*

SPORTS AND AMUSEMENTS.

BIRD, H. E. Chess novelties and their latest developments. Warne. 12°, $1.50.

DONOVAN, MIKE. The science of boxing. [*Also*] Rules and articles on training, generalship in the ring, and kindred subjects. Dick & Fitzgerald. por., il. 12°, $1; pap., 50 c.

THEOLOGY, RELIGION AND SPECULATION.

ALDEN, H. MILLS. A study of death. Harper. 12°, leath., $1.50.

DENISON, J. H. Christ's idea of the supernatural. Houghton, Mifflin. 12°, $2.

GORDON, G. A., *D.D.* The Christ of to-day. Houghton, Mifflin. 12°, $1.50.
This book has its origin in lectures delivered before the Divinity School in Yale University, in January, 1895, and before the Unitarian Association of Boston. They are now expanded into four chapters ; the first, introductory, is, to use the author's statement, " a fresh attempt to reach the absoluteness of God through the finality for mankind of the mind of Christ," and treats, among other things, of the new world into which the Church has come, and the problem before the Christian thinker of to-day ; the second is entitled " Christ in the faith of to-day," and "employs the mind of Christ as the creative and conservative principle in theology and in other intellectual movements of the time"; the third is on the "Significance to-day of a Supreme Christology," and " sees in Christ the supreme instrument of the Spirit in the moral education of the race"; and the fourth is devoted to "The place of Christ in the pulpit of to-day."

GREEN, W. H., *D.D.* The higher criticism of the Pentateuch. Scribner. 12°, $1.50.
It is the purpose of this volume to show as briefly and compactly as possible that the faith of all past ages in respect to the Pentateuch has not been mistaken. In the first chapter it is exhibited in its relation to the Old Testament as a whole. In the second the plan and contents of the Pentateuch are unfolded. In the third it is shown by a variety of arguments, both external and internal, that its author was Moses. The 4th, 5th, and 6th chapters discuss : The unity of the Pentateuch, the genuineness of the laws, and the bearing of the divisive criticism on the credibility of the Pentateuch and on supernatural religion. Author is Professor of Oriental and Old Testament Literature in Princeton Theological Seminary.

HALL, J., *D.D.*, *comp.* Light unto my path: being divine directions for daily walk; chosen and applied by J. Hall, D.D. Brentano's. sq. 16°, $1.50.
A book of devotional readings for every day in the year, adapted to the needs of communicants of the Presbyterian Church. Dr. Hall is minister of the Fifth Avenue Presbyterian Church, N. Y. Bound appropriately after designs made by Louis Tiffany & Co.

LAZARUS, JOSEPHINE. The spirit of Judaism. Dodd, Mead & Co. 12°, $1.25.
The Jewish question includes all the great questions of the day—social, political, financial, humanitarian, national, and religious. In her thoughtful papers Miss Lazarus discusses the essential spirit of Judaism chiefly from the humanitarian side. She makes a plea for justice toward moral and law-abiding citizens. Her chapters are headed : The Jewish question ; The outlook of Judaism ; Judaism old and new ; The claim of Judaism ; The task of Judaism. These essays have appeared in *The Century Magazine* and *The Jewish Messenger* since 1892.

PALMER, F. Studies in theologic definition underlying the Apostles' and Nicene creeds. Dutton. 12°, $1.25.
." " In these studies I have had in mind especially those persons who have felt a difference between the tone of the thought in which they find themselves and that to which they have been accustomed by experience or tradtion. . . . It is those, then, who, consciously or unawares, are seeking a mediator—a mode of thinking which shall reveal the inheritance of the past and claim the gifts of the present and adjust itself to the future — it is such for whom these studies are primarily intended."— *Preface.*

RECENT FRENCH AND GERMAN BOOKS.

FRENCH.

Daudet, E. Don Rafaël. 12°. Levy	$1 00
Estannie, Ed. L'Empreinte. 12°. Perrin	1 00
Ginisty, P. Le Montardier du Pape. 12°. Dentu.	1 00
Gyp. Ces bons Normands! 12°. Levy	1 00
Lepelletier, E. Les Trahisons de Marie Louise. 12°. Lib. Ill.	1 00
Lyonne, Gen. Mémoires. De Valmy à Wagram. 12°. Didot.	1 00
Maisonneuve, H. La faute de Jeanne. 12°. Plon.	1 00
Maiseroy, R. L'Ange. 12°. Lemerre.	1 00
Montepin, X. de. Sœurs Jumelles. 2 vols. 12°. Dentu.	2 00
Rosny, J. H. Résurrection. 12°. Plon.	1 00
Soiout, L. Le Directoire. 2 vols. 8°. Didot.	4 80
Tronchin, H. Le conseiller François Tronchin, et ses amis Voltaire, Grimm, Diderot, etc. 8°. Plon	$2 25

GERMAN.

Eschen, M. von. Inmitten der Bewegung. 2 vols. 12°. Reissner	2 35
Hollaender, F. Sturmwind im Westen. 12°. Fischer	1 35
Jensen, Wm. Jenseits der Alpen. Novellen. 12°. Reissner	2 00
Schulze-Smidt, B. L'Omicida, Il Bricconcello. Zwei Novellen. 12°. Reissner	1 70
Valeska, Grifin. Alte und Junge. 12°. Reissner	1 00
Zapp, A. Des Erbprinzen Weltreise. 12°. Janke	1 70

MAGAZINE ARTICLES FOR NOVEMBER.

Articles marked with an asterisk are illustrated.

ARTISTIC, MUSICAL, AND DRAMATIC.—*Century,* Mural Decoration in America,* Cortissoz; Eleanora Duse (with portrait), Towse.—*Scribner's,* Some Thanksgiving - Time Fancies (Pictures by Clinedinst, Gleeson, Leigh, McCarter, and Pyle); Wood-Engravers—Florian ;* Frederick Macmonnies,* Low.

BIOGRAPHY, CORRESPONDENCE.—*Atlantic,* A Literary Politician (Walter Bagehot), Wilson.— *Century,* The Painter Vibert, Autobiographical Sketch. — *North Am. Review,* Girlhood of an Actress, Mary Anderson de Navarro. — *Pop. Science,* Sketch of Alexander Dallas Bache (with portrait).

DESCRIPTION, TRAVEL. — *Atlantic,* After the War (Japan), Hearn. — *Cath. World,* "The Northern Athens" (Edinburgh),* O'Shea ; A Morning in Florence,* Marion A. Taggart.— *Century,* Kaiserwerth and its Founder,* Eleonora Kinnicutt.—*Chautauquan,* Among the Old Missions of California,* Connor.—*Fort. Review* (Oct.), A Roman Reverie, Alfred Austin.— *Harper's,* Out of the World at Corinto,* Davis; Recent Impressions of Anglo-Indian Life,* Weeks.—*Lippincott's,* A Brush with Kiowas, Thomson.—*Nine. Century* (Oct.), In Germany, Duchess of Sutherland. — *Scribner's,* Landmarks of Manhattan,* Cortissoz.

DOMESTIC AND SOCIAL.—*Forum,* A Generation of College Women, Frances M. Abbott.—*North Am. Review,* What Becomes of College Women? Thwing; The Rule of the Mother, Selden (Notes and Comments).

EDUCATIONAL.—*Fort. Review* (Oct.), Expressiveness of Speech, Wallace.—*Nine. Century* (Oct.), Proper Pronunciation of Greek, Gennadius; A Great University for London, Playfair. —*Pop. Science,* Recent Tendencies in the Education of Women, Mary R. Smith.

FICTION.—*Atlantic,* In Harvest-Time, Ewell; Apparition of Gran'ther Hill, R. E. Robinson; The Face of Death, Lily Dougall.—*Cath. World,* Daughter of Kings; Little Cripple of Lisfarran, Katharine Roche. — *Century,* Devotion of Enriquez,* Harte ; On Account of Emmanuel,* Taylor; Tragedy of the Comedy,* Fernald; Sir George Tressady, I., Mrs. H. Ward (with portrait).—*Harper's,* Men and Women and Horses,* Matthews; Pilgrim on the Gila,* Wister ; A Thanksgiving Breakfast, Mrs. H. P. Spofford; Blumblossom Beebe's Adventure,* Ralph.— *Lippincott's,* In Sight of the Goddess, Harriet R. Davis; A Romance in Late Fall, Marjorie Richardson.—*Scribner's,* The Late War in Europe, H. P. Robinson ; The Colonel's Tea-Party, Bessie Chandler.

HISTORY.—*Forum,* Woman's Position in Pagan Times, Boyesen.

HUMOR AND SATIRE.—*North Am. Review,* The Plague of Jocularity, H. H. Boyesen.

LITERARY.—*Century,* Robert Louis Stevenson and His Writing, Mrs. S. Van Rensselaer.— *Chautauquan,* American Humorists, Sherman. —*Fort. Review* (Oct.), Ferdinand Brunetière, Yetta Blaze de Bury ; Literary Boston Thirty Years Ago, Howells.—*Forum,* Review of Huxley's Essays, W. K. Brooks ; Studies of Notable Men, Stamboloff, Vatralsky ; Chief Influences

on My Career, Anatole France.—*Lippincott's,* A Poet, Geraldine Meyrick ; "Our Fullest Throat of Song" (J. R. Lowell), Lawton.— *Nine. Century* (Oct.), Ruskin as Master of Prose, F. Harrison ; The New Spirit in History, Lilly ; Frederick Locker-Lampson, Kernahan.—*Pop. Science,* Evolution in Folk-lore, Ellis.—*Scribner's,* Art of Living—Conduct of Life, Grant. — *West. Review* (Oct.), Gustave Flaubert, Hannigan ; A Crop of Brontë Myths, Mackay.

MEDICAL.—*Lippincott's,* Medical Education, Benedict.—*Nine. Century* (Oct.), Medical View of the Miracles at Lourdes, Berdoe.—*Pop. Science,* Consumption Considered as a Contagious Disease, Benedict.

MENTAL AND MORAL.—*Scribner's,* Logic of Mental Telegraphy, Jastrow.

NATURE AND SCIENCE. — *Cath. World,* Wonders of Old Ocean.*—*Chautauquan,* March of Invention, Shaler. — *Lippincott's,* A Hundred and Twenty Miles an Hour, Cochrane.—*Pop. Science,* Aims of Anthropology, Brinton.

POETRY. — *Atlantic,* In November, Morse.— *Cath. World,* Capital and Labor, Eleanor C. Donnelly.—*Century,* Music in Solitude, Gilder; Maid Marian's Song, Ednah P. Clarke.—*Harper's,* Two, Laura S. Portor.—*Scribner's,* To Omar's Friends at Burford Bridge, Lang; Ruin of the Year, Lampman; "They Also Serve," Bunner.

POLITICAL AND SOCIAL.—*Atlantic,* Future of Naval Warfare, Mitchell.—*Cath. World,* Study of the Sunday Question, McSweeny.—*Century,* Issues of 1896: A Republican View, Roosevelt; A Democratic View, Russell; The Armenian Question, Bryce. — *Chautauquan,* American Character in Politics, Hart. — *Forum,* Third-Term Tradition, McMaster; General Railroad Situation, Ashley; Plutocracy and Paternalism, Ward.—*North Am. Review,* Quick Transit Between New York and London, Corbin; Outlook for Republican Success, Saxton; Industrial Development of the South, Gov. of Alabama; Improvement of the Civil Service, Rice.—*Pop. Science,* Principles of Taxation, Wells; Past and Future of Gold, Ashley.—*West. Review* (Oct.), Wanted, A New Liberal Programme, Scanlon; The Labour War, H. Thomas.

THEOLOGY, RELIGION, AND SPECULATION.— *Cath. World,* Catholicism, Protestantism, and Progress, Howard.—*Fort. Review* (Oct.), Asserted Growth of Roman Catholicism in England, Farrar; Islam and Its Critics: A Rejoinder, "A Quarterly Reviewer." — *Nine. Century* (Oct.), Religion of Humanity: A Reply, Mallock; Religion of the Undergraduate, Deane. —*West. Review* (Oct.), Dawn of the Trinity, Waterer.

COMPANY.

I THOUGHT, "How terrible, if I were seen
Just as in will and deed I had always been !
And if this were the fate that I must face
At the last day, and all else were God's grace,
How must I shrink and cower before them there,
Stripped naked to the soul and beggared bare
Of every rag of seeming !" Then, "Why, no,"
I thought, "why should I, if the rest are so?"

(Harper. $2.50.) — *From Howells' "Stops of Many Quills."*

freshest News.

R. F. FENNO & Co. have nearly ready a new illustrated edition of "A Window in Thrums" and "Auld Licht Idyls," J. M. Barrie's wonderfully successful books. Mrs. Oliphant's new book, "The Story of a Governess," is noticed elsewhere in this issue. The fourth edition of "A Galloway Herd" is now ready, and shortly there will be ready "Captain Antifer," by Jules Verne, and "A Girl of the Commune," by G. A. Henty.

THE AMERICAN LIBRARY ASSOCIATION has just issued the completed "List of Books for Girls and Women and Their Clubs" which has been appearing in parts. The list contains upward of 2000 books chosen and appraised by men and women of authority. The great bulk of the drudgery in this list has been done by George Iles, who has been indefatigable in his efforts to make the list what it purports to be—a truly reliable guide to an education by reading.

LOVELL, CORYELL & Co. have just ready "A Daughter of the Tenements," the new continuous story by Edward W. Townsend of the N. Y. *Sun*, elaborately illustrated by E. W. Kemble, an absorbing story told with manifest sympathy for the denizens of the New York City tenements; "The Manhattaners," a bright story of New York society, by Edward S. Van Zile; "As the Wind Blows," by Eleanor Merron; "Eunice Quince," a story of New England in the last century, by Dane Conyngham ; and "The Sheik's White Slave," by Raymond Raife, with many illustrations.

F. WARNE & Co. have just issued "The German Emperor William II.," by Charles Lowe, in their *International Series of the Public Men of To-Day*, in which have already appeared "M. Stambuloff," by A. Hulme Beaman, noticed in our last issue ; "The Ameer," by Stephen Wheeler ; and "Li Hung Chang," by Prof. Robert K. Douglas. Among the latest books are the eighth edition of "The Legend of King Arthur and the Knights of the Round Table"; "Paul Heriot's Pictures," by Alison McLean ; "The Desert Ship," by John Bloundelle-Burton; a new revised edition of "Whist, or Bumblepuppy "; and "Chess Novelties," by H. E. Bird.

HOUGHTON, MIFFLIN & Co. have just ready Stedman's important work, "A Victorian Anthology," which has not only a rare value as a work of literature, but is also typographically beautiful; "Anima Poetæ," selections from the unpublished note-books of Samuel Taylor Coleridge, edited by Ernest H. Coleridge, uniform with Coleridge's Letters recently published by this firm; "Colonial Dames and Goodwives," by Alice Morse Earle; "Mr. Rabbit at Home," a sequel to "Little Mr. Thimblefinger," by Joel Chandler Harris; "A Question of Faith," a novel by Lily Dougall, author of "The Zeit Geist," etc.; "Little Miss Phœbe Gay," by Helen Dawes Brown, a bright, wholesome story that cannot fail to interest youthful readers and older people who have not forgotten their childhood; also a new *Birthday edition* of Dr. Holmes's "Over the Teacups."

GEORGE D. HURST, New York City, announces for his *Ambrosial Library* "The Beads of Tasmer," by Amelia E. Barr ; "The King of Honey Island," by Maurice Thompson; "The Chautauquan," by John Habberton; Le Grand's "Manual for Stamp-Collectors"; and "The Satires of Cynicus." He also calls attention to "The New Standard Electrical Dictionary of Words and Terms," by T. O'Connor Sloane, of the *Scientific American;* "The New Dictionary of Photography," by E. J. Wall; "Photography, Artistic and Scientific," by Johnson and Chatwood; "The Anchor Handy Volume Atlas of the World"; "Practical Typewriting," by Bates Torrey; a library edition suitable for the holidays of Eggleston's "The Hoosier Schoolmaster"; and two books by Susan E. Wallace—one "The Repose in Egypt," the other a new edition of "The Land of the Pueblos."

ROBERTS BROTHERS make the important announcement of an illustrated edition of Balzac's works as translated by Miss Wormeley. The edition will be in forty octavo volumes, limited to 1000 numbered sets. It will be printed on a paper specially made for this purpose, and will be illustrated with designs by L. Rossi, J. Muenier, G. Roux, Chalon, Moreau, and others, all of whom rank among the best artists in France. The designs will be reproduced in high-grade goupilgravures. In connection with these illustrations the publishers announce that they have a surprise in reserve for the subscribers to the work. The distinguishing feature of this edition will be the uniformity of the translation, which is not only thoroughly in the spirit of Balzac but is most original in treatment. The artists, also, are thoroughly imbued with the subjects they have chosen, and have treated them in the most loving as well as artistic manner. The publishers have long been contemplating the issue of this work, but have delayed it in order to insure the highest order of workmanship in every particular, and the result promises to be gratifying to lovers of Balzac as well as to bibliophiles.

G. P. PUTNAM'S SONS have in preparation "Russian Portraits," by Vicomte Melchior de Vogüé, an authorized translation, by Elisabeth L. Cary, of Vogüé's volume, recently published by Colin & Co., in France, where it achieved a signal success under the title of "Les Cœurs Russes"; "The Gold-Diggings of Cape Horn," a study of life in Tierra Del Fuego and Patagonia, by John R. Spears, fully illustrated ; "Fundamental Concepts of Economics," by H. Dunning Macleod ; "Egyptian Decorative Art," a course of lectures delivered at the Royal Institution, by Prof. W. M. Flinders Petrie, illustrated ; "A Treatise on Horsemanship," by E. L. Anderson, revised, with new material and additional illustrations ; a new novel by Miss Mead, entitled "A Princess of the Gutter, a story of life in the East End of London " ; "The Proverbial Philosophy of Confucius," an Eastern every-day book, selected and arranged by Forster H. Jenings ; and "Nymphs, Nixies, and Naiads," poems, by M. A. B. Evans. They also announce a new story by Grant Allen, entitled "The British Barbarians—a hill-top novel." The sub-title, the author explains, will in future be added to all his novels having special mental and moral importance.

NEW BOOKS AND NEW EDITIONS

————◆PUBLISHED BY◆————

GEORGE D. HURST,

114 FIFTH AVENUE, - - - NEW YORK,

and which are wholesaled to dealers. All buyable from your home bibliopole. . . . .

THE AMBROSIAL LIBRARY
OF STANDARD FICTION

For Every-Day Reading. Buckram cloth, 12mo, 75 cents.

INCLUDES NOW

THE BEADS OF TASMER.
By AMELIA E. BARR, author of "Girls of a Feather."

THE KING OF HONEY ISLAND.
By MAURICE THOMPSON, author of "A Tallahassee Girl."

THE CHAUTAUQUANS.
By JOHN HABBERTON, author of "Helen's Babies."

LE GRAND'S MANUAL FOR STAMP-COLLECTORS.
A companion to the Stamp Album. Translated from the French, annotated and adapted for American collectors by HENRI PÈNE DU BOIS, Esq. International Edition. Cloth, extra, $1.00.

THE SATIRES OF CYNICUS.
Each sketch and expression is a thought of superlative quality. "Cynicus' mighty line." Buckram cloth, square 12mo, 75 cents.

NEW STANDARD ELECTRICAL DICTIONARY
Of Words and Terms Used in the Practice of Electric Engineering. By P. O'CONOR SLOANE, of the *Scientific American*. Including 350 illustrations. Cloth, crown 8vo, $2.50.

NEW DICTIONARY OF PHOTOGRAPHY
For the Amateur and Professional Photographer. By E. J. WALL. It is recent and reliable. Cloth, crown 8vo, $2.50.

PHOTOGRAPHY, ARTISTIC AND SCIENTIFIC
By JOHNSON and CHATWOOD. With 54 illustrations. This book is entirely new and is the latest work existing on the subject. Cloth, 8vo, $2.50.

ANCHOR HANDY VOLUME ATLAS OF THE WORLD.
The world's maps compressed, then bound as a book. 72 of the latest maps (engraved) with population and statistics of a various nature included. Cloth, small 12mo, $1.50.

PRACTICAL TYPEWRITING
By the All-Finger Method, which leads to operation by touch. Arranged for self-instruction and school use. By BATES TORREY. This work also includes various combination forms showing what can be made by a repetition of a character or letter, besides a mint of ideas for the student. Cloth, quarto, $1.50.

A Library Edition (suitable for holidays) of
THE HOOSIER SCHOOLMASTER.
By EDWARD EGGLESTON. Revised with an introduction and notes on the dialect by the author, together with portrait in gravure. Cloth, crown 8vo, gold top, $1.50.

THE REPOSE IN EGYPT.
A Medley. By SUSAN E. WALLACE. New Edition. "It is a charming panorama of Oriental scenery." Buckram cloth, 12mo, 75 cents.

THE LAND OF THE PUEBLOS.
By SUSAN E. WALLACE. New Edition. "Mrs. Wallace's bright talks, with their vivid descriptions and womanly quickness in delineating detail, give information which many will be glad to possess." Buckram cloth, 12mo, 75 cents.

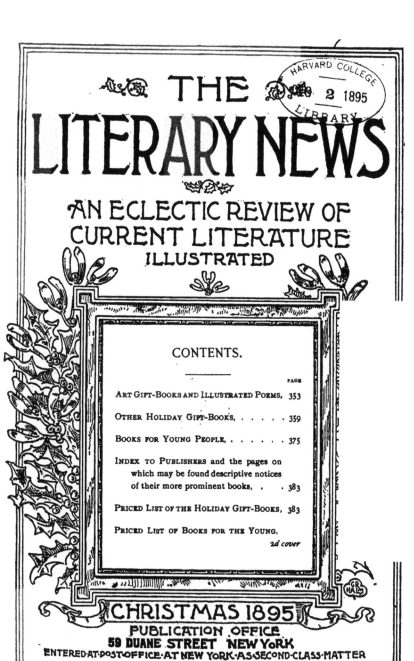

THE LITERARY NEWS

AN ECLECTIC REVIEW OF CURRENT LITERATURE
ILLUSTRATED

CONTENTS.

CHRISTMAS 1895

PUBLICATION OFFICE
59 DUANE STREET NEW YORK
ENTERED AT POST OFFICE AT NEW YORK AS SECOND CLASS MATTER

Books for Young People.

Adventures in New Texas. Stebbing. Il. $1.50..*Stokes*
Afloat in a Gypsy Van. Suffling. Il. $1.50......*Stokes*
After School. Overton. Il. $1.50..............*Stokes*
Ampthill Towers. Foster. 80c............*Nelson*
Animal Object-Book. Col. il. Bds., $1.50......*Warne*
Arabian Nights. Il. by J. D. Batten. *Second series.*
$2..............................*Putnam*
At War with Pontiac. Munroe. Il. $1.25.....*Scribner*
Aunt Louisa's Book of Common Things. Il. Bds., 50c.
..............................*Warne*
Antipas, Son of Chuza. L. S. Houghton. Il. $1.50.
..............................*Randolph*
Books on Wild Flowers for the Young. M. C. Cooke
("Uncle Matt"). 5 v. *Ea.*, 75c.; bds., 50c...*Nelson*
Boris, the Bear-Hunter. Wishaw. Il. $1.25...*Nelson*
Bunyan's Pilgrim's Progress. *One-syllable ed.*, $1;
bds., 60c..............................*Winston*
Cats and Kittens. Tucker. Col. il. by F. J. Boston.
$1.50..............................*Stokes*
Charles XII. R. Nisbet Bain. (*Heroes of the nations
ser.*, no. 15.) Il. $1.50..............*Putnam*
Charlotte's Revenge. Morgan. *Crown ser.* V. 5.
$1.50..............................*Am. Bapt. Pub. Soc*
Children's Book of Dogs and Cats. Tucker. Col. il.
by F. J. Boston. $2.50..............................*Stokes*
Children's Favorite Classics: Black beauty, by A.
Sewell; Carrots, by Mrs. Molesworth; Cuckoo clock,
by Mrs. Molesworth; Water babies, by C. Kingsley.
Il. 8° *ed.*, *ea.*, $1.25; 16° *ed.*, *ea.*, 75c....*Crowell*
Children's Friend. Il. *Ie*; bds., 75c..........*Stokes*
Children's Stories in American Literature, 1660-1860.
Wright. $1.25..............................*Scribner*
Child's Life of Christ. Hesba Stretton. *New ed.* $1.
..............................*Winston*
Chilhowee Boys in War-Time. Morrison. Il. by F.
T. Merrill. $1.50..............................*Crowell*
Christmas Stories. Heimburg; tr. by Mrs. J. W.
Davis. Il. $1.25..............................*Stokes*
Columbia Toys: 1, Tabby family at home; 2, Red
Riding-Hood; 3, Cinderella. Pap., *ea.*, 40c.; untear-
able, 65c.
Cossack Fairy-Tales and Folk-Tales; ed. and tr. by
R. N. Bain. Il. by E. W. Mitchell. $1..........*Stokes*
Cosy Corner Stories. Col. il. *Ie*..........*Dutton*
Cuore. Edmondo de Amicis; tr. by I. F. Hapgood.
New il. ed. $1..............................*Crowell*
Dear Little Marchioness. Taylor. $1..........*Crowell*
Desert Ship. Bloundelle-Burton..............*Warne*
Dogs Great and Small. Tucker. Col. il. by F. J. Bos-
ton. $1.50..............................*Stokes*
Don, by the author of "Miss Toosey's mission." $1.
..............................*Roberts*
Dora. Mrs. Read. Il. $1.25..............*Scribner*
Dorothy and Anton. Plympton. Il. by the author.
$1..............................*Roberts*
Dulcie King. Corbett-Seymour. Il. *Ie*......*Dutton*
Dutton's Holiday Annual for 1896. Il. $1.25...*Dutton*
Easy A B C Painting-Book. Col. il. Pap., 50c...*Warne*
Enchanted Butterflies. Crosby. Il. by S. H. Clark
and the author. $1.25..............................*Stokes*
Fairy Tales, far and near. "Q." $1.50..........*Stokes*
Family at Misrule. Turner. $1..........*Ward, L. & B*
Famous Leaders Among Women. Bolton. $1.50.
..............................*Crowell*
Favorite Book of Beasts, Birds, and Fishes. Il. 75c.;
bds., 50c..............................*Nelson*
Fisherman's Daughter. Benedict. $1.
..............................*Am. Bapt. Pub. Soc*
Flock of Boys and Girls. Perry. Il. by C. T. Parker.
$1.50..............................*Little, B. & Co*
Frowsle, the Runaway. Wesselhoeft. Il. by J. Mc-
Dermott. $1.25..............................*Roberts*
Garden Behind the Moon. Pyle. Il. by the author. $2.
..............................*Scribner*
Goostie. Hyde. 50c..............................*Roberts*
Great Men's Sons. Brooks. Il. $1.50..........*Putnam*
Gulliver's Travels. Il. by Browne. 80c..........*Dutton*
Half a Dozen Boys. Ray. *New il. ed.* Il. by F. T.
Merrill. $1.50..............................*Crowell*
Hallowe'en Ahoy. St. Leger. Il. $1.50..........*Scribner*
Harper's Round Table for 1895. $3..........*Harper*
Heroes of the Nations Series, vs. 15 and 16. *Ea.*, $1.50.
..............................*Putnam*
How Jack Mackenzie Won His Epaulettes. Gordon
Stables. $1.25..............................*Nelson*
How Tommy Saved the Barn. Otis. 50c......*Crowell*
Hunters Three. Knox. $1.50..............*Dutton*
In Far Japan. Sitwell. 80c..............................*Nelson*
In Taunton Town. Everett-Green. $1.75..........*Nelson*
In the Okefenokee. Pendleton. Il. $1.25......*Roberts*
In the Young World, Poems for Young People. Edith
M. Thomas. $1.50..............................*Houghton, M. & Co*
Infant's Magazine. Il. $1; bds., 75c..........*Stokes*
Jack Alden. Gross. Il. $1.50..............*Crowell*

Jacob and the Raven. Frances M. Peard. Il. $1.50.
..............................*Dutton*
Jane and Her Family. E. Lang. 50c..........*Nelson*
Joel, a Boy of Galilee. Johnston. Il. $1.50....*Roberts*
Jolly Good Summer. Smith. Il. $1.25..........*Roberts*
Joseph, the Dreamer, by the author of "Jesus, the Car-
penter of Nazareth"..............................*Scribner*
Kanter Girls. Branch. Il. $1.50..........*Scribner*
Katharine's Yesterday. Hill. Il. $1.50..........*Lothrop*
Keeper of the Salamander's Order. Shattuck. Il. $1.
..............................*Roberts*
King's Pardon. Overton. Il. $1.50..........*Stokes*
Knight of Liberty. Butterworth. Il. $1.50...*Appleton*
Knight of the White Cross. Henty. Il. $1.50.
..............................*Scribner*
Leaves from a Middy's Log. Knight. $1..........*Nelson*
Lieutenant at Eighteen. Adams ("Oliver Optic").
Il. (*Blue and the gray—on land*, v. 3.) $1.50. *Lee & S*
Life of Christ; Life of Daniel; Life of Esther; Life of
Joseph. Col. il. Bds., *ea.*, 35c..............*Nelson*
Lights Out. Overton. Il. $1.50..............*Stokes*
Little Bet. Taylor. 75c..............................*Nelson*
Little Miss Phœbe Gay. Brown. *Ie*..........*Pott*
..............................*Houghton, M. & Co*
Little Orphans. Leigh. $1..............*Nelson*
Little Susy's Six Birthdays, Six Teachers, Six Servants.
New ed., in 1 v. Il. $1..............*Randolph*
Lost Army (A). Fred Wishaw. $1.25..........*Nelson*
Master of Deeplawn. Mrs. Colter. *Crown ser.* V. 4.
$1.50..............................*Am. Bapt. Pub. Soc*
Merry Moments Painting-Book. 25c..........*Warne*
Mr. Midshipman Easy. Marryat. *Malta ed.* $2.50.
..............................*Putnam*
Mr. Rabbit at Home. Harris. Il. by O. Herford. $2.
..............................*Houghton, M. & Co*
Moving Toy-Books: 1, Moving faces. Meggendorfer.
Bds., $1; 2, In the country. Bds., $2.50......*Stokes*
Mushroom Cave. Raymond. Il. $1.50..........*Roberts*
My Honey, by the author of "Miss Toosey's mission."
..............................*Roberts*
My Strange Rescue. Oxley. Il. $1.25..........*Nelson*
Nimble Dollar. Thompson. $1..*Houghton, M. & Co*
Niram. Mitchell. Il. 75c..........*Am. Bapt. Pub. Soc*
Nono, or, the Golden Rose. 60c..............*Nelson*
Nonsense. Col. il. Bds., $1......*E. & J. B. Young*
Oakleigh. E. D. Deland. $1.25..............*Harper*
Object Painting-Book. 25c..............*Warne*
Our Darling's Surprise Pictures. Movable col. il. $1.
..............................*Dutton*
Picture Puzzle Toy-Books. Col. il. *Ea.*, 25c...*Warne*
Playtime Toy-Books. Il. Pap., *ea.*, 25c.; untearable,
40c..............................*Warne*
Pleasant Days at Maplewood. Bartlett. Il. $1.
..............................*Ireland*
Princess Louise. Temple. 60c..............*Nelson*
Rabbit Witch, and other tales. Pyle. $1.50....*Dutton*
Rex. Thompson. Il. $1.50..............*Stokes*
Robinson Crusoe. $2.50..............*Dutton*
Robinson Crusoe. Browne. $1..............*Scribner*
Royal Little People. Tucker. Il. $1.25..........*Stokes*
Secret Cave. Searchfield. 60c..............*Nelson*
Seven Wise Scholars. Hope. Il. by G. Browne. $1.50.
..............................*Scribner*
Shaven Crown. Bramston. Il. 80c. *E. & J. B. Young*
Silver Fairy-Book. Il. $2..............*Putnam*
Snow-Shoes and Sledges. Munroe. Il. $1.25.*Harper*
Something Nice to Look At. Col. il. $1.25...*Dutton*
Stand-Up A B C. 50c..............*Dutton*
Stories and Poems for Children. Thaxter; ed. by S. O.
Jewett. $1.50..............*Houghton, M. & Co*
Stories for All the Year. Rice. Il. $1.50......*Stokes*
Tales from the Field. Asbjörnsen. $1.
Three Apprentices of Moon Street. Montorgueil; tr.
by H. Smith. Il. by L. Le Révérend and P. Steck.
$1.50..............................*Crowell*
Through Forest and Plain. Russan and Boyle. Il. by
H. Barnes. $2..............................*Nelson*
Through the Russian Snows. Henty. Il. $1.50.
..............................*Scribner*
Tiger of Mysore. Henty. Il. $1.50..........*Scribner*
Tony. Mitchell. Il. 75c........*Am. Bapt. Pub. Soc*
Torch-Bearers of History. *Second series.* Sterling.
80c..............................*Nelson*
"Tuck-Up" Songs. Walton. Bds., 50c..........*Nelson*
"Tuck-Up" Tales. Aunt Dweedy. 50c..........*Nelson*
Two Gallant Rebels. Pickering. Il. $1.25....*Scribner*
Two Little Pilgrims' Progress. Burnett. Il. by R. B.
Birch. $1.50..............................*Scribner*
Under the Bonnie Blue Flag. Stables. Il.....*Nelson*
Under the Lone Star. Hazens. $2..............*Nelson*
Under the Stable Floor. Hyde. 50c..........*Roberts*
Unlessoned Girl. Tompkins. $1.25..........*Putnam*
Vivian Vansittart, R.N. Knight..............*Warne*
Yan and Nochie of Tappan Sea. Hyde. 50c...*Roberts*

THE

LITERARY NEWS

An Eclectic Review of Current Literature.

Published monthly, and containing the freshest news concerning books, and authors; lists of new publications; reviews and critical comments; characteristic extracts; sketches and anecdotes of authors; courses of reading; literary topics of the magazines; and other literary subjects.

| VOL. XVI. | *CHRISTMAS*, 1895. | No. 12 |

Art Gift=Books and Illustrated Poems.

From "The Abbey Shakespeare." Copyright, 1895, by Harper & Brothers.

MARIA, SIR ANDREW, AND SIR TOBY. ("TWELFTH NIGHT," ACT I., SCENE 3.)

(Half tone Plate from the Original Drawing, which is reproduced in the Work by Photogravure.)

The Abbey Shakespeare. — Among the most sumptuous publications of many years may be reckoned *The Comedies of Shakespeare*, with the Abbey illustrations, which month after month were a delight to the readers of *Harper's Magazine.* One hundred and thirty-one full-page photogravure reproductions of Mr. Abbey's drawings illustrate this edition of the *Comedies of Shakespeare.* The text is that of the folio of 1623, with obvious errors corrected and the orthography modernized, and the retention of passages which occur in the folio, but which many editors have omitted, will be noted with interest. These volumes should be welcomed equally by the student and reader of Shakespeare and the lover of artistic illustration. As the basis of the process of photogravure—by which these copperplate pictures are made—is photographic, all forms in the original drawings are perfectly retained and the qualities faithfully rendered, so far as the translatable portions of these superb drawings can be reproduced. Museums were ransacked for the costumes and armor of the periods; and almost forgotten bits were brought to light by the diligent search of the enthusiastic artist. Old hangings and cabinets, that may have been a part of the surroundings of the *dramatis personæ,* have been skilfully used as decorative backgrounds, and form no small part of these charming compositions. These drawings are the result of many years of careful thought. Months were spent in the study of the scenery and accessories of each play, and the student and the antiquary will find much in these illustrations to delight his eye. No other illustrator has got so near to the heart of the immortal bard. The text and illustrations of these unique volumes will average about 350 pages each. (Harper. 4 v., large 8°, hf. cl., $30.)

Standish of Standish.—One of the best historical novels of New England life, the late Jane G. Austin's "Standish of Standish," has, says *The Beacon,* "been made the subject of an exquisitely planned luxurious edition with photogravure illustrations by Frank T. Merrill. Dealing as it does with the romantic career of the famous Puritan hero, Captain Miles Standish, involving the idyllic tale of John Alden and Priscilla Molines, all set off against a care-

From "Standish of Standish."   Copyright, 1895, by Houghton,
Mifflin & Co.

"PARDON ME, MISTRESS MOLINES."

fully studied, vividly colored, unquestionably authentic background of early colonial manners and customs, this story well deserves to be regarded as a classic, and it was a happy thought on the part of the publishers to send it forth in this sumptuous holiday dress. Mr. Merrill has done a great deal of admirable work in the depiction of colonial characters and conditions, but he has done nothing that, on the whole, reflects so much credit upon his knowledge and artistic capability as the work he has put into the twenty pictures contained in these two volumes. They are positively creative in their portrayal of historical personalities, they show the peculiarities of Puritan dress and domestic surroundings with singular impressiveness, and these have a gracefulness and felicity of technique that entitle them to a high rank among the productions of contemporary illustrators. The details of typography and binding have been conscientiously attended to, and the book may be safely commended as a holiday tribute well worth buying and well worth owning." (Houghton, Mifflin & Co. 2 v., $5.)

Crowell's New Illustrated Library.—It would be impossible indeed to find better made and cheaper books than are year by year being added to this most popular and satisfactory library of standards. This year six works claim attention, all of which are gotten up in two volumes and in two styles of binding. This season something specially attractive and certainly new has been hit upon for the more elegant style of binding. The backs and corners are in white parchment cloth, richly lined in gold, and the coverings are a very pretty flowered design, with the look of rare old silk brocade. The whole effect is light and gay in an unusual degree, not exactly in keeping, perhaps, with the sombre and severe character of the work within, but certainly striking and charming. As for the books themselves they are crown octavos, showing a broad imprint in good type, though with rather narrow margins, a rubricated title, and nine illustrations (full page) in each volume. "*The Wandering Jew*" is printed from new plates made from the original Chapman & Hall edition. This romance still holds its own as one of the immortal masterpieces of French literature. The text of the edition of "*Keats's Poetical Works*" is a reprint of the latest Forman edition. It contains every line of verse as far as is known that Keats ever wrote and a biographical sketch by Nathan Haskell Dole, and would seem a peculiarly appropriate gift to offer in Keats's centennial year; and the text of the "Complete Works of Thomas Moore" has been carefully edited and printed from the author's own original ten-volume edition of 1841, and the volumes contain a biographical sketch by Nathan Haskell Dole, with notes and index to first lines, and the best-loved of household poets has seldom appeared in more bewitching exterior finish. Other books in Crowell's *New Illustrated Library* are "*The Life of Christ,*" by Dean Farrar; "*The Life of Washington,*" by Washington Irving ; and "*The Scottish Chiefs,*" by Jane Porter, which has been the delight of successive generations. (Crowell. Ea., $3, $6.)

From "Correggio : His Life, His Friends, and His Time."   Charles Scribner's Sons.

COPY OF CORREGGIO'S "REDEEMER," BY ONE OF THE CARRACCI,

In the Vatican.

Correggio: His Life, His Friends, and His Time.—This is one of the most important art-works of the day, with sixteen full-page photogravure plates and nearly two hundred text illustrations. It is translated from the Italian of Dr. Corrado Ricci, the Curator of the Museum of Parma, who, by virtue of the many years of study he has devoted to Correggio, and the extraordinary facilities granted him by the Italian Government for this purpose, stands, naturally, as the first living authority on the subject. Besides the masterly study of Correggio's works the book presents the man in the curious surroundings in which he lived and draws a splendid and fascinating picture of his time. The illustrative material is varied and rich, forming of the volume a sumptuous art-work, uniform in style with the handsome "Life of Rembrandt" by Michel, issued two years ago. (Scribner. $12.)

The Tavern of Three Virtues.—This handsome book is made of a story of Charles Delorme, who wrote under the name of "St. Juirs," and sixty drawings by Daniel Vierge, together with a criticism of his art by Edmund Gosse and a portrait of Vierge as a frontispiece, and a title-page in two colors. No more beautiful present could be devised than this. Vierge is foremost among the illustrators of Paris. His exquisite drawings display a knowledge of form, of light, of shade, of architecture, expressed with a brilliancy of handling, which has never been equalled. This fascinating story is admirably adapted to illustration, and the result is a treat

to the book-lover. The binding of this beautiful work is worthy of its contents. In size it is a large thick quarto, and it is bound in a dark buff linen. The title is stamped in gold on the front side and back, which are almost entirely covered with an attractive design in gold, heavily embossed. (Stokes. $15.)

A Cyclopædia of Works of Architecture.—This elaborate and exhaustive work on architecture in Italy, Greece, and the Levant has been some years in preparation under the editorship of Mr. William P. P. Longfellow, whose name is a guarantee both of scrupulous accuracy and of literary excellence. No pains have been spared on the part of either publishers or editor to obtain the most exact and most recently determined data concerning the many hundreds of architectural monuments described, and the book is unique both in its scope and execution. The wealth of illustration not only illuminates the descriptive text but decorates it so effectively as to produce a superb and sumptuous volume, as well as a useful and instructive dictionary of the subject. The form and presentation of the work are in keeping with its unusual and ornate character, and constitute a fitting dress for a book that has a distinctly æsthetic as well as a purely scholarly side and purpose. A bibliography and complete glossary make the work indispensable to the student and practitioner and to the cultivated public. The work has twelve full-page photogravure plates and 250 illustrations. (Scribner. $25.)

From Gilbert White's "Selborne."   Copyright, 1895, by D. Appleton & Co.

AN OLD HOP-KILN.

Gilbert White's "Natural History of Selborne." —White's study of natural history, written a century ago, has been printed and reprinted in almost innumerable editions and in every conceivable size and shape. This year it is issued as a holiday book, with a charming introduction by John Burroughs, eighty illustrations by Clifton Johnson, and the text and new letters of the *Buckland* edition. The publishers have made a beautiful work in two volumes, which seems in every way calculated to be a satisfactory and final edition. They have shown fine discrimination in choosing Burroughs and Johnson to elucidate the old text with words and pictures. No two more competent men could well be imagined. In his delightful introduction the American naturalist says : "This book of Gilbert White's has a perennial charm. It is much like country things themselves. This is one secret of White's charm. The great world is afar off ; Selborne is as snug and secluded as a chimney corner ; we get an authentic glimpse into the real life of one man there ; we see him going about intent, lovingly intent, upon every phase of nature about him. We get glimpses into humble cottages and into the ways and doings of the people ; we see the bacon drying in the chimneys ; we see the poor gathering in Wolmer Forest the sticks and twigs dropped by the rooks in building their nests ; we see them claiming the 'lop and top' when big trees are cut. Indeed, the human touches, the human figures here and there in White's pages add much to the interest. The pictures of Mr. Johnson that illustrate this edition, taken as they were from the actual scenes, bring back the memory of my visit very vividly." The photographs and the drawings form in themselves a most delightful gallery of pictures of unspoiled English rural life. All who know

with it in size and in general style, and has received from the artist the same wealth of illustrations and from the publishers and printers the care and outlay which combined with the artist's work to make " Elizabethan Songs " "one of the most exquisite specimens of the book-maker's art ever produced." The " Victorian Songs " are confined to the lyrics of the affection and of nature, and they are ushered in by a very happy introduction by Edmund Gosse. Strange as it may appear, more verse of this species has appeared in the practical Victorian age than ever in the combined Elizabethan and Jacobean ages. The Victorian epoch has been of extraordinary length. It covers not a mere generation, but much more than half a century. The word " Victorian " is used in literature to distinguish what was written after the decline of that age, of which Walter Scott, Coleridge, and Wordsworth were the survivors. Tennyson, the Victorian writer *par excellence*, had published the most individual and characteristic of his lyrics before the queen ascended the throne. The selections in this exquisite volume are chosen from about fiftv poets. The "Victorian" age has been rich indeed in singers. All the favorites are represented. Truly a collection worth possessing that contains poems from Tennyson, Swinburne, Jean Ingelow, Adelaide Procter, Christina and Dante Gabriel Rossetti, Michael Field, Norman Gale, Bryan W. Proctor, and many other sweet singers. An *édition de luxe* is also ready, consisting of 250 numbered copies—225 copies on Japan paper, with proof of the full-page plates on Japan paper, and twenty-five copies on Japan paper, with proof-plates on Japan paper, an original water-color illustration by Mr. Garrett, and preliminary title embellished with a water-color design by the artist. (Little, Brown & Co. $6–$30.)

Mr. Clifton Johnson's rare talent at catching the salient points of rural life either in animate or inanimate objects will feel certain that a rare treat awaits those who come into possession of this very beautiful combination of word-pictures and pictured words. The "Observations on Nature," which occupied the genial parson and his intimate friends for several years, are also included in these handsome volumes. This new edition cannot be neglected by any one who cares for nature or for the classics of English literature. (Appleton. 2 v. $4.)

Garrett's Victorian Songs. —Mr. Garrett's collection of " Elizabethan Songs " was universally pronounced beyond question the most beautiful holiday book in many years. It has proved to be, in addition, an acceptable volume at all seasons. The companion volume here described, "Victorian Songs," is made uniform

Tales of a Traveller, Buckthorne Edition.—Our native American fiction began with Irving. When to novelty in theme and form was added the easy serenity of an assured and confident literary touch, American fiction had clearly passed beyond the stage of apology and curiosity. All that lay within Irving, as far as the writing of fiction was concerned, he gave us; and that his success was no accident, but the nice adjustment of mind to theme, is shown by the fact that, in their way, the English sketches are as good as the American. In the many-toned "Tales of a Traveller" he showed more than almost in anything else he had written the sympathy and observant faculty which must belong to the true novelist. At first they met with severe criticism, but little by little the reading world has begun to see how much was really said in those apparently light narratives which showed close study of the life of England, France, and America in the troubled years the stories describe. The second part of these "Tales of the Traveller" is a sort of autobiography of Buckthorne, a dear old genial *cicerone* who introduces the traveller into the literary society of the day in London and makes many charming comments on the ways, methods, and characters of authors and writers. From this character the *Buckthorne* edition has been named. It is uniform in general style with the holiday editions of "The Alhambra," "Granada," "Knickerbocker," and "Sketch-Book," printed from new type, with artistically designed borders by George Wharton Edwards, and 25 illustrations from designs by Arthur Rackham, Allan Barraud, F. S. Church, George Wharton Edwards, Henry Sandham, Frederick Dielman, and others, and published in two large volumes

with ornamental borders. Young people should read Washington Irving. His style is as smooth as that of Addison or Goldsmith, he is full of the kindliest humor, and he introduces his readers into thoroughly good company, where they learn refinement of thought and deed in every sentence. (Putnam. 2 v., $6, $12.)

Illustrated Edition of "The Manxman."—Few stories lend themselves so readily to illustration as those of Hall Caine, and certainly the publishers have not gone astray in choosing this immensely popular novel to make into their leading holiday gift-book this year by illustrating its fascinating text with forty gelatin prints of actual scenes in the Isle of Man, which were selected by the author himself as the most characteristic scenes in his marvellously successful book. "In the little Isle of Man is unfolded," says *The Athenæum*, "a drama of grandiose dimensions, whether we regard the lapse of time which it occupies, the actions and passions of the principal characters, or the startling nature of the incidents and episodes in which it abounds." All the world has read "The Manxman" In this new edition charming pictures are given of the Manx harvest-home and the wedding ceremonials and the many delightful evidences of a minute and faithful study of the Manx manners and superstitions. The *édition de luxe* of "The Manxman" is in two volumes, bound in white vellum, and is limited to 250 copies, all signed by the author. Not one in a hundred of the many who will try their best to come into possession of this ideal holiday book can therefore hope to attain their wishes. (Appleton. 2 v., $15.)

From "Tales of a Traveller."   Copyright, 1895, by G. P. Putnam's Sons.

"THE OLD HALL ECHOED TO BURSTS OF ROBUSTIOUS FOX-HUNTING MERRIMENT."

Constantinople.—Edwin A. Grosvenor, Professor of European History at Amherst College, has written a very interesting work on Constantinople, which Roberts Brothers have brought out as a most sumptuous gift-book in two volumes, with an introduction by General Lew Wallace, an expert on Constantinople since his studies for "The Prince of India," and 250 Wallace and Professor Grosvenor worked over the city together through years, the former to collect material for "The Prince of India," the latter for the preparation of this book. Constantinople, in natural beauty, advantageous situation, and political importance, is the queen of the world. Everybody is interested in it; everybody has some idea of it. Yet there is no

From Grosvenor's "Constantinople."   Copyright, 1895, by Roberts Brothers.

THE YUSEK KALDERIM.

illustrations of important places, rulers, and noted people of Ancient Constantinople. Professor Grosvenor is an enthusiastic and laborious student, a long-time resident in Constantinople, familiar with its languages and customs, possessing warm friends of every rank in every nationality and of every creed, with doors open to him which are commonly shut, and no man could be better equipped for the task he had undertaken. Nor did he make his studies and researches alone, without the incentive of congenial and inspiring companionship. General Lew other European capital which is so little known. Its multiplicity of races, languages, and religions, and the peculiar, complicated variety of its history, have rendered real acquaintance almost impossible. This book endeavors to picture as much of the wonderful, cosmopolitan city as can be painted on 800 pages. It is a book for all who have interest in the world outside their own doors, for the unlearned and the learned, for the traveller, and for him who stays at home. The author has had every possible advantage. (Roberts. 2 v., $10; hf. mor., $14.)

From "Uncle Remus."   —— Copyright, 1895, by D. Appleton & Co.

Other Holiday Gift-Books.

Uncle Remus.—"There is but one 'Uncle Remus,'" says the *Commercial Advertiser*, "and he will never grow old. However, he appears this coming season in new and luxurious attire, for Mr. Joel Chandler Harris's masterpiece is brought out in a new edition, wherein are found 112 drawings by the one man best fitted for such work—Mr. A. B. Frost. It was a happy thought, that of marrying the work of Harris and Frost, and the Appletons are to be congratulated thereupon. Frost's unfailing individuality, his instant realization of types, his quaint and unexpected turns of humor, incline us to look forward with the greatest interest to this new edition of 'Uncle Remus.' There is also an *édition de luxe*, printed from new plates, containing the new pictures and rich in all the wealth of large paper and wide margins, each copy of which will be signed by the author. We are informed that this is the final, the definitive edition of Mr. Harris's masterpiece." "'Uncle Remus,' after its fifteen years of popularity," says the New York *Times*, "is found in this new edition more valuable than ever, because we are further removed by just so many years from opportunities of studying the type that has been so accurately represented by the author's extraordinary skill. Mr. Frost's pictures of animals would be an additional charm to almost any book, and in the present instance they breathe the very spirit of the text." (Appleton. $2.)

New Popular Edition of "The Three Musketeers."—By their arrangements with the French publishers, Messrs. D. Appleton & Co. are able to present a popular edition of this classic romance with Leloir's original illustrations. These illustrations are printed directly from the French blocks, and their superiority to cheap reproductions gives this authorized edition a unique value. There can be no edition equal to this in the quality of the illustrations or in the care which has been bestowed upon the translation, and it is safe to say that the final and standard English edition of "The Three Musketeers" is now presented to the public. A letter from Alexandre Dumas, *fils*, explaining the history of this world-renowned book and also giving interesting details of his celebrated father's methods, accompanies this edition. (Appleton. 2 v., $4.)

Miss K. P. Wormeley's Translations of Balzac and Molière.—The new volumes of "Balzac Novels" include "A Start in Life," "The Marriage Contract," "Beatrix," and "The Daughter of Eve." This set now numbers thirty-four volumes (*ea.*, hf. russia, $1.50). The fourth volume in the new translation of the plays of Molière, by Miss Katherine P. Wormeley, contains "L'Avare," "Don Juan," and "Les Fâcheux." It is now 227 years since "L'Avare" was first presented on the stage. "Don Juan" appeared three years later, in 1665, and "Les Fâcheux" in 1661. The frontispiece of the volume is an etched portrait of Molière printed in sepia tint. It is a handsome edition, worthy of a place in a library of standards. (Roberts. 4 v., *ea.*, $1.50.)

"Stops of Various Quills," by W. D. Howells," says the *Mail and Express*, "is a remarkable book, concerning which there will probably be considerable difference of opinion among readers of current verse, though there ought to be none, and will be none among those who are capable of looking beyond and below mere poetic technique into the thing which is poetry itself—the thought which is in the poet's mind, the feeling which is in his heart, and which, whether he has captured it in his verse, or whether it has evaded him, is individual, vital, inevitable. Mr. Howells has given us here a remarkable book, as we have said, and one which we would select as an infallible touchstone of the poetic knowledge or ignorance of its readers. If they are enamoured of perfect technique, it may not please them; but if they know what poetry is, apart from its technique, they will be profoundly touched by it and will return to it again and again." The illustrations are by Howard Pyle. There is also an *édition de luxe*, limited to fifty copies, each signed by Mr. Howells and Mr. Pyle, with illustrations printed in sepia, and the full-page illustrations on Japan proofs in black. (Harper. $2.50, $15.)

The Courtship of Miles Standish.—The Song of Hiawatha.—New and cheaper editions of both these favorite songs of Early American life are brought out this season and make fabulously cheap and very beautiful presentation volumes. "The Courtship of Miles Standish" is illustrated by ten artists, George H. Boughton, F. T. Merrill, C. S. Reinhart, Grandville Perkins, D. C. Hitchcock, S. H. Shapleigh, J. D. Smillie, J. E. Baker, Charles Copeland, and S. L. Smith. Some of the most interesting and valuable of the ornamentations given to the volume are contained in Mr. Copeland's head and tail pieces. ($1.50.) "The Song of Hiawatha" is preceded by a portait of Mr. Longfellow as he appeared in 1840, when still young and quite beardless. The other illustrations, which number twenty or more, are from designs by Frederic Remington. The poem was first published in 1855, as is explained in an introductory note, which also gives a number of historical facts in regard to the circumstances under which it was written. The illustrations very much enhance the poem and lend interest to the text of this curiously original and rhythmic Indian song. (Houghton, Mifflin & Co. $2.)

Malta Edition of "Midshipman Easy."—There is something untamed and untamable about the sea which is peculiarly fascinating; there is a sense of grandeur and vastness which is instructive. This feeling is, in large part, lost nowadays, when the sea is traversed by swift steamships, but in the period described by Captain Marryat in his famous story, "Mr. Midshipman Easy," when vessels were propelled by the mysterious force of the winds, when they were so largely at the mercy of the storm or the calm, those who went "down to the sea in ships" were more conscious of its wonders. The *Malta edition* of this standard sea-tale has been finely illustrated by R. F. Zogbaum, the well-known marine artist, and has very pretty head and tail pieces by A. W. Van Deusen. Mr. Zogbaum has given a series of stirring pictures, rendering still more attractive the narrative of the author, itself so engrossing, with its thrilling adventures, rollicking good-humor, and dramatic incidents. (Putnam. $2.50.)

Five Series of Dainty Books.—G. P. Putnam's Sons have brought together a selection of famous books which they distribute in four series. *The Elia Series* (6 v., printed on deckel-edge paper, with gilt tops, and bound in full ooze calf, in dark green, garnet, or amber, *ea.*, $2.25). *Contents:* Group 1, "The Essays of Elia," 2 v.; "A Selection of the Discourses of Epictetus" with "The Encheiridion"; "Sesame and Lilies;" "The Autobiography of Benjamin Franklin;" and "The Thoughts of the Emperor Marcus Aurelius Antoninus." 2. *The Stories of the Ages,* uniform with *The Elia Series.* *Contents:* Group 1, "Select Tales from the Gesta Romanorum;" "Headlong Hall and Nightmare Abbey;" "Cranford;" "Tales by Heinrich Zschökke;" "The Rose and the Ring;" "Undine;" and "Sintram and His Companions." (*Ea.*, $2.25.) 3, *The World's Classics,* a reissue in less expensive form of the more important volumes published under the title of *The Knickerbocker Nuggets* (39 v.,16mo, *ea.*, 50 c.). 4, *The Ballads of the Nations,* comprising a set of nine volumes, possessing value as reflecting the thought of the peoples. Profusely illustrated. (9 v., sq. 16mo, *ea.*, 75 c.); and, 5, *The Fly Leaves Series,* initiated by Calverley's "Fly Leaves," and now followed by Thackeray's "Novels by Eminent Hands" and Bayard Taylor's "The Echo Club." (Putnam. 3 v., 16mo, in box, *ea.*, $1.75.)

The Echoes of the Playhouse.—Many books have been written upon the stage, but Mr. Robins has an excellent excuse for adding yet another volume to the number. His "Echoes of the Playhouse" is written in an unconventional way; he has attempted nothing pretentious, and has carefully avoided dry or technical details. Authorities have been quoted liberally and judiciously, and the volume should appeal to both the layman and the professional. The illustrations are for the most part reproductions of quaint old engravings. (Putnam. $2.)

Nymphs, Nixies and Naiads.—A dainty volume of poems by M. A. B. Evans, author of "In Various Moods," with illustrations by William A. McCullough, comes just in time for the Christmas shoppers. Its charm is hard to explain. Rare sympathy with Nature and an imagination fired by all her many mystic sounds are gifts Miss Evans showed in her first musical collection, of which this is a fitting successor. (Putnam. $1.25.)

F. A. Stokes & Co.'s Fiction.—The publishers' first aim has been to secure works of human and contemporaneous interest. Preference has also been given to writers who deal with the incident and the romance of life rather than to the exponents of metaphysical and psychological problems. They believe that such good stories are worthy of attractive dress, and consequently these books are of convenient size, well printed, and tastefully bound. Quite a long list is ready for Christmas shoppers. Specially noticeable are the books of William Le Queux, "Zoraida" and "Stolen Souls." The author was born in London of a French father and English mother, and as his first leanings were toward art he spent some time in the Latin Quarter in Paris. He wrote a Russian story entitled "Guilty Bonds," and since then every scrap bearing his name has been ruthlessly blocked out by the Russian censor. During the past few years his really remarkable work has begun to be appreciated. The Stokes have published his "Zoraida," a story of the Harem and the Great Sahara, full of adventure and mystery, very appropriately illustrated. Mr. Le Queux made a dangerous journey over the Sahara to collect this material ($1.50). A series of stories of adventure showing his peculiar talent is entitled "Stolen Souls" ($1). Very excellent works of fiction are "The Grasshoppers," by Mrs. Andrew Dean; "Annie of Argyle, or, cavalier and covenant" ($1); "Lakewood," by Mary Harriott Norris, a description of the brilliant social life of that very popular winter resort ($1); "Bohemia Invaded," by James L. Ford, the brilliant writer of "The Literary Shop" (50 c.); "Sinners Twain," a story of the great Lone Land, by John Mackie, etc. (75 c.). These novels of the Stokes should be examined. All their books are noted for delicate workmanship, and these novels are very tempting in their colored buckram covers. Most of the books are illustrated with half-tone engravings. (F. A. Stokes Co. 50 c.—$1.50.)

Westminster.—As in the book entitled "London," of which this is the successor, Sir Walter Besant does not pretend to offer a history of Westminster. The story of the Abbey buildings, of the great functions held in the Abbey, of the monuments in the Abbey, may be found in the pages of Stanley, Loftie, Dart, and Widmore. The history of the houses of parliament belongs to the history of the country, not that of Westminster. It has been his endeavor, in these pages, (1) to show, contrary to received opinion, that the Isle of Bramble was a busy place of trade long before London existed at all. (2) To restore the vanished palaces of Westminster and Whitehall. (3) To portray the life of the Abbey, with its services, its rule, its anchorites, and its sanctuary. (4) To show the connection of Westminster with the first of English printers. And, lastly, to present the place as a town and borough, with its streets and its people. The publishers have made a fine book, with many most interesting illustrations by William Patten and others. (Stokes. $3; full gilt, $4.)

From "Lyrics of Love and Nature."   Copyright, 1895, by Frederick A. Stokes Co.

"A LOVE SONG."

choice poems relating to the ballet and the stage, illustrated by twelve fac-similes of water-color designs of the ballet by Ellen G. Emmet, one for each month of the year. Accompanying these are designs of the twelve precious stones representing the different months. Miss Emmet's pictures are very dainty and entirely unlike anything previously published. Exquisitely gotten up in three styles of binding, all equally pretty. (Stokes. $2.50, $3, $3.50.)

Volney Streamer's A Cluster of Gems.—A collection of

Lyrics of Love and Nature.—These poems by Mary Berri Chapman have almost all appeared in the *Century* and other well-known magazines, where they attracted considerable attention by their strength and beauty. They have pretty cuts in half-tone to set off their musical words, also the work of the talented author. A variety of bindings have been given the book. (Stokes. $1.50; $3)

Harper's Illustrated Descriptive Books. — "From the Black Sea Through Persia and India" consists of pictures of Eastern life in desert and bazaar, and is a volume unique in scope—the outcome of a long journey undertaken by Edwin Lord Weeks in consequence of an arrangement with Harper & Brothers. The readers of *Harper's Magazine,* in which appeared from time to time the articles now incorporated in this volume, do not require to be told how successfully Mr. Weeks has represented in picture and text some of the most fascinating scenes that the East has to offer. ($3.50.) And another beautiful volume, so timely that it may be said to have been born under a lucky star, will be naturally associated with the foregoing. It is the "Notes in Japan," by Alfred Parsons—exquisite studies of mountain and grove and temple, of flower and of quaint humanity, in a land that, suddenly and unexpectedly commanding attention, is now receiving it in large measure from all the world. The volume contains a few fresh illustrations, in addition to the series already published in *Harper's Magazine.* ($3.) "Pony Tracks," written and illustrated by Frederic Remington, chiefly devoted to camp life and sporting life in the West, is wholly charming and delightful. The text is blood-curdling at times, the illustrations profuse and very good, the print, paper, binding, etc., sumptuous. ($3.) All three of these beautiful books are illustrated by their authors, with pictures made while the experiences were fresh, and wholly different from the work of professional illustrators. Constance Fenimore Woolson has written a book on "Mentone, Cairo, and Corfu," with a novelist's privilege of letting the information conveyed come from the lips of imaginary travellers, who notice all the details of customs, occupations, and manners of the inhabitants and make vivid and often amusing comments ($1.75); Richard Harding Davis tells us "About Paris," and his descriptions of many "points" which escape the eyes of the general tourist are supplemented with excellent illustrations by Charles Dana Gibson ($1.25); the storm and stress of our Western borderland are realized in "Red Men and White," dramatic tales of adventure by Owen Wister, with illustrations by Frederic Remington ($1.50); Julian Ralph's studies of people on the East Side in New York City are now collected in a volume bearing the title "People We Pass" ($1.25); and "Dixie," a valuable and entertaining series of Southern scenes and sketches, is by the same author ($1.25).

John Galt's Novels. — "Roberts Brothers are issuing the 'Works of John Galt' in neat form, beautifully printed and illustrated. The two volumes before us contain 'Annals of the Parish' and the 'Ayrshire Legatees,' which are generally considered the best of Galt's Scotch novels, if they may be called such, with an introduction by Mr. S. R. Crockett and a memoir. The works are edited by Mr. D. Storrar Meldrum. Leisurely readers who like Scotch dialect, quiet humor, quaint and simple pictures of country life, and all that goes into the making of good old-time humdrum literature," says the *Independent,* "will be delighted with this excellent edition of Galt's works. Mr. Crockett's introductory sketch is a cleverly written bit of appreciation cast into graceful form and is, moreover, an excellent piece of light criticism in which Galt's measure is correctly taken. Mr. Crockett does not range Galt, as some English critics have tried to do, on a level with Scott, but gives him a place by himself as a happy, gossipy chronicler and letter-writer who could photograph a country parson to perfection and depict the country life of his time with precise yet interminable truthfulness." (Roberts. 8 v., *ea.,* $1.25.)

Henry Kingsley's Novels. — Ward, Lock & Bowden have ready for the holidays the now completed edition, in twelve volumes, of "Henry Kingsley's Novels," edited by Clement K. Shorter, with frontispieces by well-known artists. The twelfth volume, entitled "The Boy in Grey, and other stories," contains a biographical sketch of Henry Kingsley by his nephew, Maurice Kingsley, who by such eminent critics as James Payn, Andrew Lang, Augustus Birrell, and many others is held to have been far better as a novelist than his brother Charles, whose novels were somewhat spoiled from a literary standpoint by their important purpose. Although written a generation ago, Henry Kingsley's novels appeal to the most modern readers. Many of the stories have met with less favor than the more popular ones, but in this new uniform edition will again be read in their chronological sequence with his great successes, "Geoffrey Hamlyn," "Ravenshoe," "The Hillyars and the Burtons," "The Silcotes of Silcote," etc., and may perhaps receive a totally new distribution of relative rank by a generation of readers judging them solely on their merits and not by the reputation of the author at the time they appeared. This set of novels in handsome three-quarter morocco makes as satisfying an addition to a library as can be thought of. (Ward, Lock & Bowden. 12 v., *ea.,* $1.25; three-quarter mor., only in sets, $32.50.)

Little, Brown & Co.'s Dumas, George Sand, and Charles Lever. — In response to repeated requests Messrs. Little, Brown & Company have issued, in continuation of their standard edition of the Romances of the incomparable Dumas, six more new volumes. "Ascanio" and "The War of Women" ("La Guerre des Femmes") are among the great novelist's well-known works, and the publishers have received numerous inquiries regarding them. "Black, the Story of a Dog," and "Tales of the Caucasus" have never before been translated, but will without question commend themselves to the lovers of Dumas. (6 v., $9, $18.) George Sand's masterpieces, "François, the Waif," "The Devil's Pool," "Fadette," and "The Master Mosaic-Workers" are made into beautiful editions, which must be seen to be appreciated. There is a plain edition, a limited edition, and an *édition de luxe,* sumptuously fitted out (4 v., $6–$40); "The Novels of Adventure," by Charles Lever, with twenty etched plates by "Phiz" and E. Van Muyden, are now ready for Christmas shoppers. (6 v., $15–$39.)

G. P. Putnam's Sons' Famous Novels. —The new issues for the holiday season of 1895 in the series of "Famous Novels" are the *Waldering* edition of "At Odds," by the Baroness Tautphœus, and the *Fontainebleau* edition of "Richelieu," by G. P. R. James. The series now includes six works, comprising thirteen volumes;

the four earlier issues being as follows : " Lorna Doone : a romance of Exmoor," by R. D. Blackmore ; "The Initials," by the Baroness Tautphœus ; "The Home, or, life in Sweden," by Fredrika Bremer; and "Quits," by the Baroness Tautphœus. (*Ea.*, 2 v., in box, $2.50.)

The Heroes of the Nations Series.—In this excellent series have recently been issued four volumes of exceptional interest: "Julian, Philosopher and Emperor," by Alice Gardner ; "Louis XIV.," by Arthur Hassell; "Life of Charles XII.," by R. Nisbet Bain, and "Lorenzo de' Medici," by Edward Armstrong. The series now numbers sixteen volumes, all fully illustrated. (Putnam. *Ea.*, $1.50.)

The Story of the Nations Series. — Many years will undoubtedly pass ere a more important series of historical works will be successfully planned and carried out than *The Story of the Nations.* The plan of this series, which now comprises forty-four volumes, is to present, in graphic narratives prepared by competent historians, the stories of the different nations that have attained prominence in history. The latest volumes are "The Story of the Crusades," by T. A. Archer and Charles Kingsford, and "The Story of Vedic India," by Z. A. Ragozin. All illustrated. (*Ea.*, $1.50.)

The Doom of the Holy City. Christ and Cæsar.—Lydia Hoyt Farmer gives a picture of Jerusalem and Rome in the first century. The historical and fictitious characters, alike Jewish and Roman, are set forth with a vivid realism, while a domestic romance enlivens the shadows of the dark, historic background. The work has required painstaking research, and is full of thrilling incidents, as the characters, real and fictitious, participate in the scenes connected with the fall of the Holy City. Graphic pictures are also given of Roman life. The work is not only a romance but a carefully compiled history as well of the political, religious, and social life of the period. (Randolph. $1.50.)

Palmyra and Zenobia.—Dr. William Wright's comely volume entitled "Palmyra and Zenobia" is about evenly compounded of history, archæology, and travels. In the way of history the author naturally does not attempt to add much to what the early historians have told us of Zenobia's disastrous conflict with the Romans ; but he has nevertheless availed himself to some extent of current popular traditions, a source to which he inclines to ascribe more weight than

his predecessors have done. The explorations and incidents recorded are the fruit of a nine years' sojourn in Syria; and as the writing was done on the spot, partly in the saddle and partly in the tent, it is unusually fresh, crisp, and full

From "Heroes of the Nations."

LORENZO DE' MEDICI.

of local color. Half the volume is devoted to the ruins of Palmyra and the story of Zenobia, and the remainder to travels and adventures in Bashan and the desert. The illustrations are profuse and of much archæological interest. (Nelson. $2.50.)

Constantinople.—No living writer in English has wider knowledge of Constantinople from personal investigation than Mr. Crawford, and this book presents in condensed form all of his information in regard to that city. It is written in his most charming narrative style, so that it is admirable alike for its picturesque descriptions and for the clear manner in which it summarizes information not accessible elsewhere. The illustrations, which are the work of Edwin Lord Weeks, the greatest artist of Oriental subjects that America has produced, were drawn directly from nature and expressly for Mr. Crawford's text. (Scribner. $1.50.)

Algerian Memories.—Fanny Bullock Workman and William Hunter Workman have written an interesting account of a bicycle tour in the spring of 1894, extending the entire length of Algeria, from Oran and Plemcen on the west to the Tunisian frontier on the east, and south over the mountains to the desert. Attention is called to the beauty and grandeur of the natural scenery at different points, to the habits and customs of the people, to the important Roman remains at Tebessa, Timgad, and other places, historical facts connected with them, and to certain vivid experiences and adventures of the authors. Four chapters are devoted to the remarkable region of the Grande Kabylie, and to the history and customs of its interesting inhabitants, including an account of the life and capture of the famous brigand, Areski. (Randolph. $2.)

Little Rivers.—Dr. Van Dyke's book, which he calls "Essays in Profitable Idleness," consists of delightful sketches of outdoor life and impressions of travels, embodying the reflections of a cultivated, keen, and sympathetic observer of nature, in his rambles through the

From "Algerian Memories." Copyright, 1895, by A. D. F. Randolph & Co.

A JEWISH CHILD OF CONSTANTINE.

woods and fields in various climes, on foot and in canoes. The pages are full of unconventional observations of nature and life, and cheerful, blue-sky philosophy; beautifully illustrated by Edmund H. Garrett. (Scribner. $2.)

A. D. F. Randolph & Co's Holiday Books.— "The Chronicles of Uganda," by Rev. R. P. Ashe, is a faithful and impartial account of Uganda, its inhabitants, its resources, and its possibilities, with a portrait and twenty-six illustrations ($2); "Antipas, Son of Chuza, and others whom Jesus loved," by Louise Seymour Houghton, is a book full of hopeful religion, with fifteen full-page illustrations ($1.50); and "A (Vest) Pocket History of the Presidents of the United States," by Thomas Rand, contains a portrait of each President, a biographical sketch, the date of his election to office, and the principal features of each administration (25 c.). New editions are also ready of the old favorites —"Christmastide in Song and Story" (2 v., $2); "Pictures of Swedish life" ($3.75); "In Cairo and Jerusalem," by Mary Thorne Carpenter ($1.50); and "Gypsying Beyond the Sea," by William Bement Lent (2 v., $3). (Randolph.)

Ward, Lock & Bowden's Holiday Books.— A work eminently suitable for presentation is "The Poets' Bible," in two parts, covering the Old and New Testament sections of the Bible, a collection of verses by noted poets dealing with all the great scenes and promises and prophesies of the Bible, a most valuable collection of religious poems very neatly gotten up in simple bindings of rich color (*ea.*, $1.25); "Home Carpentry for Handy Men," by Francis Chilton-Young, with upward of 500 illustrations, is a book that would make many people who are handy with tools and full of ideas for beautifying a home perfectly delighted to gain possession of ($3); and "Practical Palmistry," by Henry Frith, with forty explanatory diagrams, appeals to almost an equally large number of people, although they must be of totally distinct character (50 c.). Good novels are also on the list of this house. "A Man's Foes," by Mrs. E. H. Strain, tells with masterly skill a tale of the siege of Londonderry in 1689, when the old-fashioned manufacturing city of Derry was so successfully defended by the Irish Protestants against James II. ($1); "Thrasna River" is the story of a townland of Australia, by John Farmer, with full-page illustrations by St. Clair Simmons, and there are many more excellent stories, titles of which appear in the list elsewhere ($1.50); and "The Story of a Baby," by Miss Ethel Turner, is a study of the results of selfishness in married life that must make its way to the front if merit far above the average and fine literary ability are any factors in success ($1).

Philip Gilbert Hamerton's Books.—Beautiful editions have been prepared of "Painting in France," covering the period after the decline of classicism, an exhaustive essay illustrated with fourteen photogravures after celebrated modern French artists ($3); and "Contemporary French Painters," an essay illustrated with sixteen photogravures after Ary Scheffer, Delaroche, Ingres, Meissonier, Bouguereau, Gérôme, etc. ($3); and there is also a volume devoted to "Imagination in Landscape Painting," with many illustrations and etched frontispiece. (Roberts. $2.)

The Faïence Library.—T. Y. Crowell & Co. have in this library, which is to include twelve little sixteenmo volumes, in either cloth or leather bindings, a new line of literary gems, carefully edited and printed, with wide margins, photogravure frontispieces, and attractive title-pages; they are daintily illustrated and bound, being in every respect models of book-making. The volumes thus far ready are "*The Faïence Violin,*" by Champfleury, translated by Helen B. Dole, which takes its place with the most highly finished masterpieces of the eighteenth century; "*La Belle Nivernaise,*" and other stories," by Alphonse Daudet, translated by Huntingdon Smith; and "*L'Avril,*" by Paul Margueritte, translated from the French by Nathan Haskell Dole, with charming descriptions of southern France. Other volumes to be added will include "*L'Abbé Constantin,*" by Halévy; "*L'Abbé Daniel,*" by Theuriet; "*Cranford,*" "*Light of Asia,*" "*Lucile,*" Lamb's "*Tales from Shakespeare,*"Daudet's "*Tartarin of Tarascon*" and "*Tartarin on the Alps,*" and "*The Vicar of Wakefield.*" (Crowell. *Ea.,* $1, $1.50.)

The Hawthorne Tree, and Other Poems. — For upward of twenty years Mr. Nathan Haskell Dole has been an occasional contributor to the pages of the *Century, The Independent,* and other periodicals. Many of his songs have been set to music. He has culled out from a large number of his published verses a representative collection of songs, sonnets, *vers de société,* and more serious pieces, making a dainty volume which will prove welcome to those who like simple, melodious poetry, untouched by the *fin-de-siècle* decadentism. The songs are spontaneous, unaffected utterances, the *vers de société* are unpretentious bits of fun, and the sonnets and other poems are for the most part marked by a cheerful optimism. They have received the warm encomiums of such judges as Mrs. Louise Chandler Moulton and Mr.

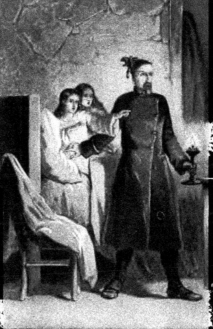

From "The Wandering Jew."

THE ALARM.

Arlo Bates, who indeed kindly helped to make the selection. (Crowell. Hf. leath., gilt top, $1.25.)

Shakespeare's Heroines on the Stage.—"A book that lovers of the drama will be sure to esteem highly, and in fact a really valuable contribution to the literature of English and American theatrical history presents a systematic account of "Shakespeare's Heroines on the Stage," by Chas. E. L. Wingate "It is an extended and brilliant galaxy of talent that Mr. Wingate reviews," says *The Beacon,* "for not only all the famous actresses of the past century and a half come within the range of his animated chronicle, but those prominent at the present day — Miss Renan, Miss Ward, Mrs. Potter, Mrs. Langtry, Miss Terry, and Miss Marlowe — are the themes of graceful and piquant comment. Mr. Wingate has the secret of disguising a vast amount of erudition under a manner that has an almost Gallic lightness and vivacity of coloring. His book is immensely readable, from the first page to the last, and it abounds in a variety of data practically inaccessible to any one who does not make a special study of theatrical annals. Of the fifty-three full-page portraits included in the volume most are copied from rare prints. The book is handsomely printed and tastefully and attractively bound." (Crowell. $2.)

The Tower, With Legends and Lyrics.—"Mrs. Emma Huntington Nason's poems," says the N. Y. *Times,* "are above the average verse that is so copiously launched upon the market. The author displays a warm and delicate fancy, and writes with a singularly happy choice of words and figures. Most of the poems in this volume show deep womanly feeling, but the touch in some of them is almost masculine in its boldness." (Houghton, Mifflin & Co. $1.25.)

A Victorian Anthology.—Mr. Edmund Clarence Stedman's "Victorian Anthology" has finally appeared from the press of Messrs. Houghton, Mifflin & Company, in a sumptuous octavo of 744 pages, with all the typographical convenience and graces for which these Boston

From Mrs. Jameson's Works.   Copyright, 1895, by
                 Houghton, Mifflin & Co.

MAGDALENE (LUCAS VAN LEYDEN).

publishers have long been noted. The "Anthology," as the qualifying adjective indicates, is limited in its scope to the yield of one nation during a single reign; its aim is "not to offer a collection of absolutely flawless poems, long since become classics and accepted as models," but to present "a truthful exhibit of the course of song during the last sixty years, as shown by the poets of Great Britain in the best of their shorter productions." In other words, while standing on its own feet, and on independent compilation, the "Anthology" is designed to supplement Mr. Stedman's "Victorian Poets"—a fact which leads us to hope that Mr. Stedman will find the time to supplement his "American Poets" by a similarly planned collection of illustrative selections. The "Anthology" is made to subserve its educational purpose still more completely by containing an appendix of concise bibliographical notes. "The 'Anthology' excellently supplements 'The Victorian Poets,'" says the Philadelphia *Telegraph.* ($2.50–$10.)

Robert Browning in One Volume.—"The Riverside Press, which has rendered so much genuine service to American literature, has done nothing better in its way," says *The Outlook,* "than the publication of one-volume standard editions of the poets. The latest body of verse which has appeared in the Cambridge edition is that of 'Robert Browning.' The publishers have succeeded in making an octavo of over a thousand pages of very comfortable weight.

The thin paper is opaque, and the text stands out on the double-column page with entire distinctness. Like its predecessors, this volume is notable for intelligence and completeness of editorial treatment. It not only contains the entire poetical work of Browning, but also reproduces his essay on Shelley, and it furnishes a biographical sketch, a series of notes, and complete indexes of titles and first lines. The volume is very appropriately prefaced by a new portrait of the poet, and the title-page is enriched with a vignette view of Asolo, which Browning loved so well, and which all his readers have come to know so well. The verse in this volume is, with one or two exceptions, arranged in chronological order. Very many of the poems are prefaced by head-notes giving interesting information with regard to their origin; and the whole volume, in its completeness and dignity, seems to us quite above criticism." (Houghton, Mifflin & Co. $3.)

Last Poems of James Russell Lowell.—"Charles Eliot Norton, who edited this slender volume of bequests from Mr. Lowell's muse, might have been less chary," says the N. Y. *Times,* "of words in his introductory note. He states that the book contains those of the author's latest poems which he himself might have wished to preserve. 'Three of them were published before his death. Of the rest, two appear here for the first time.' There is some doubt as to one of these two. The other is, of course, 'On a Bust of General Grant,' for the editor tells us in an appended note that 'this poem is the last, so far as is known, written by Mr. Lowell.' The posthumous poems of a writer so much beloved by the general public and so especially dear to the disciples of true culture as Mr. Lowell was deserved a little more generous accompaniment. No doubt Mr. Norton feared to obtrude too much of himself in a book of such small content, but it is hardly likely that any reader would have accused him of immodesty. The poems themselves are precious examples of Mr. Lowell's verse. They embody some of its very best characteristics." (Houghton, Mifflin & Co)

James Pott & Co.'s Holiday Books.—A new holiday edition is again made ready of Henry Drummond's "The Greatest Thing in the World," bound in white cloth, with cover design by Miss Knauft; and still another pretty booklet is "Little Bet," by Eliza Dean Taylor, the author of "A Cup of Loving Service." Not strictly of holiday nature, but calculated to please people who love natural lives and enjoy the quiet of nature, is a new work of fiction by Rentoul Esler, entitled "'Mid Green Pastures," made up of eight short stories, bringing home the great fact that the tragedies of life are enacted quite as often beneath the mask of a stolid exterior and "'mid green pastures" as they are in the glare of city lights. Pott & Co. run a long line of Bagster's Bibles, and the Cambridge editions of the Book of Common Prayer and of the Hymnal, all printed from entirely new plates, on pure white paper, light in weight and opaque, bound by B. Collins & Son in every variety of style, all equally beautiful as to finish and design. "The Bagster's Teachers' Bible," with colored illustrations, printed in gold color and monotint, is one of the most suitable presents for Sunday-school teachers and advanced students

Professor Geikie's Works. — James Pott & Company are publishing a most valuable work in Cunningham Geikie's "The Apostles: their lives and letters," of which two volumes are ready. The style of this learned scholar is so easy that the general reader can learn much and enjoy thoroughly while reading his fascinating pages. The first volume covers the story of the first Christians from Pentecost A.D. 30 to spring of A.D. 55, with the Epistles of St. James and 1st and 2d Thessalonians and many illustrations given in elucidation ; the second volume treats of Christianity from A.D. 55 to A.D. 64, and gives the Epistles to the Galatians, Romans, and Ephesians. This volume contains a most elaborate study of St. Paul (2 v., *ea.,* $1.50). Other works of Geikie's, "Hours with the Bible" (6 v., $7.50; hf. cf., $12), 'The Gospels" ($1.50), and "The Holy Land and the Bible" (2 v., $5), are also published by this house.

" ' *Studies in Theologic Definition Underlying the Apostles' and Nicene Creeds,'* by Frederic Palmer, is a helpful book," says the N. Y. *Commercial Advertiser.* " Any work that assists the doubter to obtain even a partial understanding of the mysteries of the Christian religion must have great value. Mr. Palmer, in his preface, dated from ' Christ Church Rectory, Andover, Mass.,' says : ' In these studies I have had in mind especially those persons who have felt a difference between the tone of the thought in which they find themselves and that to which they have been accustomed by experience or tradition. This difference is making itself felt widely in the world to-day, in some cases with suspicion and fear, in others with welcome.' Mr. Palmer is a thoughtful writer and an earnest student, and his book will be read with the greatest interest by all classes of people anxious to follow the most vital problem known to man." (Dutton. $1.25.)

Grandma's Attic Treasures.—"A very pretty illustrated edition has been made of Mary D. Brine's homely little romance in verse, 'Grandma's Attic Treasures.' Mrs. Brine sometimes twists the New England country dialect into astonishing and alien forms, but a tender sentiment runs through her stories, and they undoubtedly make their appeal to the great mass of readers, who very wisely and fortunately care more about sincerity of feeling and unselfishness of motive in what they call poetry than they do for all the laws of prosody that ever were made. " ' Grandma's Attic Treasures ' is a book," say *The Beacon,* "that has for fifteen years found a not unworthy welcome, and in its new form will doubtless prove even more acceptable than ever. The twelve pages in color are almost too finely done to harmonize with the unpretentious simplicity of the text, and the ornamental white cloth cover, showing a

very plump and youthful grandma, gayly attired in brocade satins and seated in a Chippendale easy-chair, is a really brilliant inspiration." (Dutton. $1.50.)

Reading Aloud in Missionary Societies. — " ' What I Told Dorcas ' is a story for missionary workers, by Mary E. Ireland, which will not only prove acceptable to missionary, literary, and sewing societies," says the N. Y. *Commercial Advertiser,* " but to all the home circles in which it may enter. It is the story of a foreign missionary society in a country town and is written in a light and pleasing vein. The form the author has adopted was suggested by seeing, in many years' association with missionary societies of different denominations, the need of a book for reading aloud at their meetings—a lively, suggestive, continued story yet so constructed as to be read satisfactorily in monthly or weekly instalments." " A rare book of its kind," says the N. Y. *Herald.* " It deals with mission work, and the author evidently has her wits about her and knows how to use her brains." (Dutton. $1.25.)

"I STOPPED TO CHAT AWHILE WITH DORCAS."

Illustrated Editions of Barrie. — That Mr. Barrie's racy, humorous annals of Scottish weaving and peasant life in the hamlet of Thrums lend themselves to the art of the illustrator will be conceded by all who recognize the genius of the author who has so cleverly conceived and portrayed the pathetic history. New illustrated editions of " Auld Licht Idylls " and " A Window in Thrums " have just been issued, which can hardly fail to be appreciated by Mr. Barrie's myriad of readers and furnish delight to the lovers of art and interest to the students of physiognomy and human character. The types are strong, rugged, and full of the humor and pathos that belongs to Scottish peasant life, with its canny and pauky worldliness, relieved by tender streaks of humanness, and touches of the Divine hand moving now and then with a gentle but manifest play over the human countenance. These new and artistic editions will give increased impetus to the already extensive sale of these now famous Scottish classics. (Fenno. *Ea.*, $1.25.)

Captain Antifer. — A new and original story from the magical pen of Jules Verne, whose writings have been translated into almost every modern language, may well whet the appetite of the readers of his myriad stories of marvel and adventure. The copyright of an English translation of Verne's new work, " Captain Antifer," has just been acquired by R. F. Fenno & Company, of New York, who have issued a handsome illustrated edition and placed it on the American market. The work narrates the amazing adventures of Captain Antifer, a French mariner, of St. Malo, while in search of treasure, of a fabulous amount, which was concealed on an island in the Levant during the struggle, in 1830, of the Greeks for independence and freedom from the Turkish yoke. The chief interest of the story arises from the fact that the island on which the treasure has been buried is subject to submersion, and after a period of years rises again from the waters of the Mediterranean. The book is full of thrilling incident, which transfixes the attention of the reader. (Fenno. 50 c.)

The Monthly Illustrator and Home and Country. — No lover of the beautiful in art in America, and no artist anywhere—amateur or professional—will fail to be interested in *The Monthly Illustrator and Home and Country.* Certainly nothing to compare with it in the magazine world, here or abroad, has heretofore been issued. The table of contents is grand. Delightfully American, with just enough of a foreign flavor to add zest, the latest issue of this popular magazine is a revelation. In " English Fads and Fancies," by Thomas Campbell-Copeland, with illustrations from drawings by George Du Maurier; " Kiku : the royal flower of Japan," by Lillian E. Purdy, illustrated from photos of living chrysanthemums by A. T. Spaulding, and " Cuxhaven to Constantinople," by C. W. Allers, illustrated from drawings by the author, there is a feast for the intellect and the sight which is really enjoyable. The Christmas number and those which follow will equal in beauty of illustration any of the American monthlies. (The Monthly Illustrator Publishing Co. Subs., $2 a year.)

From Jules Verne's "Captain Antifer."   Copyright, 1895, by R. F. Fenno & Co.

HE HOISTED THE SIGNAL.

From " From the Black Sea Through Persia and India "   Copyright, 1895, by Harper & Brothers.

GRAIN MARKET TEHERAN.

The Story of the Other Wise Man.—"One of the most appropriate Christmas books that has appeared is ' The Story of the Other Wise Man,' by Henry Van Dyke," says the Boston *Evening Gazette.* " This is a very touching story of Artaban, of the ancient priesthood of Magi, who went in search of the Victorious One, but who, unlike the three wise men whom all the world knows, never found him until the day of the crucifixion of Jesus Christ in Jerusalem. The adventures of this fourth pilgrim are set forth with much picturesque power and historical accuracy of detail, and the full-page pictures by F. Luis Mora, which accompany them, increase the interest of the luminous text. (Harper. $1.50.)

Sports of Long Ago.—Mr. Laurence Hutton's new volume, " Other Times and Other Seasons," contains a series of fifteen brief essays, tracing the origin of some of our modern games and customs and telling of the beginnings of the observance of some of the days we celebrate. The titles of these essays are " Foot-Ball," " Prize Fights," " Tennis," " Golf," " Boat-Races," " Transportation," " Tobacco," " Coffee," "A Gammon of Bacon," " St. Valentine's Day," " April Fool's Day," " Good Friday," " May Day," " The Fifth of November," and " Christmas Day." In each of the essays various authors. ranging from Herodotus to Brander Matthews, are relevantly quoted. (Harper. $1.)

Christmas Week at Bigler's Mill, by Dora E. W. Spratt, is a little tale depicting life in Virginia by one who evidently knows her subject well. A note informs the reader that in the country districts of Old Virginia the people celebrate not only Christmas Day, but all Christmas week, hence this title, which includes not only the great day but the preparations for it. Miss Spratt further calls her book "A Sketch in Black and White," and the delineations of negro character make one of its strongest features. (Amer. Bapt. Pub. Soc. 75 c.)

The Ambrosial Library.—George D. Hurst takes just pride in his *Ambrosial Library,* which he intends to fill with books that have been at the top wave of popularity during different times and seasons, and also with new books that shall have special aim and purpose and be demanded in good, permanent shape. Thus far the books prepared are Amelia E. Barr's " The Beads of Tasmer," Maurice Thompson's " The King of Honey Island," and John Habberton's " The Chautauquans." Each volume in the series contains a handsomely engraved title-page reproduced from an early illuminated manuscript in the British Museum, Harleian Collection. The books are neatly gotten up in serviceable buckram covers. (*Ea.,* 75 c.)

Useful Books for People with Hobbies.—George D. Hurst has an *International edition* of Le Grand's " Manual for Stamp Collectors," translated from the French and annotated and adapted for American collectors by Henri Pène du Bois, Esq. ($1); " New Standard Electrical Dictionary," by P. O'Conor Sloane, of the *Scientific American* ($2.50); " New Dictionary of Photography," for the amateur and professional photographer, by E. J. Wall ($2.50); " Photography, Artistic and Scientific," by Johnson and Chatwood, with fifty-four illustrations, an entirely new book ($2.50); and " Practical Typewriting," by the all-finger method, arranged for self-instruction and school use, by James Torrey ($1.50).

George D. Hurst's Miscellaneous Books.—When looking for gifts do not overlook the *Library edition* of " The Hoosier Schoolmaster," Edward Eggleston's pioneer contribution to local dialect literature ($1.50); new editions of Susan E. Wallace's " The Repose in Egypt " (75 c.) and " The Land of the Pueblos " (75 c.); and " The Satires of Cynicus," a new book of pointed expressions in pen and picture, showing up many of the foibles of the age (75 c.).

From " The Temptation of Katherine Gray." Copyright, 1895, by American Baptist Pub. Soc.

MARY LOWE DICKINSON.

The Temptation of Katherine Gray. — This story by Mary Lowe Dickinson, always to the front in all movements making for the improvement of women, is one that deserves special attention. In her connection with Christian Endeavor Societies, the White Cross movement, and many other elevating and helpful movements making for higher morality and purer useful life, Mrs. Dickinson has had great opportunities to study woman, her special temptations, her great power of self-sacrifice and work for those she loves, and her special danger of letting emotion and feeling get the better of principles. In a well-told story of strong narrative interest Mrs. Dickinson describes Katherine Gray, who has been a girl longing for an easy life and pretty things, who to attain that has married Robert Gray, although knowing his weak character and special temptation, which is drink. Things go from bad to worse, and finally come to a climax. Then Katherine Gray, in the hope of gaining for her child a position in the world, proves unworthy to a trust and commits a sin to attain her ends, the consequences of which follow her all her days. "The whole record," says the author, "is one long illustration of the futility of building houses upon sand, of making bricks without straw, of attempting to do noble work in any of the world's fields with the brain or hands without purity of heart and honesty of purpose ; a lesson of the value and importance of an active religious principle moving in the innermost life of every woman who longs to be a blessing in her home, and to take her share in alleviating the miseries of the world." Mrs. Dickinson has just successfully conducted the jubilee celebration of Elizabeth Cady Stanton in New York, and is in the woman's movement one of the foremost women in the land. (Amer. Bapt. Pub. Society. $1.50.)

E. P. Dutton's Illustrated Gift - Books. — Among the most beautiful this season are " Flowers of Song," selections from the poets, with twelve colored plates ($2); "Pictures from Dickens," with colored plates ($2); "Violets," "Forget-Me-Nots," "Pansies," three square gilt books beautifully illustrated and bound in white cloth (*ea.*, $1.25).

E. P. Dutton's New Year-Books. — The newcomers this year are " The Musician's Year-Book," by Margaret Reintzel (75 c.), and "The Farrar Year-Book" ($1.25), a companion to "The Phillips Brooks Year-Book," which holds its own as one of the most successful year-books ever issued ($1.25).

E. P. Dutton & Co.'s Calendars.—Every one expects from Messrs. E. P. Dutton & Co., with the advent of every new holiday season, a collection of calendars suited to the most refined tastes, and this year the house in question sends out a series that in beauty of design, perfection of coloring, and literary merit are safely to be reckoned among the finest productions of the sort ever published. Over seventy different kinds of calendars are included in the series, and they range from cheap to very expensive. Among the most beautiful of this year's calendars are "Golden Treasury Calendar," twelve leaves with selections from the leading poets and illustrations in tints ($2); "Cathedral Chimes Calendar," six leaves illustrating six English cathedrals ($2); "Sweet Nature,' landscape pictures appropriate to the season ($1.25); "The Phillips Brooks Calendar," with illustrations in color and selections from last volume of sermons ($1); "Shakespeare Calendar" (50 c.); "Dickens's Calendar" (50 c.); "The Composers' Calendar," portraits in color of six famous composers (75 c.); "Wit and Humor Calendar," twelve leaves with comic illustrations (75 c.); "Fair Calendar," twelve leaves with silk cord and tassels (50 c.); "The Circling Year," selections from Shakespeare and illustrations in color (50 c.); "My Times Are in Thy Hands Calendar," Scripture texts and illustrations in color (50 c.) ; "The Comic Calendar" (35 c.); and last, but as place of honor, "The Basket of Flowers Calendars," either pansies or chrysanthemums, the petals lifting to show the dates, exquisitely beautiful (*ea.*, 50 c.). In Block Calendars the Duttons have " The Farrar Calendar " (50 c.) ; " The Phillips Brooks Calendar " (50 c.); " Tennyson Calendar " (40 c.) ; "Christian Year Calendar " (40 c.), etc.

The Whittier Year-Book.—There are large numbers of people who are devoted to year-books and an even larger number devoted to Whittier. How they will rejoice to know that the well-loved words have been distributed by a nice hand among the 365 days of the year, and that for every birthday and remembrance day the Quaker poet will speak to them in a quiet, helpful verse or rouse them with his clarion tones to American patriotism. In a pretty binding of grayish blue, with covers and back simply lettered and decorated in silver, with an exquisitely gracious frontispiece portrait from an unfamiliar photograph, comes " The Whittier Year-Book," made up, as the title-page has it, of " passages from the verse and prose of John Greenleaf Whittier, chosen for the daily food of the lover of thought and beauty." " The writings of Whittier," says *The Beacon,* " lend themselves with peculiar adaptability to an undertaking of this sort, and the anonymous editor has produced a little anthology, filling in the most satisfactory way the object in view." (Houghton Mifflin & Co. $1.)

Westminster Abbey and the Cathedrals of England.—The large number of books that have been published describing the cathedrals of England indicates the rich and varied interest in them, both religious and secular. This general interest and the perfection to which the art of photography has been advanced in making views and in reproducing them for the purposes of illustration have suggested this additional book. The plan has been to put together the best accounts of these great cathedrals with the finest illustrations from the very best photographs obtainable. The text used has been gathered from many exhaustive writings upon the great subject of cathedrals, but chiefly from the works of Deans Farrar, Milman, Stanley, and others, who did some of their best work in historic Westminster Abbey. Upward of 100 superbly printed views are given of both exterior and interior views. Thus appear Durham's massive Norman nave ; Salisbury's uniform nave of the pointed period ; Westminster's decorated choir ; Canterbury's choir of several ages ; St. Paul's modern Renaissance interior ; York's exterior façade and rood screen ; Lincoln's noble towers and bishop's palace ; Winchester's reredos and picturesque precincts ; Salisbury's spire, cloister, and chapter-house ; and Chester's richly carved stalls. Forty of the illustrations are full-page and sixty appear in the text. None of the many books hitherto published on this subject have attempted to use, to any extent, the present high art of photography, and cannot, therefore, compare with this in the beauty and faithfulness of its pictorial representations of these monumental buildings. It is believed the work will especially interest travellers, architects, and all students of English history, and will give to the casual reader the quickest and best general idea of the great English cathedrals and the interesting monuments in them. A unique feature is the fine collection of portraits of the great church dignitaries of the past and present, with short sketches of their lives. This collection includes Deans Farrar, Milman, Church, Stanley ; Canon Liddon ; Archbishops Tait and Benson ; Bishops Lightfoot, Westcott, Wilberforce, etc. The book is carefully printed on heavy coated paper and is one of the handsomest publications of the year. The size of page is 9 x 12 inches and the binding is ornamental cloth. (John C. Winston & Co. $3.50.)

Books by Ernest Renan.—The fifth volume, completing his great " History of the People of Israel," is now ready. Viewing the five volumes as a whole, their interest centres in Renan's interpretation of Hebrew history ; and it may safely be said that nothing that he has done reveals the brilliancy of his mind and the greatness of his intellectual grasp as does this monumental work (5 v., *ea.,* $2.50). There is also a translation newly revised from the twenty-

From " Westminster Abbey."   Copyright, 1895, by John C. Winston & Co.

ST. PAUL'S FROM CHEAPSIDE.

third and final edition of Renan's " Life of Jesus " ($2.50), and a very touching biography entitled " My Sister Henrietta." The labors and privations bravely endured by this noble creature for the sake of her family, her unshrinking devotion to the task of giving her brother every possible advantage and the use of every possible moment, her abandonment of every personal wish, her entire absorption in her sisterly charity make up a life only to be compared with that of another noble sister, Eugénie de Guérin. The American edition is illustrated by portraits of the brother and sister and by views of places memorable in their lives by Henri Scheffer and Ary Renan. (Roberts. $1.25.)

Editions of Shakespeare, and Other Holiday Books.—F. Warne & Co. have on their list of books several works that year after year delight the fortunates who come into possession of them. "The Bedford Handy-Volume Shakespeare," in twelve pocket volumes, daintily printed and rubricated, is always kept ready for Christmas and birthdays in various handsome bindings and covers, including Spanish morocco, real russia and turkey, and satin-lined cases; also in cases of fine wood, with locks and keys, and trimmings in imitation of jewel-boxes ($7.50–$35). The *India paper edition* "Lansdowne Shakespeare," in six pocket volumes, is also bound and cased in choice smooth calf or turkey morocco ($8–$22.50). "Milton's Poetical Works," in four volumes, are also cased in various leathers, and are specially beautiful in a Venetian morocco case with clasps ($6). It is hard to find a better-made dictionary than "Wood's Dictionary of Quotations," taken from ancient and modern English and foreign sources, containing 30,000 references, alphabetically arranged, with an exhaustive subject index, a happy combination of what everybody knows and wishes to authenticate most practically arranged ($2.50, $4.50). A valuable contribution to English history may be found in "Abbeys, Castles, and Ancient Halls of England and Wales," in three volumes, by John Timbs and Alexander Gunn, who seem to have true feeling for the legendary lore of these historic monuments, a work embellished with twelve full-page photogravures from the newest and best views of the buildings mentioned ($7.50). Charles Knight's "Popular History of England," in nine volumes, with 1000 illustrations and 190 steel-engraved portraits, is available for generous givers in cloth or morocco ($20–$45).

D. Appleton & Co.'s New Fiction.—"The Prisoner of Zenda" proved Mr. Hope's power as the author of a fighting romance, and his pen again becomes a sword in "The Chronicles of Count Antonio," a picturesque and thrilling story of a mediæval Italian paladin, whose character will recall the Chevalier Bayard to the reader who breathlessly follows him through his adventures and dangers. ($1.50.) "Corruption," by Percy White, the author of "Mr. Bailey-Martin," illustrates phases of social and political life of the present hour, told with rare facility of expression by an author intimately acquainted with his subject. ($1.25.) "A Hard Woman" is a story in scenes, by Violet Hunt, a brilliant picture of certain types and phases of modern London life will be read and talked about for its originality and power. This study of artistic and fashionable society will be found intensely modern in spirit, bright and entertaining throughout. ($1.25.) The Boston *Beacon* says: "There is nothing in American fiction to compare with 'The Red Badge of Courage,' by Stephen Crane, in the vivid, uncompromising, almost aggressive vigor with which it depicts the strangely mingled conditions that go to make up what men call war." ($1.) Miss F. F. Montrésor, whose book "In the Highways and Hedges" proved so very successful, has now written "The One Who Looked On." Miss Montrésor's point of view is always fresh, and the originality of her new book is no less in evidence than the delicacy and truthful sentiment

which are felt throughout its pages. Its tenderness and the subtle poetic quality which characterize the story have a distinction and charm that differentiate the book from the mass of current fiction. ($1.25.) Among the recent books the best stories are Conan Doyle's "The Stark Munro Letters" ($1.50); Bram Stoker's "The Watters' Mou" (75 c.); John Oliver Hobbes's "The Gods, Some Mortals, and Lord Wickenham" ($1.50); and Chauncey C. Hotchkiss's "The American Revolution," the latter in *The Town and Country Library.* (50 c., $1.)

D. Appleton & Co.'s Miscellaneous Books.—A new volume in the *Anthropological Series*, so ably edited by Prof. Frederick Starr, is "The Beginnings of Writing," by Dr. Walter J. Hoffman. Professor Hoffman, one of the most successful workers in the field of American ethnology, presents the first steps in the development of writing from tangible reminders like quipus and wampum belts through picture writing to phonetic writing with an alphabet. These first steps are described especially as they are shown among the North American tribes. ($1.75.) "The Story of the Earth," by H. G. Seeley, is the new-comer in the *Library of Useful Stories.* When a subject so peculiarly inviting is treated so lucidly and compactly as Mr. Seeley has done, the resulting volume becomes almost indispensable for readers with any interest whatever in the stories of popular science. This book is certain to prove one of the most successful in this excellent series. (40 c.) New editions are ready of *The Music Series*, edited by George T. Ferris, in five volumes, with twenty-eight full-page portraits, consisting of biographical and anecdotal sketches of the great German, Italian, and French composers, great singers, great violinists and pianists, very prettily bound in colored silk with entirely new cover design (5 v., $4); and "The Memoirs of General Count de Ségur, 1800–1812," an aide-de-camp of Napoleon. ($2.)

Frail Children of the Air.—"In this attractive volume of nearly three hundred pages, the author of that magnificent work, 'Butterflies of the Eastern United States,' has discussed, in his felicitous manner," says *The Nation*, "most of the interesting problems which naturally arise in the study of these butterflies. As originally published, in a series of excursuses in the costly work above mentioned, they could be known and enjoyed by comparatively few persons, while, in the convenient form in which they are now presented, they will be read with delight by hundreds of lovers of nature. The young naturalist will find much in the volume that he would look for in vain in purely scientific treatises. The author has succeeded in thoroughly infusing these pages with his enthusiastic love of butterflies. The titles of some of the chapters indicate the fascinating nature of the topics discussed, for example: 'Butterflies as Botanists.' 'How Butterflies Pass the Winter,' 'Aromatic Butterflies,' 'Butterflies at Night and at Sea,' 'A Budget of Curious Facts about Chrysalids.'" "It is a great pleasure," says *The Outlook*, "to note the publication for popular use of material which bears on every page a stamp of exact observation, of thorough knowledge, and of intelligent arrangement." (Houghton, Mifflin & Co. $1.50.)

F. A. Stokes Co.'s Calendars. — One distinctive feature of the calendars published by the Stokes is that they are thoroughly American in spirit. They are the only important series of calendars designed by American artists and manufactured in this country. The publishers believe that the lithographic work on these has never been surpassed. It has been their constant aim to make them perfect fac-similes of the original water-color designs, and no expense has been spared to accomplish this. In some cases sixteen colors have been needed to produce the effect sought. Ninety different calendars to choose from, ranging in price from 10 cents to $15, after designs by such well-known

The Land of Tawny Beasts.—A most original and valuable work by Pierre Maël, translated by Elizabeth L. Carey. It describes the adventures of a party of explorers and hunters in the Himalayas. They are attacked by Hindoo fanatics and have all sorts of strange experiences in consequence. The hunting exploits of the party are also very wonderful. The book has fifty-two wood-engravings done in the best modern French style by A. Paris. The very cover speaks of daring deeds by field and flood, as it has one of the most telling scenes of the books stamped in gold and red and white and black inks on the binding of Holliston cloth. (Stokes. $2 50, $3.)

From "The Land of Tawny Beasts."   Copyright, 1895, by F A. Stokes Co.

THEY SET OUT UPON THEIR WAY.

artists as W. Granville Smith, E. Percy Moran, Maud Humphrey, Francis Day, and H. W. McVickar. The decorations of these calendars are chiefly fac-similes of water-color designs by well-known artists. The greatest care has been given to make each plate as finished as possible, and the result is that many of the plates have enough merit to warrant their preservation under glass and in frames. Among the more noteworthy of these are "The Calendar of the Brave and the Fair" (13½ x 18 in.), with designs by W. Granville Smith ($3.50); "Roses and Pansies," with designs by Newton A. Wells and Henrietta D. La Fraik ($2); "The Footlights Calendar," with designs of *premiers danseuses* in costume, by Miss E. G. Emmet ($1.50); "A Calendar of Belles," with fine studies of costume effects, by Caroline C. Lovell ($1.50), made up of portraits taken from life, each one signed by the Southern beauty it represents and mounted with the coat of arms of her State; and "A Calendar of Dogs and Cats," a fine gift to a lover of these pets, designed by Frederick J. Boston ($1.75); and "A Calendar of Elves'" is an artistic "comic" folder, by Frances Brundage (40c.), representing four little elves standing in a row, emblematic of the four seasons, and nothing can be imagined more comical than their expressions.

Fair Women of To-Day.—These poems by Dr. Samuel Minturn Peck were written especially for the publishers and have never been published before. Accompanied by twelve fac-similes of water-color drawings by Caroline C. Lovell—portraits of thirteen young Southern women celebrated below Mason an Dixon's line for their beauty. This pretty book is gotten up in different styles, in various colors of buckram and also in silk. The buckram is stamped in silver, the silk in gold. (Stokes. $2.50, $3, $3.50.)

Foster's Books on Cards.—R. F. Foster has added a book entitled "Whist Tactics" to his successful "Whist Manual." In this work the author has followed the same principles which made his manual so successful, first giving the examples with the cards and then showing the principles underlying their management. The general management of the hand is gone into, and rules are given for the best course when the plain suits and the trumps are in certain proportions. The examples consist of 112 hands at duplicate whist, played by correspondence between sixteen of the finest players in America. ($1.25.) "Hearts," the only work published on this interesting game, is a standard by which all disputes can be settled. (Stokes. 50 c.) .

Thomas Nelson & Sons' "Oxford" India Paper Editions.—Another treasure has been added to the many beautiful "Oxford" editions. This is the "Oxford Miniature Scott," similar to the "Shakespeare" brought out last year. It comprises all of Scott's poems and is issued in two forms—in five dainty little volumes, each four by three inches in size and only three inches thick, put up in a neat case, and in a single twelvemo volume, small enough for convenient handling. Not only does the "Oxford Miniature Scott" contain the longer poems, "Lady of the Lake," etc., but it includes the verses and mottoes scattered through the Waverley Novels, the adaptations from the German, and the later and little known ballads and poems. Beautifully printed on the famous Oxford India paper, which combines opacity with the utmost thinness, with red gold edges, and a binding of tasteful simplicity, the Oxford Scott and its companion Shakespeare are specimens of exquisite book-making that will delight the heart of all true book-lovers. Ranking with these beautiful miniature volumes are the Oxford "Thumb" editions, to which are added this year "The Imitation of Christ" and "The Christian Year." These, with the "Thumb" Prayer-Books, are exactly 2 x 1¼ inches in size, yet possess the legibility, the beauty of finish and workmanship that characterize the ordinary "every-day size" Oxford volumes.

Rose Porter's Year-Books.—Miss Rose Porter has issued a companion volume to her book "About Women : what men have said." In the new book, entitled "About Men : what women have said," the editor has followed the same plan as before, devoting one month to each of her twelve authors. The writers from whom quotations are made include Charlotte Brontë, George Eliot, George Sand, Mrs. Humphry Ward, Frances Burney, Maria Edgeworth, etc. The pretty little volumes are interesting from a literary point of view, and being arranged in the form of year-books they are likely to be constantly referred to. (Putnam. *Ea.*, $1.)

The Poets' Dogs.—Lovers of dogs, and their name is legion, will welcome Mrs. Richardson's compilation of verses upon this faithful friend and companion of man.

> " All poets' wit hath ever writ
> In doggerel verse of hounds."

The book includes many prime favorites, such as Burns's "The Twa Dogs," Spencer's "Beth-Gêlert," Homer's "Ulysses's Dog Argus," Goldsmith's "Elegy on the Death of a Mad Dog," and Browning's "Tray." Mrs. Richardson dedicates her volume to the memory of Pip, Pentaur, and Monk, dogs whose lot was doubtless to be envied, as her selections show that she knew how to value aright these friends of ours, whose faithfulness and devotion so often put to shame the inconstancy of man. (Putnam. $1.25.)

Lilian Whiting's "From Dreamland Sent."—Last year Lilian Whiting's "The World Beautiful" was one of the great successes among the Christmas books, and there is every reason to feel sure that "From Dreamland Sent" will take its place beside it on the shelves of all who own it. "The title of the volume," says the N.Y. *Commercial Advertiser*, "prepares one for the tender melancholy that pervades it, but it never becomes lugubrious. In these days, when good poetry is so hard to find, Miss Whiting's little book will be especially welcome. While it is not ambitious, 'From Dreamland Sent' is decidedly pleasing." (Roberts. $1.25.)

Helen Jackson's Year-Book.—"The writings of Helen Jackson in prose and verse afford an abundance of material for selection, and the compiler of 'The Helen Jackson Year-Book' has on the whole performed her task with creditable good taste and a clear appreciation of ethical and literary values," says *The Beacon*. "All of Helen Jackson's books are represented and every page has its suggestive thought, its brilliant epigram, and its expression of beautiful and uplifting imagery. Occasionally a poem is printed entire, and in this way some of the author's finest sonnets and shorter lyrics are included. The book is illustrated with pretty little vignette titles by E. H. Garrett and with reproductions of the somewhat lackadaisical, ultra-Gallic, full-page designs of Emil Bayard." (Roberts. $1.50.)

From " Unc' Edinburg."

"NOW I KNOW PUSSY ATE UP MY GOLDFISH, FOR YOU CAN SEE THE BONES
STICKING OUT OF HER CHEEKS."

Books for Young People.

Harper's Round Table.—During the year the
name of *Harper's Young People* was changed
to *Harper's Round Table.* For several years
the " Round Table " had been a very important
part of this excellent periodical. Readers of
Harper's Young People week by week turned
eagerly to the " Round Table " pages to find
questions put and questions answered of interest to their active, inquiring brains. The department became the most important part of
the paper and was given its due honor by having its name adopted for the whole publication. Since then if things could be better
done or more good things offered they have
been so A better periodical for boys and
girls, more calculated to make them think and
make them patriotic, well-posted inhabitants of
their great country, does not exist. The bound
volume for 1895 is a treasure-house of information and recreation. (Harper. $3.50.)

Oakleigh.—Mrs. Ellen Douglas Deland has
prepared a story for young people that is
simply delightful. A young stepmother is
brought home to take care of five children
ranging from a daughter of sixteen to a very
young child. The story is a simple one of home
trials and daily struggles, but the characters
are exquisitely natural and the tale is full of
bright speeches, interesting games, discussions
of plans for the future of the boys, etc. The
sixteen-year-old daughter at first is rebellious,
but her mother's love and excellent sense finally conquer all her children. Not preachy, and

often very funny. First published in *Harper's
Round Table.* (Harper. $1.25.)

Snow-Shoes and Sledges. — This story is a
sequel to " The Fur-Seal's Tooth." The principal characters in the story are : Phil Ryder,
son of John Ryder, a mining engineer ; Serge
Belcovsky, a boy of Russian parentage, whose
home is in Sitka, Alaska ; Jalep Coombs, a
typical Yankee sailor, the humorous character
of the book, and Simon Goldollar, the black
sheep of the story. " Snow-Shoes and Sledges "
opens at the point where the characters were
left at the close of " The Fur-Seal's Tooth."
The boys are on their way to Sitka, which they
hope to reach by way of the Yukon. The
captain becomes ill and Phil and Serge are left
in charge of the boat. Mr. Kirk Munroe piles
on the adventures and teaches much about our
great Western Archipelago. (Harper. $1.25.)

A Life of Christ for Young People.—" I desire
to speak of ' A Life of Christ for Young People,
in Questions and Answers,' by Mary Hastings
Foote. It contains a good map of Palestine
and a diagram of Herod's temple. It is a good
book to place in the hands of Sunday-school
teachers, and it ought to be very useful in suggesting subjects to be discussed. Of its kind,"
says Dr. Hepworth in the New York *Herald,*
" it is the best thing I have seen, for the questions are pertinent and the answers short. It
is also a book for a rainy Sunday at home, and
is without an atom of dulness." (Harper.
$1.25.)

Some of the Finest of Stokes's Juveniles.—Frederick A. Stokes Company have as usual prepared some beautiful color-books for the young people. Chief among them is "The Children's Book of Dogs and Cats," for which Frederick J. Boston prepared twelve water-color sketches, the central figures of six being dogs and the central figures of six others being cats. These have been finely reproduced in fac-simile, and Miss Elizabeth S. Tucker has written delightful stories for the pictures, which are printed in inks of different colors, enclosed in decorated borders designed by her. Two fac-similes of Mr. Boston's sketches adorn two sides of the cover. ($2.50.) This work is divided into two thinner volumes, under the titles of "Cats and Kittens" and "Dogs Great and Small," each containing just half the illustrations and half the text of the larger book and being offered in brilliant board covers. Also from the pen of Elizabeth S. Tucker and gay and bright in many colors is "Royal Little People." It consists of portraits of little princes and princesses of Scotland, Holland, Spain, France, England, and—America, dressed in the youthful costumes of the different periods to which they belonged, accompanied by original stories and verses by Miss Tucker. An unusually pretty fairy-tale with Princess Sunbeam and Princess Moonbeam as the principal characters is to be found in "The Enchanted Butterflies," by Adelaide Upton Crosby, illustrated in an original style by Susan H. Clark and the author—children were posed in the costumes of the characters in the book and photographed, and then the background of the scene was drawn about their pictures. The binding of this book is half white cloth stamped in gold and half embossed paper, a wonderful combination of violets and butterflies. This house always has a number of pretty moving toy-books, exceptionally desirable gifts for the nursery ; they have also three tiny alphabet books printed in colors. For prices consult the list.

Scribner's Sons' Holiday Juveniles. — "Two Little Pilgrims' Progress," by Frances Hodgson Burnett, with illustrations by R. B. Birch, is the largest and most notable children's book that Mrs. Burnett has written since "Fauntleroy." It is a charming story of a little boy and girl who, taking their small savings, leave home to visit the World's Fair. This is their Pilgrims' Progress; and their interesting adventures and the happy ending of it all Mrs. Burnett tells as no one else can. It is in the author's best vein, and will take place in the hearts of her readers close beside "Fauntleroy." ($1.50.) Howard Pyle, who disputes with Mrs. Burnett the favor of youthful readers, has written and illustrated a most poetically conceived fairy-tale, "The Garden Behind the Moon," a real story of the moon angel. David, its little hero, goes along the moon-path to the moon, where he is welcomed by the "man in the moon"; in "the garden behind the moon" little David witnesses things as remarkable as did "Alice in Wonderland," though perhaps not so funny, Mr. Pyle's story having beneath the surface a mystical

"LITTLE CHILDREN, BE YE KIND . . . FORGIVING ONE ANOTHER."

moral significance that gives it the dignity of true literature and recommends it to grown people. Mr. Pyle's illustrations are as graceful and artistic as usual. ($2.) G. A. Henty's powers of invention seem inexhaustible; he is in the field this year again as the author of three new books of adventure, which seem just as fresh and attractive as if he had but only now entered the lists as a writer. They are "Through Russian Snows," a story of Napoleon's retreat from Moscow;"A Knight of the White Cross," a tale of the siege of Rhodes; and "The Tiger of Mysore," a story of the war with the cruel Tippoo Saib; they all have boy heroes of seventeen years or less, who do wonderful deeds of valor under exceptionally thrilling circumstances; they are also richly and substantially bound and profusely illustrated. (*Ea.,* $1.50.) Other excellent juveniles are: "The Kanter Girls," by Mary L. B. Branch ($1.50); "At War with Pontiac," by Kirk Munroe ($1.25); "For Life and Liberty," by Gordon Stables ($1.50); "Children's Stories in American Literature," by Henrietta Christian Wright, ($1.25); and a new edition of Robert Louis Stevenson's "A Child's Garden of Verse." "College Girls," by Abbe Carter Goodloe ($1.25), and "Side Talks with Girls," by Ruth Ashmore, are books every girl should read to prevent her striving to be that dreadful combination now styled "a new woman." ($1.50.)

From "A Jolly Good Summer."   Copyright, 1895, by Roberts Bros.

SKETCHING.

The Mushroom Cave.—Evelyn Raymond, author of "The Little Lady of the Horse," is always interesting, and this new book, with its delightfully mysterious title, is no exception to its predecessors. It is a capital story of the fortunes of an old violinist and his grandchildren, who are of "the people called Quakers." The old man, wrapped up in his music and his dreams, disregards the practical things of life and the family income gradually dwindles and disappears. Then the children take hold and, turning a deserted old quarry into a mushroom garden, bring prosperity again. Their efforts to be thorough business people are varied and entertaining, and the lugubrious old family servant, Hepzibah Letitia, is a most entertaining figure in the tale. (Roberts. $1.50.)

In the Okefenokee.—Here is a stirring tale of adventure by Louis Pendleton that will win the hearts of boy readers. It is a story of wartime and of the great Georgia swamp, and tells of the adventures of two lads who run away from home in search of "experiences." Their expectations are more than fulfilled, for they have a thrilling series of hairbreadth 'scapes from death and danger, mixed in with no little fun. Of course, in the end, they reach home

safely, wiser than when they left, and the faithful ex-slave who helps them through their trials finds himself rewarded by freedom and an independence. (Roberts. $1.25.)

Roberts Brothers' Juveniles.—Miss Plympton has not yet said farewell to "Dear Daughter Dorothy," whose doings were last year chronicled in a delightful book, and this year she adds a sequel, "Dorothy and Anton" ($1), wherein Dorothy studies music in Berlin, finds a new friend in litte German Anton, and has many interesting experiences. "The Keeper of the Salamander's Order," by William Shattuck ($2), is a fairy-story of astonishing adventure, while two charming fanciful tales are "Under the Stable Floor" (50 c.), the doings of a family of rats, described by M. Carrie Hyde, and "Frowzle, the Runaway" ($1.25), a tale of a naughty dog, by Lily M. Wesselhoeft. Among the other books that will delight childish hearts are "A Jolly Good Summer" ($1.25), a new volume of the "Jolly Good Times" books, by Mary P. Wells Smith; "Through Forest and Plain," a tale of adventure, by Ashmore Russan and Frederick Boyle ($1.50); "Goostie" and "Yan and Nochie of Tappan Sea," both by M. Carrie Hyde (*ea.,* 50 c.).

The Nürnberg Stove.—If "Ouida's" unquestioned talent, and power of emotional as well as picturesque writing, had run more into the vein of "The Nürnberg Stove"—that quaint, fanciful, and most touching story for both young and old, with its tender but inspiriting

SHE LISTENED EAGERLY.

moral lesson, it would undoubtedly have been better for her literary reputation. Hardly anything could be more delightful than the qualities of heart and mind shown by Louisa de la Rame in the conception and working out of this touching tale of the little Tyrol lad's chivalrous passion for the family heirloom of the potter Hirschvogel's inspired art. Those who know "The Nürnberg Stove"—one of the gems of "Ouida's" better-nature genius, will not need to be told of its idyllic beauty, its quaint fancifulness, its imaginative and romantic charm, and above all its child-like purity and tender humanness—for all these qualities are conspicuous in the pathetic, fascinating, and impressive story. Those who do *not* know the tale have a great treat in store for them, and the treat is the richer now that the publishers have happily illustrated the story with dainty drawings, which interpret the attractive narrative with a fine vigor and poetic grace. For the coming holiday season scarcely a more exquisite story could be put in the hands of youth than this admirably illustrated edition of "Ouida's" rarely beautiful and fascinating tale of "The Nürnberg Stove." It is hard to understand the varied genius of "Ouida." She has been thoroughly misunderstood and never has condescended to explain. But when time has sifted prejudice some very flattering things will be said of "Ouida." She is the George Sand of English novelists. (Fenno. 50 c.)

G. P. Putnam's Sons' Juveniles.—G. P. Putnam's Sons have "Great Men's Sons," by Elbridge S. Brooks, the prolific writer of "Historic Boys" and "Historic Girls," and as definitely instructive as entertaining, as are all this well-known and popular writer's books. It embraces the stories of the lives of the sons of Socrates, Cicero, Alexander, Marcus Aurelius, Mahomet, Dante, Columbus, Luther, Shakespeare, Napoleon, and others famed in the world's history, and is fully illustrated. ($1.50.) A charming story for girls, with a pointed lesson, may be found in "An Unlessoned Girl," by Elizabeth Knight Tompkins—the heroine, a spoilt, undisciplined girl, with latent possibilities, is polished and reduced to a proper state of humility by being sent to an excellent boarding-school, where she learns she does not know everything and wins a Vassar scholarship. ($1.25.) A second series of tales from the Arabian Nights is contained in "More Fairy-Tales from Arabian Nights"; the volume was edited and arranged by C. Dixon, and is illustrated by J. D. Batten in his characteristic style; the stories of the "Enchanted Horse," "Ali Baba," "Aladdin," "The Fisherman and Genie," with several others equally famous, are enclosed within its handsome cover. (Two series, *ca.* $2.) "The Silver Fairy-Book" has a rich cover in silver and blue and "lots" of pictures, and comprises fairy tales from the French, Spanish, German, Servian, and other sources. ($2.) "Tales from the Field" is a series of popular tales from the Norse of P. Ch. Asbjörnsen, translated by Sir George Webb Dasent and profusely illustrated from Moyr Smith's original designs. ($1.25)

Juveniles of T. Y. Crowell & Co.—An unusual number of singularly pretty juveniles have been prepared by T. Y. Crowell & Co. Warren L. Goss has added another volume to his series of historical stories of the War for the Union. The hero of "*Jack Alden*" is a New England boy who served through the Virginia campaigns, beginning as a private in 1861 and entering Richmond as a member of a general's staff at the close of the struggle. He was wounded in the streets of Baltimore, was present at Antietam, Fredericksburg, and Chancellorsville, was a prisoner in Libby, escaped through a tunnel and served once more under the Stars and Stripes from Petersburg to Appomattox. ($1.50.) "*The Three Apprentices of Moon Street*" is a translation of George Montgorgeuil's wholesome and droll account of the doings of three mischievous boys who belong to the establishment of a Parisian jeweller. One of them, running away from the penalty of misdeeds, falls in with a travelling show, and, dressed up in feathers, serves as a savage, and has some ludicrous experiences. Numerous sketches by Louis Le Révérend and Paul Steck, show the French children sometimes in long blouses and sometimes in feathers at every stage of their amusing careers. ($1.50.) One of the most charming of children's books comes to us in Mabel F. Hapgood's translation from the thirty-ninth Italian edition of Edmondo de Amicis's "*Cuore: an Italian School-boy's Journal.*" It is the record of a year in a Turin public school, a picture of the different pupils and their names, of the school system, and of the teachers and their ways. In it are seen the pleasant side of the Italian life of the middle and lower classes, with its simplicity, naïve openness, good feeling, and charity. Some American boy may think he is much too "grown up" for that kind of a school himself, but he cannot fail to enjoy learning how the young Italians are taught. ($1.50.) *"Dear Little Marchioness"* is the story of a child's faith and love, with an introduction by Bishop Gailor, of Tennessee, brought out with wide margins, beautiful illustrations, and tasteful bindings. ($1.) " Half a Dozen Boys," by Anna Chapin Ray, published five years ago, now appears in an illustrated edition. ($1.50.) *"Chilhowee Boys in War Time,"* by Sarah E. Morrison, with three illustrations by Frank T. Merrill, shows the boys we first met as pioneers living through the exciting times of the War of 1812 ($1.50); and Mrs. Sarah K. Bolton has ready another of her valuable books of biographical sketches, dealing with *"Famous Leaders Among Women,"* profusely illustrated with portraits.

Thomas Nelson & Sons' Juveniles. — Admirable provision has been made for boys in J. Macdonald Oxley's latest books, entitled " In the Wilds of the West Coast," of which the hero is a boy of fifteen ($1.50), and " My Strange Rescue, and other stories of sport and adventure in Canada" ($1.25), containing rather more than thirty short stories, all spirited and thrilling ; in two capital books, by Fred Wishaw, entitled " Boris, the Bear-Hunter, a story of Peter the Great and his times" ($1.25), and " A Lost Army," profusely illustrated ; and in Dr. Gordon Stables's new book, " How Jack Mackenzie Won His Epaulettes" ($1.25), and Captain Basil Hall's " Voyages and Travel" ($2). Sure to please both boys and girls are " Ampthill Towers," by Albert J. Foster, dealing with the reign of Henry VIII. (80 c.); " In Far Japan," by Mrs. Isla Sitwell, a story about child-life in Japan (80 c.); " Princess Louise," a tale of the Stuarts, by Crona Temple (60 c.); and five perfectly charming books on wild floweis by "Uncle Matt" (M. C. Cooke), kept within the capacity of intelligent boys and girls of twelve years of age, splendidly illustrated throughout, and put up in very tempting illuminated board covers (*ea.,* 50 c., 75 c.). Several other books published by the Nelsons are entered in the list of Books for Young People elsewhere in this issue.

The Susy Books. — A *new edition* of the " Susy Books " — the three volumes being issued in one handsome volume with new illustrations. The title given to it is "Little Susy's Six Birthdays, Six Teachers, Six Servants." These little books have given delight for many years to thousands of little children wher-

ever the English language is spoken, and are destined in their new form to gain thousands of other little readers. (Randolph. $2.)

D. Appleton & Co.'s books for young people are few this year but exceptionally interesting. "The Knight of Liberty," by Hezekiah Butterworth ($1.50). The picturesque figure of Lafayette is the central interest of the narrative ; his adventures in Paris, in an Austrian prison, and in the American Revolution form an exciting story which verifies the facts of history. It is a fitting successor to the author's "The Patriot Schoolmaster" and "The Boys of Greenway Court," and appeals strongly, as did these stirring tales, to the patriotism and imagination of the American boy. The book is an extremely handsome one, with a half-dozen full-page illustrations. The first volume in the *Story of the West Series,* edited by Ripley Hitchcock, should interest boys as well as grown folk. It is devoted to " The Story of the Indian" ($1.50), the author being George Bird Grinnell, and carries out admirably the object of the series. Mr. Grinnell's volume has been written from an intimate knowledge of his subject.

From " The Knight of Liberty."

LAFAYETTE AND HIS FUTURE DELIVERER.

Two New Books by the Author of Miss Toosey's Mission. — The mingled pathos and humor characteristic of the author of "Miss Toosey's Mission" are delightfully blended in these two new stories. "'Don,'" says the New York *Times*, "is a pretty love-story which glows with life from the first page to the last. There are no startling adventures, but there is interest in every line, imparted by the sympathy excited in the reader for Donald Grant—the Don of the story—and Sybil, and dear, gentle Miss Whateley. How manly and natural a being Don is, and how the little waif influences his life from boyhood up, until she refuses an earl to marry her 'under-keeper,' is told in simple, straightforward terms that reach the heart." "My Honey" is also a love-tale, set in a peaceful English rectory and full of a quiet simplicity that is refreshing in these days of "purpose" novels. (Roberts. *Ea.*, $1.)

John C. Winston & Co.'s Children's Books. — "Bunyan's Pilgrim's Progress" is ready in words of one syllable for little children, and the book is printed in large type so clearly as to be tempting to the smallest child that has successfully struggled with the alphabet. It is fully illustrated with the well-known designs by Barnard and others, and has also four full-page colored plates ($1). Hesba Stretton's "The Child's Life of Christ," illustrated from the celebrated drawings by Plockhorst and Hoffmann, makes a specially appropriate Christmas gift. ($1.)

A Flock of Girls and Boys. — Like her last book, "Hope Benham," the new book by Miss Nora Perry is as much for boys as for girls, and they are certain to like it as well. To be sure the first ones, "A Flock of Girls" and "A Rosebud Garden of Girls," may well attract any boy reader of natural tastes, but there are more boys in the new books, and particularly in this delightful "Flock." There are eleven tales here of holiday times, of hearty, happy school life, and youthful struggles and triumphs, of goodness and badness, of generosities and always of high ideals and of true, simple, fine, and faithful standards of feeling and behavior. "A Flock of Girls and Boys" is illustrated in sympathetic fashion and with much technical skill by Charlotte T. Parker, a new illustrator for whom added successes may well be prophesied. (Little, Brown & Co. $1.50.)

Pleasant Days at Maplewood. — A most entertaining book for younger readers is "Pleasant Days at Maplewood," by Mrs. E. B. Bartlett, with illustrations by Florence E. Little. It relates the doings and happy movements of a city family in the country during the summer and winter months. A delightful feature is the charming little stories told by the different characters in the book. It is healthful in tone, and it will make an acceptable volume for every household where there are children. From it they can learn many ways of enjoying themselves. All children who have the great privilege of being born in the country will feel sympathy with the stories the bright little book tells them, and to the less fortunate little city girls and boys it will make very attractive some of the many delights of life, real life in the country — a very different thing from a few weeks spent at a summer hotel, dressed up in fine clothes. Few people in our busy days stop to think of the dense ignorance of city children on subjects that come to country children by intuition. They seldom learn to connect the milk and butter they consume with the cows which produced them. When they go to the country cows and chickens are carefully kept off the lawns on which they play croquet and tennis; goats never walk about near their white-capped nurses; geese are unseen, and many children really form no idea to themselves when they read of pigs, sheep, calves, oxen, etc., that these are names of animals which, when killed, become pork, lamb, mutton, veal, beef, etc. To all such children this book will be a delight, and it is specially suitable for reading aloud. (Ireland. $1.50.)

From "A Flock of Girls and Boys." Copyright, 1895, by Little, Brown & Co.

THE GREEN PAPER BASKET.

Mr. Rabbit at Home.—"Joel Chandler Harris has done no better work in his peculiar vein," says the Boston *Daily Evening Gazette*, "than in this his latest addition to holiday literature. Every child will enjoy the stories in this volume with their mixture of realism and supernaturalism. The style in which they are told enchains attention and the little groups of characters from whose mouths falls such entertaining folk-lore are strikingly individualized and leave a lasting impression." " 'Little Mr. Thimblefinger' was one of the most popular of last season's books," says the Boston *Weekly Transcript*,"and the announcement of a sequel to that original tale will create a great stir in juvenile circles. 'Mr.Thimblefinger' is a delightful host, and of course Sweetest Susan, and Buster John, and funny black Drusilla could not be expected to stay away from his house for very long." "Mr. Harris tells a fairy story well," says the N.Y. *Tribune*, "but he tells about the negroes better, and Drusilla, though she is not very prominent, reminds us of that fact when she speaks. The stories, which are just what fairy stories should be— simple, imaginative, and entirely sufficient in themselves, without anything of science, history, or hidden meaning in them—are illustrated with numerous sketches by Oliver Herford." (Houghton, Mifflin & Co. $2.)

From " Mr. Rabbit at Home."   Copyright, 1895, by Houghton, Mifflin & Co.

A PICNIC.

The Nimble Dollar.—"The small group of stories by Mr. Charles Miner Thompson, collected under the title of the first, 'The Nimble Dollar,'" says the Boston *Daily Evening Gazette*, "shows workmanship so excellent that it is to be hoped that many another group will follow. 'The Nimble Dollar,' 'The Reward of Heroes,' and 'The "Story" of Leon' have that exquisite neatness of finish, that keen vision for the inevitable that Americans were accustomed to call French until they perceived that they were as much American as Gallic, and they have humor which is entirely American. The author frankly says that he has borrowed the plot of one story from the German, leaving it to his readers to add that he has improved it even in its title. Such volumes are among the few really good reasons why the male authors of the United States should not abandon the writing of short stories to the feminine adepts—Miss Jewett, Mrs. Foote, Mrs. Wiggin, and Miss Pool." "We can heartily commend 'The Nimble Dollar' for a handful of amusing stories." says *Public Opinion*. "The actors are chiefly boys, but their adventures, though not wildly exciting, are of an unusual kind, and make as good reading for a sexagenarian as for a school-boy. The author has a goodly fund of humor." (Houghton, Mifflin & Co. $1.)

Colonial Dames and Goodwives.—Alice Morse Earle has given us a perfect picture of the olden days, drawn by one who has colonial blood in her veins and who has studied her subject so many years that her present life must seem like a reincarnation to her. She has written other works along the same lines, but this last one seems to me to be the best of all. "Under Mrs. Earle's guidance," says the New York *Times*, "the Colonial dames and goodwives again hang out their samplers on the outward walls. We know by this time a good deal about their clothing and their cookery, their amusements and their books, but Mrs. Earle appears to possess an inexhaustible store of information concerning them, and every time she puts in her spoon, as M. de Vogüé says of the Russian soup, she dips up something new and unexpected." "Every aspect of the status of womanhood," says the N. Y. *Sun*, " whether due to law or custom, is studied and depicted; we follow, with the author's help, the colonial woman through her whole life, from her girlhood and youth to her experiences in marriage and widowhood. We see her poor or rich, distinguished or low, in her household occupations and in her amusements, in business and politics, as well as in society; for we learn that, even in the colonial period, there were women who engaged in masculine employments, and took a lively interest in politics as well. The whole field of inquiry is covered in a dozen chapters. Shows clearly that women have changed little in 300 years." (Houghton, Mifflin & Co. $1.50.)

rom "Dorothy and Anton." Copyright, 1895, by Roberts Brothers.

LEARNING TO PLAY THE VIOLIN.

Joel: a Boy of Galilee.—Annie Fellows Johnston has, in this story, successfully accomplished the difficult task of weaving the life of Christ into a tale for children. Joel, a young Galilean lad, is a witness of the chief scenes in the life of Jesus, is himself healed by him, knows one of the shepherds of the Nativity in his old age, sees the crucifixion, and meets the risen Saviour. On this framework is constructed a touching tale, bringing out the chief incidents of the New Testament Gospels and handled with reverence and force. It is, most literally, a "Christmas story." (Roberts. $1.50.)

The Wood Beyond the World.—"The charm, or one of the charms, of this last book of William Morris," says the *Mail and Express*, "is more easily felt than described, and is only felt in the feelings, we think, by those who are enamoured of the invention which underlies all folklore, the element of fantasy, with or without a seeming purpose, containing in itself its excuse for being, and are enamoured at the same time of the simple, homely, idiomatic diction which characterized the early chroniclers and romancers, and of which Malory's 'Morte d'Arthur' is a fair example. At the age of sixty or thereabouts he is still pouring out his lovely things, more full of the glory of youth, more full of romantic adventure and romantic love, than any of the beautiful poems in his first volume. By the side of this exhaustless creator of youthful and lovely things, the youngest of the poets who have just appeared above the horizon seems faded and jaded." Frontispiece by Burne-Jones, printed on antique English paper with decorated cover. (Roberts. $3.)

Ward, Lock & Bowden's Juveniles.—A sequel to the "Seven Little Australians" of last year is entitled "The Family at Misrule," and it carries on the story of the wild pranks of the "little Australians" and their young stepmother. Miss Ethel Turner is naturally the author, and it is gracefully illustrated. ($1.)

E. P. Dutton & Co.'s Juveniles.—E. P. Dutton & Co. are the providers of innumerable colored picture-books and movable picture-books for the little inmates of the nursery; they have also stories of adventure and fairytales and school-life stories for larger children. Their publications as a whole are brilliant in picture covers, gayly tinted; they luxuriate, too, in pictures black and white as well as colored, and have charming reading-matter within their lovely bindings. Among their color-books the following may be mentioned: "Dutton's Holiday Annual for 1896" ($1.25); "Picture-Book Garden" ($2); "Cosy Corner Stories" ($2); "Pussy Purr" ($1.50); "Something Nice to Look At" ($1.25); "Farmyard Friends" ($1.25); "The Merry and Wise A B C Children's Spelling Bee" ($1); "Making Fun" and "Squire Squirrel and Other Animal Stories" ($1). Included in their movable picture-books are "The Model Menagerie" ($2.50); "Our Darling's Surprise Pictures" ($2); "The Children's Tableaux" ($2); "Transformation Pictures and Comical Fixtures" (75 c.), and many others equally attractive. By a mechanical device the figures in the pictures may be moved, producing many odd and laughable combinations. A new "Robinson Crusoe," in quarto shape, exhibits many full-page colored pictures ($2.50); "The Rabbit Witch, and other tales," by Catherine Poyle, is a humorous book with very original illustrations; it is of the order of Lear's "Book of Nonsense," and "Slovenly Peter," and must attract great attention ($1.50). Colonel Thomas W. Knox is the author of a capital book of sport and adventure in South Africa that boys will revel in, called "Hunters Three" ($2.50).

From "The Rabbit Witch." Copyright, 1895, by E. P. Dutton & Co.

"NOW," CRY THE RABBITS, "WE WILL PLAY"

☞ *The following names and figures refer to the publishers and to the pages on which may be found descriptive notices of their more prominent books:*

The New Books for the Holiday Season.

Abbey Shakespeare, Comedies. Il. by E. Abbey. 4 v. hf. cf., *per set*, $30 . . . . *Harper*

About Men, What Women Have Said. Comp. and arr. by R. Porter. $1 . . . . *Putnam*

Algerian Memories. F. B. and W. H. Workman. Il. *Net*, $2 . . . . *Randolph*

Anima Poetæ, Selections from the Unpublished Note-Books of S. T. Coleridge. Ed. by E. H. Coleridge. $2.50 . . . . *Houghton, M. & Co*

Art of Living. Robert Grant. Il. $2.50 . . . . . . *Scribner*

Artists' Series of Classic Prose and Poetry. 15 v. *Ea.*, $1.50 . . . . *Crowell*

At Odds, a novel. Baroness Tautphœus. *Waldering ed.* 2 v. $2.50 . . . . *Putnam*

Auld Licht Idylls. J. M. Barrie. *New il. ed.* $1.25. *Fenno*

Avril, L' Margueritte. *Fatence ed.* $1 ; leath., $1.50. *Crowell*

Baby Life. Il. $1.25 . . . . *Dutton*

Ballads of the Nations. 1, The book of British ballads, ed. by S. C. Hall ; 2, Ancient Spanish ballads, tr. with notes by J. G. Lockhart ; 3 and 4, American war ballads, ed. by C. E. Eggleston, 2 v. ; 5, French ballads, ed. by T. F. Crane ; 6, German ballads, ed. by H. S. White ; 7, 8, and 9, The Iliads of Homer, tr. from the Greek by G. Chapman, 3 v. Il. Buckram. *ea.*, 75c . . . . . . *Putnam*

Battle of the Frogs and Mice, tr. by Jane Barlow ; il. by Francis D. Bedford. $2 . . . . *Stokes*

Belle Nivernaise (La). Daudet. *Fatence ed.* $1 ; leath., $1.50 . . . . *Crowell*

British and European Butterflies and Moths. Full-p. col. pl. $7.50 . . . . *Dutton*

Browning, Robert. Complete Poetical and Dramatic Works. Por. *New Cambridge ed.* $3 ; hf cf., $5 ; tree cf. or full levant, $5.50 . . . . . . *Houghton, M. & Co*

Bulwer-Lytton's Novels. New Kenilworth ed. Pelham ; Falkland and Zicci ; Devereaux ; The disowned. *Ea.*, $1.50 . . . . *Routledge*

Burroughs, John. Works. *New Riverside ed.* Por. 9 v. $13.50 . . . . *Houghton, M. & Co*

Cameo Ed.: A chosen few, short stories by F. R. Stockton ; A little book of profitable tales, by E. Field ; Reflections of a married man, by R. Grant ; The opinions of a philosopher, by R. Grant. *Ea.*, $1.25. *Scribner*

Cats. F. J. Boston. Water-color fac-similes. Buckram, $1.75 . . . . *Stokes*

Christ in Song. *New enl. ed.* Ed. by D. S. Schaff. 2 v., *net*, $5 . . . . *Randolph*

Christmas Cards and Their Chief Designers. White. Il. $1.25 . . . . *Stokes*

Chronicles of Uganda. Rev. R. P. Ashe. Il. *Net*, $3 . . . . *Randolph*

Clarence ; and in a Hollow of the Hills. Bret Harte. 2 v. *Ea.*, $1.25 . . . . *Houghton, M. & Co*

Cluster of Gems. Streamer. Il. by fac-similes of water-color designs of the ballet by E. G. Emmet, accompanied by 12 designs of precious stones. Buckram, $3 and $2.50 ; silk, $3.50 . . . . *Stokes*

Colonial Dames and Goodwives. Alice Morse Earle. $1.50 . . . . *Houghton, M. & Co*

Constantinople. Crawford. Il. by Edwin Lord Weeks. $1.50 . . . . *Scribner*

Constantinople. Grosvenor. Introd. by Lew Wallace. Il. by Edwin Lord Weeks. 2 v. $10 ; hf. mor., $14. *Roberts*

Contemporary French Painters. Hamerton. Photogravures. $3 . . . . *Roberts*

Cooper, J. F. Works. 32 v. *Mohawk ed* , *per set*, $40 ; *per v.*, $1.25 . . . . *Putnam*

Correggio, His Life, His Friends, and His Time ; tr. from the Italian by C. Ricci. Full-p. photogravure pl. and il. *Net*, $12 . . . . *Scribner*

Courtship of Miles Standish. Longfellow. *Popular holiday ed.* Il. by G. H. Boughton, F. T. Merrill, and others. $1.50 . . . . *Houghton, M. & Co*

Crime of a Christmas Toy. Herman. Il. by G. Hutchinson. $1 . . . . *Ward, L. & B*

Crowell's Standard Library: Anna Karénina, by Count Tolstoi ; Crown of wild olive, Sesame and lilies, etc., by J. Ruskin ; Essays of Elia, by C. Lamb ; Pride and prejudice, by J. Austen ; Scottish chiefs, by J. Porter ; Sense and sensibility, by J. Austen ; Seven lamps of architecture, by J. Ruskin ; Wandering Jew, by E. Sue. 2 v. ; Westward ho!, by C. Kingsley. *Per v.*, $1. *Crowell*

Cyclopædia of Architecture in Italy, Greece, and the Levant ; ed. by W. P. P. Longfellow. Full-p. pl. and il. *Net*, $25 . . . . *Scribner*

Dogs. F. J. Boston. Water-color fac-similes. Buckram, $1.75 . . . . *Stokes*

Domestic Animals. Shaler. Il. by C. H. Leon, E. L. Weeks, and others. $2.50 . . . . *Scribner*

Don Quixote of the Mancha. Cervantes ; tr. by T. Shelton ; il. by Frank Brangwyn. 4 v. $4. *Lippincott*

Dona Perfecta. Galdós. *Odd number ser.* $1. *Harper*

Doom of the Holy City. Lydia H. Farmer. $1.50. *Randolph*

Dumas Romances, *new series*. incl.: 1, Ascanio, 2 v. ; 2, The war of women, 2 v. ; 3, Black, the story of a dog ; 4, Tales of Caucasus. 6 v., *ea.*, *per v.*, $1.25 ; hf. cf. or hf. mor., *per set*, 6 v., $18 . . . . *Little, B. & Co*

Early Venetian Printing ; with introd. by C. Castellani. Il. $7.50 . . . . *Scribner*

Earthwork Out of Tuscany. Hewlett. $1.75.*Putnam*

Echoes from the Sabine Farm. E. and R. M. Field. ll. by E. H. Garrett. $2.................................*Scribner*

Echoes of the Playhouse. E. Robins, *Jr.* 16 full-p. ll. $7..*Putnam*

Elia Series: Group I.—The essays of Elia, by C. Lamb, 2 v.; A selection from the discourses of Epictetus, with the Encheiridion, tr. by G. Long; Sesame and lilies, by J. Ruskin; The autobiography of Benjamin Franklin, ed. with notes by J. Bigelow; Thoughts of the Emperor Marcus Aurelius Antoninus, tr. with notes by G. Long. Ooze cf., *ea.*, $2.25.........*Putnam*

English Lands Letters, and Kings. Donald G. Mitchell. $1.50...*Houghton, M. & Co*

Essays in Miniature. Repplier. *New enl. ed.* $1.25.

Evolution in Art as Illustrated by the Life Histories of Designs. Haddon. ll. $1.25.................*Scribner*

Fables and Fabulists, Ancient and Modern. Newbigging. $1.50...*Stokes*

Fac-Similes of Water-Colors, by W. Granville Smith. Buckram, $5...*Stokes*

Fact and Fancy, Humorous Poems. "Cupid Jones." $1.50...*Putnam*

Fadette. Sand; from the French by J. M. Sedgwick. *Regular ed.* Por. $1.25................*Little, B. & Co*

Faience Violin Champfleury. *Faience ed.* $1: leath., $1.50...*Crowell*

Fair Women of To-Day. Peck. Poems accompanied by 12 fac-similes of water color drawings by C. C. Lovell. Por. Buckram, $3 and $3.50; silk, $3.50.........*Putnam*

Famous Leaders Among Women. Bolton. $1.50...*Crowell*

Flaubert, Gustave, as Seen in His Works and Correspondence. Tarver. Por. $4.................*Appleton*

Flowers of Song. Selections from the Poets. Full-p. col. pl. $2...*Dutton*

Fly-Leaves Series: 2, Novels by Eminent Hands, by W. M. Thackeray; 3, Echo Club, by B. Taylor. Ooze cf., *ea.*, $1.75...*Putnam*

Forget-me-nots. ll. $1.25..........................*Dutton*

Frail People of the Air, Excursions Into the World of Butterflies. Scudder. ll. $1.50.*Houghton, M. & Co*

From Dreamland Sent. Whiting. $1.25.........*Roberts*

From the Black Sea through Persia and India. Edwin Lord Weeks. ll. by the author. $3.50.......*Harper*

Front-Yard, and other Italian stories. C. F. Woolson. ll. $1.25...*Harper*

Galloway Herd. Crockett. $1: pap., 50c.........*Penno*

Galt, John, Novels, *new ll. ed.*, with an introd. by S. R. Crockett, the text rev. and ed. by D. S. Meldrum, por. and ll. from drawings by J. Wallace: The annals of the parish and the Ayrshire legatees, 2 v.; Sir Andrew Wylie, 2 v.; The provost and the last of the lairds, 2 v.; The entail, 2 v. *Ea.*, $1.25................*Roberts*

General Sherman. Force. *Great commanders ser.* $1.50..*Appleton*

Gentleman Vagabond. F. Hopkinson Smith. $1.25...*Houghton, M. & Co*

Girl of the Commune. Henty. $1.25............*Penno*

Grandma's Attic Treasures. Brine. *New ed.* Col. ll. Vellum, $1.50..*Dutton*

Gray, Thomas. Works. Ed. by E. Gosse. 4 v. ll. Buckram, $6; hf. cf., $12.....................*Stokes*

Great Men's Sons, from Socrates to Napoleon. Brooks. ll. $1.50...*Putnam*

Gwyn, Nell. Story and Sayings of Charles the Second; related and col. by P. Cunningham. ll. Por. $2.50...*Putnam*

Handy-Volume Classics: Poe's tales, Scarlet letter, and Tartarin of Tarascon. Vellum, 75c.; parti-cl. 75c.; silk, $1; hf. cf., $2.........................*Stokes*

Haunted House. Hood. ll. by Rob. Railton. $2.*Stokes*

Hawthorne-Tree, and Other Poems. Dole. $1.25...*Crowell*

Heroes of the Nations Ser.: Charles XII. and the collapse of the Swedish Empire, 1682–1719, by R. N. Bain. Lorenzo de' Medicis, by E. Armstrong. *Ea.*, $1.50; hf. leath., $1.75.......................................*Putnam*

History of Egypt from the Earliest Times to the Present. Petrie. 6 v. *Ea.*, $2.25.................*Scribner*

History of Florence for the First Two Centuries. Villari. 2 v. ll. $3.75.............................*Scribner*

Holmes, O. W. Complete Poetical Works. Por. *New Cambridge ed.* $2; hf. cf., $3.50; tree cf. or full levant, $5.50..*Houghton, M. & Co*

Hoosier Schoolmaster. Eggleston. *New rev. ed.* ll. $1.50...*G. D. Hurst*

House-Boat on the Styx. J. Kendrick Bangs. ll. $1.25...*Harper*

Huguenots and the Revocation of the Edict of Nantes. Baird. 2 v. Maps. $7.50...............*Scribner*

Humor of Russia: tr. by E. L. Voynick, with introd. by Stepniak *International humor ser.* ll. by O. Paque. $1.25..*Scribner*

Imagination in Landscape Painting. Hamerton. ll. $2..*Roberts*

Impressions and Memories. Noble. $1.50....*Putnam*

In the Land of Lorna Doone. William H. Rideing. $1. ....*Crowell*

In the Young World, Poems for Young People. Thomas. ....*Houghton, M. & Co*

Jameson's (Mrs.) Works of Art; ed. by E. M. Hurll, with a memoir of Mrs. Jameson. 5 v.: Sacred and legendary art, 2 v.; Legends of the Madonna; Legends of the monastic orders; Memoirs of the early Italian painters. *New ed.* ll. *per* v., $3.*Houghton, M. & Co*

Jude the Obscure. Hardy. ll. $1.75.............*Harper*

Keats's Poetical Works. ll. in photogravure. 2 v., $3: hf. cf., $6...*Crowell*

King, Rufus, Life and Correspondence of; ed. by C. R. King. v. 3. Hf. leath., $5.....................*Putnam*

Kingsley's (H.) Novels. *New ed.*; ed by C. K. Shorter. 12 v. *As.*, $1.25............................*Ward, L. & B*

Kingsley's Novels. 12 v. *Ea.*, $1.................*Scribner*

Knox, John. MacCunn. *English leaders of religion.* $1...*Houghton, M. & Co*

Last Poems. Lowell. $1.25.........*Houghton, M. & Co*

Later Lyrics. T. B. Aldrich. $1.*Houghton, M. & Co*

Leighton Court. Kingsley. *New uniform ed.* $1. ....*Scribner*

Lever, C. Novels of adventure, 6 v., ll. Maurice Tiernay, 2 v.; Sir Jasper Carew, 2 v.; Con Cregan, 2 v.; Roland Cashel, 2 v. ll., *per* v., $2.50; *per set*, $15; hf. cf., $27; hf. levant, $39................*Little, B. & Co*

Life of Christ. Dean Farrar. 2 v. ll. $3.....*Crowell*

Life of Nancy. Sarah Orne Jewett. $1.25. ....*Houghton, M. & Co*

Life of Washington. Irving. 2 v. ll. $3.....*Crowell*

Literary History of the English People. Jusserand. Pt. 2, From the Renaissance to Pope. $3.50....*Putnam*

Little Journeys to the Homes of Good Men and Great. Hubbard. Por...*Putnam*

Little Rivers. Van Dyke. ll. $2.50.............*Scribner*

London Idylls. Dawson. $1........................*Crowell*

Love and Friendship. Emerson. 35c............*Crowell*

Lyric Series: Century of German lyrics, sel., arr., and tr. by K. F. Kroeker; Heine's Book of songs, ed. by F. A. Stokes; The golden treasury. ll., *ea.*, $1; buckram, $1.25; hf. cf., $4; limp cf., $2.50.............*Stokes*

Lyrics and Ballads of Heine, Goethe, and Other German Poets; tr. by F. Hellman. *2d ed.* $1.50.....*Putnam*

Lyrics of Love and Nature. Chapman. ll. Cl. or buckram, $1.25; hf. buckram, $1.50; hf. cf., $2.50..*Stokes*

Madonna of the Tubs. Phelps. *New popular ed.* 75c. ....*Houghton, M. & Co*

Makers of Modern Rome. Mrs. Oliphant; ll. by J. Pennell and Rivière on wood by O. Lacour. $3. *Edition de luxe.* $8...............................*Macmillan*

Making of Manhood. Dawson. $1..............*Crowell*

Manual for Stamp Collectors. Le Grand. $1. ....*G. D. Hurst*

Manual of Greek Antiquities. Gardner and Jevons. ll. *Net,* $4..*Scribner*

Manxman (The). Hall Caine. *Edition de luxe.* ll. 2 v. $15..*Appleton*

Margaret Winthrop. Earle. $1.25...............*Putnam*

Master Mosaic-Workers. Sand; from the French by C. C. Johnston. *Regular ed.* Por. $1.25.*Little, B. & Co*

Masterpieces of Greek Sculpture. Adolf Furtwängler; with 19 full-p. text and 200 text ll. *Net,* $15. ....*Scribner*

Masterpieces of Verse and Prose: Lucile, by O. Meredith, ll. by F. M. Gregory; Lady of the lake, ll. by J. M. Gleeson. *Ea.*, 75c.; hf. cf., $1.50.............*Stokes*

Masters of Italian Music. Streatfield. *Masters of contemporary music.* $1.75.........................*Scribner*

Mentone, Cairo, and Corfu. Woolson. ll. $1.75.*Harper*

Midsummer of Italian Art, containing an examination of the works of Fra Angelico, Michael Angelo, and others. Stearns. $2.25.........................*Putnam*

Milton's Poetical Works. 4 v. ll.................*Warne*

Mimosa Leaves. Litchfield. $1.50...............*Putnam*

Modern Etching; descriptive text by C. Quentin; pl. etched by Strang, Legros, Holroyd, Cameron, and Rodin. *Limited ed.* Buckram, *net,* $15.*Little, B. & Co*

Modern Poster. H. C. Bunner, Spielmann and others; with 60 ll. 250 copies on Japan pap., *net,* $6; 750 copies on enamelled pap., *net,* $3...................*Scribner*

Moliere's Dramatic Works; tr. by K. P. Wormeley. V. 4. Leath., $1.50...........................*Roberts*
Moore's (Thomas) Poetical Works. Il. in photogravure. 2 v., $3; hf. cf., $6.......................*Crowell*
Music Series. George T. Ferris. *New il. ed.* Great German composers; Great Italian composers; Great French composers; Great singers; Great violinists and pianists. 5 v. *Per set*, $4; hf. mor.,$8....*Appleton*
My Climbs in the Alps and Caucasus. Mummery. Il. full-p. pl. *Net,* $7.50................................*Scribner*
My Sister Henrietta. Renan; tr. by A. L. Alger. Il. by H. Scheffer and A. Renan. $1.25............*Roberts*
Mystery of Witch-Face Mountain. Craddock. $1.25, ...*Houghton, M. & Co*
Napoleon, Private Life of, Memoirs of Constant; tr. from the French, with an introd., by Imbert de Saint-Amand. 4 v $5...............................*Scribner*
Natural History of Selborne. Gilbert White. Introd. by J. Burroughs. 80 il. by C. Johnson. 2 v., $4.*Appleton*
Notes in Japan. Parsons. Il. by the author. $3.*Harper*
Old Chester, with 11 etchings and 20 pen-and-ink sketches, principally full-p., etched and described by H. Crickmore. Silk, $2.50................................*Scribner*
Old Dutch and Flemish Masters, by T. Cole; a collection of wood-engravings accompanied by explanatory text by J. C. Van Dyke. $7.50........................*Century*
Old New England Town. Rev. Frank S. Child. Il. $2. *Edition de luxe,* $5....................*Scribner*
Our Edible Toadstools and Mushrooms, and How to Distinguish Them. Gibson. 30 col. pl. and 57 other il. by the author. $7.50..................................*Harper*
Painting in France, After the Decline of Classicism. Hamerton. Photogravures. $3.................*Roberts*
Painting, Sculpture, and Architecture as Representative Arts. George L. Raymond. Il. $2.25.........*Putnam*
Palmyra and Zenobia. Wright. Il. $2.50...*Nelson*
Pansies. Il. $1.25....................................*Dutton*
Pansies. H. D. La Praix. Water-color fac-similes. Buckram, $2.....................................*Stokes*
Parkman, Francis, Life and Uncollected Papers. Farnham. Por. $2.50....................*Little, B. & Co*
Peninsular War. Napier. 5 v. Maps, plans. *Per set,* $6.25...*Stokes*
People We Pass. Julian Ralph. Il. $1.25....*Harper*
Pictures from Dickens, with selections from his writings. Full-p. col. pl. $2.....................*Dutton*
Poets' Bible: Old Testament, and New Testament; comp. and ed. by W. G. Horder. 2 v. *Ea.,* $1.25. ....*Ward, L. & B*
Pony Tracks. Written and il. by F. Remington. $3. *Harper*
Queens of Society. G. and P. Wharton. *New ed.,* with pref. by J. H. McCarthy. Il. by C. A. Doyle. 2 v. *Stokes*
Red Cockade. Weyman. Il. $1.25..............*Harper*
Repose in Egypt. Susan E. Wallace. *New ed.* 75c. *G. D. Hurst*
Rhymes and Roses. Peck. *Puck series.* $1.25..*Stokes*
Rhymes of Our Planet. Carleton. Il. $1.25..*Harper*
Rip Van Winkle, ed. by J. Jefferson, being the text of the play by this actor. Il. and por. by R. Crelfelsh. *Large-pap. ed., net,* $25. *Ed. of 150 copies, net,* $10. Ordinary ed. $5....................................*Dodd*
Roses. N. A. Wells. Water-color fac-similes. Buckram, $2...*Stokes*
Rossetti, Dante Gabriel, his Family Letters, with a Memoir by W. M. Rossetti. 2 v. Por. $6.50..*Roberts*
Sand, George, Choice Works, incl. 1, François the waif, tr. by J. M. Sedgwick; 2, The Devil's Pool, tr. by J. M. Sedgwick and E. Sedgwick; 3, Fadette, tr. by M. Sedgwick; 4, The master mosaic-workers, tr. by C. C. Johnston. *Limited ed.,* 4 v., por. and il., bds., *per set, net,* $6; hf. levant mor., $14; full cf., $16; *edition de luxe,* 4 v., por. and il., bds., *net,* $14.*Little, B. & Co*
Scott, "Oxford" Miniature. 5 v., 'from $7 to $12.50; 1 v., from $1.50 to $4.50......................*Nelson*
Scottish Chiefs. Porter. 2 v. $3; hf. cf., $6.*Crowell*
Shakespeare's Heroines on the Stage. Wingate. Il. $2...*Crowell*
Side Talks with Girls. Ashmore. $1.........*Scribner*
Sindbad the Sailor and Ali Baba and the Forty Thieves. Full-p. il. by W. Strang and J. B. Clark. $2..*Scribner*
Singing Shepherd, and other poems. Annie Fields. $1.....................................*Houghton, M. & Co*
Singular Life. Phelps. $1.25.....*Houghton, M. & Co*
Sketch of Life and Work of the Painter Domenico Morelli. Willard. Il. $1.25.......*Houghton, M. & Co*

Song of Hiawatha. Longfellow. Full-p. il. and por. *Popular holiday ed.* $2............*Houghton, M. & Co*
Spring Blossoms. Mary Lowe Dickinson. Il. 75c. *Amer. Baptist Pub. Soc*
Stambuloff, M. Beaman. *Public men of to-day ser.* $1.25..*Warne*
Standish of Standish. Mrs. Austin. *Holiday ed.* 20 full-p. photogravure il. by F. T. Merrill. 2 v., $5. *Houghton, M. & Co*
Stark Munro Letters. Doyle. Il. $1.50....*Appleton*
Stevenson's Works. *New ed.* 5 v. *Ea.,* $1..*Scribner*
Stops of Various Quills. Howells. Il. by Pyle. *Edition de luxe,* on hand-made pap., sepia il., $15; *Regular ed.,* $4.50..*Harper*
Stories of the Ages: Group I—Select tales from the Gesta Romanorum; Headlong Hall and Nightmare Abbey, by T. L. Peacock; Cranford, by Mrs. Gaskell; Tales by Heinrich Zschokke; The rose and the ring, by W. M. Thackeray; Undine, and Sintram and his companions, by De La Motte Fouqué. Ooze cf., *ea.,* $2.25...*Putnam*
Stories of the Nations. *Ea.,* $1.50..............*Putnam*
Story of America, from 1492 to 1895. Hamilton W. Mabie. Il. $2.......................................*Winston*
Story of the Other Wise Man. Van Dyke. Il. $1.50. *Harper*
Tales of a Traveller. Irving. *Buckthorne ed.* 2 il. by G. W. Edwards, A. Rackham, A. Barraud, F. S. Church, and others. 2 v., $6; ¾ levant, $12..*Putnam*
Tavern of the Three Virtues. Saint-Juirs. 60 il. by D. Vièrge, and a critical essay on his art by E. Gosse. *Limited ed.* $15.....................................*Stokes*
Temptation of Katharine Gray. Dickinson. $1.50. *Am. Bapt. Pub. Soc*
Thaxter, Celia. Poems. Ed. by S. O. Jewett. $1.50. *Houghton, M. & Co*
This Goodly Frame the Earth. Francis Tiffany. $1.50. *Houghton, M. & Co*
Three Musketeers. Dumas. 250 il. by M. Leloir. *New popular ed.* 2 v. $4........................*Appleton*
Turning-Points in Successful Careers. Thayer. $1.50..*Crowell*
XXIV. Bits of Vers de Société. Il. *New ed.* Cl. or buckram, $1.75..*Stokes*
Uno' Edinburg. Page. *Il. ed.* Il. by B. W. Clinedinst. $1.50..*Scribner*
Uncle Remus, His Songs and Sayings. Harris. *Edition de luxe.* 112 il. by A. B. Frost. $10. *Library ed.* Il. $2..*Appleton*
Undine. Fouqué. Tr. by E. Gosse. Il. by photogravures by W. E. F. Britten. $6................*Stokes*
Vesper Library. 7 v. *Ea.,* 75c.................*Crowell*
Victorian Anthology, containing representative poems by the authors discussed in "Victorian Poets," sel. and ed. by E. C. Stedman. *Lib. style,* $2.50; *large-pap. ed.,* 2 v., *net,* $10.........................*Houghton, M. & Co*
Victorian Songs; collected and il. by E. H. Garrett; with introd. by E. Gosse. $6; full cf., $10; *Ed de luxe,* vellum, *net,* $15..................................*Little, B. & Co*
Vignette series: The laureates, essays by K. West, with 48 full-p. il. by F. C. Gordon; Poems and stories of Poe, il. by H. C. Edwards. Il. *Ea.,* $1.25; $1.50; $2. *Stokes*
Violets. Il. $1.25....................................*Dutton*
Voyages and Travels. Hall. Il. $2.............*Nelson*
Wandering Jew. Sue. *Il. ed.* 2 v. $3; hf. cf., $6. *Crowell*
Wanderings, Literary and Historical. Jusserand. $3.50...*Putnam*
Washington, Life of. Irving. 2 v. $3; hf. cf., $6. *Crowell*
Westminster. Walter Besant. Il. $3; $4.....*Stokes*
Westminster Abbey and the Cathedrals of England; il. from recent photographs. $3.50............*Winston*
What I Told Dorcas. Ireland. $1.25............*Dutton*
William the Silent, Prince of Orange. Ruth Putnam. 2 v. Il. *Ea.,* $3.75.................................*Putnam*
Window in Thrums. J. M. Barrie. *New il. ed.* $1.25. *Fenno*
Wits and Beaux of Society. G. and P. Wharton; pref. by J. H. McCarthy. Il. by H. K. Browne and J. Godwin. 2 v. $3..*Stokes*
Women of Colonial and Revolutionary Times: Margaret Winthrop, by A. M. Earle; Martha Washington, by A. H. Wharton; Dorothy Payne Madison, by M. W. Goodwin; Mercy Otis Warren, by A. Brown; Eliza Lucas Pinckney, by A. M. Earle. *Ea.,* $1.25..*Scribner*
Wood Beyond the World. Morris. Il. by E. Burne-Jones. $3...*Roberts*

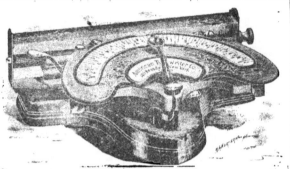

THE

LITERARY NEWS

𝔄 𝔐onthly 𝔍ournal of 𝔠urrent 𝔏iterature

[NEW SERIES.]

Vol. XVII.

1896

NEW YORK
PUBLICATION OFFICE, 59 DUANE STREET
1896

THE LITERARY NEWS.

INDEX TO VOL. XVII. (NEW SERIES) 1896.

BOOKS FOR YOUNG PEOPLE.

INDEX TO ADVERTISERS.

72

LI Y NEWS

AN ECLECTIC REVIEW OF CURRENT LITERATURE
~ILLUSTRATED~

CONTENTS.

VOL·XVII·Nº 1   JANUARY ~ 1896 $1.00 YEARLY
10 CTS. PER NO.

~ PUBLICATION OFFICE ~
59 DUANE STREET, NEW YORK
ENTERED AT THE POST OFFICE AT NEW YORK AS SECOND CLASS MATTER

The Literary News

In winter you may reade them, ad ignem, by the fireside; and in summer, ... under some shadie tree, and therewith pass away the tedious howres.

| VOL. XVII. | JANUARY, 1896. | NO. 1. |

Edwin A. Grosvenor.

EDWIN A. GROSVENOR, author of "Constantinople," was born at Newburyport, Mass., in 1845. He comes of old colonial stock, his ancestors through nine generations being clergymen or physicians, and he is tenth in descent from John Grosvenor, who was tomahawked by the Indians at Roxbury in 1691. The quaint tombstone of this remote ancestor, on which is carved the Grosvenor coat of arms — the only coat of arms in the ancient cemetery —and the tomahawk above, may still be seen in the Eustis Street graveyard in Boston. Professor Grosvenor's preparation for college was obtained mostly from his mother, a rarely gifted lady, one of the most popular writers of juvenile books in her time. She always published anonymously, but many can still remember their youthful delight on reading her "Old Red House" and "Captain Russell's Watchword."

Grosvenor graduated from Amherst College in 1867, being salutatorian and class poet, studied at Andover and Paris, and from 1873 to 1890 was Professor of History at Robert College, Constantinople. There he came into intimate relations with diplomats and scholars in the Ottoman Empire, in Greece, and throughout Europe. His vacations and absences on leave

PROF. EDWIN A. GROSVENOR.

were always devoted to some line of historical research away from the capital and read like a romance. His first vacation was passed on the plain of Troy. In another he visited all the places from Domremy to Rouen connected with Joan of Arc. In another he traced Napoleon's Italian campaign of 1796; in another Napoleon's campaign of 1814; in another the battles of Servian and Bulgarian history; in another the battlefields of Switzerland from Morgarten, and so on, all over Europe. Also he went over a great part of the route of Alexander, and of the Ten Thousand, and he followed out all the apostolic tours of Saint Paul.

But the chief thought in his mind, aside form his college work, was always his "Constantinople." Through more than fifteen years he was engaged in the collection of material and in composition. His opportunities were unequalled. Archæologists and antiquaries are often uncommunicative and suspicious of each other, but Professor Grosvenor was as willing to give as to receive, and he enjoyed the friendship of the leading authorities upon Byzantine and mediæval topics.

Resigning his position in 1890, he devoted the following year to travel in Roumania, the Balkan Peninsula, the Greek Islands, Asia

Minor, and northern Syria. Hon. Eugene Schuyler and he had planned a work in copartnership upon the Greek Islands, but the project ended on the lamented death of Mr. Schuyler.

Returning to America, he was invited to lecture on history at Amherst. In 1892 he was appointed Professor of French Language and Literature at Amherst ; meanwhile, from 1892 to 1894, he was also head of the department of history at Smith College. In July, 1895, he was made Professor of European History at Amherst.

Since his return to America Professor Grosvenor has translated and revised Duruy's " Histoire des Temps Modernes," now extensively used as a college text-book, and has contributed several hundred articles on European and Oriental subjects to Johnson's Cyclopædia. Among the more notable of these articles are those on "Constantinople," " Ravenna," " Roumania," " Mohammedanism," " Servia," " Sicily," " Syria," and " Turkey." So much of the world seen and studied and so much labor done in the class-room and outside would have been impossible had not Professor Grosvenor been a tireless worker and known the value of minutes.

If you cannot afford to buy his great work on "Constantinople" read it at the library as soon as possible. (Roberts. 2 v., $10.)

Mars.

WE have come very near entering this work under the head of Travel and Exploration, for certainly in it Mr. Lowell travels toward Mars, if not actually to Mars, and as certainly explores the surface of that planet, and maps it, in this interesting volume. His station was the Lowell Observatory at Flagstaff, Arizona.

PIAZZA DEL POPOLO.

His telescope was an 18-inch refractor, by Brashear, of Allegheny, Pa. But the instrument, he says, is of less importance than the atmosphere, and neither is of account without systematic study. From May 24, 1894, to April 3, 1895, with this instrument, at that station, and in that atmosphere, he studied this planet, made nearly a thousand drawings and sketches of it, and this handsome volume is his report.

Several considerations invest the Planet Mars with peculiar interest for us. He is of our own " cosmic kin"; no other heavenly body, save Venus and the Moon, ever comes so near the Earth, and for all practical purposes he is our nearest neighbor. His diameter is about 4215 miles ; he has a cloudless atmosphere, an apparent dearth of water, yet surface indications of a vast system of irrigation and fertilized oases. If what we call life exists on Mars, it must, however, be in many ways a different life from our own. Gravity there is only a little more than one-third what it is here, and from this fixed point Mr. Lowell ventures out upon a little ramble of amusing speculations as to the way our Martian neighbors live, move, and have their being, if any such neighbors there are. We ought not, however, to represent him as believing that Mars actually is inhabited, but only that it may be.

Mr. Lowell's book, as it is founded upon truly scientific research, is scientifically planned and constructed, and its method, clearness, and discriminating exposition of detail will please all readers who like to go slowly and cautiously through a new field, and feel sure as, to every step they take. The five chapters discuss in turn the General Characteristics of the Planet, its Atmosphere, its Water System, and its Conjectured Canals and Oases. Twenty-four illustrations, based upon telescopic photography, add greatly to the interest of the text.

While it will require close attention to understand some of Mr. Lowell's pages, much in them will appeal to the curiosity of the general reader, and the outward attractiveness of the volume will be sure to find a way for it into many hands. Mr. Lowell's great gift is clearness of style and the art of making his readers take interest even in topics somewhat beyond their grasp. (Houghton, Mifflin & Co. $2.50.)—*Boston Literary World.*

The Makers of Modern Rome.

I TURN to a solid volume of six hundred pages from the pen of Mrs. Oliphant, who claimed and kept our attention some time since

She gives the reader with a few strokes of her pen a vivid picture of personal ambition, public policy, and domestic life, which is in every

From " Makers of Modern Rome."   *Copyright, 1896, by Macmillan & Co.*
SANTA MARIO MAGGIORE.

by her work on "The Makers of Florence." The book before me is named "The Makers of Modern Rome," which means, of course, Rome since the Christian era. It is divided into four parts, the first covering nearly one hundred pages, devoted to the famous women of the city ; the second to the Popes who created the Papacy; the third to the Tribune of the people, and the fourth to the Popes who made the city. There are several illustrations, and the publishers, Macmillan & Co., have done their part with admirable skill, for the volume presents a very attractive appearance.

I don't know that I can do the work justice in the short space allotted to it, but I should be glad to at least commend it to your careful attention. Mrs. Oliphant is well known by us all, and although she does not pretend to be a historian in the strict sense of the word, she has a genius for detecting the salient incidents which are either the cause or the consequence of what has gone before. Moreover, she has an interesting style, and her chapters on Gregory the Great and the Monk Hildebrand and Innocent III. are as fascinating as a novel.

way delightful. In many instances she quotes from the diary of the individual discussed, and you feel at the end as though you had been in actual contact with him, sometimes agreeably and again rather disagreeably. I have found several hours of intellectual refreshment in the book and am more than glad to have it within easy reach. (Macmillan. $3 ; *Large-pop. ed.*, $8.)—GEORGE H. HEPWORTH, in the *N. Y. Herald.*

Andromeda.

THE smooth-worn coin and threadbare classic phrase
  Of Grecian myths that did beguile my youth
Beguile me not as in the olden days :
  I think more grief and beauty dwell with truth.
Andromeda, in fetters by the sea,
  Star-pale with anguish till young Perseus came,
Less moves me with her sufferings than she,
  The slim girl figure fettered to dark shame
That nightly haunts the park there, like a shade,
  Trailing her wretchedness from street to street.
See where she passes—neither wife nor maid.
  How all mere fiction crumbles at her feet !
Here is woe's self, and not the mask of woe;
A legend's shadow shall not move you so !

  (Houghton, Mifflin & Co. $1.) — *From Aldrich's " Later Lyrics."*

The One Who Looked On.

IN "The One Who Looked On," by F. F. Montrésor, there is none of the strangeness visible in the author's first novel. It is a simple story of an unreturned and unacknowledged love, told by the heroine, an old-fashioned, womanly little body, whose small cousins amuse by their childish frolics and naughtiness. Anything more quiet it would be difficult to imagine, but the heroine is a personage to remember long, and the hero, although sadly like John Humphrey and Guy Carleton, the beloved of all English nurseries, is a gentleman, and the book is one not likely to be soon forgotten by its readers. (Appleton. $1 ; pap., 50c.)—*Boston Gazette.*

Jude the Obscure.

THOMAS HARDY'S novel of "Jude the Obscure," which has undergone so many vicissitudes of one sort and another since it began to appear as a serial a year or more ago, is now put forth in complete and definitive form, "the present edition," says the author in his preface, "being the first in which the whole appears as originally written." Any discriminating reader who takes up the work in its latest shape, and follows it from beginning to end, will be able to see how much it suffered in the artistic sense by previous editorial revision. Like "Tess of the D'Urbervilles," the story of "Jude the Obscure" is a manifestation of the author's later manner—a manner which is a natural and almost inevitable development in a writer who possesses Mr. Hardy's extraordinary capacity for observation, profound knowledge of human nature, and philosophical ideas concerning the problem of existence. Mr. Hardy has never been an author to write novels merely for the purpose of providing entertainment, or for illustrating in more or less persuasive form some preconceived didactic proposition. He has been content to take men and women as they are, and no one in English fiction—possibly no one in the whole range of modern literature—has been able to surpass him in depicting the reaction of circumstances upon character. In this carefully reasoned, closely woven narrative of "Jude the Obscure" he sets before us the entirely natural and consistent experiences of two sensitive and impulsive creatures, who have been profoundly and disastrously affected by the changes in popular thought regarding ideals of religious faith and personal conduct; who, yielding to their thoroughly undisciplined emotions, work out for themselves a destiny full of bitterness and sorrow. It has been said that Mr. Hardy is not a writer to work on preconceived theories, but he certainly has some effective doctrines regarding the behavior of the two sexes under similar conditions, and when one comes to analyze this story one finds that a settled conviction underlies its entire texture, and this conviction is that misfortunes and disappointments, which soften the heart of man and tend to make him more considerate and charitable in his dealings with his fellows, have as a rule a contrary effect upon the heart of a woman. It would be easy to dispose of the two leading characters in "Jude the Obscure" by saying that they are two consummate fools and that they deserved all the punishment they inflicted upon themselves in their mutual folly, but the fact remains that they are representative types of a transition era and that to study them is the duty of every thoughtful and inquiring mind. Concerning the artistic quality of the book it is possible here to speak but briefly. Mr. Hardy has never written anything more richly varied in its contrasts of coloring, more significant in play of incident, or more gracefully expressive in style. The novel as a whole is the work, not only of a great literary artist in point of technique, but of a master of thought and feeling. It is a novel not only to be read, but to be studied, for it is in its way a document for the times, full of important meanings for those who are able to read it aright. (Harper & Bros. $1.75.)—*The Beacon.*

The Amazing Marriage.

IF Aminta had fled with her Lord Ormont instead of from him, the Beautiful Gorgon of the present "Amazing Marriage" might easily be identified as their child. Indeed, the whole complicated scandal of the Old Buccaneer and the beautiful, daring young Countess Fanny reminds one forcibly of "Lord Ormont and His Aminta." When at last, after forty pages of ancestral fact and fancy, the pedigree of sister and brother has been rooted in the mind of the reader as the one vital explanation of all that is to come, the events at the disposal of Dame Gossip begin to be discussed.

"A Chapter of Undercurrents with a Few Surface Flashes" is the heading of one of the chapters. It applies equally well to the whole two volumes, for the book is a philosophical study of character even more than a novel. . . .

This is the tale—not much more than the ordinary sugar and salt, flour, water, and compressed yeast of nowadays' "staff o' life," the novel. But here comes the skill of this amazing author. He dives into motives, skips from one point of view to another, calmly relates, transfixes a tragedy with an adjective, lingers for pages over a prize-fight or a pretty walk of brother and sister along a mountain-path, dashes headlong into events one can hardly grasp for the speed and hammer-and-tongs treatment, and in the end rounds, smoothes, and perfects until in wonder we find ourselves the possessors not only of a complete, well-turned novel, but of a world of men and women true as sunlight on a new country. (Scribner. 2 v., $2.50.)—*Boston Literary World.*

The Riviera.

"THE Riviera," a translation, by Dr. Charles West, of a work by Charles Lenthéric, a French engineer. An important and valuable study, after a thoroughly scientific method, and with exhaustive thoroughness, of the French Mediterranean coast from Marseilles to Ventimiglia on the Italian boundary. This coast—bold, rocky, and picturesque, looking off on the blue Mediterranean, studded with such modern towns as Hyères and Toulon, Nice, Cannes, and Mentone—is not more attractive to the present winter resident, fleeing from the United States, or the North of Europe, than it is famous for its Greek and Roman occupations and remains of olden times. And it is M. Lenthéric's purpose to explore it carefully in search of its old cities, and their sites and ruins, to recover its old aspects, to reinvest it with its old life. The beautiful maps with which the volume is illustrated, its uncut edges, its abundant historical notes, its admirable plan and methods make it a book which the scholar will rejoice in, though not the indolent, superficial reader sitting in the sunshine on the shore ; and we know of no book which we would so earnestly recommend to Mediterranean travellers who carry brains with them as we would this, especially if they are going to spend the winter at Nice, or Mentone, or anywhere along there. (Putnam. $2.) —*Boston Literary World.*

The Mediterranean Trip.

"THE MEDITERRANEAN TRIP," by Noah Brooks, is a short guide to the principal ports on the shores of the Western Mediterranean and the Levant. Descriptions are given of many cities bordering on the inland sea, as Ponta Delgada (Azores), Funchal (Madeira), with Alexandria, Jaffa, Smyrna, Constantinople, Athens, Messina, Palermo, and Naples. Mr. Brooks, who is an experienced traveller, gives just the necessary information. The volume is of the size fitted for the pocket, and there are many illustrations, with the necessary maps. (Scribner. *net*, $1.25.)—*N. Y. Tribune.*

From "The Mediterranean Trip."   Copyright, 1895, by Charles Scribner's Sons.

MALTA—THE SALUTING BATTERY.

A House-Boat on the Styx.

JOHN KENDRICK BANGS had the happy idea of reporting for us some of the high and instructive conversations on the " other shore," and the result is " A House-Boat on the Styx," The Associated Shades are a select body of im-

From "A House-Boat on the Styx." Copyright, 1896, by Harper & Bros.

A WEIRD COMPANY.

mortal ghosts who organize themselves into a club for mutual intercourse and social benefit. The house-boat, the *Nancy Nox,* anchored close to the Hades shore of the Styx, is the club; such eminent spirits as Sir Walter Raleigh, Cassius, Demosthenes, Blackstone, Dr. Johnson, and Confucius are the house committee, and old Charon is the steward and manager of the organization. Club-life on the *Nancy* seems to have been a feast of reason. Nero, Dr. Johnson, and Emerson have a spirited debate as to the authorship of Shakespeare's plays, and Bacon and the bard himself join in it. Burns and Homer discuss cooking and sculpture over a small bird and a bottle. Noah and P. T. Barnum argue about animals. Washington gives a birthday dinner. Finally the club go to see a mill between Goliah and Samson, and in their absence Capt. Kidd steals the *Nancy.* Mr. Bangs's fooling is at its highest level in this book. (Harper. $1.25.)—*Mail and Express.*

The Red Republic.

ROBERT W. CHAMBERS has written a story of nearly 500 pages, but in large print, and it is not a book for boys only, but also for older folks. The Commune was a huge tragedy, and a writer can hardly deal with it in a tame way, It must be dramatic and thrilling, or it is noth-ing. Mr. Chambers has given a good deal of study to details, and the general coloring of the narrative is satisfactory. He reproduces the spirit of these wild times with unusual success, and in the very first chapter you are transported to the streets of Paris and begin to feel as though you had lived there for years. You become a part of the incidents which occur, and partake in the dangers of which the city is full. There is a good deal of veritable history in the book, and of course a good deal of romance. The young men who constitute the most prominent characters are Americans of the dare-devil sort, and the risks they run and the narrow escapes they effect are without number. I wish Mr. Chambers had suppressed the profanity which appears now and then, for it mars the book to a certain extent, and in a story of this kind is wholly unnecessary. Perhaps I am over-critical, and so hasten to add that the work is quite worth your perusal, and will give you a fair idea of Paris during one of its most volcanic periods. (Putnam. $1.25.)—GEORGE H. HEP-WORTH in *New York Herald.*

In a Hollow of the Hills.

IN Mr. Bret Harte's new book, " In a Hollow of the Hills," he indulges himself in the unwonted luxury of an entirely unmitigated scamp, so that the book may well be regarded as remarkably original; but one does not ask originality from Mr. Harte, so long as he possesses that exquisite grace of style which would make the table of superficial measures agreeable reading. He may produce the daring yet innocent young girl with a dangerous past belonging to some of her kindred; the trusting husband of the runaway wife; the brave young man born only to be taken for some roving villain of the Sierras; the stage-driver of inexhaustible profanity, and all the rest of his little company a hundred times more if he like, and not a hand will be lacking in the applause. As for this book, the villain would make it successful, and the trusting husband is perfect. One of Mr. Harte's unique gifts is to make an upright fool seem wiser than a brilliant, handsome scoundrel, and he has exercised it very skilfully in his latest book. For some time his stanchest admirers feared that Bret Harte had lost some of his old genius, but here once more he has prepared a book that has a good plot and the old skill in its unravelling. (Houghton, Mifflin & Co. $1.25.)—*Boston Gazette.*

Aftermat'.

AGAIN the author of "Flute and Violin" and of "A Kentucky Cardinal" has given proof of his power and depth of feeling as a literary artist. "Aftermath," in spite of its forbidding title, is a pure and clean-cut romantic cameo, worthy of a name and a fame all its own. It has all the individuality and poetic feeling of "A Kentucky Cardinal," of which it is a sequel, but by no means an appendage.

Like the former story, "Aftermath" depicts the struggle in a man's heart between the love of nature and the love of woman—between the charms of the wilderness and the tyranny of civilization. The quaint and exquisite close of "A Kentucky Cardinal" left Adam and Georgiana united as lovers over the dead form of a captive redbird—the symbol of Adam's sacrifice. The new story takes up the courtship, follows it through marriage and birth until, after a year of idyllic home life, death claims the young mother.

The close of the book is not so strong as that of its predecessor. The story, indeed, is the merest thread. But it is a golden thread, strung with jewels quarried deep in the mysteries of human nature and of life. The charm of Ik Marvel is there, but Mr. Allen has a delicacy of touch, a courtly Kentucky grace, and an unerring aptness of expression peculiarly his own. His sentences are polished as diamonds, yet they never betray the labor which their conscientious author has lavished upon them.

The book depicts Kentucky life in the fifties, talks of Prentice and Clay and the gathering clouds of civil strife, and breathes the author's longing to heal the old wounds. "I know one thing," says Adam ; "if I could do my whole duty as a Kentuckian—as an American citizen—as a human being —I should have to fight on both sides." Only rarely does Mr. Allen indulge in a distinctly humorous touch, and yet there is the Irving humor all through the book, as when he remarks that if the effusive Sylvia had been Lot's wife she would not have turned to a pillar of salt, but to a geyser ; or when he hints that "Mr. Prentice's

studious regard for much of the poetry that he published was based upon the fact that he could not parse it."

The beautiful character sketch of Georgiana, the quaint idea of having one room in the house where it was not allowed even a visitor to speak ill of any living creature, the flashes of true feminine nature, the mystery and might of love and its sacrifices—all are here, and all are pervaded with the water-mark of true artistic power.

Mr. Allen writes from within. He sits within his story as within a room and deals with the heart of things, not with the surface. The world can never have too much of James Lane Allen's style of romanticism. (Harper. $1.) —*Chicago Tribune.*

British Foreign Policy.

WE have lately received two important contributions to the history of the attitude of England toward foreign countries. We shall recur at length hereafter to one of these, an historical essay on "The Growth of British Policy," by the late Sir J. R. Seeley, which covers the period from the accession of Elizabeth to the death of

From Miss Latimer's "Europe in Africa."   Copyright, 1895, by McClurg & Co.

A SULTAN.

William III. The other book to which, for the moment, we would draw attention is "The History of the Foreign Policy of Great Britain," by Capt. Montague Burrows, R. N., Professor of Modern History at Oxford, which undertakes to review the whole epoch from the reign of Elizabeth down to the present day. The main purpose of this work is to show the continuity or continuous development of British foreign policy. Now and again temporarily distorted or even reversed by dynastic interests, by careless diplomacy, by erratic statesmanship, by ecclesiastical dissensions, by foreign rivalry, or by stress of circumstances, it has, in Capt. Burrows's opinion, always reverted to the course prescribed by nature and approved by experience. This book was written to prove that, deeply implicated as England has become at certain times in the balance of power in Europe, yet she has never long lost sight of her unique position as an extra-Continental power, a position which, as her navy, her commerce, and her colonies grew, was destined to expand into that of a world-wide maritime empire. The delineation of the evolution, oscillation, and reconciliation of these two principles of national policy is the aim kept in view throughout the 350 pages of the book before us.

In the present notice we shall confine ourselves to a question of present and urgent interest, to wit, what is said by this semi-official expounder of England's foreign policy concerning her attitude toward the United States during the last hundred years. We regret that we are unable to regard all that is set down on this subject as entirely in accordance with the facts. (Putnam. $3.)—*Extract from notice in N. Y. Sun.*

England's Responsibility Towards Armenia.

THE first reports of the recent atrocities in Armenia were received with creditable incredulity, but with discreditable ignorance ; and so long as the Turkish Government is looked upon as being but another of the sisterhood of nations, so long will such ignorance continue. Yet we have been many times told, and are told again by Canon Malcolm MacColl in his new book, "England's Responsibility Towards Armenia," that Turkey's system of government is a theocracy, and consequently irreformable in every particular which touches the mutual relations of Christians and Mussulmans. The sultan, as Commander of the Faithful, conceives it his duty to reduce all mankind to the alternative either of embracing Islam or of submitting to a cruel servitude. This servitude demands, in addition to ordinary taxation, a capitation tax—for the right

to live from year to year. As Christians are excluded from Turkish military service, there is, of course, a tax in lieu of that service assessed on all males from three months old and upward. There are besides extraordinary taxes for temporary purposes, which, however, Canon MacColl tells us are never removed. Thus, in 1867 an extraordinary tax was laid on the Christians to pay the cost of the sultan's visit to England. It was promised that the tax would be levied only for that year; but the wretched Christians are obliged to pay it still. Again, Christians are sometimes made to pay their taxes a year or two in advance, on the promise of exemption from taxation in the interval. But this promise is never kept. "For instance, the Christians throughout Turkey were compelled to pay two years' taxation in advance in 1877 as a contribution toward the war against Russia ; but the taxes were exacted as usual, without the smallest remitment, during those two years." Any failure to pay any of these taxes is legally rebellion, we are informed, and involves forfeiture of property and of life. The Armenian Christians have been obliged to pay blackmail to the Turkish Kurds in order that their property and lives and the dignity of their women might be saved. What is the consequence? Not only does the Turkish Government persistently refuse to protect them so long as it can elicit this infamous blackmail, but the Christians themselves have become so impoverished as to be unable to pay the additional government taxes. Even after paying the ordinary government taxes the peasant's share of his crop is but one-third. It was in the final turning of the worm that the recent massacres in Armenia had their origin. The Christians actually had not enough money to pay the government taxes. Therefore they forfeited their right to live, and the massacres were legal. One reason why the first reports of the massacres were discredited in Turkey itself was that Christian evidence was not admissible against the Mohammedan. The uncorroborated accusation of any Mussulman is actually enough to send a Christian to prison. Another outrageous disability under which the Christians suffer is that they are not allowed to have arms. In addition to this valuable information, Canon MacColl prints many officially vouched for instances of brutality in Armenia ; indeed, he sees nothing improbable in the allegation that there is scarcely a Christian woman in Armenia who has not been outraged. No one can read these accounts of the terrible bestiality which preceded and accompanied the actual massacres without feeling the stern necessity of Christian intervention. Righteous indignation is felt here, but how much more ought it to be in England, whose responsibility toward Armenia through repeated treaties is trebly great? (Longmans, Green & Co. 75 c.)— *The Outlook.*

A Scientific Library Indeed.

THE publication of *éditions de luxe* has become almost epidemic. Books of little value in themselves are printed and bound sumptuously in limited editions, and sold at high prices with the assurance that their rarity will never be diminished. In fact, it would seem that in such cases these extraordinary editions are overdone, if not from a financial point of view, at all events from the point of one who loves books for what is in them rather than what is on them.

To produce such a sumptuous edition of scientific works is something not attempted hitherto. For that reason the undertaking of the firm of D. Appleton & Co. in the matter of its *Scientific Library* is the more to be commended.

The *Scientific Library* is worthy of all the care expended upon the volumes that compose it. In number these volumes are sixty; in scientific importance they are incalculable. Eighteen authors are represented, among whom are Huxley, Darwin, Spencer, Tyndall, Bain, Whitney, J. W. Draper, Le Conte, and Proctor, to say nothing of as many others only less well known but not less authoritative than these. The books in the library are world-famous. We congratulate the publishers on their undertaking, and the American public on having the works of the greatest scientific minds of the time, setting forth the whole of the evolutionary philosophy in a form that adds to the intrinsic value of the volumes. (Appleton. *ea.*, $1.50.)—*N. Y. Sun.*

The Shuttle of Fate.

BOOKS in matter and manner not unlike "The Shuttle of Fate" are common enough to make it wear a somewhat familiar air. It is a Lancashire story, not much better, perhaps, and certainly not worse, than many another of the genus. It contains the usual supply of dialect, of strikes and rumors of strikes. There are a stern, self-righteous parent, a

From "The Shuttle of Fate."   Frederick Warne & Co.

THE FIRST CHECK DICK FORGED.

repentant prodigal, sundry cottage interiors, and a young manager who eventually softens the heart of the mill-owner to his "hands." There is a love-affair, too, and other things not of any special importance. It is a story suitable for presentation to young folk at the Christmas season, though, for the matter of that, it need not be tabooed at any season of the year. The efforts of father and mother to shield their prodigal son are deeply touching. (Warne. $1.25.)—*The Athenæum.*

An Old Convent School in Paris.

ROMANTIC and entertaining as fiction are the five biographical papers by Miss Susan Coolidge, gathered into a volume called "An Old Convent School in Paris, and Other Papers." The characters who figure in these sketches are real personages, and the author seems to have had access to sources, in the shape of diaries, memoirs, and autobiographies, not commonly accessible. These being used with much literary art, a remarkably picturesque series of narratives is the result. The subject in each case is some person of high social or political distinction. The first two papers have to do with a Polish princess of the eighteenth century; the third with that terrible woman-emperor, Catherine II. of Russia. At her death, a sealed manuscript was found among her papers — an autobiography of the early years of her married life, written in her own hand, and addressed to her son, the Grand Duke Paul, great-grandfather of the present Czar. At first kept in the imperial archives and guarded with scrupulous care, this manuscript finally, in some unexplained manner, was copied, found its way to Paris, and into print. One of the copies, rare and hard to come by, has served Miss Coolidge as basis for "The Girlhood of an Autocrat." A story of English official life in India bears the title "Miss Eden," the authority being three volumes of delightful letters written by the sister of Lord Auckland, governor-general of India; the concluding paper takes us into the French court of Louis XIV. through the memoirs of the Duke of Saint-Simon. The book is one to instruct as well as delight, and is suited to readers old or young. (Roberts. $1.50.)—*The Dial.*

The Wonderful Visit.

AN angel—not the angel of religious feeling or of popular belief, but still an angel, as the author assures us—descends from a world where the fantastic things of our science are commonplace, where, for instance, there are griffins and dragons, and cherubim and mermaids and sphinxes, and there are no flowers upon their plants but jets of flame—he leaves all this and comes here, where he is shot by a vicar, who mistakes him for a bird. He then first feels the sensation of pain, followed by that of hunger, and being cared for by the vicar he develops a thirst for information. His celestial costume scandalizes the community, and he is equipped with mundane clothing. Then he wanders about, violating in his innocence all the conventionalities. He is introduced into society, but his social career is brief, and he becomes such an object of suspicion that his good clerical sponsor sadly comes to the conclusion that this is no world for angels. Fire and love help him out of it before he is ignominiously expelled, and he survives in village tradition only as a lunatic.

Of course all this is extravaganza of the wildest kind, although we are told with an air of whimsical gravity that it all happened last August; but there is an under-current of satire which cannot be ignored, and it compels one unwillingly to agree with the good vicar in his judgment. The author does not trouble himself to explain away difficulties in his story; being satisfied with the impossibility of the situation, he amplifies with audacity and defies criticism. It is amusing, but there is a moral there all the same. (Macmillan. $1.25.)—*Public Opinion.*

From "Fanchon the Cricket."   Copyright, 1896, by Little, Brown & Co.

FANCHON

A GAY PARTY.

Later Lyrics.

THE new book issued by Mr. Aldrich under the title of "Later Lyrics" contains no new verses, but the selection it gives from three or four of his other publications comprehends few poems which it is not a pleasure to see again. The first thing in the book, "Sweetheart, Sigh No More," is one of the most delightful songs Mr. Aldrich has written and should long ago have been reprinted from "Wyndham Towers"—a work which has not, on the whole, maintained its own. In the collection under notice there reappear the pretty "Echo-Song," the dainty stanza to "Memory," the curious and skilfully turned "Insomnia," the happy lines on "The Sailing of the Autocrat," and twice the number of other excellent performances; there are fifty poems in all, including the little verse prefixed to the collection. There are few which need to be subtracted in order to make this a thoroughly representative little anthology of the author. But a few should certainly go. The poem to Shakespeare is hopelessly inadequate, a platitude if ever there was one; and the poem at page 76, which opens thus:

> " I vex me not with brooding on the years
> That were ere I drew breath,"

does not arrive anywhere or please in its method of not arriving. For once Mr. Aldrich amazes by being obscure and only partially the workman that he is at his best. (Houghton, Mifflin & Co. $1.)—*N. Y. Tribune.*

Casa Braccio.

AMID the mass of crudities, sometimes clever and original, oftener dull and second-hand, which make up most of the literature of fiction in these days, it is a relief to come upon the work of a craftsman. Mr. Crawford has his faults—indeed, he is far from a perfect narrator of stories; but he knows how he wants to impress his readers, and how to set about it. He is one of the few writers who can really make an "atmosphere." After reading one of his stories one goes about for a time with the same sort of odd feeling of being somebody else which occasionally results from a very vivid dream. After all, this is only a roundabout way of saying that they are *interesting*—stories in which the reader is made to feel *se interfuisse.* It is a test of quality at which some may smile who think that what the story-teller has to tell is of less importance than the words in which he tells it, but it is the test of staying power. Which is the more read to-day, Dumas or Flaubert? Not that Mr. Crawford is a careless writer. On the contrary, we are not quite certain but that he, like so many others, " fancies himself " most on the side where his strength does not lie.

The real strength of the book lies in a certain Æschylean gloom. It cannot be said that the fault of Angus Dalrymple and Maria Braccio led any more inevitably, or even logically, to the misconduct of their daughter twenty years later, or to the misery caused thereby, than did the trespasses of Tantalus and Pelops to the murder of Agamemnon; and, indeed, the ultimate vengeance on Dalrymple is taken under a misconception by a man to whom he has done no great wrong. Yet under the influence of the "atmosphere" of which we have spoken, the reader is inclined to accept it all as part of the fitness of things. At the same time a little more attention to construction would have made a better book. (Macmillan. 2 v., $2.)—*The Athenæum.*

A Man's Foes.

"A MAN'S FOES," by E. H. Strain, is a work that has been the subject of considerable comment in London, and is worth reading. The fact that it is by a woman is not indicated in the way she presents her name on the title-page, and although it is written in the first person, as by a woman who went through the stirring scenes she describes, the style of diction and the vividness of narrative are almost masculine in their strength. In fact, this book will go far to prove the assumption by advanced women that their sex are the equal of man in literature as in many other fields of effort.

The story tells of the struggle between James II. and William of Orange in Ireland, and deals in particular with the siege of Derry. The scene is laid in that ancient town, and the atmosphere of the place, as well as that of the time, permeates the book. The quaint, stilted language of the eighteenth century is used, but it seems to accord well with the events described.

A more graphic picture of the period could hardly be given, and the matter-of-fact way in which the every-day life of those who were involved innocently in the disturbances is not the least part of its charm.

In "A Man's Foes" E. H. Strain does a distinct service to her sex, for she proves that a woman can write one of the strongest novels of a decade. (Ward, Lock & Bowden, Ltd. $1.25.) —*Commercial Advertiser.*

Courtship by Command.

ONE of the most charming little sketches I have found in a good while is "Courtship by Command," a story of Napoleon at play, by M. M. Blake. It is not highly colored, eulogistic, sentimental, or pedantic; it is simply a bright, moving study of an unusually interesting period in the life of Napoleon. The great little man is not the central figure in the story; his is the hand which guides and makes the puppets dance and suffer and rejoice, but he is subdominated in interest by the other characters. Augusta of Bavaria, the lovely young daughter of Prince Maximilian, is the heroine, and she is forced by the influence and power of Napoleon to marry Eugène de Beauharnais. The little noblewoman refuses, storms, weeps, and then resigns herself sorrowfully to her fate. But she falls in love with her "official lover," and they live happily—oh, very happily for a royal couple!

Josephine is deftly described, her beauty, fascination, her influence over her husband— and her wonderful worthlessness; the emperor himself is given to us with a few strokes of the pen and a few little scenes to set off his portrait, as it were. There are gorgeous glimpses of court scenes, royal betrothals, and royal weddings and festivities of all sorts. It is deliciously told, the characters are clearly, strongly, and very delicately modelled, and the odd touches of color which light up the series of pictures are most artistically done. "Courtship by Command" is (for light reading) the most satisfactory Napoleon *bonne-bouche* we have had, including even that odious Mister Barras. (Appleton. 75c.)—*Commercial Advertiser.*

Dixie.

THESE sketches, by Julian Ralph, which originally appeared in *Harper's Magazine* and *Harper's Weekly*, were worth publishing in permanent form. They not only are entertaining and amusing, but they also are instructive, containing a good deal of information about what we are pleased to call the "New South."

It would be almost safe to say that when Mr. Ralph got back to New York from his Southern journey he had finished the work he had been

Ward, Lock & Bowden, Ltd.

COVER DESIGN OF THE "NAUTILUS SERIES."

commissioned to do. It is not every man who writes for a living who can do work in that way. Mr. Ralph has carried into his literary ing a kindly interest in everybody with whom he comes in contact. (Harper. $2.50.)—*N. Y. Times.*

From "Dixie."   Copyright, 1896, by Harper & Brothers.

MOUNTAIN WOMEN IN THE SOUTH.

life the methods he worked under as a newspaper reporter. The reporting life embodies, after a fashion, the sentiment, "sufficient unto the day is the evil thereof." The day referred to, when this sentiment is applied to the reporter, is of course the day that will come with the morrow. The newspaper reporter seldom sleeps on his work. What he sees and hears to-day, he writes to-day. It may be some rough sentences will appear in his stories and more or less of error, but the chances are that he will gain in accuracy, force, and picturesqueness through the stress he is under of writing while his facts are fresh in his mind, while his impressions are strong, and while his interest is at a high pitch.

The man who talks with everybody and listens to everybody, the man whom everybody calls a good fellow, is, in that respect at least, the very sort of man to send out to describe a country, its institutions, and people. He gets among the people, sizes up their mental and moral equipments, marks their habits of thought, notes their business methods, gets at their social and political philosophy. There is no doubt that Mr. Ralph's success as a descriptive writer is due in a very large measure to his good nature and his happy faculty of tak-

AT THE BOOK-SALE.

Some people dote on spooks,
   Postage stamps, or files and books,
While to others old engravings are a feast ;
   But I much prefer the tale
   Of " A library for sale,
Collected by a gentleman deceased."

   You may never know his name,
   Or the limits of his fame,
He might have been a poet or a priest,
   But you know his little ways
   From the sermons or the plays
Collected by the gentleman deceased.

   What phrases can compare
   With the " Scarce " or " Very Rare "
What sorrow with the " Foxed " or " Soiled "
     or " Creased."
   As you read the auction mems.
   On the literary gems
Collected by the gentleman deceased ?

   If the pages aren't cut,
   If they're guiltless of a smut,
You think he never read them in the least ;
   While occasional dog's-ears,
   Or some annotation smears,
Say something for the gentleman deceased.

   It is clear, it seems to me,
   Or, at least, it ought to be,
That a history may readily be pieced
   From the books of divers kinds
   (Representing many minds)
Collected by a gentleman deceased.
         —*The Sketch.*

Napoleon from the Valet's Point of View.

To the multitude of books called forth by the revival of popular interest in Napoleon is now added an English translation of the "Recollections of the Private Life of Napoleon," by Constant, premier valet de chambre. This work, which was originally published some sixty-five years ago, has been attacked on the score both of authenticity and of truthfulness, but it is accepted as an authority by Taine, and there seems to be now an agreement of opinion that the reminiscences did emanate from the valet Constant, and that, in the main, they are trustworthy. Attached to the person of Napoleon for fifteen years, the author of this book undoubtedly had opportunities of observation such as no other man enjoyed, and if he does not always make the most of them it is because he naturally considers things from a valet's point of view. To him his master is no hero, and there is no doubt that certain aspects of Napoleon's character disclosed in the recollections tend to lower our conception of him. Constant himself maintains that, while Napoleon, seen near at hand, was no demigod, he was, nevertheless, a great man, and, what is less generally known, a man of singular amiability. The habitual kindliness of his character is the subject of frequent comment in these memoirs. After admitting that Bourrienne in his recollections may have had reason to treat with severity the emperor considered as a public man, Constant declares that in private life Napoleon was rarely unjust and almost always patient and good-natured. (Scribner, 4 v., $5; Merriam, 3 v., ea., $2.50.) —N. Y. Sun.

A Singular Life.

THE motive of a book has never made a defect in execution less defective, yet it should never be left outside an estimate of the work. If it counts when the work is well done why should it not count when the work is less satisfactory than it ought to be? Let us acknowledge, then, that the motive of Mrs. Ward's new novel is one that demands admiring recognition, even while we lament the too sentimental and gushing way in which that motive is developed. An attempt to show the consequences in an imperfect world of following the Christ life in deed and truth is no new thing in literature; and Mrs. Ward's endeavor is not particularly original in its devices. But it shows a feminine earnestness, sympathy, and nobility of feeling which win respect, disarm criticism, and almost subdue the smiles which the author's strangely overwrought phrases and hectic adjectives often call forth. The most successful character in the story is not its lofty-minded hero, but the old theological professor whose heart is so much tenderer than his

From "Among the Pueblo Indians."   Copyright, 1896, by Merriam & Co.
A GIRLS' SCHOOL.

From "On Winds of Fancy Blown."   Copyright, 1896, by Lee & Shepard.

NEW ENGLAND SCENERY.

dogmatic theories. (Houghton, Mifflin & Co. $1.25.)—*N. Y. Tribune.*

The Laureates.

The Boston Public Library contains but one book devoted exclusively to the English laureates, and that one is, to us, incomplete, as its publication, in 1853, ends the long list with Wordsworth, to the exclusion of Tennyson.

Now Tennyson is dead, and this just ended period of the "vacant chair" in official English verse made a most fitting point to stop, turn back, and review the works and lives of all those men who with varying degrees of success have occupied the most conspicuous position of poet laureateship in England.

Right in the height of this particular literary interest and research comes Kenyon West's new book, "The Laureates of England" from Ben Jonson to Alfred Tennyson, a concise, well-planned, well-executed work, with an introduction explaining the origin and history of the laureateship as a court office, biographical notes and style-criticisms of the fourteen poets, with a generous number of extracts from their works, full-page portraits, and numerous text illustrations.

Those full-page portraits! What a host of unfamiliar faces! Could any one at random give half the names of England's laureates? Here is the list with the dates of office:

Ben Jonson, 1616-1637.
Sir William Davenant, 1637-1668.
John Dryden, 1670-1689.
Thomas Shadwell, 1689-1692.
Nahum Tate, 1692-1715.
Nicholas Rowe, 1715-1718.
Lawrence Eusden, 1718-1730.
Colley Cibber, 1730-1757.
William Whitehead, 1757-1785.
Thomas Warton, 1785-1790.
Henry James Pye, 1790-1813.
Robert Southey, 1813-1843.
William Wordsworth, 1843-1850.
Alfred Tennyson, 1850-1892.

Kenyon West has scarcely chosen to show these poets only in their official capacity, but rather in general poems more representative of their authors' genius. Those extracts from some of the earlier laureates are of moral necessity short and scattered, but Southey has thirty pages, Wordsworth one hundred and sixty, and Tennyson one hundred and ten. This leaves one hundred and sixty pages for all those others back to "Rare Ben Jonson."

Altogether this is a book, a course of study, invaluable to all students of English literature, and should prove a most useful addition to every private or public library. (Stokes. $1.50.)—*Boston Literary World.*

Idyllists of the Country Side.

Mr. George H. Ellwanger has secured many friends by his faculty of agreeable observation and his vein of delightful sentiment. Under the title of "Idyllists of the Country Side." Mr. Ellwanger has published a little volume of essays devoted to out-of-door writings of Walton, Gilbert White, Thomas Hardy, Jefferies, Thoreau, and Burroughs. The title, it may be said in passing, is not quite accurate, the only idyllist, in any exact sense of the word, in this group being Jefferies. This, however, is a small matter; the chief concern of the reader is to know that Mr. Ellwanger has made a very charming book out of very charming material. He is a worshipper of nature and a lover of those who have written about nature. It is, therefore, not a critical comment which he has prepared, but an appreciation full of sympathy, insight, and affection. One of the chapters which will awaken most interest in this volume is that on "The Landscape of Thomas Hardy," a very charming bit of literary study. Mr. Ellwanger's "In Gold and Silver" and "Story of My House" should also be read by all. (Dodd, Mead & Co. $1.25. —*Independent.*

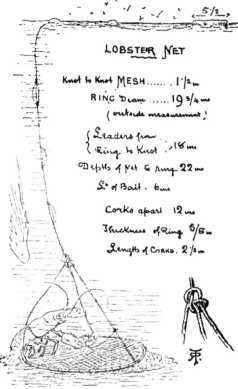

LOBSTER NET

Knot to Knot MESH...... 1·/2 in

RING Diam ...... 19 3/4 ins
(outside measurement)

{ Leaders from .
{ Ring to Knot . ·18 ins

Depth of Net to Ring 22 ins

L· of Bait . 6 ins

Corks apart 12 ins

Thickness of Ring 5/8 in

Length of Corks . 2·/2 in

From Badminton Library.   Little, Brown & Co.

THE LOBSTER NET.

Deep-Sea Fishing.

AFTER all, the main purpose of "Deep-Sea Fishing," by John Bickerdyke and others (the latest issue in the *Badminton Library*), is to instruct sea-fishing anglers at home, and the thoroughness of the counsels given is very noteworthy. A chapter on knots, whippings, and the like, carefully illustrated, will prove a serviceable beginning. Fly-fishing from land and piers, and while sailing in a small boat, attracts most fishermen, as it is free from the nauseous accompaniments of bottom fishing; and much pains have been taken with this part of the subject. Fish that love the bottom are next treated in the same practical manner— cod, haddocks, whiting, and the like, together with the appropriate lures or the unsavory

baits which each kind loves. Special attention is paid to the conger, which is not only caught in British seas of great size, but which is able to defend itself stoutly with tail and teeth when hooked. Large congers taken on reefs far from the coast are cleanly, excellent fish. Smaller ones and those near the shore are, unfortunately, fond of foul feeding, as, indeed, are eels in general, and ascend drains with the tide at watering-places. So that as food (although alder-manic turtle soup is largely made of them) they do not entirely commend themselves to *cogno-scenti*. Other fish, like pollack, swim between the rocks and the surface, and afford much sport to amateurs. Here, again, the author caters admirably for an-glers. The book ought to prove a great comfort to paterfamilias obliged to kill time at the sea-side. If he is a good sailor and can hire a steady boatman, John Bickerdyke's advice ought to furnish him with a novel sport and render the thoughts of the annual sojourn by the sea as welcome as it is too often dull and distasteful. (Little, Brown & Co. $3.50.)—*Athenæum.*

Dutch Masters.

THIRTY masterpieces of the Dutch and Flemish painters of the seventeenth century, repro-duced through the incomparable wood-engraving of Timothy Cole for the pages of the *Century Maga-zine*, have been given a permanent form by the Century Company; accompanied by Mr. Cole's comments and the critical notes of John C. Van Dyke, they make a most beautiful and artistic volume for the holiday season and "for all time" under the title of "Old Dutch and Flem-ish Masters." A thicker, richer paper and broader margins than could be given them in their original setting show them to far greater advantage, especially in the printing, the lights and shades being deeper and more distinctly marked. The volume, in its warm, cream-col-ored binding, with a delicate design in gold and with black lettering, is as charming and attractive outside as the most exacting could desire.

After his long study of Italian art, exemplified

in his "Old Italian Masters," Mr. Cole became so imbued with its classicism and ideality as to be little in sympathy with Dutch art, and scarcely prepared on his arrival in Holland to at once see all its beauties and fine points. After a year spent in Amsterdam, however, engraving the pictures chosen for reproduction from the Holland galleries, and after a long period in Paris working from the Dutch and Flemish pictures in the Louvre and elsewhere, he no longer shed tears over the "gross materialism" of these charming *genre* pictures and speaking, faithful portraits and home-like landscapes. He tells how he gradually recognized "masterpieces by the score" in a collection he had at first sight characterized as "a dreary waste." "Now," he continues enthusiastically, "I see working in these earnest Dutchmen the same spirit of sincerity and love and reverence which actuated the Italians. These honest workers tell us in their pictures that all things are miracles, and that each part and tag of anything or of any one is a miracle ; and so they paint the hair on a cow's back with the same reverence that Fra Angelico painted the flowers of paradise, and an old woman's face is as divine as that of an angel. How can there be too much fidelity and realism where nature is approached with humility and reverence ? Even the sublimity of the Italian, which lifts one to the skies, is not wanting in the landscapes of Ruisdael and Hobbema. I learn now that what charmed and fascinated in the work of the Italians holds me equally in the work of the Hollanders."

Out of the examples embraced in this volume we can only quote a few, but all are equally representative and exquisitely beautiful—great credit being due to Mr. Cole that he has missed nothing of the original charm in his work. As with his earlier engravings after the Italian masters, these engravings were made directly from the original picture, the photograph being thrown upon the block, and its insufficiencies or inequalities being corrected by consulting the original. The examples of Rembrandt, Rubens, and Van Dyck, perhaps, will inspire more general interest than those of less-known artists ; they are certainly among the most perfect specimens of art that the eye is often permitted to feast upon. From Rembrandt comes "Portrait of a Woman," making a charming frontispiece ; a detail of "The Night-Watch," from the central portion of this well-known picture ; "A Philosopher in Meditation," and his grand study of "The Supper at Emmaus" ; examples of Rubens are "Helen Fourment and Her Children," "Chapeau de Paille," and "Portrait of Jacqueline de Cordes" ; two of Van Dyck's almost perfect high-bred portraitures are

embraced in "Portrait of a Lady and Her Daughter" and "Portrait of Richardot and His Son." The volume opens with a sketch of Frans Hals, the founder of the Dutch school of painting, his style being best represented in "The Jester" and "The Jolly Man" ; following are the works of Ferdinand Bol, Govert Flinck, Nicolaes Maes, Bartholomeus Von Der Helst, Gerard Dou, Gerard Terburg, Adriaan Van Ostade, Jan ver Meer of Delft, Hobbema, Cuyp, Paul Potter, Tanier, and others. In the absence of the originals, which the majority has little opportunity to enjoy, this volume is a most delightful medium for study of the much-neglected art of the Netherlands. (Century Co. $7.50.)　　　　　　　　　　　M. M. M.

Mercedes.

UNDER a sultry, yellow sky,
On the yellow sand I lie ;
The crinkled vapors smite my brain,
I smoulder in a fiery pain.

Above the crags the condor flies,
He knows where the red gold lies ;
He knows where the diamonds shine.
If I knew, would she be mine ?

Mercedes in her hammock swings ;
In her court a palm-tree flings
Its slender shadows on the ground,
The fountain falls with silver sound.

Her lips are like this cactus cup ;
With my hand I crush it up,
I tear its flaming leaves apart ;
Would that I could tear her heart !

Last night a man was at her gate,
In the hedge I lay in wait ;
I saw Mercedes meet him there
By the fireflies in her hair.

I waited till the break of day ;
Then I rose and stole away,
But left my dagger in the gate.
Now she knows her lover's fate !

(Houghton, Mifflin & Co.　$1.50.)—*From Elisabeth Stoddard's Poems.*

The Christian's Consciousness.

"I HAVE just received a book by J. S. Black which has afforded me peculiar pleasure, and I am glad," says Dr. George H. Hepworth, "to commend it to those of my readers who require thoughtful and suggestive reading. It is entitled 'The Christian's Consciousness: Its Relation to Evolution in Morals and in Doctrine.' Mr. Black is rather original in his way of putting things, and even the ordinary reader who wants to find more or less excitement in a book will have his attention strongly attracted. Mr. Black does not strictly follow the lines of orthodox doctrine, but is nevertheless sufficiently conservative. He takes nothing for granted, but uses his common sense with the utmost freedom and liberality. He has given us a wholesome, a strong and a suggestive book. You may not always agree with him, but can hardly fail to respect him for the quiet courage with which he defends the position he has taken. Perhaps the fossiliferous among us may shrink a little at one or two of his conclusions, but he is ready to give a good and weighty reason for the faith that is in him. I like the book because there is no shirking in it, but an honest attempt to solve certain problems which have been puzzling the world ever since the Ark of Noah landed on Ararat.

"Let me give you a sample paragraph. I take it from the chapter on 'The Destiny of Man,' and you will see that whatever else Mr. Black is, he is a broad and generous thinker. Here is the paragraph: 'Christian revelation and scientific evolution unite in declaring that the world was made for man, and that man is the flower of all the centuries, and the lord of this visible creation. The end is not yet. Evolution cannot say that the processes of nature have reached their goal, and that now, or ere long, development is to give place to permanence. Evolution of the scientific kind distinctly repudiates this most unscientific assumption. Nor can evolution consistently affirm that man returns to dust, once more takes his place among elemental matter, and begins once more the mighty circle of life. It is as unscientific to suppose that evolution is a circle as to suppose that it has reached, or can reach, an ultimate or permanent form. The more thoughtful evolutionists are asking the question, "What comes next in the destiny of man?" Here or hereafter there must be something in store for him who is made a little lower than God.'

"That makes healthy and stimulating reading. Mr. Black would put what he calls Christian consciousness by the side of the Bible, harness the two together, as it were. He has given us a good book, and I hope his pen will not be idle in the future." (Lee & Shepard. $1.25.)—*N. Y. Herald.*

Domesticated Animals.

PROFESSOR SHALER'S papers on "Domesticated Animals," although widely read while passing through *Scribner's Magazine,* probably received less attention than will be given them in their new form of a handsome octavo volume, printed in uncommonly large type, and having twelve full-page illustrations and some fifty smaller pictures. Dogs, horses, horned cattle, wool-bearing animals, camels, elephants, pigs, fowls, pigeons, hawks, bees, and silkworms are the chief subjects, but an entire chapter is devoted to the rights of animals, and another to the problem of domestication. Professor Shaler would found natural reservations upon which all forms of existing animal life might be preserved, and he desires to arouse the attention of man to his duty toward the lower creatures. He holds the rational view on vivisection, believing it best that many animals should suffer rather than that the earth should be devastated by a deadly disease. His argument for the good treatment of animals is its reflex effect upon man both in securing him advantages and in developing his better nature, and his book is likely to do more toward bringing about the desired end than thousands of prize essays. (Scribner. $2.50.) —*Boston Gazette.*

The American Indian.

A NEW collection of books relating to American history, to be called the *Story of the West Series,* has been projected by the Appletons, and is to be edited by Mr. Ripley Hitchcock. The series begins attractively and usefully with the volume called "The Story of the Indian," by George Bird Grinnell. This book is based on recollections of actual Indian life; it is obvious, indeed, that only an author qualified by personal experience could offer us a profitable study of a race so alien from our own as is the Indian in thought, feeling, and culture. Only long association with Indians can enable a white man measurably to comprehend their thoughts and enter into their feelings. Such association has been Mr. Grinnell's, and the conclusion to which it has brought him is that, while the red man is a savage and consequently has savage qualities, yet the most striking characteristic of the Indian is his reproduction of the child period in the life of his white brother. In his simplicity, his vanity, his sensitiveness to ridicule, his thirst for revenge, and his fear of the supernatural, he is, all his life, a child, and acts like one. No attempt is made by the author of this volume to suggest to the Federal legislators a solution of the Indian problem. His aim is to place them at the intelligent and sympathetic point of view from which alone is attainable a solution worthy of a powerful, enlightened, and humane nation. We are to act; he is simply a narrator. He warns us, however, in his preface not to forget that the red men are human like ourselves; that they are fathers and mothers, husbands and wives, brothers and sisters; men and women with emotions and passions like our own, even though these feelings are not well regulated and directed in the calm, smoothly flowing channels of civilized life. Not until more of us are brought to recognize this common humanity can we attain a right comprehension of the character of the Indian and deal with him as we ought to deal in legislation. (Appleton. $1.50.)—*The Sun.*

Stedman's Victorian Anthology.

MR. STEDMAN'S "Victorian Anthology" is different in character from any other collection of verse we know. It is more than a charming assemblage of poems, reflecting the personal taste of the editor. Its good qualities are chiefly due to the scientific criticism which makes Mr. Stedman's "Victorian Poets" a source of authority. The book is critical and historical. It is divided into three sections, and it is in the instructive character of these sections that the book finds a large part of its value. A collection of Victorian verse might easily be made which would include everything Mr. Stedman has included, and yet not prove half so interesting, for the present volume is intended as an amplification of the author's prose survey of the period illustrated, and he aims to show in both books not merely the bulk but the organic development of English poetry in the reign of Victoria. The poets who have encircled the Parnassus of England during that reign have stood on various levels, but they have been linked together by the strain of thought which, broadly speaking, makes modern poetry modern. Mr. Stedman never loses sight of the connecting links. He begins his book on the serenely chanted note of Landor and closes it on the tunings and tinklings of the minor poets of yesterday and to-day, English and colonial. The march is long, but it is unbroken, and this latter fact becomes intensely interesting as the editorial scheme of the anthology is apprehended. (Houghton, Mifflin & Co. $2.50; *Large-pap. ed.,* 2 v., *net,* $10.)—*N. Y. Tribune.*

Anima Poetæ.

"ANIMA POETÆ" is edited by Ernest Hartley Coleridge. In the words of the preface, Coleridge "in earlier and happier days, had been eager not merely to record, but to communicate to the few who would listen or might understand the ceaseless and curious workings of his ever-shaping imagination, but from youth to age note-books and pocket-books were his silent confidants, his never-failing friends by night and day." It is impossible in the space at command to describe the contents of this heterogeneous volume. It is enough to say that it contains the jottings of Coleridge the poet, the philosopher, the theologian, the religious dreamer. Of course, there are some, perhaps many things here for no better reason than that Coleridge wrote them, sparks that could start a flame in his own mind and in no other, but the great bulk of the book is suggestive to all true lovers of letters and sure to reward the thinking reader. A good index guides the eye to the treasures of the volume, which is a good example of the book-maker's art. (Houghton, Mifflin & Co. $2.50.)—*N. Y. Observer.*

The Book-Hunter in London.

MR. W. ROBERTS's book is one that would have been dear to the heart of the late Eugene Field. Indeed, one does not need to be a bibliomaniac to appreciate much of the work—anecdotes, historical incidents, and odd happenings relating to book-making, bookselling, and book-hunting. The collection of literary curiosities is large, and entertaining in a high degree. What might by another writer have been made a mere dry-as-dust compilation is by Mr. Roberts infused with spirit and life. In form the book is really delightfully choice. The process cut of an ideal book-hunter on the cover is a particularly delicate and well-executed piece of illustrative work. Reproductions of rare prints, portraits of famous bookish men, and charming bits of English architecture are scattered throughout. The charm of books about books cannot be explained to those who are not already charmed. A book of this kind awakens a greedy covetousness in the soul of the true book-lover. (McClurg. $8; *Large-pap. ed.,* $13.50.)—*N. Y. Observer.*

TO EUGENE FIELD.

THERE's a little girl's heart that was broken to-night,
　　When I told her of Little Boy Blue,
And that the one who wrote so tender of him
　　Had "sailed off in his wooden shoe."
"Sailed on a river of misty light,"
　　Never for us to view,
Quickly and swiftly into the night,
　　And into his "sea of dew."

There's a little boy's heart that was broken to-night,
　　As he left his trinkets and play;
And I told him the prince of his story-books
　　Was sleeping the night away—
"Sailed on a river of misty light,"
　　While in his land of Nod—
Quickly and swiftly into the night,
　　Touched by an angel of God.

There's an old fellow's heart that is sad to-night,
　　As he reads them over again,
The "Dutch Lullaby" and "Trumpet and Drum,"
　　And the tracings of his pen,
"Sailed on a river of misty light,"
　　Out from the Shores of Now,
And safe on the sands of Over There
　　Has grounded the Boatman's prow.

There's many a heart that is sad to-night
　　As we look on the printed page,
And the merry jingle for boy and girl,
　　The wit of the mask and sage—
"Sailed on a river of misty light,"
　　But happy is he over there,
For a Gentle Shepherd has kept for him
　　A Boy Blue and Golden Hair.

　　　　—GEORGE R. BARKER, in the *Detroit Free Press.*

Che Literary News.

An Eclectic Monthly Review of Current Literature.

EDITED BY A. H. LEYPOLDT.

JANUARY, 1896.

PROFITABLE READING.

An unusually active publishing year has come to a close. Upward of 5000 titles were entered in the official record of *The Publishers' Weekly.* The average merit of these publications was higher than in any previous year, but no one book made for itself the record that "Trilby" or "The Manxman" did in 1894. Several volumes of lasting importance were contributed to the solving of questions now uppermost in the minds of men in all countries— the Eastern question; the woman question; American finance, and the peculiar characteristics, mental, moral, and physical, of the closing century. Biography and history were strongly represented, and several new volumes added to the Napoleonic literature, which was one of the chief features of 1894.

Finely made editions of standard works were brought out by many publishers, and all book-lovers must rejoice to see their favorite authors put into such tempting shape at the very reasonable price that the publishers have striven to combine with expert editing and generous manufacture.

People have talked "hard times" since time immemorial, but the great bulk of men and women, in spite of "hard times" and many difficulties, manage to attain what they really put their energies to getting.

We sincerely wish the day might come when books should take their rightful place in the proportionate expenditure of cultivated and reading people.

Books still are ranked far too much as luxuries, and as luxuries not so eagerly striven for as many less profitable ones.

The causes of this well-known fact have been set forth in most able treatises by many skilful pens with much show of reason. The busy unrest of the American people, the tired, overwrought minds, the magazine and newspaper habit, etc., etc., have all been explained. All these certainly lead to the superficiality and lack of thoroughness and of individuality so characteristic of the hour, or, perhaps, are caused by the state of mind and heart and life that makes them possible.

Cause and effect—effect and cause are hard to sunder and to judge aright.

One and all, we try to do too much. The average reader first thinks of reading all his neighbor has devoured, regardless of the fitness for his needs of the ideas and opinions and information and recreation he thus accumulates Everything is done to help along the hurry of the day. Books are condensed and popularized and criticised, and by the time these helps have been dealt with no time remains for the original book and but little capacity has been gained for personal, individual estimate. We sincerely hope the many editions of standard books now put within the reach of all may lead to more "solid" reading, especially among our young people.

Although many more young people than formerly can claim college education and can talk glibly of some things best left unmentioned, the standard of true culture and the earnestness of purpose in acquiring information are not as high as in the old days when things were not made easy and when every mind was obliged to do its own thinking.

A great part of the reading furnished to be talked about is as machine-made as the many imitations of the other arts provided for the same class of custom.

If readers would make it a rule to own every book they read, they would very soon be much more careful in selecting their mental food, and they would in a very short time have a distinct influence upon the books published.

It is a good rule. Try it during 1896.

The New Poet Laureate.

Alfred Austin, poet, novelist, critic, and journalist, has been appointed Poet Laureate by the Queen, an office which has been vacant since the death of Tennyson, October 6, 1892. Alfred Austin was born in Headlingley, near Leeds, May 30, 1835.

His father was a merchant and magistrate of the borough of Leeds, and his mother was the sister of Joseph Locke, the eminent civil engineer and M.P. for the borough of Honiton, of which he was lord of the manor. Both his parents being Roman Catholics, he was sent to Stonyhurst College, and afterward to St. Mary's College, Oscott. From Oscott he took his degree at the University of London in 1853, and in 1857 he was called to the bar of the Inner Temple.

The publication, although anonymously, of a poem entitled "Randolph," when he was eighteen, showed the bent of his disposition, and it may be said, on the authority of Mr. Austin himself, that he ostensibly embraced the study of law in deference only to the wishes of his parents, and from his earliest years was imbued with the desire and determination to devote his life mainly to literature.

On the death of his father, in 1861, he quitted the Northern Circuit and went to Italy. His first acknowledged volume of verse, " The Season : a satire," appeared in 1861. A third and revised edition of " The Season" appeared in 1869.

His other poetical productions are : " The Human Tragedy " (1862), republished in an amended form in 1876, and again finally revised in 1889; " The Golden Age : a satire," 1871; " Interludes," 1872; " Rome or Death," 1873; " Madonna's Child," 1873; " The Tower of Babel," a drama, 1874; " Leszko, the Bastard : a tale of Polish grief," 1877; " Savonarola," a tragedy, 1881; " Soliloquies in Song," "At the Gate of the Convent," " Love's Widowhood, and other poems," " Prince Lucifer," and " English Lyrics," all published between 1881 and 1890. He has published three novels —" Five Years of It," 1858; " An Artist's Proof," 1864; and " Won by a Head," 1866; also " The Poetry of the Period," reprinted from *Temple Bar*, 1870, and " A Vindication of Lord Byron," 1869, occasioned by Mrs. Stowe's article, " The Story of Lord Byron's Life."

He has written much for *The Standard* and for *The Quarterly Review.*

His political writings include " Russia Before Europe," 1876; " Tory Horrors," 1876, a reply to Mr. Gladstone's " Bulgarian Horrors," and " England's Policy and Peril," a letter to the Earl of Beaconsfield, 1877. In 1883, in conjunction with W. J. Courthope, he founded *The National Review,* and continued to edit that periodical till the summer of 1893. In 1892 Macmillan & Co. issued a collected edition of his poems in six volumes, since which time they have published " Fortunatus, the Pessimist," and " England's Darling, and other poems," and a prose work entitled " The Garden That I Love."

FOR A BOOK BY THOMAS HARDY.

WITH searching feet, through dark circuitous ways,
    I plunged and stumbled ; round me, far and near,
    Quaint hordes of eyeless phantoms did appear,
Twisting and turning in a bootless chase—
When, like an exile given by God's grace
    To feel once more a human atmosphere,
    I caught the world's first murmur, large and clear,
Flung from a singing river's endless race.

Then, through a magic twilight from below,
    I heard its grand sad song as in a dream :
Life's wild infinity of mirth and woe
It sang me ; and, with many a changing gleam,
Across the music of its onward flow,
    I saw the cottage lights of Wessex beam.

—EDWIN ARLINGTON ROBINSON, in *The Critic.*

MAGAZINE ARTICLES FOR DECEMBER AND JANUARY.

Articles marked with an asterisk are illustrated.

ARTISTIC, MUSICAL, AND DRAMATIC.—*Century* (Dec.), Humperdinck's " Hänsel und Gretel,"* Stavenhagen; Titian's " Flora," Eng. by Closson; Tissot's " Life of Christ,"* Edith Coues.—*Forum* (Jan.), Development of Sculpture in America, Partridge.—*Lippincott's* (Jan.), Some Women in Doublet and Hose, Weeks; Architecture in America : A Forecast, Stewardson.—*Nine. Century* (Nov.), Art Connoisseurship in England, Sir Chas. Robinson.—*Scribner's* (Dec.), Laurens Alma-Tadema, R.A.,* Monkhouse; Wood-Engravers,* A. Lepère*; (Jan.), Decorative Painting by Robert Blum.*

BIOGRAPHY, CORRESPONDENCE, ETC.—*Chautauquan* (Dec.), Pasteur and His Life-Work, Oswald.—*Cosmopolitan* (Dec.), Actresses Who Have Become Peeresses,* A. C. Wheeler.—*Pop. Science* (Dec.), David Dale Owen ; (Jan.), Ebenezer Emmons (Por.).

DESCRIPTION, TRAVEL.—*Atlantic* (Jan.), The Fête de Gayant, Agnes Repplier.—*World* (Dec.), Armenia, Past and Present,* Hyvernat.—*Century* (Dec.), The Passion-Play at Vorder-Thiersee,* Annie S. Peck; (Jan.), A Kaleidoscope of Rome,* Crawford; The First Landing on the Antarctic Continent,* Borchgrevink; Tribal Life Among the Omahas,* Alice C. Fletcher.—*Cosmopolitan* (Dec.), Christmas Legend of King Arthur's Country,* A. Warren and J. L. Williams.—*Harper's* (Dec.), On Snow-Shoes to the Barren Grounds,* Whitney; From the Hebrid Isles,* Fiona Macleod; The Paris of South America * (Caracas), R. H. Davis; (Jan.), London's Underground Railways,* Eliz. R. Pennell.—*Outing* (Dec.), Touring Bermuda Awheel,* Dowden.—*Scribner's* (Jan.), The New Building of the Boston Public Library,* T. R. Sullivan; Water-Ways from the Ocean to the Lakes,* Thos. C. Clarke.

DOMESTIC AND SOCIAL.—*North Am. Review* (Jan.), A Study in Husbands, by "Marion Harland," Mrs. Burton Harrison, Eliz. Bisland.

EDUCATIONAL.—*Atlantic* (Jan.), The Schoolhouse as a Centre, H. E. Scudder.—*Chautauquan* (Dec.), Student Life at Oxford, Eng.,* F. Grundy.—*Pop. Science* (Jan.), Scientific Temperance, David S. Jordan.

FICTION.—*Arena* (Jan.), The Valley Path, Will Allen Dromgoole.—*Atlantic* (Dec.), Witchcraft, L. Dougall; Dorothy, Harriet L. Bradley; (Jan.), Country of the Pointed Firs, Sarah Orne Jewett; Pirate Gold, I., F. J. Stimson.—*Cath. World* (Dec.), A Round Year, Marion A. Taggart.—*Century* (Dec.), Captain Eli's Best Ear,* F. R. Stockton; Tom Grogan, I.,* F. Hopkinson Smith; The Brushwood Boy, Kipling (Jan.), A Slender Romance, Ruth McE. Stuart.—*Chautauquan* (Dec.), A Colonial Christmas in the Red Hills of Georgia, E. F. Andrews.—*Cosmopolitan* (Dec.), The Great North Road,* R. L. Stevenson; A Momentary Indiscretion,* Sarah Grand; Tonia,* "Ouida." — *Harper's* (Dec.), Interview with Miss Marlenspuyk,* Brander Matthews; Briseis, I.*, Wm. Black; (Jan.), Story of Miss Pi,* Julian Ralph; Twentyfour,* Eliz. Stuart Phelps; Courtship of Colonel Bill, J. J. Eakins.—*Lippincott's* (Dec.), The Old Silver Trail, Mary E. Stickney; Three Fates,

Virna Woods; (Jan.), Mrs. Crichton's Creditor, "Mrs. Alexander."—*Outing* (Dec.), A River Between,* Florence Guertin ; (Jan.), Sweet Marjory,* Sara B. Kennedy; The Stranger at the Anchor,* M. F. S. Williams.—*Scribner's* (Dec.), A White Blot—Story of a Picture,* H. Van Dyke; The Colonel's "Nigger Dog," J. C. Harris; The Kinetoscope of Time,* Brander Matthews; Staying Power of Sir Rohan,* F. R. Stockton; (Jan.), Sentimental Tommy, I.,* J. M. Barrie; Madame Annalena, Bliss Perry.

HISTORY.—*Atlantic* (Dec.), Starving Time in Old Virginia, J. Fiske; Defeat of the Spanish Armada, W. F. Tilton.—*Harper's*, (Jan.), In Washington's Day,* W. Wilson —*Lippincott's* (Dec.), English Mediæval Life, A. F. Sanborn.

LITERARY.—*Arena* (Dec.), Personal Recollections of America's Seven Great Poets, First Series, by Savage, Chadwick, Sanborn, and others; (Jan), A Few Latter-Day Notes on Walt Whitman, Traubel; Glimpse of Longfellow, Savage.—*Atlantic* (Jan.), The Johnson Club, G. B. Hill.—*Fort. Review* (Nov.), Book-Collecting as a Fine Art, J. Moore; How to Counteract the " Penny Dreadful," H. Chisholm; (Dec.), Gustave Flaubert, E. Newman.—*Forum* (Dec.), Trail of " Trilby," A. D. Vandam; Editorship as a Career for Women, Marg. E. Sangster; Carlyle: His Work and Influence, Wm. R. Thayer; (Jan.), Matthew Arnold's Letters, H. W. Paul.—*Lippincott's* (Jan.), Longfellow, R. H. Stoddard.—*Nine. Century* (Nov.), Author, Agent, and Publisher, T. W. Laurie; (Dec.), The Society of Authors, Sir W. M. Conway; The Literary Agent, Sir W. Besant.—*Scribner's* (Jan.), Frederick Locker, Por., A. Birrell. —*West. Review* (Nov.), A Gallery of Australasian Singers, O. Smeaton; Russian Fictional Literature, R. G. Burton; (Dec.), Paul Bourget: Novelist, Poet, and Critic, M. Todhunter.

NATURE AND SCIENCE. — *Atlantic* (Dec.), A New England Woodpile, R. E. Robinson.— *Lippincott's* (Jan.), Landmarks, C. C. Abbott. —*Pop. Science* (Dec.), New Evidence of Glacial Man in Ohio,* G. F. Wright. — *Scribner's*, (Dec.), Wild Beasts as They Live,* C. J. Melliss.

POETRY.—*Atlantic* (Dec.), Song of a Shepherd-Boy at Bethlehem, Josephine P. Peabody; (Jan.), The Awakening, Marion C. Smith.— *Century* (Dec.), A Woodland Dream,* Sarah D. Hobart; " Hear, O Israel," Harriet P. Spofford; (Jan.), To A. V. Williams Jackson, G. E. Woodberry.—*Lippincott's* (Dec.), Shrived, Marg. G. George.—*Scribner's* (Dec.), The Joy of the Hills, C. E. Markham ; On a Forgotten By-Way—From an Office Window, A. E. Watrous.

POLITICAL AND SOCIAL.—*Arena* (Dec.), Government Control of the Telegraph, R. T. Ely and W. Clark; Shall Women Vote?, Helen H. Gardener; (Jan.), Government Control of the Telegraph, Abbott, Wilson, and Parsons. —*Atlantic* (Jan.), The Children of the Road, J. Flynt; Emancipation of the Post-Office, J. R. Procter.—*Fort. Review* (Nov.), Improvement of Working-Class Homes, H. M. Bompas; The Beginnings of a Republic, I., A. D. Vandam; (Dec.), England in Nicaragua and Venezuela, G. H. D. Gossip; Turkey or Russia?, M. MacColl.—*Forum* (Dec.), Conditions for American Commercial and Financial Supremacy, P. Leroy-Beaulieu; Nature of Liberty, W. D. How-

ells; Thos. B. Reed and the Fifty-First Congress, T. Roosevelt; The Monroe Doctrine: Defence not Defiance, A. C. Cassatt; (Jan.), Some Suggestions on Currency and Banking, A. Ladenburg; Railroad Rate Wars, J. W. Midgley; Naval Aspects of the Japan-China War, Sir E. R. Freemantle; Federal Census, C. D. Wright.—*Harper's* (Jan.), The United States Naval Academy, T. R. Lounsbury.— *Nine. Century* (Dec.), The Eastern Question, by Prof. Geffcken, Mme. Novikoff, and R. Ahmad; University Settlements, S. A. Barnett.—*North Am. Review* (Dec.), Work of the Next Congress, by M. W. Hazeltine, A. C. Catchings, J. P. Dolliver, and others; The Last Gift of the Century, N. S. Shaler; House of Representatives and the House of Commons, R. F. D. Palgrave; (Jan.), War and Its Modern Instruments, by W. S. Aldrich, P. H. Colomb, S. B. Luce, and J. K. Cree; The Crisis in the East, K. Blind; Central America and Its Resources, A. Gosling.—*Pop. Science* (Dec.), Principles of Taxation, I., D. A. Wells.— *West. Review*(Dec.), Politics and Culture, H. Seal.

SPORTS AND AMUSEMENTS. — *Lippincott's* (Dec.), Athletic Sports of Ancient Days, T. J. de la Hunt.—*Outing* (Dec.), Skating,* E. W. Sandys; Two Hours Over Decoys, E. A. Shepherd, Characteristics of Canadian Football,* A. C. Kingstone and C. A. S. Boddy; (Jan.), Winter Fishing,* E. W. Sandys.—*Scribner's* (Jan.), A New Sport * (Tobogganing).

THEOLOGY, RELIGION, AND SPECULATION.— *Cath. World* (Dec.), The Church and the New Sociology, G. McDermot.—*Forum* (Dec.), The Pilgrim Principle and the Pilgrim Heritage, Wm. DeW. Hyde.—*Nine. Century* (Nov.), The Rigidity of Rome, W. Ward.—*North Am. Review* (Dec.), Christianity's Millstone, Goldwin Smith; (Jan.), The Future Life and the Condition of Man Therein, I., W. E. Gladstone; Foreign Missions in the Light of Fact, Judson Smith.— *Pop. Science* (Dec.), Sir John Lubbock and the Religion of Savages, J. Carmichael.— *West. Review* (Nov.), The Persistence of Dogmatic Theology, G. Greenwood.

Literary Miscellany.

" MISCELLANEOUS STUDIES," by Walter Pater (Macmillan), contains a complete bibliography of his works, beginning with the paper on Coleridge, which appeared in 1866.

FOR true religion comes not by violence, but chiefly, I think, from being brought up with good men, reverencing their ways and words. —*From " The Men of the Moss Hags."*

SOME persons may have looked on the map of Scotland for Ian Maclaren's (the Rev. John Watson's) " Drumtochty," but of course have failed to find it. It is not a village nor a parish, but we learn from *The Bookman* that it is an estate, for many generations that of the Lairds of Logie, but now the property of the wealthy Earl Mansfield. It is about twelve miles northwest of Perth.

A LITTLE PARABLE.—" The little cheesemites held debate," it runs, " as to who made the cheese. Some thought that they had no data to go upon, and some that it had come together by a solidification of vapor, or by the centrifugal attraction of atoms. A few surmised that the platter might have something to do with it ; but the wisest of them could not deduce the existence of a cow."

A subtle parable—and perfect.—*From A. Conan Doyle's Stark Munro Letters.*

WOMEN AS BOOK - LOVERS.—An English writer says of women as book-lovers : " Women love books just as much as men do ; but they love them in a different way. With men books are more a crutch and a prop than they are with women. Women need no such help. Great knowledge is not expected of a woman, and wit she has by nature. A Frenchman once said very truly that ' there are two witty men in a hundred, and one woman who is not witty in a hundred.' Any woman with a trained intelligence talks of books with better taste than a man, and she is rarely so foolish as to spend money upon first editions and large-paper copies. A woman who went stall-hunting would at once cease to be charming, for this is not a woman's method. A man's method is to amass, while a woman has keener affinities — she chooses."

ANTHONY HOPE HAWKINS, the author of " The Prisoner of Zenda," is thirty-two years old. There is an almost boyish look, we are told, in the long, oval, clean-shaven face, but in the gray eyes which gaze at one so intently there is deep earnestness of purpose and marked resolution. His alertness of movement reminds the observer that Mr. Hawkins (Hope) won no small reputation at Oxford as an athlete. Football he chiefly delighted in. Mr. Hawkins is enthusiastic in his commendation of the work done by Mr. Rose in dramatizing his novel. He likes particularly the prologue, which is entirely the work of Mr. Rose. The author says he has no fixed intention of coming to this country, though he has received many invitations to make a lecturing tour. Some day, he adds, he may come, " but there is plenty of time for that."

THE sudden death of the well-known Russian author, Sergius Stepniak, is one of the most melancholy of recent events. As Mr. Stepniak was walking to a friend's house at Chiswick, England, he attempted to cross a railway track at grade, and as he stepped on the track a train, unnoticed by him, struck and killed him. It may not be known that the Russian refugee came of a semi-noble Cossack family. He studied at Kiev, and published several works in the Little Russian dialect which were promptly prohibited by the government. In 1865 he became a " docent " in the University of Kiev, and in 1870 a professor, but three years later was removed from his chair by the government. In 1876 he was exiled. He settled in Geneva and afterward in England. His principal books are: " The Turks Within and Without," " ' Tyrannicide in Russia," " Little Russian Internationalism," " Little Russian Folk Songs," and " King Stork and King Log : a study of modern Russia."

THE THOMAS PAINE EXHIBITION IN LONDON. — Moncure D. Conway while editing the " Works of Thomas Paine," published by G. P. Putnam's Sons, worked up the idea of an exhibition of the many interesting relics relating to his life, with the assistance of Edward Smith (biographer of Cobbett), Clair J. Grece, George Jacob Holyoake, G. Julian Harney, and Edward Truelove. The exhibition took place last month in South Place Chapel, London. It was successful beyond our expectations, the catalogue enumerating 485 exhibits and really representing more than 600; many tokens, manuscripts, etc., being included under one or another single label. In the evenings the exhibition took the form of a soirée; there were addresses from eminent men, and songs of the old period, some composed by Paine, were sung. Among the exhibitors were some eminent Conservatives; and among the exhibits were pamphlets, caricatures, and tokens hostile to Paine. The aim of the exhibition was purely historical and without any purpose of propagandism.

CHAUTAUQUA READING CIRCLE LITERATURE FOR 1895-96.—In the course of reading selected for the Chautauqua Circle, America has special prominence. " Initial studies in American letters," by Henry A. Beers, is the " Outline sketch of American literature " published in 1887, reissued in 1891 under the title " Initial Studies," and now revised and supplied with marginal catchwords and a new chapter bringing selections from representative American writers up to date. " The Growth of the American Nation," by Harry Pratt Judson, tells in the form of a continuous narrative of the development of the American nation from the scattered colonies along the Atlantic coast into a great people bound together in national unity by the constant forces of modern civilization; and " The Industrial Evolution of the United States," by Carroll D. Wright, shows how American industries have developed from the colonial period to the present day. The author is United States Commissioner of Labor. No American can know enough about America. It is satisfactory to think so large a circle of readers are studying its great achievements in industry, literature, and growth.

LECTURES BY MISS KINGSLEY.—Miss Kingsley, who will visit America this winter, with a view to lecturing upon modern French art, and some other subjects, is the elder daughter of the late Charles Kingsley. Miss Kingsley has been much in France, and has for some years taken a special interest in modern French art. Her first paper on the subject was written in 1889, after a study of the peasant painters, J. F. Millet, Courbet, Bastien Lepage, Lhermite, etc., and the landscape painters of the Barbizon school, as represented by the Paris Universal Exhibition of that year. For this paper the French Government in 1890 conferred upon her the decoration of *officier d'Académie.* She has continued her studies, assisted by the courtesy of the French authorities, who have afforded her every facility for seeing such pictures as she desired, whether in public galleries, the collections of private owners, or the studios of artists. The result of these studies Miss Kingsley has embodied in a course of lectures on French pictures and painters of the nineteenth century, which she delivered in London during the season of 1894, and is giving this autumn in various large towns. Miss Kingsley has also prepared a lecture entitled " Shakespeare in Warwickshire," designed to show the influence which the scenery and dialect of his native county exerted upon the mind of the poet.

Survey of Current Literature.

☞ *Order through your bookseller.*—"*There is no worthier or surer pledge of the intelligence and the purity of any community than their general purchase of books; nor is there any one who does more to further the attainment and possession of these qualities than a good bookseller.*"—PROF. DUNN

ART, MUSIC, DRAMA.

RAYMOND, G. LANSING. Painting, sculpture, and architecture as representative arts: an essay on comparative æsthetics. Putnam. 8°, $2.50.

BIOGRAPHY, CORRESPONDENCE, ETC.

ARNOLD, MATTHEW. The letters of Matthew Arnold, 1848–1888; collected and arr. by G. W. E. Russell. Macmillan. 2 v., 8°, $3.

BLACKWELL, ELIZ., *M.D.* Pioneer work in opening the medical profession to women: autobiographical sketches. Longmans, Green & Co. 12°, $1.50.

BOLTON, *Mrs.* SARAH KNOWLES. Famous leaders among women. Crowell. pors. 12°, $1.50.
Nine biographical sketches, the subjects being Madame de Maintenon, Catharine II. of Russia, Madame le Brun, Dolly Madison, Catherine Booth, Lucy Stone, Lady Henry Somerset, Julia Ward Howe, Queen Victoria.

CONSTANT, [L. Constant Wairy.] Memoirs of Constant (first valet de chambre of the emperor) on the private life of Napoleon, his family, and his court; tr. by Eliz. Gilbert Martin; with a preface to the English ed. by Imbert de Saint-Amand. Scribner. 4 v., 12°, $5.
Napoleon was a hero to his valet de chambre, whose full name is Louis Constant Wairy, and Constant's account of his master, from whom he was separated but a few days in the years that passed between Marengo and Fontainebleau, is as sympathetic as it is interesting. One of the most intimate memoirs in Napoleonic literature, into which every historian, biographer, or critic of Napoleon has delved. It gives a definite portrait of Napoleon as a man, of his family life, his personal appearance and habits, his manner of dealing with people, his conduct during his campaigns, etc.

CONSTANT, [L. Constant Wairy.] Recollections of the private life of Napoleon; by Constant, valet de chambre; tr. by Walter Clark. In 3 v. V. 1, 2. The Merriam Co. por. 8°, *ea.*, $2.50.

GIBERNE, AGNES. A lady of England: the life and letters of Charlotte Maria Tucker, [A. L. O. E.] Armstrong & Son. por. 8°, $1.75.

HILDEBURN, C. R. Sketches of printers and printing in Colonial New York. *Limited ed.* Dodd, Mead & Co. il. 16°, bds. *net*, $6.50.
Biographical sketches of William Bradford, the founder of the press in the Middle Colonies, and of his successors, the Zengers, more especially John Peter Zenger; the Parkers, and the minor presses of the middle of the century—Henry De Foreest, Samuel Brown, William Weyman, Samuel Farley, Benjamin Mecom, and Samuel Campbell; Hugh Gaine, the Irish printer; the Holts and the Robertsons; James Rivington; the ante-Revolutionary printers—Inslee & Car, Hodge & Shober, John Anderson, and Samuel Loudon; and the Loyalist printers of the Revolution—Macdonald & Cameron, Mills & Hicks, William Lewis, Morton T. Horner, and Christopher Sower 3d. Indexed.

LAMON, WARD HILL. Recollections of Abraham Lincoln, 1847–1865; ed. by Dorothy Lamon. McClurg. por. 12°, $1.50.

LOWE, C. The German Emperor William II. Warne. por. 12°, (Public men of to-day ser.) $1.25.

OBER, F. A. Josephine, Empress of the French. The Merriam Co. por. il. 8°, $2.
In this biography is given for the first time the full and authentic history of the youth of Josephine on the Island of Martinique; with these details the author has interwoven accurate descriptions of the tropical scenery, anecdotes of her home life, etc. Her life as Empress of the French is written in the light of recent research.

ROSSETTI, DANTE GABRIEL. Dante Gabriel Rossetti, his family letters; with a memoir by W. Michael Rossetti. Roberts Bros. 2 v., pors. 8°, $6.50.

WOOLSEY, *Miss* SARAH CHAUNCEY, ["Susan Coolidge," *pseud.*] An old convent school in Paris, and other papers. Roberts Bros. 12°, $1.50.
"An old convent school in Paris" and "The Countess Potocki" contain the biography of the Princesse Hélène Massalski, who entered the famous Abbaye au Bois in 1771, at the age of eight, and left it at fourteen to marry the Prince de Ligne. She afterward became the Countess Potocki. "The girlhood of an autocrat" refers to the early life of Catherine the Great. "Miss Eden" was the sister of Baron Aukland, appointed governor-general of India in 1835; and "The Duc de Saint-Simon" passed his brilliant career in the court-circle of Louis XIV.

DESCRIPTION, GEOGRAPHY, TRAVEL, ETC.

ADOLPHUS, F. Some memories of Paris. Holt. 12°, buckram, $1.50.
Contents: The streets forty years ago; 29th January, 1853; Two balls at the Hôtel de Ville; The last day of the empire; The English food gifts after the siege; The entry of the Germans; The Commune; Mr. Worth; General Boulanger; The opera; Indoor life.

BROOKS, NOAH. The Mediterranean trip: a short guide to the principal points on the shores of the western Mediterranean and the Levant. Scribner. map, il. 16°, *net*, $1.25.

LENTHÉRIC, CHARLES. The Riviera, ancient and modern; tr. by C. West, M.D. Putnam. 8°, $2.

MORRIS, J. Advance Japan: a nation thoroughly in earnest. Lippincott. il. 8°, $4.50.

RALPH, JULIAN. Dixie; or, Southern scenes and sketches. Harper. 8°, $2.50.

RALPH, JULIAN. People we pass: stories of life among the masses of New York City. Harper. il. 12°, $1.25.

SMALL, HERBERT, *comp.* Handbook of the New Public Library in Boston; comp. by Herbert Small, with contributions by C. Howard

Walker and Lindsay Swift. Curtis & Co. il. pap., 10 c.

A full description of the New Public Library of Boston, its various rooms, their purpose, the paintings, architecture, etc. Mr. Walker writes on the architecture, Mr. Swift on the significance of the library.

SPEARS, J. R. The gold diggings of Cape Horn: a study of life in Tierra del Fuego and Patagonia. Putnam. il. 12°, $1.75.

The author visited the places he describes as reporter for the New York *Sun*. He now groups his facts according to the subjects to which they relate, and not geographically or quite chronologically. The aborigines of Patagonia, a branch of the red aborigines of the Americas, are vividly described, and their customs and manners and the mission work among them have been closely studied.

TIFFANY, FRANCIS. This goodly frame the earth: stray impressions of scenes, incidents, and persons in a journey touching Japan, China, Egypt, Palestine, and Greece. Houghton, Mifflin & Co. 12°, $1.50.

Mr. Tiffany leaves the beaten path of travel description to others, while he condenses into a book of positive value the deeper impressions which his recent circumnavigation of the globe have brought him. The peculiar customs, usages, occupations, manners, and religions of the various peoples he encountered are not described in detail, but sufficiently to indicate how carefully and in what a generous spirit he studied them, and how just we may regard the conclusions he draws concerning the varied civilizations he observed and the future of the nations he traversed.

DOMESTIC AND SOCIAL.

GRANT, ROB. The art of living; il by C. D. Gibson, B. West Clinedinst, and W. H. Hyde. Scribner. 12°, $2.50.

Mr. Grant discusses practically and amusingly the problems that beset the American of limited income who wishes to live as near as he can to the opportunities of our civilization, without running into its extravagances, the subjects being: income; the dwelling; house-furnishing and the commissariat; education; occupation; the use of time; the summer problem.

RONALD, MARY. The century cook-book. Century Co. interleaved, il. 8°, leath., $2.

EDUCATION, LANGUAGE, ETC.

FROEBEL, F. The songs and music of Friedrich Froebel's "Mother play" (*Mutter und Rose lieder*); songs newly translated and furnished with new music; prepared and arr. by Susan E. Blow. Appleton. il. 12°, (International education ser., no. 32.) $1.50.

The publishers divided Froebel's "Mother play" in order to bring it into volumes of convenient size. The edition of Wichard Lange and the former English translations have the form and style of a music-book. In separating the contents, the mottoes, commentaries, and mother communings have been placed in the first volume, which may be called the mother's volume. The songs and music are reserved for the present volume, which is the children's volume. What it contains is suitable for children's ears and voices. The il. are reproduced from the cuts of the Wichard Lange ed., long out of print.

WIGGIN, KATE DOUGLAS, [*now Mrs.* G. C. Riggs,]*and* Smith, Nora Archibald. Froebel's gifts. Houghton, Mifflin & Co. 12°, (The republic of childhood, v. I.) $1.

The first book in a series of three volumes which are devoted to and will bear the title of "The republic of childhood," having for its motto Froebel's remark, "The kindergarten is the free republic of childhood." The volumes are the outcome of talks and conferences on Froebel's educational principles with successive groups of earnest young women for fifteen years past. The books are meant to be popular and helpful; the second will deal with the occupations, the third with the educational theories of Froebel.

FICTION.

ALLEN, GRANT. The British barbarians: a hill-top novel. Putnam. 16°, $1.

Grant Allen has here begun a set of stories in which he will criticise the world as he sees it from the hill-top of experience and study. A wonderfully handsome man suddenly arrives in England and studies British subjects as he has already studied the barbarians of other lands. He is writing a book on "taboos" and "fetishes," and finds wonderful specimens to describe in the daily life of conventional Englishmen. A short episode reminds the reader of the theories which produced "The woman who did."

ALLEN, JA. LANE. Aftermath. Pt. 2 of a "Kentucky cardinal." Harper. 16°, (Harper's little novels.) $1.

In "A Kentucky cardinal" the volume closes with the betrothal of Adam Moss and Georgiana Cobb. It is but a few days after their troth is plighted that "Aftermath" begins. Their married life is described, and Adam's views on nature and many other subjects noted. The story ends with a tragedy.

AUSTIN, MAUDE MASON. 'Cension: a sketch from Paso del Norte. Harper. il. 16°, (Harper's little novels.) $1.

A simple love-tale and sketch of ranch life near Paso del Norte, where the slothful Mexicans are somewhat excited over the railroads which the enterprising Americans are building. 'Cension, the young daughter of a wealthy and easy-going owner of a ranch not far from Paso del Norte, loves Eduardo Lerma, a bold, coarsely handsome man of thirty-eight. Simple, pure in heart, unselfish, and trustful, this beautiful Mexican girl is in direct contrast to the man upon whom she bestows her love. Her brother saves her from the man's wiles by proving his true character.

BALZAC, HONORÉ DE. A daughter of Eve; tr. by Katherine Prescott Wormeley. Roberts. 12°, $1.50.

BARR, *Mrs.* AMELIA E. Bernicia. Dodd, Mead & Co. 12°, $1.25.

Bernicia is the ancient name for Northumberland, where Bernicia, daughter of Sir William Cresswell, lived until her father losing his life in the cause of the Stuarts she finds refuge in London, in the house of a sister's husband, Lord John Pomfret, apparently a stanch defender of the house of Hanover. Thereafter Bernicia's history, being closely identified with such notable events of the eighteenth century as the Jacobite ascendancy and the great revival movement in English Methodism promulgated by George Whitfield, has singular interests.

BLACK, ALEX. Miss Jerry. Scribner. il. 16°, $1.
A little love-story of to-day, with its scene in New York City. The heroine takes up journalism at a crisis in her father's affairs. The story is somewhat enlarged from its first form, when used by the author as a reading for a public entertainment accompanied by a rapid succession of pictures from life illustrating its scene, thrown by the stereopticon; a selection of these photographs is given in the text.

BLACKMORE, R. D. Slain by the Doones, and other stories. Dodd, Mead & Co. 12°, $1.25.
Contents: Slain by the Doones; Frida, or, the lover's leap; George Bowring; Crocker's hole.

BLAKE, M. M. Courtship by command: a story of Napoleon at play. Appleton. 12°, 75 c.

BUCHAN, J. Sir Quixote of the moors: being some account of an episode in the life of the Sieur de Rohaine. Holt. 1 il. nar. 16°, (Buckram ser.) 75 c.
The romantic experiences of Jean de Rohaine, a gentleman of France, while travelling over the Scottish moors when the English were hunting the Covenanters. His French impressions of the zeal of the devoted men of that day are full of suggestion. The heroine, Anne, almost proved a stumbling-block to the strict code of honor the French exile had always made his boast.

COBBAN, J. MACLAREN. The king of Andaman: a saviour of society. Appleton. 12°, (Appleton's town and country lib., no. 180.) $1; pap., 50 c.

CRAWFORD, F. MARION. Casa Braccio; il. by A. Castaigne. Macmillan. 2 v., 12°, buckram, $2.
Opens in a small town in Italy, Subiaco, near Tivoli, in the year 1844; here Angus Dalrymple, a Scotch tourist and physician, comes for a brief stay, and falls in love and elopes with a nun, Sister Maria Addolorata, under very dramatic circumstances. Many years afterward, her death having occurred in Scotland, Dalrymple returns to Rome with their daughter Gloria; her ill-fated marriage and death are the chief events of an intense story. Paul Griggs, who was first seen in "Katharine Lauderdale" and "The Ralstons," has his early life related and his unhappy love for Gloria.

CHAMBERS, ROB. W. The red republic: a romance of the Commune. Putnam. 12°, $1.25.
The scene of the story is laid in Paris during the exciting winter and spring of 1871, just after the German siege, and when Paris was in possession of the Communists. With the dramatic scene of the Commune as a background, the reader is presented with an idyl of love and art as developed in a quiet studio and a secluded garden in the old quarter of Paris. By the author of "The king in yellow."

COUCH, ARTHUR T. QUILLER, ["Q," *pseud.*] Ia: a love-story. Scribner. 16°, 75 c.

FOOTE, MARY HALLOCK. The cup of trembling, and other stories. Houghton, Mifflin & Co. 12°, $1.25.

FORD, JA. L. Bohemia invaded, and other stories; with frontispiece by A. W. B. Lincoln. Stokes. 16°, (Bijou ser.) 50 c.
Contents: Bohemia invaded; Wedded bliss; High etiquette in Harlem; The talent in the napkin; A dinner in Poverty Flat; The better element; The squarer; The joke that failed;

Dan Briordy's gitaway shadder; The wardman's wooing; The change of the luck; Mr. Synick's anti-bad-break; Freaks and kings.

FORD, JA. L. Dolly Dillenbeck: a portrayal of certain phases of metropolitan life and character; il. by Francis Day. G. H. Richmond & Co. 12°, $1.
The career of a pretty young country girl, who comes to New York City with the intention of going on the stage, and finds a financial backer in T. Adolphus Dillenbeck, a reputed millionaire, is painted in this novel. The girl, who is clever and heartless, rises to the top of the ladder of fame, while "Dolly Dillenbeck" goes mad through his dissipations, loses his fortune, and ends his life in an insane asylum. The worried theatrical manager, various types of actors and actresses and society men are depicted. By the author of "The literary shop."

FRANCIS, M. E., [*pseud.* for *Mrs.* M. E. Blundell.] The story of Dan. Houghton, Mifflin & Co. 16°, (Riverside pap. ser.) pap., 50 c.

GRIBBLE, FRANCIS. The red spell; with frontispiece by F. M. Gregory. Stokes. 1 il. nar. 16°, (Bijou ser.) buckram, 50 c.
Paris in 1871, during the Commune, is the scene. The story centres in the action of Ernest Durand, a young Communist; introduces scenes from his love episode with a Parisian shop-girl, whom he finally forsakes that he may fight under the red standard of the socialists. The policy of Delescluze, Jules Ferry, and other notable characters of the French Republic is seen.

HARDY, T. Jude the obscure. Harper. il. 12°, $1.75.

HARTE, FRANCIS BRET. In a hollow of the hills. Houghton, Mifflin & Co. 12°, $1.25.

HERMAN, H. The crime of a Christmas toy: a detective story; il. by G. Hutchinson. Ward, Lock & Bowden, Ltd. 12°, $1.
A well-worked-up story of a murder, in which two innocent people are suspected. The scene is principally London, and the mystery is well concealed to the end.

HOLDSWORTH, ANNIE E. The years that the locust hath eaten. Macmillan & Co. 12°, $1.25.

HOPE, ANTHONY. [*pseud.* for Anthony Hope Hawkins.] The chronicles of Count Antonio; with photogravure frontispiece by S. W. Van Schaick. Appleton. 12°, $1.50.
Somewhat in the vein of "The prisoner of Zenda," this story deals with romance and adventure in an imaginary kingdom and country, seemingly mediæval Italy; it tells of the love of Count Antonio (a sort of Chevalier Bayard) for the Lady Lucia, who is promised to another, and his banishment in consequence by the duke, and how he fled to the hills and there gathered other outlaws around him, all engaging in daring deeds.

HUNT, VIOLET. A hard woman: a story in scenes. Appleton. 12°, $1.25.
A study of a very unlovely type of the modern woman. A Manchester girl, with a small fortune, marries a celebrated artist on account of his social position. She does about everything she should not do, proving herself utterly selfish and heartless. At the end, when she has nearly wrecked her life, and her husband gen-

erously comes to her rescue, she sees his worth and loves him—but he does not care for her any longer.

JEBB, *Mrs.* J. GLADWYN. Some unconventional people. Roberts. 12°, $1.25.

LANG, ANDREW. A monk of Fife: a romance of the days of Jeanne D'Arc, done into English from the manuscript in the Scots College of Ratisbon. Longmans, Green & Co. il. 12°, $1.25.

MACLAREN, IAN, [*pseud.* for *Rev.* J. Maclaren Watson.] Beside the bonnie briar bush. Dodd, Mead & Co. 16°, 15 c.

MACLAREN, IAN, [*pseud.* for *Rev.* J. Maclaren Watson.] The days of auld lang syne. Dodd, Mead & Co. 12°, $1.25.
A companion volume to " Beside the bonnie briar bush," telling again in ten short stories of Drumtochty and its canny and kindly "fouk." Like their predecessors, the tales are full of dry Scotch humor, of pathos, and of "humanness." They are called: A triumph in diplomacy; For conscience' sake; A manifest judgment; Drumsheugh's love-story; Past redemption; Good news from a far country; Jamie; A servant lass; Milton's conversion; Oor lang hame.

MACMAHON, ELLA. A pitiless passion. Macmillan. 12°, $1.25.
Norman Grain, a young Englishman of good social position, marries Georgie Fitzroy, with whom he believes himself to be very much in love. After his marriage he is slowly brought to the realization that his wife is a confirmed inebriate. Norman has scarcely recovered from the shock of this revelation when he awakens to the fact that another woman has supplanted his erring wife in his affection. Several social problems are fearlessly treated.

MARCHMONT, ARTHUR W. Sir Jaffray's wife: a novel. Warne. 12°, bds., 80 c.

MEREDITH, G. The amazing marriage. Scribner. 2 v., 12°, $2.50.

MERRIAM, H. SETON, [*pseud.* for H. S. Scott.] The sowers: a novel. Harper. 12°, $1.25.
Prince Alexis, son of a Russian princess and an English father, attempts to assist his starving tenants by means of a Charity League, of which the existence is unknown to the Russian Government. The secret is sold to the authorities, and the prince flies to London with his faithful agent. He marries a designing woman, who is in the power of a French diplomatist with whom rests the plot of the story. Strong scenes are the visit of the prince to cholera patients, home-coming in a snow-storm, a bear-hunt, a peasant meeting, and an attack of peasants on a Russian castle. By the author of " With edged tools."

MITCHELL, J. A. Amos Judd. Scribner. 16°, 75 c.
The editor of *Life* has done an original thing in his first novel. He has transplanted a Rajah from northern India into the quaint environment of an old Connecticut town. He appears as a very small boy, and is given a typical New England education, including a course at Harvard. The novel concerns itself principally with the love-story of his young manhood, which is a pretty idyl with touches of humor.

MONTRÉSOR, FRANCES FREDERICA. The one who looked on. Appleton. 16°, $1.25.

MORRIS, MARY HARRIOTT. Lakewood: a story of to-day; il. by Louise L. Heustis. Stokes. 12°, $1.

MURFREE, *Miss* MARY N., [*pseud.* for Charles Egbert Craddock.] The mystery of Witch-face mountain, and other stories. Houghton, Mifflin & Co. 12°, $1.25.

PATER, WALTER. The child in the house: an imaginary portrait. Copeland & Day. 12°, pap., $1.50.

PEMBERTON, MAX. Jewel mysteries I have known; from a dealer's note-book; il. by R. Caton Woodville and F. Barnard. Ward, Lock & Bowden, Ltd. 8°, $1.50.
Contents: The opal of Carmalovitch; The necklace of green diamonds; The comedy of the jewelled links; Treasure of White Creek; The accursed gems; The watch and the scimitar; The seven emeralds; The pursuit of the topaz; The ripening rubies; My lady of the sapphires.

PRAED, *Mrs.* R. M. CAMPBELL. Mrs. Tregaskiss: a novel of Anglo-Australian life. Appleton. 12°, (Appleton's town and country lib., no. 181.) $1; pap., 50 c.
The heroine was born in Australia, but a greater part of her young life was spent in England. Her father's dishonorable bankruptcy and suicide and her disappointment in making a fine social marriage lead her to accept Keith Tregaskiss, a rough Australian rancher. Her story opens in Australia after she has borne her husband several children and finds her weary of life and her surroundings and patiently enduring her husband. Another man comes into her life and they love each other —the tragical death of her little girl alone preventing her eloping with him. Mrs. Trekaskiss is presented as a type of the new woman shrinking from wifehood and motherhood.

RAYMOND, WALTER, [" Tom Cobbleigh," *pseud.*] In the smoke of war: a story of civil strife. Macmillan. 16°, $1.25.
The civil strife is the war between the Church and the Covenanters. The story opens in 1645 in a tall stone wind-mill near the edge of the low moorlands of Somersetshire. The heroine is a strong, noble woman who suffers many hardships for her devotion to her country and her lover, one of the bravest of the Covenanters. Gives a stirring account of the battles and intrigues of that stormy period of English history.

SAVAGE (A) of civilization. J. Selwin Tait & Sons. 12°, $1.
John Robarts, a young artisan of good character and ability, is living at home with his mother, whom he believes to be a widow, when he suddenly learns of his illegitimacy, through a scapegrace uncle. Having obtained the name of his father through the same source, he heartlessly leaves his mother and starts to wreak his vengeance on his father, a wealthy manufacturer in a distant city, called New Manchester. He obtains employment at the Lotus Works, belonging to his father, under the name of Nomanson, and gets intimate with a Russian anarchist, and is the cause of some scenes of violence by inciting his fellow-workmen to riot.

SCHEFFEL, JOS. VICTOR V. Ekkehard: a tale of the tenth century; from the German with all the notes of the 138th ed. Crowell. 2 v., il. 16°, $2.50.
Von Scheffel's " Ekkehard " stands in the

forefront of historical novels. It appeared in 1855 and has reached its 150th edition. It is a tale of Lake Constance at the time of the great Hun invasion in the tenth century. The present translation is practically new, and a series of illustrations by German artists adds greatly to the interest and value of this edition. Neatly bound in imitation of the German classics.

SETOUN, GABRIEL. Sunshine and haar: some further glimpses of life at Barncraig. Harper. 12°, $1.25.

SMITH, F. HOPKINSON. A gentleman vagabond and some others. Houghton, Mifflin & Co. 12°, $1.25; *Large-paper ed., net,* $3.
Contains the following stories: A gentleman vagabond; A knight of the Legion of Honor; John Sanders, laborer; Bläder; The lady of Lucerne; Jonathan; Along the Bronx; Another dog; Brockway's Hulk.

STOWE, *Mrs.* HARRIET BEECHER. Uncle Tom's cabin; with introductory sketch, notes, etc. Houghton, Mifflin & Co. 12°, (Riverside lit. ser., no. 88, quadruple no.) *net,* 60 c.; pap., 50 c.

STRAIN, E. H. A man's foes. Ward, Lock & Bowden, Ltd. 12°, (Colonial lib.) $1.25.
The story tells of the struggle between James II. and William of Orange in Ireland and deals in particular with the siege of Derry. The scene is laid in the ancient town, and the atmosphere of the place, as well as that of the time, permeates the book. The quaint stilted language of the eighteenth century is used, and it is a woman who tells the story.

TODD, G. EYRE. Anne of Argyle; or, cavalier and covenant. Stokes. 1 il. 12°, (West End ser.) buckram, $1.
The historical romance begins in Glasgow Cathedral in 1650 at the moment it is announced to the worshippers that Charles II. is to be allowed to sit upon his father's throne. The crafty and diplomatic Marquis of Argyle, bent upon securing the domination of the Presbyterian form of church government, offers the king his daughter Anne to win concessions in favor of his party.

TURNER, ETHEL S. The story of a baby. Ward, Lock & Bowden, Ltd. il. 16°, (Nautilus ser., no. 1.) 75 c.

VAN ZILE, E. S. The Manhattaners: a story of the hour. Lovell, Coryell & Co. 12°, $1.
New York is the scene. The characters are two prominent newspaper men and people well known in Gotham society. The interesting issues of the novel are a Platonic friendship between Mrs. Percy-Bartlett and Richard Stoughton, a rising young reporter, and a romantic episode between Gertrude Van Vleck, a New York belle, and John Fenton, a *blasé* journalist interested in social problems. ——

WALFORD, *Mrs.* L. B. Frederick: a novel. Macmillan. 12°, $1.25.

WEYMAN, STANLEY J. The king's stratagem, and other stories. Blatt & Bruce. 1 il., nar. 16°, 50 c.
Contents: The king's stratagem; The body birds of court; In Cupid's toils; The drift of fate; A Blore manor episode; The fatal letter.

WEYMAN, STANLEY J. The red cockade: a novel. Harper. il. 12°, $1.50.

A stirring romance of the early days of the French Revolution.

WHITE, PERCY. Corruption: a novel. Appleton. 12°, $1.25.
The author of " Mr. Bailey-Martin " has again written a story showing the corruption of English politics and of the marriage relations between people brought together by motives of interest, greed, ambition, and the thousand and one other causes that bring about unions in the unnatural life of large cities. The plot is complicated. Full of epigrammatic sentences of pessimistic tendency.

WOOLSON, *Miss* CONSTANCE FENIMORE. Dorothy, and other Italian stories. Harper. il. 12°, $1.25.
Contents: Dorothy; The waitress; The transplanted boy; A Florentine experiment; At the Château of Corinne. All of these stories but " A Florentine experiment" were originally published in *Harper's Magazine ;* the latter appeared in the *Atlantic Monthly.*

HISTORY.

BETTANY, G. T. A popular history of the Reformation and modern Protestantism. Ward, Lock & Bowden, Ltd. pors. il. 8°, $2.
This is, as the title says, " a popular history of the Reformation," profusely illustrated. Chapters on: Causes of the Reformation; Early English reformers; John Wyclif, John Huss, the Waldenses, Savonarola, Luther, Calvin, John Knox, etc.

BRADLEY, E. T., [*now Mrs.* A. Murray Smith.] Annals of Westminster Abbey; il. by H. M. Paget and W. Hatherell; preface by Dean Bradley and a chapter by J. P. Micklethwaite. Appleton. 4°, $15.

DODGE, THEODORE AYRAULT. Gustavus Adolphus: a history of the art of war from its revival after the Middle Ages to the end of the Spanish Succession War, with a detailed account of the campaigns of the great Swede, and the most famous campaigns of Turenne, Condé, Eugene, and Marlborough; with 234 charts, maps, plans of battles and tactical manœuvres, and cuts of uniforms and weapons. Houghton, Mifflin & Co. 8°, (Great captains ser.) $5.

LATIMER, ELIZ. WORMELEY. Europe in Africa in the nineteenth century. McClurg. map. pors. il. 8°, $2.50.

LEROY-BEAULIEU, ANATOLE. Israel among the nations: a study of the Jews and anti-semitism; tr. by Frances Hellman. Putnam. 12°, $1.75.
Contents: Number and distribution of the Jews in different countries; The oldest grievance against the Jews, the religious grievance; The Jews, Christianity, and modern ideas; The Jews and the national grievance—Aryans and Semites; Are the Jews pure Semites?; The Jew is the product of his tradition and his law; Physiology of the Jew; Jewish genius; The Jewish spirit; The duration and the signs of Jewish particularism; The nationalization of the Jew; The cosmopolitanism and the fraternization of the Israelites. Index. The writer is entirely free from prejudice; shows neither intolerance nor race-hatred.

MINES, J. FLAVEL, [" Felix Oldboy," *pseud.*] Walks in our churchyards, old New York,

Trinity parish. G. Gottsberger Peck. il. 12°,
$1.25.
A series of papers published some years ago
in the *Trinity Record*; they are historical reminiscences of those who were prominent in public and private life, and now rest in the churchyards of Trinity Parish.

OLIPHANT, *Mrs.* MARG. O. W. The makers of
modern Rome. Macmillan. 12°, $3; *Large-
pap. ed.*, 8°, $8.

HUMOR AND SATIRE.

BANGS, J. KENDRICK. A house-boat on the
Styx: being some account of the divers doings of the Associated Shades. Harper. il.
16°, $1.25.

LITERATURE, MISCELLANEOUS AND COL-
LECTED WORKS.

AMERICAN LIBRARY ASSOCIATION. List of sub-
ject-headings for use in dictionary catalogues;
prepared by a committee of the American
Library Association, [Gardner M. Jones, G.
E. Wire, and C. A. Cutter.] Library Bureau.
8°, $2.

BOOK-LOVERS' ALMANAC FOR 1896. [*4th year.*]
Duprat & Co. il. 12°, 400 copies on plate
pap., $3; 100 copies on Japan pap., $6.
Contains, among other contributions, a sketch
on "Illustrated posters," by Clarence Cook;
"Books of emblems," by O. A. Bierstadt; "The
old and the new," an article on the types of Jen-
son and Bodoni, by Theo. L. De Vinne, and
"A bibliography of Frederick Locker-Lampson," by E. D. North. Among the illustrations
are four artotype reproductions of original
drawings by George H. Boughton, Edmond
Morin, and Louis Titz, in unique books in private New York collections; posters by Jean Gi-
goux, Ch. Jacque, Grandville, Gavarni, and
Manet; curious emblems from de Bry and by
Gravelot and Cochin; a new border by Louis J.
Rhead; various title-pages, vignettes, ornaments, printers' marks, portraits, and ex-libris.

BURROUGHS, J. Works. Houghton, Mifflin &
Co. 9 v., pors. 12°, *per set, net,* $13.50;
hf. cf., *net,* $27.

DOWDEN, E. Introduction to Shakespeare.
Scribner. 16°, *net,* 75 c.

ELLWANGER, G. H. Idyllists of the country-
side: being six commentaries concerning some
of those who have apostrophized the joys of
the open air. Dodd, Mead & Co. 16°, $1.25.
Contents: The wand of Walton; Gilbert
White's pastoral; The landscape of Thomas
Hardy; Afield with Jefferies; The sphere of
Thoreau; A ramble with Burroughs.

FULLER, SARAH MARGARET, [*Marchioness* Os-
soli.] Margaret and her friends; or, ten conversations with Margaret Fuller upon the mythology of the Greeks and its expression in
art, held at the house of Rev. George Ripley,
Bedford Place, Boston, beginning March 1,
1841; reported by Caroline W. Healey. Roberts Bros. 12°, $1.

GODKIN, EDWIN LAWRENCE. Reflections and
comments, 1865-1895. Scribner. 8°, $2.

GOODWIN, T. A., *D.D.* Lovers three thousand
years ago as indicated by the Song of Solomon. Open Court Pub. Co. 8°, bds., 50 c.

GRISWOLD, W. M., *comp.* A descriptive list of
books for the young. W. M. Griswold. 8°,
pap., $1; $1.25.
An excellent list of books for young readers

classified as follows: General; Amusements and
occupations; Anatomy and physiology; Behavior and language; Biography; Exploration;
Geography and history, these two subjects being
subdivided by countries; Literature; Natural
science; Natural history; Poetry; Animal
stories; Fairy stories; Fanciful tales; Impossible stories; American stories. There are two
pages of books not mentioned in the text recommended by Mr. Gardner M. Jones, of the
Salem Public Library, a list of authors and a
subject index.

GRISWOLD, W. M., *comp.* A descriptive list of
international novels. [*New enl. ed.*] W. M.
Griswold. 8°, pap., 75 c.
Increased by some forty pages inserted in the
main alphabet.

GROWOLL, A. The profession of bookselling:
a handbook of practical hints for the apprentice and bookseller. In 3 pts. Pt. 2. Office
of *The Publishers' Weekly.* il. 8°, interleaved,
bds., *net,* $2.
Contents: Insurance; Moving and taking
stock; How to keep a stock of music; Care and
arrangement of paper-bound stock issued in
series; Newspapers, magazines, and books issued
in parts; The circulating library, giving a short
list of fiction and dealing with location, selection of books, paper-covered books, shelving
and counters, dusting and cleaning, book-covers,
dating slip, catalogues, charging systems, etc.;
Bookbinding — practical and historical, incl.
specifications for bindings, cost of binding,
bindings of single books, historical notes, and
glossary of technical terms and implements
used in bookbinding. Illustrated with specimens of representative bindings.

HOWE, *Mrs.* JULIA WARD. Is polite society
polite? and other essays. Lamson, Wolffe &
Co. por. sq. 8°, $1.50.
Contents: Is polite society polite?; Paris;
Greece revisited; The salon in America; Aris-
tophanes; The halfness of nature; Dante and
Beatrice. Lectures delivered by Mrs. Howe in
many parts of the world.

JUSSERAND, JEAN ADRIAN ANTOINE JULES.
English essays from a French pen. Putnam.
il. sq. 12°, $2.25.
Contents: The forbidden pastimes of a recluse—England, 12th century; A journey to
Scotland in the year 1435; Paul Scarron; A
journey to England in the year 1663; One more
document concerning Voltaire's visit to England.

MATTHEWS, JA. BRANDER. Bookbindings old
and new; notes of a book-lover, with an account of the Grolier Club of New York.
Macmillan. il. 12°, $3.

NOBLE, J. ASHCROFT. Impressions and memories. Putnam. 12°, $1.50.

ROBERTS, W. The book-hunter in London:
historical and other studies of collectors and
collecting. McClurg. il. 8°, *net,* $5.
The author after a general introduction on
the subject describes early book-hunting;
book-hunting after the introduction of printing; transition from the old to the new; book
auctions and sales; book-stalls and book-stall-
ing; some book-hunting localities; women as
book collectors; book thieves, borrowers, and
knock-outs; some humors of book catalogues;
and some modern collectors. The volume is

liberally illustrated with portraits of collectors, booksellers, and librarians, sketches of noted book-shops, specimen pages of rare books and bookbindings, many of which have not been published before. Well indexed.

SAINTSBURY, G. Essays in English literature, 1780 — 1860 ; second series. Imported by Scribner. 12°, $2.

STEARNS, FRANK PRESTON. Sketches from Concord and Appledore. Putnam. il. 12°, $2. Concord thirty years ago. Sketches of Nathaniel Hawthorne, Louisa M. Alcott, Ralph Waldo Emerson, Matthew Arnold, David A. Wasson, Wendell Phillips, John Greenleaf Whittier, Appledore and its visitors.

WEST, KENYON. The laureates of England from Ben Jonson to Alfred Tennyson ; with selections from their works and an introd. dealing with the origin and significance of the English laureateship. *Vignette ed.*, il. by F. C. Gordon. Stokes. por. 12°, buckram, $1.50 ; hf. cf., $3.

WOLFE, THEODORE F., *M.D.* A literary pilgrimage among the haunts of famous British authors. Lippincott. il. 12°, $1.25.

WOLFE, THEODORE F., *M.D.* Literary shrines: the haunts of some famous American authors. Lippincott. il. 12°, $1.25.

MENTAL AND MORAL PHILOSOPHY.

DAWSON, W. J. The making of manhood. Crowell. 12°, $1.
Fourteen addresses : entitled The duty of right thinking; The power of the ideal; The power of purpose; The madness of youth; Courage ; The gains of drudgery; Money; Gambling; The empty mind; Patriotism; Leisure and holidays; The ministry of books; The price of perfection; A young man's religion.

GLADDEN, WASHINGTON. Ruling ideas of the present age. Houghton, M. & Co. 12°, $1.25.

MATSON, H. Knowledge and culture. McClurg. 12°, 75 c.

NATURE AND SCIENCE.

BENJAMIN, PARK. The intellectual rise in electricity: a history. Appleton. por. 8°, $4.

COCHRANE. C. H. The wonders of modern mechanism: a résumé of recent progress in mechanical, physical, and engineering science. Lippincott. il. 8°, $2.

LOWELL, PERCIVAL. Mars. Houghton, Mifflin & Co. il. 8°, $2.50.

SEELEY, H. G. The story of the earth in past ages. Appleton. 16°, (Library of useful stories.) 40 c.

SHALER, NATHANIEL SOUTHGATE. Domesticated animals; their relation to man and to his advancement in civilization. Scribner. il. 8°, $2.50.
Papers dealing chiefly with the horse, the dog, the familiar beasts of burden, and domesticated birds and insects; rich in apt illustration, anecdote, ingenious clearing up of difficult points, and otherwise entertaining reading on a topic full of attraction. There are articles on "The rights of animals" and "The problem of domestication." The illustrations have been done by some master hands. Delort, of Paris, the late famous artist in this field, drew the horses; Herrmann Léon, the dogs; Ernest E. Thompson, the Canadian ornithologist, the

birds, and Edwin Lord Weeks, the beasts of burden.

POETRY.

AUSTIN, ALFRED. In Veronica's garden. Macmillan & Co. il. 8°, $2.50.

FIELD, EUGENE *and* ROSWELL MARTIN. Echoes from the Sabine farm. Scribner. 8°, $2.
Translation and adaptations in metrical shape of Horace's Odes.

FIELDS, *Mrs.* ANNIE. Singing shepherd, and other poems. Houghton, Mifflin & Co. 16°, $1.

RICHARDSON, ELIZ., *comp.* Poets' dogs ; collected and arr. by Eliz. Richardson. Putnam. 16°, $1.25.
Sixty-seven poems that famous poets have written about their favorite dogs.

ROCHE, JA. JEFFREY. Ballads of blue water, and other poems. Houghton, Mifflin & Co. 12°, $1.25.
Poems of the sea ; appropriately bound in white cloth, a long pennant in red, white, and blue being stamped on front cover.

STODDARD, *Mrs.* ELIZ. Poems. Houghton, Mifflin & Co. 12°, $1.50.
The first volume printed of Mrs. Stoddard's poems contributed to magazines.

THOREAU, H. D. Poems of nature; selected and ed. by H. S. Salt and Frank B. Sanborn. Houghton, Mifflin & Co. 16°, $1.50.

POLITICAL AND SOCIAL.

BASCOM, J. Social theory: a grouping of social facts and principles. Crowell & Co. 12°, (Crowell's lib. of economics and politics, v. 7.) $1.75.

BISMARCK-SCHÖNHAUSEN, C. E. LEOP. O., *Prince* v. Bismarck's table-talk; ed. with notes and introd. by C. Lowe. Lippincott. por. 12°, $2.

BURROWS, MONTAGU. The history of the foreign policy of Great Britain. Putnam. 8°, $2.

GORDON, ARMISTEAD C. Congressional currency: an outline of the federal money system. Putnam. 12°, (Questions of the day ser., no. 85.) $1.25.

SCOTT, EBEN GREENOUGH. Reconstruction during the Civil War in the United States of America. Houghton, Mifflin & Co. 8°, $2.

SHAW, ALBERT. Municipal government in Continental Europe. Century Co. 8°, $2.

WHEELER, D. HILTON. Our industrial Utopia and its unhappy citizens. McClurg. 12°, $1 25.
The rights and wrongs both of the capitalist and the wage-earner are set forth in a plain and pleasant style. Not too scientific for the general reader.

WHITE, HORACE. Money and banking illustrated by American history. Ginn & Co. il. 12°, $1.50.
Begins with the first settlement at Jamestown, and traces the course of the tobacco currency of Virginia and Maryland, the commodity currencies of New England. New York, and South Carolina, the introduction of Spanish coins and the different valuations of the same in the different colonies, and the final establishment of the money of account of the United States. The subjects of coinage, of legal tender, and of the gold standard are treated in both

their local and their general aspects, and a chapter is given to the Brussels Monetary Conference. The subject of representative money is divided into two parts, viz.: fiat money and bank-notes. Colonial bills of credit, continental money, greenbacks, treasury notes, and silver dollars are separately treated. The course of banking development forms the concluding part.

WOODS, ROB. A., ELSING, W. T., RIIS, JACOB, [*and others.*] The poor in great cities, their problems, and what is doing to solve them; il. by Hugh Thomson, Otto H. Bacher, C. Broughton, [*and others.*] Scribner. il. 8°, $3.

THEOLOGY, RELIGION, AND SPECULATION.

CORNILL, C. H. The prophets of Israel: popular sketches from Old Testament history; tr. by Sutton F. Corkran. The Open Court Pub. Co. 1 il., 8°, $1.
Prof. Cornill is an orthodox Christian, holding the chair of Old Testament history in the venerable University of Königsberg; he is also a scientist, and he has applied the methods of science to his investigations. The book grew out of a course of lectures delivered by the author; as a whole it may be viewed as a brief popular sketch, giving only the salient and important outlines of the religious history of Israel from Moses down to the time of the Maccabees.

HARNACK, ADOLF. History of dogma; tr. from the 3d German ed. by Neil Buchanan. V. 1. Roberts Bros. 8°, $2.50.
The author is Professor of Church History in the University of Berlin. His great work first appeared in 1885, and reached its third edition in 1893. He has written a preface for this English translation, which is issued in conjunction with Williams & Norgate, of London. The translation is made under the supervision of Professor A. B. Bruce, of the Free Church College, Glasgow. In his account of the genesis of ecclesiastical dogma the author gives room only to those doctrines of Christian writers which were authoritative in wide circles, or which furthered the advance of the development of dogma. The work includes the articles on Neoplatonism and Manichæism furnished by Dr. Harnack to the Encyclopædia Britannica.

HORDER, *Rev.* W. GARRETT, *ed. and comp.* The poets' Bible. In 2 v. V. 1, Old Testament section. V. 2, New Testament section. Ward, Lock & Bowden, Ltd. 12°, *ea.*, $1.25.
Collections of poems by various English and European writers on the various events in the Old and New Testaments. Lists of authors. Indexes of first lines.

MOOREHEAD, W. G., *D.D.* Studies in the Mosaic institutions: the tabernacle, the priesthood, the sacrifices, the feasts of ancient Israel. W. J. Shuey, [United Brethren Pub. House.] il. 12°, *net*, $1.25.

Books for the Young.

AMICIS, EDMONDO DE. Cuore; an Italian school-boy's journal: a book for boys; from the thirty-ninth Italian ed. by Isabel F. Hapgood. Crowell. 12°, $1.50.
BROOKS, ELBRIDGE S. Great men's sons, who they were and what they did, and how they

turned out: a glimpse at the sons of the world's mightiest men from Socrates to Napoleon. Putnam. il. 12°, $1.50.
The seventeen great men whose sons are described are: Socrates, Alexander the Great, Cicero, Marcus Aurelius, Constantine, Mahomet, Charlemagne, Alfred the Great, William the Conqueror, Saladin, Dante, Tamerlane, Columbus, Luther, Shakespeare, Cromwell, and Napoleon. Six of these sketches have appeared in *Harper's Round Table.*

FENN, G. MANVILLE. The young castellan: a tale of the English civil war. Lippincott. il. 12°, $1.50.
While Sir Granby Royland was fighting for the cause of Charles I. of England, during that king's war with Parliament, his castle was attacked by Parliamentarians, and notwithstanding the brave defence of his only son was seized and confiscated. The story gives incidents of the long exile of the Roylands, and tells how Roy Royland regained his ancestral home.

FOOTE, MARY HASTINGS. A life of Christ for young people; in questions and answers. Harper. 12°, $1.25.

FOSTER, *Mrs.* I. H., ["Faye Huntington," *pseud.*] The Boynton neighborhood. Congregational S. S. and Pub. Soc. il. 12°, $1.
When Samuel Boynton returned to the Boynton neighborhood, after an absence of many years, he was pained to see that there was a great laxity of religious principle in that section of the country. Acting on the suggestion of a friend he organized a home class, the main object of which was Bible study. His results are given for the purpose of helping Home Department workers and inciting those who live in outlying country districts to take up the same line of work.

GOODLOE, ABBE CARTER. College girls; il. by C. Dana Gibson. Scribner. 12°, $1.25.
Contents: A photograph; an aquarelle; "La belle Hélène"; As told by her; A short career; An episode; Her decision; Revenge; The college beauty; A telephoned telegram; "Miss Rose"; A short study in evolution; The genius of Bowlder Bluff; Time and tide. These stories embrace romantic episodes in which college girls largely figure.

GRINNELL, G. BIRD. The story of the Indian. Appleton. il. 12°, (Story of the west ser., no. 1.) $1.50.

KNOX, T. W. In wild Africa: adventures of two youths in a journey through the Sahara Desert; il. by H. Burgess. W. A. Wilde & Co. 12°, (Travel adventure ser.) $1.50.
Northern Africa, a region comparatively unknown to even the explorer, is the country traversed by Mr. Whitney and his travel-loving nephews; the incidents of their adventurous journey, the strange and barbarous country through which they travel, and the habits and superstitions of the native people are accurately described.

MARDEN, ORISON SWETT. Architects of fate; or, steps to success and power; a book designed to inspire youth to character-building, self-culture, and noble achievement. Houghton, Mifflin & Co. pors. 12°, $1.50.
A companion volume to "Pushing to the

front "; a series of telling anecdotes and quotations of wise and witty sayings gathered together under such headings as " Wanted a Man," " Dare," " The will and the way," " Success under difficulties," " Sowing and reaping," " Wealth in economy," " Rich without money," " Decision," " Books," etc. The 26 chapters are illustrated with 26 portraits of prominent men.

NORTON, C. LEDYARD. Jack Benson's log; or, afloat with the flag in '61 ; il. by G. Gibbs. W. A. Wilde & Co. il. 12°, (Fighting for the flag ser.) $1.25.
Jack Benson shipped first in accordance with the wishes of his guardian, on the United States ship *Constitution* (" Old Ironsides"), after the firing of the first gun at Fort Sumter. He played an important part in saving " Old Ironsides " from the Secessionists in the harbor of Annapolis (1861), after which he shipped on the *Otter*, doing blockade service for the North. Jack being either a participator or spectator in all the notable naval events of the Civil War, his adventures are unusually interesting.

POLEVOI, P. NIKOLAEVICH. Russian fairy-tales from the " Skazki " of Polevoi, by R. Nisbet Bain ; il. by C. M. Gere. Way & Williams. 8°, $1.50.
The original source of these stories is the vast collection of Afanasiev, who did for the Russian what Asbjörnsen has done for the Norwegian folk-tale. A selection of about three dozen was made by the eminent Russian historian and archæologist Polevoi, and worked over into a fairy-tale book, which was published in 1874 at St. Petersburg, under the title of " Popular Russian Märchen." It is from this volume the present selection of 24 tales was made by Mr. Ralston, and now translated for the first time into English. Polevoi made the stories wholly his own, so admirably has he adapted their quaint wisdom and unique humor to nursery purposes.

SEAWELL, MOLLY ELLIOT. Quarterdeck and fok'sle : stories of the sea. W. A. Wilde & Co. il. 12°, $1.25.
There are two complete stories in the volume of the navy written for boys, but of equal interest to girls. The first story tells how a young fellow, who hated study and had never been made to go to school, learned through bitter experience the lesson of self-control. The second story deals with a famous incident of the English occupation of Newport, R. I., during the Revolutionary War, when General Prescott was captured in his own house by a handful of Americans.

TAIT, J. SELWIN. Wayne and his friends. J. Selwin Tait & Sons. il. 12°, $1.25.
Nine short stories of dreams and fairy adventure, written for the amusement of a little boy.

THAXTER, *Mrs.* CELIA. Stories and poems for children. Houghton, Mifflin & Co. il., 12°, $1.50.
The stories and poems here gathered are varied in subject, but all appeal strongly to boys and girls. Bound in a richly decorated cover, with gilt edges.

THOMAS, EDITH M. In the young world. Houghton, Mifflin & Co. 12°, $1.50.

NEW BOOKS

VIII . 472

LITERARY NEWS

AN ECLECTIC REVIEW OF
CURRENT LITERATURE
~ILLUSTRATED~

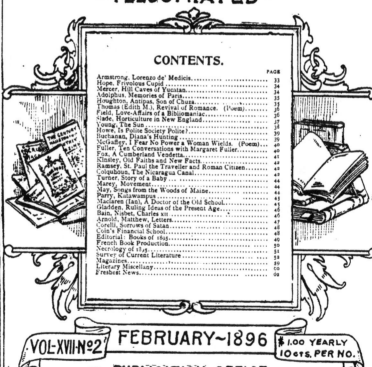

CONTENTS.

VOL-XVII-N°2   FEBRUARY~1896 $1.00 YEARLY   10 CTS. PER NO.

~PUBLICATION OFFICE~
59 DUANE STREET, NEW YORK
ENTERED AT THE POST OFFICE AT NEW YORK AS SECOND CLASS MATTER

The Literary News

In winter you may reade them, ab ignem, by the fireside; and in summer, ab umbram, under some shadie tree, and therewith pass away the tedious howres.

| VOL. XVII. | FEBRUARY, 1896. | No. 2. |

Lorenzo de' Medicis.

IN Edward Armstrong's volume upon "Lorenzo de' Medicis" in *The Heroes of the Nations Se-* Pope Sixtus IV. In 1484 Pope Sixtus IV. was succeeded by Innocent VIII., who became a

From "Lorenzo de' Medici," Copyright, 1895, by G. P. Putnam's Sons.

PALLAS, BY SANDRO BOTTICELLI.

ries is presented a glowing picture of this prince of Florence, who was surnamed "The Magnificent." Lorenzo narrowly escaped death at the hands of assassins hired by the Pazzi family in conjunction with the Archbishop of Pisa and stanch ally of Lorenzo, under whose beneficent rule Florence enjoyed great prosperity.

Mr. Armstrong's volume is exceptionally well illustrated. The picture here presented is in the private apartments of the Pitti Palace, Florence.

It has been recently discovered and is believed to commemorate the return of Lorenzo to Naples in 1480. It represents the triumph of Medicean civilization and peace over anarchy and war. Pallas is wreathed with olive branches. It is reproduced from a photograph by Alinari. (Putnam. $1.50.)

A Frivolous Cupid.

THE man who wrote "The Prisoner of Zenda," Anthony Hope, has been turning his talents to short-story writing, and has produced a small volume of them under the title of "A Frivolous Cupid." He has a light and sure touch, and in these stories his sparkle and brilliancy have not deserted him. They are not magazine stories by any means, and therefore they have a charming style about them. In one called "Reluctance" the process of what is commonly called "puppy" love is happily described with the inevitable result. The youngster in a few years passed by the married woman he once loved and actually did not know her. The stories are written in the author's best vein. (Platt, Bruce & Co. 75 c.)—*Commercial Advertiser.*

From "A Frivolous Cupid."   Copyright, 1896, by Platt, Bruce & Co.

THE DECREE.

"For every man over 21 years of age to find himself a wife."

The Hill Caves of Yucatan.

A SCIENTIFIC book which is equally interesting to the scientist and the lay reader is a *rara avis* indeed, but in "The Hill Caves of Yucatan," by Mr. Henry C. Mercer, we have found such a book. The lay reader cannot but be charmed with the vivid pictures of Yucatan scenery and customs, as well as with the clear and careful explanations of the methods pursued in cave explorations; while to the scientist the importance of the minute details of the latest investigations in "culture layers" in Central America can hardly be exaggerated. Yucatan has for many years attracted the imagination of historians and archæologists; its ruins, its scattered remains of manuscripts, its hieroglyphs, all speak of a civilization at least equalling, perhaps surpassing, any other existing in the New World at the time of its discovery. The problem of man's antiquity in Yucatan engaged the attention of the Corwith Expedition. Ten caves were searched for evidence of an earlier race of men than those who built the ruins and left the hieroglyphs whose form has given rise to the legend that the Mayas were the only original ten lost tribes of Israel. No such evidence was found. These caves are important as natural and original sources of water-supply at certain times. The first comer must have visited them or perished; and, if there was any value in the test of cave layers anywhere, these layers should have proved the presence, not of one race only, but of all the races that ever visited the peninsula.

This inference is only fair, and we may consider Mr. Mercer's investigations as conclusive, at least as conclusive as anything ever is in science. Mr. Mercer says:

"A people generally identical with the builders of the ruins had come to the cave. Reaching the region in geologically modern times, and always associated with still existing animals, they had not developed their culture there, but had brought it with them. No human visitor had preceded them."

Among other curious contributions to our knowledge of the ancient Mayas resultant from these cave excavations is the probability that they were cannibals. The illustrations in Mr. Mercer's volume are interesting. (Lippincott. $3.50.)—*Boston Literary World.*

A FORD OF THE JORDAN.

Memories of Paris.

MR. F. ADOLPHUS's "Memories of Paris" is an exceedingly readable book. In the opening chapter the writer describes the Paris of forty years ago, before the Haussmann reconstruction, and he passes thence to a recital of his recollections of the city under the Empire and during and immediately after the siege by the Germans. The entry of the latter is graphically described, as are the later scenes incident to the rise and fall of the Commune—this chapter making one realize how perfectly capable modern Paris is of repeating, under due conditions, the revolutionary excesses of a century ago. The Communards of 1871 were, in capacity for evil and the brute instinct of destructiveness, plainly no whit behind the ferocious rabble by means of which the Jacobin extremists swayed, saved, and dishonored the great Revolution. Among other dramatic episodes of the time the author witnessed the pulling down of the Vendôme Column—one of the many insensate performances of the latter-day *Sans-Culottes.* The first attempt had failed, the great structure steadily resisting the strain of rope and windlass. But after an hour's delay, says the author, "I had become conscious, after a particularly savage jerk on the ropes, that the line between the chimney and the statue was not exactly straight. Slowly—very slowly—the statue swerved past the chimney ; slowly the great column bowed toward me—never did any one receive so superb a salutation ; slowly it descended, so slowly that it almost seemed to hesitate : in a great haze of spurting dust it fell. . . . With a wild rush and frantic shouts the people dashed past the sentries into the Place Vendôme, leaped upon the dislocated fragments, and howled coarse insults at them." Allowing for a rather pronounced tendency to overcolor in his more dramatic passages, we think Mr. Adolphus (who was evidently at Paris as a press correspondent) may be accepted as a trustworthy narrator. An amusing chapter is devoted to Mr. Worth, and another to General Boulanger. (Holt. $1.50.)—*The Dial.*

Antipas, Son of Chuza, and Others Whom Jesus Loved.

IN this story by Louise Seymour Houghton, primarily designed for young people, but which will attract older readers as well, the author has tried to show the real nature of the Messianic hope held by the various classes from which our Lord's followers were drawn—the devout, the worldly, the patriots, the ecclesiastical party—and to trace the gradual change in the views of those who loved him, as his life and teachings led them more and more near to a true apprehension of his Messianic calling. That nearly all the principal characters are children does not argue that the story was written for children only. Its deepest meaning is, indeed, for their elders, and the key to it lies in the motto on the title-page: "Except ye be converted and become as little children ye cannot enter into the Kingdom of Heaven." Fifteen full-page illustrations. (Randolph. $1.50.)

REVIVAL OF ROMANCE.

Too long, too long we keep the level plain,
   The tilled tame fields, the bending orchard bough !
   The byre, the barn, the threshing-floor, the plough
Too long have been our theme and our refrain !
Enough, my brothers, of this Doric strain !
   Lift up your spirits, and record a vow
   To gather laurel from the mountain's brow,
And bring the era of rich verse again !
Ye painters, paint great Nature at her height—
   Seas, forests, cliffs upreared in liquid air,
   And touch with glamour all things rough and crude.
And ye who fiction weave for our delight,
   Give us brave men, and women good as fair—
   And shame our hollow Sadducean mood !
     —*Edith M. Thomas, in The Century Magazine.*

The Love-Affairs of a Bibliomaniac.

EUGENE FIELD wrote "The Love-Affairs of a Bibliomaniac" just before he died, and, as his brother tells us in a pleasant introduction of half a dozen pages, he put into the work all the enthusiasm and bibliomaniacal tenderness of his long experience as a collector of books and a lover of them. Often a man is one of these two things before he is the other, often he is only one of the two ; but with Field there seems to have been a fusion of both characters at the very beginning. When, in the company of little Captivity Waite, he first discovered the delights of the famous "New England Primer," he may not have attempted at once to make the book the nucleus of a library. But the instinct of the bibliomaniac was already in his heart as he turned the quaint pages with Captivity at his side. She herself, he says, "approached closely to a realization of the ideals of a book—a sixteenmo, if you please—fair to look upon, of clear, clean type, well ordered and well edited, amply margined, neatly bound ; a human book, whose text, as represented by her disposition and her mind, corresponded felicitously with the comeliness of her exterior." "I never think or speak of the 'New England Primer,'" says this amusing bibliomaniac, "that I do not recall Captivity Waite." The episode might be taken as a fair illustration of what Field's love-affairs as a bibliomaniac were from beginning to end. The book before us opens on this charming "first love," and as the chapters go on they present the same winning mixture of bookish with more artless sentiments, of bibliomaniacal with sunny human feelings. Field conceived the volume as recording the talk and recollections of a collector of mature years, looking back fondly upon the passions of his life and passing them on to his fellows with modesty, but withal a conviction that he who makes two bibliomaniacs to grow frenzied where only one was mad before is a benefactor to the human race. There is a Judge Methuen in the book, the author's companion in a bibliomaniacal crime, and between the two we get a dis-cursive account of their dealings with the tender passion that the poets prate of, but the tenderest passion of all, the one for which men go hungry, content with a certain leathery smell, a certain aroma of old ink, old paper, and old binding, which comes from, say, the Quintus Horatius Flaccus or from some kindred source. "The New England Primer" was Field's first love. "Robinson Crusoe" was his second, and about this time he fell in with Grimm's fairy-tales. In consequence, we find him in his third chapter talking about one of the bibliomaniac's most characteristic pleasures, "the luxury of reading in bed," and it is fairy lore that this particular bibliomaniac is reading. The combination was irresistible to him, and it proves the same to his reader, though the bibliomaniac's sister, Miss Susan, insists that such practices make him "the most exasperating man in the world." We had forgot Miss Susan. She, too, was a collector, and though she thought her bibliomaniacal brother foolish enough for his passion of accumulation, she had her own treasures, and would not give them up. Her brother's mania was fastidious. He kept good company. He fell in love with good books.

Field was good-humored, if ever a bibliomaniac was, and there is no acid in this book of love-affairs ; but he was dearly fond of a story like that just quoted, and he tells another, better, if anything, which carries a similar point. That he founded it on fact, in all probability, is in no way calculated to diminish its fun. . . . Throughout this book there is an air of drollery, of gay enjoyment, which will place the pages permanently among the best that Field ever wrote. They have his personal attraction to the full, reflect his kindliness, his quaint wit, his love of trifles, his really profound love of books. When he writes of "Baldness and Intellectuality," aiming to show that the two go together, one can see him pointing to his own cranium with comic pride ; and there is the same atmosphere of pure frolic in his chapters on "The Malady Called Catalogitis," "The Delights of Fender-Fishing," and "The Odors Which My Books Exhale." The strong sub-current of a book-lover's true enthusiasm is never missing, however, and, no matter how uproarious his vein, Field portrays himself as a worthy bibliomaniac, one who deserved to possess the treasures he adored. There is soon to be published a complete edition of his work in prose and verse. This book, which is written in his most engaging style, and is accompanied by several sets of his merry rhymes, will form a welcome number of the uniform set of ten delightful volumes. (Scribner. $1.25.)—*N. Y. Tribune.*

Horticulture in New England.

HORTICULTURE means the cultivation of fruits, vegetables, herbs, or flowers within a certain limited enclosure, and that area, be it large or small, we call a garden. Garden is distinctly of Anglo-Saxon origin, "*gyrdan*" meaning to enclose. Orchard is then an *ort geard*, or a fruit enclosure, and so *wyrt geard* would mean an enclosure where herbs or vegetables were cultivated.

Mr. Slade shows briefly the acquaintance Greeks and Romans had with gardens. Long before there was an Athens or a Rome the Egyptians had their gardens, for they have left us plans with pictures of them. We derive our taste for horticulture from the English, and so we have to trace gardens as far back as the early Briton. As the Roman knew Britain, we are to believe that the islanders did not cultivate the cereals, but this probably was an error. Across the Channel were the Gauls, who certainly knew how to cultivate some kinds of grain, and it looks as if the Druids were gardeners. Strabo says that the southern Britons had gardens adjacent to their houses and cultivated vegetables and fruits. It seems as if the rose and violet were brought to England by the Romans.

In England before the middle of the sixteenth century there had been many books issued treating of horticulture, and Mr. Slade gives an excellent summary of the works of Gerarde (1597); Lawson (1615); Markham (1613); Parkinson (1600); Sir Hugh Platt (1570); Worlidge, Evelyn, and others. These authors wrote generally of the formal mathematical character of the gardens of the wealthy, and of "stately terraces with gilded balustrades and curious quincunx, obelisks, and pyramids." The natural was in a measure shunned and the nearest admissible approach was the making of a heath or desert, which

might, through art, represent "a wilderness." Sir William Temple, imitative of the Dutch, carried stiffness in garden to a climax.

Worlidge, however, though he was a formalist, nevertheless appreciated what was within the possibilities of those who had but little means, and so he told about the beauty of the cottage garden. "There is scarce a cottage in most of the southern parts of England but hath not its proportionable garden." Worlidge then says how "nuptials, feasts, funerals" could be supplied "with the products of these gardens." What Worlidge wrote, says Mr. Slade, is interesting to us, because the Puritans and Pilgrims from various parts of England used to reproduce in their new homes the cottage gardens of old England. Mr. Slade's volume is pleasantly conceived. (Putnam.)—*N. Y. Times.*

From "Chilhowee Boys in War-Time." Copyright, 1895, by T. Y. Crowell & Co.
"TRY BEEF TALLER FOR THEM SORE HEELS."

The Sun.

THE *International Scientific Series* of books, which comes from the press of D. Appleton & Co., ought to have a place in every well-stocked library. Over seventy volumes have already been published, and they treat of subjects which have a peculiar interest for every thoughtful man, whether he is a professional scholar or a merchant. Indeed, these books form a library in themselves, and cover nearly every topic on which scientific research is engaged. For example, there is Tyndall's "Forms of Water in Clouds, Ice, and Glaciers," Pettigrew's "Animal Locomotion," Vogel's "Chemistry of Light and Photography," Whitney's "Life and Growth of Language," and others too numerous to mention. The best thoughts of the best men are within reach of all, and at a very moderate price.

From "The Sun."   Copyright, 1895, by D. Appleton & Co.

CORONA OF 1893.

I have on my table at this moment two volumes in this series which seem to me to have a peculiar fascination. The first is entitled "The Sun." Its author, Professor Young, of Princeton University, is a man to whom every one gives a respectful hearing, a careful and painstaking scientist, whose words are always well considered and whose style is as free from technical terms as the circumstances of the case permit.

Professor Young wrote on the sun as far back as 1881, and his book at once received the attention it merited, but fifteen years have wrought great changes, and the little volume needed revision. The progress of discovery has been both continuous and rapid, and a book of astronomy that is even five years old must needs be behind the times in many important respects. Professor Young, in his successive editions, added foot-notes in abundance, but at last it became necessary to recast the whole book, and we have the results of his labor in this attractive volume.

The chapters on the Spectroscope and the Solar Spectrum, on The Methods and Apparatus for Studying the Surface of the Sun, and on The Sun's Light and Heat, have been materially altered, and now embody all the new information which is at present available. We find a succinct account of recent advances and discoveries in solar spectroscopy and spectro photography, a wonderfully interesting statement of the latest theories concerning sun-spots, a subject which still remains a puzzle, and many facts concerning the corona which are based on recent eclipses. In a word, it is a thoroughly satisfactory volume, finely illustrated and furnishing the ordinary reader with an answer to the many questions which his curiosity has propounded. It is unnecessary to commend it, for the name of Professor Young always insures a large hearing among all classes. (Appleton. $2.)—*N. Y. Herald.*

From "The Sun."   Copyright, 1895, by D. Appleton & Co.

SIZE OF MOON'S ORBIT.

Lectures by Mrs. Julia Ward Howe.

I REMEMBER that, quite late in the fifties, I mentioned to Theodore Parker the desire which I began to feel to give living expression to my thoughts, and to lend to my written words the interpretation of my voice.

Parker, who had taken a friendly interest in the publication of my first volumes, " Passion Flowers" and "Words for the Hour," gave his approval also to this new project of mine. "The great desire of the age," he said, "is for vocal expression. People are scarcely satisfied with the printed page alone; they crave for their instruction the living voice and the living presence."

At the time of which I write no names of women were found in the lists of lecture courses. Lucy Stone had graduated from Oberlin and was beginning to be known as an advocate of temperance and as an anti-slavery

From "Is Polite Society Polite!"   Copyright, 1895, by Lamson, Wolffe & Co.

MRS. JULIA WARD HOWE.

speaker. Lucretia Mott had carried her eloquent pleading outside the limits of her Quaker belonging. Antoinette Brown Blackwell occupied the pulpit of a Congregational church, while Abby Kelly Foster and the Grimke sisters stood forth as strenuous pleaders for the abolition of slavery. Of these ladies I knew little at the time of which I speak, and my studies and endeavors occupied a field remote from that in which they fought the good fight of faith. My thoughts ran upon the importance of a helpful philosophy of life, and my heart's desire was to assist the efforts of those who sought for this philosophy.

Gradually these wishes took shape in some essays, which I read to companies of invited friends. Somewhat later I entered the lecture field, and journeyed hither and yon, as I was invited.

The papers collected in the present volume have been heard in many parts of our vast country. As is evident, they have been written for popular audiences, with a sense of the limitations which such audiences necessarily impose. With the burthen of increasing years, the freedom of locomotion naturally tends to diminish, and I must be thankful to be read where I have in other days been heard. I shall be glad indeed if it may be granted to these pages to carry the message which I myself have been glad to bear — the message of the good hope of humanity, despite the faults and limitations of individuals.

That hope casts its light over the efforts of years that are past, and gilds for me, with ineffaceable glow, the future of our race.

The lecture, " Is Polite Society Polite ? " was written for a course of lectures given some years ago by the New England Women's Club of Boston. "Greece Revisited " was first read before the Town and Country Club of Newport, R. I. "Aristophanes" and "Dante and Beatrice" were written for the Summer School of Philosophy at Concord, Mass. The "Halfness of Nature" was first read before the Boston Radical Club. "The Salon in America" was written for the Contemporary Club in Philadelphia. (Lamson, Wolffe & Co. $1.50.)—*Preface of "Is Polite Society Polite? and Other Essays."*

Diana's Hunting.

IN Robert Buchanan's latest novel the hero is a successful playwright, the heroine a popular actress who has made a great "hit" in the hero's latest play. The scene is constantly among the London theatres and clubs in the realm called "Bohemia." Diana Meredith

DIANA.

the actress, seeks to win the playwright, Frank
Horsham, from his wife and carry him away
with her to America; there is a brief struggle,
an apparent yielding, but duty triumphs in the
end.   One of the pretty *Twentieth Century
Series*. (Stokes.   75 c.)

I FEAR NO POWER A WOMAN WIELDS.

I'FEAR no power a woman wields
While I can have the woods and fields,
With comradeship alone of gun,
Gray marsh-wastes and the burning sun.

For aye the heart's most poignant pain
Will wear away 'neath hail and rain,
And rush of winds through branches bare
With something still to do and dare.

The lonely watch beside.the shore,
The wild-fowl's cry, the sweep of oar,
And paths of virgin sky to scan
Untrod, and so uncursed by man.

Grammercy for thy haunting face,
Thy charm of voice and lissome grace !
I fear no power a woman wields
While I can have the woods and fields.

(Dodd, Mead & Co. $1.25.)—*From " Poems
by Ernest McGaffey."*

Ten Conversations with Margaret Fuller.

THESE ten conversations were held by Margaret Fuller at the house of the Rev. George
Ripley in Boston in 1841. The other end of the
conversation was sustained by Emerson, Al-
cott, Elizabeth Peabody, the Ripleys, and
others of the coterie—twenty-odd in all ; and
Caroline Healey, considerably younger than
the others, was the chiel that took the notes.
The book will not edify the classical student.
Even after allowance is made for the growth
since that day of philological science, Miss
Fuller's inspiration, if we may rely on the present document, was remarkably untrammelled
by knowledge. Her notions of Greek mythology, as here reported, were based on local
collections of casts, gems, etc., interpreted
chiefly by the light of Ovid's poems ! She apparently held that the myths originated in the
age of Plato (see page 29) ; she thought "the
' Odyssey' was written when Homer was young
and romantic," and she used interchangeably
the Greek and Latin names of the gods.

With such data as these, Margaret and her
friends sat themselves cheerfully down to
"spiritualize" the myths. A familiar event
is thus described : " The Indomitable Will
had dethroned Time, and, acting with Productive Energy, .   .   .   had driven back the
sensual passions to the bowels of the earth,
while it produced Perfect Wisdom, Genius,
Beauty, and Love ; results which were more
excellent if not more powerful than their
Cause." Frank Shaw felt a not ungrounded
misgiving as to how these personifications
" suggested themselves in that barbarous age,"
and "it was acknowledged, as a matter of
course, that only a few preserved any consciousness of the original significance of the
mythology." In fact, the book serves as a
mile-stone to show how the penchant for facts
has advanced in the last half-century. There
is a very wide conviction to-day, among wom-
en as well as men, that, before speaking *ex
cathedra* on any subject, it is better to burden
one's self with the facts. The magazines are
inclined to think that, by her pursuit of information, the college woman has choked the
muse ; at all events, she and all of us hold with
him who sings that " parting with knowledge
we have not got is the hardest parting of all."

It is a far cry from Margaret Fuller to Jane
Harrison. But the student of psychology will
be interested in the effect of a little acquaintance with ancient art on a fine and impressionable mind, and to note how nearly Miss Fuller
possessed the gifts that Rousseau bestowed on
his ideal woman: " Du goût sans étude, des
talents sans art, du jugement sans connois-
sances." (Roberts. $1.)—*The Nation.*

A Cumberland Vendetta.

WE have, in "A Cumberland Vendetta, and other stories," by John Fox, Jr., a series of studies of American life and character of a kind which, when its ends are accomplished, is a better example of the success that our authors have attained in fiction than any and all their ambitious and elaborate novels put together. There have been many attempts to write the American Novel, as there were many attempts in the early years of the century to write the American Poem. The social conditions of the people of the United States are not favorable to the creation of a great novel, and for many reasons, among which is the absence of a National Character, in the large sense that appeals to us in the fictions of Balzac and Thackeray; the fluctuating movements of life in our great cities and large towns; the conflicting temperaments of various European races which have sought a home among us in order to better their fortunes, while their hearts are in the fatherlands, to which most of their habits and ways of thinking still conform; to which might be added our want of comprehension of what we are, and of what, except our individual selves, we may fairly be supposed to represent in the history of mankind. We are a heterogeneous mass of many peoples, but, except politically, not a nation. There is no unity in our life, but a diversity of lives, one kind, and that a changing one of late years, in the New England States, another on the Pacific shores, and divers others scattered through the Southern and Western States.

What New England was rather than is we have seen in the stories of Judd, of Mrs. Stowe, of Mrs. Stoddard, of Miss Jewett, and Miss Wilkins. What Western life was we have seen in many stories, notably those of Mr. Eggleston; what Georgia life, in the stories of Col. Johnson; what Louisiana life, in the stories of Mr. Cable and Miss King; and what phases of Virginia life, in the stories of Mr. Page. Mr. Fox's stories belong to the special studies which we have in mind, and of which they are good examples. He has the advantage of writing about a wild and rugged region of country such as we see nowhere in the neighborhood of our Northern cities, or rustic characters in keeping with such primitive regions, men, women, and children, who, as compared with those we see about us, may be said to be in a state of nature, a law to themselves, impulsive alike in their good and evil qualities, simple, hardy, free of speech, quick to give blows and take blows, kind, generous, cruel, revengeful, brutal. But the reader must make their acquaintance for himself, and through Mr. Fox, who knows them much better than we can, their lives, their joys and sorrows, their tenderness, their pathos, and in such bitter feuds as he relates in "A Cumberland Vendetta" and "The Last Section." (Harper. $1.25.)— *Mail and Express.*

FOXHOUNDS OF THE IMPERIAL KENNELS.

Old Faiths and New Facts.

"OLD FAITHS AND NEW FACTS" is the title of a suggestive work by W. W. Kinsley. In this timely and important book the author aims to show how far facts, brought to light by modern scientific research, modify and how confirm the time-honored faiths of Christendom. He applies the new tests to those three most vital questions of the hour: Does prayer avail? Was Christ divine? Is man immortal? The first he finds to include: Can God interfere without abrogating any law or destroying any force? Has He? Will He for us? Will He because we ask Him? Are reasonably and rightfully offered prayers certain of favorable answer? The second: Does man's worth warrant Christ's coming? Was His coming essential to complete world-evolution? Are His life and teachings explicable if not divine? The third: Is there a life beyond? What will that life be? Has not the plan of evolution already been sufficiently carried out and the trend of creative thought been sufficiently revealed to afford grounds for safe predictions as to essential details in ultimate human destiny? These general subjects, with the many subjects which they include, are discussed in entirely modern spirit, with a freshness and range of knowledge which render the book instructive, stimulating, and immediately valuable. (Appleton. $1.50.) —*Philadelphia Press.*

The Nicaragua Canal.

A BULKY volume of over 400 pages on a matter which has occupied public attention for a great many years. Mr. Colquhoun gives us a very carefully prepared history of the various attempts which have been made to pierce the isthmus and get to the Pacific without making the long and dangerous journey around Cape Horn. He tells us, in a pleasant, chatty way, about the Panama Railroad, a scheme in which a few—but only a few—engineers have confidence in these days, and about the Panama Canal, which brought De Lesseps to comparative poverty and embittered his last days.

That a railroad can be constructed which will transport a big ship bodily from shore to shore without danger to the vessel seems a good deal like talking of miracles, but the plan has advocates, and is therefore beyond the reach of ridicule. Whether the Panama Canal will ever be finished is a puzzle which no one can solve. It is the most pathetic and most disastrous problem, financially and otherwise, that has been undertaken in modern times. The Nicaragua Canal is a much easier adventure, but for some reason there is a degree of indifference on the part of the public which, for the present, will render successful action impossible.

This is an admirable book of reference, and its effect will be to force the subject on the attention of Englishmen, and increase their desire to take hold of the enterprise financially, in order that they may ultimately obtain control of it. If that was the purpose of the author he will go far toward achieving it. Nevertheless, it is a valuable contribution to the literature of the subject, and is, on the whole, the best book of its kind that I have seen. (Longmans, G. $7.)—*Dr. Hepworth, in N. Y. Herald.*

St. Paul the Traveller and the Roman Citizen.

THIS volume is composed of the "Morgan Lectures," delivered by Professor Ramsay at Auburn Theological Seminary, in 1894, and the "Mansfield College Lectures," in 1895. Lectures delivered at Harvard, Johns Hopkins, and Union Theological Seminary are also worked up in it. Though some parts of the volume are older, it is the most recent of Professor Ramsay's publications, and represents the conclusions drawn from all his previous work. The material for these lectures and the basis upon which they stand are mainly published in the author's "Church of the Roman Empire" and "The Cities and Bishoprics of Phrygia." The point to which all this enormous amount of material is applied in "St. Paul the Traveller and the Roman Citizen" is the illustration and corroboration of the Book of the Acts and the parallel history of Paul as contained in his Epistles.

We by no means commit ourselves to all the positions taken by this most ingenious and prolific student. His treatment of the Manuscript Texts sometimes seems dictated by *à priori* rather than strictly critical considerations. It may not be proven that Paul's thorn in the flesh was some form of the scourge of the country, now as then, malaria. Paul may or may not have belonged to some ancient and honorable family from whom, in his later years, property came to him which enabled him to bear the expense, at which he very certainly was, if the account in the Acts is to be trusted. We are even inclined to suspect that Professor Ramsay's ingenuity gets away with him in his argument to prove that in the Gospel of Luke and in the Acts we have but two parts of an unfinished historic trilogy, which was to have been finished in three parts, and to have carried the history down to the death of Paul. . . . Great and important as this view of the subject is, we doubt whether, after all, it will prove as useful or furnish as much support to

From Julia A. Shedd's, "Famous Painters." Copyright, 1896, by Houghton, Mifflin & Co.

REMBRANDT.

faith as the endless minor corroborations and general clearance of the history throughout its ordinary course from doubt. This is a service which can be appreciated only by one who is familiar with the strong points of the Tübingen theory and knows with what a grip they have seized on some of the best minds in the Church. On the other hand, it is also a service which can only be measured by studying the volume itself, in which all the clues and threads of the argument are gathered up by a master hand, and to which we would gladly send our readers. (Putnam. $3.)—*The Independent.*

Architects of Fate.

UNDER this title Mr. Marden has published another volume, which possesses the same qualities as those which procured for "Pushing to the Front" so hearty a welcome from the press and the public. The press pronounced that one of the best books ever written of its kind; and the verdict has been justified by the public, which has absorbed many editions. It has been adopted in the public schools of Boston and other cities, and has received hearty commendation from other countries.

The aim of this volume, as of the former, is to incite youth to high achievement and lofty purpose by inspiring examples of perseverance and consequent success, of the struggles and triumphs of those who have led the world toward the heights attained by the Washingtons, Lincolns, and Gladstones. Among its subjects are: Wanted—a Man, Dare, Will and the Way, One Aim, Self-Help, Work and Wait, Grit, The Grandest Thing in the World, Rich without Money, The Might of Trifles, Guard Your Weak Point, Nature's Little Bill, Decision, Curse of Idleness, Integrity, Ideals, etc. Rev. Edward A. Horton, of Boston, pronounces the book "a storehouse of incentives, a treasury of precious sayings, a granary of seed-thoughts capable of a fine character harvest" President Warren, of Boston University, says: "Dr. Marden's power of pithy statement and pertinent illustration seems inexhaustible." Rev. C. L. Goodell, Boston, observes: "These two books place Dr. Marden at the head of helpful writers for the young." The book is packed from cover to cover with the most stirring examples of noble achievement in all history. It is as fascinating as a romance; there is intense magnetism in every page. (Houghton, Mifflin & Co. $1.50.)

Animals in Motion.

"MOVEMENT" is hardly a happy title, though it may lend itself to the speculation of the curious. The subject matter of the book, however, is the graphic representation of the various movements of animals, and of the time taken to do them, together with a description of the apparatus employed for registering and recording these. Everybody is familiar with the highly interesting instantaneous photographs, by Mr. Muybridge, of the movements of animals, more especially of those of the horse. It is evident that considerable interest is added to such photographs if they are accompanied by a graphic representation of the time taken by the animal to change from one position to another. The chief method by which this double result is obtained is that known as chronophotography, and we have in this most interesting book a full description of its application to the movements of man, animals, birds, reptiles, fishes, insects, and even inanimate objects, accompanied by numerous and often highly entertaining illustrations. M. Marey writes as a popular expounder of scientific facts, but the most enjoyable as well as the most valuable chapter in his volume is that which treats of the subject from the artist's standpoint. Music is represented by, in the first chapter, a graphic time record (not a chronophotographic one) given of two airs played on the keyboard of a harmonium. All who wish to know more of this interesting subject should undoubtedly read this highly entertaining and instructive work. It is admirably printed and excellently illustrated. (D. Appleton & Co. $1.75.)—*Bookselling.*

Songs from the Woods of Maine.

IF merit had the unerring knack of meeting with desert in the proper proportion, some books that come unheeded, only to go unheeded, would be sure of the acceptance which belongs to them of right. We have received complaints from American poets that their volumes of verse obtain but scant courtesy in the English press, and our own observations cause us to admit the justice of the grumble. The London papers find it no easy task to keep pace with the home-grown poetical product, so the temptation to resort to a policy of protection is sometimes too hard to be resisted. Take one instance. If James Whitcomb Riley had been an Englishman how he would have been lauded, puffed, dined, interviewed, photographed, and paragraphed! The Authors' Club would have made him free of its soup; the Vagabonds would have given him of their mutton. To think that a want of free trade in letters should keep such a delightful poet from

enjoying a wide circulation in England! Mrs. May has a less claim upon our attention, but it is safe to say that she will not meet with due recognition; and this is to be regretted, for she has a most winning way of preaching pluck for a creed. Easy of speech, bright with hope, glowing with a belief in the eventful purging of the base, she sings her songs of the courageous heart so sweetly and so quaintly that we desire to record our personal thanks. We might write a column without providing as much evidence as is contained in the three following verses:

"A STAR CAN BE AS PERFECT AS A SUN.

"Because you cannot be
An overhanging bow,
Whose promise all the world can see,
Why are you grieving so?
A dewdrop holds the seven colors too;
Can you not be a perfect drop of dew?

"Because you cannot be
Resplendent Sirius,
Whose shining all the world can see,
Why are you grieving thus?
One tiny ray will reach out very far;
Can you not be a perfect *little* star?

"The smallest, faintest star
That dots the Milky-Way
And sends one glimmer where you are
Gives forth a faultless ray;
Learn then this lesson, oh, discouraged one!
A star can be as perfect as the sun."

How kindly it is! How cleverly the reproach is concealed, and yet how vigorous the lesson! It is a triumphant illustration of how to be didactic, and, despite one of the sections of the Decalogue, we are unable not to be unenvious. Mrs. May often writes better poetry, but in our opinion she is best employed when she makes a union of good cheer and good advice. (Putnam.)—*Norman Gale, in The Athenæum.*

The Story of a Baby.

THE ingenuousness of "The Story of a Baby" endears the book from its first page, but the ingenuousness is only of the surface. By and by, round about the baby, and all because of the baby, there begins to enact itself a very real, human, and touching story. Dot and Larrie drift apart. At first the breaches are so small that they can be bridged over, but at last comes one so wide that Dot and Larrie, standing on opposite sides, cannot hear each other's voices, or see each other's faces properly. As it all begins with the baby, so it all ends with the baby, who crows and coos and "googuls" his way, all unknowing, through the miseries of those bigger children his parents. Endless are the stories of unhappy husbands and wives, but seldom has there been one treated with the purity and tenderness and truth of this. Not once is a discordant note struck. The quarrels are very real; Dot's tears and Larrie's grim honesty of determination appeal to the reader's outworn heart; but there is absolutely no vulgarity of touch or sentiment —a thing so dangerously ready to creep into stories of this kind. There is just enough of local Australian color to give freshness of scene to the freshest of simple narratives. (Ward, Lock & Bowden. 75 c.)—*The Academy.*

Katawampus.

A NOVEL and amusing story, of the kind that children love to listen to at the story-telling hour, just before the sandman comes, is " Katawampus: its treatment and cure," by Judge Edward Abbott Parry. According to this persuasive chronicle, the perplexed father of four unruly children happens to meet and confide in a little dwarf, called Krab, the Cave Man, who says that the children have a disease called "Katawampus," which he can cure by taking them to his cave for repairs, a business of which he makes a specialty, as might be seen from his professional card, bearing this inscription: "Children repaired with neatness and despatch. New manners in all styles. Good tempers supplied and a liberal allowance made for old ones." In the narrative that follows the four children go to the cave for treatment, and then have a singular voyage home in a boat commanded by a duck captain, with four-and-twenty white mice for sailors, and a white kitten with nine tails to keep the mice in order. The story fairly bubbles over with humor and is simple enough to be enjoyed by a child of five. The verses from " Pater's Book of Rhymes " are very funny, and the illustrations, by Archie Macgregor, are even more ingenious than the text. Apt quotations from this delightful nonsense will help a family bring harmony out of conflicting tempers. (Macmillan. $1.25.)— *The Beacon.*

A Doctor of the Old School.

IT was a happy thought, that of bringing together under the title of " A Doctor of the Old School," Ian Maclaren's delightful sketches of the life and death of William MacClure, embellished as they are with a series of admirably expressive illustrations by Frederick C. Gordon. The story of the rough-featured, uncouth, great-hearted doctor of Drumtochty is safely to be reckoned as the finest thing in the artistic sense that its author has yet published, and is indeed one of the select masterpieces of modern literature. Its tender yet manly portrayal of a character that with less discriminating treatment might have been rendered ab-

From "The Sheik's White Slave."   Copyright 1895, by Lovell, Coryell & Co.
EASTERN WARRIORS.

surd through over-sentimentality, its depth of pathos, its frequent gleams of humor, its simplicity of narration—all these qualities united make a singularly vivid impression and give to the work an individuality no less distinct than it is charming. One would, in fact, be perfectly safe in saying that "A Doctor of the Old School" will hold its place in literature side by side with Goldsmith's "Vicar of Wakefield." This edition is in every way a desirable one to own or to utilize for gift purposes. The author himself vouches for the fidelity of Mr. Gordon's designs, which are over fifty in number, and which are certainly full of thought and expression; and in typography, paper, and binding the book is wholly unexceptionable. (Dodd, Mead & Co. $2.)— *The Beacon.*

Ruling Ideas of the Present Age.

DR. WASHINGTON GLADDEN has written quite a number of books on social questions, undertaking to apply Christianity to the problems of the day. He says: "The regulative truths which are working themselves out in the experience of every generation are often and but imperfectly articulate, and it is a good service if one can help his neighbors to discern the meaning of the intellectual and ethical movements that are going on around them." This essay, which won the prize offered by the Fletcher trust of Dartmouth College, is intended to apply Christianity to our social life, and it has the merit of pointing out, within safe lines, the principles which are behind the right working of our social forces. Dr. Gladden has studied this subject all his life, and after his first chapters, which are chiefly of an elementary character, he enters into some of the deeper questions of our time, though his treatment is so unaffected that it does not seem so thorough as it really is. In the chapter on "The Law of Property" the principle is laid down that the rights of property are seated in the very foundations of our ethical and spiritual being, and that every attempt to gain it by infringing upon the rights of others is an injustice. Again, in the chapter on "Religion and Politics," he insists strongly upon the need of a deep and genuine religious preparation for the discharge of all the more important duties of citizenship. Under the head of "Public Opinion" he says: "We Americans give ten times as much thought, in our politics, to the construction of political machinery as we do to the provision of adequate and well-directed power to move it. But public opinion is far more to the republic than power is to machinery." As the volume reaches its conclusion Dr. Gladden shows up the weakness of those who cover up their wrong-doings by benevolent action. He points out that human progress is largely due to forces that limit and check each, and thus, by their reactions, strengthen and support each other. In the closing chapter the ruling ideas are brought together to show that they express the immanence of the Christ among men. It is assumed in this work that the relations of men to one another in society are vital and organic, and that the kingdom of God is here, its essential forces in active operation, though its completion is yet to come. Dr. Gladden thinks that the social conditions are preparing for a revelation to the world of the glory of Christ which will be overpowering when the truth is better understood than it is now. His book is full of optimism and will be helpful to a great many people in placing emphasis on the ruling ideas of the present age, but it lacks that power of fresh style which carries the reader impetuously along from sentence to sentence. Its chief merit is its clearness and simplicity. It is a valuable exposition of the truths which are foremost in our own time. (Houghton, Mifflin & Co. $1.25.)—*Providence Sunday Journal.*

Charles XII.

"CHARLES XII. and the Collapse of the Swedish Empire," by R. Nisbet Bain, is the latest issue of the *Heroes of the Nations* series of historical biographies, and the work is fully the equal of the other volumes which have appeared. The author observes quite properly that it would be impossible within the space allotted to present anything like an exhaustive history of the subject of this study, which occupied such a large place in the annals of his time. The purpose has been to present the leading facts of the notable career of Charles XII. in the light of the latest investigations, and it endeavors to dissipate the many erroneous and unjust ideas for which French history in this respect is mainly responsible. The Swedish hero was a remarkable man in every respect, and Professor Bain, having thoroughly acquainted himself with the original documents, was abundantly qualified to do the work assigned him. The book is written in familiar style, and gives a concise account of Swedish history as well as a running commentary on the life and character of the soldier king. The purpose, aside from presenting the main facts, is to place Charles before the readers of modern times in an honorable light; to vindicate his memory, while at the same time recording the true story of a notable career. The work abounds in graphic pen portraitures of men and scenes of notable men and accounts of scenes and incidents. (Putnam. $1.75.)— *Philadelphia Telegraph.*

Letters of Matthew Arnold.

WRITING to his sister in 1859 Matthew Arnold observes that "in Paris there is certainly a larger body of people than in London who treat foreign politics as a science, as a matter to know upon before feeling upon." To go through these two volumes is for the reader to have it brought home to him that in all the relations of life Arnold held to the principle or habit which he admired so much in the French. He "knew upon" a thing before "feeling upon" it. This does not make him less humanly interesting. His letters show the man in him with a revelation of his tenderness and warm genuineness of heart such as those who have considered him in his work alone must meet with considerable surprise. But the first impression they leave, and the last, is of a man born out of his time, of a man who comes nearer to the ideal which he himself recognized and admired in Marcus Aurelius than any other figure of English literature and English life. He has streaks of infinite human sweetness in him, of almost boyish fun, and a reliance upon family ties which makes his letters to his wife, mother, sisters, and children among the most delightful ever printed; but he remains in every letter here given the clear-eyed, stern-souled type, the son of his father, with an intense justification of the hereditary idea, only more austere, perhaps, than the Arnold of Rugby because more absolutely lucid of intellect, more serenely poised. The one overpowering passion of his life seems to have been living the truth. It is his consecration to this ideal that calls to mind the Roman Emperor whom he studied.

There is not a dull line in his correspondence. This is because he played many parts, because he was critic, man of the world, playful friend, incessant traveller, endlessly lovable husband and father, and a thousand other things. But most of all it is his poetic strain that brings a spell within his pages, a strain of imaginative divination, a strain of feeling for beauty in all

things. It does not come out in any obvious way, but that was because poetic inspiration for Matthew Arnold was not an obvious matter. You feel it in his letters, in their indescribable touches of poetic grace, of an imagination seizing upon the thought, the impulse, most delicate, most urbane, most charming. It was in this vein that he came in contact with all the

Reproduced from "Die Gesellschaft."

GUSTAV FREYTAG.

elements of a career that was far more than that of a mere literary man, a mere scholar. He sought unremittingly for the loveliness in life, the finer grain, the subtler emotion, the higher ideal, and, without qualification, he found it. One might know this from the texture of his letters alone. Their substance is of the rarest in epistolary literature and their style is unique, for in the smallest matters as in the greatest Matthew Arnold gave the best of himself to his task; even as a letter-writer his motto was "Noblesse Oblige." (Macmillan. 2 v., $3.)—*N. Y. Tribune.*

The Sorrows of Satan.

MISS CORELLI is thoroughly in earnest. She has convictions which carry her along on a strenuous tide of declamation and description. She is highly sorrowful and painfully serious in her mission of exposing the iniquities of the critics who have not accepted her as a heaven-born genius, and of a world that has not yet stoned the critics for their temerity. No single touch of humor ever comes to relieve the black shadows of her picture, no breath of self-distrust ever brings her to question the absorbing importance of what she has to say. With the solemnity of a Hebrew prophet, she cries out to the world to witness the sorrows of a misunderstood Satan and the wrongs of Marie Corelli.

If the devil worshippers of Asia have half so admirable a god as her Satan the high character which they sustain among the neighbors is not to be wondered at. It is man in general, and the critics of Marie Corelli in particular, who are responsible for the evils of the world. Satan tempts them, but he tempts more in sorrow than in anger, obedient to what the Greeks would have called an "inexorable necessity"; he does not like his work, hopes that people will resist him, and when they do resist reverently kisses their hands. Satan is a fallen angel, but an angel nevertheless, and an angel awaiting redemption. He is bound by an oath to keep men from doing good, but every unwilling success takes him away from his goal, and every good deed of man brings him nearer to it. He is not getting much nearer, according to the interpreter of his sorrows. About all he has to contend with in his diabolical enterprise is the Prince of Wales and a literary woman named Mavis Clare, who can be none other than the author herself, with her virtues and charms toned down to suit a character of fiction.

The English critics, it appears, have corruptly failed to appreciate the author of "The Sorrows of Satan," and have found fault with previous books. If they buy this one—they will not get it otherwise, for she is resolved not to throw away good literature on people only fit for chicken feed—they may, perhaps, learn how much they have been mistaken. Do they want impassioned prose? Here are almost five hundred pages of it rich in volcanic splendors and prophetic frenzy. Do they want evil denounced? They will find here not mere assertion, but bristling proofs put in foot-notes. Do they want mystery? Let them visit the other world with Geoffrey Tempest and the "Angel-Foe whose eyes are wild with an eternity of sorrows," hear the spirits talk Latin amid the thunders, and see pallid skeletons and "Immortal Despair." Do they want tragedy? Let them stay with the poisoned Sibyl as she writes with her dead hand her awful thoughts. Do they want philosophy? The theory of a man-redeemed Satan is a prodigy of abstract thought. Do they want novelty? They here get the information that society is selfish and sensual, that the world loves riches and follows not the ways of righteousness, that hypocrites abound, and that only in the conquest of the world, the flesh, and the critics is there eternal happiness.

This ought to prove her case whatever the critics may say. They always miss the good books anyway. They missed Keats. They missed Shelley. They missed her. She is a classic. As the Monk of Cluny said, the world is very evil—and so are the critics. (Lippincott. $1.50.)—*N. Y. Tribune.*

"COIN'S FINANCIAL FOOL."

HIS SOLILOQUY.

I WANT a bogus dollar, just based on mere pretence;
I hate the "gold-bug's" gold one that is worth a hundred cents;
For I'm a "Silver Beetle," as all the world can see,
And except my precious humbug, you will find no bugs on me.

I can give you learned statistics from Rome to Adam Smith,
And quite a miscellaneous lot of fallacies therewith,
To prove that all our troubles in panics new or old
Are but the rank production of a dollar made from gold.

I brook no British meddling with the "white" stuff that I laud,
For what care we for England or the folks who live "abroad"?
They tell us two and two make four, as sure as I'm alive,
And so to be "American" I vow that they make five.

Does anybody think the Yankee Nation cannot say
That anything's a dollar and make its value stay?
Should England ever dare to, by the Revolution's birth,
We will suddenly "annex her" or "wipe her from the earth."

We need a pile of money, and it isn't England's right
To refuse the kind we offer. If she does I want to fight.
For if we Yankees legislate that water runs up hill,
In spite of all creation I will bet you that it will.

I know the silver bullion that the people had to buy,
Piled up, would make a monument broad-based and six miles high,
Besides the minted silver, which nobody takes away,
But we ought to keep on buying it in spite of what they say.

I don't care a continental for Wall Street or Grover C.,
For all the bloated "gold-bugs" are as mean as they can be;
So I've sent broadcast my pamphlet as a sort of "Summer School,"
To show the folks the wisdom of "Coin's Financial Fool."

—*Joel Benton, in Harper's Weekly.*

The Literary News.

An Eclectic Monthly Review of Current Literature.

EDITED BY A. H. LEYPOLDT.

FEBRUARY, 1896.

NOTABLE BOOKS OF 1895.

STATISTICS have some of the characteristics of "the little girl who had a little curl right in the middle of her forehead." To those whose mind absorbs and assimilates them they are "very, very good"; to those to whom they convey no definite idea they are "horrid." We shall go into no special detail about the causes of the figures it is our habit to offer once a year, but simply let the tables tell their own story of the increase or decrease in certain lines of publication during 1895, both in England and America.

CLASSIFICATIONS.	1894. New Books	1894. New Editions	1895. New Books	1895. New Editions
Fiction	573	256	1050	64
Law	440	45	480	51
Theology and Religion	442	26	471	35
Education and Language	426	16	456	32
Literary History and Miscellany	208	29	455	13
Juvenile	315	29	365	10
Political and Social Science	233	21	313	22
Poetry	131	133	294	15
Physical and Mathematical Science	141	24	108	24
History	163	24	185	8
Biography, etc.	140	21	167	13
Medical Science, Hygiene	118	42	141	22
Description, Travel	116	28	124	27
Fine Arts and Illustrated Books	127	11	133	7
Useful Arts	118	20	100	11
Mental and Moral Philosophy	42	7	55	6
Domestic and Rural	42	9	48	4
Sports and Amusements	50	6	34	4
Humor and Satire	10		32	
Totals	3837	647	5101	368
		3837		5101
		4484		5469

The London *Publishers' Circular* presents the following analytical table of the books published in England during the past year:

DIVISIONS.	1894. New Books	1894. New Editions	1895. New Books	1895. New Editions
Theology, Sermons, Biblical, etc.	476	80	501	69
Educational, Classical, and Philological	615	127	660	111
Novels, Tales, and Juvenile Works	1584	366	1544	347
Law, Jurisprudence, etc.	126	23	57	33
Political and Social Economy, Trade and Commerce	141	21	163	23
Arts, Sciences, and Illustrated Works	98	39	96	16
Voyages, Travels, Geographical Research	282	68	263	75
History, Biography, etc.	256	58	353	68
Poetry and the Drama	160	21	231	16
Year-Books and Serials in Volumes	318	2	311	
Medicine, Surgery, etc.	97	59	153	33
Belles-Lettres, Essays, Monographs, etc.	370	113	430	42
Miscellaneous, including Pamphlets, not Sermons	767	215	749	182
Totals	5300	1183	5581	935
		5300		5581
		6483		6416

So many of the books published in this country are of English parentage that we shall not attempt to separate them, but say a few words of the more notable works in both lists under their classifications by subject.

Fiction leads the list in both countries in point of numbers. Almost every phase of human life, every problem of society, every line of theory and speculation is now handled in fiction, as it has been proved the most efficacious way of reaching a class of readers of influence in righting wrongs and forming opinions, who cannot be overlooked and who cannot be reached except under cover of romance. One of the most important books of the year in point of subject covered, with a great mission to bring home to full-grown men and women the growing danger lurking in theories and impressions, in self-study and self-indulgence which do not rest upon a solid basis of knowledge, truth, education, self-control, and aspiration toward spiritual conquests, is Thomas Hardy's "Jude the Obscure." Only four characters play important parts in this gloomy tragedy: Jude, who has his aspirations for higher culture wrecked by his uncontrolled physical desires; Arabella, his coarse, wholly uneducated wife; Sue, his cousin, the victim and outcome of semi-education; and the schoolmaster, the product of unromantic, selfish cramming. What does Hardy try to prove? All may read a different lesson. He puts no curb upon his imagination in planning out his blood-curdling scenes, and he puts no curb upon his pen in tracing the words that are shocking in themselves as well as descriptive of shocking scenes. We cannot but think that perhaps Hardy might have accomplished much more by saying much less. But he has written a powerful book that has made all honest critics pause. They know Hardy has given of his best; they are studying to determine whether the reading world would be better or worse without his gift. No other author gave a novel last year which touched this in strength.

Among the novels of the year showing originality of subject and treatment were:

WARD, Mrs. Humphry. Story of Bessie Costrell.
CRAWFORD, F. Marion. Casa Braccio.
ZANGWILL, Israel. The Master.
DOYLE, A. Conan. The Stark Munro Letters.
HICHENS, Robert S. The Story of an Egyptian Sphinx.
CROCKETT, S. R. A Galloway Herd; Men of the Moss-Hags.
HOCKING, Joseph. All Men are Liars.
PHELPS, Elizabeth Stuart. A Singular Life.
HASTINGS, Elizabeth. An Experiment in Altruism.
CRANE, Stephen. The Red Badge of Courage.
BARRETT, Frank. A Set of Rogues.
WELLS, H. S. The Time Machine; The Wonderful Visit.
PHILPOTTS, Eden. A Deal with the Devil.
TURNER, Ethel S. The Story of a Baby.

WHITE, Eliza Orne. The Coming of Theodora.
PENDLETON, Louis. The Sons of Ham.
BARLOW, Jane. Maureen's Fairing.
LE QUEUX. Zoraida.
HOLDSWORTH, Annie E. The Years the Locust Hath Eaten.
CECIL, Lady Gwendolen. The Curse of Intellect.
HUNT, Violet. A Hard Woman.
MERRIMAN, Henry Seton. The Sowers.
CORELLI, Marie. The Sorrows of Satan.

The most discussed novels of the year were:
"Jude the Obscure," by Thomas Hardy; "The
Gods, Some Mortals, and Lord Wickenham,"
by John Oliver Hobbes; "The Amazing Marriage," by George Meredith ; "My Japanese
Wife," by Clive Holland; "His Egyptian Wife,"
by Hill Hilton; and "Chimmie Fadden," two
series of funny anecdotes about New York City
low life, by Edward W. Townsend, which have
been widely read and quoted and from which
a successful drama has now been made.

Short stories were abundant and specially
good during 1895.

The most important works in Biography, Me-
moirs, and Correspondence were "The Letters
of Matthew Arnold"; "Letters of Samuel
Coleridge"; "Dante Gabriel Rossetti: His
Family Letters"; "Life and Letters of E. A.
Freeman"; "Senator Sherman's Recollections
of Forty Years"; "Life of Samuel J. Tilden";
"Gustave Flaubert," by John Charles Tarver;
"The German Emperor," by Charles Lowe;
"Great Astronomers," by Sir Robert Ball; and
"The Vailaima Letters," by R. L. Stevenson.

Descriptive and historical works were unusually good. Four books appeared on Constantinople : "Guide to Constantinople," by De-
metrius Coufopoulos ; "Constantinople," by
Mrs. Clara Erskine Clement ; "Constantinople," by F. Marion Crawford ; and Prof. Grosvenor's monumental work, "Constantinople,"
in two sumptuous illustrated volumes. "Westminster Abbey" was described in three works :
"Westminster," by Walter Besant ; "Westminster Abbey and the Cathedrals of England,"
made up from the writings of Archdeacon Farrar, Canon Milman, and others ; and "Annals
of Westminster Abbey," by Emily Tennyson
Bradley Smith, illustrated by Paget, with preface by Dean Bradley. Many valuable works
were brought out by the Eastern question.
Notable books on China and Japan were : "Peoples and Politics of the Far East," by Henry
Norman ; "Out of the East," studies in New
Japan, by Lafcadio Hearn ; "Notes in Japan,"
by Alfred Parsons ; "The Real Chinaman," by
Chester Holcombe ; "Lotus Time in Japan,"
by Henry T. Finck ; and "The Religions of
Japan," by William Elliott Griffis.

In Theology and Religion "The Foundations
of Belief," by Arthur James Balfour, "That

Monster, the Higher Critic," by Marvin R.
Vincent, "The Oxford Church Movement,"
by G. Wakeling, and "A Study of Death," by
Henry Alden, were the most important.

The question of bimetallism led to a large
number of pamphlets and books, many of them
of great influence. W. H. Harvey published
many popular expositions advocating silver,
the most talked of being "Coin's Financial
School," which led to a host of replies and
imitations, some serious and many successfully humorous. Books on taxation much
commented upon were "Double Taxation in
the United States," by Francis Walker, and
"Natural Taxation," by Thomas G. Shearman.

Among the many books of literary criticism
issued perhaps the one which had the most
influence and led to the most writing in
almost every department of literature was
Max Nordau's "Degeneration." William
John Courthope issued the first volume of
an exhaustive work on "The History of
English Poetry," covering the period of the
Middle Ages and has convinced all his readers
that his vast subject is in expert hands.
The first volume of Jusserand's "A Literary
History of the English People," covering from
the beginnings to the Renaissance, promises a
work of rare quality to be completed in three
volumes.

Books which have not yet received the attention which must lead to their full appreciation
are Vida D. Scudder's "Life of the Spirit in
the Modern English Poets"; Mary Fisher's
"Twenty-five Letters on English Authors";
and Gilbert M. Tucker's "Our Common
Speech," a book full of information on the history of English words and of the ideas for which
they stand, presented with rare art in an almost
perfect style.

The year brought several prizes to book-col-
lectors: E. C. Stedman's "A Victorian Anthol-
ogy, 1837-1895;" "Greater Victorian Poets,"
by Hugh Walker; "The Growth of the Idylls
of the King," by Richard Jones; "A Book of
Elizabethan Lyrics," selected and edited by
Felix E. Schelling; "The Literature of the
Georgian Era," by William Minto; Ditchfield's
"Books Fatal to Their Authors;" "The Lau-
reates of England," by Kenyon West; and
Brander Matthews's "Bookbindings Old and
New."

A distinctive feature of the year was the
"fad" of posters. Among the books devoted
to this art were "The Reign of the Poster," by
Charles Knowles Bolton; "The Modern Poster," by Arsène Alexander and others ; "Picture Posters," by Charles Hiatt; and "A Collection of Posters," edited by Edward Bela.

BOOK PRODUCTION IN FRANCE IN 1895.

ACCORDING to the *Bibliographie de la France* the number of books issued in France during 1895 was 12,927, showing a decrease of 80 works, compared with the total of 13,007 in 1894. The number of musical compositions was 6446, or 774 less than in 1894, and the number of engravings, lithographs, and photographs was 1483, or 47 more than in 1894.

NECROLOGY OF 1895.

BLACKIE, Prof. J. S., b. 1809. Greek chair at the University of Edinburgh.

Rawlinson, Sir Henry, b. 1810. Assyriology.

Badeau, Gen. Adam, b. 1831. Journalist. Editor of books on General Ulysses S. Grant and the Civil War.

Coppée, Henry, b. 1821. President Lehigh University. English Literature.

Ballou, Maturin M., b. 1820. Traveller, author, founder of Boston *Globe.*

Dana, Prof. James D., b. 1813. Mineralogist and geologist of Yale University.

Plon, Eugène, b. 1837. Publisher. Author of life of Thorwaldsen.

Fréytag, Gustav, b. 1816. Historic fiction. essays, plays.

Faithfull, Emily, b. 1835. English economist and philanthropist.

Locker-Lampson, Frederick, b. 1821. Compiler of "Lyra Elegantiarum." Society verse.

Huxley, Prof. Thomas Henry, b. 1825. Scientist. Writings on evolution and ethics.

Gneist, Rudolph, b. 1816. Professor of jurisprudence in University of Berlin.

Paull, Mrs. Minnie E. Children's stories.

Sybel, Heinrich v., b. 1817. History.

Tauchnitz, Christian Bernard, b. 1816. German publisher of English novels.

McClelland, Miss M. G. Southern novelist.

Hurlbert, Henry M., b. 1827. Journalist. Letters to *The Sun* signed "An American Traveller."

Pasteur, Louis, b. 1822. Discoverer of treatment for cure of rabies. Investigator of microbe theory.

Story, William Wetmore, b. 1819. Sculptor and author.

Boyesen, H. H., b. 1848. Professor of Germanic languages and literature at Columbia College. Voluminous writer.

Field, Eugene, b. 1850. Poet and humorist. Bibliophile.

Droz, Gustave. Painter; afterwards novelist.

Dumas, Alex. (*fils*), b. 1827. Dramatist.

Frothingham, O. B., b. 1822. Unitarian minister; afterwards biographer and literary essayist.

Barthelemy-Saint-Hilaire, b. 1805. French statesman, philosopher, and orientalist.

Sala, George Augustus Hare, b. 1827. Distinguished journalist and author.

Cosmopolis, the new international magazine, must look for its support to English, French, and German readers of culture and broad interests. The editors say definitely: "We will have no translations," and all articles printed in the magazine must be originally written in one of those three languages. (George Brandes, who contributed a most excellent article on Alexandre Dumas *fils,* was obliged to write it in French instead of his Danish mother-tongue.)

The first issue is about equally divided into three sections. Each part begins with a continued story, then follows a special article on some question of timely interest by an expert; then a review of the times, a review of the theatre, and a review of literature. In the English part are represented Henry James, Sir Charles Dilke, who writes of the origin of the war of 1870, Andrew Lang, who deals with passing events, A. B. Walkley, who writes the theatrical review, and Edmund Gosse, who writes of literature. In the same order of subject the French contributors are Bourget, Anatole France, Geo. Brandes, Edouard Rod, and Francisque Sarcey. In the German portion are found Ernst von Wildenbruch, Erich Schmidt, Theodor Mommsen, Friedrich Spielhagen, Anton Bettleheim, and Neumann-Hofer. The magazine is gotten up on fine paper in excellent type, and makes a sumptuous appearance. Libraries should certainly add it to their list of periodicals. We sincerely hope this ambitious magazine may have a long, successful career. Even those who only understand one or two languages will fully get their money's worth, and all cultured people should give material support to such an educating and broadening influence. The International News Co. are the agents in America.

WITH WEYMAN IN OLD FRANCE.

THE wind moans round about the eaves;
    Against the reeking pane
The rain is dashed; the whirling leaves
    To rest are never fain.
Within the room the fire's bright beams
    Midst elfin shadows dance;
Their mellow gleams shine o'er my dreams
    And o'er the fields of France.

And I with eager eyes see naught
    But autumn wood and field;
And in my dream the perfume's caught
    That roadside blossoms yield.
With bated breath through leafy way
    I tread with stealthy glance;
The sun doth play on rapier gay
    And o'er the fields of France.

I turn the page: the castle looms
    Above me in the night;
The bell from out a turret booms;
    The steeds are shod for flight.
And now, away at headlong speed—
    For foes ride close, perchance—
O'er hill and mead, through paths that lead
    Beside the fields of France.

Moan on, O blasts, and do your worst!
    Against the dim blurred pane
The whirling torrents beat and burst.
    I heed nor wind nor rain;
But here, the cheerful hearth beside,
    Deep in my brave romance,
Whatever betide, I gayly ride
    With Weyman in Old France.
      —*Richard Stillman Powell, in Lippincott's.*

Survey of Current Literature.

☞ *Order through your bookseller.*—"*There is no worthier or surer pledge of the intelligence and the purity of any community than their general purchase of books; nor is there any one who does more to further the attainment and possession of these qualities than a good bookseller.*"—Prof. Dunn

ART, MUSIC, DRAMA.

HIATT, C. Picture posters: a short history of the illustrated placard; with many reproductions of the most artistic examples in all countries; with upward of 150 examples of picture posters of England, France, Germany, and America, many published here for the first time. Macmillan. 8°, *net*, $4.

ISSEN, H. Prose dramas. United States Book Co. 2 v., 12°, (Lakewood ser., nos. 22, 23.) pap., *ea.*, 50 c.
Contents: V. 1, A doll's house, and other plays; tr. by W. Archer, and others. With a biographical and critical introd. by Edmund Gosse. V. 2, The lady from the sea, and other plays; tr. by Clara Bell, and others.

LEARS, LORENZO. The history of oratory from the age of Pericles to the present time. S. C. Griggs & Co. 12°, $1.50.
Contents: Traces of oratory in early literature; Forensic oratory in Sicily; Professional speech-writers; Attic orators; Political orators; Aristotle, the rhetorician; Early Roman orators; Cicero and his successors; Greek and Latin patristic oratory; Mediæval preachers; Preachers of the Crusades; Eccentric eloquence; Savonarola; Oratory of the Reformation; Three French orators in reign of Louis XIV.; Oratory of the French Revolution; Orators of the Restoration; British Parliamentary oratory; Mansfield-Burke; Sheridan-Fox; Daniel Webster; Charles Sumner; Wendell Phillips.

PEMBERTON, T. EDGAR. John Hare, comedian, 1865-1895: a biography. Routledge. pap., 50 c.
The story of Mr. Hare's thirty years' professional career as a comedian at the Garrick Theatre, St. James', The Court, and the Prince of Wales's Theatre, London.

PENNELL, JOS. Modern illustrations; profusely illustrated with examples of illustrations of Europe and America; reproduced from various sources, many inaccessible and out of print and some printed here for the first time from unpublished drawings. Macmillan. 16°, (Ex-libris ser.) satin, *net*, $3.50.

REINHARDT, C. W. Lettering for draftsmen, engineers, and students: a practical system of free-hand lettering for working drawings. Van Nostrand. 8 pl., obl. 8°, bds., $1.
The writer has endeavored to set forth the proper methods of forming purely free-hand lettering in a simple, easily acquired way, giving at the same time the proper safeguards against the errors most commonly committed. The letters exhibited are actual free-hand work and can readily be copied. The system outlined is the result of the writer's experience during years of practice as chief draftsman on *The Engineering News.*

SIEDENBURG, ANNA. Glass painting: an instruction in the different kinds of this art. Bruno Hessling. nar. 12°, pap. 75 c.
A manual for the amateur who would paint on glass. Chapters on: Stained glass painting; The old method of glass painting; Swiss cabinet painting on glass, etc.

SHEDLOCK, J. S. The pianoforte sonata, its origin and development. Imported by Scribner. pl., 12°, $2.

WALDSTEIN, C. The study of art in universities. Harper. sq. 16°, $1.25.

BIOGRAPHY, CORRESPONDENCE, ETC.

MANNING, ANNE, [*Mrs.* Rathbone.] The household of Sir Thomas More; with an introd. by W. H. Hutton. Scribner. por. il. 12°, $2.25.

PALMER, A. H. The life of Joseph Wolf, animal painter. Longmans, Green & Co. por. il. 8°, $7.

TUCKERMAN, C. K. Personal recollections of notable people. Dodd, M. & Co. 2 v., 8°, $5.

DESCRIPTION, GEOGRAPHY, TRAVEL, ETC.

LUTAUD, A. Aux États-Unis. *New 2d ed.* Brentano's. 12°, pap., 88 c.
Describes with enthusiasm the sights of the United States as seen by an educated and fairminded Frenchman. Railroads, buildings, natural scenery, large cities, systems of government, religious communities (Quakers, Shakers, Mormons, the Oneida settlement, etc.) are critically pictured. Dr. Lutaud intends to come again and travel in the far West.

MEREDITH, ROB. Around the world on sixty dollars. Laird & Lee. por. il. 12°, (Pastime ser., no. 21.) 75 c., pap., 25 c.
It cost the writer really $225 to travel around the world—$60 of this he had with him when he started, the rest he earned on the way; he travelled in the humblest manner and endured many privations, but he saw the world; his journey occupied a year and six days. His observations about the poor of great cities are quite interesting.

QUILLINAN, *Mrs.* E., [Dora Wordsworth.] Journal of a few months' residence in Portugal and glimpses of the south of Spain; ed. with memoir by Edmund Lee. Longmans, Green & Co. por., 12°, $2.

WOOLSON, CONSTANCE FENIMORE. Mentone, Cairo, and Corfu. Harper. il. 12°, $1.75.
The part on Mentone is in the form of fiction. Among the descriptions the making of olive-oil and Monaco and the gambling are the best. Cairo and Corfu are described in sketches of travel. The descriptions of Cairo, the great Gizeh Museum, the school in the mosque, the harem of the Khedive are excellent word-pictures. Most of these sketches appeared in *Harper's Magazine,* 1884–1892. Much material,

however, has been added to the descriptions of Corfu.

EDUCATION, LANGUAGE, ETC.

CARPENTER, ELIZABETH. The student's guide to general literature. Arnold & Co. 11 cards in an envelope, *per set*, $1.
A series of eleven charts or cards, intended as an aid to study, in the arrangement of contemporaneous history and literature, and as a help to varied reading upon any given period from 1066 A.D. to 1893.

PAYNE, W. MORTON, *ed.* English in American universities. 12°, (Heath's pedagogical lib.) $1.
With the exception of the articles upon Johns Hopkins University and the University of Minnesota the papers are reprinted, with revisions, from *The Dial*, for which they were originally written; they consist mainly of a series of eighteen articles upon the teaching of English in as many American colleges and universities, prepared in each case by one of the leading department professors of the institution in question, and of an appendix which includes a few communications and discussions germane to the subject. The institutions represented are: Yale, Columbia, Harvard, Stanford, Cornell, Virginia, Illinois, Lafayette, Iowa, Chicago, Indiana, California, Amherst, Michigan, Nebraska, Pennsylvania, Wisconsin, Wellesley.

SARDOU, ALFRED. The French language with or without a teacher: the exact pronunciation in English sounds under every word ; French verbs conquered; all verbs, regular and irregular, at a glance and the difficulties of tenses simply solved. Jenkins. 3 pts. with chart, 12°, $5.
A practical method for learning to speak, read, and write French correctly, arranged in fifty conversation-lessons.

FICTION.

ABBOTT, C. CONRAD, *M.D.* A colonial wooing. Lippincott. 12°, $1.
The facts relating to the courtship of Ruth Davenport, a Quakeress, by John Bishop, likewise a Friend, are supposed to be gathered from a record of colonial days found in an old desk. Ruth coming to live in the vicinity of Burlington, (N. J.), a few years after the Quaker settlement of Pennsylvania, in Philadelphia, excites the admiration of John Bishop, and at the same time the anger of her stepfather, Matthew Watson, who refuses to favor the wedding of the lovers until fate and Robert Pearson interfere, and the result is a quaint love-story which describes some scenes of colonial days and introduces well-known friends living in the seventeenth century.

BARLOW, JANE. Strangers at Lisconnel: a second series of Irish idylls. Dodd, Mead & Co. 12°, $1.25.
Contents : Out of the way ; Jerry Dunne's basket ; Mrs. Kilfoyle's cloak ; A good turn ; Forecasts ; A fairing ; Mr. Polymathers ; Honoris causa ; Boys' wages ; Con the quare one ; Mad Bell ; A flitting ; A return ; Good luck.

BROWN, ANNA ROBESON. The black lamb. Lippincott. 12°, $1.25.
"A well-constructed and agreeably written novel, which we judge well likely to attain popular-

ity. It possibly labors under a too great complexity of plot, but this, if a fault, is one in the right direction in a time when most novelists are given to analysis rather than to real story-telling. The action in 'The black lamb' is, at all events, rapid, and the story is told brightly and well. The characters are for the most part allowed to show their own characteristics, in dialogue, and, as all experienced novel-readers know, this is one of the most difficult and unusual points in the art. Miss (or should we say Mrs?) Bowen has clearly a vocation in this direction."— *Philadelphia Telegraph.*

BURRAGE, H. S., *D. D.* True to the end : a story of the Swiss Reformation. American Baptist Pub. Soc. il. 12°, 90 c.

DU BOIS, CONSTANCE GODDARD. The shield of the fleur de lis: a novel. Merriam Co. 12°, $1.50.
At the close of a May day in the year 1434, a stranger came for shelter to a miserable inn in the village where Jeanne Darc was born. Three years before she had been burned at the stake. The stranger learns all the details of her life, and these form the story.

EASTWICK, JA. The new *Centurion :* a tale of automatic war. Longmans, Green & Co. 12°, pap, 40 c.
The author through a naval story illustrates his views about fighting with automatic guns; he takes the old English *Centurion* and refits her according to his plan, and tests her in battles with other ships. The plan is seriously offered for the consideration of naval architects.

FARRAR, F. W. (*Dean*). Gathering clouds: a tale of the days of St. Chrysostom. Longmans, Green & Co. 8°, $2.

GRIFFIN, WALTER T. Grandmont: stories of an old monastery. Hunt & Eaton. il. 8°, $1.00.
Limoges in the eleventh century is the scene. The Count de Thiers, determining that his son Etienne shall become a soldier, sends him to Rome in the service of the Comte de Clermont; in Rome he is greatly impressed by the preaching and the death of Paulus, the evangelist; he returns to France, where he founds Grandmont, a well-known monastery of mediæval France. Incidents in the history of this monastery and from the personal history of Hugues, a well-known French monk, are given.

HALL, OWEN. The track of a storm. Lippincott. 12°, $1.25.
The robbery of a stage-coach and the murder of one of the passengers by a dashing highwayman in 1832 in England is the startling incident. The merchant who is the loser of money and diamonds does some detective business on his own account, and believes he has had arrested and convicted the real criminal, who is sent to Australia. But there is a mistake—the supposed criminal is suffering for the sins of a twin brother, and is finally vindicated. A woman plays a part in the story, which has many scenes from convict life in Australia.

HAMILTON, M. A self-denying ordinance. Appleton. 12°, (Appleton's town and country lib., no. 183.) $1; pap., 50 c.

JONES, ALICE ILGENFRITZ. Beatrice of Bayou Tèche. McClurg & Co. 12°, $1.25.
"A tale of Creole life is 'Beatrice of Bayou

Têche,' by Alice Ilgenfritz Jones. It is more than ordinarily well written, full of fanciful turns of phrase and short, charming pen pastels, and would be agreeable reading even were the story a less pulse-quickening one. The author's style has the natural grace and charm of a cultivated Southerner's conversation, and is characterized by a quaint and delicate humor."— *Chicago Tribune.*

KEDDIE, HENRIETTA, [" Sarah Tytler," *pseud.*] A bubble fortune. Lippincott. 12°, (Lippincott's select novels, no. 176.) $1; pap., 50 c.

McCLELLAND, M. G. Mammy Mystic. The Merriam Co. 1 il. nar. 16°, 75c.
A novel founded on an incident of New Orleans life, supposed to have occurred before the emancipation of the slaves.

MACKIE, J. Sinners twain: a romance of the great lóne land; il. by A. Hencke. Stokes. il. 12°, (Twentieth century ser.) 75 c.
The wild Canadian northwest is the scene. The story deals with smugglers, mounted police, and gives a series of excellent pen-pictures of life on the remote frontier. By the author of " The devil's playground."

McNEILL, ORANGE. A Jesuit of to-day. J. Selwin Tait & Sons. 12°, $1.
A young Yale College man is the hero of a love-story of the present: he gives up the girl he fancies, to become a priest of the Roman Catholic Church.

SLADEN, DOUGLAS. A Japanese marriage. Macmillan. 12°, $1.25.

SMITH, TITUS K. Altruria. Altruria Publishing Co. 12°, 50 c.; pap., 25 c.
Altruria is supposed to be a western settlement run upon strict principles of love to one's neighbor. A young New Yorker goes there and is instructed in the details of the new systems of finance, religion, co-operation in work, care of criminals, etc. Returning to New York in twenty years' time he finds the new theories have spread and New York is also run upon Altrurian principles.

WEYMAN, STANLEY J. A little wizard. R. F. Fenno & Co. por. il. nar. 16°, 50 c.
A tale of Yorkshire, England, in the time of Cromwell, just after the battles of Marston Moor and Naseby, and before the surrender by the Scot's army of Charles I.

HISTORY.

ANDERSON, *Rev.* DUNCAN. Scottish folk-lore; or, reminiscences of Aberdeenshire from pinafore to gown. J. Selwin Tait & Sons. 16°, $1.
A faithful picture of a quiet Aberdeenshire village and parish, about forty or fifty years ago. The author's own reminiscences of his childhood.
" Not a story-book, nor yet a book of essays, but something between the two, commingling the best elements of both in such a way that you cannot help being charmed. There is a little dry Scotch wit, and a great many interesting facts concerning the poor folk of the parish, and a deal of information which I haven't seen elsewhere. It is just the book for a quiet afternoon, when you have a couple of leisure hours ahead. And when you lay it down you will thank me for bringing it to your attention."—*New York Herald.*

BAIN, R. NISBET. Charles XII. and the collapse of the Swedish Empire, 1682–1719. Putnam. maps, pors. il. 12°, (Heroes of the nations ser., no. 15.) $1.50; hf. mor., $1.75.

CHITTENDEN, HIRAM MARTIN. The Yellowstone National Park: historical and descriptive. The Robert Clarke Co. maps, pors. il. 8°, *net*, $1.50.

HESDIN, RAOUL, (*pseud.*) The journal of a spy: spy in Paris during the reign of terror, January–July, 1794. Harper. 12°, $1.25.

HIDDEN, ALEX. W. The Ottoman dynasty. E. W. Nash. il. 12°, $2.
A concise history of the sultans of Turkey from the foundation of their dynasty in 1299 to the present day. The author's father occupied an important official position under the Ottoman Government for fifty-five years, during which the writer was born and studied the peculiar conditions from the inside. Specially designed to call English attention to the many wrongs for which the Turk is responsible.

KRASINSKA, FRANÇOISE (*Countess.*) The journal of Countess Françoise Krasinska, great-grandmother of Victor Emmanuel; from the Polish by Kasimir Dziekonska. McClurg. por. 16°, $1.25.

McLAUGHLIN, M. LOUISE. The second Madame: a memoir of Elizabeth Charlotte, Duchesse d'Orleans. Putnam. 12°, $1.25.
" The second Madame" was the daughter of Charles, the Elector Palatine, and was brought to France in 1671 to become the second wife of Philippe Duc d'Orleans, or Monsieur as he was called—the brother of Louis XIV. Madame had a long and romantic career at the French court, and was often very unhappy; she was a voluminous correspondent, and it is from her letters, covering a period of over fifty years and describing the most minute incidents of her life, that this little book is made up.

MARTIN, W. G. WOOD. Pagan Ireland: an archæological sketch: a handbook of Irish pre-Christian antiquities. Longmans, Green & Co. il. 12°, $5.

MERCER, H. C. The hill-caves of Yucatan: a search for evidence of man's antiquity in the caverns of Central America. Lippincott. 8°, $2.

ONGANIA, FERD. Venice: the early art of printing. Lamson, Wolffe & Co. 8°, *net*, $5.50.

RAND, T., *comp*. A pocket history of the presidents and information about the United States. A. D. F. Randolph & Co. size 2¼ x 2¼ in., 25 c.
A tiny book in white cloth, decorated in red and blue, containing brief sketches and portraits of the presidents; also some information about choosing a president, about the U. S. Treasury, Army, Navy, etc.

RICHARD, E., [" An Acadian," *pseud.*] Acadia: missing links of a lost chapter in American history. Home Book Co. 2 v., 8°, pap., $2.
The writer is ex-member of the House of Commons of Canada. His work is an investigation into the true history of the deportation of the French settlers in Nova Scotia by the British in 1755. Many of the accusations made against them and sustained by Parkman and

other historians he shows to be untrue. His history is based upon new documents and traditions in the families of the descendants of the deported Nova Scotians.

TRASK, CAROLINE W. Reference handbook of Roman history from the earliest times to the times of Commodus, 753 B.C.–192 A.D., by the library method for schools and colleges. Lee & Shepard. 12°, *net,* 40 c.

LITERATURE, MISCELLANEOUS AND COLLECTED WORKS.

BELL, D. C., *ed.* The reader's Shakespeare: his dramatic works condensed, connected, and emphasized for school, college, parlor, and platform. In 3 v. V. 1, Historical plays, English and Roman. Funk & Wagnalls Co. 12°, $1.50.
These condensations are specially intended for reading aloud. By means of explanatory notes, narratives historical and literary, elucidatory remarks, etc., the condensations and collations of the text do not impair the import of Shakespeare unabridged. The historical plays occupy the first volume; the next will contain all the tragedies and romantic plays; and the third volume all the comedies. The editor of the work is author of several successful books for students of elocution.

BERDOE, E., *ed.* Browning studies: being select papers by members of the Browning Society; ed. with an introd. by E. Berdoe. Macmillan. 8°, $2.25.

CHENEY, J. VANCE. That dome in air: thoughts on poetry and the poets. McClurg. 12°, $1.25.
Contents: The relation of poetry to life, with special reference to religion; Ralph Waldo Emerson; James Russell Lowell; John Greenleaf Whittier; Henry Wadsworth Longfellow; William Cullen Bryant; Walt Whitman; William Blake; William Cowper; William Wordsworth; A forgotten volume.

DARMESTETER, *Mrs.* AGNES MARY FRANCES ROBINSON. Froissart; from the French by E. Frances Poynter. Imported by Scribner. pl. pors. 8°, $3.
" It is very seldom, indeed, that the fortunate reader obtains a historical book of general interest built upon so sound a basis of information and written in so engaging a manner as this by Mme. Darmesteter, whose opportunities have been as unusual as are her gifts. As a specimen of book-making, too, the volume is a delight to the eye and to the hand, with its heavy pages, its admirable cover, and the illustrations taken from antique sources."—*N. Y. Times.*

HURST, J. FLETCHER. Literature of theology: classified bibliography of theological and general religious literature. Hunt & Eaton. 8°, *net,* $4.
Based on the author's " Bibliotheca theologica," published in 1882. New departments have been treated, many subordinate rubrics have been introduced. every title has been gone over anew, and, in recognition of the vast increase in theological publications since 1882, many hundreds of new works have been supplied and many undesirable works have been eliminated. " The literature of theology " may therefore fairly claim to be a new work. The

author is an American bishop of the Methodist Episcopal Church and a writer on church history. Contains full author and subject indexes.

JONES, H. Browning as a philosophical and religious teacher. Macmillan. 12°, $2.25.

LUCE, MORTON. A handbook to the works of Alfred Lord Tennyson. Macmillan. 16°, 75 c.

MARTIN, E. SANDFORD. Cousin Anthony and I: some views of ours about divers matters and various aspects of life. Scribner. 12°, $1.25.
Contents: Cousin Anthony and his book; Readers and reading; Work and the Yankee; Chores; Considerations matrimonial; Love, friendship, and gossip; Woman suffrage; The knowledge of good and evil; Civilization and culture; Arcadia and Belgravia; Ourselves and other people; Profit and loss; Certain assets of age; The after-dinner speech; Cousin Anthony's address to the trained nurse.

RALEIGH, WALTER. Robert Louis Stevenson. E. Arnold. 12°, $1.

REYNARD, the fox; ed. with introd. and notes by Jos. Jacobs; done into pictures by W. Frank Calderon. Macmillan. 12°, (Cranford ser.) $2.

ROBERTS, W. Rare books and their prices; with chapters on pictures, pottery, porcelain, and postage stamps. Longmans, Green & Co. 12°, (Collector ser.) $1.50.

SHAKESPEARE, W. The Arden Shakespeare; ed. by E. K. Chambers. Heath. 6 v., 16°, (Heath's English classics.) *ea.,* 40 c.
Contents: Hamlet; Macbeth; Julius Cæsar; Twelfth night; As you like it; Richard II. These are the plays so far issued. An attempt in this edition is made to present the greater plays of the dramatist in their literary aspect and not merely as material for the study of philology or grammar; criticism purely verbal and textual has only been included to such an extent as may serve to help the student in the appreciation of the essential poetry. Questions of date and literary history have been fully dealt with in the introductions. Every volume of the series has been provided with a glossary, an essay upon metre, an index and appendices. The text is based on the *Globe edition* of Shakespeare.

SPIELMANN, M. H. The history of *Punch.* Cassell Pub. Co. pors. il. 8°, $4.
Mr. Spielmann has been engaged upon this work for four years; during that time " hardly a man living," he says, " whom I suspected of having worked for *Punch* but I have communicated with." The immense amount of information thus obtained has been sifted down into chapters dealing with: *Punch's* birth and parentage; *Punch's* early progress and the *Punch* Club; *Punch* as a politician; " Charivarieties "; *Punch's* jokes—their origin, pedigree, and appropriation; Cartoons — cartoonists and their work; Cartoons and their effect; *Punch* on the warpath; *Punch's* writers, from 1841 to 1894, and *Punch's* artists, covering the same period.

TAYLOR, I. Names and their histories alphabetically arranged as a handbook of historical geography and topographical nomenclature. Macmillan. 12°, $2.

MENTAL.

WINSLOW, FORBES. Youthful eccentricity, a precursor of crime. Funk & Wagnalls Co. 16°, 50 c.

Advocates a most careful study of children from their earliest years, with a view of repressing firmly but kindly all unnatural, morbid, or cruel thoughts and actions. The author, who is Physician to the British Hospital for Mental Disorders, dwells specially upon the necessity of educating the heart as well as the head of young children. He also lays special stress upon the value of religion in education.

NATURE AND SCIENCE.

BRIGHTWEN, *Mrs.* ELIZA. [*formerly* Eliza Elder.] Inmates of my house and garden; il. by Theo. Carreras. Macmillan. 12°, $1.25.

Studies of lemurs (monkeys of Madagascar), squirrels, birds, the brown owl, willow-wrens, tame doves, etc., with chapters on feeding wild birds in winter; starving tortoises; teaching children to be humane; studying nature; insect observation; solitary bees and wasps; the praying mantis; the clothes moth; the death-watch; cheese-mites and flies, etc.

SLADE, DAN. DENISON. The evolution of horticulture in New England. Putnam. 16°, hf. shp., $1.50.

WILLIAMS, H. SHALER. Geological biology: an introduction to the geological history of organisms. Holt. 8°, buckram, $2.80.

YOUNG, C. A. The sun. *New. rev. ed.* Appleton. il. 12°, (International sc'entific ser., no. 34.) $2.

POETRY.

BLACKMORE, R. DODDRIDGE. Fringilla; or, tales in verse; with sundry decorative picturings by Will H. Bradley. The Burrows Bros. Co. 8°, $3.50; *Special ed.*, $6.

GUNSAULUS, FRANK W. Songs of night and day. McClurg. sq. 12°, $1.50.

Forty-eight short poems.

POLITICAL AND SOCIAL.

COLQUHOUN, ARCHIBALD ROSS. The key of the Pacific: the Nicaragua Canal. Longmans, Green & Co. folding map, il. 8°, $7.

HARDING, S. B. The minimum principle in the tariff of 1828 and its recent revival. American Acad. of Political and Social Science. 8°, (Publications of the society, no. 153.) pap., 25 c.

The Act of 1828, for the first time in the history of our tariff legislation, established a series of duties graduated according to the value of a group of goods. This series of duties rests upon what is known as the "graduated minimum" of the woollen schedule of the act of that year, the principle of which was revived and largely extended in the Act of 1890, and the traces of which have not been entirely banished from the tariff of 1894. Mr. Harding's paper traces the origin and operation of these provisions of the earlier act and sketches briefly their later revival.

ROGERS, JA. TAYLOR. Scientific money. Ja. Taylor Rogers. por., sq. 16°, pap., 25 c.

SCHOENHOF, J. A history of money and prices: being an inquiry into their relations from the thirteenth century to the present time. Putnam. 12°, (Questions of the day, no. 86.) $1.50.

"It is needless to say that Schoenhof has no confidence in the scheme of regulating prices by artificial changes in the volume of currency. His book is, in fact, a demonstration that prices are the result of very complex causes, in which the amount of currency has only a subordinate part, and that arbitrary interference with the currency must be mischievous and mischievous only. This he illustrates with a wealth of material, thoroughly verified and carefully analyzed."— *New York Times.*

SPORTS AND AMUSEMENTS.

GROVE, *Mrs.* LILLY, [*and others.*] Dancing. Longmans, Green & Co. il. 12°, (Badminton lib.) $3.50.

THEOLOGY, RELIGION, AND SPECULATION.

BROOKS, PHILLIPS (*Bp.*) Sermons for the principal festivals and fasts of the church year; ed. by Rev. J. Cotton Brooks. *7th ser.* Dutton. 12°, $1.75.

BROWN, *Rev.* W. MONTGOMERY. The church for Americans. Whittaker. 1 il. 12°, $1.25.

Seven lectures, entitled : Church membership; Our controversy with Romanists ; Our controversy with denominationalists ; The mother church of England ; The American Church ; Objections to the Episcopal church; Why Americans should be Episcopalians. Appendices and introduction. The author is Archdeacon of Ohio; Lecturer at Bexley Hall, the Theological Seminary of Kenyon College.

BURTON, ERNEST DE WITT. The records and letters of the apostolic age : the New Testament, Acts, Epistles, and Revelation in the version of 1881 ; arranged for historical study. Scribner. 8°, *net,* $1.50.

"The purpose of this book is to promote the historical study of the Apostolic Age. It aims to perform in respect to the early history of the Christian Church a service corresponding to that which the 'Harmony of the gospels,' recently put out by Prof. W. Arnold Stevens and myself, sought to render in respect to the life of Christ. Like that book, it endeavors, not to indicate the solution of all the historical problems presented by the New Testament documents pertaining to the period under consideration, but to present the material in convenient form for historical study." Author is Professor of New Testament Interpretation in the University of Chicago.

CARPENTER, W. BOYD (*Bp.*) The great charter of Christ : being studies on the Sermon on the Mount. Whittaker. 12°, $1.50.

CRAFTS, *Rev.* WILBUR F. Practical Christian sociology : a series of special lectures before Princeton Theological Seminary and Marietta College ; with supplemental notes and appendixes ; with an introd. by Jos. Cooke. Funk & Wagnalls. pors. 12°, $1.50.

Discusses on the basis of the latest facts and figures, temperance, Sabbath reform, gambling, purity, civil service, ballot reform, municipal reform, education, immigration, divorce, woman suffrage, and all the other social problems, not separately but in their relations to each other as parts of one great problem, which is presented from the standpoints, first, of the church; second, of the family and education ; third, of capital and labor ; and fourth, of citizenship.

The appendixes take a large portion of the book and include chronological data of progress from the beginning of the second century, closing with a record of reform progress in 1895. There are a number of valuable statistics. A Bible index, an index of modern authors quoted, and an index of places sociologically considered. Full topical index. Contains a brief reading course in practical Christian sociology (6 p.).

GREEN, W. H. *D.D.* The unity of the Book of Genesis. Scribner. 12°, $3.
A critical study of Genesis from beginning to end, chapter by chapter and section by section, the purpose being to demonstrate the unity of the Book of Genesis as opposed to the critical hypothesis that the Pentateuch is not the continuous production of one author, but a compilation from various documents belonging to widely different ages long posterior to the time of Moses.

MOOREHEAD, W. G., *D.D.* Studies in the Mosaic institutions, the tabernacle, the priesthood, the sacrifices, the feasts of ancient Israel. United Presb. Bd. of Pub. il. 12°, $1.
These studies aim to show that the essential truths of Christianity were imbedded in the rites established by Moses. Judaism was a prophecy of the gospel. The book is occupied with the main features of ancient Judaism : The place of worship, the ministry of worship, means of worship, and seasons of worship. The author is Professor of the United Presbyterian Theological Seminary, Xenia, Ohio.

MURPHY, T., *D.D.* The messages to the seven churches of Asia: being the inaugural of the enthroned king : a beacon on Oriental shores. Presb. Bd. of Pub. map, 8°, $3.
Relates to the two chapters of the Apocalypse which contain the messages of God to the seven churches of Asia Minor. Dr. Murphy makes a profound study of them and their meaning and importance, and gives a history of the land, the seven cities in which the churches were located, the people, etc. These seven churches are to be considered as types of all church life, and therefore the messages are held up as beacons that all would be able to understand in all ages of the world.

RAMSAY, W. M. St. Paul the traveller and the Roman citizen. Putnam. folding map, 8°, $3.
Author is professor of humanity in the University of Aberdeen; wrote "The historical geography of Asia Minor," etc. These chapters on St. Paul comprise the Morgan lectures in the Theological Seminary of Auburn, in the State of New York, 1894, and the Mansfield College lectures, 1895.

SMITH, W. ROBERTSON. The prophets of Israel and their place in history to the close of the eighth century B.C. *New ed.*, with introd. and additional notes by the Rev. T. K. Cheyne, D.D. Macmillan. 12°, $3.50.

Books for the Young.

ELIOT, GEORGE, [*pseud.* for *Mrs. J. W. Cross.*] Child sketches from George Eliot: glimpses at the boys and girls in the romances of the great novelist by Julia Magruder; il. by R. B. Birch and Amy Brooks. Lothrop. il. 8°, $1.25.
Contents : The childhood of George Eliot; The Poyser children, from "Adam Bede"; Tom and Maggie Tulliver, from "The mill on the floss"; "The story of Eppie," from "Silas Marner"; Lillo and Ninna, from "Romola"; Job Tudge, from "Felix Holt"; Brother and sister, a personal poem ; The Garths, from "Middlemarch"; The little Cohens, from "Daniel Deronda"; Other boys and girls, from miscellaneous stories.

FESTETITS, KATE NEELY. A year at Dangerfield. Amer. Baptist Pub. Soc. il., 12°, $1.25.
The Dangerfield Military Institute is an American academy for young men and boys ; the story has its scene here ; the plot has to do with a reckless joke played by one of the students upon another, thereby ruining his career for the time being ; a year passes before the truth is explained and the young man vindicated from any suspicion of dishonorable conduct.

HAVENS, HERBERT. Under the lone star : a story of the revolution in Nicaragua ; il. by W. S. Stacey. Nelson. 12°, $2.
The story of Walker's filibustering expedition to Central America in 1855. The narrative is given by an English boy of sixteen, who enlists under Walker in San Francisco, and serves under the "Lone Star" flag in Nicaragua until Walker is captured and shot.

LAURIE, ANDRÉ. School-boy days in Japan; tr. by Laura E. Kendall. Estes & Lauriat. il. 8°, (College life in all countries.) $1.50.
A French *savant*, with his son and daughter and a Japanese youth, in making the ascent of Mt. Ravacha in Nippon, the principal island of Japan, meet with an accident which for the time renders the daughter helpless. Chance gives them refuge in a Daimio's castle, where the little boy is introduced who afterward becomes a pupil of the Imperial University of Tokio. Some political history is introduced and Japanese studies and methods of teaching described.

LOVEJOY, MARY I., *comp.* Nature in verse: a poetry reader for children. Silver, Burdett & Co. 12°, $1.
The need of a nature-poetry reader for the lower school grades has long been felt, and it was to meet this obvious want that the present volume has been compiled. It is intended to cover the first four years of school work. The selections have been carefully graded. They are divided into songs of spring, summer, autumn, and winter.

NORTON, C. ELIOT, *ed.* The heart of oak books. Heath. 6 v., 12°, Bk. 1, 25 c.; Bk. 2, 45 c.; Bk. 3, 55 c.; Bk. 4, 60 c.; Bk. 5, 65 c.; Bk. 6, 70 c.
These six volumes embrace "a collection of traditional rhymes and stories for children, and of masterpieces of poetry and prose for use at home and at school, chosen with special reference to the cultivation of the imagination and the development of a taste for good reading."

PARRY, E. ABBOTT. Katawampus: its treatment and cure; il. by Archie Macgregor. Macmillan. 4°, $1.25.

RIPLEY, *Mrs.* MARY ANNA, [*formerly* M. A. Paull.] Hildebrand and Cicely; or, the monk of Tavystoke Abbaye. Cranston & Curts. il. 12°, $1.

Friar Hildebrand, through whose journal the story is told, was an English Augustinian monk of the sixteenth century, who while yet a young man sought the shelter and solitude of the old abbey and its rigorous vows. A temptation comes to him in the person of "sweet Cicely," and it is related how heroically he kept his vows. English life just at the dawn of the Reformation is well described.

UPTON, FLORENCE K. The adventures of two Dutch dolls and a golliwogg. Longmans, Green & Co. obl. 12°, bds., $2.

At twelve o'clock on a frosty Christmas eve, that being the hour, according to the story, "when dolls and toys taste human joys," Peggy Deutchland and Sarah Jane awake from their wooden sleep on a toy-shop counter and make the circuit of the shop, their most notable adventure being their meeting with a golliwogg (a black gnome). The calamities which befel the trio after this time are graphically pictured in rhyme.

WILLIAMSON, *Mrs.* MARY L. The life of Gen. Robert E. Lee for children; in easy words. [*Also*] Gen. R. E. Lee's farewell address to his soldiers. The Baughman Stationery Co. col. il. 8°, bds., 75 c.

KNOX, T. W. Captain John Crane, 1800–1815. Merriam Co. il., 12°, $1.50.

The story of a Boston boy who became a sailor on a merchantman and in three years was a captain; he has many adventures with British war-ships, Algerine pirates, etc., serves through the War of 1812, is made a prisoner, and is imprisoned at Plymouth and Dartmoor, etc.

MARRYAT, F. Peter Simple; il. by J. Ayton Symington; with an introd. by D. Hannay. Macmillan. 12°, (Macmillan's illustrated standard novels.) $1.25.

SAUNDERS, MARSHALL. Charles and his lamb; written for the little ones of the household. American Baptist Pub. Soc. il. 12°, bds., 75 c.

The author of "Beautiful Joe" presents for little folks sketches and scenes in the real life of a baby-boy, and the story of the influences of a little child whose kindness of heart and love for animals is prettily shown.

RECENT FRENCH AND GERMAN BOOKS.

FRENCH.

Bonnefont, Gaston. Les Parisiennes chez elles. Mademoiselle Bartet. In-4, $1................Paris, *Flammarion*

Bourgeois, Emile. Le Grand siècle Louis XIV., les arts, les idées, d'après Voltaire, Saint-Simon, Spanheim, Mme de Sévigné, etc. Gr. in-8 avec 500 grav. et 22 pl., $9 .... Paris, *Hachette*

Franklin, B. Comment on devient un homme. Mémoires de Benjamin Franklin. Traduction nouvelle par F.-A. Changeur. In-8, 60c......Paris, *Flachbacher*

Gilbert, Eugène. Le Roman en France pendant le dix-neuvième siècle. In-12, $1 ....Paris, *Plon*

Grand-Carteret, John. Vieux papiers, vieilles images. Cartons d'un collectionneur. Gr. in-8 avec 461 grav. et 6 pl. hors texte, $7.50......................Paris, *Le Vasseur*

Lafenestre, Georges. La fontaine. In-12, 60c. Paris, *Hachette*

Mael, Pierre. Les derniers hommes rouges. Gr. in-8 illustré, $2.40 ....Paris, *F. Didot*

Maindron, Ernest. Les affiches illustrées (1886–1895). Ouvrage orné de 64 lithographies en couleur et de 102 reproductions en noir et en couleur. In-4, $20. Paris, *Boudet*

Neukomm, Edmond. Les dompteurs de la mer. Les Normands en Amérique depuis le Xe jusqu'au XVe siècle. Gr. in-8 illustré, $2.10..............Paris, *Hetzel*

Nordau, Max. Paradoxes psychologiques. In-12, 75c. Paris, *Alcan*

Robida, A. Le vingtième siècle. Roman d'une Parisienne d'après-demain. In-12, $1. Paris, *Librairie illustrée*

Schulz, Jeanne. Les fiançailles de Gabrielle. In-12, $1......................................Paris, *C. Lévy*

Verne, Jules. L'Ile à hélice. Gr. in-8 avec 80 illustrations par Benett, $2.70 ....Paris, *Hetzel*

GERMAN.

Dincklage-Campe, Frdr. Frhr. v. Kriegs-Erinnerungen; Wie wir unser eisern Kreuz erwarben. Nach persönl. Berichten bearb. Illustr. v. ersten deutschen Künstlern. 4°, vii, 360 p., 15 chromolithographs, cloth, $3.30........Berlin, *Deutsches Verlagshaus Bong & Co*

Ebers, Geo. Die Uebersetzlichen. Ein Märchen. Illustr. v. Arpad Schmidhammer, 4°, vii, 61 p., cloth, gilt edges, $3.30........Stuttgart, *Deutsche-Verlagsanstalt*

Ehrlich, Heinr. Modernes Musikleben. Studien. 2. Aufl. 8°, v, 326 p., hf. mor., $2. Berlin, *Allgemeiner Verein f. deutsche Litteratur*

Engelmann, Emil. Nordland-Sagen. Nord'sch-ger man. Lieder u. Mären, f. das deutsche Haus bearb. Mit vielen Bildern nach Zeichngn. v. G. Closs, C. Häberlin, Th. Hoffmann, R. E. Kepler, u. U. Lex.-8°, 343 p., cloth, $2.65...............Stuttgart, *P. Neff, Verl*

Erhard, Emile. Aus Fortunios Erinnerungen. Illustr. von Hertha v. Warburg. 8°, ix, 148 p., $1. Stuttgart, *Deutsche Verlagsanstalt*

Flügel, Fel., Prof. Im. Schmidt u. G. Tanger, D.D. Wörterbuch der englischen u. deutschen Sprache f. Hand- u. Schulgebrauch. Unter besond. Benutzg. v. F.'s allgemeinen englisch-deutschem u. deutsch-englischem Wörterbuch bearb. v. S u T. 2 vols. Lex.-8°, x, 968 and ix, 1006 p., hf. mor , $4.50. N. Y., *Lemcke & Buechner*

Grazie, M. E. delle. Gedichte. With portrait. 8°, iv, 193 p , cloth, $1.35 ....Leipzig, *Breitkopf & Härtel*

Hilty, Prof. 'Dr. C. Lesen u. Reden. 8°, 116 p., cloth. 80c........... .. ..Leipzig, *J. C. Hinrichs' Verl*

Kunstler-Monographien. In Verbindg. m. Andern hrsg. v. H. Knackfuss. IX. u. X. Lex.-8°, boards. IX. A. v. Werner. Von. Adf. Rosenberg. Illustr. 128 p. and portrait, $1.—X. Murillo. Von H. Knackfuss. Illustr. 76 p., 70c ....Bielefeld, *Belhagen & Klasing*

Lauff, Jos. Der Münch v. Sankt Sebald. Eine Nürnberger Geschichte aus der Reformationszeit. Roman. 8°, vi, 419 p., $2 ; cloth, $2.55............Köln, *A. Ahn*

Minerva. Jahrbuch der gelehrten Welt. Hrsg. v. Dr. R. Kukula u. K. Trübner. 5. Jahrg. 1895–1896. 12°, xix, 989 p. and 1 portrait, hf. parchment, $2. Strassburg, *K. J. Trübner, Verl*

Oppel, Dr. Karl. Das Buch der Eltern. Praktische Anleitg. zur häusl. Erziehg der Kinder vom frühesten Alter bis zur Selbständigkeit. 8°, vi, 768 p., cloth, $1.35. Frankfurt a. M., *M. Diesterweg*

Renatus, Johs. (Joh. A. Frhr. v. Wagner). Lebensskizzen aus ernsten u. heiteren Tagen. Erzählend gezeichnet. 2 vols. 8°, xi, 228 and iv, 397 p., bd. in 1 vol., cloth, $1.35............Dresden, *Zahn & Jaensch*

Reuter, Fritz. Briefe an seinen Vater aus der Schüler-, Studenten- u. Festungszeit. (1827–1841). Hrsg. v. Dr. Frz. Engel. 2 vols. 8°, viii, 232 and viii, 267 p., cloth, $2 ....Braunschweig, *G. Westermann*

Salomon, Ludw. Signora Francesca. Eine Geschichte aus Paul Flemings Leben. 8°, 159 p., cloth, $1.20. Gotha, *F. A. Perthes*

Schubin, Ossip. Con fiocchi. Roman. 8°, 240 p. and portrait, $1.20...................Dresden, *H. Minden*

Stettenheim, Jul. Heitere Erinnerungen. Keine Biographie. 8°, 316 p., cloth, $1.50. Berlin, *S. Fischer, Ver*

MAGAZINE ARTICLES FOR JANUARY AND FEBRUARY.

Articles marked with an asterisk are illustrated.

ARTISTIC, MUSICAL, AND DRAMATIC.—*Arena*, Madness as Portrayed by Shakspere, Winslow.—*Cath. World*, A Golden Age and Its People,* Edselas.—*Century*, The Convent Under Arms ; The Wonderful Sauce; The Night School, pictures by the author, J. G. Vibert; Puvis de Chavannes,* Cox. — *Fort. Review* (Jan.), Alexander Dumas *fils* and His Plays, Mme. Van de Velde.—*Godey's*, Studio Life in Paris,* L. Jerrold and A. Hornblow; "The Heart of Maryland,"* Fletcher.—*New England*, John Rogers. the People's Sculptor,* W. O. Partridge.—*Scribner's*, Design in Bookbinding,* Prideaux.

BIOGRAPHY, CORRESPONDENCE, ETC.—*Chautauquan*, Theodore Roosevelt, F. Morris.—*Forum*, Victoria, Queen and Empress, Edwin Arnold.—*Pop. Science*, Andrew Dickson White (Por.).

DESCRIPTION, TRAVEL.—*Arena*, The Land of the Noonday Sun* (Mexico), W. Clark.—*Cath. World*, The City of Redemption* (Jerusalem), Ryan. — *Century*, Pope Leo XIII. and His Household,* F. M. Crawford.—*Fort. Review* (Jan.), The Sultan and His Priests, Davey.—*Harper's*, The New Baltimore,* Bonsal.—*New England*, Passing of the New England Fisherman,* W. M. Thompson.—*Nine. Century* (Jan.), In the Wild West of China, Alicia B. Little.—*Scribner's*, Life in the Altitudes—The Colorado Health Plateau,* Iddings.

DOMESTIC AND SOCIAL.—*New England*, Home Culture for Americans, N. Hapgood.—*North Amer. Review*, Discontented Women, Amelia E. Barr ; Does the Ideal Husband Exist? Mary A. Livermore.

EDUCATIONAL.—*Fort. Review* (Jan.), School Boards and Denominational Schools : The Educational Outlook for 1896, J. R. Diggle ; Our Educational Finance, J. Dundas White. — *Godey's*, The Dumb Speak,* Lillian A. North.

FICTION.—*Atlantic*, Glasses, Henry James ; A Little Domestic, Mary H. Catherwood.—*Chautauquan*, The Greatest Man in the Country, H. D. Ward.—*Cath. World*, Story of Consolation Jones, O'Connor.—*Century*, How " The Kid " Won His Medal, Wilson ; Perdita's Candle, Martha Young.—*Godey's*, Something New Under the Sun,* Lucy Cleveland ; Liz Bascom's Revenge,* R. Clarke. — *Harper's*, A Snipe-Hunt,* M. E. M. Davis ; A Mother in Israel, H. H. Boyesen; Her Boy, R. Stewart.—*Lippincott's*, Ground-Swells, Jeanette H. Walworth ; Fifteen, Marjorie Richardson.—*Scribner's*, Sevillana,* Mabel Thayer ; A Long Chase, Hall ; Hopper's Old Man, Meyers.

HISTORY.—*Century*, Certain Worthies and Dames of Old Maryland,* J. W. Palmer ; Nelson at Cape St. Vincent,* A. T. Mahan ; *Harper's*, St. Clair's Defeat,* T. Roosevelt.

HYGIENIC AND SANITARY. — *Chautauquan*, Composition of Food and Its Use in the Body, T. G. Allen.—*Forum*, Notable Sanitary Experiments in Massachusetts, W. T. Sedgwick.

INDUSTRIAL.—*Pop. Science*, Gathering Naval Stores,* L. J. Vance.

LITERARY.—*Atlantic*, Some Memories of Hawthorne, I., Rose Hawthorne Lathrop; The Bibliotaph, L. H. Vincent; Don Quixote, H. D. Sedgwick, Jr. — *Century*, Three Unpublished Letters (Lowell's), Introd. by Mary A. Clarke. — *Fort. Review* (Jan.), Matthew Arnold, Bailey. — *Forum*, The French Academy, Houssaye. — *Godey's*, O Rare 'Gene Field, Moffett. — *Lippincott's*, Paralyzers of Style, Bird.—*New England*, Ibsen at Home,* E. O. Achorn.—*Nine. Centu·y* (Jan.), Advantage of Fiction, M. G. Tuttlett. — *West. Review* (Jan.), Matthew Arnold's Letters, Hannigan.

MENTAL AND MORAL.— *Forum*, The Stage from a Clergyman's Standpoint, T. P. Hughes.

NATURE AND SCIENCE.—*Atlantic*, Some Tennessee Bird Notes, Torrey.—*Godey's*,The Pranks of Nature,* I., Humphrey. — *North Amer. Review*, Is the Human Race Deteriorating?, Mulhall ; The Newest Telescope, Young.—*Pop. Science*, Lord Salisbury on Evolution, Spencer.

POETRY.—*Arena*, Brotherhood, B. Arnold. — *Atlantic*, A Tear Bottle, F. D. Sherman ; The Caravansary, R. H. Stoddard. — *Century*, The Little Mothers, R. Burton; The Fisher-Maiden's Song, H. H. Boyesen.— *Harper's*, Pæstum, J. Hay ; The Acknowledgment, L. I. Guiney.—*Scribner's*, The Hermit and the Pilgrim, C. Howard ; The Singer, M. L. Van Vorst ; Wood Songs, A. S. Hardy.

POLITICAL AND SOCIAL.—*Arena*, A Half Century of Progress, Mary L. Dickinson ; New System of State Warrants, H. L. Weed.—*Cath. World*, A Homeless City (New York), O'Shea; Catholic Schools and Charities Under the New Constitution, McDonough.—*Century*, Story of the Development of Africa, H. M. Stanley ; Palmerston Ideal in Diplomacy, E. M. Chapman.—*Chautauquan*, Turks in Armenia, De Pressensé ; Industrial Conditions of the South Before 1860, Edmonds ; The Monroe Doctrine and Some of Its Applications, Woodburn.—*Fort. Review* (Jan.), Object Lesson in Christian Democracy, Crawford ; Boer, Africander and Briton in the Transvaal, II., Ricarde-Seaver.—*Forum*, Some Aspects of Civilization in America, Norton ; Our Monetary Programme, Laughlin ; The Venezuelan Crisis : The President's Monroe Doctrine, Woolsey ; Lord Salisbury and the Monroe Doctrine, Straus ; Duty of Congress, Rice ; "German-Americans" and the Lord's Day, Doane.—*Harper's*, Passing of the Fur-Seal, Nelson.—*Nine. Century* (Jan.), The Issue Between Great Britain and America, H. M. Stanley ; Common Sense and Venezuela, E. Dicey ; Ugliness of Modern Life, "Ouida."—*North Amer. Review*.—The Venezuelan Difficulty, Carnegie ; The British Feeling, Bryce ; Study of War, Taylor ; Follies and Horrors of War, Doane ; How a War Begins, Lathrop.—*Pop. Science*, Stamping Out of Crime, Oppenheim.—*West. Review* (Jan.), Canada, Britain, and the United States, "Cosmopolite."

SPORTS AND AMUSEMENTS. — *Godey's*, What the Bicycle Does for the Muscles,* H. E. Morrow.—*Scribner's*, Hunting Musk-Ox with the Dog Ribs,* F. Russell.;

THEOLOGY, RELIGION, AND SPECULATION.—*North Amer. Review*, The Future Life, II., Gladstone. — *West. Review* (Jan.), Doctrine of Immortality in the Old Testament in the Light of the Higher Criticism, S. Holmes.

Literary Miscellany.

THE SOUTH AMERICAN QUESTION. — John Bach McMaster contributed an interesting article to the *N. Y. Times* on the Venezuelan imbroglio, and in it gave a clear exposition of the history and meaning of the Monroe doctrine. Other works bearing on this question are Johnson's "The Nicaragua Canal," Keasby's "The Nicaragua Canal," and Miler's "Advantages of the Nicaragua Canal."

THE illustrations which accompany Marion Crawford's article on "Pope Leo XIII. and His Household," in the February *Century*, are made from photographs taken by a private chamberlain of the Pope and a personal friend of Mr. Crawford. So far as known they are the only pictures ever made of the inner rooms of the Vatican. They were taken with the consent of the Pope, who moved from room to room to make way for the photographer.

THE CENTURY CO. has arranged with General Horace Porter for the publication in *The Century Magazine* of his personal reminiscences of General Grant during the war. The papers consist of General Porter's memoirs of his intercourse with the great commander, both in the line of duty as his staff officer and as a friend who shared his confidence to the end of his life. From the beginning of the intimacy General Porter made notes of important conversations bearing on military acts, and of the recollections and anecdotes which, contrary to his reputation as a silent man, were characteristic of Grant's moments of relaxation. The author, whose terse and anecdotal style is well known through his public speaking, has been engaged on the work for several years, and it is now nearly a year since the serial and book rights were secured by The Century Co.

CINDERELLA APPEARS IN SACRED HINDU BOOKS.—The origin of Cinderella is to be found in the Vedas, the four sacred books of the Hindus. According to them Cinderella is a dawn maiden, her sisters being the Powers of Darkness, who compel her to wait upon them, keeping her hidden from sight. The dawn maiden breaks from her bonds, and captivates the sun, remaining with him for a time. But she cannot linger with him in the heavens; she can remain only until a certain hour. Once she lingers too long, and, hurrying back, leaves on the path she has taken a token of her visit, in the form of a fleecy cloud, which had borne her aloft when she left the regions of darkness. The sun, determined to find her, sends out his emissaries (the rays of light), but does not find her until she appears before him as the evening twilight. In the Vedas the Prince is called Mitra, which is one of the names given to the sun.

THE MS. of "Trilby" is preserved in a locked glass case at the rooms of the Fine Art Society of London. It is written in little exercisebooks, each of which cost a penny, and is not entirely in Mr. Du Maurier's prim, upright hand. That author has a pet superstition to the effect that all the members of his family should take a small part in the work of writing out his imaginings. Consequently the MS. exhibits various calligraphies. It is said that the author sold it for a sum which many other novelists would be only too glad to receive for entire serial and book rights. Du Maurier, it is also said, delights in writing, but considers the production of the illustrations a toil. A translation of "Trilby" has lately appeared in Russia, with Du Maurier's illustrations. It is printed under the title of "Katia" and is ascribed to one "Teminoff"; and all the names are altered to Russian ones—the three immortal Companions of the Brush being turned into Russians.

A BOOK-LOVER'S PASTIME.—The getting together of rare and curious prints to insert in some favorite book has long been the pastime of book-lovers. Sometimes years have passed before the collection was completed, second-hand book-stores have been haunted and collections ransacked. One man that I know possesses "Stones of Venice" and "Seven Lamps of Architecture," enriched with old prints. A lady has recently inherited a book of colored fashion plates, taken from magazines of thirty, forty, and fifty years ago by her mother. And it is bound in a yellowed satin breadth of the mother's wedding-gown, appliquéd with figures from the lace bertha that draped her shoulders. Another lady has the history of the battle in which her father fell in the Civil War, made up of scattered magazine articles, chapters from histories, old prints, newspaper descriptions, and lists of killed and wounded, all the precious documents, and bound in all that was left of his faded uniform.

EVER since the first chapters of the "Personal Recollections of Joan of Arc" appeared in *Harper's Magazine* there have been guesses in private and public as to who the author might be. The majority have been in favor of Mark Twain. The correctness of this guess seems to be confirmed by the announcement that the publishers of the "National Cyclopædia of American Biography," that in the VIth volume, containing a biography of Mark Twain, enumerates the "Personal Recollections of Joan of Arc" among the humorist's writings. We doubt whether the publishers of the "Recollections" will ever reveal the author's name. The author is said to be a prominent one, who believes the "Personal Recollections" to be his or her masterpiece, and who is waiting for final judgment from the public before acknowledging the work. If the consensus of opinion among intelligent readers should indorse his or her own, it is highly probable that the authorship will be fully revealed. Otherwise it will continue to be kept a secret.

THE FRENCH ACADEMY.—There are now thirty-seven "Immortals." They are: Sully-Prudhomme, Léon Say, Pierre Loti, Gerard, Ernest Legouvé, Joseph Bertrand, Victorien Sardou, Henri Houssaye, Brunetière, Thoreau-Dargin, Paul Bourget, De Bornier, Duc de Broglie, Lavisse, Sorel, De Vogüé, Freycinet, Pailleron, D'Haussonville, Mezières, Challemel-Lacour, Cherbuliez, Edouard Herve, Emile Ollivier, De Heredia, Rousse, D'Audeffret, Pasquier, Meilhac, Coppée, Gaston Bossier, Duc d'Aumale, Bishop Perrand, Ludovic Halévy, Jules Simon, Jules Clarétie, and Anatole France. The chairs of Camille Doucet, Louis Pasteur, and Alexandre Dumas are still empty. The Paris *Figaro* whispers that Zola may, after his many attempts, perhaps be awarded the chair of Dumas. Zola is certainly one of the most distinguished figures of latter-day France, and has personified the claims of the novel in himself. The Dean of the Academy, Ernest Legouvé, will celebrate the 89th anniversary of his birthday on February 14.

MRS. RITCHIE MET HER HUSBAND THE DAY HE WAS BORN.—"One of the most surprising things to American women in England," says the *Commercial Advertiser,* "is the number of English women who marry men from five to twenty years younger than themselves. The action of the Baroness Burdett-Coutts in taking so young a husband as Mr. Bartlett is by no means uncommon in all grades of English society, and a bit of a shock to the romantic-minded American, who prefers to let her husband have quite the advantage of her in point of years at least. It was with almost a little gasp of horror a sentimental little American was told of the first meeting between Mrs. Ritchie, Thackeray's daughter, and her present husband. His mother was a dear friend of Miss Anne Thackeray, who, one day, when about 20 years old, dropping into the Ritchie home, received the interesting information of a brand new arrival in the household. Proud Mrs. Ritchie herself placed the wee Richard in Miss Thackeray's arms, as that young lady remarked with a laugh : ' So it is another pink little boy come to make the Ritchie family happy.' It was the same Richard Ritchie who in after years made Miss Anne Thackeray his wife."

THE GOVERNESS IN NOVELS.—Walter Besant says: "I was looking over the pages of ' Martin Chuzzlewit,' a book which surely contains all the faults as well as all the virtues of its author, and my mind went suddenly back to the period when the woes of the governess were a stock subject for the novelist. I read the burning yet self-restrained words of that amazing character, Tom Pinch, and my mind went back, I say, to the old-fashioned governess of the novel. She was down-trodden, she was despised, the servants insulted her, she was bullied—do you remember? Most of the novelists produced her in that guise; Dickens and Charlotte Brontë, for example. She was used to stimulate wrath and contempt for the purse-proud. Thackeray produced her, however, in quite another guise—you remember Elizabeth and the governess in the country house. Oh, she was too much with us, the governess. She has now totally disappeared from fiction. Why? Well, first of all, because she has almost disappeared from life. She exists in country places, but not in the middle-class society. She is now a high-school mistress, not so well paid as she ought to be, but better than she was, and the middle-class girl now goes to school instead of having a governess at home."

KARL VON DEINES, writing of "Stepniak" in the New York *Evening Post,* says: "For many years this man's real name was unknown to the public, and even to this day there are many curious errors concerning it. The day after his death I saw an obituary sketch of him in a leading English paper, which stated that he was really Sergius Michael Dragomanoff, and it related the story of his earlier life as such. The fact is Dragomanoff was a

very different man, a college professor, who died in Sophia, Bulgaria, nearly a year ago. Others say that ' Stepniak's' identity has never been disclosed. That, too, is a gross error. Five or six years ago he threw off the veil of secrecy, and let it be known to all who cared to know it that his true name was Serge Michael Kravchinsky. ' Stepniak' was born in the Ukraine about forty-three years ago, and was educated for a military career. He served, indeed, for some time in the artillery. In the army he began his propagandist efforts on behalf of the wretched millions of the Ukraine. He was arrested in 1874 on suspicion while so engaged. On his way to prison he escaped and made his way to Odessa. During 1875 and 1876 he was in St. Petersburg, where he organized the escape of Prince Kropotkin. In 1877 he went to Geneva, which he left to go to Paris and afterward to London." "It is an open secret," says the London *Publishers' Circular,* "that Stepniak collaborated with Hesba Stretton in the production of ' The Highway of Sorrow.' This work, which has met with a very wide welcome in this country, is a novel based on the 'Stundists,' a religious body in Russia which has suffered greatly from persecution."

ANATOLE FRANCE A MEMBER OF THE FRENCH ACADEMY.—Anatole France has been elected to membership in the French Academy, to fill the vacancy caused by the death of Ferdinand de Lesseps. The election of Anatole France should please all. It will meet with favor from his fellow-writers, because they recognize M. France's work is full of the most exquisite poetry; it will humor the philosophers, because the elect's work reveals at every instant the habit of serious meditation; it will regain for the institute the entire esteem of psychologists, because Anatole France has written the most subtle descriptions of the movements of various complex minds. His work exhales love for good literature: it is full of tenderness and it is adorned by irony. He is the son of a bookseller whom all the great book-lovers of Paris liked. He was born in 1844, and, although the public think that profound learning is an old man's affair, he is a *savant.* Anatole France is profoundly learned. He is Librarian of the French Senate. He was the writer of the literary reviews of *Le Temps* before Deschamps. His first book, a biography of Alfred de Vigny, was published in 1868. He published "Les Poêmes Dorés" in 1873, and "Les Noces Corinthiennes," poems, in 1876. He published his first novel, " Jocaste et le Chat Maigre," in 1879. Harper & Brothers have published a translation by Lafcadio Hearn of his first famous novel, "Le Crime de Sylvestre Bonnard," issued in 1881, laureated by the Académie Française. Since then Anatole France has been celebrated among the first writers of France. Among his works must be recalled "Balthazar," 1889 ; "Thaïs," 1890 ; "Jerome Cogniard," 1891 ; "La Rôtisserie de la Reine Pedaugue," 1892 ; "L'Etui de Nacre," 1893 ; "Le Jardin d' Epicure," 1894; "Le Lys Rouge," wherein the late Paul Verlaine is immortalized as Choulette, 1895. It is difficult to appreciate the literature of France without consulting the volumes wherein were reunited under the title of "La Vie Littéraire" the literary reviews written by Anatole France.

Freshest News.

ROBERTS BROTHERS have issued Ernest Renan's "Life of Jesus"; "Dante Gabriel Rossetti: his family letters" in two volumes, with a memoir by William Michael Rossetti; "The Entail, or, The Lairds of Grippy," in two volumes, the latest addition to the Galt Novels; "Cavalry in the Waterloo Campaign," by Lieut.-Gen. Sir Evelyn Wood, the third volume in *The Pall Mall Gazette Library*; and "The Religion of Hope," by Philip Moxom. Edwin A. Grosvenor's "Constantinople," issued recently, is daily meeting with commendation from the critics in high places.

CHARLES SCRIBNER'S SONS have just issued "Letters and Verses of Arthur Penrhyn Stanley," edited by Rowland E. Prothero, covering the years between 1829 and 1881, and brought out uniform with the first edition of "Life and Letters of Dean Stanley"; a new and cheaper edition of the two volumes of "The Life and Adventures of George Augustus Sala," which is sure of a large sale, coming so soon after the death of that interesting figure in literary life; "Wandering Heath," a charming collection of stories, studies, and sketches, by "Q" (Arthur T. Quiller-Couch); and a fourth edition of Murray's "Handbook for Japan." "The Love-Affairs of a Bibliomaniac," that gem of writing left by the lamented Eugene Field, is noticed elsewhere in this issue

D. APPLETON & CO. have ready "Studies of Childhood," the delightful articles of Prof. Sully which have appeared in the *Popular Science Monthly* during the year just ended; "The Story of the Solar System," by George F. Chambers, a concise but comprehensive handbook of popular scientific information; "Stone-pastures," by Eleanor Stuart, an American novel, describing life among the laborers in a Pennsylvania mining and manufacturing town; and three new volumes in the *Town and Country Library:* "A Self-Denying Ordinance," by M. Hamilton, a clever social study of fashionable and Irish country life; "Successors to the Title," by Mrs. L. B. Walford; and "The Lost Stradivarius," by J. M. Falkner. "Old Faiths and New Facts," by William W. Kinsley; "Movement," by E. J. Marey; "Criminal Sociology," by Enrico Ferri; and a new and revised edition of "The Sun," by C. A. Young, are noticed elsewhere in this issue.

HOUGHTON, MIFFLIN & CO. have ready several books, of which the titles are irresistible temptations. "Joan of Arc," by Francis C. Lowell, is a thorough study of the Maid of Orleans, the author's experience as a lawyer giving great value to his treatment of her trial and sentence; "Kokoro: hints of the Japanese inner life," by Lafcadio Hearn, is a valuable contribution to the understanding of the China-Japan war; "Bayard Taylor," by Albert H. Smyth, appears in the series of *American Men of Letters;* and a work of commanding interest is "The Life of Thomas Hutchinson," Royal Governor of the Province of Massachusetts Bay, by James K. Hosmer. A volume of discourses preached by the Rt. Rev. William Lawrence, bishop of the diocese of Massachusetts, entitled "Visions and Service," will be eagerly read by all who know the manly, direct, stimulating qualities of the teachings of this worthy successor of Phillips Brooks.

G. P. PUTNAM'S SONS have among their new books some works of unusual interest. "Regeneration," by an author who for the moment prefers to remain anonymous, is a reply to Max Nordau's rather morbid "Degeneration." It has an introduction by Nicholas Murray Butler, Professor of Philosophy, Ethics, and Physiology in Columbia College, New York City, and its tenor emphasizes the considerations which make for progress and hopefulness, while frankly admitting the serious evils and difficulties presented by modern civilization. Quite an original compilation is offered in "A Metrical History of the Life and Times of Napoleon Bonaparte," compiled and arranged with introductory notes by William J. Hillis, who has so carefully studied the poetry of a century that he has been able to find a song or a poem covering almost every event in the life of the ambitious Corsican. The book is sumptuously gotten up, and contains about twenty-five illustrations in photogravure. "The Rights of Man" and "The Age of Reason" are the new volumes in the edition of Thomas Paine, edited by Moncure D. Conway; "Renaissance Fancies and Studies," by Vernon Lee, is a sequel to "Euphorion: studies of antique and mediæval in Renaissance"; and "Russian Portraits," translated by Elizabeth L. Cary from the French of Vicomte E. Melchior de Vogüé, forms the sixth volume in the *Autonym Library*. The Putnams are also issuing a complete edition of James Fenimore Cooper's works in thirty-two volumes, printed from new plates and bound in the general style of the new *Hudson edition* of Washington Irving. It will be known as the *Mohawk edition*.

NEW BOOKS.

ROBERTS' JANUARY BOOKS

LITERARY NEWS

AN ECLECTIC REVIEW OF
CURRENT LITERATURE
~ILLUSTRATED~

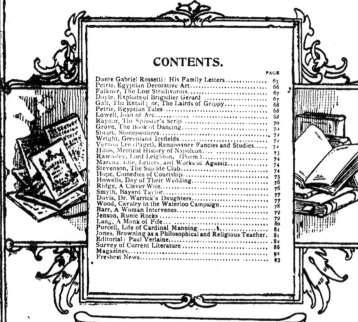

CONTENTS.

VOL·XVII·N°3 **MARCH ~ 1896** **$1.00 YEARLY**
10 CTS. PER NO.

~PUBLICATION OFFICE~
59 DUANE STREET, NEW YORK

ENTERED AT THE POST OFFICE AT NEW YORK AS SECOND CLASS MATTER

The Literary News

𝔍𝔫 𝔴𝔦𝔫𝔱𝔢𝔯 𝔶𝔬𝔲 𝔪𝔞𝔶 𝔯𝔢𝔞𝔡𝔢 𝔱𝔥𝔢𝔪, 𝔞𝔰 𝔦𝔤𝔫𝔢𝔪, 𝔟𝔶 𝔱𝔥𝔢 𝔣𝔦𝔯𝔢𝔰𝔦𝔡𝔢; 𝔞𝔫𝔡 𝔦𝔫 𝔰𝔲𝔪𝔪𝔢𝔯, 𝔞𝔰 𝔲𝔪𝔟𝔯𝔞𝔪, 𝔲𝔫𝔡𝔢𝔯 𝔰𝔬𝔪𝔢 𝔰𝔥𝔞𝔡𝔦𝔢 𝔱𝔯𝔢𝔢,
𝔞𝔫𝔡 𝔱𝔥𝔢𝔯𝔢𝔴𝔦𝔱𝔥 𝔭𝔞𝔰𝔰 𝔞𝔴𝔞𝔶 𝔱𝔥𝔢 𝔱𝔢𝔡𝔦𝔬𝔲𝔰 𝔥𝔬𝔴𝔯𝔢𝔰.

| VOL. XVII. | MARCH, 1896. | No. 3. |

Dante Gabriel Rossetti: His Family Letters.

IT was proper enough for Mr. William Rossetti to give precedence in the title of this work to the Letters, yet this arrangement of the

Dante Gabriel Rossetti, as he was called in later years, Gabriel Charles Dante Rossetti, as the name really ran, was born in London on

From "Dante Gabriel Rossetti."   Roberts Bros.

GABRIELE ROSSETTI. [By his son, D. G. Rossetti, 1853.]

title-page is somewhat misleading, as the entire first volume, which is the larger of the two, is occupied by the memoir, while there are copious notes to the letters inserted in the second volume. There is, therefore, found to be considerably more memoirs than letters.

the 12th of May, 1828, the second of four children born within as many years, all of whom inherited their father's interest in intellectual pursuits. . . .

As one sees Dante Rossetti through the medium of his brother's account of him and still more through his own letters to his family, his was not only an interesting but an unusually lovable personality. His letters are quite free from the element of self-satisfaction often to be found in men of somewhat capricious genius; his tone toward his family is unceasingly frank and affectionate, and his lively interest in the affairs of others and in little daily happenings of life is noticeably free from the taint of gossip. One closes the covers feeling that Dante Gabriel Rossetti was more thoroughly natural, more companionable, even more to be respected in spite of his weaknesses and errors, than would be gathered from many other descriptions of him that have been written. Since Mr. William Rossetti has accomplished this result his work cannot be said to have missed its aim, in spite of multitudinous faults of style and judgment. The illustrations in the two volumes are very beautiful reproductions, and are of exceptional interest. (Roberts. 2 v., $6.50.)—*N. Y. Times.*

Egyptian Decorative Art.

PROF. PETRIE is the most active popularizer of Egyptological subjects at the present time, and is, in this line, a worthy successor of the late Amelia B. Edwards, for whom his professorial chair is named. He lacks something of the literary charm which belonged to his patron, but the greater stores of his special and detailed knowledge make ample atonement in the mind of those who desire first-hand facts more than figures of speech. His own diction, moreover, has often a personal and rugged character, resembling a natural conversational tone, which is not lacking in attractiveness.

Prof. Petrie won his spurs as an explorer and excavator rather than as a professor, and has paid special attention to the forms of characters, signs, art-motives, and architectural designs, with a view to discovering their origin and genesis. We are all familiar with most of the artistic forms and devices portrayed by him in this volume, and the charm of his treatment is to be found in the tracing of artistic motives from their historical origination down through their successive stages of development and then into the art of other lands. This last is done to only a limited degree, yet sufficiently to show that a wide, varied, and interesting field is opened to view. The stages of decoration treated are the geometrical, the natural, the structural, and the symbolic. In each case the text is well illustrated with appropriate drawings taken from printed books, public and private collections, and from a fund of personal knowledge which has resulted from long-continued and varied observation at home and afield. (Putnam. $1.50.)—*The Nation.*

The Lost Stradivarius.

IN "The Lost Stradivarius," which is a story having for foundation a theme that is far

From "The Rule of the Turk."   Putnam's Sons.   Kindness of *Harper's Weekly.*
A BURIAL-PIT IN ARMENIA.

removed from the usual, Mr. Meade Falkner has succeeded in supplying us with a book of note. The story deals with a mysterious influence for which it is impossible to discover proper terms, and it is so treated by the will of the author that the reader is sensible of mental pressure arising from the indefinable communion between the quick and the dead as recorded in these able chapters. This air of disaster, this overhanging dread, is maintained from beginning to end, so that it is possible for all, save the dense and wholly unimaginative, to experience a thrill while learning the events which pushed Sir John Maltravers on to his early death. At the time when this story commences Sir John was an undergraduate at Oxford, where his chief friend was a young musician named Gaskell. Together these two were in the habit of trying many a piece written for violin and piano, and so continually did they play that we, knowing something of Oxford impatience, marvel that their neigh-

From Conan Doyle's "Brigadier Gerard."   Copyright, 1896, by D. Appleton & Co.

"THE EMPEROR WAS STANDING BEFORE ME."

bors on the staircase did not protest in several practical ways. In an evil hour they became acquainted with Graziani's "Areopagita" *suite,* which contained a *Gagliarda,* that is, music for a certain licentious dance. One day it happened that Sir John moved some old bookshelves in his room, in the course of which proceeding he discovered a secret cupboard, in which he found a Stradivarius violin covered with dust and cobwebs. The finding of this treasure only increased the gloom which was gradually spreading over Sir John's face and heart. He saw visions, he dreamt dreams, and at last he saw the sight which had blasted the lives of two men before him. Mr. Falkner uses nothing revolting. His are simple expedients, but, nevertheless, he has the secret of commanding our nerves. (Appleton. pap., 50 c.; $1.)—*London Literary World.*

The Exploits of Brigadier Gerard.

THERE is a flavor of Dumas's Musketeers in the life of the redoubtable Brigadier Gerard, a typical Napoleonic soldier, more fortunate than many of his compeers because some of his Homeric exploits were accomplished under the personal observation of the Emperor. His delightfully romantic career included an oddly characteristic glimpse of England, and his adventures ranged from the battlefield to secret service. In picturing the experiences of his fearless, hard-fighting, and hard-drinking hero, the author of "The White Company" has given us a book which absorbs the interest and quickens the pulse of every reader. The hand which penned the exploits of Sherlock Holmes has not lost its cunning. Conan Doyle's romances rest upon a sure foundation of scientific accuracy. (Appleton. $1.50.)

The Entail; or, The Lairds of Grippy.

THE seventh and eighth volumes of the new edition of the works of John Galt are given up to that one of his novels in which, Mr. Crockett thinks, his faults, limitations, and peculiarities "are more insistent and apparent than in any of his other important Scottish books." Yet Mr. Crockett considers it "a delightful chronicle, wayward and wimplesome." He insists that its second title, "The Lairds of Grippy," is enough. It is the simple history of three generations of a Scotch family. When it was written fashionable novelists affected such generalizing titles as "Marriage," "Destiny," "Precaution," and "Eccentricity"; wherefore, "The Entail."

Byron was particularly fond of this work. Perhaps readers will be found at this late day fond enough of truth in the form of fiction to agree with him and Mr. Crockett in appreciation of the diverting qualities of Leddy Grippy, Cornelius Luke and his wife, Mr. Walkinshaw, Kilfuddy, Keelevin, and Betty Bodle.

The best of Galt's novels are now before a public that has hitherto scarcely known his name, in a perfect form as regards text and typography. The work of the editor has been admirably done, while Mr. Crockett's speeches before the curtain, so to speak, are alone worth the price of admission. (Roberts. 2 v., $2.50.) —*N. Y. Times.*

Egyptian Tales.

W. M. FLINDERS PETRIE, the eminent professor of Egyptology, has collected "Egyptian Tales," in which he gives us specimens of the oldest literature and fiction of the world. In translating these documents into English Mr. Petrie has freely used the various translations already published in other languages, but in all cases more or less revision of the original has been made. As far as possible, the style and tone of Egypt have been preserved, and the edition adopted is the oldest that could be used without affectation. It will be noticed how the growth of the novel is shadowed forth in the varied grounds and treatment of the tales. The earliest is purely a collection of marvels of fabulous incidents of the simplest kind. Then we advance to contracts between town and country, between Egypt and foreign lands. Then personal adventure and the interest in schemes and successes become the staple material, while only in the later periods does character come in as the groundwork. The same may be seen in English literature—first the tales of wonders and strange lands, then the novel of adventure, and, lastly, the novel of character. The work is very remarkable and complete. (Stokes. 2 v., *ea.*, $1.50.)—*Philadelphia Telegraph.*

Joan of Arc.

I HAVE just finished reading a charming book, more interesting than any novel of the day, entitled "Joan of Arc." Its author, Francis C. Lowell, is by no means unknown to my readers. He is one of the few men who can write history as though it was a prolonged romance, and in this book he has had ample opportunity to display his peculiar gift.

Of course, we have had scores of lives of the Maid of Orleans, but I know of none which deals as fully as does this one with that period of the Maid's life which preceded her wonderful military career, and in these days, when visions and dreams and supernatural appearances are as readily accepted as they were in the fifteenth century, the early life of Joan will have a special fascination. It has been the habit of some critics to account for these visions on natural grounds, to attribute them to a wild imagination and to a physical condition akin to hysteria, but Mr. Lowell looks upon them with a more serious eye, and though he does not actually commit himself to a belief in their heavenly origin, he leaves it to be strongly inferred.

Up to the time when she entered her teens Joan was surrounded by the thick and suffocating air of warfare—not clean and civilized warfare, but the kind which in modern phrase is known as guerilla warfare. Domremy was ravaged again and again, and its inhabitants were robbed on every possible occasion. Joan's father, a well-to-do farmer, suffered loss of crops and cattle, and the soldiers of the brutal La Hire, "under pretence of blackmail, seized men, women, and little children; violated women and girls; killed husbands and fathers before their wives and daughters." That was the air which Joan breathed, and the effect on her childish mind may well be imagined.

When the Maid was thirteen years old she was one day in her father's garden, which adjoined the church, and she there saw "a great light, and had a vision of the Archangel Michael, surrounded by other angels." She was frightened, and did not know what manner of disease affected her vision. This revelation, however, recurred again and again, until she became used to it. The archangel at length spoke to her, promised that she should see others of the heavenly host, naming some of them, and this promise was, later on, fulfilled. Afterward her communications with these beings became constant. As Mr. Lowell says, "Two things only are certain; first, that she was sincere, and second, that no trick was played upon her by others." During the three following years she heard these voices constantly, and their purport was that she was to free France from the English. At seventeen she was sought in marriage, but she said that "God had called her to do a work, impossible of accomplishment if she married, and, therefore, she vowed to remain a virgin so long as He should please."

The first step was to reach the Dauphin, and she applied to Baudricourt, a sensual

by the clergy, but no fault was found with her orthodoxy. Still, there was hesitation and doubt. The examiners wanted a sign, some miracle. "In God's name," she replied, "I have not come to show signs, but lead me to Orleans, and I will show you the signs for which I am sent." Still further hesitation fol-

From Mrs. Jameson's "Legends of the Madonnas."   Houghton, Mifflin & Co.

MADONNA OF THE INK-HORN (BOTTICELLI).

rogue, who told Laxart "to take her back to her father's house and give her a sound whipping." Still she persisted. "I must be with the Dauphin," she said, "though I have to wear my legs down to my knees."

At last, after a thousand difficulties, which would have broken the heart of most persons, she reached Chinon, where Charles held his court. But Charles was "lazy, luxurious, and cowardly, which was natural enough, since he was the son of a crazy father and a licentious mother." He sent a messenger to her, and she returned answer that "she had two commands laid upon her by the King of Heaven; one, to raise the siege of Orleans, the other, to lead Charles to Rheims, that he might be crowned and consecrated there." A strange picture—this contemptible, sensual Charles, and that wonderful maid. "Gentle Dauphin," she said, when she was face to face with him, "I have come to you on a message from God, to bring help to you and your kingdom."

Then she was examined and cross-examined

lowed, but at last the condition of France became so desperate that even Charles saw that something must be done, and he gave a reluctant consent to allow Joan to head a certain number of troops. She was then on the very threshold of great things. The banner, which she had made, was worthy of her. "In the midst of it God was painted, holding the world and sitting upon the clouds; on either side an angel knelt; the motto was Jesus Maria."

The rest of her story is thoroughly well known to all of us. We have followed her a hundred times and know her career by heart. It is not, therefore, necessary to say more. Her volume will find a welcome place in many a library, and, if I mistake not, it will be read with delight by every one who buys it. I have had a full day's enjoyment with it, and commend it very heartily, and without a mental reservation, to all my readers. (Houghton, Mifflin & Co. $2.)—*Dr. Hepworth in N. Y. Herald.*

From "Dancing" (Badminton Library).   Little, Brown & Co.

A DANCING DRESS IN CENTRAL BRAZIL.

The Spinster's Scrip.

"THE Spinster's Scrip," compiled by Cecil Raynor, seems to have been devised as a book of consolation for the unmarried. It is made up of a formidable array of quotations from a variety of eminent sources, all the way from Spenser and Swift to Sarah Grand and Ian Maclaren, all directed in a humorous, satirical or openly condemnatory way at the possibilities of matrimony. Here are a few examples :

"When a woman falls in love you can't make her believe all men are alike ; and when she has been married ten years you can't make her believe that they are not."—*Anon.*

"Give warning ! Going to be married ! Why, cook, I did not even know that you were engaged." "Which I am not, mum ; but I am of that easy disposition that I am ready to be 'appy with any man."—*Punch.*

"Marriage—monotony multiplied by two."—*George Meredith.*

"Men cannot read women's character from their faces. It is well that they are denied this fact, or the race would become extinct."—*S. Baring-Gould.*

"There are men made of such stuff that an angel could hardly live with them without some deceit."—*Anthony Trollope.*

"It is impossible for a man to marry a clever woman."—*I. Zangwill.*

"She loved him, but probably no woman could live with a man for many years without having an indulgent contempt for him and wondering how he is considered a good man of business."—*J. M. Barrie.*

The compiler has shown a great deal of discrimination in making his selections and the two sexes seem to fare about equally well or equally ill at his hands. The author most frequently cited is George Meredith, and the whole month of June—for there is one quotation for every day in the year—is given up to extracts from his writings. The book is neatly got up, though with rather an unnecessary display of white paper, for occasionally there is only one short quotation to the long and narrow page. The proof-reading has been a little careless. Thus Junius Henri Brown figures as "Junius Henroln Brown"; Vauvenargues appears as "Vaubenargues," and La Rochefoucauld figures sometimes without the "La," sometimes with it. (Macmillan. $1.)—*The Beacon.*

The Book of Dancing.

THE handsome and exhaustive treatise, "Dancing," which Mrs. Lilly Grove and other writers have compiled, forms a volume in the far-famed *Badminton Library*, and it is safe to say that nothing having the slighest bearing on the subject has been neglected by the authors. Of the work itself, as of the subject, it is possible to treat at extreme length or by the briefest mention. The principle editorially followed has been to trace the dance from antiquity—although precisely what a young lady of the present day illustrating the skirt dance is doing in this classic section we are at a loss to understand—down to the present time, dwelling, by the way, on the various Terpsichorean forms and customs adopted in different parts of the world. That such a work is instructive goes without saying, and it is even more curious. What modern young lady could fail, for instance, to be frankly astonished at the representation and description on page 79 of a dancing dress in Central Brazil? It looks rather like a badly constructed haystack, with two naked and somewhat clumsy feet showing below. This is not the only instance the book supplies in support of our contention that the dance is not necessarily a thing of beauty. Nothing more grotesque can be imagined than the " Bear Dance " or the " Snow-shoe Dance " of the North American Indians, unless it be the cotillon of France or the minuet of the early Victorian age. To show the exhaustive nature of the book, we find record of Janet Ker and sundry other ladies who were charged, and not seldom executed, for "dancing with the devil," though precisely what step was used at these festive gatherings is not recorded. Another dance which hardly sounds attractive is that which is described as common in Tibet, where the lady "stands alone in the middle of a circle, swinging a sabre rapidly round and round." From time to time one of the men darts forward, and pretends to seize her by the hem of her dress, and, it is gravely recorded, " if the woman is awkward, and the man not very agile, a hand or finger is cut off ; though the accidents occur frequently, the people are very fond of the amusement." Possibly they have acquired a taste for it ; but for our part we should decline an invitation to a dance of that description. Mention is even made of the famous dance of one William Kemp,

who in 1599 footed it merrily from London to Norwich. But space forbids us to dwell on these and other curious items as well as on the more usual and certainly the more pleasing aspects of the subject. The work is illustrated with a profusion of drawings and reproductions of old prints, and has the further advantage of several musical passages to illustrate the author's meaning. As a work on the subject of dancing it is exhaustive and unique, and will cover ground that has never before been so satisfactorily and thoroughly exploited. The cuts have been certainly reproduced from the printed book. (Little, Brown & Co. $3.50.)—*London Literary World.*

From " Dancing " (Badminton Library).   Little, Brown & Co.

THE MINUET, 1720.

Stonepastures.

"STONEPASTURES" is a most masculine book, so grim and hard and adamantine is it, and yet when you study it just here and there come in the little faint touches which only a woman could conceive. Hard or not hard, the force and vigor of the story are masculine traits, and, taking a topic which was not to be wheedled or coaxed, Eleanor Stuart gives it a vigorous whack, as if with a sledge-hammer, and splits it open. Soot City is a mining town blacker than the English Black Country. Eleanor Stuart does not pretend to redress workmen's wrongs. It is not the work which is wrong, but the men who are. In Soot Town accidents are common. Men suffer daily from what are known as "blasts." A man is blasted because of want of precaution in firing dynamite, which tears out the hard ore. If the man thus blasted escapes with his life he lives to be about as inanimate as the hard gang itself.

Emma Butte is not a prepossessing girl, but a masterful one and an honest one. She carried on a curious trade. She was a barber, cunning in the stropping of razors, in lathering chins, and reaping the stubble, and she loved the gentlest of Swedes, August Jarlsen, a great big honest fellow, who brought to Soot City, all begrimed as it was, a bit of Swedish sunlight. Then Quarry, a dissolute wretch, envied Jarlsen his happiness, and on his and Emma's marriage-day, Quarry, without giving the Swede warning, fired a mine, and poor August was blasted. Then Emma had no wedding-day, but months of sorrow. Would the merry August ever sing for her again? If he were blind he still perhaps might hear her voice. It is the dead earnestness of Eleanor Stuart's "Stonepastures" which scores it into the reader's consciousness. (Appleton. 75 c.)—N. Y. Times.

Greenland Icefields.

THE immediate impulse to the preparation of this volume arose in connection with a trip to Greenland by Professor G. Frederick Wright in the summer of 1894 on the steamer *Miranda*. While preparing to make the most of this excursion much difficulty was encountered in collecting the facts which one would most like to know concerning this still mysterious land. The work therefore aims to give within moderate limits a comprehensive view of the scenery, the glacial phenomena, the natural history, the people, and the explorations of Greenland. The photographs, some sixty in number, are all original, and the maps have been prepared to show the latest state of knowledge concerning the region. The chapters treat of The Ice of the Labrador Current; The Coast of Labrador; Spitzbergen Ice in Davis Strait; The Author's Excursions on the Coast; The Coast in Detail; The Greenland Eskimos; Europeans in Greenland; Explorations of the Inland Ice; The Plants of Greenland; The Animals of Greenland; Changes of Level since the Advent of the Glacial Period; and a final chapter giving a summary of the bearing of the the facts upon glacial theories. The work is of both popular and scientific interest. There is no other work upon the subject so comprehensive. (Appleton. $2.)

From "Greenland Icefields." Copyright, 1896, by D. Appleton & Co.
ESKIMO HOUSEHOLD SERVANTS. MARRIED AND UNMARRIED.

Renaissance Fancies and Studies.

"RENAISSANCE Fancies and Studies," by Vernon Lee, is a most delightful and satisfying volume. You can see the scope of the book in the table of contents. The love of the saints is a charming chapter, full of vigor and noble criticism, strong and manly, interesting and suggestive. The chapters on Tuscan sculpture and the imaginative art of the Renaissance are full of beauty. One feels that he is sitting at the feet of a worthy teacher, who has made himself master of his subject by years of patient study. "The Life of Domenico Neroni," at the end of the volume, is a chapter to be read more than once. It is full to the brim with a charm of its own. As a criticism of the times in which Domenico lived it is admirable, for the author takes the reader on many a pleasant excursion into places and ideas which are more or less irrelevant to the subject in hand, and when he has done all this he leaves this reader saturated with the spirit of that early age. I am extrav-

and no dictionary of writers or of subjects seemed able to help me out of my difficulty. In my search for the poem wanted, and ultimately unearthed, I found so many others relating to the French Revolution, the consulate, and the empire, which were before unknown to me, that I determined to preserve in my hunt for these fugitive verses, and to make a collection of those found for the purpose of adding the volume, in manuscript, to my own private library, consisting mainly of works concerning the wonderful Corsican and his most remark-

From "Lorenzo de' Medici."　　　Copyright, 1895, by G. P. Putnam's Sons.

A FLORENTINE WEDDING.

agant, perhaps, but I have enjoyed the book immensely. (Putnam. $1.25.)—*Dr. Hepworth in the N. Y. Herald.*

A Metrical History of Napoleon.

"A METRICAL History of the Life and Times of Napoleon" is certainly something unique in the literature of biography, and the idea could hardly have occurred to any one but of an original mind. In his preface the compiler, Mr. William J. Hillis, tells how it came about. "Some years ago," he says, "long before the present Napoleonic fever had taken hold of the people, I had occasion to use a certain little poem relating to the death of the illustrious exile at St. Helena. Much to my surprise, when I came to look for it I could not find it. My friends were in the same quandary. They knew the poem but could not locate the author,

able career. When my collection was as complete as I could make it, I discovered I had a poem for nearly every incident of note in the life and history of Napoleon, from his birth to his second funeral, and the idea struck me that, by arranging the poems in chronological order as to the dates of the incidents portrayed, and by introducing each with a brief recital of the facts upon which the poem was based, I might make for myself a novel, if not a perfectly reliable, history."

The volume contains selections not only from the standard poets—Byron, Scott, Campbell, Victor Hugo, Southey, Browning, and others, but from those of lesser note. They are made with judgment in the main. The volume is elegantly printed on heavy paper and is profusely illustrated with etched and engraved portraits. (Putnam. $5.)—*Boston Transcript.*

*IN MEMORY OF LORD LEIGHTON, PRESIDENT
OF THE ROYAL ACADEMY.*

Crrv of Lilies, by the Arno's tide,
　Thou hast remembered well six hundred years
　The glad procession and triumphant cheers
That went with Cimabue, in its pride,
To bear the Mother of the Crucified
　To Rucellai's altar; now with tears,
　Not soon to pass, thy heart in sorrow hears
How he who told thy triumphing has died.

For of thy sons a son, tho' Western born,
　He worked with Lionardo, had the fear
　Of mighty Raphael still before his eyes,
He mixed his colors 'with the golden morn,
　And, finding lack of gorgeous glory here,
　He has gone forth right glad to Paradise.
　　　—H. D. Rawnsley in The Athenæum.

Life, Letters, and Works of Louis Agassiz.

A NEW biography of one of our greatest
naturalists comes in two volumes from the
press of Macmillan & Co., entitled "Life,
Letters, and Works of Louis Agassiz." It is
by Jules Marcou, who "enjoyed his friendship
during almost thirty years," and is "the last
survivor of the small band of European naturalists who came to America with him." It
may be fairly said of the author that he was
thoroughly equipped for the work he undertook, and, moreover, though his "admiration
for the man is not concealed," he has been entirely impartial in his criticisms.

Mrs. Agassiz wrote a life of her husband
many years ago, a tribute to his memory, giving us an insight into his character, by means
of nearly a hundred letters, which were very
largely confined to family affairs, though some
were written to the representative savants of
the day. We have, however, for a long while
been looking for a life of Agassiz, viewed from
the standpoint of the naturalist only, and Mr.
Marcou has done us that service. It is a well-
known fact that Agassiz had an enormous
correspondence. He was in constant communication with Humboldt, Cuvier, Buckland,
Lyell, and a dozen others, who were authorities on the subjects to which he devoted his
life. We have heard that hardly a day passed
in which he did not write half a dozen letters
for the purpose of comparing notes with his
confrères in scientific research. Mr. Marcou
had access to these letters, and has given us a
good many of them.

Those of us who knew Agassiz will give a
hearty welcome to these two volumes, for they
bring back a host of reminiscences. Agassiz
was greatly beloved, not only in Harvard University, but by every one who knew him.
"His faults were small, while his genius was
great." He was absorbed to a remarkable
degree in his vocation, and though he had
many opportunities to prosper' financially by

his researches he persistently declared that he
had no time for mere money-making.

The work will, of course, find a place in the
library of every scientific man in the country,
for although we have got far beyond some of
the theories which were in vogue in his time,
his life, like that of Humboldt and Cuvier, is a
milestone in the journey of scientific progress.

Agassiz passed his youth in Heidelberg,
Neuchâtel, and Paris. His life-work was suggested by his early environment. As Mr.
Marcou says, "Born and educated in such a
place as Motier, surrounded by water and
marshes, with the Oberland always in full
view in front, and the summit of the Jura in
the rear, it is no wonder that Agassiz became
an ichthyologist and a glacialist." Moreover,
his father was a clergyman, and naturally
afforded his gifted son every opportunity for
investigation. He had scarcely gotten out of
his teens before he began to make a name for
himself, and long before he reached Boston,
in 1847, he was recognized as one of the master
minds of the age.

It is impossible to do justice to this valuable
work in a short space. It must suffice to say
that the two volumes are exceedingly attractive in their outward form, are properly illustrated, and will give a great many hours of
pleasure to the reader. In every way, in the
matter of style, in the arrangement of incidents, in the impartial criticism of the work
of Agassiz, it is altogether charming, and I
feel free to assert that it is one of the most delightful biographies I have ever read. (Macmillan. 2 v. $4.)—*Dr. Hepworth in the N. Y.
Herald.*

The Suicide Club.

THE original "New Arabian Nights" of
Robert Louis Stevenson concerned the remarkable history of the discovery by Prince
Florizel of Bohemia of the existence in the
heart of London of a suicides' club, the members of which, with the exception of the president and owner (for it was a proprietary club),
were tired of life and anxious to find an easy
way out of it. Most of them were very young
men. Prince Florizel, of course, is a lineal
descendant of Shakespeare's Perdita and that
prince whose wooing caused her grief when his
royal father discovered it. He has an adventurous disposition and extraordinary influence with the British authorities, and he is
almost as whimsical and entertaining as Ha-
roun al Raschid.

There is a great deal of grim humor in "The
Suicide Club," which is now republished as a
volume of the *Ivory Series*, and no lack of
subtle irony, while as an example of plot weav-

ing and invention it compares favorably with some of Stevenson's later work. The "New Arabian Nights" were afterward extended to include more remarkable adventures of Prince Florizel and his faithful ally, Col. Geraldine, but none of them excelled in audacity those here related.

To be sure, the advantages of the club of suicides were greatly overrated. A member never kills himself. He was invariably murdered by another member. The member to whose lot the act of killing fell was not to be envied. The most ingenious murderer cannot always evade the police, and the danger of being captured and hanged was very great. No self-respecting suicide would care to be legally hanged.· (Scribner. 75 c.)—*N. Y. Times.*

Comedies of Courtship.

MR. ANTHONY HOPE'S "Comedies of Courtship" has more of the quality that abounded in his "Dolly Dialogues" than that which made his "Prisoner of Zenda" such a brilliant success. It is characteristic of the author that you never feel that you require to criticise or compare his work; it is good to read as a complete and thorough relaxation, and when a writer can present himself, or herself, in this attitude, the necessity for analytical observations, whether real or imaginary, is overlooked. Mr. Hope's "Comedies" are real comedies, and, as the title leads us to expect, they are played out by sundry young people in a way that would simply paralyze the old-fashioned hero and heroine. The first story in the book, "The Wheel of Love," is perhaps the best of

the half-dozen before us by reason of its unexpectedness. There is a good, healthy touch of pure cussedness about the respective couples concerned in the story, that illustrates the average human mind to perfection, although the

"WHO IS THIS MAN, AND WHAT HAS HE TO DO WITH YOU?"

virtues of constancy and firmness be quoted from a whole stack of three-volume novels against such heresy. "It is the unexpected that happens" may be said of Mr. Hope's stories, which are worked out with a knowledge of men and women and manners that is all too rare in these days of voluminous fiction. (Scribner. $1.50.) — *London Literary World.*

The Day of Their Wedding.

"LORENZO," asks Althea in this tale, "what was it made you feel foolish about me in the first place?" Thus does the nun-like girl try to have the shy Lorenzo tell what were the first symptoms of his love. Mr. Howells's "The Day of Their Wedding" may be the least bit of a laugh at bucolic manners, for Althea Brown and her lover, Lorenzo Weever, are country folk, absolutely unsophisticated.

The two are Shakers, and have just escaped from the Family at Harshire, and somehow, although Lorenzo prides himself on having broken away from the Shakers, Althea scarcely forgives herself for the escapade. Mutual liking has, however, made the two run away, and they have agreed to be married. Mr. Howells is a most observant chronicler when he tells what befell Althea and Lorenzo on their wedding day.

The two are the sweetest and most innocent of human beings. Lorenzo's worldliness is only the experience of a few days, and Althea is the little dove, making her first flight from her nest, and she flutters in blissful ignorance. The young fellow, who is manly enough, meets Althea in the cars. There is their rendezvous. It has been agreed that they shall go to Sara-

From "The Day of their Wedding."   Copyright, 1896, by Harper & Brothers
"A'N'T YOU GOING TO LET ME SET WITH YOU, ALTHEA?"

toga and be married there. It is the great plunge. Althea has her coal-scuttle bonnet, and is dressed in the original straight-laced clothes of the Shakers, but there is just a suspicion of Eve about her. . . .

"The Day of Their Wedding" is the tenderest of idyls, with a sad conclusion, and has a tinge of mysticism about it. It is, however, truly American. Perfect as a picture, it is handled with that delicacy of touch of which the author is past master. There is a psychological study in it. We call woman *volage*, fickle, and yet she is the more conservative of the two sexes. Shakerism, once absorbed by Althea, was never to be thrown off. Her "foolishness" was only a passing episode. She had conquered what was a fugitive passion. But there is one matter which might have entirely changed all Althea's nature. If only her hair had been longer. As a philosopher has said, "The addition of a fraction of an inch to Cleopatra's nose would have changed the destinies of the world." (Harper. $1.25.)—*N. Y. Times.*

A Clever Wife.

No one ever heard before of W. Pett Ridge, and the name suggests an ill-chosen pseudonym. But it will hereafter be held pleasantly in the memory by all who read this bright and thoroughly entertaining story. We infer that W. Pett Ridge is a woman, from evidence inherent in the story, especially from the delineation of male character. One must not be too positive, though.

Here is a story which, if its elements had been proclaimed in advance, any well-seasoned novel-reader would have avoided. One's interest is stimulated at the very beginning by the freshness of the author's narrative style and the appreciable if somewhat trivial wit displayed in the early passages. The things that provoke smiles are not, perhaps, such as would shine brightly apart from their context. "Don't smoke stationery," says a veteran to a youth who is rolling a cigarette, "have a cigar." "I am turning Republican," says a young man who is short of money, "and am getting rid of my last sovereign." "Needy actors" are said to "eke out a livelihood by borrowing half crowns of each other." Here is a short dialogue between a "man of the world" and a callow youth:

"Never been in love?"
"Heavens, no!"
"What's her name?"

Together with this modern flippancy, which is not at all disagreeable, there is a seemingly unconscious imitation in some descriptive passages of the manner of Dickens, or one of his manners, which is not at all bad. The reader finds himself well along in the story, and bound to finish it, before he thoroughly realizes that this is still another novel of the "art life" of London, with Fleet Street editorial offices, the theatres, the semi-fashionable "musical and literary evenings," and the picture galleries all in evidence again, and that hitherto detestable personage the "new woman" is the protagonist.

The book is lively and inspiriting from beginning to end. Its *ensemble* passages, so to speak, are admirably graphic and original. Its pictures of London and Paris life have the "local color" well applied. It is free from pessimism and other mental maladies. It treats of young love in a wholesome and charming way, and its pathos and its humor are alike unforced. Wherefore "A Clever Wife" is worth reading. (Harper. $1.25.) — *N. Y. Times.*

From Smyth's "Bayard Taylor." Copyright, 1896, by Houghton, Mifflin & Co.

Bayard Taylor.

THE study of "Bayard Taylor," by Albert H. Smyth, which makes a new volume in the *American Men of Letters Series*, is a thoroughly praiseworthy performance. Mr. Smyth had a great abundance of material at his disposal in the more or less autobiographical writings of Taylor himself, and in the elaborate "Life and Letters" edited by his widow and Mr. Scudder, but the author of the present monograph has not been contented with making a summary of previously existing literature dealing with his theme; he has been able to secure from many of Taylor's friends and colleagues a considerable quantity of instructive reminiscences, and he has given particular attention to the analyzing of the changing intellectual and social conditions amid which Taylor lived and wrote during the thirty years of his active literary career. Mr. Smyth starts out with an exceed-

ingly comprehensive though brief chapter on the literary history of Pennsylvania, and he succeeds in making quite clear the influence of ancestry and tradition in the evolution of Taylor's peculiar qualities of mind. In the six chapters that follow are sketched the early life of Taylor; his experiences as reporter and traveller, lecturer and land-owner; his experiments in novel-writing; and his striking series of German studies that culminated in the translation of "Faust." Mr. Smyth gives a separate chapter to Taylor's poems and plays —a chapter containing no small amount of sane and wholesome criticism—and he winds up with a touching narrative of hopes unfulfilled in setting forth briefly the details of Taylor's last days and death. Mr. Smyth is very systematic in his analysis of the literary productions of Taylor and his estimate of this author's rank in literature, and when he passes judgment it is with a persuasive reasonableness, the validity of which no one will be inclined to question. He certainly touches acutely upon the cardinal defect in Taylor's verse, when he says that it lacks spontaneity. "His poetry is all intended. It is carefully built up by the intellect. The reader searches in vain for an escape from the intellectual; Taylor never gives the rein to the spirit." Elsewhere, in a paragraph well worth quoting, Mr. Smyth gives in an appendix a full bibliography of Taylor. The book is well indexed and has a finely executed frontispiece portrait. (Houghton, Mifflin & Co. $1.25.)— *The Beacon.*

Dr. Warrick's Daughters.

THERE were two of Dr. Warrick's daughters, the elder Mildred, the younger Anne, and their father was of Luxborough. If Luxborough, in Pennsylvania, was not exactly a Little Pedlington, there were resemblances. It was a stuck-up place, and the Luxboroughans assumed many airs, which Philadelphia did not even presume to have. There was an immensely

From " Doctor Warrick's Daughters."   Copyright, 1896, by Harper & Brothers.

"SHE TRACED THE MARKS IN THE BRICKS."

rich old woman in the place, Eliza Joyce, who was always just going to die, and she was a distant relative of the Warricks.

There was no end to the money Eliza Joyce was supposed to have. Mildred, who is a managing person, encourages Eliza with the hope of being her heir. The Joyce woman dies and leaves Mildred a beggarly $500. Mrs. Davis has a difficult task in depicting Mildred. The girl herself suffers from self-delusion; she thinks she is making a sacrifice of herself for her needy and careless father. Dr. Warrick never has done anything; he dreams as to what he might do. The other sister, Anne, is made of better material than Mildred.

The romance drifts from Pennsylvania to Louisiana, and the Southern plantation life of the bayou is described. Mildred engages herself to John Soudé, a planter, with a sugar estate, and then throws him over and marries the fat and uninteresting Dave Plunkett, who is an oil millionaire. Then Mrs. Plunkett goes to Paris and becomes a speculator. Her husband has only three or four million dollars. She wants him to be the possessor of a hundred millions. Anne, after many uncertainties, be-

comes the wife of Brooke Calhoun, who is half lawyer and half farmer.

Mrs. Rebecca Harding Davis is always interesting when she writes a story, and she always has a story to tell. (Harper. $1 50.)—N. Y. Times.

Cavalry in the Waterloo Campaign.

GEN. WOOD is not one of those who think that the cavalry has seen its best days, and that because of the great improvements that have been made in what are called the "cowardly" weapons, shock tactics no longer are to be considered in laying plans for battles and in the study of the arts of war. The theory of those whose opinion Gen. Wood opposes is that long before a body of cavalry could reach the enemy upon which it would hurl itself, its potentiality would be reduced to insignificance. It is chiefly for the purpose of showing the possible uses of cavalry that Gen. Wood has written his work about the Waterloo campaign. He endeavors to show when and in what conditions cavalry attacks succeeded, and in cases of failure, to point out the causes, in order that his readers may draw some deductions that shall bear on the mooted question whether it is worth while for a country to spend money in the creation of strong bodies of mounted troops. Military critics will disagree in their judgments as to the strength of the argument Gen. Wood makes in favor of his proposition, that the cavalry is quite as valuable and necessary as ever it was.

In one case we have a body of infantry standing like a wall against a cavalry force. There is nothing absolute that may be offered in explanation of the failure of horsemen to stampede the foot soldiers. It comes down to a question of the merits of theories when we undertake to discover why the infantry did not turn its back to the cavalry, nor allow itself to be trampled over and cut to pieces. It is the same thing, if we consider an instance of the other sort.

But while Gen. Wood does not settle everything, he certainly throws light upon an interesting question, and the judgment of the unprejudiced reader will be that he gives substantial support to the estimate he puts on the value of the mounted soldier in the field. (Roberts. $1.25.)—N. Y. Times.

A Woman Intervenes.

THIS bright little story contrasts two girls whose intervention on several occasions influences the fortunes of two ingenuous youths (an accountant and a mining engineer) in their speculation in the matter of certain Canadian mines. The idea of setting a romance in a commercial framework is highly modern, and the part played by the ladies equally " up-to-date." Of the contrasted pair, Jennie Brewster, the American, who plays the part of special " commissioner " to a New York paper with admirable *verve* and considerable freedom from scruple, is more interesting than the equally business-like, but less unconventional English damsel, whose wits are pitted against her. One of the best scenes in the book is that in which Jennie seeks an interview with the man she has endeavored to out-manœuvre on the eventful voyage from America, ostensibly to seek information about the mine, but really to re-establish herself in his and her own good opinion. But, throughout, Jennie's pluck and power of repartee, her trenchant but kindly criticism of English ways and people, her womanliness, which lies so close to the surface of worldly callousness, make her one of the completest types of femininity the author has described. She is none the less charming in that she is exceptional, even among her countrywomen, in maintaining the best points of her sex in spite of the hardening influences of her encounter with the " inhuman turmoil " of the world. The plot is ingenious, if slight, and the dialogue lively as usual. (Stokes. 75 c.) — *The Athenæum.*

Runic Rocks.

" RUNIC Rocks " is the first of the many books of the Frisian writer, Wilhelm Jensen, which has found an English translator; and Miss Suckling has performed a labor of love in a manner which, I should imagine, does no injustice to the original work. It will certainly quicken the desire of the best English readers for further acquaintance with a romance which might be described as of imagination all compact, did not its purely imaginative quality gain weight and momentum from the infusion of a very in-teresting and suggestive intellectual element. In form and treatment " Runic Rocks " will remind many readers of the most characteristic work of Björnson; but Jensen is a thinker as well as an artist, and it is the molten metal of thought as well as of imagination which is run into an artistic mould. The young man in the opening chapter, which strikes the keynote of the book, has a vision of the three mystic women who sit upon the runic rocks. One of them sees only the solemn endlessness of life, another its trivial emptiness, a third its pathetic brevity; and in his story of the island in the northern sea the grouping of these three types of character and temperament provides the material for strange comedy and sombre tragedy. The burden of the book is one which it is impossible briefly either to

From " The Woman Intervenes."   Copyright, 1896, by Frederick A. Stokes Co.
" HE CHANGED HIS STEP TO SUIT HERS."

expound or to discuss, nor, indeed, is this the place for such exposition or discussion. There is not even room for detailed criticism of "Runic Rocks" as a contribution to creative literature; but as such it is a book of great beauty and worth, which certainly takes a very high place in the imaginative literature of the present decade. It is to be hoped that other translations from Jensen will follow in due course, and those who read German will turn eagerly to the originals. It puts still another book of excellent fiction on the list of Stokes publications. Every novel issued by this firm has elements of marked originality, and their general "get-up" is such that they please at first sight. (Stokes. 75 c.)—*The Academy.*

A Monk of Fife.

THE recent revival of interest in the Maid of Orleans has resulted in the production of a considerable amount of romantic fiction, of which the most important example is Mr. Lang's "A Monk of Fife." The subject is one almost ideally suited to Mr. Lang's hand, appealing, as it does, to his deepest interests and intellectual sympathies — how warmly the noble poem in his latest volume of verse may witness. The romance before us pretends to be a translation of a French manuscript in the Ratisbons Scots College. Whether this pretence be wholly a bit of mystification we are not concerned to inquire; for all practical purposes "A Monk of Fife" is an original work of Mr. Lang's imagination, although it follows historical fact more closely than such fiction is wont to do. As to the style of the book, it may be described, in Mr. Lang's own words, as "not imitating, in manner, the almost contemporary English of the 'Paston Letters,' or the somewhat earlier English style of the Regent Bedford, but merely attempting to give a moderately old air to his (Mr. Lang's) version of a French which, genuine or imitative, is certainly, in character and spelling, antique." The story is told in the first person, and is essentially the narrative of a young Scotsman, fleeing from his own country in consequence of a brawl, and finding service with the French at such a time as to be concerned in the siege of Orleans, and to become closely associated with the fortunes of the Maid. The narrative is at times labored, as the result of a wish to omit no historical fact of importance, but is for the most part highly readable, giving a vivid impression of the stirring life of early fifteenth-century France. (Longmans, Green & Co. $1.25.)— *The Dial.*

From "A Monk of Fife."   Copyright, 1896, by Longmans, Green & Co.

"REELING SHE FELL INTO MY ARMS."

Life of Cardinal Manning.

ANOTHER has now been added by Edmund Sheridan Purcell to the great series of full-length portraits, which is gradually nearing completion, of the men who have moulded English religious life during this century. They are painted by different hands, by the hands of men who had far different opportunities of studying their subjects, and have only one main basis of unity. They are all, however, finished in detail, but studies for the greater historical picture which will some day show the progress of religious life since George III. was king.

Cardinal Manning's biography presents exceptional possibilities of interest. His life is divided into two almost equal periods by a sharp severance—forty-four years Anglican, forty-one Roman ; and the two bulky volumes wh'ch describe it follow the same partition. It can hardly be necessary to recapitulate its course, which ended only four years ago, and which we are unwilling to believe is forgotten already ; nor would the task of epitomizing 1500 octavo pages in a column of *The Critic* be an easy one. It is more to the point to give those who desire to increase their knowledge of the subject an idea of what help they may expect from the labors of the biographer. Mr. Purcell enjoyed unusual opportunities of learning the cardinal's own view of the events of his life, and had access to all the letters, diaries, and notes which could assist him. With the minor exception of frequent repetitions, this part of the work is well done, and, as it renders accessible a vast amount of first-hand material, it is extremely valuable.

We are grateful for the fuller knowledge which the cardinal is allowed to give us, in such detail, of some of the most notable events of our time. Perhaps the most valuable new light is that thrown on the Vatican Council, of which he was so distinguished a member, and to whose outcome he contributed more important services than is generally known. History from the Anglican side, which usually repeats the statement that his allegiance to the Church of England was shaken by the Gorham Judgment, will be corrected by the publication of his private letters to Robert Wilberforce, which show that the case had little to do with it, and that for years before that date he had been coming definitely to the conviction that he was outside the communion of the Apostles. In fact, the ample documents given all through the book will prove most fascinating reading to all who (whether from the Roman or Anglican standpoint) have an interest in the religious history of England. We mentioned above a good deal which might have been left out ; and

it remains to say that the space thus gained might have been profitably filled by some of Manning's letters of spiritual counsel, of which only a few are given. He was a great statesman, but we do not want to forget that he was also a great guide of souls, and, since so much of an intimate nature has been printed, it would have done no harm to let us see more of him in this aspect. (Macmillan. 2 vols., $6.)—*The Critic.*

Browning as a Philosophical and Religious Teacher.

THE devoted students of Browning who seek in his verse for philosophy rather than for pleasure, and who insist upon recognizing in him not the sometimes admirable and sometimes defective artist, but always and everywhere a great preacher and instructor, will be glad to see a book published by the Macmillans, and entitled " Browning as a Philosophical and Religious Teacher," by Henry Jones, Professor of Moral Philosophy in the University of Glasgow. The author takes his subject and himself most seriously. He proclaims Browning one of that class of poets who were also prophets. "He was never merely," we are told, "the idle singer of an empty day, but one who spoke 'in numbers' because they were for him the necessary vehicle of inspiring thought." Accordingly, separate chapters are devoted to Browning's optimism, to his idealism, to his agnosticism, and to his solution of the problem of evil. There is this much reason for such an examination of the poet's writings, that, in his later works, he raised philosophical problems, and discussed them with no little dialectical skill. But Mr. Jones finds himself in the end constrained to acknowledge the impossibility of evolving from Browning's poetry a coherent system of philosophy. The ideas of the poet, like those of many a smaller man, underwent profound and even revolutionary changes during the course of his long life. What else, indeed, could be expected from one who began to write long before the publication of the " Origin of Species," and who continued to write long after that epoch-making book had sunk into the mind of the civilized world ? There is no evidence, indeed, that, even in his later years, Browning deliberately strove to evolve for himself a co-ordinated philosophic system. Although, in his later years, he now and then employed his intellect in mooting and solving metaphysical riddles, it is evident to the last, as from the first, that, in his more powerful compositions, Browning, like other poets of the first or second rank, thought rather with his heart than with his head, and beheld truth through a mist of emotion. (Macmillan. $2.25.)—*The Sun.*

The Literary News.

An Eclectic Monthly Review of Current Literature.

EDITED BY A. H. LEYPOLDT.

MARCH, 1896.

PAUL VERLAINE.

MIDDLE-AGED, fair-minded readers of the poetry and fiction written within the past ten or fifteen years have reached a state of mind most uncomfortable to be in and almost impossible to describe.

Turning from the pages of the "realists," the "symbolists," the "impressionists," the "Parnassians," the "decadents," in prose and verse, to the pages of their admiring or disgusted critics, the confusion and uncertainty of mind become intensified. Why should the writings which have conveyed almost nothing to the conventionally-trained mind call forth such delight or such detestation? What faculty in the cultured reader of the recognized masters of poetry and fiction of eight decades of the nineteenth century has become extinct in judging the poets and novelists of its closing decades who, without some special power, could hardly arouse such violent partisanship in adulation or reproof

The first clear thought which comes to the reader of these works, dealing almost wholly with the emotions, is a large measure of curiosity concerning the lives and idiosyncrasies of these writers who, with such infinite pains, show themselves so exaggerated, affected, restless, strained, unworthy, insincere. This curiosity has been discovered and fed by caterers of news, leaning chiefly to gossip and scandal, and often leading to almost unpardonable indiscretions.

Seldom has this been carried further than in the case of Paul Verlaine, the French "symbolist" poet, who died in Paris on January 8. Max Nordau in his great book, "Degeneration," has devoted a long chapter to Paul Verlaine and the symbolists, and has said many rather hard things about their private lives. The still unconfessed author of "Regeneration" says in his appeal against the hopelessness of Max Nordau's views:

"Nordau, in obedience to his professional prejudices, looks for no other causes, no other influences than those that can be found in the mechanism of their brains. This is all the more amazing, as he over and over again recognizes that external circumstances, conditions of life and habits, exercise a strong influence on the brain, or, in other words, that the mechanism which connects the *Ego* with matter may be influenced by the *Ego*. The result of his criticism presents, therefore, a want of fairness which, to the English mind, is especially objectionable. The manner in which he pries into the private life of Paul Verlaine, and the indelicate manner in which he refers to the personal appearance of the poet, impress us English people as so many unfair means of giving plausibility to his conclusions. When a hunchback is good-humored enough to make fun of his own deformity, those of gentle feelings sympathize all the more with his misfortune, and become all the more anxious not to refer to it. When a poet, in his love of truth and in his anxiety to rouse a certain emotion, makes confessions, when he instances his own sad experiences and failings, when he, so to say, throws himself into the flames on the altar of truth, we in England count it indelicate and unfair to base criticism on the facts thus revealed. Had Nordau read Verlaine's poetry with an unbiassed mind, he could not have failed to be struck by the extent to which the poet typifies the movement going on around him: his failing, his errors, and maybe his bad habits—all this is the fate of millions who have been induced by the materialist tendencies of recent times to disregard personal responsibility, and who, after rejecting such guides as the nobler instincts of humanity had proffered, attempt to follow the dictates of the lower instincts and animal impulses. His terrible remorse and despair while he is still unmoved by religion bear witness to aspirations which the materialist would fain deny. His instinctive groping for the consolations of religion shows to what extent he attributes his failings to an irreligious life, and that he experiences within him yearnings for a happiness which the gratification of the senses, prompted by atheism, has never afforded him."

Unhappiness would seem to be the keynote of the poetry of the "symbolists." There is not a touch of humor, not a ray of hope, not a touch of resignation even, in its constant recapitulation of despairing thoughts and its reiteration of phrases or rhymes. And when we turn from the work of the unhappy poets and study their characters, their surroundings, and their daily lives, we are almost sure to come upon human beings whose physical, mental, and moral manhood has been wrecked by uncontrolled self-indulgence in physical, mental, and moral dissipation. Everything about these poets is weak—their will-power, their pure, disinterested affection, their knowledge of facts, their interest in their fellow-men. Conscious of this weakness, without trained knowledge of its causes, without the trained endurance to master their effects, the first impulse of these poets leads them to resort to stimulants—physical, mental, and moral. In their peculiar condition of body and mind they do not assimilate the nourishment provided in healthy food, work, study, experience, duty. good literature, and pure, restful recreation, and they fly to absinthe, to wild orgies followed by enervating reactions, and to literature and hood was spent in following his father and mother from one garrison town to another, until the captain retired and settled in Paris in a modest apartment at the Batignolles. The child was sent to boarding-school. After years

PAUL VERLAINE.
Printed by courtesy of Stone & Kimball

drama provided by brains and souls as wrecked and morbid as their own.

The similarities of the life histories of the well-known "symbolists" in prose and verse is in itself full of meaning.

Listen to the facts in the life of Paul Verlaine, in whom, perhaps, the physical, mental, and moral symptoms of the "symbolists" have reached their climax. He has told them himself with great frankness in the pages of *Fin de Siècle.*

Paul Verlaine was born at Metz in 1844. His father was a captain of engineers. His child-

in which the imaginative boy and youth suffered intensely in the cold and gloomy surroundings, Verlaine was admitted to pass his examination for the bachelor's degree. which a good proportion of the middle class consider the end of study, and he passed it successfully, with excellent marks in literature and pretty low marks in science. He was obliged to find something to do, and he entered the municipal service of Paris as a copyist. Verlaine soon married the daughter of a talented musician, M. de Sivry, who continued his friend through all his misspent life. Soon afterward the

Franco-German War broke out, the Commune came, and during this period Verlaine was in charge of the Press Bureau. Then came the reaction and the repression and quiet which to Verlaine were terrible. At this time Verlaine took his fate into his home in the person of Rimbaud, a young poet only sixteen years of age, full of imagination, yet at the same time hysterical to excess and of most villanous habits.

With this comrade Verlaine set out for a journey to Belgium without even leaving word to his wife. There they lived wild lives, and one night, in a drunken spree, Verlaine stabbed his young friend. For weeks Rimbaud lay at the point of death. During this time Paul Verlaine had been tried and condemned to two years' imprisonment at Mons, Belgium. Rimbaud went to Africa. After ten years he turned up again at Marseilles, and while lying ill returned to the faith of his childhood and "died like a saint." In prison Verlaine also faced himself and, like Rimbaud, found hope and comfort in the faith of his childhood. But upon his return to the world he again led his wholly irresponsible life, following his lowest instincts for a long period, then suddenly repenting and indulging for a time in the ecstatics of the ascetic. "Verlaine believes in the Roman Catholic Church," says Jules Lemaître, "as earnestly as the Pope himself; but in Verlaine there is only belief—practice is wholly wanting in him."

Verlaine's favorite resort is said to have been the Café du Soleil, where he could generally be found an hour or two before dinner, seated at a little table, with a glass of absinthe within easy reach, engaged in smoking a pipe, reading the newspapers and jotting down memoranda or bits of verse. He was usually ill-clad, dirty, unkempt; and yet the other habitués of the place. knowing his ability and impressed by his widening fame, regarded him with a respect that was in nowise impaired even when the effects of a long evening's imbibition of absinthe and inhalation of the smoky atmosphere of the café were such as to make it impossible for him to find his way to his wretched "lodging for a night" without their guidance and support. The café, the jail, the hospital—these were his three homes.

Of late years he managed to have his own garret, where he spent most of his days in bed writing, and at night wandered out to drink absinthe and to forget. And this life came to an end on January 8, and many of the younger writers who had admired and imitated his art followed him to the grave.

What has Paul Verlaine left us of his work that will live when all this wretched story of his squandered talents is forgotten !

A list of Verlaine's works includes thirteen volumes of poetry—" Poèmes Saturniens," his first published work, 1866; "La Bonne Parole," "Romances Sans Paroles," " Jadis et Naguère," "Sagesse," his best work, etc., six volumes of prose. and a one-act comedy in verse. The best study thus far made of his work is that of Jules Lemaître in volume 4 of his "Les Contemporains." Almost everything that has appeared on Verlaine since his recent death is founded on Lemaître.

Of Verlaine's great influence on the poetry of France there can be no doubt. He defied every rule which had been binding in the making of correct, inflexible French verse. He was a great artist in words. The setting of his thoughts was faultless. Whether they were worth this exquisite mounting time alone can decide. His "Sagesse" has been likened to "The Imitation" of Thomas à Kempis, but such a comparison is only possible to those to whom church and religion are identical. "Sagesse," says Lemaître, "is one of the most curious books in existence. The poet has sinned, has been punished, has repented. In his distress he has turned to God. What God? The God of his childhood, the God of his first communion. 'Sagesse' is perhaps the only book of Roman Catholic poetry (not only Christian and religious) that I know."

In Verlaine's school of versification every sound has color and music as well as defined meaning. The symbolists have taught us: "A is black; E, white; I, blue; O, red; U, yellow. Black is the organ; white, the harp; blue, the violin; red, the trumpet; yellow, the flute. The organ expresses monotony, doubt, and simplicity; the harp, serenity; the violin, passion and prayer; the trumpet, triumph and ovation; the flute, ingenuousness and smiles. This is called poetic instrumentation. It is a most difficult art, and has been carried to its highest perfection by Paul Verlaine. But this can appeal only to those who understand every shade of meaning of the language in which the "symbolists" write.

It is almost impossible to convey the beauty of Verlaine's poetry in translation. A collection of about fifty of his most noted poems has been translated by Gertrude Hall, herself an artist in words ; but the sound of Verlaine's verse is perhaps more important than their sense, and this specialty of his art is necessarily lost, and much of his verse becomes rubbish when robbed of its music. Even Max Nordau has said of "Chanson d'Automne" that there are few poems in French literature that can rival it. Here it is in French and in English :

CHANSON D'AUTOMNE.

Les sanglots longs
Des violons
    De l'automne,
Blessent mon cœur
D'une langueur
    Monotone.

Tout suffocant
Et blême quand
    Sonne l'heure,
Je me souviens
Des jours anciens
    Et je pleurs.

Et je m'en vais
Au vent mauvais
    Qui m'emporte
De çà, de là
Pareil à la
    Feuille morte.

CHANSON D'AUTOMNE.

Leaf-strewing gales
Utter low wails
    Like violins,
Till on my soul
Their creeping dole
    Stealthily wins.

Days long gone by !
In such hour, I,
    Choking and pale,
Call you to mind.
Then like the wind
    Weep I and wail.

And, as by wind
Harsh and unkind,
    Driven by grief,
Go I, here, there,
Recking not where,
    Like the dead leaf.

The *technique* of this little work of art is perfect ; but *technique* in itself can only be appreciated by those who realize the difficulties overcome. Almost all the verse of the symbolists describes moods, generally sad and vague, longings. This tone does not attract healthy human nature. The love of sad things and delight in painful emotions, felt or betrayed by others, are only acquired under unnatural conditions. Humor appeals to all men, because it is warm and closely allied to pity, and of humor there is no trace in the symbolists. Carlyle has told us that "humor is justly regarded as the finest perfection of poetic genius."

The men who have become immortal in literature, art, and music have all appealed to something in the soul of man that was there before any language was spoken, and will be there when the meanings of decadent, symbolist, saturnien, Parnassian, impressionist, sensitivist, etc., are wholly forgotten.

Time will show how much of this enduring life has been breathed into the magic verse of Paul Verlaine and his followers.

TO WILLIAM SHAKESPEARE, DRAMATIST.

(*After having read Henrik Ibsen, dramatist.*)

Forgive me, ample soul, in whom man's joy
    Finds room for laughter, as his grief for sighs,
    If e'er I leave thee for an hour's emprise
Where live but souls made sick with life's annoy.
I bartered Time's best coin without alloy,
    And sailed with him within an inlet's rise
    Where stricken ghosts, with tragic voice and guise,
Made thy world seem a dire fantastic toy.

O Ocean, take me back to thee, and fill
    My sails once more with elemental breath—
    With wind that haunts thy choric world-wide spell ;
Some truth may say, "All's well," or "All is ill,"
    But on thine azure line 'twixt life and death
    The whole of truth speaks clear : "All shall be well."
        —*F. W. Gunsaulus in The Dial.*

POETRY AND MUSIC.

SHELLEY AND SCHUBERT.

Man's soul itself with songs of sky entrancing
Makes life a lyric field, bright dews enhancing,
Where lily-sounds in wild enchantment growing
Throng close, like stars, on vaulted darkness blowing.

ROSSETTI AND CHOPIN.

Far murmuring seas upon the white sand glistened.
Two full-toned souls for faint woe-accents listened.
When eddied passion's pains to calm were sinking,
These seized the concords, mate to mate re-linking.

BROWNING AND WAGNER.

Thunders and whispers sway the jubilation ;
Crashes of pains long past and joys from earth sweep
        near ;
Then sobs and wails in rhythmic modulation
Breathe radiant, surgent song within a tear.

SHAKESPEARE AND BEETHOVEN.

What God wrote deepest in the soul is spoken.
Fair vase of tears and loves they brought unbroken ;
Found every thread of secret joy or grieving ;
Wrought out the dream, immortal mazes weaving.

(A. C. McClurg. $1.50.)—*From Frank W. Gunsaulus's " Songs of Day and Night."*

OBITUARY NOTES.

Rev. John Owen died at the vicarage of East Anstey in Somerset, Eng., on February 2. He was born in Pembroke in 1833. Among his published works his " Evenings with the Sceptics " is probably the best known.

Arsène Houssaye, the celebrated French *littérateur*, died February 26. He was born at Bruyères, in the department of Aisne, on March 28, 1815. When about 20 years of age he went to Paris and was soon upon friendly terms with some of the leaders in the French literary world. His first books quickly attracted attention and led in a short time to his becoming celebrated. In 1849 he became director of the Théâtre Français, and under the Empire was appointed Inspector-General of the museums. Among his works are " Philosophes et Comédiennes," " Les Filles d'Eve," " Sous la Régence et Sous la Terreur," " Blanche et Marguerite," " Nos Grandes Dames," " History of the Forty-first Fauteuil of the French Academy," " King Voltaire," and " History of French Art."

Survey of Current Literature.

☞ *Order through your bookseller.*—"*There is no worthier or surer pledge of the intelligence and the purity of any community than their general purchase of books; nor is there any one who does more to further the attainment and possession of these qualities than a good bookseller.*"—PROF. DUNN.

ART, MUSIC, DRAMA.

ARCHITECTURAL masterpieces of Belgium, Holland, etc. Bruno Hessling. 96 pl. 4°, bds., $10.

ESPOUY, H. d', *ed.* Details of architecture in the antiquity taken up and reconstructed by prominent architects of the "Académie de la France à Rome." In 10 pts. Pt. 1. Bruno Hessling. 10 pl. f°, bds., $4.50.

PETRIE, W. M. FLINDERS. Egyptian decorative art : a course of lectures delivered at the Royal Institution. Putnam. 12°, $1.50.

BIOGRAPHY, CORRESPONDENCE, ETC.

BROWN, ALEX. The Cabells and their kin : a memorial volume, historical, biographical, and genealogical, on Dr. W. Cabell, the founder of the family in Virginia, and his descendants and kinsfolk. Houghton, Mifflin & Co. por. 8°, *net,* $7.50.

GOUNOD, C. FRANÇOIS. Memoirs of an artist: an autobiography, rendered into English by Annette E. Crocker. Rand, McNally. por. 12°, $1.25.

HARE, A. J. C. Biographical sketches. Dodd, Mead & Co. 12°, *net,* $2.50.
Memorials of Arthur Penrhyn Stanley, Dean of Westminster ; Henry Alford, Dean of Canterbury ; and Mrs. Duncan Stewart ; with a descriptive sketch of Paray Le Monial; this last-named article is reprinted from *Evening Hours*, and the two first appeared originally in *Macmillan's Magazine* and *Good Words*.

KING, RUFUS. The life and correspondence of Rufus King ; comprising his letters, private and official, his public documents, and his speeches ; *ed.* by his grandson, C. R. King, M.D. In 5 v. V. 3. Putnam. por. 8°, $5.

PURCELL, EDMUND SHERIDAN. Life of Cardinal Manning, Archbishop of Westminster. Macmillan. 2 v., pors., 8°, $6.

ROMANES, G. J. The life and letters of George John Romanes, written and *ed.* by his wife. Longmans, Green & Co. 8°, $4.

ROSSETTI, DANTE GABRIEL. Dante Gabriel Rossetti, his family letters; with a memoir by W. Michael Rossetti. Roberts. 2 v., pors., 8°, $6.50.

SALA, G. A. The life and adventures of George Augustus Sala, written by himself. [*New cheaper ed.*] Scribner. 2 v., pors., 8°, $3.

SCHWABE, *Mrs.* SALIS, *comp.* Reminiscences of Richard Cobden; with a preface by Lord Farrar. Imported by G. P. Putnam's Sons. 8°, $6.

SMYTH, ALBERT H. Bayard Taylor. Houghton, Mifflin & Co. 12°, (American men of letters.) $1.25.

DESCRIPTION, GEOGRAPHY, TRAVEL, ETC.

APPLETONS' handbook of winter resorts for tourists and invalids. *New ed. rev.* to date. Appleton. maps, il. 12°, pap., 50 c.

SPEARS, J. R. The gold diggings of Cape Horn: a study of life in Tierra del Fuego and Patagonia. G. P. Putnam's Sons. map, 8°, $1.75.

DOMESTIC AND SOCIAL.

FLETCHER, JULIA CONSTANT, ["George Fleming," *pseud.*] For plain women only. The Merriam Co. 12°, (The Mayfair set, no. 4.) $1.25.
Conversations between a clever, witty old lady and her nephew. She starts with the assertion that "no woman under forty has the moral right to look irrecoverably plain "; how to achieve good looks is suggested in amusing discussions on mirrors, bonnets, ruffles, the superfluous, bead trimmings, waistbands, tailor-made women, looks, "an excursion and alarms," and "the case for the defence."

WELCH, DESHLER. The bachelor and the chafing-dish; with a dissertation on chums. F. Tennyson Neely. il. 12°, $1.
Clever papers on the pleasures of cooking, especially certain things, in the chafing dish — more than a hundred recipes being given for the latter; among other topics discussed are the language of the menu, sayings of Savarin, salads and sauces, etc.

EDUCATION, LANGUAGE, ETC.

DARBISHIRE, HERBERT DUKINFIELD. Relliquiæ philologicæ ; or, essays in comparative philology ; ed. by R. S. Conway; with biographical notice by J. E. Sandys. Macmillan. 8°, *net,* $2.

SCHMIDT, IMMANUEL, *and* TANGER, GUSTAVE, *eds.* Flügel-Schmidt-Tanger's Dictionary of the German and English languages, for home and school ; with special reference to Dr. Felix Flügel's "Universal English-German and German-English dictionary." In 2 pts. : pt. 1, English-German ; pt. 2, German-English. Lemcke & Buechner. 4°, hf. leath., $4.50; the German-English pt. separately, $2.60.
As regards the relation of this work to Dr. Flügel's "Universal dictionary," published in 1891, the editors explain that for the English-German part they have used it more as a starting-point than as a basis, and that their work is by no means a mere abstract from, or adaptation of, Dr. Flügel's larger work. Wherever it seemed desirable they followed their own way, whether as regards the matter or form, the development or arrangement of definitions, or the marking of pronunciations. And while this is true of the first part of the work it holds good to a still greater extent concerning the German-English section, which claims to be considered as an entirely independent work. Being in-

tended for "home and school," the editors have not aimed at absolute completeness.

FICTION.

ASBJÖRNSEN, P. CH. Tales from the fjeld : popular tales from the Norse by Sir G. Dasent. *New ed.*, il. by Moyr Smith. Putnam. il. 12°, $1.75.

ATHERTON, *Mrs.* GERTRUDE FRANKLIN, ["Frank Lin," *pseud.*] A whirl asunder ; with frontispiece by E. Frederick. Stokes. il. 16°, 50 c.
Owin Clive, an Englishman of fine physique and unusual attainments, comes to California to keep his troth with Mary Gordon, who is a young countrywoman of Owin's. Soon after his arrival he is thrown into constant companionship with Helena Belmont, whose singular characteristics both repel and attract him. After a series of unconventional scenes that occur in the redwood forest the pair tacitly agree that they love each other. This confession is attended with surprising results and a final tragedy.

BALZAC, HONORÉ DE. Novels. V. 7, Ursule Mirouët ; tr. by Clara Bell ; ed. with a preface by G. Saintsbury ; il. by D. Murray-Smith. Macmillan & Co. 12°, silk, $1.50.

BUCHANAN, ROB. Diana's hunting ; il. by Edwin B. Child. Stokes. 1 il. nar. 16°, (Twentieth century ser.) buckram, 75 c.

CHRISTIAN, SYDNEY. Persis Yorke. Macmillan. 12°, $1.25.

CRAWFORD, F. MARION. A tale of a lonely parish. Macmillan & Co. 12° (Macmillan's novelists' lib., v. 1, no. 11.) pap., 50 c.

CAINE, T. H. HALL. The bondman. *New ed.* Appleton. 12°, (Appleton's town and country lib., no. 5½.) $1 ; pap., 50 c.

COUCH, ARTHUR T. QUILLER, [" Q," *pseud.*] Wandering heath : stories, studies, and sketches. Scribner. 12°, $1.25.
Contents : The roll-call of the reef ; The Love Die-Hards ; My grandfather, Hendry Watty ; Jetsom ; Wrestlers ; The Bishop of Eucalyptus ; Widdershins ; Visitors at the Gunnel Rock ; Letters from Troy ; Legends ; Experiments.

DAGGETT, *Mrs.* C. STEWART. Mariposilla : a novel. Rand, McNally. 12°, $1.25.
"Mariposilla" was a beautiful young Spanish girl of southern California. Her story is related by a New York lady who spent the season in San Gabriel on account of her invalid daughter. She makes the acquaintance of a Mrs. Sanderson and her handsome blond son, who between them break the heart of "Mariposilla."

DAVIS, REBECCA HARDING. Doctor Warrick's daughters : a novel. Harper. 12°, $1.50.

DELAND, *Mrs.* MARGARET. Philip and his wife. Houghton, Mifflin & Co. 16°, (Riverside pap. ser.) pap., 50 c.

FALKNER, J. MEADE. The lost Stradivarius. Appleton. 12°, (Appleton's town and country lib., no. 185.) $1 ; pap., 50 c.

FIELD, EUGENE. The love-affairs of a bibliomaniac. Scribner. 12°, $1.25.

GALT, J. Novels ; ed. by D. Storrar Meldrum. [*New il. ed.*] In 8 v. V. 5 and 6, The entail ; or, the lairds of Grippy ; with introd. by S. R. Crockett ; il. by J. Wallace. Roberts. il. 12°, $2.50.

GISSING, G. The paying guest. Dodd, Mead & Co. nar. 16°, 75 c.

HAMILTON, KATE W. The parson's proxy. Houghton, Mifflin & Co. 12°, $1.25.

HORNUNG, E. W. Irralie's bushranger : a story of Australian adventure. Scribner. nar. 16°, 75 c.

HOUGH, E. The singing mouse stories. Forest and Stream Pub. Co. 16°, $1.

HOUSMAN, CLEMENCE. The were-wolf ; il. by Laurence Housman. Way & Williams. sq. 12°, $1.25.

HOWELLS, W. DEAN. The day of their wedding : a novel. Harper. 12°, $1.25.

HUNGERFORD, *Mrs.* MARG. HAMILTON, ["The Duchess," *pseud.*; *formerly Mrs.* Argles.] A point of conscience. Lippincott. 12°, $1.

HUNGERFORD, *Mrs.* MARG. HAMILTON, ["The Duchess," *pseud.*; *formerly Mrs.* Argles.] The professor's experiment. R. F. Fenno. 8°, $1.25 ; pap., 50 c.

KOMPERT, LEOPOLD. Christian and Leah, and other Ghetto stories ; tr. by Alfred S. Arnold ; il. by F. Hamilton Jackson. Macmillan. 12°, (Iris ser.) *net,* 75 c.

McCLELLAN, M. Vanna : a Scotch story. Putnam. 12°, $1.

MIMOSA, (*pseud.*) Told on the pagoda ; tales of Burmah. Putnam. 16°, $1.

MOLLOY, J. FITZGERALD. An excellent knave. Lovell, Coryell & Co. 12°, (Belmore ser., no. 40.) pap., 50 c.
Two thousand pounds won at Monte Carlo is the cause of the hero's death ; he is followed to England by "an excellent knave," a man of some refinement and education, who covets the money, and who chloroforms him in a railway car between Dover and London and robs him ; he had not intended to commit murder, that event being an accident. An innocent man is suspected of the crime, and is only cleared by the efforts of a celebrated London detective, who cleverly clears up the mystery.

MONCRIEFF, F. The X Jewel : a Scottish romance of the days of James I. Harper. 12°, $1.25.

READ, OPIE P., ["Arkansaw traveller," *pseud.*] The Jucklings : a novel. Laird & Lee. il. 12°, $1.

RIDGE, W. PETT. A clever wife : a novel. Harper. 12°, $1.25.

SMITH, EDGAR MAURICE. A daughter of humanity. Arena Pub. Co. 12°, $1.25 ; pap., 50 c.
Helen Richmond, a Boston heiress, becoming interested in the life of the saleswomen in the large dry-goods establishments of New York, obtains a situation under a feigned name in a large store, where she remains for seven months, living the life of a working-girl, forming friendships with other girls, winning their confidences, and learning at first hand the terri-

ble evils and temptations of their lot. The tragical fate of several girls working at starvation wages is told. Miss Richmond relates her experience finally from the lecture platform.

SMITH, *Mrs.* ELIZ. THOMAS, [*formerly* L. T. Meade.] A princess of the gutter. Putnam. 12°, $1.25.
A girl of twenty-two, just after leaving Girton, inherits from an uncle a large fortune; the uncle had lived a selfish life, and tells her before his death that he has been "an unfaithful steward," and that she must rectify his mistakes when she receives his money. To do this she lives among the very poor of London, using her life and strength and money in their service, and tears down the dreadful houses on her property, building in their place sanitary tenements. Martha Mace, the "Princess," her helper, is a fine character.

STEVENSON, ROB. L. The Suicide Club. C. Scribner's Sons. 16°, (Ivory ser., no. 3.) 75 c.
Contents : Story of the young man with the cream tarts; Story of the physician and the Saratoga trunk; The adventures of the hansom cab. These stories appeared in the "New Arabian nights" under the title of "The Suicide Club."

STUART, ELEANOR, (*pseud.*) Stonepastures. Appleton. nar. 12°, 75 c.
This graphic picture of quaint characters belongs to the class of specialized American fiction which has been headed by the work of Miss Wilkins, Mr. Cable, Colonel Johnston, Mr. Garland, and others. The author has studied the peculiar and almost unknown life of the laborers in a Pennsylvania mining and manufacturing town with a keenness of observation and an abundant sense of humor which will give her book a permanent place among the *genre* studies of American life.

TOWNSEND, MARY ASHLEY, [" Xariffa," *pseud.*] Down the bayou, the captain's story; and other poems. [*New issue.*] Lippincott. por. 12°, $1.50.

VOGÜÉ, EUGÈNE MARIE MELCHIOR DE (*Vicomte.*) Russian portraits tr. by Eliz. L. Cary. Putnam. nar. 12°, 50 c.
Tales of Russian peasant character: Winter tales ; Uncle Fédia ; Pétrouchka, the fifer ; Barbara Afanasiévna ; Days of serfdom.

WALFORD, *Mrs.* LUCY BETHIA. Successors to the title. Appleton. 12°, (Appleton's town and country lib., no. 184.) $1 ; pap., 50 c.
Three direct heirs to the earldom of St. Bees dying in quick succession, "Dolly" Feverll, a distant cousin and a "nobody," becomes, to his own great surprise as well as that of others, Lord St. Bees. He has only been married a few years to a little Scotch wife with some fortune— but also a "nobody." The way they accept their inheritance, their coming to the great castle, the shock their youth and ignorance give their neighbors, and the methods adopted to polish and instruct them, make the story. Readers of the best contemporary fiction know how to appreciate this popular author's lightness of touch and unfailing humor.

HISTORY.

BARING-GOULD, SABINE. Curiosities of olden times. T. Whittaker. 12°, $1.50.

BRADFORD, W. The history of the Plimoth plantation : written by William Bradford, one of the founders and second governor of that colony : reproduced in fac-simile, by photography of the original manuscript; with an introduction by John A. Doyle. Houghton, Mifflin & Co. 4°, *net*, $25.

CHAMBERLAIN, ALEX. FRANCIS. The child and childhood in folk-thought, (The child in primitive culture.) Macmillan. 8°, *net*, $3.

CHESNEY, *Sir* G. TOMKYNS. The battle of Dorking ; the German conquest of England : reminiscences of a volunteer, describing the arrival of the German Armada, the destruction of the British fleet, decisive battle of Dorking, the capture of London, downfall of the British empire. Way & Williams. 12°, 25 c.
An imaginary narrative of the invasion and conquest of England by a foreign army ; written in 1871, and published anonymously. The original title was "Battle of Dorking, or, reminiscences of a volunteer, by an eye-witness in 1925." "The strained relations of America with England growing out of the Venezuelan boundary dispute on the one hand, and of England with Germany due to complications in South Africa on the other," the publishers say, "will give a peculiar and timely interest to this reprint of 'The battle of Dorking.'"

DU HAUSSET, *Madame.* The private memoirs of Louis XV., taken from the "Memoirs of Madame Du Hausset," lady's maid to Madame de Pompadour. Imported by Scribner. 8°, *net*, $5.

GODLEY, A. D. Socrates and Athenian society in his day : a biographical sketch. Macmillan. 12°, $1.75.

HAZLITT, W. CAREW. The coin collector. Longmans, Green & Co. 8°, (The collector ser.) *net*, $2.25.

LOWELL, FRANCIS C. Joan of Arc. Houghton, Mifflin & Co. 8°, $2.

MACKINNON, JA. The union of England and Scotland : a study of international history. Longmans, Green & Co. 8°, $5.

MAHAFFY, J. P. The empire of the Ptolemies. Macmillan & Co. 12°, $3.50.

MARCH, T. The history of the Paris Commune of 1871. Macmillan. 8°, $2.

SCHUYLER, *Rev.* HAMILTON. Studies in English church history ; with an introd. by the Rev. T. Richey. Crothers & Korth. 12°, *net*, $1.
Contents ; The planting of the church in Britain ; The mediæval church and Roman supremacy ; The Reformation, its causes and results ; The rise and progress of Dissent ; The Anglo-Catholic revival. Lectures delivered before the congregation of Trinity Church, Newport, R. I., during the Lenten season of 1895.

SECRET memoirs of the court of St. Petersburg, particularly toward the end of the reign of Catharine II. and the commencement of that of Paul I.; from the French. Imported by Scribner. por. 8°, *net*, $5.

TYLER, J. M. The whence and whither of man; a brief history of his origin and development though conformity to environment : being the Morse lectures of 1895. Scribner. 12°, $1.75.

WOOD, *Sir* EVELYN. Cavalry in the Waterloo campaign. Roberts. il. 12°, (Pall Mall magazine lib.) $1.25.
Contents: Organization of the French army; The French cavalry leaders, and how they crossed the Sambre River; Battle of Ligny, 16th June; Quatre Bras and Genappe; Waterloo, 18th June. List of books consulted (1 p.).

LITERATURE, MISCELLANEOUS AND COLLECTED WORKS.

BURTON, ROB. The anatomy of melancholy: what it is, with the kinds, causes, symptoms, prognostics, and several cures of it. *New ed.* Warne. 8°, $2.75.

CURTIS, G. W. Emerson. Putnam. 16°, (Little Journeys to the homes of American authors, v. 1, no. 1.) pap., 5 c.

ENOCH. The book of the secrets of Enoch; tr. from the Slavonic by W. R. Morfill; ed. with introd., notes, and indices, by R. H. Charles. Macmillan. 8°, *net*, $2.

FORD, J. Works; ed. by W. Gifford; with additions by Rev. Alexander Dyce; now reissued with further additions. Imported by Scribner. 3 v., 12°, *net*, $8.50.

GOETHE, J. WOLF. v., *and* SCHILLER, J. F. v. Goethe and Schiller's Xenions; selected and tr. by Paul Carus. The Open Court Pub. Co. pors.obl. 24°, $1.
Satirical epigrams mostly directed against the literary men of Goethe and Schiller's day; given both in German and English and grouped under subjects. Preceded by a history of the Xenions.

HANSSON, OLA. Young Ofeg's ditties : sketches and meditations from the Swedish by George Egerton ; with title-page and cover by Aubrey Beardsley. Roberts Bros. 16°, $1.25.

KIRKLAND, CAROLINE H. Bryant. Putnam. 16°, (Little journeys to the homes of American authors, v. 2, no. 2.) pap., 5 c.

LABOUCHERE, NORNA. Ladies' book-plates: an illustrated handbook for collectors and booklovers. Macmillan. 12°, (Ex-libris ser.) *net*, $3.

MOULTON, R. GREEN. The literary study of the Bible: an account of the leading forms of literature represented in the sacred writings; intended for English readers. Heath. 12°, $2.
This book deals with the Bible as literature, without reference to theological or distinctively religious matters, or to the historical analysis which has come to be known as "the higher criticism." *Contents:* Introduction—The Book of Job and the various kinds of literary interest represented by it: bk. 1, Literary classification applied to the sacred literature ; bk. 2, Lyric poetry of the Bible ; bk. 3. Biblical history and epic ; bk. 4, The philosophy of the Bible, or wisdom literature ; bk. 5, Biblical literature of prophecy; bk. 6, Biblical literature of rhetoric. Appendices : 1, Literary index to the Bible ; 2, Tables of literary form ; 3. On the structural printing of scripture ; 4, Use of the digression in "Wisdom."

MOULTON, R. GREEN, *ed.* The modern reader's Bible : a series of works from the sacred scriptures in modern literary form. V. 2, Ecclesiasticus ; ed. with introd. and notes. Macmillan. 24°, (Wisdom ser.) 50 c.

NICOLL, W. ROBERTSON, *ed.* Literary anecdotes of the nineteenth century, v. 1. Dodd, Mead & Co. 8°, *net*, $8.

PAGET, VIOLET, ["Vernon Lee," *pseud.*] Renaissance fancies and studies : being a sequel to "Euphorion." Putnam. 12°, $1.25.
Essays: The love of the saints; The imaginative art of the Renaissance ; Tuscan sculpture ; A seeker of pagan perfection, being the life of Domenico Neroni, pictor sacrilegus.

RAYNOR, CECIL, *comp.* The spinster's scrip. Macmillan & Co. nar. 16°, $1.

SAINTSBURY, G. A history of nineteenth century literature, 1780–1895. Macmillan & Co. 12°, $1.50.

MENTAL.

REGENERATION : a reply to Max Nordau ; with introd. by N. Murray Butler. Putnam. 8°, $2.
A vigorous analysis of the morbid pessimism of Nordau's "Degeneration." The author, who prefers to remain anonymous, presents a calm and wholesome view of the actual status of modern civilization, and while frankly admitting the serious evils and difficulties, emphasizes the considerations which make for progress and for hopefulness.

SULLY, JA. Studies of childhood. N. Y., Appleton. 12°, $2.50.
Studies dealing with certain aspects of children's minds which happened to have come under the author's notice and to have had a special interest for him. Their subjects are : The age of imagination ; The dawn of reason ; Products of child-thought ; The little linguist ; Subject to fear ; Raw material of morality ; Under law ; The child as artist ; The young draughtsman ; Extracts from a father's diary ; George Sand's childhood. Bibliography (3 p.). Index.

WOOD, H. Studies in the thought world ; or, practical mind art. Lee & Shepard. 12°, $1.25.
Twenty-two lectures and essays, by the author of "The political economy of natural law." Some of the subjects are as follows : Ownership through idealism ; The evolutionary climb of man ; A great art museum ; The vital energy and its increase ; A corrected standpoint in psychical research ; Our relations to environment ; Divinity and humanity ; The education of thought ; The psychology of crime, etc.

NATURE AND SCIENCE.

CHAMBERS, G. F. The story of the solar system, simply told for general readers. Appleton. il. 16°, (Library of useful stories.) 40 c.
As this little volume is intended for general readers, rather than for educational or technical purposes, statistical details and numerical expressions have been kept within very narrow limits.

COPE, E. D. The primary factors of organic evolution. The Open Court Pub. Co. 12°, $2.
Prof. Cope calls this "an attempt to select

from the mass of facts accumulated by biologists those which, in the author's opinion, throw a clear light on the problem of organic evolution, and especially that of the animal kingdom." As the actual lines of descent can be finally demonstrated chiefly from paleontologic research, he has drawn from this source a large part of his evidence. Contains a list of papers by American authors who have contributed to the evidence used in this book.

MAREY, ETIENNE JULES. Movement; tr. by Eric Pritchard. Appleton. il. 12°, (International scientific ser., no. 73.) $1.75.

POETRY.

BLOEDE, GERTRUDE, ["Stuart Sterne," pseud.] Angelo: a poem. New ed. Houghton, Mifflin & Co. 18°, $1.

DALMON, C. W. Song favours. Imported by Way & Williams. 16°, $1.25.

DANTE ALIGHIERI. The divine comedy; the Inferno; or, Hell: a version in the nine-line metre of Spenser by G. Musgrave. Macmillan. 12°, $1.50.

DAVIDSON, J. Fleet Street eclogues. Dodd, Mead & Co. 16°, $1.25.
By the author of "Sentences and paragraphs." The American edition contains the first as well as the second series of "Fleet Street eclogues," giving the poems their proper sequence.

DONNELLY, ELEANOR CECILIA. Tuscan Magdalen, and other legends and poems. H. L. Kilner & Co. 8°, net, 75 c.; gilt edges, net, $1.25.
Miss Donnelly is a Philadelphia authoress, who has produced many volumes of poems and prose, often exhibiting a sentiment quite devout; the present volume contains some of her best efforts; the legends are picturesque and refined, and tell a story directly and gracefully.

HILLIS, W. J. A metrical history of the life and times of Napoleon Bonaparte. Putnam's Sons. pors. 8°, $5.
A collection of poems and songs, many from obscure and anonymous sources, selected and arranged with introductory notes and connecting narrative, forming a consecutive history of Napoleon Bonaparte.

McGAFFEY, ERNEST. Poems. Dodd, Mead & Co. 16°, $1.25.
Classified as: Songs and lyrics; Outdoors; Warp and woof; Foam-wraiths and driftwood; My chapter; In the sunset lands.

ROSSETTI, CHRISTINA. New poems, hitherto unpublished or uncollected; ed. by W. Michael Rossetti; with por. from a pencil drawing by Dante Gabriel Rossetti. Macmillan. 12°, $1.75; large-pap. ed., net, $3.50.

ROSSETTI, DANTE GABRIEL. Hand and soul. Way & Williams. 12°, $3.50.

POLITICAL AND SOCIAL.

BENEDETTI, VINCENT DE (Count.) Studies in diplomacy; from the French. Macmillan. por. 8°, $3.

BISMARCK-SCHÖNHAUSEN, C. E. LEOP. O., Prince v. Bismarck's table-talk; ed. with an introd. and notes by C. Lowe. Lippincott Co. por. 12°, $.
Based on Herr von Poschinger's Fürst Bis-

marck, und die Parlamentarier and Fürst Bismarck, Neue Tischgespräche und Interviews, bulky works recently published and carefully compiled from a variety of sources and private communications, etc., presenting the great German Chancellor in his most human and interesting light, in familiar intercourse with his friends, to whom he unbosoms himself on men and things in general.

CHAMBERS, H. E. Constitutional history of Hawaii. The Johns Hopkins Press. 8°, (Johns Hopkins University studies, 14th ser., no. 1.) pap., 25 c.
Opens with a sketch of the position and importance of the Hawaiian Islands, their discovery and early history, and goes on to consider the following points: The establishment of governmental unity; The arrival of the missionaries; The first Hawaiian constitution; The organic acts of 1845; The constitution of 1852; The constitution of 1864; The revolution of 1887; The constitution of 1887; The revolution of 1893; The republic of Hawaii.

DEL MAR, ALEX. History of monetary systems: record of actual experiments made by various states of the ancient and modern world, as drawn from their statutes, customs, treaties, mining regulations, jurisprudence, history, archæology, coins, and other sources of information. Brentano's. 8°, $5.

FERRI, ENRICO. Criminal sociology. Appleton. 12°, (Criminology ser., no. 2.) $1.50.
The first chapter, on "The data of criminal anthropology," is an inquiry into the individual conditions which tend to produce criminal habits of mind and action. The second chapter, on "The data of criminal statistics," is an examination of the adverse social conditions which tend to drive certain sections of the population into crime. The last chapter, on "Practical reforms," is intended to show how criminal law and prison administration may be made more effective for purposes of social defence.

HOBSON, J. A., ed. Co-operative labour upon the land, and other papers. Imported by Scribner. 12°, $1.

HOWARD, M. W. The American plutocracy. il. by A. A. Cobb. Holland Pub. Co. 12°, (Holland lib. no. 4.) $1; pap., 50 c.

KEASBEY, LINDLEY M. The Nicaragua Canal and the Monroe doctrine. American Acad. of Political and Social Science. 8°, (Publications of the society, no. 164.) pap., 50 c.

MERRITT, FRANKLIN T., comp. Merritt's ready reference encyclopædia. The Schuldt-Gathmann Co. 24°, 25 c.; 50 c.; flex. leath., 75 c.
Covering in alphabetical order over fifteen thousand subjects, including law, business, mechanics, geography, biography, history, medicine, chemistry, zoölogy, botany, etc. Compiled from the latest statistics and researches with regard to modern requirements.

MILLER, J. W. The advantages of the Nicaragua route. American Acad. of Political and Social Science. 8°, (Publications of the society, no. 165.) pap., 15 c.

MINOT, ROB. S. Our money. Damrell & Upham. 8°, pap., 10 c.
"The purpose of this article is to apply the theory of monometallism rigidly, but simply,

briefly, and practically, to the actual condition of our ' money,' so-called."—*Preface.*

PATTEN, SIMON N. The theory of social forces. American Acad. of Political and Social Science. 8°, (Publications of the society, no. 163.) pap., $1.

SPORTS AND AMUSEMENTS.

GROVE, *Mrs.* LILY, [*and others.*] Dancing, with musical examples ; il. by Percy Macquoid. Little, Brown & Co. pl. 12°, (Badminton lib.) $3.50.

ROOSEVELT, THEODORE, *and* GRINNELL, G. BIRD, *eds.* Hunting in many lands : the book of the Boone and Crockett Club. [V. 2.] Forest and Stream Pub. Co. il. 8°, $2.50.
The first volume published by the Boone and Crockett Club, under the title " American big-game hunting," confined itself, as its title implied, to sport on this continent. In the second volume a number of sketches are included written by members who have hunted big game in other lands, such as China, Tibet, Africa, etc.

WHITE, MARY. The book of a hundred games. Scribner. 12°, $1.

THEOLOGY, RELIGION, AND SPECULATION.

COYLE, J. PATTERSON, *D.D.* The spirit in literature and life : the E. D. Rand lectures in Iowa College for the year 1894. Houghton, Mifflin & Co. 12°, $1.50.

KINSLEY, W. W. Old faiths and new facts. Appleton. 12°, $1.50.
The author of " Views on vexed questions" discusses the efficacy of prayer, the divinity of Jesus Christ, and man's immortality from an orthodox Christian standpoint that is intelligent, helpful, and cognizant of the facts revealed by modern scientific research, in three papers entitled : Science and prayer; Science and Christ; Science and the life beyond.

LAWRENCE, W. Visions and service : fourteen discourses delivered in college chapels. Houghton, Mifflin & Co. 12°, $1.25.

MOXOM, *Rev.* PHILIP STAFFORD. The religion of hope. Roberts. 12°, $1.25.
Seventeen sermons selected from those given by the author during his eight and a half years of labor in a Boston pulpit. He has written " The aim of life," " From Jerusalem to Nicæa," etc.

RANDOLPH, B. W. The law of Sinai: being devotional addresses on the Ten Commandments. Longmans, Green & Co. 12°, $1.25.

RENAN, ERNEST. Life of Jesus ; tr. newly rev. from the 23d and final ed. Roberts Bros. 8°, $2.50.
"In this revised version the two best-known English translations have been freely used, while nearly every sentence has been recast, and the whole has been scrupulously weighed, phrase by phrase, with the original. The scripture references have been made more precise, and some of them corrected ; attention has been called to several points of recent criticism which appear to qualify the author's judgment; and additions have been made here and there, in footnotes, as seemed to be required."—*Editor's note.* An index has been added.

WATSON, *Rev.* J. MACLAREN, [" Ian Maclaren," *pseud.*] The upper room. Dodd, Mead & Co. nar. 12°, (Little books on religion, ed. by W. Robertson Nicoll.) flex. cl., *net,* 50 c.
Seven religious papers: The goodman of the house ; The guest-chamber of the soul ; The twelve ; The shadow of the cross ; A lost wish ; The bequest of Jesus ; The Lord's tryste.

Books for the Young.

AGUILAR, GRACE. The days of Bruce: a story from Scottish history. Warne. 12°, $1.50.

BARTLETT, *Mrs.* E. B. Pleasant days at Maplewood ; il. by Florence E. Little. J. Ireland. 12°, $1.50.

READ, *Mrs.* R. H. Dora, a girl without a home. C. Scribner's Sons. 12°, $1.25.

RECENT FRENCH AND GERMAN BOOKS.

FRENCH.

Beaume, G. Les Vendanges. 12°. Plon........ $1 00
Bonnefont, G. Nos belles mondaines : Liane de Pougy. Ill. 8°. Flammarion.................... 1 00
Cadol, E. Madeleine Houlard. 12°. Ollendorff.. 1 00
Daudet, E. Drapeaux ennemis. 12°. Plon...... 1 00
Davont, Maréchal. Operations du 3e Corps, 1806-7. 8°. Levy.. 2 25
Delard, Eug. Bélicerté. 12°. Levy............. 1 00
Dictionnaire de la danse. Cloth, 12°. Quantin.. 1 65
Ennery, A. d'. Markariantz. 12°. Ollendorff.. 1 00
Floran, Mary. La faim et la soif. 12°. Levy... 1 00
Gautbies. L'Italie du 16e siècle L'Aretin. 12°. Hachette... 1 00
Goudeau, E. Chansons de Paris et d'ailleurs. 12°. Charpentier............... .... 1 00
Gyp. Le bonheur de Ginette. 12°. Levy......... 1 00
Laurent, E. Sensations d'Orient. 12°. Flammarion.. .... 1 00
Le Roux, Hughes. O mon passé. 12°. Levy... 1 00
Lescot, Mde. Un peu, beaucoup, passionément. Cloth, 12°. Hachette............................ 1 50
Mael, I. Erreur d'amour. 12°. Ollendorff...... 1 00

Marx, A. Rives benies. De Marseille à Naples. 12°. Quantin $1 00
Napoleon. D'Après les peintres, les sculpteurs, et les graveurs. Album in 4° oblong. Hachette. 3 00
O'Monroy, R. Les propos de Mme. Manchaballe. 12°. Levy 1 00
Queyssie, Eug. de la. Acte de foi. 12°. Plon.. 1 00
Reibrach, J. Par l'amour. 12°. Ollendorff..... 1 00
Rod, Ed. Dernier refuge. 12°. Perrin.......... 1 00
Sales, P. Miracle d'amour. 12°. Flammarion... 1 00
Scholl, A. Tableaux vivantes. 12°. Charpentier. 1 00
Spuller, E. Hommes et choses de la Révolution. 12°. Alcan.. 1 00
Theuriet, A. Années de printemps. 12°. Ollendorff 60

GERMAN.

Friedmann. Der Hemmschuh. 8°. Schottlaender......... .... 1 35
Neumann, K. E. Die Reden Gotamo Buddho's. 1. Lief. (To be issued in 5 Lief.) 8°. Friedrich. 2 00
Schubin, O. " Con fiocchi." 12°. Minden...... 1 20
Torresani, Carl Baron. Aus drei Weltstädten. 12°. Pierson...................................... 1 70

MAGAZINE ARTICLES FOR MARCH.

Articles marked with an asterisk are illustrated.

ARTISTIC, MUSICAL, AND DRAMATIC.—*Century*, J. G. Vibert's Paintings* ; The Century's Printer on the Century's Type, De Vinne (Open Letters).— *Fort. Review* (Feb.), George Henry Lewes and the Stage, Archer. — *Lippincott's*, The Tall Office Building Artistically Considered, L. H. Sullivan.—*Scribner's*, Miss Mary Cassatt,* Walton; French Binders of To-Day,* Prideaux ; High Buildings ; The Pennsylvania Academy's Exhibition ; Gustave Flaubert ; John P. Davis (Field of Art); Photograph in History (Point of View).

BIOGRAPHY, CORRESPONDENCE, ETC.—*Catholic World*, Life of Cardinal Manning, Hewitt. — *Century*, John Randolph of Roanoke, Bouldin; The Elder Dumas,* Emily Crawford.—*Fort. Review* (Feb.), Barthelemy St. Hilaire, Marie Belloc-Lowndes.—*Harper's*, Colonel Washington,* Wilson.—*Nine. Century* (Feb.), Life of Cardinal Manning, Vaughan; Meynell.

DESCRIPTION, TRAVEL. — *Arena*, Mexico in Midwinter,* Clark.—*Atlantic*, A Holy Island (Lindisfarne) Pilgrimage, Eugenia Skelding ; French Roads, Mary H. Catherwood.—*Catholic World*, Boston Half a Century Ago,* Edselas ; An Impression of Holland,* Kennedy. — *Century*, A Personally Conducted Arrest in Constantinople,* Hopkinson-Smith.—*Forum*, Manners and Customs of the Boers, White.—*Outing*, The Balearics ;* Across the Mesaba.*—*Scribner's*, Florentine Villas,* Lee Bacon.

DOMESTIC AND SOCIAL. — *Forum*, Family Life in America, Th. Bentzon.

EDUCATION, LANGUAGE. — *Arena*, Educational Crisis in Chicago, Washburne.—*Century*, The Perils of Small Talk, Hamilton ; College Women and Matrimony, Frances M. Abbott (Open Letters). — *Forum*, The Best Thing College Does for Man, Thwing : The Manitoba Schools Question, Goldwin Smith.

FICTION. — *Atlantic*, A Public Confession, Ellen Mackubin.—*Century*, A Winter House-Party, Mrs. Burton Harrison ; Enter the Earl of Tyne, Fernald.—*Chautauquan*, A Romance of the Stars, Mary Proctor.—*Harper's*, Where Fancy was Bred, Owen Wister ; Jane Hubb's Salvation, Helen Huntington ; The Boss of Ling-Foo,* Julian Ralph.—*Lippincott's*, A Whim and a Chance, Nichols. — *Scribner's*, The Lost Child,* Bunner ; A Chameleon, Vachell.

HYGIENIC AND SANITARY. — *Arena*, Desirability of Disposing of Infected Bodies by Cremation, Dr. J. Heber Smith.

INDUSTRIAL.—*Harper's*, Arcadian Bee-Ranching,* Ninetta Eames. — *Nine. Century* (Feb.), Dairy Farming, Vernon. — *No. Amer. Review*, Recent Photographic Invention, Wallace.

LITERARY. — *Catholic World*, The New Poet Laureate,* O'Shea. — *Century*, On an Author's Choice of Company, Wilson.—*Fort. Review* (Feb.), Shakespeare, Falstaff, and Queen Elizabeth, Kennedy ; Criticism as Theft, Knight.—*Scribner's*, Matthew Arnold's Letters ; On a Saying of Burns (Point of View).— *West. Review* (Feb.), Thomas Hardy's Latest Novel, Hannigan ; Cataloguing and Empire, Ling Roth ; Enduring Characteristics of Macaulay, Bradfield ; The Voice of Woman, Harvey.

MENTAL AND MORAL.— *Arena*, Maeterlinck and Emerson, Dr. Hamilton Osgood. — *Fort. Review* (Feb.), Reflex Action, Instinct and Reason, Archdall-Reid.

NATURE AND SCIENCE.—*No. Amer. Review*, The Natural History of Warfare, Shaler ; A Guerilla Eden, Oswald ; Chemists as Leaders, Ansten. — *Scribner's*, Carnations,* Connelly.

POETRY AND DRAMA. — *Atlantic*, An Elegy, Louise I. Guiney.—*Catholic World*, Ingratitude, Eleanor C. Donnelly ; To the Sultan, Rooney. —*Century*, Kennst Du ?, Stedman ; Desolate, Minnie Leona Upton. — *Harper's*, The Gospel of the Ground. Cheney ; A Water-Lily, Z. D. Underhill. — *Lippincott's*, The Pilgrims, Scollard. — *Nine. Century* (Feb.), Robert Burns, Swinburne.— *Scribner's*, Sarasate, Van Vorst ; The Spring, Hughes.

POLITICAL AND SOCIAL. — *Arena*, Successful Experiment for the Maintenance of Self-respecting Manhood, Flower ; The Telegraph Monopoly, Parsons; Bishop Doane and Woman Suffrage, Margaret Noble Lee; Wealth Production and Consumption by the Nation, Waldron. —*Catholic World*, The Causes of the Present War in Cuba,* De Zayas.—*Century*, Stamping Out the London Slums,* Marshall; Our Foreign Trade, Newbery ; The Anachronism of War; A New Force in Politics; Plenty of Gold in the World (Topics of the Time).—*Fort. Review* (Feb.), A Lesson in German, "Genosse Aegir" ; The Two Eastern Questions : The Germans in South Africa, Greswell; The Venezuelan Dispute, Thwaite ; England's Policy in Turkey; Armenia, and the Transvaal, MacColl ; The Isolation of England, Dicey.—*Forum*, The Nicaragua Canal an Impracticable Scheme, Nimmo, Jr. ; Some Municipal Problems, Bemis; Cost of an Anglo-American War, Atkinson ; The European Situation, Geffcken. — *Harper's*, The Nerves of a War-Ship, Park Benjamin ; Money Borrowers, Junius Henri Browne.— *Lippincott's*, The Horse or the Motor, McKee. —*Nine. Century*, Facts About the Venezuela Boundary, Bolton ; Relations of France and England, Pressensé; Corn-Stores for War-Times, Marston ; Proposed German Barrier Across Africa, Gregory ; Slavery Under the British Flag, Lugard.—*No. Amer. Review*, Our Foreign Trade and Our Consular Service, Warner; The Excise Question, Warner Miller; Bishop Doane ; Our Defenceless Coasts, Southwick; Free Silver and the Savings Banks; Congress and Its Critics, Hansbrough, Dingley, *and others*; Woman's Wages, Grace Stephens. —*Outing*, The National Guard of Nevada.— *Scribner's*, British Opinion of America, Whiteing.— *West. Review* (Feb.), An American View of the Venezuelan Dispute, Shriver; The Real Interest of the Public in International Affairs, Farquharson ; Divorce and Re-Marriage, Sewell; Bimetallism, Marischal.

SPORTS AND AMUSEMENTS.—*Forum*, Spirit of Racing in America, Speed.—*No. Amer. Review*, Revival of the Olympian Games, Horton.— *Outing*, Cycling in Trinidad*; Russian Bear*; Hunting the Sambur*; Duck-Shooting on the Savannah.*

THEOLOGY, RELIGION, AND SPECULATION.— *Arena*, The Social Value of Individual Failure, Herron.—*Catholic World*, How the Celtic Revival Arose, O'Byrne.— *West. Review* (Feb.), Denominational Education, Herzfeld.

Freshest News.

JOHN OLIVER HOBBES'S new novelette is entitled " The Herb Moon."

W. S. FORTESCUE & Co., Philadelphia, will publish shortly a novel by M. W. Lewis, entitled " The Wife's Vow."

HARPER & BROTHERS will publish shortly Mrs. Mary Anderson de Navarro's reminiscences under the title of " A Few Memoirs."

EDMUND GOSSE is collecting a new volume of his essays, to be entitled " Critical Kit-Cats." The book will be ready this spring.

THIS is a good time to be reading Mr. Frank Vincent's " Actual Africa." Its account of the Transvaal is full and clear, and it will place the reader at the centre of the present difficulty there.

THE Messrs. Crowell announce that they will issue a companion volume to Charles E. L. Wingate's "Shakespeare's Heroines on the Stage." It will be called "Shakespeare's Heroes on the Stage."

SOME of Prof. Richard T. Ely's works on sociological questions have been translated into Japanese. His book, "The Outlines of Economics," has been printed in raised characters for the use of the blind.

HENRY HOLT & Co. announce "Emma Lou, Her Book," edited by Miss Mary M. Mears. It is the diary, during her sixteenth year, of an ingenious Western girl, who by her highly serious and lofty views of life supplies an unconscious element of humor. They will also publish at once "On Parody," an essay on the art by Arthur Shadwell Martin, with numerous selections from its masters, beginning with the Greeks and Romans. Most of the earlier pieces are inaccessible to readers of to-day.

JUSTIN MCCARTHY is at work on a monograph dealing with the present Pope, more than half of which is finished ; and a new novel, and a collection of short stories, both of which may be published before the fall. He has also started writing his own " Reminiscences," which cannot fail to be of wide interest.

SIR JOHN E. MILLAIS, one of the founders and one of the seven members of the Pre-Raphaelite Brotherhood, has been elected to succeed the late Lord Leighton as president of the Royal Academy. It is not generally known that Sir John is the brother of Mrs. Lester Wallack, of New York, the widow of the late famous actor-manager.

THE CASSELL PUBLISHING Co. have just ready a new novel by Frank Frankfort Moore entitled "Phyllis of Philistia "; " Official, Diplomatic, and Social Etiquette of Washington," compiled by Katherine Elwes Thomas, with an introductory note by Mrs. John A. Logan ; and in their *Union Square Library* " Old Maids and Young," by Elsa d'Esterre-Keeling.

IN connection with the coming Burns Centenary, Messrs. J. and M. Tregaskis are issuing for Mr. Herbert Graham a "Centenary Commemoration" statuette in bronze of the poet, by Mr. Paul R. Montford. Copies in terra-cotta can also be obtained at a much cheaper rate. In the meantime the centenary literature grows apace, the latest addition being "Burns at Galston and Ecclefechan," which will be published by Mr. John Muir almost immediately.

MACMILLAN & Co. have in press a volume of essays by W. H. Mallock, in which he discusses the distribution of wealth (controverting the principles laid down by Karl Marx), the minimum of humane living, wages, the products of work, and the census and the people. They will publish in the spring the edition of the works of Bishop Butler, upon which Mr. Gladstone has for some time been engaged.

RALPH B. KENYON, Tribune Building, New York City, has just ready "Mosby's Rangers," a history of the 43d Battalion, Virginia Cavalry (Mosby's Command), from its organization to the surrender, by J. J. Williamson, of Company A. This missing chapter of history is made up from the author's diary, supplemented with official reports of Federal officers, also of Mosby. It contains over 200 illustrations, including portraits of many of Mosby's men.

MR. G. F. SCOTT ELLIOT, whose account of his journey to the Mountains of the Moon and Tanganyika is published under the title of " A Naturalist in Mid-Africa," is likely, says *The Academy*, to raise something of a laugh by his suggestion for a suitable literary addition to the baggage of every well-equipped traveller. This is the list :

Shakespeare, Bible, R. Browning, Kipling, Wolseley (" Soldier's Pocket-book "), " Hints to Travellers," &c.

There is, perhaps, a saving grace in that " &c.," though without leaving any margin for it, the cost of a thorough outfit, we note with some surprise, is as near £100 as possible.

A. D. F. RANDOLPH & Co. will publish immediately a new and cheap edition of Mrs. Prentiss's " Stepping Heavenward," neatly bound, with eight full-page illustrations ; and a new edition in six volumes of her "Susy Books." The first and second volumes of " First Corinthians " will be ready in the *Biblical Illustrator* ; the first volume of " Psalms " will be added to the *Pulpit Commentary*, and " Landmarks of Church History to the Reformation," by Dr. Henry Cowan, will be the new volume in the *Guild Library*. A novel by Katrina Trask, the author of "Under King Constantin," " Sonnets and Lyrics," and other poetical works, is in preparation, to be issued in specially dainty dress under the title " White Satin and Homespun."

FREDERICK WARNE & Co. have nearly ready " The Right Hon. Joseph Chamberlain," by S. H. Jeyes, editor of the *Public Men of To-Day Series;* "Sport in Ashanti, or, Melinda the Caboceer," a tale of the Gold Coast, by J. A. Skertchly; also a story by Fergus Hume, to be entitled " The Carbuncle Club "; " An Original Wager," by " A Vagabond," illustrated by George Michelet, a story of six weeks in France, during wh'ch the hero raced on foot, on bicycle, and on horseback, against the champion lady bicyclist of the world ; and " The Shuttle of Fate," by Mrs. Whitehead, a book full of good sense and bright reading, with illustrations by

94   THE LITERARY NEWS.   [March, 1896

Lancelot Speed, adding interest to this powerful story of the Lancashire cotton-mills ; and the fifth edition of "Electricity Up to Date," by John B. Verity, is now ready.

THE number of books printed in Italy during 1894 was 9416 works, of which 7646 were handled by the book trade. This total shows a falling off of 73 works compared with the output of 1893, and a falling off of 721 works compared with the total issued in 1891, in which year 10,311 works were printed, of which 8327 were handled by the trade. The decrease in 1894 was in history and geography 68 works, in philology and literary history 47 works, in fiction 46 works, and in popular literature 32 works. An increase was shown in the department of medicine 74 works, drama 67 works, political economy 43 works, education 30 works, and military and naval science 29 works. In literary activity the province of Lombardy takes the lead, followed by Piedmont, Tuscany, Venetia, and Latium, in the order named.

CHARLES SCRIBNER'S SONS will publish early in March a volume of "Vailima Table-Talk," by Mrs. Strong and Lloyd Osbourne. Mrs. Strong, it may be remembered, was Mr. Stevenson's amanuensis, and Mr. Osbourne, as is better known, collaborated with him in several of his stories. This "Table-Talk" was taken down while it was fresh in the memory of both, and with the consent of Mr. Stevenson. The Scribners have also nearly ready a volume of short stories by Richard Harding Davis entitled "La Cinderella, and other stories," which will contain five stories, a new Van Bibber story being among the number. They have made arrangements to publish Paul Bourget's "A Tragic Idyll," which was published serially in the New York Herald; Julian Hawthorne's $10,000 Herald prize story, "A Fool of Nature," and Miss Edith Carpenter's Herald prize story, "Your Money or Your Life."

THE PERSONAL LITERATURE OF CAMBRIDGE. —It is gratifying to see, says the N. Y. Tribune, "that what might be called the personal literature of Cambridge in its palmiest days is being written, edited, and put into permanent form. It began with the correspondence of Emerson and Carlyle. Not long ago Mr. Norton gave Lowell's delightful letters to the world. And now in the same week with the publication of Mr. Marcou's life of Agassiz it is announced that there will soon be printed a biography of the Autocrat, in two volumes, with many

letters. Holmes had a humor unlike that of any of his contemporaries, and he never lost it. It irradiates his entire life and work. All those autobiographical revelations which he made in his lifetime carried with them an indescribable beauty of spiritual and intellectual sunshine, and the new books by Mr. John T. Morse, Jr., ought to prove an unqualified pleasure to every reader of Holmes—which is to say to every lover of the man."

HOUGHTON, MIFFLIN & Co. have just ready a work entitled "Moral Evolution," by Prof. George Harris, D.D., of Andover, which is described as "a contribution of positive value to the higher thought and literature"; "The Life of Thomas Hutchinson, last Royal Governor of the Province of Massachusetts Bay," by James K. Hosmer, whose work adds materially to our knowledge of the Revolutionary era; "In New England Fields and Woods," by Rowland E. Robinson, who writes with minute observation, and an interest in nature so deep as to be truly affectionate ; a new Birthday edition, from new plates, of Oliver Wendell Holmes's "Over the Teacups"; also new editions of Harriet Beecher Stowe's "Pink and White Tyranny," and of Julia A. Shedd's "Famous Painters and Paintings" and "Famous Sculptors and Sculpture." The two latter have been considerably enlarged and are published at a reduced price. Houghton, Mifflin & Co. are also to be the American publishers of the long-desired and "definitive" edition of Burns, edited by William Ernest Henley and T. F. Henderson. The work will be in four octavo volumes.

MR. WATSON'S SONNET TO AMERICA.

O TOWERING daughter, Titan of the West,
  Behind a thousand leagues of foam secure,
  Thou toward whom our inmost heart is pure
Of all intent, although thou threatenest
With most unfilial hand thy mother's breast,
  Not for one breathing space may earth endure
  The thought of war's intolerable cure
For such vague pains as vex to day thy rest.
But if thou hast more strength than thou canst spend
  In tasks of Peace, and find'st her yoke too tame,
Help us to smite the cruel, and befriend
  The succorless, and put the false to shame :
  So shall the ages laud thee, and thy name
Be lovely among nations to the end.
—*The Dial.*

MOSBY'S RANGERS:

A History of the Forty-third Battalion Virginia Cavalry (Mosby's Command), from Its Organization to the Surrender. By J. J. WILLIAMSON, of Company A. 8vo, cloth, about 500 pp., illustrated, $3.50.

THE MISSING CHAPTER OF WAR HISTORY.

From the author's diary, supplemented with official reports of Federal officers, also of Mosby. Contains over 200 illustrations, including portraits of many of

"**MOSBY'S MEN,**"

and of Federal officers with whom they came in contact, views, engagements, etc., also maps of "Mosby's Confederacy" and of localities in which he operated ; accounts of skirmishes, dashing raids, and daring adventures.

Specimen pages, with table of contents, list of illustrations, etc., free.

RALPH B. KENYON, Publisher, Tribune Building, NEW YORK.

Roberts' New Books.

JUST OUT.

BALZAC IN ENGLISH.

THE GALLERY OF ANTIQUITIES.

By HONORE DE BALZAC.   12mo, half russia, $1.50.

NOBODY'S FAULT.

By NETTA LYRETT.   (Keynote Series.)   16mo, cloth, $1.00.

SIX MODERN WOMEN.

Psychological Sketches. By LAURA MARHOLM HANSSON. Translated from the German by Hermione Ramsden. 12mo, cloth, $1.25. Contents:

    I.   THE LEARNED WOMAN: SONIA KOVALEVSKY.
   II.   NEUROTIC KEYNOTES: GEORGE EGERTON.
  III.   THE MODERN WOMAN ON THE STAGE: ELEONORA DUSE.
  IV.   THE WOMAN NATURALIST: AMALIE SKRAM.
   V.   A YOUNG GIRL'S TRAGEDY: MARIE BASHKIRTSEFF.
  VI.   THE WOMAN'S RIGHTS WOMAN: A. CH. EDGREN-LEFFLER.

"There are some hidden peculiarities in woman's soul which I have traced in the lives of these six representative women, and I have written them down for the benefit of those who have not had the opportunity of discovering them for themselves.

"There is only one point which I should like to emphasize in these six types of modern womanhood, and that is the manifestation of their womanly feelings. I want to show how it asserts itself in spite of everything—in spite of the theories on which they build up their lives, in spite of the opinions of which they were the teachers, and in spite of the success which crowned their efforts, and bound them by stronger chains than might have been the case had their lives been passed in obscurity."—*From the Preface.*

RECENTLY PUBLISHED.

LIFE OF JESUS.

By ERNEST RENAN, author of "History of the People of Israel," "The Future of Science." Translation newly revised from the twenty-third and final edition. 8vo, cloth, $2.50.

DANTE GABRIEL ROSSETTI.

His Family Letters. With a Memoir by WILLIAM MICHAEL ROSSETTI. Portraits. 2 vols., 8vo, cloth, $6.50.

    Vol. I. Memoirs.
    Vol. II. Family Letters.

With Introductory Notes by W. M. Rossetti. With ten portraits by D. G. Rossetti of himself and other members of the family, including his father, mother, wife, brother and sister, uncle and aunt.

The memoir is of very substantial length, and readers will find in it a great deal of new matter, much of which could only be supplied by his brother.

THE ENTAIL;
or, The Lairds of Grippy.

By JOHN GALT, author of the "Annals of the Parish," "Sir Andrew Wylie," "The Provost," etc. 2 vols , 16mo, cloth, gilt, $2.50.

CAVALRY IN THE WATERLOO CAMPAIGN.

By Lieut.-General Sir EVELYN WOOD, V.C., etc. Forming the third volume in the "Pall Mall Magazine Library." With portraits, maps, and plans. 12mo, cloth, $1.25.

THE RELIGION OF HOPE.

By PHILIP S. MOXOM, author of "The Aim of Life," "From Jerusalem to Nicæa." 16mo, cloth, $1.25.

FOR SALE BY ALL BOOKSELLERS.

ROBERTS BROTHERS, Publishers, Boston.

LITERARY NEWS

AN ECLECTIC REVIEW OF
CURRENT LITERATURE
~ILLUSTRATED~

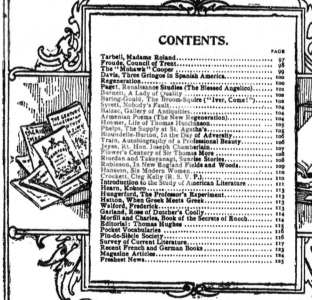

CONTENTS.

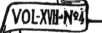

VOL. XVII-Nº 4   APRIL ~ 1896 $1.00 YEARLY
10 CTS. PER NO.

~PUBLICATION OFFICE~
59 DUANE STREET, NEW YORK
ENTERED AT THE POST OFFICE AT NEW YORK AS SECOND CLASS MATTER

The Litera  News

In winter you may reade them, ad ignem, by the fireside; and in summer, ad umbram, under some shadie tree, and therewith pass away the tedious howres.

| Vol. XVII. | APRIL, 1896. | No. 4. |

Madame Roland.

Some eight years ago Miss Tarbell undertook a study of the women of the French Revo-

MADAME ROLAND. [By Jules Goupil.]

lution, her object being merely to satisfy herself as to the value of their public services in that period. In the course of her studies Miss Tarbell became particularly interested in Madame Roland, and when five years ago she found herself in Paris for an extended period, she decided to use her leisure in making a more careful investigation of Madame Roland's life and times than she had been able to do in America. The result of that study is condensed in this volume.

Much of the material used in the book Miss

Tarbell has obtained from the descendants of Madame Roland, now living in Paris. Her relations with them came about through that distinguished scholar and gentleman, the late James Darmesteter. In May, 1892, she spent a fortnight at Le Clos, the family home of the Rolands, where Madame Roland passed her happiest, most natural years. The old place is ripe with memories of its former mistress, and it was there and afterwards in Villefranche that Miss Tarbell found material for chapters 4 and 5, which are of special interest. Miss Tarbell writes with enthusiasm and gives a vivid picture of those troubled days in French history. The publishers have supplied the book with illustrations of great interest. (Scribner. $1.50.)

For Plain Women Only.

GEORGE FLEMING's dialogues between an aunt and a nephew—"For Plain Women Only"—have already appeared in the *Pall Mall Gazette;* but they were certainly worth reprinting in the present form. The two talkers are amusingly sketched by their conversation, and the aunt, who is rather like a wicked old French *marquise,* is especially charming, while the jerky and allusive style of rejoinder and repartee must be more comprehensive here than in the weekly instalments. The object of the book is most excellent, and has a moral which might well be studied in England; it is a reminder to plain women that their want of attraction depends largely on themselves, and that if only women would devote some intelligent study to the dress and fashion which become them, they might make the world look less ugly than they do, and largely enhance their own personal sphere of attraction and influence. George Fleming, in the course of her moralizings, involves in well-merited condemnation such abominations as tailor-made dresses and unmeaning ruffles and decorations of the person, and pleads for the same uniformity in tone in a dress as we expect in a tasteful room. (The Merriam Co. $1.25.)—*The Athenæum.*

The Council of Trent.

To read history is one thing; to make history is another. The history reader is more or less accurately informed beforehand as to the outcome of events. With an air of superior wisdom he can criticise his betters who have long passed away. He can wonder why they took one course of action when an opposite or, at least, a different course was so obvious. But the maker of history always works in the dark. He does not know what the outcome of his acts or the acts of others will be. His conduct is guided by circumstances, and it is only when he can look back over his life that he sees how it all came about. This difference between history read and history in the making is the text of these lectures of Froude on the Council of Trent.

He endeavored to put his hearers in a position where they could sympathize with the hopes, the fears, and the uncertainties of the men who shared and the men who opposed the Reformation, and also of the men, still more harassed, who tried to keep the peace of Europe. The task he set for himself was not an easy one. He was an eager partisan of the Reformation, particularly in the form that it took in England under Henry VIII., and sometimes he praised in the reformers what he condemned in the adherents of the ancient Church. The idea seems to be advanced that when Luther and his associates went in for minute hair-splitting about doctrines they were forced to do this by the dogmatism of their adversaries, while the eagerness of the bishops and others in the Council of Trent to plunge into the mysteries was only a political dodge to evade awkward questions about the immoralities of churchmen.

It is not necessary to follow Froude in the brief study that he makes of Luther's origin, of his visit to Rome, and of the question of indulgences. He adds nothing to what is already known. But he lays emphasis on two points. In the first place, Luther, of his own wish, would never have gone beyond the question of indulgences. In the second place, the Reformation, as it began, "was not a question of faith. It was a question whether the Pope by his own arbitrary will was to impose his own pleasure upon Christendom." It was more than this. It involved—and nobody was more astounded than Luther himself to find this out —the whole question of the relations between the plain people and their superiors, both lay and clerical. Froude makes out a good case against the clergy.

It was out of all these diverse movements that the Council of Trent grew into a reality. It was the distrust which the diversity created that made the Council a failure. Nobody was satisfied. The reformers were opposed to the whole machinery of the Church. The bishops were eager to recover the powers which the Papacy had wrested from them. Statesmen wished to encourage the growth of national feeling. Men like Erasmus vainly hoped for peace. Pope succeeded Pope, and yet the Roman court remained untouched. Rome was sacked by German Lutherans and Spanish Catholics; both factions pleased to carry ruin into the hated city, and to treat the princes of the Church with ribald contempt. Only one man in Europe really felt that a council could be of any use. But that one was the Emperor Charles V. If he could have had such a council as he desired, in which laymen should be present as well as bishops, with free discussion of all the abuses in the Church, he might have prevented schism. At least he imagined so.

This forgetfulness on the part of modern historians is one of the things of which Froude complains. He quotes some as saying that "the Reformation settled nothing." On the contrary, in his opinion, it settled everything that could be settled. "Everywhere in Catholic countries, as in Protestant, the practices have been abandoned which the laity then rose to protest against. Popes no longer depose princes, dispense with oaths, or absolve subjects from their allegiance. Appeals are not any more carried to Rome from the national tribunals, nor justice sold there to the highest bidder. The clergy have ceased to pass laws which bind the laity and to enforce them with spiritual censures. Felonious priests suffer for their crimes like unconsecrated mortals. Too zealous prelates cannot call poor creatures before them ex-officio, cross-question them on their beliefs, fine, imprison, or burn them at the stake. Excommunications are kept in bounds by the law of libel. Itinerant pardon-vendors no longer hawk through Europe their unprofitable wares. Cardinals cannot now add see to see that they may have princes' revenues, or private clergy buy benefices as they would buy farms, and buy along with them dispensations to neglect their duties." Above all, he adds, the world has learned that "men can disagree in religion without wishing to destroy each other." (Scribner. $2.)—*N. Y. Tribune.*

From "The Spy."

G. P. Putnam's Sons.

THE VIRGINIANS SWEPT ACROSS THE PLAIN.

The "Mohawk" Cooper.

THE Messrs. Putnam's uniform *Mohawk edition* of the works of James Fenimore Cooper is sure of a welcome. It is generously conceived, the typography is bold, clear, and elegant, and the several works comprised in the thirty-two large 12mo volumes are to be had separately at a very reasonable price. There is no editorial apparatus. If we may judge from "The Spy," which leads off, there will be a frontispiece illustration in each volume, and a vignette upon the rubricated title-page. The binding is in a tasteful red cloth, and the new series is designed to range on the shelf beside the *Hudson edition* of Irving. (Putnam. 32 v., *ea.* $1.25.)—*The Nation.*

Three Gringos in Spanish America.

So much interest is felt just now in the relations between the United States and the Central and South American republics, that the newly published volume by Richard Harding Davis, called "Three Gringos in Venezuela and Central America," has a timeliness which will undoubtedly tend to enhance its importance in the eyes of American readers. The three gringos were Mr. Davis, H. S. Somerset, son of Lady Henry Somerset, and Lloyd Griscom, who later became *attaché* of the American embassy in London. They landed at Belize in British Honduras, travelled t h e n c e along the coast to Porto Cortez in Honduras proper, made the journey on horseback across the mountains to Amapala on the Pacific coast, visited Corinto and made a s o m e w h a t extended excursion into Nicaragua, then went along the coast to Panama, crossed the Isthmus, and voyaged

From "Three Gringos in Venezuela and Central America."—Copyright, 1896, by Harper & Brothers.

SIMON BOLIVAR.

thence to Caracas, which city the three travellers unhesitatingly agreed to be quite worthy of the title of "The Paris of South America." The journey throughout abounded in incident and was not lacking in experiences that demanded a degree of endurance bordering on heroism, and Mr. Davis unfolds the narrative in his well-known style of straightforward and unaffected ease. The travellers had interviews with a number of the leading men of the countries they visited, and of each of these notabilities Mr. Davis gives a vivid and suggestive portrait. The account he gives of President Crespo, of Venezuela, is highly favorable to the character of that liberal-minded ruler, although it is said of him that he is "more at home when fighting in the field than in the council-chamber." Mr. Davis naturally touches upon the controversy concerning the Venezuela boundary, and he is so kind as to inform his readers that, personally, he is not in favor of intruding the Monroe doctrine in the matter at all. The book is profusely and handsomely illustrated, and is sure to have a very wide reading. (Harper. $1.50.)—*The Beacon.*

Regeneration.

IN its issue of the 6th of April, 1895, the *Literary World* said of Max Nordau's "Degeneration" :

"It is in the main a most salutary indictment which he brings against the corrupting tendencies of contemporary literature, and what he says deserves the careful consideration of Wagner, Tolstoï, Ibsen, Whitman, Zola, and lesser teachers of degeneracy."

After r e a d i n g "Regeneration," the reply to "Degeneration," we see no reason seriously to modify the above opinion.

"Regeneration" is an anonymous work, presented to American readers with the benefit of an introduction by Professor Butler, of Columbia College. It bears every internal evidence of being the work of an Englishman, of one who has no love for Germany or the Germans, and yet of one who is well acquainted w i t h Continental lines of thought and well read in Continental literature. He has written what is in many ways an intelligent, thoughtful, earnest, spirited, and vigorous criticism of Max Nordau's book, which assaults it severely, but does not do it serious damage. It is the writing of a man of considerable ability, who has read Nordau with care, and who is on a level with him intellectually, though not in scientific knowledge and precision, and whose failure to carry his case, if he fails, is due not to the poor quality of his weapons or his clumsiness in the use of them, but to the invulnerability of his antagonist.

Without in the least abating the qualifications attached to our last year's judgment of "Degeneration," we think the verdict of those best fitted to pronounce one will be that the author of "Regeneration" has made a bold and powerful attack, and been repulsed.

The book is in twelve chapters, which take up Nordau's positions one by one. The first chapter is a personal one upon Nordau himself —accuses him of being a German, and argues the impossibility of a German doing justice to the art and literature of his time. The second chapter is a defence of modern society, and chapter third a similar defence of modern art. The fourth chapter claims the bankruptcy of science in its account with religion as embodied in the church. The next four chapters are apologetic in turn for the French poets, for Tolstoï, for Ibsen, and for Wagner, whose respective virtues, merits, and various good traits, personal and professional, are sounded with a good deal of ingenuity and force. The remainder of the book goes to show the impracticability of anything like a public censorship of art and letters, and loudly voices the prerogative of England to lead and save the world.

There will be curiosity to know who the author of "Regeneration" is, for he is a critic not to be despised, and we should not be at all surprised if, when disclosure came, it should reveal some person well known in the controversial world. He is a virile writer, whoever he is, accustomed to call a spade a spade. Our guess is that the author of "Regeneration" is not a member of the company of those who use that word of high meanings in its traditional sense, but rather that he is one of the Philistines. We shall see. (Putnam. $2.)—*Literary World.*

The Blessed Angelico.

LEST some one take Puritanic umbrage at my remarks on early Italian art, and deprecate the notion that religious painters could be so very human, I shall say a few parting words about the religious painter, the saint *par excellence*, I mean the Blessed Angelico. Heaven forbid I should attempt to turn him into a brother Lippo, of the Landor or Browning pattern! He was very far indeed, let alone from profanity, even from such flesh and blood feeling as that of Jacopone and scores of other blessed ones. He was, emotionally, rather bloodless; and whatsoever energy he had probably went in tussles with the technical problems of the day, of which he knew much more, for all his cloistered look, than I suspected when I wrote of him before. Angelico, to return to the question, was not a St. Francis, a Fra Jacopone. But even Angelico had his passionately human side, though it was only the humanness of a nice child. In a life of hard study, and perhaps hard penance, that childish blessed one nourished childish desires—desires for green grass and flowers, for gay clothes,* for prettily dressed pink and lilac playfellows, for the kissing and hugging in which he had no share, for the games of the children outside the convent gate. How human, how ineffably full of a good child's longing, is not his vision of Paradise! The gayly-dressed angels are leading the little cowled monks—little baby black and white things, with pink faces like sugar lambs and Easter rabbits—into deep, deep grass quite full of flowers, the sort of grass every child on

*Mme Darmesteter's charming essays, "The End of the Middle Ages," contain some amusing instances of such repressed love of finery on the part of saints. Compare Fioretti xx., "And these garments of such fair cloth, which we wear (in Heaven) are given us by God in exchange for our rough frocks."

From "Three Gringos in Venezuela and Central America."　　　Copyright, 1896, by Harper & Brothers.

THE CUYUNI RIVER.

this wicked earth has been cruelly forbidden to wade in ! They fall into those angels' arms, hugging them with the fervor of children in the act of *loving* a cat or a dog. They join hands with those angels, outside the radiant pink and blue toy-box towers of the celestial Jerusalem, and go singing " Round the Mulberry Bush" much more like the babies in Kate Greenaway's books than like the Fathers of the Church in Dante. The joys of Paradise, for this dear man of God, are not confined to sitting *ad dexteram domini.* (Putnam. $1.25.)— *From Vernon Lee's " Renaissance Fancies and Studies."*

A Lady of Quality.

THE professional reviewer of works of fiction in these days rarely has opportunities for the exercise of his powers of judgment and the display of his literary equipment so alluring and invigorating as those enjoyed by his predecessors in the middle years of this century, when a new novel by Mr. Dickens or Mr. Thackeray, by Anthony Trollope or Wilkie Collins gave him a good week's employment in the mere perusal, and opened up for his appreciation a new little world, with a host of animated human beings between whom and the author of their existence, on the one hand, and that ever mysterious and unclassified " reading public " on the other, he was an accredited interpreter.

The best of our novelists of to-day are sparing alike of their imaginations and their physical energies. Mr. Meredith and Mr. Hardy, to be sure, tax the reviewer's abilities as well as his temper not a little, but even "An Amazing Marriage" and " Jude the Obscure" are miniatures compared with the big, crowded canvases of Scott and Bulwer and the other great novelists of a past age.

"A Lady of Quality" is an excellent specimen of the modern novel. It is a book that will be talked about all the year ; that will surely be dramatized, with the result of disappointing all who have read it admiringly, and at the same time securing for it a host of new readers ; that will be discussed vaguely but persistently from every point of view, possible or impossible, in the discussion of literary art, particularly the moral and the religious. It will be attacked with vehemence, it will be praised intolerantly. As a picture of an interesting historical epoch—the age of Bolingbroke and the Churchills, of Addison, Steele, and Pope—it will be diligently examined for flaws, which will doubtless be found. It will be weighed in the balance against " Esmond " and " The Spectator " and the interesting writings of Mr. Addington Symonds. It will be read by everybody who reads fiction of the higher

class and probably by many others. In short, it will be a " book of the year."

Yet in the 365 pages of "A Lady of Quality " Mrs. Burnett treats of a whole lifetime, from the hour of birth to death in green old age; of the development and transformation of an odd, strong character, and all the states and moods through which it passes ; of town and country life, of London polite society in the dawn of the eighteenth century, of the court and of the slums, of love and hate, piety and sin, revenge and expiation, lust and debauchery, purity and charity. And Clorinda is its one distinguished personage, its sole luminary.

Neither Hardy nor Meredith has imagined a more remarkable woman. She is never vulgarly probable, yet she is always splendidly human. Whether ordinary men, reading of her, will fall in love with her is doubtful. She is a creature quite too bright and good for human nature's daily food. Women will certainly like her. But we shall not injure her chances with a single reader by telling any part of her story in advance.

In the manner of its telling this story is a modern antique. Like " Esmond," it is told in the language of *The Tatler*, but its literary likeness to "Esmond" ends there. The story triumphs in spite of its style, not because of it. The phraseology often seems affected, and the author is always thinking more of the traits and moods of her heroine than of the fashions and manners of the time in which she lived. (Scribner. $1.50.)—*N. Y. Times.*

Iver, Come !

KNEELING behind Thor's Stone, with the steel barrel of his gun laid on the anvil, and pointed in the direction whence came Iver's voice, he waited till his rival should appear, and draw within range, that he might shoot him through the heart.

"Summon him again," he whispered.

"Iver—come !" called Mehetabel.

Then through the illuminated haze, like an atmosphere of glow-worm's light, himself black against a background of shining water, appeared the young man.

Jonas had his teeth clenched ; his breath hissed like the threat of a serpent, as he drew a long inspiration through them.

"You are there !" shouted Iver, joyously, and ran forward.

She felt a thrill run through the barrel, on which she had laid her hand ; she saw a movement of the shoulder of Jonas, and was aware that he was preparing to fire.

Instantly she snatched the gun to her, laid the muzzle against her own side, and said : "Fire!" She spoke again. "So all will be well."

From "The Broom-Squire."   Copyright, 1896, by Frederick A. Stokes Co.

SHE LAID THE MUZZLE AGAINST HER OWN SIDE.

Then she cried in piercing tones, "Iver! run! run! he is here, and he seeks to kill you."

Jonas sprang to his feet with a curse, and endeavored to wrest the gun from Mehetabel's hand. But she held it fast. She clung to it with tenacity, with the whole of her strength, so that he was unable to pluck it away.

And still she cried, "Run, Iver, run ; he will kill you!"

"Let go!" yelled Bideabout. He set his foot against Thor's Stone ; he twisted the gun about, he turned it this way, that way, to wrench it out of her hands.

"I will not!" she gasped.

"It is loaded! It will go off!"

"I care not."

"Oh, no! so long as it shoots me."

"Send the lead into my heart!"

"Then let go. But no! The bullet is not for you. Let go, I say, or I will brain you with the butt end, and then shoot him!"

"I will not! Kill me if you will!"

Strong, athletic, lithe in her movements, Mehetabel was a match for the small muscular Jonas. If he succeeded for a moment in twisting the gun out of her hands it was but for an instant. She had caught the barrel again at another point.

He strove to beat her knuckles against Thor's Stone, but she was too dexterous for him. By a twist she brought his hand against the block instead of her own.

With an oath he cast himself upon her, by the impact, by the weight, to throw her down. Under the burden she fell on her knees, but did not relinquish her hold on the gun. On the contrary, she obtained greater power over it, and held the barrel athwart her bosom, and wove her arms around it.

Iver was hastening to her assistance. He saw that some contest was going on, but was not able to discern either with whom Mehetabel was grappling nor what was the meaning of the struggle.

In his attempt to approach, Iver was regardless where he trod. He sank over his knees in the mire, and was obliged to extricate himself before he could advance.

With difficulty, by means of oziers, he succeeded in reaching firm soil, and then, with more circumspection, he sought a way by which he might come to the help of Mehetabel.

Meanwhile, regardless of the contest of human passion raging close by, the great bird swung like a pendulum above the mere, and its shadow swayed below it.

"Let go! I will murder you if you do not!" hissed Jonas. "You think I will kill him. So I will, but I will kill you first."

"Iver! help!" cried Mehetabel; her strength was abandoning her.

The Broom-Squire dragged his kneeling wife forward, and then thrust her back. He held the gun by the stock and the end of the barrel. The rest was grappled by her, close to her bosom.

He sought to throw her on her face, then on her back. So only could he wrench the gun away.

"Ah, ah!" with a shout of triumph.

He had disengaged the barrel from her arm. He turned it sharply upward, to twist it out of her hold she had with the other arm.

Then—suddenly—an explosion, a flash, a report, a cry; and Bideabout staggered back and fell.

A rush of wings.

The large bird that had vibrated over the water had been alarmed, and now flew away. (Stokes. $1.25.)—*From Baring-Gould's " The Broom-Squire."*

Nobody's Fault.

BRIDGET RUAN'S father was "in beer"; that is to say, Bridget's father was a publican, and kept a first-class house of entertainment at Rilchester, and was quite well-to-do. Bridget's mother had certain social aspirations, and determined that Bridget should have all the advantages of a first-class education, and so her girl was sent to a fashionable London school, and there Bridget took in ideas. When she came home to Rilchester she could not find her place. The silly girls, the simpering youths disgusted her. She could take no interest in what they said or did. Mrs. Ruan was made unhappy and Mr. Ruan showed temper.

To escape them Bridget married Travers, a cynic and a man of letters, who had written a book, and Bridget had fascinated him by her beauty. But he soon tired of his wife, and as to Bridget, in time she despised him. Then she left him, and came near ruining herself with Carey, a *littérateur* of merit and a really good fellow. But Bridget stopped just in time. She remembered that, though her mother and father had been "in beer," they were honest people, and so the fear of disgracing them held her back. The story of "Nobody's Fault" is well written, and the character of an impetuous young woman, maddened by disappointments, is cleverly told. (Roberts. $1.)—*N. Y. Times.*

The Gallery of Antiquities.

"THE Gallery of Antiquities" is the thirty sixth in the series of De Balzac's novels issued by Roberts Bros. It is uniform with others in the series. The translations are by Miss Kath-

erine P. Wormeley, which have called out the best words of commendation from the readers of De Balzac in the original. This handsome series will make American readers better acquainted with the great author, who, like Dumas, had a fault—he wrote too much. Briefly, "The Gallery of Antiquities" recites life in the salon of the Marquis d Esgrignon. The Marquis, his sister Mlle. Armande, and his son Victurnien, are the principal characters, and the rise and fall of the latter furnish the dramatic features. This salon was composed of royalists mostly without fortune, and the old and proud Marquis was upon a throne of his own, unmindful of the changes time and events had wrought; and in opposition thereto was the bourgeoisie faction of Liberals, centred about the Hôtel de Crosier. It was a courteous war, but one carried to ultimate victory and vengeance by the latter. Some of the characters of the story are unusually good. That of Chesnol, the servitor, is the finest De Balzac ever created. His virtues and heroism are beautiful creations. (Roberts. $1.50.)—*Chicago Inter-Ocean.*

Phyllis of Philistia.

SARCASM is a pretty good vehicle for smartness, but it is possible to get too much of it in a novel. Too much of it and the invention of situations that might be found in actual life, but seem too strange and improbable for fiction, are almost the only faults the reader is likely to find with "Phyllis of Philistia," by Frank Frankfort Moore. A young woman of more than common intelligence, but extremely conventional, and who is as a little child in religion—which is the orthodox ideal—is the heroine. Engaged to a popular young clergyman, chiefly because all the other girls seemed to want him, she breaks with him because he published a startling work in the line of the higher biblical criticism—attacking the character of the patriarchs and their wives and even Ruth, and at last denying that Christianity owed any duty to the Jews, but insisting that Christianity was in fact a protest against the whole Mosaic history. Eventually she marries a man who was virtually an atheist and whom she had saved from eloping with the wife of his best friend. This wife, after supposing herself madly in love with her husband's best friend, discovers instantly on the death of her husband that her heart had been always wholly devoted to her husband. The reader must have some difficulty in accepting these conclusions of the novelist. Still, the characters are strongly drawn and the book is well written and constantly interesting. (Cassell. $1.)—*N. Y. Commercial Advertiser.*

The Life of Thomas Hutchinson.

LESSING once projected a series of papers to which he proposed to give the name of "Rettungen" (Rescues), his design being to vindicate from obloquy great men of the past to whom harsh measure had been dealt out. It was a generous thought of a most just and courageous mind, and deserves imitation in every age. The history of America, like that of every land, has its *bêtes noires*, characters remembered, for the most part, only to be execrated, some of whom certainly do not deserve their bad fame ; and of these there is no more pathetic example than Thomas Hutchinson, the last royal Governor of Massachusetts Bay before the futile effort of England to divide with the sword the perplexities of the oncoming Revolution.

Among Tories there was no one so illustrious, through his position and abilities, as Thomas Hutchinson. His historical writings give him a respectable place in the literature of his century. "His learning even in the science of the law was highly respectable, and, when we consider his early education, was indeed remarkable," said the Hon. Charles Deane. As a financier, John Adams celebrated Hutchinson thirty years after his death: "If I was the Witch of Endor I would wake the ghost of Hutchinson and give him absolute power over the currency of the United States and every part of it, provided always that he should meddle with nothing but the currency. I will acknowledge that he understood the subject of coin and commerce better than any man I ever knew in this country."

There is no lack of material for a biography of Hutchinson. Hutchinson pervaded the life of his time in a most remarkable way, standing out as a leading figure in the most various spheres. While an exile in England in his old age, Hutchinson prepared an autobiographical sketch recounting his career from childhood to the troubles of the Revolution. At that point his history is taken up in many manuscripts preserved in the historical societies of Massa-chusetts. Dr. Hosmer's book is written with fairness and from full information. He specially brings out that Governor Hutchinson, while loyal to the crown, was true to the best interests of the colony, and that because he was a loyalist but scant justice has been done by Americans to his sterling virtues. Dr. Hosmer dedicates his book to John Fiske, his

HE HAD BEEN INVITED TO SUPPLY AT ST. AGATHA'S.

life-long friend. It forms an excellent history of the American Revolution. (Houghton, Mifflin & Co. $4.)

The Supply at St. Agatha's.

Is there any need of urging people to read a story by Miss Phelps? The hundreds of thousands who have read and been profoundly moved by "The Gates Ajar" ; the additional scores of thousands who have read and are reading with the deepest interest her latest novel, "A Singular Life"—these certainly re-

quire no prompting to read or re-read her story
of "The Supply at Saint Agatha's." For it is,
in fact, one of the strongest, most suggestive,
most illuminating of all the stories Miss Phelps
has written. The setting of the story is vigorous and skilful, the narrative is rapid and engrossingly interesting, and the revelation of
the "Supply" reaches to the inmost thoughts
and emotions of men. This story appears
most appropriately as an Easter issue, complete in a single volume, appropriately illustrated by Mr. and Mrs. Charles H. Woodbury.
who have rendered with exquisite feeling the
delicate sentiment of the author. Tastefully
and fitly bound, it will form a peculiarly suitable Easter gift. "The Supply at St. Agatha's"
once more emphasizes the truth that behind all
preaching there must be a preacher with personal magnetism, a pure life, a warm heart for
the most unlovable of humanity, if the words
spoken are to bring about peace and righteousness. How deeply Miss Phelps feels this need
she has told us in "A Singular Life," and now
recalls to mind in this little literary cameo.
(Houghton, Mifflin & Co. $1.)

From "A Professional Beauty." Copyright, 1896, by
          J. B. Lippincott Co.
"WHAT ARE YOU DOING, MR. TRESHAM?"

Autobiography of a Professional Beauty.

MISS TRAIN'S first long story is now reprinted
as a companion volume to "A Social Highwayman," which obtained the dignity of book form
after its success in a dramatization. "A Professional Beauty" is more rational and not less
pleasing than the latter tale. Its plot is ample
and well thought out, and bears a strong relation to that of "A Social Highwayman."
But in this story the author is never hampered by her plot. It develops easily and
naturally, and is of secondary importance to
slight but appreciable character study and vivacious dialogue and narrative. (Lippincott.
75 c.)—N. Y. Times.

In the Day of Adversity.

THE reader who begins Mr. Bloundelle-
Burton's latest story, "In the Day of Adversity," will not be content until he has unravelled
the mystery that surrounds its hero, one
Georges St. Georges, a lieutenant in the
chevaux légers of the Nivernois, about the year
1687, in the reign of Louis XIV., known in history as "the Great." The tortuous thread of
the story gives the author plenty of scope for
descriptions of life at that period, and it is not
too much to say that he enables us to realize
that past—now as far removed from us almost
as the time of King Solomon, owing to the immense material advances made during the
nineteenth century—with a vividness unsurpassed by any other writer we can recall. The
corrupt and tyrannical *régime* of Louis, under
which no man's life or honor was safe from
secret accusation and silent but swift punishment, is laid bare in the thrilling account of St.
Georges' relations with Louvois, the king's
chief minister. The book simply teems with
adventure, duels, murders, hairbreadth escapes,
and intrigues jostling each other in its pages.
Yet throughout there is a clear object in view—
the discovery of St. Georges' identity with
the heir of a great nobleman and the restoration
to him of his stolen daughter, the little Dorine.
The hero may appear rather too devil-may-care
for so affectionate a father, but his misfortunes
were certainly of a kind to make the interest in
him "breathless" and keep the reader en-
chained till the end. The author's inspiration
for the tale, as we learn from the preface, was
drawn from "Mémoires Secrets de M. Le
Comte de Bussy-Rabutin," and from Rousset's
"Histoire de Louvois," and he may be warmly
congratulated on the use he has made of his
materials. It deserves to rank high among the
best historical novels we possess. (Appleton.
$1; pap., 50 c.)—London Literary World.

From Jeyes's " Joseph Chamberlain."   Frederick Warne & Co.

RT. HON. JOSEPH CHAMBERLAIN.

Honorable Joseph Chamberlain.

MR. S. H. JEYES is the editor of a series of volumes known as *Public Men of the Day*, and he has been announced for some time as preparing for it a monograph on the present Secretary of State for the Colonies. His work is completed and published at a most opportune moment—a moment when its subject is beyond question the man most prominently in the public eye. With Mr. Chamberlain as a party politician we have here, of course, nothing to do, and, even from the point of view of party, friends and opponents alike have recently joined in a chorus of praise of the minister's recent exhibition of statesmanship.

But, although not concerned with Mr. Chamberlain as a political force, we cannot refrain from complimenting the author of this volume upon the impartial manner in which—writing from an avowedly Conservative standpoint—

he has dealt with the career of his subject. We learn from Mr. Jeyes that his hero was born in 1836 in Camberwell; that he comes of a stock in which Nonconformist traditions had been hereditary, and that his father was a boot manufacturer in the City. Educated at first at a private school, and later at University College School, young Joseph Chamberlain was brought up for a commercial career. At the age of eighteen he went to Birmingham to represent his father in a manufacturing business with which his name has long been familiar. His rise was rapid, and he was able to retire at the age of thirty-eight. He early took a prominent part in municipal affairs in Birmingham, and then in 1876 he was elected as one of the Members of that town. Thenceforward he has been always more or less prominently before the public, and Mr. Jeyes in this volume follows the details of his public career with con-

GUTENBERG.

siderable care and discrimination. The volume is not so much a biography of Mr. Chamberlain as a study of his career, first, as a public-spirited leader in his adopted town, later as a member of the Radical party, and Cabinet Minister in Mr. Gladstone's Administrations, and now as one of the most popular ministers in the Coalition Cabinet. We have been so struck by the impartiality and clearness of Mr. Jeyes's monograph that we have no hesitation in recommending it to all who take an intelligent interest in the management of public affairs, whether they be, in a political sense, followers or opponents of one who has known what it is to be, to use his own words, "the best abused man in England." (Warne. $1.25.) —*London Literary World.*

The Century of Sir Thomas More.

SIR THOMAS MORE was born when the twilight of mediævalism was paling before the dawn of modern times. Feudalism had lived its day ; there were everywhere the signs of a coming storm. The conditions of the poor had grown most pitiful. The ambition of kings had received a strange new impulse ; the superior rulers surged forward toward absolute power, with a confidence and recklessness which cowed the feudal lords. The popes, as we have seen, in many instances were secular potentates rather than spiritual fathers. Dreams of conquest swelled in the breasts of those born to the ermine, those who had risen to the scarlet cap, and those who had achieved position and power by the possession of military genius and daring, aided by the fortunes of war. But while the anarchy of feudal brigandage was giving way before a more centralized and (in a

way) orderly rule, while kings were engrossed with plans for personal aggrandizement, scholars, scientists, and skilled artisans were intoxicated by an intellectual stimulation seldom if ever equalled in the history of the race. Some were revelling in the rediscovered treasures of ancient Greece ; some were brooding over the wonder-stories of the far East. Artists and sculptors were transferring to canvas and marble the marvellous dreams which haunted their imagination. Gutenberg had recently invented the printing-press, Copernicus was interrogating the stars, and another profound dreamer was gazing upon the western ocean with a question and a hope—one of which would not be silenced, the other so big as to appear wild and absurd to the imagination of small minds. At this momentous time, when the clock of the ages was ringing in the advent of an epoch which should mark a tremendous onward stride in the advance of humanity—at this time when change was written over every great door of thought or research throughout civilization, Sir Thomas More was born. (Arena Pub. Co. $1 50.)—*From B. O. Flower's "The Century of Sir Thomas More."*

The Bamboo-Cutter.

AN old bamboo-cutter, who had finished his day's work on the hills near Biwa, and tied up his fagot, bethought him to cut an extra cane to serve for a staff on his way down tne snow-clad slopes of the mountain. Astonished to see light streaming from the incision made by his knife, he carefully laid open the hollow joint and found within it an infant from whose tiny body came the supernatural radiance. He took the prodigy home and she grew to be a famous beauty. Suitors came from all directions, and even from the Imperial City. But not caring to accept the addresses of any of

ZWINGLI.

them, the Bamboo Maiden set them impossible tasks to perform, pretending that her object was to test the sincerity of their professions. One soon returned with an old silver cup, gray from oxidation, which he had bought at an extravagant price from a Buddhist monk as the legendary vessel that he had been required to discover. But the sharp-witted maiden immediately scoured it and brought out an inscription showing that it was of comparatively modern manufacture. Another had been despatched to seek an enchanted island where grew a golden tree bearing jewels for fruit. This gentleman came back after a longer interval, with a moving tale of shipwreck and disaster and a branch which he had had made by a jeweller in Kioto. His golden branch had not the requisite magic virtues, however, and a sharp cross-examination developed serious flaws in his story. A third, himself deceived by a merchant into buying for a great price a blue foxskin, said to be uninflammable, saw his gift consigned to the flames, where it perished in an instant; and a fourth, the only suitor who had honestly attempted the task assigned him, had the worst luck of all, for he fell from the sheer rock that he was to seek, and broke his neck.

The fame of the wise but dangerous beauty at last reached the Emperor, and he set out in his august bullock-cart to visit her. A flame at once sprang up between the two, but the maiden was proof against even the attractions of love in a palace. Having fulfilled the period of her exile, she returned to the moon, whence she had come, leaving an example of obstinate virtue, which unfortunately is "unapproachable by mortal women." The "Bamboo-Cutter" is a fairy-story that reminds one of the "Moral Tales" of the witty Count Hamilton. (Scribner. $1.50.)—*From Riordan and Takayanagi's "Sunrise Stories."*

In New England Fields and Woods.

AMONG books of degeneration and regeneration there now and then appear—jostled by science and elbowed by art—inoffensive little manuals of outdoor life that are quite refreshing to the reader who retains his taste for simple bread-and-milk diet. The volume at hand is written by Rowland E. Robinson in a vein

JAPANESE DANCER.

of gentle reminiscence, and gives evidence of quick observation and much sentiment on the part of the author. The scene is laid oftenest in field or forest, and the *dramatis personæ* are the mink, the woodchuck, the gartersnake, the toad, the bobolink, the bullfrog, etc. The action is never intense, save when the sportsman enters with his gun; but there is a great deal made of the background, the patches of moss on gray rocks and tree-trunks, the purple-budded maples; the odorous white sea of buckwheat, the tasselling corn, and the rich loam.

It is not for the cockney that such intimate studies of nature are written; only those who have lived close to the earth will get the smell of it from their somewhat prosy little pages; a few will cherish them as they cherish sundry pre-Raphaelite drawings of old tree-stumps and tangled grasses, because they are " the thing itself," microscopically observed, and the readers who do not cherish may at least find a moment's bliss in having their thoughts turned to the birds of the forest and the lilies of the field, away from the whirl of the nineteenth-century civilization. (Houghton, Mifflin & Co. $1.25.)—*N. Y. Times.*

Six Modern Women.

EVERY intelligent woman in the United States should read "Six Modern Women," by Laura Marholm Hansson, a book which is sure to become a lasting and valuable contribution to psychological literature. Its present-day mission is many-sided, serving, as it does, as a healthy mental antidote for several different classes of those overdosed with the " woman question." It contains, nevertheless, an inspiring message for the timid and halting ones, who would fain scale heights if they but dared. While for all there is uncovered, with a true and sympathetic touch, the intricate and diversified folds that disclose at last one throbbing, living centre — the sensitive heart, the soul of woman.

Mrs. Hansson has selected strong types for her sketches of the modern women, Sonia Kovalevsky taking the lead. In the fifty pages devoted to this remarkable character we learn more than in all the volumes her biographers have given us. It is a study of the suffering and high-spirited woman — a mystic creature despite all her learning, and we pity her. It is as if the masculine and stronger half of her nature were constantly waging battle upon the weaker half, and in the end overcame it, while still the wailing feminine cry for love rang on.

" Neurotic Keynotes " is a subtle designation for the second sketch, which fairly vibrates with the sounds drawn from the delicate organism, the nervous personality of the woman author, George Egerton. In this paper and that succeeding, called " The Modern Woman on the Stage," Eleonora Duse, the writer concentrates her best powers. So penetrating is she, employing such perfect understanding of her character in hand, together with a mastery of expression, that her word-pictures are clearer than any we remember, actually bring-

ing the naked soul to our complete understanding. Complete, do we say? Hardly so. Even Mrs. Hansson, for all her marvellously intuitive gift, cannot fathom quite all the mysteries of woman's soul. But what is possible for mortal to do she has accomplished.

Sketches of Amalia Skram, " The Woman Naturalist," Marie Bashkirtseff and "The Woman's Rights Woman," Fru Edgren - Leffler, who will be recognized as Sonia Kovalevsky's biographer, follow in succession. The authoress is less in harmony with the subject of the last sketch than with any other. She better understands and sympathizes with the emotional nature of Marie Bashkirtseff, or even the honest Amalia Skram.

Throughout the reading of this remarkable book one unnamed personality is felt strongly, an invisible presence, as a sustained and sweet note, or the lingering fragrance of a hidden flower. It is the seventh modern woman, the " Woman Critic," the author of the book, who unconsciously leaves an unwritten record of her own tender sensibility on every page. (Roberts. $1.25.)—*Boston Transcript.*

R.S.V.P.

A GREAT event happened in the back-kitchen of Bailie Holden. The postman had brought a letter with a fine monogram—a very stiff, square letter, for Miss Janet Urquhart. The table-maid, who considered herself quite as good as a governess, examined it as though there must needs be some mistake in the address. The housemaid turned it about and looked at it endways and upside down, to see if there might not be another name concealed somewhere. She rubbed it with her apron to see if the top would come off and something be revealed beneath. The cook, into whose hands the missive next passed, left a perfect tracing of her thumb and fore-finger upon it, done in oils, and very well executed, too.

In this condition it reached the back-kitchen at last, and the hands of Janet of Inverness. As she took the letter in her little damp fingers, she grew pale to the lips. What she feared, I cannot tell—probably only the coming true of some of her dreams.

In a cluster around the door stood the housemaid, the table-maid, and family cat—the one which went habitually on four legs, I mean. The cook moved indignantly about the range, clattering tongs, pans, and other instruments of music, as it is the immemorial use of all cooks when the bird in the breast does not sing sweetly. She was, of course, quite above curiosity as to what Janet's letter might contain.

"Likely it's an invitation !" sneered the housemaid.

"Aye, frae the police !" added the table-maid from the doorway. She was plain, and Cleaver's boy never stopped to gossip with her. Not that she cared or would have stood talking with the likes of him.

The cook banged the top of the range, like Tubal-cain when Naamah vexed him in that original stithy, near by the city of Enoch in the land of Nod.

Janet of Inverness opened the letter. Scarcely could she believe her eyes. It was a formal invitation upon a beautifully written card, and contained a wish on the part of Mr. Greg Tennant and Miss Tennant that Miss Janet Urquhart would favor them with her company at Aurelia Villa on the evening of Friday, the 17th, at eight o'clock. R.S.V.P.

Janet sank into a seat speechless, still holding the invitation. The table-maid came and looked over her shoulder.

"Goodness me !" she exclaimed, as she read the card.

" She's been tellin' the truth after a'," said the housemaid, who, having some claims to beauty, was glad of Janet's good fortune, and hoped that the like might happen to herself.

"I dinna believe a word o't!" said the cook, indignantly. "I'se warrant she wrote it hersel' !"

But Janet had not written it herself. She could not even bring herself to write the answer, though she had received a sound School Board education. But the three R's do not contemplate the answering of invitations upon thick cardboard, ending "R. S. V. P." They stop at the spelling of "trigonometry" and the solving of vulgar fractions.

In spite of her silks and satins and her vaunted experience, Janet did not know the meaning of "R.S.V.P." But the housemaid had not ,brushed clothes ten years for nothing.

"It means 'Reply shortly, v e r y pleased'!" said she. Which, being substantially correct, settled the question. (Appleton. $1.50.)—*From Crockett's " Cleg Kelly."*

Introduction to Study of American Literature.

THE study of literature in our secondary schools is a subject that has of late attracted much attention from teachers, and is likely to attract still more. Whether such study should be confined to the reading, with suitable annotations, of a few great classics, or should include, in addition, a survey of the chief facts of literary history in a formal manual, may be cited as points in the problem on which those who have thought most deeply will probably be least dogmatic; but whatever the position we may take with regard to these mooted matters, few of us will fail to agree that a book like this of Professor Brander Matthews's ought to be used with success in every school in the country. For it is certainly nothing less

From Crockett's " Cleg Kelly."   Copyright, 1896, by D. Appleton & Co.

WHEN " THE WARRIOR " CAME.

than a shame, in view of the fact that so many of our youth terminate their education with the high school, that girls and boys should be allowed to enter on active life with little or no knowledge of the literature that has shaped and is shaping the life of the society of which they are to become members.

With regard to Mr. Matthews's thorough success in treating his subject I am in as little doubt as I am with regard to the value of that subject from an educational point of view. He has laid his chief stress on the great names, and omitted every detail that would tend to obscure for the pupil the personality of the writer described. In other words, Mr. Matthews has shown himself to be an adept in child-psychology, for persons appeal more to the young than things, and books are things to the average young mind. Strings of dates, lists of books and names, long-winded paragraphs of criticism find, therefore, no place in this excellent volume. Needful apparatus is given, however, in the shape of practical bibliographies, questions for examination, chronological tables, etc., as well as in admirable illustrations, which include authentic portraits of all our chief writers, views of their birthplaces or homes, and last, but not least, fac-similes of portions of their important manuscripts. In the latter particulars the publishers have seconded the author admirably, and as they have more than done their duty with regard to strictly typographical details, we have been given a volume that ought to delight every pupil in whose hands it is placed. . . .

Indeed, if I could fairly choose one quality of this book, and only one, for commendation, I should point to its geniality—a quality that young people love, and that his friends always associate with Mr. Matthews. (American Book Co. $1.)—*W. P. Trent in the Educational Review.*

Handbook to the Works of Lord Tennyson.

THE plan and distinct purpose of Mr. Luce's volume do not call for, even if they would admit, illustrations, but it has the attraction of superior typography, that combination of softly tinted and opaque paper, exquisitely cut and harmoniously proportioned type, untrimmed edges, and chaste binding which go to make up the perfect book mechanically viewed. What is the indescribable something which stamps the English-made book of high grade with its unmistakable individuality? In all its outward features this one, unassuming and modest as is its appearance, belongs to the true nobility of literature.

Mr. Luce's method is as explicitly critical as

Mr. Waugh's is biographical. The first chapter alone has anything approaching suggestions for a life, and these are only a few paragraphs giving the barest outline. The greater part of the chapter is occupied with acute observations on Tennyson's times for the purpose of defining his place in English literature, and with critical remarks upon his characteristics in general. His religious faith, it is claimed, was in a transitional state, but his ethical point of view was high and firm. The same, though in a less degree, was true of his political and social principles. From science he expected much, as likewise from commerce and conquest, but evolution he regarded with caution. He painted England minutely, beautifully, and lovely, though perhaps not so freshly as some others have done. He sketches his figures first, and then fills in his landscape. The question of his honor is a debated one, and not yet settled. And so on for about fifty pages. Then we take up the poems themselves, one by one, for close examination and careful running criticism, with frequent illustrative extracts, and occasional footnotes, and a generally intelligent interpretation and instructive comment upon the text. The poems are followed in their chronological order, and each being given its number, references in the index are made easy. "The Princess" gets nearly 40 pages of attention, "In Memoriam" 17, "Idylls of the King" 43, and others in proportion. A chronological list of the poems and a good index complete the volume. There have been frequent inquiries the past few years for such a handbook as this, and a very large number of students of English poetry will welcome it with gratitude. It will not answer all questions, but it will many, and where it is baffied in its interpretations of the poet's thought it will help the reader materially in explaining allusions and circumstances. (Macmillan. $1.75.)—*Boston Literary World.*

ON READING THE LETTERS OF MATTHEW ARNOLD.

WAS it not well you should no longer stay,
  Seeing we know you better than before!
You whose true heart was tender to the core
And clear as those pellucid brooks that stray
Hid in the Chiltern grasses. Not a spray
  Of bright may-blossom or of diamond frore
  But wove its rainbows for you; from the shore
To Fairfield's crown you have honored Nature's way.

Breathed from these letters, like the south wind, come
  Sweet thoughts for others, purpose high and pure,
    Hope inexhaustible and holy will
  To help the nation, patience to endure,
    A love of all that keeps us England still
Filled with the dear felicities of home.
(Macmillan.)—*H. D. Rawnsley in The Athenæum.*

Kokoro.

A VERY charming book and one which you will find it difficult to lay down until the last page has been reached. Mr. Hearn we all know, not personally, perhaps, but through his work. He is an observant and a conscientious writer. His style is attractive, and although there is nothing of the Paul Pry about him, he has a quick eye, and, what is of more importance, he has a quick appreciation of incidents. I have followed him in his travels, and can cheerfully say that if you desire to look at a truthful picture of the domestic and social life of the Japanese, Mr. Hearn will furnish you with an ample opportunity. The chapter on certain tendencies among the Japanese is peculiarly interesting, while that on the Japanese idea of pre-existence has the charm of a bit of romance. I like the book thoroughly, and if you read it you will thank me for calling your attention to it. (Houghton, Mifflin & Co. $1.25.)—*George H. Hepworth in N. Y. Herald.*

The Professor's Experiment.

MRS. HUNGERFORD has never written a more delightful book than "The Professor's Experiment." The Professor himself dies at the end of the second chapter; and his experiment has little to do with the story, beyond serving to introduce to us the two most prominent characters—Paul Wyndham, a barrister, and Ella Moore, a mysterious orphan. As with all books written by the author of "Molly Bawn," the style is crisp, the characters life-like, and the tone healthy throughout; and having thus thoroughly commended the book as a whole, we are at liberty to draw attention to features which leave something to be desired. Paul Wyndham is much too cross-grained a character either to enlist our sympathies or to make us suppose it possible that Ella could really have fallen in love with him. Again, the Burkes are a charming family, but a good deal too much space is devoted to them. Family prattle faithfully reported is apt to become dull; the repartees are rude rather than witty, the jokes are of the practical order, and the play is for the most part equine. As for the final solution of the mystery—the secret drawer containing marriage certificates, family papers, etc., such as we all of us are well known to keep locked up at home, in order to prove our identity in case of being lost or mislaid—the indulgent reader will, no doubt, forgive a trifling poverty of conception in his delight at coming across a thoroughly lively, cheerful story. (Lippincott. $1.25.)—*The Academy.*

When Greek Meets Greek.

WE feel that we are in for a stirring and breathless story of adventure from the opening chapters of "When Greek Meets Greek," and subsequent investigation confirms our prophetic impression. There is no need to waste time and space over it, because when we have heartily recommended it to our readers nothing much remains to be said, and it is a story that will require to be read for itself; no reviewing, however descriptive, will compensate for the actual narrative. "When Greek Meets Greek" is a story of the Revolution of 1792, with a strong historical plot, held together and rendered fresh and attractive by the introduction of pure fiction subtly interwoven with it. It is told as Mr. Hatton knows how to tell a story, and from the time young Jaffray Ellicott invades the apartment of the police spy's daughter, in escaping from the Communists, to the final peaceful happiness which follows the escape to England of the characters chiefly concerned, the interest is so well sustained that it is safe to aver no reader of ordinary emotions will consent to lay aside the book until the climax is reached. The history is of minor importance, but something is due to the skilful way in which Mr. Hatton has interwoven it with his fiction, and the striking features of what life was during the Reign of Terror come to us more vividly through his agency than from any quantity of cut-and-dried historical essays. We live it over again with the characters, noble and simple, matron and maid, lover and brother, to whom Mr. Hatton introduces us, and we cannot say more than that for any fiction that is brought before us. (Lippincott. $1.50.)—*London Literary World.*

Frederick.

As once before in "Mr. Smith," so now in "Frederick," Mrs. Walford has justified herself in choosing a hero whom the average author, and also many others, would have passed by as quite unworthy of dissection. Frederick is a country gentleman of a truly gentle type, kind to everybody, devoted to sport, immensely interested in all the little concerns of his neighbors, and beloved and indulged by his neighbors in return. First he was looked after by his father; now he is looked after by his elder brother, Sir William; he has no responsibilities; nobody expects anything from him but his unfailing good-humored acquiescence in life; and so he remains, at nearly forty, just the sweetest-natured and best-behaved child anybody ever met. But into his placid existence there come, all on a sudden, Aline Carey, smarting under a thwarted love-affair, and her scheming cousin, the barrister, Horace Carey. The characters of these three, and their action and reaction on one another, are presented with all the verisimilitude of Mrs. Walford's facile style, just tipped with humor as of old. Real life and real love dawn on Frederick, Aline discovers how overhastily she had thought she loved, and Horace —he discovers several unpleasant things. This book, with "Mr. Smith" and "The Baby's Grandmother," stand out from the rest of Mrs. Walford's work on a height apart. (Lippincott. $1.25.)—*The Academy.*

Rose of Dutcher's Coolly.

I CHERISH with a grateful sense of the high pleasure they have given me Mr. Garland's splendid achievements in objective fiction. In that sort his stories, "Main Travelled Roads," are monumental, but "Rose of Dutcher's Coolly" is not wholly in that sort. The scheme of it has apparently been so dear to the author, the lesson he wished to convey has seemed so important, that he has somewhat sacrificed the free movement of his characters to them ; he has not wholly taken his hand from them; he has not let them go their own gait ; they act from his hypnotic suggestion.

That is, at times. At any other times they have their being from him, or apparently free of him, for at best this freedom of one's creatures is an illusion which one must strive by all means to produce, but which is still only the finest illusion. There is a frankness in his portrayal of the rustic conditions which Rose springs from, very uncommon in our fiction, and there is an acknowledgment of facts and influences usually blinked. But along with this valuable truth there is a strain of sentimentality which discredits it ; and the reader is left in an uncertainty as to the author's meaning in one essential which is at least discomfiting. If fiction is to deal with things hitherto not dealt with in the evolution of character, it must be explicit. From anything less we have the haunting sense of something unwholesome, which taints the whole after-life of the personage for the reader, and avails nothing for the author's real purpose. This purpose in the present case is to prove that a woman may live down her past as a man may. But I remain unconvinced that a woman can live down her past, for I do not believe that a man can live down his past. Our past becomes part of us, whether we are women or whether we are men; if there has been an error in it, we may disown it by owning it; if we do not, it remains a wound and a source of moral disease and

death. This may be very hard, but it seems the intention of

" La somma Sapienza e il primo Amore,"

and we cannot help it. I do not find that Rose owned her whole past to the man who married her, and so I cannot quite accept her upon the author's terms.

There are beautiful passages in the book, and the life that it reports is almost as new to fiction as if it were new to fact. It is the country life of the great middle West, both in its rustic environment and in its self-translation to the city, which in this case is Chicago. I get a less vivid impression of the city people than of the country girl who has come to them : she is always, except upon the most intended side, strongly and attractively realized, but she is less interesting and charming to me in her Chicago phase than in her student avatar in Madison. That whole part of the book relating to the university, and to the young aspirations and ambitions which form its soul, with the light of actual and potential passion over all, is beautiful, and in despair of fresher terms I must call it a contribution to literature. That alone would justify the being of the book, though even that is troubled with the effect of some things the author wished to be rather than really were. A touch of the ideal can be felt in it by the nerves which no one more than Mr. Garland has striven to render sensitive to impressions of the real and the unreal. (Stone & Kimball. $1.50.)—*W. D. Howells in Harper's Weekly.*

Book of the Secrets of Enoch.

THE "Book of the Secrets of Enoch," edited by W. R. Morfill and R. H. Charles, is an interesting addition to pre-Christian pseudepigraphic literature. Though abundantly cited by early Christian writers, it exists at present, so far as is known, only in Slavic versions. It appears to have been written by an orthodox but free-minded Jew, who not only sets down current Jewish opinions about religion, but adopts ideas from the Persian, Egyptian, and Greek thought of the time (between B.C. 50 and A.D. 50). He imitates the form of the Book of Enoch, but has noteworthy opinions of his own on the soul, the origin of death, the millennium, angels, Seraphim (*Chalkidri*), cosmography, and ethics. Mr. Morfill has given an English translation based on a text carefully constructed from the various Slavic versions, and Mr. Charles (the well-known translator of Enoch) has added critical and historical notes and a general introduction. The names of these two gentlemen are a guarantee of the good performance of the editorial work. (Macmillan. *net*, $2.)—*The Nation.*

Che Literary News.

An Eclectic Monthly Review of Current Literature.

EDITED BY A. H. LEYPOLDT.

APRIL, 1896.

THOMAS HUGHES.

ON Sunday, March 22, the busy life of Thomas Hughes came to an end, the life he had faithfully spent in trying "to make things a little better and honester" about him. Thomas Hughes is most widely known as the author of "Tom Brown's School-Days at Rugby," in which he preached delightfully the principles of manliness, courage, honesty, and true democracy, which have governed his life.

This book, which certainly needs no description, was first published in the fall of 1856, and after thirty years, amidst totally changed conditions, still holds its own as one of the few books all parents and teachers desire their boys to read, and all healthy, manly boys delight in. It fulfils the conditions of a successful book for young people, it deals with their daily lives and their troubles and pleasures, shows how close together lie the good and evil in impulsive young hearts, and dwells above all things upon the influence of companionship and the power of hero-worship. Thomas Hughes spent his eight years at Rugby under Dr. Thomas Arnold, and in his fascinating book has paid him tribute as Dean Stanley did. The latter appears as a school-boy in "Tom Brown," and is the great power for good in the story.

Three critical decades have changed many of the wrongs and prejudices attacked by Thomas Hughes, but there is yet need of many of his stirring words regarding the universal brotherhood of man, and his rights and duties in his special place in the world. Tom Brown's father "held the belief that a man is to be valued solely for that which he is in himself, for that which stands up in the four fleshly walls of him, apart from clothes, rank, fortune, and all externals whatsoever. Which belief I take to be a wholesome corrective of all political opinions, and if held sincerely, to make all opinions equally harmless, whether they be blue, red, or green. As a necessary corollary to this belief, Squire Brown held further that it didn't matter a straw whether his son associated with lords' or ploughmen's sons provided they were brave and honest." "Class amusements, be they for dukes or ploughboys, always become nuisances and curses to a country." "The object of all schools is not to ram Latin and Greek into boys, but to make them good English boys, good future citizens; and by far the most important part of that work must be

done or not done out of school hours. To leave it in the hands of inferior men is just giving up the highest and hardest part of the work of education. Were I a private schoolmaster, I should say, let who will hear the boys their lessons, but let me live with them when they are at play and rest." "One's own—what a charm there is in the words! How long it takes boy and man to find out their worth! How fast most of us hold on to them! When shall we learn that he who multiplieth possessions multiplieth troubles, and that the one single use of things which we call our own is that they may be his who hath need of them."

These are the principles that ruled the life of Thomas Hughes; to spread which he labored without ceasing. He was born at Uffington, Berkshire, England, in 1822. In 1830 he was sent to school at Twyford, near Winchester, and in 1833 he was removed to Rugby. From there he went to Oriel College, Oxford, where he took his B.A. degree in 1845. He early turned his attention to political problems, and when he left Oxford was an advanced Liberal. He was called to the bar in 1848, and was appointed a queen's counsel in 1869. Judge Hughes entered the House of Commons as a representative for the borough of Frome, and continued for the same constituency until 1874. While in Parliament he took prominent parts in debates relating to trades-unions and the amendment of the law of master and servant. He was always an energetic friend of the working classes, bent upon their social and educational improvement. After leaving Oxford he had been closely associated with Charles Kingsley and Frederick Denison Maurice in their "state socialism," and had assisted in the early days of Maurice's workingman's college. Hughes also supported the bills for disestablishing the church in Ireland, secularizing the universities and admitting dissenters to fellowship in Oxford and Cambridge.

After a visit to America Hughes founded the colony of Rugby in Tennessee, intending to develop a community in a healthful and natural way, with regard for each other's rights and a sense of the common interests of all. Provision was made for the mental and religious culture of the residents, who worship in one church, the services being alternately after the ritual of the Protestant Episcopal Church, and the simpler plan of other Protestant denominations. The colony has not been the success hoped for, owing to lack of enthusiasm in those in charge.

Almost all Thomas Hughes's writings are directed to special purposes, and he has produced much fearless work. He was a typical

Englishman of the best sort who proved a stanch friend of America in the days of war. He believed in "Muscular Christianity" and excelled in all athletic exercises. He has drawn a faithful portrait of himself in his own Tom Brown. And who does not love Tom Brown !

Among the more important of Thomas Hughes's writings may be briefly summed up : "Tom Brown's School-Days," 1856; "The Scouring of the White Horse," 1858; "Tom Brown at Oxford," 1861; "The Cause of Freedom," "Alfred the Great," "The Old Church : what shall we do with it?" 1878; "The Condition and Prospects of the Church of England," 1878; "The Manliness of Christ," 1879; "The Rugby Settlement," 1881; "A Memoir of Daniel Macmillan," 1882; "Gone·to Texas," "Tracts for Priests and People," 1861; "Religio Laici," reprinted as "A Layman's Faith" in 1868. In 1859 Mr. Hughes edited Lowell's "Bigelow Papers"; and when he visited us for the second time, in 1880, endeavored earnestly to impress Americans with the fact that they had neglected Lowell as an author.

Pocket Vocabularies.

A SERVICEABLE substitute for style in literature has been found in such a collection of language ready for use as may be likened to a portable vocabulary. It is suited to the manners of a day that has produced salad-dressing in bottles, and many other devices for the saving of processes. Fill me such a volume full of "graphic" things, of "quaint" things and "weird," of "crisp" or "sturdy" Anglo-Saxon, of the material for "word-painting" (is not that the way of it?), and it will serve the turn. Especially did the Teutonic fury fill full these common little hoards of language. It seemed, doubtless, to the professor of the New Literature, that if anything could convince him of his own success it must be the energy of his Teutonicisms and his avoidance of languid Latin derivatives, fit only for the pedants of the eighteenth century. Literature doubtless is made of words. What then is needful, he seems to ask, besides a knack of beautiful words? Unluckily for him, he has achieved, not style, but slang. Unluckily for him, words are not style, phrases are not style. "The man is style." O good French language, cunning and good, that lets me read the sentence in obverse or converse as I will ! And I read it as declaring that the whole man, the very whole of him, is his style. The literature of a man of letters worthy the name is rooted in all his qualities, with little fibres running invisibly into the smallest qualities he has. He who is not a man of letters simply is not one; it is not too audacious a paradox to affirm that doing will not avail him who fails in being. "Lay your deadly doing down," sang once some old hymn known to Calvinists. Certain poets, a certain time ago, ransacked the language for words full of life and beauty, made a vocabulary out of them, and out of wantonness wrote them to death. To change somewhat the

simile, they scented out a word—an earlyish word by preference—ran it to earth, unearthed it, dug it out, and killed it. And then their followers bagged it. The very word that lives, "new every morning," miraculously new in the literature of a man of letters, they killed and put into their bag. And, in like manner, the emotion that should have caused the word is dead for those, and for those only, who abuse its expression. For the maker of a portable vocabulary is not content to turn his words up there; he turns up his feelings also, alphabetically or otherwise. Wonderful how much sensibility is at hand in such round words as the New Literature loves. Do you want a generous emotion? Pull forth the little language. Find out moonshine, find out moonshine ! (Copeland & Day. $1.25.)—*From Alice Meynell's "Essays."*

Fin-de-Siecle Society.

"OH, tell me about the people to-night, Trelawney! Remember I'm out of it. What's the set ?"

"Well, there'll be the usual lot, no doubt—Blandford, Eversleigh, Archie Morefield, and that young ass Trilling, I suppose."

"Don't know any of them. What do they do ?"

"Tell them you never heard of them ! Trilling will say, 'How exquisitely subtle !' or, if it's Eversleigh, 'How symbolic !'"

"Of what ?"

"Oh ! anything, nothing. Ask them that, too, and they'll hurl paradoxes and epigrams at you till you'll begin to doubt your own sanity. You'll soon see how it's done; you may even learn to do it yourself. It's not difficult. Merely remember what a normal man says when he's asked a plain question, invert it, season to taste with a few passion-colored adjectives, and serve up as languidly as possible."

"Ah ! a few passion-colored adjectives may be useful, I imagine, if that's the set. Well, go on." (Roberts. $1.)—*From Syrett's "Nobody's Fault."*

THE NEW GENERATION.

WHEN the mother with sore travail,
    To the world a man-child gives,
Let a sharp sword from his father
    Be the first gift he receives.

As he grows, instead of playthings,
    Toys for childish sport and game,
Let his father give him, rather,
    A good gun of deadly aim.

When his time is come for schooling,
    Let him to the sword give heed,
Teach him first to wield his weapon,
    After, let him learn to read.

Skill of reading, craft of writing,
    Is a useful thing and good ;
But at the examinations
    Ask him first, "Canst thou shed blood ?"

Hope ye in no other manner
    Poor Armenia to save,
Ill the beggar's part beseemeth
    Independent men and brave.

(Roberts. $1.25.)—*From "Armenian Poems."*

Survey of Current Literature.

☞ *Order through your bookseller.*—*"There is no worthier or surer pledge of the intelligence and the purity of any community than their general purchase of books; nor is there any one who does more to further the attainment and possession of these qualities than a good bookseller."*—PROF. DUNN.

ART, MUSIC, DRAMA.

BERENSON, BERNHARD. The Florentine painters of the Renaissance; with an index to their works. Putnam. por. 12°, (The Italian painters of the Renaissance, v. 2.) $1.
The first volume of this series is "The Venetian painters of the Renaissance," published first in 1894. The series, to be completed in four uniform volumes, aims at presenting the significant facts of an historical or æsthetical nature connected with the great schools of Italian painting in such a way that the reader shall be brought immediately and vitally into contact with the great masters of Italy and their works. The index to the works of the principal Florentine painters covers nearly fifty pages.

HUMPHREYS, FRANK LANDON. The evolution of church music; with preface by Bp. H. C. Potter. Scribner. 12°, *net*, $1.75.

SHEDD, *Mrs.* JULIA ANN. Famous painters and paintings. *New rev. enl. ed.*, with new il. Houghton, Mifflin & Co. 12°, $2.

SHEDD, *Mrs.* JULIA ANN. Famous sculptors and sculpture. *New rev. enl. ed.* Houghton, Mifflin & Co. 12°, $2.

BIOGRAPHY, CORRESPONDENCE, ETC.

JEYES, S. H. The Right Hon. Joseph Chamberlain. Warne. por. 12°, (Public men of today.) $1.25.

ROMANES, G. J. The life and letters of George John Romanes, M.A., LL.D., F.R.S.; written and ed. by his wife. Longmans, Green & Co. por. 8°, $4.

SMYTH, ALBERT H. Bayard Taylor. Houghton, Mifflin & Co. por. 12°, (American men of letters.) $1.25.

DESCRIPTION, GEOGRAPHY, TRAVEL, ETC.

BALFOUR, ALICE BLANCHE. Twelve hundred miles in an ox-wagon. Arnold. 8°, $3.50.
Mrs. Balfour is an English lady with a taste for art and adventure. On the 11th of April she started for Cape Town, and for five weeks drove about the wilds of Africa. She has illustrated her vivid descriptions most conscientiously.

BOISSIER, GASTON. Rome and Pompeii: archæological rambles; tr. by D. Havelock Fisher. Putnam. maps, 8°, $2.50.

DAVIS, R. HARDING. Three gringos in Venezuela and Central America. Harper. il. pors. map, 12°, $1.50.

HEARN, LAFCADIO. Kokoro: hints and echoes of Japanese inner·life. Houghton, Mifflin & Co. 12°, $1.25.
Contents: At a railway station; The genius of Japanese civilization; A street singer; From a travelling diary; The nun of the Temple of Amida; After the war; Haru; A glimpse of tendencies; By force of Karma; A conservative; In the twilight of the gods; The idea of pre-existence; In cholera-time; Some thoughts about ancestor-worship; Kimino. Three popular ballads. These papers treat of the inner rather than of the outer life of Japan, for which reason they have been grouped under the title *Kokoro* (heart).

GREELY, A. W. Handbook of Arctic discoveries. Roberts. por. maps, 16°, (Columbian knowledge ser., no. 3.) $1.
A succinct account of all important Arctic voyages and explorations and such minor explorations as are of popular interest. At the conclusion of each chapter lists are given of the more important books on the subject that may interest the general reader. There is a chapter at the end entitled "Bibliography," which considers briefly sources of detailed information.

HOGARTH, D. G. A wandering scholar in the Levant. Scribner. map, il. 8°, $2.50.

WRIGHT, G. F., *D.D., and* UPHAM, WARREN. Greenland ice-fields and life in the North Atlantic; with a new discussion of the causes of the ice age. Appleton. maps, il. 12°, $2.

DOMESTIC AND SOCIAL.

EWING, EMMA P. Art of cookery: a manual for homes and schools. Flood & Vincent. [The Chautauqua Century Press,] por. il. 8°, buckram, $1.75.
"A great need exists in our homes and schools for more intelligent instruction in regard to the preparation of food. This book was written to supply that need. In it the principles underlying the art of cookery are clearly explained, and with its aid any person of ordinary intelligence ought to be able to select, prepare, and serve in a scientific and skilful manner such articles of food as are in general use."—*Preface.*

EDUCATION, LANGUAGE, ETC.

BALDWIN, JA. Old stories of the East. American Book Co. 12°, (Eclectic school readings.) 45 c.
Twelve stories that have come to us from antiquity through the medium of the Hebrew Scriptures. It has been the aim of the author to retell these stories from a literary standpoint and in exactly the same manner as he would relate other stories pertaining to the infancy of the human race.

CORSON, HIRAM. The voice and spiritual education. Macmillan. 24°, (Macmillan's miniature ser.) 75 c.

DEFOE, DAN. Robinson Crusoe; with biographical sketches, notes, etc. Houghton, Mifflin & Co. 12°, (Riverside lit. ser., no. 87, quadruple no.) *net*, 60 c. ; pap., *net*, 50 c.

FITZGERALD, JOS. Pitfalls in English: a manual of customary errors in the use of words. J. Fitzgerald & Co. 12°, (Bookshelf ser., no. I.) 50 c. ; pap., 25 c.

HARDY, G. E. The schoolmaster: the president's address delivered before the New York State Teachers' Association at Saratoga, Monday, July 9, 1894. D. C. Heath & Co. 12°, pap., 25 c.
A plea for the liberal education of the schoolmaster.

HAWTHORNE, NATHANIEL. House of the seven gables. Houghton, Mifflin & Co. 12°, (Riverside lit. ser., no. 91, quadruple no.) pap., *net*, 50 c. ; *net*, 60 c.

MATTHEWS, JA. BRANDER. An introduction to the study of American literature. American Book Co. il. 12°, $1.

SWIFT, JONATHAN. Gulliver's travels. Houghton, Mifflin & Co. 2 v., 16°, (Riverside lit. ser., nos. 89 and 90.) *ea.*, *net*, 15 c. ; or 2 pts. in 1 v., *net*, 40 c.

TAYLOR, F. LILIAN. The Werner primer for beginners in reading. The Werner Co. il. sq. 12°, bds., 30 c.
The primer is beautifully illustrated in colors, and is based upon the kindergarten idea as taught by Froebel. It outlines for the teacher's use all the work for the first term or half year, including reading, writing, language, science, literature, and occupations. Full instructions for the teacher's guidance are given in the "suggestions" and notes.

UNDER the greenwood tree: children's play; words and music given. Edgar S. Werner. 16°, pap., 25 c.

UNWIN, MARY LOUISA HERMIONE. A manual of clay-modelling, for teachers and scholars; with 66 il. and a preface by T. G. Rooper. Longmans, Green & Co. 12°, $1.

FICTION.

ARNOLD, EDWIN LESTER. The story of Ulla. Longmans, Green & Co. 12°, $1.25.
"There is barbaric pathos and a poetical strain sad in the extreme. Ulla was a Viking of Sweden and fell in love with an English maiden who was present at the wedding of the King of Norway. She returned Ulla's love, but her uncle bore her back to England, and for ten years her disconsolate lover did nothing but pillage and burn the coast towns of Albion in the vain hope of finding her. After putting the torch to a beautiful town and murdering many of the inhabitants in his endeavors to carry away many maidens for slaves, he at last found his sweetheart high in the citadel amid the flames. He reached her, seized her in his arms, and sprang into the sea. He was picked up alive, but the maiden was dead. Ulla became a convert to Christianity and also a monk. There are nine other interesting stories by the same author in this book."—*N. Y. Commercial Advertiser.*

BARR, ROB. A woman intervenes; or, the mistress of the mine; il. by Hal Hurst. Stokes. 12°, $1.25.

BURNETT, *Mrs.* FRANCES HODGSON. A lady of quality: being a most curious, hitherto unknown history as related by Mr. Isaac Bickerstaff but not presented to the world of fashion through the pages of *The Tatler* and now for the first time written down. Scribner. 12°, $1.50.

BURTON, J. BLOUNDELLE. In the days of adversity : a romance. Appleton. 12°. (Appleton's town and country lib., no. 187.) $1 ; pap., 50 c.

CAREY, ROSA NOUCHETTE. Mrs. Romney. Lippincott. 12°, (Lippincott's select novels, no. 178.) $1; pap., 50 c.

CHRISTIAN, SIDNEY. Persis Yorke. Macmillan. 12°, buckram, $1.25.
A cheap, sordid little house in London is the home of Persis Yorke; her mother has just died in an hospital, and her father, a worthless scamp, has just deserted her and her sister, carrying away with him all the movable valuables, intending to marry a rich woman. The sister runs away with a man who has no intention of marrying her, and Persis is left distracted, ashamed, poor, and alone. Her troubles do not end here, both members of her family returning to her after she has earned a little money, and they in their turn are destitute. Her bitterness over her apparently endless misfortunes is in the end turned to joy by the love of a good man.

CORELLI, MARIE. Cameos. Lippincott. 12°, $1.
Ten short stories : "Three wise men of Gotham;" Angel's wickedness; The distant voice ; The withering of a rose ; Nehemiah P. Hoskins, artist; An old bundle; "Mademoiselle Zéphyr;" Tiny tramps; The lady with the carnations; My wonderful wife.

DANVERS (The) jewels, and Sir Charles Danvers. [*New ed.*] Harper. 8°, $1.
Two stories now published in one volume. The first few chapters ("The Danvers jewels") of the book are taken up with a thrilling history of the family jewels, involving a story of theft and detection. The sequel ("Sir Charles Danvers") is an entertaining love-story.

DOYLE, ARTHUR CONAN. The exploits of Brigadier Gerard. Appleton. il. 12°, $1.50.

EBERS, G. MORITZ. In the Blue Pike : a romance of German civilization at the commencement of the sixteenth century. Appleton. sq. 16°, 75 c.; pap., 40 c.

FIELD, EUGENE. The holy cross, and other tales ; with decorations by J. L. Rhead. Stone & Kimball. 16°, *net*, $1.25.

FRITH, WALTER. In search of quiet : a country journal, May–July. Harper. 12°, $1.25.

GERARD, DOROTHEA. The wrong man : a novel. Appleton. 12°, (Appleton's town and country lib., no. 186.) $1 ; pap., 50 c.
A duel fought by two young officers of the Austrian army, under a misunderstanding, results in one of them having the muscles of his

right arm severed—his career in the army being thus ended forever; he returns to the home of his father, a poor priest, and teaches a village school. The man who has injured him is rich and his superior socially; he is consumed with remorse and can think of nothing but making atonement for the great wrong he has committed. All his overtures are rejected by his old comrade, for whom fate had yet another bitter experience in store. The scene is an Austrian village.

GRIBBLE, FRANCIS. The things that matter. Putnam. 12°, (Hudson lib.) $1; pap., 50 c.

HALDANE, WINIFRED AGNES. A chord from a violin. Laird & Lee. 1 il., 16°, 50 c.
"Winifred Agnes Haldane, a 16-year-old miss of this city, is the author of an attractive brochure entitled 'A chord from a violin.' The story is simply but charmingly told. It is that of the experiences and observations of a violin from its first appearance as an entity in the shop of its maker through several hands into those of a young man who laid down his life in the rescue of a lady whom he loved. Of course the violin is made to speak well of itself. It is a superior instrument, capable of producing the sweetest music at the will of one who knew how to play well upon it, and the story fittingly closes with the practical tribute to the memory of the hero: 'No other hand shall make me sing as yours has done or awaken the sleeping melodies within my soul.'"—*Chicago Tribune.*

HAMILTON, KATE W. The parson's proxy. Houghton, Mifflin & Co. 12°, $1.25.

HARDY, T. The hand of Ethelberta. *New uniform ed.*, with etched frontispiece. Harper. 8°, $1.50.

HARDY, T. The woodlanders: a novel. *New uniform ed.* Harper. 8°, $1.50.

HARVEY, COCKBURN. The light that lies. Lippincott. il. 16°, 75 c.
Mr. Harry Merton's weakness and undoing was his pursuit of "the light that lies in woman's eyes." After several aimless flirtations, described quite humorously, he finds himself engaged to two women; the result is a rather dramatic ending to the story.

HATTON, JOSEPH. When Greek meets Greek: a tale of love and war; il. by B. West Clinedinst. Lippincott. il. 12°, $1.50.

HORNUNG, E. W. Irralie's bushranger: a story of Australian adventure. Scribner. nar. 16°, 75 c.

HOUGH, E. The singing mouse stories. Forest and Stream Pub. Co. il. nar. 16°, $1.
About sixteen little imaginative sketches, gracefully written and poetically conceived, about life and nature, etc.; for grown people's reading; a prettily made book with marginal sketches.

HUME, FERGUS W. The carbuncle clue: a mystery. Warne. 12°, $1.25.

IN a silent world: the love-story of a deaf-mute. Dodd, Mead & Co. nar. 16°, (The feather lib.) 75 c.

JOHNSTON, H. Dr. Congalton's legacy: a chronicle of North Country byways. Scribner. 12°, $1.25.

KEELING, ELSA D'ESTERRE. Old maids and young. Cassell. 12°, (Cassell's Union sq. lib., no. 11.) pap., 50 c.
Three young girls and two elderly spinsters are the interesting figures in a novel which gives the reader a chance to study diverse femininity in youth and middle age. The male element is characteristic, consisting of the blind Lord Warham, a sturdy young Elishman with democratic views, and young Archdale, who attracts attention chiefly because he is a "cad," and on account of marrying one of the trio of young maids.

LE QUEUX, W. The temptress. Stokes. 12°, $1.
"This is a bit of startling and sensational and spectacular work. Like the other books of Le Queux, it is, in some parts, painfully dramatic, and in all parts interesting. It does not belong to a high order of literature, and yet, if you like to have your blood boil and your nerves tingle once in awhile, this volume will help you to that consummation. There are murder, and gory plots and hypocrisy, and first-class villany, and all the other stimulants to keep you awake. When you begin to read the time will pass quickly."—*N. Y. Herald.*

LLOYD, J. URI. Etidorhpa; or, the end of earth: the strange history of a mysterious being and the account of a remarkable journey as communicated in manuscript to Llewellyn Drury, who promised to print the same, but finally evaded the responsibility; with many il. by J. A. Knapp. [*New cheaper*] 2d ed. The Robert Clarke Co. 4°, *subs., net*, $2.

MASON, A. E. W. A romance of Wastdale. Stokes. 12°, $1.25.

MONCRIEFF, F. The X jewel: a Scottish romance of the days of James VI. Harper. 12°, $1.25.
King James the First of England and Sixth of Scotland, having lost a jewelled St. Andrew's cross of great value, commissions Captain Andrew Evlot, a Scotch soldier of fortune, to find it. The captain goes to the castle of the Earl of Arran, one of the king's favorites, where he meets Jean Uchiltree, an heiress and a ward of the earl. He recovers the jewel only to have it stolen from him. He is challenged by a friend of the Countess of Arran, whom he kills in the duel, and has other exciting adventures.

MORE, E. ANSON, *jr.* Out of the past. Arena Pub. Co. 12°, $1.25; pap., 50 c.
"This story is in the nature of an allegory, where the good contends with the evil. It is full of incident and fine descriptions, and all told fascinatingly. It is the possible life the Brahmin led in ancient times. The incidents are brought out in the story of two college-bred young men who, while travelling in India, lose their guide from the bite of a cobra. One goes for help; the other meantime entering a cavern discovers in the pillow of a mummy old writings which he takes to a priest for translation, and he learns that from the Hindu point of view women are 'the cause of all trouble,' that even Indra finds them 'subtle in wickedness beyond his cunning.' The author treats the origin of Suttee—burning the wife with her

dead husband — and other customs, many of which are still practised."—*Boston Transcript.*

O'GRADY, STANDISH. Ulrick the Ready: a romance of Elizabethan Ireland. Dodd, Mead & Co. 12°, $1.25.

OTTOLENGUI, RODRIGUES. The crime of the century. Putnam. 12°, $1; pap., 50 c.

PHELPS, ELIZ. STUART, [*now* Mrs. Herbert D. Ward.] The supply at St. Agatha's; il. by E. Boyd Smith and Marcia Oakes Woodbury. Houghton, Mifflin & Co. 8°, $1.

PRESCOTT, E. LIVINGSTON. The apotheosis of Mr. Tyrawley. Harper. 12°, $1.25.
"There is the material here for a fine bit of writing. Tyrawley is a good-natured sort of vagabond, a fellow whom it would never do to tie to, since the chief peculiarities he inherited from his father were a love of gambling and a well-developed ability to cheat at cards. He saves a girl from drowning, falls in love with her, and straightway becomes disgusted with his previous life. He therefore makes some strenuous efforts to earn an honest living, but is discouraged by the hypocrites who pretend to be too pious to help such a man, but are willing to let him slide down hill. At last—but I must not anticipate. You get a glimpse, and that is all you need. The book is in some chapters very strong, and the character of Paget, the goody-goody rogue, is well portrayed. Altogether you will find the story very companionable."—*N. Y. Herald.*

RHOSCOMYL, OWEN. Battlement and tower. Longmans, Green & Co. 12°, $1.25.

ROSSETTI, DANTE GABRIEL. Hand and soul. Way & Williams. 24°, parchment, $3.50.

SKERTCHLY, J. A. Sport in Ashanti; or, Melinda the Caboceer: a tale of the Gold coast in the days of King Koffee Kalcalil; with original il. Warne. 12°, $1.50.

SMITH, GERTRUDE. Dedora Heywood. Dodd, Mead & Co. nar. 16°, (The feather lib.) 75 c.
A little New England village is the scene of the love-story of Dedora Heywood and David Loring; for almost twenty years they are separated by religious differences; a change of view on Dedora's part brings them together again, only to be separated in a little while by death.

SNAITH, J. C. Mistress Dorothy Marvin. Appleton. 12°, (Appleton's town and country lib.) $1; pap., 50 c.
This stirring historical romance pictures the stormy career of a hero who took part in the events of the latter part of the seventeenth century in England. The reader shares in the adventures attendant upon Monmouth's Rebellion and the coming of William of Orange. It is a story of narrow escapes, of excellent fighting, and of continued and breathless interest.

SPENDER, HAROLD. At the sign of the guillotine. The Merriam Co. 12°, $1.
The story has its scene chiefly in Paris during the Reign of Terror. It has to do with the fall of Robespierre and his friends, which is largely brought about by a young deputy that Robespierre endeavors to send to the guillotine

because he loves and is loved in return by a young girl that the great man has hoped to win for himself.

STEEL, *Mrs.* FLORA ANNIE. Miss Stuart's legacy. Macmillan. 12°, (Macmillan's novelists' lib., v. 1, no. 12.) pap., 50 c.

STOWE, *Mrs.* HARRIET BEECHER. Pink and white tyranny. *New ed.* Houghton, Mifflin & Co. 16°, $1.25.

SYRETT, NETTA. Nobody's fault. Roberts. 16°, (Keynotes ser., no. 19.) $1.

THURBER, ALWYN M. Quaint Crippen, commercial traveller: a novel. A. C. McClurg. 12°, $1.

TRAIN, ELIZ. PHIPPS. The autobiography of a professional beauty. Lippincott. il. 16°, (Lotos lib.) 75 c.

WATSON, H. B. MARRIOTT. Galloping Dick; being chapters from the life and fortunes of Richard Ryder, sometime gentleman of the road. Stone & Kimball. 16°, $1.25.

WHEELER, IDA WARDEN. Siegfried the mystic: a novel. Arena Pub. Co. 12°, $1.25; pap., 50 c.
This story is written to "acquaint the public with psychic and occult phenomena. . . . The central figure is Siegfried the mystic, whose main purpose in life is to better the condition of his less fortunate fellow-men, chiefly by inducing them to resolve to be stronger, braver, truer, more loving, and more kind."

HISTORY.

FRASER, *Sir* W. Recollections of Napoleon III. Scribner. 12°, $2.

FROUDE, JA. ANTHONY. Lectures on the Council of Trent, delivered at Oxford, 1892–3. Scribner. 8°, $2.
Contents: The condition of the church; The indulgences; The edict of Worms; Clement VII.; Paul III.; The diet of Ratisbon; The demands of Germany; The council in session; Definitions of doctrine; The flight to Bologna; The German envoys; Summary and conclusion. These lectures formed the first of three courses delivered by Mr. Froude during his Regius Professorship of Modern History at Oxford; the other two being on Erasmus and on the English seamen of the sixteenth century.

GREGORY, *Rev.* J. Puritanism in the old world and in the new; from its inception in the reign of Elizabeth to the establishment of the Puritan theocracy in New England: a historical handbook; with introd. by Amory H. Bradford, D.D. Revell. 8°, $2.

HENNE AM RHYN, OTTO. The Jesuits: their history, constitution, moral teaching, political principles, religion, and science. J. Fitzgerald & Co. 12°, (Bookshelf ser., no. 3.) 30 c.; pap., 15 c.

HENNE AM RHYN, OTTO. Mysteria: history of the secret doctrines and mystic rites of ancient religions and mediæval and modern secret orders. J. Fitzgerald & Co. 12°, (Bookshelf ser., no. 2.) 75 c.; pap., 50 c.

HOSMER JA. K. The life of Thomas Hutchinson, royal governor of the province of Massachusetts Bay. Houghton, Mifflin & Co. por. 8°, $4.

SLATIN *Pasha*, RUDOLPH C. Fire and sword in the Sudan: a personal narrative of fighting and serving the Dervishes, 1879–1895; tr. by F. R. Wingate; il. by R. Talbot Kelly. E. Arnold. pors. il. folding map, 8°, $5.

HUMOR AND SATIRE.

BANGS, J. KENDRICK. The bicyclers, and three other farces. Harper. 12°, $1.25.

LITERATURE, MISCELLANEOUS AND COLLECTED WORKS.

BALDWIN, JA. A guide to systematic readings in the Encyclopædia Britannica. Werner Co. 12°, $2.

BURNS, ROB. Complete works; ed. by W. E. Henley and T. F. Henderson. *Centenary de luxe ed.* In 4 v. V. 1. Houghton, Mifflin & Co. portraits, fac-similes of manuscript, etc. 8°, per v., $4. Ed. limited to 150 copies.

FISKE, AMOS KIDDER. The Jewish scriptures: the books of the Old Testament in the light of their origin and history. Scribner. 12°, $1.50.
"Mr. Fiske's work presents its information in so convenient a form and is, withal, written in so lucid and manly a style that it will surely win its way in quarters where anything savoring of the 'higher criticism' is still under suspicion. If it serves in even a slight degree to break down the absurd wall which superstition and prejudice have built around the ancient Hebrew literature, the author can honestly feel that he has done something to make the world better."—*Boston Gazette.*

FLETCHER, W. I., *and* BOWKER, R. R. The annual literary index, 1895: including periodicals, American and English; essays, book chapters, etc.; with author-index, bibliographies, and necrology; ed. with the co-operation of members of the American Library Association and of the *Library Journal* staff. Office of *The Publishers' Weekly.* 8°, $3.50.

HOGG, JA., *ed.* De Quincey and his friends: personal recollections, souvenirs, and anecdotes of Thomas De Quincey, his friends and associates; written and collected by James Hogg; with fac-similes of some of De Quincey's letters. Scribner. por. 8°, hf. roan, $3.

LAWTON, W. CRANSTON. Art and humanity in Homer. Macmillan. 12°, (Macmillan's miniature series.) 75 c.
Seven lectures: The Iliad as a work of art; Womanhood in the Iliad; Closing scenes of the Iliad; The plot of the Odyssey; The Homeric underworld; Odysseus and Nausicaa; Post-Homeric accretions to the Trojan myth.

MACDONELL, ANNIE. Thomas Hardy. Dodd, Mead & Co. 16°, (Contemporary writers ser.) *net*, $1.

RIORDAN, ROGER, *and* TAKAYANAGI. TOZO. Sunrise stories: a glance at the literature of Japan. Scribner. il. 12°, $1.50.

MENTAL AND MORAL.

HANSON, LAURA MARHOLM. Six modern women: psychological sketches; from the Ger-

man by Hermione Ramsden. Roberts. 12°, $1.25.

HARLEY, FANNY M. Sermonettes from Mother Goose: for big folks. F. M. Harley Pub. Co. 16°, $1; pap., 50 c.
Taking nine of the familiar ditties of the nursery as texts, the author preaches nine excellent sermons on every-day shortcomings that are rich in wisdom and advice. They must not be thought funny, as they are not, although the writer draws her inspiration from "There was a man in our town," "There was an old woman, and what do you think?" "Cross Patch," "Three wise men of Gotham," etc.

HARRIS, G. Moral evolution. Houghton, Mifflin & Co. 12°, $2.
Prof. Harris, of the Andover Theological Seminary, presents in sixteen chapters the results of his long and profound study on the ethical and religious development of the individual and of society: Evolution and ethics; Personality in society; The moral ideal, the good; The moral law, the right; The happiness theory; Self-realization and altruism; Ethics and evolution; Morality and religion; The Christian ideal, personal; The Christian ideal, social; Degeneration; Personal regeneration; Social regeneration, economics; Social regeneration, institutions; Ethics and theology; Christianity and evolution.

NATURE AND SCIENCE.

BRIGGS, H. MEAD. By tangled paths: stray leaves from nature's byways. Warne. il. 12°, $1.25.
Articles depicting various phases of English landscape: A skipper bold; In the heart of Surrey; An incorrigible rogue; April showers; Riverside wanderings; Happy days; When hearts are young; As twilight falls; A woodland path; Autumn; When summer pales; Winter, etc.

BURROUGHS, J. A bunch of herbs, and other papers; with a biographical sketch and notes. Houghton, Mifflin & Co. 16°, (Riverside lit. ser., no. 92.) pap., *net,* 15 c.

ROBINSON, ROWLAND E. In New England fields and woods. Houghton, Mifflin & Co. 12°, $1.25.
"A most charming and in every way delightful little volume. It was evidently written by one who is a lover of nature and a careful observer of the changes of the seasons. There is a breath of the south wind in it, and you cannot resist its charm. Wherever you may happen to go this next summer, you will need this neat book as a daily companion. It will tell you of the birds and the plants that belong to every month of the year, and do it in such way that you will feel once more the glamour of this beautiful earth and wish to live forever. It is a quiet little book, not at all pretentious or intrusive, but for true companionship I commend it more heartily than I have words to express."—*N. Y. Herald.*

TYLER, J. M. The whence and whither of man; a brief history of his origin and development through conformity to environment; being the Morse lectures of 1895. Scribner. 12°, $1.75.
Contents: The problem, the mode of its solu-

tion ; Protozoa to worms, cells, tissues, and organs ; Worms to vertebrates, skeleton, and head ; Vertebrates, backbone, and brain ; The history of mental development and its sequence of functions ; Natural selection and environment ; Conformity to environment ; Man ; The teachings of the Bible ; Present aspects of the theory of evolution. Index.

VERITY, J. B. Electricity up-to-date for light, power, and traction. [*New 5th ed. rev. and enl.*] Warne. il. 12°, $1.
In the present edition the work has once more been enlarged and many illustrations have been added, while to justify its title the contents have again been revised.

POETRY AND DRAMA.

PLUMMER, MARY WRIGHT. Verses. Cleveland and N. Y., printed at the De Vinne Press for Paul Lemperly, F. A. Hilliard, and Frank E. Hopkins. 12°, bds.. $1.25.
A small collection of poetry, mostly sonnets, by the librarian of the Pratt Library ; they are smoothly and gracefully written and refined in sentiment ; a pretty book with wide margins and uncut edges.

WATSON, W. The father of the forest, and other poems, Stone & Kimball. 12°, $1.25.

POLITICAL AND SOCIAL.

COMMONS, J. R. Proportional representation. Crowell. 12°, (Lib. of economics and politics, no. 8.) $1.75.
Prof. Commons argues that as the legislature controls the very life-blood of the city, the state, and the nation, it therefore ought to be eminently representative. He traces the recent evil phases of American political life directly or indirectly to the century-old system of electing single representatives from limited districts. He is in favor of the plan adopted and recommended by the American Proportional Representation League, of which he was the founder. He illustrates it by example taken from the European countries wh'ch have successfully tried it. He believes that proportional representation will secure the independence of the voter and freedom from the rule of the party machine ; that it will do away with the spoils system and result in the purification of our politics ; and that it will be an effective agent in municipal and social reform.

HOWARD, M. W. The American plutocracy ; il. by A. A. Cobb. Holland Pub. Co. 12°, (Holland lib., no. 4.) $1 ; pap., 50 c.
The author is member of Congress in Alabama and an advocate of free coinage of silver. He attributes all the financial troubles of the country to the maintenance of the gold standard. This, he says, has fostered trusts and combinations and made the rich richer and the poor poorer ; he gives some startling statistics as to the wealth of the country and as to the poverty. The rapid concentration of wealth in the hands of a few he considers the most alarming sign of the times.

INGLE, E. Southern side-lights ; a picture of social and economic life in the South a generation before the war. Crowell. 12°, (Library of economics aud politics.) $1.75.

WEEKS, STEPHEN B. Southern Quakers and slavery: a study in institutional history. The John Hopkins Press. folding map, 8°, (Johns Hopkins Univ. studies, extra v. 15.) $2.
This volume deals with the Society of Friends in Virginia, North Carolina, South Carolina. Georgia, and Tennessee. It has been entitled " Southern Quakers and slavery," for the reason that slavery was *the* object which differentiated Friends in the South from other religious bodies. A bibliography of Southern Quakerism is given (16 p.). Index.

SPORTS AND AMUSEMENTS.

CULIN, STEWART. Korean games; with notes on the corresponding games of China and Japan. 153 il. and 22 colored plates by native artists. Univ. of Pennsylvania. sq. 4°, lim. ed., $7.50.
A comprehensive account of the games of Korea, comprising 97 titles, including the amusements of children, tops, kites, and football, and dice, dominoes, playing cards, backgammon, and chess, with detailed descriptions of several hundred more or less related games in other parts of eastern Asia. The introduction presents a new theory of the origin of games in divination; offers an explanation of the distribution of games, and indicates the value of their study in the science of ethnology. The chapter on Korean chess is by W. H. Wilkinson, late H. B. M. Consul-General at Seoul.

WHITE, MARY. The book of a hundred games. Scribner. 12°, $1.
The object of this little book is to give, to those who need them, a number of new games, with changes rung on the old favorites.

THEOLOGY, RELIGION, AND SPECULATION.

CHURCH CLUB of New York. Christian unity and the Bishops' declaration : lectures delivered in 1895, under the auspices of the Church Club of New York. E. & J. B. Young. 12°, *net,* 50 c.
Contents : Christian unity—the Master's word and the Church's act, by T. F. Gailor, D.D.; The Holy Scriptures as the rule and ultimate standard of faith, by C. E. W. Body, D.D.; The two creeds, by C. S. Olmsted (Archdeacon); The two great sacraments, by A. St. J. Chambre (Archdeacon); The historic Episcopate, by Rev. Francis J. Hall.

COYLE, J. PATTERSON, *D.D.* The spirit in literature and life: the E. D. Rand lectures in Iowa College for the year 1894. Houghton, Mifflin & Co. 12°, $1.50.

GOULD, *Rev.* EZRA P. A critical and exegetical commentary on the Gospel according to St. Mark. Scribner. 8°, (International critical commentary.) *net,* $2.50.

LAWRENCE, W. Visions and service: fourteen discourses delivered in college chapels. Houghton, Mifflin & Co. 12°, $1.25.
Contents: The young man's vision; The challenge of Jesus; The fixedness of character; The worth of one fact; A skilful defence; The unchangeableness and the changeableness of faith; The priests' taunt; Three characters; The university man in active life; Jesus in his own city; Heavenly mindedness; Privilege and helpfulness; A keynote of college life; A servant of his own generation.

LEA, H. C. A history of confession and indulgences in the Latin church. In 3 v. V. I] Lea Bros. & Co. 8°, $3.

SCHURMAN, JACOB GOULD. Agnosticism and religion. C. Scribner's Sons. 16°, $1.

The author is president of Cornell University; he takes Prof. Huxley's well-known position as a starting-point and proceeds to exhibit systematically the arrogance and illogicality of absolute agnosticism. A plea for retaining relations with church organizations, even when creeds cease to be convincing, is a noteworthy and original contribution to the discussion of the subject.

STACKPOLE, EVERETT S. Prophecy; or, speaking for God. Crowell. 16°, 75 c.

Consists of seven chapters dealing, in order, with the following topics: Prophecy defined; The prophetic call and character; The prophetic message; Prophetic inspiration; Predictive prophecy; Messianic prophecy; and The prophet as moral reformer.

Books for the Young.

BELL, *Mrs.* A. F. Victor in Buzzland: a nature fairy story. A. Flanagan. il. 12°, bds., 25 c.

Gives in the form of a fairy-tale information about the insect world; can be used as a reader.

BURT, MARY E., *ed.* Little nature studies for little people; from the essays of J. Burroughs.

V. 1, A primer and a first reader. *New rev. ed.* Ginn & Co. il. 12°, 30 c.

After "Little nature studies" was first published in the early part of 1895, it was sent to leading teachers in the United States, with the request that they criticise it. One of the return requests was that more notice should be given to diacritical marking, and also that more of the simple lessons should be placed in the front of the book, while the longer and harder lessons at the back should be bound in another cover for the higher grade. These suggestions were adopted—hence this is now v. 1 and a primer, covering less ground than the first edition.

LEE, ALBERT. Tommy Toddles; il. by P. S. Newell. Harper. 12°, $1.25.

LOTHROP, *Mrs.* HARRIET MULFORD. ["Margaret Sidney," *pseud.*] The old town pump: a story of east and west. Lothrop Pub. Co. il. 12°, $1.25.

On a memorable Thanksgiving Day the old town pump at Haytown is the scene of what is rumored about the staid New England village as an attack on the patron saint of the town, Miss Nancy Harkness. Later developments, however, show that facts have been misrepresented by a village hypocrite, and an unsuspected mystery in the Harkness family is revealed; after this Betty and Simon, with other principal characters, emigrate to the West, a graphic description being given of a race for possession in the "boomers' section."

RECENT FRENCH AND GERMAN BOOKS.

FRENCH.

Adam, P. La force du mal. 12°. Colin......... $1 00

Basserie, I. P. La conjuration de Cinq-Mars. 12°. Perrin..................................... 1 00

Bats, Baron de. Un conspirateur royaliste pendant la terreur. 8°. Plon.................. 2 25

Bonnefont, G. Nos grandes dames: Mme. la duchesse d'Uzès. Ill. 8°. Flammarion........ 1 00

Bonnioeau-Gesmon. Domestiques et maîtres: Question sociale. 12°. Lemerre............ 1 00

Bovet, M. A. de. Roman de femmes. 12°. Lemerre. 1 00

Broglie, Le duc de. La mission de M. de Gontant-Biron à Berlin 12°. Levy.......... 1 00

Cadol, E. L'archduchesse. 12°. Levy.......... 1 00

D'Avenel, G. Le mecanisme de la vie moderne. 12°. Colin..................................... 1 00

Deschamps, G. Chemin fleuri. 12°. Levy..... 1 00

Desjardins, A. P. J. Proudhon. Sa vie, etc. 2 vols. 12°. Perrin.......................... 2 00

Feuillet, O. Souvenirs et confidences. 8°. Levy. 2 25

Franklin, A. La vie privée d'autrefois: L'enfant. 12°. Plon.......................... 1 00

Goncourt, E. de. L'art japonais du 18ieme siècle: Hokousaï. 12°. Charpentier............ 1 00

Hervieu, P. Le petit Duc. 12°. Lemerre..... 1 00

Isambert. La vie à Paris pendant une année de la révolution (1791–1792) 12°. Alcan....... 1 00

Les magasins de nouveautes. III. 12°. Plon.... 1 00

Maeterlinck, M. Le trésor, des humbles. 12°. Mercure..................................... 1 07

Manheimer, E. Le Nouveau monde Sud Africain: La vie au Transvaal. 12°. Flammarion.. 1 00

Metenier, O. Raphaela. 12°. Dentu.......... 1 00

Mourey, G. L'œuvre nuptial. 12°. Lemerre... 1 00

Navarre, Marguerite de. Les dernières poesies de. 8°. Colin............................. 3 60

Pierret, E. La fin d'un flirt. 12°. Lemerre..... 1 00

Prevost, M. Le mariage de Juliette. 24°. Lemerre..................................... 60

Rochefort, H. Les aventures de ma vie. Vol. 1. 12°. Dupont............................. $1 00

Saint Chamas, Cte. de. Mémoires. Aide de camp du Maréchal Soult. 1802–1832. 8°. Plon.. 2 25

Sassenay, Le Marq. de. Les derniers mois de Murat. 12°. Lemerre...................... 1 00

Secretan, C. Essais de philosophie et de littérature. 12°. Alcan......................... 1 00

Sudermann, H. Le moulin silencieux. 12°. Levy. 1 00

Theuriet, A. Fleur de Nice. 12°. Ollendorf... 1 00

GERMAN.

Berkow, K. Unsere Backfische. 12°. Janke.... 45

Bobertag, B. Mit allen Waffen. 3 vols. 12°. Pierson..................................... 2 65

Borchardt, F. Lavastroeme. 12°. Duncker.... 1 20

Cotta, J. Ehefolter. 12°. Dieckmann.......... 70

— Verweibt. 12°. Dieckmann................ 70

Friedmann, F. Grifin Ilse. 12°. Duncker..... 85

Gersdorff, A. v. Am Arbeitsmarkt. 2 vols. 12°. Reissner................................... 2 35

Hartmann, E. v. Tagesfragen. 8°. Haacke... 2 00

Hedenstierna, A. v. Der Majoratsherr von Halleborg. 12°. Meyer.................... 70

Jokai, M. Es giebt keinen Teufel. 12°. Janke.. 70

— Die reichen Armen. 12°. Janke............ 70

— Schwarzes Blut. 12°. Janke............... 70

Nessen, J. Heine's Familienleben. 8°. Fulda. 80

Niemann, A. Die Erbinnen. 2 vols. 12°. Pierson..................................... 2 00

Raimund, G. Ein deutsches Weib. 12°. Janke. 40

Schoenthan. Stickluft. 12°. Reissner......... 1 20

Suttner, B. v. High-Life. 12°. Pierson........ 1 70

Werther, C. W. Zum Victoria Nyanza. 8°. Paetel..................................... 2 00

Wildenbruch, E. v. Heinrich und Heinrich's Geschlecht. 12°. Freund & Jeckel......... 1 00

Zapp, A. Offizierstöchter. 2 vols. 12°. Reissner. 1 70

Zeitgenoss, E. Moralische Träumereien. 12°. Schwabe.................................. 55

Zobeltitz, F. v. An der Wende. 12°. Janke.... 40

MAGAZINE ARTICLES FOR APRIL.

Articles marked with an asterisk are illustrated.

ARTISTIC, MUSICAL, AND DRAMATIC.—*Century*, Japanese War Posters,* W. D. Howells; George De Forest Brush, J. C. Van Dyke; The Delights of Art (Coquelin),* Vibert.—*Fort. Review*(Mar.), Monticelli, Drage.—*Godey's*, Mrs. Clio Hinton Huneker, Sculptoress,* Robard; Chimmie Fadden on the Stage,* Beaumont Fletcher; W. W. Gilchrist (Music in America, XII.), Rupert Hughes; Julia Marlowe Taber, Severance; Pappenheim and Gerster, Parks.— *Nine. Century* (Mar.), Lord Leighton and His Art, W. B. Richmond.—*Scribner's*, Lord Leighton,* Cosmo Monkhouse; Recent Discoveries at Lake Nemi*; Colored Shadows*; Studio Furnishings; The Artists' Work and Theory*; An Epoch of Opera.*

BIOGRAPHY, CORRESPONDENCE, ETC.—*Atlantic*, Some Memories of Hawthorne, by Rose Lathrop.—*Godey's*, The Most Eccentric Man in the World (George Francis Train).* Willetts.— *Harper's*, Mr. Lowell in England, Smalley.

DESCRIPTION, TRAVEL, ETC.—*Atlantic*, Latter-Day Cranford, Alice Brown; An Archer's Sojourn in the Okefenokee, Maurice Thompson.— Old-Time Sugar-Making, Robinson.—*Catholic World*, In the Land of the Jesuit Martyrs,* O'Hagan; John Harvard's Parish Church,* Locke.— *Century*, Churches of Périgneux and Angoulême,* Van Rensselaer.— *Fort. Review* (Mar.), In the Land of the Northernmost Eskimo, Astrup.—*No. Amer. Review*, Gold-mining Activity in Colorado, Richard; North Polar Problem, Markham, R. N.—*West. Review* (Mar.), Pilgrimage to the Temples of Java, Rivington.

EDUCATION, LANGUAGE, ETC. — *Arena*, The Educational Value of Instructive and Artistic Entertainments which Appeal to the Non-Theatre-going Public,* Flower. — *Atlantic*, The Training of the Teacher, Atkinson.—*Fort. Review* (Mar.), An Educational Interlude, Mrs. Fred. Harrison.—*Forum*, Teaching: a Trade or a Profession?, Schurman.—*Harper's*, Phase of Modern College Life,* H. T. Fowler.—*Nine. Century* (Mar.), The Encroachment of Women, Whibley; Self-help Among Amer. College Girls, Eliz. L. Banks.

FICTION.—*Atlantic*, The Old Things, Pts. i.-iv., Henry James; A Son of the Revolution, Octave Thanet; Zilpah Treat's Confession.—*Century*, The Little Bell of Honor, Gilbert Parker; The Mutiny on the "Jimmy Aiken," Whitmarsh.— *Godey's*,—A Burglar, a Bicycle, and a Storm,* Ransom; Rosalind a-Wheel, Comstock.—*Harper's*, The Voice of Authority,* Alexander; A Spring Flood in Broadway,* Brander Matthews; The Missionary Sheriff,* Octave Thanet. — *Lippincott's*, Flotsam, Owen Hall; Dreaming Bob, Abbott.—*Scribner's*, A Day at Olympia,* Duffield Osborne; Cinderella, R. H. Davis; A Baby in the Siege, J. C. Harris.

HISTORY.—*Catholic World*, Early Labors of the Printing-Press, Currier.—*Century*, Four Lincoln Conspiracies,* V. L. Mason.—*Harper's*, Mad Anthony Wayne's Victory,* Roosevelt.—*Lippincott's*, The Washingtons in Virginia Life, Wharton.—*No. Amer. Review* Recollections of Lincoln's Assassination, Seaton Munroe.

HYGIENIC AND SANITARY.—*Godey's*, Woman's Cycle, Mary L. Bisland; Is Bicycling Harmful?, Arthur Bird, M.D.—*West. Review* (Mar.), Practicability of Vegetarianism.

LITERARY.—*Atlantic*, A Book-Lovers' Paradise.—*Harper's*, Incomes of Authors; Judge and Poet (Editor's Study).—*Nine. Century* (Mar.), Matthew Arnold, Fred. Harrison; Poisoning the Wells of Catholic Criticism, Edmund S. Purcell.—*West. Review*, The New Poet Laureate, D. F. Hannigan; Edward Fitzgerald, Maurice Todhunter.

MENTAL AND MORAL.—*Atlantic*, The Scotch Element in the Amer. People, Shaler.—*Century*, Who Are Our Brethren?, Howells.—*Forum*, Holland's Care for Its Poor, J. H. Gore.

NATURE AND SCIENCE.—*Catholic World*, Amer. Museum of Natural History,* Seton.—*Forum*, The Cathode Ray, A. W. Wright.—*Nine. Century* (Mar.), Recent Science (Röntgen's Rays— The Erect Ape Man), Kropotkin.—*No. Amer. Review*, Pygmy Races of Men, Starr; Birds and the Atmosphere, Baines.—*Scribner's*, New Photography by Cathode Rays,* Trowbridge.

POETRY AND DRAMA. — *Century*, Arborside, Guiney; Ballad of Laughing Sally, Roberts; The One Desire, Frank Dempster Sherman; A Wound, De Vere. — *Harper's*, A Night and Morning in Jerusalem,* Katrina Trask; A Dream, Margaret E. Sangster.—*Scribner's*, The Dreamer, Scollard; Sonnet, George Cabot Lodge.

POLITICAL AND SOCIAL. — *Arena*, Government by Brewery, Gates.—*Atlantic*, The Alaska Boundary Line, Mendenhall; China and the Western World, Hearn.—*Catholic World*, For the Party, for the State, or for the Nation.— *Century*, Possibilities of Permanent Arbitration —Patriotism that Costs (Topics of the Times).— *Fort. Review* (Mar.), The Fiasco in Armenia, Dillon; Venezuela Before Europe and America, Gossip; The Modern Jew and the New Judaism, I., Cohen; Rhodes and Jameson, Verschoyle. —*Forum*, Deficiency of Revenue the Cause of Our Financial Ills, Sen. Sherman; Two South African Constitutions, Hon. James Bryce; Present Outlook of Socialism in England, William Morris; Rumors of War and Resultant Duties, J. W. Miller; Foibles of the New Woman, Ella W. Winston.—*No. Amer. Review*, Great Britain and the United States: Their True Relations, David A. Wells; Possible Complications of the Cuban Question, Hazeltine; Problems of the Transvaal, Karl Blind; Governor Morton as a Presidential Candidate (Platt, Depew, Warner Miller, etc.); The Regeneration of Russia, A. W. Sherman.—*Scribner's*, The Ethics of Modern Journalism, Gorren; The Quarrel of the English-Speaking Peoples, Henry Norman.—*West. Review* (Mar.), The Monroe Doctrine, Henriques; German Competition, Newcomen; "Merrie England," Scanlon; A Living Wage, Thomas.

SPORTS AND AMUSEMENTS. — *Century*, The Old Olympic Games,* Marquand.—*Godey's*, The Work of Wheelmen for Better Roads, Potter; A Cycle Show in Little,* Humphrey.—*Scribner's*, The Revival of the Olympic Games,* Richardson.

THEOLOGY, RELIGION, SPECULATION.— *Lippincott's*, Holy Week in Mexico, by O. L.

Freshest News.

A. E. CLUETT & CO., New York City, announce "Conjugal Amenities," by "Delta," obviously a *nom de plume.* The book has already met with success in England and is endorsed as exceptionally bright by *The Lady, The Court Journal, The Sketch,* etc. It is the story of a luxurious and high-spirited young woman who married an English nobleman, and gave him serious cause for anxiety by her greedy desire to make the most of the pleasures of life. There will also later on appear a novel by Adeline Sergeant, to be entitled "Marjory Moore," and to deal with English home life, in the sketching of which the author is specially successful.

CHARLES SCRIBNER'S SONS have just ready one of Eugene Field's last books entitled "The House, an episode in the lives of Reuben Baker, astronomer, and his wife Alice," which will appeal irresistibly to every one who has passed through the fever of house-building; Miss Ida M. Tarbell's biography of "Madame Roland"; also, Julian Hawthorne's New York *Herald* $10,000 Prize Story, "A Fool of Nature," in which the author has drawn some interesting types of character in metropolitan society, both in its most select and its Bohemian circles. They have added to their dainty and attractive *Ivory Series* Harriet Prescott Spofford's poetical musical story, "A Master Spirit," and George W. Cable's lovely story, "Madame Delphine."

THE FREDERICK A. STOKES CO. have just ready "A Woman Intervenes," by Robert Barr, telling of an astute New York woman reporter who managed to glean secrets from unsuspecting ship companions ; "The Broom-Squire," a study of English life full of stirring scenes, by S. Baring-Gould ; "A Woman with a Future," by Mrs. Andrew Dean; and "A Rogue's Daughter," by Adeline Sergeant. They have recently added "Diana's Hunting," by Robert Buchanan ; and "I Married a Wife," by John Strange Winter, to their *Twentieth Century Series;* and "Stolen Souls," by William Le Queux ; "Anne of Argyle," by George Eyre-Todd ; "A Comedy in Spasms," by Iota ; and "A Whirl Asunder," by Gertrude Atherton, to their *West End Series.*

D. APPLETON & CO. have just ready S. R. Crockett's new story, "Cleg Kelly, Arab of the City, his progress and adventures," in which the lights and shadows of curious phases of Edinburgh life and of Scotch farm and railroad life are pictured with an intimate sympathy, richness of humor, and truthful pathos ; "Voice Building and Tone Placing," showing a new method of relieving injured vocal chords by tone exercise, by Dr. H. Holbrook Curtis ; "Sleeping Fires," a new story by George Gissing ; "In the Blue Pike," a romance of German life in the beginning of the 16th century, by Dr. Georg Ebers ; and "Mistress Dorothy Marvin," a historical romance of the time of Monmouth's Rebellion and the coming of William of Orange, by J. C. Snaith.

ROBERTS BROTHERS have had some remarkable books recently, several of them hardly within the compass of the "reading public," but sure in time to make their way to the shelves of connoisseurs and careful students of the literature of psychology and reflections upon the state of the world at the close of the nineteenth century. A book deserving most careful reading is "Young Ofeg's Ditties," delicate prose poems full of thought and mystery, by Ola Hansson, translated by George Egerton, author of "Keynotes," whose innate sympathy with her author and her great talent at word-painting make her rendering of the difficult phrases a rare work of art as a translation. Ola Hansson is the husband of Mrs. Hansson who has written "Six Modern Women," also a very remarkable study, very ably put into English. The third number of the *Columbian Knowledge Series* is ready—the "Handbook of Arctic Discoveries," by A. W. Greely.

G. P. PUTNAM'S SONS have just ready the long-promised volume on "Lorenzo de' Medici, and Florence in the Fifteenth Century," by E. Armstrong, which forms the 16th volume of the *Heroes of the Nations* series. They have also just ready "The Rule of the Turk," a revised and enlarged edition of "The Armenian Crisis," by Frederick Davis Greene. They announce a novel by Jean Porter Rudd entitled "The Tower of the Old Schloss"; and "At Wellesley—Legend for '96," stories and studies by the senior class of Wellesley College. G. P. Putnam's Sons will also soon bring out in co-operation with John Murray, the English publisher, a new edition of the works of George Borrow. The first work in the set is "The Bible in Spain, or, the journeys, adventures, and imprisonments of an Englishman in an attempt to circulate the Scriptures in the Peninsula." This new edition is edited, with notes and a glossary, by Ulick Ralph Burke, M.A., author of "A History of Spain," etc. It will be completed in two volumes, and will contain a map and four etchings. The same publishers have in press for early publication the book of the Hastings Chess Tournament; the volume will contain the full official record of the 230 games played by the 22 competitors at this international congress.

HOUGHTON, MIFFLIN & CO. have just ready Miss Elizabeth Stuart Phelps's new story,'" The Supply at Saint Agatha's"; the first volume of the new limited *Centenary edition* of the complete works of Robert Burns, edited by William E. Henley and T. F. Henderson; "Kokoro: hints and echoes of the Japanese inner life," by Lafcadio Hearn ; the ninth volume of Sargent's monumental work on "The Silva of North America"; a fac-simile of Gov. William Bradford's account of "The History of the Plimoth Plantation," with introduction by John A. Doyle ; the 1896 edition of "A Satchel Guide for the Vacation Tourist in Europe"; and, in the *Riverside Literature Series,* "A Bunch of Herbs, and other papers," by John Burroughs, with biographical sketch and notes. Houghton, Mifflin & Co. are preparing for publication next fall an entirely new *Riverside edition* of the writings of Mrs. Harriet Beecher Stowe. It will comprise, probably, sixteen twelvemo volumes, very carefully edited, with bibliographical introductions and whatever notes are needed. It will contain portraits of Mrs. Stowe and engraved title-pages, and in all details will be equal to the best previous *Riverside editions* of great American authors. A limited large-paper edition will contain as a special feature Mrs. Stowe's autograph, which she has written for each copy.

Roberts' Spring Announcements

HOUGHTON, MIFFLIN & COMPANY,

4 Park Street, Boston;   11 East 17th Street, New York.

TOM GROGAN.

A Novel. By F. HOPKINSON SMITH, author of "Colonel Carter of Cartersville," "A Gentleman Vagabond," etc. With 20 illustrations by Charles S. Reinhart. In a strikingly decorative binding. 12mo, $1.50. (*April* 18.)

"Tom Grogan" is, thus far, the crowning achievement of Mr. Smith's genius as a novelist. It has attracted marked attention in its serial appearance, both because of the delightful qualities of the story and its style, and also because of its frank attitude on certain phases of the labor question, in which multitudes are interested. It is sure to cause warm discussion, and equally sure to win a very large circle of readers who know by experience or by hearsay how charmingly Mr. Smith's stories are told.

Pirate Gold.

A Novel. By F. J. STIMSON. 16mo, $1.25. (*In April.*)

Mr. Stimson (" J. S. of Dale ") is no novice in story-telling. He has won an enviable reputation, which will be emphasized by "Pirate Gold," a story of Boston in the middle of this century. It is not an historical novel, but reproduces with great fidelity and charm the social atmosphere of the place and time. The season will bring few brighter, more readable novels.

Spring Notes from Tennessee.

By BRADFORD TORREY, author of "A Florida Sketch-Book," "Birds in the Bush," "A Rambler's Lease," "The Foot-path Way." 16mo, $1.25. (*April.*)

A delightful group of papers containing observations of birds and scenery in Tennessee, many of them on famous battlefields—Chickamauga, Lookout Mountain, etc. Several of the papers have not before been printed, and all are very charming.

THE SUPPLY AT SAINT AGATHA'S.

By ELIZABETH STUART PHELPS, author of "A Singular Life," "The Gates Ajar," etc. Printed on deckel-edge paper of high quality, and artistically bound in cloth with a distinctive cover design by Mrs. Whitman. With illustrations. Square 12mo, gilt top, $1.00.

This is one of the strongest, most suggestive, most illuminating of all the stories Miss Phelps has written. The setting of the story is vigorous and skilful, the narrative is engrossingly interesting, and the revelation of the "Supply" at once startles and uplifts. The book is every way artistic and is admirable for an Easter gift.

By Oak and Thorn:

A Record of English Days. By ALICE BROWN, author of "Fools of Nature," "Meadow Grass," etc.   16mo, $1.25. (*April* 11.)

A very pleasant book of travel and observation in England, notably in Devon, one of the most picturesque counties.

A Satchel Guide

For the Vacation Tourist in Europe. Edition for 1896, carefully revised to date, both the text and maps. 16mo, roan, flexible, $1.50, *net*.

This guide-book covers the portions of Europe commonly visited by vacation tourists, and contains just the information they desire, in thoroughly reliable form.

THE EXPANSION OF RELIGION.

By E. WINCHESTER DONALD, D.D., Rector of Trinity Church, Boston. 12mo, $1.50.

Here is a volume which cannot fail to be regarded as a valuable contribution to the religious literature of the day. Dr. Donald aims to show that religion is not to be confounded with ecclesiasticism, but is a permanent force in human affairs; and he attempts to trace its conpection to-day with industrialism, socialism, education, organized Christianity, and the enlargement of human life.

HISTORY OF PRUSSIA UNDER FREDERICK THE GREAT. 1756-1757.

By HERBERT TUTTLE, late Professor in Cornell University. With a Biographical Sketch by Professor Herbert B. Adams. 1 vol., crown 8vo, $1.50.

This volume contains the addition made to his work on "The History of Prussia" by Professor Tuttle when his hand was arrested by fatal disease. It covers the early part of the great Seven Years' War, and is a distinct addition to the admirable work he had already achieved in such a style as to win the emphatic praise of the foremost authorities.

FOR SALE BY YOUR BOOKSELLER.

LITERARY NEWS

AN ECLECTIC REVIEW OF
CURRENT LITERATURE
~ILLUSTRATED~

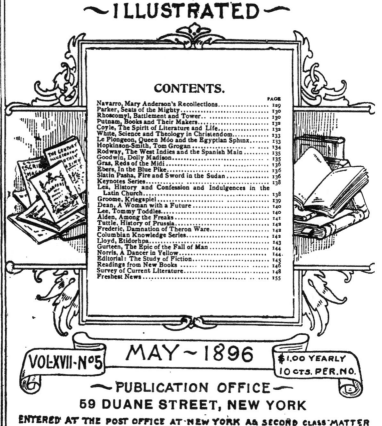

CONTENTS.

MAY ~ 1896

VOL. XVII · No 5

$1.00 YEARLY
10 CTS. PER. NO.

~ PUBLICATION OFFICE ~
59 DUANE STREET, NEW YORK
ENTERED AT THE POST OFFICE AT NEW YORK AS SECOND CLASS MATTER

The Literary News

In winter you may reade them, ab igneм, by the fireside; and in summer, ab umbram, under some shadie tree, and therewith pass away the tedious howres.

VOL. XVII.	MAY, 1896.	No. 5.

Mary Anderson's Recollections.

IN the first chapter of this book Miss Anderson explains her purpose in writing for publication. "I have written these pages," she says,
the same readers continue through ten chapters more, until the end is reached, the odds are that they will consider Miss Anderson's

From "A Few Memories."   Harper & Bros.
(Copyright, 1896, by Mary Anderson de Navarro.)
MME. DE NAVARRO. (1895.)
[From the portrait in photogravure.]

"more for young girls (who may have the same ambitions that I had) than for any one else, to show them that the glitter of the stage is not all gold, and thus do a little toward making them realize how serious an undertaking it is to adopt a life so full of hardships, humiliations, and even dangers." This is a noble ambition, but to have realized it Miss Anderson should have ended her book at the sixth or seventh chapter. This would leave the "young girls" with a convincing sense of the hardships to which the author alludes. But if
triumph cheaply bought. She suffered in winning fame, but it came to her early in life, and when the prize was attained it brought recompense with it in experiences for which many would gladly undergo pains as bitter as those with which she became acquainted during her apprenticeship. It is no small thing to have enjoyed the companionship of such men and women as are celebrated in the pages of this book. Certainly Miss Anderson dwells more upon the sunny side of her life than upon its trying episodes, and she has

From "The Seats of the Mighty."   Copyright, 1896, by D.
                    Appleton & Co.

GENERAL WOLFE.

more to say to those who read for enterain-
ment than to those who read for instruction.
Her memories may be few in number, but
they cover a wide range of social experience
and give many attractive pictures of life if
they do not give much about art.

The whole trend of these recollections, indeed, is far less toward the philosophical elucidation of an artist's life than toward the
pleased narration of a successful woman's
career.

Miss Anderson does not burden her pages
with trivial matters.   Nearly everything that
she has to say of the people she has met is not
merely in good taste, but interesting, and she
reports conversation with the utmost discretion,
quoting things that are worth quotation.

There is not a dull page in the book.   The
latter is well indexed, and the student of the
dramatic or literary or merely celebrated roll-
call of England and America during the last
ten or fifteen years will find in that index promises of enjoyment which scrutiny of the narrative itself does not disappoint.   Typographically, the volume has been well finished and there
are some interesting portraits of Miss Anderson
finely reproduced.   It is a simple and an admirably written work of reminiscence and ought
to be widely appreciated.   The year thus far
has been specially rich in volumes of biographical interest, and this may fairly take its place
among books that make for hope and encouragement.   (Harper & Brothers. $2.50.)—*N. Y.
Tribune.*

The Seats of the Mighty.

In Gilbert Parker's new romance, "The Seats
of the Mighty," the author has chosen for the
time of his story the most absorbing period of the
romantic eighteenth-century history of Quebec.
The curtain rises soon after General Braddock's
defeat in Virginia, and the hero, a prisoner in
Quebec, curiously entangled in the intrigues of
La Pompadour, becomes a part of a strange history, full of adventure and the stress of peril,
which culminates only after Wolfe's victory
over Montcalm.   The illustrations preserve the
atmosphere of the text, for they present the famous buildings, gates, and battle-grounds as
they appeared at the time of the hero's imprisonment in Quebec.   (Appleton. $1.50.)—*The
American.*

"I Felt He Was no Common Man."

"How now, young sir?" demanded he with
austere severity.   "What meaneth this brawl
in the public streets?"

"As to that, most noble sir," replied the lieutenant steadily, "this brawl, as you term it, is
assuredly not of mine own seeking.   I know
not why I should answer you further, saving
that, having already a sufficient enemy in front,
even I do not want another in rear.   Therefore
I pause to explain that I am a plain gentleman
of Wales, come hither hastily to perform an
errand.   Some of these wits in front did pass a
scurvy trick upon my squire and page, and
when they got the return fell out with drawn steel
upon them.   As soon as they found their bad-
ger was a wolf, they raised that rabble yonder."

From "The Seats of the Mighty."   Copyright, 1896, by D.
                    Appleton & Co.

GENERAL MONTCALM.

"But you may know what a mean spirit an idle mob hath, for already, seeing you but listen to me, they fear the result and are trailing away like smoke. 'S death! sir, none of the common sort will bide the shock, as you can see, and only one of the wits. Gad! I take that one for a gentleman, for he seemeth ashamed of his position, as a gentleman would be. I must e'en offer to fight him, I suppose, to restore his self-respect and end the quarrel mannerly."

The penultimate part of this speech exactly described what had taken place, and the gravity of the new-comer's glance increased to sternness as it rested upon the one who remained, a spruce young fellow of somewhere between twenty-five and thirty. Riding forward he addressed him in a tone of high displeasure as he stood with downbent head and doffed beaver.

"A pretty business for the Lord Warrendon, truly. But since you have so little courtesy to strangers, I warn you that your own safety shall answer for that of this gentleman and his people, so long as they remain in the same place with you. And for you, bold sir," turning to our lieutenant, who had kept at his bridle-elbow; "be not so ready with your blade in the streets: keep it for the field, where there is such sore need of its like."

"I thank you for your aid, most noble sir, and, touching my blade, it has proved itself in the field already more than once and will do so again, I hope."

"You hope!" A deep sadness settled in the leader's eyes for an instant while he gazed dreamily at the lieutenant. Then, starting, with a half sigh, he hastily resumed the rein his abstraction had dropped and once more put his horse in motion. "Give you good-day, young sir," said he, bowing with kingly courtesy as he rode on.

"God keep you, noble sir," replied Howel, impressed to an answering courtesy by the other's bearing.

He held his horse in check till the leader and

"WHAT MEANETH THIS BRAWL?"

his party, followed by their troop, turned out of sight, and then, seeing the one addressed as Lord Warrendon still standing by, he demanded to know what officer it was whose coming had caused such swift change in what had promised so bloody a fray.

"That is the king," replied Warrendon, moodily.

"The king!" exclaimed Howel. "Od's death! and yet I felt he was no common man. Egad! I am glad I spoke to him so civilly, or he might have taken my message all awry when I came to deliver it." (Longmans, Green & Co. $1.25.)—*From Rhoscomyl's "Battlement and Tower."*

Books and Their Makers.

It is not often that we publish even a syllabus of the contents of a new book passing under review, but Mr. George H. Putnam's "Books and Their Makers During the Middle Ages" must make an exception to the rule, and the following paragraph will show the succession of topics in the first volume:

Volume I., 476–1500. Part I.—Books in Manuscript. I.—The Making of Books in the Monasteries. Introductory.—Cassiodorus and S. Benedict.—The Earlier Monkish Scribes.—The Ecclesiastical Schools and the Clerics as Scribes.—Terms Used for Scribe Work.—S. Columba, the Apostle to Caledonia.—Nuns as Scribes.—Monkish Chroniclers.—The Work of the Scriptorium.—The Influence of the Scriptorium.—The Literary Monks of England.—The Earlier Monastery Schools.—The Benedictines of the Continent.—The Libraries of the Monasteries and Their Arrangements for the Exchange of Books. II.—Some Libraries of the Manuscript Period. III.—The Making of Books in the Early Universities. IV.—The Book Trade in the Manuscript Period. Italy.—Books in Spain.—The Manuscript Trade in France.—Manuscript Dealers in Germany. Part II.—The Earlier Printed Books. I.—The Renaissance as the Forerunner of the Printing-Press. II.—The Invention of Printing and the Work of the First Printers of Holland and Germany. III.—The Printer-Publishers of Italy.

We also lay before our readers thus early the course of topics in the second volume, which is yet in press, but will shortly appear: Volume II., 1500–1709. IV.—The Printer-Publishers of France. V.—The Later Estiennes and Casaubon. VI.—Caxton and the Introduction of Printing into England. VII.—The Kobergers of Nüremberg. VIII.—Froben of Basel. IX.—Erasmus and His Books. X.—Luther as an Author. XI.—Plantin of Antwerp. XII.—The Elzevirs of Leyden and Amsterdam. XIII.—Italy: Privileges and Censorship. XIV.—Germany: Privileges and Book-Trade Regulations. XV.—France: Privileges, Censorship, and Legislation. XVI.—England: Privileges, Censorship, and Legislation. XVII.—Conclusion: The Development of the Conception of Literary Property.

Speaking now of the first volume only, Mr. Putnam has done a useful and interesting work and done it well. He has filled upwards of 450 pages with a carefully studied and readable history of early book production, beginning with the multiplication of manuscripts, chiefly in the monasteries and later in the universities, taking in the first achievement of the printing-press, and ending with the great printers of Germany, Holland, and Italy. A bibliography of works cited or referred to as authorities alone occupies some ten pages, most of them, of course, being in French or German, though a few English works are included.

We cannot in the space at our command give more than the most general idea of the contents of this richly stored volume, which accumulates from countless sources a mass of information which it would be hard to find elsewhere in any such form. For all persons of literary tastes, for all librarians and collectors, for all authors and publishers, for all readers who would like to follow the evolution of thought into manuscript, and of manuscript into books, and of books into literature, and of literature into a profession and a business, the work will have an irresistible fascination. The amount of original research that has gone into it is simply enormous and the materials have been most thoroughly assimilated and methodically presented. (Putnam. 2 v., *ea.*, $2.50.) —*Boston Literary World.*

The Spirit in Literature and Life.

We are seldom privileged to read a more interesting and at the same time so instructive a book as "The Spirit in Literature and Life," by the late Dr. Coyle. The volume contains six lectures originally delivered by Dr. Coyle in 1894 in Iowa College. It requires and will amply repay careful reading. It is a strong and thoughtful book, showing great originality of thought and amazing research. In writing of this work Prof. Herbert B. Adams, of Johns Hopkins, speaks of it as the latest gospel of sweetness and light, much finer in spirit than Matthew Arnold's "Literature and Dogma" and more hopeful. This is well-merited praise from a man whose opinion carries so much weight. In this book we follow out the workings and manifestations through the history and literature of the world of the spirit of Judaism and of Christianity, retaining the idea that the latter is the fullest fruition of the former and so indissolubly connected with it. The revision of this volume was the last literary work of Dr. Coyle. His widow has given the book to the publisher as her husband left it. Denver unfortunately knew Dr. Coyle but a short time, but still long enough for him to make a strong impression on the community as being a man of great intellectual power. In those who knew him he inspired warm affection and great admiration of his character, and to these this book will be of peculiar interest. In fact, the book deserves an honored place in every library. (Houghton, Mifflin & Co. $1.) —*The Book-Leaf.*

Science and Theology in Christendom.

"A HISTORY of the Warfare of Science with Theology in Christendom" is the full title of the important work by the Hon. Andrew D. White, which is just published. In this book the author "simply tries to let the light of historical truth into that decaying mass of outworn thought which attaches the modern world to mediæval conceptions of Christianity, and which still lingers among us—a most serious barrier to religion and morals, and a menace to the whole normal evolution of society. . . . My belief is that in the field left to them—their proper field—the clergy will more and more, as they cease to struggle against scientific methods and conclusions, do work even nobler and more beautiful than anything they have heretofore done. And this is saying much. My conviction is that science, though it has evidently conquered dogmatic theology based on biblical texts and ancient modes of thought, will go hand in hand with religion; and that, although theological control will continue to diminish, religion, as seen in the recognition of a ' Power in the universe, not ourselves, which makes for righteousness,' and in the love of God and of our neighbor, will steadily grow stronger, not only in the American institutions of learning but in the world at large." The reader of the *Popular Science Monthly* need not be informed of the exceeding interest of these papers. (Appleton. $1.50)—*Philadelphia Press.*

Queen Móo and the Egyptian Sphinx.

"THIS is not a book of romance or imagination; but a work—one of a series—intended to give ancient America its proper place in the universal history of the world. The study of the relics of the ancient Mayas has revealed such striking similarities between their language, their religious conceptions, their cosmognic notions, their manners and customs, their traditions, their architecture, and the language, the religious conceptions, the cosmognic notions, the manners and customs, the traditions, the architecture of the ancient civilized nations of Asia, Africa, and Europe, of which we have any knowledge, that it has become evident, to my mind at least, that such similarities are not merely effects of hazard, but the result of intimate communications that must have existed between all of them." These words of Dr. Le Plongeon's preface sufficiently explain the task he has undertaken. The book takes its name from one of the facts he claims to have discovered. Queen Móo, driven from her American dominion by her cruel husband-brother, settled among the Mayas of Egypt and there perhaps created the Egyptian Sphinx which has proved so puzzling to all scholars. The book is full of information which can be assimilated even without accepting the author's theories. Based on studies of monuments and sculptures made under great difficulty by Dr. Le Plongeon and his wife. (Rob. Clarke & Co. $5)

From "Queen Moo and the Egyptian Sphinx."   Copyright, 1896, by Augustus Le Plongeon.
SERPENT HEADS FOUND IN CAY'S MAUSOLEUM, CHICHEN.

Tom Grogan.

AT the foot of the derrick, within ten feet of Babcock, stood a woman perhaps thirty-five years of age, with large, clear gray eyes, made all the more luminous by the deep rich color of her sunburnt skin. Her teeth were snow-white, and her light brown hair was neatly parted over a wide forehead. She wore a long ulster half concealing her well-rounded, muscular figure, and a black silk hood rolled back from her face, the strings falling over her broad shoulders, revealing a red silk scarf loosely wound about her throat, the two ends tucked in her bosom. Her feet were shod in thick-soled shoes laced around her well-turned ankles, and her hands were covered by buckskin gauntlets creased with wear. From the outside breast-pocket of her ulster protruded a time-book, from which dangled a pencil fastened to a hempen string. Every movement indicated a great physical strength, perfect health, and a thorough control of herself and her surroundings.

Coupled with this was a dignity and repose unmistakable to those who have watched the handling of large bodies of workingmen by some one leading spirit, master in every tone of the voice and every gesture of the body. The woman gave Babcock a quick glance of interrogation as he entered, and, receiving no answer, forgot him instantly.

" Come, now, ye blatherin' Dagos "—this time

" I'LL . . . HAND HIM THIS LETTER."

to two Italian shovellers filling the buckets— " shall I throw one of ye overboard to wake ye up, or will I take a hand meself? Another shovel there—that bucket's not half full "— drawing one hand from her side-pocket and pointing with an authoritative gesture, breaking as suddenly into a good-humored laugh over the awkwardness of their movements. Babcock, with all his curiosity aroused, watched her for a moment, forgetting for the time his own anxieties. He liked a skilled hand, and he liked push and grit. This woman seemed to possess all three. He was amazed at the way in which she handled her men. He wished somebody as clear-headed and as capable were unloading his boat. He began to wonder who she might be.

There was no mistaking her nationality. Slight as was her accent, her direct descent from the land of the shamrock and the shillalah was not to be doubted. The very tones of her voice seemed saturated with its national spirit—" a flower for you when you agree with me, and a broken head when you don't." But underneath all these outward indications of dominant power and great physical strength he detected in the lines of the mouth and eyes a certain refinement of nature.

There was, too, a fresh, rosy wholesomeness, a sweet cleanliness about the woman. These, added to the noble lines of her figure, would have appealed to one as beauty, and only that, had it not been that the firm mouth, well-set chin, and deep, penetrating glance of the eye overpowered all other impressions.

Babcock moved down beside her. "Can you tell me, madam, where I can find Thomas Grogan?"

" Right in front of ye," she answered, turning quickly, with a toss of her head like that of a great hound baffled in hunt. "I'm Tom Grogan. What can I do for ye?"

"Not Grogan the stevedore?" Babcock asked in astonishment.

"Yes, Grogan the stevedore. Come! Make it short—what can I do for ye?"

"Then this must be my boat. I came down——"

"Ye're not the boss?"—looking him over slowly from his feet up, a good-natured smile irradiating her face, her eyes beaming, every tooth glistening. "There's me hand. I'm glad to see ye. I've worked for ye off and on for four years, and niver laid eyes on ye till this minute. Don't say a word. I know it. I've kept the concrete gangs back half a day, but I couldn't help it." (Houghton, Mifflin & Co. $1.50.)—*From Hopkinson Smith's " Tom Grogan."*

The West Indies and the Spanish Main.

THE story of the West Indies and the Spanish Main is one to stir the hearts of many nations. The shores of the Caribbean Sea have been the scene of marvellous adventures, of intense struggles between races and peoples, of pain, trouble, and disaster of almost every description. From " Robinson Crusoe " to Marryat's genial stories, and down to "Westward Ho!" and "Treasure Island," old and young have been entranced for many generations with its stories of shipwrecks, pirates, sea-fights, and treasure-seekers. Yet with all this the field has not been exhausted, for hardly a year passes without a new romance dealing more or less with the "Indies."

. . . Latterly the West Indies have sunk into neglect by Europe. Except for the difficulties of the planters their history is almost a blank sheet. Few know anything about the beautiful islands or the grand forests of the mainland. Even the discovery of gold in Guiana, which goes to confirm the reports of Raleigh, three centuries ago, is only known to a few. Ruin and desolation have fallen upon them since the peace of 1815 and the emancipation. Even the negro—the protégé of the benevolent—is no longer the object of interest he once was. Cane-sugar is gradually being ousted by that from the beet, and hardly anything has been done to replace its cultivation by other tropical products.

Yet the islands are still as lovely as they were four centuries ago, and on the continent is a wealth of interest to the naturalist and lover of the beautiful. Now and again a tourist goes the rounds of the islands and publishes the result in a book of travel; but the countries are out of the track of civilization and progress. Possibly if the Panama or Nicaragua Canal is ever finished things may be a little better, but at present the outlook is very dismal.

In attempting to compress the story of the West Indies and the Spanish Main within the covers of one volume we have undertaken a task by no means easy. Every island and every province has its own tale, and to do them all justice would require a hundred books. Every West Indian will find something missing—some event unmentioned which is of the greatest importance to his particular community. This is only to be expected, yet we believe that the reader will get a fairer idea of their importance when they are comprehended in one great whole. The photoblock illustrations are numerous and well selected, and the book is charming in subject and execution. (Putnam. $1.75.) *Preface to Rodway's "The West Indies and the Spanish Main."*

From "Tom Grogan." Copyright, 1896, by Houghton, Mifflin & Co.

"ABOVE THEIR HEADS THE BRANCHES TWINED."

Dolly Madison.

THACKERAY, in the beginning of his lectures on the Four Georges, makes loving mention of a charming lady of the old school, whose life extended far back into the last century. "I have often thought," he says, "as I took my kind old friend's hand, how with it I held on to the old society of wits and men of the world." Even such a link with the past, to those of us at least who have reached middle age, is Mrs. Madison. This life of hers, which almost or quite touched ours, touched also the lives of Alexander Hamilton and Aaron Burr, of Decatur and Somers and Paul Jones, of Talleyrand and Lafayette and Jefferson, while she was "dear Dolly," to the spouse of Washington himself. Her life was so deeply influenced by its environment, and its significance depended so largely upon the people and events with which it was connected, that I feel that no apology is necessary for the effort I have made to present in this volume less a formal biography than a sketch of the social and domestic life of the epoch as it affected Dolly Madison. (Scribner. $1.25.)—*From Maud Wilder Goodwin's "Dolly Madison."*

FÉLIX GRAS.

The Reds of the Midi.

IN all French history there is no more inspiring episode than that with which M. Gras
deals in this story: the march to Paris, and
the doings in Paris of that Marseilles Battalion
made up of men who were sworn to cast down
"the tyrant" and who "knew how to die."
And he has been as happy, I think, in his
choice of method as in his choice of subject.
Had his hero been a grown man, or other than
a peasant, there would have been more reasoning in the story and less directness. But
this delightful peasant-boy Pascalet—so simple and brave and honest, and altogether lovable—knows very little about reasoning. To
him the French Revolution is but the opportunity that he has longed for to avenge the
wrongs done to his peasant father; and he is
eager to capture "the King's Castle" and to
overthrow "the tyrant," because he understands—though vaguely: for the castle he believes to be only a day's march across the
mountains from Avignon, and the tyrant is a
very hazy concept in his little mind—that somewhere along these lines of spirited action harm
will come to the particular marquis against
whom his grievance lies. And so he joins the
Marseilles Battalion and goes with it on his
conquering way; and through his uninstructed
but very wide open eyes we see all that happens on, and all that flows from, that heroic
march. Nor are the standards and convictions which accompanied the action changed
in the narration. Pascalet has become old
Pascal; but he is still a peasant, and he still
regards the events which he tells about from
the peasant's point of view.

It is this point of view, with its necessarily
highly objective scheme of treatment, which
gives to M. Gras's story a place entirely apart
from all the fiction of the French Revolution
with which I am acquainted. The loving
touch that is so evident in the setting of the
story comes naturally, for there the author is
writing of his own people and his own home.
This prose is the prose of a poet, yet racy and
strong. (Appleton. $1.50.)—*From Janvier's
Preface to "Reds of the Midi."*

In the Blue Pike.

EGYPT having been exhausted, Ebers now
devotes himself to presenting the manner of
the Germans of the sixteenth century. "The
Blue Pike" is a famous hostelry in Nüremberg, and Deitel, the old waiter, is the important personage there. In the long guest-room
of the house of entertainment there is a party
of strollers. The interest centres in Kuni,
who, once a graceful rope-dancer, is now
crippled from an accident. Once Kuni was
beautiful, but, worn out and lame, she is suffering from consumption. Long before she
came to Nüremberg she had loved the noble
gentleman Lienhard Groland. Once Kuni had
found a jewelled necklace, and it looked as if
the girl had stolen it, but Groland had been
merciful as one of the magistrates, and Kuni
had been released. Ebers introduces the
clerics and humanists of the time, and conspicuous among them is Wilibald Pirckheimer.
Kuni takes to religion, and dies a repenting
sinner. No one could be more familiar than is
Ebers with the period he writes about, and so
his volume is an interesting one, at least in a
historical sense. (Appleton. 75 c.; pap., 40 c.)

Fire and Sword in the Sudan.

IN a large octavo volume of 630 pages, entitled "Fire and Sword in the Sudan," by
Rudolf C. Slatin Pasha, we have an autobiographical account of the sixteen years spent by
the author in the Sudan, during twelve of
which he was a captive of the Mahdi and of
the latter's successor, Khalifa Abdullahi. Considered merely as a record of personal adventure and suffering, the narrative is one of
thrilling interest, but it is also of great historical value, affording, as it does, the sole authentic and tolerably exhaustive description of the
rise and course of the remarkable religious
movement which still dominates large sections
of northeastern Africa. As Governor-General
of Darfur, the author was in a position to
understand and explain the ethnological, social,
and political conditions which made the triumph of the Mahdi possible, and during his
long captivity at Omdurman he was an eye-
witness of the ruin which the revolution brought
on the greater part of the native population.
Through long and intimate contact with the
Mahdi himself, and with the inheritor of his
power, the Khalifa Abdullahi, he has been en-

abled to give us a more intelligible and minute account of their personal characteristics, their religious aims, and their methods of government than has hitherto been accessible to the appointed by Gordon Financial Inspector, Mudir of Dara, and, ultimately, Governor-General of Darfur. The greater part of the first nine chapters of the book are. devoted to the

From " Fire and Sword in the Sudan."   Copyright, 1895, by E. Arnold & Co.

THE DEATH OF HICKS PASHA.

Western world. We add that the English translation is by Major F. R. Wingate, of the Egyptian army, and that to the present volume is prefixed an introductory note by Father Ohrwalder, who for ten years was a fellow-captive of Slatin Pasha's in the Mahdist camp.

Rudolf Slatin is an Austrian by birth, and in July, 1878, was serving as a lieutenant in the Crown Prince Rudolph's regiment on the Bosnian frontier when he received a letter from Gen. Gordon inviting him to come to the Sudan and take service with the Egyptian Government under his direction. To account for this invitation we should mention that previously, in 1874, Slatin had undertaken a journey to the Sudan, reaching Khartum in October of that year. There he made the acquaintance of Emin Pasha (then Dr. Emin), who had recently arrived from Egypt. Gen. Gordon, who at that time was residing at Lado as governor-general of the equatorial provinces, invited Emin and Slatin to visit him, but the latter was unable to go, being obliged to complete his military service at home during the following year. Slatin longed, he tells us, to return to the Sudan in some official capacity, but it was not till December, 1878, that he received permission, as an officer of the reserves, to set out once more for Africa. He arrived at Khartum on Jan. 15, 1879, and was successively

author's experiences in Darfur and to his energetic but eventually fruitless attempts to stem the tide of Mahdism, which, starting in Kordofan, had swept westward over the first-named province. We pass over the record of this unavailing struggle, merely noting that, toward the end, Slatin, finding that his defeats were ascribed by his officers and men to the fact that he was a Christian, decided to nominally adopt the Mohammedan religion. The decision undoubtedly saved his life when he was forced to surrender at Dara, not long before the siege of Khartum. (Edward Arnold. $5.)—*N. Y. Sun.*

THE DIVINE RIGHT OF KINGS.

THE right divine! What king that hath it not?—
The right to look through all his realm and see
What fever courses in the people's veins,
And lay thereon the balm of kingly hands;
To turn aside the treasonable blade,
And make a friend of him who carries it ;
To bind up public wounds ; to put away
The screens wherewith men hide accusing truth,
And speak grave words when these befit the time ;
To sow the land so full of happiness,
Of peace and justice, love and courtesy,
That ships bound seaward unto fabled shores
Shall never tempt his people otherwhere—
Such right divine as this hath every king.

(Lemperly ; Hilliard ; Hopkins. $1.25.)—
From " Verses " by Mary Wright Plummer.

The Keynotes Series.

IN 1893 there was a book published in London with the extraordinary title of "Keynotes." Three thousand copies were sold in the course of a few months, and the unknown author became a celebrity. Soon afterwards the portrait of a lady appeared in "The Sketch." She had a small, delicate face, with a pained and rather tired expression, and a curious, questioning look in the eyes; it was an attractive face, very gentle and womanly, and yet there was something disillusioned and unsatisfied about it. This lady wrote under the pseudonym of George Egerton and "'Keynotes' was her first book. It was a strange book! too good a book to become famous all at once," as is also Mrs. Hansson's "Six Modern Women," from which we have taken the above facts. Later on it became known that the author of this collection of scenes from woman's most individual experience was Mrs. Claremonte; and about a year later she gave her waiting public another volume entitled "Discords," covering much the same ground, but falling short of reaching the perfection of method of the first sketches. Since then Mrs. Claremonte has translated "Young Ofeg's Ditties," by Ola Hansson, the husband of the woman who gives her so glowing a chapter in

"Six Modern Women," and in this most difficult work she has distanced even her "Keynotes" in her rare art of making music of language.

Mrs. Clairemonte's book gave its name to a series devoted to stories and tales dealing especially with psychological and social problems. Twenty-one volumes are now published and two more thus far announced. For these books Aubrey Beardsley drew some of his most characteristic title-pages, and these the Roberts are now bringing out in a portfolio. The separate books have led to endless discussion in literary circles, but it is agreed, however one may differ with authors who dwell almost exclusively upon unhappy moments in the lives of their characters, the literary work on almost every individual one of the books is of the highest order.

1. Egerton, George. Keynotes.
2. Farr, Florence. The Dancing Faun.
3. Dostoievsky, Fedor. Poor Folk.
4. Adams, Francis. A Child of the Age.
5. Machen, Arthur. The Great God Pan and the Inmost Light.
6. Egerton, George. Discords.
7. Shiel, M. P. Prince Zaleski.
8. Allen, Grant. The Woman Who Did.
9. Lowry, H. D. Woman's Tragedies.
10. Harland, Henry. Gray Roses.
11. Watson, H. B. Marriott. At the First Corner.
12. D'Arcy, Ella. Monochromes.
13. Sharp, Evelyn. At the Relton Arms.
14. Dix, Gertrude. The Girl from the Farm.
15. Makower, Stanley V. The Mirror of Music.
16. Dawe, W. Carlton. Yellow and White.
17. Macleod, Fiona. The Mountain Lovers.
18. Machen, Arthur. The Three Impostors.
19. Syrett, Netta. Nobody's Fault.
20. Nesbit, E. In Homespun.
21. Smith, John. Platonic Affections.
22. Taylor, Una A. Nets for the Wind.
23. Lipsett, Caldwell. When the Atlantic Meets the Land. (Roberts. ea., $1.)

Title-page of "Keynotes."　　　Copyright, 1893, by Roberts Bros.

History of Confession and Indulgences in the Latin Church.

AFTER an interval of eight years Dr. Henry Charles Lea continues his special and prolific studies, so brilliantly begun in the "History of the Inquisition of the Middle Ages," with the first volume of an extensive "History of Auricular Confession and Indulgences in the Latin Church." It would be idle to ignore alike the delicate nature of the subject and the author's instructive treatment of it. For, although it is certainly true that there is an entire absence of controversial tone in Dr. Lea's book, and that in his desire to escape the imputation of having written a polemical treatise, he has abstained from consulting Protestant writers and has confined himself exclusively to original sources and to Catholic authorities (being thus confident, as he says, "that what might be lost in completeness would be compensated by accuracy and impartiality"), yet the simple facts of history as they are adroitly arrayed by Dr. Lea constitute in themselves a sufficiently formidable assault.

Within the wide range of his research nothing seems to have escaped his attention—the writings of the early fathers, the codes of secular and canon law, the decrees of the popes, the labors of the schoolmen who remodelled ·heology throughout the Middle Ages, the records of the chroniclers, the interminable treatises of modern theologians, and the popular manuals of devotion which show how theory is reduced to practice. Step by step the evolution of the power of the keys is followed, showing how the priest was interposed between the sinner and his God, and how the simple intercessory prayer to God for pardon became the awful sacrament which controls the portals of hell and heaven. The present volume treats of the theory and practice of the primitive Church, the successive beliefs as to the pardon of sin, the rise and development of the power of the keys, the introduction of auricular confession and its establishment as an obligatory duty, giving rise to various subsidiary and complicated questions, the practices of the confessional and its abuses, and the development of the absolution by which the priest, acting as God, pardons the sinner. The second volume, which will follow shortly, will treat of the conditions on which absolution is granted and the numerous questions connected with the injunction and performance of penance. The third volume will be devoted to the subject of indulgences, showing how they originated and the use made of them as a financial resource prior to the Reformation, and subsequently as a means of strengthening the tie between the faithful and the Papacy.

The serious student of ecclesiastical history will be profoundly interested in these pages; they will but amuse the secular reader who, in his profane sophistication, will see in all the cumulative evidence marshalled by Dr. Lea against auricular confession and indulgences a mere tilting against windmills. The author handles his voluminous material with great readiness and skill, and serves it with his customary dignity and grace. (Lea Brothers & Co. Vol. I, $3.)—*Philadelphia Press.*

Kriegspiel.

A NOVEL dealing largely with gypsy life by a writer particularly conversant with gypsies demands a somewhat special attention, for, thanks largely to railways, the true gypsies are fast dying out. Although novelists, dramatists, and poets are particularly fond of trying to paint the gypsies, it cannot be said that many of them have been successful in their delineations. And this is because the inner and the outer life of a proscribed race must necessarily be unlike each other. Those who join us in loving that most delightful of all romances, "Guy

Title-page of "The Great God Pan." Copyright, 1894, by Roberts Bros.

Mannering," may be shocked at being told that Meg Merrilies is as a gypsy as great a failure as the other gypsies of fict'on. One of the finest and rarest and most poetical female characters in imaginative literature she is undoubtedly. But as we have said before when discussing the place of the Romany woman in fiction, Meg Merrilies is no more a gypsy than is Borrow's delightful Isopel Berners. Scott's Meg is a Scotch woman of a peculiarly noble and picturesque type who, like Isopel, leads a gypsy life.

The central idea of Mr. Groome's story, "Kriegspiel," the vanishing of Sir Charles Glemham, and the finding of his dead body a year after in the family vault, is founded, if we mistake not, on a tradition told of the ancestor of a living baronet. The situation is striking, but the scene where the dreadful discovery is made by the murdered man's son should have been amplified. Indeed, all that this story needed in order to become a really powerful tale was a more ingenious construction, a better method of arranging and evolving the imaginative material at the writer's command.

Carlyle's remark that, given the imaginative material contained within the lines of "Hamlet," it would still require a Shakespeare to make, by power of construction, the play vital, is not, perhaps, so true of "Hamlet" as of certain other great works, but it is generally admirable, and applies to all imaginative literature. This lack of constructive power on the part of the writer of "Kriegspiel" is not unlikely to stand in the way of his tale's prosperity with the general novel-reader.

But whatever may be the temporary success of any work of fiction, the quality by which it really passes into literature is that of truth of organic detail. The incidents, the manners, and the scenery must be so true that they seem to be a natural growth. Here is Mr. Groome's strength. His pictures of East Anglia and the lights and shades of East Anglian character and manners are worthy of the writer of "Two Suffolk Friends"; and as regards the pictures of gypsy life, the book is full of touches which could only have come from a writer who has had intimate personal contact with the Romanies, and who was at the same time deeply versed in their traditional lore. This enables him to introduce touches that seem to spring up as naturally as flowers from the soil.

As a gypsy novel, as a novel depicting gypsy life, "Kriegspiel" is unrivalled. (Ward, Lock & Bowden, Ltd. $1.50.)—*The Athenæum.*

A Woman with a Future.

A NEW book by the author of "The Grasshoppers" will be gladly welcomed by all who delight in the quiet descriptive style of which Mrs. Dean is so finished a master. Family life with its petty but irritating little troubles and misfortunes is her specialty. Little schemes for eking out small incomes, little plans of housekeeping, little details of daily life she works into little scenes that could be easily transformed by a painter into most captivating pictures of home-life.

In her latest book Mrs. Dean draws two portraits of women: one an old-fashioned, duty-loving, devoted mother; the other a young wife of the period, devoted to pleasure and flirtation, who takes no interest in her husband's life-work, and all but ruins him by her careless extravagance. This woman has not had much past, but she prepares for herself a future of which the two ingenious letters with which the book closes give a very distinct forecast.

Mrs. Dean has read the present style of novels to good purpose. She pictures the style of home created by a woman who has for years delighted in decadent poets, impressionist painters, and novels which treat of "new woman" and the "higher life." The story is so slight, that were it told the reader would be cheated of some pleasure; still the charm rests not in the plot, but in the little touches by which Mrs. Dean brings out the characters and peculiarities of the actors in the little drawing-room drama. (Stokes. 75 c.)

From "A Woman with a Future." Copyright, 1896, by
F. A. Stokes Co.

HESPERIA.

Preparing the Banquet.

"I GUESS they take us for a pair of animals," observed Tommy, as he glanced about at the peaceful beasts. "Some new kind," he added.

"That must be it," said the ex-Pirate, absent-mindedly; "but I wish we could find the Sheep."

"In this crowd!" exclaimed the Gopher, who

From "Tommy Toddles."　　　　　　　　　　Copyright, 1896, by Harper & Brothers.

"THEY WON'T LET HIM PLAY, BECAUSE HE'S A CHEETAH."

came up at that moment. "Why, that's like looking for a beetle in a smoke-stack."

The three walked along for some time in silence, and they saw all sorts of queer things as they went. In a retired corner the Hippopotamus was shaving himself with a razor-backed Hog, who kept up a perpetual snorting and grunting. Near by an old mother Pig was putting her little Pigs' tails up in curl-papers for the night. Further along the Armadillo, the Turtles, the Hedge-Hog, the Porcupine, squatted on the floor together, were playing dominoes. A Leopard-like creature sat near by, watching the game, looking very much diappointed and mournful.

"They won't let him play," volunteered the Gopher, "because he's a Cheetah." All this time there was much bustle and preparation going on in the middle of the hall. The Monkey tribe, of which there must have been a hundred, were bringing up tables and stools and benches from down below somewhere, and were stretching these out the entire length of the big room. They made a banqueting-board much longer than Tommy had ever seen before, and then they laid plates and mugs along the edges, enough to accommodate all. The Monkeys made first-rate waiters, and the big Gorillas bossed them around, and kept them working "just like real waiters in a restaurant," thought Tommy.

"There's the Sheep!" shouted the ex-Pirate suddenly, and he pointed out their old friend,

sitting on a bench about a third of the way down from the head of the long table. They hastened towards him, for the animals were taking seats rapidly. (Harper. $1.25.)—*From Lee's "Tommy Toddles."*

Among the Freaks.

MR. W. L. ALDEN has been to Chicago for his latest volume. He represents himself as having made the acquaintance of the proprietor of a dime museum there, who was induced to part with sundry incidents in his career. The dime museum is essentially an American institution. We get an occasional "skeleton man" or "fat woman" in the booths of a country fair, but the "Freak Show," as such, is only to be seen to perfection across the Atlantic. The "freaks," by reason of their peculiarities, lend themselves readily to Mr. Alden's treatment, and their loves and hates, their sentiments and passions, are sufficiently ridiculous for a humorist of quite average ability to make capital from, without any gross exaggeration. Of course, the best stories occur with the manufactured articles, who are always in danger of detection, and who generally get "given away" at some particularly nopportune moment. Mr. J. F. Sullivan and Miss Florence K. Upton, help out the text admirably with their genuinely funny illustrations. (Longmans, Green & Co. $1.25.)—*London Literary World.*

History of Prussia.

THE concluding volume of the "History of Prussia Under Frederic the Great," by the late Professor Herbert Tuttle, of Cornell University, leaves unfinished a work which in its wealth of erudition, scientific exactitude and philosophical tone is acknowledged by eminent authorities to stand among the foremost productions of modern historical literature. The book now published contains the first three chapters of the third volume of Professor Tuttle's "Frederic," or the fourth of his "History of Prussia." It opens with the march into Saxony, in the autumn of 1756, reviews the general aspect of European affairs, as they were affected by Saxon subjugation, and follows in detail the progress of the memorable "Year of Battles," from the battle of Prague to that of Leuthen. In spite of the illness with which the author was stricken, and which finally brought his life to an end, these three chapters show no trace of weakness in thought or manner, but are as logical in their marshalling of events and as vigorous in the judgment passed upon men and affairs as were any of the preceding volumes. Professor Herbert B. Adams, in a sympathetic biographical sketch included in the volume, speaks of Professor Tuttle as "perhaps the only original American scholar in the domain of Prussian history." In fact, it is probably not too much to say that he has given a new reading to many incidents that have hitherto been partially obscured or sadly misinterpreted. All the vast literature that has grown up since Carlyle's day he had completely mastered, and his command of the original authorities enabled him, as Professor Adams observes, to clear away many historical delusions which Carlyle and Macaulay had perpetuated. The story of his life, as Professor Adams concisely gives it, is that of the ideal scholar, who never spared himself in his search after truth, and who sacrificed health and strength and a career of future usefulness in his persistent and tireless pursuit of his chosen studies. He was a man of many friends, whose recollections add much to the interest of the biography. (Houghton, Mifflin & Co. $1.50.)—*The Beacon.*

The Damnation of Theron Ware.

FOR his latest novel, "The Damnation of Theron Ware," Harold Frederic has taken for his theme a subject somewhat analogous to that which Mr. Howells treated in "A Modern Instance." The story deals with the career of a young Methodist minister, who had not strength of character enough to withstand the influences of a new theological and social environment, and who went to pieces with a rapidity of degeneration that will be surprising only to those who have never met a Theron Ware in the flesh. Mr. Frederic's story is very carefully worked out, and it presents an effective series of contrasts in its portrayal of militant Methodism on the one hand, and of a tranquil, easy-going Catholicism on the other. In presenting this picture Mr. Frederic has brought out effects that are entirely new in American fiction, and his characters, nearly all of them, stand out with lifelike impressiveness. Theron Ware himself is undoubtedly a type, but in Mr. Frederic's hands he has distinct individuality. He has that fatal gift of persuasive oratory so often associated with lack of moral stamina, and when he casts off his traditional beliefs and tries to become a man of the world, his downfall is only the outward and visible sign of an innate tendency. Mr. Frederic has undoubtedly produced a book that will be read with conflicting emotions by a widely divergent class of readers, and though some of them may question the validity of some of the scenes which he depicts, no one can question the essential veracity of the whole picture. Given such and such characters and such and such conditions, and the story works itself out in its own way, and leads up to a sequel that is grimly humorous in its inevitability. "The Damnation of Theron Ware" is not likely to be a popular novel, as novels go, but there have been few American stories in recent years better worthy the attention of those who seek for originality and artistic power. (Stone & Kimball. $1.50.)—*The Beacon.*

The Columbian Knowledge Series.

THE editor of the *Columbian Knowledge* series has been singularly happy in the selection of subjects for the volumes that have thus far appeared. "Total Eclipses of the Sun," "Public Libraries in America," and "Arctic Discoveries" are all subjects of timely interest, and each is, in a sense, complete in itself; that is, deserving of special treatment, although really but a part of some larger subject. General A. W. Greely's "Handbook of Arctic Discoveries" is essentially a manual of facts, concisely stated and well arranged, condensed from the 50,000 pages of narrative that have grown up about the subject, mostly during the past half-century. The book is divided into a series of sketches, under separate chapters, devoted to special lines of exploration regardless of chronological bearing. It is well supplied with maps, and will be found in every way helpful to those interested in Arctic exploration. (Roberts. *ea.,* $1.)—*The Dial.*

From "Etidorhpa."   Copyright, 1896, by Robert Clarke & Co.

ETIDORHPA.

Etidorhpa.

UPON a first examination *The Inter-Ocean* pronounced it the strongest fiction of a decade and its author a literary genius. While it abounds in romance and adventure that taxes the imagination, yet the author never for a moment loses sight of the truths of science which he unfolds with grace and beauty. The style is severely simple and the theories so bold and so well executed to a finish as to charm the reader. The volume has no impure teaching in all its chapters. Faith in God and all things pure and true and beautiful shine out in white light all through the pages. It is the strangest mixing of science, mythology, theosophy, and morals the reader will anywhere find, and told in such a Jules Verne style as to constantly call out the wonder of the reader. The first edition of the work was speedily exhausted, and Messrs. Robert Clarke & Co. have issued a beautiful edition at a reduced price. The artist deserves also a special commendation for the excellence of his artistic work. (Robert Clarke & Co. $2.)—*The Inter-Ocean.*

· The Epic of the Fall of Man.

DR. GURTEEN's new work, " The Epic of the Fall of Man," though highly interesting from other points of view, is more especially so from the fact that it brings together in close com-

JEANNE D'ARC.

parison the two most remarkable poets in English sacred literature—Cædmon and Milton—the monk-poet of the seventh century and the puritan-poet of the seventeenth. The author's object is to show the points of similarity and divergence between these two men of genius in their mode of treating the subject of " Paradise Lost," and by comparison of passages from their respective works to emphasize the correspondence that at times exists between the two poems in the invention of incident, and, at times, even in the wording of some impassioned speech.

Dr. Gurteen, in the last chapter, gives a translation of the Anglo-Saxon poem in blank verse, and it is this translation which the author uses throughout his work to enable the reader of modern English only to compare the two poems, side by side. The book is a full comparative study of Cædmon's and Milton's account of the rebellion in heaven; the expulsion of the rebel hosts from the empyrean; the creation of the starry universe; the council in hell; the fall of man; and the banishment from Eden. There is, besides, a characteristic chapter on the "Angel of Presumption and Other Devils"; and another equally suggestive one on "The Three Poetic Hells." In the latter chapter Dr. Gurteen introduces the "Inferno" of Dante, and shows the difference between the early legendary hell of Cædmon, the mediæval, philosophical hell of Dante, and the modern traditional hell of Milton.

The plates in this work (twenty-six) give a distinctive character to the book. The volume contains, in addition, a number of diagrams explanatory of the comparative study. (Putnam. $2.50.)

A Dancer in Yellow.

WE are well content to read Mr. Norris's smooth and unruffling fictions as long as he is pleased to send them forth so well finished and, as far as they go, perfect. His characters never appear to be very real, their passions are not strong, but everything is expressed in admirable proportion, and there is never any rudeness or vehemence to throw the picture out of key. This story is a most agreeable specimen of his art ; the hero is the young man to whom Mr. Norris has accustomed us, weak and impressionable, possibly a somewhat dull fellow, but redeemed from commonplace by the rare distinction of being a perfect gentleman. Mr. Norris is eminently restful, and none of his books has surpassed "The Dancer in Yellow" in this his peculiar quality. (Appleton. $1 ; pap., 50 c.)—*The Athenæum.*

The Literary News.

An Eclectic Monthly Review of Current Literature.

EDITED BY A. H. LEYPOLDT

MAY, 1896.

THE STUDY OF FICTION.

SLOWLY, but surely, fiction in the form of novels has made for itself a place in literature, and literature has been recognized as an art to be studied as music, painting, sculpture, and architecture are studied. It has now been conceded that the finest essence of literary ability is to be found in our novels, and no one can now lay claim to a liberal education who has not read Thackeray. Dickens, Scott, Reade, Kingsley, and George Eliot, not to speak of the living novelists whose masterpieces do not yield in rank even to those of the greatest masters.

Critically considered, the writing of novels now is what the writing of plays was in the age of Elizabeth, and while there is not much prospect of another Shakespeare or another Ben Jonson, there is no reason why the noble art which they created and developed should be belittled as it is, since its chief object, which was to hold the mirror up to nature, remains, and always must remain, what it was. The aim of the Victorian novelist should not be less than the aim of the Elizabethan dramatist, which was to delineate the hearts and souls, the emotions and conduct of men and women. The drama was the novel in action, the novel is the drama in narration.

The modern novel has had to outgrow the disrepute into which it had fallen. It is not so very long ago when to read a novel was thought a frivolous waste of time, and to read the bulk of the novels now published would still be a frivolous waste of time. But in fictitious form our great writers are now teaching history, biography, social science, psychology, and all that makes for human progress and happiness, and there is need that the line should be sharply drawn between the novels that waste time and enervate the reader, and the novels that teach, inspire, and strengthen.

The question so often discussed whether purpose has place in fiction does not enter here. The fact is established that all the problems of our day are brought before us in the form of fiction, and it has become necessary to seek direction and study the aim, the cause, and the effect of the novels we are reading.

Many have begun to realize this. For two seasons the study of fiction has been a course in the curriculum of Yale University. Under the direction of a competent professor such a study is full of possibilities, and it is with regret we notice that it is to be given up. Taste in fiction needs training. It can be cultivated only by reading and re-reading the works of the great masters. Such training will determine whether fiction shall be a dissipation or a mental and moral food.

The practical problem is to find modes of studying fiction which can fit themselves into the routine of ordinary busy life. Some excellent suggestions in this direction are given in "Four Years of Novel-Reading: an account of an experiment in popularizing the study of fiction," edited with an introduction by Richard G. Moulton, Professor of Literature in English in the University of Chicago. Some hard work is called for by Prof. Moulton, but his ideas, carried out under intelligent guidance, would educate the readers of novels in systematic thinking, and open up to them a view of life that would widen their sympathies and increase their personal influence and usefulness.

The only way to get rid of the trashy fiction is to cultivate the minds and hearts of readers until it becomes an abomination to them. Taste in music, in painting, in sculpture, is cultivated by constantly hearing and seeing what is good. Why should this not hold good in the art of literature? Read with understanding and cultivate the critical faculty. Trained readers of fiction will be an inestimable benefit to authors, many of whom are now content to furnish only what a large proportion of their readers are satisfied with—false pictures of false life, excitement and enervating reaction.

Homer, Virgil, the Parables of the Bible, what are they but fiction? Tennyson, Browning, William Morris have presented us systems of philosophy in fictitious setting. In other arts we have been taught to study the old. Why not apply the same rule in literature? Training in fiction does not mean to be able to discuss glibly the latest novel, but to have so read the masters that you know at a glance where the author has found his subject, and just how much of himself he has put into his art.

The technique of fiction and poetry is almost perfect in the hands of literary artists, and we have a right to demand a soul and a message as well as correct literary form. But we must be taught to look for it. The earnest study of fiction to-day is really a study of life. Men and women may see the life they are leading and may reflect upon the conditions of society which they are helping to bring about. It is an open question whether the earnest study of life is not about as good a study as any college can take up.

Readings from New Books.

TRILBY.

O LIVING image of eternal youth!
Wrought with such large simplicity of truth
That, now the pattern's made and on the shelf,
Each vows he might have cut it for himself;
Nor marvels that we sang of empty days,
Of rank grown laurel and imprimèd bays,
While yet in all this lovely Crusoe land,
The Trilby footprints had not touched the sand.
Here's a new carelessness of Titan play,
Here's Ariel's witchery to lead the way
In such sweet artifice of dainty wit
That men shall die of imitating it.
Now every man's old grief turns in its bed,
And bleeds a drop or two, divinely red ;
Fair baby joys do rouse them one by one,
Dancing a lightsome sound, though love be done ;
And Memory takes off her frontlet dim,
To bind a bit of tinsel round the rim.
Dreams come to life and faint foreshadowings
Flutter anear as on reluctant wings.
But not one pang, nay, though 'twere gall of bliss,
And not one such awakening would we miss.
Oh, comrades, here's true stuff ! ours to adore,
And swear we'll carve our cherry-stones no more.

—From Alice Brown's " The Road to Castelay."
(Copeland & Day. $1.)

Democracy and Literature.

MANY causes have been assigned for this intellectual sterility, continuing long after America had taken her place among the great nations of the world. Tocqueville believed that there was no country with less intellectual independence and less real liberty of discussion than America, or in which the expression of unpopular opinion was more bitterly resented ; and he said that there were no great American writers because "literary genius cannot exist without liberty of thought, and there is no liberty of thought in America." Mill, expanding another passage from Tocqueville, described America as, "intellectually speaking, a province of England—a province in which the occupation of the inhabitants is making money, because for that they have peculiar facilities, and are, therefore, like the people of Manchester or Birmingham, for the most part contented to receive the higher branches of knowledge ready-made from the capital." Maine attributed much to the long refusal of the Congress to grant us international copyright, the want of copyright effectually crushed American authorship in the home market by the competition of the unpaid and appropriated works of British authors, and "condemned the whole American community to a literary servitude unparalleled in the history of thought." In all this there is much truth, but it must, be added that modern democracy is not favorable to the higher forms of intellectual life. Democracy levels down quite as much as it levels up. The belief in the equality of man, the total absence of the spirit of reverence, the apotheosis of the average judgment, the fever and the haste, and the advertising and sensational spirit which American life so abundantly generates, and which the American press so vividly reflects, are all little favorable to the production of great works of beauty or of thought, of long meditation, of sober taste, of serious, uninterrupted study. Such works have been produced in America, but in small numbers and under adverse conditions. The habit, too, which has so long existed in America, and which is rapidly growing in England, of treating the private lives of eminent men as if they were public property; of forcing their opinions on all subjects into constant publicity by newspaper interviews; of multiplying demands upon their time for public functions for which they have no special aptitude, adds greatly to the evil. Among the advantages which England derives from her aristocracy, not the least is the service it renders to literature by providing a class of men who are admirably fitted for presidential and other public functions, which in another society would have been largely thrown on men of letters. No one can fail to observe how large a proportion of the Americans who have shown distinguished talent in literature and art have sought in European life a more congenial atmosphere than they could find at home. (Longmans. 2 v., $5.)—*From Lecky's " Democracy and Liberty."*

Woman vs. Man as Cook and Gourmet.

I HAVE always wondered that woman could be so glib in claiming equality with man. In such trifling matters as politics and science and industry, I doubt if there be much to choose between the two sexes. But in the cultivation and practice of an art which concerns life more seriously, woman has hitherto proved an inferior creature.

For centuries the kitchen has been her appointed sphere of action. And yet, here, as in the studio and the study, she has allowed man to carry off the laurels. Vatel, Carême, Ude, Dumas, Gouffé, Etienne, these are some of the immortal cooks of history; the kitchen still waits its Sappho. Mrs. Glasse, at first, might be thought a notable exception; but it is not so much the merit of her book as its extreme rarity in the first edition which has made it famous.

Woman, moreover, has eaten with as little distinction as she has cooked. It seems almost—much as I deplore the admission—as if she were of coarser clay than man, lacking the more artistic instincts, the subtler, daintier emotions.

I think, therefore, the great interest of the following papers lies in the fact that they are written by a woman—a greedy woman. The collection evidently does not pretend to be a "Cook's Manual," or a "Housewife's Companion"; already the diligent, in numbers, have catalogued recipes with more or less exactness. It is rather a guide to the beauty, the poetry that exists in the perfect dish, even as in the masterpiece of a Titian or a Swinburne. Surely hope need not be abandoned when there is found one woman who can eat, with understanding, the "Feasts of Autolycus." (Merriam. $1.25.)—*From Preface to Eliz. R. Pennell's " The Feasts of Autolycus."*

Ja. A. Froude Among His Friends.

LAST night I turned over many letters of Froude's; all long letters; some very long, written just as gracefully as what he wrote to be printed, and some of them frankly stating his feeling towards the gravest things which can be. It was odd to mark the old-fashioned courtesy which in his very first letter apologized for beginning "Dear Sir," and then to see how speedily it became "My dear Boyd." Also how "Yours faithfully" soon passed into "Yours very affectionately." Englishmen write more warmly than Scotch folk do. And their cordiality warms up and draws out us who are not chilly but *blate*. . . . If I can get permission I hope when I come to speak of Froude more fully to give some specimens of his letters. I could hardly give one throughout. Not merely for intimate expression of views and feelings; far more because the great man, desiring to cheer a humble friend, spoke of his friend's merits as no mortal else ever did. Such as knew nothing earthly about Froude save through his books have talked of him as "saturnine." Never was a man more outspokenly frank, more warmly affectionate. One always felt there was something of the kindest woman's nature in Froude, though he was so brave a man. As for his playful kindness, inquire of those who were children at 78 Great King Street thirty-three years ago; on that first visit to Scotland I have never read so fair and complete a description of him as in the attractive "Table-Talk," which has come out in these dark days of his old friend (and I am proud to say mine) Dr. John Skelton. ("The Table-Talk of Shirley." Edinburgh, 1895.) But I think I may say that Skelton was more to Froude than any living person, save only Carlyle. And the relations with Carlyle were quite different in nature. Froude was content to drive out with his hero, the greatest Scotsman (he wrote to me) except John Knox alone; and having unluckily named a certain Home Secretary, to see Carlyle turn his face to the open window of the carriage, and pour forth, through all the rest of the drive, a stream of anathemas beside which the Council of Trent would grow pale. No one else durst have tried that. I am keeping what I have to say of Froude till further on. (Longmans, Green & Co. $5.)—*From Boyd's "The Last Years of St. Andrews, 1890–1895."*

Quartette and Boy-Choirs.

THERE is no denying that a fine quartette choir can produce most beautiful harmony; so beautiful, indeed, that in listening the congregation becomes entirely absorbed in the intellectual or the sensual appreciation of it. Its spiritual significance is so overshadowed that none but the most devout can keep sight of it. The quartette choir often gives us a very finished performance of chamber-music ; but as church-music it is paralyzing to congregational worship—it promotes spiritual dulness and death.

But at present there is some danger of our drifting to another extreme. From accounts published from time to time in the parochial news-columns of our church papers one would suppose that what is properly called a "boy-choir" is the only choir that can fitly sing the church's music. Thus it is told with deep satisfaction that St. Harmonium's parish has at last attained a vested choir, which made its first appearance upon such a date, and under such and such circumstances; and from the way the affair is written up it is easily seen how happy the good priest is at his success, whether the people may be or not. One would almost imagine that some pressing doctrinal principles were absolutely dependent upon having a surpliced choir. The idea has seized upon the community that it is more devotional that the soprano parts should be rendered by boys' and not women's voices, and the fancy has swept the country, capturing parish after parish, without regard to the many limitations which must regulate and modify the usage. The popular idea seems to be that all that is needed to obtain a boy-choir is to gather a mob of urchins from the streets, give them books and a few rehearsals, put vestments on them, and turn them into the stalls. They may sing flat and sing sharp, they may murder the service and drag through the hymns, they may shout and scream with voices that would scratch glass, they may rattle the windows with the Nunc Dimittis— but the parish has a boy-choir, and the rector is happy, even though the long-suffering congregation be literally sung out of doors.

A poor boy-choir is the worst kind of a choir. A good one, outside of the large cities, is, under ordinary circumstances, an impossibility. There may arrive a time when the musical taste and knowledge of the mass of our people will reach a level high enough to make it possible for every village church to have its well-trained, vested choir; but that time has not yet arrived, nor is there much hope of its coming for several generations yet. (Scribner. $1.75.)—*From Humphrey's "Evolution of Church Music."*

A "Hill-Top" Mother.

AND when Lucy (the housemaid) came creeping softly up, as commanded, to watch by Lionel's bedside, she found the little fellow sleeping, with traces of tears glistening on his pale cheeks, and his aspect was so touching and solemn in its innocence and sorrow and helplessness, that being nothing but a woman, and a warm-hearted woman, too, she took out her handkerchief and had a good, quiet cry all to herself. "How could she—how *could* she leave the little dear !" she wondered, dolefully, as she thought of the reckless and shameful flight of her recent mistress. "To leave *him*"—meaning Mr. Valliscourt—"isn't so surprising howsomever it's wished, for he's a handful to live with and no mistake !—but to leave her own boy—that's real downright bad of her !—that it is !" Poor Lucy ! She had never read the works of Ibsen, and was entirely ignorant of the "new morality," as inculcated by Mr. Grant Allen. Had she been taught these modern ethics she would have recognized in Mrs. Valliscourt's conduct merely a "noble" outbreak of "white purity" and virtue. But she had "barbaric" notions of motherhood—she believed in its sacredness in quite an obstinate, prejudiced, and old-fashioned way. She was nothing but a "child of nature," poor, simple, Ibsen-less housemaid Lucy !—and throughout all creation, Nature makes mother-love a law, and mother-duty paramount. (Lippincott. $1.25.)— *From Corelli's "The Mighty Atom."*

Survey of Current Literature.

☞ *Order through your bookseller.*—"*There is no worthier or surer pledge of the intelligence and the purity of any community than their general purchase of books; nor is there any one who does more to further the attainment and possession of these qualities than a good bookseller.*"—PROF. DUNN.

ART, MUSIC, DRAMA.

CURTIS. H. HOLBROOK, *M.D.* Voice building and tone placing ; showing a new method of relieving injured vocal chords by tone exercises. Appleton. il. 12°, $2.
Contents : The origin of music ; The anatomy and physiology of the larynx; Respiration ; The vocal resonators ; Tone and overtones ; The registers of the human voice ; Tone placing ; Voice building ; Voice figures. Dr. Curtis has had a wide experience among singers in his capacity of physician. The author is curator of voices at the Metropolitan Opera House.

HAMLIN, A. D. F. Text-book of the history of architecture. Longmans, Green & Co. il. 12°, $2.

NAVARRO, *Mrs.* MARY ANDERSON DE. A few memories. Harper. il. 8°, $2.50.

RENNER, A. L., (*pseud.*) Sarah Bernhardt : artist and woman ; with numerous autograph pages, especially written by Sarah Bernhardt; with sixtv il., fac-similes, and complete scenery of " Izeyl." A. Blanck. sq. 8°, pap., $1.
The great actress's stage career is chiefly described, and an account given of her chief rôles; many of the illustrations are full-page ; printed on rich, smooth paper, the page enclosed in a tinted border.

BIOGRAPHY, CORRESPONDENCE, ETC.

BOYD, ANDREW KENNEDY HUTCHINSON, [" Country Parson," *pseud.*] The last years of St. Andrews, September. 1890, to September, 1895. Longmans, Green & Co. 8°, $5.

BRIGGS, C. F. Lowell. Putnam. 16°, (Little journeys to the homes of American authors.) pap., 5 c.

CONSTANT, [L. Constant Wairy.] Recollections of the private life of Napoleon; by Constant, valet de chambre; tr. by Walter Clark. In 3 v. V. 3. Merriam. 8°, $2.50.

HILLARD, G. S. Prescott. Putnam. 16°, (Little journeys to the homes of American authors.) pap., 5 c.

RENAN, ERNEST *and* HENRIETTE. Brother and sister: a memoir and the letters of Ernest and Henriette Renan; tr. by Lady Mary Loyd. Macmillan. pors. il. 8°, $2.25.

DESCRIPTION, GEOGRAPHY, TRAVEL, ETC.

ARMOUR, MARGARET. The home and early haunts of Robert Louis Stevenson; il. by W. Brown Macdougall. Scribner. 18°, $1.40.

ARNOLD, *Sir* EDWIN. East and west; being papers reprinted from the *Daily Telegraph* and other sources; il. by R. T. Pritchett. Longmans, Green & Co. 8°, $4.

BORROW, G. The Bible in Spain ; or, the journeys, adventures, and imprisonments of an Englishman in an attempt to circulate the Scriptures in the Peninsula; ed. with notes and a glossary by Ulick Ralph Burke. Putnam. 2 v., il. 12°, $4.

CURTIS, W. ELEROY. Venezuela: a land where it's always summer. Harper. maps, 12°, $1.25.
" We have in this volume the work of an intelligent traveller. Mr. Curtis tells how to go to Venezuela, gives a brief history of the nation and its rulers, and much information about the principal cities, the government, the characteristics of the Venezuelan people, their religion, manners, customs, morals, and peculiarities. The volume also contains a chapter on the disputed territory in Guiana and an appendix giving the message of President Cleveland concerning the boundary dispute and the correspondence of Secretary Olney and the Marquis of Salisbury. Accompanying the book is a carefully prepared map showing the various disputed boundary lines between Venezuela and British Guiana."—*N. Y. Observer.*

DYER, *Mrs.* D. B. Fort Reno; or, picturesque Cheyenne and Arrapahoe army life before the opening of Oklahoma. G. W. Dillingham. por. il. 12°, $1.
Mrs. Dyer, as the wife of an Indian agent, spent a leng time at Fort Reno, in the Cheyenne and Arrapahoe Reservation, some ten years ago or more. Her book is an intelligent study of Indian life and character of the tribes that surrounded her, with many valuable details of customs, etc. Some personal adventures are included, and some encounters between our troops and the Indians described. Also space is given to army life.

GRENFELL, WILFRED T. Vikings of to-day; or, life and medical work among the fishermen of Labrador. Revell. il. 12°, $1.25.
Gives a general account of the country and people of Labrador, and summarizes the efforts made by the Council of the Mission to Deep Sea Fishermen, during the past three years, to brighten the lives of the many brave toilers of the sea on that desolate coast.

HOLMES, OLIVER WENDELL. Our hundred days in Europe. Houghton, Mifflin & Co. 16°, (Riverside pap. ser., extra no. 69.) pap., 50 c.

RODNEY, JA. The West Indies and the Spanish Main. Putnam. 8°, $1.75.

SATCHEL guide for the vacation tourist in Europe. *Ed. for* 1896, *rev.* to date. Houghton, Mifflin & Co. folding maps, interleaved, 16°, flex. roan, $1.50.

DOMESTIC AND SOCIAL.

PENNELL, ELIZ. ROBBINS. The feasts of Autolycus. Merriam. 12°, (The Mayfair set, no. 5.) $1.25.

SCHMIDT, W., [" The only William," *pseud.*] Fancy drinks and popular beverages; over five hundred recipes for preparing popular beverages, by the only William. Dick & Fitzgerald. 16°, 75 c.; pap., 50 c.

EDUCATION, LANGUAGE, ETC.

HAWTHORNE, NATHANIEL. Twice-told tales; with introductory note by G. Parsons Lathrop. Houghton, Mifflin & Co. 12°, (Riverside literature ser., quadruple no. 82.) 60 c. ; pap., 50 c.

HOLMAN, H. Education: an introduction to its principles and their psychological foundations. Dodd, Mead & Co. 12°, $1.50.

HERVEY, WALTER L. Picture-work for teachers and mothers. Flood & Vincent, (Chautauqua Century Press.) 16°, (Monographs of the new education in the church ser., no. 3.) pap., 30 c.
Points out interesting methods, by the use of pictures and story-telling, of holding the attention of pupils, especially in Sunday-schools; the author is president of the Teachers' College of New York City. A useful chapter is given on "Books, pictures, and illustrative material," with the full titles, prices, and publishers of the books, etc., recommended for teachers' use.

WIGGIN, *Mrs.* KATE DOUGLAS, [*Mrs.* G. Christopher Riggs,] *and* Smith, Nora Archibald. Froebel's occupations. Houghton, Mifflin & Co. 16°, (The republic of childhood, no. 2.) $1.

FICTION.

BARING-GOULD, SABINE. The broom-squire. Stokes. 12°, $1.25.

BECKE, L: The ebbing of the tide: South Sea stories. Lippincott. 12°, $1.25.
Contents : "Luliban of the pool"; Ninia; Baldwin's Loisé; At a Kava-drinking; Mrs. Liardet—a South Sea trading episode; Kennedy the boat-steerer; A dead loss; Hickson, a half-caste; A boating party of two; "The best asset in a fool's estate"; Deschard of Oneaka; Nell of Mulliner's camp; Anicki Reef; At the ebbing of the tide; The fallacies of Hilliard; A tale of a mask; The cook of the "Spreetoo Santoo"; Lupton's guest; In Nouméa; The feast at Pentecost; An honor to the service.

BOOTHBY, GUY. The beautiful white devil: a novel. Ward, Lock & Bowden, Ltd. 12°, $1.

BOWCHER, HAVERING. The C major of life. Stokes. 8°, $1.50.

CARPENTER, EDITH. Your money or your life: a story. Scribner. 12°, $1.25.
Tom Norrie, a Harvard graduate, was the junior partner of an old and well-established business making millions; at twenty-eight he is sick of life and money-making, dyspeptic, and not able to sleep at nights; the girl he loves finds him slow, cautious, fussy, and, she thinks, cowardly, and rejects him. He takes a sudden resolution, deserts his business, and going west leads a life of wild adventure in which train-robbing is included. Finally he and his old lady-love are reunited, and they resolve that mere money-getting is not living — that they will be satisfied with a moderate income, and spend it in study and travel, enjoying their lives.

CHAMBERS, JULIUS. Missing: a romance. Transatlantic Pub. Co. 16°, $1.

CLIFFORD, *Mrs.* LUCY LANE, [*Mrs.* W. K. Clifford.] A flash of summer : the story of a simple woman's life. Appleton. 12°, (Appleton's town and country lib., no. 189.) cl., $1 ; pap., 50 c.

CORELLI, MARIE. The mighty atom. Lippincott Co. 12°, $1.25.

CROCKETT, S. RUTHERFORD. Cleg Kelly, Arab of the city ; his progress and adventures. Appleton. il. 12°, $1.50.

DAVIS, MARTHA CAROLY. The refiner's fire. Pott & Co. il. 12°, $1.25.

DICKINSON, MARY LOWE. From hollow to hilltop. Amer. Bapt. Pub. Soc. il. 12°, 50 c.
An Easter story with its scene in New Hampshire. Mrs. Burke had spent several years of her girlhood as a teacher in a small mill-town, to which she returns as a widow; here she does missionary work in a gentle, unobtrusive way.

ELMSLIE, THEODORA, ["Baynton Foster," *pseud.*] His life's magnet. Warne & Co. *New edition.* 12°, (Warne's star ser.) $1.

FIELD, EUGENE. The house : an episode in the lives of Reuben Baker, astronomer, and of his wife Alice. Scribner. 12°, $1.25.
It was the ardent desire of Mrs. Reuben Baker to own a house of her own; her husband encouraged her dreams, but as he was thoroughly impractical in money matters his encouragement did not aid her very much. It was not until they had quite a family that Mrs. Baker carried out her plan of buying a house ; the story that is then told of their various troubles before they can take possession, their repairs and changes, their furnishing and planting, etc., is full of amusement.

FOOTE, MARY HALLOCK. The chosen valley: a novel. Houghton, Mifflin & Co. 16°, (Riverside pap. ser., no. 69.) pap., 50 c.

GARBE, R. The redemption of the Brahmin : a novel. The Open Court Pub. Co. 12°, (Religion of science lib., no. 17.) pap., 25 c.
Scene laid in Benares, in October of the year 1840. Deals with the religious superstitions of the Hindus, especially those regarding early marriages and the cruel laws concerning widows.

GARDNER, E. C. The house that Jill built, after Jack's had proved a failure: a book on home architecture, with illustrations. *New ed.* W. F. Adams Co. il. 12°, $1.
First published in 1882 by the Our Continent Publishing Co. The aim of the work is to show what an ideal home is, from a woman's point of view. After "Jack," the husband, has built a house and failed from a practical standpoint, "Jill," the wife, who has received a blank check from her father for a wedding present, to be filled in with the sum necessary to build such a house as she wants, takes up the task. How her plans are finally evolved is amusingly and instructively shown. The present edition contains two new chapters, describing changes "Jill" would make, after a half dozen years' experiences.

GISSING, G. Sleeping fires. Appleton. nar. 12°, 75 c.
"Mr. Gissing is subtle in this romance, to which he has given an archæological coloring. The main idea is not so exactly complex as is the

mechanism of it. The topic, a difficult one, is delicately treated with much special pleading introduced in extenuation of Langley's mistake."—*N. Y. Times.*

"As always, Mr. Gissing gives every thought its fitting word, every motive its appropriate act, and every act its inevitable consequences."—*London Academy.*

GOBEL, HARVEY. On the shelf; il. by C. Paterson. Warne. 12°, $1.

Some volumes of well-known books, of various degrees of merit, gathered by chance together in the window of a second-hand bookseller's shop, are the tellers of the stories; the incidents they relate having come to them while circulating from hand to hand. The stories, six in number, are pathetic and realistic, being largely among the poor of London.

GRAS, FÉLIX. The reds of the Midi: an episode of the French Revolution; tr. from the Provençal by Catharine A. Janvier; with an introd. by T. A. Janvier. Appleton. 16°, $1.

GROOME, FRANCIS HINDES. Kriegspiel: the war. game. Ward, Lock & Bowden, Ltd. por. 12°, $1.50.

HARDY, T. A Laodicean: a novel. *New uniform ed.* Harper. 12°, $1.50.

HAWTHORNE, JULIAN. A fool of nature. Scribner. 16°, $1.25.

"A fool of nature" was written by Mr. Hawthorne for the competition of stories instituted by the *New York Herald* in 1895, and obtained the first prize of $10,000. The hero's parentage is obscured by a great deal of mystery, which it takes the larger part of the book to explain; he is supposed to be the descendant of an illustrious line of ancestors, but he fails to obtain his degree at college, is fond of low company and not overburthened with brains, but physically is a fine specimen of manhood, and has his share of virtues.

HECTOR, *Mrs.* ANNIE F., [" *Mrs.* Alexander," *pseud.*] A fight with fate: a novel. Lippincott. 12°, $1.25.

HOWELLS, W. DEAN. A parting and a meeting: story. Harper. il. 24° (Harper's little novel ser.) $1.

"A pathetic although by no means a morbid story, in which Mr. Howells shows the power of religious fervor over love. There is a quaint atmosphere to the tale, the scene of which is laid in a Shaker village, for the most part in the early period of this century."—*N. Y. Tribune.*

HUME, FERGUS W. The crime of the '*Lisa Jane*; il. by G. Hutchinson. Ward, Lock & Bowden, Ltd. 12°, $1.

An ocean tramp going up the Channel to London, in June of 1891, picks up a small pleasure-boat, the '*Lisa Jane*, in which is the dead body of a man, bound hand and foot to the bottom of the boat; there is a wound in his left breast, over which is tattooed the inscription "Down with tyrants." This is the starting-point of a sensational tale, rich in the most puzzling mysteries. The characters are anarchists, journalists, actresses, detectives, etc.

KOVALEVSKY, SONIA KRUKOVSKY. Vera Vorontzoff; rendered into English by Anna

Von Rydingsvärd, (Baroness Von Proschwitz.) Lamson, Wolffe & Co. 16°, $1.25.

Vera Vorontzoff was eight years old in 1859 when on February 15 the manifesto liberating the Russian serfs was read in all the churches of St. Petersburg. The story deals with the consequences of this great change in Russia's condition and with Vera's relations from her fifteenth year with a man working for social equality whose labors banished him to Siberia. Vera, the scion of a proud race of noblemen, works to carry out the principles this man had taught; and the tale leaves her departing for Siberia to cheer and work for the exiles in the year 1876.

LE QUEUX, W. The great war in England in 1897. Stokes. 8°. $2.

LUMMIS, C. F. The gold fish of Gran Chimú; il. by H. Sandham. Lamson, Wolffe & Co. il. 16°, $1.50.

"The quest of hidden treasure and the adventures which befall those who are searching is the theme of Mr. Charles F. Lummis's story 'The gold fish of Gran Chimú.' The scene is laid in Peru, and the matter of the tale rests on a legend which is to the effect that Atahualpa being a prisoner, his captor, Cajamarco, agreed to release him upon his filling a certain room with treasure. This the war chief assented to, but as his messengers were bringing the gold they heard of the death of their chief, and not knowing what to do with their precious burden, buried it in the Gran Chimú. The story passed current for 350 years, and it remained for the party of adventurers, who are the heroes of Mr. Lummis's story, to prove its authenticity. A fortunate misadventure, in which the boy Gonzalo is the lonely protagonist, brings the priceless treasure to light. The story is told with considerable constructive skill."—*N. Y. Tribune.*

MAETERLINCK, MAURICE, ECKHOUD G., [*and others.*] The massacre of the innocents, and other tales by Belgian writers: tr. by Edith Wingate Rinder. Stone & Kimball. 16°, (Green tree lib.) $1.25.

Contents: The massacre of the innocents, by Maurice Maeterlinck; Kors Davie, Ex-Voto, and Hiep-Hioup, three stories, by Georges Eckhoud; Fleur-De-Ble and Saint Nicholas Eve, by Camille Lemonnier; Trompe-La-Mort, by Auguste Jenart; Pierre-De-La-Baraque, by L. Delattre; The shadowy bourne, by Stephane Richelle; Jacclard, by G. Ganir; The denial of Saint Peter, by Eugene Demolder; The Mountebanks, by Hubert Krains.

MALLOCK, W. H. The heart of life: *New rev. cheaper ed.* Putnam. 12°, (Hudson lib., no. 14.) pap., 50 c.

MANN, MARY E. Susannah: a novel. Harper. 12°, $1.25.

"The plot of 'Susannah' should give a fillip to the palate of the most jaded of novel-readers, for the theme is refreshingly new and piquant. A young English girl, born and bred a lady, is yet compelled, through stress of circumstances, to go out to service as a London 'slavy.' The situation is treated with vigorous realism, and an unusually strong love interest supplies the romance."—*Chic. Tribune.*

MATHER, MARSHALL. Lancashire idylls. Warne. 12°, $1.50.

Contents: Mr. Penrose's new parish; The

money-lender; Amanda Stott; Saved as by fire ; Winter sketches ; Miriam's motherhood ; How Malachi o' th' mount won his wife ; Mr. Penrose brings home a bride. The stern Puritanism of the hill sects of Lancashire is illustrated in these idylls.

MEARS, MARY M. Emma Lou: her book. Holt. 12°, buckram, $1.

"This volume contains the neatest, closest, and most accurate description of village life in exactly the way an uncommonly bright girl would see it. It is so cleverly precise that it sounds as if it were autobiographical. It is its exceeding naturalness which is so taking. There are all the ludicrous little accidents about dress which a masculine mind never could have seized. Emma Lou is half girl, half woman, and just at that age when mistakes are made, when the true discipline of life begins. The girl is keen, sharp, and honest, and she is a typical American. Emma Lou will certainly interest any intelligent girl, and the mothers will understand it. We are inclined to give to the book the highest of encomiums as a sound, wholesome, and most amusing story."—*N. Y. Times.*

NORRIS, W. E. The dancer in yellow. Appleton. 12°, (Appleton's town and country lib., no. 190.) $1; pap., 50 c.

RIDEING, W. H. The captured Cunarder : an episode of the Atlantic. Copeland & Day. nar. 16°, 75 c.

To revenge Ireland's wrongs Capt. O'Grady, a daring and patriotic Irishman, conceives the bold plan of capturing a Cunarder and using it for preying upon England's commerce. He is captain of the steamer *Rosario*, upon which he is carrying to Venezuela the armament of a fast cruiser; with this he first seizes the *Grampania*, then puts his guns and men aboard of her, transferring her passengers to the *Rosario*, and begins his war on the Atlantic liners. He captures six before his career comes to an end.

RIDGE, W. PETT. The second opportunity of Mr. Staplehurst. Harper. 12°, $1.25.

Mr. Gilbert Staplehurst is furnished with a second opportunity to go through life on earth by the author invoking a supernatural agency which restores him—a middle-aged and successful literary man—to youth. Gilbert makes a dismal failure of his second opportunity and willingly returns to his former condition. By the author of "A clever wife."

ROBERTS, C. G. D. Earth's enigmas: a volume of stories. Lamson, Wolffe & Co. 16°, buckram, $1.25.

ROD, E. The white rocks: a novel; from the French; il. by E. Boyd Smith. Crowell. 12°, $1.25.

Edouard Rod is a distinguished French novelist of the psychological school. His *Les roches blanches* has gone through fifteen editions in France. It has a distinct ethical motive. The theme is love and renunciation. The scene is a little Swiss town, to which comes a new minister, an unworldly youth of peasant origin, fresh from the seminary, with his faithful, shrewd-minded old mother. He has great eloquence and exalted ideals. His temptation comes through his sympathy with a cultivated married woman—but both the lovers remain true to principles.

SCOTT, DUNCAN CAMPBELL. In the village of Viger. Copeland & Day. nar. 16°, $1.

The French village of Viger is the scene of the following short stories : The little milliner; The Desjardins; The wooing of Monsieur Cuerrier; Sedan; No. 68 Rue Alfred de Musset; The bobolink; The tragedy of the seigniory; Josephine Labrosse; The pedler; Paul Farlotte.

SERGEANT, ADELINE. The failure of Sibyl Fletcher: a novel. Lippincott. 12°, (Lippincott's select novels, no. 179.) $1 ; pap., 50 c.

SERGEANT, ADELINE. Marjory Moore. A. E. Cluett. 12°, $1.

Marjory Moore as a child displays great talent for music. A rich squire of Surrey hears her playing the violin by accident, and offers to pay for lessons and send her to Leipsic to finish, that she may make for herself a career. Squire Hyde is passionately fond of music, and has been disappointed in his nephew, who, though the owner of a beautiful tenor voice, refuses to become a professional musician, preferring to study medicine. He makes his will, hoping to force the young people to marry; many perplexing circumstances grow out of this.

SPOFFORD, HARRIET PRESCOTT. A master spirit. Scribner. nar. 16°, (The ivory ser., no. 5.) 75 c.

STIMSON, F. J., ["J. S. of Dale," *pseud.*] Pirate gold. Houghton, Mifflin & Co. 16°, $1.25.

A story of Boston in the early days of the century. One of the ships of the great banking house of James Bowdoin's Sons returns to Boston in 1829, with several captured pirates on board; as the captives are leaving the vessel one hands a bag of gold to young James Bowdoin, who is watching the landing, and another, a beautiful yellow-haired child to an old and trusted clerk. The child is adopted by the latter, and the gold placed in the bank; both are factors in the story and strong influences on the old clerk.

THOMES, W. H. Ocean rovers. Laird & Lee. 12°, (Pastime ser., no. 29.) pap., 25 c.

A story of the War of 1812; the scene is laid mostly on board an American privateersman. The ms. of this work was bought from M. Thomes's heirs shortly after his death, and is for the first time published.

WENDELL, BARRETT. The Duchess Emilia : a romance. [*New issue.*] Scribner. 12°, $1 ; pap., 50 c.

WENDELL, BARRETT. Rankell's remains : an American novel. [*New issue.*] Scribner. 12°, $1; pap., 50 c.

WHITE, W. HALE, ["Mark Rutherford," *pseud.*] Clara Hopgood; by Mark Rutherford; ed. by his friend Reuben Shapcott. Dodd, Mead & Co. 12°, $1.25.

Clara Hopgood's part in the story is uncomplaining self-sacrifice ; when a lover comes into her life and the life of her sister, whom she might have loved, but whom her sister does love, she effaces herself, and goes to Italy to work with Mazzini for Italian liberty. Madge Hopgood—Clara's sister—is a mother, though not a wife, and persistently refuses to marry her betrayer, on the ground that she no longer loves him; the man she does marry knows and forgives her history.

WINTER, JOHN STRANGE, (*pseud.* for *Mrs.* H. E. V. Stannard.) I married a wife. Stokes. nar. 16°, (Twentieth century ser.) buckram, 75 c.

WOLF, ALICE S. A house of cards. Stone & Kimball. 16°, (Peacock lib.) $1.25.

HISTORY.

CAMPBELL, H. COLIN. Exploration of Lake Superior : the voyages of Radisson and Grosseilliers. H. E. Haferkorn. 8°, (Parkman Club publications, no. 2.) pap., 30 c.

For more than two hundred years the two Frenchmen who were the pioneer explorers of Lake Superior have remained nameless. It is now certain they were Pierre-Esprit Radisson and Medard Chouart des Grosseilliers. This pamphlet offers details of their lives and explorations, not only of Lake Superior, but of other western regions. A bibliography (1 p.).

LE NORMAND, M. A. The historical and secret memoirs of the Empress Josephine. Scribner. 2 v., il. 8°, $10.

OLD South leaflets. Directors of the Old South Work, Old South Meeting-House. 2 v. 12°, (General ser., v. 1, nos. 1–25, v. 2, nos. 26–50.) ea., $1.50.

Contents: V. 1—no. 1, Constitution of the United States ; 2. Articles of confederation ; 3, Declaration of Independence ; 4. Washington's farewell address ; 5, Magna Charta ; 6, The "Healing question" ; 7, Charter of Massachusetts Bay ; 8, Fundamental orders of Ct.; 9. Franklin's plan of union ; 10, Washington's inaugurals; 11, Lincoln's inaugurals and emancipation proclamations; 12, The Federalist, nos. 1 and 2 ; 13, The ordinance of 1787 ; 14, The constitution of Ohio ; 15, Washington's circular letter to the governors of the states, 1783 ; 16, Washington's letter to Benjamin Harrison, 1784 ; 17, Verrazzano's voyage ; 18, The Swiss constitution ; 19, Bill of rights ; 20. Coronado's letter to Mendoza, 1540 ; 21, Eliot's narrative, 1670 ; 22, Wheelock's narrative, 1762 ; 23, Petition of rights; 24. The grand remonstrance; 25, The Scottish national covenant. V. 2—26. Agreement of the people ; 27, Instrument of government ; 28, Cromwell's first speech to his parliament ; 29, Discovery of America, from life of Columbus ; 30, Strabo's introduction to geography; 31, Voyages to Vinland ; 32, Marco Polo's account of Japan and Java ; 33, Columbus's letter to Gabriel Sanchez ; 34. Amerigo Vespucci's account of his first voyage ; 35, Cortes's account of the city of Mexico ; 36. The death of De Soto ; 37. Early notices of the voyage of the Cabots ; 38, Henry Lee's funeral oration on Washington ; 39 De Vaca's account of his journey to New Mexico ; 40, Manasseh Cutler's description of Ohio ; 41, Washington's journal of his tour to the Ohio, 1770 ; 42, Garfield's address on the Northwest Territory and the Western Reserve ; 43. G. Rogers Clark's account of the capture of Vincennes ; 44. Jefferson's Life of Captain Meriwether Lewis ; 45, Fremont's account of his ascent of Fremont's Peak ; 46, Father Marquette at Chicago ; 47, Washington's account of the army at Cambridge ; 48, Bradford's Memoir of Elder Brewster ; 49, Bradford's first dialogue ; 50, Winthrop's Conclusions for the plantation in New England.

RILEY, F. L. Colonial origins of New England senates. The Johns Hopkins Press. 8°, (Johns Hopkins University studies, 14th ser., no. 3.) pap., 50 c.

Traces the evolution of state senates from the colonial councils, which exercised a power which was threefold—executive, judicial, and legislative ; the study is confined to the New England colonies—Massachusetts, Connecticut, New Hampshire, and Rhode Island.

RODWAY, JA. The West Indies and the Spanish Main. Putnam. il. 12°, $2.50.

TUTTLE, HERBERT. History of Prussia under Frederic the Great, 1756–1757; with a biographical sketch of the author by Herbert B. Adams. Houghton, Mifflin & Co. 12°, $1.50.

WEST, B. B. A financial atonement. Longmans, Green & Co. 12°, $2.

WILLIAMSON, JA. J. Mosby's rangers: a record of the operations of the Forty-third Battalion Virginia Cavalry. from its organization to the surrender. Ralph B. Kenyon. pors. il. maps, 8°, $3.50.

From the diary of a private, supplemented and verified with official reports of Federal officers, and also of Mosby; with personal reminiscences, sketches of skirmishes, battles and bivouacs, dashing raids and daring adventures, scenes and incidents in the history of Mosby's command. Contains over 200 illustrations, including portraits of many of Mosby's men and of Federal officers with whom they came in contact, views, engagements, etc., maps of Mosby's Confederacy and localities in which he operated, muster-rolls. occupation and present whereabouts of surviving members.

HUMOR AND SATIRE.

ALDEN, W. L. Among the freaks; il. by J. F. Sullivan and Francis K. Upton. Longmans, Green & Co. 12°, $1.25.

McVICKAR, H. WHITNEY. The evolution of woman. Harper. il. sq. 8°, $2.

"In this clever brochure, half humorous and half satirical, Mr. McVickar takes lovely woman from her first appearance in the Garden of Eden, and pictures the evolution of the sex to the end of the nineteenth century. From the days of the ancient Egyptians and Greeks. she is brought forward through the mediæval times, when she was something between a hindrance and a help, to the present century, when, all professions being open to her, she is holding her own with her alleged lord and master, and, if her physique develops as Mr. McVickar foreshadows in his closing sketches, she is destined to make a bigger sensation than the Roentgen rays. But in all these changes she is still lovely woman; and in her golf and bicycle dresses she is certainly a thing of beauty and a joy forever."—*N. Y. Herald.*

LITERATURE, MISCELLANEOUS AND COL-LECTED WORKS.

BOAS, F. S. Shakspere and his predecessors. Scribner. 12°, (University ser.) $1.50.

Treats of the writings of the dramatists in their approximate chronological order. *Contents:* The mediæval drama; The early renaissance drama; The rise of the theatres — Marlowe's dramatic reform; Kyd, Lyly, and Peele; Robert Greene; Shakspere at Stratford;

Shakspere in London — the sonnets; Shakspere's dramatic apprenticeship; Shakspere's poems; The early period of comedy; Shakspere Italianate; The chief group of chronicle-history plays; The golden prime of comedy; The problem-plays; The climax of tragedy; The Plutarch series of plays; The dramatic romances.

BURNS, ROB. Life and works; ed. by Rob. Chambers; rev. by W. Wallace. In 4 v. V. 1. Longmans, Green & Co. 8°, $2.50.

DIXON, W. MACNEILE. A Tennyson primer with a critical essay. Dodd, Mead & Co. 12°, $1.25.

HOLMES, OLIVER WENDELL. The autocrat of the breakfast-table; every man his own Boswell; with biographical sketch. Houghton, Mifflin & Co. 12°, (Riverside literature ser., triple no. 81.) 50 c.; pap., 45 c.

LAMB, C. Old china, and other essays of Elia; with biographical sketch and notes. Houghton, Mifflin & Co. 12°, (Riverside literature ser., no. 79.) pap., 15 c.

MEYNELL, ALICE. The rhythm of life, and other essays. Copeland & Day. 16°, $1.25. *Contents:* The rhythm of life; Decivilized; A remembrance; The sun; The flower; Unstable equilibrium; The unit of the world; By the railway side; Pocket vocabularies; Pathos; The point of honour; Composure; Dr. Oliver Wendell Holmes; James Russell Lowell; Mr. Coventry Patmore's odes, etc.

PUTNAM, G. HAVEN. Books and their makers during the middle ages : a study of the conditions of the production and distribution of literature from the fall of the Roman Empire to the close of the seventeenth century. In 2 v. V. 1, 476–1600. Putnam. 8°, $2.50.

REES, T., *M.D.* Reminiscences of literary London, from 1779–1853; with interesting anecdotes of publishers, authors, and book auctioneers of that period, etc.; with extensive additions by J. Britton; ed. by A book-lover. F. P. Harper. il. sq. 16°, $1.

ROBERTS, W., *ed.* Book-verse : an anthology of poems of books and bookmen from the earliest times to recent years. Armstrong. 16°, (The book-lover's lib.) $1.25. The present volume is the pendant to "Book-song," edited by Gleeson White and published in the *Book-lover's library series* two years ago. The arrangement is chronological. Notes. Index.

WARREN, F. M. A history of the novel previous to the seventeenth century. Holt. 12°, $1.75.

MENTAL AND MORAL.

HIBBEN, J. GRIER. Inductive logic. Scribner. 12°, $1.50. Dr. Hibben has emphasized the necessity of a thorough knowledge of the principles of inductive logic in order to comprehend the material as well as the formal elements of inference. He insists that the inductive and deductive are mutually dependent and simply different phases of the same logical procedure, and it is to provide the means of pursuing their study co-ordinately that the present treatise has been written. Author is Professor of Logic in Princeton University.

WHITE, ALEXANDER, *D.D.* The four temperaments. Dodd, Mead & Co. nar. 12°, (Little books on religion.) 50 c. Dr. Whyte, minister of Free St. George's Church, Edinburgh, discusses in a half-humorous manner, with a vein of deep underlying earnestness, the relative differences and effects of the four distinct temperaments — the sanguine, the choleric, the phlegmatic, and the melancholy — which are characteristic of mankind.

NATURE AND SCIENCE.

MILLER, *Mrs.* OLIVE THORNE. Four-handed folk. Houghton, Mifflin & Co. 16°, $1.25.

TORREY, BRADFORD. Spring notes from Tennessee. Houghton, Mifflin & Co. 16°, $1.25. Several of these papers describing the birds and natural charms of the most picturesque and historic section of Tennessee appeared in the *Atlantic Monthly.* Contents: An idler on Missionary Ridge ; Lookout Mountain ; Chickamauga ; Orchard Knob and the Natural Cemetery; An afternoon by the river : A morning in the North Woods ; A week on Walden's Ridge ; Some Tennessee bird notes. A list of birds found in the neighborhood of Chattanooga. Index.

POETRY AND DRAMA.

AUSTIN, ALFRED. England's darling, and other poems. Macmillan. por. 12°, $1.25.

BLACKWELL, ALICE STONE, *comp.* and *tr.* Armenian poems rendered into English verse. Roberts. por. 12°, $1.25. Selections from the poems of Bedros Tourian, Michael Nalbandian, Archbishop Khorène Nar Bey De Lusignan, Mugurditch Beshiktashlian, Raphael Patkanian, Leo Alishan, and other Armenian poets.

MARTIN, ARTHUR SHADWELL. On parody. Holt. 12°, buckram, $1.25. Opens with a short historical and critical sketch of the art of parody ; followed by poetical examples gathered from every source.

SCOLLARD, CLINTON. Hills of song. [Verses.] Copeland & Day. 16°, $1.25. "The forty poems comprised in the ' Hills of song ' are in a little volume that will fit nicely into your pocket, and you will carry it with you probably till you know most of its contents by heart."—*N. Y. Commercial Advertiser.*

SUDERMANN, HERMANN. Magda: a play in four acts; from the German by C. E. Amory Winslow. Lamson, Wolffe & Co. 16°, (Sock and buskin lib.) $1. Called in the original *Heimat;* considered Sudermann's masterpiece. Magda is an interesting psychological study; the scene is laid in a provincial German town, in the home of a retired half-pay officer—a man of integrity, but narrow of vision and exercising his parental authority with an iron hand. Magda has fled from this home in her youth; she returns to it a rich, successful prima donna. The modern conflict between the old and the new is painfully illustrated.

POLITICAL AND SOCIAL.

CHIROL, VALENTINE. The far Eastern question. Macmillan. il. maps, 8°, $3.50.

FLINT. ROB., *D.D.* Socialism. Lippincott. 8°, $3.25.

GIDDINGS, FRANKLIN H. The principles of sociology: an analysis of the phenomena of association and of social organization. Macmillan. 8°, $3.

LECKY, W. E. HARTPOLE. Democracy and liberty. Longmans, Green & Co. 2 v., 12°, $5.

NICHOLSON, J. SHIELD. Strikes and social problems. 12°, $1.25.

TAUBENECK, H. E. The condition of the American farmer. The Schulte Pub. Co. 12°, (Ariel lib. ser., no. 8.) pap., 25 c.
The subjects considered are: the farmer's income; depreciation of farm property; increase of tenant farmers; decadence of home-ownership; depreciation of farm products; the overproduction fallacy; the cause; the remedy.

WILLOUGHBY, WESTEL WOODBURY. An examination of the nature of a state: a study in political philosophy. Macmillan. 8°, $3.

SPORTS AND AMUSEMENTS.

DAVIS, S. T., *M.D.*, ["Shongo," *pseud.*] Caribou shooting in Newfoundland; with a history of England's oldest colony from 1001 to 1895. The New Era Printing House. il. maps, 8°, bds., $1.25.
Besides some wonderful accounts of caribou shooting and adventures. the book contains chapters on the physical features of Newfoundland, its fauna and flora, the fisheries, agriculture, mineral resources, government and finance, education, aborigines, etc. The island contains more reindeer or caribou than can be found in any other portion of the world, and the waters surrounding it are rich in every kind of fish. The author offers good advice to overworked literary men.

DRAYSON, A. W. Whist laws and whist decisions; with upwards of 150 cases illustrating the laws; also remarks on the American laws of whist and cases by which the reader's knowledge of the English laws my be tested by himself. Harper. 24°, $1.
The English laws of whist are first set forth and are followed by a page or two on the etiquette of whist and a few pages of pertinent and unprejudiced remarks on the comparative merits of the English and American laws. The main feature of the book (pp. 46–162) is the series of 154 cases illustrative of questions likely to arise under the laws, each case being followed by a careful and somewhat elaborate decision. These cases are culled from the author's long experience at the whist-table. Reference to these cases is facilitated by a concise and comprehensive index. The book also includes the 39 Laws of Whist as adopted by the American Whist League.

LOCKYER, J. NORMAN, *and* RUTHERFORD, W. The rules of golf. Macmillan. 24°, interleaved, 75 c.

PATTON, F. JARVIS. How to win at draw-poker, showing all the chances of the game. Dick & Fitzgerald. 16°, pap., 25 c.

SANDEMAN, FRANK. Angling travels in Norway. Scribner. il. 8°, $6.40.

THEOLOGY, RELIGION, AND SPECULATION.

DALE, ROB. W. Christ and the future life. Dodd, Mead & Co. nar. 12°, (Little books on religion.) 50 c.

DONALD, *Rev.* E. WINCHESTER. The expansion of religion : six lectures delivered before the Lowell Institute. Houghton, Mifflin & Co. 12°, $1.50.
"Dr. Donald has produced one of the most suggestive, persuasive, and stimulating books of the decade—a book that is sure to set men to thinking along lines which at first sight seem strange. There is nothing controversial in Dr. Donald's book ; it seeks to pick no quarrels, but rather to explain away misunderstandings which have been the causes of quarrels. No book was ever written in a manlier, more modest, and more generous spirit."—*Boston Gazette.*

ECKENSTEIN, LINA. Woman under monasticism: chapters on saint lore and convent life between 500 and 1500. Macmillan. 8°, *net*, $4.

FISHER, G. PARK, *D.D.* History of Christian doctrine. Scribner's Sons. 8°, (International theological lib., no. 4.) $2.50.
The author is Professor of Ecclesiastical History in Yale University. His present work is a history not only of dogma as laid down by recognized authority, but also of doctrine as held by various Christian sects and bodies to the present day. The primary aim has been to present in an objective way and in an impartial spirit the course of theological thought respecting the religion of the Gospel. The author holds that all must become better Christians before they can be great theologians. "A theology which is the creation of a poor and degraded religious life will have neither stability nor grandeur." Full index.

HEPWORTH, G. H. The farmer and the Lord. Dutton. 12°, 75 c.
"Those who read 'Hiram Golf's religion,' by the Rev. Dr. George H. Hepworth, will be glad to know that another book by him in a somewhat similar vein, entitled 'The farmer and the Lord,' has just appeared. The principal character is a rugged and obstinate old New England farmer named Elijah Tomkins, who did not believe in the church or religion, but whose life in many respects was a contradiction of his negative creed; for he exercised the Christian virtues without knowing that they were Christian. How he and his Christian neighbor, Rastus, disputed together about life and death and God, and what Samanthy, the wife of 'Lige, and his strapping son Sam, thought and said and did are recorded by Dr. Hepworth with great fidelity to truth and sympathetic insight. As a graphic story of homely New England life it is well worth a perusal; but in addition to that it presents the problem of scepticism and faith as it is worked out by the rural New Englander with such truth to life that it reads like a shorthand report."—*N. Y. Tribune.*

LEA, H. C. A history of auricular confession and indulgences in the Latin church. In 3 v. V. 1. Confession and absolution. Lea Bros. & Co. 8°, $3.

SOULSBY, LUCY H. M. Stray thoughts for invalids. New ed. Longmans, Green & Co. 16°, 75 c.

WHITE, ANDREW D. A history of the warfare of science with theology in Christendom. Appleton. 2 v., 8°, $5.

Freshest News.

ROBERTS BROTHERS have issued "Platonic Affections," by John Smith, a new volume in the *Keynotes Series;* "The Gallery of Antiquities," the latest addition to their works of Balzac; and "Effie Hetherington," by Robert Buchanan.

R. F. FENNO & Co. have ready "A Bride from the Desert," by Grant Allen; "A New Note," by Ella McMahon; "The Unclassed," by George Gissing; "The Heart of a Mystery," by T. W. Speight; the fifth edition of "A Little Wizard," by Stanley J. Weyman; and a third edition of Mrs. Hungerford's "The Professor's Experiment," which by inadvertence was last month credited to the Lippincotts.

THE HOME PUBLISHING Co. have just ready "Her Senator," by Archibald Clavering Gunter, who seems to keep up his phenomenal popularity with every new story; and "The Love Adventures of Al-Mansur," translated from the Persian by Omar-El-Aziz and edited by Archibald Clavering Gunter. These two widely different pieces of work show Mr. Gunter's great literary cleverness to fine advantage.

LONGMANS, GREEN & Co. have just issued "Democracy and Liberty," by William Edward Hartpole Lecky, one of the notable books of a decade; "East and West," essays by Sir Edwin Arnold, with forty-one illustrations by R. T. Pritchett; a new and revised edition of "Problems of the Far East," by George N. Curzon; and "Among the Freaks," by W. L. Alden, formerly the writer of humorous editorials on the N. Y. *Times.*

WARD, LOCK & BOWDEN, LTD., will shortly begin a series, to be entitled *The Nineteenth Century Classics,* a collection of desirable books to be issued, in uniform style, under the general editorship of Clement K. Shorter. The first volumes announced are Carlyle's "Sartor Rpsartus," with an introduction by Edward Dowden; and Matthew Arnold's "Alaric at Rome, and other poems," with an introduction by Richard Garrett.

FREDERICK WARNE & Co. have just issued "Señor Castelar," by David Hannay, the new volume in the *Public Men of To-day Series;* a second series of "Wayside and Woodland Blossoms," by Edward Step ; "By Tangled Paths," stray leaves from Nature's byways, by H. Meade Briggs; "Robert Urquhart," by Gabriel Setoun, a delightful story of Scottish rural life, introducing a quite original school-teacher; and "The Carbuncle Clue," one of Fergus Hume's always delightful tales of mystery.

D. APPLETON & Co. have just issued a suggestive and instructive work in "The Warfare of Science and Theology," by Andrew D. White, who ably words his conviction "that science, though it has evidently conquered dogmatic theology based on biblical texts, will go hand in hand with religion"; "The School System of Ontario," by Hon. George W. Ross, a new volume in the *International Education Series;* "Chronicles of Martin Hewitt," by Arthur Morrison, an addition to the *Town and Country Library;* a new edition, revised and enlarged by Cady Staley, of William M. Gillespie's "Treatise on Surveying"; and a new edition of John B. Henck's standard "Field-Book for Railway Engineers," which has been entirely rewritten and revised.

G. P. PUTNAM'S SONS have just ready Part 3 of "The Empire of the Tsars," by Anatole-Beaulieu, which is devoted to "Religion" and completes a work which is one of the literary events of the times. They will also issue at once "Buddhism : its history and literature," by T. W. Rhys-Davids; "The Epic of the Fall of Man," by S. Humphreys Gurteen, a comparative study of Cædmon, Dante, and Milton; and "Jeanne d'Arc : her life and death," by Mrs. Oliphant. In fiction are announced "A King and a Few Dukes," a new romance by Robert W. Chambers, author of "The King in Yellow"; and "The Broken Ring," by Elizabeth Knight Tompkins, author of "Her Majesty"; and "An Unlessoned Girl," the new volume in the *Hudson Library.*

HOUGHTON, MIFFLIN & Co. report a good demand for Mr. Hopkinson Smith's new story, "Tom Grogan," the orders before publication being over six thousand copies. They have a rather unusually rich variety of books this week, including, in addition to "Tom Grogan," Mr. Stimson's capital story of Boston, "Pirate Gold"; Bradford Torrey's new collection of outdoor observations, entitled "Spring Notes from Tennessee"; another of Mrs. Olive Thorne Miller's delightful books, entitled "Four-Handed Folk"; "Froebel's Occupations," the second volume in the *Republic of Childhood,* by Mrs. Wiggin and her sister, Miss Smith; and a new and very desirable popular edition of "Tom Brown's School-Days," and the "Life of Elias Boudinot" of Revolutionary times, including addresses and letters by him.

HENRY HOLT & Co. announce for speedy publication a one-volume edition of "Fyffe's History of Modern Europe" (1792–1878) from new plates; this work, which is generally acknowledged to be a classic in its field, has heretofore been accessible only in a three-volume edition. They have in press a work entitled "In India," by André Chevrillon, translated by William Marchant. The author does not see Kipling's India, but the less known mystic Hindu land, which he describes in a poetic and picturesque vein like Loti's. "Russian Politics," by Herbert M. Thompson, attempts to put the English reader in a position to understand the conditions of life and the problems of government that exist in the Russia of to-day. "Emma Lou : her book," by Mary M. Mears, is an unusually bright book of girlish confidences.

ANSON D. F. RANDOLPH & Co. have just ready "Simon Ryan, the Peterite," by Augustus Jessopp, who distinctly proves in this clever and entertaining sketch of a wholly original character that the hand that penned "The Trials of a Country Parson" has lost none of its cunning. The special doctrines of Paul and Peter are contrasted in a telling way, and the humor and pathos of the little plot are exquisite. Another work of fiction is "White Satin and Homespun," by Katrina Trask, as yet only known to readers by her poetry. This is an altruistic story, intended to bring out character regardless of outside appearances. Mrs. Trask proved in "King Constantine" that she is master of English, and in her present story she shows much common sense as well as poetic feeling. "No Place for Repentance," by Ellen F. Pinsent, is a powerful story of sacrifice and of struggle against temptations.

SOME TIMELY BOOKS.

NEW BOOKS

Some Spring Books.

Armenian Poems.

Rendered into English Verse by ALICE STONE BLACKWELL. 12mo, cloth, $1.25.

" A timely volume."—*Boston Transcript.*

Life of Jesus.

By ERNEST RENAN, author of " History of the People of Israel," " The Future of Science." Translation newly revised from the twenty-third and final edition. 8vo, cloth, $2.50.

" Eloquent the book certainly is ; and there have been few Oriental scholars who possessed the magnificent equipment of Renan."—*Philadelphia Bulletin.*

" Remarkable work which has become a classic. . . . Reverent and appreciative."—*Woman's Journal.*

Dante Gabriel Rossetti.

His Family Letters. With a Memoir by WILL-IAM MICHAEL ROSSETTI. Portraits. 2 vols., 8vo, cloth, $6.50.

Vol. I. Memoir. Vol. II. Family Letters. With introductory notes by W. M. Rossetti. With ten portraits by D. G. Rossetti of himself and other members of the family.

" One of the most notable of recent biographical works . . . replete with interest."—*Brooklyn Life.*

" The first account of the life of Rossetti that can pretend to any considerable degree of accuracy and completeness."—*Beacon.*

The Religion of Hope.

By PHILIP S. MOXOM, author of " The Aim of Life," " From Jerusalem to Nicæa." 16mo, cloth, $1.25.

" We cannot have too much of this preaching."—*Phila. American.*

" He has already proved his helpfulness to many."—*Christian Register.*

Cavalry in the Waterloo Campaign.

By Lieut.-General Sir EVELYN WOOD, V.C., etc. Forming the third volume in the " Pall Mall Magazine Library." With portraits, maps, and plans. 12mo, cloth, $1.25.

" Spirited and vividly written little book."—*London News.*

Handbook of Arctic Discoveries.

By A. W. GREELY, Brigadier-General United States Army. 16mo, cloth, gilt, $1.00.

Instead of the usual chronological treatment, the book is divided into a series of sketches, under separate chapters, devoted to special lines of exploration ; in this manner are treated distinctly Bering Strait, Spitzbergen, the Northwest Passage, the Franklin Search, Smith's Sound, the Northeast Passage, Greenland, and Dr. Nansen's novel journey.

New Volumes of the Keynotes Series.

Nobody's Fault. By NETTA SYRETT.

" An interesting and suggestive story."—*Woman's Journal.*

" Clearly and ably put."—*Cleveland World.*

Platonic Affections. By JOHN SMITH. Title-pages by Aubrey Beardsley. Each, 16mo, cloth, $1.00.

Six Modern Women.

Psychological Sketches. By LAURA MARHOLM HANSSON. Translated from the German by Hermione Ramsden. 12mo, cloth, $1.25.

CONTENTS : Sonia Kovalevsky. — George Egerton. — Eleonora Duse.—Amalie Skram.—Marie Bashkirtseff.— A. Ch. Edgren-Leffler.

" Strong, healthy, and truly womanly."—*N. Y. Times.*

" A thoughtful, earnest writer."—*Commercial Advertiser.*

" A keen, interesting study."—*Chicago Inter-Ocean.*

" A novel theme in such competent hands."—*Boston Journal.*

Effie Hetherington.

By ROBERT BUCHANAN, author of " The Shadow of the Sword." 12mo, cloth, $1.50.

An unusual and intensely interesting story.

The Gallery of Antiquities.

By HONORÉ DE BALZAC. Translated by Katharine Prescott Wormeley. 12mo, half russia, $1.50.

ROBERTS BROTHERS, Publishers, Boston.

LITERARY NEWS

AN ECLECTIC REVIEW OF CURRENT LITERATURE

~ILLUSTRATED~

CONTENTS.

VOL. XVII—No 6   **JUNE~1896** $1.00 YEARLY
                                    10 CTS. PER. NO.

~PUBLICATION OFFICE~
59 DUANE STREET, NEW YORK

ENTERED AT THE POST OFFICE AT NEW YORK AS SECOND-CLASS MATTER

The Literary News

Jn winter you may reade them, ab ignem, by the fireside; and in summer, ab umbram, under some shadie tree, and therewith pass away the tedious howres.

| VOL. XVII | JUNE, 1896. | No. 6. |

Confidences of Locker-Lampson.

To a certain extent this book disarms criticism. It is not, we are told, intended as a contribution to literature but simply to preserve for the writer's own descendants such little notices and anecdotes of two or three of their progenitors as will probably be interesting to them, if not to the public ; and if they are printed in a volume, instead of being left in manuscript, it is because this is the only way to assure their preservation.

Mr. Locker came of a family respectable rather than distinguished— London men of business, with some literary tastes. His grandfather entered the navy, rose in the service, at one time had both Nelson and Collingwood under his command, and seems to have been one of the best specimens of that lost type, the old sea-captain. Mr. Locker's father was attached to the navy in a civil capacity, and an interesting letter from him is here given, describing an interview with Napoleon at Elba.

Mr. Locker himself was born at Greenwich Hospital, of which his father was a resident commissioner, in 1821. His parents intended him for a professional career, but the boy, though a good cricketer, and with rather a

From "My Confidences."   Charles Scribner's Sons.

FREDERICK LOCKER-LAMPSON.

[From a photograph taken in July, 1892, by Dickinson & Foster.]

knack of turning off English verses, could never take kindly to Latin; so that scheme had to be given up, and a clerkship was obtained for him in the Admiralty. Here it was that he made his first public venture in poetry with "London Lyrics," light, easy, and graceful pieces, which are still pleasantly remembered, and deserve to be. These brought him to the notice of Thackeray, who asked him to write for the *Cornhill*. His marriage, in 1850, to Lady Charlotte Bruce, a great favorite at court, introduced him to very distinguished people indeed, and seems to have wrought an improvement in his fortunes, as the Admiralty drops out of sight, and we find him travelling like a man of leisure, wintering in Italy, and collecting rare majolica and *editiones principes*, to say nothing of paying £100 for a missing leaf of the First Folio. Even early in the sixties this sort of thing took a long purse.

The last chapter, in which he describes himself in a pleasant country home, cheerfully awaiting the end, is at once pleasing and touching ; and the whole book leaves one with a distinct image of a bright, cheery, and amiable personality. (Scribner. $5.00.)—*The Nation.*

His Honour and a Lady.

ENGLISH people at home still largely think of their countrymen in India as typified by Thackeray's Joe Sedley, or the red-faced, irascible, and dyspeptic but kind-hearted uncle of Charles Surface in Sheridan's "School for Scandal," or by the equally amusing Anglo-Indian who figures in the "Private Secretary." They are not without excuse, for it must be acknowledged that among the retired members of the Indian services to be met with in the clubs in London these types are still represented.

It is not to the Anglo-Indian of the Joe Sedley order, the shelved and mummified variety, that Mrs. Everard Cotes (who still uses her former name, Sara Jeannette Duncan) introduces us in "His Honour and a Lady," but to the Anglo-Indian on active service, in his temporary home on the Gangetic Plain, or rather in the City of Palaces (so called), for which Mr. Kipling has borrowed the far more appropriate name of the "City of Dreadful Night." Mrs. Cotes writes of Calcutta very much as if it were some English town. She does not waste many pages on local description, it is true, but the impression she conveys all the while is that it is rather a desirable place to reside in.

There is not very much in the story, and yet it holds one; indeed, when we had read to the end at a sitting prolonged into the early hours, we could not help wondering how the author contrived to weave so breathless a tale out of such slender materials. But what we are most curious about is to know whether Ancram represents a real person or is a mere figment. We are convinced that such a person lived and was known to Mrs. Cotes, but we imagine she has raised him to the lieutenant-governorship without warrant. That the Indian civil service may have contained such a cur is a sad possibility.

Mrs. Church is a woman for whom we feel a modified sympathy. Her acceptance of Ancram's attentions puts a great strain on it, but the way in which she punishes him in the end half atones for her weakness. Rhoda Daye and her vulgar mother are for the most part unreal characters. But the scene in which Rhoda plays the part of involuntary eavesdropper, and the earlier one in which Rhoda foils Ancram in his attempt to make her break off her engagement possesses verisimilitude. On the whole, however, the plot is subordinated to the delineation of life in the most exclusive section of Calcutta society, and this Mrs. Cotes has achieved with marvellous success. We were frequently reminded, while perusing this one, of that delightful former book of hers, "The Strange Adventures of a Mem Sahib." (Appleton. $1.50.)—London Literary World.

Madelon.

AT the present time there is not, perhaps, in all American literature, a man or woman who has a better title to be termed original than has Miss Mary E. Wilkins, the author of "A Humble Romance," "Jane Field," and "Pembroke." Miss Wilkins has stepped forth into a region hitherto neglected by most of the American writers of the present day, who are, or call themselves, realists; and she has stepped forth boldly, one might say masculinely, in her chosen path, and become almost a mind-reader of New England character.

"Madelon," her last attempt in sustained realism, introduces the reader to one of those little New England villages, shut in by hills and mountains, where the germs of conscience, brought over by our stern Puritan forebears, took root and flourished with such amazing strength. Narrow and hard and proud are these little villagers among their hills, following their code of morals and fashion. It is old England battling with primeval nature. Pride, hampered by labor almost menial; morals of the finest and firmest, fighting against passions strong as death; civilization hemmed in by a wilderness—such were the forces that helped to mould these people into types of unbending strength, only vaguely understood by the city-bred populations.

The scene of "Madelon" is laid in the past— at a time when our great-grandmothers disported themselves in quilted satins, wore shoes of the same material, enormous bonnets, and wadded mantles trimmed with swansdown. Their motions are restrained and stately, as befits their costumes, and as they move they exhale faint, clean odors of lavender and rose-leaves. There are lanes, cool and shady, and poplar trees; a village store; and a great house with stately Doric pillars. The mise en scène is drawn admirably, and the characters are painted no less truthfully.

All the familiar village types are to be met in "Madelon," each playing his or her own particular part, and serving, as in artistic fiction subordinate characters always must, to set off the person and conduct of the principal actors. Of these there are three in Miss Wilkins's last story: Madelon Hautville, Lot Gordon, and Burr Gordon. They are subtilely differentiated, presented vividly, and the person of the heroine is depicted in most attractive colors. Madelon is not of pure New England stock; there is a strain of French blood in her nature which accounts for a certain wilfulness, and explains, in part, that peculiar panther-like beauty on which the author lays so much stress. "Madelon" is a work cordially recommended to our readers. (Harper. $1.25.)—The Examiner.

"HE SPENT MUCH TIME WITH THE BOWRINGS."

Adam Johnstone's Son.

F. MARION CRAWFORD has never displayed greater deftness in telling a simple, straightforward love-story in such a way as to rivet the reader's attention than in "Adam Johnstone's Son." The tale is modern in the fullest degree; there is nothing inherently improbable in the situations; yet the originality of the plot is singularly striking and bold. A husband and wife, having been divorced, both make second marriages; a son of the one and a daughter of the other by these second marriages meet in ignorance of the facts, and finally love one another. This is the bare situation ; how Mr. Crawford handles it is what makes the story a fascinating one. Both Adam Johnstone and his son are men "with a past," and the inevitable question as to the world's way of looking differently at men and women who have violated the moral law is constantly suggested, but never directly argued out. Mr. Crawford, with the privilege of the novelist, makes both men essentially lovable and true to their own standards of honor; in real life it more often happens that such men deteriorate in all points when once they have thrown aside ultimate standards of morality and replaced them by the world's conventionalities. The few characters of the story are all drawn with admirable clearness, and the analysis of motive is keen and consistent. We think that none of Mr. Crawford's recent novels has been better adapted to please and interest a large circle of readers than this slight story. (Macmillan. $1.50.)—*The Outlook.*

Rome.

To a man of Zola's temperament idleness is an impossibility. No sooner had he finished "Dr. Pascal," and thereby concluded his *Rougon-Macquart Series*, than he cast about him for fresh occupation. And the outcome was the scheming of a trilogy in three volumes to be called "Lourdes," "Rome," and "Paris." The first was published last year, and its central idea was the great revival in the belief in supernatural agencies which distinguishes the end of the century. At the same time it sought to show that this revival has gone too far, and if persisted in would bring us back to the grossest forms of superstition. Yet Zola, impartially respecting the beliefs of others, was careful to point out how great is the solace which the human mind derives from faith in the divine, and whatever attacks his book may have contained on certain cults and certain abuses, it was, broadly, an explanation and even a defence of religious feeling. Zola began life, I should say, as a disciple of Auguste Comte; for years he displayed the most uncompromising Positivism; but he has ended by acknowledging that a belief in the Divine and in futurity are necessary to humanity in the present state of its development. He has never wilfully attacked religion; but he has undoubtedly attacked certain of its ministers for greed, fraud, and the leading of impure lives. Now, in "Rome," the second volume of his trilogy, he deals with religion as nowadays practised in the Roman Catholic Church. The central figure of his narrative is Abbé Pierre Froment, the young priest who was previously the central figure of "Lourdes"; and he opens with a bird's-eye sketch of the Eternal City and of the purpose which takes Abbé Froment thither. And in this connection he calls, in impressive language, for a return to the old organization of Christendom, for a return to the pure unadulterated gospel of Christ. Of course, being a Roman Catholic by baptism, a native of a Roman Catholic country, he writes mainly with regard to Roman Catholicism and in connection with that reunion of the churches of which we have heard so much. Now and again he expresses on these religious questions opinions which the reader may not absolutely share, but every sentence is dictated by impartiality, and couched in restrained, yet feeling language. Zola's great argument is that if the churches of Christendom were united, and the teaching of the Gospel followed, there might yet be a peaceful issue to that great social struggle which slowly but surely proceeds in our very midst, and which will rend the world atwain if not efficiently coped with. Then, however, he presents to us the Papal Court of Rome, its dignitaries, its ideas, and its ambitions, and by facts and examples shows how far or how little one may venture to look to it to work the necessary change.

Yet "Rome," despite this religious exordium and the undercurrent of religiosity running through it, is by no means what is known as a "religious novel." It will appeal, no doubt, to the higher feelings of many, but it will also more than content those who seek purely human interest in a story. Some of its characters are admirably drawn. Among the numerous feminine characters, all of exceptional interest, are two young women, both very lovable and very beautiful; one a true daughter of Rome, descended from proud, passionate ancestors, married, yet no wife, and awaiting the dissolution of her nominal marriage at the hands of the Holy Father in order that she may espouse the one man whom her heart cherishes. And the other, a budding lily, a Juliet of the present day, daughter of a Roman prince and a high-born English lady, also deeply in love, but with a man whom her parents refuse her. Innocent, maidenly though she is, she divines that the true mission of life is love, and proclaims it, intuitively giving expression to the

one great law, the new commandment given by Christ, which, were it universally followed, would forever stay all our social warfares and bring true peace and brotherhood into the world. Later will come "Paris," with its menace of universal upheaval and destruction through Anarchy, should men persist in hardening their hearts. (Macmillan. 2 v., $2.)—*Ernest Alfred Vizetelly in Book Reviews.*

The Madonna of a Day.

MISS DOUGALL'S "The Madonna of a Day" attracted much attention as it appeared from month to month in *Temple Bar*; and now, when one sees it for the first time as a whole, one's impression of its value as a work of art is both heightened and deepened. From an entirely new standpoint, and with a subtlety all its own, it lights up one aspect of the great vexed, unsettled, unsettleable woman question. There is in it not a word of the abuse which generally gives flavor to stories dealing with this subject, not a word of preaching, not an indication of the writer's view. It merely places a certain situation before the reader, on which he must perforce reflect and meditate; and all this with a charm of style, and a power of realizing and presenting a scene or a character, which grow stronger with each book Miss Dougall produces. The description of the vast snowy solitudes of the mountains, and of the impression they make on the eager, unrestful mind of Mary Howard, who is lost among them, is an achievement that will have its place in literature. But everything in the book is subordinate to the wonderful conception of Mary's influence on the dwarf—her half-romantic and half-tragic, half-artificial and half-real relations with that singular creature —into whose vicious life the simple, reverent character she has assumed comes as a revelation and an ideal. (Appleton. $1; pap., 50 c.) —*The Academy.*

Joan of Arc.

ACCORDING to Louis Kossuth, "since the writing of human history began, Joan of Arc is the only person of either sex who has ever held supreme command of the military forces of a nation at the age of seventeen." Very true, and equally true is it that since the writing of human history began, Mark Twain is the only humorist of either sex who has ever given to the world a historical novel of any value or interest. Reference is here made to the "Personal Recollections of Joan of Arc." The title-page a-sures us that the book is from the pen of the Sieur Louis De Conte (Joan of Arc's page and secretary) and that it has been freely translated by Jean François Alden, out of the ancient French into modern English from the original unpublished manuscript in the national archives of France. Many persons were for some time puzzled as to the identity of Jean François Alden and finally were on the point of placing him in the same category with the mysterious Teufelsdrock of Carlyle's "Sartor Resartus," when lo! the problem was solved and it became known that Mark Twain was the author of the "Personal Recollections of Joan of Arc."

Now there is no reason why a humorist should not write a good historical novel. A humorist is not necessarily always cracking jokes or on the alert for incongruous episodes and incidents. Dean Swift was a wit and a good deal of a humorist, but he was also much more. In like manner, in the book before us, Mark Twain gives ample evidence of his ability to write an interesting historical novel. His admirers may claim that his work in this direction cannot rank· with his work as a humorist, and possibly they are right. Still, the fact remains that he has given us here a very readable book. The task which Mark Twain set before him was a difficult one, and he has accomplished it astonishingly well. If he were not a great humorist he might have become a famous writer of historical novels. (Harper. $2.50.)—*N. Y. Herald.*

Excursions in Libraria.

"EXCURSIONS in Libraria" is a delightful volume of essays, by G. H. Powell, on various bookish subjects, and well worth reading. It also is full of capital illustrations from sixteenth-century books. Mr. Powell is deeply read in

From Mark Twain's "Joan of Arc."　　　Copyright, 1896, by Harper & Brothers.

IN THE FOREST.

the lore of the thirteenth, fourteenth, and fifteenth centuries, and he has stores of entertaining information to impart to his readers. Two of the essays are particularly amusing, "The Paradise of Pirates" and "The Wit of History." Mr. Powell has gathered together an astonishing number of stories of the celebrated pirates of those days, and the essay is very entertaining. The whole volume is an admirable addition to the "curiosities of literature." (Scribner. $2.25.)—*Boston Literary World.*

THE LOVERS SHOULD HAVE A LITTLE QUIET TALK.

Pirate Gold.

THE old - fashioned Boston merchant has waited long for a worthy painter of his portrait, but the artist appears at last in the person of Mr. F. J. Stimson, whose "Pirate Gold," although a woman is the mainspring of the action, is a story of men, of a firm of Boston merchants and their book-keeper. The former characters are perfect portraits; keen-witted as lawyers ; generous as kings, as kings in a proverb; delicate in feeling as women, and yet pitiless in their humor; perfectly understanding their dull wives but indulging all their whims, the Bowdoins, grandsire and son, will be fitted with half a dozen real names by Bostonians whose memory extends backwards sixty years. There were so many clever, gallant, witty, white-haired old gentlemen on India Wharf in those days. There were so many Boston families in which the boys spent four years nominally at Harvard, chiefly in earning and enjoying rustication, that certainty in regard to the Bowdoins is difficult, but they are as real as the Hardies or the Osbornes of English fiction. The little book-keeper is "Dickensy," as one of his employers calls him, not only in appearance, but his devotion, which belongs to the unsophisticated days when novelists were not sceptical as to the creation of man a little lower than the angels, and did not insist upon giving their good characters too many redeeming weaknesses. The heroine and the villain are commonplace, but the three Bowdoins, the third emancipated from commerce and sent into the navy by the war, are perfect. There is some amazing chronology in the book, and an anach-ronism or two of which "Veritas" and "A Constant Reader" will promptly notify the daily papers, and Mr. Bowdoin once "extends" a piece of news in a manner worthy of a telegraph editor, adding matter sure to dismay the serious-minded and to lead them to write to the author. Nevertheless, "Pirate Gold" is an excellent little novel. (Houghton, Mifflin & Co. $1.25.)—*Boston Pilot.*

Out of Town.

"OUT of Town," by an unnamed author, gives a series of pictures of suburban life drawn without any idealization and with not too much exaggeration to make them seem unreal. The book deals with such familiar subjects as the railroad humorist, a lawn-tennis match, village theatricals, house repairs and the like, and through each of the chapters smoothly runs the tiny thread of a love-story that ends, as all suburban stories should, on the piazza of a vine-clad cottage. The humor is of a human sort, and the studies of character, while not, perhaps, profound, yet serve to exhibit certain easily recognizable figures of the environs of New York. It is existence without the glamour, but comfortable withal, and worth the while, and rounded out with incidents petty in themselves and yet of a kind that appeals to the reader with a kindly aspect of verisimilitude. The book has the advantage of illustrations of more than ordinary spirit by Rosina Emmet Sherwood. As a whole, it may be set down as an interesting sketch of the manners of the time. (Harper. $1.25.)—*N. Y. Mail and Express.*

Life on the Mantel.

THIS funny tenant of my mantel never washed face nor hands, and paid no attention to his coat, with one exception—his tail. This apparently useless appendage, twice as long as he was, which usually hung straight down, or stood straight out, gave him much concern, and was evidently the one point on which he prided himself. To dress it he brought it up before him, held it with one hand and combed it violently with the claws of the other—the wrong way of the fur. When he got too far up in his operations to reach while sitting (for the tail towered above his head like a flagpole) he rose to his feet, and stretched up in a ludicrous way. It never seemed to occur to him to draw the prim tail down. In fact, he acted as if it belonged to somebody else. He often sat and held it up before his face, contemplating it with a grave interest and curiosity, as who should say, "What is this that I see before me?" In fright, the beautiful silky hair of his head rose so much as to change his expression, while that on the tail stood out all around and in anger the member itself was "swished" like that on an angry cat. In fact, although he was afraid of people, when he was really cornered he became savage, and showed that, notwithstanding he was a pet and lived on the mantel, he might be a very unpleasant beast to manage, a genuine wild monkey.

As the weather grew colder in the fall the little monkey hardly came out at all from his warm corner under the blanket. One day I bethought me of trying to comfort him with a foot-stove. I got a flat stone three or four inches square and an inch thick. This I put on the kitchen range till it was very warm, then wrapped it in a flannel and laid it in the path of the shivering little fellow. When he came out to breakfast and stepped on it he instantly stopped, and nothing would induce him to leave it till it grew cold. After that I kept it heated for him all the time he was awake, and he hugged it as a freezing person would hug a stove.

But as the weeks went on he grew more and more sleepy and dull, so that he was no longer amusing, and I knew he would not brighten up till the summer came. So I moved his quarters to another place, and never again tried to keep a monkey on the mantel. (Houghton, Mifflin & Co. $1.25.) — *From Mrs. Olive Thorne Miller's " Four-Handed Folk."*

The Lad was Nancy Barker.

JUST then the breeze freshened for a minute into a strange little sucking, swirling gust, the smoke lifted, and there, close alongside, lay the ship that we were fighting. Our deck was a slaughter-house, but so was theirs as well, and her sails were ribbons, her mainmast gone, and she was afire.

Cheer ! How the poor lads tried to cheer when we saw it, but the noise was more like gasping. Afire she was, and her men running about like mad devils, working over the flames; but none the less we saw that she was coming aboard and that her boarders were gathered in the bows. I saw Blakely turn and hold his hand to McKnight, and then "Stand by to repel boarders," came along the deck.

'Twas like the resurrection trumpet.

From Miller's " Four-Handed Folk." Copyright, 1896, by Houghton, Mifflin & Co.

THE MARMOSETS.

Men who were lying half stunned and faint from blood staggered onto their feet, gripping the bulwarks or whatever came handy to steady by. Pikemen and marines who'd lain close waiting for this moment jumped up. Poor beggars, they'd seen their friends die around 'em by the score, and no hand in the game themselves. But now their turn had come, and as the frigate's bow cut upon our port quarter and her great bowsprit ripped and tore among our ropes and tackle, they ran yelling to the point where already the British were pouring aboard. They'd stored their fight so long, our lads, they'd boiled and raged so long inside, that they were madmen. I was with them; every man left of the port battery was there, for the guns had gone, and our chance now lay in cutlass and pike.

'Twas desperate hard fighting. Twice we beat 'em back, but the third time they came again and stronger yet. We were driven aft, inch by inch; in a minute they'd ha' been in possession of the ship, when the Lord sent the mizzentop, shot through and through, and heavy as lead with its weight of dead topmen, thundering into the very midst of them. Some were killed outright, some sprang into the sea to escape, some were cut off from the others and left to us, and we gave account for each man. The two ships were parallel, for the push of the frigate's bow had straightened our course, so that we were lying in the wallow of the sea, side by side. 'Twas our own chance to board, and Blakely knew it. "Boarders away," he roared, and up we swarmed.

I say swarmed, 'tis but a word I use because it comes handy. There was no swarm of us, the Lord knows. But what were there were true "wasps," and had stings. Some of the lads jumped for their deck. I made a dash at an open port whose gun had been knocked off its truck. I thought there were others behind me. I heard some one climbing and panting. Some one passed me quickly, and in the smoke of the musketry that rattled from their decks, in the smoke and flying cinders of the smouldering fire, for the British had put out the flames, a figure like a boy's jumped by me into the open port.

I thought 'twas John Rawlins, a lad of but eighteen; we had a number of such aboard, and I yelled and followed after. When, as I jumped, and landed by the dismounted gun, the figure turned, and like a flash a cutlass swung and struck me over the head. I fell like a log. but before the blow took me I saw the lad was none but Nancy Barker. (Putnam.　75 c.) *From Rogers' "Will o' the Wasp."*

Training for Home Secretary.

"DID you think really that your family began with the Judge, Sir George?"

"Well, I never heard much about his predecessors, except that story of the lost diamonds."

"Now you see. The first man of whom we know anything builds this fine house, lines it with cedar and rosewood and oak wainscoting; adorns it with wood-carving——"

"That overmantel work might belong to a later time," I interrupted. "It looks like grinning Gibbons, though. He may have done it—or perhaps one of his scholars."

From Rogers' " Will o' the Wasp."　　　　　

THE GREAT FIGHT.

From " The Master Craftsman."   Copyright, 1896, by F. A. Stokes Co.

SIR WALTER BESANT.

One side of the room was completely spoiled as regards the original intention of him who clothed it with cedar by the introduction of a bookcase covering the whole wall, and fitted with books. There was a central table littered with papers, and a smaller table with a row of books. And there were only two chairs, both of them wooden chairs with arms —the student's chair. The books, one might observe, had the external appearance of having been read and well used; the bindings being cracked or creased and robbed of their pristine shininess. I looked at them. Heavens ! What a serious library of solid reading ! Herbert Spencer, Mill, Hallam, Freeman, Stubbs, Hamilton, Spinoza, Bagehot, Seeley, Lecky, and a crowd of others for history; Darwin, Huxley, Tyndall, Wallace, and more for science; rows of books on the institutions of the country and on the questions of the day.

"These are my books." Robert pointed to them with undisguised pride. "I don't believe there's a better collection this side of the Tower. I collected them all myself. You see, my people were never given much to books. My father in the evening smoked his pipe. His father smoked his pipe in the evening. The girls of the family did their sewing all the time. They didn't want to read. All the books we had stood in two shelves in a cupboard. They were chiefly devotional books. 'Meditations among the Tombs,' 'Sermons,' 'Reflections for the Serious,' ' Pilgrim's Progress,' and such-like—mighty useful to me. So I had to collect my own books. And, mind you, no rubbish among them all—no silly novels and poetry and stuff—all good and useful books. And, what's more, I've read them every one, and I know them all."

I now began to understand how he had been training for the post of Home Secretary. (Stokes. $1.50.)—*From Besant's "The Master Craftsman."*

Mosby's Rangers.

From "Mosby's Rangers." Copyright, 1896, by R. Kenyon, N. Y.

A MOSBY SCOUT IN SIGHT OF THE ENEMY.

THE Virginia commander of the Rangers, as described by James J. Williamson, of Co. A, of the 43d Battalion of Virginia Cavalry, was a redoubtable foe, and a capital type of the quick - moving cavalryman, who should be here and everywhere, ready to strike a blow, and never offer resistance when the odds were too strong against him. " To destroy supply-trains, to break up the means of conveying intelligence, thus isolating an army from its base, as well as its different corps from each other, to confuse plans by capturing despatches, are the objects of partisan warfare," and for these special duties no one was more fully prepared than was Mosby.

In war times names go for a great deal, and vary according to the sides from whence they emanate. So if Mosby's men were called "guerrillas, bushwhackers, freebooters," the reply is that these cavalrymen were mustered into Confederate service under the partisan ranger law, and were as regularly soldiers as were any others. Their business was to raid and harry, and raid and harry they did. Mosby was acting under orders from Gen. Stuart up to the time of Stuart's death, and then under those of Gen. Lee. He had a genius for the work, with an absolute reliance on himself, and certainly he had under him a set of dare-devils who put the most implicit faith in their commander, because he ever was at the head of his little column. The particular thing which gave Mosby his notoriety was the capture of Brig.-Gen. Stoughton. It may be called one of the boldest episodes of the war. Col. Mosby described it all. in 1892, as if it were a huge joke, for in war, as in anything else, he who wins laughs.

It has been generally supposed that the Rangers were made up of any kind of material which presented itself. This was by no means the case. If the force was a minute one, Mosby was careful as to the choice of his men. A man had to be cool, intelligent, and of good character before he could be enrolled. Mr. Williamson, who joined Mosby in 1863, tells modestly the many adventures and exploits of Mosby and his men. At Fauquier, Va., on April 21, 1865, Mosby disbanded his organization, preferring that to a surrender. In time he made his peace with the United States, and to-day there is no more loyal American. The last meeting of the Mosby men was at a reunion, held in August of last year, when the old Rangers were well represented. The volume is fully illustrated. (Kenyon, N. Y. $3.50.)— *N. Y. Times.*

Weir of Hermiston.

"WEIR of Hermiston," which is appearing serially in Mr. Unwin's new *Cosmopolis*, comes to us, unhappily, as a fragment. The book was barely more than a third done when the end came. But the six chapters which I have already seen give me the bitterest and most implacable grievance against death that I have ever felt. " Weir of Hermiston " would have been one of the great books of the language, and its abrupt interruption is a loss to literature comparable only to one of those savage destructions of big libraries which blacken the barbaric chasm between classical Rome and Alexandria and the Europe of the Renaissance. Indeed, there is a more intimate sense of personal loss in the knowledge that it can never be a completed whole than is aroused by all the devastations charged upon Goths and Vandals. Their torches must have rid mankind of a tremendous mountain of monkish and occult rubbish, along with some good things. But here there is no compensating thought of dross going with the treasure. " Weir of Hermiston " is all gold.

. . . "Weir of Hermiston" reveals a Stevenson we had hardly known before. There may have been some hair-breadth and blood-curdling business in the author's projects for the tale. But these opening six chapters spread out a broad and rich field of serious work, with a dozen noteworthy personages, great and little, painted with extraordinary mastery of character and the promise of a real story among them which should be worth a hundred " romances of adventure." The figures of the Lord Justice Clerk and his son Archie are as fine as anything in Stevenson's whole gallery of men folk, but much more striking still is the young girl, Christina Elliot, whom the sixth chapter brings in the foreground. For the first time there is a Stevenson heroine who interests and wholly pleases her creator. The " Catriona " who preceded her was an empty shadow, but this Christina is glowing with life. In fact, Stevenson at forty-four had just attained the point where he could paint a woman as well as men—and then at a stroke the hand stiffens and the brush falls. Oh, the irreparable pity of it ! (Scribner. $1.50.)—*Harold Frederic in the N. Y. Times.*

Lincoln's Campaign, 1860.

"THE political campaign of 1860 will go down in history as one of intense excitement. It was composed of four tumultuous and exciting conventions, each nominating candidates for President and Vice-President of the United States. The Republican candidates were Lincoln and Hamlin. The Democratic party was flying with two wings, Douglas and Johnson representing the North, Breckinridge and Lane the South; finally Bell and Everett stood for the 'Constitutional Union Party.'

"It has been our aim to give a correct and impartial history of these conventions, together with their platforms. The material has been gathered from the *New York Herald*, *Springfield Journal*, Illinois, and from other authentic sources of information, and it is confidently claimed that the volume will be useful as a book of reference of historical worth.

"We have reproduced many of the badges, medals, songs, and other emblems that formed so prominent a part in the great campaign of 1860, the second in date but the first in importance in the history of the Republican party, and hope they will be interesting as an illustration of the make-up of a presidential canvass.

"In 1860 the men whose names were presented to the convention were: William H. Seward, of New York ; Abraham Lincoln, of Illinois ; Simon Cameron, of Pennsylvania ; Edward Bates, of Missouri ; William L. Dayton, of New Jersey; John L. McLean and Salmon P. Chase, of Ohio.

"Mr. Lincoln called into his first cabinet four of the candidates who were before the convention for the Presidency — William H. Seward, Secretary of State ; Simon Cameron, Secretary of War ; Salmon P. Chase, Secretary of the Treasury ; and Edward Bates, Attorney-General. Caleb B. Smith, Secretary of the Interior, and Gideon Welles, Secretary of the Navy, took an active part in the convention, and Montgomery Blair, Postmaster-General, was not present.

"Many of the prominent men who were in the convention were rewarded with good appointments, although nearly all of them were in opposition to Mr. Lincoln during the balloting. William L. Dayton was sent as minister to France, Thomas Corwin to Mexico, N. B. Judd to Prussia, Cassius M. Clay to Russia, Carl Schurz to Spain, David K. Carter to Bolivia, Frederick Hassaurek to Ecuador.

"Abraham Lincoln was called to guide the ship of state that rocked on the turbulent waves of war, commencing soon after his election and lasting until he died in the fulness of his fame."

Thus writes Osborn H. Oldroyd in his introduction to a book of great interest to all patriotic politicians. It is full of anecdotes, campaign songs and documents, and many things one forgets in course of years and likes to see gathered together and put in readiness if they should be wanted. (Laird & Lee. 75 c.; pap., 25 c.)

From Oldroyd's "Lincoln's Campaign."　　　Copyright, 1896, by Laird & Lee.

AN HONEST MAN IS FOUND.

The Secret of the Sea.

SUDDENLY I became aware of some one standing by my side, and, turning my head, I discovered it was none other than the Beautiful White Devil herself. She was still dressed in black, with a sort of mantilla of soft lace draped about her head.

"What a supreme fascination there is about the sea at night, isn't there?" she said, softly, looking down at the sparkling water. I noticed the beauty of the little white hand upon the rail as I replied in appropriate terms.

"I can never look at it enough," she continued, almost unconsciously. "Oh, you black, mysterious, unfathomable depths, what future do you hold for me? My fate is wrapped up in you. I was born on you; I was brought up on you; and if my fate holds good, I shall die and be buried in you."

"At any rate, you need give no thought to that contingency for very many years to come,"

From "The Beautiful White Devil." Copyright, 1896, by Ward, Lock & Bowden, Ltd.

"FOLLOWED BY THE ENORMOUS BULL-DOG."

I answered bluntly. "Besides, what possible reason can you have for thinking you will end your days at sea?"

"I don't know, Dr. De Normanville. It would puzzle me to tell you. But I feel as certain of finding my grave in the waves as I am that I shall be alive to-morrow! You don't know what the sea has been to me. She has

been my good and my evil genius. I love her in every mood, and I don't think I could hope for a better end than to be buried in her breast. Oh, you beautiful, beautiful water, how I love you—how I love you !"

As she spoke she stretched her arms out to where the stars were paling in anticipation of the rising moon. In any other woman such a gesture would have been theatrical and unreal in the extreme. But in her case it seemed only what one might expect from such a glorious creature.

"There is somebody," she continued, "who says that 'the sea belongs to Eternity, and not Time, and of that it sings its monotonous song for ever and ever.'"

· "That is a very beautiful idea," I answered, "but don't you think there are others that fully equal it? What do you say to 'The sea complains upon a thousand shores'?"

"Or your English poet Wordsworth, 'The sea that bares her bosom to the wind'?"

"Let me meet you with an American : 'The sea tosses and foams to find its way up to the cloud and wind.' Could anything be finer than that? There you have the true picture — the utter restlessness and the striving of the untamed sea."

"'Would'st thou,' so that helmsman answered,
'Learn the secret of the sea?
Only those who brave its dangers
Comprehend its mystery !'"

"Bravo ! That caps all."

For some seconds my companion stood silent, gazing across the deep. Then she said, very softly :

"And who is better able to speak about its dangers than I, whose home it is? Dr. De Normanville, I think if I were to tell you some of the dangers through which I have passed you would hardly believe me."

"I think I could believe anything you told me." (Ward, Lock & Bowden, Ltd. $1.)—*From Boothby's "The Beautiful White Devil."*

Marjory Moore.

"MARJORY MOORE," another of Miss Adeline Sergeant's stories of life in the great middle class of English society, differs from "A Rogue's Daughter," recently noticed in these columns, in being less sombre in tone. One may trace a passing resemblance between the innocent girl who suffered for her father's sins and the child-woman whose husband's misdoings brought to her so much sorrow and shame, in that both exemplify how much the woman who loves can and will endure from the man she loves. Marjory Moore is a girl of musical temperament, an orphan and alone in the world, and dowered with a nature that craves love and home ties and is especially subject to environment. In the middle-aged master of Redwood Hall she finds a friend, and in his nephew Felix a champion and eventually a lover. But she marries the wrong man as girls have a way of doing outside of fiction, and pays dearly for her hasty act. It may be questioned whether it was really necessary to make Archie Severne quite such an abominable cad and coward, but as these qualities eventually lead to his ultimate taking-off to nobody's regret, and pave the way to the reward of patience, love, and faith which always is expected in books, the reader is perfectly reconciled. The story is pleasant, the interest well sustained, and the *dénouement* acceptable to Marjory's well-wishers. (Cluett. $1.)—*Detroit Free Press.*

Eclogues of Fleet Street.

IT may be doubted whether Mr. Davidson has really succeeded in naturalizing the eclogue in the nineteenth century. The Elizabethan pastoral, indeed, derived its inspiration less from the countryman's appreciation of his familiar meadows than from the *desiderium* of the citizen for the remembered scenes of childhood or of holiday. And in this point Mr. Davidson preserves the tradition. His singers are journalists who weary among their "Fleet Street wires" and "the jangle of the printing press" for the refreshment of lands where "the night-jar haunts the dark," or where

> "Deep in the Chiltern woodland glows
> The purple pasque anemone."

But after all, the rue is worn with a difference. Mr. Davidson is a modern of the moderns, and the brave Elizabethan carelessness cannot be his. He can never surrender his spirit wholly to the Dorian mood, nor betake himself to his pipe and crook with an unfettered blitheness. The world is too much with him, and the problems and the causes which he has at heart must needs break in upon the bucolic strain, to disturb its easy harmonies:

> HERBERT.
> " I hear the lark and linnet sing;
> I hear the whitethroat's alto ring."

> MENZIES.
> " I hear the idle workman sigh;
> I hear his hungry children cry."

The spiritual equilibrium of the pastoral has been changed; and the city, whose presence in the background once gave the piquancy of contrast, has come somewhat insolently into the foreground. But, shepherd or no shepherd, there can be no doubt that Mr. Davidson has given us another volume of fine thought, fine feeling, and fine expression. These eclogues have all that spontaneity of song which we are coming to look upon as his especial prerogative. And amongst the speakers we greet an old friend who has not forgotten to be "perfervid."

From "Nature and Culture." Copyright, 1896, by Dodd, Mead & Co.

HAMILTON W. MABIE.

But Ninian's attitude to nature is introspective, and therefore hardly pastoral:

> "I am besieged by things that I have seen;
> Followed and watched by rivers; snared and held
> In labyrinthine woods and tangled meads;
> Hemmed in by mountains; waylaid by the sun;
> Environed and beset by moon and stars;
> Whispered by winds and summoned by the sea."

Those are greatly fashioned lines, and so, too are the closing ones of the same poem:

> "—the restless moon
> Swung low to light us; clouds; the limpid sky;
> The bourdon of the great ground-bee, athwart
> A lonely hill-side, vibrant on the air,
> And subtler than the scent of violets;
> Sonorous winds, storm, thunder, and the sea "

Mr. Davidson gives his readers credit for wide literary culture and many of his allusions send us to the bookcases. (Dodd, Mead & Co. $1.25.)—*The Athenæum.*

A King and a Few Dukes.

MR. ROBERT W. CHAMBERS is not only telling just now the best stories written by any American, but he is telling them with progressive skill. " The King in Yellow " was distinctively good; " The Red Republic " was better; " A King and a Few Dukes " is much the best of the three. Mr. Chambers has previously exhibited rare powers of imagination and conspicuous ability in the handling of delicate dramatic situations. In this latest romance, while there is no diminution of these qualities, there is demonstrated the possession of a rich fund of sterling humor. If at the outset of the story, which concerns the frustrated attempt of an American, in conjunction with the " King of Caucasia," to reseat on his throne one King Theobald of " Hoznovia," there seems to ring through the pages an echo of " The Prisoner of Zenda," this soon dies out and in the rush of adventure and the sparkle of dialogue we discern not the disciple but the peer of Anthony Hope. What is most extraordinary about Mr. Chambers is the extent and variety of his special information and interests, such as the knowledge of military and diplomatic affairs he displayed in " The Red Republic," and continues to display, though in a different way, in the present book. That he is a close observer of the minutest phases of outdoor life is also clear. But his art of telling his stories directly and without flourish or apparent effort, and of making them instinct with life and motion, and brilliant with wit—this is the great thing about Mr. Chambers, and it is a thing to be said of few living story-tellers throughout the world. (Putnam. $1.25.)—*Philadelphia Press.*

The Man Who Became a Savage.

" THE Man Who Became a Savage," by Mr. W. T. Hornaday, is a story with a purpose. The author "is willing to let it go at that." So we may, if we like, improve our minds by the contemplation of the perjury, the strikes, the drunkenness, and the profligacy of the States, from which Mr. Rock, the disgusted man of business, finds a refuge in the heart of Borneo, among the gentlemanly Dyaks and the blameless orangoutans. But most readers will be content to regale themselves with a well-imagined story of adventure, and will not advert much to the author's principles, except to find a reason for the atrocious cruelty with which the liquor-seller Bugsby is put to death. The notion of confining a man in a cage and furnishing him with drink, that he may execute himself by slow suicide *coram populo*, is just such a gentle expedient as would occur to a fanatic. But the author's general level is far above this. We admire the courageous Elinor, and can forgive and even applaud her attempted homicide; her honest friend, the cowboy Cheyenne Jim, is much to our mind; and we recognize a desire to do justice to the filibustering Englishman Cumberson, though it is too bad, even granting him to be related to some sort of lord, to put a kind of coster dialect into his mouth. The book is, of course, written in that of America. It is well illustrated, though there seems an unnatural smoothness about the Dyaks. (Peter Paul Book Co. $1.50.)—*The Athenæum.*

Robert Urquhart.

COMPLAINT is sometimes made that novelists rarely deal with professions as professions, and show the effect a man's work and surroundings have upon his character. From this point of view it is a pity that Mr. Gabriel Setoun makes the hero of " Robert Urquhart " finally abandon his work as schoolmaster in a country parish in Scotland, for the strength of the novel, and it is considerable, lies largely in the vivid picture given of a schoolmaster's life. And worse remains behind. The hero is allotted nothing more original in the way of a new career than literature. Fortunately his literary experiences are a minor feature in the story compared with his experiences as a teacher, whose official position complicates even affairs of the heart, for his rival is a member of the school board, and the girl he loves, having seen a good deal in Edinburgh of young teachers, dislikes them as a class. This prejudice would be reasonable were teachers fairly represented by a young philologist, who figures in " Robert Urquhart," and who wants pruning badly. He is neither as pleasant nor as amusing company as the village characters introduced. Excellent people some of the latter are, with a sincere, though quaintly expressed, love of literature and respect for education. The villain of the story is an ambitious minister, whose victim has gone mad, and recovers her senses enough t recognize him while he is preachi·.g at a special Christmas service. We have said enough to show that " Robert Urquhart " is not lacking in sensational interest, and, we may add, it is full of homely morals, handled and expressed in a manner that will appeal to many who are weary of subtle discussions of obscure and complicated ethical problems. In conversations carried on in the midst of every-day family life the author is particularly strong, and many unusually interesting extracts might be made for reading aloud. (Warne. $1.50.) — *London Literary News.*

The White Rocks.

THIS work, the latest production of one of the most gifted of the younger French novelists, Edouard Rod, is said to have been received with such favor in France that it ran through fifteen editions in the brief term of a few months. It is a work of originality and power, having a distinct ethical motive, as impressive in its way as Hawthorne's "Scarlet Letter," though treated in a very different manner. The theme is love and renunciation. The scene is a little Swiss town, to which comes a new minister, an unworldly youth of peasant origin, fresh from the seminary, with his faithful, shrewd-minded old mother. He immediately comes into contact with the conventional, sordid notions of his people, who have no conception of his exalted ideals, but who, nevertheless, are captivated by his eloquence.

He is introduced to the wealthy Massod family, and a peculiar sympathy discovers itself between him and Mme. de Massod. This ripens into a master-passion which almost carries them away, and which overwhelms them with unhappiness. But both the minister and the wife are too firmly fixed in their principles to yield as the lovers do in the "Scarlet Letter." Their struggles to hide from each other, and even from themselves, the true state of affairs are detailed with graphic vividness, and the name of the story is justified in the skilful use which the author makes of the legend attaching to the White Rocks, where the accidental betrayal of their mutual secret takes place. The construction of the story is most dramatic, while the portrayal of character shows rare artistic ability. (Crowell. $1.25.)—*Chicago Inter-Ocean.*

Effie Hetherington.

MR. ROBERT BUCHANAN, who is endowed with a strong and vigorous style, has a peculiar penchant for the writing of unpleasant romances. In "Effie Hetherington" all is stress and storm, illumined by the fitful flare of lightning.

Richard Douglas, the laird, is a "dour" and sour "chiel." With the best blood in Scotland running through his veins, he holds himself aloof from all social intercourse. He lives in a gloomy old house on the seashore, not far from Castle Lindsay. His only friend is his old serving-woman, Elspeth. Why Douglas should be such a cynic you can hardly tell. He has travelled all over the world, has ac-quired much learning, and with it a contempt for humanity. At Castle Lindsay lives the Earl of Durmshairu, a grim, melancholy man.

There is some slight intercourse kept up between the earl and Douglas, for, had the laird so willed it, he would have been a welcomed guest at the Castle. One stormy night a small cavalcade asks shelter of the laird. The party is composed of Miss Effie Hetherington, Lady Bell, and Mr. Arthur Lamont. Effie afterward disappears, abandoning her child, and Douglas fathers it. Some eighteen years afterward, taking the child, who is now a young lady, to Paris, Douglas sees Effie in a theatre. His former enchantress is now an abandoned woman. A floating corpse drawn out of the Seine terminates the career of this wretch. Even then, notwithstanding all her crimes, Douglas saves her from exposure in the morgue. Some novels are written to amuse, others to impart a moral. If the latter is Mr. Buchanan's intention it has been carried out by massing together many horrors. (Roberts. $1.50.)—*N. Y. Times.*

From Galt's "The Last of the Lairds."   Roberts.

A SURPRISE.

The Literary News.

An Eclectic Monthly Review of Current Literature.

EDITED BY A. H. LEYPOLDT.

JUNE, 1896.

THE BIOGRAPHY OF OLIVER WENDELL HOLMES.

To write a good biography would seem to be one of the most difficult achievements of authorship. To be just and generous, truthful and discreet, accurate and interesting, critical and appreciative, surely calls for a combination of head, heart, and knowledge not given to the many. It was formerly supposed that almost any one could gather facts, hearsay, letters, papers, family reminiscences of some man or woman who had made a mark in art, history, literature, or any of the sciences, and condense all this heterogeneous material into a book which by courtesy was then called a biography.

But more and more it is being realized that the great importance and perhaps only real value of a biography depends upon the man who writes it. If he is not in sympathy with his subject, not competent to judge the great underlying purpose of the life which he is to lay before his readers, his work must remain simply a compilation of unconnected events and circumstances.

During the past six months some very remarkable biographies have been published which almost without exception show skilled authorship or trained editing. It is in itself notable that within half a year the reading world

From "Life and Letters of Holmes." Copyright, 1896, by Houghton, Mifflin & Co.

OLIVER WENDELL HOLMES [1892].

should have been put in possession of biographies and correspondence of Matthew Arnold, Dante Gabriel Rossetti, Cardinal Manning, Louis Agassiz, J. G. Romanes, Thomas Hutchinson, Laurence Sterne, Thomas Carlyle, Shelley, Coleridge, Sheridan, Sir John Franklin, Locker-Lampson, Elias Boudinot, Bayard Taylor, and Oliver Wendell Holmes, besides at least a dozen others on a smaller scale on Agnes Giberne, Richard Cobden, Madame Roland, Frederick A. P. Barnard, Gounod, Sarah Bernhardt, Mary Anderson, Allan Ramsay, etc.

In interest of subject " The Life and Letters of Oliver Wendell Holmes" can hardly compete with the memoirs of Arnold, Rossetti, Shelley, Sheridan, Sterne, and Manning, but John T. Morse, Jr., may confidently take his place among the authors and editors to whom the greater lights have been entrusted, for he has performed his onerous task in a most competent manner.

William D. Howells says :

"I wish I could know what impression of Dr. Holmes's growth and final measure Mr. John T. Morse's volumes of his biography and correspondence would give one who had not been personally a witness of his life, and who preferably was not of his time. This means posterity, of course, and externality, and these, when I come to think of it, both have their disadvantages. Perhaps what I really desire for a criticism of the man is the judgment of some contemporary and acquaintance who could miraculously, not to say impossibly, liberate himself from the influence of a personality singularly penetrating and powerful, and from the wonder of a development which was as nearly the image of an intellectual palingenesis as anything I know of in the history of literature. I will frankly own that I am not qualified to do this, and so far I feel my judgment disabled; yet I will hazard the opinion that these volumes will arrange for the reader a perspective in which Oliver Wendell Holmes will be more justly and truly seen than ever before. Mr. Morse's admirable work has been done quietly and modestly throughout."

"The reading world," says the rather exacting *Dial*, " has awaited these volumes with unusual interest, and they will disappoint no reasonable anticipations. The work is, all in all, the best of the several biographies of American men of letters that have appeared in recent years. Taken together, the Memoir and the Letters form a complete and most engaging piece of literary portraiture—one which the reader finishes with a gratified sense of having learned all that one needs know and has a right to know of the career and personality of the kindly 'Autocrat.'"

" Over and above his own contribution as critic and interpreter," says the *Atlantic Monthly*, " we must value the great service Mr. Morse has rendered in his judicious selections from and groupings of Dr. Holmes's correspondence, and the clear manner in which he has put at the disposal of the reader the means for forming his own conception of the fine spirit which lay behind the prose and verse of the complete works, and of the development of that spirit in the course of a long life of singular tranquillity in outward conditions, of great activity in the realm of thought."

It had been rumored that Dr. Holmes had during recent years prepared autobiographic notes to be a fund of material for his biographer. But all the notes found were meagre, and related only to his college years. He also was not given to letter-writing, and his gathered correspondence hardly fills two-thirds of one volume in Mr. Morse's book. The letters to Motley, written during our Civil War just after the publication of "The Dutch Republic," are full of patriotism and keen appreciation of the great work finished by his life-long friend. In letters to Mrs. Stowe and to James William Kimball he told the story of his mental struggles from orthodoxy to an all-abiding faith in a personal God and a total disregard of humanly manufactured creeds and church organizations; and to James Russell Lowell, Mrs. Elizabeth Phelps Ward, and Whittier he gave of his finest thought.

The serene story of the wise and witty Autocrat's life is told with artistic simplicity in these volumes. H. E. Scudder says Oliver Wendell Holmes will remain a gracious figure in American letters after his entire writings have been reduced to "The Autocrat," "The Chambered Nautilus," and "The Last Leaf." Of this we here give two verses in fac-simile:

FAC-SIMILE OF COPY FOR "THE LAST LEAF."

Sheridan.

"WHAT could be done for Sheridan," writes Lord Dufferin in his introduction to these two handsome volumes, "has been done by Mr. Fraser Rae." It has; and the biography makes a genuine addition to literature. Occasionally it becomes, as was almost inevitable, a commentary on Moore, and Mr. Rae has sometimes gone out of his way to trounce certain minor delinquents—Mr. Percy Fitzgerald, for example. Still, its combativeness does the book no harm. It gives its readers the real Sheridan, or, at any rate, a far more genuine presentment than they ever had before. And nobody can quarrel with Lord Dufferin's statement that such a record cannot fail to excite the sympathies of the English-speaking race, since its subject has many claims on their admiration and gratitude.

Mr. Fraser Rae has made numerous and important discoveries in the family papers, and to them we propose mainly to devote our space. We cannot find, indeed, that he has provided many material additions to our knowledge of Sheridan's grandfather, the friend of Swift, of his gifted mother, or of his queer father—actor, elocutionist, lexicographer, and what not. But some school-boy letters from Harrow are amusing, and there is much interesting information about Sheridan's youthful collaborations with Halhed.

Mr. Rae's contributions to our information as to Sheridan's efforts to make a living by his pen, even to the production of "The Rivals," do not call for particular comment. As to the means whereby Sheridan was enabled to become a proprietor of Drury Lane, Mr. Rae adopts Mr. Brander Matthews's solution, that his hero pledged the income of the theatre for the payment of annuities. It is ingenious, but it depends unfortunately on some assertions by that most inaccurate of biographers, Watkins. The documents dealing with "The School for Scandal" will be interesting to textual critics. It is by no means surprising that Mr. Fraser Rae should have detected Moore in tampering freely with the poem whence Sheridan extracted Sir Benjamin Backbite's verses on Lady Betty Curricle. The two acts of "The School" prepared by Sheridan for publication are curious as showing that he was perpetually striving after finish. The most important change is the elimination of "the widow of a City knight" from Snake's speech to Lady Sneerwell. We may add that the chapter on Sheridan's "Characteristics as a Dramatist" in Mr. Fraser Rae's second volume contains much sound criticism. But the judgment, "the greatest dramatist since Shakespeare," fairly makes the reader gasp. To ignore the whole of the later Elizabethans and all the Restoration stage is surely startling, even when an enthusiast is concerned.

The book vindicates Sheridan as completely and successfully as did Mr. Forrest's researches into the career of his mighty antagonist Warren Hastings.

A word of praise is due to the publishers for the fine reproductions they have inserted of many interesting portraits as well as for the excellent fac-similes. (Holt. 2 v., $7.)—*The Athenæum.*

Guns and Cavalry.

To a book which is neither written wholly for professional soldiers, nor yet in a style which appeals to popular taste alone, some few words by way of preface seem demanded. To one class of readers I must often appear to dwell on matters which are already obvious and need no explanation, while I may occasionally weary another with details and considerations which are too technical to be attractive. Yet all soldiers are not students, and many laborious civilians in their hours of relaxation are very capable soldiers indeed.

That some words on the action of guns and cavalry may not, however, just now be superfluous, when the problem of their application is far more complicated than it was before scientific ingenuity had invaded successfully the realm of the gun-constructor, is shown by the interest the subject has within the last year or two aroused, and, moreover, there is a special attraction which always hangs about the tactics of these arms. No branch of the art of war is more difficult; none calls for the exhibition of more soldierlike qualities, physical as well as mental, on the part of a leader, and in none are so many noble chances offered to aspiring youth. The story of cavalry and of artillery co-operating with it is a record studded with the names of young and resolute men, low down in the scale of precedence according to rank or age, who climbed to fame by such deeds as have ever delighted soldiers. Many of them never rose to high dignities; many were killed or died when comparatively young: Norman Ramsay was but a brevet-major when he fell at Waterloo; Brandling and Von Woldersdorf were captains when they influenced considerably the fate of a serious combat; Lasalle was thirty-four when he was killed at Wagram; Murat was only four years his senior; and Kellerman, when he, "inspired by a happy and sudden resolve, threw himself on the Austrian column," and won Marengo for Bonaparte, was no more than thirty. The unexpected, sudden, and fleeting opportunities offered by the circumstances under which cavalry and guns engage, are indeed the very ones to give a young man an opportunity, and he who snatches it must be something more than medi- ocre and painstaking. It is because of this that there is a greater halo of romance round these arms than any others, and that they at- tract so much of the admiration and attention of the general public. (Roberts. $1.25.)— *Preface by E. S. May.*

Democracy and Liberty.

FOR the English historian Lecky to raise his voice against absolute democracy does not re- quire so much courage as it would for an American. In England universal suffrage is a comparatively recent institution, not yet in its teens, while we are taught from earliest child- hood that absolute democracy is a quasi-sacred institution, a panacea for all evils. Lecky's purpose is to study "the present aspects and tendencies of the political world." Thus he does not confine his attention to the Anglo- Saxon states, but studies the workings of uni- versal suffrage in all countries. After a keen and admirable analysis of the vote in a demo- cratic state, he says : " One of the great divi- sions of politics in our day is coming to be whether, at the last resort, the world should be governed by its ignorance or by its intelli- gence." With Maine, he looks with dismay at the rule of mere numbers, saying that the day will come when "it will appear one of the strangest facts in the history of human folly that such a theory was regarded as liberal and progressive." This is significant, for, remem- ber, it is the author of the history of rational- ism who is speaking. Thus, this work is an arraignment of Rousseauism and Jeffersonism, and an appeal to the English public not to be led away by *a priori* philosophy, but to be guided, as heretofore, by reason and experi- ence in introducing changes into the body poli- tic. This has always been a marked char- acteristic of English statesmen, as contrasted with those of France.

Mr. Lecky teaches the lesson that political liberty, or the right to aid in creating the gov- ernment, is much less important than civil liberty, which protects the individual from the government he creates. His criticism of the tendencies in English political life is very pes- simistic.

The work as a whole is very stimulating to thought. It is a keen analysis of modern po- litical tendencies, full of trenchant criticisms and valuable suggestions. Its spirit is that of one who has the interests of civilization most closely at heart. And as a result of the au- thor's earnestness, the literary quality of the work is a decided improvement upon that of

his "History of England." The language is limpid, forcible, and very rarely commonplace. From page after page one would like to cull compact sentences, pregnant with meaning. The work is not a systematic treatise, such as a political scientist would write ; it is written, rather, from the standpoint of a scholar and statesman combined. Its main fault is that it is almost purely destructive. The remedies Mr. Lecky proposes for the evils that are springing up in England, if efficacious at all, would be only partially remedial. Proportional representation, "fancy franchises," the refer- endum, would not go to the root of the trouble. Mr. Lecky is too practical a man to propose such a heroic remedy as restriction of the suf- frage, for he knows too well that, although universal suffrage was granted before the peo- ple were fully ripe for it, yet it would be abso- lutely impossible to restrict it now, unless, per- haps, by violent revolution. And then the cure would be worse than the evil. Universal suffrage must be taken as a permanently es- tablished institution, and the only way to cure the many evils that have followed in its wake is through the political education of the masses.

But Mr. Lecky does not believe in the spread of popular education. Like Prof. Goldwin Smith, he contends that in every society a large number of the people must perform purely physical tasks, requiring but little intelligence, and that education unfits men for work of this nature. Such work is, however, absolutely es- sential. Some one must handle the spade and clean the streets. Besides, the half-education that the lower classes always inevitably receive makes them very apt to take hold of glittering Utopias, and converts an unintelligent and negatively dangerous voter into one positively so. Thus Mr. Lecky's work is excessively gloomy, for he has reached an unsurmountable barrier. This fact is in harmony both with his opinion that "King Hazard" exercises a pow- erful influence over the destinies of humanity, and with his rejection of the views of the evo- lutionary school of historians, who, naturally, are all optimists. The evils that he points out are undoubtedly not exaggerated, and their cause is truly indicated; and yet we maintain that pure democracy is a decided step in ad- vance in historical evolution. The trouble has been that the suffrage was granted too hastily, and the optimistic and also, as we think, the scientific view is that the people, after a long- er apprenticeship, will be able to exercise the suffrage honestly, seriously, and intelligently. We are living, unfortunately, in the beginning of this period, for in historical evolution a few decades count for naught. (Longmans, Green & Co. 2 v., $5.)—*The Critic.*

Survey of Current Literature.

☞ *Order through your bookseller.*—"*There is no worthier or surer pledge of the intelligence and the purity of any community than their general purchase of books ; nor is there any one who does more to further the attainment and possession of these qualities than a good bookseller.*"—PROF. DUNN.

ART, MUSIC, DRAMA.

COHEN, ALFRED J., ["Alan Dale," *pseud.*] Queens of the stage. Dillingham. pors. 12°, (Dillingham's Globe lib.) 50 c.

CROWEST, F. JA. The story of British music, (from the earliest times to the Tudor period.) Imported by Scribner. 8°, $3.50.

KLECZYNSKI, JEAN. Chopin's greater works: ballads, nocturnes, polonaises, mazurkas; how they should be understood ; tr. with additions by Natalie Janotha. Imported by Scribner. pors. fac-similes, 12°, $1.75.

BIOGRAPHY, CORRESPONDENCE, ETC.

BARRAS, PAUL FRANÇOIS J. N. (*Comte*) DE. Memoirs of Barras, member of the Directorate ; ed. with a general introd , prefaces, and appendices by G. Duroy. In 4 v. V. 3 and 4; tr. by C. E. Roche. Harper. pors., fac-similes, plans, 8°, *ea.*, $3.75.
The third volume of the memoirs of Barras comprises the period extending from the *coup d'état* of the 18th Fructidor, year v. (4th September, 1797), to the *coup d'état* of the 18th Brumaire, year VIII. (9th November, 1799). It has, like the second volume, been composed to some extent from the notes jotted down by Barras at the close of each sitting of the Directorate. V. 4 comprises the Consulate, the Empire, the first Restoration, and the greater portion of the second.

BOUDINOT, JANE J., *ed.* The life, public services, addresses, and letters of Elias Boudinot, LL.D., President of the Continental Congress. Houghton, Mifflin & Co. 2 v., pors. 8°, *net*, $6.
Elias Boudinot was born at Philadelphia, May 2, 1740; died at Burlington, N. J., October 24, 1821; he was the friend of Washington, an ardent patriot and philanthropist, and President of the Continental Congress; he gave the greater part of a long life to the service of his country. This volume aims to place before the reader his services, speeches, and letters in such chronological sequence that they shall tell the history of his life.

FITZGERALD, PERCY. The life of Laurence Sterne. Imported by Scribner. 2 v., por. 16°, $3.

FULTON, J. Memoirs of Frederick A. P. Barnard, tenth president of Columbia College in the city of New York. Macmillan. 8°, (Columbia University Press ser.) $4.

GOODWIN, *Mrs.* MAUD WILDER. Dolly Madison. Scribner. 12°, (Women of Colonial and Revolutionary times, no. 2.) $1.25.

HANNAY, D. RODNEY. Don Emilio Castelar; with a frontispiece. Warne. 12°, (Public men of to-day ser.) $1.25.

LODGE, R. Richelieu. Macmillan. 12°, 75 c.

MORSE, J. TORREY, *jr.* Life and letters of Oliver Wendell Holmes. Houghton, Mifflin & Co. 2 v., pors. 12°, $4 ; hf. cf. or hf. polished mor., $7. *Large-pap. ed.*, 2 v., 8°, *net*, $10.

RAE, W. FRASER. Sheridan . a biography ; with an introd. by Sheridan's great-grandson, the Marquess of Dufferin and Ava. Holt. 2 v., pors. fac-similes, 8°, buckram, $7.

SALT, H. STEPHENS. Percy Bysshe Shelley, poet and pioneer: a biographical study. Imported by Scribner. 16°, $1.50.

SMEATON, OLIPHANT. Allan Ramsay. Imported by Scribner. 12°, (Famous Scots ser.) 75 c.

DESCRIPTION, GEOGRAPHY, TRAVEL.

BEYNON, W. G. L. With Kelly to Chitral. E. Arnold. maps, il. 8°, $1.75.

BROWN, ALICE. By oak and thorn: a record of English days. Houghton, Mifflin & Co. 12°, $1.25.

CHANLER, W. ASTOR. Through jungle and desert: travels in eastern Africa; with numerous il. and photographs taken by the author. Macmillan. 8°, $5.

CHEVRILLON, ANDRÉ. In India ; from the French by W. Marchant. Holt. il. 12°, $1.50.
A vivid and poetical description of Hindu India. *Contents :* At sea; Ceylon, Buddhism, Pondichéry, Calcutta ; The Himalaya, Dargiling ; Benares, Bramahnism, Hindulsm ; Lucknow, Cawnpur, Agra ; Delhi, Jaipur ; Bombay ; Ellora; The voyage.

McALLISTER, AGNES. A lone woman in Africa: six years on the Kroo coast. Hunt & Eaton. por. il 12°, *net*, $1.
Miss McAllister had charge of Garaway Mission Station on Kroo coast, west Africa, for nearly eight years. Her book tells of all she saw and accomplished there.

TORREY, BRADFORD. Spring notes from Tennessee. Houghton, Mifflin & Co. 12°, $1.25.

TRUMBLE, ALFRED. In jail with Charles Dickens. Harper. 1 il., 12°, $1.25.
Descriptions of Newgate without and within, the Fleet prison, the Marshalsea, the King's Bench. the New York Tombs, and Philadelphia's Bastile—the Eastern State Penitentiary. The author owes to Dickens's books many very strong passages of description, which he quotes at length. He also obtained much information from a personal inspection of some of the prisons, and is indebted to the old English chronicles.

WARD, JULIUS H. The White Mountains : a guide to their interpretation. *2d ed. rev. and enl.* Houghton, Mifflin & Co. il., map, 12°, $1.25.

In the present edition, besides much revision, the following chapters have been added : The gateway at North Woodstock, The mountain colors, Snow-shoeing on Osceola, and the Winnipesaukee region.

DOMESTIC AND SOCIAL.

HORTON, ROB. F. On the art of living together. Dodd, Mead & Co. 12°, 50 c.

YSAGUIRRE AND LA MARCA. Cold dishes for hot weather. Harper. 16°, $1.

EDUCATION, LANGUAGE, ETC.

HINSDALE, B. A. Studies in education, science, art, history. The Werner School-Book Co. 12°, $1.
Twenty essays and addresses. Some of the titles are: Sources of human cultivation ; The dogma of formal discipline; The laws of mental congruence and energy applied to some pedagogical problems ; The science and the art of teaching ; Calvinism and averaging in education; The pedagogical chair in the university and college ; The American school superintendent ; History teaching in schools ; Moral and religious training of children; Twenty years of public schools in Rome ; Religious instruction in the schools of Germany ; Education in Switzerland.

FICTION.

ALLEN, GRANT. A bride from the desert. [*Also*] Dr. Greatrex's engagement, and The backslider. Fenno. nar. 16°, 50 c.

BAILEY, ALICE WARD. Mark Heffron: a novel. Harper. 12°, $1.25.

BARNES, JA. For king or country: a story of the American Revolution. Harper. 12°, $1.50.
George and William Frothingham were twins and constantly mistaken for each other. This led to many remarkable adventures when George volunteered in the Continental Army and William entered the British Army. A story specially suited for boys. The description of the old " Sugar-House " prison in New York and of the secret patriot societies in the city while under British rule — both historical — are of especial interest.

BARNES, WILLIS. Dame Fortune smiled: the doctor's story. Arena Pub. Co. 12°, $1.25; pap., 50 c.
The story is a retrospect from the year 1900; the aim of the doctor's narrative is to show the reasonableness of giving during life; he is physician to a number of New York millionaires suffering from nervous prostration; he succeeds in leading them to adopt his views and cures them; the use of mental suggestion as a therapeutic agent is freely used.

BIRCHENOUGH, *Mrs.* MABEL C., [*formerly* M. C. Bradley.] Disturbing elements [a novel]. Macmillan & Co. 12°, $1.25.

BLODGETT, MABEL FULLER. Fairy tales; pictures by Ethel Reed. Lamson, Wolffe & Co. 8°, $2.
Contents : The Story of Prince Peppermint and Princess Sarsaparilla; The witch's daughter;

The blue emerald; Princess Sunbeam and the horned toad; The moon lady; How Olaf fought the ogre; The silver song; The magic violets; The good goblin; The Sultan's pepper-box; Dame Elfrida's bees; How Gold-wing found the fairy queen.

BOOTHBY, GUY. The beautiful white devil. Ward, Lock & Bowden, Ltd. il. 12°, $1.

BUCHANAN, ROB. Effie Hetherington. Roberts. 12°, $1.50.

CHAMBERS, ROB. W. A king and a few dukes: a romance. Putnam. 12°, $1.25.

CLEMENS, S. LANGHORNE, [" Mark Twain," *pseud.*] Personal recollections of Joan of Arc, by The Sieur Louis de Conte (her page and secretary), freely translated out of the ancient French into modern English from the original unpublished manuscript in the national archives of France by Jean François Alden; il. from original drawings by F. V. Du Mond. Harper. 8°, $2.50.

COTES, *Mrs.* SARA JEANNETTE DUNCAN, [*Mrs.* Everard Cotes.] His Honour and a lady. Appleton. 12°, $1.50.

CRAWFORD, FRANCIS MARION. Adam Johnstone's son. Macmillan & Co. il. 12°, $1.50.

DAVIS, R. HARDING. Cinderella, and other stories. Scribner. il. 12°, $1.
Contents : Cinderella; Miss Delamar's understudy; The editor's story; An assisted emigrant; The reporter who made himself king. These stories have appeared in *Scribner's Magazine, Harper's Magazine, Weekly,* and *Young People.*

DIDIER, C. PEALE. 'Twixt Cupid and Crœsus; or, the exhibits in an attachment suit: [il. by C. Peale Didier.] Press of J. H. Williams Co. unp. il. 4°, leatherette, *net*, $1.50. (*Corr. title.*)
Fac-similes of telegrams, notes, letters, and newspaper clippings tell a little story in which there are three characters, viz., a handsome young woman of Gotham, her intended husband Jack Garnet, and F. Clarence Bleaker, a millionaire, who is also in love with the girl. Her hesitancy between the two suitors and a mistake in directing two letters are almost fatal. Between the " exhibits " of letters, etc., are eighteen full-page pictures illustrating the story.

FREDERIC, HAROLD. The damnation of Theron Ware. Stone & Kimball. 12°, $1.50.

GISSING, G. The unclassed. Fenno. il. 12°, (Fenno's illustrated ser.) $1.25; pap., 50 c.

GOODWIN, *Mrs.* MAUD WILDER. White aprons: a romance of Bacon's Rebellion, Virginia, 1676. Little, Brown & Co. 12°, $1.25.

HOLLAND, CLIVE. The lure of fame. New Amsterdam Book Co. il. 12°, cl., $1.50.

HUME, FERGUS W. The dwarf's chamber, and other stories; il. by Percy F. S. Spence, Ja. Creig, and others. Ward, Lock & Bowden, Ltd. 12°, $1.

HUNGERFORD, *Mrs.* MARG. HAMILTON, [" The Duchess," *pseud.*, *formerly Mrs.* Argles.] An unsatisfactory lover. Lippincott. 12°, (Lippincott's select novels, no. 180.) $1; pap., 50 c.

KEIGHTLEY, S. R. The cavaliers: a novel. Harper. il. 12°, $1.50.
Story introduces Cromwell. The author has based his facts upon Green's " History of the English people." The romance of the love of Tom Duncombe, a loyal follower of the king, and Melody Leigh, the daughter of his father's nearest neighbor, runs through the story of plots and counterplots against Cavaliers and Roundheads. The characters of Charles I., Cromwell, Mazarin, and other figures of that day are drawn with skill. By the author of " The crimson sign."

KING, K. DOUGLAS. The scripture-reader of St. Mark's. The Merriam Co. I il., 12°, (Waldorf ser., no 26.) pap., 50 c.

KING, PAULINE. Alida Craig; il. by T. K. Hanna. jr. G. H. Richmond. il. 12°, $1.25.
Alida Craig is a young girl painter who has established herself in a studio building in New York City and begun to be successful after a hard experience in learning her art. Among her friends and patrons is a man who, after confessing his love for her, tells her of his previous engagement to a celebrated actress. The story gives the outcome of this young man's love troubles, and ends with a surprising revelation. Some very delightful women, married and unmarried, in every class of society, are skilfully brought into the tale.

LOVER, S., JESSOP, G. H., BARLOW, JANE, [and others.] Stories by English authors: Ireland. Scribner. por. 16°, 75 c.
Contents : The gridiron, by S. Lover; The emergency men, by G. H. Jessop; A lost recruit, by Jane Barlow; The rival dreamers, by John Banim; Neal Malone, by W. Carleton; The banshee.

MACLEOD, FIONA. The sin eater, and other tales and episodes. Stone & Kimball. 16°, $1.

MACMAHON, ELLA. A new note; il. by Willard Bonte. Fenno. il. 12°, $1.25; pap., 50 c.

MARCHBANK, AGNES. Ruth Farmer: a story. Cassell. 12°, $1.

MARTEL DE JANVILLE, SIBYLLE GABRIELLE MARIE ANTOINETTE (Comtesse) DE, ["Gyp." pseud.] Those good Normans ; from the French by Marie Jussen. Rand, McNally & Co. 16°, $1.
The fortunes of the Dutrac family are here related in a series of sharp, witty dialogues ; their great desire is to get into society and they buy a châlet at a Norman watering-place, with a view to embarking Dutrac père on a political career. They are natives of Normandy, however, and mean to get the worth of their millions made in trade by establishing cordial relations with the nobility and gentry of the neighborhood. All the members of the Dutrac family are sharply sketched ; also their daughter's marriage and incidents of their intercourse with their neighbors.

MORRISON, ARTHUR. Chronicles of Martin Hewitt. Appleton. 12°, (Appleton's town and country lib., no. 191.) $1; pap., 50 c.
Six detective stories : The Ivy Cottage mystery ; The Nicobar bullion case ; The Halford will case ; The case of the missing hand ; The case of Lake, absconded ; The case of the lost foreigner.

NEVINSON, H. W. In the valley of Tophet. Holt. 12°, buckram, $1.
Short stories.

OUT of town; il. by Rosina Emmet Sherwood. Harper. il. 12°, $1.25.

PEATTIE, ELIA W. A mountain woman. Way & Williams. 12°, $1.25.
Short stories.

PEEL, Sir ROBERT. An engagement ; with frontispiece by E. Frederick. Stokes. I il., nar. 16°, 50 c.
Arthur Hopetoun, a young Englishman, having a salary of £500 a year from the Foreign Office, and the promised patronage of his uncle, Lord Drillingham, believing himself very much in love with the poor but beautiful Bella Carstairs, proposes to her and is accepted, chiefly on the grounds of Lord Drillingham's promises; these failing to materialize, and Arthur, wishing to hasten his prospective marriage, hits upon a plan in which Lord Drillingham's daughter is to be his chief aid and abettor. It is needless to say that his scheme works admirably.

PEMBERTON, MAX. A gentleman's gentleman : being certain pages from the life and strange adventures of Sir Nicolas Steele, Bart., as related by his valet, Hildebrand Bigg. Harper. 12°, $1.25.

POSTGATE, J. W. The mystery of Paul Chadwick: a bachelor's story. Laird & Lee. 12°, (Pinkerton's detective ser., no. 27.) pap., 25 c.

POUSHKIN, ALEX. Prose tales ; tr. from the Russian by T. Keane. Macmillan. 12°, (Bohn's standard lib.) net, $1.

READE, C., ROBINSON, F. W., EDWARDS, AMELIA B., [and others.] Stories by English authors: England. Scribner. por. 16°, 75 c.
Contents : The box tunnel, by C. Reade; Minions of the moon, by F. W. Robinson ; The four-fifteen express, by Amelia B. Edwards ; The wrong black bag, by Angelo Lewis ; The three strangers, by T. Hardy; Mr. Linsmore and the widow, by Wilkie Collins ; The philosopher in the apple-orchard, by Anthony Hope.

ROBERTS, MARG. On the edge of the storm. New ed. Warne. 12°, $1.25.

SEAWELL, MOLLY ELLIOT. A strange sad comedy. The Century Co. il. 12°, $1.25.

SERGEANT, ADELINE. A rogue's daughter. Stokes. 12°, $1.
The rogue is the defaulting secretary of a bogus mining company, who has for years lived in luxury upon invested funds. His son and daughter are thrown upon the world and change their name. The daughter becomes companion to a lady and marries well. The son marries beneath him from noble motives. His wife betrays the fact that the rogue's children are enjoying prosperity under new names. Much trouble follows, but in the end it is proved that the rogue's descendants are most competent and lovable people.

SETOUN, GABRIEL. Robert Urquhart. Warne. 12°, $1.50.
Robert Urquhart after leaving college becomes schoolmaster in a rural Scottish town. He boards with ladies who have a friend with

them who has had a sad experience in life. Robert falls in love and finds his sweetheart's story involved with that of this poor lady. There are many scenes that bring out strongly the faithfulness and loyalty of Scotch character.

SHIEL, M. P. The rajah's sapphire, from a plot given him *vivâ voce.* by W. T. Stead. Ward, Lock & Bowden, Ltd. il. 16°, 75 c.

SIMMONS, *Mrs.* VESTA S., ["V. Schallenberger," *pseud.*] A village drama. Cassell. nar. 12°, (Unknown lib., no.   ) 50 c.
The drama is enacted in a California village.

SMITH, F. HOPKINSON. Tom Grogan; il. by Charles S. Reinhart. Houghton, Mifflin & Co. 12°, $1.50.

SMITH, J. Platonic affections. Roberts. 16°, (Keynotes ser., no. 21.) $1.
A Devonshire story full of local color. One of the characters is a parson of a school now almost extinct, who hunts, drinks, and smuggles, but has a heart as big as his vast frame. He had been George Heaton's tutor in the past, and when George feels his life has burnt out he seeks him again. George Heaton had buried his heart in the grave of a married woman, and believed it impossible for him to love again. He meets a young widow in Devon, and a mutual liking grows up. They agree to go through a marriage ceremony, but live together as brother and sister. This experiment has an unexpected ending.

THURBER, ALWYN M. Quaint Crippen, commercial traveller. A. C. McClurg & Co. 12°, $1; pap., 50 c.

TRAIN, ELIZ. PHIPPS. Doctor Lamar. *New cheaper ed.* Crowell. 12°, pap., 50 c.

WHEELWRIGHT, J. T. A bad penny; il. by F. G. Atwood. Lamson, Wolffe & Co. 12°, (Papyrus ser.) $1.25.
The events worked into the story took place in an unprosperous, out-of-the-way Massachusetts sea-board town about eighty years ago. The son of an old sea-captain whom he destined for the ministry had far stronger leanings towards the sea. The turning up of "a bad penny," an uncle formerly the family scapegrace changes all the plans of the sedate old people of Olbury, and James, the hero, goes to sea and falls in love and inherits a fortune, and all ends happily.

WILKINS, MARY ELEANOR. Madelon: a novel. Harper. 12°, $1.25.

HISTORY.

ESTES, STANLEY J., *ed.* The story of New Sweden as told at the quarter centennial celebration of the founding of the Swedish colony in the woods of Maine, June 25, 1895. Loring, Short & Harmon. pors. il. 8°, 50 c.; pap., 25 c.
New Sweden was the first successful colony of Swedes settled in the wilds of Maine, twenty-five years ago; from a very small beginning it has grown into a large thriving town. The opening address made by Frank Oscar Landgrane, on the celebration of its twenty-fifth anniversary, gives a full history of its inception

and growth. Other addresses and letters from prominent men complete the volume.

HOWELL-AP-HOWELLS. The birthplace and childhood of Napoleon. Scribner. il. 12°, $1.50.

JOHNSON, CLIFTON. What they say in New England: a book of signs, sayings, and superstitions. Lee & Shepard. il. 12°, $1.25.
Mr. Johnson has gathered and given in the language in which he received them the odd sayings, rhymes, and superstitions which are or have been current in New England. The volume was begun with the idea of collecting for private entertainment the remnants of folklore which are in constant use in many New England households. For convenience the matter is classified under numerous headings, such as money, luck, warts, tea - grounds, snakes, love and sentiment, weather, etc., each of which is introduced by an appropriate design.

KNIGHT, E. F. Madagascar in war-time: the *Times* special correspondent's experiences among the Hovas during the French invasion of 1895. Longmans, Green & Co. il. 8°, $4.

LEROY-BEAULIEU, H. J. BAPT. ANATOLE. The Empire of the Tsars and the Russians; tr. from the 3d French ed.; with annot. by Zénaïde Ragozin. Pt. 3, The religion. Putnam. 8°, $3.
This, the concluding volume of the work, is entirely devoted to religion and matters bearing on religion. It is divided into four parts, viz., Bk. 1, Religion and religious feeling in Russia; Bk. 2, The Russian orthodox church; Bk. 3, The Raskòl (Schism) and the sects; Bk. 4, Religious liberty and the dissident creeds. Index.

MASPERO, G. The dawn of civilization (Egypt and Chaldæa); ed. by A. H. Sayce; tr. by M. L. McClure; rev. and brought up-to-date by the author. 2d *ed.* Appleton. map, il. 4°, $7.50.

PASTON letters, 1422 – 1509 A.D.: a new ed. first published in 1874; cont. upwards of four hundred letters, etc., hitherto unpublished; ed. by Ja. Gairdner. Macmillan. 3 v., 12°, $6.

POTE, W., *jr.* The journal of Captain W. Pote, jr., during his captivity in the French and Indian war. from May, 1745, to August, 1747. Dodd, Mead & Co. folded map in separate binding, il. por. 8°, $15. [Ed. limited to 375 copies.]
Mr. J. Fletcher Hurst, who acquired the MS. volume of this journal in Geneva, Switzerland, in August of 1890, says: "It supplies many missing links, and reconciles contradictions which had hitherto defied the student of American colonial history. In addition, it throws full light on entire departments of that important struggle between the French and English for the possession, not of Canada alone, but of North America in general. It records incursions related to Pote by the captives themselves; gives memoranda of marriages, illnesses, deaths, and many other minute facts relating to the captives; and contains the best and fullest account of Donahew's exploit in Tatmegouche Bay."

INDUSTRIAL.

SILK: its origin and culture. Nonotuck Silk Co. il. 16°, pap., 10 c.

Contains an account of the discovery and introduction of silk and of the silkworm, reeling the silk from the cocoons, and how silk is manufactured.

LITERATURE, MISCELLANEOUS AND COLLECTED WORKS.

BARTLETT, *Rev.* T. E. The English Bible in American eloquence. American Baptist Pub. Soc. 16°, leatherette, 10 c.

BROWN, ALICE. By oak and thorn: a record of English days. Houghton, Mifflin & Co. 12°, $1.25.

Descriptions of journeyings through England, largely in Devon, one of its most fascinating and picturesque districts. The writer, who is the author of " Meadow grass," weaves into her appreciative sketches of nature a wide knowledge of English literature.

EGBERT, JA. C., *jr.* Introduction to the study of Latin inscriptions. Am. Book Co. il. 12°, hf. leath., $3.50.

The purpose determining the plan of this work has been to combine abundant introductory and explanatory matter with numerous examples for illustration and for practice in reading. The inscriptions, with the single exception of those from movable articles, have been printed in the type ordinarily used for Latin texts, since this form has been considered more satisfactory than any attempt at a typographical imitation of the original letters. A bibliography of epigraphy covering books, periodical literature, collections, etc., is included in the introduction.

GURTEEN, S. HUMPHREYS. The epic of the fall of man: a comparative study of Cædmon, Dante, and Milton. Putnam. il. 8°, $2.50.

This volume contains, in addition to the subject-matter proper, a new translation in blank verse of that part of Cædmon's paraphrase which treats of the fall of man. Also fac-similes of 26 illustrations from the Junian manuscript in the Bodleian Library at Oxford, England.

IRVING, WASHINGTON, WEBSTER, DAN., *and* EMERSON, RALPH WALDO. Select American classics: being selections from Irving's " Sketch-book," Webster's " Orations," and Emerson's " Essays " as published in the " Eclectic English classics." Am. Book Co. por. 12°, 90 c.

LAMPSON, F. LOCKER. My confidences: an autobiographical sketch addressed to my descendants. Imported by Scribner. 8°, $5.

LE GALLIENNE, R. Retrospective reviews: a literary log. In 2 v. V. 1, 1891–1893; v. 2, 1893–1895. Imported by Dodd, Mead & Co. 12°, $3.50.

MABIE, HAMILTON WRIGHT. Essays on nature and culture. Dodd, Mead & Co. por. 12°, $1.25.

PUTNAM, G. HAVEN, *comp.* The question of copyright; comprising the text of the copyright law of the United States, a summary of the copyright laws at present in force in the chief countries of the world, with a report of the legislation now pending in Great Britain, a sketch of the contest in the United States, 1837–1891, in behalf of international copyright, etc. *2d ed. rev. and enl.* Putnam. 12°, $1.75.

The additional material brings the work down to 1896; it consists of the Hicks Bill, the Covert amendment, the Cummings amendment, and the Treloar Bill; papers on: Results of the Copyright Law of 1891, considered in Jan., 1894; A summary of International Copyright cases and decisions since the act of 1891; States which have become parties to the Convention of Berne, Jan. 1896; Summary of the existing copyright laws of the more important countries of the world, Jan., 1896; The status of Canada in regard to copyright, Jan., 1896.

QUILLER-COUCH, ARTHUR T., [" Q," *pseud.*] Adventures in criticism. Scribner. 12°, buckram, $1.50.

⊗ Short articles on Chaucer; " The passionate pilgrim "; Shakespeare's lyrics; S. Daniel; W. Browne; T. Carew; " Robinson Crusoe "; Sterne; Scott and Burns; C. Reade; H. Kingsley; Rob. L. Stevenson; Zola; The popular conception of a poet; The poor little penny dreadful; Ibsen's " Peer Gynt "; George Moore; Hall Caine; Margaret L. Woods; Anthony Hope; Mr. Stockton, etc.

SHEPHERD, R. HERNE. The bibliography of Tennyson: a bibliographical history of the published and privately printed writings of Alfred (*Lord*) Tennyson, poet laureate, from 1827–1894 inclusive, with his contributions to annuals, magazines, newspapers, etc. Imported by Scribner. 16°, net, $2.50.

SHERWOOD, S. V., BATCHELDER, J. H., [*and others.*] At Wellesley, legenda for 1896; published for the senior class of Wellesley College. Putnam. 12°, $1.

Contents: A question of science, by S. V. Sherwood; Lake Waban, by S. V. Sherwood; Mental telegraphy, by J. H. Batchelder; The rime of the sophomore, by I. H. Fiske; A smile of fortune, by S. V. Sherwood; At the first floor centre, by J. S. Parker; The claim of the heathen, by S. V. Sherwood; An experiment, by J. S. Parker and I. H. Fiske. Stories and poems by students of Wellesley College.

SWIFT, JONATHAN. Travels into several remote nations of the world in four parts, by Lemuel Gulliver, first a surgeon and then a captain of several ships. Longmans, Green & Co. 8°, $1.

MENTAL AND MORAL.

BLAIR, T. S. Human progress: what can man do to further it? W. R. Jenkins. 12°, $1.50.

The author of this treatise, taking up the above question and finding the present state of human knowledge inadequate to furnish an answer, reasons that the complexity of the facts of human experience has proved too much for the philosophers, and looks about for an instance of better results elsewhere. This he finds in the case of the successful man of affairs. The present work is simply a report of the conclusions reached through the application of business common-sense methods to the inquiry in hand.

FLOWER, SYDNEY. Hypnotism up to date. Kerr. 12°, (Unity lib., no. 56.) pap., 25 c.

NATURE AND SCIENCE.

CHESTER, A. H. Dictionary of the names of minerals, including their history and etymology. Wiley. 8°, $3.50.

KEELEY, LESLIE E., *M.D.* The non-heredity of inebriety. Griggs. 12°, $1.50.
In this volume Dr. Keeley for the first time publishes his theory of the causes, nature, and treatment of inebriety, taking the ground that it is a disease which is not hereditary. The various agencies for the suppression of drunkenness, the question of prohibition, the duty of the state to inebriates, and kindred topics of vital importance are discussed in a manner that makes this work of exceptional value to the general reader and to all who are, by legislation or otherwise, endeavoring to correct the evils of intemperance.

PINCHOT, GIFFORD, *and* GRAVES, H. S. The white pine: a study with tables of volume and yield. The Century Co. il. 12°, $1.
A valuable contribution to the natural history of the most important lumbering tree in North America. The motive that prompted its preparation was a desire to assist in making clear the real nature of forestry and to hasten the general introduction of right methods of forest management. Mr. Pinchot's work as a consulting forester is best known in connection with the management of Mr. Vanderbilt's Biltmore Forest in North Carolina. Tables showing the percentage of merchantable timber in comparison with the diameter of the tree, the yield for a given area, the height of a forest pine at a given age, etc.

WEISMANN, A. On germinal selection as a source of definite variation. The Open Court Pub. Co. 8°, (Religion of science lib., no. 19.) pap., 25 c.
A paper read in the first general meeting of the International Congress of Zoölogists at Leyden on September 16, 1895. Several points, which for reasons of brevity were omitted when the paper was read, have been re-embodied in the text, and an appendix has been added where a number of topics receive fuller treatment. The basal idea of the essay — the existence of germinal selection — was propounded by the author some time since, but it is here for the first time fully set forth and tentatively shown to be the necessary complement of the process of selection.

PHYSICAL AND MATHEMATICAL.

KEENE, J. HARRINGTON, ["Grapho," *pseud.*] The mystery of handwriting: a handbook of graphology; il. by the author, and with autographs of celebrated persons. Lee & Shepard. por. obl. 12°, $2.
Contents: Graphology, what it is and can do; Physical qualities indicated by writing; Directions for reading character from handwriting; The general indication in writing; Signification in letters considered singly; Qualities and aptitudes alphabetically arranged; Characteristic flourishes; Some graphological demonstrations. All these papers are illustrated with fac-simile autographs of celebrated persons. While Mr. Keene does not claim that graphology is an exact science, he makes out a very interesting case.

SHELDON, W. L. An ethical movement: lectures. Macmillan. 12°, $1.75.

POETRY AND DRAMA.

DUER, CAROLINE *and* ALICE. Poems. G. H. Richmond. 12°, $1.25.
Thirty-five short poems, of which twenty-five are by Caroline, nine by Alice, and one by the two authors together. The subjects are varied and the treatment shows strength and taste.

FULLER, H. B. The puppet-booth: twelve plays. The Century Co. 12°, $1.25.
In this book Mr. Fuller enters a field which has not been occupied by any American writer. "The puppet-booth" contains twelve highly imaginative plays, each confined to a single act. One is obviously a parody on Ibsen and another a sly hit at Weyman and Anthony Hope.

KEATS, J. Poems; ed. with introduction and notes by Arlo Bates. Ginn. 12°, (Athenæum Press ser.) $1.10.

KIMBALL, HANNAH PARKER. Soul and sense. [Poems.] Copeland & Day. 16°, bds., 75 c.

LAMPMAN, ARCHIBALD. Lyrics of earth. [Poems.] Copeland & Day. 16°, bds., $1.

MACKAY, ERIC. Song of the sea, My lady of dreams, and other poems. Stone & Kimball. 16°, $1.25.

MITCHELL, SILAS WEIR, *M.D.* The collected poems. The Century Co. 12°, $1.75.
The collection includes the dramatic poems "Philip Vernon," "Francis Drake," "The cup of youth," etc., as well as miscellaneous and occasional verse. These poems were previously scattered through several volumes and published by different houses.

PRENTISS, CAROLINE EDWARDS. Sunshine and shadow. [Poems.] Putnam. 12°, ooze, $1.50.

POLITICAL AND SOCIAL.

BASSETT, J. SPENCER. Slavery and servitude in the Colony of North Carolina. The Johns Hopkins Press. 8°, (Johns Hopkins University studies, 14th ser., no. 4–5.) pap., 50 c.
Contents: The introduction of slavery; The legal status of slavery; Religious and social life of the slaves; The free negro and Indian slaves; White servitude. Authorities used (1 p.).

BIDDLE, JACOB A. Social regeneration. Student Pub. Co. 12°, $1.

CABRERA, RAIMUNDO. Cuba and the Cubans; tr. from the 8th Spanish edition of *Cuba y sus jueces*, by Laura Guiteras; rev. and ed. by L. E. Levy, and completed with a supplementary appendix by the editor. The Levytype Co. il. map, 12°, $1.50.
A comprehensive statement of the Cuban question. Señor Cabrera deals with his subject-matter from the vantage-ground of an acknowledged leadership of the Autonomist party of Cuba, and his work, although voicing the demands of the Cuban people for reforms, has

commanded the recognition and the respect of Spanish statesmen. As the work was published in 1887, before the present difficulty, it is free from the bitterness of party rancor.

CONANT, C. A. A history of modern banks of issue ; with an account of the economic crises of the present century. Putnam. 8°, $3.

DEL MAR, ALEX. History of monetary systems. C. H. Kerr & Co. 12°, $2.
Record of actual experiments in money made by various states of the ancient and modern world as drawn from their statutes, customs, treaties, mining regulations, jurisprudence, history, archæology, coins, nummulary systems, and other sources of information. A bibliography on monetary systems and money (6 p.), finance, etc.

EDE, W. MOORE (*Canon*). The attitude of the church to some of the social problems of town life; with a preface by the Lord Bishop of Durham. Macmillan & Co. 12°, (Hulsean lectures, 1895.) *net*, 70 c.

GOODE, JA. B. The modern banker: a story of his rapid rise and dangerous designs. C. H. Kerr & Co. 12°, (Lib. of progress, no. 18.) pap., 25 c.
An attack on the financial policy of the government in the form of a story.

HADLEY, ARTHUR TWINING. Economics : an account of the relations between private property and public welfare. Putnam. 8°, $2.50.
An attempt to apply the methods of modern science to the problems of modern business. Large investments of capital in factories and railroads have developed new problems in business life and special attention is given to the important work of the speculator. He studies closely the effect of combinations upon the interests of the consumers and of the laborers, and examines the results of meeting organizations of capital with organizations of labor and of controlling them by special legislation or by direct government ownership. He tries to make the study of practical problems a means of developing and explaining scientific theories. Full index. List of authorities at the head of every chapter. Intended specially for earnest students of economics.

HOWE, F. C. Taxation and taxes in the United States under the Internal revenue system, 1791–1895 : an historical sketch of the organization, development, and later modification of direct and excise taxation under the constitution. Crowell. 12°, (Lib. of economics and politics, no. 11.) $1.75.

JOHNSTON, ALEX., *ed.* American orations: studies in American political history ; ed. with introds. by Alex. Johnston ; re-edited with historical and textual notes by Ja. Albert Woodburn. [*New rev. ed.*] In 4 v. V. I. Putnam. 12°, $1.25.
First published in 1884 in three volumes. The changes in the revision are chiefly in the way of additions which have made necessary a fourth volume. By the revision the volumes will be confined entirely to political oratory. Notable American orations on literature and religion are excluded. To the first volume have been added selections from Otis, Samuel Adams, Gallatin, and Benton, and from it have been omitted Washington's Inaugural and President Nott's oration on the death of Hamilton. Madison's speech on the adoption of the Constitution has been substituted for Patrick Henry's oration on the same subject.

LECKY, W. E. HARTPOLE. Democracy and liberty. Longmans. 2 v., 12°, $5.

LEE's vest-pocket pointers for busy people: quick and accurate answers to all questions. Laird & Lee. 1 il., nar. 16°, leath., 50 c.
Twenty thousand facts of importance; the prominent events of history; area, population, location, and rulers of all nations; states of the Union, population, area, capitals, and cities of over 10,000 inhabitants; all the largest cities of the world; the great battles; chief rivers, lakes, etc.; postal regulations; parliamentary rules; constitution of the United States; biographical dates; foreign, legal, and scientific lexicon; alphabetically arranged.

LEWIS, EUGENE C. A history of the American tariff, 1789–1860. C. H. Kerr & Co. 12°, (Unity lib., no. 54.) pap., 25 c.

MAN or dollar, which ? a novel; by a newspaper man. C. H. Kerr & Co. 12°, (Unity lib., no. 55.) pap., 25 c.
The story opens in the year 1983; it shows what may be made of this nation when man thinks more of his own physical and mental development than of accumulating wealth. A retrospect is taken, giving a picture of the present times and the various changes and improvements which led up to the conditions described as existing a hundred years since.

PRICE, L. L. Money and its relations to prices: being an inquiry into the causes, measurement, and effects of changes in general prices. Imported by Scribner. 12°, $1.

ROUSIERS, PAUL DE. The labor question in Britain; with a preface by H. De Tourville; tr. by F. L. D. Herbertston. Macmillan. 8°, $4.

STIMSON, F. JESSUP, ["J. S. of Dale," *pseud.*] Handbook to the labor law of the United States. Scribner. 12°, $1.50.
Sets forth, as it exists in the United States today, that law of labor disputes and the regulation of industrial affairs and protection of employees which has had its greatest development in the last few years. While the work is sufficiently full and accurate to serve as a legal textbook, the author's chief object has been to make it a clear and trustworthy guide for laboring men and their several organizations throughout the United States.

TANDY, FRANCIS DASHWOOD. Voluntary socialism: a sketch. Francis D. Tandy. 16°, (Ideal lib., no. 3.) $1; pap., 50 c.
Chapters on Evolution ; Egoism ; The state ; Equal freedom ; Defence of person and property; Value and surplus value ; Money and interest; Mutual banks of issue; Free land ; Special privileges ; Profit ; Transportation, etc.; Methods ; The prospect. " A few books for subsequent reading," on all the subjects treated, covers 6 pages.

THOMPSON, HERBERT M. Russian politics. Holt. maps, 8°, $2.

Contents: Physical aspects of Russia, and the racial descent of her peoples; Historical sketch up to the death of Peter the Great, and from Peter the Great to the Crimean War; The peasantry, their emancipation from serfdom and subsequent treatment and conditions of life ; Account of other reforms undertaken in the sixties, and their subsequent partial undoing; Religions and religious persecutions ; Dramatis personæ on the political stage of modern Russia ; Question of the extradition of prisoners to Russia. A list of books to which reference is made (2 p.).

WALDRON, G. B. A handbook on currency and wealth ; with numerous tables and diagrams. Funk & Wagnalls Co. nar. 12°. 50 c.

Contains among other things descriptions in full of the money systems of the United States, present and past ; The money systems and finances of the world; The relation of gold and silver, as to production, prices, and wages ; Wealth and its ownership, including its production, distribution, and consumption ; also the extent of debts of all kinds ; Facts relative to railroads, telegraphs, and telephones, strikes and lockouts, land and population, immigration and foreign-born, the liquor traffic, and the last vote for president.

THEOLOGY, RELIGION, AND SPECULATION.

ATKINSON, J., *D.D.* The beginnings of the Wesleyan movement in America and the establishment therein of Methodism. Hunt & Eaton. 8°, $3.

" The story related in this volume has never before been told. The period commencing with the origin of the Wesleyan movements here, and closing with the conference held in Philadelphia in the midsummer of 1773, was a momentous one. The struggles and victories of the Wesleyan heroes and heroines of those seven years made possible all the achievements and triumphs of Methodism on this continent that have followed."—*Preface.*

BANKS, L. ALBERT, *D.D.* The fisherman and his friends: a series of revival sermons. Funk & Wagnalls Co. il. 12°, $1.50.

The thirty-two sermons in this volume were delivered in Hanson Place Methodist Episcopal Church, Brooklyn, N. Y., during the month of January, 1896, in a series of revival meetings.

DAVIDS, T. W. RHYS. Buddhism, its history and literature. Putnam. 12°. (American lectures on the history of religions, no. 1, 1st ser., 1894-1895.) $1.50.

Contents: 1, Development of religious belief in India previous to Buddhism ; 2, The Buddhist sacred books : 3, Life of the Buddha ; 4, The secret of Buddhism. Pt. I.: The four truths, the chain of life, and the ideal ; 5, The secret of Buddhism. Pt. II.: Mystic trance and Arahatship; 6, Later developments of Buddhism. The great and little vehicle.

ELMENDORF, *Rev.* J. Ja. The word and the book : letters on the higher criticism. The Young Churchman Co. 8°, *net*, 50 c.

GREGORY, DAN. S., *D.D.* Christ's trumpet-call to the ministry; or, the preacher and the preaching for the present crisis. Funk & Wagnalls Co. 12°, $1.25.

Contents: The preacher's present commission : The preacher's message ; The preacher and his furnishing; The preaching for these times; The preacher as a pastor in these times.

KENT, C. FOSTER. A history of the Hebrew people from the settlement in Canaan to the division of the kingdom. Scribner. 12°, $1.25.

Author is associate professor of biblical literature and history, Brown University. The purpose of his work is to introduce the general as well as the technical Bible student to the essential features of the political, social, and religious life of the Hebrew people. Appendix contains " The authorities upon Hebrew history " (4 p.), " Books of reference " (1 p.), and " References " to sources of study (6 p.).

LEA, H. C. A history of auricular confession and indulgences in the Latin church. In 3 v. V. 2, Confession and absolution (*continued*). Lea Bros. & Co. 8°, $3.

WATSON, J. MACLAREN, *D.D.*, ["Ian Maclaren," *pseud.*] The mind of the master. Dodd, Mead & Co. 12°, $1.50.

Fifteen papers on: Jesus our supreme teacher; The development of truth ; The sovereignty of character; Ageless life ; Sin an act of self-will ; The culture of the cross ; Faith the sixth sense; The law of spiritual gravitation; Devotion to a person the dynamic of religion ; Judgment according to type; Optimism the attitude of faith; Fatherhood the final idea of God; The foresight of faith ; The continuity of life ; The kingdom of God.

Books for the Young.

CASTLEMON, HARRY, [*pseud.* for C. Austin Fosdick.] The house-boat boys. Coates. il. 12°, $1.25.

Two Western boys, in order to gain money to pay for a university education, build a house-boat for themselves; they float in it down the Ohio into the Mississippi River, fishing and trapping and selling their game. There is a mystery about the parents of one of the boys, which is gradually revealed; after many serious adventures he discovers his father in a rich Southern planter.

CHEEVER, *Mrs.* HARRIET A. A rescued madonna. Congregational S. S. and Pub. Soc. 1 il. 12°, 60 c.

A short Easter story, showing how two lives, almost infinitely distant from each other in worldly condition, were influenced and brought together in a helpful way by a picture of the Madonna and child. By the author of " Little Jolliby's Christmas." Bound in white, with a lily design in gold and lettering in pale green.

ELLIS, E. S. Stories from American history. A. Flanagan. il. 12°, 50 c.; bds., 35 c.

The object is to interest children in the history of their country.

RECENT FRENCH AND GERMAN BOOKS.

FRENCH.

Avrillon, Mlle. Mémoires sur la vie privée de Joséphine. 12°. Garnier........................ $1 00
Bazin, R. En province. 12°. Levy.............. 1 00
Blaze, S. Mémoires d'un aide-major sous le premier empire. 8°. Flammarion..... .... 1 80
Brunetiere, F. Le renaissance de l'Idéalisme. 12° Didot. 15
Daudet, A. Contes d'Hiver (Coll. Guillaume). 32°. Borel........ 30
Dragomanov. Correspondence de M. Bakounine 12°. Perrin...... .... 1 00
Gounod, C. Mémoires d'un artiste. 12°. Levy. 1 00
Hugo, G. Souvenirs d'un matelot. 12°. Charpentier........ .... 1 00
Lecomte, G. Espagne. 12°. Charpentier...... 1 00
Marguerite, P. L'eau qui dort. 12°. Colin.... 1 00
Ohnet, G. I. Inutile richesse. 12°. Ollendorff. 1 00
O'Monroy, R. Quand j'étais capitaine. 12°. Levy.. 1 00
Renan, Henriette, *and* E. Renan. Lettres intimes. 8°. Levy.................................. 2 25

Ricard, J. Le chemin de la paix. 12°. Levy... $1 00
Ritter, E. La famille et la jeunesse de J. J. Rousseau. 12°. Hachette....................... 1 00
Sales, P. Le petit charbonnier. 12°. Flammarion.. 1 00
Simon, J. Quatre portraits. 12°. Levy........ 1 00
Vanderheym, I. G. Le negous Ménélik. 12°. Hachette... 1 20
Wodzinski, A. Srebro père et fils. 12°. Levy...... .... 1 00
Zola, E. Rome 12°. Charpentier.............. 90

GERMAN.

Elcho, R. Die Pflicht des Starken. 12°. Bong & Co... 1 70
Juncker, E. Unter Kosacken. 12°. Janke..... 2 00
Suttner, G. von. Darrdjan. 12°. Pierson...... 1 35
Telmann. Unter römischem Himmel. 12°. Reissner... 2 35
Wichert, E. Die Schwestern. 12°. Reissner.. 70
Wildenbruch, E. von. Der Junge von Hennersdorf. 12°. Freund & Jeckel................ 70

BOOKS FOR SUMMER TRAVELLERS.

AMERICAN BOOK COMPANY, New York.

Gray's Manual of Botany. Tourists' ed. $2.00.

D. APPLETON & CO., New York,

Appletons' General Guide to the United States. With numerous maps and illustrations. 12mo, flexible morocco, with tuck, $2.50. (Part I., separately, NEW ENGLAND AND MIDDLE STATES AND CANADA; cloth, $1.25. Part II., SOUTHERN AND WESTERN STATES; cloth, $1.25.)

Appletons' Canadian Guide-Book. A guide for tourist and sportsman, from Newfoundland to the Pacific. With maps and illustrations. 12mo, flexible cloth, $1.50.

Appletons' Guide-Book to Alaska. By Miss A. R. Scidmore. With maps and illustrations. 12mo, flexible cloth, $1.25.

Appletons' Handbook of American Summer Resorts. With maps, illustrations, table of railroad fares, etc. 12mo, paper, 50 cents.

Appletons' Dictionary of New York. 16mo, paper, 30 cents; cloth, 60 cents.

THE CASSELL PUBLISHING CO., New York.

Cassell's Pocket Guide to Europe for 1896. With maps, etc. Bound in leather, $1.50.
The model book of its kind for accuracy, fulness, legibility of text and maps, compact beauty and usefulness, and very moderate price.

HOUGHTON, MIFFLIN & CO., Bost.

Bacon's Dictionary of Boston. $1.50; boards, $1.00.
Boston Illustrated. Paper, 50 cents.
Satchel Guide to Europe. Edition for 1895. $1.50.
England Without and Within. By Richard Grant White. $2.00.
Sweetser's New England. $1.50.
Sweetser's White Mountains. $1.50.
Sweetser's Maritime Provinces. $1.50.
Nantucket Scraps. By Jane G. Austin. $1.50.
Mrs. Thaxter's Among the Isles of Shoals. $1.25.
Jenness' Isles of Shoals (History). $1.50.
Julius H. Ward's White Mountains. $1.50.
Mrs. Woodman's Picturesque Alaska. $1.00.

THOMAS NELSON & SONS, New York.

English Scenery. 120 views. 4to, cloth, $2.50.
Souvenir of Scotland. Its cities, lakes, and mountains. 120 chromo views. 4to, $2.50; and $4.00.
Ramblers in Rome. By S. Russell Forbes. With maps, plans, and illustrations. 12mo, cloth extra, $1.50.

THOMAS NELSON & SONS.—Continued.

Rambles in Naples. By S. Russell Forbes. With maps, plans, and illustrations. 12mo, cloth, extra, $1.25.

ROBERTS BROTHERS, Boston.

Jackson (Helen ["H. H."]). Glimpses of Three Coasts. 12mo, $1.50.
These are "Bits of Travel" in California and Oregon, Scotland and England, and Norway, Denmark, and Germany.
—— **Ramona.** A Story. 12mo, $1.50.
Most delightful glimpses of So. California.
—— **Bits of Travel.** Illustrated. Square 18mo, $1.25.
—— **Bits of Travel at Home.** Square 18mo, $1.50.
Drake (Samuel Adams). Old Landmarks and Historic Personages of Boston. With 93 illustrations. 12mo, $2.00.
—— **Old Landmarks and Historic Fields of Middlesex.** With 39 illustrations and maps. 12mo, $2.00.
Aloha. (A Hawaiian Salutation.) By G. L. Chaney. Travels in the Sandwich Islands. With illustrations and map. 16mo, $1.50.
Constantinople. By Edwin A. Grosvenor. With an introduction by Gen. Lew. Wallace. With 250 illustrations. 2 vols., 8vo, cloth, gilt top, $10.00.

GEORGE ROUTLEDGE & SONS, Ltd., 29 W. 23d St., New York.

Hare's (A. J. C.) Books of Travel.
Edwards's (A. B.) A Thousand Miles Up the Nile. Profusely illustrated. 8vo, $2.50.
—— **Untrodden Peaks and Unfrequented Valleys.** A Midsummer Ramble in the Dolomites. Maps and illustrations. 8vo, $2.50.
Caine's Picturesque India. 200 illustrations and map. 8vo, cloth, $4.00.

Send for Complete Catalogue.

WARD, LOCK & BOWDEN, Ltd., New York.

On the Cars and Off. Being the Journal of a Pilgrimage along the Queen's Highway to the East, from Halifax, in Nova Scotia, to Victoria, in Vancouver's Island. By Douglas Sladen. Profusely and beautifully illustrated. 8vo, cloth, $6.00.

BRADLEE WHIDDEN, Boston, Mass.

Knobel's Guides in Natural History. Trees and Shrubs. Ferns and Evergreens. Day Butterflies. The Beetles. The Moths. Fresh-water Fishes. Each 12mo, *net*, 50 cents.
Emerton's Life on the Seashore. Illustrated. 12mo, cloth, $1.50.

In the June Magazines.

The Atlantic Monthly contains the second instalment of George Birkbeck Hill's criticism of the Rossetti Letters; a criticism of the " Works of Orestes Brownson," and an epitome of his spiritual life from transcendentalism to the Catholic Church, by George Parsons Lathrop; a description of the home of George Sand, now in the possession of her granddaughter, by Mary Argyle Taylor, entitled " In a Famous French Home "; " The Politician and the Public School," by H. L. Jones; " Restriction of Emigration," by Francis A. Walker; " Lord Howe's Commission to Pacify the Colonies," by Paul Leicester Ford, and several short stories and verses of the usual high order of merit.

The Century contains " Notes on City Government in St. Louis," by Dr. Albert Shaw; " Humor and Pathos of Presidential Conventions," by Joseph R. Bishop; " Impressions of South Africa," by James Bryce; " Lights and Shadows of the Alhambra," written by Mrs. Elizabeth Robins Pennell and illustrated by her artist husband; " Sargent and His Painting," with particular reference to Boston Public Library decorations, with text by William A. Coffin and reproductions of the paintings, which include two wood-cuts by Coles.

The Forum contents include " Elections of Senators by Popular Vote," by John H. Mitchell; " The Fallacy of Territorial Extension," by W. G. Sumner; " A Keats Manuscript," by Thomas Wentworth Higginson; " Armenia's Impending Doom: Our Duty," by M. M. Mangasarian; " The Democratization of England," by Thomas Davidson; " Ego, et Rex Meus: a study of royalty," by Ouida; and " The Isolation of Music," by Waldo S. Pratt.

Harper's Magazine includes " A Visit to Athens," by Bishop Doane, with illustrations by Guy Rose; " The Greatest Painter of Modern Germany (Adolf Menzel)," by Dr. Charles Waldstein (illustrated) ; " The Ouanoniche and Its Canadian Environment," by E. T. D. Chambers, with thirteen illustrations ; the first instalment of a story by John Kendrick Bangs entitled "A Rebellious Heroine"; a short story by Brander Matthews, called " A Wall Street Wooing," illustrated by W. T. Smedley ; " Evelina's Garden," and a story by Mary E. Wilkins, illustrated by Clifford Carleton.

Scribner's Magazine for June contains " In the Balkans—the Chessboard of Europe," by Henry Norman, illustrated from photographs ; "Vailima Table-Talk—Robert Louis Stevenson in His Home Life," by Isabel Strong ; " A Letter to Town — Urban and Suburban Sketches," by H. C. Bunner ; short stories of Grace Ellery Channing, Mary T. Earle, and Harry C. Hale ; poems by Edith M. Thomas, Louise Betts Edwards and Emily Dickinson, and short essays on " Thomas Hughes " and " The Rule of the Bicycle " in " The Point of View."

The Westminster Review (May) contains " History of Hindu Civilization Under British Rule," by J. F. Hewitt ; " The Victorian Age of Literature and Its Critics," by D. F. Hannigan; and " The Note-Books of Samuel Taylor Coleridge," by F. W. Wiltshire.

Literary Miscellany.

THE PEOPLE—AND HAWKINS.—A correspondent sends us a rhyme that he says was very popular at Balliol when the author of " The Prisoner of Zenda " was there:

> There was a young fellow named Hawkins
> Who bossed all the Radical talkin's ;
> His idea it was great,
> He'd smash Church and State,
> And leave but the People—and Hawkins !

A BRILLIANT vindication of " Dean Swift " will shortly appear from the hand of the novelist, Richard Ashe King; and later Sir Charles Gavan Duffy's " Life of Thomas Davis," a long-promised book, will be published. " The early association of Duffy with the gifted young Irish poet and patriot," says the London *Literary World*, " will probably give the public an insight into much of Davis's life that is as yet unknown. Mr. King, by the way, has left the Emerald Isle, and, like many of his literary compatriots, has taken up his residence near London."

AN AMERICAN AND ENGLISH ROBERT BRIDGES. —*The Critic's* " Lounger " says: " It seems to disturb the British reviewers that *Life's* genial ' Droch ' should be named Robert Bridges. They have a Robert Bridges of their own in England, and resent ours. They want him to indicate by some means, when he publishes a book in England, that he is not their British Bridges. Unfortunately he is not a woman, or he might change his name to oblige them. I really do not see what he can do about it, unless he has printed on the title-pages of his English editions—Robert Bridges : ' Made in America.'"

NOTABLE WOMEN OF THE PRESENT CENTURY. —1. What woman did much of the drudgery of astronomical work for her older brother, and was later appointed assistant astronomer to George III. and member of the Royal Astronomical Society?

2. What woman in the early part of this century far surpassed all others in mathematical and scientific attainments?

3. What woman has gained great fame by her paintings of horses?

4. Of what woman was it said, "She belongs by birth to New England, by marriage to Italy, and by genius to the whole world"?

5. Who is the best-known woman writer on the subject of political economy?

6. What American novelist—a woman — has recently died who gained fame by stories of colonial days?

7. What American novelist—a woman — has recently died in Italy whose fame rests upon stories of the present day?

8. What American novelist—a woman — whose grave is near the summit of a high mountain, has done much by her stories to benefit an oppressed nation?

9. What woman, born on American soil, had one husband who was executed and a second who died in exile? She was wife of one emperor and grandmother of another.

10. What woman, who was for many years highest authority in points of fashion and etiquette, has passed the last of her life in exile?
— *Emily W. Tapley in the Outlook.*

Freshest News.

THE NEW AMSTERDAM BOOK CO. announce " A Husband's Ordeal, a romance of Queensland," by Percy Russell; and " Political Parties of the United States, their history and influence, 1789-1896," by J. Harris Patton, author of " Four Hundred Years of American History," etc.

BRENTANO'S have a timely, up-to-date book in " Bicycling for Ladies," by Maria E. Ward, a most practical treatise on the sport now recognized as the ideal outdoor exercise, properly illustrated with drawings giving details of pedalling, dress, and necessary tools for the care of the bicycle.

THE KELMSCOTT PRESS has just ready for issue Mr. William Morris's new romance, " The Well at the World's End," printed in double columns, with entirely new borders and ornaments by the author, and four illustrations designed by Sir E. Burne-Jones. The edition is limited to 350 copies on paper and eight on vellum.

LEMPERLY, HILLIARD AND HOPKINS, New York City, have ready " The Way a Soul Dies," by Orville E. Watson, an Episcopalian clergyman of Cleveland, Ohio, a strong essay on the sinfulness of hate; " Verses," by Mary Wright Plummer; " Little Rhymes for Little People," by Anna M. Pratt; and " Lincoln and His Cabinet," a lecture of great historical value, by Charles A. Dana, editor of *The Sun.*

THE BURROWS BROTHERS COMPANY, Cleveland, O., will publish in August of this year the first volume of their reprint of " The Jesuit Relations and Allied Documents," edited by Reuben Gold Thwaites. The work will be an exact *verbatim et literatim* reprint of the very rare French, Latin, and Italian originals, both MS. and printed, accompanied page for page by a complete English translation, by John Cutler Covert, assisted by Mary Sifton Pepper and others. It will be in sixty volumes, illustrated with numerous *fac-similes,* portraits, maps, etc. The edition will be limited to 750 numbered sets.

CHARLES SCRIBNER'S SONS have now ready Robert Louis Stevenson's " Weir of Hermiston," the unpublished romance to which Sidney Colwin has furnished an elaborate editorial note indicative of its natural close; and also " Poems and Ballads," gathering into one volume " A Child's Garden of Verses," " Underwoods," and " Ballads." A new volume is added to the *Women of Colonial and Revolutionary Times,* devoted to " Eliza Pinckney," written by Harriott Horry Ravenel, with facsimile reproduction of a letter ; two volumes are added to *Stories from English Authors,* one dealing with " France," one with " London " ; and the first of the series of *American Summer Resorts* is issued, devoted to the " North Shore of Massachusetts," written by Robert Grant and illustrated by W. T. Smedley.

D. APPLETON & CO. have just ready " With the Fathers," a chapter on the Monroe doctrine and other studies in United States History, by Prof. J. B. McMaster, with treatise on the third term in the presidency from the historical point of view; " Wages and Capital," an examination of the wages fund doctrine, by Prof. F. W. Taussig, of Harvard University; and " Ice Work, Present and Past," by T. G. Bonney. professor of geology at University College. London, the new volume in the *International Scientific Series.* In lighter vein they have ready for summer trunks " The Picture of Las Cruces," by Christian Reid, a dramatic story of Mexico; " Maggie, a Girl of the Streets," by Stephen Crane. author of " The Red Badge of Courage "; " False Coin or True ?" by F. F. Montrésor; " Green Gates," by Mrs. K. M. C. Meredith (Johanna Staats); and " The Folly of Eustace," by R. S. Hichens. All " Appletons' Guide-Books " are also ready for travellers, having undergone their thorough annual revision.

FRANCIS P. HARPER has just published two books of great interest. One is entitled " Reminiscences of Literary London from 1779 to 1853," and is from the pen of Dr. Thomas Rees, with extensive additions by John Britton, F.S.A., and the other is entitled " In Jail with Charles Dickens," and is from the pen of Alfred Trumble. Attractive titles these, but not more attractive than the books themselves. London has always been the Mecca of English-speaking men of letters, and hence any book that adds to our information concerning the London publishers, authors, and booksellers of the past deserves a cordial welcome. " In Jail with Charles Dickens " is another entertaining and instructive book, the author describing fully the notable London and American prisons mentioned in the works of the famous novelist. Thus he gives us distinct pictures of Newgate, the Fleet Prison, the Marshalsea, the King's Bench, the Tombs of this city, and the Eastern District Penitentiary in Philadelphia. This book contains a great deal of useful information, and may fitly be regarded as an authority on the places on which it deals.

G. P. PUTNAM'S SONS announce for immediate publication a volume which will be issued under the general title of " The United States and Great Britain," and which will contain three monographs, as follows: (1) " The Relations Between the United States and Great Britain," by David A. Wells, a reprint (issued under the authorization of the publishers of the *North American Review*) of the article by Mr. Wells, printed in the April number of the *Review,* rewritten and augmented ; (2) " The True Monroe Doctrine," by Edmund S. Phelps, LL.D., late minister to Great Britain, a reprint of the address delivered some weeks back by Dr. Phelps in Brooklyn, also rewritten with important additions; and (3) " Arbitration," by Carl Schurz, a reprint, with a few changes, of the address recently delivered by Mr. Schurz in Washington. The Putnams will publish at once " A Venetian June," by Anna Fuller, to be issued uniform in general style with the author's " A Literary Courtship," and to be illustrated by George Sloane. They have nearly ready "Will o' the Wasp," a sea-yarn of the War of 1812, by Robert Cameron Rogers, author of " The Wind in the Clearing," with a frontispiece prepared by R. F. Zogbaum; and " Abraham Lincoln, a poem," by the Rev. Lyman Whitney Allen, which won the $1000 prize in the recent *New York Herald* competition.

LITERARY NEWS

AN ECLECTIC REVIEW OF
CURRENT LITERATURE
~ILLUSTRATED~

VOL. XVII-N° 7   JULY ~ 1896 $ 1.00 YEARLY
10 CTS. PER NO.

~ PUBLICATION OFFICE ~
59 DUANE STREET, NEW YORK
ENTERED AT THE POST OFFICE AT NEW YORK AS SECOND CLASS MATTER

BOOK The Literary News

In winter you may reade them, ab ignem, by the fireside; and in summer, ab umbram, under some shadie tree, and therewith pass away the tedious howres.

| VOL. XVII. | JULY, 1896. | No. 7. |

The Life and Letters of Charles Bulfinch.

FROM time to time, ever since the death of my grandfather, inquiries have been made of the family regarding the chief facts of his life

From "Life and Letters of Charles Bulfinch." Copyright, 1896, by Houghton, Mifflin & Co.

CHARLES BULFINCH.

and work, and several biographical notices have appeared.

Since the death of his immediate descendants left the family papers to the care of my mother, and especially since the enlargement of the State House in Boston led to a search for the architect's original plans, I have become gradually familiar with their contents, and have believed that material existed for a more complete and permanent memorial.

My grandfather was not only a builder with wood and stone. For twenty years, as chairman of the selectmen, he stood at the head of the town government of Boston, called by Henry Cabot Lodge "the most famous municipal organization of America," and contributed his share towards moulding its character and institutions, so that an historic interest, apart from his artistic career, attaches to his name. Senator George F. Hoar has written, in an address delivered before the Worcester Fire Society in 1893: "If the artist who fashions a

great statue, or who paints a great picture, leave behind him an enviable fame and a fragrant memory, surely the men who have helped fashion and adorn a great city, who have laid its foundations and builded its walls, who have given it its character and guided the currents of its history, who have made Boston Boston and Worcester Worcester, have a far better title to grateful remembrance."

In the preparation of this volume I have made use of a narrative written by my father, Rev. S. G. Bulfinch, twenty-five years ago, at the request of the Boston Society of Architects, and published in the *Daily Advertiser* of February 20, 1869, under the title "Our First Architect"; and also of the papers referring to my grandfather in the "Memorial History of Boston," vol. iv., prepared by Mr. Charles A. Cummings, and in the *New England Magazine* for November, 1890, by Mr. Ashton R. Willard. The episode of the discoveries on the northwest coast was frequently alluded to in my childhood, but I find slight mention of it in the letters, and am therefore indebted to the graphic description of Rev. Edward G. Porter. A recent number of the *Architectural Review*, vol. iii., No. 3, contains a notice by Mr. Cummings of Mr. Bulfinch's architectural works; and the history of the Massachusetts State House is treated at length by Mr. T. A. Fox in the *American Architect* for June 29, 1895.

I have printed practically entire, although in separate sections, the autobiographical sketch that Charles Bulfinch left, in his own compact and even handwriting, and I have given selections from his letters and those of other members of the family, with the correspondence relating to his removal to Washington to take charge of the work of completing the capitol.

The gap left in his own correspondence, during the years most heavily burdened with labor and anxiety, is partially filled by his mother's letters, in which we catch sight of his own activities and the life of Boston at that period.

My grandfather died before my birth, but I have been glad to profit by my mother's clear recollections of his personal appearance and way of life when she knew him in his old age.

A very few passages, of a confidential character and of no general interest, have been omitted from Mr. William Lee's letters regarding the position of architect at Washington. No mention is made of Mr. Bulfinch ever meeting Mr. Latrobe, his predecessor, there; but Mr. Lee, who always expresses a high admiration for Mr. Latrobe, remarks on his friendship for my grandfather, a regard which was without doubt cordially reciprocated by the architect from Boston. The story of the building of the capitol at Washington has never been fully illustrated by original documents, and towards this end it is hoped the present volume may make some contribution. (Houghton, Mifflin & Co. $5.)—*Ellen Susan Bulfinch's Preface to "The Life and Letters of Charles Bulfinch."*

On Snow-Shoes to the Barren Grounds.

"YE gods! it was a relief to be started!" The gusto with which these words are uttered by Mr. Whitney, on the edge of the Barren Grounds, with hardships before him that would quench the spirit in most men, is the secret of his having produced a more than readable book about his adventures. He interests not so much by what he tells as by his evident enjoyment of the things he describes. The volume is not, indeed, so much a matter of minute memoranda of the sort dear to sportsmen and

NATIVE "SNOW-GLASSES."

travellers as it is an impression, an enthusiastic celebration of achievements which imply a love of outdoor life even more than a desire to gain specific trophies. Suppose Mr. Whitney had not seen a single specimen of the wood-bison or of the musk-ox, two animals whom he left New York and travelled far into the bitter regions of the Northwest to hunt. He would, nevertheless, have revelled in his journey and made his reader revel with him.

There is nothing more delightful about this book than its preservation of the atmosphere in which its substance was attained. "Wherever I looked," writes Mr. Whitney, as he directs the vision out upon the bleak wastes stretching up to Coronation Gulf and the beginnings of the Arctic Sea, "north, south, east, west— nothing showed but that terrible stretch of silent, grinning white." The last adjective is a little masterpiece, and it is the more striking because it is perfectly plain that Mr. Whitney was not thinking of adjectives when he set it down. He was thinking with all his heart of "the awful ghastliness of the whiteness that encircled us for miles and miles," and he gets the ghastliness itself, the cold, the bitter cold, into his straightforward text. The various episodes of his narrative, his Indian comrades, the animals he saw or killed, stand in an environment so thoroughly their own that the reader is at home with them at once. Mr. Whitney had not only enthusiasm but pluck and endurance to qualify him for his enterprise. He went into training before he left New York, and, though he suffered extremely, his strength held out to the end, bringing him triumphantly home.

The bulk of Mr. Whitney's book is provocative of the quickest sympathy, for it is full of hearty enjoyment, it is wholesome, plucky, and brimming over with cold northern air. The record is of an excessively difficult task successfully performed, and the reader will find himself taking a personal interest in Mr. Whitney's exploits and good fortune before he has turned half a dozen pages. (Harper. $3.50.)—*N. Y. Tribune.*

A WAR-BONNET.

Spring Notes from Tennessee.

MR. BRADFORD TORREY is an ornithologist of distinguished merit, who, looking out for his birds, visits the great battlefields of Chattanooga, Missionary Ridge, Lookout Mountain, etc. His attention is called from the raging battles of the past, with their boom of cannon and rattle of musketry, to the chirp and twitter of the birds which he sees in what were once the horrid scenes of human strife. He tells how changed is the aspect of Lookout Mountain. "The place was spoiled, I thought. About the fine inn were cheap cottages, as if one had come to a second-class summer resort; while the lower slopes of the mountain, directly under Lookout Point, on the side toward the city, were given up to a squalid negro settlement, and, of all things, a patent-medicine factory—a shameful desecration, it seemed to me." When talking to a bronzed Confederate veteran, the author suddenly hears the sweet notes of a Bachmans finch, and the soldier's story is entirely lost. So, wandering from place to place, the tourist gives many happy descriptions of the birds. At the conclusion of the volume is a check-list of ninety-three birds found in the neighborhood of Chattanooga from April 27 to May 18 1894. There are a dozen varieties of warblers, with numerous woodpeckers and the mocking - bird. (Houghton, Mifflin & Co. $1.25.)—*N. Y. Times.*

In India.

"IN India," translated from the French of André Chevrillon by William Marchant, is a delightful book to read. In giving it an English dress the author has paid more attention to the substance than to the form and done his best to translate the French sparkle and dramatic vivacity. The result is something new; certainly not ungrammatical, not defiance of grammar, and not at all unpleasing, and it is wonderfully vital. The author looks at things with the eye of an artist, and writes about them as he sees them. His tone is that of sympathetic appreciation, mildly critical occasionally, but in general the tone of a man who has no theories or ideas of his own, but only a vast capacity of absorption for whatever circumambient environment he is plunged in. This is no new recipe for the production of a book that reads well; and certainly it has raised in this case the art of the writer to something like a fascination. Under this lightness of touch is concealed much hard thinking. The mental conditions of the refined and the still uncivilized inhabitants especially is closely studied and in his comparisons between the Hindus and the men of other nations the author shows a wide range of reading and a subtile comprehension of the most differing national characteristics of the races. (Holt. $1.50.)— *The Independent.*

From "On Snow-Shoes to the Barren Grounds."   Copyright, 1896, by Harper & Brothers.

SOUR GRAPES.

From "A Venetian June." Copyright, 1896, by G. P. Putnam's Sons.

AT TORCELLO.

Painting and Dreaming.

GEOFFREY DAYMOND discovered that when he was making believe paint pictures, in the first freshness of early morning, or when he was smoking his after-dinner cigar, in the lingering June twilight, the face that interfered with the one occupation and lent charm to the other, was not framed in golden hair, nor animated with the lively and bird-like intelligence which he found so amusing. And not only was it Pauline Beverly's face, with its softly blending colors, and its quiet, indwelling light, that floated before his mental vision, but he found that he remembered her words, and even the tones of her voice, when the gay and occasionally witty talk of the others had gone the way of mortal breath. He somehow came to associate certain inflections of her voice with the sweet sounds that make the undertone of Venetian life; the plash of the oar, the cooing of doves about the Salute, the bells of Murano, softened in the distance, the sound of the surf beating outside the Lido of a still evening, when one floats far out on the lagoon, and the familiar, every day world seems farther away than those other worlds shining overhead. He speculated a good deal over this new occupation, and more still over the sense of passive content that had come to be associated with it.

For Geof was an active temperament and possessed of but scant talent for repose. This was his first real vacation in seven years, yet in spite of his good resolve to idle away a month in Venice for his mother's sake, he had been on the point of finding an outlet for his surplus energies in that tramp in the Cadore, when—just what was it that had deterred him from carrying out the plan? He believed, at the time, that it was merely the prospect of better acquaintance with the prettiest and brightest girl it had yet been vouchsafed him to meet. As he had since heard May remark—for having once adopted an opinion, she was fond of testing it in more than one direction—it is such a comfort to get hold of anything superlative! He was not aware that the elder sister, who certainly could not claim a single superlative quality, had played any part at all in that first impression; yet the thought of her had gradually come to be the hourly companion of his solitude. And now, for the first time in his life, he found himself luxuriating, not only in solitude but in idleness. (Putnam. $1.)—*From Fuller's "A Venetian June."*

PEACE.

From Lampman's "Lyrics of Earth." (Copeland & Day.)

PEACE, peace.
　　But where?
　　Everywhere.
In the air;
In the torrent's roar
　　And brook's soft sweep;
In things that soar
　　And things that creep;
Where gardens bloom,
　　In desert sand;
Where pine-trees gloom,
　　Where vineyards stand;
In a crowded street,
　　On trackless hill;
In motions fleet
　　And trances still;
In sailing clouds
　　And ocean's green;
In chilly shrouds
　　And bright eyes' sheen;
In noontide bright
And darkest night;
Peace, peace,
　　But where?
　　Everywhere
To him who reads aright.

From "A Venetian June." Copyright, 1896, by G. P. Putnam's Sons.

THE SALUTE.

Cyrus W. Field.

"CYRUS W. FIELD: His Life and Work," by his daughter, Isabella Field Judson, is a carefully compiled narrative, overburdened, as American biographies are apt to be, with a superfluity of trivial detail, lacking in coherency of form, and making but a vague presentation of the more intimate traits of character of the one whose personality it undertakes to portray. It contains, however, in a crude and undigested form, ample material for a definite study of Cyrus W. Field and his career, and in competent literary hands could be made the basis for a really fascinating volume. Only little more than fifty pages are given to the first thirty-eight years of Field's life up to the date of the laying of the first cable. These first four chapters give all due attention to genealogical data, present a few entertaining reminiscences, and derive their chief value from the selections made from Field's early letters relating to his mercantile experiences in New York. Various cable enterprises, in which Field was engaged from 1853 to the close of the war, are the theme of nearly half of the book, and here Mrs. Judson's determination to include every scrap of documentary evidence shows to excellent advantage, for the book gives what is by far the most systematic, exhaustive, and trustworthy account of the laying of the Atlantic cable that has ever been published ; and the finer qualities of Field— his inventive resources, his boundless patience, and his sublime faith in the success of his aims—stand out in a most impressive way. A chapter is given to Field's work in behalf of rapid transit in New York, to his participation in the Pacific cable scheme, and still another to his last days, in which eulogies pronounced at the time are freely quoted. Mrs. Judson's account of her father's personal traits fills just a page and a half of the volume. (Harper. $2.) — *The Beacon.*

From "Cyrus W. Field."   Harper & Brothers.
(Copyright, 1896, by Isabella Field Judson.)
CYRUS W. FIELD.
[From the portrait in photogravure.]

In Homespun.

IT is many a long day since we had the pleasure of reading and reviewing a volume of stories so much to our taste as "In Homespun," by Mrs. E. Nesbit. For the most part Mrs. Nesbit is content to dwell among themes devoid of extravagant tragedy, and in her hands the simple annals of poor folk in Kent are made to yield a plentiful supply of pleasure, being full of tenderness and truth to nature. Nothing could be more wholesome and contenting than the matter and manner of the tale which holds the place of honor in this book. It is entitled "The Bristol Bowl," and it tells us of the strange device whereby Jane's Aunt Maria was kept from the knowledge of Jane's misfortune with the treasured piece of old ware. Each of the three chief personages in the story is drawn with skill. There is no hesitation in Mrs. Nesbit's analysis of character, no false deductions, no tendency to spend undue time in elaboration. Her touch is firm and final, with the result that we are persuaded at once. Very little of bloodshed finds room in this volume, the title of which at once suggests mildness of conduct, but when Mrs. Nesbit is obliged to use the knife she is not found wanting. In "Barring the Way" the death of Ellen's callous seducer is put before us both strongly and temperately, without the authoress smacking her lips over a lot of gruesome details, as is the way of many who try to extract bread and cheese by penning fiction. The loves of young people come thickly into these Kentish memorials, and we have the usual number of kisses given, of regrets experienced, of obstacles surmounted, and of eventual babies. Wherever we turn in "In Homespun" we discover reasons for applause, and we can safely recommend Mrs. Nesbit's contribution to the *Keynotes Series* as one of the most refreshing. (Roberts. $1.) — *London Literary World.*

Charles Gounod.

THESE memoirs, which extend from the early youth of Gounod down to the time of the first production of his opera "Faust," reveal an intellect uncommonly keen and versatile. Much of their charm arises from the many-sidedness of the great master's genius, which renders him equally entertaining in the rôles of literary and art critic and musician. When it became necessary to choose a profession, Gounod's talent for drawing claimed notice. M. Ingres, director of the French Academy in Rome, urged his pupil to discard music and develop his taste for color and form ; but the youth's preference was for music, which he loved and understood as a mere child. He describes vividly his first rapt hearing of Rossini's "Othello," which transformed the schoolboy into an incipient composer. Mozart's "Don Juan" added to the exhilaration of purely musical delight, a knowledge of true expression and perfect beauty combined. Rome seemed, at first, unattractive to Gounod ; and it offered no musical advantages outside the Sistine Chapel. But in the end he awoke fully to the interest of the Italian cities, and some of his most brilliant writing is descriptive of the scenery and the famous galleries of Florence, Naples, and Venice. The artist's sojourn in Italy and Germany saw the rise of his fame as a composer of masses. In Rome he met Madame Henzel, who played for him many of the

From " Memoirs of an Artist."   Copyright, 1896, by Rand,
McNally & Co.

CHARLES FRANÇOIS GOUNOD.

masterpieces of German music, and when he went to Leipzig he bore a letter of introduction to Mendelssohn, whose attentions he acknowledges with much feeling. In relation to his own works Gounod writes but little, and that is generally in praise of some other genius, as when he alludes to the power of Goethe's "Faust," a copy of which he carried with him constantly, in the seventeen years wh·ch elapsed before he completed his opera. A noticeable trait in the writer is the genuine modesty shown in his habit of effacing himself out of love for the theme which he discusses. The tone of the original has been faithfully preserved by the translator, Miss Annette E. Crocker. (Rand, McNally & Co. $1.25.) — *Philadelphia Press.*

Briseis.

WHEN we take up a new novel by Mr. Black we are at least not in a state of alarmed expectation of violent surprises. We know fairly well what we may look for. There will be a certain amount of yachting, or salmon-fishing, or both; for he, too, like Mr. Lang, is endowed " with ink-pot and with rod," nor are the two ever very far apart. We have seen so much of him on the heather that we find an occasional visit to London a trifle refreshing; and in " Briseis," though the salmon and the stag are pursued as hotly as of yore, we are allowed to spend some time amid metropolitan excitements. Among these come a visit to a club of " advanced " ladies, and therein an encounter with a very startling poetess of passion, the memory of whom almost induces us to retract our opening words. There is, also—for Mr. Black is quite literary in this book—a formidable critic who, we hope, is not drawn from life. But these are episodes.

The story opens attractively with the delightful Briseis, half Greek, half Scotch, rambling over the hills in attendance on her old uncle and his passion for botany. . . .

Let us be reassuring before we close; at the worst the book reads well, and these constructive defects are more apparent on subsequent reflection. Moreover, there are several exceedingly good situations, one or two of them good enough to outweigh several faults. Exceptionally sure and firm is the treatment of the difficult situation where Briseis, driven frantic by the persecution of the blackmailer, goes in her innocence direct to Gordon's chambers to clear herself before him. The whole scene, from the moment when the excellent aunt walks in, and by intuition says exactly the right thing without the hesitation of a second, is little short of masterly. On the whole, then, any one who has not read one of Mr. Black's novels for a year or so, and will promise not to be too critical with this, can be safely trusted to read "Briseis" with considerable pleasure. (Harper. $1.75.)—*The Critic.*

sions, and ought not to have been found in a work so painstaking and generally acceptable as Mr. Martin's undoubtedly is. (Holt. $1.25.) —*The Dial.*

From "Briseis"　　　　　　　　　　　Copyright, 1896, by Harper & Brothers

SHE FOLLOWED THE DIRECTION OF HIS FINGER.

On Parody.

MR. A. S. MARTIN'S book "On Parody" takes us into one of the pleasant byways of literature, giving us a historical essay upon the subject and an abundant sheaf of illustrative examples. Parody, like all other literary forms, began with the Greeks, and the author of the "Batrachomyomachia" was, in a sense at least, the first great parodist. Aristophanes, of course, revelled in parody, and numerous others of the ancients tried their hands at it. It is extremely interesting to trace the influence of this literary form down through the Middle Ages to modern times, and Mr. Martin has pursued the task with industry and a keen scent. His examples are taken from a wide range of English poetry, but we are surprised to find that they do not include what are unquestionably the best parodies in the language —those published by Mr. Swinburne in his "Heptalogia." This is all the more surprising from the fact that Mr. Martin quotes from the "Heptalogia" in his prefatory essay, so that he cannot be charged with ignorance of its existence. Calverley, too, although quoted from, is not illustrated by his best work, "The Cock and the Bull." These are serious omis-

Out of Bounds.

"OUT of Bounds," by A. Garry, which is further described as being "The Adventures of an Unadventurous Young Man," is a brief and very amusing little story, in which the vagaries of "young Mr. Stephen Ayres" are duly set forth. Stephen Ayres is a particularly correct young man of influential middle-class position and exceedingly wealthy. His life is lived in an atmosphere of business, social ties, and benevolent cares. For the purposes of the story he kicks over the traces for a brief two days, and contrives to get more excitement out of the revolt than falls to the lot of many men in a whole twelve-month. "Out of Bounds" is brief, pithy, and pleasant; it abounds in humorous situations and happy developments, with just a touch of wholesome sentiment in it to hold it together and give consistency to the breezy freshness of the adventures of this particularly unadventurous young man. (75 c.) "Wisdom's Folly," by A. V. Dutton ($1), is, we are told, "a study in feminine development." We discover for ourselves that it is a bright and sympathetic study of female life, darkened for a time, but brightened again at the close. (Holt.)—*London Literary World.*

Bicycling for Ladies.

BRENTANO'S publishing house has issued Maria E. Ward's "Bicycling for Ladies," profusely illustrated and crammed full of knowledge. The author modestly disclaims any attempt to treat her subjects exhaustively, but says she has endeavored to place them comprehensively before her readers. She has gone deeply enough into the various laws which affect the bicyclist to arouse one's admiration at the thoroughness of her information. She says : " The needs of the bicyclist are an intelligent comprehension of the bicycle as a machine, an appreciative knowledge of the human machine that propels it, and a realization of the fact that rider and bicycle form one combined mechanism. For this a knowledge of the laws that determine the limits and possibilities of both mechanisms is necessary. Moreover, the cyclist is limited not only by laws physiological and mechanical which determine when and for how long he may travel, but he is restricted by the laws and ordinances of county, town, and village as to how and where he may travel. A knowledge of these laws is also necessary." Miss Ward dissects the wheel inch by inch, and puts it together again, explaining as she goes in a way that is positively startling. One really ought to be able to learn even to make a bicycle by reading this book, not to mention taking complete care of one. She has a chapter for beginners, one on dress, discusses all the problems that are likely to come up, lectures on tools and their use, all with the same decisive air. Her hints on temporary repairs are especially valuable, covering as they do almost every possible accident. (Brentano's. $1.50.) — *Springfield Republican.*

The Flaw in the Marble.

"THE Flaw in the Marble" is another story of human disappointment and unsatisfied desires. It is French in character and setting, and deals with artistic life in Paris, in the course of which the unfolding of the love-tragedy of a clever but morbid and somewhat boorish young sculptor is portrayed with considerable skill and vigor. At first Paul Lanthony is an artist to the exclusion of everything else; nature exists solely to be interpreted on canvas, and humanity is troublesome and offensive except it lends itself to the conception of ideals in marble. A beautiful actress, an enigma to her acquaintances and a stumbling-block in the lives of all men who are brought into contact with her, awakens him to a perception of life's possibilities. The woman seems to love him, and when he is supposed to be dying she acknowledges as much. This declaration is more powerful than the skill of all the doctors; but when the confession has worked its purpose she denies its reality as the outcome of a fevered brain and a disordered imagination. Paul's remedy is small, but delightfully human; he buys back the masterpiece which, inspired by her beauty and his love, has brought him fame, and attacks it savagely with a coal-hammer until marble splinters are all that remain of the "Circe" that a few months before all Paris was talking of. After that he returns to his first love, Art and the old Greek masters, and the lady dies at Vienna, an enigma still. The book is a dainty volume, and has the advantage of some clever illustrations scattered amongst its pages. (Stokes. 75 c.)—*London Literary World.*

American Summer Resorts.

As the first of a projected series of monographs on *American Summer Resorts* comes a brilliantly written little volume on "The North Shore of Massachusetts," by Robert Grant, illustrated by W. T. Smedley. It was not to be expected that Judge Grant would do anything in the guide-book way in dealing with a subject like this, and in fact what he gives is really a series of impressionistic sketches, in which the scenic qualities and social characteristics of the different localities between Nahant and the end of Cape Ann are set forth with the fine comprehension of one to the manor born and the felicitous expressiveness of the genuine literary artist.

It is suggested that the casual observer may be wrong in supposing that the only subjects of really vital importance on the North Shore are horses and yachts, but Judge Grant is perfectly willing to acknowledge that there are but scant indications in the region under notice of the frivolity that gives a frankly human aspect to Newport and Bar Harbor. It may be that this absence of the volatile features of American summer resort life generally is due to a certain spirit of self-complacent exclusiveness, but there is undoubtedly something in Judge Grant's contention that the people who have settled the North Shore have done so, not to fulfil social obligations or ambitions, but to make themselves and their families supremely comfortable, on a stretch of coast which in natural beauty and acquired advantages has not its like in the world. The book is handsomely printed and Mr. Smedley's illustrations are all that could be desired.

The second volume is "Newport," by W. C. Brownell, with illustrations by W. S. Vanderbilt Allen ; and the other volumes already in preparation cover "Bar Harbor," by F. Marion Crawford, with illustrations by C. S. Reinhart ; and "Lenox," by George A. Hibbard, with illustrations by W. S. Vanderbilt Allen. (Scribner. *ea.*, 75 c.)—*The Beacon.*

From "The North Shore of Massachusetts." Copyright, 1896, by Charles Scribner's Sons.

"I WILL STEER."

The Tale of Balen.

THE character of Balen of Northumberland is one of the weirdest in Arthurian legend. His deeds lie on the surface of life, as is the case with most of the knights of Camelot ; and his prowess, though marvellous, is not supernatural. He is not mysterious as Merlin is mysterious. Yet Arthur's seer himself is not more forbiddingly attractive than the hero whom Mr. Swinburne has taken from Malory as the central figure for his latest book. On Balen's face there is flung at the beginning shadow of a great doom ; all the incidents of his brief career, as they are recorded in the second book of the "Morte Darthur," make for a sinister conclusion; and not all the poetry of Malory's romance, not all the romance of Mr. Swinburne's poetry, can remove the atmosphere of gloom which hems round their knight. That Balen should exert the charm which is unquestionably his is partially due to the beauty inherent in a tragic fate, but it is rooted still more deeply in the wildwood magic of the time and place in which his days were set. Mr. Swinburne was wise in choosing the unfortunate knight of the two swords for his theme, and in taking his reader back into the world of "golden-tongued romance," Arthur's world, the world that is so old and yet ever new.

The rhymed measures in which the poet has worked do not belong to the literature of the ballad, accurately speaking ; but he has evidently sought the ballad rhythm, the reiterative music which fits as no other the conditions of adventurous narrative. In employing that music, moreover, he has avoided more successfully than some of his later work might have seemed to promise, the rigidity of feeling, the opacity of tone which an inelastic arbitrary metre so often brings upon a poet's head. What he has to say fills out the swinging lines, ardent sympathy makes them supple, and they illustrate in a degree that power of verse which means an exact balance between thought and expression. Mr. Swinburne's faculty of characterization, which is so frequently invalidated by his lyrical madness, in the present instance keeps pace with the movement of his verse.

This being so, it is for a moment puzzling that the poem as a whole should leave one cold. With all his gifts, with all his opulence of fine resonant words, Mr. Swinburne is not Malory. There is so much that is alert, clear, and ringing in Mr. Swinburne's verse that for a few pages it seems as if he had actually inhaled the deep breaths of the sea and the forest that he celebrates in swift, spontaneous, tactfully alliterative lines. Then the light fades, and the reader goes back to Caxton's text—not that he loves Mr. Swinburne less, but that he loves Malory more. (Scribner. $1.)—*N. Y. Tribune.*

Footpaths in America.

MR. BURROUGHS — especially when he is published in the dainty little Douglas duodecimos—is one of the authors whose books a busy man reserves for a pocket-luxury of travel. So it was that, a belated reader, I came across his lament over our pathlessness, some years after my having had a hand—or a foot, as you might say—in the making of a certain cross-lots footway which led me to study the windings and turnings of the longer country-sidewalks until I got the idea of writing "The Story of a Path." I am sorry to contradict Mr. Burroughs, but, if there are no footpaths in America, what becomes of the many good golden hours that I have spent in well-tracked woodland ways and in narrow foot-lanes through the wind-swept meadow-grass? I cannot give these up ; I can only wish that Mr. Burrows had been my companion in them.

A footpath is the most human thing in inanimate nature. Even as the print of his thumb reveals the old offender to

From Bunner's "Jersey Street and Jersey Lane." Copyright, 1896, by Charles Scribner's Sons.

A REST FOR THE FOOT-SORE.

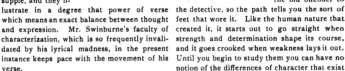

the detective, so the path tells you the sort of feet that wore it. Like the human nature that created it, it starts out to go straight when strength and determination shape its course, and it goes crooked when weakness lays it out. Until you begin to study them you can have no notion of the differences of character that exist among footpaths. One line of trodden earth seems to you the same as another. But look ! Is the path you are walking on fairly straight from point to point, yet deflected to avoid short rises and falls, *and is it worn to grade?* That is, does it plough a deep way through little humps and hillocks something as a street is cut down to grade? If you see this path before you, you may be sure that it is made by the heavy shuffle of workingmen's feet. A path that wavers *from* side to side, especially if the turns be from one bush to another, and that is only a light trail making an even line of wear over the inequalities of the ground—that is a path that children make. The path made by the business man—the man who is anxious to get to his work at one end of the day, and anxious to get to his home at the other—is generally a good piece of engineering. This type of man makes more paths in this country than he does in any other. He carries his intelligence and his energy into every act of life, and even in the half-unconscious business of making his own private trail he generally manages to find the line of least resistance in getting from one given point to another. (Scribner. $1.25.)—*From Bunner's "Jersey Street and Jersey Lane."*

Eliza Pinckney.

" In ending this account of the life and labors of this Southern matron of the old time, I cannot refrain from saying one word in behalf of the bygone civilization, and especially of the class which she exemplified. It was, as we are often told, indolent, ignorant, self-indulgent, cruel, overbearing. Does this life (and such were the lives of many) show these faults? Is it not, rather, active, useful, and merciful, accepting without hesitation the conditions it found, and doing its utmost to make those conditions good?

" If I have succeeded in making this plain, then I have not written in vain. The women of all the colonies had committed to them a great though an unsuspected charge; to fit themselves and their sons to meet the coming change (self-government) in law and soberness; not in riot and anarchy, as did the unhappy women of the French Revolution.

" Those of the Southern States had more to do. They had to train and teach a race of savages—a race which had never known even the rudiments of decency, civilization, or religion; a race which, despite the labors of colonists and missionaries, remains in Africa to-day as it was a thousand years ago; but a race which, influenced by these lives, taught by these Southern people for six generations, proved in the day of trial the most faithful, the most devoted of servants, and was declared in 1863 by the Northern people worthy to be its equal in civil and political rights."

Thus Mrs. Ravenel concludes her admirable little biography of a woman from whom she is justly proud to claim descent. Eliza Pinckney did none of those things which the world is wont to call great, but she was the mother of great men and a woman of a type to which this nation owes much. In the bitter days when the fight against slavery was on, it used to be the custom here in the North to ascribe South Carolina's acknowledged fertility in statesmanship to the fact that she had a leisure class

which owed its being to the existence of "the peculiar institution." The effect was credited to the wrong cause. It existed not by virtue of but in spite of slavery. Plantations cultivated by bond labor required the most careful of superintendence, and, if the men of the ruling class had not been blessed with assistants far more faithful and painstaking than the best of salaried overseers, they would have found no time to devote to statecraft; their wives and mothers were the real directors of South Carolina's industries, for it was to the women that the practical management of the plantations was left, and the wonderful prosperity which the State enjoyed, up to the moment of her great political mistake, shows how intelligently the work was done. The task of watching the actual tilling of the fields might be left to overseers, but the training of the laborers and the

THROUGH THE RICH MAN'S COUNTRY.

control of the finances were almost exclusively in the hands of these women.

Mrs. Ravenel deserves both praise and thanks for the workmanlike manner in which she has fulfilled her pious task. There is a womanly strength in her literary touch which admirably

From "The Victory of Ezry Gardner." Copyright, 1896, by
T. Y. Crowell & Co.

WITH THE SWEET EXPANSE OF THE MOORS
ABOUT THEM.

suits the subject. Her book is fully the equal
of its predecessors in a most interesting series,
and to say that is to pass a very high en-
comium; for Alice Morse Earle's "Margaret
Winthrop" and Maude Wilder Goodwin's
"Dolly Madison" are among the best short
biographies ever written by Americans. (Scribner. $1.25.)—*Boston Saturday Evening Gazette.*

The Victory of Ezry Gardner.

A DELIGHTFULLY told story of the agony suffered by a man who, with the noblest impulses
and the most poetic love of nature and all
things beautiful, was a great physical coward.
The circumstances which led to Ezry's finally
joining the army and the misery of fear he endured while a soldier are told with rare artist
touch.

On one occasion his soul conquered his
body and this is the victory told of in the
story. He rescued a man from drowning and
was rewarded by the admiration of a child.
Love of nature was a passion with Ezry, and
his lonely heart found much solace from the
companionship of a white pony, to whom he
confessed his carefully guarded secret of
cowardice. (Crowell. 75 c.)

White Aprons.

MRS. GOODWIN'S new romance takes us back
to a period in Colonial Virginia somewhat later
than the period to which her "The Head of a
Hundred" related. The latter work belonged
to the era of colonization when the Indian
and the white man were first making each
other's acquaintance. Indeed, one of the stirring episodes of that work pertained to a massacre of the whites. In the present volume
we are on much later, but not less sangui-
nary, ground. Two-thirds of a century have
passed, and royal governors have come and
gone. One royal governor, magnifying his office, now finds himself confronted with rebellion,
puts it down with blood, and then gets recalled
to London.

About this rebellion, which took its name
from the leader, Nathaniel Bacon, runs the
course of this particular history related by Mrs.
Goodwin. The scene opens at Rosemary Hall,
which stood at the head of a winding creek tributary to the York River, and was counted in
its time "the finest mansion in tide-water Virginia." Characteristic of its period was it also,
for its posts and beams "were hewn from the
giant pines of the primeval forest, and were of
a size and thickness to put our modern cardboard frames to shame." Beginning sadly in
such a home, the romance ends happily on a
scaffold. Hero and heroine there meet after a
long separation, the hero having his life saved
through a pardon brought by the heroine from
no less a personage than his sacred majesty,
Charles II.

Not less charming than the colonial scenes
depicted is the description of life in London
which we read—that strangely distorted social
fabric to which the heroine was introduced by
her uncle, our ancient friend, but no hero,
Samuel Pepys. It had been a strange life for
her to enter, even had it been cleaner and
nobler, for of Penelope Payne we are told,
"long of limb was she, with the lithe, far-
reaching stride of some wild thing of the forest
who had never learned the mincing gait of the
civilized world."

How she conducted herself in that social
world, how she was presented to Dryden in the
Abbey, to Charles II. at a masked ball in Whitehall, to Buckingham, to my Lady Castlemaine
and the Duchess of Cleveland, all this is told
and told deftly, accurately as to the period and
cleverly in a literary sense. With "The Head
of a Hundred" we were charmed and surprised.
With "White Aprons" we are charmed and
surprised again. It is a beautiful little story—
sweet and inspiring, not less than clever and
true. (Little, Brown & Co. $1.25.)—*The New
York Times.*

The Unclassed.

GEORGE GISSING'S novels usually treat of some social problem, but one would not say that they are of the morbid kind. One gets the idea rather that his purpose is to show that the debased and the exalted have like longings, like aspirations, like souls. In his novel of "The Unclassed," the heroine is an outcast who is led by her love for a man who has unselfishly befriended her to turn from her old life and to undergo hardship and privation to win his esteem. He, knowing all the circumstances of her life, grows to love her and in the end marries her. Thus, the heroine is something like Tess, but the hero is not an Angel Clare. Neither of the characters is typical. The life led by such a woman as Ida Starr speedily destroys strength of character and refinement. To preserve them argues a rare nature—one of the most opposing qualities. But the principal idea in the book, though it is not obtruded in Sarah Grand's brutal fashion, is that a man risks no more in marrying a woman that has fallen from grace than a woman risks in the very common case of marrying a man who has repeatedly yielded to temptation. The book is written with fine skill, the characters are drawn with power, and are quick with life, and one obtains an inkling of the struggle of the "odd women" in London. George Gissing has made a scientific study of men and women and their relation to the artificial life of the end of the nineteenth century. He is fearless and true, but he has kept the element of hope and lets his readers share it with him. All his stories teach by their influence the great lesson of self-conquest and self-sacrifice. In these days of wild writing about the new woman, her sphere and her mission, it is good to read a dispassionate statement on the woman question. (Fenno. $1.)—*Buffalo Courier.*

In the Valley of Tophet.

"IN the Valley of Tophet" is a really strong volume of semi-detached stories of a coal-mining country, written by Henry W. Nevinson, and is well worth reading. Some of the stories, such as "An Old Red Rag" and "Miss Rachel," are admirable, and "An Anti-Social Offender" is capital throughout, but all contain strong situations and real humor or pathos. Mr. Nevinson has struck quite a new vein, and it is one well worth working. His touch is masterly, and we do not know when we have taken up the work of a totally unknown author and been so struck with his talent and literary skill. Mr. Nevinson is no novice, and it must be that he is a contributor to English magazines which have escaped our notice, for his work is too clean cut to be a first attempt. (Holt. $1.)—*Boston Literary World.*

From Gissing's "The Unclassed."

SHE WOULD SIT FOR HOURS WITH NO COMPANION SAVE HER THOUGHTS.

What They Say in New England.

THOUGH we would not for the world confess it, many of us believe in some superstition or other. Of course we laugh at those who acknowledge that they would not like to pass under a ladder or to sit at table with twelve other persons, but when it comes to the point, do not some of us shun the ladder and use every expedient by which we may avoid the mysterious influence of the number thirteen at the dinner-table? Heartily and rightly we scoff at many an old worn-out superstition, but the glamour of them has still some potency, and impresses us, though we may not be conscious of it. In New England there are many such curious old fancies, as can be seen from a book by Clifton Johnston. In this dainty little book, which is entitled "What They Say in New England," we find an admirable collection of ancient superstitions, many of which are now mere nursery rhymes, but all of which were regarded at one time with more or less awe. We smile now as we read this quaint doggerel and these mystic predictions, and, if we are utter sceptics, we become half angry at the thought that our forefathers guided their lives to some extent in accordance with the rules laid down by these unknown sibyls. Well, any book that makes us smile is welcome in these days, when so many books tempt us to yawn, and if only for this reason, a good word should be said for Mr. Johnston's work. But there is another and a more excellent reason why this little book should be commended. Folk-lore has of late years become a subject of intense interest to many persons, who believe that there is far more significance in it than appears on the surface, and as a contribution to folk-lore this collection of old New England sayings is of no mean value. (Lee & Shepard. $1.25.)—*N. Y. Herald.*

Among the Freaks.

MR. W. L. ALDEN had a happy idea when he started to chronicle the adventures of dime-museum exhibits, "Among the Freaks." It is not Mr. Alden, but the manager of the museum, from whom we hear of the love-affairs, the jealousies, and the heartburnings of the fat woman, gorilla, living skeleton, dwarf, Abyssinian giant, and the rest of the happy family. And what a life that poor manager led! He was the one in whom all the freaks confided, and on whom they all depended. He had to rescue the dwarf when the fat woman sat down on him; he was the man who saved the gorilla's life after the strong lady had hurled him thirty feet through the air, and he it was who rescued the giant from an elopement upon which the fat woman had determined. There is a great deal of clever, humorous work in "Among the Freaks," but in spots the fun is attenuated. It is not a book one would wish to read through at a sitting, but it would furnish several half-hours of laughter, especially if read aloud. The illustrations are excellent. (Longmans, Green & Co. $1.25.)—*Mail and Express.*

Mrs. Meynell's Selections from Coventry Patmore.

IN making her selections from the works of Coventry Patmore Mrs. Meynell's task has been not merely to copy out for the printer all the loveliest passages to be found in the volume of the poet's writing, but to bring forward only poems and fragments devoted to sorrow and delight. Never had an editor a nobler motive. We shall not be accused of a want of charity if we express a fear that the large majority of those responsible for the birth of anthologies consider the private guinea rather than the advantage likely to accrue to the singing folks who have helped them to make a book. With Mrs. Meynell it is different. Of the several links that join her to Coventry Patmore (we are only referring to the similarity between their spiritual energies) all wise observers are aware. What more becoming than that the younger should strive to win a wider recognition for the greatness of the elder? Mrs. Meynell's desire is to show the world of educated people how much they miss each day that they neglect Coventry Patmore. Eloquent as are her words by way of preface, they have in them not one-thousandth part of the entreaty which is contained in the poems themselves. Strange and little luminaries have been worshipped while the great poetic gods have been passed by. In outrages of this sort it may be seen how history repeats itself. But, after all, the mighty can wait in ironical silence; for their hour must come, and with the rest Coventry Patmore will march into his kingdom. (Scribner. $1.25.)—*London Literary World.*

The Life of James McCosh.

PROF. SLOANE, in the midst of labors connected with the publication of his biography of Napoleon, has been able to turn aside long enough to prepare this memoir of one whom all Princeton men, along with him, may be said truly to revere. The volume, however, is not presented as a critical estimate of Dr. McCosh's life and work; the time has not yet come for that; but as "a permanent record of the facts and dates," such as Princeton men and the general public have naturally desired. Prof. Sloane sets off in an impressive passage the claims which Dr. McCosh has to public interest. "To have seen a century rise and wane," he says: "to have spent threescore years of active, influential life in its very noon; to have moulded in some degree the thought of two generations in three lands; to have shared in Scotland's latest struggle for religious liberty; to have wrought in the great enterprise of Ireland's intellectual emancipation; to have led a powerful educational movement in America, and to have regenerated one of her most ancient universities—these are the titles of James McCosh to public distinction. He was a philosopher, but no dreamer; a scholar, but no recluse; a preacher, but no idealogue; a teacher, but no martinet; he was a thinker, a public leader, and a practical man of affairs."

The record is properly described as "chiefly autobiographical." Dr. McCosh wrote the autobiographical portions of it in his last years, by request of Princeton men. The style is so free and simple as to be almost colloquial. As a piece of writing the work has the charm which simplicity in such matters commonly gives, if joined to the other necessary qualities. One feels that Dr. McCosh might have greatly extended the work, and that its interest would have continued with its length. It is obvious that no special effort was made to make the work exhaustive or finished. Indeed, it comprises such things as the writer might have set forth in conversation with a friend, a stenographer meanwhile taking down the recollections as he proceeded with them. Prof. Sloane has arranged the passages with skill and appreciation, making the book a satisfactory one. The reader will lay it down with a new sense of the strength, the brightness, and the humanity of James McCosh. Much of what Scotland gives to her sons was in him, and, for the good of our land as well as for the good of an older land, it was permitted to come out of him, to bless two generations of young men.

When Dr. McCosh came to Princeton he had passed his fifty-seventh birthday, and yet such was the spirit of consecration in which he came that he accepted his election in these words: "I devote myself and my remaining life under God to old Princeton and the religious and literary interests with which it is identified,

and, I fancy, will leave my bones in your graveyard beside the great and good men who are buried there, hoping that my spirit may mount to communion with them in heaven."

Joseph H. Dulles has provided a bibliography for the volume covering a period of sixty-one years, from the time Dr. McCosh was twenty-two years old until the year of his death. It is arranged chronologically and this constitutes an exposé of his literary life. The list embraces three classes: books, papers read before learned societies, and articles contributed to various periodicals, and distinct pamphlets. (Scribner. *net*, $2.50.)—*N. Y. Times.*

TO THE MEMORY OF DR. JAMES McCOSH.

Che Literary News.

An Eclectic Monthly Review of Current Literature.

EDITED BY A. H. LEYPOLDT.

JULY, 1896.

ROBERT BURNS.

" But yet the light that led astray
Was light from Heaven."

ONE hundred years have gone by since Robert Burns died on July 21, 1796, haunted to the last moment of consciousness by fears of the debtor's prison and despair for the future of his wife and children. Born January 25, 1759, his hard and unsuccessful struggle for the mere necessaries of life was abandoned before he had numbered thirty - seven years.

Many biographies and many papers have been written to explain the short life and account for the outward, wayward way of Robert Burns, and the great army of poets have one and all told us of the great gift of poesy which was entrusted to his untutored keeping.

Thomas Moore was seven years old when Burns was born. Byron was six years old when Burns died. Within forty years Ireland, Scotland, and England had produced the three poets whose verse is always music.

Byron and Moore had great opportunities given them with the royal gift of genius. Burns had nothing but his muse. One and all they failed to reach their highest possibilities; one and all they lacked the foundation of all greatness—the mastery of mental and physical self.

From " Poems of Robert Burns."   Copyright by T. Y. Crowell & Co.

ROBERT BURNS.

Earnest, impartial study of time, circumstances, and special qualities of organization would seem to lead to the opinion that Burns perhaps may be entitled to more lenient judgment than his Irish and English brother poets.

Carlyle has pointed out the great principle in which Burns excelled Byron and Moore—his sincerity, his indisputable air of truth. In his criticism of Lockhart's "Life of Burns," now generally recognized as the best summary of the weakness and strength of Burns as man and poet, Carlyle says: "Here are no fabulous woes or joys; no hollow, fantastic sentimentalities; no wire-drawn repinings, either in thought or feeling ; the passion that is traced before us has glowed in a living heart ; the opinion he utters has risen in his own understanding and been a light to his own steps. He does not write from hearsay, but from sight and experience ; it is the scenes that he has lived and labored amidst that he describes; those scenes, rude and humble as they are, have kindled beautiful emotions in his soul, noble thoughts and definite resolves; and he speaks forth what is in him, not from any outward call of vanity or of interest, but because his heart is too full to be silent. He speaks it in such melody and modulation as he can, 'in homely, rustic jingle,' but it is his own and genuine. This is the grand secret for finding readers and retaining them : let him who would move and convince others, be first moved and convinced himself."

"This may appear a very simple principle, and one which Burns had little merit in discovering. Byron was no common man; yet if we examine his poetry with this view, we shall find it far from faultless. Generally speaking we should say that it is not true. Perhaps 'Don Juan,' especially the latter parts of it, is the only thing approaching to a sincere work he ever wrote, the only work where he showed himself in any measure as he was, and seemed so intent upon his subject as, for moments to forget himself. We recollect no poet of Burns's susceptibility—who comes before us from the first, and abides with us to the last with such a total want of affectation. He is an honest man and an honest writer. In his successes and his failures, in his greatness and his littleness, he is ever clear, simple, true, and glitters with no lustre but his own. It is the poetry of Burns to which we allude."

A celebration of the centenary of his death in loving memory of Burns will attract many this year to Scotland, where, in the places which Burns made famous there will be elaborate ceremonies. At Edinburgh and Glasgow especially there will be programs of memorial exercises that will include literary, musical, and convivial features. By many men of many minds will be retold the well-known story of the poet's birth at Ayr on January 25, 1759, of his childhood, in which he absorbed from his mother the Scotch songs and traditions which he was to preserve for all time for all people; of his youth, when in spite of hard physical toil he was "the gayest, brightest, most fantastic, fascinating being to be found in the world," and of his few short years of manhood when he struggled for daily bread at the most unpoetic, most uncongenial work of an excise customs collector. Perhaps some kindred spirit may give some new reading to the sad story of uncontrolled emotions, desires, and tastes which undermined physical and mental health, and kept a great mind and heart from accomplishing the work for which they were endowed.

The heresies towards the established church, and the biting, sometimes very rough handling of its representatives cannot shock as they did a century ago when they were of such fatal import in Burns's history.

In the beautiful city of Edinburgh it will no doubt be told how Burns came to Edinburgh after the publication of a few poems had saved him from immediate ruin and exile to the West Indies. If only here he could have found a friend who could have comprehended the temptations of his nature and from whom he would have accepted restraint and correction. His exuberant, unbridled nature needed guidance. Coming from almost absolute want into the society for which he had hungered, fêted as a poet, and even more as a prodigy, what wonder that the young ploughman, whose passionate,

pleasure-loving, artistic nature had been thus far starved, should plunge into dissipation and excess. When all has again been told, all excuses made, all inconsistencies accounted for, Burns will remain to those who love him what he has been for one hundred years—a great national poet and a man whose many-sided character brought him much joy and more sorrow.

In view of this coming celebration several more have been added to the almost innumerable editions of Burns. Houghton, Mifflin & Co. have published the first volume of an edition of " The Complete Works of Robert Burns " ed. by W. E. Henley and T. F. Henderson, *Centenary de luxe ed.* In 4 volumes, per volume, $4. The beauty of detail in this edition grows upon one hourly. Longmans, Green & Co. have ready the first two volumes of "Life and Works of Robert Burns," edited by R. Chambers, revised by William Wallace. In 4 v., *ea.*, $2.50; and also "The Poetical Works of Robert Burns," ed. by John Fawside, $1; Frederick Warne & Co., "The National" [*new Centenary ed.*], edited with glossary, notes, etc., really the cheapest edition that can be imagined; and J. B. Lippincott Co. bring out "The Poems, Epistles, Songs, Epigrams, and Epitaphs," edited by James A. Manson [*Kilmarnock ed.*]. 2 v., $2. They already have on their list "The Complete Poetical Works," chronologically arranged, with notes, glossaries, and index, by W. S. Douglas. 3 v., $2.25–$5. T. Y. Crowell & Co. also have "The Complete Works," edited by A. Smith, in their *Red Line Poets*, and to them we are indebted for the above portrait.

THE MASTER'S PEN—A CONFESSION.

In my collection famed of curios
I have, as every bookman knows,
A pen that Thackeray once used.
　　　　To be amused,
I thought I'd " take that pen in hand,"
And see what came of it—what grand
Inspired lines 'twou d write,
　　　　One Sunday night.

I dipped it in the ink,
And tried to think,
　　　　" Just what shall I indite?"
And do you know, that pen went fairly mad :
A dreadful time with it I had.
It spluttered, spattered, scratched, and blotted so,
I had to give it up, you know.
It really wouldn't work for me,
And so I put it down ; but last night, after tea,
I took it up again,
And equally in vain.
　　　　The hours sped ;
　　　　I went to bed,
And in my dreams the pen came up to me and said :
" Here is the list of Asses who have tried
To take up pens the Master laid aside ;
Look thou !" I looked and lo!—perhaps you've
　　guessed—
My name, like Abou Ben's, led all the rest !
　　　　　　　　—From Harper's Weekly.

Dr. Watson Mystifies the Gypsies.

From Groome's "Kriegspiel." (Ward, Lock & Bowden.)

"'WHO are my co-operators?' you will ask, perhaps: I answer, 'Any one, everybody.' If you ask me next, 'What are they?' my answer is, 'Holders of secrets.' Now, there are some who receive secrets *ex officio,* as it were—doc-. tors, confessors, procuresses, lawyers, bankers, telegraph-clerks, and money-lenders. There are others who receive them unofficially—wives, mistresses, valets, ladies'-maids, *id genus omne.* My original bait for most of these is money; afterwards comes in fear of exposure, fear of jail, fear of the gallows, and so forth. Your excellent father, now, there is nothing he would not do for me, because he fears me as a dread magician, and because he knows too that I could consign him to-morrow to Portland, that is, if I felt mercifully disposed. With him the bait was not money, but revenge.

"As to which of all these classes is the most useful, that depends. Doctors might be, unquestionably, but they so seldom will, at least the better class. No, there was one young man of high promise, from whom I looked for great things, and whom I accordingly established in a neighborhood where I had particular need of a co-operator. I advanced him the money for the purchase of his practice; his house was furnished with my money; and on my money he married. Yet, would you believe it, he chose to affect indignation the very first time I put a question, quite an innocent question, to him about one of his patients. *He* had to come under, though, for I had another hold on him than money—ye-e-es.

"Confessors, again, the few whom I have employed, have been men on whose word I could place no kind of dependence. They will tell you this and that about any one, but 'this' will be always false, and 'that' very seldom true.

"Money-lenders, on the other hand, are safe. No man ever goes to a money-lender quite openly: there is always some one he would not wish to know of it. You will have had no dealings with the tribe, but you have probably heard of the mythical 'friend in the City.' . . .

"Then there are the Gypsies: I omitted to mention them, but they fall between the two classes. Themselves most credulous, they are objects of credulity; and their women, as fortune-tellers, are the recipients of numberless secrets. But to me the chief value of the Gypsies is their ubiquity. They may go anywhere, stop any time, and depart at the shortest notice, without exciting surprise or suspicion; and I may visit them in the capacity of doctor, or, disguised as the blackguard who guided you to the encampment, may accompany them in their wanderings. I can disappear in one place, and reappear in another, a hundred, two hundred miles distant. The secret of my power over them, the reason they are willing to serve my ends, is ridiculously simple: I know their language, I can *rokka Romanes.** They guard it jealously, but there is one rare work, from which I acquired a knowledge of its mysteries. The Gypsies, however, have never heard of that work, and so they ascribe my knowledge to omniscience. Yes; I re-

---

* Speak Gypsy.

member the very first Gypsy who ever came to consult me; it is thirty years since now. I challenged him to test me, told him I should know what he said, though he said it in French or Italian. 'But you won't know what *bongo grei* means,' he said, and I answered, 'lame horse'—that Gypsy was an uncle of your father's, Sempronius Stanley. In my grandfather's time—he had hardly any dealings with the Gypsies—they had their 'wise men' dotted all over England and Wales; to-day they have only one, Dr. Robert Watson, to consult whom they would journey from Land's End to John o' Groats. . . .

"Again there are my unintelligent agents: not that the foregoing are by any means always intelligent. There are old newspapers, old magazines, and the like. One time and another I have gone through the whole of the *Annual Register* from its commencement; and whenever I am about to settle in a new place, I always go for some days before to the British Museum, and run over the files of the local newspaper for years and years back, noting down carefully old crimes, old accidents, any strange events generally. In this way I am able to tell men of things that happened in their native place fifty years before, a hundred years before, with a fulness and a precision that amaze them."

Man and Nature.

From Hamilton Mabie's "Essays on Nature and Culture." (Dodd, Mead & Co.)

MAN is incomprehensible without Nature, and Nature is incomprehensible apart from man. For the delicate loveliness of the flower is as much in the human eye as in its own fragile petals, and the splendor of the heavens as much in the imagination that kindles at the touch of their glory as in the shining of countless worlds. Nature would be incomprehensible without her interpreter, whose senses supplement her own wonderful being; whose imagination travels to the far-off boundaries of her activity; whose thought masters and demonstrates her order; whose skill utilizes her forces; and whose patient intelligence brought to bear century after century on her vast and all-embracing life, has not, it is true, uncovered the source of her vitality, but has gone far to discern its methods of manifestation. Man, on the other hand, cannot comprehend a single chapter of his history without appealing to Nature; cannot trace a single developed faculty back to its rudimentary stage without finding Nature present at every step in that evolution and largely directing it; cannot retrace the course of any skill, art, industry, trade, or occupation without coming upon Nature at every turn. The story of his slow rise from barbarism to civilization is very largely the story of his contact with Nature; and when he turns to his inward life and studies the religions, sciences, and arts by which he lives and expresses himself and his energy, he finds Nature everywhere present as the chief influence, the constant companion, or the authoritative and commanding teacher.

This slow education of the race at the foot of Nature is not the only training to which men have been subdued, but it has been so constant, so gradual, so intimate, that by a true process of absorption man has become a part of Nature and Nature a part of man. They have lived together so many thousands of years, and in such substantial unity, that they are no longer separable. They are bound together in the great order or movement of the universe; the inexorable obedience of Nature to the law of her being has become character in her companion and pupil; the beauty of her landscape is reproduced in his arts; the changes of her seasons, which constantly set his life in a new framework, are recorded in his poetry; the majesty, mystery, and order of her manifold life underlie his religions; her products and forces sustain his life, spread the roof over his head, furnish the materials for all his fabrics, and turn the wheels which transform them into things of beauty and of use. All that man is and has done, has depended largely upon his relationship with the sublime power which kindled the stars above the cradle of his infancy, and, now in his maturity, makes him master of forces which are lifting him above drudgery and making him poet, artist, and creator.

A Virginia Grandfather.

From Seawell's "A Strange, Sad Comedy." (Century Co.)

ARRIVED in their seats, which were near the other party, Letty settled herself with an ecstatic air of enjoyment to hear the play. The overture was unmixed delight. So was the first quarter of the first act. But in about ten minutes "the fun began," as Farebrother afterward ruefully expressed it. The play was one of the larkiest descriptions of larky French comedy.

At the first *risqué* situation, Farebrother, whose heart was in his mouth, saw the colonel's eye flash, and an angry dull red creep into his fine old face. Letty was blissfully unconscious of the whole thing, and remained so much longer than the colonel. But when the curtain came down on the first act her cheeks were blazing, and she turned a pair of indignant eyes full on Farebrother, who felt like a thief, a sneak, and a liar. What made Letty blush never frightened her in the least, but simply angered her, so that she was always able to take care of herself. Farebrother, whose ruddy face was crimson, and who struggled between a wild disposition to swear and to laugh, leaned over toward the colonel, and said in an agonized whisper, that Letty caught distinctly:

"For Heaven's sake, colonel, don't think that I brought you knowingly to see this thing. I had never seen it myself, and merely went by the advertisement in the papers."

"Your intentions were no doubt good, my young friend," replied the colonel, stiffly, "but you should exercise greater care in the selection of plays to which you ask innocent young women."

At that Farebrother would have been thankful if the floor had opened and swallowed him up. But Letty had evidently heard his few words of explanation, and they had mollified her. She felt sorry for Mr. Farebrother and pitied his chagrin.

"Nevertheless, sir," continued the colonel, in a savage whisper, "if this sort of thing continues I shall deem it my duty to withdraw my granddaughter."

Farebrother was in an agony, and looking around he saw Mr. Romaine's bright eyes fixed on him gleaming with malicious amusement. Poor Farebrother at that moment was truly to be pitied. But disaster followed disaster, and worse ever seemed to remain behind. The second act was simply outrageous, and Farebrother, although he had more than the average masculine tolerance for *risqué* and amusing plays, was so disconcerted by the colonel's scowl and Letty's discomfort that he fixed his eyes on his programme and studied it as if it were the most fascinating composition he had ever read. Not so the colonel. He kept his attention closely upon the stage, and at one point which brought down the house with roars of laughter and applause, the colonel rose, with a snort, and with a countenance like a thunder-cloud, offering his arm to Letty, stalked down the main aisle of the theatre, with Farebrother, utterly crestfallen, following them. Not only was Farebrother deeply annoyed at having brought his innocent Virginia friends to such a play, but the absurdity of his own position and the illimitable chaff he would have to put up with on account of it at the club and at masculine dinners was a serious consideration with him.

And there was no room for misunderstanding the reason of their departure. The colonel's face was a study of virtuous indignation. Letty was crimson, and her eyes persistently sought the floor, particularly as they passed the Romaine party, while poor Farebrother's hang-dog look was simply pitiable. He glanced wofully at Mr. Romaine and Dr. Chessingham; both of them were grinning broadly, while a particular chum of his, who had an end seat, actually winked and poked a stick at him as he followed his friends out.

In the carriage he laid his hand upon the knee of the colonel, who had maintained a terrible and portentous silence, and said, earnestly:

"Pray, Colonel Corbin, forgive me for my mistake in taking you and Miss Corbin there. Of course I didn't dream that anything would be given which would offend you, and I am more sorry than I can express."

The colonel cleared his throat and responded:

"I can well believe, my dear sir, that your mistake came from the head, not the heart, and as such I fully condone it. But I could not allow my granddaughter to remain and see and hear things that no young girl, or any woman for that matter, should see or hear, and so I felt compelled to take some decisive step. I am prodigiously concerned at treating your hospitable intention to give us pleasure in this manner. But I ask you, as a man of the world, what was I to do?"

Nationality in Smoking.

"HE got up rather late, and promptly marched out upon the terrace under the vines, smoking a brier-root pipe with that solemn air whereby the Englishman abroad proclaims to the world that he owns the scenery. There is something almost phenomenal about an Englishman's solid self-satisfaction when he is alone with his pipe. Every nation has its own way of smoking. There is a hasty and vicious manner about the Frenchman's little cigarette of pungent black tobacco; the Italian dreams over his rat-tail cigar; the American either eats half of his Havana while he smokes the other, or else he takes a frivolous delight in smoking delicately and keeping the white ash whole to the end; the German surrounds himself with a cloud, and, godlike, meditates within it; there is a sacrificial air about the Asiatic's narghileh, as the thin spire rises steadily and spreads above his head; but the Englishman's short brier-root pipe has a powerful individuality of its own. Its simplicity is Gothic, its solidity is of the Stone Age, he smokes it in the face of the higher civilization, and it is the badge of the conqueror. A man who asserts that he has a right to smoke a pipe anywhere practically asserts that he has a right to everything. And it will be admitted that Englishmen get a good deal." (Macmillan. $1.50.)—*From Crawford's "Adam Johnstone's Son."*

Father and Aunt of a New Woman.

From McMahon's "A New Note." (*Fenno*)

" Now, can you not understand, Dora? Don't you see that I dare not, with a temperament like Victoria's, take any other course? With the other girls" (he alluded to his elder daughters) "it did very well, but Victoria is Victoria, and God forbid that I should repeat my mother's mistake with her!"

" But this career! this absurd, preposterous notion of a professional career? I hate it, George! What has your daughter to do with such things?"

" Providence, Dora, I assure you, took no pains to ascertain my wishes on the subject before making me the father of an artist."

" Tut!" with a swift return of her old manner; "let her be an artist as much as she pleases, in private—insist upon its being in private."

" Ah!" that is precisely what an artist can never be. Your artist, Dora, pants for notoriety, popularity, fame."

" I have no patience with such *panting* in a woman; in a man, I suppose——"

" Then a woman should not be an artist?"

" No," said the old lady, popping beautifully into the trap.

" Dora," said her tempter, with inimitable gravity, "you really should have been the author of the universe, and the creator of its creatures."

" Sneer if you like," she retorted, "and as much as you like, but no man ever yet got Dora Payne to see that black was white. I suppose I am out of the way of the world. I am an old woman who, thank God, was brought up in an age which had some respect left for the decencies of life. In these days I find myself completely at fault. No good ever came yet of men and women deliberately renouncing that station of life to which it has pleased God to call them. Oh! you may smile. I dare say it's very amusing indeed to hear an old woman repeating the catechism; only I happen to *believe* in the catechism, and it seems to me that the young men and women of the present day will go anywhere and do anything except their duty in that state of life in which God has placed them."

He smiled broadly, with the warm good-humor which had made for him many friends and preserved him from almost a single enemy.

Nothing pleased him better than a war of words with this redoubtable kinswoman, whose tongue was as a sharp sword while her heart was as a silken cushion.

" My dear Dora!"

" Don't ' my dear Dora ' me!"

" Very well, I won't then. Only let me remind you that, admirable as your contention is, were it carried to its logical conclusion—its *logical* conclusion, Dora—the world would have been deprived of some of its greatest sons and daughters, some of its noblest treasures in every branch of human knowledge."

" Human knowledge," remarked this dreadful old lady, with a perversity of which perhaps only a vigorous feminine mind could be capable, "is well enough in its way, but there are better things than human knowledge. No, you *won't* persuade me! Go and tell the House of Commons that black is white, and evil is good, and I have no doubt it will believe you, that it will be delighted to believe you. But I say, and will always say, that for your daughter to deliberately enter upon a mode of life for which Providence plainly never intended her, thereby to satisfy the caprice or the craving of an unhealthy ambition, is wrong, inexcusable, improper in the highest degree. There, I have done. I dare say "—her voice changed suddenly —"I have said too much. I am laying down the law where I have no business to lay it down. But the child is very dear to me." The break in her voice touched him.

" Look here, Dora," he said, gently, "I agree with you in part. But you will not misunderstand me when I say that the ruling principles of one age do not always meet the requirements of another. When you and I were young, and looked at life as the present generation look at it to-day, our *milieu*, so to speak, was entirely different. The tide of existence has now set in another direction. The best we can do is to fit our young people to sail with it. I won't say that it is better or worse than its predecessor, only that it is different. But it is so, and the generation of to-day must reckon with it. The barriers of civilization and social conditions have widened, and are widening more and more; and after all, if civilization was to be true to its name, if it was to really justify its existence, this must be so. Victoria—to come back from the general to the particular, because that is what concerns us most nearly— is a child of the age, emphatically and perhaps typically so. My other children are not. Edmund belongs to the old order, which you would fain keep within the old rigid boundaries. Perhaps that is a good thing, as he is my eldest son, although——" He paused.

" Edmund," interposed his hearer, "is a respectable noodle; and his wife is a prig—a female prig—starched too, but not blue!"

Mr. Leathley laughed.

Bravo, my cousin! give a woman time, and she will be certain to turn upon her most cherished convictions. I mean to give Victoria time to do likewise.

The Price of the Bristol Bowl.

From Nisbet's "In Homespun." (*Roberts.*)

I was up to my elbows in the suds, 'doing aunt's bit of washing for her, when I heard a step on the brick path, and there was that old gentleman coming round by the water-butt to the back-door.

"Well?" says he. "Anything fresh happened?"

"For any sake," says I in a whisper, "get out of this. She'll hear if I say more than two words to you."

"But," he says in a whisper, "just let me into the parlor for five minutes to have a look around and see what the rest of the bowl is like."

I squeezed my hands out of the suds, and rolled them into my apron, and went in and him after me.

You never see a man go on as he did. It's my belief he was hours in that room, going round and round like a squirrel in a cage, picking up first one bit of trumpery and then another, with two fingers and a thumb, as carefully as if it had been a *tulle* bonnet just home from the drapers, and setting everything down on the very exact spot he took them up from.

More than once I thought that I had entertained a loony unawares, when I saw him turn up the cups and plates and look twice as long at the bottoms of them as he had at the pretty parts that were meant to show, and all the time he kept saying—"Unique, by Gad, perfectly unique!" or "Bristol, as I'm a sinner," and when he came to the large blue dish that stands at the back of the bureau, I thought he would have gone down on his knees to it and worshipped it.

"Square-marked Worcester!" he said to himself in a whisper, speaking very slowly, as if the words were pleasant in his mouth. "Square-marked Worcester—an eighteen-inch dish!"

He had a brown paper parcel with him, a big one, and I thought to myself, "Suppose he's brought his bowl and is wishful to sell it."

"Now, look here," he said, "I want you—I must—oh, I don't know which way to begin, I have so many things to say. I want to see your aunt and ask her to let me buy her china."

"You may save your trouble," I said, "for she'll never do it. She's left her china to me in her will," I said.

The old gentleman put down his brown paper parcel on the porch seat as careful as if it had been a sick child, and said:

"But your aunt won't leave you anything if she knows you have broken the bowl, will she?"

"No," I said, "she won't, that's true, and you can tell her if you like."

"Well," says he, speaking very slowly "if I lent you my bowl, you could pretend it's hers and she'll never know the difference, for they are as like as two peas. I can tell the difference, of course, but then I'm a collector. If I lend you the bowl will you promise and vow in writing, and sign it with your name, to sell all that china to me directly it comes into your possession?"

That was a sad moment for me. I might have taken the bowl and promised and vowed, and then when the china came to me I might have told him I hadn't the power to sell it; but that wouldn't have looked well if any one had come to know of it. So I just said straight out:

"The only condition of my having my aunt's money is, that I never part with the china."

He was silent a minute, looking out of the porch at the green trees waving about in the sunshine over the grave-stones, and then he says:

"Look here, you seem an honorable girl. I am a collector. I buy china and keep it in cases and look at it, and it's more to me than meat, or drink, or wife, or child, or fire—do you understand? And I can no more bear to think of that china being lost to the world in a cottage instead of being in my collection than you can bear to think of your aunt's finding out about the bowl, and leaving the money to your cousin Sarah."

"Well?" I said, for I saw that he had something more on his mind.

"I'm an old man," he went on, "but that need not stand in the way. Rather the contrary, for I shall be less trouble to you than a young husband. Will you marry me out of hand? And then when your aunt dies, the china will be mine and you will be well provided for."

"And the bowl?" I said.

"Of course I'll lend you my bowl, and you shall give me the pieces of the old one. Lord Worsley's specimen has twenty-five rivets in it."

"Well, sir," I said, "it seems to be a way out of it that might suit both of us. So, if you'll speak to mother, and if your circumstances is as you represent, I'll accept your offer, and I'll be your good lady."

IN MEMORIAM—TOM HUGHES.

CLOSE up, close up, as the ranks grow thin,
  As the daylight deepens, the sun goes down!
Though faint and bleeding, too few to win,
  We may help others to wear the crown.

Ah, fatal shot! Did ye mark that fall?
  'Twas he, O brothers, strong heart, true brain;
And a splendid fighter; his breezy call
  Rang forth, and the world grew young again;

With the boys at battle, the boys at play,
  In the old School-close, 'neath the old School-bell,
And the great old Master, who led the fray
  With the earnest brow and the sacred spell;

All fighters, all—and there's one more gone,
  With his gallant bearing, his lofty crest;
And we must not stay, for the fight goes on;
  This world is for fighting, the next for rest.

So, just one look as we pass him by!
  And just one tear as we turn the sod!
And a star the less in a darkened sky!
  And a prayer as we leave his soul with God!

Then close up closer! yet nearer stand,
  As in those school-days that he loved so well,
And fill up the gap, a united band,
  And step in the place where a comrade fell!

And onward still with your faces set
  To the sunbright thought of a younger day!
For a soul is alive in the old world yet,
  And a spirit astir in its bonds of clay.

And all together! Ye shall not fail—
  To doubt were coward, to halt were crime—
With God and with man to uplift the veil,
  And win out light from the gloom of time.

    —A. G. B. *in The Spectator.*

Survey of Current Literature.

☞ *Order through your bookseller.*—"*There is no worthier or surer pledge of the intelligence and the purity of any community than their general purchase of books; nor is there any one who does more to further the attainment and possession of these qualities than a good bookseller.*"—PROF. DUNN.

ART, MUSIC, DRAMA.

EVANS, E. P. Animal symbolism in ecclesiastical architecture; with a bibliography and 78 il. Holt. il. 12°, *net*, $2.

FENOLLOSA, ERNEST F. Mural painting in the Boston Public Library. Curtis & Co. 12°, pap., 25 c.
A critique on Abbey's, Sargent's, and Chavenne's designs.

NAYLOR, E. W. Shakespeare and music; with illustrations from the music of the sixteenth and seventeenth centuries. 12°, (Temple Shakespeare manuals.) $1.25.

BIOGRAPHY, CORRESPONDENCE, ETC.

BRYANT, W. CULLEN. Simms. Putnam. 16°, (Little journeys to the homes of American authors, v. 11, no. 5.) pap., 5 c.

BULFINCH, C. The life and letters of Charles Bulfinch, architect, with other family papers; ed. by his granddaughter, Ellen Susan Bulfinch; with an introd. by C. A. Cummings. Houghton, Mifflin & Co. por. 8°, *net*, $5.

JUDSON, ISABELLA FIELD, *ed.* Cyrus W. Field, his life and work. Harper. il. 12°, $2.

McCOSH, JA. The life of James McCosh: a record chiefly autobiographical; ed. by W. Milligan Sloane. Scribner. por. 8°, *net*, $2.50.

MITCHELL, MARIA. Maria Mitchell: life, letters, and journals; comp. by Phebe Mitchell Kendall. Lee & Shepard. por. 12°, $2.
A memorial of the American astronomer, prepared by her sister, Mrs. Kendall. Maria Mitchell was born in Nantucket, Mass., in 1818, and died June 28, 1889; she was professor of astronomy at Vassar College and was the first woman elected a member of the American Academy of Arts and Sciences. Her strong character and personality and valuable services not only to Vassar College and its pupils, but to women generally, make this volume unusually interesting.

OLIPHANT, *Mrs.* MARG. O. W. Jeanne D'Arc, her life and death. Putnam. il. 12°.(Heroes of the nations ser., no 17.) $1.50; hf. mor., $1.75.

RAVENEL, HARRIOTT HORRY. Eliza Pinckney; with fac-simile reproduction. Scribner. 12°, (Women of Colonial and Revolutionary times, no. 3.) $1.25.

WAERN, CECILIA. John La Farge, artist and writer. Macmillan. il. 8°, (The portfolio, no. 26.) pap., *net*, $1.25.
"Miss Waern has done her work modestly and with very little attempt at criticism. Where it was possible, she has, by extracts from notebooks and published writings, let Mr. La Farge speak for himself. She has made some slight effort to trace the strains of influence that have united in the mature product of his ripe years; but, in the main, she has let the panorama of suggestive facts unroll itself, without obtruding her own impressions upon the spectator, and she could hardly have done more wisely. We should perhaps be grateful that so many reproductions of Mr. La Farge's paintings and windows have been collected for us in this convenient form, and we are certainly not prepared to say that they are not valuable as memoranda. But so much is lost in losing the color and personal touch that, while the reality is close at hand or even clear in memory, the reproduction is an aggravation rather than a joy."—*N. Y. Times.*

DESCRIPTION, GEOGRAPHY, TRAVEL, ETC.

BROWNELL, W. C. Newport; il. by W. S. Vanderbilt Allen. Scribner. il. map, 16°,(American summer resorts, no. 2.) 75 c.

CORNEY, PETER. Voyages in the northern Pacific. Honolulu, H. I., T. G. Thrum. 12°, $1.25.
Narrative of several trading voyages from 1813 to 1818 between the northwest coast of America, the Hawaiian Islands, and China, with a description of the Russian establishments on the northwest coast, interesting early account of Kamehameha's realm, manners and customs of the people, etc., and a sketch of a cruise in the service of the Independents of South America in 1819; with preface and appendix of valuable confirmatory letters prepared by W. D. Alexander. This narrative, reprinted from the *London Literary Gazette* of 1821, is now published in a separate form for the first time.

GRANT, ROB. The north shore of Massachusetts; il. by W. T. Smedley. Scribner. 16°, (American summer resorts, no. 1.) map, 75 c.

MAURY, NANNIE BELLE. Whalers and whaling. H. S. Hutchinson & Co. il. obl. 12°, *net*, $1.
The whale ship as it starts out on its voyage, the life aboard her, and her appearance as she returns home are the subjects of this little sketch.

RIDEING, W. H. At Hawarden with Mr. Gladstone, and other transatlantic experiences. Crowell. 16°, $1.
Seven papers, of which the first gives title to the book. The others are called: A run ashore at Queenstown; The route of the Wild Irishman; Quaint old Yarmouth; Law, lawyers, and law-courts; The House of Commons; Old and new on the Atlantic.

WHITNEY, CASPAR W. On snow-shoes to the Barren Grounds: 2800 miles after musk-oxen and wood-bison. Harper. il. 8°, $3.50.

EDUCATION, LANGUAGE, ETC.

HINSDALE, BURKE AARON. Teaching the language-arts, speech, reading, composition. Appleton. 12°.(International education ser., no. 34.) $1.
"The book is a collection of fine thoughts on language—its use, its growth, the study of its

mechanics, its grammatical and logical structures, the order of mastering its use in speaking, reading, and writing—first in the primary, next in the grammar school, and after in the high school and college; its place in the cultivation of the powers of thought, the study of literary works of art, the significance of philology among the sciences."—*Preface.*

FICTION.

ALLEN, JA. LANE. Summer in Arcady: a tale of nature. Macmillan. 16°, $1.25.

ANDREAE, PERCY. The vanished emperor. Rand, McNally. 12°, $1.25.
The German Emperor William II. is introduced as Willibald II. the Arminian Emperor. The rumor goes through Brandenburgh (Berlin) that the emperor has disappeared. The complications which ensue, owing to the young monarch's idiosyncrasies, self-will, and misunderstood government policies, are set before the reader with knowledge of the various perils which threaten Germany if at any moment any catastrophe should befall the Kaiser. There is only the form of fiction. It is a study in German political history as controlled by William II.

BALZAC. HONORE DE. Gobseck; tr. by Katharine Prescott Wormeley. Roberts. 12°, hf. rus., $1.50.
Contents: Gobseck; The secrets of the Princesse de Cadignan; Unconscious comedians; Another study of woman; Comedies played gratis. These scenes from Parisian life are included in Balzac's "The comedy of human life." Gobseck is a miser. The study of women is a treatise on what the French mean by " *une femme comme il faut.*"

BARLOW, JANE. Mrs. Martin's Company, and other stories. Macmillan. 12°, (Iris ser.) 75 c.

BELL, LILIAN. The under side of things: a novel. Harper. por. 12°, $1.25.
By the author of " Love-affairs of an old maid." A pleasant story of West Point and the town of Stockbridge, Pennsylvania, in which love and marriage have a large part.

BLACK, W. Briseis: a novel; il. by W. T. Smedley. Harper. 12°, $1.75.

BLAND, *Mrs.* HERBERT, ["Edith Nesbit,"*pseud.*] In homespun. Roberts. 16°, (Keynotes ser., no. 22.) $1.
Contents: The Bristol bowl; Barring the way; Grandsire Triples; A death-bed confession; Her marriage lines; Acting for the best; Guilty; Son and heir; One way of love; Coals of fire.

CLARK, IMOGEN. The victory of Ezry Gardner. Crowell. il. 16°, 75 c.

CRANE, STEPHEN. George's mother. Arnold. 12°, 75 c.

CRANE, STEPHEN. Maggie: a girl of the streets. Appleton. 12°, 75 c.
"The conviction is forced upon one that by writing ' Maggie' Mr. Crane has made for himself a permanent place in literature. It matters not if he continues to grind out grotesque verse and slipshod short stories. These may injure him temporarily so far as money returns are concerned. But it is enough that he has written ' Maggie'—one of the most powerful, terrible,

and hideous studies of the dregs of humanity that have been produced in the English language."—*Henry Edward Rood in the Mail and Express.*

DOUGALL, LILY. The Madonna of a day. Appleton. 12°, (Appleton's town and country lib., no. 194.) $1; pap., 50 c.

DUTTON, A. V. Wisdom's folly: a study in feminine development. Holt. 16°, $1.
The rector of a rural parish in England, devoted to the collecting of early editions and materials for a history of early printing, had seven children—two sons and five daughters. Miss Romeston, the second daughter, for years had charge of the busy household and was her father's standby in all his "isms" and "specialties." When she and all the world had given her over to spinsterhood she married the owner of the park and estate of Chesney. Her married life proved full of dangers.

ESLER, E. RENTOUL. The way they loved at Grimpat: village idylls. *Authorized ed.* Holt. 12°, $1.
Contents: Kitty; Eunice; Linnet's lover; Naomi; Good for nothing; Betty's luck; Alice; Daisy Wynn; Bessie.

GARRY, A. Out of bounds: being the adventures of an unadventurous young man. Holt. 1 il., nar. 16°, buckram, 75 c.

HAMILTON, M. A. Across an Ulster bog. Arnold. 12°, $1.
"An interesting story of the North of Ireland. The author is familiar with the dialect and customs of the district whence he has drawn his plot, and with the party spirit which has now existed for over 200 years. Though inferior in humor to the admirable tales of Carlton, there is much in the book to remind us of that most original of Ulster chroniclers. We are introduced to the northern peasant in his true colors, so totally at variance with the Irishman of fiction and of the stage, and we are touched by the true pathos, the keynote of these who are at once the most humorous and the saddest of the nations of the earth."—*N. Y. Herald.*

HENEY, T. The girl at Birrell's: a pastoral of the Paroo: an Australian story. Ward, Lock & Bowden, Ltd. il. 12°, $1.
The scene is laid in the western division of New South Wales on a huge sheep-raising estate worked as two separate stations. The heroine is a pretty, illiterate girl, the daughter of a man keeping a public-house, and is the barmaid of the place. A good picture of Australian life.

HICHENS, ROB. S. The folly of Eustace, and other stories. Appleton. 12°, 75 c.
Contents: The folly of Eustace; The return of the soul; The collaborators.

HONOR ORMTHWAITE: a novel; by the author of "Lady Jean's vagaries." Harper. 12°, $1.

HUME, FERGUS W. The dwarf's chamber, and other stories; il. by Percy F. S. Spence, James Greig, and others. Ward, Lock & Bowden, Ltd. il. 12°, $1.
Contents: The dwarf's chamber; Miss Jonathan; The dead man's diamonds; The tale of the turquoise skull; The green-stone god and the stockbroker; The justice and the Mexican

coin; The rainbow Camellia; The ivory leg and the twenty-four diamonds; My cousin from France.

JENNINGS, MARY ELIZ. Asa of Bethlehem and his household, B.C. IV.–A.D. XXX. A. D. F. Randolph & Co. 12°, $1.25.
The story of the life of Jesus Christ told in the form of fiction. Based chiefly on Edersheim's "Life and times of Jesus the Messiah" and Andrews's "Life of our Lord."

KOCH, RICHERT V. Camilla: a novel; from the Swedish and Danish; il. by Edmund H. Garrett. Crowell. 12°, $1.25.
The scene is laid in Stockholm. Camilla is a Danish girl, highly educated, who startles the Crusenborg family, who are staid conservative and aristocratic Swedes, with her heresies on all social and religious topics. She shows character and heart. As a foil to Camilla, Anna Crusenborg shows the same strength of character by joining the Salvation Army. Some of the scenes in which the girls do good give valuable details of domestic Swedish life.

LILLARD, J. F. B., *ed.* Poker stories, as told by statesmen, soldiers, lawyers, etc.; embracing the most remarkable games, 1845–95. E. P. Harper. 12°, $1; pap., 50 c.
Stories and anecdotes relating to the game of poker, arranged under the following chapter headings: Stories told of statesmen; Mississippi river stories; Stories told from the effete east; Stories from the wild and woolly west; Pacific coast stories; Stories of war-times; Stories of high stakes, superstitions, and hoodoos; Told at the Ananias Club, etc.

LOW, C. R. Tales of old ocean. *New ed.* Warne. il. 12°, $1.

MARSHALL, *Mrs.* EMMA. An escape from the tower: a story of the Jacobite rising of 1715. Macmillan. 12°, $1.25.

MEREDITH, *Mrs.* KATHARINE MARY CHEEVER, ["Johanna Staats," *p eud.*] Green Gates: an analysis of foolishness. Appleton. 16°, $1.25.

MONTRÉSOR, FRANCES FREDERICA. False coin or true? Appleton. 16°, $1.25.

MONTRÉSOR, FRANCES FREDERICA. Worth while. Arnold. 16°, 75 c.

PAYNE, WILL. Jerry the dreamer: a novel. Harper. 12°, $1.25.
Jerry Drew came to Chicago from a small country village and gradually worked himself into a good position on a newspaper. He met Georgie, the daughter of Judge House, and ran away with her. After his marriage he became insanely jealous of Sidney Bane, his wife's cousin, and at the same time developed socialistic theories. Gradually he drifted away from his wife and lost his position, and the socialistic newspaper in which he had an interest failed. The story paints a man who dreams, who is without any logical power, and who torments himself.

PRATT, CORNELIA ATWOOD. The daughter of a stoic. Macmillan. 16°, $1.25.
Arria James was given her name in honor of the Roman matron who inflicted death upon herself to teach her husband how to die under the same conditions stoically. Arria's mother having had a singularly unhappy life consoles herself with the teachings of Marcus Aurelius

and strives to inculcate her principles into the life of her daughter, who, grafting some individual theories on her mother's philosophy, becomes the heroine of a rather dramatic story.

PRENTISS, *Mrs.* ELIZ., ["Aunt Susan," *pseud.*] Stepping heavenward. *New ed.*, with a sketch of the author. A. D. F. Randolph & Co. il. 16°, 50 c.
First published in 1869. This diary of the religious experiences of a young girl is now printed from new electrotype plates.

ROGERS, ROB. CAMERON. Will o' the *Wasp:* a sea-yarn of the War of '12; ed. by H. Lawrence, and now brought before the public for the first time. Putnam. il. 12°, $1.25.
The *Wasp* was an American man-of-war, which had a notable career in the War of 1812; after taking and burning a dozen prizes, after fighting and whipping the *Reindeer* and sinking the *Avon,* she disappeared—no one ever knew how or where. This story aims to elucidate the mystery, and brings in the many dramatic incidents of her cruise.

ROWLANDS, EFFIE ADELAIDE. A faithful traitor. Lippincott. 12°, (Lippincott's select novels, no. 181.) cl., $1; pap., 25 c.

SARDOU, VICTORIEN. Alice de Beaurepaire; a romance of Napoleon; unabridged tr. from the French by I. G. Burnham. C. Brown & Co. il. 12°, $1; pap., 50 c.
Covers the career of Napoleon from the birth of the King of Rome until the end of the retreat from Moscow: "Madame Sans-Gêne" is again introduced as the Duchess of Dantzig: Alice de Beaurepaire is a beautiful young girl betrothed to the duchess's adopted son Henriot. The emperor falls in love with the girl, who remains innocent, but her lover suspects her and swears vengeance against Napoleon and is the centre of a conspiracy against him.

SCOTT, H. S. ["H. Seton Merriman," *pseud.*] Flotsam: the study of a life. Longmans, Green & Co. il. 12°, $1.25.
The "flotsam" is a boy left orphaned in India, who at three years of age is taken to England and shifted from the care of an adventurer to that of a strait-laced English banker. His youth is stormy, his affections unregulated. Misunderstood, sinning and sinned against, he becomes a wanderer. During this life he fights in the American War and in the Indian Mutiny.

STANNARD, *Mrs.* HENRIETTA ELIZA VAUGHAN, ["J. Strange Winter," *pseud.*] The truthtellers: a novel. Lippincott. 12°, (Lippincott's select novels, no. 182.) $1; pap., 50 c.
Elinor Mortimer, spinster, living alone in a fashionable part of London, finds her life of ease interrupted by the advent of her dead brother's five children, of whom she had been made sole guardian. These five clever, beautiful children are the "truth-tellers." Brought up on one of the Shetland Islands in an utterly unconventional way, and taught by their father to tell the bare unadorned truth on all occasions, their contact with artificial life brings about some funny episodes.

STEVENSON, ROB. L. Weir of Hermiston: an unfinished romance. Scribner. 12°, $1.50.

STORIES by English authors : France. Scribner. por. 16°, 75 c.
Contents : A lodging for the night, by Rob. L.

Stevenson ; A leaf in the storm, by " Ouida " (Louise de la Rame); A terrib'y strange bed, by Wilkie Collins; Michel Lorio's cross, by Hesba Stretton; A perilous amour, by Stanley J. Weyman.

STORIES by English authors : London. Scribner. por. 16°, 75 c.
Contents : The inconsiderate waiter, by J. M. Barrie; The black poodle, by F. Anstey. Guthrie; That brute Simmons, by Arthur Morrison; A rose of the Ghetto, by I. Zangwill; An idyll of London, by Beatrice Harraden; The omnibus, by "Q" (Arthur T. Quiller Couch); The hired baby, by Marie Corelli.

TAYLOR, UNA. Nets for the wind. Roberts. 16° (Keynote ser., no. 23.) $1.
Contents : Nets for the wind; The sword of Michel; A scarlet shadow; The knight of the Blessed Mary; Black snow; Seed of the sun; The king's mountebank; The truce of God; A rose of Paradise; Poor Satan; The crazy pilgrim.

TIERNAN, FRANCES C. FISHER, ["Christian Reid," *pseud.*] The picture of Las Cruces : a romance of Mexico. Appleton. 12°, (Appleton's town and country lib., no. 193.) $1; pap., 50 c.
A story of an artist in Mexico.

TOMPKINS, ELIZABETH KNIGHT. The broken ring : a romance. Putnam. 16°, (Hudson lib., no. 15.) $1; pap., 50 c.

TRASK, KATRINA, [*Mrs.* Spencer Trask.] White satin and homespun. A. D. F. Randolph & Co. nar. 16°, 75 c.
Morton Hunnewell, a New Yorker, awakened and aroused to an overpowering sense of the miseries of his fellow-men, sold what he had and moved to Delancey Street into the house of a cabinet-maker. Miss Katharine van Santlandt, reared in luxury, goes to hear Hunnewell lecture disguised as a washerwoman, and little by little becomes his valuable assistant. After many of her outings "in homespun" Katharine agrees to give up all and live with Hunnewell among the poor.

VACHELL, HORACE ANNESLEY. The quicksands of Pactolus ; a novel. Holt. 12°, $1.
Rufus Barrington, a New Englander, immigrating to California when gold was first discovered in that state, invests his money skilfully, and later founds a bank, becoming a financial power after his wealth is almost as countless as the golden sands of the mythical river for which the story is named. The history of Rufus and family is noteworthy, because it illustrates the social effects of rapid wealth accumulation on the Pacific slope.

ZOLA EMILE. Rome. International News Co. 16°, pap. 90 c.

ZOLA, EMILE. Rome: sole authorized version in the English language; tr. by Ernest Alfred Vizetelly. Macmillan. 2 v., 12°, $2.

YONGE, CHARLOTTE MARIA. The release; or, Caroline's French kindred. Macmillan. 12°, $1.

HISTORY.

ABBOTT, E. A paragraph history of the United States from the discovery of the continent to the present time; with brief notes on contemporaneous events chronologically arranged. *New ed.* Roberts. 12°, 50 c.
A little book written more than twenty years ago. The new edition is brought up to date.

BEERBOHM, MAX. The works of Max Beerbohm. 12°, $1.25.
Contents : Essays on Dandies and dandies; A good prince; Eighteen hundred and eighty (1880); King George the Fourth; The pervasion of rouge ; Poor Romeo; Diminuendo.

BLISS, W. ROOT. Quaint Nantucket. Houghton, Mifflin & Co. 12°, $1.50.
Relates to the "quaint Nantucket" of two hundred years ago, before the island was discovered by the "summer boarder." The materials from which it has been written comprise the original town and court records, various letters, account-books, sea-journals, and other private manuscripts, including the record-books of the Quaker Society of Nantucket. *Contents :* The beginning of all things; The triumph of John Gardner; The Nantucket Indian; The dominion of the Quakers; The missionary from Boston, etc.

BROWN, ABRAM ENGLISH. Beneath old rooftrees. Lee & Shepard. il. 12°, (Footprints of the patriots.) $1.50.
A view of the opening of the Revolution. The author has, through ten years of reportorial work, come in touch with scores of New England people still living on old homesteads occupied by their parents or grandparents at the time of the alarm of April 19, 1775, and there he has heard the story of personal experience reported by the descendants of those who at their own doors or in the highway faced the army of the king. While delineating in his characteristic manner the story of Lexington and Concord, he has most happily shown the part taken by other towns· in that memorable day's experience.

DANA, C. ANDERSON. Lincoln and his cabinet: a lecture delivered on Tuesday, March 10, 1896, before the New Haven Colony Historical Society. Printed at the De Vinne Press for Paul Lemperly, F. A. Hilliard, and Frank E. Hopkins. por. 1 il. 12°, bds., $1.50. [Ed. limited to 350 copies.]
As Assistant Secretary of War during Lincoln's administration Mr. Dana, of the New York *Sun,* had exceptional opportunities for studying the President and the members of his cabinet. His interesting views are found in this little book, with a number of details that readers will find quite new. Contains a reproduction of Frank B. Carpenter's painting, "The first reading of the emancipation proclamation."

ENGELBACH, ALFRED H. The Danes in England : a tale of the days of King Alfred. *New ed.* Warne. 12°, 75 c.

ENGLISH, W. HAYDEN. Conquest of the country northwest of the river Ohio, 1778-1783; and, Life of Gen. George Rogers Clark, with numerous sketches of men who served under Clark, and full list of those allotted lands in Clark's grant for service in the campaigns against the British posts, showing exact land allotted each. The Bowen-Merrill Co. pors. 4°, $6; hf. leath., $8; leath., $10.
This work grew out of a history of Indiana which the author has been preparing for years. His material had grown so voluminous that it

was determined to publish at once in convenient form the matter in relation to the conquest of the country northwest of the river Ohio; this necessarily included the life of George Rogers Clark, who successfully planned and executed the campaigns against the British posts. Much of the matter had never before been published. Numerous historical letters, papers, etc., are reproduced in fac-simile or otherwise. Mr. English is president of the Indiana Historical Society.

HILL, GEORGIANA. Women in English life from mediæval to modern times. Macmillan. 2 v., 8°, $7.50.

McMASTER, J. BACH. With the fathers : studies in the history of the United States. Appleton. 1 il., 12°, $1.50.
Contents : The Monroe doctrine; The third-term tradition; The political depravity of the fathers; The riotous career of the Know Nothings; The framers and framing of the constitution; Washington's inauguration, A century of constitutional interpretation; A century's struggle for silver; Is sound finance possible under popular government?; Franklin in France; How the British left New York; The struggle for territory; Four centuries of progress.

MAY, E. S. Guns and calvary: their performances in the past and their prospects in the future. Roberts Bros. por. il. plans, 12°, $1.25.

ROOSEVELT, THEODORE. The winning of the west. V. 4, Louisiana and the northwest, 1791-1807. Putnam. 8°, $2.50.
"This volume covers the period which opened with the checkered but finally successful war waged by the United States Government against the northwestern Indians, and closed with the acquisition and exploration of the vast region that lay beyond the Mississippi. It was during this period that the west rose to real power in the Union."—*Preface.*

LITERATURE, MISCELLANEOUS AND COLLECTED WORKS.

COMENIUS, J. AMOS. The great didactic of John Amos Comenius ; now for the first time Englished ; with introds., biographical and historical, by M. W. Keatinge. Macmillan. 8°, *net*, $2.

GOSSE, EDMUND W. Critical kit-kats. Dodd, Mead & Co. 12°, $1.50.
Gosse borrows from graphic art the title for this volume of essays; painters of the last century called their half-length portraits "kit-kats." *Contents :* The sonnets from the Portuguese ; Keats in 1894 ; Thomas Lovell Beddoes ; Edward Fitzgerald ; Walt Whitman ; Count Lyof Tolstoi ; Christina Rossetti ; Lord De Tabley ; Toru Dutt ; M. Jose-Maria de Heredia ; Walter Pater ; Robert Louis Stevenson.

HARE, A. J. CUTHBERT. Works. *New ed.* Macmillan. 13 v., *ea. about* 300 p. il. 12°, *prices from* $1-$3.50.

QUACKENBOS, J. DUNCAN, *M.D.* Practical rhetoric. American Book Co. 12°, $1.
Contents : The æsthetic basis of rhetorical principles ; Literary invention ; Literary style ; Figurative speech ; Functions and technic of standard prose forms ; Poetry and the principles of versification—poetical forms. Each lesson is followed by a group of works of reference.

SANBORN, KATHARINE ABBOTT. My literary zoo. Appleton. 16°, 75 c.
In four chapters called "Everybody's pets," "Devoted to dogs," "Cats," and "All sorts," Miss Sanborn tells of the various pets that have been cherished by literary people or have been written about by them ; with numerous anecdotes in this same line.

NATURE AND SCIENCE.

BONNEY, T. G. Ice-work present and past. Appleton. il. 12°, (International scientific ser., no. 84.) $1.50.
Contents : Pt. 1, "Existing evidence," treats of "Alpine glaciers, past and present," and "Arctic and Antarctic ice-sheets"; Pt. 2, "Traces of the glacial epoch," is devoted to a consideration of "Lake basins and their relation to glaciers—the parallel roads of Glenroy, Eskers, etc.," "Ice-work in Great Britain and Ireland—the deposits and their significance." "Ice-work in Europe and other parts of the world " ; Pt. 3, under " Theoretical questions " are chapters on : Temperature in the glacial epoch ; Possible causes of a glacial epoch; The number of glacial epochs ; Glacial deposits and general principles of interpretation.

CODY, SHERWIN. In the heart of the hills : a book of the country. Macmillan. 12°, $1.25.

SINNETT, A. P. The rationale of mesmerism. *2d ed.* New Amsterdam Book Co. 12°, $1.

WITCHELL, C. A. The evolution of bird-song ; with observations on the influence of heredity and imitation. Macmillan. 12°, $1.75.

POETRY AND DRAMA.

MacCULLOCH, HUNTER. Robert Burns: an ode on the centenary of his death, 1796-1896. The Rose and Thistle Pub. Co. il. 8°, 20 c.

SPENSER, EDMUND. Faerie queene ; pictured and decorated by L. Fairfax-Muckley ; with an introd. by J. W. Hales. In 13 or 14 pts. Pt. 1. Macmillan. 12°, *Limited ed.*, pap., $1.

STEVENSON, ROB. L. Poems and ballads. Scribner. por. 12°, $1.50.
Contains besides the poems published in separate volumes under the titles of "A child's garden of verses," "Underwoods," and "Ballads," forty additional poems written since the volumes were published, forming the third book of "Underwoods."

SWINBURNE, ALGERNON C. The tale of Balen. Scribner. 12°, $1.

WORDSWORTH, W. Lyrical poems ; ed. by Ernest Rhys. Macmillan. 12°, (Lyric poets.) $1.

YOUNG, E. Poetical works; with a memoir by Rev. J. Mitford. *Aldine ed.* 2 v., 12°, cl., *net, ea.,* 75 c.

POLITICAL AND SOCIAL.

DURAND, E. DANA. Political and municipal legislation in 1895. American Acad. of Political and Social Science. 8°, (Publications of the society, no. 173.) pap., 15 c.
A summary of the recent legislation on questions of state and local government by the various states. The subjects discussed are the restriction of the suffrage, ballot reform, voting machines, the corrupt practices acts, reform in modes of nomination, limitations on legislatures,

and county government, and in conclusion the author gives a summary of the legislation concerning municipalities.

GIDDINGS, FRANKLIN H. The principles of sociology: an analysis of the phenomena of association and social organization. *2d ed.* Macmillan. 8°, *net*, $3.

GILES, FAYETTE STRATTON. The industrial army. The Baker & Taylor Co. 12°, $1.25. Contains a discussion of certain proposed means of relieving and eliminating poverty and crime. These means are intended to confer upon the individual economic and locative freedom, personal freedom and equality of opportunity, and through these to achieve a higher civilization and a greater human happiness, consequent upon the proposed attainment of higher moral, mental, and physical development of the individual.

HERSHEY, AMOS S. The recognition of Cuban belligerency. American Academy of Political and Social Science. 8°, (Publications of the society, no. 175.) pap., 15 c. The purpose is "to demonstrate the undoubted right and propriety on the part of the United States Government to accord belligerent rights to the Cuban insurgents."

JAMES, EDMUND J. A review of Bryce's "American commonwealth": a study in American constitutional law. American Academy of Political and Social Science. 8°, (Publications of the society, no. 172.) pap., 25 c. This paper deals exclusively with the first volume of the third edition. Criticism is made on five general points. First, the author's statement as to the basis of the classification of the distribution of functions between state and nation ; second, his remarks on the subject of the responsibility of officials ; third, his exposition of the judicial power of the United States ; fourth, his formulation of the principles of constitutional interpretation; fifth, his views as to the final authority in interpreting the constitution.

LUCY, H. W. A diary of the Home Rule Parliament, 1892-1895. Cassell. 1 il. 12°, $2. The English general election of 1892 placed Mr. Gladstone in power with a majority of forty pledged to carry a Home Rule bill for Ireland. The course of this bill, during the following three years in the House of Commons, with its many attending dramatic incidents and final defeat, is admirably and graphically portrayed in this diary. Mr. Gladstone's appearance from day to day is noted, Lord Randolph Churchill's physical breakdown and death recorded, and interesting details given of Chamberlain, Keir-Hardie, and other leaders.

McKINLEY, W. McKinley's masterpieces : selections from the public addresses in and out of Congress; ed. by R. L. Paget. Joseph Knight Co. por. 16°, (Famous men ser.) 75 c. Opens with a brief account of McKinley's life. Following are selections from his speeches on the subjects of The Republican party ; The protective tariff ; The purity of the ballot ; Finance ; The interests of labor ; also on Educational topics, Religion, and Memorial day and and patriotism. Miscellaneous and occasional addresses. Eulogies.

OLDROYD, OSBORN H. Lincoln's campaign; or, the political revolution of 1860. Laird & Lee. por. il. 12°, (The pastime ser., no. 40.) 75 c., pap., 25 c.

PATTON, JAC. HARRIS. Political parties in the United States : their history and influence. New Amsterdam Book Co. 12°, $1.25.

TAUSSIG, FRANK W. Wages and capital : an examination of the wages fund doctrine. Appleton. 12°, $1.50. "Prof. F. W. Taussig, of Harvard University, examines the relations of capital to wages, and concludes that wages are paid from capital, but not from a predetermined fund of capital. He examines and rejects the doctrine that wages are paid from the laborer's own product. The bearing of this general reasoning on practical problems, such as strikes and trades unions, and on general economic theory, is then considered. In the second part of the book the literary history of the wages fund doctrine and of the discussion of wages and capital is followed in detail. This important and searching contribution to economic theory may have a wide-reaching effect on the development of political economy in the future, and probably will be of great value for all who teach or investigate general economic theory."—*Evening Post.*

SPORTS AND AMUSEMENTS.

BADDELEY, WILFRED. Lawn tennis. Routledge. il. 12°, (The oval ser.) flex., 50 c.

BIDLAKE, F. T. Cycling. Routledge. 12°, (The oval ser.) flex., 50 c.

ELLIS, EDWIN J. Riding. Routledge. il. 12°, (The oval ser.) flex., 50 c.

KNOWLES, R. G., *and* Morton R. Baseball. Routledge. il. diagrams, 12°, (The "Oval" ser. of games, no. 8.) pap., 40 c. In a prefatory note the authors say: "We have endeavored to make this little volume a handbook of practical utility to the student and amateur. Further than that, our object has been to show the present position of the game in the United States, and to record its recent rise into popularity in England."

PARK, W., *jr.* The game of golf. Longmans, Green & Co. 12°, $2.50.

TRACK athletics in detail; comp. by the editor of "Interscholastic sport" in *Harper's Round Table*; il. from instantaneous photographs. Harper. 8°, $1.25. Gives clearly and concisely the best available information concerning the methods of training, for track and field events, practised by college and school athletes. The events treated are limited to those recognized as standards by intercollegiate and interscholastic associations. A chapter on "Bicycling for men" and one on "Bicycling for women" have been added to the descriptions of the track athletics.

WARD, MARIA E. Bicycling for ladies; with hints as to the art of wheeling; advice to beginners; dress; care of the bicycle; mechanics; training, exercises, etc., etc. Brentano's. 8°, $1.50. *Contents:* Possibilities; What the bicycle does; On wheels in general and bicycles in particular; For beginners ; How to make progress ; Helping and teaching ; A few things to remember : The art of wheeling on a bicycle ; Position and

power; Difficulties to overcome; Dress; Watch
and cyclometer ; Women and tools ; Tools and
how to use them ; Where to keep a bicycle ;
Tires; Mechanics of bicycling; Exercise; Training ; Breathlessness. Illustrated with thirty-
four full-page pictures, giving the various positions, etc.

THEOLOGY, RELIGION, AND SPECULATION.

BRIGHTMAN, F. E., *ed.* Liturgies eastern and
western: being the texts, original or translated,
of the principal liturgies of the church; ed.
with introds. and appendices by F. E. Brightman, on the basis of the former work by C.
E. Hammond. V. 1, Eastern liturgies. Macmillan. 8°, *net,* $5.

HERRON, G. D. Social meanings of religious
experiences. Crowell. 12°, 75 c.
Contents : The affections as social energies ;
Economics and religion ; The leadership of social faith ; Repentance unto service ; Material
world and social spirit ; The appeal of redemption to progress.

KENNARD, H. MARTYN. The veil lifted: a new
light on the world's history. Lippincott. 8°,
$2.
" I shall point out that the Biblical narratives
are based upon authentic archives and run parallel with the monumental inscriptions. That the

races of Shem, Ham, and Japheth have dominated Europe, Asia, and northern Africa since
the first dawn of history. That the Hamites
and the Semites were the Hebrews and Israelites of the Old Testament. That all the prominent Biblical characters were reigning monarchs, etc., etc."—*Introduction.*

LEWIS, *Rev.* W. SUNDERLAND, *and* BOOTH, *Rev.*
H. M. A critical commentary on the Gospel
according to St. Matthew. Funk & Wagnalls.
4°, (Preacher's complete commentary, v. 1.)
$3.
The first volume of an extensive work in
eleven volumes, printed from imported plates.
The entire work is already issued in London.

MOULTON, R. GREEN, *ed.* The modern reader's Bible: a series of works from the sacred
scriptures in modern literary form. V. 3,
The Book of Job; ed. with introd. and notes.
Macmillan. 24°, (Wisdom ser.) 50 c.

OTTLEY, ROB. L. The doctrine of the incarnation. In 2 v. V. 1, To the Council of
Nicea. V. 2. To the present day. Macmillan. 8°, *net,* $3.25.

PAINE, T. The age of reason : being an investigation of true and fabulous theology ;
ed. by Moncure D. Conway. Putnam. 8°,
$1.25.

RECENT FRENCH AND GERMAN BOOKS.

FRENCH.

Bastard, G. Le Chaloupier. 12°. Lemerre..... $1 00
Benjamin, E. Cœur malade. 12°. Lemerre.... 1 00
Chaperon, P. La confession de Jacques. 12°.
  Lemerre... 1 00
Chibra, J. de. La princesse des ténébres. 12°.
  Levy...... .... 1 00
Claretie, J. La vie à Paris. 12°. Charpentier.. 1 00
Decourcelles, P. Les deux gosses. 2 vols. 12°.
  Dentu 2 00
Dostoievsky, T. L'eternel mari. 12°. Plon.... 1 00
Ferry, A. de. Les épines ont des roses. 12°. Levy. 1 00
Flat, P. Figures de rêve. 12°. Lemerre........ 1 00
Fogazzaro, A. Daniel Cortis, trad. de l'Italien.
  12°. Levy... 1 00
Fransay, G. Mlle. Huguette. 12°. Colin....... 1 00
Gebhart, E. Moines et Papes. 12°. Hachette.. 1 00
Ghika, Marie-Gregoire. Fatalité. 12°. Levy... 1 00
Greville, H. Céphise. 12°. Plon............... 1 00
Lavedon, H. Petites fêtes, 12°. Levy......... 1 00
Leneveu, G. La Gueuse. 12°. Lemerre........ 1 00
Lovenjoue, S. de. Un roman d'amour. 12°.
  Levy.. 1 00
Maizeroy, R. Le reflet. 12°. Flammarion..... 1 00
Mendes, C. Gog. 2 vols. 12°. Charpentier... 2 00
Naurouse, J. A travers la tourmente. 12°.
  Colin.. 1 00
Noel, E. Rosie. 12°. Charpentier............ 1 00
Peyrebrune, G. de. La Margotte. 12°. Le-
  merre 1 00
Rameau, Jean. Le cœur de Régine. 12°. Ol-
  lendorff.. 1 00
Richepin, J. Grandes amoureuses. 12°. Char-
  pentier... 1 00
Rosny, J. H. Le serment. 12°. Ollendorff..... 60
Senechal, C. Lettres d'honnêtes femmes. 12°.
  Lemerre... 1 00

Vogue, M. de. Devant le siècle. 12°. Colin. . 1 00

GERMAN.

Bertz, E. Das Sabinergut. Cloth, 12°. Schall &
  Gruad 2 00

Bobertag, B. Mit allen Waffen. 3 vols. 12°.
  Pierson.. $2 65
Bock, A. Dora Peters. 12°. Fontane........... 1 70
Hedenstierna, A. v. Der Majoratsherr v. Halle-
  borg. 12°. Meyer............................... 70
— Im Swedischen Bauernheim. 12°. Meyer...... 70
Heyse, P. Abenteuer eines Blaustrümpfchens.
  8°. Krabbe.. 70
— Einer von Hunderten, etc. 24°. Franck....... 40
Hoecker, P. O. Polnische Wirthschaft. 12°.
  Bong & Co... 1 70
Kirstein, P. A. Eine Bekanntschaft. 12°. Pier-
  son.. 1 20
Lindau, R. Erzählungen eines Effendi. 12°.
  Fontane 70
Mackay, J. H. Der kleine Finger. 12°. Fischer. 50
Meyer, E. Eifersucht der Seelen. 12°. Janke.. 40
Mors, O. Ein Revolutionär. 12°. Janke....... 40
Niemann, A. Die Erbinnen. 2 vols. 12°. Pier-
  son.. 2 60
Postumus, C. In deutscher Hand. 12°. Janke. 70
Reichenbach, I. von. Ein reiches Mädchen.
  12°. Reissner..................................... 1 00
Rittland, K. Ihr Sieg. 12°. Fontane.......... 1 70
Rosegger, P. Alpengeschichten. 12°. Krabbe. 40
Rosenberg, M. von. Die Kugelsucherin. 12°.
  Fontane... 1 70
Schumacher, H. V. Das Hungerloos. 12°.
  Hong & Co... 1 00
Suttner, B v. High-life. 12°. Pierson......... 1 70
Treumann, J. Was ein Weib will. 2 vols. 12°.
  Rünsheimer.. 1 35
Wachenhusern, H. Eine Frauenschuld 12°.
  Janke 70
Wald-Zedwitz, v. Kein Erbarmen. 12°. Janke. 70
Werther, J. von. Eine anständige Frau. 12°.
  Honz 1 20
Wurzburg, L. Arkanum. 12°. Janke........... 40
Zapp, A. Der tolle Schmettwitz. 12°. Deutsche
  Verlagsanst........................... .. .... 1 35

In the June Magazines.

The Atlantic Monthly devotes a third of its space to weighty articles on history and government. "The Real Problems of Democracy" are treated by E. L. Godkin; "A Century's Progress in Science," by John Fiske; "Arbitration and Our Relations with England," by E. J. Phelps; and "The United States and the Anglo-Saxon Future," by George Burton Adams. In lighter vein are "The Speculations of a Story-Teller," by G. W. Cable; "To the Housatonic at Stockbridge," by Robert U. Johnson; "Young America in Feathers," by Olive Thorne Miller; and "Confessions of Public School Teachers." The Contributors' Club contains articles on "A City by Starlight" (Algiers); "Who was the Imitator, Dickens or Thackeray?"; "The Area of Patriotism," and "The Real Paul and Virginia."

The Century Magazine opens with a description of St. Peter's at Rome, by F. Marion Crawford. W. D. Howells begins a story entitled "An Open-Eyed Conspiracy," an idyl of Saratoga; and there are short stories by Richard Malcolm Johnston, and Chester Bailey Fernald. Sloane's "Napoleon" and Mrs. Humphry Ward's "Sir George Tressidy" are continued on the usual strong lines; James Bryce describes south Africa; "Glimpses of Venezuela and Guiana" are given by W. Nephew King; the Topics of the Time cover "The Folly of Bi-Metallism, President Cleveland's Emancipation Proclamation," and "Fears for Democracy"; and the Open Letters deal chiefly with the Treloar bill and musical copyright. The frontispiece shows Hans von Bülow.

Harper's Magazine offers a very interesting number. Among its most important contents may be mentioned "General Washington," by Woodrow Wilson, with eight illustrations from drawings by Howard Pyle, Harry Fenn, and C. C. Curran, and from a portrait by Rembrandt Peale; "Literary Landmarks of Venice," by Laurence Hutton, with nine illustrations by F. V. Du Mond; "English Elections," by Henry Cabot Lodge; and "Ohio," by Charles F. Thwing, with seven illustrations from drawings by Carlton T. Chapman, W. A. Rogers, George Wharton Edwards, and Harry Fenn. There are short stories by W. E. Norris, Octave Thanet, and Julian Ralph; and poems by Margaret E. Sangster, George Cabot Lodge, and Alice Archer Sewall. Bangs's story, "A Rebellious Heroine," is concluded; and Langdon Elwyn Mitchell begins a new tale under the title "Two Mormons from Muddlety."

Lippincott's publishes as a complete story "A Judicial Error," by Marion Manville Pope; and poems by Florence Earle Coates, Margaret Gilman George, Jenny Terrill Ruprecht, and Grace F. Pennypacker. Of literary interest is "Decadence of Modern Russian Literature," by "A Russian," who fiercely arraigns the government for the dearth of men of letters of original minds. A posthumous article of Hjalmar Hjorth Boyesen's is entitled "My Rural Experiences."

Scribner's Magazine has descriptive articles on Coney Island by Julian Ralph, illustrated by Henry McCarter; and on "A Thousand Miles Through the Alps," by Sir W. Martin Conway, illustrated by Edwin Lord Weeks. Other articles of interest are "On the Poetry of Place Names," by Brander Matthews; "Ars et Vita," by T. R. Sullivan, illustrated by Albert E. Sterner; "A New Art" (Taxidermy), by J. Carter Beard, with illustrations of the work of American taxidermists; "Some Portraits of J. M. W. Turner," by Cosmo Monkhouse, illustrated from photographs of paintings and drawings; and "A French Friend of Browning" (Joseph Milsand), by Th. Bentzon. Clinton Ross has a short story entitled "The Confession of Colonel Sylvester," illustrated by C. S. Reinhart; and W. D. Ellwanger has written "The Lay of the Grolierite," which is enshrined in decorative borders.

Literary Miscellany.

ACCORDING to Hamilton W. Mabie, "The Scarlet Letter" and "Pembroke" are the best American novels.

MME. CALMANN-LÉVY, widow of the famous Parisian publisher, has bought Ernest Renan's library and will make a present of it to the State.

ANOTHER BOOK ON AFRICA EXPECTED.—Prof. R. L. Garner, of monkey-language fame, and Frank Hegger, the New York dealer in photographs, with twenty others, are to make an excursion into Darkest Africa with a view to hunting the big game of that country. A complete photographic outfit will be taken and an illustrated book will no doubt be the outcome of the picnic.

OWEN WISTER'S TALENTS.—Owen Wister did not begin his working life as a writer of fiction. He was a Harvard student specially devoted to music, and accomplished a great deal in the study as his graduation record shows. He even undertook a musical career, and made some preparation for it during a visit in Europe; but he soon gave up the idea—fortunately for the readers of his clever Western sketches.

MASTERS OF "IAN MACLAREN."—The Rev. John Watson (Ian Maclaren) says, according to a letter in the *Bookman*, that the first writer who left any impression on his mind was Scott, whom he read very eagerly. Another stage of his development was crowned by the name of Thomas Carlyle, and still another by that of Matthew Arnold. Four authors he singles out as his masters: Scott, Carlyle, Matthew Arnold, and Sir John Seeley, the author of "Ecce Homo."

POSTHUMOUS WORKS OF PAUL VERLAINE.—It is a question what will become of the posthumous works of Paul Verlaine. The manuscripts are at the moment in the house where he died in the home of his friend Mlle. Krantz. The valise which contains them has not been sealed, and Mlle. Krantz refuses to deliver it, as she is a creditor of Verlaine's to the amount of 320 fr. She has intimated her intention of consulting some literary woman and turning over to her the work of classifying and publishing the manuscripts. Many will anxiously await assurance that this work has been put into the proper hands.

Freshest News.

R. F. FENNO & CO. will publish at once "Daireen," by Frank Frankfort Moore. They have nearly ready a new novel by B. L. Farjeon, entitled "The Betrayal of John Fordham."

ESTES & LAURIAT have just ready three notable books—"A Parisian in America," by S. C. de Soissons, described as "a painstaking attempt on the part of an intelligent Frenchman to get at the real distinctive characteristics of [the American] people"; "A Voyage to Viking-Land," by Thomas Sedgwick Steele, who describes a trip that has just recently begun to be taken by travellers as a novel summer outing to the "Land of the Midnight Sun"; and "My Fire Opal," a collection of stories of prison life, by Sarah Warner Brooks.

THE MACMILLAN CO. have just ready a new novel by Henry James, entitled "Embarrassments." They have also ready "Christmas Stories," which completes the set of Dickens's novels in twenty volumes. The texts of this edition are accurate reprints of the first edition. All the original illustrations are reproduced, and each volume contains a valuable introduction by Charles Dickens the younger. The volumes are printed in readable type on good paper, and form the most attractive cheap edition of Dickens at present in the market.

HENRY HOLT & CO. have just ready a volume entitled "Social Forces in German Literature, a study in the history of civilization," by Kuno Francke, assistant professor of German literature in Harvard University, who treats the subject from the point of view of the student of civilization rather than from that of the linguist or the literary critic. They have also just ready in their *Protean Series*, No. 5, "The Touch of Sorrow," a story of life among the English upper classes; and No. 6, "A Stumbler in Wide Shoes," a story of temptation and sacrifice.

G. P. PUTNAM'S SONS have just published "A Venetian June," a series of prose sketches of life in Venice, by Anna Fuller; and "America and Europe," a new volume in the *Questions of the Day* series, containing three essays: (1) "The United States and Great Britain," by David A. Wells; (2) "The Monroe Doctrine," by Edward J. Phelps; and (3) "Arbitration in International Disputes," by Carl Schurz. They have also just ready six volumes in the second section of the *Mohawk edition* of Cooper's works, including: "The Pilot," "Red Rover," "Wing and Wing," "The Water Witch," "The Two Admirals," and "The Sea Lions."

LONGMANS, GREEN & CO. have just ready "The Paget Papers," the diplomatic and other correspondence of the Rt. Hon. Sir Arthur Paget, 1794-1807, with two appendixes, 1808-1829, arranged and edited by his son, Sir Augustus B., with notes by Mrs. J. R. Green; "Madagascar in War-Time," the experiences of the London *Times* correspondent (E. F. Knight) with the Hovas during the French invasion of 1895; "The Speaker of the House of Representatives," describing the office, its powers and duties, by M. F. Follet, with an introduction by Albert Bushnell; and "The Hare," five essays by leading authorities on its natural history, shooting, coursing, hunting, and cookery, illustrated with eight full-page plates.

ROBERTS BROTHERS have in preparation for early publication "Poems," by Johanna Ambrosius, translated by Mary J. Safford, of which the Philadelphia *Telegraph* says: "Nothing so precious has come from the Fatherland since the hymns of Luther and the writings of Goethe." The author was a laborer in the fields and by sheer force of genius has risen to be one of Germany's most popular poets. During the summer will be brought out "Maris Stella," by Marie Clothilde Balfour; "Shapes in the Fire," a midwinter entertainment, by M. P. Shiel; "Day-Books," chronicles of good and evil, by Mabel E. Wotton; "In Scarlet and Grey," stories of soldiers and civilians, by Florence Henniker, with "The Spectre of the Real," by Thomas Hardy and Florence Henniker, in collaboration; and "An Ugly Idol," by Claud Nicholson.

CHARLES SCRIBNER'S SONS have ready a "History of Philosophy," by Prof. Alfred Weber, of the University of Strasburg, translated with the consent of the author from the fifth French edition by Prof. Frank Thilly, of the University of Missouri; "Jersey Street and Jersey Lane," six attractive and sympathetic "urban and suburban sketches," alternating in scene between New York City and the country, by the late H. C. Bunner, with illustrations by A. B. Frost, B. West Clinedinst, Irving R. Wiles, and Kenneth Frazier; two new volumes in the series of *Stories by English Authors*—"Africa," six stories, by A. Conan Doyle, H. Rider Haggard, J. Landers, W. C. Scully, Percy Hemingway, and one by an anonymous writer; and "Italy," five stories, by James Payn, W. E. Norris, A. Mary F. Robinson, Laurence Oliphant, and Anthony Trollope; also two volumes in the series of *The Oxford Manuals of English History*—"The Making of the English Nation, B.C. 55-1135 A.D.," by C. G. Robertson, and "King and Baronage, 1135-1327 A.D.," by W. H. Hutton.

D. APPLETON & CO. have ready some works of fiction of more than average merit. "Yekl," by A. Cahan, is a tale of the New York Ghetto or Jewish quarter, giving humorous and pathetic pictures of life among the abject poor, and the methods by which they earn the bare necessaries of life, notably by sewing in "sweatshops"; and "Maggie: a girl of the streets," by Stephen Crane, the much-discussed author of "The Red Badge of Courage," also pictures certain realities of life in overcrowded cities, which are almost too ghastly to be handled in fiction. "Green Gates," by Mrs. K. M. C. Meredith (Johanna Staats), describes a Long Island country-house and hunting life and social incidents in New York City; "The Sentimental Sex," by Gertrude Warden, is the story of an Australian's introduction to certain phases of London life, and "Sir Mark," by Anna Robeson Brown, introduces Washington, Jefferson, and Franklin, and gives the reader an insight into the social and political life of Philadelphia—the first capital of the United States. In more serious vein are "Teaching the Language-Arts," speech, reading, composition, by Prof. B. A. Hinsdale, of the University of Michigan; "The Story of a Piece of Coal," by Edward A. Martin, a new volume in the *Library of Useful Stories;* and "My Literary Zoo," by Kate Sanborn. Appletons' Guidebooks for Canada, Alaska, and the Summer Resorts are also all revised up to date.

BOOKS FOR SUMMER TRAVELLERS.

LITERARY NEWS

AN ECLECTIC REVIEW OF
CURRENT LITERATURE
~ILLUSTRATED~

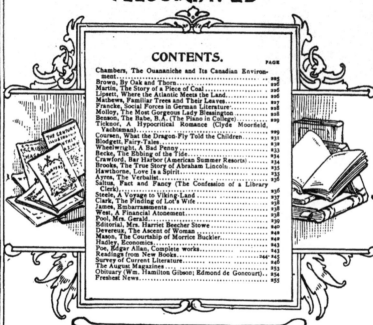

CONTENTS.

VOL. XVII-No 8   AUGUST~1896 $1.00 YEARLY
10 CTS. PER NO.

~PUBLICATION OFFICE~
59 DUANE STREET, NEW YORK

The Literary News

In winter you may reade them, ab ignem, by the fireside; and in summer, ab umbram, under some shadie tree, and therewith pass away the tedious howres.

| VOL. XVII. | AUGUST, 1896. | No. 8. |

From "The Ouananiche"   Copyright, 1896, by Harper & Brothers.

THE LITTLE SAGUENAY NEAR ST. RAYMOND.

The Ouananiche and Its Canadian Environment.

THIS book of the ouananiche is the result of repeated requests to the author for a treatise upon the fish and its environment on the part of many anglers and others who have been among the readers of his contributions to the pages of periodical literature. The book is the outcome of years of observation and study. It contains brief records of the experiences and opinions of many of those best qualified to speak of the fish, and especially of its game qualities and geographical distribution. It also embodies references to all that is of special interest in the literature of the subject.

It is a popular fallacy that the ouananiche is a land-locked salmon, prevented from returning to salt water by some upheaval of nature that has raised an impassable barrier at Chicontimi—a fall of some sixty or seventy feet in height. To support this absurd theory it became necessary to insist upon one of the hugest blunders committed in the whole realm of natural history, namely, that the ouananiche—one of the most universally distributed of the inhabitants of Labrador waters — was peculiar to Lake St. John and its feeders and outlet, for it could scarcely be pretended that the fish of the rivers that flow into the Ungava Bay, Hamil-

ton Inlet, and the Gulf of St. Lawrence were prevented by a fall at Chicontimi, on the Saguenay, from running down to the sea. Yet ouananiche are found in all these waters. Much of the information contained in the chapter on the Montagnais Indians and their folk-lore will reach readers for the first time. The superstitions, legends, and language of this interesting people have engaged the attention of the author for many years past, and he has been fortunate in having had the assistance of some old missionaries and officials of the Hudson's Bay Company. Valuable old manuscripts relating to tribal characteristics which have thus far escaped even Schoolcraft and Morse have been studied and their treasures of information set before readers in a most attractive way.

From the original intention of writing a simple angling book, the author has drifted to dealing with the whole Canadian environment of the ouananiche, well aware that portions of this environment are as little known, even to Canadians, as is the interior of Africa.

The publishers have put all this fascinating information into a beautiful book. (Harper. $2.)—*From Preface to Chambers's " The Ouananiche."*

By Oak and Thorn.

MISS BROWN possesses that rare faculty of enthusiastic description which is at once the delight and the despair of imaginative readers. Her exquisite word-pictures of rural English scenery, landmarks, and people might safely be guaranteed to infect with the travelling fever all except the most stolid of chronic stay-at-homes. She feels the gypsy's wandering instinct herself and imparts it to anybody who has the good fortune to peruse her charming little book in an amiable spirit. She has tramped over the Devon moorland in the footsteps of Charles Kingsley and R. D. Blackmore, marking each spot made memorable by episodes in " Westward Ho!" or " Lorna Doone." She has looked upon the landscapes that used to greet the eyes of William Shakespeare, and followed the track of Washington Irving into the quaint lanes of oldest London. With true antiquarian fervor she has gazed at the ruins of Glastonbury Abbey, and striven to locate the spot where Camelot, King Arthur's capital, once stood. She is too accurate a student of history to give herself up utterly to that innocent credulity which accepts hazy tradition as clear fact, but never ceases to wish that the brave old times and men and places were in reality as the story-tellers have made them. " By Oak and Thorn" is a volume for those who have explored the field of English literature pretty widely and are, moreover, endowed with that comfortable gift, a lively fancy. (Houghton, Mifflin & Co. $1.25.)—*Daily Evening Gazette.*

The Story of a Piece of Coal.

THE knowledge of the marvels which a piece of coal possesses within itself, and which in obedience to processes of man's invention it is always willing to exhibit to an observant inquirer, is not so widespread, perhaps, as it

From Martin's "The Story of a Piece of Coal."　Copyright, 1896, by D. Appleton & Co.

ENCRINITES : VARIOUS.　MOUNTAIN LIMESTONE.

should be, and the aim of this little book, this record of one page of geological history, has been to bring together the principal facts and wonders connected with it into the focus of a few pages, where, side by side, would be found the record of its vegetable and mineral history, its discovery and early use, its bearings on the great fog-problem, its useful illuminating gas and oils, the question of the possible exhaustion of British supplies, and other important and interesting bearings on coal or its products.

In the whole realm of natural history, in the widest sense of the term, there is nothing which could be cited which has so benefited, so interested, I might almost say so excited mankind, as have the wonderful discoveries of the various products distilled from gas-tar, itself a distillate of coal.

Coal touches the interests of the botanist, the geologist, and the physicist, the chemist, the sanitarian, and the merchant.

In the little work now before the reader I have endeavored to recount, without going into unnecessary detail, the wonderful story of a piece of coal. (Appleton. 40 c.)—*From Martin's " The Story of a Piece of Coal."*

Where the Atlantic Meets the Land.

IN this new member of the "Keynote" family readers of a not too exacting disposition will find themselves catered for in a manner likely to give them satisfaction, while those of a more particular kind will come upon occasional passages good enough to obtain forgiveness for the parts which are not conspicuous for merit. Mr. Lipsett shifts from excellence to mediocrity so easily and frequently, and back again from his best to his worst so suddenly, that we find it difficult to make up our minds about him. We believe "Where the Atlantic Meets the Land" to be his first venture, and, as hasty verdicts are often falsified by an author's second attempt, we prefer to await the appearance of other work from Mr. Lipsett's pen before endeavoring to give him his peculiar place among the thousands who now write for fame or bread. The volume before us contains sixteen stories dealing with life among the peasants of Ireland. Of these the first is perhaps the best; it is entitled "The Unforgiven Sin," and tells very tenderly how mightily Terry Gallagher came to love Bella Sweeny. But men propose and women dispose. "The Legend of Barnesmore Gap " tells how an astute highwayman was outwitted by an oaf whose head was rather short of brains, but who had intervals of cunning, as is often the case with creatures hovering between sanity and insanity. Other taking stories will be found in this book. (Roberts. $1.)—*London Literary World.*

Familiar Trees and Their Leaves.

PERHAPS the noblest tribute ever paid to trees was given by him who once said that old friends were like them. It is true of both that they shelter and refresh us. Prof. Bailey, who writes an introduction to Mr. Mathews's book, justly remarks of trees that nothing in nature "would leave the earth so bare of loveliness if they were to be removed." May the same not be said of friends —were they to be removed?

Mr. Mathews, as do the botanists generally (for there lie the keys), writes mainly of the leaves of trees, and it is these that he illustrates. How enormous is the number of leaves a single tree may support he shows in an estimate he has made. Near his cottage grows a large sugar-maple, to which he credits in one season no fewer than 432,000 leaves. The leaf is the worker that builds the tree, and bears the most intimate relation to the tree from outermost stem down to the roots. From it proceeds downward all the way what may be called a nerve. "It leads a life of endurance, effort, and various success, issuing in various beauty," says Ruskin, "and it connects itself with the whole previous edifice by one sustaining thread, continuing its appointed piece of work all the way from top to root."

Apart from the forms and color of leaves, the author gives much other information that is interesting and often will be new. The wood so extensively used in interior work for houses, and called whitewood (probably because it is not white), is the well-known tulip-tree of the lower Wabash Valley. It is not wholly unknown in this locality. Indeed, the finest specimen the author has seen grows in Englewood. The common basswood, which we often despise for its softness, might secure a better hold on our esteem did we remember that it has a better name, and a name not neglected by the poets — linden. The graceful elm, which never looks so well as in a large meadow, standing alone against an adjacent upland and seen from some distance, has not only beauty, but strength, for out of it are made hubs, yokes, and saddle-trees.

The horse-chestnut was so recently introduced here that in Yonkers may still be seen what is believed to be the original importation, made about 1750. A sugar-maple tapped in the spring will yield about twenty-five gallons of its life-blood, and still live to put forth its leaves and grow as if it had not met a loss. The author for twenty-five years has watched the effect of tapping on scores of trees, and he cannot see that they have lost any of their vigor. The hoary alder is the trout's best friend, and has earned from it "an enormous debt of gratitude for hiding his cool and pebbly retreat and untangling the angler's fly."

This book is a companion volume to "Familiar Flowers," which last season gave intense pleasure to all nature-lovers fortunate enough to come into possession of it. (Appleton. $1.75.)—*Public Opinion.*

From Mathews's " Familiar Trees." Copyright, 1896, by D. Appleton & Co.
THE PAINTED BEECH.

Social Forces in German Literature.

KUNO FRANCKE, Ph.D., is the assistant professor of literature in Harvard University. We have forgotten for the moment who is the head professor in that institution of learning, but he must be a good man if he outclasses his assistant. The mental altitude which he is called upon to overtop may be determined from a book entitled "Social Forces in German Literature," which Professor Francke has just published. The sub-title of this book is "A Study in the History of Civilization." Title and sub-title give an idea of the task which Professor Francke has set before him. He has not aimed at a mere chronological chain of biographies of German writers, nor at a mere series of criticisms of individual styles and methods. He has gone deeper. His effort has been to show how the literature of a great nation is not only a natural evolution from its life, but is also a factor in the evolution of that life, for life and literature are mutually interdependent, and if events shape and determine literature, literature in its turn predicts influences and directs events.

He shows how the influx of the Germanic barbarians into the decaying civilization of the Roman Empire—a civilization in which their ancestral faith, customs, and institutions have no authority—brings them face to face for the first time with the conflict between universal law and individual passion, and results poetically in the German epic with its colossal types of heroic devotion, greed, and guilt.

The feudal system, the crusades, the long struggle, first between the empire and the papacy, and then between Protestantism and Catholicity, each finds expression in the literature of its own period.

But the reformation which had begun with a grand movement for popular freedom seems to end by establishing more firmly than ever the absolutism, religious as well as political, of the territorial princes. For the all-embracing mediæval Church has been substituted a host of narrow, warring sects, for the united empire a weltering chaos of rival states. The national spirit, the national religion, the national literature seem dead. In reality they are only dormant. "Debarred from active participation in public life, hemmed in by narrow surroundings, out of contact with the nation at large, Germany's best men now turn all the more eagerly to the cultivation of the inner self. Reorganization of the national body through regeneration of the individual mind—this now becomes the great task of literature. Pietism and Rationalism, Sentimentalism and Storm-and-Stress, Classicism and Romanticism, co-operate in this common task of building up and rounding out the individual life." And so begins the last great movement of German thought in which Goethe, Schiller, and their kin point beyond individual freedom and culture toward a communion of interests in the new order, built upon the ruins of the old. This movement is epitomized in the masterwork of the period, Goethe's "Faust," which Francke rightly characterizes as a complete embodiment of the modern ideas of personality as related to social environment. "Restless endeavor, incessant striving from lower spheres of life to higher ones, from the sensuous to the spiritual, from enjoyment to work, from creed to deed, from self to humanity — this is the moving thought of the whole drama." And that is also the moving thought of all the splendid literature of which Goethe was the dominant figure. (Holt. *net*, $2.)—*N. Y. Herald.*

The Most Gorgeous Lady Blessington.

THE Messrs. Scribner have published in two volumes an entertaining book by Mr. J. Fitzgerald Molloy, who is tolerably well known as the compiler of historical and biographical anecdotes. The title of the book is "The Most Gorgeous Lady Blessington"; the author of the adjective applied to the beautiful Irish woman was the learned Dr. Parr. There is no doubt that Lady Blessington had a singularly romantic life, and that she may have suggested to Mrs. Burnett the heroine of her latest novel. That she possessed a most engaging personality we know on the evidence of the best judges of her time, for there was hardly any distinguished man in England, France, or Italy, who did not regard her with admiration, if not always with respect. When one considers how meagre were her early educational advantages, it seems surprising that she should have acquired so much knowledge and so much taste as to make of her drawing-room a veritable salon of the type with which Paris was familiar in the last century. She became an excellent critic in literature and art, and her own literary performances were of no mean order. Of sympathy and generosity she gave innumerable proofs, and the only serious blot upon her character, after her marriage to Lord Blessington, was her acquiescence in the marriage of her husband's daughter to Count D'Orsay and the equivocal relation in which she and her son-in-law subsequently lived. In the volume before us Lady Blessington herself is only the central figure. We hear also a great deal about her friends, including Byron, Landor, Bulwer, Disraeli, and Prince Louis Napoleon. (Scribner. 2 v., $4.)—*N. Y. Sun.*

The Piano in College.

EALING'S powers of execution on the piano were limited. He could play hymn-tunes or other compositions, where the next chord to the one he was engaged on followed as a corollary from it, and anything in the world which went so slowly as to enable him to glance from the music to his hands between each chord, however complicated it was, provided it did not contain a double sharp, which he always played wrong. He could also, by dint of long practice, play "Father O'Flynn" and the first verse of "Off to Philadelphia in the Morning;" and there seemed to be no reason why, with industry, he should not be able to acquire the power of playing the other verses, in which he considered the chords to be most irregular and unexpected, deserting the air at the most crucial points. Reggie, however, was far more accomplished. He had got past hymn-tunes. The Intermezzo in *Cavaleria Rusticana*—even the palpitating part—was from force of repetition mere child's play to him, and he aspired to the slow movements out of Beethoven's Sonatas.

The hours in which each might practice, therefore, demanded careful arrangement. College regulations forbade the use of the pianos altogether between nine in the morning and two in the afternoon, since it was popularly supposed by the authorities who framed this rule—and who shall say them nay?—that all undergraduates worked between these hours, and that the sound of a piano would disturb them. Consequently, Ealing was allowed to play between eight A.M. and nine A.M. every morning, a privilege which he used intermittently during

CLARE COLLEGE AND BRIDGE.

breakfast, and by which he drove Reggie, daily, to the verge of insanity, and Reggie between two P.M and three P.M. Ealing again might play between three and five, and Reggie from five to seven. During these hours the temporary captain of the pianos, even if he did not wish to play himself, might stop the other from playing except with the soft pedal down. It had been found impossible to regulate the hours after dinner, and they often played simultaneously on their several pianos, and produced thereby very curious and interesting effects, which sounded Wagnerian at a sufficient distance. Finally, the use of the piano was totally prohibited by common consent between two A.M. and eight A.M. (Putnam. $1.)— *From Benson's "The Babe, B.A."*

Clyde Moorfield, Yachtsman.

THERE were two things, besides himself, of which Clyde Moorfield was passionately fond, and these were yachting and young ladies. It was a lamentable fact that his two preferences were often hard to reconcile, because the young ladies who suited his fastidious taste were apt to care little for his favorite sport; nevertheless, he generally managed to find one or two who were first-class sailors and who interested him as well, though the combination of these two requirements often gave him no small amount of trouble. His definition of happi-

From "A Hypocritical Romance." Copyright, 1896, by Jos. Knight Pub. Co.

NO BUSINESS TO-MORROW, MY DEAR.

ness was a fine sailing breeze, a boat built after the most approved models (one which could win him two or three prizes every year), and a pretty girl who could help him and be entrusted with the tiller from time to time.

He had been disappointed in respect to this last requisition so many times that he had come to make it a point not to become interested in any girl until he found out whether or not she was what he styled "a true salt." If, after an introduction, he received a negative reply to his invariable question, "Are you fond of yachting?" he soon excused himself, and studiously avoided further advances in so unprofitable a direction.

Moorfield had been studying law so assidu-ously for two or three years that during the

winter seasons he allowed himself very little recreation, refusing all invitations, and shun-ning society conscientiously. In summer time, however, he tried to make up for all this self-denial, and he usually succeeded in having a blissfully selfish time. He knew that he was very selfish, but he gloried in it; he revelled in pleasing himself exclusively, and he did not care whether other people liked it or not. He would not play euchre, nor help the older ladies out on whist, nor make up a set of ten-nis, nor, in fact, do anything but suit Mr. Clyde Moorfield; and he considered that the sooner the majority of bores found this out the better. He had not come away to spend his vacation in en-tertaining people who did not interest him, and he did not propose to do it.

He was handsome and lazy, and, in spite of his failure to appreciate them as he should have done, the girls sim-ply adored him. Moorfield was a su-perb waltzer; but he said that "he didn't care to dance in summer," and only strolled into the dancing-hall occa-sionally to look on, when he would sit and converse with the fortunate girl who pleased his fancy, knowing full well that she would very much like to dance, but never asking her to do so, because he didn't care about it.

He never took out parties in his boat, having a perfect horror of being sur-rounded by a lot of people who lost off their hats and screamed whenever the boat went about, and who brought lemons out with them to prevent seasickness. He had no patience with people who were seasick; and a girl lost all charm for him who was not proof against a ground-swell. He felt no sympathy for the poor sufferers who begged to be al-lowed to lie down in the bottom of the boat; he only despised them.

The fortunate young woman upon whom he smiled did not fail to appreciate the favor, and an invitation to sail with him was never re-fused—it was too great an honor; moreover, the lucky recipient of it always took care to be promptly on hand at the appointed hour, for Mr. Clyde Moorfield did not like to be kept waiting.

He had demonstrated this fact on a memora-ble occasion when one independent damsel upon whom he had showered much attention had kept him striding up and down the pier for a whole half-hour. When she finally appeared she found him calm and affable as ever, and even more entertaining and happy-go-lucky than usual, so that she experienced a slight feeling of disappointment, having hoped to ruffle him somewhat by the delay, which none of the other girls would have dared to inflict. Nevertheless, she thought she recognized in this amiability a greater depth of devotion to her than she had even dreamed of. Alas, her satisfaction was but short-lived, for never again did Clyde Moorfield ask her to step over the gunwale of his dainty craft. He was polite, and even provokingly agreeable whenever they met, but that was all; he never joined her in her promenade on the piazza, never sat beside her in the dance-hall; in fact, he showed plainly from that day that her society was no longer an item on his nautical programme. But after that few girls ever kept the imperious yachtsman waiting; and if by chance anything delayed them a moment beyond the appointed time they were profuse in their apologies. (Knight. $1.)—*From Ticknor's "A Hypocritical Romance."*

What the Dragon-Fly Told the Children.

NEARLY all children are poetic. They live near the heart of things in the early springtide of life when "birds and buds and they are happy peers." They have also a natural love of rhyme and rhythm and the melody of verse. Mother Goose ministers to this need of their natures for the first two or three years of life ; but immediately after that comes generally nothing in the way of poetry. Why should not the God-given instinct be further cultivated by reading to them at such an age selections from the poets, culling here and there, where in simple, lovely words the great singers have sung simple, lovely thoughts fit for children's ears, and likely to delight their imaginations?

It would indeed be well to have the names of our greatest poets familiar household words even to the children. In the belief that such a thing could be, and should be, and that the children would enjoy and be greatly benefited by such reading, this little book of selected bits from the poets is offered.

It is meant to lie on the table ready to be picked up when the children beg Mamma or Auntie to read to them "just a little bit." Though a light thread of continuous narrative runs through the book, by which to hold the attention of the youngest readers, it is only a thread on which to string the poems ; the poetry itself is the bait by which we hope to catch the children. Bits of decorative illustration are scattered through the text and there are numerous portraits of poets given. Six friendly little cousins came to Edgehurst to visit grandpa and grandma. There was only one boy among them, but he was kept in mind while the Dragon-Fly chose poetry for them. (Lothrop Pub. Co. $1.50.) — *From the Preface of Coursen's "What the Dragon-Fly Told the Children."*

THEY ALL MARCHED AFTER HER THROUGH THE WOODS.

THE PRINCESS SARSAPARILLA.

Fairy-Tales.

FIDELITY to an established ideal and a general dislike of literary novelties are characteristic attributes of "really truly" children, such as played in our grandmothers' attics and dug in our grandmothers' gardens. What child would have a new story if he could get an old one, and what child would hear the story of an every-day human being if he could listen to the adventures of a king or prince? Mrs. Blodgett's rehash of well-known themes will, therefore, find a welcome, unless Mr. Kipling and Mr. Lang have so salted and prepared the taste of the present-day children that the old dishes no longer find favor.

We are in honor bound to look at this collection of stories from the children's point of view —a point of view in which suspicions of plagiarism are not considered, and, if we remember rightly, it is very much the sort of thing that children like; but we are not so sure about the pictures. Miss Ethel Reed has undoubted talent, and disposes her Japanese patterns effectively. She is clever in the massing of her blacks, and she gets action and expression into her figures and her queer little paper-doll faces; but the style of work she has undertaken makes very strenuous demands upon the artist. If she is serious—and there is certainly no indication in her pictures that she is not—she will suffer from a noble discontent until she has more nearly approached the Japanese standard of line. Her illustrations "make" the book for the grown-ups, whether or not the children accept them. (Lamson, Wolffe & Co. $2.)— *N. Y. Times.*

A Bad Penny.

THE romance that lightened the sombre life of the Puritan residents of New England at the beginning of this century helps much to make any story of that time interesting. "A Bad Penny" is a fascinating presentation of life in a Massachusetts seaport town, in which all the romance of the period has been utilized. We have an old retired sea-captain, with a harum-scarum boy, who also wants to be a sailor. The old gentleman has settled it that his son shall be a minister. There is a prim maiden aunt, to whom the lad is a perpetual torment, and there is a bad sailor brother of hers, who comes back from sea when he was supposed to be dead, and who disturbs the quiet New England household as such bad brothers and uncles have a way of doing. The bad uncle has robbed a hard old deacon in the town thirteen years before, and the deacon chases him to his ship when he finds that the thief is in town. The uncle escapes, and is prevailed on to restore to the deacon the silverware he stole so many years before, and which has been secreted in the neighborhood ever since. The boy, James Woodbury, takes the silver to the deacon's house in the night, and is mistaken for a burglar. Then the boy goes to sea, and fights on the *Chesapeake* against the British

ship *Shannon*. Everything ends happily. James marries his own true love, and settles down as a ship-builder, and the reader thinks what a fine fellow he is.

The scapegrace uncle? Oh, he dies as the result of a wound received on the *Chesapeake* from British boarders. He has the satisfaction of giving his life for his country, and this partly condones his offences against her laws.

The story is told with much spirit. The description of the engagement between the *Chesapeake* and *Shannon* is splendid, while in the quiet, domestic scenes, the author proves that he possesses the true story-teller's instinct for making effective contrasts. Every character is well drawn, and the local color is so faithful as to prove that the author knows New England coast towns as they are to-day, which enables him to picture them in the early days of this republic.

While "A Bad Penny" is the sort of book that every healthy boy will devour, it is so well written and has so ingenious a plot that the boy's father will read it, too.

The publishers have given the tale a handsome setting. It is printed on heavy finished paper, in clear type, and bound tastefully in cloth. It is one of the firm's *Papyrus Series*, and the suggestion of Egyptian literature is carried out by three of the Pyramids pictured in gold on the cover. The illustrations by F. G. Attwood are exceedingly good. (Lamson, Wolffe & Co. $1.25.)—*N. Y. Commercial Advertiser.*

A BOY WHO NEVER WAS A BOY.

The Ebbing of the Tide.

"THE Ebbing of the Tide," by Louis Becke, is a set of South Sea stories marked by all the poetic insight and story-telling faculty which

From Crawford's "Bar Harbor."   Copyright, 1896, by Charles Scribner's Sons.
ON THE CORNICHE ROAD.

characterized this author's "By Reef and Palm," which was one of the book successes of last year. Mr. Becke is decidedly one of the new writers who claim attention, and this book will go far towards putting him definitely on his feet among the authors who are "worth while." The stories not infrequently remind the reader of Stevenson, not from any want of originality in Mr. Becke, but because these writers have a similar way of looking at life. The stories are mostly brief, and there are over twenty in the volume. There is a singularly high average of merit in them; but a few may be particularized as perhaps standing out beyond their fellows—such as "Lubban of the Pool," "A Dead Loss," "Auriki Reef," and "A Tale of a Mask." Imagination and style are blended in Mr. Becke's work. (Lippincott. $1.25.)— *Philadelphia Evening Telegraph.*

Bar Harbor.

AN element of the picturesque is supplied by an Indian camp, which used for years to be pitched in a marshy field known as Squaw Hollow ; but with the advent of a Village Improvement Society certain new-fangled and disturbing ideas as to sanitary conditions obtained a hearing, and the Indians were banished to a back road out of the way of sensitive eyes and noses. They claim to be of the Passamaquoddy tribe, speak their own language, and follow the peaceful trades of basket-weaving and moccasin-making and the building of birch-bark canoes. Their little dwellings — some of them tents, some of them shanties covered with tar-paper and strips of bark — are scattered about, and in the shadow of one of them sits a lady of enormous girth, who calls herself their queen, and who wears, perhaps as a badge of sovereignty, a huge fur cap even in the hottest weather. She is not less industrious than other "regular royal" queens, for she sells baskets and tells fortunes even more flattering than the fabled tale of Hope. Some of the young men are fine, swarthy, taciturn creatures, who look as though they knew how to put a knife to other uses than whittling the frame of a canoe ; but one does not feel tempted to rush upon Fate for the sake of any of the dumpy and greasy-looking damsels who will soon become like their even dumpier and greasier mothers.

The whole encampment is pungent with the acrid smoke of green wood, and many children roll about in close friendship with queer little dogs in which the absence of breed produces a family likeness. It is curious to see in the characteristic work of these people the survival of the instinctive taste of semi-savage races and the total lack of it in everything else. The designs cut on the bark of their canoes are thoroughly good in their way ; but contact with a higher civilization seems to have affected them as it has the Japanese, turning their attention chiefly to making napkin-rings and collar-boxes, and to a hideous delight in tawdry finery, which is fondly, though distantly, modelled on current American fashions. (Scribner. 75 c.)—*From Crawford's "Bar Harbor."*

The True Story of Abraham Lincoln.

COLUMBUS, the discoverer of our country, and Washington, the father of our country— these two famous ones has this series of *Children's Lives of Great Men* recalled for young Americans. Now comes the third and crowning figure in the series—that of Abraham Lincoln, the savior of his country, and, above all others—the American.

His story is as marvellous as a fairy-tale, and yet as simple as the truth. Sprung from nothing he rose to the highest eminence, and died a martyr for liberty, Union, and the rights of man. Upon his life, through four terrible years, hung the destinies of this republic and the redemption of a race. To-day the world reveres him as one of the most eminent rulers of any time; the future will yet place him where he rightly belongs—one of the world's greatest men, perhaps the greatest.

For the boys and girls of America brought up in the atmosphere of liberty, of justice, and of patriotism, Abraham Lincoln, the man of the people, has an especial claim to reverence. He stands as a type—as before all others *the* American.

In the preface to "The True Story of George Washington" the writer quoted for boys and girls a sentiment from one of the noblest of American thinkers and authors, James Russell Lowell. This introduction to "The True Story of Abraham Lincoln" cannot be more fittingly closed than with the splendid tribute of the same prophetic poet, in his noble "Commemorative Ode," which every boy and girl of America should some day read:

> "These all are gone ; and standing like a tower,
>   Our children shall behold his fame,
>   The kindly, earnest, brave, far-seeing man,
>   Sagacious, patient, dreading praise, not blame,
>   New birth of our new soil, the first American."

(Lothrop. $1.50.)—*From Preface to Brooks's "The True Story of Abraham Lincoln."*

Love Is a Spirit.

JULIAN HAWTHORNE's new novel, "Love Is a Spirit," is a whimsical affair, yet by no means unserious. No one who has read "Archibald Malmaison" is unacquainted with Hawthorne's marvellous power for touching in just the right way the mysterious regions that lie just beyond the realm of what we call the natural. The supernatural, or quasi-natural, if you will, has for him, as it had for his father, a deep and a fertile fascination. Angus Hugh Strathspey, a married man, separated from his wife—they hate each other—meets a girl, Yolande, on an island in the tropics, and the two fall in love. He conceals from her the fact that he is married, and she confesses her love. Leaving her, he struggles with himself whether he will

From Brooks's " The True Story of Abraham Lincoln."   Copyright, 1896, by The Lothrop Pub. Co.

HE BORROWED EVERY BOOK IN NEW SALEM.

marry her, knowing it will be no marriage, and,
in revolt at the idea, determines to kill himself.
He receives a letter from his wife, written a
day or two before her death, and believes he
can marry Yolande. Then the memory that
he had kissed her when he thought he was a
married man makes him understand he is
too vile. After a short illness he rides towards
Yolande's house in order to tell her the truth.
He meets her on horseback, and they talk.
After a few hours she vanishes, and he realizes
that he has been talking to her spirit, and that
she is dead. The book closes with Angus on
his knees beside Yolande's body. No other tale
by the author is so suggestive of the eerie subtlety of his great father's method and style.
(Harper. $1.25.)—*Brooklyn Times.*

The Verbalist.

A COMPARISON of the second edition of "The
Verbalist," that excellent little manual devoted
to brief discussions of the right and the wrong
use of words, by Alfred Ayres, with the work
in its original form, as it appeared in 1882, shows
many marked improvements. The number of
pages has been increased by more than one-
half, and where the substance of the original
text has been retained the wording has been in
many cases entirely recast. The author has
also greatly added to the value of his book by
making free use of illustrative quotations.
Sometimes Mr. Ayres finds occasion to modify
his earlier opinions: for instance, on page 26
he inserts this suggestive paragraph, after a
wholesale denunciation of nouns ending in
" ess ": " On the other hand there are those
that think the use of ' authoress ' should be left
to individual tastes. It cannot be denied, however, that we could get on quite as well without it." The two or three pages that Mr. Ayres
gives to the subject of " noun construction "
are new and timely, and deserve to receive the
careful attention of the student of contemporary
English. The author seems to have taken
something like a malicious pleasure in making
up the warning extracts under this heading
largely from the columns of that self-confessed
champion of linguistic purity, the New York
Sun. Another noteworthy feature of this
second edition of "The Verbalist " is a full discussion of the use of the relative pronouns; Mr.
Ayres is also happily explicit with regard to the
employment of the auxiliaries " will " and
" would," and he expands the section on " is
being built" to a general discussion of "is
being." It is pleasant to find that Mr. Ayres, in
his pursuit and denunciation of verbal mon-
strosities and distortions, has not failed to take
note of the recent tendencies to use the word
" unique " in the sense of " beautiful"; he has

neglected, however, to comment on the unpardonable employment of the phrase " to a degree," or the comparatively recent usage in the
newspapers, and even in official documents, of
" issuance " for issue. One is more than glad
to discover that Mr. Ayres still clings to the
opinion, so pungently expressed in the first edition of "The Verbalist," that "pants are worn
by gents, who eat lunches and open wine, and
trousers are worn by gentlemen, who eat lunch-
eons and order wine." There is no more handy,
compact, trustworthy, and comprehensive guide
to the elements of good English than Mr.
Ayres's "Verbalist," and this new and enlarged
edition of the book will be cordially welcomed
by those who continue to have a regard for
sound, expressive, and correct diction. (Appleton. $1.25.)—*The Beacon.*

THE CONFESSION OF A LIBRARY CLERK.

BY CUPID JONES (*pseud.* OF FRANCIS S. SALTUS).

EACH day, with locks well oiled, I stand,
  A literary Mentor,
And greet with smiles serene and bland
  Our patrons as they enter.

'Tis not alone to give a book
  To any who demand it,
But 'tis the manner and the look
  And the sweet way I hand it.

And then it is a well-known fact,
  When making a selection,
I show a most discerning tact
  And judgment in perfection.

So, when old fogies come to get
  Of novel new the lightest,
I hand them over *Not Dead Yet,*
  And calmly smile my brightest ;

Or vaguely hint of *Dead Men's Shoes.*
  And if they prove not docile,
I give them, for their instant use,
  Some treatise on the fossil !

And should my tailor to me bend
  And say, "You are my debtor,"
I hand him *To the Bitter End,*
  To make his nature better.

When a rich girl comes in all bent
  A passion strong to foster
For some young man without a cent,
  I hand her *What He Cost Her.*

And to all crusty, mean old men,
  Who say they'll marry never,
I offer, while I twirl my pen,
  The book, *Deceivers Ever.*

My mind, to make a joke a shade
  More witty, has never tarried,
For when I see a gaunt old maid
  I give her *Safely Married.*

And it has always been my forte
  To hand out, without shrinking,
A copy new of *Wrecked in Port*
  To old men fond of drinking.

Played Out I give to those whose store
  Of gold is lost at euchre,
And *Birds of Prey* I lay before
  Fat brokers gorged with lucre.

And thus the happy days go by,
  While I strain brains and fibres
To please the world and satisfy
  Our numerous subscribers.

—*From the volume called " Fact and Fancy."*
(Putnam.)

A NORWEGIAN "MAUD MÜLLER."

A Voyage to Viking-Land.

MR. STEELE sailed from New York on the *Normannia* and was present at the opening of the Kiel Canal, which was celebrated with great pomp by the war-ships of all nations, before he started on his pleasant tour through Viking-Land.

The following pages are all an "introduction" to one of the loveliest countries of the Old World which it has been the pleasure of the writer to visit. It is the itinerary of a most delightful voyage along the coast of Norway of a happy party of tourists, who on pleasure bent were blessed with an excellent steamer, fine weather, good appetites, and a capacity for enjoyment only limited by the daily supply which the circumstances offered.

It was like cruising in one's own yacht, without its responsibilities and cares. The glories of the silent fjord, the wonderful glaciers, and the majestic waterfalls were seen to their very best advantage, while few tourists to this region obtain such unobstructed views of the splendors of the midnight sun. With the exception of the portraits, almost all of the illustrations are from photographs taken on the trip, the larger portion from the steamer's deck while sailing through the fjords and along the shores. — (Estes & Lauriat. $2.) — *From Steele's "A Voyage to Viking-Land."*

The Finding of Lot's Wife.

MR. ALFRED CLARK has written a novel that has an interesting plot, and summer idlers will find in it material for several hours of self-forgetfulness. "The Finding of Lot's Wife" is not strikingly original, the characters are somewhat conventional, and, with one exception, the situations appeal to the memory rather than to the imagination ; but nevertheless the book is worth the reading. The best-drawn character is that of Ayeda, the Arab girl, and there is more than a suggestion of real pathos in her devotion to Yorke. The heroine, Isha, however, is an old friend that has paraded through many novels without convincing anybody that she is real flesh and blood. The men are lay figures to be found in the studio of any professional writer, and, with a change of attire and attitude, ready to figure in any conceivable situation with credit. There is a certain dramatic power revealed in the chapters leading up to the discovery of Lot's wife, but a good deal of the effect is marred by a mingling of petty realism with poetic imagination. It is impossible to describe a miracle in scientific language, and any attempt at making it definite robs it of its effect. The chronic novel-reader might also object to the unnecessary tragedy in the story. Good and interesting people die in our real world, but they do not do it with deliberation, and one feels that Ayeda goes to her grave simply because she was an Arab girl and might shock English society if she married Yorke. With all its faults there are but few dull pages in the book, the plot uninterruptedly progresses, and is thrilling enough to hold the reader's attention to the end. (Stokes. $1.)—*Boston Evening Gazette.*

Embarrassments.

HENRY JAMES requires plenty of room "to turn round in." This may be partly the consequence of his elaborate thinking; it is certainly due to his elaborate literary style. A goodly sized volume entitled "Embarrassments" contains four of his "short" stories. Mr. James is not a writer for the frivolous, the superficial, or the dull-witted. It is true that the plots of Mr. James's stories are often frivolous and puerile, but he has the gift of investing them with an air of ponderous gravity that rather awes one at first. As the reader follows the careful unfolding of the narrative—which reminds one of a Supreme Court judge trying to be playful without compromising his dignity —one begins to see his way through the interstices of Mr. James's closely woven argument and to admire the beauty of his syntax.

The best of the four stories is "The Way It Came." It is the last in the volume. The commonest of spiritual manifestations for which practical every-day people will vouch is the appearance of a man or woman at the moment of his or her death to some other man or woman. Why these appearances is not often explained. Generally they seem to be merely whimsical, without any serious purpose. The main point is that there are thousands of people, reputed to possess well-balanced intellects, who will tell you that they have been favored by those visitations.

Nothing could be more natural, from Mr. James's point of view, than for such ghost-seers to be mysteriously attracted toward each other. They do not meet in life, but they become acquainted when the lady dies, and—her husband having departed this life some years previously—she comes to see the young man frequently. The diary girl is jealous, and breaks off her engagement. The dead woman and her living lover—for such he has become—enjoy each other's society on nether ground for six years. Then the young man crosses the river to join his spiritual bride.

"Glasses" and "The Next Time" are the other two stories. They are of somewhat lighter purpose than the first and last, although both are good examples of the author's mellifluous, graceful story-telling. After all it is not so much what he says as his exquisite manner of saying it that makes Henry James one of the most brilliant exponents of light literature that this century has seen. He is the Addison of his day. (Macmillan. $1.50.) —*N. Y. Herald.*

A Financial Atonement.

MR. WEST has drawn a curious study. Arthur Brigges is born in London, and early in life has suffered from the pinches of poverty. Educated at the Soapboilers, he shows little ability. What brains he may have he carefully hides. His aim is to be a promoter, a builder of visionary schemes, by means of which he shall fleece the public. Mr. West is highly ingenious in the construction of the many companies Brigges invents. You have the entire list presented, some twenty-two of them. One is the "Parental Sweetmeats Automatic," another "The Musical Omnibus," another the "Old Clo'." This latter company is semireligious in character. Christians are to crowd out the Jews in the business of buying and selling old frippery, and the sons of Moses, then being driven to the wall, must become Christians or starve.

"The Waste Land's Reclamation," capital £4,000,000, 20,000 shares, £3 paid, is a noble enterprise. London curbstones are to be pulled up and to be replaced with borders of marrow-fat peas, scarlet runners, and Jerusalem arti-chokes. Brigges, as promoter in chief, has for his tools "the sterling Joseph Hicks, honest Robert Jones, sagacious Jonadab Shuffles, transparent Daniel Ruggles, and blunt Thomas Grogges," all men of straw. After running his course Arthur Brigges comes to grief, and all his companies go into liquidation. There are millions to be accounted for. Brigges, as cool as a cucumber, faces a thousand or so of the fleeced ones at a public meeting, and tells his angry creditors that he will pay every cent owed, and then he disappears.

Mr. B. B. West now launches into the sea of speculation, and a peculiar man appears at the bottom of all. There are corners and squeezes in every part of the world. This remarkable person will murder, cheat, be a traitor, gamble, so that there is money in it. It is Brigges who is at work in Asia, Africa, India, and America. When the coup is struck the main actor invari-ably disappears, leaves no sign, and so does the money. Finally, Brigges, having amassed millions, returns to England, satisfies his cred-itors, principal and interest, and dies. "A Financial Atonement" has a moral to it, though in the construction of the story there may be much which is disjointed. Evidently written by a man who has studied the great commer-cial systems of the day. (Longmans, Green & Co. $2.)—*N. Y. Times.*

Mrs. Gerald.

To readers of mature years Miss Maria Louise Pool's novels are a delight which the younger generation can scarcely appreciate. In the first place her descriptive powers are so wonderful, and men, women, and scenery drawn with her sure, practised, artistic touch must bring back to older people all the details of the places with which their brightest, best hours are associated. For about ten years Miss Pool has been writing, and she has steadily im-proved. The Ransome sketches for the *N. Y. Tribune* and some travel sketches for the *Even-ing Post* first attracted literary readers; since then "Roweny," "Roweny in Boston," "A Vacation in a Buggy," "Dally," "In a Dyke Shanty," "The Two Salomes," "Against Hu-man Nature," and now "Mrs. Gerald," have shown a steady increase of imagination and artistic setting.

"Mrs. Gerald" is another of those studies of strong individual womanhood that Miss Pool has made her artistic specialty.

Mrs. Gerald starts as a poor girl, working in a factory and supporting her discouraged mother and her shiftless, useless father, who squanders all the family savings in remedies for an imaginary liver complaint. (This father and mother are works of art.) The battle of life makes her hard, and she does not show the beautiful, affectionate side of her complex nat-ure. She becomes Mrs. Gerald to help her family. (Harper. $1.50.)

JUDITH'S FATHER AND HER FRIEND.

Che Literary News.

An Eclectic Monthly Review of Current Literature.

EDITED BY A. H. LEYPOLDT.

AUGUST, 1896.

THE AUTHOR OF "UNCLE TOM'S CABIN."

THE author of "Uncle Tom's Cabin" passed quietly out of this life on July 1. To many the fact that Mrs. Stowe had been living until this year was a surprise. Her chief work is so connected with a time long past that its author has been thought of, especially by younger people, as one whose life on earth was ended years ago. How many realize to-day that John Ruskin and Florence Nightingale still walk among us, their work done and waiting to be called ?

Thirty-three years have rolled by since the Emancipation Proclamation, which nine years before, when Mrs. Stowe published "Uncle Tom's Cabin" in book-form, seemed beyond the outlook of even the most optimistic and enthusiastic workers in the cause of abolition. It has been conceded by those who watched and studied and worked and suffered to educate the American people and make them realize the incongruousness of slavery in a free country, and to bring home to them the inherent dangers of the slave system, both to master and bondsman, that Mrs. Stowe's "Uncle Tom's Cabin" did more than they all to wake up the people and bring home to them the facts and possibilities of the great wrong they were committing or condoning. .

In spite of its fabulous success there is reason to doubt that "Uncle Tom's Cabin" will take its place among the great and permanent works of literature. It was a purpose novel written to rouse the world's resentment against a mighty wrong, and it had the great advantage of introducing to the reading world a race of human beings practically new to literature. It appealed to the heart more than the head, and it touched the universal heart by its pathos and its humor. Marked literary ability cannot be denied to Mrs. Stowe, but she has shown this far more in her lesser-known books, notably in "The Minister's Wooing," "The Pearl of Orr's Island," and "Old Town Folks."

Mrs. Stowe was so carried away by her subject that her great appeal to the civilized nations often lacks proportion and repose and that intangible, almost indefinable something that we have been taught to call style. When all the conditions of which the book was born have become ancient history it will, however, remain a work of permanent value for the student of American men and women, customs and manners, and social and political conditions of an independent republic then not a century old. Whatever may have been said and written claiming that Mrs. Stowe was responsible for much hard feeling between North and South, that she distorted facts and wrote a wild, partisan, war-breathing novel no one can read

From "Mrs. Stowe's Complete Works." Copyright, by Houghton, Mifflin & Co.

MRS. HARRIET BEECHER STOWE.

the book quietly and find any such spirit in it. All through the book Mrs. Stowe's most earnest censure falls upon the North, which, recognizing the evils of slavery, still for its own grasping greed of wealth made use of a system it publicly execrated, and upon Christian ministers who stood and apologized for or ignored a condition wholly incompatible with the religion they preached : " Love thy neighbor as thyself." She showed delightful characters among the Southerners and in the words she let St. Clare speak to his uncompromising Vermont cousin gave a clear view of the Southern point of view, and never blamed individuals but always the system which to weak and bad characters gave power for evil and of which even the conscientious and the good felt the trammels.

The phenomenal success of this book had a great influence on Mrs. Stowe and all with whom she came in contact. The money she received for the first time made it possible for the hard-working woman to get beyond the limits of her New England home. She travelled, met all who were working for humanity and progress, saw all the works of art of which she had read and dreamed, and came back to her own land full of new ideas and capable of a much wider outlook upon the themes she put into books that with all their literary shortcomings have been powers for good and full of comfort, especially to good women.

Since the death of Mrs. Stowe the magazines and papers have given the few biographical facts of her quiet, useful life. In January, 1889, THE LITERARY NEWS gave these in connection with a portrait reproduced from a painting by Dora Wheeler. Some of these notices and reminiscences of Mrs. Stowe have been of great interest and all are written in a tone of personal affection. *The Atlantic,* for August, has some delightful glimpses of the days the *fêted* author of the most widely read book of the century spent among choice spirits in Italy. These are from the pen of Mrs. James T. Fields, the wife of the publisher whose name stood on the title-pages of the works which first gave America a place in the world's literature. *The Outlook,* which, as *The Christian Union,* was for many years under the special care of the Beechers, contains in its magazine number for July 25 an article by John R. Howard, to which are appended personal recollections by Edward Everett Hale, Julia Ward Howe, Richard Malcolm Johnson, Charles Dudley Warner, and Mrs. James T. Fields, the latter quoted from the article in *The Atlantic* already mentioned.

A most interesting collection of portraits make *The Outlook* contribution very valuable. Especially noteworthy are the portraits of Mrs.

Stowe's parents—Dr. Lyman Beecher and Roxana Foote. A study of their beautiful old faces is a lesson on the value of ancestry, and on the solemn duties of fathers and mothers. Mrs. Beecher's calm, serene beauty recalls a sentence from " Uncle Tom's Cabin " in Mrs. Stowe's description of the lovely Quaker friend of the slaves, Rachel Halliday : " So much has been said and sung of the beauty of young girls, why don't somebody wake up to the beauty of old women ? " Every one of the children of these parents has accomplished something in this world that tended to make it a better world for those who should live after them. In her books, in her daily life, and in her talks with girls especially Mrs. Stowe has always dwelt upon the privileges and duties of home life. She believed in homes and in mothers, and in the great influence for good of true womanliness.

The quickened demand for the works of Mrs. Stowe, consequent upon her death, will be happily met by the new and definitive edition of her complete writings, which her publishers, Messrs. Houghton, Mifflin & Co., have for some time had in preparation, to comprise sixteen volumes in their excellent *Riverside* editions of standard authors. The first volume will have a biographical sketch, and all the volumes are to be thoroughly edited and furnished with notes when necessary. Each of the volumes will have a frontispiece and a vignette, including several portraits, views of Mrs. Stowe's homes, and other interesting designs. There is to be a limited large-paper edition, each set of which will contain Mrs. Stowe's autograph written by her expressly for this purpose a few months ago.

In the volume of this edition devoted to " Uncle Tom's Cabin," will appear the bibliography of the work prepared by George Bullen, keeper of the department of printed books in the British Museum, together with an introductory account of the work. This bibliography occupies sixteen pages. It shows that Mrs. Stowe's book has been translated into twenty different languages, among them many obscure ones, languages it would seem hard for popularity to penetrate. These languages in alphabetical order are as follows : Armenian, Bohemian, Danish, Dutch, Finnish, Flemish, French, German, Hungarian or Magyar, Illyrian or Wendish, Polish, Portuguese, Romaic or modern Greek, Russian, Servian, Spanish, Swedish, Wallachian, and Welsh.

A book that could appeal to people of every race and clime has something in it that will live, something that appeals to the universal heart of man, the one thing that will remain the same under every system of government throughout all generations.

The Ascent of Woman.

"THE Ascent of Woman," by Roy Devereux, sounds modest and simple and innocent enough, doesn't it? One would expect nothing more terrifying than a little preamble about Mrs. Eve and her frock of fig leaves, and then paragraphs pirouetting along the ages through all the stages of "degradation" and delusion, up to the present g-l-o-r-i-o-u-s epoch of college professorships, of feminine surgeons, of women plumbers, and of masculine mothers!

But this book is not that kind of a bore at all. In fact, it isn't a bore, and the conservative gentlemen of the old school who write book critiques and portion out the household expenses every Monday morning to their "truly womanly wives" have waxed wroth over the audacity of this gossipy, cynical, amusing screed of Roy Devereux.

"The Ascent of Woman" doesn't include the New Woman. Her love for fine lingerie died when her aversion to being "bossed" was born. The properly constituted "ascended" woman prefers lace on her skirts to a husband, and sees nothing essentially antithetical between a dress made by a Doucet and a love of literature.

Apropos of literature here is a rather *naif* idea of the child-woman. "She has regarded books as her rivals, possessing over the soul of man an influence antithetical to her own, so that the poet who acknowledged that his only books were women's looks paid her as fair a tribute as any since the world began."

The following explanation of mankind's objection to woman's advancement is not a bad one :

"He has prepared a dish of love for her since the world began. It is the only plate he knows how to cook, and now for the first time she has no appetite for the banquet. That it is badly cooked, so overdone that no piquancy is left in it, never occurs to him, nor that woman has turned to more ethereal food out of sheer disgust at a diurnal *réchauffé*. If the modern Eve is a sexless creature, man has largely his own clumsiness to thank for it. . . . Having starved for centuries, she has now to recover from the surfeit of intellectual dainties to which she has helped herself with both hands."

I wish the women who write ponderously of commonplace ideas would take a peep at these amusing, clever, and thoughtful essays, where wit and style and theories go hand in hand and even tolerate discussions on dress at the end of the book. A spade is certainly called a spade here, but it is used to make the "ascent" and not to serve up sentimental nonsense or probe emotions born of want of exercise.

Absurd diatribes against, or cloying, maudlin arguments for matrimony and motherhood usually fill the decadent book. Roy Devereux says of those ancient estates, "Neither at least was ever intended as a profession for the unemployed."

Surely this fresh, bright book is far cleaner, broad and sweeping though its theories may be, than the nonsensical novel with an erotic heroine and a wild-eyed hero who never could or should or will be understood. (Roberts. $1.25.)—*N. Y. Commercial Advertiser.*

The Courtship of Morrice Buckler.

MANY months have passed away since good luck brought us such an inspiriting romance as "The Courtship of Morrice Buckler." After a perusal of its absorbing chapters we do not hesitate to say that our Parkers, our Weymans, and our Hopes must look to their laurels. We will even go further. While reading any book by any one of the three authors just mentioned, we never remember to have been more delighted than we have been by Mr. Mason's record of an English gentleman's adventures in two most eventful years of his life. The merest tyro amongst those whose duty it is to dole out praise or blame to the thousands of men and women who make bids for fortune by means of writing novels, will be able to detect with half a glance the undoubted merits of the narrative now before us. Whether we closely consider the skill evinced in the management of the plot, or the swiftness of the recital, or the admirable sense of proportion which has been employed by the author, we are only the more convinced that we here have a book to which all readers who revel in bright love and valorous deeds will turn to-day and return to-morrow. Nor does Mr. Mason fail when we jealously inspect his prose and his drawing of characters, though in these two respects he displays occasional lapses. It appears to us that when he started to write "The Courtship of Morrice Buckler" a tremendous zeal animated him, which gradually changed from a flame to a steady glow. We have come to this conclusion because in the first two or three chapters we find from time to time a distinction of phrasing which does not continue throughout the book, although the writing is always kept at an honorable level. All the characters may be commended, save only Culverton. He is undoubtedly worked up from ejaculatory predecessors and is a blemish on the book. This is the more to be regretted in view of his absolute unimportance. But where is there a sun without spots?

The story is one of the very best, compelling

attention from the opening to the concluding page.

Beyond a disclosure of the fact that the countess turned out to be a successful blood-hound (if we may speak of a lovely lady as a dog), we do not intend to go, as we feel certain that our remarks will induce some of our readers to travel straight to the source of pleasure. They will never regret such a pilgrimage. (Macmillan. $1.25.)—*London Literary World.*

Economics.

PROFESSOR HADLEY's book is an elaborate application of the methods of modern science to the problems of modern business. Such a work would be useless without a most carefully digested plan systematically carried out, but by division into fourteen sections the author has been able to produce a clear elucidation of his views. His first chapter is on public and private wealth, followed by others on economic responsibility, competition, speculation, investment of capital, combination of capital, money, credit, profit, wages, machinery and labor, co-operation, protective legislation, and government revenue.

The general correctness of the views expressed on trusts and combinations are, we think, borne out by the results. Ground is taken as to the unwisdom of laws limiting profits, for the good reason that they do not cause reduction in rates whether such laws are obeyed or evaded. Upon limitation of rates the author looks with somewhat more favor, although he admits the uncertainties attending that plan from the difficulty of estimating cost. One of his axioms is that interest is not paid by society to the capitalists, but by one group of capitalists to another, and that it must not be supposed that a low rate of interest due to increased security represents an unmixed good for society, for risk is an incident of progress and great security may be obtainable only at the price of general stagnation. Another is that the whole country becomes poorer under conditions which prevent conservative borrowing and safe investment. The author's plan for diminishing the evils of prison labor (from an economic point of view) is to distribute it among different industries in such a way that no one trade shall suffer unduly from a sudden influx of prison competition. On the immigration question he is in favor of removing the restrictions, and makes the statement that voluntary and unassisted immigration is generally of a pretty high grade.

We are aware that this is an inadequate *résumé* of only a part of Professor Hadley's book, but it is one of those works which cover so much ground and in which distinctions are so carefully defined that none other is possible in the limited space which we are able to give. The style is perspicuous, although at times he appears to be overcautious in the expressions of his opinions. (Putnam. $2.50.)—*Public Opinion.*

The Works of Edgar Allan Poe.

THE fine edition of the "Works of Edgar Allan Poe" is now complete in ten volumes—five of tales, four of literary criticism and miscellaneous writings, and one of poems. Mr. Woodberry's notes on the criticisms supply names of periodicals in which the articles appeared, dates, and in fact all the information that can be desired by the most curious. Longfellow's letter, exculpating himself from the charge of plagiarizing Motherwell's ballad, "Bonnie George Campbell," shows that Poe might have gathered from the New England poet some salutary ideas about his own specialty—taste in literary composition. With the notes on the poems a complete variorum is printed for the first time, the editors having thought this desirable, "partly because there is no such illustration in literature of the elaboration of poetry through long-continued and minute verbal processes, and partly because so large a portion of the verse written by Poe perished in those processes." Mr. Stedman's introductions to these two divisions of the Works are as interesting, thoughtful, and discriminating as is that to the Tales. For the preservation of Poe's critical writings apart from those which deal with what it is art's function to express and the technique of expression, he gives perhaps the only very good reason, saying that though they might not have been worth much if produced in any other period, "in consideration of the man and the time—as a part of our literary history—they have a very decided value." After considering the nature and quality of Poe's lyrical genius and the violently different opinions about it expressed by authoritative writers, Mr. Stedman concludes definitely that "a distinctive melody is the element in Poe's verse that first and last has told on every class of readers—a rhythmical effect which, be it of much or little worth, was its author's own ; and to add even one constituent to the resources of an art is what few succeed in doing." The bibliography of English and foreign editions is careful, and even the index has not been slighted. If a glimpse of the edition could be wafted to the poet, "within the distant Aidenn," the perfection of its make-up might almost persuade him to forgive the unflattering justice of some of the comments on his life and works. (Stone & Kimball. *ea.,* $1.50.)—*The Nation.*

The Water-Finder.

ONCE in awhile there is a rare person who is endowed by nature with the power to discover where it is best to dig a spring or a well. This person, if you employ him, walks about your premises with a branch of witch-hazel in his hand. At such spots as water can be struck without deep digging, the hazel branch droops downward, even if the medium attempts to prevent its doing so. By the way the twig twists and turns can be determined the exact spot where it will be best for you to dig.

A witch-hazel crotch is the favorite instrument of the water-finders. But there is a variation in preference. Some claim it doesn't matter what sort of a tree the crotch comes from. One old man I heard of used an apple-tree crotch. He demonstrated that he could locate water-pipes at the farm where he worked with no previous knowledge of where they were. Every time he came over a pipe the crotch bent downward. He really was able to tell just where the pipes were in spite of their crooked curves. He was a simple, mild old laborer, and was not to be suspected of sleight-of-hand. He said he couldn't prevent the downward inclination of the crotch if he tried to, but had no explanation to offer of the queer performance of the twig in his hand.

One man gifted with this water-finding power is a minister. It is his idea that this is not a special gift, but that all of us have it. He once followed back an underground water-course to where another water-course branched away from it. Here a well was dug that gave a most plenteous and never-failing supply of water. He said that by careful calculation a person could determine how deep the water lay. For instance, notice the inclination of the crotch and the spot where the pull of the water first asserts itself. Then discover the spot that brings you right over it. A calculation can be made from the angle and the distance from the place where the pull was first felt that will show just how much digging is necessary.

A water-finder who uses an elm crotch says any one can find water in this way who has warm hands. This man was something of a professional, and his charge was three dollars for each time he was employed.

He says he has never failed but once in his water searching, and that was when the man didn't dig where he told him to. (Lee & Shepard. $1.25.)—*From Clifton Johnson's "What They Say in New England."*

The Hindu Mind in Shelley.

WE have had Hindu minds in Europe. In England, where man is so valiant and so active, where personality is so strong and stable, where poetry is so subjective, where religion is a monotheism so Hebraic, Shelley was almost such. Critics have long since noted in him faculties analogous to those which wove the Vedic myths. No poetry is more impersonal, no sympathetic imagination more capable of reproducing the elemental sensations of elemental beings—the gladness of the earth revolving in the light of space, with its girdle of seas and continents, its forests, its clouds, its humid blue atmosphere; the peace of the splendid cloud floating in the warm ether, then laughing in the thunder and falling in the rain, mother of future harvests; the ecstasy of the lark, intoxicated with the sight of the luminous plains, quivering with joy, throbbing invisible in space,

"Like an unbodied joy whose race has just begun,"

and the timid affection of the fragile plant dreaming of its future buds. Shelley became earth with the earth, a flower with the flower, a brook with the brook, and his poetry is a changeful reflection of changeful nature. He was destitute of that durable emotion on which personality is founded; the sensation of the Me, with him, was reduced to its minimum. He is always speaking of that ecstasy in which the observer becomes one with the object contemplated. His soul is not distinct, isolated in nature, but is all scattered through it. Hence, all natural objects appear to him to be alive and to have a soul; to be capable of sensations; and, moreover, to be constantly in motion, ever changing, always undergoing transformation. The sensation of Life—of Life at the same time one and multiple—this is what his poetry expresses. He recognizes a soul of the universe, a soul of which we are the thoughts, into which death absorbs us, which quivers in the worm and in the star; a soul of which nature is the mystic garment, hidden under the things which are seen, and, at rare moments, shining through beautiful and noble forms, as a pale flame within a vase of translucent alabaster. Let a man re-read "Prometheus Unbound," where all beings unite in chorus, and especially that marvellous dialogue of the Earth and the Moon, and let him say if the poet were not intoxicated with that universal, eternally upspringing life which circulates through all things; if he were not transported by the vision of the living Bráhma displayed in sounds and perfumes and colors. Beyond this, Shelley never went. He never perceived the neuter Bráhma, motionless, without qualities. Of the two stages of Hindu intelligence and feeling, he passed through the first only. He knew the dream, the gayety, the ecstasy of the Vedic poets; he never attained to the inertia of the gymnosophists. A pantheist he was, but with a joyous pantheism, and he remained valiant and sound. (Holt. $1.50.)—*From Chevrillon's "In India."*

W. E. H. Lecky Judges America.

ANOTHER consideration, which has hardly, I think, been sufficiently recognized among the guiding influences of American politics, is the complete separation of church and state. American writers, probably with good reason, consider this one of the great successes of their government. In spite of the Episcopal Church establishment that once existed in Virginia, and the intensely theocratic character which New England governments for a long time presented, the idea of the connection of church and state did not strike root in America, and public opinion, within as well as without the churches, seems cordially to approve of the separation. But one consequence has been to diminish greatly the interest in national politics. Every one who honors England knows how large a proportion of the best men who are interested in politics are mainly interested in their ecclesiastical aspects, in questions directly or indirectly connected with establishment or disestablishment.

All this class of questions is in America removed from the sphere of politics.

That public opinion can be powerfully aroused there in a worthy cause no one will question. Nowhere in the present century has it acquired a greater volume and momentum than in the War of Secession. The self-sacrifice, the unanimity, the tenacity of purpose, the indomitable courage displayed on each side by the vast citizen armies in that long and terrible struggle, form one of the most splendid pages in nineteenth-century history. I can well recollect how Laurence Oliphant, who had excellent means of judging both wars, was accustomed to say that no fighting in the Franco-German War was comparable to the tenacity with which in America every village, almost every house, was defended or assailed; and the appalling sacrifice of life during the struggle goes far to justify this judgment. Nor were the nob'er qualities of the American people less clearly manifested by the sequel of the war. The manner in which those gigantic armies melted away into the civil population, casting aside, without apparent effort, all military tastes and habits, and throwing themselves into the vast fields of industry that were opened by the peace, forms one of the most striking spectacles in history; and the noble humanity shown to the vanquished enemy is a not less decisive proof of the high moral level of American opinion.

It was especially admirable in the very trying moments that followed the assassination of Lincoln, and it forms a memorable contrast to the extreme vindictiveness displayed by their forefathers, in the days of the Revolution, towards their loyalist fellow-countrymen. America arose at this time to a new place and dignity in the concert of nations. Europe had long seen in her little more than an amorphous, ill-cemented industrial population. It now learned to recognize the true characteristics of a great nation. There was exaggeration, but there was also no little truth, in the words of Lowell :

" Earth's biggest country got her soul.
And risen up Earth's greatest nation."

Jobbing and corruption and fraud flourished, indeed, abundantly during the war, but the lines of national greatness and genuine patriotism were far more conspicuous. In times of peace, no nation has ever been more distinguished than America for the generosity shown by her citizens in supporting public institutions and public causes. (Longmans, Green & Co. 2 v., $5.)—*From "Democracy and Liberty."*

A Perfect Treasure.

A FEW days after the exchange of these letters in 1886, a young man inquired of the porter, who sits like a modern Argus beneath Tom Tower, the way to Mr. Englefield's rooms.

I compare the porter to Argus rather than to Cerberus, partly because it has never been done before, and partly because the latter was, according to Mrs. Malaprop, " three gentlemen at once," so it seems inappropriate.

The stranger was of medium height, with a very pale face, a long nose, receding chin, and shallow, bluish-gray eyes, which looked at you without any penetration. His expression was rather sad, indicative of a chastened sorrow, and he appeared anæmic ; but his manner was the last extreme of respectful self-possession, and in his neat, black tail-coat, gray trousers, and irreproachable bowler hat, he was every inch the self-respecting servant out of livery.

He presented himself at the door of the Don's rooms, and after a short interval took a note from him to the bursar's, which resulted in his being engaged by the college as a scout, to serve his apprenticeship under Peter on the Tutor's staircase, much to the jealous indignation of many other under-scouts, who scowled at him with undisguised aversion, and regarded the whole proceeding as the flagrant job it undoubtedly was.

The history of scoutland has yet to be written, and must remain a blank page until some literary genius becomes a servitor, or is generated by this particular form of labor ; when that happens the result will be interesting reading. Who, that has never carried a luncheon-tray across a quadrangle, or polished pewters in a buttery, can hope to describe the infinite gradations of that under-world society, and distinguish properly between the social stations of a scout, a messenger, and a porter? What novelist of the present day could state accurately the pretensions of a kitchen clerk or a college gardener, or turn out even a plausible article on manciples and cooks ?

Suffice it to say, that human nature is much the same everywhere, and variety of character as obvious amongst a row of retainers as it is in a company of the Guards, and, it may be observed, their social customs, having the force of law, are as numerous and complicated as any which regulate the conduct of their superiors.

On the border-line where master and man meet, the moral advantage is unquestionably with the man : much of the comfort of his masters rests with the scout, and his opportunities of becoming acquainted with their most private affairs, when they have any, increase his sense of power. He overhears their conversation, sees most of their visitors, reads all the invitation cards stuck into the looking-glass over the chimney-piece, knows what letters they receive, and, not uncommonly, their contents also ; gauges their financial position, and can estimate to a shilling what they will give him at the end of term.

Too often the nature of his service depends upon the latter consideration, and it is not unusual to hear the strictly just clamoring for his food long after his more lavish neighbor has sat down to table. This, again, is human nature. Tom or William naturally prefers carrying pies and chickens to Mr. Nokes and his party to hastening up another flight of stairs with Mr. Stokes's bread and cheese. The latter will disappear down Mr. Stokes's throat, whereas something substantial will remain on Mr. Nokes's table at two o'clock, to be put into the little covered basket which is Tom's or William's *vade-mecum.* So day after day Mr. Stokes shouts while Mr. Nokes entertains. (Routledge. $1.25.)—*From Bradnock Hall's "A Rough Mischance."*

Survey of Current Literature.

☞ *Order through your bookseller.*—"*There is no worthier or surer pledge of the intelligence and the purity of any community than their general purchase of books; nor is there any one who does more to further the attainment and possession of these qualities than a good bookseller.*"—PROF. DUNN.

ART, MUSIC, DRAMA.

BOOTH, JOSIAH. Everybody's guide to music; with illustrated chapters on singing and cultivation of the voice, full and explicit helps to the piano and organ, complete dictionary of musical terms. [*New ed.*] G. W. Jacobs & Co. 24°, flex. leath., 50 c.

CHATWOOD, A. B. The new photography. Scribner. il. 12°, 40 c.

EDWARDS, T. G. The history of Mendelssohn's "Elijah"; with introd. by Sir G. Grove. Scribner. il. pors. 8°, $1.50.

FLETCHER, BANISTER, *and* BANISTER, F. History of architecture for the student, craftsman, and amateur : being a comparative view of the historical styles from the earliest period. Scribner. il. 12°, $4.50.

HIPKINS, A. J. Description and history of the pianoforte, and of the older keyboard stringed instruments. Scribner. il. 8°, bds., $1.25.

JACKSON, FRANK G. Theory and practice of design: an advanced text-book on decorative art. Scribner. il. 8°, $2.50.

SMOLIAN, ARTHUR. The themes of Tannhäuser; from the German by W. A. Ellis. Scribner. 12°, pap., 50 c.

WOLZOGEN, HANS V. A key to Parsifal; with thematic musical illustrations; from the German by W. A. Ellis. Scribner. 12°, pap., $1.

BIOGRAPHY, CORRESPONDENCE, ETC.

BASKERVILL, W. MALONE. Joel Chandler Harris. Publishing House M. E. Church, South. 16°, (Southern writers : biographical and critical studies, no. 1.) pap., 10 c.

CURTIS, G. W. Hawthorne. Putnam. 16°, (Little journeys to the homes of American authors.) pap., 5 c.

GROVE, G. Beethoven and his nine symphonies. Scribner. 12°, $2.40.

HUBBARD, ELBERT. Walt Whitman. Putnam. 16°, (Little journeys to the homes of American authors) pap., 5 c.

JOYCE, F. W. The life of Rev. Sir F. A. G. Ouseley ; with two chapters appreciative of Sir Ouseley as a musician, by G. R. Sinclair. Scribner. il. pors. 8°, $3.

KUHE, W. My musical recollections. Scribner. 8°, $5 60.

LEASK, W. KEITH. Hugh Miller. Scribner. 12°, (Famous Scots.) 75 c.

PAGET, *Sir* ARTHUR. The Paget papers; diplomatic and other correspondence of the Right Hon. Sir Arthur Paget, G.C.B., 1794–1807; with two appendices, 1808 and 1821–1829; arr. and ed. by his son, Sir A. B. Paget; with

notes by Mrs. J. R. Green. Longmans, Green & Co. pors. 8°, $10.

SALT, H. STEPHENS. Henry David Thoreau ; with bibliography by J. P. Anderson. Scribner. 12°, (Great writers ser.) $1.

DESCRIPTION, GEOGRAPHY, TRAVEL, ETC.

CLEMENS, S. LANGHORNE, ["Mark Twain," *pseud.*] Life on the Mississippi. [*New lib. ed.*] Harper. 8°, $1.75.

CRAWFORD, FRANCIS MARION. Bar Harbor; il. by S. C. Reinhart. Scribner. 16°, (American summer resorts, no. 3.) 75 c.

FLETCHER, J. S. Life in Arcadia ; il. by Patten Wilson. Macmillan. 12°, (Arcady lib.) $1.75.

HENRY, STUART. Paris days and evenings. Lippincott. por. 12°, $2.
Twenty-five sketches of Parisian life grouped as "Phases of life," "Letters and colours," "Opera and theatre," and "The Latin Quarter."

INGERSOLL, ERNEST. Rand, McNally & Co.'s handy guide to Washington and the District of Columbia. Rand, McN. il. maps, 16°, 50 c.; pap., 25 c.
Contents : An introduction to Washington ; A tour of the Capitol ; The new building for the Library of Congress ; On Capitol Hill ; From the Capitol to the White House; At the Executive Mansion ; The executive departments ; From the monument to the museum ; Historic and picturesque Washington ; Official etiquette at the capital ; Churches, art galleries, theatres, clubs, etc. Excursions about Washington. List of the diplomatic corps.

MAZAMA : a record of mountaineering in the Pacific Northwest. V. 1. No. 1. Published by The Mazamas. il. 8°, pap., 75 c.
"Mazama" is the Indian name for the American chamois or mountain goat. It is the name taken by a society of Portland, Oregon, devoted to mountain climbing and exploration. This present book, besides some original poems, contains papers giving the history of the Mazamas, its presidents' addresses, the flora of Mount Adams, the glaciers and ice caves, and an account of the Klamath Mountains, etc. Contains a bibliography (4 p.) of the most important things that have been published concerning the territory thus far explored by the Mazamas.

PARR, H. New wheels in old ruts: a pilgrimage to Canterbury *via* the ancient pilgrim's way; with pen-and-ink sketches by F. W. R. Adams. Lippincott. map, 12°, $1.50.

RAND, McNALLY & Co.'s handy guide to the country around New York : for the wheelman, driver, and excursionist. Rand, McN. il. maps, 50 c.; pap., 25 c.
Describes bicycling and steamboat and rail-

road routes in Westchester County, on Long Island, Staten Island, suburban New Jersey, and central and seaside New Jersey.

RAND, McNALLY & CO.'s road maps and cycling guide to Westchester County, N. Y. folding maps, nar. 8°, pap., 50 c.

STEELE, T. SEDGWICK. A voyage to Vikingland; 89 il., also map of Norway and Spitzbergen. Estes & Lauriat. 12°, $2.

TRAILL, H. DUFF. From Cairo to the Soudan frontier. Way & Williams. 12°, $1.50.
A record of impressions derived from a couple of brief tours in Egypt during the winters of 1893-4 and 1895-6.

DOMESTIC AND SOCIAL.

C., M. Everybody's book of correct conduct: being the etiquette of every-day life. *2d ed.* G. W. Jacobs & Co. 24°, flex. leath., 50 c.

DEVEREUX, ROY. The ascent of woman. Roberts. 12°, $1.25.

EVERYBODY'S cookery and household guide, with recipes for every description of table dishes, drinks, etc. G. W. Jacobs & Co. 24°, flex. leath., 50 c.

EDUCATION, LANGUAGE, ETC.

FARNHAM, AMOS W. The Oswego normal method of teaching geography; prepared for the practice department of the Oswego State Normal and Training School of Oswego. Bardeen. 16°, 50 c.

RIVERSIDE SCHOOL LIBRARY. Houghton, Mifflin & Co. 16° and 12°, hf. leath., prices 50 c. 60 c., and 70 c.
The first 10 v. are: Lambs' Tales from Shakespeare, 60 c.; Franklin's Autobiography, 50 c.; Scudder's George Washington, 60 c.; Fiske's War of Independence, 60 c.; Andersen's Stories, 50 c.; Scott's Ivanhoe, 70 c.; Holmes's Autocrat of the breakfast-table, 60 c.; Mrs. Stowe's Uncle Tom's cabin, 70 c.; Goldsmith's Vicar of Wakefield, 50 c., Cooper's The last of the Mohicans, 70 c.

FICTION.

ALDEN, *Mrs.* ISABELLA MACDONALD, ["Pansy," *pseud.*] Making fate. Lothrop. il. 12°, $1.50.
Ralph Bramlett, innately cowardly and selfish, believing himself in love with Marjorie Edmonds, who is noted for her strength of character, is induced by Estelle Douglass to an act of discourtesy, which annoys Marjorie, when a series of misfortunes follow this impulsive act. Ralph Bramlett attributes his misfortunes to the intervention of fate. The author tries to show that every one makes his own fate.

BARR, ROB. From whose bourne; il. by Frank M. Gregory. Stokes. il. nar. 16°, (Twentieth century ser.) 75 c.

BESANT, *Sir* WALTER. The master-craftsman: a novel. Stokes. por. 12°, $1.50.
Extract in June issue.

BROWN, ANNA ROBESON. Sir Mark: a tale of the first capital. Appleton. nar. 12°, 75 c.

BUCHANAN, ROB. A marriage by capture: a romance of to-day. Lippincott. 1 il., nar. 16°, (Lotos lib.) buckram, 75 c.
In the year 1890 Catherine Power, living in Newport, County Mayo, Ireland, declares her preference for the old-time custom marriage by capture, announcing in the presence of a rejected suitor her intention of marrying only under this condition. Immediately after this strange declaration Kate Power mysteriously disappears, and her cousin, likewise an aspirant for her hand, is arrested on the suspicion that he knows of the whereabouts of the missing heiress; at this crisis Miss Power returns, and surprising revelations follow.

BUNNER, H. CUYLER. Jersey Street and Jersey Lane: urban and suburban sketches; il. by A. B. Frost, B. West Clinedinst, Irving R. Wiles, and Kenneth Frazier. Scribner. 12°, $1.25.
A charming mingling of fact and fiction are found in the following six sketches: Jersey and Mulberry; Tiemann's to Tubby Hook; The Bowery and Bohemia; The story of a path; The lost child; A letter to town. Extract in July issue.

CAHAN, A. Yekl: a tale of the New York Ghetto. Appleton. 12°, $1.
Yekl was a cloakmaker in a sweat-shop in the Jewish quarter of New York City. In three years after landing he had become Americanized enough to dread the arrival of his wife and child among the people who admired his swaggering ways. But Gitl came and the consequences were disastrous.

CLARK, ALFRED. The finding of Lot's wife. Stokes. 12°, $1.

COCKE, JA. R., *M.D.* Blind leaders of the blind: the romance of a blind lawyer. Lee & Shepard. por. 12°, $1.50.

CROSS, *Mrs.* ADA CAMBRIDGE. A humble enterprise. Appleton. 12°, (Appleton's town and country lib.) $1; pap., 50 c.
Joseph Liddon, senior clerk of the firm of Churchill & Sons, Melbourne, is suddenly killed while crossing the railway track, and his eldest daughter, seeing no other means of support for herself and the remaining family, determines to start a tea-parlor. Little Collins Street is the scene of Jennie Liddon's business venture and of the quaint love-story in which Anthony Churchill plays an important part.

DAVIS, ARLINE E. The romance of Guardamonte. J. Selwin Tait & Sons. 16°, $1.

DAVIS, HARRIET RIDDLE. In sight of the goddess: a tale of Washington life. Lippincott. 1 il., nar. 16°, (Lotos lib.) 75 c.
The story is told alternately by the hero and heroine. The hero is the private secretary of a member of the cabinet at Washington and falls in love with the Honorable Secretary's daughter. The time is the present. The complications of plot are not profound, but the story is fresh and pure and gives a good picture of Washington social life.

FULLER, ANNA. A Venetian June; il. by G. Sloane. Putnam. 16°, $1.
The romance of a charming young couple, of American origin, is acted out in Venice in the beautiful month of June, and the reader learns much of this delightful old city and its many attractions. As a background is the romance of Col. Steele, the uncle of the girl and an old soldier of the Civil War, who has been hopelessly in love for years with the widowed mother of the hero.

HARDY, T. Wessex tales. *New uniform ed.* Harper. il. 8°, $1.50.

HAWTHORNE, JULIAN. Love is a spirit. Harper. 12°, $1.25.

JAMES, H. Embarrassments. The Macmillan Co. 12°, $1.50.
Four stories: The figure in the carpet; Glasses; The next time; The way it came.

KAYVE, MARVEL. Vashti, old and new; or, the eternal feminine : a romance of the wheel : a dramatic idyl. Authors' Publishing House. 12°, $1 ; pap., 50 c.

KEIGHTLEY, S. R. The crimson sign: a narrative of the adventures of Mr. Gervase Orme, sometime lieutenant in Mountjoy's regiment of foot. Harper. il. 12°, $1.50.

KING, C. An army wife. Neely. il. 12°, $1.25.

LE FANU, JA. SHERIDAN, YOUNG, *Sir* C., [*and others.*] A stable for nightmares; or, weird tales. New Amsterdam Book Co. 1 il., 16°, 75 c.
Contents: Dickon the Devil; A debt of honor; Devereux's dream; Catherine's quest; Haunted; Fichon and Sons, of the Croix Rousse ; The phantom fourth ; The spirits whisper ; Dr. Peversham's story; The secret of the two plaster casts; What was it ?

LIPSETT, CALDWELL. Where the Atlantic meets the land. Roberts. 16°, (Keynotes ser., no. 23.) $1.

LYALL, D. Heather from the brae : Scottish character sketches. Revell. 12°, 75 c.

McCARTHY, JUSTIN. The riddle ring. Appleton. 12°, (Appleton's town and country lib., no. 195.) $1; pap., 50 c.

McMANUS, L. The silk of the kine. Harper. 12°, $1.

MARRYAT, F. Novels. *New lib. ed.,* ed. by Reginald Brimley Johnson; il. with 150 full-p. etchings by W. Wrightbooth, D. Murray Smith, C. O. Murray, etc. In 24 v. V. 1-12. Little, Brown & Co. 8°, *subs., per v.,* $3.50. [Ed. limited to 750 sets.]

MATTHEWS, JA. BRANDER. Tales of fantasy and fact. Harper. il. 12°, $1.25.
A collection of seven short stories, in which the author illustrates the contrast between pure imagination and realism. They are entitled: A primer of imaginary geography; The kinetoscope of time; The dreamgown of the Japanese ambassador; The rival ghosts; Sixteen years without a birthday; The twinkling of an eye; A confidential postscript.

MOORE, FRANK FRANKFORT. Daireen. Fenno. il. 12°, $1.25.

POOL, MARIA LOUISE. Mrs. Gerald: a novel. il. by W. A. Rogers. Harper. 12°, $1.50.

RIVERS, G. R. R. The governor's garden: a relation of some passages in the life of His Excellency Thomas Hutchinson, sometime Captain-General and Governor-in-chief of His Majesty's Province of Massachusetts Bay. Joseph Knight Co. 8°, bds., $1.50.

STORIES by English authors: Africa. Scribner. por. 16°, 75 c.
Contents: The mystery of Sasassa Valley, by A. Conan Doyle; Long odds, by H. Rider Hag-

gard; King Remba's point, by J. Landers; Ghamba, by W. C. Scully; Mary Musgrave, Anonymous; Gregorio, by Percy Hemingway.

STORIES by English authors: Italy. Scribner. por. 16°, 75 c.
Contents: A faithful retainer, by Ja. Payn; Bianca, by W. E. Norris; Goneril, by A. Mary F. Robinson; the brigand's bride, by Laurence Oliphant; Mrs. General Talboys, by Anthony Trollope.

STORIES by English authors: the Orient. Scribner. por. 16°, 75 c.
Contents: The man who would be king, by Rudyard Kipling; Tajima, by Miss Mitford; A Chinese girl graduate, by R. K. Douglas; The revenge of her race, by Mary Beaumont; King Billy of Ballarat, by Morley Roberts; Thy heart's desire, by Netta Syrett.

STORIES by English authors: Scotland. Scribner. por. 16°, 75 c.
Contents: The courting of T'now Head's Bell, by J. M. Barrie; The heather lintie, by S. R. Crockett; A doctor of the old school, by Ian Maclaren; Wandering Willie's tale, by Sir Walter Scott; The Glenmutchkin railway, by Professor Aytoun; Thrawn Janet, by R. L. Stevenson.

STUMBLER (A) in wide shoes. Holt. 12°, (Protean ser., no. 6.) buckram, $1.
"In the intense competition among writers of fiction for new and striking titles, it is nothing wonderful if curiously compounded phrases sometimes appear. The relationship between a copyrighted title and the romance to which it is attached is sometimes hard to discover. 'A stumbler in wide shoes' is the story of a spendthrift young artist of Amsterdam and the complicated conspiracy that is formed to ruin him by a Jew money-lender, because the artist, having married an English girl, is unable to wed the usurer's daughter, who fancied him. The Jew is a sort of Shylock up to date, modernized in manners at least, if not in morals, and, of course, he is properly routed and put to confusion by the agency of the English wife. Daria, the beauty of Amsterdam, his daughter, is fascinating, but not so charming as Jessica, of Venice. There is a rescue from drowning, a double diamond robbery, plenty of incident with interest well sustained, and the story on the whole is right cleverly told. It is published anonymously in the *Protean Series.*"—*Commercial Advertiser.*

TINSEAU, LÉON DE. In quest of the ideal: a novel; from the French by Florence Belknap Gilmour. *Authorized ed.* Lippincott. 12°, $1.

TOUCH (The) of sorrow: a study. Holt. 12°, (Protean ser., no. 5.) buckram, $1.

VENUS and Cupid; or, a trip from Mount Olympus to London, by The personal conductor of the party: a new fantastic romance, by the author of "The fight at Dame Europa's school." Lippincott. 12°, $1.
Some of the gods and goddesses of Olympus wishing to take a personally conducted tour of the earth, Ganymede effects an arrangement with an agent of Messrs. Thomas Cook & Sons, who, agreeing to the terms of the Boy-god, is taken by a novel conveyance into the presence of the divine tourists. Soon organizing his party of celestial travellers, they start. While *en route,* Bacchus drinks *vin ordinaire,* Diana

obeys her hunting propensity and comes to grief, and Cupid and Venus figure in other ungodlike pranks, which are given with the deductions of the conductor.

WARDEN, GERTRUDE. The sentimental sex. Appleton. 12°, $1.

An innocent, warm-hearted Australian reads a volume of verses composed by "Iris" and sees her portrait. He immediately goes to London and is shocked to find the writer a woman of thirty, cynical, and very free in conversation, who has already been twice married. He is rich and "Iris" marries him, although she thinks him a savage and a bore. She is all shallowness and modern slang and he is desperately in earnest and of what his wife insists is the "sentimental sex." The end is tragic.

WHEELER, A., (*pseud.*) Wheels: a bicycle romance. Dillingham. 12°, (Dillingham's metropolitan lib.) pap., 50 c.

WOODWARD, G. A. The diary of a peculiar girl. Peter Paul Book Co. 16°, pap., 50 c.

WOODWARD, R. PITCHER. Trains that met in the blizzard: a composite romance; being a chronicle of the extraordinary adventures of a party of twelve men and one woman in the great American blizzard, March 12, 1888; il. by Dan Beard, J. Carter Beard, Harry L. Parkhurst, and the Artist of the party. Salmagundi Pub. Co. 12°, $1.25.

HISTORY.

ELLIS, E. S. Epochs in American history. A. Flanagan. 12°, (American history ser., nos. 1, 2.) *ea.*, 50 c.

Sets forth in simple language the leading events in American history, such as the settlements of Jamestown and Plymouth, the battles of Quebec and Lexington, the Declaration of Independence, framing and adoption of the constitution, invention of the cotton-gin, the steamboat, invention of the electro-magnetic telegraph, bombardment of Fort Sumter, Gettysburg, etc.

FISHER, W. E. G. The Transvaal and the Boers: a brief history. Scribner. 12°, $2.40.

HABBEN, F. H. London street names: their origin, signification, and historic value; with divers notes and observations. Lippincott. 12°, $2.

HARRIS, T. L. The Trent affair, including a review of the English and American relations at the beginning of the Civil War, with an introduction by Ja. A. Woodburn. Bowen-Merrill. 12°, $1.50.

"A remarkable contribution to the history of English and American relations at the beginning of the Civil War. There is not a superfluous sentence in it, and no town or college library which desires to help in the creation of American citizens, as distinguished from Anglo-maniacs, can afford to dispense with Mr. Harris's book."—*M. W. H. in N. Y. Sun.*

HOW, W. W., and LEIGH, H. D. A history of Rome to the death of Cæsar. Longmans, Green & Co. map, il. 12°, $2.

HUTTON, W. HOLDEN. King and baronage, (A.D. 1135–1327.) Scribner. 16°, (Oxford manuals of English history, no. 2.) *net*, 50 c.

LUTZOW, FRANCIS (*Count*). Bohemia: an historical sketch. Scribner. 8°, $3.

NADAILLAC, J. FRANCIS ALBERT DU POUGET (*Marquis*) DE. Prehistoric Americans. McBride. 16°, 50 c.

Two papers on "The mound-builders" and "The cliff-dwellers," giving a *résumé* of all that can be known of these prehistoric Americans, as shown in the remains of their constructions, habitations, industry, manners, and style of life, etc.

PROTHERO, G. WASHINGTON, *ed.* Ireland, 1494–1868; with two introductory chapters by W. O'Connor Morris. Macmillan. 12°, (Cambridge historical ser.) *net*, $1.60.

ROBERTSON, C. G. The making of the English nation, (B C. 55–1135.) Scribner. 16°, (Oxford manuals of English history, ed. by C. W. C. Oman, no. 1.) *net*, 50 c.

The "Oxford manuals," of which this is the first issue, are designed to occupy a place between general histories and "epochs" or "periods." Six volumes are announced, each part complete in itself, but as the volumes carefully fit into one another, the whole will form together a single continuous history of England. All the volumes are written by resident members of the University of Oxford, actively engaged in teaching in the Final School of Modern History.

WAKELING, G. H. King and Parliament, (A.D. 1603–1714.) Scribner. 16°, (Oxford manuals of English history, no. 5.) *net*, 50 c.

LITERATURE, MISCELLANEOUS AND COLLECTED WORKS.

ARCHER, W., and LOWE, R. W., *eds.* Dramatic essays. [Uncollected essays of Leigh Hunt, W. Hazlitt, J. Forster, and G. H. Lewes.] Scribner. 3 v., 8°, $3.75.

FRANCKE, KUNO. Social forces in German literature: a study in the history of civilization. Holt. 8°, *net*, $2.

HERFORD, C. H., *ed.* English literary criticism; with an introd. by C. E. Vaughan. Scribner. 8°, (Warwick lib., ed. by C. H. Herford.) $1.50.

HERFORD, C. H., *ed.* English pastorals; with introd. by Edmund K. Chambers. Scribner. 8°, (Warwick lib., ed. by C. H. Herford.) $1.50.

HOWE, W. H., *comp.* Everybody's book of epitaphs; being for the most part what the living think of the dead. G. W. Jacobs. 24°, leath., 50 c.

MEYNELL, ALICE. The colour of life, and other essays on things seen and heard. Way & Williams. 16°, $1.25.

Fourteen essays: The colour of life; A point of biography; Cloud; Winds of the world; The honours of mortality; At monastery gates; Rushes and reeds; Eleonora Duse; Donkey races; Grass; A woman in grey; Symmetry and incident; The illusion of historic time; Eyes.

NOBLE, J. ASHCROFT. The sonnet in England, and other essays. Way & Williams. 12°, $1.50.

Contents: The sonnet in England; A pre-Raphaelite magazine; Leigh Hunt, the man and the writer; The poetry of common sense; Robert Buchanan as poet; Hawker of Morwenstow.

WESTON, JESSIE L. The legends of the Wagner drama : studies in mythology and romance. Scribner. 12°, $2.25.

MENTAL AND MORAL.

BRIDGER, A. E. Depression ; what it is, and how to cure it. Scribner. 16°, bds., 40 c.

WEBER, ALFRED. History of philosophy; authorized tr. by Frank Thilly; from the 5th French ed. Scribner. 8°, *net*, $2.50.
The translator says in his preface: "There is, in my opinion, no book so admirably fitted for acquainting the student with the development of thought as the able work of Prof. Weber, of the University of Strasburg. The author combines in his person the best elements of French and German scholarship. His knowledge of the subject is thorough and extensive, his judgment sound, his manner of expression simple, clear, and precise." Bibliography (7 p.).

NATURE AND SCIENCE.

CHAMBERS, E. T. D. The ouananiche and its Canadian environment. Harper. il. 8°, $2.

CORNISH, C. J. Animals at work and play, their activities and emotions. Macmillan. 8°, $1.75.

HILLIARD, CAROLINE E. Lessons in botany. Jenkins. interleaved, 8°, 75 c.
The exercises have been arranged for use in connection with Gray's "How plants grow." So far as possible the lessons are based upon careful study of specimens. Blank pages are inserted for drawings and records of observations. Designed for children 12 and 13 years of age, but can easily be adapted to older pupils.

MARTIN, E. A. The story of a piece of coal: what it is, whence it comes, and whither it goes. Appleton. il. 16°, (Library of useful stories.) 40 c.

MATHEWS, FERDINAND SCHUYLER. Familiar trees and their leaves; with over 200 drawings by the author, and an introd. by L. H. Bailey. Appleton. il. 12°, $1.75.

MORLEY, MARGARET WARNER. Seed-babies. Ginn & Co. il. 12°, bds., 30 c.
The most elementary information about the planting and growing of beans, sweet-peas, peanuts, melons and their cousins, nuts, appleseeds, clover, etc. Also chapters on bumblebees, frogs, etc. The information is elicited through conversations between two little boys and the seeds.

WARNER, H. H. Everybody's gardening; containing chapters on the cultivation of flowers, fruits, and vegetables, for every description of gardening for all seasons of the year: indispensable to amateurs. Jacobs. 24°, flex. leath., 50 c.

PHYSICAL AND MATHEMATICAL.

OSTERBERG, MAX. Synopsis of current electrical literature ; comp. from technical journals and magazines during 1895. Van Nostrand. 8°, $1.
Gives the titles and names of authors of the more important articles pertaining to electricity published in the English, German, and French languages during the past year. Generally brief but sometimes quite lengthy remarks follow the titles, giving the line of thought followed by the author, or offering a clue to the method of treatment pursued. About 29 journals have

been indexed ; the subjects under which the titles are classified number 59.

POWELL, J. WESLEY, SHALER, N. S., RUSSELL, I. C., [*and others.*] The physiography of the United States : ten monographs. American Book Co. 4°, $2.50.
Contents: Physiographic processes, by J. W. Powell ; Physiographic features, by J. W. Powell : Physiographic regions of the United States, by J. W. Powell ; Present and extinct lakes of Nevada, by I. C. Russell ; Beaches and tidal marshes of the Atlantic coast, by N. S. Shaler ; The northern Appalachians, by Bailey Willis ; Niagara Falls and their history, by G. K. Gilbert ; Mount Shasta, a typical volcano, by J. S. Diller; The physical geography of southern New England, by W. M. Davis ; The southern Appalachians, by C. Willard Hayes. Originally published separately in paper.

SPARK, J. J. Scientific and intuitional palmistry. Scribner. 12°, $1.

POETRY AND DRAMA.

CRAWFURD, OSWALD, *ed.* Lyrical verse from Elizabeth to Victoria ; with notes and index. Scribner. 16°, $1.25.

DIXON, W. M. English poetry from Blake to Browning. Scribner. 12°, (University extension ser.) $1.

ECHEGARAY, JOSÉ. The great Galeoto [*and*] Folly or saintliness : two plays done from the verse of José Echegaray into English prose by Hannah Lynch. Lamson, Wolffe. 8°, *net*, $1.50.

OMAR KHAYYÁM. Rubáiyat ; English, French, and German translations, comparatively arranged in accordance with the text of Edward Fitzgerald's version ; with further selections, notes, biographies, bibliography, and other material collected and ed. by Nathan Haskell Dole. Knight. 2 v., por. 12°, $3.50.

POPE, ALEXANDER. The rape of the lock: an heroi-comical poem in five cantos ; embroidered with nine drawings by Aubrey Beardsley. [imported by Lippincott.] 12°, $3.50.
Illustrated with nine full-page pictures in Aubrey Beardsley's characteristic style.

SHARP, ELIZ. A., *ed.* Lyric Celtica: an anthology of representative Celtic poetry; with introd. and notes by W. Sharp. Scribner. 12°, $2.25.

WATSON, W. The purple East: a series of sonnets on England's desertion of Armenia. Stone & Kimball. 12°, bds., 75 c.

POLITICAL AND SOCIAL.

AMERICAN Conference on International Arbitration held in Washington, D. C., April 22 and 23, 1896. Baker & Taylor. 4°, bds., $1.50.
Full report of the proceedings, including addresses by Hon. John W. Foster, Hon. George F. Edmunds, Rev. L. T. Chamberlain, D.D., Hon. Carl Schurz, Mr. Edward Atkinson, and others. The conference was held for the specific purpose of promoting the establishment of a permanent system of arbitration between the United States and Great Britain, and thus for the general purpose of promoting the application to international disagreements of the legal principles and procedures which already prevail in all civilized society.

FOLLETT, M. P. The speaker of the House of Representatives; with an introd. by Albert

Bushnell Hart. Longmans, Green & Co. 12°, $1.75.

REMSEN, DAN. S. The fusion of political parties: the automatic method in Australia. Am. Acad. of Pol. and Soc. Sci. 8°, (Publications of the society.) pap., 15 c.
Relates to a bill before the New York Legislature, by which the minority vote, which is now utterly lost in an election, may be counted; the scheme is to allow voters to mark their ballot for a first and second choice.

RICHARDSON, G. A. King Mammon and the heir-apparent. Arena Pub. Co. 12°, $1.25; pap., 50 c.
A treatise dealing mainly with the question of the inheritance of wealth. The author contends that the inheritance of wealth, beyond a certain modest amount at least, is a fundamental wrong, and should be abolished. The contention he bases on two main principles: the right of every human being to a fair opportunity to labor; and the wrong involved in all claims to wealth that are not based upon some form of productive effort. The inheritance of wealth, he contends, violates both these principles.

ROBERTS, I. Wages, fixed incomes, and the free coinage of silver; or, danger involved in the free coinage of silver at the ratio of 16–1 to all wage-earners and workingmen, to clerks and persons holding salaried positions, and to all persons with fixed incomes. Highlands. 12°, pap., 25 c.

TOWNE, H. R., HALSEY, F. A., *and* TAYLOR, F. W. The adjustment of wages to efficiency: three papers, on Gain-sharing: The premium plan; A piece-rate system. Macmillan. 8°, (Economic studies, v. 1, no. 2.)pap., 50 c.

WALKER, FRANCIS A. International bimetallism. Holt. 12°, $1.25.
The material embodied in this work was originally given in the form of lectures to the students of Harvard University. It is now divided into chapters with the titles : The early production of the precious metals; Augustus to Columbus; Bimetallism in England, 1666 to 1816; French and American bimetallism to 1851; French bimetallism to 1873; Demonetization; The great debate; Review and summary. Prof. Walker is a bimetallist of the international type.

WELLS, D. A., PHELPS, E. J., *and* SCHURZ, C. America and Europe: a study of international relations. 1, The United States and Great Britain, by D. A. Wells; 2, The Monroe doctrine, by E. J. Phelps; 3. Arbitration in international disputes, by C. Schurz. Putnam. 12°, (Questions of the day, no. 87.) $1.

SPORTS AND AMUSEMENTS.

FREEBOROUGH, E., *ed.* Chess endings: a companion to chess openings, ancient and modern. Scribner. 8°, $3.

LASKER, EMANUEL. Common sense in chess. Scribner. 12°, pap., $1.

QUALTROUGH, E. F. The boat-sailer's manual. Scribner. il. 24°, *net*, $1.50.
Directions for the management of sailing boats of all kinds and under all conditions of weather; contains also concise descriptions of the various rigs in general use at home and abroad, directions for handling sailing canoes, and the rudiments of cutter and sloop sailing.

THEOLOGY, RELIGION, AND SPECULATION.

BACHES, WALTER, *ed.* Everybody's Bible dictionary. Jacobs. 24°, 50 c.; leath., $1.

DRYER, G. H., *D.D.* History of the Christian church. In 4 or 5 v. V. 1, The founding of the new world, 1–600 A.D. Curts & Jennings. il. 12°, $1.50.
Written for popular use. This volume covers the period to the reign of Constantine. The second volume, now under way, will reach the period of the Reformation. The literature of the period and the sources consulted cover about ten pages.

MOULTON, R. GREEN, *ed.* The modern reader's Bible: a series of works from the sacred Scriptures presented in modern literary form. V. 4. Deuteronomy; ed. with introd. and notes. Macmillan. 24°, (Wisdom ser.), 50 c. mor., 60 c.

NEWTON, R., *D.D.* Cyclopedia of Bible illustrations: being a storehouse of similes, allegories, and anecdotes; with an introd. and a copious index. [*New issue.*] Jacobs. 12°, $1.

PERCIVAL, H. R., *D.D.* The invocation of saints, treated theologically and historically. Longmans, Green & Co. 12°, $1.75.

PRATT, *Rev.* S. W. The life and epistles of St. Paul harmonized and chronologically arranged in scripture language. A. D. F. Randolph & Co. 16°, $1.
The plan has been to construct, after the inductive method, a complete scriptural life of St. Paul, following in general the record of Luke in the Acts, and presenting in addition thereto and in chronological order whatever the apostle himself has written in his epistles concerning the same facts and events, and whatever he has written about other parts of his life and work. The chronological arrangement of the book is that of Conybeare and Howson.

PROTESTANT EPISCOPAL CHURCH. The altar-book : containing the order for the celebration of the Holy Eucharist, according to the use of the American Church, 1892. Daniel Berkeley Updike, [The Merrymount Press.] unp. F. pigskin, $75. [Ed. limited to 350 copies.]

SCHECHTER, S. Studies in Judaism. Macmillan. 12°, $1.75.

SHIELDS, C. W., *D.D.*, ANDREWS, E. B., HURST, J. F., *D.D.*, [*and others.*] Church unity: five lectures delivered in the Union Theological Seminary, New York, during the winter of 1896. Scribner. 12°, $1.
Contents : The general principles of church unity, by C. W. Shields, D.D. ; The sin of schism, by Rev. E. Benjamin Andrews ; The Irenic movements since the Reformation, by Bishop J. F. Hurst, D.D.; The Chicago-Lambeth articles, by Bishop H. C. Potter, D.D.; The unity of the spirit—a world-wide necessity, by Amory A. Bradford, D.D.

TRUMBULL, H. CLAY. The threshold covenant; or, the beginning of religious rites. Scribner. 8°, *net*, $2.

VINCENT, MARVIN R., *D.D.* The age of Hildebrand. The Christian Literature Co. 12°, (Ten epochs of church history, v. 5.) $1.50,

Books for the Young.

BEAL, MARY BARNES. The boys of Clovernook: the story of five boys on a farm; il. by Etheldred B. Barry. Lothrop. il. 8°, $1.50.

The deafness which caused John Atherton to give up his professorship in a western college and go to live with his family at Clovernook turned out to be a special boon to the young people; the many good times they had upon the farm are related in detail for very youthful readers.

BROOKS, ELBRIDGE STREETER. The true story of Abraham Lincoln, the American, told for boys and girls. Lothrop. por. il. 8°, $1.50.

CLEMENS, S. LANGHORNE, ["Mark Twain," *pseud.*] The prince and the pauper: a tale for young people of all ages. [*New lib. ed.*] Harper. il. 8°, $1.75.

COURSEN, FRANCES BELL. What the dragonfly told the children; il. by Amy Brooks. Lothrop. 8°, $1.50.

Through a little framework of fiction children are introduced to a number of well-known poets and some of their familiar verses particularly treating of nature. The dragon-fly sings these measures to a group of little children as they play in the fields. Each chapter is devoted to a different poet, and is illustrated with his portrait and appropriate pictures.

FERRES, ARTHUR. His first kangaroo: an Australian story for boys. Scribner. 12°, (Scribner-Blackie ser.) $1.25.

HILLIARD, ANDREW. Under the Black Eagle; or, through chains to freedom: a boy's adventures in Russia. Scribner. 12°, (Scribner-Blackie ser.) $1.

HUGHES, T. Tom Brown's school-days. *New ed.* Houghton, Mifflin & Co. 12°, $1.

KENYON, F. G. The Brownings for the young. Macmillan. 16°, 40 c.

LILLIE, LUCY CECIL WHITE. Ruth Endicott's way; or, Hargrave's mission. H. T. Coates & Co. il. 12°, (Honest Endeavor lib.) $1.25.

The news that her father has just died reaches Ruth Endicott on the day that her school life ends. Up to that moment she had been supposed to be a very rich young girl, having been indulged in every way. She comes to New York and learns from the family lawyer that she is almost penniless. She obtains a position as secretary to a wealthy man threatened with blindness, and makes a little home for herself with an elderly relative. Her "way" is to help all with whom she comes in contact—utter disregard of self being the keynote of her character.

PRATT, ANNA M. Little rhymes for little people. N. Y., printed at the De Vinne Press, for Paul Lemperly, F. A. Hilliard, and Frank E. Hopkins. 8°, $2. [Ed. limited to 220 copies.]

Most of these rhymes appeared in *The Sunday-School Advocate, The Youth's Companion,* and *St. Nicholas.* They are short and witty, and their gracefulness will appeal to grown folks as well as to little people.

RECENT FRENCH AND GERMAN BOOKS.

FRENCH.

Bentzon, Th. Une double épreuve. 12°. Levy. $1 00
Bire. La légende des Girondins. 12°. Perrin... 1 00
Boschot, A. Pierre Rovert. 12°. Perrin....... 1 02
Bourget, P. Une idylle tragique. 12°. Lemerre. 1 00
Brada. Les épouseurs. 12°. Levy.............. 1 00
Champol. Le Mari de Simone. 12°. Plon...... 1 00
Champsaur, F. L'epouvante. 12°. Ollendorff.. 1 00
Coppee, F. Mon franc parler. 4ième serie. 12°. Lemerre................................ 1 00
Corday, M. Mariés Jeunes. 12°. Simones Empis................................ 1 00
Dash, Ctsse. Mémoires des autres. Vol. I. 12°. Librairie Ill....................... 1 00
Daudet, A. L'énterrement d'une étoile. 24°. Guilliaume............................ 30
Doucet, C. A l'institut. 12°. Levy.......... 1 00
Filon, A. Le Théâtre Anglais. 12°. Levy.... 1 00
Genevoix, G. Ce qu'elles font. 12°. Plon..... 1 00
Geoffroy, L. Napoléon apocryphe. 12°. Librarie Ill.............................. 1 00
Goncourt, E. and J. de. Première Amoureuse. 12°. Borel.............................. 30
Henaes, I. P. Les actes de Diotine. 12°. Levy. 1 00
La Jeunesse, E. Les nuits, les ennuis et les âmes de nos plus notoires contemporains. 14°. Perrin............................... 1 00
Margueritte, P. L'Essor. 12°. Chailly...... 1 00
Pigeon, A. Un ami du peuple. 12°. Colin..... 1 60
Pouvillon, E. Mdlle Clémence. 12°. Ollendorff................................. 1 00
Richebourg, E. Le secret d'une tombe. 12°. Flammarion............................ 1 00
Rothschild, H. de. Notes Africaines. Levy. 1 00
Rouvre, Ch. de. A deux. 12°. Colin......... 1 00
Tinseau, L. de. Bien folle est qui s'y fie! 12°. Levy................................. 1 00
Vandererem, F. La patronne. 12°. Ollendorff. 60

GERMAN.

Baierlein, Z. Oberpfälzische Geschichten. 12°. Deutsche Verlag........................ 1 35

Biller, C. Señorita Paz. 12°. Reissner.. .... $1 00
Brewits, C. v. Vergiftete Pfeile. 12°. Deutsche Verlag............................. 1 35
Ebner-Eschenbach, M. v. Rittmeister Brand. Paetel................................ 2 00
Eschstruth, N. v. Der Stern des Glücks. 2 vols. 12°. List.............................. 3 35
Fransos, K. E. Leib Weihnachtskuchen. 12°. Concordia.............................. 1 70
Fulda, L. Robinsons Eiland. 12°. Cotta...... 70
Heiberg, H. Zwischen enge Gassen. 12°. Deutsche Verlag........................ 1 35
Janitschek, M. Vom Weibe. 12°. Fischer.... 70
Jokai, M. Der Fluch des Priesters. 12°. Janke. 70
— Der Seelenbändiger. 12°. Janke.......... 70
— 2000 Yahre unter dem Eise. 12°. Janke....... 70
Lang, H. Gedankensünde. 12°. Reissner...... 1 00
Nansen, P. Eine glückliche Ehe. 12°. Fischer. 70
— Maria. 12°. Fischer.................... 70
Noeldechen, W. Sonderbare Schwärmer. 12°. Reissner.............................. 70
Ortmann, R. Schatten der Vergangenheit. 12°. Deutsche Verlag........................ 1 35
Osterloh. Oberlehrer Gesenius. 12°. Deutsche Verlag............................... 1 35
Ottmer, F. Das Adoptivkind. 12°. Concordia. 1 35
Perfall, A. v. Schüchterchen. 12°. Deutsche Verlag............................... 1 35
Reisner, V. von. Jural Dragutinowitsch. 12°. Fischer.............................. 1 35
Rens, B. Hamburger Geschichten. 12°. Deutsche Verlag............................. 1 35
Spielhagen, F. Selbstgerecht. 2 vols. 12°. Engelhorn............................. 40
Telmann, K. Mann und Frau. 12°. Concordia................................ 70
Wilbrandt, A. Vater und Sohn. 12°. Cotta.. 1 00
Zingeler, K T. Zollern-Nürnberg. 12°. Deutsche Verlag........................... 1 35

In the August Magazines.

The Atlantic Monthly opens with a timely paper by Mrs. James T. Fields, entitled "Days with Mrs. Stowe," giving a sympathetic insight into the character and career of Mrs. Stowe by a friend whose intimacy covered the whole period of her fame. Other articles of literary importance are "Present Conditions of Literary Production," by Paul Shorey, of the Chicago University; "Poetic Rhythms in Prose," by E. E. Hale, Jr.; "A Holiday with Montaigne," by Henry D. Sedgwick, Jr.; "A Literary Model," by Mary Boardman Sheldon, giving some suggestive hints to writers in the form of a story; "Eugene Field and His Work," an unsigned criticisms and reviews of Miss Wilkins's "Madelon"; Frederic's "The Damnation of Theron Ware"; Mrs. Burnett's "A Lady of Quality," and Parker's "Seats of the Mighty." "What Factory Girls Read" and "An Unworked Field of Romance" are the literary features of the Contributors' Club. It is good for the writers in *The Atlantic* that they can hold and express opinions untrammelled by considerations of illustrations.

THE August issue of *The Century* appears in a distinctive cover. The opening paper, "An Island without Death," by Miss E. R. Scidmore, the author of "Jinrikisha Days," gives an account of a visit to Miyajima, a sacred island in the Inland Sea, one of the three great sights of Japan. A paper on "The Viceroy Li Hung Chang" is contributed by the Hon. John W. Foster, who, it will be remembered, was lately confidential adviser to the Emperor of China, and in that capacity accompanied the viceroy to Japan, where the treaty of Shimonoseki was negotiated. There is printed the first of a group of articles from the journals of the late E. J. Glave, who crossed Africa in the service of *The Century* in exploration of the slave trade.

The Chautauquan contains articles on "The Justices of the Supreme Court," by David Hilton Wheeler; "Where Do the Immigrants Go?" by Cyrus C. Adams; "Our Annual Travel to Europe," by Franklin Matthews; "Some Present Aspects of Art in America," by Clarence Cook; and "The Bank of England," by Horace Townsend. Of special interest to women will be "The Evolution of the Piano," by J. Torrey Connor; "Tennyson's Women," by Eugene Parsons; "Diamonds," by Sarah Brentworth; and "How Porcelain Grows," by Mrs. William H. Wait.

THE contents of *The Fortnightly Review* for July include "Stray Thoughts on South Africa," by Olive Schreiner; "Coincidences," by Max Müller; "The Muddle of Irish Land Tenure," by W. E. Bear; "A Highway Robber," by Ouida, an arraignment of railroads which run their tracks for tramways along highways and streets; "Public Sentiment in America on the Silver Question," by Francis H. Hardy; "The Salons," by Claude Phillips; "The Analytical Humorist," by H. D. Traill; and "A Chat About Jules Simon," by Albert D. Vandam.

The Forum has articles of value for the education of the people in the present political turmoil. The most important papers are: "Mr. Godkin on the West: a protest," by Charles S. Gleed, of Topeka, Kansas; "The Financial Bronco," by T. S. Van Dyke; "Altruism in Economics," by W. H. Mallock; "The Free-Silver Epidemic," by Senator Justin S. Morrill; "Blunders of a Democratic Administration," by Senator S. M. Cullom; and "What the Republican Party Stands For," by General Horace Porter. Other timely papers are "Harriet Beecher Stowe," by Julius Ward, and "The Social and Economic Influence of the Bicycle," by J. B. Bishop.

Harper's Magazine opens with an appreciative article on "Longfellow," by William Dean Howells, with eight illustrations, followed by "Stuart Lansdowne's Portrait of Washington," by Charles Henry Hart, with five illustrations; "Peeps into Barbary," by J. E. Budgett Meakin, with ten illustrations; "The Strange Days That Came to Jennie Friday," written and illustrated by Frederic Remington; and "Door-Step Neighbors," in which the late regretted W. Hamilton Gibson has written of and drawn all manner of common insects. The illustrated stories in this issue are "Tom Sawyer, Detective," by Mark Twain, illustrated by A. B. Frost; "Her Prerogative," a story by E. A. Alexander, illustrated by John W. Alexander; and "The Silent Voice," a play by Laurence Alma Tadema, with illustrations by E. A. Addey. There are also short stories by John Kendrick Bangs, Sarah Barnwell Elliott, Professor Simon Newcomb, and John Hay.

Lippincott's contains as its complete novel 'The Great K. and A. Train Robbery," by Paul Leicester Ford, the author of "The Honorable Peter Stirling," one of the best novels of recent years; "Immigration Evils," by Rhoda Gale; "Heraldry in America," by Eugene Zieber; and "The Woman Question in the Middle Ages," by Emily Baily Stone.

The Nineteenth Century for July contains "Russia, Persia, and England," by Sir Lepel Griffin; "A Warning to Imperialists," by Mrs. Lecky; "The Bab and Babism," by J. D. Rees; "The Woman Movement in Germany," by Mrs. Bertrand Russell; "Alvar Nuñez," by R. B. Cunninghame Graham, and "Are Manners Disappearing from Great Britain?" by the Earl of Meath.

The Outlook for July 25 is full of interesting and timely matter. Short biographies of the presidential candidates are given: "William McKinley," by Murat Halstead, and "William Jennings Bryan," by Richard Linthicum. A sketch of Harriet Beecher Stowe, from the pen of John R. Howard, is illustrated with fourteen pictures of peculiar interest. Other articles of importance are "Higher Life in Philadelphia," by Talcott Williams; and "Rev. Francis E. Clark," the founder of the Christian Endeavor movement, by J. Willis Baer, with eleven illustrations.

Scribner's Magazine is the annual fiction number. The authors represented include George W. Cable, R. H. Stoddard, Alice Morse Earle, George Cabot Lodge, Mrs. James T. Fields, Clinton Scollard, Annie Eliot, Rollo Ogden, Henrietta Christian Wright, Bliss Perry, Eleanor Stuart, and J. A. Mitchell. August F. Jaccaci begins a story called "On the Trail of Don Quixote," with illustrations by Vierge. The cover of this number of *Scribner's* is a wonderful piece of color-printing which will bear the closest examination.

Obituary.

WILLIAM HAMILTON GIBSON, the artist and author, died in Washington, Conn., on the 16th inst. Mr. Gibson was born at Sandy Hook, Conn., Oct. 5, 1850. After his Connecticut schooling Mr. Gibson attended the Polytechnic Institute, Brooklyn. Having decided to devote himself to art as an illustrator, he became a specialist in botanical drawing for the *American Agriculturist* and *The Hearth and Home.* He drew natural history subjects for the "American Cyclopedia" and furnished illustrations for magazine articles. He obtained a foothold with the Harpers by an illustrated article on "Birds of Plumage." Thereafter he was a frequent and valued contributor to *Harper's Magazine.* His literary composition was as carefully prepared as were his sketches, which in natural history and botany were drawn with microscopic fidelity. He published several volumes, including "A Winter Idyl," "Springtime," "The Heart of the White Mountains," "Pictorial Edition of Longfellow," "In Berkshire with the Wild Flowers," written by Dora and Elaine Goodale; "Camp Life in the Woods" and the "Tricks of Trapping and Trap-Making," "Complete American Trapper," "Highways and Byways, or, saunterings in New England," "Sharp Eyes, a Rambler's Calendar of Fifty-two Weeks Among Insects, Birds, and Flowers," "Happy Hunting Grounds, a Tribute to the Woods and Fields," and "Our Edible Mushrooms," his last book.

EDMOND LOUIS ANTOINE HUOT DE GONCOURT died on the 16th inst., at the residence of his life-long friend Alphonse Daudet, at Champrosay, Department of Seine-et-Oise. He was born in Nancy, May 26, 1822, and was joint founder, with his brother Jean, of the school of naturalistic fiction that has been developed in France by Emile Zola and in England by Thomas Hardy. It is impossible to write of Edmond without including his brother Jean (who was born in Paris, December 17, 1830, and died there in 1870), for it was in collaboration chiefly that they are known to the world of literature. Though their works of fiction are widely known their literary reputation will very likely rest on the series of studies on the society and art of the eighteenth century in France. The following is a list of the works of the two brothers: "Salon de 1852," "Les Mystères des Théâtres," and "La Lorette," 1853; "Histoire de la société française pendant la Revolution," 1854; "En 185–," 1854; "La Révolution dans les mœurs," 1854; "La Société française pendant le Directoire," 1855; "La Peinture a l'Exposition Universelle de 1855"; "Les Actrices" and "Une Voiture de Masques," 1856, republished in 1876 under the title of "Quelques Créatures de ce Temps"; "Portraits intimes du XVIIIe Siècle," 2 series, 1856–8; "Sophie Arnould, d'après sa Correspondance et ses Mémoires Inédits," 1857; "Histoire de Marie Antoinette," 1858; "Les Maîtresses de Louis XV." and "Les Hommes des lettres," 1860; a novel, republished under the title of "Charles Demailly," 1869; "Sœur Philomène," a novel, 1861; "La Femme au XVIIIe Siècle," 1862, reprinted in 1877 with the addition of a chapter entitled "L'Amour au XVIIIe Siècle"; "Renée Mauperin," a novel, 1864; "Germinie Lacerteux," 1865; "Idées et Sensations," 1866;

"Manette Salomon," 1867; "Madame Gervaisais," 1869; "Gavarni l'Homme et l'Artiste," 1873; "L'Art au XVIIIe Siècle," three volumes, 1874, and three dramas, "Henriette Maréchal," 1865; "La Patrie en Danger," 1873; and "Germinie Lacerteux," a piece based upon the novel issued in 1865. Since the death of his brother M. Edmond de Goncourt had published under his own name "L'Oeuvre de Watteau," a classified catalogue, in 1876; "L'Oeuvre de Prudhon," 1877; "La Fille Elisa," a novel, 1878; "Les Frères Zemganno," a novel, 1879; "La Maison d'un Artist," 1881; "La Faustine, roman," 1882; "Cherie, roman," 1884; "Madame Saint-Huberty, biographie de la chanteuse," 1885; "Mademoiselle Clairon, biographie de la tragédienne," 1890; "Journal des Goncourt, Mémoires de la Vie Littéraire." 1851–70; and in March, 1890, he commenced the publication of a second series extending from 1870 to 1890.

"ONE, TWO, THREE."

IT was an old, old, old, old lady,
  And a boy that was half-past three,
And the way that they played together
  Was beautiful to see.

She couldn't go running and jumping
  And the boy, no more could he ;
For he was a thin little fellow,
  With a thin little twisted knee.

They sat in the yellow sunlight,
  Out under the maple-tree ;
And the game that they played I'll tell you,
  Just as it was told to me.

It was Hide-and-Go-Seek they were playing,
  Though you'd never have known it to be—
With an old, old, old, old lady
  And a boy with a twisted knee.

The boy would bend his face down
  On his one little sound right knee,
And he'd guess where she was hiding
  In guesses One, Two, Three.

" You are in the china closet !"
  He would cry and laugh with glee—
It wasn't the china closet,
  But he still had Two and Three.

" You are up in papa's big bedroom,
  In the chest with the queer old key,"
And she said : " You are warm and warmer ;
  But you're not quite right," said she.

" It can't be the little cupboard
  Where mamma's things used to be—
So it must be the clothes'-press, Gran'ma,"
  And he found her with his Three.

Then she covered her face with her fingers,
  They were wrinkled and white and wee,
And she guessed where the boy was hiding,
  With a One and a Two and a Three.

And they never had stirred from their places,
  Right under the maple-tree—
This old, old, old, old lady
  And the boy with the lame little knee—
This dear, dear, dear old lady
  And the boy who was half-past three.

  —*H. C. Bunner in Boston Transcript.*

freshest News.

ROBERTS BROTHERS will publish shortly the volume of short stories upon which Thomas Hardy and Mrs. Henniker Heaton (Lord Houghton's daughter) have been collaborating.

DODD, MEAD & CO. have in preparation the "Memoirs of Signor Arditi," the greatest of operatic directors of the present time. The book will contain portraits and autographs of the numerous celebrities with whom Arditi has had relations, among whom are Albani, Sontag, Grisi, Mario, Patti, Verdi, Gounod, Garibaldi, Minnie Hauk, Ole Bull, Lillie Lehmann, and many others.

THE THEOSOPHICAL PUBLISHING CO., of London, will shortly publish a new book by A. P. Sinnett, entitled "The Growth of the Soul," being a sequel to his "Esoteric Buddhism." It is said to embody the author's researches in spiritual science during the last thirteen years, and conveys a comprehensive statement of the conditions under which human consciousness may be unfolded on the higher planes of nature.

D. APPLETON & CO. will publish at once an important and timely book by Logan G. McPherson on "The Monetary and Banking Problem", a new edition, in paper covers, of John Jacob Astor's romance, "A Journey in Other Worlds"; and a new edition of Mrs. Eliza McHatten-Ripley's "From Flag to Flag," a vivid picture of a woman's experiences in the South during the war, in Mexico, and in Cuba, and the account of Cuban experiences should have a special interest for readers at present.

T. Y. CROWELL & CO. have arranged with the Brotherhood Publishing Company, of London, to issue simultaneously the translation of the summary of Count Tolstoï's "Four Gospels Harmonized and Translated." The original work is in three volumes of about 400 pages each; the summary, which is the work of Count Tolstoï himself, is intended to present the results arrived at in the larger work, but in a form suitable for the general public. It consists of a paraphrase in simple modern language of the doctrinal parts of the Gospels grouped in logical sequence, and the Count appends to each chapter all the passages paraphrased in the chapter.

J. B. LIPPINCOTT CO. have just ready a fantastic romance by the author of "The Fight at Dame Europa's School," entitled "Venus and Cupid, or, a trip from Mount Olympus to London"; "In the Wake of King James, or, Dun-Randal on the Sea," an historical romance, by Standish O'Grady, author of "Finn and His Companions"; "New Wheels in Old Ruts," in which Henry Parr describes a pilgrimage to Canterbury *via* the ancient pilgrim's way, to which F. W. R. Adams contributes a number of happy pen-and-ink sketches; and an account of "The Downfall of Prempeh," the Ashanti chief, by Major R. S. S Baden-Powell, which is fully illustrated, and contains a chapter on the political and commercial position of Ashanti by Sir George Baden-Powell.

FLOOD & VINCENT, Meadville, Pa., publishers of the text-books of the Chautauqua Literary and Scientific Circle, announce for early publi-
cation the following volumes, which will constitute the Chautauqua course of reading for the French-Greek year, 1896–97, which begins in the early fall: "The Growth of the French Nation, by Prof. George B. Adams, of Yale University; "French Traits," by W. C. Brownell, published by arrangement with Charles Scribner's Sons; "A Study of the Sky," by Prof. H. A. Howe, Director of Chamberlin Observatory, University of Denver; "A Survey of Greek Civilization," by Prof. J. P. Mahaffy, noticed in our last week's issue; and "A History of Greek Art," by Prof. Frank B. Tarbell, of the University of Chicago.

CHARLES SCRIBNER'S SONS have just issued two new volumes of their *Stories by English Authors*, of which the one contains stories of Scotland by J. M. Barrie, S. R. Crockett, Ian Maclaren, Sir Walter Scott, Prof. Aytoun, and R. L. Stevenson, with a fine portrait of Ian Maclaren, the other stories of the Orient by Rudyard Kipling (whose portrait is given as a frontispiece), Miss Mitford, R. K. Douglas, Mary Beaumont, Morley Roberts, and Netta Syrett; "Bar Harbor," by F. Marion Crawford, with illustrations by C. S. Reinhart, a new volume in their charming series of *American Summer Resorts*; "King and Parliament, A.D. 1603–1714," by G. H. Wakeling, of Brasenose College, in their *Oxford Manuals of English History*; the first volume of a series of *Psychological Methods of Teaching and Studying Languages*, in which "The Facts of Life" (*les faits de la vie*) are idiomatically described and systematically arranged to form a complete dictionary of the objective language, by Victor Bétis, director of the Normal School of Languages of Boston, and Howard Swan, director of the Central School of Foreign Tongues of London; and a revised edition of Edward F. Qualtrough's "Boat-Sailer's Manual."

HARPER & BROTHERS will publish shortly "Shakespeare the Boy," by W. J. Rolfe, with a number of illustrations; also, "A Story of the Heavenly Camp-Fires," by "One with a New Name." They have in preparation "Harper's Dictionary of Classical Literature and Antiquities," edited by Harry Thurston Peck, of Columbia College, with the co-operation of many special contributors. The dictionary will present within the limits of a single volume and under a single alphabet the subjects that have usually been treated of in separate works. Its topics comprise Greek and Roman antiquities in the conventional meaning of the word, including subjects falling under these various heads: Amusements, Architecture, Art, Costume, Domestic Life, Drama, Law, Music, Numismatics, Philosophy, Religion and Rhetoric, each important article giving a selected list of the best and most recent works relating to the subject, and thus directing the student to a fuller course of supplementary reading; Biography, including not only the personages of ancient history, but sketches of great classical scholars and philologists down to the present century, Geography, History, Literature—the great works of classical literature given as separate titles, with a list of the best editions; Mythology, General Information—a great many articles on topics which no single work has yet systematically collected for general treatment. The volume will contain 1000 illustrations and a number of maps.

BOOKS FOR SUMMER TRAVELLERS.

AMERICAN BOOK COMPANY, New York.

Gray's Manual of Botany. Tourists' ed. $2.00.

D. APPLETON & CO., New York,

Appletons' General Guide to the United States. With numerous maps and illustrations. 12mo, flexible morocco, with tuck, $2.50. (Part I., separately, NEW ENGLAND AND MIDDLE STATES AND CANADA; cloth, $1.25. Part II., SOUTHERN AND WESTERN STATES; cloth, $1.25.)

Appletons' Canadian Guide-Book. A guide for tourist and sportsman, from Newfoundland to the Pacific. With maps and illustrations. 12mo, flexible cloth, $1.50.

Appletons' Guide-Book to Alaska. By Miss E. R. Scidmore. With maps and illustrations. 12mo, flexible cloth, $1.25.

Appletons' Handbook of American Summer Resorts. With maps, illustrations, table of railroad fares, etc. 12mo, paper, 50 cents.

Appletons' Dictionary of New York. 16mo, paper, 30 cents; cloth, 60 cents.

THE CASSELL PUBLISHING CO., New York.

Cassell's Pocket Guide to Europe for 1896. With maps, etc. Bound in leather. $1.50.
The model book of its kind for accuracy, fulness, legibility of text and maps, compact beauty and usefulness, and very moderate price.

HOUGHTON, MIFFLIN & CO., Bost.

Bacon's Dictionary of Boston. $1.50; boards, $1.00.

Boston Illustrated. Paper, 50 cents.

Satchel Guide to Europe. Edition for 1895. $1.50.

England Without and Within. By Richard Grant White. $2.00.

Sweetser's New England. $1.50.

Sweetser's White Mountains. $1.50.

Sweetser's Maritime Provinces. $1.50.

Nantucket Scraps. By Jane G. Austin. $1.50.

Mrs. Thaxter's Among the Isles of Shoals. $1.25.

Jenness' Isles of Shoals (History). $1.50.

Julius H. Ward's White Mountains. $1.25.

Mrs. Woodman's Picturesque Alaska. $1.00.

THOMAS NELSON & SONS, New York.

English Scenery. 170 views. 4to, cloth, $2.50.

Souvenir of Scotland. Its cities, lakes, and mountains. 120 chromo views. 4to, $2.50; and $4.00.

Ramblers in Rome. By S. Russell Forbes. With maps, plans, and illustrations. 12mo, cloth extra, $1.50.

THOMAS NELSON & SONS.—*Continued.*

Rambles in Naples. By S. Russell Forbes. With maps, plans, and illustrations. 12mo, cloth, extra, $1.25.

ROBERTS BROTHERS, Boston.

Jackson (Helen ["H. H."]). Glimpses of Three Coasts. 12mo, $1.50.
These are "Bits of Travel" in California and Oregon, Scotland and England, and Norway, Denmark, and Germany.

— **Ramona.** A Story. 12mo, $1.50.
Most delightful glimpses of So. California.

— **Bits of Travel.** Illustrated. Square 18mo, $1.25.

— **Bits of Travel at Home.** Square 18mo, $1.50.

Drake (Samuel Adams). Old Landmarks and Historic Personages of Boston. With 93 illustrations. 12mo, $2.00.

— **Old Landmarks and Historic Fields of Middlesex.** With 39 illustrations and maps. 12mo, $2.00.

Aloha. (A Hawaiian Salutation.) By G. L. Chaney. Travels in the Sandwich Islands. With illustrations and map. 16mo, $1.50.

Constantinople. By Edwin A. Grosvenor. With an introduction by Gen. Lew. Wallace. With 250 illustrations. 2 vols., 8vo, cloth, gilt top, $6.00.

GEORGE ROUTLEDGE & SONS, Ltd., 29 W. 23d St., New York.

Hare's (A. J. C.) Books of Travel.

Edwards's (A. B.) A Thousand Miles Up the Nile. Profusely illustrated. 8vo, $2.50.

— **Untrodden Peaks and Unfrequented Valleys.** A Midsummer Ramble in the Dolomites. Maps and illustrations. 8vo, $2.50.

Caine's Picturesque India. 200 illustrations and map. 8vo, cloth, $4.00.

Send for Complete Catalogue.

WARD, LOCK & BOWDEN, Ltd., New York.

On the Cars and Off. Being the Journal of a Pilgrimage along the Queen's Highway to the East, from Halifax, in Nova Scotia, to Victoria, in Vancouver's Island. By Douglas Sladen. Profusely and beautifully illustrated. 8vo, cloth, $6.00.

BRADLEE WHIDDEN, Boston, Mass.

Knobel's Guides in Natural History. Trees and Shrubs. Ferns and Evergreens. Day Butterflies. The Beetles. The Moths. Fresh-water Fishes. Each 12mo, *net*, 50 cents.

Emerton's Life on the Seashore. Illustrated. 12mo, cloth, $1.50.

A Handbook for Teachers.

THE

American Educational Catalogue for 1896,

Issued annually since 1870, includes a price-list of school and text books in use in the United States, arranged alphabetically by author's or editor's name, and a detailed subject-index, referring from each specific subject to authors of books on that subject, so that the advantages of both *a finding-list for the trade* and *a class-catalogue for the use of schools* are combined.

8°, 60 pages, bound in leatherette, 50 cents.

Office of THE PUBLISHERS' WEEKLY,

P. O. Box 943.   59 DUANE STREET, NEW YORK.

LITERARY NEWS

AN ECLECTIC REVIEW OF
CURRENT LITERATURE
~ILLUSTRATED~

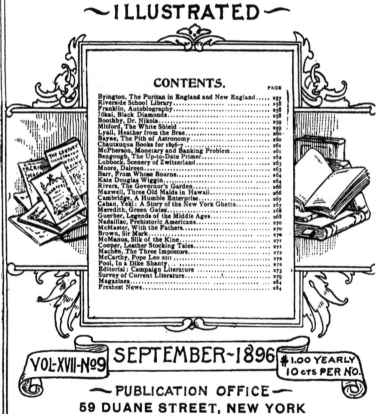

CONTENTS.

VOL. XVII–N°9   SEPTEMBER~1896 $1.00 YEARLY
10 cts PER NO.

~PUBLICATION OFFICE~
59 DUANE STREET, NEW YORK

The Literary News

In winter you may reade them, ad ignem, by the fireside; and in summer, ad umbram, under some shadie tree, and therewith pass away the tedious howres.

| VOL. XVII. | SEPTEMBER, 1896. | No. 9. |

The Puritan in England and New England.

THE Puritan has been a prominent figure in the literature of the last few years. His history and environment, in Old and New Eng-

~William Pynchon~

land, his beliefs, manners and customs, his every-day occupations and mournful Sunday rites have been described so fully by recent writers that even common mortals have learned to know the difference between Pilgrims and Puritans. In this series of historical studies Dr. Byington traces the history of the Puritan party from its beginnings in the mother-country to its sturdy development in the New World. In simple and direct language he sets forth the record of the Puritans in England, the funda-

mental differences between Puritans and Pilgrims, and the fortunes of the New England settlements, and he presents a vivid and most interesting picture of the social, domestic, and religious life of the Puritan colonies. Especially interesting are the chapters on "The Early Ministers of New England" and "The Family and Social Life of the Puritans." The strict regulations by which social and religious virtue was, as it were, hedged in from worldly contamination, the laws as to church attendance, the prohibition of smoking within two miles of a meeting-house, the style of music, the week-day lectures, the unwritten laws as to dress, decorum, and amusement— all these furnish a graphic portrayal of every-day New England life two centuries ago. Much curious and instructive information has Dr. Byington gathered into this modest volume ; he has had recourse, in many cases, to original and little-known sources for his data; and with the conscientious painstaking of the historical student he combines a direct and vigorous style that lends strength and fascination to his narrative. The book is the outgrowth of a series of papers read before various historical societies ; the variety of its contents is, perhaps, best shown by a list of the subjects covered, which include "The Puritan in England," "The Pilgrim and the Puritan, Which ?" "The Early Ministers of New England," "William Pynchon, Gent.," "The Family and Social Life of the Puritans," "Religious Opinions of the Fathers of New England," "The Case of Rev. Robert Buck," and "Religious Life in the Eighteenth Century in Northern New England." Aside from the direct historical usefulness of the work, it should prove a valuable aid to a fuller public knowledge and appreciation of the meaning and magnitude of the work begun by our fore-fathers in the planting of New England. (Roberts. $2.)

The Riverside School Library.

HARDLY any praise can be too strong for this series of volumes peculiarly suited for school libraries. They are chosen largely from the best literature which has stood the test of the world's judgment, and yet is as fresh and inviting to-day as when first published. The assistance and advice of more than a hundred eminent educators have been availed of in the selection of this library. The volumes are edited with great care, and contain biographical sketches of the authors, and in most cases portraits of them; also notes and glossaries wherever needed. They are thoroughly well printed and bound substantially in dark red half leather, with cloth sides. In every respect they commend themselves to all who wish that pupils, as well as households, may have the best, most interesting, and most salutary reading. This library now numbers fifty volumes and from it alone may be drawn a liberal education. (Houghton, Mifflin & Co. *Ea.* from 50 c. to 70 c.)

The Autobiography of Benjamin Franklin.

WHEN Franklin was born in 1706 Queen Anne was on the English throne, and Swift

and Defoe were pamphleteering; the one had not yet written "Gulliver's Travels," nor the other "Robinson Crusoe." Pope was only eighteen years old, and Addison and Steele had not begun *The Spectator.* One more decade will complete two hundred years since the birth of the greatest man America has produced. It is only in thinking back through all these years and dwelling step by step upon the scientific, the social and political evolutions that have taken place within that limit of time, that we can estimate the power of that great brain which saw to-day and its problems as clearly as his own days two centuries ago. The auto-biography of this great American statesman, patriot, scientist, and reformer is ideal reading to put into the hands of future citizens. The American Book Co. have brought out an edition for this special purpose. (American Book Co. 35 c.)

Black Diamonds.

A FAMOUS story by Jókai is the one entitled "Black Diamonds," which has just been published in English by Harper & Brothers, the translation having been made by Frances A. Gerard. A strong story it is; admirable both as regards plot and construction. The hero is Ivan Behrend, the owner of a coal-mine in Hungary and a man of much inventive skill. A thorough man of the world, also, he proves himself to be when circumstances take him into the world, but he prefers the seclusion of the country, and is never happier than when he is working with his own miners in the bowels of the earth. This Ivan becomes interested in Evila, one of the girls employed in the mine, and for a time seriously thinks of making her his wife. From the world's point of view this would have been the worst possible *mésalli-ance*, but Ivan cares nothing for the world's opinion. Felix Kaulman, a banker, is also fascinated by Evila's wonderful beauty, and takes her with him to the capital. Soon afterward Ivan mixes in society, fights a duel, wins the love of Princess Angela, a charming woman, and, finally, disgusted with the world, returns to his mine. There he nearly becomes the victim of a gigantic stock jobbing deal, managed by Felix Kaulman. He escapes, however, and when the mine catches fire he discovers a means of extinguishing the flames, and thus restores prosperity to the workers and also saves from ruin many who had invested their entire capital in the stock of the coal company. In the meantime Evila has become an actress and the wife, in name only, of Felix. When the latter commits suicide in consequence of the failure of his wildcat speculations she returns to the mine and Ivan marries her.

Only a dim idea of the beauty and power of the book can be obtained from this brief sketch. There are other characters—notably the ambitious but conscientious Abbé Samuel, the horrible Saffran known as "the man-eater," the covetous old miser who lost his all in the Bondavara coal-mine collapse, and the eccentric Countess Theudelinde, whose glory was that she was an old maid—which are a study in themselves, and the duplicates of which it would be impossible to find in any other work. In conclusion it may be said that this English version of "Black Diamonds" is excellent, and I have little doubt that, after reading it, many persons will thank Messrs. Harper & Brothers for publishing this Hungarian masterpiece. ($1.50.)

Dr. Nikola.

MR. BOOTHBY'S protagonist may irresistibly remind some of his American readers of Prof. Herrmann, the magician, but the resemblance will serve only to make him more interesting. Dr. Nikola is a wonderful fellow, whose eyes look straight through you, and whose knowledge of occult mysteries is profound. He is an adept in hypnotism and sleight-of-hand. Still, he yearns for more knowledge. There is a Buddhist monastery on a mountain-peak in Thibet wherein important information concerning life, death, and the great hereafter is closely guarded. Nikola wants to get in there and learn all that the brothers know of the mysteries of this and other worlds, and to want to do a thing is, with Nikola, to do it. Wilfred Bruce, an impoverished Englishman in China, is his chosen confederate.

"Dr. Nikola" is a story of adventure in the Rider Haggard manner. The things these two companions do in Shanghai, Tientsin, Pekin, the Llamaserai, and Thibet are quite beyond belief; the things they see are scarcely comprehensible by mortal man. But the story has motion, swing, and dash, and these qualities, in such a work, more than compensate for its somewhat commonplace literary style. Guy Boothby shows imagination in all he writes, and this quality seems inexhaustible. (Appleton. 50 c.; $1.)—*The N. Y. Times.*

The White Shield.

AFRICA, although so much written about and so much a power in the strifes now threatening the thrones of all civilized Europe, is still an al-

"GREETING, CHIEF OF THE BLUE CATTLE!"

most undiscovered country and full of new things that may be worked into fiction.

Bertram Mitford has hit a happy note in "The White Shield," the story of which and its great import to its carriers is told in a romance of the Scheherizada type. An old, mysterious man tells the story to a white man and two Zulus resting for the night in an African mountain fastness. It is a tradition of magic feats and magic arms wholly heroic and three parts mythical. The illustrations by David B. Keeler are full of life, and add to the interest of the book. The narrative is given in the fascinating Eastern style, full of allegory and word-pictures, which the drawings fitly supplement. The publishers are making a specialty of most readable novels. (Stokes. $1.25.)

Heather from the Brae.

This little volume is nicely written, though perhaps it would never have been written at all had not Mr. Barrie recorded the humors of Thrums and Ian Maclaren and Dr. Crockett the pathos of other Scotch villages. One meets the old clergyman and the young minister, the lass who went wrong, the good doctor, the brothers who quarrel and make up, the hard farmer and the gentle widow, and all the other characters of modern Scottish fiction. Of these familiar persons and of equally familiar things David Lyall writes pleasantly and sympathetically. It is evident that he has been a part of the life he describes. Perhaps, after all, Dr. Robertson Nicoll did well to hail this young writer as a worthy peer of the three novelists to whom reference has been made.

The atmosphere of these stories is charming. It is pleasant to imagine that life among the lowly, in Scotland at all events, is thus gentle, pure, self-sacrificing, and kindly. Not one evil character throws a shadow across the pages. Even the lass who goes wrong is righted in the end. It would seem that life at Faulds, even at its worst, was an argument for the millennium.

Probably Mr. Lyall himself holds no illusions as to what life really is in a mining village in his native land. He knows that even in the Free Church there is no special and exceptional virtue. Life in the heather has all the imperfections of life in the gaslit streets and other imperfections, whereof the city dweller knoweth not.

In choosing the best, however, he is quite within his right. One man studies the loam ; another studies the flowers that grow from it. Perhaps in recent fiction there has been too much digging about the roots. The chief distinction of the new Scottish school is its disregard for the manure heap. Crockett, Barrie, Maclaren, Miss M'Leod, and many others have brought back to fiction the grace and sweetness of wholesome, healthy life. They have in nowise concerned themselves with the dark corners. After a half hour in Drumtochty or Thrums or Faulds one feels anew the beauty of manly duty and Christian living.

If this impression is strong, as it unquestionably is, it is absurd to quibble over the "art." It is unpretentious work, but even when pathos drifts into pseudo-pathos, as now and again it does, still one never doubts that it is sincere work.

The incidents which Mr. Lyall has strung together are not especially novel, but they have a vast sincerity and an immense tenderness, better it may be than the smartest novelty. One comes to know his characters as though one had lived with them, had met them at farm or cottage, kirk or shop. (Revell. 75 c.)—*N. Y. Commercial Advertiser.*

The Pith of Astronomy.

In the "Pith of Astronomy" the reader wholly unfamiliar with the science of the heavens will find a little manual filled with elementary information, but freed from signs, Greek letters, and the mathematical features that figure so largely and alarmingly in the large text-books devoted to the subject. This knowledge, possible to be easily acquired, may wile the reader to more serious investigation of astronomy, and it can, at all events, be readily retained in the memory should the busy or frivolous being care to go no further. The least scientific person likes to recognize the constellations and fixed stars, to know their names, their times of appearance, and something of their history. This the little volume helps to do—and it offers a larger help to minds constituted to receive it. (Harper. $1.)—*Providence Sunday Journal.*

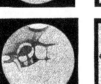

From "The Pith of Astronomy."—Copyright, 1896, by Harper & Brothers

OBSERVATIONS OF MARS SHOWING ITS CHANGES.

Chautauqua Books for 1896-7.

READERS of the Chautauqua course for 1896-7 will have a treat in the studies prepared for them. The course includes five books, as usual, two of which are devoted to a study of the French, two to the study of Greece, and one to the study of astronomy. Each of these five books is written by an authority and in a thoroughly comprehensive manner, as well as in popular style. One cannot read them without having a good general knowledge of the subjects treated, even if the details are sometimes lacking.

"The Growth of the French Nation" is written by George B. Adams, professor of history in Yale University. It traces the gradual unification of the French people from the scattered elements of the feudal system into the centralized nation of the present time. A companion piece to this work is "French Traits," a collection of essays by W. C. Brownell, who, though an American, had lived for a number of years

From "Story of the Sky."   Copyright, 1896, by Flood and Vincent.
THE CHAMBERLIN TELESCOPE OF THE UNIVERSITY OF DENVER.

in France, and was thoroughly conversant with the subject. This book, originally published several years ago, has been added to the *Chautauqua Series.* Prof. J. P. Mahaffy, who is well known to Chautauquans, and who is the wisest living man on subjects pertaining to Greece, has prepared the book dealing with "Greek Civilization." He presents a decidedly interesting picture of Hellenic civilization. Prof. Frank B. Tarbell, of the University of Chicago, has written a "History of Greek Art." This book is finely illustrated with some 200 reproductions of Greek architecture, sculpture and painting. In a "Study of the Sky" Prof. Herbert A. Howe, director of the Chamberlin Observatory, University of Denver, presents an outline of the science of astronomy, aided by many illustrations. These books will be of much interest even to those who are not pursuing the regular Chautauqua course. French, Greek, and Astronomy in one year is a combination of studies that must delight all earnest readers, and the books that are to make them at home in these studies are specially well selected; not one is dry and all are interesting far beyond the Chautauqua average. (Flood & Vincent. *Ea.*, $1.)—*Buffalo Express.*

The Monetary and Banking Problem.

THIS slender volume is an amplification of several essays contributed by Mr. McPherson to the *Popular Science Monthly.* The original papers form the second, third, and fifth chapters of the present work, to which have been added two essays on bimetallism and the standard of value. It is not, of course, an exhaustive treatise on finance, but a careful perusal of Mr. McPherson's volume justifies us in saying that he has rendered an important service to those seeking illumination on the most importunate problem of the hour. His style is simple and persuasive, and he unfolds his subject with the unaffected dignity and masterly directness characteristic of the impartial and conservative scholar. In a brief and captivating introduction the author develops the familiar thought of the intertwining of human effort, shows how it runs through all avenues of our endeavor, and points out that it has made possible the civilization which is enjoyed to-day. The author then considers the origin of money, and traces the development of the monetary problem. In this chapter he refers to the simplest conditions, presents a picture of the prehistoric man, who "knew not money and needed

AIR TO RENT.

not money," and discusses what followed upon the necessary division of labor. We learn why the precious metals were coined and the mission and importance of banks are briefly considered. "In the evolution of social organism, banks," he points out, "become the ganglia through which the action of the different parts of the organism is measured and made reciprocal." The succeeding paper forms a scholarly statement of the grave monetary problem before the nation, and is followed by a chapter on bimetallism.

We shall give, in the author's language, almost in full, the conclusions reached in the essays before us: "From the propositions that the maintenance and forwarding of civilization depend upon the exchange of human effort, and that money is the means whereby human effort is exchanged, is derived the corollary that there should be at all times sufficient money to further the exchange of human effort up to the full limit of that production and consumption which at any time is determined by the law of supply and demand. There should be sufficient coin for the small retail transactions, and as the coin necessary to this end is measurably constant in quantity and governmental issue tends to preserve uniformity in the quality and cognizability of coins, there is probably no reason that governments should not continue to be the sole sources whence coins are emitted. There should be sufficient paper currency for the transactions of greater value effected by its use. As the needful amount of such currency is variable, as its supply in adequate amount and its expansion and contraction are difficult, if not impracticable under governmental issue, but these requisites can be fulfilled under a well-adjusted banking system, it follows that the power to issue such notes should lie with banks under such restrictions as will assure

WORK FOR WORK.

their security and proper expansion in quantity. And it follows that under a well-adjusted banking system banking facilities will be provided for all communities, whether near to or remote from business centres.. In this manner can be provided that sufficiency of currency which fallacious reasoning leads many who are struggling for a livelihood, especially the farmer and the laborer in the South and Southwest, to believe can only be obtained by the free coinage of silver.

"As gold and silver, which for centuries have served as the medium of exchange, have undergone fluctuations in their relative values, which have been especially frequent and marked in recent years, and as all paper representatives of value are generally so regarded only to the extent that they are based upon and redeemable in coin of one metal or the other, it follows that, so long as coin is considered to be the basis of money, the stability of value which is necessary to commerce can the more nearly be maintained by the use as the standard of value of that metal the value of which is the least subject to fluctuation. The metal at present is gold." (Appleton. $1.)—*Phila. Ev. Bulletin.*

The Up-to-Date Primer.

A VERY ingenious little text-book in words of one syllable has been prepared as a school-reader for the future little political economists and voters of the land. Older people also may find the knotty problems of industry and finance made clear by means of clear thought and most unvarnished expression. The little pictures at the head of each lesson each tell a story that will impress itself upon the minds of the readers that spell out the weighty little words with difficulty. J. W. Bengough, the author, specially impresses that first and last all honest money must be bought by honest labor. (Funk & Wagnalls. 25 c.)

From Bengough "Up-to-Date Primer." Copyright, 1896,
by Funk & Wagnalls Co.

THE HEAD AND THE LIMBS.

The Scenery of Switzerland.

SIR JOHN LUBBOCK tells us that, from the time he visited Switzerland with Huxley and Tyndall, in 1861, his attention was directed to the physical geography of the country. "I longed," he says, "to know what forces had raised the mountains, had hollowed the lakes, and directed the rivers." Since then thousands of travellers have experienced that hunger of the mind, yet, so far as we know, this is the first plain man's manual to satisfy it. Experts have still to solve a good many problems of detail, but the main course of the physical history is now clear. Sir John, into five hundred pages of handsome letterpress, fairly teeming with illustrative diagrams, sections, profiles, and maps, has compressed the results of his own investigations and those of his fellow - savants. "The Scenery of Switzerland" is both a luminous text-book of the easier sort for amateurs, and quite a perfect *compagnon de voyage* for the intelligent traveller, whose convenience has been consulted by presenting it in a form that will not be a burden to the lightest equipment.

Two classes of readers should welcome the book. As an elementary yet thorough manual to the comprehension of the genesis of mountain and valley and their main details of structure it is quite admirable. The dullest armchair reader, who has never had sight of an Alpine peak, must find it pellucid. To travel in Switzerland, after making the book his own, is to endow the tourist with second sight. He need not quit the safe tracks to find it the very mentor he most needs.

We must decline to pick out tit-bits about glaciers and avalanches, aiguilles and ice-falls, and the rest. Our readers who care for such things will obtain the volume, which an experience of more years than we care to reckon— does not the first edition of Murray's "Knapsack" tell the story?—enables us to recommend as a rare book. It ought to accompany every educated English-speaking visitor to the Playground of Europe. (Macmillan. $1.50.)—*London Literary World.*

Daireen.

"DAIREEN," by Frank Frankfort Moore, is a novel that will be intensely enjoyed by the large class who like plenty of incident of the dramatic sort, and plenty of character to match,

From "Daireen."   Copyright, 1896, by A. F. Fenno & Co.
DRESSED ACCORDING TO MR. GLASTON'S IDEAS.

with a generous spicing of love and cross-purposes. The quieter student of character and of history will like best the first chapters that introduce us to the modern descendant of the Macnamaras and O'Dermots who, in all the pride of an hereditary King of Munster, and with such pomp as the degenerated times and conditions allow, lives in the tumbling down old castle at Innishdermot. It is an amusing picture, albeit a pitiful one—that of the old Irishman trying to keep up the dignity of his ancestors. But the love-story—and a very pretty one it is—soon sweeps us away from the Irish hills to a voyage to Cape Town. The voyage itself holds a large place in the story, for the beautiful Irish heroine, who is as free from the world's guile as a bird, is placed in the care of a designing old Major's wife who thinks it her duty to make a desirable match for her before she reaches her father in the distant colony; and she makes a fine muddle of it all, for the real lover is the Macnamara's son, who, unknown to them all, has shipped on the vessel as a sailor, for the sole purpose of being near her. It all works itself out at the Cape, in the curious and diversified society to be found there. (R. F. Fenno & Co. $1.25.)

From Whose Bourne.

WE have received from the Frederick A. Stokes Company a little book entitled "From Whose Bourne," written by Robert Barr. As the title was copyrighted first in 1888 we imagine that the story was written previous to that date; but after having read it we are at a loss to understand why half a dozen years should have elapsed before publication. For this is a good story, filled with action moving rapidly. The central idea of "From Whose Bourne" is a novel one. William Brenton, of Cincinnati,

From "From Whose Bourne." Copyright, 1896, by Frederick A. Stokes Co.

"SHE RAN BLINDLY TO THE STAIRWAY AND THERE FELL FAINTING ON THE FLOOR."

the principal character, goes to sleep and awakens to find himself dead and in another world. Just what world it is the reader does not know; for while no lake of fire and brimstone is encountered, yet Brenton feels very unhappy over having to leave his young wife on this earth. He revisits his home in a day or two and finds that he is supposed to have been murdered; his wife is charged with the crime and is in prison awaiting trial. Brenton's horror at this situation well may be imagined, for he is aware of the fact that neither she nor any one else murdered him. But try as he did in every way possible, he was unable to communicate with her or with any other mortal. Several friendly spirits came to his aid, among them that of Lecocq, the famous French detective, and they lay out a regular campaign to find Brenton's murderer and aid in his apprehension by the Cincinnati police authorities. It is not within bounds to tell what they did, and we will leave the reader to ascertain that for himself. Sufficient is it to say that the developments are curious and surprising, and they are unravelled at the end with much skill. Whether Mr. Barr intends in this little book to illustrate the danger of convicting and executing innocent persons through the use of circumstantial evidence we do not know. But he has written a comical, lively, original story, and it is worth reading. (Stokes, 75 c.)—*Mail and Express.*

Kate Douglas Wiggin.

IT is safe to say that Mrs. Kate Douglas Wiggin is one of the most popular American writers. Her stories of child-life, "The Birds' Christmas Carol" and "The Story of Patsy" particularly, have been very widely read. These two stories have reached a greater number of editions than any other recent American fiction. The secret of their popularity is that they appeal strongly to the good sense, the sympathies and susceptibilities of the reader. They play in a very forceful and wholesome manner upon the fundamental emotions of human nature: the mother's love for her child, sympathy with the unfortunate, and the combined humor and pathos of child experience. Of "Timothy's Quest," the *London Times* said: "The tale is told with a rare combination of feeling and humor. By this felicitous sketch Mrs. Wiggin has firmly established her literary reputation." Of "The Birds' Christmas Carol," which has sold well into its second hundred thousand, the *New York Evening Post* remarked: "One could hardly imagine how it would be possible to write a sweeter story."

Having achieved such remarkable success, it is not strange that Mrs. Wiggin should attempt

KATE DOUGLAS WIGGIN.

a larger book, a more elaborate and ambitious piece of fiction. This she has done, and the novel, now completed, has been secured by the *Atlantic Monthly,* and will appear in the numbers for September, October, and November. This novel, "Marm Lisa," is partly a story of child-life, but is much more. Marm Lisa, the central figure of the story, is a defective child, who has "all the cares of maternity with none of its compensating joys." Although she does not occupy as much space as some of the other characters, she is the motive-power of the narrative.

The sweet influence of Mistress Mary, Lisa's self-appointed guardian, adds a charm to the story, and every life it shines upon reflects the more clearly the truth of Goethe's saying, "The eternal womanly ever leadeth us." The story is not sweetness and light only, for the deliciously whimsical Mrs. S. Cora Grubb, whose philanthropy is hysteria, and whose good works are so many spasms, and the small twin reprobates, Atlantic and Pacific, furnish a refreshing element of humor. (Houghton, Mifflin & Co.)

THE MANUSCRIPT RETURNED.

Poor little wanderer!
　　Fate was unkind to thee!
Patient hope's squanderer!
　　Fame has been blind to thee!
Back from rude editors,
　　Lynx eyed their scrutiny,
All thy discreditors;
　　Thine not to mutiny.
　　Rest in obscurity,
　　Till, in futurity,
Laws may be passed
　　Decreeing it jailable
　　To write "not available"
"Genius" to blast;
　　Then with no stint o' space,
　　Thou'lt at a sprinter's pace
　　Come from the printer's case
Published—at last!
　　　—*E. Copinger Ward in New York Herald.*

THE BASS FISHERIES.

The Governor's Garden.

MR. GEORGE A. RIVERS deserves credit for the careful manner in which he has written his novel of "The Governor's Garden." Unfortunately, however, historical accuracy in details is not sufficient in a work of fiction; and one could spare the painstaking accuracy if its place were taken by imagination. There is no local color, no atmosphere in Mr. Rivers's story, his characters have no rounded individuality, they are silhouettes like his drawings of them and as a consequence they arouse only an unwilling sympathy. The story is told rather than acted, and it is told somewhat coldly. Comparison is not criticism, but it will save space to note that all the characteristics that make Hawthorne a master craftsman are the characteristics that are absent from Mr. Rivers's work. The opening chapter shows his limitations.

He gives us a description of an old tavern that might be useful in a guide-book but is surely overprosaic for a work of imagination. The details are all set down, but they are not fused together by the heat of imagination, and they remain details, and nothing more, to the end. The characters are described but we never come to know them; they speak but their voices have the hollowness and machine regularity of an automaton. It would seem as if Mr. Rivers persuaded himself that good intentions could supply the place of absent talents and imagination; but his readers remain unpersuaded although they recognize his honesty of intention and his courage.

Even in description Mr. Rivers cannot be heartily praised; he is as concise as a man writing a history of the universe in one small volume, and the important details are generally missing. As a good example of an all-pervading fault we refer to chapter XXVII., "in which the reader witnesses a naval engagement." The "naval engagement" consists of one well-directed shot and it reads like a telegraphic report in the daily newspapers. Mr. Rivers does not write as a master, but his book is sufficiently interesting to carry the reader on to the last chapter, and to cause him to respect if not to admire the author.

In mechanical get-up the book is charming; in its quaint chapter headings and its type it suggests an eighteenth century book; and it is so attractive to the eye and so comfortable to the hand that one regrets that the art of the author was not of the same high quality as the art of the printer, and it deserves to be honorably mentioned that the book was set up and printed by D. B. Updike, of Boston. (Knight. $1.50.)—*Boston Gazette.*

Three Old Maids in Hawaii.

OF the three, one was tall, one was short, and one neither tall nor short, but just such height as pleased those who loved her.

Of the three, one was plain and one was pretty, and one neither plain nor pretty, but altogether charming.

Of the three, one was rich and one was poor, and one neither rich nor poor, but very content with what she had.

In regard to the happy state of old-maidism it may be said that one is born to it, or one may achieve it, or it may be thrust upon one.

Belinda Mays, tall and plain, had been born an old maid; her niece Belinda, short and pretty, had achieved old-maidism at the age of twenty-three, and Judith Melrose, neither tall nor short, neither pretty nor plain, neither old nor young, had had her old-maidism thrust upon her.

These old maids started out from San Francisco to see for themselves the beauties of the Hawaiian Islands. The descriptive parts of the book are full of interest, but the thread of story that runs through it all is also delightfully drawn out, and we see the old maids gradually lose their stern judgment of men, and begin to act as is seeming for maidens blessed with good health, good spirits, and good incomes. (Eaton & Mains. $1.50.)—*From Maxwell's "Three Old Maids in Hawaii."*

A Humble Enterprise.

BECAUSE of bygone experiences of a delightful nature, we always sit down to the perusal of a book by Ada Cambridge with a marked inclination in the direction of praise, and we usually find a justification for the sentiment long before we have reached the conclusion of each volume. Feeling sure that gratification would follow close upon our reading of "A Humble Enterprise," we began this story with avidity, and reaped the customary reward, for this addition to Ada Cambridge's successes may, without any exaggeration, be described as charming. It is as simple as simple can be, uncontaminated by rascalities of any sort, innocent of aught approaching disaster. Its characters belong to flesh and blood; their troubles are our troubles, their joys our joys. The book begins at the sad moment when the Liddon family is suddenly deprived of its head by reason of a railway accident in which the master of the house was fatally injured. A few days after the burial the remaining members of the family started their humble enterprise. (Appleton. $1; pap., 50 c.)— *London Literary World.*

Yekl: A Story of the New York Ghetto.

"YEKL," by A. Cahan, is a curious study of life among the Polish and Russian Jews of New York, from the pen of one thoroughly familiar with the subject. As a story it amounts to little, but as a series of vivid pictures of a strange people who, though "among us, are not of us," it merits more than usual attention. The quarter devoted to these people in New York—the Ghetto—is in the very heart of the East Side, and one of the most densely populated places on the face of the earth—a seething human sea fed by streams, streamlets, and rills of immigration flowing from all the Yiddish (Jewish) speaking centres of Europe. Hardly a block, says the author, "but shelters Jews from every nook and corner of Russia, Poland, Galicia, Hungary, Roumania; Lithuanian Jews, Volhynian Jews, south Russian Jews,

From "Three Old Maids in Hawaii."   Copyright, 1896, by Eaton & Mains

THE VOLCANO ROAD.

A. CAHAN.

Bessarabian Jews; Jews crowded out of the 'pale of Jewish settlement'; Russified Jews expelled from Moscow, St. Petersburg, Kieff, or Saratoff; Jewish runaways from justice, Jewish refugees from crying political injustice, people torn from a hard-gained foothold in life and from deep-rooted attachments by the caprice of intolerance or the wiles of a demagogue—innocent scapegoats of a guilty government for its outraged populace to misspend its blind fury upon; students shut out of the Russian universities, and come to these shores in quest of learning; artisans, teachers, merchants, rabbies, artists, beggars—all come in search of fortune. Nor is there a tenement-house but harbors in its bosom specimens of all the whimsical metamorphoses wrought upon the children of Israel of the great modern exodus by the vicissitudes of life in this their Promised Land of to-day. You find there Jews born to plenty, whom the new conditions have delivered up to the clutches of penury; Jews reared in the straits of need, who have here risen to prosperity, good people morally degraded in the struggle for success amid an unwonted environment; moral outcasts lifted from the mire, purified, and imbued with self respect; educated men and women with their intellectual polish tarnished in the inclement weather of adversity; ignorant sons of toil grown enlightened—in fine, people with all sorts of antecedents, tastes, habits, inclinations, and speaking all sorts of sub-dialects of the same jargon, thrown pellmell into one social caldron—a human hodgepodge with its component parts changed but not yet fused into one homogeneous whole." It is this people and their social life that the author attempts to depict, and he does it with marvellous success. The book is one for the sociologist rather than the summer vacationist, but even the latter will find it of interest. A touch of pathos also enters into the author's most humorous descriptions. (Appleton. $1.)—Boston Transcript.

Green Gates.

EVIDENTLY Katherine Cheever Meredith has the art of story-telling. "Green Gates" is a quiet little story, simple in its construction, with no special points of adventure or incident, yet there is in its opening chapter a subtle suggestion of something unusual which the story is leading up to, conveyed by apparently careless touches in character painting, which, nevertheless, are so pointed that they at once impress upon the reader a definite idea of every actor that figures in the story. Green Gates is an English country-house owned by Willing Jones, a man of fortune and family. His wife has staying with her Tony, her eighteen-year-old sister, just returned from Paris, and about Tony the author manages to throw a weird and mysterious fascination, in spite of the fact that she is a cripple—indeed, her canes and her slight limp are made to add to her charm. She has two lovers, who constantly visit her, one of whom, an old bachelor, is, in his way, as interesting a study as Tony. The pictures of country-house life and social distractions are very well done, the dialogue is vivacious, and the book, in spite of the pathos of Tony's highly strung and morbid character, is as entertaining as it is well written. (Appleton. $1.25.)—The Beacon.

Legends of the Middle Ages.

THE object of this work is to familiarize young students with the legends which form the staple of mediæval literature.

While they may owe more than is apparent at first sight to the classical writings of the palmy days of Greece and Rome, these legends are very characteristic of the people who told them, and they are the best exponents of the customs, manners, and beliefs of the time to which they belong. They have been repeated in poetry and prose with endless variations, and some of our greatest modern writers have deemed them worthy of a new dress, as is seen in Tennyson's "Idyls of the King," Goethe's "Reineke Fuchs," Tegnér's "Frithiof Saga,"

KATHERINE CHEEVER MEREDITH.

Wieland's "Oberon," Morris's "Story of Sigurd," and many shorter works by these and
less noted writers.

　These mediæval legends form a sort of liter-

This book is, therefore, not a manual of mediæval literature, or a series of critical essays,
but rather a synopsis of some of the epics and
romances which formed the main part of the

From " Legends of the Middle Ages."　　Copyright, 1896, by The American Book Co.

ISEULT SIGNALS TRISTAN.

ary quarry, from which, consciously or unconsciously, each writer takes some stones
wherewith to build his own edifice. Many allusions in the literature of our own day lose
much of their force simply because these legends
are not available to the general reader.

　It is the aim of this volume to bring them
within reach of all, and to condense them
so that they may readily be understood. Of
course in so limited a space only an outline of
each legend can be given, with a few short quotations from ancient and modern writings to
illustrate the style of the poem in which they
are embodied, or to lend additional force to
some point in the story.

culture of those days. Very little prominence
has been given to the obscure early versions,
all disquisitions have been carefully avoided,
and explanations have been given only where
they seemed essential.

　The wealth and variety of imagination displayed in these legends will, I hope, prove that
the epoch to which they belong has been greatly maligned by the term "dark ages," often
applied to it. Such was the favor which the
legendary style of composition enjoyed with our
ancestors that several of the poems analyzed in
this volume were among the first books printed
for general circulation in Europe. (American
Book Co. $1.50.)—*From the Preface.*

Prehistoric Americans.

THIS is a neat pocket edition of a book divided into two studies—first of the "Mound Builders," second of the "Cliff Dwellers." The introduction gives a brief review of human life on the American continent at the time of its discovery by Columbus in 1492, and as seen by other observers during a century afterward. Our author, judging from every standpoint, of physical features, psychological, and language, says it leads to but one conclusion, "that the physical differences existing in the varieties of men can be adequately explained by climatic and other local influences, and that all ground for affirming the existence of several human species evolved from different sources will disappear." The pages are about equally divided between the Mound Builders, scattered all over our land, and the Cliff Dwellers, over a more limited area. The subjects have interested scholars for the past few years, but while they have enriched museums with the relics and handiwork of both, accurate historical knowledge of these buried nations has been scarce. The volume is a *résumé* of what has been discovered, and contains but little that is new to the antiquarian expert, who has kept abreast of the subject. (McBride. 50 c.)—*Chicago Inter-Ocean.*

With the Fathers.

UNDER this title Professor McMaster collects thirteen of his historical sketches which have been printed in the *Atlantic, Century, Harper's,* and *Forum,* and the New York *Times* and *Press.* While they all deal with American history, there is a wide range taken ; from Washington's inauguration to the career of the Know Nothings ; from the political depravity of the fathers to a century's struggle for silver, and the third-term tradition. There is a clear exposition of the Monroe doctrine with the opinions of the English press at the time of its promulgation given at length, and a sound pro-American conclusion. Indeed it is a pleasure to note the manly, patriotic tone, never degenerating into spread-eagleism, which characterizes the studies, very different from the line of thought some of our educators have followed. It is also comforting to be told that the widespread belief that politicians and legislators are more corrupt now than they were in the early days of the century is a pure delusion. A chapter—all too short—is given to "Four Centuries of Progress," setting forth the marvellous changes and abounding with robust optimism, for to him it seems "wicked to talk of degeneration and decay."

Professor McMaster has a forceful way of making his statements. As he thinks Arthur Lee was a black-hearted traitor, he says so, for he is not of the school of historians whose sphere is confined to the unadorned record of events and dates. America has reason to be proud of her historians and to be satisfied that Professor McMaster is one of them. (Appleton. $1.50.)—*Public Opinion.*

Sir Mark.

"SIR MARK," as a title for a story, has a suggestion of knightly prowess not unmixed with possibilities of villany, for about the name there cluster reflections of doughty deeds and shadows of dark ones. The tale to which Anna Robeson Brown gives this title fulfils every promise of it, for a knightlier knight, when all is done, one would not desire than Sir Mark of Lyonesse, or more villanous villany than the plot against the government of the United States. The second title of the book is "A Tale of the First Capital," and although it is a far cry from the ruined castle of Lyonesse to the well-ordered house of a Philadelphia merchant, the sequence of events seems perfectly natural, and the descriptions of President Washington and his surroundings make a most striking contrast to the Old World fortunes of Sir Brian's son. The story is in two parts. The first is a picture of wild adventure and recklessness, and shows how Sir Mark, having buried his fugitive and disreputable father on the Continent, makes a flying visit to England to recover so much of his family wealth as he can lay his hands on, and how he does it in an extraordinary night scene with his cousin Maud, at the risk of his life. Drawn swords, buried jewels, a forsaken castle, and many adjuncts of the stirring romance which is popular in these days, figure in this introduction to the real story. This first part is told by Sir Mark himself. The second part is told by Mr. David Blaythwait, to whom is confided, by a business friend in England, the reception in Philadelphia of the young man who has chosen the brand new republic to spend his fortune in. Historical incidents are suggested by this part of the story, the episodes occurring during the first term of Gen. Washington as President. The descriptions of the President and Vice-President Adams and other notable persons are suggestive and excellent, and the social and political atmospheres of the Philadelphia of that day are capitally given. The chief interest lies in the love of Sir Mark for Mr. Blaythwait's orphaned niece, how he came near losing her through his folly and ambition in joining a foul conspiracy against the government, and how Mr. Blaythwait and Letty saved him in spite of himself. It is a remarkably pretty story, with enough real romance and enough fighting and rescuing to please the lover of lovers of the days of chivalry, and the interview which Mr. Blaythwait and "Mr. Lyonesse" have with Gen. Washington is a remarkably graphic and happy little scene. The publishers have printed "Sir Mark" in one of their prettiest forms, and it makes a delightful bit of summer reading. (Appleton. 75 c.)—*Mail and Express.*

Silk of the Kine.

THIS rather obscure title Mr. McManus has elected to give a very charming little story — a romance dealing with the doings of Cromwell's soldiery in Ireland after the battles of Wexford and Drogheda. The heroine is Margery Ny Guire, a flaxen-haired young lady, with sloeblack eyes (scarcely an Irish type of beauty, by the way), who is the daughter of Fermanagh, and amongst the "Transplanted" from Monaghan to Connaught. The love of the English soldier, Piers Ottley, is prettily developed; but the author is hardly successful with Margery, who marries from gratitude, and afterwards displays a tardy affection for the gallant young man (who has risked more than his all for her sake), in a very unconvincing and ungracious manner. One brief page is all that Mr. McManus devotes to what might have been a very tender and eloquent part of his book ; indeed, a sense of restraint— of nervousness, rather—strikes one from first to last. However, the appendix assures us that he has chapter and verse for the outlines of the story, and although we think that the author might, with advantage, have left facts more in the background, and allowed his imagination more unfettered play, there is no doubt that the reader can spend a very pleasant and entertaining hour with the "Silk of the Kine." (Harper. $1.)—*Bookselling.*

Leather Stocking Tales.

THIS new issue of the most popular and famous of Cooper's works will be brought out in five handsome volumes, sold separately or in sets. A noteworthy, interesting, and valuable

From "The Last of the Mohicans."   Copyright, 1896, by T. Y. Crowell & Co.

IN THE FOREST.

feature of this edition consists in a carefully prepared and appreciative introduction by Professor Brander Matthews, of Columbia University. The illustrations are fifteen full-page photogravures (three in each volume) by Frank T. Merrill, the well-known artist, who has sought to combine historical accuracy with dramatic and poetic qualities. The vignette titlepages have been designed by the same skilled artist, who has taken deep pride in furnishing a series of illustrations that may well satisfy the most ardent and exacting admirer of Cooper's wonderful tales. (Crowell. 5 v., *ea..* $1.50.)

The Three Impostors.

"THE Three Impostors, or, the transmutations," by Arthur Machen, begins with a prologue in which some horrible crime is suggested, and in successive chapters, which are evidently planned in imitation of Stevenson's "New Arabian Nights," different people who have been more or less concerned in the tragedy relate their experiences. The pages that follow contain much that is gloomy and disagreeable, and some incidents that are unspeakably revolting, ending up with a description of a murder that rivals anything in Foxe's "Book of Martyrs." There are people who like to revel in sensational newspaper crimes, and who gloat over the most disgusting details, so there must be those who will read "The Three Impostors," and, possibly, find some merit in the book; but to the rational, thinking man or woman it will seem a most melancholy waste of time to read it, and wicked use both of time and talent on the part of the author to give it the possibilities of print. (Roberts. $1.)—*The Beacon.*

Pope Leo XIII.

IT is not easy to appreciate the effect of a man's life and work while he is himself alive and in harness, but Mr. Justin McCarthy has, at any rate, succeeded, and with considerable art, in drawing a very striking and interesting portrait of an undoubtedly great man. The present Pope Vincenzo Gioacchino Pecci was born on the 2d of March, 1810, at Carpineto in the diocese of Anagni, in the State of the Church. He was elected Pope in 1878. In two or three chapters, the second, third, sixth, we get a good idea of the personal character of the Pope, and the secrets, both personal and ecclesiastical, of his influence. Then one by one the leading episodes of his papal career are told. The Kulter-Kamp in Germany, the Education Question in Belgium and France, Ireland, Slavery, The Labor Question, Politics and Religion in general, the Appeal to England and, last of all, the contemptible and insignificant Prince Ferdinand of Bulgaria's surrender of his son to a religion that he professed to believe to be untrue, in order to secure the temporal support of Russia, are all well and interestingly told. There are one or two points over which we should be inclined to challenge Mr. McCarthy's views. For instance, it is quite true that Mazzini believed in Nationalism, but it was the making of a nation out of many allied principalities, and kindred tribes if we may use the word. He would have been aghast at a nation resolving itself again into a lot of quasi-independent principalities. It is hardly the time to write controversially about reunion, but, while we fully appreciate the charity of the Pope's appeal to England, we cannot see how the Archbishop of Canterbury could have given a more encouraging answer than he did. He was bound, with his belief in his canonical position, to lay down as his fundamental requirement that the English Church should be recognized as being really an integral part of the one Catholic Church Christ founded. The book, however, is fairly written. It is one of the *International Series of Public Men of To-Day.* An admirable portrait of the Pope forms the frontispiece. The book has just received the friendly appreciation of Mr. Gladstone. (Warne. $1.25.)—*Bookselling.*

In a Dike Shanty.

A STORY that fires one with a desire to emulate the author's example is "In a Dike Shanty," by Maria Louise Pool. The narrator professedly comes into possession of a tract of dike land skirting the town of Marshfield, which is situated on the seacoast of Massachusetts. With a friend she takes possession of a shanty that adorns her broad acres, and then and there she is whirled into the seething vortex of Marshfield life.

Miss Pool is a native of New England, and knows her people well. In this instance it pleases her to serve them to her readers much after the style in which Sally Pratt McLain immortalized "Cape Cod Folks." Society in the village of Marshfield is full of drolleries as seen by this author's eyes, and so she depicts it, not forgetting to offer a touch of pathos here and there to balance the story. Mar Baker, with her "idjit" son, has a world of tragedy pressed behind her firm set lips, and the pitifulness of Mrs. Peake's death with her husband's mad repentance is a drama in itself, if it were more elaborated. Virginia Dance, who is "kinder" Southern by birth, is a very tantalizing girl, an innocent mischief-maker, whose languorous glances make trouble for the unhappy swains unfortunate enough to come within range of her vision, and our interest is only whetted by the fact that we are left in doubt as to which of her lovers she really loves. Miss Pool's touch is of the lightest; often she merely indicates a witticism, and her whimsical "notions" drip from her pen without any consciousness apparently on her part. Her style is fresh and crisp and her wit never stings. "In a Dike Shanty" is a wholly charming little book, bubbling over with the best kind of humor, and through its entire length there is not one dull line. (Stone & Kimball. $1.25.)—*Chicago Evening Post.*

The Literary News.

An Eclectic Monthly Review of Current Literature.

EDITED BY A. H. LEYPOLDT

SEPTEMBER, 1896.

CAMPAIGN LITERATURE.

THE nominations of Presidential candidates have been made, and throughout the land the voters are making up their minds on the merits of the principles, policy, and methods for which these candidates stand.

Perhaps more than ever before voters are intending to be free agents, untrammelled by party traditions and party influence.

In order to decide a question even for one-self it is necessary to know both sides of it and to weigh carefully what those in authority, by virtue of knowledge and experience, have decided after careful study.

The publishers are manufacturing campaign literature every hour and it is necessary to have a guide in its selection for personal use. The following list includes books dealing chiefly with the money question, which this year seems paramount in importance ; but it also covers the literature dealing with the problems which during the past five years have led to the splitting up of parties, and have called the individual attention of voters to the causes of the spirit of dissatisfaction and unrest which is abroad and spreading.

The list includes chiefly books and pamphlets published since 1890, and only such as are written for general readers. Other lists of campaign literature have been prepared by Baker & Taylor Co., A. C. McClurg & Co., Pet r Paul Book Co., St. Paul Book and Stationery Co., and Charles Scribner's Sons. *The Monthly Bulletin* of the Providence Public Library for August is also devoted to "Labor and Allied Subjects" ; *The Arena* has begun a Bibliography of Literature dealing with Vital Social and Economic Questions, the August number covering Land and Land Tenure ; and No. 3 of the *Economic Studies,* published by The Macmillan Co., is devoted to "The Populist Movement" and has a seven-page index to the periodical literature of the subject, by Frank L. McVey.

Women as well as men should make a point of knowing the reason for what is going on about them, and a careful reading of the books on both sides of the issues of the present campaign is the best way to acquire knowledge and reasonable arguments towards enforcing the conclusions to which reading brings the reader. Campaign literature being of so ephemeral a character, it has been difficult always to verify the date and place of publication.

ANARCHISM.

Dubois, F. Anarchist peril. '94. $1.75.
N. Y., *Scribner*

Lum, D. D. Economics of anarchy : study of the industrial type. '91. 10c.....N. Y., *Twentieth Century*

Mackay, J. H. Anarchists. '91. 25c.
N. Y., *B: R. Tucker*

Pentecost, H. O. Evolution and social reform ; anarchistic method. '90. 20c .... Boston, *J. H. West*

Salter, W. M. Anarchy or government ? '95. $1.75.
Boston, *Crowell*

Tucker, B: R. Instead of a book, by a man too busy to write one : exposition of philosophical anarchism. '93. $1 ; 50c......................N. Y., *B: R. Tucker*

Van Ornum, W: H. Why government at all ? '92. $1.50 ; 50c ....Chicago, *Kerr*

BIMETALLISM.

Adams, B. Law of civilization and decay. (International bimetallism.) $2.50..................N. Y., *Beall*

Andrews, E. B. An honest dollar. (Plea for bimetallism.) $1 ; 50c..............Hartford, *Student Pub. Co*

Barclay, R. Disturbance of the standard of value. '96. 70c..N. Y.
Favors international bimetallism.

Barker, W. Bimetallism ; or, the evils of monometallism and the benefits of bimetallism. '96. $1 ; 50c.
Phila., *Barker Pub Co*
Favors free coinage.

Barrows, H. D. International bimetallism. '91. 10c.
Los Angeles, Cal., *Stoll & Thayer*
Scientific bimetallism.

Giffen, R. Case against bimetallism. '92. $2.
N. Y., *Macmillan*
Favors silver.

Helm, E. Joint standard : plain statement of monetary principles and of the monetary controversy. '94. net, $1.10..N. Y., *Macmillan*
Favors silver.

Laughlin, J. L. History of bimetallism in the United States. *New ed.* '96. $2.25 ....N. Y., *Appleton*

MacLeod, H. D. Bimetallism. '94. $1.75.
N. Y., *Longmans*
Favors gold. .

Noailles, *Duc de.* How to save bimetallism. '95. 15c.
Phila., *Am. Acad. Pol Sci*
Parallel and independent bimetallism without proportion or ratio.

Peabody, H. W. Opposition to bimetallism. '95. 10c.
Cambridge, Mass., *H. W. Peabody*

Peeples, W. O. Gold and silver. '95. 25c.
Chattanooga, Tenn., *Gold and Silver Pub*
Favors free coinage.

Rothwell, R: P. Universal bimetallism and an international monetary clearing-house. World's statistics of gold and silver. '93. 75c..N. Y., *Scientific Pub. Co*

Smith, R. H: Silver question settled by enactment into law of a proposed bill to establish a gold currency and a silver currency on a basis of interchangeable value. '94. 50c......................N. Y, *Baker & T*

Smith, W. H. The effects of the gold standard. '96. 25c..Chic., *Kerr*
A plea for bimetallism.

Stokes, A. P. Joint metallism : plan by which gold and silver together may be made the basis of a sound currency. '94. 75c. *Same,* 3d ed. enl. '95. $2.
N. Y., *Putnam*

Teller, J. H. Battle of the standards. '96. 25c.
Chicago, *Schulte*
Favors free coinage.

Walker, F. A. International bimetallism. '96. $1.25.
N. Y., *Holt*
Favors scientific bimetallism.

Walsh, W. J. Bimetallism and monometallism. '95. 25c........Chicago, *Coin Pub. Co.;* N. Y., *Am. News Co*
Advocates bimetallism.

Wheeler, E. P. Real bimetallism ; or, true coin *vs.* false coin : a lesson for Coin's financial school. '95. 75c..N. Y., *Putnam*
Favors gold.

CAPITAL AND LABOR.

Aveling, E. B. *and* E. M. Working-class movement in America. 2d ed. '91. $1...............N. Y., *Scribner*

Banks, L: A. White slaves ; or, the oppression of the worthy poor. '91. $1.50............Boston, *Lee & S*

Brentano, L. Relation of labor to the law of to-day. '91. $1.50.................................N. Y., *Putnam*

Clark, J: B. Surplus gains of labor. ['93.] 15c. Phila., *Am. Acad. Pol. Sci*

Cowdrey, A. H. A tramp in society. '91. 25c. Chic., *Schulte* A plea for the labor movement.

Crocker, U. H. Cause of hard times. '95. 50c. Boston, *Little, B. & Co*

Cunningham, W: Use and abuse of money. '91. $1. N. Y., *Macmillan* Capital in its relation to social progress.

Davenport, B R. Crime of caste in our country. '92. subs., $1........................Phila., *Keystone Pub. Ho* Dogs and the fleas; by one of the dogs: [satire.] '93. $1; 50c.............................Chicago, *McCallum*

Drage, G. The unemployed. '94. $1.50. N. Y., *Macmillan*

Dyer, H. Evolution of industry. '95. $1.50. N. Y., *Macmillan*

George, H: Condition of labor. '95. 30c. N. Y., *Sterling Pub*

Godard, J: G. Poverty: its genius and exodus. '92 $1 .... N. Y., *Scribner*

Gould, E. R. L. Social condition of labor. '93. 50c. Baltimore, *Johns Hopkins*

Hadfield, R. A., *and* Gibbins, H: de B. Shorter working day. '92. $1........................N. Y., *Scribner*

Hobhouse, L. T. Labor movement. '93. $1.25. N. Y., *Putnam*

Hobson, J: A. Evolution of modern capitalism: study of machine production. '94. $1.25....N. Y., *Scribner*

Howell, G: Handy book of the labor laws. 3d ed. '95 $1.50 ....N. Y., *Macmillan*

Hubbard, L. C. Coming climax in the destinies of America. 2d ed. '92. 50c................Chicago, *Kerr*

Jacobson, A: Next step forward; or, better times for us all. '92. 15c................Chicago, *Schulte* — Ounce of prevention to save America from a government of the few, by the few, and for the few. '92. 50c. Chicago, *Kerr*

Jelley, S. M. Voice of labor. '91. 50c. Chicago, *H. J. Smith*

Jocelyn, R. W. Rights of labor: relation of employer and employed. '94. 25c................Chicago, *Kerr*

Krebs, S. L. Poverty's factory. '95. 75c.; 25c. Boston, *Arena*

Mallock, W. H. Labor and the popular welfare. '93. $2. *Same,* new cheaper ed. '94. 50c. N. Y., *Macmillan*

Marx, K: Capital; critical analysis of capitalist production. ['90.] 4 pts. *ea.,* 30c......N. Y., *Humboldt*

New republic: scheme to abolish poverty; anti poverty society on the American plan: social democracy. '94· 25c ....N. Y., *New Era Pub.*

Palmer, F. L. Wealth of labor. ['95.] $1. N. Y., *Baker & T*

Rae, J: Eight hours for work. '94· $1.25. N. Y., *Macmillan*

Robertson, J: M. Eight hours question. '93. $1. N. Y., *Scribner*

Sayward, W. H. Thought on the relations of employer and workman. '93· 10c...........N. Y., *Funk*

Schaffle, A. E. T. Theory and policy of labor protection. '94· $1........................N. Y., *Scribner*

Seymour, H. W. Government & Co. limited: an examination of the tendencies of privilege in the U. S. '95· 75c......................Chicago, *McClurg*

Stimson, F. J. Labor law of the United States. '96· $1.50......................N. Y., *Scribner* — Labor in its relation to law. '95· 75c..N.Y., *Scribner*

Trumbull, M. M. Wheelbarrow articles and discussions on currency and the labor question. '90· $1. *Same.* '95· 30c...............Chicago, *Open Court*

Webb, S., *and* Cox, H. Eight hours day. '91. 50c. N. Y., *A Lovell*

Wheeler, D: H. Our industrial Utopia and its unhappy citizens. '95· $1.25.........Chicago, *McClurg*

Worthington, T. L. Dwellings of the poor and weekly wage-earners in and around towns. '93. $1. N. Y., *Scribner*

Wright, Carroll D. Industrial evolution of the United States. '95· $1...........Meadville, Pa , *Flood & V*

Yerser, J: Labor as money. '94. $1.25.; 50c. Boston, *Arena*

COMMERCE AND CREDIT.

Baird, H: C. Money and bank credit in the U. S., France, and Great Britain, and their effects on the people. '91. 10c...........................Phila., *Baird*

Bastable, C: F. Commerce of nations. '92. $1. N. Y., *Scribner*

Bowley, A. L. Short account of England's foreign trade in the 19th century; its economic and social results. '93. $1......................N. Y., *Scribner*

Earling, R. P. Whom to trust : a treatise on mercantile credits. New issue. '96· $5. Chicago, *Rand, McNally & Co*

Edwards, I: Treatise on bills of exchange and promissory notes. 2d ed. '91. $10.N. Y. and Albany, *Banks*

Gibbins, H: de B. History of commerce in Europe. '91. 90c..............................N. Y., *Macmillan*

Gilbert, F. N. Boards of trade, business men's association-, and chambers of commerce : forms and laws for their organization in the U. S. and Canada. '91. 50c......................Albany, *Weed*

Hyndman, H: M. Commercial crises of the 19th century. '92. $1 ....N. Y., *Scribner*

Lewis, R. Modern industries and commerce: information readers, no. 4. '91. 60c........*Bost. Sch. Sup.*

Macleod, H: D. Theory of credit. '94· $3.50. N. Y., *Longmans*

Mun, T: England's treasure by foreign trade. '95. 75c............................N. Y., *Macmillan*

Rabbeno, Ugo. Amer. commercial policy. '95. $3.25. N. Y., *Macmillan*

Williams, H: W. Money and bank credit in the United States. ['95.] 25c..Phila., *Am. Acad. Pol. Sci*

FARMERS.

Bentley, A. F. Condition of the western farmer, as illustrated by economic history of a Nebraska township. '93· $1................Baltimore, *Johns Hopkins*

Chase, H: S. Letters to farmers' sons on the questions of the day : talks on political economy. '91. 50c.; 25c. N. Y., *Twentieth Century*

Cunning, J: N. New constitution: how the farmer may pay off his mortgage and the working-man become his own master. '90.50c.; 25c. Chicago, *Donahue*

Free silver and its effect on the farmer and wage-earner. '96. 10c......................Chicago, *M. J. Sullivan* Advocates gold.

Kebbel, T: E. Agricultural laborer. '93· $1. N. Y., *Scribner*

Peffer, W. A. The farmer's side: his troubles and their remedy. '91. $1..............N. Y., *Appleton*

Strange, D. Farmer's tariff manual. '92· $1.25. N. Y., *Putnam*

Taubeneck, H. E. Condition of the Am. farmer. '96· 25c ....Chicago, *Schulte* Favors silver.

Ville, G. The perplexed farmer: how is he to meet alien competition. '91. $1.75........N. Y., *Longmans*

FINANCE.

Bastable, C: Fs. Public finance. '92. $4. N. Y., *Macmillan*

Blanchard, C: E. Uncle Sam's homilies on finance. '95. 25c. ......Cleveland, O, *Current Events*

Blunden, G. H. Local taxation and finance. '95· $1. N. Y., *Scribner*

Bowler, R. B. Decisions of Comptroller of the Treasury. May, '93; Sept., '94· No price..........*Gov. Pr*

Bullock, C: J. Finances of the United States from 1785–1789. '95· 75c.Madison, Wis., *Univ. of Wisconsin*

Burke, W. E. Federal finances; or, the income of the U. S. '91. $1.25................Chicago, *Schulte*

Cargill, J: F. Freak in finance : a reply to Coin's financial school: history of bimetallism in the United States. '95· 25c............Chicago, *Rand, McN. & Co* Favors gold.

Carroll, E: Principles and practice of finance. '95. $1.75................................N. Y., *Putnam* Favors gold.

Cohn, G. Science of finance. '95· $3.50. Chicago, *Univ. of Chicago*

Coin's financial series. Nos 1–6. ['95.] 6 v. *ea.,* $1 ; 50c. *Same* (pop. ed.), 6 v., *ea.,* 25c.; 10c. Chicago, *Coin Pub. Co.; N. Y., Am. News*

Dunbar, C: F. Laws of the U. S. relating to currency, finance, and banking. '95. $1.25....N. Y., *Putnam*

Harvey, W. H. Coin's financial school. '95· $1 : 50c. (Pop. ed.) 25c. Chicago, *Coin Pub. Co.; N. Y., Am. News* — *Same*; [also] Coin's financial school up to date. '95· $1 ....Chicago, *Coin Pub. Co* — Coin's financial school up to date. ['95.] $1; 50c. (Pop. ed.) 25c. Chicago, *Coin Pub. Co.; N. Y., Am. News* — — handbook. '94· 10c. Chicago, *Coin Pub. Co.; N. Y., Am. News*

Harvey, W. H. Tale of two nations. $1; 25c.
Chicago, *Coin Pub. Co.;* N. Y., *Amer. News Co*
Harvey advocates free coinage of silver.

Honest Money, S. (*pseud.*) Base coin exposed; the
arrest, exposure, and confession of W. H. H. Money,
and the dismissal of the so-called Coin's financial
school. ['95.] 25c.....................Chicago, *Weeks*
Opposes free coinage.

How, R. G., *and* **Harvey, W. H.** Great debate on the
financial question. 50c.......Chicago, *Debate Pub. Co*
Both sides of the question.

Johnson, R. P. B. United States money. ['92.] 5c.
N. Y., *Twentieth Century*

Norton, S. F. Ten men of Money Island. Primer of
finance. '95. 25c.....................Chicago, *Schulte*
Favors silver.

Roberts, G. E. Coin at school in finance. ['05.] 25c.
Chicago, *Conkey*
Favors gold.

Scott, W: A. Repudiation of state debts: study in the
financial hist. of Miss., Florida, Alabama, etc. '93.
$1.50.....................................Boston, *Crowell*

United States. *Congress.* Laws of the United States
relating to currency, finance, and banking, 1789–1890.
'91. $2.50....................................Boston, *Ginn*

Westrup, A. B. Financial problem: its relation to
labor reform and prosperity. '91. 10c.
Chicago, *Mutual Bank*

White, Horace. Coin's financial fool; or, the artful
dodger exposed. ['95.] 25c...............N. Y., *Ogilvie*
Opposes free silver.

Wisner, E: Cash *vs.* coin: an answer to Coin's
financial school. '95. 25c...............Chicago, *Kerr*
Favors gold.

Wood, Stanley. Answer to Coin's financial school.
25c.....................................Chicago, *Sherwood*
Favors gold.

GOLD AND SILVER.

Adams, B. Gold standard: a hist. study; rev. to April,
1895. '95. 50c..................Washington, D. C., *Beall*
Favors silver.

Astor, W: Waldorf. Case for gold. [93.] 25c.
N. Y., *Routledge*

Barclay, R. Silver question and the gold question.
'94. 90c.
Favors international bimetallism.

Coffin, G: M. Silver from 1849 to 1892. '92. 50c.
Washington, D. C., *McGill*

Crime of 1873. Who was the criminal? 25c.
N. Y., *Indust. Pub. Co.*
Favors silver.

Cunts, J. H. Plain words about silver money. 15c.
N. Y., *Reform Club*
Favors gold.

Dell, S. Free silver. 25c...............Boston, *Arena*
Advocates free coinage.

Dollar worth a dollar. 15c.........N. Y., *Reform Club*
Favors gold.

Economic books, including the writings of Henry C.
Carey and Henry Carey Baird..............Phil., *Baird*
All oppose single gold standard.

Ehrich, L. R. Question of silver. '92. $1. *Same*,
rev. ed., '96. 75c.; 40c...................N. Y., *Putnam*
Favors gold.

Eilstaetter, K. Indian silver currency, tr. by J. L.
Laughlin. $1.25.............Chicago, *Univ. of Chicago*
Favors gold.

Ford, W. C. Gold and foreign exchanges, 1894–1895.
'95. no price...............Washington, D. C., *Gov. Pr*

Gold and silver question at a glance. '96. 10c.
N. Y., *Excelsior Pub. House*

Hadley, O. A. Danger line reached. 25c..Chic., *Weeks*
Argument for the free and independent coinage of
silver.

Halstead, Murat. White dollar. '95. 15c.
Phila., *Franklin News*

Hertwig, J. G. Silver question. '95. 10c.
Cincinnati, O., *J. G. Hertwig*

Horton, S. D. Silver and gold and their relation to the
problem of resumption. New ed. '95. $1.50.
Cincinnati, O., *Clarke*
Favors silver.

— Silver in Europe. 2d ed. enl. '92. $1.50.
N. Y., *Macmillan*
Favors bimetallism.

Jackson, C. C. Has gold appreciated? '94. 25c.
Bost., *Little, Brown & Co*
Favors gold.

Landon, M. D. Money: gold, silver, or bimetallism.
'95. 25c...................................Chicago, *Kerr*
Against free silver.

Lowry, R: Shall the United States alone undertake
the free coinage of silver at the ratio of 16 to 1? '96.
25c...*Kerr*

Mead, C. F. The silver issue. 25c....Chicago, *Weeks*
Advocates gold.

Miller, H: G. Chapters on silver. '94. 25c.
Chicago, *Coin Pub. Co.;* N. Y., *Am. News*
Advocates gold.

Miller, M. A. Gold or silver? '96. 25c..N. Y., *Neely*
Advocates gold.

Mitchell, W. B. Dollars or what? A little common
sense applied to silver as money. '96. 25c.
N. Y., *Am. News Co.;* Chattanooga, Tenn., *H. C. Adler*
Against free coinage.

Osgood, W: N. Bug *vs.* Bug (both sides of the silver
question). ['95.] 50c.; 25c......Boston, C: *E. Brown*

Schilling, R. Silver question. '91. 10c.
Milwaukee, Wis., *South Side*

Solid money: arguments of W: C. Whitney, John G.
Carlisle, David B. Hill, Wm. McKinley, and others.
'96...N. Y., *Neely*
Favors gold.

Stevans, C. M. Free silver. Democratic campaign
handbook. $1.............................Chicago, *Laird*
Advocates free coinage of silver.

— Silver *vs.* gold. '96.....................N. Y., *Neely*
Favors silver.

Suess, E. Future of silver. '93. no price.
Washington, D. C., *Gov. Pr*

Taussig, F. W: Silver situation in the United States.
'92. 75c.........................Baltimore, *Am. Econ. Assoc*

— *Same.* 2d rev. ed. '93. 75c..............N. Y., *Putnam*
Favors gold.

Todd, Mrs. M. Pizarro and John Sherman. ['91.] 25c.
Chicago, *Schulte*

Vickers, R. H. Fiat silver: its ruinous effects shown
in history. 25c........................Chicago, *Sergel*
Opposes free silver.

Weissinger, Rozel. What is money? Discussion of
the silver question. '95. 25c.
Louisville, Ky., *Courier-Journal*

White, Horace. Gold standard; hist. sketch with reflections thereon. '93. 5c...........N. Y., *Eve. Post*

Woodford, A. B. On the use of silver as money in
the U. S. ['93.] 35c.........Phila., *Am. Acad. Pol. Sci*

MONEY, COINAGE, AND BANKING.

Bagehot, W. English and American money. 75c.
N. Y., *Longmans*

Baird, H: C. Money and bank credit in the U. S.,
France, and Great Britain, and their effects on the
people. '91. 10c.........................Phila., *Baird*

Bennett, J. W. Breed of barren metal, or currency
and interest. 25c.......................Chicago, *Kerr*
Advocates paper money.

Bossevain, G. M. Monetary question. '91. $1.
N. Y., *Macmillan*

Brooks, F. A. Objections legal and practical to our
national currency system. '93. 25c.
Boston, G. B. *Reed*

Brough, W: Natural law of money; successive steps in
the growth of money. '94. $1...........N. Y., *Putnam*
Favors gold.

Cheap-money experiments in past and present times.
'92. 50c.................................N. Y., *Century Co*

Conant, C: A. Modern banks of issue. '96. $3.
N. Y., *Putnam*

Cornwell, W: C. Currency and the banking law of the
Dominion of Canada considered with reference to currency reform in the U. S. '95. 75c...N. Y., *Putnam*

Cowperthwait, J: H. Money, silver, and finance.
'92. $1.25................................N. Y., *Putnam*
Advocates gold.

Crandall, O. A. Currency primer. '94. 25c.
Sedalia, Mo., *Dexter Bk*
Favors gold.

Dana, C: A. Proudhon and his Bank of the people.
Defence of great French anarchist. Advocates free
and mutual banking. By a veteran journalist. '95.
25c.; 10c.......................N. Y., *Benj. R. Tucker*

Del Mar, Alex. A history of monetary systems of the
world. '95. $6............................Chic., *Kerr*
Favors bimetallism and free coinage of silver.

Donnelly, I. American people's money. '95. 50c.;
25c...................................Chicago, *Laird & L*
Favors free coinage of silver.

Du Bois, W: B. Fiat money lunatics. '92. 10c.
N. Y., *Twentieth Century*

Dunbar, C: F. Theory and history of banking. '95·
$1.25...N.Y., *Putnam*
Favors gold.

Elvis, R. Uncle Sam's dream. 25c....Chicago, *Weeks*
Favors free coinage.

Evans, G: G. Evans' illustrated hist. of the U. S.
mint, and descriptions of all Am. coins issued. New
rev. ed. '92· 50c.; $1: $3 ....Phila., *G: G. Evans*

Fonda, A. I: Honest money. '95· c. $1.
N. Y., *Macmillan*
Opposes present gold standard.

Foote, A. R. Sound currency and the banking system.
'95· 75c.................................N.Y., *Putnam*
Favors gold.

Fraser, J: A., jr., *and* Sergel, C: H. Sound money.
'95· 50c.; 25c........................Chicago, *Sergel*
Gold and silver coinage under the Constitution: laws
enacted thereon by Congress. '96· 50c.
Chicago, *Rand, McN. & Co*

Goode, J. B. Modern banker: a story of his rapid rise
and dangerous designs. '96· 25c...... Chicago, *Kerr*
Advocates free silver and government control of banks.

Gordon, A. C. Congressional currency. '95· $1.25.
N. Y., *Putnam*
Favors gold.
— Outline of the federal money system. '95· $1.25.
N. Y., *Putnam*
Favors gold.

Gunn, O. B. Bullion vs. coin. '95· 25c.
Kansas City, Mo., *Hailmann*

Harvey, W: H., *and others.* Money of the people. '95·
25c..................................Chicago, *Sergel*
Articles on the free silver side.

Haslitt, W: C. Coinage of the European continent.
'93· $5.................................N.Y., *Macmillan*

Hill, T: E. Money found: recovered from its hiding-
places, and put into circulation through confidence in
government banks. Glossary of financial terms. '94·
50c.; 25c..........................Chicago, *Kerr*
Advocates government banks.

Jevons, W. S. Money and the mechanism of exchange. $1.75.................... N. Y., *Appleton*

Johnson, R. P. B. United States money. ['02.] 5c.
N. Y., *Twentieth Century*

Kellogg, E: New monetary system the only means of
securing the respective rights of labor and property
and protecting the public from financial revulsions.
New ed. '95· 25c.................N.Y., *U. S. B'k Co*
Advocates paper money.

Kinley, David. Independent treasury system of the
United States. $1.50....................Bost., *Crowell*

Kitson, A. Scientific solution of the money question.
'04· $1.25: 50c.........................Boston, *Arena*
Favors a government paper currency.

Laughlin, J. L. Facts about money. '95· 50c.
Chicago, *Weeks*
Advocates gold.

Leavitt, S. Our money wars: example and warning of
Am. finance. '94· 50c.................. Boston, *Arena*
Favors free coinage.

Lotz, W. Monetary situation in Germany. ['93.] 25c.
Phila., *Am. Acad. Pol. Sci*

McClung, D. W. Money talks: some of the things it
says when it speaks. ['94.] $1....Cincinnati, *Clarke*
Favors gold.

MacLeod, H: D. Elements of banking. '95· $1.25.
N. Y., *Longmans*
— Theory and practice of banking. 2 v. $9.50
N. Y., *Longmans*

McPherson, L. G. Monetary and banking problem.
'96· $1.................................N. Y., *Appleton*
Advocates gold.

Mason, J. H., *and* Sergel, C: H: Sound money. 25c.
Chicago, *Sergel*
Advocates gold.

Minot, R. S. Our money. '96· 10c.
Boston, *Damrell & U*
Favors gold.

Muhleman, M. L. Monetary systems of the world.
'95· $2..N. V., *Nicoll*
— Money of the U. S. 50c.................N. Y., *Nicoll*
Favors gold.

Nelson, H: L. Money we need. '95· 50c.
N. Y., *Harper*
Favors gold.

Nicholson, J. S. Treatise on money, and essays on
monetary problems. '95· $2........N. Y., *Macmillan*
Favors silver.

Norman, J: H. Complete guide to the world's twenty-
nine metal monetary systems. '92· $2.25.
N. Y., *Putnam*

Onstad, E. J., McGee, C: A. A., *and others.* The
truth about money; with introd. by Hon. J: Johnston.
'96· 50c ....Milwaukee, *C. N. Caspar*

Peabody, H: W. Sound money. '95· 10c.
Cambridge, Mass., *H: W. Peabody*

Peters, E. T. Monetary standard. '95· 10c.
Washington, D. C., *Economic Pub*

Phin, J: Common-sense currency: practical treatise on
money in its relations to national wealth and prosperity. '94· $1 ....N. Y., *Indust. Pub. Co*

Poland, L. Money: an essay. '95· 25c.
Cincinnati, *Clarke*

Potts, W: Monetary problem. '92· 10c.
N. Y., *Appleton*
Favors bimetallism, but opposes free coinage of silver.

Preston, R. E. Monetary legislation and currency
system of the U. S. '96· 25c.; 50c........Phila., *McVey*
Favors gold.

Rae, G: The country banker, his clients, cares, and
work. Am. preface by Brayton Ives. '91· $2.50
N. Y., *Scribner*

Rogers, J. T. Scientific money. '95· 25c.
San Francisco, Cal., *J. T. Rogers*

Schoenhof, J. History of money and prices. '95·
$1.50...................................N. Y., *Putnam*
Favors gold.

Schuckers, J. W. N. Y. national bank presidents'
conspiracy against industry and property. '96· 25c.
Chicago, *Am. Bimetallic*

Shaw, W. A. History of currency, 1252-1894. '95· net,
$3 75 ....N. Y., *Putnam*
Favors gold.

Sherwood, S. History and theory of money. '93· $2.
Phila., *Lippincott*

Smith, J. A. Multiple money standard. '96· 50c.
Phila., *Am. Acad. Pol. Sci*

Sound currency, 1895. '95· $1.....N. Y., *Reform Club*
Advocates gold.

Sumner's American currency. $3.........N. Y., *Holt*

Thorpe, T: M. What is money? popular remedies for
popular ills. '96· 25c...................N. Y., *Ogilvie*
Advocates free coinage and a $52 per capita volume of
currency.

Trenholm, W. L. The people's money. '93· $1.50.
N. Y., *Scribner*
Favors gold.

Upton, J. K. Coin catechism. '96· 50c.; 25c.
Chicago, *Werner School F'k Co*
Opposes free coinage.

Walker, F. A. Money, trade, and industry. $1.25.
N. Y., *Holt*
— Money. $2......................................N.Y., *Holt*

Walker, J. H. Money, trade, and banking. New ed.
'94· 50c..................Boston, *Houghton, M. & Co*
Favors gold.

Waterloo, Stanley. Honest money. '95· 25c.
Chicago, *Equitable Pub. Co*
Favors gold.

Webster, S. Misuse of legal tender. '93· $1.
N. Y., *Appleton*
Favors gold.

Wells, D: A. Robinson Crusoe's money; or, the remarkable financial fortunes and misfortunes of a remote island community. Il. by Thomas Nast. '96·
15c................................. .N. Y., *Harper*

White, Horace. Money and banking illustrated by
Am. history. '95· $1.50; 50c..........Boston, *Ginn*
Advocates gold.

Williams, H. W. Money and bank credit in the U. S.
['95.] 25c....................Phila., *Am. Acad. Pol. Sci*

Wolff, H: W. People's banks: a record of social and
economic success. $2.50..............N. Y., *Longmans*

PANICS.

Juglar, C. Brief hist. of panics and their periodical
occurrence in the U. S. '93· $1.........N. Y., *Putnam*

PRESIDENTIAL CANDIDATES.

Andrews, Byron. One of the people: life and speeches
of Wm. McKinley; with a brief sketch of Garret A.
Hobart. '96· 50c.........................N. Y., *Neely*

Bryan, Sewall, and honest money. Up to date. '96·
25c....................................N. Y., *Derby & Miller*

McKinley, W: McKinley's masterpieces: selections
from the public addresses in and out of congress; edited by R. L. Paget. '96· 75c.......Boston, *J. Knight*

March to victory: sound money, protection, prosperity.
The great Republican campaign, 1860-1896. Speeches
and platform of McKinley and Hobart '96· 25c.
Chicago, *Laird & L*

Ogilvie, J: S., *ed.* Life and speeches of McKinley and Hobart. '96· $1; 25c..... ....N. Y., *Ogilvie*
— Life and speeches of Bryan and Sewall. '96. $1; 25c..N. Y., *Ogilvie*
Our country's honor: McKinley and Hobart the standard bearers for sound money, protection, and prosperity. 10c...............................Chic., *Laird & L*
Stevens, C. M. Bryan and Sewall and the great issue of 1896. '96· 50c........................ N. Y., *Neely*

PRICES AND VALUES.

Benner, S: Prophecies of future ups and downs in prices. 10th ed. 4 v. ea., $1......Cincinnatti, *Clarke*
Bohm-Bawerk, E. v. Ultimate standard of value. ['94.] 50c...................Phila., *Am. Acad. Pol. Sci*
Green, D: I. Wieser's natural value. '95. 25c.
          Phila., *Am. Acad. Pol. Sci*
Harger, C. G. True standard of value. '95· 10c.
          Washington, D. C., *Hartmann*
Jordan. Standard of value. $2. ....N. Y., *Longmans*
Mac Vane, S. M. Austrian theory of value. ['94·] 25c................Phila., *Am Acad. Pol. Sci*
Patten, S. N. Cost and expense. ['93.] 25c.
          Phila., *Am. Acad Pol. Sci*
— Cost and utility. '93· 25c..Phila., *Am. Acad. Pol. Sci*
Price, L. L. Money and its relation to prices. '96· $1.
          N. Y., *Scribner*
    Favors gold.
Smart, W. Introduction to the theory of value on the lines of Menger, Wieser, and Bohm-Bawerk. '91. $1.25..N. Y., *Macmillan*
Wieser, F: v. Natural value. '93. $3.25.
          N. Y., *Macmillan*

PROBLEMS IN POLITICS.

Andrews, E. B. Duty of a public spirit. '92. 10c.
          N. Y., *Appleton*
Armstrong, K. L. The little statesman: a middle-of-the-road manual for Am. voters. '95. 25c.
          Chicago, *Schulte*
Armstrong, Leroy. An Indiana man. 25c.
          Chicago, *Schulte*
    Favors silver.
Blatchford, R., ["Nunquam."] Merrie England: exposition of socialism, what it is and what it is not. '95. 10c......................N. Y., *Commonwealth*
Champernowne, H: The boss: essay upon the art of governing American cities. '94· $1.25.
          Detroit, Mich, *Richmond Backus*
Commons, J. R. State supervision for cities. '95. 15c..........................Phila., *Am. Acad. Pol. Sci*
Craven, H. W. Errors of populism '96· 25c
          Seattle, Wash, *Lowman*
Daly, J: B. Dawn of radicalism. '92· $1.
          N. Y., *Scribner*
Donisthorpe, W. Individualism: system of politics. '94· $4.50........................N. Y., *Macmillan*
Ely, R. T. Socialism. '94· $1.50......Boston, *Crowell*
Eternal peace, views of a statesman: how the critical, social, and political problem of the world may be solved in the present century. '91. 25c.
          San Francisco, *Bancroft*
Foote, A. R. Prosperity and politics. '93· 50c.
          Washington, D. C., *Kittington*
Fox, D. M. Political parties. '95· $2.
          Des Moines, Iowa, *D. M. Fox*
Gilman, N: P. Socialism and the American spirit. $1.50..................Boston, *Houghton, M. & Co*
Green. Are we losing the West? '95· 10c.
          Boston, *C: E. Brown*
Gregory, C: N. Corrupt use of money in politics, and laws for its prevention. '93· 25c.
          Madison, Wis., *Univ. of Wis*
    Favors free coinage.
Gronlund, L. Co-operative commonwealth. New ed. '90. $1; 50c......................Boston, *Lee & S*
Hilliard, H: W. Politics and pen pictures at home and abroad. '92. $3....................N. Y., *Putnam*
Hoffman, F. S. Sphere of the state; or, the people as a body politic. '94· $1.50............N. Y., *Putnam*
Jacobson, A: The crisis of a party. (Arraignment of Republican party.) '92· 25c........Chicago, *Schulte*
Jenks, J. W. Social basis of representation. '95· 15c.
          Phila., *Am. Acad. Pol. Sci*
McPherson, E. Handbook of politics. 3 v. '90–'94· ea., $2................Washington, D. C., *Beall; Chapman*
Naquet, A. J. Collectivism and the socialism of the liberal school. '92. $1..................N. Y., *Scribner*
Norton, C: L. Political Americanisms. '90. $1.
          N. Y., *Longmans*

Patton, J. H. Political parties in the U. S.: their history and influence, 1789–1896. '96. $1.25.
          N. Y., *New Amsterdam Bk. Co*
Peters, M. C. Wrongs to be righted: fearless speeches on live questions. '94· 25c.......N. Y., *Artistic Pub*
Rae, J. Contemporary socialism. 2d ed. '91. $2.50.
          N. Y., *Scribner*
Remsen, D. S. Fusion of political parties. '96· 15c.
          Phila., *Am. Acad. Pol. Sci*
Shaw, G: B. Socialism: the Fabian essays, with an essay on the Fabian Society. '94· 75c.
          Boston. *C. E. Brown*
Smith, Goldwin. False hopes; or, fallacies socialistic and semi-socialistic briefly answered. '90. 20c.
          N. Y., *Lovell, C. & Co*
Strong, J. Our country: its possible future and its present crisis. Rev. ed. '91· 60c.; 30c.
          N. Y., *Baker & T*
Thompson, D. G. Politics in a democracy. '93·
$1.25......................................N. Y., *Longmans*
Tyler, L. G. Parties and patronage in the United States. '91· $1 ....N. Y., *Putnam*
Upton, J. K. Money in politics. '95· $1.25; 50c.
          Boston, *Lothrop*
Warner, A. D. A brief in the High Court of Justice: the ballot box of 1896. The people (*plaintiffs*) *vs.* the gold-bugs (*defendants*). '96· 25c.............. *Kerr*
Wilson, J. Radical wrongs in the precepts and practices of civilized man. '92· $1; 60c.Newark, *J. Wilson*

STRIKES.

Ashley, W. J. Railroad strike of 1894: statements of the Pullman Company and report of commissioner; with a bibliography. '95. 10c.
          Boston, *Church Soc. Union*
Carwardine, W. H. Pullman strike. '94· 50c.
          Chicago, *Kerr*
Cogley, T: S. Law of strikes, lockouts, and labor organizations. '94· $4.
          Washington, D. C., *Lowdermilk*
Cunningham, W. Strikes. '95· 10c.
          Boston, *Church Soc. Union*
Holbrook, Z. S. American republic and the Debs insurrection. '94· 35c...........Oberlin, O., *Bibliotheca*
Miller, M. R. Is a man worth as much as a horse? with a condensed report of the federal labor commissioner on the great strike. 2d ed. '95· 10c.
          Chicago, *Rockwell & Rupel*
Nicholson, J. S. Strikes and social problems. $1.25.
          N. Y., *Macmillan*
Swinton, J: Striking for life: labor's side of the labor question. '94· subs., $1.50; $2.........Phila., *Keller*

TAXATION AND TARIFF.

Atkinson, E: Taxation and work. '92. $1.25.
          N. Y., *Putnam*
Beatty, J: McKinleyism as it appears to a non-partisan. '92· $1 ; 50c.........Columbus, O., *Smythe*
Blunden, G. H. Local taxation and finance. '95· $1.
          N. Y., *Scribner*
Both sides of the tariff question by the world's leading men ; with biog. sketches. '91· $4.50..N. Y., *Peniston*
Bracken, F., *and* Grimes, E. B. Income tax law. '95. 50c...Phila., *Kay*
Carver, T. N. Ethical basis of distribution. '95·
          Phila., *Am. Acad. Pol. Sci*
Curtiss, G: B. Protection and prosperity : tariff legislation and its effect in Europe and America ; with introd. by Wm. McKinley, L. P. Morton, and T. B. Reed. '96· $3.75 ; $6...........N. Y., *Pan-Am. Pub*
Ely, R. T. Taxation in American states and cities. $1.75......................................Boston, *Crowell*
Farquhar, A. B. *and* H: Economic and industrial delusions: discussion of the case for protection. '91·
$1.50......................................N. Y., *Putnam*
Foster, R. *and* Abbot, E. V. Treatise on the federal income tax under the act of 1894. '95· $3.50.
          Boston *Bk*
George, H: Protection or free trade; with special regard to the interests of labor. '91· 25c.
          Washington, D. C., *Sterling Pub*
Gould, J: M., *and* Tucker, G. F. Federal income tax. '94· net, $2...............Boston, *Little, B. & Co*
Grey, Earl. Commercial policy of the British Colonies and the McKinley tariff. '92· 30c..N. Y., *Macmillan*
Gunton, G: Taxation and revenue : the protectionist's view. '92· 10c...........................N. Y., *Appleton*
Hall, B. Who pays your taxes? question of taxation. '92· $1.25............................N. Y., *Putnam*
Hewes, F. W., *and* McKinley, W: What are the facts? Protection and reciprocity illustrated : questions of to-day answered in 100 graphic studies. '92. $1.50.
          N. Y., *H. F. Clark*

Howe, F: C. Federal revenues and the income tax. '94· 25c.....................Phila., *Am. Acad. Pol. Sci*
— Taxation and taxes in the U. S. under the internal revenue system. '96· $1.75..........Boston, *Crowell*
Johnson, E. R. Relation of taxation to monopolies. '94· 25c.....................Phila., *Am. Acad. Pol. Sci*
Lewis, Eugene C. History of the American tariff, 1789–1860. '96· 25c. ....*Kerr*
McKinley, W: McKinley customs administrative act. '90. gratis...................... ....N. Y., *Downing*
— *Same* in German. '90· 50c...............N. Y., *Steiger*
Mason, D: H. A short tariff history of the United States. '96· 25c....................Chicago, *Kerr*
Shearman, J. G. Taxation and revenue: the free-trade view. '92. 10c......................N. Y., *Appleton*
Seligmann, E. R. A. Taxation. '95· $3.
                                        N. Y., *Macmillan*
Sherman, P. Tariff primer: effects of protection upon the farmer and laborer. '91· 25c.......N. Y., *Putnam*
Tiedeman, C. G. Income tax decisions. '95· 15c.
                                        Phila., *Am. Acad. Pol. Sci*
Trumbull, M. M. Free trade struggle in England. $1; 25c.....................Chic., *Open Court*
United States. *Congress.* Income tax laws of Aug. 24, 1894. '95· $1 ....*Banks*
— *Same* with speech of D: B. Hill. '95· 10c.
                                        N. Y., *Brentano's*
— — — Wilson tariff bill as passed by Congress, Aug., 1894. '95· 10c.........N. Y., *Vandegrift*
— *Same.* German. 20c...............N. Y., *Steiger*
— — *Treasury Dept.* Latest tariff law. '94· 10c.
                                        Boston, *Franklin Pub. Co*
Walker, F. Double taxation in the United States. 75c.............N. Y., *Seligman;* N. Y., *Macmillan*
Weyl, W. E., *and others.* Equitable taxation. 75c.
                                        Boston, *Crowell*
Wyman, F. A. United States income tax law simplified for business men. '95· 50c..........*Wilkins*
— *Same.* 3d ed. '95· 1................Boston, *Wyman*

TRUSTS AND MONOPOLIES.

Dabney, W. D. Basis of the demand for public regulation of industries. '92. 50c.
                                        Phila., *Am. Acad. Pol. Sci*
Johnson, E. R. Relation of taxation to monopolies. '94· 25c.....................Phila., *Am. Acad. Pol. Sci*
Halle, E. v. Trusts; or, Industrial combinations and coalitions in the U. S. '95· $1.25...N. Y., *Macmillan*
Jeans, J. S. Trusts, pools, and corners as affecting commerce and industries. '94· $1.....N. Y., *Scribner*
Knapp, A. One thousand dollars a day: studies in practical economics. ['95.] $1; 50c....Boston, *Arena*
Lloyd, H. D. Wealth against commonwealth. '94· $2.50.............................N. Y., *Harper*
Spelling, T: C. Treatise on trusts and monopolies. '93. $3.50............Boston, *Little, Brown & Co*

UNITED STATES POLITICAL ECONOMY AND GOVERNMENT.

Adams, H. C. Interpretation of the social movements of our time. '95· 10c......Boston, *Church Soc. Union*
Altgeld, J: P. Live questions, including our penal machinery and its victims. '90. $1.Chicago, *Donohue*
Bengough, J. W. The up-to-date primer. '96· 25c.
                                        N. Y., *Funk & W. Co*
Boies, H: M. Prisoners and paupers: study of the increase of criminals and of pauperism in the United States. '93. $1.50..................N. Y., *Putnam*
Bourinot, J: G. Elected or appointed officials? '95· 25c.....................Phila., *Am. Acad. Pol. Sci*
Bowker, R: R. Economics for the people. 4th ed. '93· 75c.......................N. Y., *Harper*
— *and* Iles, G:, *eds.* Reader's guide in economic, social, and political science. '91· $1; 50c.....N. Y., *Putnam*
Bradford, G. Reform of our state governments. '94. 25c.....................Phila., *Am. Acad. Pol. Sci*
Brooks, E. S. Century book for young Americans. '94· $1.50 ....N. Y., *Century Co*
Brooks, N. How the republic is governed. '95· 75c.
                                        N. Y., *Scribner*
— Short studies in party politics. '95· $1.25.
                                        N. Y., *Scribner*
Carnegie, A. Triumphant democracy. '93· $3.
                                        N. Y., *Scribner*
Carus, P. Nature of the state. '94· 15c.
                                        Chicago, *Open Court*

Clark, A. A. Beneath the dome: a novel. '94· $1.25.
                                        Chicago, *Schulte*
Claims private ownership of land is at the root of all industrial troubles.
Cleveland, S. G. Principles and purposes of our government as set forth in the public papers of Grover Cleveland. '92. 75c.; 25c...........N. Y., *G. G. Peck*
Cree, N. Direct legislation by the people. '92· 75c.
                                        Chicago, *McClurg*
Donisthorpe, W. Law in a free state. $2.
                                        N. Y., *Macmillan*
Fiske, J: Civil government in the U. S. '90. net, $1.
                                        Boston, *Houghton, M. & Co*
Flower, B: O. New time: plea for the union of the moral forces for practical progress. '94· $1; 50c.
                                        Boston, *Arena*
Follett. Speaker of the House of Representatives. $1.75......................N. Y., *Longmans*
George, H: Progress and poverty. '95· $1; $3; 35c.
                                        N. Y., *Sterling Pub*
— Social problems. '95· $1; $3; 35c.
                                        N. Y., *Sterling Pub*
Gladden, W. Tools and the man: property and industry under the Christian law. '93· $1.25
                                        Boston, *Houghton, M. & Co*
Gronlund, L. Our destiny: influence of nationalism on morals and religion. $1; 50c......Boston, *Lee & S*
Guyot, Y. Tyranny of socialism. '94· $1.
                                        N. Y., *Scribner*
Hart, A. B. Introduction to the study of federal government. '91· $1.10.....................Boston, *Ginn*
— Practical essays on Am. government. '93· $1.50.
                                        N. Y., *Longmans*
Hinsdale, B. A. American government, national and state. '93· 75c........Ann Arbor, Mich., *Register Pub*
Kinnaird, P. The science of legal robbery. '96· 25c.
                                        Chicago, *Schulte*
Knox, J. J. United States notes. $1.50.N. Y., *Scribner*
Larrabee, W. The railroad question. 50c.
                                        Chicago, *Schulte*
Lindsay, S. M. Social work at the Krupp foundries. '93· 35c............ ....Phila., *Am. Acad. Pol. Sci*
McArthur, J. N. Government. '92· $1.25.
                                        N. Y., *Longmans*
Mackay, T: Plea for liberty: argument against socialism. '91· $2.25..................N. Y., *Appleton*
Man or dollar, which By a newspaper man. 25c.
                                        Kerr
A story in which a man living in 1983 tells the history of the present crisis.
Mead, E. D. Representative government. '92· 10c.
                                        N. Y., *Appleton*
Moffett, S. E. Suggestions on government. '94· $1; 50c......................Chicago, *Rand, McN. & Co*
Moore, J. W. The American Congress: a history of national legislation and political events, 1774–1895. '96· $3.........................N. Y., *Harper*
Morgan, T: J. Patriotic citizenship. '94· $1.
                                        N. Y., *Amer. Bk. Co*
Ostrander, D. Social growth and stability. '95· $1.
                                        Chicago, *Griggs*
Patten, S. N. Economic causes of moral progress. ['92.] 25c..................Phila., *Am. Acad. Pol. Sci*
— Educational value of political economy. '90. 75c.
                                        Phila., *Am. Econ. Assoc*
Patton, J. H. Political economy for American youth. ['92.] $1.....................N. Y., *A. Lovell*
Rand, B: Bibliography of economics. '95· $1.25.
                                        J: W. Wilson (Camb.)
Ritchie, D. G. National rights. '95· net, $1.75.
                                        N. Y., *Macmillan*
Robinson, E. V. Nature of the federal state. '93· 25c.....................Phila., *Am. Acad. Pol. Sci*
Scott, W. A. Repudiation of state debts in the U. S. $1.50......................Boston, *Crowell*
Thompson, D. G. Politics in a democracy. $1.25.
                                        N. Y., *Longmans*
Trumbull, W. W. Earl Grey on reciprocity and civil service reform. 10c...........Chicago, *Open Court*
Walker, F. A. Tide of economic thought. '91· n. p.
                                        Phila., *Am. Econ. Assoc*
Wells, D. A. Recent economc changes. $2.
                                        Appleton
Why I ams: an economic symposium. 2d ed. 15c.
                                        N. Y., *Twentieth Century*

WAGES.

Atkinson, E: Food and feeding considered as a factor in making the rate of wages or earnings. '91· 10c.
                                        Boston, *Damrell & U*
Brassey, T:, *Baron.* Work and wages. '94· $1.75.
                                        N. Y., *Longmans*

Brentano, L. Hours and wages in relation to production. '94. $1......................N. Y., *Scribner*

Cope, R. Distribution of wealth; or, the economic laws by which wages and profits are determined. '90. $2..................................Phila., *Lippincott*

Hull-House maps and papers; presentation of nationalities and wages in a congested district of Chicago. ['95.] $2.50; $3 50..................Boston, *Crowell*

Nicholson, J. S. Effects of machinery in wages. '92. $1..................................N. Y., *Scribner*

Richards, J: Law of wages: the rate and amount. ['90] 25c..........Des Moines, Iowa, *Indust. Pub, Co*

Roberts, I: Wages, fixed incomes, and free coinage of silver. '96. 25c..................Phila., *Highlands* Advocates gold.

Rogers, T. Work and wages. 25c...N. Y., *Humboldt*

Schloss, D: F. Methods of industrial remuneration. '92. $1.50..................................N. Y., *Putnam*

Schoenhof, J. Economy of high wages: an inquiry into the cause of high wages and their effect on methods and cost of production. '92. $1.50. N. Y., *Putnam*

Taussig, F. W. Wages and capital. '96. $1.50. N. Y., *Appleton* Favors gold.

Thompson, H. M. Theory of wages and its application to the eight-hour question and other labor problems. '92. $1..................................N. Y., *Macmillan*

Towne, H: R., Halsey, F. A., *and* Taylor, F. W. The adjustment of wages to efficiency; On gain sharing; The premium plan; A piece-rate system. '96. 50c. Baltimore, *Am. Econ. Assoc.; N. Y., Macmillan*

WEALTH.

Andrews, E. B: Wealth and moral law. '94. $1. *Hartford Sem. Press*

Baker, J. M. Wealth. '92. 25c. Chicago, *Cranston & Curts*

Commons, J: R. Distribution of wealth. '93. $1.75. N. Y., *Macmillan*

Hopkins, A. A. Wealth and waste: principles of political economy. '95. $1..................N. Y., *Funk*

Howard, M. W. American plutocracy. '96. $1; 50c. N. Y., *Holland* Favors silver.

Lloyd, H. D. Wealth against commonwealth. '96. $1..................................N. Y., *Harper*

Osborne, G. P. Principles of economics; the satisfaction of human wants in so far as their satisfaction depends on material resources. '93. $2. Cincinnati, O., *Clarke*

Robertson, J: M. Fallacy of saving. '92. $1. N. Y., *Scribner*

Smart, W: Effects of consumption of wealth on distribution. '93. 35c.........Phila., *Am. Acad. Pol. Sci*

Spahr, C. B. Present distribution of wealth in the United States. $1.50..................Boston, *Crowell*

Thompson, H. M. The purse and the conscience: an attempt to show the connection between economics and ethics. '91. $1..................N. Y., *Macmillan*

Waldron, G. B. Currency and wealth. '96. 50c. N. Y., *Funk & Wagnalls Co*

Worthington, S. Politics and property; or, phronocracy: a compromise between democracy and plutocracy. '91. $1.50 ....N. Y., *Putnam*

Survey of Current Literature.

☞ *Order through your bookseller.*—"*There is no worthier or surer pledge of the intelligence and the purity of any community than their general purchase of books; nor is there any one who does more to further the attainment and possession of these qualities than a good bookseller.*"—PROF. DUNN.

ART, MUSIC, DRAMA.

JAMES, R. N. Painters and their works: a dictionary of great artists who are not now alive, giving their names, lives, and the prices paid for their works at auction. In 3 v. V. 1, Aalst to Hayre. Scribner. 12°, $5.

LA MARA, —, *comp.* Thoughts of great musicians. Scribner. 12°, $1.

MCARTHUR, ALEX. Anton Rubinstein: a biographical sketch. Scribner. 12°, $1.25.

TARBELL, F. B. A history of Greek art; with an introductory chapter on art in Egypt and Mesopotamia. Flood & Vincent. (Chautauqua-Century Press.) il. 12°, (Chautauqua reading circle literature.) $1.

BIOGRAPHY, CORRESPONDENCE, ETC.

FRANKLIN, B. Autobiography. Amer. Book Co. por. 12°, (Eclectic English classics.) bds., 35 c.

MASSIE, D. MEAD. Nathaniel Massie: a pioneer of Ohio: a sketch of his life and selections from his correspondence. Robert Clarke Co. 8°, $2.

Soon after the founding of Manchester (1791) and Chillicothe (1796) General Massie and his Virginia followers settled in the northwestern section of Ohio, the scene of the bitter conflict between Governor St. Clair and General Massie. This ended in the removal of St. Clair from the governorship, the framing of a state constitution, and the admission of Ohio into the Union. It is claimed that this is the first historical record of this old political struggle between the Federalists and Republicans in Ohio.

MEDILL, Jos. A typical American—Benjamin Franklin: an address delivered before the Old-Time Printers' Association of Chicago, January 17, 1896. The Ben Franklin Co. il. 8°, pap., 25 c.; *large pap. ed.*, $1.

Address spoken at the celebration of the 190th anniversary of the birth of Franklin. It especially points out how many-sided was the mind of Franklin, and how varied his natural gifts and his acquired accomplishments. It is hoped by its circulation to stimulate young men to a thorough study of the life and teachings of the great printer, philosopher, scientist, and patriot. The speaker ranks Franklin with Washington, far beyond all the other makers of the United States.

SETOUN, GABRIEL. Robert Burns. Scribner. 12°, (Famous Scots ser.) 75 c.

SIME, JA. Lessing: his life and writings. *New cheaper ed.* Scribner. 2 v. 8°, (English and foreign philosophical lib.) $4.50.

DESCRIPTION, GEOGRAPHY, TRAVEL, ETC.

GORDON, Sir T. E. Persia revisited, 1895. E. Arnold. map, il. 8°, $3.

SMITH, LEE S. Through Egypt to Palestine. Revell. il. 12°, $1.25.

STRACHEY, Sir J. India. *Rev. ed.* Scribner. 12°, $1.25.

DOMESTIC AND SOCIAL.

AU FAIT, (*pseud.*) Social observances: a series of essays on practical etiquette. Warne. 12°, $1.

These forty-six essays have been written, the author tells us, "with a view to exemplify existing rules of etiquette rather than to lay down these rules." They refer to English social functions and tell when to arrive, when to leave, entertaining on Sundays, points in card-leaving, society in the country, when is chaperonage required ?, shooting-parties, an afternoon tea, etc.

BROWNELL, W. C. French traits : an essay in comparative criticism. Flood & Vincent, (The Chautauqua-Century Press.) 12°, (Chautauqua reading circle literature.) $1.
Originally published by C. Scribner's Sons, 1888. Essays on: The social instinct; Morality; Intelligence ; Sense and sentiment ; Manners ; Women ; The art instinct ; The provincial spirit; Democracy ; New York after Paris. The author is an American who lived many years in Paris.

EDUCATION, LANGUAGE, ETC.

HERBART, J. F. Herbart's A B C of sense-perception, and minor pedagogical works ; tr. with introd., notes, and commentary by W. J. Eckoff. Appleton. 12°, (International education ser., no 36.) $1.50.
Herbart's system of pedagogy deals with educative instruction. "Education of man by man is impossible, except through instruction. That instruction is valueless in the acquisition of which no education or—in psychologic language —no apperception occurs." Education should produce right intellects and right characters, and the æsthetic presentation of the universe should be its chief office. The translator has chosen from the works of Herbart and presented his theories in a way that may be of practical use to instructors. Special knowledge of facts does not necessarily make a good instructor, and the talent to impart facts does not necessarily make a good educator, are the keynotes of Herbartism.

FICTION.

ANNUNZIO, GABRIELE D'. Episcopo & Company ; tr. [from the Italian] by Myrta Leonora Jones. Herbert S. Stone & Co. 16°, $1.25.

BENSON. E. F. The Babe, B.A.; being the uneventful history of a young gentleman at Cambridge University. Putnam. il. 12°, (University ser., no. 3.) $1.
What has been done for our American colleges, Harvard and Yale, in two preceding volumes of the series. is done in this story for Cambridge and English university life. Time-honored customs of Kings and Trinity Colleges as re-enacted by the typical student are humorously described. The interest centres in the action of three undergraduates, notably in that of Babe, B.A., so-called because it seemed impossible for him to outgrow an ingenuous countenance. By the author of " Dodo."

BLOSSOM, H. M., jr. Checkers : a hard-luck story. Herbert S. Stone & Co. 16°, $1.25.

BOGGS, MARTHA FRYE. A romance of the New Virginia. Arena. 12°, $1.25; pap., 50 c.

BOOTHBY, GUY. Dr. Nikola. Appleton. 12°, (Appleton's town and country lib., no. 197.) $1; pap., 50 c.

BOURGET, PAUL. A living lie. [Mensonges;] from the French by J. De Villiers. Fenno. 12°, $1.25.

BOWEN, HELEN M. A daughter of Cuba. The Merriam Co. 12°, (Waldorf ser., no. 28,) pap., 50 c.

BUNNER, H. CUYLER. The suburban sage : stray notes and comments on his simple life ; il. by C. J. Taylor. Keppler & Schwarzmann. il. 12°, $1; pap., 50 c.
Sixteen short stories first published in Puck. The titles of the most noteworthy are : Mr. Chedby on a regular nuisance; Early stages of the bloomer fever; The suburban horse ; The building craze ; The society church ; The suburban dog ; The evolution of the suburbanite.

COCHRAN, Mrs. M. A. Posie ; or, from reveille to retreat : an army story. The Robert Clarke Co. il. 16°, $1.25.
Describes exciting scenes which happened to a northern captain and his southern wife at Fort Harney, Oregon, while the Bannock and Piute prisoners of war were held there. Incidents of life at other isolated Western military posts are also given ; with an episode of the Civil War which occurred in St. Augustine, Florida.

CONRAD, JOS. An outcast of the islands. Appleton. 12°, (Appleton's town and country lib., no. 198.) $1 ; pap., 50 c.

EDDY, DAN. C., D.D. Saxenhurst: a story of the old world and new. American Bapt. Pub. Soc. il. 12°, $1.50.
Saxenhurst. an old manor in Kent, was built by Sir John Baker, during the reign of Edward VI. The strictly historical story describes the manor after political affairs have forced Robert, Earl of Dorset, to seek its retirement. Roger Williams and others prominent in the non-conformist movement are chief characters. Roger Williams's emigration to America and the incidental history of his founding the first Baptist church in America in 1639 are among the important events.

FLAW (The) in the marble; il. by Harry C. Edwards. Stokes. nar. 16°, (Twentieth century ser.) 75 c.

JOKAI, MAURUS. Black diamonds: a novel; tr. by Frances A. Gerard. Harper. 12°, (Odd number ser.) $1.50.

O'GRADY, STANDISH. In the wake of King James; or, Dun-Randal on the sea. Lippincott. 12°, $1.25.
A soldier who had fought on the side of William III. against James II. decided to visit his Jacobite cousins in the far west of Ireland. The author describes the dreary waste King James had left behind him when he left his followers and fled to France. In an old, crumbling castle on the wild Irish coast the hero met with stirring adventures in which dungeons, midnight escapes, treachery, underground dwellings, and a beautiful woman are described.

POST, MELVILLE DAVISSON. The strange schemes of Randolph Mason. Putnam. sq. 16°, (Hudson lib., no. 16.) $1; pap., 50 c.
A collection of stories based upon the present criminal law of New York, showing its loopholes and weak points, and pointing out how a dishonorable man might commit almost any crime and escape punishment, with the advice

of an unscrupulous lawyer. Randolph Mason is this kind of a lawyer, and he successfully aids his clients to commit murder, robbery, and other criminal deeds, and also to escape punishment.

PRITCHARD, MARTIN J. Without sin: a novel. Herbert S. Stone & Co. 12°, $1.25.

STIMSON, F. JESUP, ["J. S. of Dale."] King Noanett: a story of old Virginia and the Massachusetts Bay. Lamson, Wolff & Co. il. 8°, $2.

STURGIS, JULIAN RUSSELL. A master of fortune. Stokes. il. nar. 16°, (Newport ser.) 75 c.

TICKNOR. CAROLINE. A hypocritical romance, and other stories. Joseph Knight Co. il. 16°, $1.25.
Contents: A hypocritical romance; The fate of Clyde Moorfield, yachtsman; The judgment of Paris reversed; A little study in common sense; Mr. Hurd's holiday; The evolution of a bonnet; Mrs. Hudson's picnic; A bag of popcorn; The romance of a spoon; The history of a happy thought; A furnished cottage by the sea; A hallowe'en party. Some of the stories attracted much attention when they appeared first in *Harper's*, *The Cosmopolitan*, and *The New England Magazine*.

THORP, ABNER, *M.D.* A child of nature. Curts & Jennings. il. 12°, 75 c.
The scene is Cincinnati. Incidents in the lives of two girl companions of entirely different characteristics are given for the purpose of showing by contrast some of the social and moral consequences of following the dictates of a misguided will.

WHISTLER, C. W. A Thane of Essex: a story of the great viking raids into Somerset. Scribner. 12°, $1.25.

HISTORY.

ADAMS, G. BURTON. The growth of the French nation. Flood & Vincent, (The Chautauqua-Century Press.) il. por. map. 12°, (Chautauqua reading circle literature.) $1.

MAHAFFY, J. P., *D.D.* A survey of Greek civilization. Flood & Vincent, (The Chautauqua-Century Press.) il. 12°, (Chautauqua reading circle literature.) $1.

POWELL, R. S. S. BADEN-. The downfall of Prempeh a diary of life with the native levy in Ashanti, 1895-96; with a chapter on the political and commercial position of Ashanti by Sir G. Baden-Powell. Lippincott. il. map, 8°, $3.50.
Major Baden-Powell, of the 13th Hussars, was commander of the native levy. Since the installation of Prempeh as King of Ashanti the government had stood, in the way of trade, of civilization, and of the interests of the people. Inter-tribal disputes had led to massacres and outrages, and the author justifies the interference of England. The chapter on the wealth of Ashanti and the policy of government is suggestive of the inestimable benefits that might accrue to the natives and to England by judicious, civilizing government.

ROSS, EDMUND G. History of the impeachment of Andrew Johnson, President of the United States, by the House of Representatives, and his trial by the Senate for high crimes and misdemeanors in office, 1868. [H. B. Philbrook.] 8°, $1.25.
Andrew Johnson, who had become President after the assassination of Abraham Lincoln, came into controversy with Congress as to the restoration and preservation of the Union. It was decided to make use of the constitutional power to impeach and remove the President which had lain dormant since the organization of the government. The accusations were that the acting President had corruptly used the appointing power, the pardoning power, and the veto power, and had corruptly disposed of public property of the United States. This volume gives the whole trial. President Johnson was declared not guilty by the court of the Senate before which he was tried.

HUMOR AND SATIRE.

ILLUSTRATED first reader in social economics for backward pupils. C. H. Kerr & Co. il. 12°, (New occasions, no. 24.) pap., 10 c.
Consists of short lessons in words of one syllable, each dealing in a satirical way with some of the social phenomena of the day, such as bargain counters, tramps, safety deposit vaults, etc.

MURRAY, J. FISHER. Father Tom and the Pope; or, a night at the Vatican; [*also*,] History of the Pope's mule; freely tr. from the French of Alphonse Daudet. Eckler. il. 12°, (Lib. of liberal classics, v. 2, no. 14.) pap., 25 c.

LITERATURE, MISCELLANEOUS AND COLLECTED WORKS.

BROWN, J. T. T. The authorship of "The Kingis Quair": a new criticism. Macmillan. 8°, $1.50.
After an elaborate examination of the contents of the unique ms. copy of this poem, now in the Bodleian Library, the author has come to the conclusion that this copy is much later in date than the time of James I., to whom its authorship has generally been traced. The date of the Bodleian manuscript cannot be earlier than 1488 and James was assassinated in 1437. From this the author deduces that King James cannot be the author of "The Kingis Quair." In stating his argument he deals first with the historical or external evidence, *viz.:* A, The Bodleian manuscript, and B, The testimony of historians; and, second, with the internal evidence, *viz.:* A, The dialect; B, The court of love, and C, The autobiography of the poem.

GUERBER, H. A. Legends of the Middle Ages, narrated with special reference to literature and art. Amer. Book Co. il. 12°, $1.50.
Contents: Beowulf; Gudrun; Reynard the fox; The Nibelungenlied; Langobardian cycle of myths; The Amelings; Dietrich von Bern; Charlemagne and his paladins; The sons of Amon; Huon of Bordeaux; Titurel and the holy grail; Merlin; The round table; Tristan and Iseult; The story of Frithiof; Radnar Lodbrok; The Cid; General survey of romance literature.

HARDWICKE, H. History of oratory and orators: a study of the influence of oratory upon politics and literature, with special reference to certain orators selected as representative of their several epochs, from the earliest dawn of Grecian civilization down to the present day. Putnam. 8°, $3.

Contents: Oratory in Greece; Oratory in Rome; Modern oratory; Oratory in England; Oratory in France; Oratory in America. The great orators of the world are presented with extracts from noted speeches; their methods of study and manner of preparing speeches, with many interesting personal descriptions and biographical details, are given.

LE GALLIENNE, R. Prose fancies. 2d ser. Herbert S. Stone & Co. 16°, $1.25.

Essays on: A seventh-story heaven; Spring by parcel post; The great merry-go-round; The burial of Romeo and Juliet; Variations upon whitebait; The answer of the rose; About the securities; The boom in yellow; Letter to an unsuccessful literary man; A poet in the city; Brown roses; The donkey that loved a star; On loving one's enemies; The dramatic art of life; The arbitrary classification of sex, etc.

NIETZSCHE, F. Collected works: ed. by Alex. Tille. V. 8, Thus spake Zarathustra: a book for all and none; tr. by Alex. Tille. Macmillan. 8°, $2.50.

MENTAL AND MORAL.

CALDWELL, W. Schopenhauer's system in its philosophical significance. Scribner. 8°, *net*, $3.

JORDAN, D. STARR. The care and culture of men: a series of addresses on the higher education. The Whitaker & Ray Co. 8°, $1.

Contents: The value of higher education; The evolution of the college curriculum; The nation's need of men; The care and culture of men; The scholar in the community; The school and the state; The higher education of women; The training of the physician; Law schools and lawyers; The practical education; Science in the high school; Science and the colleges; Procession of life; The growth of man; The social order; The saving of time; The new university; A castle in Spain. Originally delivered to teachers and students, and first published in the *Forum*, *Popular Science*, etc.; most of the articles have been retouched.

NATURE AND SCIENCE.

BAYNE, S. G. The pith of astronomy (without mathematics); the latest facts and figures as developed by the giant telescopes. Harper. il. 16°, $1.

The object of this little book is to put the main astronomical figures and facts in the most simple and direct way, so that they may be easily grasped and remembered by a beginner, and so that one who has some knowledge of astronomy can refresh his memory and find what he needs in a moment, without searching voluminous works on the subject. The facts are drawn from the latest observations, calculations, and discoveries made through the use of our large modern telescopes, thus bringing all the information up to date.

HOWE, HERBERT A. A study of the sky. Flood & Vincent, (The Chautauqua-Century

Press. il. 12°, (Chautauqua reading circle literature.) $1.

A popular astronomy by the director of Chamberlin Observatory, University of Denver. It presents with the aid of 150 practical illustrations an outline of the science of astronomy, introducing concrete material in such abundance as to avoid giving the work a technical and abstract form.

LUBBOCK, *Sir* J. The scenery of Switzerland and causes to which it is due. Macmillan. il. map, 12°, $1.50.

LYDEKKER, R., *ed.* The royal natural history. Warne. il. 8°, (Warne's lib. of natural history, in 36 nos., nos. 26-28.) *subs.*, pap., *ea.*, 50 c.

No. 26 completes the information on tortoises, and treats of the scaled reptiles, with the lizards and chameleons, the geckos, agamas, the iguanas, the snake-like lizards, etc., and commences the snakes, giving a chapter on their characteristics and studies of pythons and boas. No. 27 continues the snakes, with water snakes, tree snakes, adders, and vipers, and commences the amphibians with the frogs and toads, etc. No. 28 treats of newts and salamanders, also commences the fishes with the lung fishes, mud fishes, etc., giving the characteristics of these and species of the spinney finned group, beginning with mullets, mackerel, etc.

ST. HILL, CATHARINE. Palmistry: hands of celebrities: or, studies in palmistry. Scribner. il. 12°, $1.40.

POETRY AND DRAMA.

ALLEN, LYMAN WHITNEY. Abraham Lincoln: a poem. Putnam. 12°, $1.

The poem that won the $1000 prize offered by the *N. Y. Herald* for the best poem dealing with American history. A revised edition of the poem as it appeared in the *Herald*, Dec. 15, 1895.

ROSSETTI, OLIVIA, *ed.* The Rossetti birthday-book. Macmillan. 24°, 75 c.

Poetical selections for the days of the year, accompanied by the usual blank spaces for the inscription of autographs.

POLITICAL AND SOCIAL.

ANDREWS, BYRON. One of the people: life and speeches of William McKinley, citizen, soldier, congressman, governor, and presidential candidate; embracing a complete report of the proceedings of the St. Louis Convention; to which is added a brief sketch of Garret A. Hobart. F. Tennyson Neely. 12°, (Neely's popular lib., no. 69.) pap., 50 c.

The presidential candidate of the Republican party was born in 1843. His career occupies one-half of the book; the remaining half is taken up with a full report of the St. Louis Convention at which he was nominated, with McKinley's views on many political questions and speeches he has made as tributes to national heroes. The compiler is an earnest advocate of protection. Intended as a campaign biography.

BARKER, WHARTON. Bimetallism; or, the evils of gold monometallism and the benefits of bimetallism. Barker Pub. Co. 8°, $1; pap., 50 c.

CRAVEN, HERMON W. Errors of populism. Lowman & Hanford. 12°, pap., 25 c.

The main purpose of this book is to call attention to the errors and misrepresentations made in Populist books and pamphlets about United States financial history. This falsifying of facts is shown as the cause of many of the incorrect political theories now in circulation. The teachings of Populism as set forth by representative party leaders are given, and also references to standard historical and financial works and government reports, which sustain the statements and arguments advanced.

FARRAND, MAX. The legislation of Congress for the government of the organized territories of the United States, 1789–1895. W. A. Baker. 8°, pap., 75 c.

In 1784 Thomas Jefferson submitted a plan for the government of the territories ceded by the original states, which was adopted with modifications. Later this was considered unconstitutional, and a plan proposed by Governor Randolph at the opening of the First Constitutional Convention in 1787 was adopted. In 1789 the same ordinance which gives Congress power of governing the western territories was re-enacted with modifications and made constitutional by the First Congress. Since then Congress has legislated for the territories. It is the object of this paper to trace the changes in legislation and to show that territorial government of to-day is directly developed from the ordinance of 1787.

GOLD and silver coinage under the Constitution laws enacted thereon by Congress from the organization of the Federal Government to the present time. Rand, McNally & Co. 12°, (Rialto ser., no. 72.) pap., 50 c.

The work, which is intended as an aid for voters and a handy reference-book for public men, is divided in three parts: the first part treating of the laws relating to United States coins; the second part dealing with the laws of foreign coins, and the third part giving the laws relating to gold and silver certificates. The laws contained in each part are published in chronological order, beginning with the earliest date. Index. The laws are simply given without comment or criticism.

HUNT, RANDELL. Selected arguments, lectures, and miscellaneous papers of Randell Hunt; ed. by his nephew, W. H. Hunt. F. F. Hansell. 12°, $2.

The name of Randell Hunt was for a half century, from 1832 to 1882, identified with many of the chief events in the history of the southern states. He was a constitutional lawyer of reputation and learning and a professor of law in the University of Louisiana. Some of the names of papers given are: A court, a temple of justice; An historical discourse upon the United States; The Louisiana returning board of 1876; Citizenship and allegiance; Political affairs in Louisiana; The rights of the states; The Louisiana state lottery; The Republican party in Louisiana; Counting the electoral vote.

McPHERSON, LOGAN G. The monetary and banking prob'em. Appleton. 12°, $1.

Three essays which have appeared in *Appleton's Popular Science Magazine* during the current year form the second, third, and fifth chapters of this volume. Other chapters necessary to complete the exposition of the subject in popular form have been added, and the work now treats from a practical and theoretical standpoint the problem of which the solution is the immediate and important task of the nation. The development of the monetary problem, the monetary problem, bimetallism, the banking system, and the standard of value are lucidly explained.

MASON, D. H. A short tariff history of the United States, 1783 to 1789, with a preliminary view. C. H. Kerr. 12°, (Unity lib., no. 59.) pap., 25 c.

The sub-title reads: " Disastrous outcome of the only trial of nearly absolute free trade between the United States and foreign countries.— Nature and extent of the power, with proofs that the power, as conferred in the constitution, was alien to every purpose of raising a revenue." Mr. Mason is late tariff editor of the Chicago *Inter-Ocean*.

MILLER, MARCUS A. Gold or silver? . . . a political economy . . . with pen pictures of the times. F. Tennyson Neely. 12°, (Neely's popular lib., no. 68.) pap., 25 c.

OGILVIE, J. S. Life and speeches of McKinley and Hobart. Ogilvie. 12°, $1; pap., 25 c.

ONSTAD, ERICK J., McGEE, C. A. A., [and others.] The truth about money : a practical and impartial investigation of the money question; with introd. by Hon. J. Johnston. Finance Pub. Co., [C. N. Caspar.] 12°, pap., 50 c.

STEVANS, C. M. Bryan and Sewall and the great issue of 1896. F. Tennyson Neely. 16°, (Neely's pop. lib., no. 70.) $1; pap., 50 c.

Contains a complete report of the Democratic Convention at Chicago which nominated Bryan and Sewall—speeches, platform, etc., with an account of the lives of the two candidates, extracts from speeches, etc., and a number of papers by prominent silverites on the silver question. Illustrated with portraits.

TELLER, JA. H. The battle of the standards; with an introd. by H. M. Teller. Schulte. 12°, (Ariel lib. ser., no. 9.) pap., 25 c.

WHITE, HORACE. Money and banking illustrated by American history. [*New popular ed.*] Ginn. 12°, pap., 50 c.

WILCOX, DELOS F. Municipal government in Michigan and Ohio : a study in the relations of city and commonwealth. [Macmillan.] 8°, (Columbia College studies in history, economics, and public law, v. 5, no 3.) pap., $1.

" In order that improvement may come in government or business, the first thing needful is to know the precise existing condition of affairs, and the leading causes that have operated to bring such condition about. Reformers too often forget that no matter what ideal state we are coming *to*, we must get there *from* our present position." In studying the questions of municipal government and the constitutional phase of the city problem, the author has taken Michigan and Ohio as typical states, because they are free from the conservatism attaching to the old thirteen and are old enough to have had experience which has not been distorted by the all-commanding presence of some one great metropolis, like New York, Philadelphia, and Chicago.

In the September Magazines.

Appleton's Popular Science contains a paper on "The Definition, Object, and Sphere of Taxation," by David A. Wells, in which he points out many popular errors regarding this subject.

The Arena has some timely articles of interest, namely: "The Currency Question," by the Hon. Wm. J. Bryan; "Evils of Land Monopoly," by the Rev. W. B. Williams; "Right of Women to the Ballot," by Charles H. Chapman; and "Free Silver and Prosperity," by Wm. P. St. John.

THE September *Atlantic Monthly* has for its opening paper "The Problem of the West," by Prof. Fred. J. Turner, of the University of Wisconsin. It is an explanation of sentiment in the West and of the relations of the sections to each other, with special reference to questions of the present campaign. Also, "The Election of the President," by J. B. McMaster, has a timely bearing. Of literary interest is Charles Dudley Warner's "Story of Uncle Tom's Cabin." "Marm Lisa" is a new serial by Kate Douglas Wiggin, and is said to be the author's most ambitious effort in fiction. "Girls in a Factory Valley," by Lillie B. Chace Wyman, shows the hardships which come to young women who belong to factory families.

The Catholic World has "Some Features of the New Issue: silver or gold," a timely paper by Robert J. Mahon. An illustrated article on "A Great Christian Socialist: Viscount De Melun," by the Rev. F. X. McGowan, is of interest.

The Chautauquan has for an opening paper "The City by the Golden Gate," by George H. Fitch, descriptive of San Francisco ; "Different Forms of the Ballot," by Lee J. Vance; "Joining the Atlantic to the Pacific," by George E. Walsh; "Alaska," by J. C. Brady; and "A Transition in Civilization," by Harvey L. Biddle.

The Fortnightly Review for August includes among other papers "Bimetallism and the Nature of Money," by W. H. Mallock; "Sunday Closing in Operation," by H. L. Stephen; and "The Making of a President," by Francis H. Hardy.

THE contents of *Lippincott's Magazine* are "A Marital Liability," by Eliz. Phipps Train, which constitutes the complete novel for the issue; "The Natural History of Fiatism," by Fred. Perry Powers; "Advantages of International Exhibitions," by Theodore Stanton; and "The Life of a Medical Student," by A. L. Benedict.

THE August number of *The Nineteenth Century* has "The Decline of Cobdenism," by Sidney Low; "The Battle of the Standards in America: war to the knife," by W. L. Alden; and "Suggestions for a Compromise," by Wm. Dillon. The paper entitled "Li Hung Chang," by A. Michie, formerly the *London Times* correspondent in China, is of special interest at this time.

The Westminster Review for August contains "Ivan Turgenev," by Maurice Todhunter; "English Industry and the Gold Standard," by Tyrrell Bayler; "A Claim for the Art of Fiction," by E. G. Wheelwright; and "Influence of an Aristocracy," by John Storr Hewitt.

Freshest News.

FREDERICK A. STOKES CO. continue to turn out most readable novels, gotten up in a very attractive style. Among the newest volumes are "The Heart of Princess Osra," by Anthony Hope, with sixteen full-page illustrations by H. C. Edwards; "The Herb-Moon," by John Oliver Hobbes (Mrs. Craigie) a witty love-story by this brilliant writer; "The White Shield," by Bertram Mitford, a book of adventure and war, with scene laid in South Africa; "Vawder's Understudy," by James Knapp Reeve, a study of platonic affection, of which the larger part plays in Washington: "One Day's Courtship," by Robert Barr, the story of an English artist and a Boston girl; and "Sweetheart Travellers," by S. R. Crockett, with illustrations by Gordon Browne and W. H. Groome. The last is a book for children, but its great beauty will be beyond their comprehension.

HOUGHTON, MIFFLIN & CO. are getting out "The Writings of Harriet Beecher Stowe" in a new *Riverside edition*, from new plates, thoroughly edited and rearranged with a biographical sketch and notes, with portraits, views of Mrs. Stowe's homes, and other illustrations, and engraved title-pages. It will be a handsome and every way desirable edition in sixteen volumes. The volumes promised for September will include "The Minister's Wooing," "Agnes of Sorrento," and "The Pearl of Orr's Island." "William H. Seward," by Thornton K. Lothrop, will be the new volume in *The American Statesmen's Series*; Marie Ada Molineaux has prepared "A Phrase-Book from the Poetic and Dramatic Works of Robert Browning"; and the other important books in preparation are: "The Spiritual Sense of Dante's 'Divina Commedia,'" by William T. Harris; "Talks on Writing English," by Arlo Bates; "A Second Century of Charades," by William Bellamy; "Kindegarten Principles and Practice," by Kate Douglas Wiggin and Nora Archibald Smith; and "A Primer of American Literature," by Charles F. Richardson.

LAIRD & LEE are making a specialty this fall of books in sets suitable for presentation. *The Young America Series* will have four volumes which will contain excellent juvenile literature. The separate titles of the new and recent books are "Air Castle Don," "Dick and Jack's Adventures on Sable Island," and "Tan Pile Jim," all three by B. Freeman Ashley, and "Cuore, or, the heart of a boy," by Edmondo di Amicis, and will be bound with special cover designs and neatly boxed. Opie Read's famous stories, "My Young Master," "The Jucklins," "A Kentucky Colonel," "On the Suwanee River," and "A Tennessee Judge," will also be neatly boxed as a set; as will also Wm. H. Thomes's novels in ten volumes; and *Lee's Pony Reference Library*, containing "The Modern Webster Dictionary," "Lee's Priceless Recipes," an enlarged edition of "Conklin's Handy Manual," "Lee's Pocket Encyclopædia Britannica," and "Lee's Home and Business Instructor." Last season's great success, "Yellow Beauty," a story about cats, by Marion Martin, with illustrations by Madame Ronner, will also be among the books made ready for the holidays.

Campaign Literature.

D. APPLETON & CO., New York.
Adams (H. G.). Public Debts. $2.00.
Jevons (W. S.). Money and the Mechanism of Exchange. $1.75.
Laughlin (J. L.). History of Bimetallism in the United States. New edition. '96. $2.25.
McPherson (L. G.). Monetary and Banking Problem. '96. $1.00.
Taussig (F. W.). Wages and Capital. '96. $1.50.
Wells (D. A.). Recent Economic Changes. $2.00.
White (A. D.). Fiat Money Inflation in France. New edition. 10 cents.

HENRY CAREY BAIRD & CO., Philadelphia.
Economic Books, including the writings of Henry C. Carey and Henry Carey Baird, opposing the single gold standard. Catalogue free.

CHAS. E. BROWN & CO., Boston.
Green. Are We Losing the West? 10 cents.
Osgood (W. N.). Bug vs. Bug (both sides of the silver question). ['95.] 50 cents; 25 cents.
Shaw. Socialism—Fabian Essays. 75 cents.

ROBERT CLARKE CO., Cincinnati.
Horton (S. D.). Silver and Gold and Their Relation to the Problem of Resumption New ed. '95. $1.50.

T. Y. CROWELL & CO., New York.
Ely (R. T.). Problems of To-Day. $1.50.
— Taxation in American States and Cities. $1.75.
Howe (F. C.). Taxation and Taxes in the United States Under the Internal Revenue System. $1.75.
Kinley (David). Independent Treasury System of the United States. $1.50.
Salter (Wm. M.). Anarchy or Government? 75 cents.
Scott (W. A.). Repudiation of State Debts in the U. S. $1.50.
Spahr (C. B.). Present Distribution of Wealth in the United States. $1.50.
Weyl (W. E.), and others. Equitable Taxation. 75 cents.

DERBY & MILLER COMPANY, New York.
"Common Sense Library, No. 2," Bryan, Sewall, and Honest Money. Up to date. '96. 25 cents.

ECONOMIC PUBLISHING AGENCY, Box 255, Washington, D. C.
Peters (E. T.). Monetary Standard. '95. 10 cents.

FUNK & WAGNALLS CO., New York.
Waldron (G. B.). Currency and Wealth. '96. 50 cents.

GINN & CO., Boston.
White (Horace). Money and Banking. '96. Popular ed. 50 cents.

HARTFORD SEMINARY PRESS, Hartford, Conn.
Andrews (E. B.). Wealth and Moral Law. '94. $1.00.

HENRY HOLT & CO., New York.
Walker's Bimetallism. 12mo, $1.25.
— Money. 12mo, $2.00.
— Money, Trade, and Industry. 12mo, $1.25.
— Political Economy. Elementary Course. 12mo, $1.00, net.
Sumner's American Currency. $3.00.

INDUSTRIAL PUBLICATION CO., New York.
The "Crime of 1873"! Who Was the Criminal? 25 cents.
Phin (J.). Common Sense Currency; a Practical Treatise on Money in Its Relations to National Wealth and Prosperity. '94. $1.00.

CHARLES H. KERR & CO., Chicago.
Del Mar (Alexander). A History of Monetary Systems. '95. $2.00.
Smith (Dr. W. H.). The Effects of the Gold Standard. '96. 25 cents.

LITTLE, BROWN & CO., Boston.
Jackson (Charles C.). Has Gold Appreciated? 8vo, paper, 25 cents.

LONGMANS, GREEN & CO., New York.
Bagehot (W.). English and American Money. 75 cents.
Brassey (T., Baron). Work and Wages. $1.75.
Follett. Speaker of the House of Representatives. $1.75.
Hart (A. B.). Practical Essays on American Government. $1.50.
Jordan. Standard of Value. $2.00.
Macleod (H. D.). Theory of Credit. Vol 1, $3.50; vol. 2, parts 1 and 2, each, $3.50.
— Bimetallism. $1.75.
Norton. Political Americanisms. $1.00.
Thompson (D. G.). Politics in a Democracy. $1.25.

LOTHROP PUBLISHING CO., Boston.
Upton (Hon. J. K.). Money in Politics. 338 pages, 12mo, $1.25.

JOHN JOS. McVEY, Philadelphia.
Preston (Hon. Robert E.). History of the Monetary Legislation and of the Currency of the U. S. '96. Paper, 25 cents; cloth, 50 cents.

J. S. OGILVIE CO., New York.
Ogilvie (J. S.). Life and Speeches of McKinley and Hobart. '96. Cloth, $1.00; paper, 25 cents.
— Life and Speeches of Bryan and Sewall. '96. Cloth, $1.00; paper, 25 cents.
Thorpe (T. M.). What Is Money? Popular Remedies for Popular Ills. '96. 25 cents.
White (Horace). Coin's Financial Fool; or, The Artful Dodger Exposed. ['95.] 25 cents.

OPEN COURT PUB. CO., Chicago.
Carus (P.). Nature of the State. '94. 15 cents.
Trumbull (M. M.). Wheelbarrow Articles and Discussions on Currency and the Labor Question. Cloth, $1.00; paper, 35 cents.
— Free Trade Struggle in England. Cloth, $1.00; paper, 25 cents.
— Earl Grey on Reciprocity and Civil Service Reform. Paper, 10 cents.

G. P. PUTNAM'S SONS, New York.
Atkinson (E.). Taxation and Work. '92. $1.25.
Brough (W.). Natural Law of Money: Successive Steps in the Growth of Money. '94. $1.00.
Carroll (E.). Principles and Practice of Finance. '95. $1.75.
Conant (C. A.). Modern Banks of Issue. '96. $3.00.
Ehrich (L. R.). Question of Silver. Revised ed. '96. Cloth, 75 cents; paper, 40 cents.
Foote (A. R.). Sound Currency and the Banking System. '95. 75 cents.
Gordon (A. C.). Congressional Currency. '95. $1.25.

G. P. PUTNAM'S SONS.—Continued.

Schoenhof (J.). Economy of High Wages: An Inquiry into the Cause of High Wages and Their Effect on Methods and Cost of Production. '92. $1.50.

—— **History of Money and Prices.** '95. $1.50.

Shaw (W. A.). History of Currency, 1252 –1894. '95. *Net*, $3 75.

Stokes (A. P.). Joint Metallism: Plan by Which Gold and Silver Together May be Made the Metallic Basis of a Sound Currency. '94. 75 cents. *Same*, 3d ed. enl., '95. $1.00.

Taussig (F. W.). Silver Situation in the United States. 3d rev. ed. '96. 75 cents.

Wheeler (E. P.). Real Bimetallism; or, True Coin *vs.* False Coin: a Lesson for "Coin's Financial School." '95. 75 cents.

Special terms on campaign editions for "missionary distribution."

SCHULTE PUBLISHING CO., Chicago.

Armstrong (K. L.). The Little Statesman: A Manual for American Voters. 25 cents.

Armstrong (Le Roy). An Indiana Man. 25 cents.

Clark (A.). Beneath the Dome. 50 cents.

Cowdrey (R. H.). A Tramp in Society. 25 cents.

Kinnaird (F.). The Science of Legal Robbery. '96. 25 cents.

Larrabee (Wm.). The Railroad Question. 50 cents.

Norton (S. F.). Ten Men of Money Island: A Primer of Finance. 25 cents.

Taubeneck (H. E.). Condition of Am. Farmer. 10 cents.

Teller (H. M. and J. H.). Battle of the Standards. '96. 25 cents. (German edition at same price.)

CHARLES SCRIBNER'S SONS, New York.

Trenholm (W. L.). The People's Money. '93. $1.50.

CHARLES SCRIBNER'S SONS.—Continued.

Roe (George). The Country Banker. His Clients, Cares, and Work. With a preface by Brayton Ives. $1.50.

Roe (John). Contemporary Socialism. '91. $2.50.

Cunningham (Dr. W.). The Use and Abuse of Money. $1.00, *net*.

Knox (John Jay). United States Notes. A History of the Various Issues of Paper Money by the Government of the United States. 94. $1.50.

Stimson (F. J.). A Handbook to the Labor Law of the United States. '96. $1.50, *net*

—— **Labor in Its Relation to Law.** '95. 75 cents, *net*.

Rogers (Therold). Work and Wages. $1.00.

Jeans (J. Stephen). Trusts, Pools, and Corners. '94. $1.00.

Brentano (Lujo). Hours, Wages, and Production. '94. $1.00.

Ellssard (W.). The Ethic of Usury and Interest. '92. $1.00.

Robertson (John M.) The Fallacy of Saving. '92. $1.00.

Nicholson (J. Shield). The Effects of Machinery on Wages. '92. $1.00.

Bladen (G. H.). Local Taxation and Finance. '95. $1.00.

Hyndman (H. M.). Commercial Crises of the Nineteenth Century. '92. $1.00.

Price (L. T.). Money and Its Relation to Prices. '96. $1.00.

CHAS. H. SERGEL CO., Chicago.

Frazer (J: A., jr.), and Sergel (C: H.). Sound Money. '96. 25 cents.

Harvey (W: H.), and Bryan (W. J.). Money of the People. '96. 25 cents.

STUDENT PUB. CO., Hartford.

Andrews (E. B.). An Honest Dollar. 3d edition, Sept. 1. (Plea for bimetallism.) $1 : 50 cents.

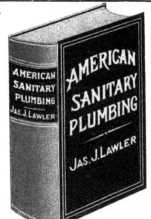

HOUGHTON, MIFFLIN & COMPANY,

4 Park Street, Boston; 11 East 17th Street, New York.

SEPTEMBER BOOKS.

The Writings of Harriet Beecher Stowe.

New *Riverside Edition*, from new plates. Thoroughly edited and rearranged, with a Biographical Sketch and Notes. With Portraits, Views of Mrs. Stowe's Homes, and other illustrations, and engraved title-pages. In 16 volumes, crown 8vo, handsomely bound, cloth, gilt top, $1.50 each.

This will be a handsome, everyway desirable edition of the writings of one of the greatest and most famous of American women. It is edited with great care, printed from new plates, clear, large type, and bound in fine library style.

READY IN SEPTEMBER.

THE MINISTER'S WOOING. AGNES OF SORRENTO. THE PEARL OF ORR'S ISLAND.

Large-paper Edition, limited to 250 copies, printed on the best of paper. *Each set has Mrs. Stowe's autograph, written a few months ago expressly for this edition.*

WILLIAM H. SEWARD.

By THORNTON K. LOTHROP. In the American Statesmen Series. 16mo, gilt top, $1.25.

As Governor of New York, United States Senator, and Secretary of State, Mr. Seward was obliged to deal with questions of great importance and of serious practical difficulty; and he brought to these the grasp of a true statesman as well as a high degree of intellectual power. Mr. Lothrop tells the story of his career and achievements with generous appreciation.

THE SPIRITUAL SENSE OF DANTE'S DIVINA COMMEDIA.

By WILLIAM T. HARRIS, LL.D., United States Commissioner of Education. *New Edition.* 12mo, $1.25.

As the work of such a scholar and thinker as Dr. Harris, this book, which embodies long and thorough study of Dante, commends itself primarily to all students of Dante, and hardly less to all serious-minded readers.

TALKS ON WRITING ENGLISH.

By ARLO BATES, Litt.D., Professor of English in the Massachusetts Institute of Technology. Crown 8vo, $1.50.

This is an admirable book for those who wish to learn to write naturally and effectively. It is simple, clear, full of helpful suggestions and illustrations which emphasize the author's statements. Mr. Bates has two rare qualifications for writing such a book—he knows very well what he wants to say, and he knows how to say it in an easy, colloquial, attractive style.

A PRIMER OF AMERICAN LITERATURE.

By CHARLES F. RICHARDSON, Professor of Literature in Dartmouth College. *New Edition*, rewritten and brought up to date. With portraits of eight authors, views of their homes, and a full index, 18mo, 35 cents, *net*.

This is an excellent, concise account of American writers and their works from early colonial days to the present time, valuable for reference and for use in schools.

A PHRASE-BOOK FROM THE POETIC AND DRAMATIC WORKS OF ROBERT BROWNING.

To which is added an index containing the significant words not elsewhere noted. By MARIE ADA MOLINEAUX, A M., Ph.D. 1 vol., 8vo, $3.00.

This book contains the quotable passages of Browning's works, arranged and indexed under leading words; also a list of all the notable proper names, compounds, rare words, and peculiarities of Browning's diction, with references to the poems and passages in which they occur. These references are to the Riverside Edition of Browning in six volumes, and to the Cambridge Edition in one.

A SECOND CENTURY of CHARADES.

By WILLIAM BELLAMY, author of "A Century of Charades." 18mo, $1.00. [*October*.

Mr. Bellamy's former book has fairly established itself as a classic in its peculiar department. The new hundred Charades are of the same unique character as the former—thoughtful, ingenious, brilliant, delightfully puzzling, and very satisfactory when guessed.

KINDERGARTEN PRINCIPLES AND PRACTICE.

By KATE DOUGLAS WIGGIN and NORA ARCHIBALD SMITH, authors of "Froebel's Gifts," "Froebel's Occupations," etc. 1 vol., 16mo, $1.00.

This book is the third and concluding part of *The Republic of Childhood*, the general title under which the three books above mentioned will be known. The first was devoted to those gifts which properly attract and train the mind of the child; the second, to those occupations which continue the child's scientific development and enlist the interest; and the third discusses the cardinal principles and the normal practice of the kindergarten—the whole forming a remarkably full and clear Handbook for the Kindergartner, and hardly less valuable and helpful to the mother of young children.

FOR SALE BY BOOKSELLERS.

LITERARY NEWS

AN ECLECTIC REVIEW OF CURRENT LITERATURE

~ILLUSTRATED~

VOL·XVII·No·10 OCTOBER~1896 $1.00 YEARLY
10 CTS PER NO.

~PUBLICATION OFFICE~
59 DUANE STREET, NEW YORK

ENTERED AT THE POST OFFICE AT NEW.YORK AS SECOND CLASS MATTER.

The Literary News

In winter you may reade them, ad ignem, by the fireside; and in summer, ad umbram, under some shadie tree, and therewith pass away the tedious howres.

VOL. XVII.   OCTOBER, 1896.   NO. 10.

From "A Year in the Fields."   Copyright, 1896. by Houghton, Mifflin & Co.

A CATSKILL ROADWAY.

A Year in the Fields.

THE happy idea has come to John Burroughs's publishers to make a gift-book of selections from his outdoor papers, covering the rural year, for which his friend Clifton Johnson has furnished twenty half-tone illustrations from photographs taken of the scenes which have been so delightfully brought before us in A Snow-storm, Winter neighbors, A Spring relish. April, Birch browsing, A bunch of herbs—fragrant wild flowers and weeds—Autumn-tides, and A sharp lookout. The book contains an introduction by Mr. Burroughs and is a most fitting souvenir to present to friends who have wandered through the fields with him in all the seasons of the year. "It is not alone the wholesome and alluring tang of the wilderness, nor the fine observing faculty bent upon Nature and her operations, nor yet the sturdy and stirring quality of his style, that so wins us to Mr. Burroughs." said Edith M. Thomas in *The Century Magazine*, ten years ago. "'Tis the strong heart-beat, the generous glow of sympathy felt in all he writes, that completes the charm for us." Though seldom making use of the usual adjuncts of poetry—rhyme and verse—

John Burroughs is essentially a poet. His great human emotional heart steadily pumps healthy, sympathetic blood into every tissue of his writing, which appeals to his reader's heart before his mind has realized how much brain-force has gone into John Burroughs's well-balanced work. To many superficial readers Burroughs appears an imitator of Thoreau, but their love of nature and accuracy in stating facts of natural history are all they have in common, and this identity of subject only serves to bring out distinctly their radical constitutional difference.

Winter and summer the essays of Burroughs are books to have about you, to pick up at any moment. and they are most suitable for reading aloud, and in this little volume have been gathered the very rarest bits of his inspiring thoughts on the little details of the life of birds, flowers, and trees, of the soft effect of the protecting snow and the glorious beauty of the autumn woods. Clifton Johnson, who loves every inch of wood and field as Burroughs does himself, is a fitting illustrator for this tasteful book. (Houghton, Mifflin & Co. $1.50.)

Johanna Ambrosius.

In Gross Wersmeninken, a little German village of East Prussia, almost on the border of Russia, more hopeless in its poverty than

From "Poems of Johanna Ambrosius."   Copyright, 1896, by Roberts Brothers.

the surrounding villages even, is the little house in which has been discovered a German Burns. Until a year and a half ago the name of Johanna Ambrosius was not known outside this little hamlet, where its bearer, as the wife of a poor peasant, led a humble and monotonous existence.

Through the newspapers Prof. Karl Weiss-Schrattenthal became acquainted with the poems of this poor peasant woman. He entered into communication with her and printed a number of her poems. The first edition of this collection appeared at Christmas-time, 1894; in less than three months the fourth edition was published. To-day her poems have passed through the twenty-seventh edition and she is hailed throughout Germany as a lyric genius,

destined to play an important part in the literary revival which has been so brilliantly initiated by the dramatic achievements of Sudermann and his associates. These poems fell into the hands of the Empress of Germany, who sent from her palace to learn the surroundings in which this peasant woman had learned the secret of a lofty spiritual life. The messenger found a woman of forty, but bent and worn to sixty, with scarred, toil-hardened hands that lay idle outside the cover of a poor bed in a snow-darkened cottage. Johanna had fallen a victim to pneumonia. The facts of her life have now been given to the world, gathered from the famous physician sent by the Empress to one who had been ill all her life and never had had the relief of medicine; from letters to Herr Schrattenthal from a sister who was caring for the poetess in what was thought to be her last illness; from a book of travels in East Prussia, Lithuania, and Poland; and from a sketch by Herman Grimm in the *Deutsche Rundschau.*

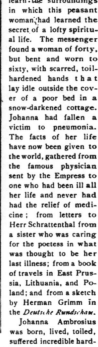

Johanna Ambrosius was born, lived, toiled, suffered incredible hardships and privations, hungered in body, thirsted in soul, wept for knowledge unattainable, gained the highest knowledge of spiritual things, and almost died before the messenger of the Empress found her. Herman Grimm says: "She was born, her cradle was rocked by the waterfall of a curious device of a wheel attached to the rocker, while her mother toiled in the slope, carrying soil to the naked rocks. She mended her father's nets in winter, oiled his great boots so that he could stand in the icy water to fish, dug the potatoes, cut the scanty wheat, gathered pine-needles to fill the beds, sheared the sheep, spun and wove, looked forward all the year to the splendid candles of Christmas that dispelled the long night in the snow-buried cottage." She married a playmate, and her children were born to be rocked by the waterfall as she had been.

Not a word does she tell of these external things herself. She says when she writes she feels an indescribable exaltation. Hunger and thirst, darkness, cold, and pain afflict her no more.

She writes of simple things—the death of a child, its toys laid in the coffin; the infrequent flowers, every birdnote, waited for uring ten months of the year. Wherever a flower grew was holy ground to Johanna Ambrosius.

Through the *Gartenlaube*, which she denied herself much to buy, she learned of the spiritual brotherhood of mankind, the sorrow of a nation for the death of a king, the striving and straining for freedom, the longing for peace that assails mankind. She longed to comfort those who mourn. She has not left her bleak home, but she now has books, pictures, leisure —all the things she had dreamed of—and fair white paper on which to speak to the hearts of all.

Roberts Brothers have published a translation of her poems, by Mary J. Safford, who has perhaps done as well as can be done with the task of rendering in another tongue an author whose great charm is her exquisite feeling for the finest shades of meaning of the language in which she writes. But, even translated, the thought is there. Only a Longfellow could translate Johanna Ambrosius musically and with full appreciation. (Roberts. $1 50.)

Shakespeare the Boy.

TWO years ago, at the request of the editors of the *Youth's Companion*, I wrote for that periodical a series of four familiar articles on the boyhood of Shakespeare. It was understood at the time that I might afterwards expand them into a book, and this plan is carried out in the present volume. The papers have been carefully revised and enlarged to thrice their original compass, and a new fifth chapter has been added.

The sources from which I have drawn my material are often mentioned in the text and the notes. I have been particularly indebted to Halliwell-Phillipps's "Outlines of the Life of Shakespeare," Knight's "Biography of Shakespeare," Furnivall's Introduction to the *Leopold* edition of Shakespeare, his "Babees Book," and his edition of Harrison's "Description of England," Sidney Lee's "Stratford-on-Avon," Strutt's "Sports and Pastimes," Brand's "Popular Antiquities," and Dyer's "Folk-Lore of Shakespeare."

I hope that the book may serve to give the young folk some glimpses of rural life in England when Shakespeare was a boy, and also to help them—and possibly their elders—to a better understanding of many allusions in his works. (Harper. $1.25.)—*From preface by W. J. Rolfe.*

The First Violin.

DURING the holiday season for 1878 appeared an anonymous novel entitled "The First Violin," which had found its way into the carefully selected *Leisure Hour Series*, published by Henry Holt & Co. It was a novel describing the life of students of music in Germany, and since the great success of Miss Sheppard's "Charles Anchester," in 1863, no musical novel had so pleased the public. It was soon traced to Miss Jessie Fothergill, who had already published, under her own name, "Healey," in 1875, and "Aldyth," in 1877. Miss Fothergill herself told us shortly before her death in 1890: "I went to the firm which had brought out my two former unlucky efforts ('Healey' and 'Aldyth'), but they kindly and patiently advised me, for the sake of whatever literary reputation I might have obtained, not to publish this novel. Much

From "Shakespeare the Boy."   Copyright, 1896, by Harper & Brothers.

SHAKESPEARE THE BOY.

THE SISTERS.

nettled, I replied somewhat petulantly that I acknowledged their right to refuse it, but not advise me in the matter, and added that I *would* publish it. Another firm 'made it a rule never to bring out novels except those of some promise.' Mine was said to be 'up in the clouds,' while at the same time 'below their mark.' Finally Mr. Bentley took pity on it and ran it through *Temple Bar*. Since that time I have never experienced any difficulty in disposing of my wares."

After nearly twenty years the possibilities for illustration of "The First Violin" have been discovered, and Brentano's have made an *Illustrated Library Edition* of this deservedly popular story. George W. Brenneman, of the Salmagundi Club, has made wood drawings of the high-spirited, artistic heroine and her surroundings in the typical German music centre in which she studied the art of song. These have been reproduced in fifty photogravures and etchings, the latter by G. M. Deschamps, made and printed under the direction of G. W. H. Ritchie. The book is in two volumes, with covers in cloth designed by H. L. Parkhurst, also in half calf, half polished morocco, etc., and, besides, there is an *édition de luxe*, limited to 100 copies.

In spite of its touch of sentimentality and the rather morbid sense of honor of the hero, the "first violin" of a remarkably trained orches-

tra, this novel is healthy in tone and gives a most interesting insight into the daily life and the high ideals and many sacrifices of those who, forsaking friends and family, go among strangers, speaking a strange language, to learn the art of music. The book is also really instructive in its criticisms of orchestral performances and the methods of instruction pursued by acknowledged leaders of taste in musical circles. The plot is simple but affords room for many descriptions of nature and of scenes of bohemian life among artists and writers. The book should take another long lease of life, and it will most surely do so. (Brentano. 2 v., $6–$15.)

"The Spirit of Power, Love, and Soberness."

THEN I became conscious of a sensation of acute physical pain, and, looking down, I saw that the Bishop had grasped my wrist, and that his strong fingers had closed on it in a grip that seemed to drive the flesh into the bone. I understood what that grasp meant when I looked at his face. He was pale as death, and the features were fixed in a sternness that struck cold to my heart.

And all this time the revivalist shouted to the sobbing, swaying crowd.

"Come," he cried, "come, all who would be saved from hell! Here is one who has the grace. Who will join her? Who will save his soul to-night? This is the only way, and this may be the only moment! Who comes forward for salvation?"

The Bishop was breathing heavily, with long trembling breaths, but I noticed that the expression had changed. It was no longer stern. It was strange and sad, and his look was fixed on something far away—far beyond the blackness of the black woods behind the madman who shrieked upon the platform. I felt a sudden fear, and turned toward Jack.

He was not by my side. I looked round and saw him at the rail that enclosed the clearing. He was placing a white-faced child in a woman's arms, and I saw by his gestures that he was forcing her to leave that place of horror. In a moment he was back, and, with one glance at me, he sat down on the other side of the

Bishop and laid his steady hand on the old man's arm.

"Come!" screamed the man on the platform. "Come, and choose between the Lord and hell! Every soul here is hanging over the fires of hell eternal. Come and be saved!"

But already, on the bench, under it, and on all sides of it lay a score of struggling, agonized human beings, beating the ground tearing their very flesh in the exaltation of fear and frenzy, choking, gasping, and through it all shrieking mad and awful appeals to the Most High; while the crowd around them, all on their feet, shouted and yelled in incoherent delirium.

"Come! come!" the voice on the platform rose above the din. "Be saved while there is yet time."

"Almighty God—"

My heart stood still. The Bishop had risen to his feet, and his gigantic figure towered up as he spread out his hands above the crowd; and, as his deep tones rang out clear and dominant in that hideous Babel, a sudden silence fell upon them all.

"—The Father of our Lord Jesus Christ, who desireth not the death of a sinner, but rather that he may turn from his wickedness and live, hath given power, and commandment, to his ministers, to declare and pronounce to his people, being penitent, the absolution and remission of their sins. He pardoneth and absolveth all those who truly repent, and unfeignedly believe his holy Gospel."

The madness had gone—utterly gone—out of that stricken throng. The struggling figures around the bench ceased to struggle. They raised their heads as they lay upon the ground, and every face in the clearing was turned toward the Bishop, wearing a look of eager wonderment which I shall never forget. The Bishop, his eyes still far away, his hands stretched out over the people, went on:

"—Wherefore let us beseech him to grant us

true repentance, and his Holy Spirit, that those things may please him which we do at this present; and that the rest of our lives hereafter may be pure and holy; so that at the last we may come to his eternal joy; through Jesus Christ our Lord."

And the people answered, "Amen."

When he had finished he steadied himself by my shoulder, at first with a nervous pressure ; but in a moment I felt the tension of his muscles relax. Then, in a voice that was almost feeble, so tender had it grown, he turned toward the east, and, in that abiding silence he pronounced the Benediction.

From "Love in Old Cloathes"   Copyright, 1896, by Charles Scribner's Sons.

AS ONE HAVING AUTHORITY.

For a moment, until they began to disperse softly and silently, the Bishop stood erect, then he sank back into his seat, with one arm around my neck and one around Jack's. (Scribner. $1.50.)—*From Bunner's "Love in Old Cloathes."*

WHERE ROBERT BROWN-
ING DIED.

Was Shakespeare in Venice?

SHAKESPEARE, who wrote much about Venice, and who probably never saw it, remarked once that all the world's a stage. Venice, even now, is a grand spectacular show; and no drama ever written is more dramatic than Venice itself. Mr. Howells prefaces his "Venetian Life" by an account of the play, and the by-play which he once saw from a stage-box in the little theatre in Padua, when the prompters and, the scene-shifters and the actors in the wings were as prominent to him as were the trage-dians and comedians who strutted, and mouthed, and sawed the air with their hands in full view of the house; and he adds: "It has sometimes seemed to me as if fortune had given me a stage-box at another and grander spectacle, and that I had been suffered to see this Venice, which is to other cities like the pleasant improbability of the theatre to every-day, commonplace life, to much the same effect as that melodrama in Padua." It has been my own good fortune to spend, at various seasons, a short time in the pit—"on a standee ticket"—just to drop in for a moment, now and then, when the performance is nearly over, and to look not so much at the broken-down stage and its worn-out settings, not so much at the actors and the acting, as to study the audiences, the crowds of men and women in parquet, gallery, and boxes, who have been sitting for centuries through the different thrilling acts of the great plays played here, and have applauded or hissed as the case may be.

So strange and so strong is the power of fiction over truth in Venice, as elsewhere, that Portia and Emilia, Cassio, Antonia and Iago appear to have been more real here than are the women and men of real life. We see, on the Rialto, Shylock first and then its history and its associations; and the Council Chamber of the Palace of the Doges is chiefly interesting as being the scene of Othello's eloquent defence of himself.

It is a curious fact, recorded by Th. Elze, and quoted by Mr. Horace Howard Furness in his Appendix to "The Merchant of Venice," that

THE COUNCIL CHAMBER IN OTHELLO'S TIME.

at the time of the action of that drama, in Shakespeare's own day, there was living in Padua a professor of the university; whose characteristics fully and entirely corresponded with all the qualities of "Old Bellario," and with all the requisites of the play. In his concluding passages Elze described the University of Padua at the close of the sixteenth century, when there were representatives of twenty-three nations among its students. He said that not a few Englishmen took up their abode in Padua, for a longer or a shorter time, for the purposes of study, all of whom must naturally have visited Venice. "And," he added, "if it has been hitherto impossible to prove that Shakespeare drew his knowledge of Venice and Padua, and the region about, from personal observation, it is quite possible to suppose that he obtained it by word of mouth, either from Italians living in England or from Englishmen who had pursued their studies at Padua." (Harper. $1.)—*From Hutton's "Literary Landmarks of Venice."*

All Mankind Was in Love with Princess Osra.

THUS the heart of Princess Osra found its haven and its rest; for a month later she was married to the Grand Duke of Mittenheim in the Cathedral of Streslau, having utterly refused to take any other place for her wedding. Again she and he rode forth together through the Western Gate, and the King rode with them on the way till they came to the woods. Here he paused and all the crowd that accompanied him stopped also; and they all waited till the sombre depths of the glades hid Osra and her lover from their sight. Then, leaving them thus riding together to their happiness, the people returned home, sad for the loss of their darling Princess. But for consolation, and that their minds might the less feel her absence, they had her name often on their lips; and the poets and story-tellers composed many stories about her, not grounded on fact, as are those which have been here set forth, but the fabric of idle imaginings, wrought to please the fancy of lovers or to wake the memories of older folks. So that, if a stranger goes now to Streslau, he may be pardoned if it seem to him that all mankind was in love with Princess Osra. Nay, and those stories so pass all fair bounds that if you listen to them you will come near to believing that the Princess also had found some love for all the men who had given her their love. Thus to many she is less a woman who once lived and breathed, than some sweet image under whose name they fondly group all the virtues and the charms of her whom they love best, each man fashioning

HE TOOK IT AND DRAINED IT.

for himself from his own chosen model her whom he calls his Princess. Yet it may be that for some of them who so truly loved her, her heart had a moment's tenderness. Who shall tell all the short-lived dreams that come and go, the promptings and stirrings of a vagrant inclination? And who would pry too closely into these secret matters? May we not more properly give thanks to heaven that the thing is as it is? For surely it makes greatly for the increase of joy and entertainment in the world, and of courtesy and true tenderness, that the heart of Princess Osra—or of what lady you may choose, sir, to call by her name—should flutter in pretty hesitation here and there and to and fro a little, before it flies on a straight wing to its destined and desired home. There have been many such, and still there is laughter as well as tears in the tune to which the world spins round :

" But still a Ruby kindles in the Vine,
And many a Garden by the Water blows."

From "Mist on the Moors."   Copyright, 1896, by R. F. Fenno & Co.

SHE LOOKED OUT INTO THE DARKNESS.

Wear your willow, then, as the Marquis de Mérosailles wore his, lightly and yet most courteously ; or like the Bishop of Modenstein (for so many say), with courage and self-mastery. That is, if wear it you must. You remember what the Miller of Hofbau thought ? (Stokes. $1.50.)—*From Hope's " The Heart of Princess Osra."*

Dreardown's Window.

PRESENTLY my heart gave a bound, for I saw the young girl enter. At first I could not see her features plainly, for she walked to and fro the room, and thus turned only the side of her face towards me. By and by, however, she came to the window and looked out. I was only twenty feet from her, while the branch of the tree on which I stood placed me on a level with the room in which she was. I saw her plainly now. The light of the lamp revealed every feature. She remained a long time, too, looking steadfastly out into the darkness.

She did not look more than twenty, perhaps barely that. In the lamplight both her hair and eyes looked as black as the raven's wing, the former being tossed in curling tresses back from her forehead, and the latter shining like stars. I learned afterwards that neither were her hair or eyes black, but a rich dark brown. Her face was very pale; it looked unhealthy in the pale lamplight, but the features were to me more beautiful than any I had ever seen.

I looked long and steadfastly, and as I looked I realized that the dream of my life was fulfilled. I saw the fulfilment of my heart's desire; I saw one whom I felt sure responded to the deepest cravings of my heart.

But oh the sadness, the utter hopeless misery that rested on her features ! Never did I think a face could tell such a story as hers told!

It was with difficulty that I refrained from jumping to the ground, going into the house, and demanding her liberty. I soon realized the foolishness of such an act, however. My new-found love gave me discretion, I think, and told me to be wise. For the throbbing of my heart, the hunger of my soul told me that I did love her, that I should love her until my heart ceased to beat, until the wheels of my life stood still.

The world became changed to me from that moment. (Fenno. 75 c.)— *From Hocking's "Mist on the Moors."*

THE JERSEY COAST.

Washington's State Dinners.

GENERAL WASHINGTON always liked to have company at dinner, for he was very hospitable, and, besides this, he considered it his duty to become acquainted with his officers and with the people of the neighborhood; and sometimes as many as thirty persons sat down at the table. Even if the various articles of food were not of the finest quality, they were well cooked and well served. While in Middlebrook, Washington desired a dinner service of white queen's-ware, and he wrote to Philadelphia to obtain it. Among the articles he mentioned in his order were eight dozen shallow plates and three dozen soup-plates, which gives an idea of the size of his dinner-parties. But although Philadelphia was searched from one end to the other, no queen's-ware of the kind could be found, and at last Washington was told that he could get what he wanted in New Brunswick, and there he bought his queen's-ware.

Among other things which he ordered at that time were "six tolerably genteel but not expensive candlesticks"; and he also wrote for a new hat, stating, "I do not wish by any means to be in the extreme of fashion, either in the size or manner of cocking it."

At these dinners there was a good deal of state and ceremony, although the heads of the family were very courteous and attentive to their guests. As this was a military establishment, everything was done promptly and according to rule. Washington never waited longer than five minutes for any guest who was late. When such a person did arrive after the company had seated themselves at table, he would always try to put him at his ease by some pleasant saying, sometimes saying that he had a cook "who never asks whether the company has come, but whether the hour has come."

During this winter a great entertainment was given by General Knox and some other officers, and it was said to be the finest thing of the kind ever seen in that part of the State. It may be thought, and probably there were people who thought it then, that at a time when money was so much needed, and provisions were so hard to get, a great and expensive festival like this was extravagant and out of place; but it is likely that the gayety of that great day had a good and encouraging effect upon the army as well as the people of the country. They knew why the day had been celebrated, and because of the general rejoicings they believed there was reason to rejoice; and when people believe that there is a good thing coming they are much more ready to fight for it than if they had no such belief. [American Book Co. 80 c.)—*From Stockton's "Stories of New Jersey."*

A NEW JERSEY KITCHEN.

From Barnes's "Midshipman Farragut."   Copyright, 1896, by D. Appleton & Co.
THE BOATSWAIN'S MATE DISCOURSES.

going to be cut and run, and fire fast, I tell you, Mr. Farragut. Ain't they beauties, them two vessels!"

He swept his hand out toward the *President* off the port bow and then to the little *Hornet*, swinging a quarter of a mile or so astern.

David turned around and looked back on the deck of his own ship. Although it was in somewhat of confusion owing to the great hurry and bustle incident to getting in commission for a long cruise, any one with half an eye could see that the *Essex* was commanded by a sailor, that her crew were sailors, and that her officers were able. There was little of bawling or shouting of orders; every man seemed to do his duty and to know his place. All the loose running gear was flemished down and lay in neat flat coils on the decks as if ready for Sunday inspection.

"It's my idee that

The Boatswain and the "Middies."

THERE is no reason why a boatswain's mate may not be allowed to tell stories to midshipmen, and many a long tale had David and his friends, Midshipmen Dashiell and Cowan, listened to in the night-watches.

As soon as the boy was within earshot the old sailor began to talk. It was only a week or so since the news had reached New York of the declaration of war against England. It was the uppermost thing in everybody's mind, and, of course, was the only subject of discussion on shipboard.

"This 'ere war," began old Bill, as a matter of course, "is a war of shootin' and sailin'. There ain't a-goin' to be no big fleets tyin' up to one another, and boardin' and grapplin'. It's

we can teach them Johnny Bulls somethin' about ships, Mr. Farragut," said old Kingsbury, with an accent of pride. "And I tell you what, sir, there ain't a man on board but what would jump into the chain-hold head first for Captain Porter."

On the 21st of June the other vessels sailed out to sea, but the *Essex* remained a few days in port overhauling her rigging and re-storing her hold. These were busy and tiresome times, and everybody on board longed for the hour when she would have put the headland behind and have the blue sea beneath and behind her.

For three successive days the declaration of war with Great Britain was read by Captain Porter to the crew assembled in the waist, and each time after reading he inquired if there was any one on board who objected to fighting on the plea of being a British subject.

On the last day there came a sensation, a man stepped forward and said he was an Englishman. A murmur ran through the crew, and the midshipmen will never forget the dramatic scene that followed. No sooner had the man made his declaration than another sailor stepped to the mast beside him.

"This man lies!" he said. "I know him well. We were brought up together, man and boy, at Barnstable."

The murmur grew louder.

"Step back among the crew," said Captain Porter, to both men.

The man who had claimed to be an Englishman paled. He hesitated about obeying the order, for three or four of the foremast hands stepped forward to meet him. It was with difficulty that they could be restrained.

However, Captain Porter allowed them to wreak a little vengeance, for just before the vessel sailed the man was put ashore, as he had requested to be. He was, however, dressed in a unique costume for that season of the year— it was composed of tar and feathers. (Appleton. $1.)— *From Barnes's "Midshipman Farragut."*

On the Irrawaddy.

WITH the exception of the terrible retreat from Afghanistan, none of England's many little wars have been so fatal in proportion to the number of those engaged as our first expedition to Burma. It was undertaken without any due comprehension of the difficulties to be encountered from the effects of climate and the deficiency of transport; the power, and still more the obstinacy and arrogance of the court of Ava, were altogether underrated; and it was considered that our possession of her ports would assuredly bring the enemy, who had wantonly forced the struggle upon us, to submission. Events, however, proved the completeness of the error. The Burman policy of carrying off every boat on the river, laying waste the whole country, and driving away the inhabitants and the herds, maintained our army as prisoners in Rangoon through the first wet season, and caused the loss of half the white officers and men first sent there. The subsequent campaign was no less fatal, and although large reinforcements had been sent, fifty per cent. of the whole died, so that less than two thousand fighting men remained in the ranks when the expedition arrived within a short distance of Ava. Not until the last Burmese army had been scattered did the court of Ava submit to the by no means onerous terms we imposed. Great, indeed, was the contrast presented by this first invasion of the country with the last war in 1885, which brought about the final annexation

STANLEY CUT DOWN THE MAN.

of Burma. Then a fleet of steamers conveyed the troops up the noble river, while in 1824 a solitary steamer was all that India could furnish to aid the flotilla of rowboats. No worse government has ever existed than that of Burma, when with the boast that she intended to drive the British out of India she began the war; no people were ever kept down by a more grinding tyranny, and the occupation of the country by the British has been an even greater blessing to the population than has that of India. Several works, some by eye-witnesses, others compiled from official documents, appeared after the war. They differ remarkably in the relation of details. I have chiefly followed those given in the narratives of Mr. H. H. Wilson, and of Major Snodgrass, the military secretary to the commander of the expedition. (Scribner. $1.50.)—*From Henty's " On the Irrawaddy."*

A BOOK.

THERE is no frigate like a book
  To take us lands away,
Nor any coursers like a page
  Of prancing poetry.
This traverse may the poorest take
  Without oppress of toll ;
How frugal is the chariot
  That bears a human soul !

(Roberts. $1.25.)—*From "Emily Dickinson's Poems."*

The Flora of Madeira.

TURNING now to the flora of the island, let us review the names of some of the principal fruits which grow in abundance. They are bananas, loquots, figs, guava, grapes, pears, peaches, apples, apricots, plums, cattley quava, custard apple, mangos, pitanga, alligator or avocado pear, oranges, pineapples, tangierine oranges, lemons, dates, citrons, grandillas, tabiaba, gooseberries, and red bananas.

The flowering plants of a Tunchal garden include fuchsias, begonias, pelargoniums, cannas,

A FAMILY PARTY.

mesembryanthema, the lily of the Nile, amaryllis, and the geraniums and various other varieties. Geraniums, by the way, grow in Madeira somewhat as daisies grow in America, They are ubiquitous to the soil and grow anywhere and everywhere.

There are two marked differences, however. between our cultivated geraniums and Madeira's wild ones. The general rule regarding wild flowers is that the cultivation of them improves and makes them larger and more beautiful.

The geranium, however, seems to contradict this rule. It grows in its perfection in Madeira, the flowers being much larger and the plants themselves often obtaining the height of ten and twelve feet from the ground.

When growing by the side of a wall, or a house, the geranium takes the form of a vine,

A FAMILY AT BREAKFAST.

and quickly spreads its twining branches upward in all directions.

So may I, perhaps, best conclude in the beautiful language of Diniz, the grand old Portuguese
poet: "*Filha do oceano, Do undoso campo flor,
gentil Madeira.*"

Bowdich said: "If Homer's beautiful description of the Phœacian Isle, where fruit succeeded
fruit and flower followed flower in rich and endless variety, be applicable to any modern one,
it is Madeira." (Drexel Biddle & Bradley Pub.
Co. $2.)—*From Barnes's " The Madeira Islands."*

A Cycle of Cathay.

THE Rev. W. A. P. Martin, president emeri-
tus of the Imperial Tungwen College, has
written a book on China which is to be earnestly commended for its liberality of view, wealth
of information, and clear knowledge of the
scope and limitations of
Chinese character. "A Cy-
cle of Cathay" Dr. Martin
calls his book and in it he
takes a survey of the history
of the empire during the
last sixty years. For three-
fourths of that period he
was a resident of China,
travelling in the double
capacity of missionary and
agent of the Chinese Gov-
ernment ; and during the
critical treaty negotiations
leading up to the opening
of Pekin he was in the diplomatic service of the United
States. Dr. Martin writes
at length and in an entertaining and instructive way
of the manners and cus-
toms of the Chinese, their
language and religions,
sketches the Taiping rebellion and the Arrow war, and

gives a full and rather humorous account of the
Tientsin negotiations. The most valuable portion of the book, however, is that wherein the
author narrates his experiences at Pekin, the
founding of the Tungwen College, his relations
with the mandarins and leading members of the
government, and the organization of the customs service under Sir Robert Hart. In a suggestive chapter on the missionary question Dr.
Martin declares unreservedly that the riots are
due entirely to local prejudice against the influx
of foreign ideas, and not in the least to religious
differences. On this point he says :

"If it be asked how long it is likely to be before the
nations of Christendom can safely withdraw from their
missionaries and native Christians even the semblance
of a protectorate, I answer that it may be withdrawn as
soon as they are prepared to renounce extra-territorial
privileges for all their citizens, and to trust life and
property to the jurisdiction of Chinese courts. China
must first revolutionize her judicial system, and show
that her entire government is penetrated with the modern spirit."

The illustrations in "A Cycle of Cathay,"
largely from drawings by Chinese artists, are
of rather exceptional interest. Dr. Martin
made the speech of welcome to Li Hung Chang
at the banquet at The Waldorf, New York City.
(Revell. $2.)—*The Beacon.*

IRRIGATING RICE-FIELDS.

From "Dick and Jack." Copyright, 1896, by Laird & Lee.

A HAIRBREADTH ESCAPE.

The Young America Series.

B. FREEMAN ASHLEY, who has already proved a capital story-writer for boys in his "Tan-Pile Jim" and "Dick and Jack" has now ready "Air Castle Don ; or, from dreamland to hard pan," telling the adventures of a manly little fellow left to fight his way up alone in one of the largest American cities. There is a breeziness about this tale that makes it very attractive. The characters are real flesh and blood, and there is a simplicity and earnestness in the telling that touches the best part of a healthy boy's nature. This series deserves great praise. It is profusely illustrated. It now includes four books, three by Mr. Ashley already mentioned above, and Amicis's little classic "Cuore; or. the heart of a boy," the story of the little Italian boy who has so endeared himself around the whole world. (Laird & Lee. *Set,* 4 v., $4.)

March Hares.

"MARCH HARES" is the latest book of that capable American novelist, Harold Frederic. It was first published under a pen-name, and none of the English critics suspected its authorship. This was natural enough. It is not in the Frederic vein. Indeed, it is such a light and pretty trifle that one might easily have been tempted to lay it—like a nameless child — at the door of Anthony Hope-Hawkins, who is a trifler.

It is a new vein for Harold Frederic, but a vein entirely delightful.

It is lightly written—a fanciful and mocking little love-story. One unusual feat Mr. Frederic has accomplished. He, being a Yankee, has yet succeeded in depicting two thoroughly Scottish Scots. David Mosscrop and Lord Drumpipes are quite as good as anything Barrie or Crockett or John Watson have done—and they are less maudlin. From a careful perusal of the recent Scotch fiction one is led to imagine that the average Scot spends his time comforting the widow and arguing with the minister over the doctrine of predestination. Mr. Frederic's view of the Scot is more reasonable, and is, in a way, reassuring. There still be cakes and ale in the bonnie land.

The story of "March Hares" is exquisitely simple. Mr. David Mosscrop is a young and erudite Scot, given to an indulgence in too much drink. One morning, in a melancholy and repentant mood, he is lounging on Westminster Bridge, when a young woman, with lemon-colored hair, comes by. Since they are both frequenters of the reading-room in the British Museum, they have some knowledge of each other. Together they walk away to breakfast. Love takes its usual eccentric gait, but in the end there is the noise of wedding bells.

Taken all in all "March Hares" is capital fiction. (Appleton. $1.25.)—*N. Y. Commercial Advertiser.*

Day-Books.

THE last story is the most notable of those contained in "Day-Books," a *Keynotes* volume, by Mabel E. Wotton. A sense of deep but carefully restrained pathos, a knowledge of the heart and feelings of an elderly, poor, but far from commonplace woman, and the man who uses her talents and friendship for his own literary advancement, give some of the value that pertains to a real study of human nature, however slight. The next best is the first of the batch. It tells of a girl and of two men who love her in different ways, and each of whom supplies, in sentiment or conduct, something the other lacks. So far as the woman is concerned, one is merely the complement of the other. As she is not able to admire them "simultaneous," they succeed one another in her regard. Indeed, history so far repeats itself that the heroine, rediscovering the true state of her feelings, returns to her first love. Here the story breaks off; had it been continued it is not unlikely that the second man would have been found once more in the ascendant. That this unfailing and generous devotion is practically appreciated is evident from the fact that on her departure she leaves her child in the keeping of the man who is not its father. The warm, tangible, but unworthy love of the one and the deep, undemonstrative affection of the other are well tested by this impulsive and rather empty-headed creature. The two other stories are trivial enough. "The Hour of Her Life" and "An Acquaintance Renewed" seem to have got sandwiched by mistake between better things. No matter what may be said of this series, it contains brilliantly written books, but they have a morbid touch almost without exception. Still they are notable specimens of a phase of fiction-writing that appeals to present unrest. (Roberts. $1.)— *London Literary World.*

Three Little Daughters of the Revolution.

THIS is a very attractive book, containing three of the most popular of Miss Nora Perry's stories for girls—"Dorothy," "Patty," and "Betty Boston's Fourth of July." Miss Perry's forte lay in writing stories for girls. She understood her audience perfectly—perhaps she preserved the heart of the girl throughout her life; she knew what girls are interested in; she sympathized fully with them. And having a lively imagination, humor, and a charming style, she could hardly fail to write unusually good stories for them. The unanimous verdict was that her stories were among the very best written for girls, and the tone of them was so fresh and wholesome that mothers were glad to have their daughters read them—indeed, they themselves read them with hardly less eagerness. The book is illustrated by Frank T. Merrill. (Houghton, M. & Co. 75 c.)

From "Three Little Daughters of the Revolution." Copyright, 1896, by Houghton, Mifflin & Co.

"YANKEE DOODLE."

Che Literary News.

An Eclectic Monthly Review of Current Literature.
EDITED BY A. H. LEYPOLDT.

OCTOBER, 1896.

HERMAN MELVILLE.

JUST fifty years ago a book called "Typee" introduced to readers of his day an author who for ten years held his audience spellbound

Herman Melville

Liverpool before the mast. He liked his experience and shipped on a whaler bound to the Pacific in 1841, in the great whaling days when the American flag was to be seen on every sea. In 1842 he deserted his ship, *The Marquesas*, owing to the tyranny of the captain, and fell into the hands of a warlike race inhabiting the valley of Typee in the island Nukaheva. His adventures there formed the basis of "Typee." He was rescued by a whaler as described in "Omoo," which contains a remarkably accurate description of the condition of Tahiti. In this book Melville spoke very frankly of the missionaries of the region, and his book raised much hostile comment. The hero of "Omoo" shipped for home on a whaler, but Melville really left Tahiti on the frigate *United States*, and on her found the material for "White Jacket," in which he described many abuses endured by sailors, and especially the cruel injustice of flogging as practised by hot-tempered, intoxicated captains. Besides the three novels above mentioned Melville wrote "Mardi," in 1849; "Redburn," in the same year, a plain description of his first voyage to Liverpool; "Moby Dick," in 1850; "Pierre, or, the ambiguities," in 1852; "Israel Potter," in 1855, a narrative of the real adventures of an American sailor of that name; "The Piazza Tales," in 1856, which had first appeared in *Putnam's Magazine*; and "The Confidence Man," in 1857, an entertaining story of life on the Mississippi during its golden days. After nine years of silence, spent among the Berkshire Hills, appeared a volume of poems entitled "Battle Pieces and Aspects of the War," in 1866, and ten years after, in 1876, "Clarel" was published, and with this story of the Holy Land ended the literary career of Captain Melville, although he lived until 1891. "When

while he related to them adventures of the most thrilling character, which grew in interest when it became known that their writer had lived them all himself.

Herman Melville was born in New York in 1819, and at the age of seventeen sailed to he was drawing on his own memories," says the *Springfield Republican*, in noticing the new issue of his works, "Melville was almost unsurpassable as a chronicler of sea life and adventure. The chapters on forecastle life in ' Typee ' and ' Omoo ' can hardly be equalled; ' Moby Dick ' is an unparalleled mine of information on whaling in the South Seas, and in its soberer parts is excellent literary work; ' White Jacket ' is probably the best picture extant of life before the mast in the American navy during the closing years of the old *régime* of wooden sailing vessels. It is among seafaring men, and especially among those who have visited the South Seas of which he wrote, that his reputation now stands highest. These men are able to separate fact from fancy, and are unrestrained in their admiration of the truth and vigor of his descriptions."

Readers of the present day would do well to buy and read the works of Melville, now again issued in attractive form by The American Publishers Corporation. Books are turned out so fast by the publishers to-day that it becomes more and more necessary to point out to a new generation the stories that have been enjoyed and must always be enjoyed for their lasting merit. Captain Melville was a great reader, and sometimes in later years his own fund of knowledge led him to put into the conversation of his characters words that seem unnatural; but aside from this blemish from an artistic standpoint, his writing is full of life and color and his books make real a phase of life that has passed—the days of wooden vessels and the romance of the sea before steam and iron had crowded out individuality, lonely days in hidden places in out-of-the-way islands, and hard work in storm and stress above and below decks on well-loved ships.

OCTOBER.

AGAINST the winter's heav'n of white
      the blood
Of earth runs very quick and hot to-day ;
A storm of fiery leaves are out at play
Around the lingering sunse of the wood.
Where rows of blackberries unnoticed stood,
   Run streams of ruddy color wildly gay ;
   The golden lane half dreaming picks its way
Through 'whelming vines, as through a
      gleaming flood.

O warm, outspoken earth, a little space
   Against thy beating heart my heart shall
      beat,
   A little while they twain shall bleed and
      burn,
And then the cold touch and the gray, gray
      face,
   The frozen pulse, the drifted winding sheet,
   And speechlessness, and the chill burial
      urn.

(Lamson, Wolffe & Co. $1.)—*From Wetherald's "The House of Trees."*

My Lady's Heart.

IN " My Lady's Heart," by Ellis Markoe, we have a charming little love-story, told with grace, sincerity, and artistic taste. Perverse human nature refuses to sympathize fully with the perfect hero who seems superhuman in the sense with which he struggles against temptation. He is too fully rounded in character, and we estimate our fellow-creatures by their angularities. And yet his love for the married Muriel is most delicately and humanly drawn, and Muriel herself is lovably human. The story is as a landscape seen in a midsummer haze, reality pleasantly magnified by the mist of romance. One reads it delightfully as one inhales wholesome air, and even the touch of pain is invigorating. We have been told that the world no longer holds the heroic, so much more the need then for high art to build up the heroic for our admiration and our imitation. We have had so many immoral messages dealt out to us by recent fiction, that, perhaps, this moral of "My Lady's Heart" will attract attention by its novelty : " But the time came when it brought to her only a message of peace and consolation, when she knew that her life with all its dreariness was far, far better than it could have been if, with the sweetness of love, it had known the tinge of shame. Oh, wonderful strength ! His manhood had been sufficient for her weakness. Oh. true and loyal lover ! With a mighty forgetfulness of his own happiness he had saved her from her own folly and from herself." (Roberts. $1.)—*Boston Evening Gazette.*

In Search of Truth.

VAWDER was a writer of stories. He had won, perhaps, the most distinct niche in the Temple of Fame which had yet been accorded to any of this coterie. Regarding his work, the critics said he possessed a keen insight, that he understood men and women, that his portrayals of life, of the petty follies and passions of the little human manikins who danced briefly across his pages, was exact and not fanciful. In this they were more correct than is usually the case with critics.

Vawder himself was correct. He was painstaking. His stories never left his hand until he was satisfied his characters were true types; that they talked, acted, felt, and even thought as real people would under the same circumstances—under the conditions which he pictured for their environment. Withal, he was a very rapid worker, for his material was usually well digested before he put pen to paper.

But he had been working on one thing now for a long time, and it annoyed him to have it drag so. This thing that was troubling him was a story in which he was endeavoring to show how near the danger-line a man and woman might go in the way of friendship, of platonic affection, if that term is not too badly worn, without tumbling over to the wrong side. He had been observing some of the people he knew, and had laughed softly to himself at thinking what pertinent illustrations they would afford for one side of his subject. Unfortunately, for the wrong side, for most of them seemed to have overstepped the danger-line, to have gotten already on the thither side of safety.

He was not getting just what he wanted. no matter how closely he applied his powers of observation. He could see what these people did and hear them talk, sometimes. But he reasoned that the talk which would really be the key to the situation was that which passed between each couplet of these friends alone. No third could hope to be admitted to the sanctuary of their friendship, to lay bare with the keen scalpel of the anatomist their most sacred relations. So in the nature of things he was unable to take the manuscript that he wanted from life, and he was growing a trifle moody at the thought of defeat. (Stokes. 75 c.) —*From Reeve's " Vawder's Understudy."*

without introducing something novel and original; and here in these pages we are made acquainted with a wonderful syndicate of three whose business is to act as jackals for the great speculative lions of Lothbury by scouring the world in search of openings for the investment of capital.

" In old days," said Sir Francis Rose, the leader of this dauntless three, " when a discoverer found out a new promise of wealth in some far-off region, he annexed it for his king or he sold it to his king. Now the plan," as Sir Francis pointed out in eloquent and glowing terms, " was to sell the discovery to a capitalist, or to a syndicate of capitalists, and let the capitalists annex it or exhaust it for themselves."

Everything reads pleasantly and ends pleasantly, though many readers will be inclined to think that Jim Conrad, with his five hundred a year and lazy aspirations after success in authorship, is but an idle and good-for-little hero after all, and not half worthy of the wife he wins; nor will they believe in the fulfilment of the resolution which he and his wife agree upon forming, "that he shall not live a useless life—that he shall be 'not a shadow among shadows, but a man among men.'" (Appleton. $1; 50 c.)—*London Academy.*

The Riddle Ring.

NOBODY will begrudge Mr. Justin McCarthy praise for the qualities of either industry or versatility. In the midst of his biographical and other labors he has found time to throw off, as it were, another of those delightful efforts in fiction which, whatever their theme, are pretty sure to please. "The Riddle Ring" is not a sensational story, such as we had not long ago from the same pen; no enormous fortunes are at stake, and no murderous villains figure in its pages, the worst character in this respect being only incited to an attempt at murder by a genuine bit of jealousy evoked by his own wife. Nor is it a novel of the society type; it might be more fitly described as of the hotel and private flat kind, most of the incidents occurring between a few individuals at meeting-places of that sort. The ring which furnishes its name to the book is picked up in the Bois de Boulogne by a discarded lover and broken-hearted young London clubman, Jim Conrad, who weaves a fanciful romance around the cryptographic letters engraved on its outside. Its real story becomes known to him through an acquaintance casually made at the Grand Hotel in Paris with Mrs. Morefield, her daughter Gertrude, and their friend, Miss Clelia Vine. But Mr. McCarthy never writes

In Scarlet and Grey.

THE misfortunes and sorrows of misplaced love are the theme of four out of the six stories making up the collection called *In Scarlet and Grey*, by Florence Henniker, and the same theme is dealt with in the tale entitled "The Spectre of the Real," by Thomas Hardy and Florence Henniker, bound up in the same volume. This last-named story shows unmistakably Mr. Hardy's characteristic touch, and is strongly worked out to a dramatic and irresistible conclusion. A clandestine marriage and the results that come of it supply the immediate framework of the tale, in which the personality of the three leading actors stands out with vivid intensity. Of Mrs. Henniker's own stories it can be said in all truthfulness that they exhibit a quality of imagination and technique far superior to the average run of fiction. Mrs. Henniker seems to partake fully of Mr. Hardy's views regarding the lottery of love, and she exploits them quite fearlessly, especially in the glowing and tragic tale, " At the Sign of the Startled Fawn." Mrs. Henniker's humor is admirably unfeminine, and in "A Successful Intrusion," recording the experiences of a company of pious British tourists in Rome with a clever adventurer, it attains delightful effects. (Roberts. $1.)—*The Beacon.*

REMEMBRANCE.

REMEMBRANCE has a rear and front—
'Tis something like a house;
It has a garret also
For refuse and the mouse,
Besides, the deepest cellar
That ever mason hewed;
Look to it, by its fathoms
Ourselves be not pursued.

(Roberts. $1.25.)—*From "Emily Dickinson's Poems."*

Denounced.

THE bicentennial issue of *Appletons' Town and Country Library* has come to us in a historical romance by J. Bloundelle-Burton, entitled "Denounced," and we think that lovers of good contemporaneous fiction will agree with us that the event is worthy of notice. In their *Town and Country Library*, as it is known familiarly, the Messrs. Appleton have been remarkably successful, both in preserving a good standard and in the matter of popularity. Presumably this is one of the very few efforts of the kind which have been successful for more than a few months. And we think the secret of continued success lies in the discrimination used in selecting tales that are clean, pure, and withal of interest to the average reader's intelligence; and, furthermore, to the fact that the editors have been using American stories more and more frequently. More than one well-known author owes his first success to the *Town and Country*, and that is another reason for congratulation. (Appleton. $1; pap., 50 c.) —*Mail and Express.*

An Outcast of the Islands.

"AN Outcast of the Islands," by Joseph Conrad, is one of the most remarkable novels that we have read for years, though it may not be one for which ordinary novel-readers will care much. It is a profound study of character, which is fairly described when we say that its elements are essentially base, treacherous, ungrateful, and selfish, and that the nature in whom it is embodied is apparently no more responsible for himself and his actions than a cunning reptile for its subtle noxiousness, or for its malice, which defends itself and perishes from its own poison, like the baffled scorpion from its own sting. To benefit such a creature from motives of humanity is to reveal a tenderness of feeling which is incomprehensible to him from his knowledge of himself, and of which he proceeds to take advantage, holding it and its silly possessor in contempt and hatred and as things made for his own use. which he would be worse than a fool not to use. If outcasts like this one who figures here are ever conscious of their own baseness, which is hardly probable, they are never at a loss for reasons for it, the most potent of which is generally the injustice of the world of which they are the victims, and which in self-defence they naturally resent. Villains like Iago are never without excuses for their villany, or no more without excuses than financiers of the Tweed order are for their peculations, the complacent justification of such scoundrels being wonder at their moderation and indignation at their detection. "The Outcast of the Islands" is a profound study of character, as we have said, but rather begins here, for all the subordinate characters in this dark drama are more or less of the same sinister type, and the stage itself, which is about and along the Pacific coast, is suggestive of the strange actors who skulk in its pathless forests and steal in and out of its secret rivers—Malays, Arabs, savage natives, the whole forming a phantasmal panorama of tropic growths and moral glooms. The background of barbaric life and customs before which these figures move is so marvellously drawn and colored that it is not likely to be forgotten, though the figures themselves may, perhaps, fade from the crowded gallery of contemporary characters of fiction. Mr. Conrad is a man of genius. (Appleton. $1; pap., 50 c.) —*Mail and Express.*

MY SONG.

My song I will not sell for gold;
  Nor fame nor honor'll buy it:
I sing it for myself alone,
  Or praise ye or decry it.
No master e'er hath taught the art
  Nor have I learned one feature;
The music came direct from God,
  The words were writ by Nature.

Full oft the breeze ot morning b.ars
  A page from distant regions;
I marvel when I note th-things
  Which men must learn in legions.
If rhyme be faulty, all condemn;
  And if 'tis not quite flawless,
One poet's work another blames
  With judgment far too lawless.

A foot's here missing, there a rhyme;
  Then undue flourish grieves them.
Full eagerly they strive and toil
  Until the turf receives them.
My song of solitude I sing,
  With all its many errors;
'Tis for myself and for my God:
  The critic hath no terrors.

Therefore, kind friends, strive not to teach
  Me learning's strict rules narrow;
The nightingale's notes do not ask
  From throat of northern sparrow.
Yet thanks I give for fame and praise,
  With all their fleeting glitter;
From practice as a cook, I know
  The laurel's leaf is bitter.

(Roberts. $2.)—*From "Poems" by Johanna Ambrosius.*

Survey of Current Literature.

☞ *Order through your bookseller.*—"*There is no worthier or surer pledge of the intelligence and the purity of any community than their general purchase of books ; nor is there any one who does more to further the attainment and possession of these qualities than a good bookseller.*"—PROF. DUNN.

ART, MUSIC, DRAMA.

PHIPSON, T. L. Famous violinists and fine violins: historical notes, anecdotes, and reminiscences. Scribner. 12°, *net,* $1.75.

BIOGRAPHY, CORRESPONDENCE, ETC.

DOUGLAS, ROB. B. Life and times of Madame du Barry. Scribner. 8°, *net,* $6.40.

GODWIN, PARKE. Audubon. Putnam. 16°, (Little journeys to the homes of American authors, v. 2, no. 8.) pap., 5 c.

HUTCHINSON, J. WALLACE. Story of the Hutchinsons (Tribe of Jesse); comp. and ed. by C. E. Mann; with introd. by F. Douglass. Lee & Shepard. 2 v., il. 8°, $5.
The Hutchinson family during over fifty years, from 1839 to 1892, bore an important part in the history of the country, singing for abolition, temperance, woman suffrage, and all other moral reforms. They were often mobbed, driven from large cities by pro-slavery officials, and had various exciting and strange experiences. There were thirteen members of this family of singers known to the public. They came in contact not only with the great people of this country but of Europe. Their stories are here told with a mass of interesting anecdotes and descriptive matter concerning many of the most important incidents in the life of the nation for half a century.

McCARTHY, JUSTIN. Pope Leo XIII. F. Warne & Co. 12°, (Public men of to-day ser.) $1.25.

MORLEY, J. The life of Richard Cobden. *New ed.* Macmillan. 2 v., 8°, $3.

MORLEY, J. Life of Richard Cobden. Roberts. 8°, *reduced to* $1.

O'CONNOR, T. POWER. Napoleon. Scribner. 12°, $3.

ROLFE, W. JA. Shakespeare the boy; with sketches of the home and school life, the games and sports, the manners, customs, and folk-lore of the time. Harper. il. 12°, $1.25.

SOUTHEY, ROB. Southey's life of Nelson; ed. with notes and an introd. by Edwin L. Miller. Longmans, G. 12°, (Longmans' English classics.) 75 c.

DESCRIPTION, GEOGRAPHY, TRAVEL, ETC.

FITZGERALD, E. A. Climbs in the New Zealand Alps : an account of travel and discovery; il. in photogravure and other processes by Joseph Pennell, H. G. Willink, and from photographs; with contributions by Sir W. M. Conway and others. Scribner. 8°, *net,* $7.50.

HIBBARD, G. A. Lenox, Mass.; il. by W. S. Vanderbilt Allen. Scribner. 16°, (American summer resorts ser.) 75 c.

HUTTON, LAURENCE. Literary landmarks of Venice. Harper. il. 12°, $1.

ROBERTSON, ALEX., *D.D.* Through the Dolomites, from Venice to Toblach. Scribner. il. 12°, $3.

WILCOX, WALTER DWIGHT. Camping in the Canadian Rockies; with 25 full-page photogravures and many text il. from photographs by the author. Putnam. 4°, $4.

WHYMPER, E. Travels amongst the Great Andes of the Equator. Scribner. maps, il. 8°, (Library of contemporary exploration and adventure.) $2.50.

DOMESTIC AND SOCIAL.

GUIDE to good living : a pocket dictionary of the French terms employed in cookery, confectionery, and kindred arts, and on menus or bills of fare. The Industrial Publication Co. 32°, pap., 10 c.
Gives the meaning, pronunciation, and grammatical relations of each word according to the best authorities.

HERBERT, A. KENNEY, ["Wyvern," *pseud.*] Fifty lunches. E. Arnold. 12°.

RYDER, H. P. Knickerbocker stockings for cycling and shooting : how to knit them with plain and fancy turn-over tops. Macmillan. 4°, bds., 75 c.

SANGSTER, *Mrs.* MARG. ELIZ. MUNSON. With my neighbors. Harper. 12°, $1.25.
This is a reprint of a number of articles first published either in the *Congregationalist* or the *Christian Intelligencer*. They consist of short essays on homely topics relating to every-day life, and the lessons sought to be conveyed are often illustrated by some pithy anecdote. In addition to the "talks," as the author calls these little essays, she has reprinted—by request —some of her poems.

FICTION.

BALZAC, HONORÉ DE. The lesser bourgeoisie. Roberts. 12°, hf. mor., $1.50.

BRAY, CLAUDE. The king's revenge. Appleton. 12°, (Appleton's town and country lib., no. 199.) $1; pap., 50 c.
The story is told in the first person by Aubrey de Mauleverer, the son of a poor knight, who had been faithful to the fortunes of King Edward I. The incidents have to do with the wars of the Roses between the Houses of York and Lancaster; the personal career of the hero is full of adventure and some love-making.

BUNNER, H. C. Love in old cloathes, and other stories; il. by W. T. Smedley, Orson Lowell, and Andre Castaigne. Scribner. 12°, $1.50.

BURNETT, *Mrs.* FRANCES HODGSON. That lass o' Lowrie's. [*New ed.*] Scribner. 12°, $1.25.

BURTON, J. BLOUNDELLE. Denounced : a romance. Appleton. 12°, (Appleton's town and country lib., no. 200.) $1; pap., 50 c.
The days which followed the Jacobite ris-

ing of 1745 are included in the period of this stirring historical romance. The scene alternates between France and England, the young Pretender Charles Edward being one of the characters. Life in the Bastile is well described. The events of the story result from the love of two men for the same woman. They are both followers of Charles Edward, but one goes over to the Hanoverian side, and seeks the life of the other by denouncing him while in England.

CARLETON, WILL. The old infant and similar stories. Harper. 12°, $1.25.
Contents : The old infant; The vestal virgin; Lost—two young ladies; The one-ring circus; The Christmas car; A business flirtation; Old bottle's bui glars.

FARJEON, B. LEOPOLD. The betrayal of John Fordham. Fenno. 12°, (Fenno's select ser., no. 20.) $1.25; pap., 50 c.

FREDERIC, HAROLD. March hares. Appleton. 16°, $1 25.

GUTHRIE, F. ANSTEY, ["F. Anstey," *pseud.*] The statement of Stella Maberly. Appleton. 16°, $1.25.

HARDY, T., *and* HENNIKER, FLORENCE. In scarlet and grey : stories of soldiers and others, by Florence Henniker; and The spectre of the real, by Thomas Hardy and Florence Henniker. Roberts. 16°, (Keynotes ser., no. 24.) $1.
Contents : The heart of the color sergeant; Bad and worthless; A successful intrusion; A page from a vicar's history; At the sign of the Startled Fawn; In the infirmary; The spectre of the real.

HAWKINS, ANTHONY HOPE. The heart of Princess Osra; il. Stokes. $1.50.

HOBBES, JOHN OLIVER, [Mrs. Craigie.] The herb-moon. Stokes. 12°, $1.25.

LINDSEY, W. Cinder-path tales. Copel nd & Day. 16°, $1.
Seven stories which introduce incidents of sporting life on the sprinting track are entitled: My first for money; The hollow hammer; How Kitty queered the "mile"; Paddy the leaper's probation; Atherton's last "half"; A Virginia jumper; And every one a winner.

MARKOE, ELLIS. My lady's heart: a sketch. Roberts. 16°, $1.

MEREDITH, G. Novels. Roberts. 12 v., 16°. Eng. cl., uncut, *ea. reduced to* $1.50. *Popular Amer. ed.*, 16°, *ea. reduced to* $1.

MITFORD, BERTRAM. The white shield; il. by D. Keeler. F. A. Stokes Co. 12°, $1.25.

MUNROE, KIRK. Through swamp and glade: a tale of the Seminole war; il. by Victor Perard. Scribner. 12°, $1.25.

POOL. MARIA LOUISA. In a dike shanty. Stone & Kimball. 12°, $1.25.

PORTER, D. D. Allan Dare and Robert le Diable: a romance. *New ed.* Appleton. 8°, $2.
"All wonderfully vivid, exciting, and picturesque, with enough plot and incident all ready to furnish out some half-dozen ordinary novels. It rivets the attention and holds it steadily

by its force, originality, and daring."—*Boston Saturday Evening Gazette.*

REEVE, JA. KNAPP. Vawder's understudy: a study in platonic affection; il. by Louise L. Heustis. F. A. Stokes Co. nar. 16°, (Twentieth century ser.) buckram, 75 c.

STOCKTON, FRANK R. Stories of New Jersey. Amer. Book Co. il. 12°, 80 c.

STORIES by English authors: The sea. Scribner. 16°, 75 c.
Contents : The extraordinary adventure of a chief mate, by W. Clark Russell; Quarantine Island, by Sir Walter Besant; The rock scorpions (anonymous); The master of the *Chrysolite*, by G. B. O'Halloran; *Petrel* and the *Black Swan* (anonymous); Melissa's tour, by Grant Allen; Vanderdecken's message home (anonymous).

STOWE, HARRIET BEECHER The writings of Harriet Beecher Stowe. *New Riverside edition* from new plates. Houghton, Mifflin & Co. 16 v., *ea.*, $1.50.
The minister's wooing; Agnes of Sorrento; The Pearl of Orr's Island.

WELLS, H. G. The island of Doctor Moreau: a possibility. Stone & Kimball. 16°, $1.25.

WARD, Mrs. MARY AUGUSTA, [Mrs. T. Humphry Ward.] Sir George Tressady. Macmillan. 2 v. $2.

WOTTON, MABEL E. Day-books. Roberts. 16°, (Keynotes ser., no. 25.) $1.
Four stories—" . . . . chronicles of good and evil" to quote from the title-page. Their titles are: Morrison's heir; An acquaintance renewed; The hour of her life; The fifth edition.

HISTORY.

BIDDLE, ANTHONY J. DREXEL. The Madeira Islands. Drexel Biddle & Bradley. il. 12°, $2.

BYINGTON, EZRA HOYT, *D.D.* The Puritan in England and New England: with an introd. by Alex. McKenzie, D.D. Roberts. 8°, $2.

COFFIN, VICTOR. The province of Quebec and the early American Revolution : a study in English-American colonial history. University of Wisconsin. 8°. (Bulletin of the university, economics, political science, and history ser., v. 1, no 3.) pap., 75 c.
List of the author's sources of information covers five pages—no attempt being made to furnish a complete bibliography. The main study is based almost entirely on the manuscript copies of British state papers in the Canadian archives.

GUIZOT, FRANÇOIS PIERRE GUILLAUME. General history of civilization in Europe; ed. with critical and supplementary notes by G. Wells Knight. *New issue.* Appleton. 12°, $1.50.

MARTIN, W. ALEX. PARSONS. A cycle of Cathay; or, China South and North with personal rem niscences. Revell. il. map, 12°, $2.

PARMELE, Mrs. MARY PLATT. The evolution of an empire : a brief historical sketch of the United States. W. Beverley Harison. 12°, (Evolution of empire ser., no. 4.) 75 c.
A broad outline of the history of our country from the birth of Christopher Columbus to the election of Grover Cleveland. The volume follows the previous issues of the series in dealing with conditions and results rather than details. Only leading facts are considered, so that the

student obtains a clear story of the growth of the empire of the western hemisphere.

WARD, *Mrs.* MARY ALDEN. Old Colony days. Roberts. 16°, $1.25.

LITERATURE, MISCELLANEOUS AND COLLECTED WORKS.

STEARNS, FRANK PRESTON. The real and ideal in literature. [*New issue.*] Putnam. 12°, $1.25.

Essays on: Real and ideal; Classic and romantic; Romance, humor, and realism; The modern novel; Idols; The art conscience; Herman Grimm; Emerson as a poet; A poetic autobiography; The Muller and Whitney controversy; The science of thought; also, Two sonnets and a poem and a chapter on Fred W. Loring, to whose memory the volume is dedicated. First published in 1892 by J. G. Cupples Co.

MENTAL AND MORAL.

COMPAYRÉ, GABRIEL. The intellectual and moral development of the child. Pt. I, containing the chapters on perception, emotion, memory, imagination, and consciousness; from the French by Mary E. Wilson. Appleton. 12°, (International education ser., no. 35.) $1.50.

The present volume contains the first half of the translation of the work of Prof. Gabriel Compayré, entitled *L'Evolution intellectuelle morale de l'enfant.* The object of the work is to bring together in a systematic pedagogical form what is known regarding the development of infant children so far as the facts have any bearing upon early education.

NATURE AND SCIENCE.

BREHM, ALFRED EDMUND. The animals of the world: a complete natural history for popular home instruction and for the use of schools. In 3 v. V. I, Mammalia; tr. from the *3d German ed., rev. and abr.* by R. Schmidtlein. A. N. Marquis. il. folio, $6 ; hf. mor., $7.

HOFFMAN, F. L. Race traits and tendencies of the American negro. Macmillan. 8°, (Publications of the society, v. II, nos. 1–3.) $2; pap., $1.25.

MUNRO, J. The story of electricity. Appleton. il. 16°, (Library of useful stories.) 40 c.

Contents : The electricity of friction; The electricity of chemistry; The electricity of heat; The electricity of magnetism; Electrolysis; The telegraph and telephone; Electric light and heat; Electric power; Minor uses of electricity. List of books on electricity (1 p.).

TROWBRIDGE. J. What is electricity? Appleton. 12°, (International scientific ser., no. 75.) $1.50.

"I am often asked the question, 'What is electricity?' and I have endeavored in this book to give in a popular manner the present views of scientific men in regard to this question. According to modern ideas, the continuance of all life on the earth is due to the electrical energy which we receive from the sun; and physics, in general, can be defined as that subject which treats of the transformations of energy. I have therefore presented the varied phenomena of electricity in such a manner that the reader can perceive the physicist's reasons for supposing that all space is filled with a medium that transmits electromagnetic waves to us from the sun."—*Preface.*

POETRY AND DRAMA.

CRAIGIE, W. A. A primer of Burns. Scribner. 12°, $1.

DICKINSON, EMILY. Poems; ed. by Mabel Loomis Todd. *3d ser.* Roberts. 16°, $1.25.

This third volume of Emily Dickinson's verses is put forth in response to the repeated wish of the admirers of her peculiar genius. It consists of poems often of four lines only on a page grouped under "Life," "Love," "Nature," and "Time and Eternity."

POLITICAL AND SOCIAL.

COPLEY square ser., works on economic problems. Arena Pub. Co. 8 v., 16°, pap., *ea.*, 25 c.

HOUGH, L. S. The principles of coinage and currency as applied to the late crisis, and as preventive of future ones; also setting forth a uniform basis for the money values of the world; or, true bimetallism, for the consideration of an international congress, leading financiers, and business people generally. *2d ed. enl.* L. S. Hough. 12°, pap., 25 c.

LOWRY, R. Shall the United States undertake alone the free coinage of silver at the ratio of sixteen to one? C. H. Kerr & Co. 12°, (L·b. of progress, no. 20.) pap., 25 c.

The question is answered affirmatively. *Contents:* Depression the condition that confronts us; Examination of the coinage laws of the U. S.; How the crime of 1873 was committed; Evidences of the crime; The case against the banks; Panics; Prices; The truth about Mexico, Japan, China, Russia; The case of India; The case of France; Money; The endless chain; The remedy.

ROBY, H. R. Gold and silver question at a glance: cont. valuable and desirable information for the million; with a comprehensive vocabulary and catechism of pertinent questions. Excelsior Pub. House. 32°, pap., 10 c.

A convenient little book for the sound-money man to carry in his vest-pocket. It is divided into chapters with the following headings: Hot shot for the silver camp; Mint Director Preston's explanation of 16 to 1; Free coinage catechism; Questions and answers; Vocabulary.

SPAHR, C. B. An essay on the present distribution of wealth in the United States. Crowell. 12°, (Lib. of economics and politics, no. 12.) $1.50.

Dr. Spahr's essay is written for the instruction of the instructed classes. While he presents many statistics and tables he is careful to draw from them conclusions that coincide with the common observations of common people. He claims that less than two per cent. of the families of Great Britain hold three times as much private property as all the remainder. The same concentration of wealth in the hands of a few is rapidly taking place in the United States. As to taxation he shows that the wealthy class pays less than one-tenth of the indirect taxes, the well-to-do class less than one-quarter, and the relatively poorer classes more than two-thirds. He believes that the awakened conscience of the country will demand a progressive income tax.

SPELLING, T. C. Won on a silver basis: a story founded on current politics. Hartwell, Mitchell & Willis. 16°, (The good times ser., no. 1.) pap., 25 c.

On a mere thread of a story are given statistics and arguments in favor of the free coinage of silver.

WHITE, ANDREW D. Fiat money inflation in France: how it came, what it brought, and how it ended. *New rev. ed.* Appleton. 16°, pap., 25 c.

"There is perhaps a special reason for issuing this new edition, in the fact that the principle involved in the proposed unlimited coinage of silver is, at bottom, identical with the idea which led to the fearful wreck of public and private prosperity in France. And there is an added reason in the fact that the utterances of the Chicago nominee and of the Populist platform point clearly and unmistakably to unlimited issues of paper money hereafter. . . . I have taken all pains to be exact, giving the authority for every important statement."— *From the Author's Preface.* An extract is added to this edition from Macaulay showing the results of tampering with the currency in England.

SPORTS AND AMUSEMENTS.

BRITISH (The) draughts-player: a course of studies on the principles and practice of the game of draughts (checkers); being an analysis of all the openings, with copious notes and instructions to learners and students ; by various authors. Warne. 16°, $1.50.

CHESHIRE, HORACE F., *ed.* The Hastings chess tournament, 1895. Putnam. pors. 12°, $1.75.

Contains the authorized accounts of the 230 games played at the international Chess Congress, at Hastings, England, August–September, 1895; with annotations by Pillsbury, Lasker, Tarrasch, Steinitz, Schiffers, Teichmann, Bardeleben, Blackburne, Gunsberg, Tinsley, Mason, and Albin, and biographical sketches of the 22 chess masters who contested at the tournament. Includes autographs, rules, diagrams of situations, appendix.

GROHMAN, W. A. BAILLIE. Sport in the Alps in the past and present : an account of the chase of the chamois, red-deer, bouquetin, roe-deer, capercaillie, and black-cock; with personal adventures and historical notes, and some sporting reminiscences of H. R. H., Duke of Saxe-Coburg-Gotha. Scribner. il. 8°, $5.

SACHS, EDWIN. Sleight of hand: a practice manual of legerdermain for amateurs and others. *2d enl. ed.* Scribner. 12°, $2.60.

THEOLOGY, RELIGION, AND SPECULATION.

BOWERMAN, G. FRANKLIN, *comp.* A selected bibliography of the religious denominations of the United States ; with a list of the most important Catholic works of the world as an appendix ; comp. by Rev. Jos. H. McMahon. Cathedral Library Assoc. 8°, leatherette, 75 c.

COIT, J. OWEN. The religion of manhood. Putnam. 12°, 75 c.

Short essays on religious subects ; with quotations from the poetry and prose of the best American and foreign authors.

DU BOSE, W. P. The ecumenical councils. Christian Literature Co. 8°, (Ten epochs of church history, no. 3.) $1.50.

LEA, H. C. A history of auricular confession and indulgences in the Latin church. In 3 v. V. 3. Indulgences. Lea Bros. & Co. 8°, $3.

McCRIE, C. G., *D.D.* The free church of Scotland: her ancestry, her claims, and her conflicts. Scribner. 24°, (Bible-class primers.) pap., 25 c.

MOULTON, R. GREEN, *ed.* The modern reader's Bible : a series of works from the sacred scriptures in modern literary form. V. 5, Biblical idyls ; V. 6, Genesis ; V. 7, Ecclesiastes ; ed. with introd. and notes. Macmillan. 24°, (Wisdom ser.) *ea.,* 50 c.

NEEDHAM, G. C. Shadow and substance: an exposition of the Tabernacle types. [*New issue.*] Amer. Bapt. Pub. Soc. 12°, 75 c.

NEWBOLT, *Rev.* W. C. E. The gospel of experience; or, the witness of human life to the truth of revelation; being the Boyle lectures for 1895. Longmans. 12°, $1.50.

STORY of the heavenly camp-fires ; by one with a new name. Harper. 12°, $1.25.

A thoughtful and religious speculation concerning existence in heaven ; the speaking characters are largely chosen from the well-known names of history, such as Dante, Milton, Cromwell, King Alfred, Gustavus Adolphus, Bunyan, etc. These spirits gather about the "heavenly camp-fires" and discuss the various religious, moral, and ethical questions that have interested them during their former terrestrial existence. All these discussions are carried on in a pious, devout, and philosophical strain which presents the abstruse speculation in a form that is at once simple and comprehensive.

USHER, E. P. Protestantism: a study in the direction of religious truth and Christian unity. Lee & Shepard. 8°, $1.50.

An answer to the question, "What is the Christian religion?" The author is a Harvard graduate, who has given his leisure time for nearly fifteen years to the preparation of the work. Christianity is set forth not as sacramental or theological or hierarchical, but as purely ethical and spiritual. The author believes Christianity rightly understood is the final religion of mankind, but that it has been perverted so that it exists to-day in conventional form, of which the various churches are visible expression; the churches, he believes, stand in a large measure in the way of real Christianity.

Books for the Young.

BROOKS, ELBRIDGE S. Under the Tamaracks; or, a summer with General Grant at the Thousand Islands. Penn Pub. Co. il. 12°, $1.25.

A story for boys and girls. It represents a summer's outing of young people among the Thousand Islands. It is timed to include the visit of General Grant at Alexandria Bay, and space is devoted to illustration of the great general's character.

REID, T. MAYNE. The boy hunter; or, adventures in search of a white buffalo. *Nimrod ed.* Putnam. il. 12°, $1.25.

REID, T. MAYNE. The bush boys; or, the history and adventures of a Cape farmer in the wild karoos of Southern Africa. *Nimrod ed.* Putnam. il. 12°, $1.25.

In the October Magazines.

The Arena opens its current number with an article on the engrossing subject of the hour, "Silver—A Money Metal," by U. S. Senator J. T. Morgan. Other articles are "Municipal Reform," by Wm. Howe Tolman, "Dual Suffrage," by Mrs. E. O. Norton, and "Free Silver *vs.* Free Gold," by Prof. Frank Parsons.

The Atlantic Monthly for October contains "Five American Contributions to Civilization," by Prof. C. W. Eliot, viz.: The practice of arbitration, the increase of religious toleration, the safe development of manhood suffrage, the proof that people of a variety of nations are fit for political freedom, and fifth, the diffusion of well-being among the population in general. "The Political Menace of the Discontented" is a study of the campaign and some of its deeper social meanings. Agnes Repplier contributes "Cakes and Ale," a study in older English literature.

The Catholic World begins its sixty-fourth volume with the October issue. The opening article is by Bishop Chatard, entitled "Pius VI. and the French Directory." Henry Austin Adams has the first of a series of papers the title of which is "Pillars of Salt." Other papers are "Development, not Evolution," by Alex. McDonald; "The Housing of the People in Great Cities," a social science article dealing with the important question of house-rents; and the first set of a series of brief biographical sketches of Catholic authors with their portraits.

The Century contains "A Study of Mental Epidemics," by Boris Sidis, who explains the theory of mental suggestion or hypnotism by which susceptible people give themselves up to a popular delusion. The Hon. G. W. Julian writes on John P. Hale, "A Presidential Candidate of 1852." Mme. Blanccon tributes a paper "About French Children," noting the differences between their characteristics and those of English and American children. It is profusely illustrated. Short stories in an amusing vein are "A Little Fool," by Agnes Blake Poor, and "Sonny 'Keepin' Company," by Rut McEnery Stuar. The third paper from the journals of the late E. J. Glave appears with the title "Glave in the Heart of Afric ."

The Chautauquan contains two important papers bearing on the great political question of the day, "The Free Coinage of Silver," by Gen. James B. Weaver, and "The Single Gold Standard," by Prof. W. G. Sumner, of Yale University. Of literary interest is the paper of Prof. W. M. Baskerville on "Joel Chandler Harris," the famous writer of negro dialect.

In the October *Forum* will be found a noteworthy article by Ex-President Harrison on the silver question. "Free Coinage and the Farmer" is from the pen of Hon. John M. Stahl. Prof. Thos. Davidson has contributed a timely article on "The Creed of the Sultan: its future." Having spent two years in the East, his opinions should have much force. Edmond de Goncourt is the subject of an appreciative paper by Henri Frantz, a well-known Parisian editor. An entertaining article entitled "Princeton College and Patriotism" is by Prof. Hibben, of Princeton.

THE October issue of *Godey's Magazine* contains the first chapter of a short life of Benjamin Franklin, by George C. Lay. In this number he treats of "Franklin the Apprentice, the Printer, and the Philosopher," in a very readable manner. "The Present Campaign in Cartoon" reflects in newspaper pictures the political sentiment throughout the country.

Harper's Magazine has the opening chapters of a new novel by George Du Maurier entitled "The Martian," with five illustrations by the author. The most important article is on "Electricity," the 12th of *Great American Industries*, edited by R. R. Bowker; it is profusely illustrated and will be read with interest. Other papers are "The Blue Quail of the Cactus," by Fred. Remington, "A Recovered Chapter in American History," by Walter Clark, and short stories by Octave Thanet, Ruth McEnery Stuart, Zoe D. Underhill, Martha McCulloch-Williams, and Sarah Barnwell Elliott.

THE novel of the October number of *Lippincott's* is by Edward S. Van Zile, with the title "The Crown Prince of Rexania." It contains in addition "The Last Resort in Art," by Ellen Olney Kirk; "Russian Girls and Boys at School," by Isabel F. Hapgood; a descriptive article of "The Quays of Paris," by A. F. Sanborn, and the usual short stories.

Scribner's Magazine is strong in American subjects of immediate interest, including in its contents a powerful and satirical essay by E. L. Godkin on "The Expenditure of Rich Men"; "The Government of Greater New York," by Col. F. V. Greene; a paper on the way in which "The New York Working-Girl" has organized to take care of herself, by Mary Gay Humphreys, with illustrations from life. "Siena—the City of the Virgin," by E. H. and E. W. Blashfield, is the opening article, and illustrated by one of the authors.

Freshest News.

THE HOME PUBLISHING CO. have just issued "Her Foreign Conquest," another of Col. Richard Henry Savage's stirring novels of fashionable life. It opens at Homburg during the height of the season of 1893. Tourists from all parts of the world are gathered there. A typical self-made American and his friends and relatives are the chief characters. Col. Savage never gives attractive pictures of the world's four hundred, and the usual note of pessimism as regards true virtue in high places runs through his latest book. But there is no denying his talent as a story-teller, and to those who have spent summers among the "sights" of Germany the book will recall some happy days and hours. They have also ready "The Love Adventures of Al-Mansur," a choice selection of charming Persian tales with original illustrations, edited by Archibald Clavering Gunter, very neatly bound in currant cloth, with gold dies.

THE PETER PAUL BOOK COMPANY recently published "The Man Who Became a Savage," a cheery story by William T. Hornaday, with illustrations by Charles B. Hudson, which in the crowding one upon the other of new, newer, and newest books has not yet had a chance to get at the popularity its contents merit. Mr. W. T. Hornaday is also in luck on the other side of the water with his "Man Who Became a Savage." Messrs. Kegan Paul, Trench, Trübier & Co. have secured the copyright of the novel for Great Britain and the British colonies on terms that are very liberal to the author, and the first English edition will soon appear. It is said to be the settled policy of that house to publish no novels save those which they consider to possess unusual merit and interest, and it will be interesting to see how the English public receives a novel so intensely American throughout as is "The Man Who Became a Savage." In anticipation of a large sale the London publishers will print the book from their own plates. To be approved of in England is still a rare tribute for American authors.

THE NEW AMSTERDAM BOOK COMPANY announce "Nephelé," a mystical music-novel, by Francis William Bourdillon, author of the charming song, "The Night Has a Thousand Eves and the Day but One." The Glasgow *Herald* says: "Bourdillon's story is a beautiful prose poem, of which the transcendental or allegorical meaning will come with especial force and charm to the skilled musician. But no one, whether musical or not, can read it without being thrilled through and through by its weird and delicate suggestions Nephelé is a real woman and the hero a real man, who meet for the first time in the world of trance, which the modern world has agreed to call

telepathic feeling. It is in the region of music that the simple tragedy is laid. The event on which the story is founded may be impossible, but the author has made a most natural story. Mr. Bourdillon believes in the higher meanings and significance of music with a faith that is absolute, and he manages to proselyte the least musical of his readers.

THE CENTURY CO. have prepared a most interesting set of books for the fall and holiday season, all of which may now be found at the book-stores. The holiday books will be mentioned in later issues. They include some fascinating juveniles. Among the books of interest at all times are "Impressions of South Africa," by James Bryce; "American Highways," by Prof. N. S. Shaler; "Quotations for Occasions," a collection of about 1500 clever and appropriate quotations for use on dinner menus, invitations, concert programmes. etc. "Daphne," the libretto of a comic opera, by Marguerite Merington, author of Mr. Sothern's play, "Captain Letterblair"; and "Without Prejudice," by I. Zangwill, a collection of satirical essays on men, women, and books, written with a trenchant pen. In fiction the new books include "The Metropolitans," a novel of New York society, by Jeanie Drake; "Gold," a Dutch-Indian novel, by Annie Linden; "Stories of a Sanctified Town," the religious experiences of a Kentucky community; and "Sonny," a book of stories, by Ruth McEnery Stuart, having a continuous thread of narrative.

D. APPLETON & CO.'S NEW BOOKS.

Genius and Degeneration.

A Study in Psychology. By Dr. WILLIAM HIRSCH. With a Preface by Prof. Dr. E. Mendel. Translated from the second edition of the German work. Uniform with "Degeneration." Large 8vo, cloth, $3.50.

Dr. Hirsch's acute and suggestive study of modern tendencies was begun before "Degeneration" was published, with the purpose of presenting entirely opposite deductions and conclusions. The appearance of Dr. Nordau's famous book, with its criticisms upon Dr. Hirsch's position, enabled the latter to extend the scope of his work, which becomes a scientific answer to Dr. Nordau, although this was not its specific purpose originally. Dr. Nordau has startled the reading world by his cry of "Degeneration"; Dr. Hirsch opposes his conclusions by demonstrating the difference between "Genius" and "Degeneration," and analyzing the social, literary, and artistic manifestations of the day dispassionately and with a wealth of suggestive illustrations. In a brilliant explanation of the psychology of genius he shows that Lombroso and Nordau make no distinction between scientific genius based upon hard work and artistic genius; nor between ge ius and talent. He points to Goethe as an example of a perfectly developed genius. He answers specifically Nordau's claim that this is an age of hysterical disorder, and after an extended, bril iant, and informing discussion of Art and Insanity, in which he shows himself a confirmed Wagnerian, he summarizes his conclusions by absolutely declining to accept Nordau's point of view. It is safe to say that the book is one which must be read by every reader of Nordau, and should be read by every intelligent person who wishes to understand the spirit of his time and the lessons which history teach the psychologist.

General History of Civilization in Europe.

By FRANÇOIS PIERRE GUILLAUME GUIZOT. Edited, with Critical and Supplementary Notes, by George Wells Knight, Ph.D., Professor of History and Political Science in Ohio State University. *New revised edition.* 12mo, cloth, $1.50.

This work has been a source of inspiration to historical students, teachers, and writers for more than half a century. It is to-day as inspiring to the student as when the lectures were first delivered. The object in the preparation of this edition has been, without changing the original form of the lectures, to adapt the work more exactly to the needs of college and university classes to day.

Fiat Money Inflation in France.

How it Came, What it Brought, and How it Ended. By ANDREW D. WHITE, LL.D. (Yale), L.H.D. (Columbia), Ph.Dr. (Jena), late President and Professor of History at Cornell University. To which is added an extract from Macaulay showing the results of tampering with the currency in England. 12mo, paper, 25 cents.

The Statement of Stella Maberly.

By F. ANSTEY, author of "Vice Versa," "The Giant's Robe," etc. 16mo, special binding, $1.25.

Mr. Anstey's original and impressive story has called from the *London Bookman* the comment that Hawthorne or Poe might have chosen such a theme; while the *London Times*, in speaking of this "very noteworthy" novel has said, "There is something approaching genius in the hallucination which makes the fantastical impress us like the real."

What Is Electricity?

By JOHN TROWBRIDGE, S.D., Rumford Professor and Lecturer on the Applications of Science to the Useful Arts, Harvard University. Vol. 76, International Scientific Series. Illustrated. 12mo, cloth, $1.50.

"I am often asked, 'Where can one find a popular account of the views of scientific men in regard to the question, "What is Electricity?"' and, from my inability to recommend any treatise which answers this question, I have endeavored to explain in a popular manner the electromagnetic theory of light and heat; and I have devoted much attention to the subject of periodic currents and electric waves. The answer to the question 'What is Electricity?' must be sought in the study of transformations of energy, and in a consideration of the various hypotheses of movements in the ether or medium surrounding us. The modern applications of electricity illustrate in a peculiarly suggestive manner the great subject of the transformation of energy, and I have endeavored to simplify forms of apparatus and methods of exhibiting new phenomena so that the apparatus and the methods should be within the reach of the ordinary demonstrator. The reader of the treatise will perceive that the attention of the scientific investigator in electricity is now being devoted more than ever to the medium surrounding a wire carrying a current of electricity rather than to the wire."—*From a Note by the Author.*

When William IV. was King.

By JOHN ASHTON, author of "Social Life in the Reign of Queen Anne," etc. With 47 illustrations. 8vo, cloth, $3.50.

In this entertaining volume of social and political history and personal anecdotes Mr. Ashton sketches the manners and customs of the time when the first passenger railway was opened and steam navigation began to be general. Like a modern Pepys, although not a contemporary of his characters, he sketches the subjects of interest in the reign of the sailor king, pictures the social aspects, and introduces us to the notable personages of a most interesting time.

SECOND EDITION.

March Hares.

By HAROLD FREDERIC, author of "The Damnation of Theron Ware," "In the Valley," etc. 16mo, cloth, special binding, $1.25.

"One of the most cheerful novels we have chanced upon for many a day. It has much of the rapidity and vigor of a smartly written farce with a pervading freshness a smartly written farce rarely possesses. . . . A book decidedly worth reading."—*London Saturday Review.*

The Idol-Maker.

By ADELINE SERGEANT, author of "Out of Due Season," "The Mistress of Quest," etc. No. 202, Town and Country Library. 12mo, paper, 50 cents ; cloth, $1.00.

In this strong story, one of the best that the popular author has given us, she presents a character new to most readers of fiction, who provides the title for a book distinguished throughout by sustained force and interest.

A Court Intrigue.

By BASIL THOMPSON. No. 201, Town and Country Library. 12mo, paper, 50 cents ; cloth, $1.00.

In this striking and original story there are adventures as strange as those which happened at Zenda, and there is a constant maintenance of lively interest until the unexpected *dénouement* is reached.

FOR SALE BY ALL BOOKSELLERS.

D. APPLETON & CO., 72 Fifth Avenue, N. Y.

SOME SEPTEMBER BOOKS.

EMILY DICKINSON'S POEMS. Third Series.

Edited by MABEL LOOMIS TODD. 16mo, cloth, uniform with First and Second Series, $1.25 ; white and gold, $1.50.

"The intellectual activity of Emily Dickinson was so great that a large and characteristic choice is still possible among her literary material."—*Introduction.*

MODERN FRENCH LITERATURE.

By BENJAMIN W. WELLS, Ph.D., author of "Modern German Literature." 12mo, cloth, $1.50.

"Dr. Wells brings to his work a clear vision, sound thought, and careful study, and a love for the subject that makes everything fresh and refreshing."—*Springfield Republican.*

POEMS BY JOHANNA AMBROSIUS.

Translated from the Twenty-sixth German Edition by MARY J. SAFFORD. Portrait. 16mo, cloth, $1.50.

"How she acquired the exquisite literary style she possesses will not be explained this side of the hereafter."—*Philadelphia Telegraph.*

NEW VOLUMES IN THE KEYNOTES SERIES.

16mo, cloth, $1.00 each.

DAY-BOOKS. Chronicles of Good and Evil. By MABEL E. WOTTON.

IN SCARLET AND GREY. Stories of Soldiers and Others. By FLORENCE HENNIKER; with

THE SPECTRE OF THE REAL. By THOMAS HARDY and FLORENCE HENNIKER.

UGLY IDOL. By CLAUDE NICHOLSON.

THE WORLD BEAUTIFUL. Second Series.

By LILIAN WHITING, author of "The World Beautiful" and "From Dreamland Sent." 16mo, cloth, $1.00 ; white and gold, $1.25.

THE PURITAN IN ENGLAND AND NEW ENGLAND.

By EZRA HOYT BYINGTON, D.D., Member of the American Society of Church History. With an Introduction by ALEXANDER MCKENZIE, D.D., Minister of the First Church in Cambridge, U. S. A. Three illustrations. 8vo, cloth, $2.00.

OLD COLONY DAYS.

By MAY ALDEN WARD, author of "Dante," "Petrarch," etc. 16mo, cloth, $1.25.

MY LADY'S HEART.

A Story. By ELLIS MARKOE. 16mo, cloth, $1.00.

A charming, romantic little love-story, written with rare simplicity and grace.

NUGÆ LITTERARIÆ ;

OR, BRIEF ESSAYS ON LITERARY, SOCIAL, AND OTHER THEMES. By WILLIAM MATTHEWS, author of "Getting On in the World," etc. 12mo, cloth, $1.50.

A REDUCTION IN PRICE.

GEORGE MEREDITH'S NOVELS.

"Mr. George Meredith is the greatest English novelist living : he is probably the greatest novelist of our time. He is a man of genius, a literary artist, and a truly great writer."—*The Beacon.*

The Ordeal of Richard Feverel.	The Shaving of Shagpat and Farina	Rhoda Fleming.
Evan Harrington.	Sandra Belloni.	The Egoist.
Harry Richmond.	Vittoria.	One of our Conquerors.
Diana of the Crossways.	Beauchamp's Career.	The Tragic Comedians.

Twelve uniform volumes. English cloth, uncut, reduced to $1.50 each. Popular American edition, 16mo, cloth, reduced to $1.00 each.

The above volumes, published with the author's sanction, include his earliest and best-known books, and are printed as originally written, without mutilation.

THE LIFE OF RICHARD COBDEN.

By JOHN MORLEY. With steel portrait. 8vo, cloth, 655 pages, reduced from $3.00 to $1.00.

"Mr. Trevelyan's 'Life of Macaulay' is very properly regarded as one of the best biographies dealing with the present century that have lately been written ; but Mr. Morley's 'Life of Cobden' is superior to it. He has written not only a very honest and very able memoir of Cobden, but also a valuable contribution to contemporary history and to the study of contemporary politics."—*London Athenæum.*

FOR SALE BY ALL BOOKSELLERS.

ROBERTS BROTHERS, Publishers, Boston.

Campaign Literature.

AMERICAN ACADEMY OF POLITICAL AND SOCIAL SCIENCE, Philadelphia.

Woodford (A. B.). **Use of Silver as Money in the U. S.** An Historical Sketch. 50 cents.

Ross (E. A.). **Standard of Deferred Payments.** 15 cents.

Molesworth (Sir G. L.). **Indian Currency.** 35 cents.

Smith (J. A.). **Multiple Money Standard.** 50 cents.

Special list ready of books on political topics.

D. APPLETON & CO., New York.

Adams (H. G.). **Public Debts.** $2.00.

Jevons (W. S.). **Money and the Mechanism of Exchange.** $1.75

Laughlin (J. L.). **History of Bimetallism in the United States.** New edition. '96. $2.25.

McPherson (L. G.). **Monetary and Banking Problem.** '96. $1.00.

Taussig (F. W:). **Wages and Capital.** '96. $1.50

Wells (D: A.). **Recent Economic Changes.** $2.00.

White (A. D.). **Fiat Money Inflation in France.** New edition. 25 cents.

HENRY CAREY BAIRD & CO., Philadelphia.

Economic Books, including the writings of Henry C. Carey and Henry Carey Baird, opposing the single gold standard. Catalogue free.

CHAS. E BROWN & CO., Boston.

Green. **Are We Losing the West?** 10 cents.

Osgood (W: N.). **Bug vs. Bug** (both sides of the silver question). ['95] 50 cents; 25 cents.

Shaw. **Socialism**—Fabian Essays. 75 cents.

THE CENTURY CO., New York.

Cheap Money Experiments. New and Revised edition. 5 cents a copy; $3.50 a hundred. Cloth edition, 75 cents a copy.

ROBERT CLARKE CO., Cincinnati.

Horton (S. D.). **Silver and Gold and Their Relation to the Problem of Resumption.** New ed. '95. $1.50.

T. Y. CROWELL & CO., New York.

Ely (R. T.). **Problems of To-Day.** $1.50.

—— **Taxation in American States and Cities.** $1.75.

Howe (F. C.). **Taxation and Taxes in the United States Under the Internal Revenue System.** $1.75.

Kinley (David). **Independent Treasury System of the United States.** $1.50.

Salter (Wm. M.). **Anarchy or Government?** 75 cents.

Scott (W. A.). **Repudiation of State Debts in the U. S.** $1.50.

Spahr (C. B.). **Present Distribution of Wealth in the United States.** $1.50.

Weyl (W. E.), and others. **Equitable Taxation.** 75 cents.

DERBY & MILLER COMPANY, New York.

"Common Sense Library, No. 2," **Bryan, Sewall, and Honest Money.** Up to date. '96. 25 cents.

ECONOMIC PUB. AG., Box 255, Washington, D. C.

Peters (E. T.). **Monetary Standard.** '95. 10 cents in cash or postage stamps.

FUNK & WAGNALLS CO., New York.

Waldron (G. B.). **Currency and Wealth.** '96. 50 cents.

GINN & CO., Boston.

White (Horace). **Money and Banking.** '96. Popular ed. 50 cents.

HARTFORD SEMINARY PRESS, Hartford, Conn.

Andrews (E. B:). **Wealth and Moral Law.** '94. Cloth, $1.00 ; paper, 50 cents.

HENRY HOLT & CO., New York.

Walker's Bimetallism. 12mo, $1.25.

—— **Money.** 12mo, $2.00.

—— **Money, Trade, and Industry.** 12mo, $1.25.

—— **Political Economy.** Elementary Course. 12mo, *net*, $1.00.

Sumner's American Currency. $3.00.

INDUSTRIAL PUBLICATION CO., New York.

Phin (J.). **Pocket Dictionary of Monetary and Coinage Terms.** Facts and Figures for Both Sides. '96. 10 cents.

—— **Common Sense Currency:** a Practical Treatise on Money in Its Relations to National Wealth and Prosperity. '94. $1.00.

CHARLES H. KERR & CO., Chicago.

Del Mar (Alexander). **A History of Monetary Systems.** '95. $2 00.

Smith (Dr. W. H.). **The Effects of the Gold Standard.** '96. 25 cents.

LITTLE, BROWN & CO., Boston.

Jackson (Charles C.). **Has Gold Appreciated?** 8vo. paper, 25 cents.

LONGMANS, GREEN & CO., New York.

Bagehot (W.). **English and American Money.** 75 cents.

Brassey (T:, Baron). **Work and Wages.** $1.75.

Follett. **Speaker of the House of Representatives.** $1.75.

Hart (A. B.). **Practical Essays on American Government.** $1.50.

Jordan. **Standard of Value.** $2.00.

Macleod (H: D.). **Theory of Credit.** Vol 1, $3.50; vol. 2, parts 1 and 2, each, $3.50.

—— **Bimetallism.** $1.75.

Norton (C: L.). **Political Americanisms.** $1.00.

Thompson (D. G.). **Politics in a Democracy.** $1.25.

LOTHROP PUBLISHING CO., Boston.

Upton (Hon. J. K.). **Money in Politics.** 222 pages, 12mo, paper, 50 cents; cloth, $1.25.

JOHN JOS. McVEY, Philadelphia.

Preston (Hon. Robert E.). **History of the Monetary Legislation and of the Currency System of the U. S.** '96. Paper, 25 cents; cloth, 50 cents.

J. S. OGILVIE CO., New York.

Ogilvie (J: S.). **Life and Speeches of McKinley and Hobart.** '96. Cloth, $1.00; 25 cents.

—— **Life and Speeches of Bryan and Sewall.** '96. Cloth, $1.00; paper, 25 cents.

Thorpe (T: M.). **What Is Money?** Popular Remedies for Popular Ills. '96. 25 cents.

White (Horace). **Coin's Financial Fool;** or, The Artful Dodger Exposed. ['95.] 25 cents.

OPEN COURT PUB. CO., Chicago.

Carus (P.). **Nature of the State.** '94. 15 cents.

Trumbull (M. M.). **Wheelbarrow, Articles and Discussions on Currency and the Labor Question.** Cloth, $1.00; paper, 35 cents.

—— **Free Trade Struggle in England.** Cloth, $1.00 ; paper, 25 cents.

—— **Earl Grey on Reciprocity and Civil Service Reform.** Paper, 10 cents.

G. P. PUTNAM'S SONS, New York.

Atkinson (E:). **Taxation and Work.** '92. $1.25.

Brough (W:). **Natural Law of Money:** Successive Steps in the Growth of Money. '94. $1.00.

Carroll (E:). **Principles and Practice of Finance.** $1.75.

Conant (C: A.). **Modern Banks of Issue.** '96. $3.00.

Ehrich (L. R.). **Question of Silver.** Revised ed. '96. Cloth, 75 cents; paper, 40 cents.

LITERARY NEWS

AN ECLECTIC REVIEW OF
CURRENT LITERATURE
~ILLUSTRATED~

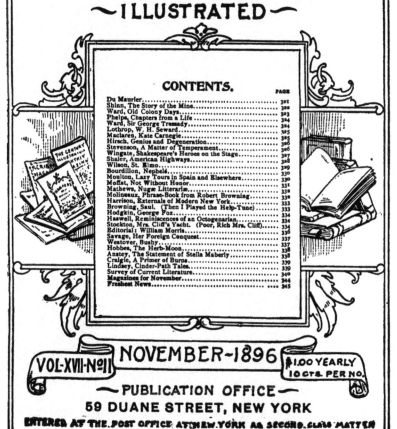

CONTENTS.

NOVEMBER~1896

VOL·XVII·Nº11

$1.00 YEARLY
10 CTS. PER NO.

~PUBLICATION OFFICE~
59 DUANE STREET, NEW YORK

ENTERED AT THE POST OFFICE AT NEW YORK AS SECOND-CLASS MATTER

The Literary News

In winter you may reade them, ab ignem, by the fireside; and in summer, ab umbram, under some shadie tree, and therewith pass away the tedious howres.

Vol. XVII.   NOVEMBER, 1896.   No. 11.

Du Maurier.

GEORGE DU MAURIER, the artist and novelist, died on the morning of October 8 at his London home.   Never strong, and troubled all his life with an affection of the eyes which made him dread a blind old age, Du Maurier's chief characteristic w a s energy. To the very end of his last illness, an affection of the heart brought about by an attack of pneumonia, he was able to converse with his friends about his work, and he confided to them that he had planned several new works of fiction. Du Maurier's death has caused widespread sorrow. He was a strong personality, and his active interest in life, in art, and in humanity was visible in every feature.

It is by his novels "Peter Ibbetson," "Trilby," and "The Martian," now running in *Harper's Magazine*, that Du Maurier became popular in America, but his chief and enduring reputation has rested and will rest upon his work as an artist.

George Louis Pamela Busson Du Maurier, for that was his full name, was born in Paris, March 6, 1834. His grandfather was one of the minor nobility of the province of Anjou, a manufacturer of glass—a trade which was reserved to the gentry in France at that time. Du Maurier's father was born in England, whither his grandfather had fled from France to escape the guillotine. His grandfather returned to France in 1816, and died as a schoolmaster at Tours. Du Maurier's father recovered the ancestral glass-works and married an English woman in Paris, where he

From Harper's Magazine.   Copyright, 1896, by Harper & Brothers.
DU MAURIER.

lived as a small *rentier*. Du Maurier's father and mother are idealized as the parents of the hero in "Peter Ibbetson," and it is a fact that the elder Du Maurier had an extremely fine voice, which would doubtless have won him fame and fortune had not family prejudices prevented him from going upon the stage. Du Maurier himself desired to study music but his father discouraged him, and was more pleased with an early proficiency the son showed in drawing.

Du Maurier's father died in 1856, having lived for some time in England. Du Maurier and his mother returned to France, and he first studied art in Glayre's studio, which he has described in "Trilby." "From Paris I passed to Antwerp," Du Maurier has told us, "where I met with a serious accident, which entirely deprived me of the sight of one eye, and for fifteen years I was only allowed to work two hours a day. I began to draw pictures for English magazines in 1860, illustrating *Once a Week*, and sending now and again to *Punch*. In 1864, a few days after Leech's death, I sat down to my first *Punch* dinner, and was formally enrolled a member of the staff. I got my cue from Mark Lemon, who was editor when I joined. 'Don't do funny things,' said Lemon ; 'do the graceful side of life ; be the tenor in *Punch's* opera-bouffe.'" Acting upon this cue of his genial chief, Du Maurier speedily made a name for himself. From that time up to the beginning of his fatal illness his drawings gave a stamp and character to *Punch*. His studies of contemporary life were always apt and amusing. They were regarded as mirrors of the times, particularly as they portrayed drawing-room life, and the legends which accompanied the pictures had a graceful, satirical style which foreshadowed in a way the success Du Maurier was afterwards to make in literature.

A writer in *The Tribune* says : " He is true to nature, always. You may find in English society the prototypes of his Sir Gorgias Middas, his Duchess of Towers, his Postlethwaite, and Mrs. Cimabue Brown. He is a close observer and a most accomplished draughtsman. With his clear and artistic vision and his admirable technique he has told the truth about the objects of his satire. But he has also thrown over them the mantle of his own individuality, he has kept himself invariably between his public and his personages, without disturbing the one or doing injustice to the other."

He was, excepting Sir John Tenniel, the best of the famous caricaturists of *Punch*, and this school of caricature, as well as his own peculiar school of literature, will perish with him. Nowhere will he be more missed than in the office of *Punch.*

Literary work came from Du Maurier late in life. This is not the time or place to discuss his ultimate place in the world of authorship. It is sufficient to refer to the extraordinary popularity of his stories. "Peter Ibbetson," his first novel, published in 1891, was a surprise to those who had not suspected his literary capacities, and his " Trilby," as everybody knows, commanded an enormous sale, and in its dramatic form is still filling theatres on both sides of the Atlantic. The novel elicited the most widespread criticism and this was collected by the N. Y. *Critic*, of November 17, 1895, and afterwards published in book form under the title " Trilbyana."

A very excellent criticism of " Trilby " appeared in the *Westminster Review* for October, written by Mary Gilliland Husband. It is said that of no publication issued in this country, except Hawthorne's " Scarlet Letter " and Mrs. Stowe's " Uncle Tom's Cabin," have so many copies been sold as of " Trilby." It even outran " Ben-Hur," the other wonderfully successful book published by the Harpers. An extended review of Du Maurier's works as an artist and novelist appeared also in the New York *Tribune* of October 4.

Du Maurier died when his fame was greatest, and the regret of his readers that he should not have lived longer to enjoy the fortune which came to him late in life is unfeigned and general.

The Story of the Mine.

In accordance with the plan of the *Story of the West Series* for the presentation of the characteristic phases and types offered by the evolution of the real West—the great country lying for the most part beyond the Missouri—Mr. Shinn, out of a singularly complete personal knowledge, tells in this volume "The Story of the Mine." Like Mr. Grinnell, in his " Story of the Indian," Mr. Shinn does not aim at a comprehensive history, but he illuminates its salient points. There are allusions in his pages which afford glimpses into this romantic and varied history from the Toltec legends, the Aztec discoveries, the fierce treasure hunts of the Spaniards, the desultory quests of later Anglo-Saxons, the epoch-making event at Sutter's Mill, the development of the great Comstock lode, and the feverish searching from the Sierra Madre to Alaska, which at one time and another has brought before the world the gold fields of Idaho or the blanket deposits of Tombstone, the rich silver ores of Leadville or the wealth of Butte and Helena, the placers of California, or the silver of Cripple Creek. These glimpses show us the figures of the prospector and the miner, types different yet still closely related despite the vast modern changes in conditions and methods. By dwelling particularly upon the life history of one great lode Mr. Shinn has succeeded in bringing these figures out in clear relief, and also in presenting some of the more significant aspects of the evolution of the mining industry. It is not easy for one who has camped with eager prospectors, who has followed the miner's candle through dark galleries, and has seen the sharp contrasts of mining life, to introduce such a narrative as this without emphasizing, perhaps unduly, its romantic interest. That interest is constant, but there is also the interest belonging rightfully to a great industry which energy and science have developed to a high point of perfection. Nowhere else on this continent has this development been better illustrated than on the Comstock lode. Nowhere else could the author have found a happier means of exemplifying the entire range of mining life.

The picture of this life drawn by Mr. Shinn is of lasting as well as timely interest. He has not written to advocate any theory, nor to deal with any special issue. He has simply told the actual story, and it is such writing which is needed for a better understanding of the conditions met with and the splendid energy and resourcefulness displayed in the building of our West. Within the last few years expansion westward has been checked and the reaction has brought problems which may seem serious, though no true American can be doubtful as to the ultimate destiny of our country. Many of the typical figures of Western development have passed, and their preservation as historical types is the object of this series. The miner, though transformed in many ways, is a figure of the present as well as the past, and in presenting him and his work in this volume Mr. Shinn has not only contributed to American history something of lasting value but he has also furnished for those who sometimes read between the lines another reason for pride in the qualities which have conquered this continent and an aid to the understanding and sympathy which make for a perfect national unity. (Appleton. $1.50.)—*From Preface to "The Story of the Mine."*

Old Colony Days.

THERE is of late much delving among old manuscripts and family papers, not yet corrupted by the moth and rust of time and neglect, for details concerning the personality of different ones among the little band of pioneers whose story in its general outline is so well known to us. "This," says the New York *Times*, "has brought old journals and letters before the eyes of the public, familiarized them with the daily life of those who sowed seed from which we have reaped a curious harvest, and has very appreciably vivified the general impression gathered from school histories of wooden Pilgrims who resembled nothing so much as the Shem, Ham, and Japhet of an old-fashioned Noah's ark.

"The latest of these humanizing volumes is in some respects the best of all that have come to our notice. Mrs. Ward has the historian's instinct, and gives her facts without feeling the necessity of breaking into ejaculations over their picturesqueness. Her good training as a writer tells as training always ought to tell, and her five papers on subjects connected with our Colonial history are written in a style both reticent and lively.

From "The Story of the Mine."   Copyright, 1896, by D. Appleton & Co.

THE BOTTOM OF A SHAFT.

"Those amazing ancestors of our Yankee race, so superb in their heroism, so absurd—so unlike ourselves, that is—in their strained conventions, may well remind us that the soil on which we rear our monuments was first broken by men who were not afraid of perishing by starvation that their consciences might be fed.

"This book consists of five admirably-written sketches of prominent figures in old New England history strongly outlined on the dark background of the seventeenth century." "The author, Mrs. Ward, is a direct descendant of the Pilgrims," says *The Boston Gazette*, "her research has been careful and thorough, and she writes with an enthusiasm that excites and holds the interest of the reader." (Roberts. $1.25.)

Chapters from a Life.

THIS is a remarkably attractive book of biographical and literary interest. Miss Phelps tells with more or less fulness of her girlhood in the beautiful town of Andover, and of the impression made upon her by the theological professors and students. She gives very graphic outline portraits of her distinguished father and saintly mother, of Professor Park and other Andover celebrities, including Mrs. Stowe, whom she names as "the greatest of American women." She describes her own entrance into the charmed world of literature; how she wrote her famous story, "The Gates Ajar"; and how pleasant and satisfactory on the whole, though occasionally trying, she has found the literary career. Peculiarly interesting chapters give glimpses, sometimes full views, of Longfellow, Holmes,

From Phelps's "Chapters from a Life." Copyright, 1896, by Houghton, Mifflin & Co.

MRS. ELIZ. STUART PHELPS WARD.

Whittier, Mr. Fields, Bishop Brooks, Mrs. Thaxter, Miss Larcom, Mrs. Lydia Maria Child, and others. She tells how she discovered the beautiful spot in East Gloucester which was her home for many summers, and which figures in one of her books as "An Old Maid's Paradise." Indeed, every chapter is fresh and exceedingly readable, and the book cannot fail to gratify the large circle of Miss Phelps's readers, and to deepen their admiration and love for her. (Houghton, Mifflin & Co. $1.50.)

Sir George Tressady.

'THERE can be no question," says the *Athenæum*, "that Mrs. Ward is a puzzle to the conscientious critic. This has partly resulted from the history of her career as a novelist. If we leave 'Miss Bretherton' out of the reckoning, we may say that she seemed to be sprung upon

the reading world with an exaggerated form of that sort of success which somebody has called a *succès Gladstone*—a rather dangerous pre-eminence, in which, if she has a rival, it is (as his advertisements remind us) Mr. Hall Caine. School-girls at once spoke of her with awe, and many persons of influence—people interested in religious and philanthropic developments, whose literary judgment was not necessarily above the level of the school-girls. On the other hand, a section of the *illuminati*, chiefly because she dealt with these religious and social matters—legitimate subjects, if any were, for dramatic treatment—at once set her down for a prig and a pedant, and would have no more to do with her. All this tends to the confusion of the moderate and modest critic. Has he to do with a sort of cleansed and refined Zola, he asks himself, or only a more philosophical Edna Lyall? It must make the application of the heaven-descended maxim not easy to the distinguished author herself.

"In the present case the critic might well get rid of his difficulties by indiscriminate praise of Mrs. Ward's 'Sir George Tressady,' were such a course fair to any one concerned. There is so much that is good throughout, and the latter part especially is so fine and moving, that fault-finding is disarmed. Most of the qualities which distinguished 'Marcella' far above the run of its contemporaries are present again here. We have nothing so fully understood and so finely handled as the village life in the previous volume—nothing so poetical as the description of Hurd's poaching, or so affecting as the night of Hurd's execution spent by Marcella in the cottage with his wife. But the glimpses we get here of the laboring classes, their ways and thoughts, whether in East-End London or in the mining village in the Midlands, are well realized and now and then are startlingly effective."

"Those who have read 'Marcella,'" says the *London Literary World*, "will at once recognize that 'Sir George Tressady' is a sequel to that work, and will find keener pleasure from it, we imagine, than those who approach it without the introduction which the earlier story affords. It is not only that the heroine is the same in both works—for Marcella, if she divides that honor with Letty Tressady, is the dominating character throughout the greater part of the present story—but that the problems she discusses with such skill are almost identical. And here we must say that we feel the same uncertainty regarding Mrs. Ward's real sentiments on the topics she introduces as we did after reading 'Marcella.' To some readers, whose sympathies are strong on one side or the other, this will appear a defect, engendering, possibly, some feeling of annoyance. The great and pressing problems that cluster round the labor question are presented with unusual skill, the arguments *pro* and *con* being put into the mouths of her characters in such a way as to make it a greater puzzle than ever to discover the author's personal opinions. If it had been her special design to conceal her views she could not have done it better than by connecting the opposing opinions with the private characters and habits of the speakers, and by showing the play of concealed motives in current politics." (Macmillan. 2 v., $2.)

William H. Seward.

"In the excellent series, *American Statesmen*, the volume "W. H. Seward," by Thornton Kirkland Lothrop, will find an honored place," says the Chicago *Inter-Ocean*. "Few American statesmen, so long in the very front of political battles, whose reputation will so surely stand the test of the white light of history. Seward was born in Florida, a village of New York, on May 16, 1801, and died in Auburn, N. Y., October 10, 1892. He entered public life when about twenty-eight years of age, and, with short respites, he was, in one position and another, continually called to serve the public in capacities which called for scholarship, manhood, wisdom, and the highest statesmanship. Often criticised by his enemies, he yet held at all times a high and sure place in the hearts of the American people. His public career, though long, was without a shadow of stain, and his state papers, speeches, and decisions mark him as the safe, wise, and prudent statesman. Sew-

ard was an all-round American of the best type of manhood. Loved for his fine personal qualities, honored for his great abilities, with his integrity unsullied amid the most trying scenes, he rightfully belongs not only to the series of *American Statesmen* but is eminent in the series."

Living through the administrations of Fillmore, Pierce, and Lincoln, the biography of Seward covers some of the most important events in the history of the United States. (Houghton, Mifflin & Co. $1.25.)

Ian Maclaren and Kate Carnegie.

Not only Mr. Barrie, but the Rev. John Watson, the latter better known as Ian Maclaren, is at present on a visit to this country, and Mr. Watson has for his object something more serious than to "amuse" himself. He is here, among other things, to wrestle with the very momentous question of accepting or declining the call of the Broadway Congregational Church, New York, to become its pastor. That church, having in years gone by made a hit by

From "Kate Carnegie." Copyright, 1896, by Dodd, Mead & Co

A TALL, BONY, FORBIDDING WOMAN.

the importation of one pastor from a suburb of Liverpool, the late Rev. Dr. Taylor, now naturally turns its eyes in the same direction for another, for Mr. Watson is a minister of Liverpool itself. Some friends of ours who heard him in his own pulpit last June were greatly pleased with the man and his matter. And if he preaches as he writes, he must have the first secret of the preacher, which, next to telling the truth, is to be interesting. "Kate Carnegie" is at least that, however the critics may differ as to the rank they give it. The story has been running as a serial in the *Outlook*, but is now about ready in book form, as a set of the advance sheets from the publishers testify. A handsome book these sheets will make when properly bound up, with their 358 pages, their many effective illustrations, and all their regard for a fine typography. "Kate Carnegie" is the sort of story one would expect from a Scotch Presbyterian, full of the scenery of that fascinating land, of its dialect, of its theology, of its ecclesiastical history, and of its quaint, picturesque, strongly-marked characters. The man and woman who meet in the first chapter are mated in the last, and the reader who gets as far as the closing scene will admit that Mr. Watson knows how to sketch the scene of all scenes between a pair of lovers as if to the manner born; and that he is that no one will doubt who looks into the kindly, honest, cultivated, genuine face that meets us in the frontispiece. (Dodd, Mead & Co. $1.50.)—*Boston Literary World.*

Genius and Degeneration.

DR. HIRSCH'S acute and suggestive study of modern tendencies was begun before "Degeneration" was published, with the purpose of presenting entirely opposite deductions and conclusions. The appearance of Dr. Nordau's famous book, with its criticisms upon Dr. Hirsch's position, enabled the latter to extend the scope of his work, which becomes a scientific answer to Dr. Nordau, although this was not its specific purpose originally. Dr. Nordau has startled the reading world by his cry of "Degeneration"; Dr. Hirsch opposes his conclusions by demonstrating the difference between "Genius" and "Degeneration," and analyzing the social, literary, and artistic manifestations of the day dispassionately and with a wealth of suggestive illustrations. In a brilliant explanation of the psychology of genius he shows that Lombroso and Nordau make no distinction between scientific genius based upon hard work and artistic genius; nor between genius and talent. He points to Goethe as an example of a perfectly developed genius. He answers specifically Nordau's claim that this is ——are of hysterical disorder, and after an ex-

tended, brilliant, and informing discussion of Art and Insanity, in which he shows himself a confirmed Wagnerian, he summarizes his conclusions by absolutely declining to accept Nordau's point of view. It is safe to say that the book is one which must be read by every reader of Nordau, and should be read by every intelligent person who wishes to understand the spirit of his time and the lessons which history teaches the psychologist.

"The warm reception given to Dr. William Hirsch's 'Genius and Degeneration' on this side of the water," says the *N. Y. Herald*, "is but an echo of the approval accorded to the original German edition in the doctor's native country. The leading papers, lay and medical, of Berlin, Frankfort, Dresden. and Hamburg have welcomed it as a complete refutation of Nordau's theory that the race is on the point of perishing in madness and deterioration and that nearly all our leading artists, musicians, and writers are degenerates. Amid this chorus of praise only one dissenting voice has been heard. And whose is that? Why, Max Nordau's, of course."

Dr. Hirsch, the author of the book which has aroused all this discussion, is a German by birth, who studied medicine and practised it in Berlin, but who, for the last two years, has been a resident practitioner in New York. (Appleton. $3.50.)

A Matter of Temperament.

THIS classically-written novel portrays one phase of music's relation to morals. A terrible moral tragedy is enacted, and love, music, and the stage are each involved. The epoch is the middle of the present century, a time marked by the influence and success of Meyerbeer, and by the deep impression made by the master on the composers of the school of Germany. Meyerbeer himself is encountered in the first part of the novel. The story is sustained with painful interest to the end. It supplies a valuable study of a direct and grave impeachment of music, as also, directly and indirectly, against its exponents. As such, "A Matter of Temperament" should be read and considered by every adult musician, professional or amateur.

Both quantity and quality are factors in music. A little of the best, whether considered from the standpoint of execution or of influence, goes a long way, and a little of the worst is equally effective. Neither are all influenced alike by the same causes; effects are dissimilar in degree and in kind, yet there are, undoubtedly, airs which, without words, excite the baser possibilities of human nature, so also there are airs which, used with moderation, can but be productive of good and not of evil. Immoderation, however, is apt to result in weakness, or frenzy, and frenzy is a species of insanity.

Good, soul-stirring music, whether sacred or secular in composition, has its beneficent mission on earth. If it finds response in the passions unassociated with the exercise, there, of living moral principles, the perturbed waters are apt to cast up mire and dirt. Familiarity and custom, even in the cases of the most skilful of professional performers, have, in some instances, as is shown in this book, a hardening effect, and wherein the best music fails either to arouse or cultivate the better emotions of our nature. It is nevertheless true that "Music is the universal language of mankind," also that

"The man that hath no music
     in himself
 And is not moved with con-
     cord of sweet sounds
 Is fit for treason, stratagems,
     and spoils."

In a forceful manner the author illustrates the moral instability of the artistic temperament. By induction the book emphasizes music's moral force and spiritual excellence.

The moral lessons of this novel should be pondered by every one interested in the art or science of music, and by every lover of its grave, gay, or sympathetic strains.

Mr. Stevenson at first called his book "Janus," the name of the Latin Deity having two similar faces looking in opposite directions, but has changed it to that of "A Matter of Temperament." (American Publishers Corporation. $1; pap., 50 c.)

Shakespeare's Heroes on the Stage.

A COMPANION volume to his deservedly popular "Shakespeare's Heroines on the Stage" has been prepared by Charles E. L. Wingate, dealing with "Shakespeare's Heroes on the Stage." The heroes selected are Othello, Iago, Lear, Shylock, Coriolanus, Macbeth, Hamlet,

and Richard III. The actors identified with one or the other of these heroes are Edmund Kean, Richard Burbage, George Frederick Cooke, Gustavus V. Brooke, E. L. Davenport, Tommaso Salvini, Edwin Booth, David Garrick, Edwin Forrest, Charles Macklin, Junius Brutus Booth, Henry Irving, Lawrence Barrett, Thomas Abthorpe Cooper, John McCullough, James Quin, W. C. Macready, Samuel Phelps, Thomas Betterton, John Philip Kemble, Charles

From "Shakespeare's Heroes on the Stage."   Copyright, 1896, by T. Y. Crowell & Co.

JUNIUS BRUTUS BOOTH AS KING RICHARD III.

Fechter and Richard Mansfield. The book, like the "Heroines," is not intended exclusively for the professed lovers of theatrical literature. It is written to entertain the masses of people who read Shakespeare's works and see them played, and who naturally feel interested in knowing how the great actors of the past and present, in England and America, have interpreted the famous characters on the stage. Scores of books have been written about Shakespeare's

From " American Highways."   Copyright, 1896, by The Century Co.

HUNTINGTON PARK AVENUE, PHILADELPHIA.

plays, and about theatrical performers, but no book exactly like this has been published to show how the plays were presented by performers and what incidents accompanied the presentations. A field, therefore, is open to a book of this kind, and no more acceptable Christmas souvenir can be offered by a young man to the girl who has honored him by accompanying him to see Shakespeare's plays as they are performed in the present day. Portraits of all the actors make a most valuable feature of the book. The old-time pictures are, for the most part, from the collection of Mr. John Bouvé Clapp, of Boston, and in a number of cases they reproduce rare prints. (Crowell. $2)

American Highways.

THE historian of this country for the century which is now drawing to its close is likely to note the fact that the people of the United States bore, in a singularly patient manner, with the evils arising from poor carriage roads until near the end of the tenth decade, and that they then were suddenly aroused to a sense of the sore tax the ill condition of these necessary features of civilization had long inflicted upon them. Let us hope that he may be able to say that in approaching this great economic problem they did so in a manner which showed that they were well informed as to the conditions under which they could deal with it in the light of the previous experience of men, and with the help which the resources of modern science could afford them.

It seems fit that the writer should explain in brief the experience which has made it proper for him to undertake the work which is here set forth. This in outline is as follows: During the Civil War he was in a position to learn the meaning of wheelways in the critical work of campaigns; since that time he has been much interested in road-making and in geological work carried on in different parts of this country and Europe, and has paid close attention to the physical conditions of such ways. For more than four years he has been engaged as one of the three members of the Massachusetts Highway Commission in studying the condition of the roads in that commonwealth, and developing a plan for their betterment by State constructions. In connection with his colleagues he has had to do with the laying out and constructing of about one hundred roads, and has been particularly engaged in a study of the relations of the road-building materials to the needs of these ways. He has had, moreover, to do with planning, in the Scientific School of Harvard University, a system for the instruction of engineers in road-making, a course which is carried on under the direction of William E. McClintock, one of the members of the above-mentioned Highway Commission. He has prepared two reports for the United States Geological Survey, one entitled " The Geology of Highway Materials," and the other " The Road-Building Materials of Massachusetts."

Those who desire more detailed statements concerning the methods of constructing and maintaining particular kinds of roads than are given in the following chapters may advantageously consult the list of works which is given in the Appendix. This list contains, with few exceptions, only works in English, and includes those only which have some value to the non-professional reader. (Century Co. $1.50.)—*From Preface to .V. S. Shaler's "American Highways."*

St. Elmo.

IT came to pass in the year 1866, that a certain humble scribe indited the tale of "St. Elmo," the publisher whereof (George W. Carleton) made haste to scatter it abroad. But the Chief Priests and Rulers who governed the kingdom of letters in that day lifted up their pens and smote that scribe—and set forth a decree that the tale was full of all unwisdom—was *anathema maranatha*.

Nevertheless, many young men and young maidens, and some baldheads, disobeyed the edict, and did buy the foolish book, which was like unto the leaven which was hid in three measures of meal, so that after a time it came to the ears of those Chief Priests that a multitude had broken the decree. Then the Rulers waxed wroth and ground their teeth, and one among their number jeered and mocked that tale, and sent out a cunning and most powerful emissary named "St. Twelmo," and heard the shouts of the people who had gone astray in their reading, as they rent their garments, crying: "Ephraim is joined to idols !"

But the hearts of the publishers were made glad and they issued proclamation : "Go to ! The voice of the people is lifted for us, and the young and the old are on our side—and from lands beyond the sea —from the farthest isles of the great deep, and even from the shores of Australia come messages unto us, and unto that scribe, saying, 'Blessed be St. Elmo !' "

So, as the years passed and the book was sold, lo ! the metal plates wore away, so that no more copies could be made, and as the people of the land still came to buy, those publishers resolved to cut new plates of metal whereon to engrave that tale, and to order most skilful workers to adorn it with pictures, and thus make the people's book " a thing of beauty and a joy forever."

And behold ! it was done.

The result is the *Magnolia edition* of "St. Elmo" in two octavo volumes, embellished with thirty full-page photogravure and half-tone illustrations, from drawings by Louise L. Heustis and G. S. Snell, made especially for the work. More than 125,000 copies of "St. Elmo" have been sold and there is no doubt it will take a new lease of life in its present form of a holiday presentation gift-book. (G. W. Dillingham Co. 2 v., $6.)—*Preface to "St. Elmo."*

From "St. Elmo.'   Copyright, 1896, by G. W. Dillingham Co.

LOOKING DOWN ON THE MASS OF MANUSCRIPT.

Nephelé.

"NEPHELÉ," by the author of one of the most lovely and also—which is singular—one of the most popular little songs of the present generation ["The night has a thousand eyes and the day but one"], which first appeared upwards of twenty-two years ago, is a romance of cloudland, the cloudland of mystical musical sympathies. Yet it is a very stirring and poetical romance, too, without any of that rhetorical rhodomontade of "deep no-meaning" about it which the first Lord Lytton used to affect. . . . Nephelé is a real woman, and not a mere cloud lit up by the prismatic rays of dawn or sunset, and the hero is a real man, though they meet for the first time, without any previous knowledge of each other, in that world of trance and musical mystery which the modern world has spoiled for all human purposes by giving it the pedantic name of telepathic feeling. Mr. Gerard, the hero of the little story, is playing on the organ of the college chapel [? Winchester] where he is at school:

"I set the hydraulic power to work, mounted to the organ loft, pulled out a few stops, and laid my fingers on the keys. Open in front of me was Mendelssohn's sixth organ concerto, at the *andante* movement; and I was about to begin to play this, when something prompted me to turn aside my will; my fingers fell on the notes in a rich, soft chord, and half unconsciously, wholly unintentionally, I found myself playing a strange, unknown air. I knew quite certainly that it was something I had never heard before, and yet it seemed half familiar, as if I might have heard it in dreams. Very sweet it was, and plaintive, full of human feeling, and with so much of the sense of song about it that I could almost imagine words were being sung to it as I played. Once I played it, and again; and to make sure that I should not forget it I had begun it a third time, when a strange sensation came over me. I was conscious that some one else was somewhere near me. I turned around, while I was playing, to see if any one had come up into the organ loft. But no, there was only room for one or two persons besides the player, and there was certainly no one there. I rose and went down into the chapel, but it was quite empty; and indeed I had turned the key in the lock, and no one could have come in without knocking at the door for me to let him in. Yet I had still a strong impression of some one near me; whether in the body of the chapel or in the organ loft, I could not say, but very near me. . . . And as my fingers still played on, I found they were now no longer content with the simple air, but were beginning to entwine it with lovely variations; variations that never obscured the original air, but seemed to mingle with it, and to be the echoes that it woke in all things or people that heard it. Then I became conscious that this girl-presence, whose mysteriousness had at first terrified me, was awakening a new sense, not of dread—that my whole soul was being flooded with its sympathies and graces, and that the unexplained desire, 'the desire of the moth for the star,' that we call Love, was quickening within me. And with this feeling the music—that I myself was playing—grew more tumultuous, the pure, clear air sounding through a passionate surge of harmonies and discords, while a wild, ecstatic yearning thrilled me, that was neither grief nor joy, but an unutterable intermingling of both."

This volume is more of a prose poem than of a mere tale, and yet it has all the interest, and much more than the vividness and simplicity, of an exciting tale. Mr. Bourdillon believes in the higher meanings and significance of music with a faith that is almost spiritual, and manages to engrave his conviction on even the least musical of his readers. (New Amsterdam Book Co. $1.)

Lazy Tours in Spain and Elsewhere.

THERE is an attraction in the very title of Mrs. Moulton's travel sketches. One is sure not to find in a volume with such an appellation any trace of that perfunctory zest for guidebook detail which is so often the besetting sin of the sight-seer in foreign lands. Mrs. Moulton in these sketches goes largely over beaten paths, but she is in search of impressions, not of exterior facts, and the one great charm of her book is that it reflects in a thoroughly spontaneous way the individuality of its author. Mrs. Moulton's tour in Spain was undertaken in spite of many discouragements, but she found it eminently worth while, and it will be strange if many a reluctant explorer is not tempted by her glowing descriptions to brave the terrors of the Spanish cuisine and the discomforts of the Spanish railways for the sake of seeing the Alhambra by moonlight as Mrs. Moulton saw it, of wandering among the aisles of the great cathedral at Cordova, or plucking roses in the sultana's garden there, or subjecting oneself in acquiescent mood to what Mrs. Moulton calls the "seductive consolations" of Seville. Mrs. Moulton's unstudied itinerary takes her into southern Italy, to Naples, Sorrento, Amalfi, and to a sojourn in Rome, with a leisurely pause at Florence on the way back to Paris. Treasures of art and architecture naturally occupy a great deal of Mrs. Moulton's attention, but she seems always to look at them in the unconventional light, and whether climbing Vesuvius, or standing amid the ruins of Pompeii, or treading the classic ground of the Eternal City, she does not fail to give her narrative a warm human interest by taking due note of the people with whom she is thrown in contact. At Paris Mrs. Moulton is chiefly occupied with the pictures of the impressionist painters, and as a guide in making her investigations she has the assistance of the alert and sagacious poet-critic, Stéphane Mallarmé. Her rambles in Switzerland take her to Lucerne and to Geneva, over the Tete Noire to Chillon, and to the little-known village of Ragatz, which is depicted as a veritable paradise. As for the chapters on the French and German water-cures, from Aix-les-Bains to Wiesbaden, the invalid will read them with eager attention for the many practical hints which they contain, and the general reader for their humorous and winning descriptions of life and manners. A glimpse at Tunbridge Wells and an excursion into Yorkshire bring to a close a series of tours full of instruction and entertainment for those fortunate enough to make them in Mrs. Moulton's gracious company. (Roberts. $1.50.) —*The Beacon.*

every one will recognize at once as being distinctively American. The story is chiefly concerned with the experiences of a country lad with literary aspirations, who goes to New York intent on making a name for himself, and because of his sensitive, idealistic temperament finds great difficulty in mastering the details of practical affairs. His efforts at newspaper work are amusingly described, and his introduction to characteristic features of city life is attended with some rather startling adventures. Mr. Moffat has unquestionably depicted in Pennington Rae a youth who will be at once accepted as of fine if not heroic mould, and one, moreover, whose traits and

HOW MUCH HE LOOKS LIKE HIS FATHER.

Not Without Honor.

"NOT Without Honor," by William D. Moffat, is a story for boys that should achieve a wide popularity, for it is capitally written, with abundance of incident and a firm adherence to dramatic form, while at the same time it keeps close to scenes and characters of every-day life, and while abounding in vivid contrasts never lapses into mere sensationalism. Mr. Moffat has evidently not forgotten how boys think and feel about the problems that confront them at the outset of a career, and he shows a fine knowledge of character in portraying a number of authentic types that

ideals have seldom been so sympathetically set forth in the guise of fiction. There are elements of mystery and romance in the tale, and these are well contrived to sustain the interest. "Not Without Honor" is a straightforward, honest, manly book, full of wholesome suggestions to the boy reader. Perhaps in asking us to believe that a lad of twenty can leap into fame at a bound, as a successful novelist and magazine writer, Mr. Moffat is straining somewhat the limits of probability, but the novice in literature ought to be welcome to all the encouragement he can get from such a picture. (Arnold & Co. $1.25.)—*The Beacon.*

From "Saul."   Copyright, 1896, by T. Y. Crowell & Co.
THEN I PLAYED THE HELP-TUNE.

Nugæ Litterariæ.

MR. WILLIAM MATHEWS has preserved in "Nugæ Litterariæ" the substance of a wide range of miscellaneous reading on his part, and while he cannot be said to have produced literature in it, he has contrived to produce the appearance of literature in the selection of topics about which he writes, in a rambling, desultory way, and which he illustrates by quotations from the writings of famous authors, and by the relation of incidents in their lives, anecdotes, clever sayings, and other personal trifles. We meet with many old friends in his pages, and we are glad to meet with them again, for the least of them are of a kind that one would not willingly forget, and are not likely to forget hereafter, for in addition to these, and arm-in-arm with them, as we say, we meet with others of their kind which we had not known before, and which we shall associate with them in days to come. Mr. Mathews belongs to the same class of writers as the elder Disraeli, with the difference of being more compact and less pedantic, and that the topics upon which he touches come closer to the bosoms and business of men than the verbose discussions which form the staple of the "Curiosities of Literature." He is readable, he is amusing, and when one is in the mood to enjoy light thought and easy chat one cannot do better than skim over his book, where he will find an abundance of both. (Roberts. $1.50.)—*Mail and Express.*

Phrase-Book from Robert Browning.

MISS MARIE ADA MOLINEAUX has compiled "A Phrase-Book from the Poetic and Dramatic Works of Robert Browning," and a beautiful octavo it makes. We should not have supposed that Browning was sufficiently read to render such a book necessary, but then we know nothing about the various Browning societies which have sprung up in this country within the last decade or two, and, consequently, know nothing about the circulation of his writings, either in single volumes or in complete editions, of which Messrs. Houghton, Mifflin & Co. publish two, one in six volumes crown octavo, and another in one volume, the last being what they call the *Cambridge edition;* so we are not in a position to form an opinion in this matter. For ourselves, we have never felt the need of "A Phrase-Book," for when we remember anything of Browning's, we remember at the same time the poem in which it occurs, and, more often than not, the page on which it is printed in the edition with which we are familiar; but the memory of others who admire Browning ardently enough to establish societies for the elucidation of his observations is probably less worthy of trust than our rambling recollections, and it is for those that this "Phrase-Book" was designed. We can testify to its accuracy, not only as regards the exact words which are quoted, but also as regards the title of the poem in which they are found, and the very place in the poem, for the lines are enumerated, as they should be, if a "Phrase-Book" like this is to be a help and not a hindrance. Miss Molineaux's work is a marvel of correctness. (Houghton, Mifflin & Co. $3.) —*Mail and Express.*

Externals of Modern New York.

IN bringing down to date the general history of New York since 1880, at which point the able and conscientious chronicle of Mrs. Lamb came to a halt, it has been found possible to touch, within the limits of a single chapter, upon only such salient features of a great city's rapid strides in civilization as may prove interesting to the casual student of the time.

For the same obvious reason, want of space, it has been decided to tell the story of the last fifth of the century by "thumb-nail" sketches of the various departments of the city's work, and by a brief summary of progress in social development, rather than to attempt to recite incidents chronologically and separately. We shall mention externals, chiefly—things that catch the eye. With the deeper issues of religion and morality; with details of the fluctuations of society attributable to reinforcements from abroad and from other quarters of our own country; with meditations suggested by the fact that, as Guizot once said of the relation of France to the rest of Europe, all institutions of civilization must pass through New York before they are accepted elsewhere in America; with suggestions for the future to be found in centralizing here the influences of literature and art; with accounts of our struggle for great wealth, and with what is to be learned from the dropping out of public consideration of those who do not maintain it; with the annals of political abuses and party warfare; with the fret and fever of speculation, and financial questions of the hour, there will be no attempt to deal. It is enough to try to outline only the most noticeable, to a looker-on, of the model differences between the New York of fifteen or sixteen years ago and the metropolis of to-day. Mrs. Burton Harrison has added the chapter on the present city, which has been published as a separate volume, profusely illustrated (A. S. Barnes. $3.)

THEN I PLAYED THE HELP-TUNE.

THEN I played the help-tune of our reapers, their wine-song, when hand

Grasps at hand, eye lights eye in good friendship, and great hearts expand

And grow one in the sense of this world's life.—And then, the last song

When the dead man is praised on his journey—"Bear, bear him along

With his few faults shut up like dead flowerets! Are balm seeds not here

To console us? The land has none left such as he on the bier.

Oh, would we might keep thee, my brother!"—And then, the glad chaunt

Of the marriage,—first go the young maidens, next, she whom we vaunt

As the beauty, the pride of our dwelling—And then, the great march

Wherein man runs to man to assist him and buttress an arch

Nought can break; who shall harm them, our friends? Then, the chorus intoned

As the Levites go up to the altar in glory enthroned.

But I stopped here : for here in the darkness Saul groaned

(Crowell. $1 50.)—*From Browning's "Saul."*

LEO XIII.

George Fox.

"GEORGE FOX," by Thomas Hodgkin, is a biography of unusual interest. To an extent that is simply marvellous this unlearned enthusiast of the seventeenth century anticipated the religious thought of the close of the nineteenth. His doctrine of the "inner light" was but another expression of the faith in the "immanence of God" which is to-day the centre of the creed of so many religious evolutionists. Fox was as far from a bibliolator as the boldest of the deeply religious minds of our own time. In fact, the first imprisonment he suffered was for his condemnation of the teaching that the Scriptures furnished the one rule of faith. "I could not hold," he says, "but was made to cry out and say, 'Oh, no, it is not the Scriptures'; and I told them what it was, namely, the Holy Spirit by which the holy men of God gave forth the Scriptures, whereby opinions, religions, and judgments were to be tried, for it led into all truth." Towards the Catholics, whose doctrines were antipodal to his own, he was so full of charity as to be called at one time a Jesuit in disguise. His test of true religion was not doctrinal, but related to the "tenderness" of the spirit of the men who professed it. Upon social and industrial relationships he was a believer in brotherhood to an extent that would satisfy the most socialistic of modern Christians. Dr. Hodgkin, the biographer, is in faith a Friend, but while his biography is sympathetic, as one would wish it to be, he does not allow his sympathies to exclude the unattractive and purely fanatical sides of Fox's life and teachings.— (Houghton, Mifflin & Co. $1.)—*The Outlook.*

Reminiscences of an Octogenarian.

SINCE the publication of Philip Hone's "Diary," some eight or ten years ago, there has not been so good, authoritative a book about New York as this one by the last man in the world from whom such a work might have been expected. Felix Oldboy did some excellent things in the same field, and had some grace in writing. Mr. Haswell makes no pretensions whatever to literary style. He has been known for the best years of his life as the author of an indispensable engineering manual, and, considered strictly as a writer, it may be said that he writes like an engineer to this day. But his book has a great deal of talk in it, mere discursive talk, and in that our author is one of the most entertaining of historical companions. It is useless for him to protest that he is not writing history. He describes the events and manners of his time, and no matter how he describes them, they are the material of history. When he states that "as late as

1820 I, in company with an elder relative, occasionally practised pistol-shooting at a target on a fence" in Canal Street, he may be reviving memories which are not altogether unfamiliar to readers in New York; but he is a serious contributor to the literature of our development as a city when he sets down the street cries of eighty years ago and tells us the ins and outs of the daily life of our grandfathers. The book contains a mass of historical notes, put together with some chronological symmetry, but otherwise arranged in a miscellaneous way. One is constantly discovering quaint fragments of "ana" in the rambling story. . . .

The volume is a perfect mine of topographical information. It has something to say about innumerable landmarks, about the streets and their names, about restaurants and places of amusement noted in their day, about the thousand and one things which gave New York its physiognomy, about the thousand and one celebrities who were prominent in the making of the city. But the work is too encyclopædic, too miscellaneous, to be extensively cited or even consecutively analyzed. It is a book to dip into; one, moreover, in which the casual reader will never fail to find something worth having paused to scan. The illustrations are numerous, well chosen, and well executed. To the older generation pictures and text will recall much that it has well-nigh forgotten, and to the younger public it offers a store of anecdotes as instructive as they are amusing. (Harper. $3.)—*N. Y. Tribune.*

Poor, Rich Mrs. Cliff.

ONE thing Mrs. Cliff had determined upon—her money should not come between her and those who loved her and who were loved by her. No matter what she might do or what she might not do, she would not look down upon people simply because she was rich, and oh, the blessed thought which followed that! There would be nobody who could look down upon her because she was not rich!

She did not intend to be a fine new woman; she did not intend to build a fine new house. She was going to be the same Mrs. Cliff that she used to be—she was going to live in the same house. To be sure, she would add to it. She would have a new dining-room and a guest's chamber over it, and she would do a great many other things which were needed, but she would live in her old home, where she and her husband had been so happy, and where she hoped he would look down from heaven and see her happy until the end of her days.

As she thought of the things she intended to do, and of the manner in which she intended to do them, Mrs. Cliff rose and walked the floor. She felt as if she were a bird, a common-sized bird, perhaps, but with enormous wings, which seemed to grow and grow the more she thought of them, until they were able to carry her so far and so high that her mind lost its power of directing them.

She determined to cease to think of the future, of what was going to be, and to let her mind rest and quiet itself with what really existed. Here she was in a great city full of wonders and delights, of comforts, conveniences, luxuries, necessities, and all within her power. Almost anything she could think of she might have ; almost anything she wanted to do she might do. A feeling of potentiality seemed to swell and throb within her veins. She was possessed of an overpowering desire to do something now, this moment, to try the power of her wealth.

Near her on the richly-papered wall was a little button. Should she touch this and order — what should she order? A carriage and prancing pair to take her to drive? She did not care to drive. A cab to take her to the shops, or an order to merchants to send her samples of their wares that here, in her own room, like a queen or a princess, she might choose what she wanted and think nothing of the cost? But no, she did not wish to buy anything. She had purchased in Paris everything that she cared to carry to Plainton.

She went and stood by the electric button. She must touch it, and must have something ! Her gold must give her an instant proof that it could minister to her desires, but what should she ask for? Her mind travelled over the

whole field of the desirable, and yet not one salient object presented itself. There was absolutely nothing she could think of that she wished to ask for at that moment. She was

"DOES MRS. CLIFF LIVE HERE?"

like a poor girl in a fairy-tale, to whom the good fairy comes and asks her to make one wish and it shall be granted, and who stands hesitating and trembling, not being able to decide what is the one great thing for which she should ask. What should she want?

In her agitation she touched the bell. Half frightened at what she had done, she stepped back and sat down. In a few minutes there was a knock, the door opened, a servant entered. "Bring me a cup of tea," said Mrs. Cliff. (Scribner. $1.50.)—*From Stockton's "Mrs. Cliff's Yacht."*

The Literary News.

An Eclectic Monthly Review of Current Literature.
EDITED BY A. H. LEYPOLDT.

NOVEMBER, 1896.

WILLIAM MORRIS.

THE death of William Morris leaves only Swinburne remaining of the great quartette of poets who have shed lustre upon the Victorian era. Without having enjoyed the popularity

William Morris

that was Tennyson's for nearly half a century, and although he never inspired the profound study that has been accorded the works of Browning, Morris nevertheless did his best and most lasting work as a poet. For the moment he stands before the popular mind more as a capitalist, an employer of labor, a reformer in

the art and business world, and as a writer of fiction difficult to understand by reason of its technique. But time will take care of Morris, as it has of all the world's great workers, and after all political differences and all social problems and all fashions of taste have passed away, the thoughts Morris has put into glowing English will remain moving, inspiring, helpful to all men, and these thoughts, whether written with or without versification, will always rank him among the poets.

Morris was a man of such manifold activities and such startling originality of plan and purpose, and also had such far-reaching, constant influence on so many men, that it would seem almost impossible that he should have accomplished all his varied work inside of sixty-two years. In the midst of his busy life his health suddenly began to decline, diabetes with its complications had seized him, and after unavailing efforts to re-establish his health by rest and change of scene, he finally succumbed to an almost painless death on the morning of October 3, in his own beautiful home in Hammersmith.

William Morris was born in Walthamstown, a little village of Essex, England, in 1834. His father was an enterprising business man, and from his birth William Morris was secured against all anxiety for material comforts, and all his life was surrounded with everything that makes for culture and progress. He was highly talented in many directions, a fact which for some years kept him from finding his true vocation. In 1848 the Morris family moved to Marlborough, and William went to college and began to show interest in art and archæology. He was specially fond of memorial brasses. In 1852 he entered Oxford at Exeter College, at a time when the University was in the midst of a mediæval revival, which was fostered on the one hand by the Tractarian College of John Henry Newman, and on the other by the artistic guild of the pre-Raphaelite Brotherhood— Holman Hunt, D. G. Rossetti, and John E. Millais. Under their influence. William Morris and his college chum, E. Burne-Jones, became students of the Middle Ages. This period of Morris's life is delightfully covered in "Dante Gabriel Rossetti : his family and letters," edited by William Rossetti, published this year by Roberts Brothers. In 1856 Morris started *The Oxford and Cambridge Magazine*, and wrote for it a series of mediæval romances which showed his poetic imagination and his great literary facility. Morris then studied architecture, but afterwards abandoned it. Later he studied painting and artistic decoration, and in this art and in his writing he finally found the means of expression for his healthy, virile idealism. In 1861 he joined Ford Madox Brown, E. Burne-Jones, D. G. Rossetti, and Philip Webb in forming an art firm, with the intent of designing and manufacturing stained-glass mosaics, wall-papers, artistic furniture, and general household decorations. Of late years William Morris has declared himself a socialist, and has written and spoken much in defence of socialism. He led Burne-Jones to a deep sympathy with socialism, and inspired Walter Crane, Cobden-Sanderson, and many of the other designers and workers in wood and metal who have organized the annual Arts and Crafts Exhibition. Recently Morris has busied himself as a printer, issuing from the Kelmscott Press a series of sumptuous reprints of old works. All through his busy career as poet, artist, prophet, and reformer Morris wrote rapidly and well. The list of his works is a very long one. Those which gained him his place in literature are: "The Defence of Guenevere," 1858; "The Life and Death of Jason," 1867; "The Earthly Paradise," 1868; "The Story of Sigurd the Volsung," 1875; "The Decorative Arts and Modern Life and Progress," 1878; "Hopes and Fears for Art," 1882; "A Tale of the House of the Wolfings and all the Kindreds of the Mark," 1888; "The Roots of the Mountains," 1889; "The Story of the Glittering Plain"; "News from Nowhere," 1890; "Poems by the Way," 1892; and "The Wood Beyond the World," 1895. Messrs. Roberts Brothers introduced Morris to American readers. A new book entitled "The Well at the End of the World" has just been issued by Longmans, Green & Co. Morris was wholly unconventional, and in all things a law unto himself. He was strongly opposed to routine and mammon rule, and labored earnestly to educate all who came within his influence to strive for independence and individuality, and to honor labor and do healthy, hopeful work for human progress and human happiness.

Her Foreign Conquest.

COL. RICHARD HENRY SAVAGE is never at a loss for exciting incidents in the lives of the characters he creates to enact the plots he evolves from his active imagination. This is the story of two wealthy and beautiful American girls to whom modern readers are introduced at Hamburg, surrounded by the gay society of a fashionable European watering-place. These girls both fall in love with a German count, who gives his affection to the elder girl. Maddened by jealousy, the younger girl strives to belittle her sister in the estimation of her lover, and even resorts to misrepresentation to prove the favored girl an illegitimate adopted child. Much of the story revolves around this calumny and the measures taken to prove the sister's true position Colonel Savage proves in "My Official Wife" that he knows the characteristics and foibles of the German and other European nobility, and he continues to make all the information he has gained available for his readers. (Home Publishing Co. pap., 50 c.; $1.)

Bushy.

MISS CYNTHIA M. WESTOVER, well known as a singer and journalist, has written a remarkable novel, which one might almost suppose to be autobiographical in part. It tells of the adventures of a little girl named "Bushy," after whom the book is called, in the mining regions of the West. The widowed father of the little girl, a geologist, cannot bring himself to leave her behind at his former home in Iowa when he sets out for a prospecting tour in the Rocky Mountains.

While the exciting episodes that one naturally expects to find in such a book are in this the principal feature, the author finds opportunity in reciting them to reflect many profound traits of human nature and to impart in her diction certain touches of tenderness which show how intimately she has lived in her theme. Could anything of the kind be sweeter than this little scene, on the last night spent by the child, Bushy, in the Iowa village ?

"That night in putting Bushy to bed old Mrs. Golden hovered over her longer than usual.

"'Come, dear, say your prayers,' said the old lady, as she secured the last button on the 'nightie.' 'You won't forget to kneel down and say your little verse every evening while away from auntie, will you, darling?'

"'Dess I won't, tause I tant s'eep when I fordet,' was the lisped reply. Then dropping on her dimpled knees she placed her head in Mrs. Golden's lap, clasped her little hands, and began the prayer :

" ' Now I lay me down to s'eep—but I ain't a-layin' down to s'eep, auntie !'

" She lifted her head and peered inquiringly into Mrs. Golden's face.

" ' It means that you will go to sleep in just a minute, dear.'

" ' Oh !' said Bushy, and down her head rested again on the old lady's knee.

" ' Now I lay me down to s'eep—auntie, tan I say sumpin else ?' A second time the head was raised and the little one looked into the auntie's eyes.

" ' Certainly, my dear, if you want to.'

" Snuggling so close was the little face now in the folds of Mrs. Golden's dress that it was with some difficulty the old lady heard the quaint prayer offered by her tiny charge.

" ' Now I lay me down to s'eep, tause I must dit up awful early, tause I'm doin' away wiv my papa.

" ' I pray the Lord my soul to teep away from all the bad sings what Tommy Tiddles said would eat me up—the bears—and—and—sings like dat.'

" There was a pause ; then the wee voice inquired :

" ' What tomes next, auntie ?'

" ' If I should die——'

" ' If I should die before I wake,' broke in the child's voice—' but I'm not doin' to die, tause I must dit up awful early. I'll tell Tommy Tiddles he don't know nuffin 'bout where I'm doin', and if I say my prayers no bears'll eat me up.

" ' I pray the Lord my soul to take wiv my papa's tachel (satchel). Amen.'

" ' Now, auntie, lay me down to s'eep,' she cried, jumping to her feet, and, pulling up her nightgown, she examined her knees to see how the red spots looked. The red spots that came through her kneeling always amused Bushy, and she examined them as regularly as she said her prayers."

And this is the little girl who learns to " shoot straight " on the frontier, to excel in harum-scarum riding, and kills Indians and wild beasts to save her father's, Tom Tiddles', and her own life. The book is, indeed, fascinating. (The Morse Co. $1.50.)—*N. Y. Commercial Advertiser.*

The Herb-Moon.

THE invocation of Prospero, in the fourth act of " The Tempest," rises to the lips as one approaches the author of " The Herb-Moon." " Come with a thought. I thank thee, Ariel; come." And the response of John Oliver Hobbes, her immediate fulfilment of all the tricksy, whimsical, mischievous, and yet lovable conditions which go to make up the world of her Shakespearian prototype, leaves the reader with a sense of witchery that is full of pleasurable excitement and equally pleasurable repose. For the fantasticality of this author is also wise. She is capricious, paradoxical, even a little cynical; but underneath the audacious drollery of her pages there runs a steady stream of right feeling about many things in life which too many novels are disposed to treat with cant phrases, under the pretence that they are standing up for good morals and good taste. John Oliver Hobbes plainly has a conviction that to have taste in the matter of morals is as necessary as to have morals in matters of taste; and she talks as a woman of the world, who can deal with that world on its own terms—as she must—without sacrificing any of the bloom which means a stainless mind. She can set forth a sequence of most surprising situations, as in " The Herb-Moon," which seems somehow enveloped from the first to the last in an atmosphere of improbability, yet all the time she keeps the white principles of life in sight and shows the reader how these will carry eccentric and even improbable characters straight to the honorable conclusion. Thus her cynicism, it must be called, has nothing in common with the arid flippancy which so often goes by the same name. The mere scoffer would protest that such a " Fantasia " as this should be permitted all the poetic license of a fantasia to the end, and that the characters should be bundled off the stage with only such a finishing touch being given to their careers as the wayward fancy of their creator should prefer. But, we repeat, the fantasticality of John Oliver Hobbes is very wise. She is the most freakish writer in contemporary fiction, but there is no novelist living who is, on the whole, more human.

" The Herb-Moon " is a brilliant little book. Knowledge and sympathy are mingled in its pages with imagination and a rippling wit. For the sheer pleasure of being amused on the serious side of one's nature, there is nothing in late fiction which is so effective. (Stokes. $1.25.)—*N. Y. Tribune.*

The Statement of Stella Maberly.

" THE Statement of Stella Maberly," by F. Anstey, belongs to a kind of fiction of which Poe and Hawthorne were masters, but which, even in their hands, is not so much story-telling as analysis of character and feeling. The world with which this fiction concerns itself is not the world in which we live, move, and have our being, but an imaginary world on the " night side " of nature, the inhabitants of which are so strangely unlike the men and women whom we know that if they are not absolutely mad, they are certainly not quite sane. "The Statement of Stella Maberly," which purports to be written by herself, is a record. of her life, as she remembers it, or thinks she remembers it, at the time of writing, and it is so simply and clearly related that it does not occur to us while we are reading it to doubt its entire veracity. If she had merely cared to interest us in her life, we think she would have exercised her inventive faculties oftener, and if she had been solicitous of our good opinion, she would have painted herself in more engaging colors than she has. We accept her as she accepts herself, frankly, if not favorably; we sympathize with her in her troubles, even when they are of her own making; and when she is of the belief that it is not her dead friend and benefactress who is restored to life, but an evil spirit who has entered into her form, we share her belief, whether we will or no, we are so bewitched by her strange personality. By and by, however, we begin to think that we have been deluded, but whether by our credulity or her cunning we are uncertain. Did the things that she has described really happen, or did she only imagine that they happened as she has described? We put these questions to ourselves, and are unable to answer them, which we take to be a proof of the art of the writer, whose object, like that of Poe and Hawthorne in similar autobiographies, was to excite rather than satisfy us, the possibilities of unknown motives surpassing the potentialities of actual catastrophes. "The Statement of Stella Maberly" is a remarkable psychological study, the spirit of which will haunt its readers long after its letter has vanished from their recollections. (Appleton. $1.25.)—*Mail and Express.*

A Primer of Burns.

AT a rough guess, one would say that the Burns Centenary had witnessed—say within the last twelve months—at least as many new editions of the poet's works. However, we are not left to conjecture; since, by turning to the bibliography appended to Mr. Craigie's "Primer," we find precise statistics. Taking 1895 and 1896 together, there have been published eleven different Complete, or Selected Works, which, with other kindred matter, run to a total of twenty-four volumes appearing in honor of the occasion. The latest, but by no means the least worthy edition issues from the critical pen of Mr. Lang—*facile princeps* of living writers on this special subject. One word as to the poetical contents. They are, we believe, "Complete" and unexpurgated, including the unpublished poems and those which have come to light in later years. The arrangement is chron-

ological—after all the best—beginning with the juvenilia of 1773, of which "Handsome Nell" takes the lead as the poet's acknowledged "first performance," and ending with "Fairest Maid on Devon Banks," written only nine days before his death. The text is accompanied by foot-notes, giving the history (where known) of each piece, with glossarial explanations, in addition to a "Reference" glossary at the end of the volume. In short, nothing could be more completely equipped. Mr. Lang's "Introduction" is a valuable study on the poet's life and writings, which, considered as a biography, tells the oft-told tale with consummate skill. At its conclusion, the writer notices Carlyle's regret that circumstances had not allowed Burns an university education. "We might as well wish," says Mr. Lang, "that Jeanne D'Arc had been trained at St. Cyr! He had, probably, as much schooling as Shakespeare, and better Scots poetry Burns could not have written had he been a Craven scholar. Burns—one cannot say it too strongly—*is quite good eno' as he is!*" No! the great regret is not that Burns had no classical education, but that his life was so soon terminated. Mr. Craigie's "Primer of Burns" is a timely subsidiary aid to the student of the poet's life and writings. It maps out his career into its natural periods, and follows with a more extended enumeration and critique of his principal works; giving, throughout, so much of Burns's personal history as is necessary to an understanding of his poems. Annexed to this is, as we have already observed, a complete bibliography of Burns and Burnsiana. (Scribner. $1.)—*Bookseller.*

Cinder-Path Tales.

IF "Cinder-Path Tales," by William Lindsey, shall succeed in reaching the audience which is fitted to appreciate them, it will be a large one, for it will embrace whoever is interested in the multitudinous bodily activities which, once content to be called games and sports, now arrogate to themselves the more dignified name of athletics, concerning which Mr. Lindsey assumes to be an authority, writing in the person of an English teacher of the various branches thereof, particularly those that obtain in collegiate circles, where muscles are cultivated while metaphysics are neglected, and prizes are given for pedestrianism and not for poetry. There are seven of these "Tales," the majority of which deal with incidents and episodes of athletic life. They are good for one reading, if for no more, even among those who care nothing for athletics, for here and there they contain genuine literary touches. (Copeland & Day. $1.)—*Mail and Express.*

Survey of Current Literature.

☞ *Order through your bookseller.*—"*There is no worthier or surer pledge of the intelligence and the purity of any community than their general purchase of books ; nor is there any one who does more to further the attainment and possession of these qualities than a good bookseller.*"—PROF. DUNN.

ART, MUSIC, DRAMA.

McKAY, F. E., *and* WINGATE, C. E. L., *eds.* Famous American actors of to-day. Crowell. 12°, $2.

MARQUAND, ALLAN, *and* FROTHINGHAM, ARTHUR L., *jr.* A text-book of the history of sculpture. Longmans, G. & Co. 12°, $1.50.

MUTHER, R. The history of modern painting ; with 1300 il. Macmillan. 3 v., 8°, $20.

WINGATE, C. E. L. Shakespeare's heroes on the stage. Crowell. 12°, $2.

BIOGRAPHY, CORRESPONDENCE, ETC.

BALDRY, ALFRED LYS. Albert Moore, his life and works ; with photogravures and numerous il. Macmillan. 4°, $9.

BOLTON, *Mrs.* SARAH KNOWLES. Famous givers and their gifts. Crowell. 12°, $1.50.

GEDDIE, J. The balladists. Scribner. 12°, (Famous Scots ser.) 75 c.

HASWELL, C. H. Reminiscences of an octogenarian of the city of New York, 1816–1860. Harper. pors. il. 8°, $3.

HAYES, I. ISRAEL, *M.D.* An Arctic boat journey in the autumn of 1854. [*New ed.*] Houghton, Mifflin & Co. il. maps, 12°, $1.50.
"An excellent book for boys, not a story, is Dr. Hayes's 'An Arctic boat journey,' just republished in view of the interest excited by the Nansen and other recent Polar explorations. No book in its day received a wider reading than this, and no story of hardship and courage was ever told in a more interesting way."—*The Outlook.*

HODGKIN, T. George Fox. Houghton, Mifflin & Co. 12°, (Leaders of religion ser.) $1.

IRVING, WASHINGTON. Columbus, his life and voyages; (condensed by the author from his larger work.) Putnam. 12°, (Heroes of the nations ser., no. 18.) $1.50; $1.75.

LANG, ANDREW. Life and letters of John Gibson Lockhart, by Andrew Lang; from Abbotsford and Milton Lockhart mss. and other original sources. Scribner. 2 v., 4°, $12.50.

LITTLE journeys to the homes of American authors. Putnam. pors. il. 16°, $1.75.

LOCKHART, J. GIBSON. Life of Sir Walter Scott; with prefatory letter by J. R. Hope Scott. Crowell. 2 v., pors. il. 12°, $3; hf. cf., $6.

LOTHROP, THORNTON KIRKLAND. William Henry Seward. Houghton, Mifflin & Co. 12°, (American statesmen ser.) $1.25.

McKAY, F. E., *and* Wingate, C. E. L., *eds.* Famous American actors of to-day. Crowell. pors. 12°, $2.

SMITH, G. BARNETT. William Tyndale, the translator of the English Bible. Revell. il. 12°, (Popular biographies.) 75 c.

WINGATE, C. E. L. Shakespeare's heroes on the stage. Crowell. pors. il. 12°, $2.

YOUMANS, W. JAY. Pioneers of science in America: sketches of their lives and scientific work ; reprinted with additions from the *Popular Science Monthly,* edited and revised. Appleton. 8°, $4.

DESCRIPTION, GEOGRAPHY, TRAVEL, ETC.

EARLE, *Mrs.* ALICE MORSE. Colonial days in old New York. Scribner. 12°, $1.25.

MOULTON, *Mrs.* LOUISE CHANDLER. Lazy tours in Spain and elsewhere. Roberts. 8°, $1.50.

SHALER, N. S. American highways: a popular account of their condition and of the means by which they may be bettered. Century Co. il. diagrams, 12°, $1.50.

WHYMPER, E. Chamonix and the range of Mount Blanc: a guide. Scribner. 12°, *net,* $1.20.

DOMESTIC AND SOCIAL.

BROWN, ANNA ROBERTSON. Culture and reform. Crowell. 12°, leatherette, 35 c.

DOLE, *Rev.* C. F. The golden rule in business. Crowell. 12°, leatherette, 35 c.
In "The golden rule in business" Dr. Dole has applied to a difficult problem the open sesame of common sense. It is more than an exposition of the old max'm that "honesty is the best policy." It calls for something even higher than honesty, for brotherhood, generosity, fairness, and sympathy.

FARRAR, F. W., (*Dean.*) The paths of duty: counsels to young men. Crowell. 12°, leatherette, 35 c.

EDUCATION, LANGUAGE, ETC.

WIGGIN, *Mrs.* KATE DOUGLAS, [*now Mrs.* G. Christopher Riggs,] *and* SMITH, NORA ARCHIBALD. Kindergarten principles and practice. Houghton Mifflin & Co. 12°, (The republic of childhood ser., no. 3.) $1.

FICTION.

BARR, ROB., ["Luke Sharp," *pseud.*] One day's courtship; [*and*] The Heralds of fame; with frontispiece by E. Frederick. Stokes. nar. 16°, (Newport ser.) 75 c.

BOURDILLON, FRANCIS W. Nephelé. New Amsterdam Book Co. 12°, $1.

BRODHEAD. *Mrs.* EVA WILDER, [*formerly* Eva Wilder McGlasson.] One of the Visconti: a novelette. Scribner. nar. 16°, 75 c.
"Exceptionally well told, and, besides possessing many positive virtues, there are so many disagreeable things the author does not do that one must pronounce her very wise. She does not bore one with tedious observations. She is crisp and bright, and her little story is no more

nor less than it was intended to be—a very attractive, entertaining bit of work. The scene is Naples."

CAREY, ROSA NOUCHETTE. The mistress of Brae Farm: a novel. Lippincott. 12°, $1.25.

CRAIGIE, *Mrs.* M., ["John Oliver Hobbes," *pseud*] The herb-moon : a fantasia. Stokes. 16°, $1.25.

CROCKETT, S. RUTHERFORD. The gray man: a novel. Harper. Il. 12°, $1.50.

DOUGLAS, THEO. Iras: a mystery. Harper. 12°, $1.

DRAKE, JEANIE. The Metropolitans. Century. 12°, $1.25.

EARLE, MARY TRACY. The wonderful wheel. Century. 12°, $1.25.
A romance, with its scenes among the Creoles of Louisiana. The title is taken from a luminous wheel that awoke superstitious fears in the minds of the ignorant Creoles, who, sometimes, with bated breath, saw it revolve in the dead of night. The development of the story is concerned with the efforts of the owner of the wheel to live down the "hoodoo" that it brings upon him, his little daughter, and her fair cousin. The story is full of local coloring, and is imaginative and humorous in its character.

EDWARDS, G. WHARTON. Break o' day, and other stories. Century. il. 32°, (Thumb-nail ser.) leath., $1.
Seven sketches of the sturdy fisher-folk living on the islands that lie off the coast of Maine. *Contents:* A watch and chain; A mole or not; Manley; A protégé; Pop's yaller fiddle; Break o' day; A matter of will.

FENN, G. MANVILLE. Beneath the sea: a story of the Cornish coast. Crowell. il. 12°, $1.25.

HERVEY, MAURICE H. Amyas Egerton, cavalier; il. by J. Skelton. Harper. 12°, $1.50.

HOCKING, JOS. The mist on the moors: a romance of North Cornwall. Fenno. il. 12°, 75 c.

HORNUNG, ERNEST W. The rogue's march : a romance. Scribner. 12°, $1.50.
Gives a vivid picture of life within the walls of old Newgate, and the life of a convict in Australia in 1837, full of cruel details. Tom Erichsen, a young man of wasted opportunities, is through strong circumstantial evidence, convicted of a murder of which he is innocent, and his sentence of hanging is commuted to penal servitude for life. The woman he loves follows him to the colonies, where after many dramatic events his innocence is made clear.

LINDEN, ANNIE. Gold : a Dutch-Indian story. Century. 12°, $1.25.
The story opens with a picture of the quiet life of Holland, in the family of a retired East Indian merchant, who lives only among his books. His son, the hero of the story, whose mind is somewhat unsettled by the religious unrest of the day, is sent to Java to take charge of business interests. At Genoa he meets a young lady bound for the same destination. During the long sea voyage they are thrown into close intimacy, and friendship gradually ripens into love. To test the depth and permanence of the affection, the hero plunges into the wilds of

Java in search of a mountain of gold described in the traditions of the natives.

MAGRUDER, JULIA. The violet ; with il. by C. Dana Gibson. Longmans. 12°, $1.25.
The author of "The Princess Sonia" tells a story of fashionable New York. "The violet," named so by admiring friends, is a Mrs. Bertrand, an English woman come over to chaperon Louise Wendell in her first season in society. She is highly recommended, but has evidently a story, as she shrinks from all unnecessary contact with society. Louise's cousin and guardian, Pembroke Jerome, a rich widower, falls in love with Mrs. Bertrand, and by degrees her unhappy past is unravelled.

MANNING, *Mrs.* ANNE. Cherry and Violet : a tale of the great plague. *New ed.* with an introd. by Rev. W. H. Hutton, and 26 ll. by J. Jellicoe and Herbert Railton. Scribner. 12°, $2.25.

MAYNARD, CORA. Some modern heretics : a novel. Roberts. 8°, $1.50.

MILLER, JA. RUSSELL, *D.D.* A gentle heart. Crowell. 12°, leatherette, 35 c.

MORRIS, W. The well at the world's end : a tale. Longmans. 2 v., 8°, $7.50.

RIDGE, W. PETT. An important man and others. Ward, L. & B. 12°, 40 c.

ROBERTS, C. G. DOUGLAS. Around the campfire; il. by C. Copeland. Crowell. 8°, $1.50.

RUDD, JEAN PORTER. The tower of the old schloss. Putnam. 12°, $1.25.

SEAWELL, MOLLY ELLIOT. The sprightly romance of Marsac ; il. by Gustave Verbeek. Scribner. 16°, $1.25.

SERGEANT, ADELINE. The idol-maker: a novel. Appleton. 12°,(Appleton's town and country lib., no. 202.) $1; pap., 50 c.

STOCKTON, FRANK R. Mrs. Cliff's yacht; il. by A. Forestier. Scribner. 12°, $1.50.

THOMPSON, BASIL. A court intrigue. Appleton. 12°, (Appleton's town and country lib., no. 201.) $1; pap., 50 c.
The chief character is a bicycle rider, who finds himself in an out-of-the-way part of Belgium; here he is attracted by an old chateau, which he visits. To his surprise he finds the house occupied by a dethroned monarch, the King of Ethuria, who is surrounded with all the circumstances of a court. There are many amusing incidents, and also a conspiracy, which nearly ends in a tragedy. The secret of the chateau is worth reading for.

WARD, *Mrs.* MARY AUGUSTA, [*Mrs.* T. Humphry Ward.] Sir George Tressady. Macmillan. 12°, $2.

WESTOVER, CYNTHIA M., [*now Mrs.* J. Alden.] Bushy: a romance founded on fact; il. by J. A. Walker. Morse Co. 12°, $1.50.

HISTORY.

ABRAHAMS, ISRAEL. Jewish life in the Middle Ages. Macmillan. 8°, $1.75.

ANDREWS, C. MCLEAN. The historical development of modern Europe, from the Congress of Vienna to the present time. In 2 v. V. I, 1815–1850. Putnam. 8°, $2.50.
Contents: The French Revolution; Napoleon Bonaparte; Reconstruction and the European

system; France during the Restoration; The struggle against absolutism in Italy; The liberal movement in Germany; The July monarchy to 1840; The revolution of 1848 in France; Revolution and reaction in central Europe.

GRAY, G. ZABRISKIE, *D.D.* The children's crusade: an episode of the thirteenth century. [*New ed.*] Houghton, Mifflin & Co. il. 12°, $1.50.
"A new edition of a valuable book is always welcome, because it indicates that the reading public has discrimination. 'The children's crusade,' by George Zabriskie Gray, has appeared in the eleventh edition, and will be read now by hundreds of readers of all ages, who will follow these children of the past in their pathetic and futile enthusiasms."—*The Outlook.*

HASSALL, ARTHUR. The making of the British Empire, (A.D. 1714–1832.) Scribner. 16°, (Oxford manuals of English history, no. 6.) *net*, 50 c.

RATZEL, F. The history of mankind; tr. from the 2d German ed. by A. J. Butler, with introd. by E. B. Tyler. Macmillan. pl. maps, il. 8°, $4.

LITERARY MISCELLANY, COLLECTED WORKS, ETC.

BATES, ARLO. Talks on writing English. Houghton, Mifflin & Co. 12°, $1.50.

CHAMBERLIN, JOS. EDGAR. The listener in the country. Copeland & Day. 16°, 75 c.

ELIOT, C. W. The happy life. Crowell. 12°, leatherette, 35 c.
An essay to young people by the president of Harvard University.

GOETHE, J. WOLF. v., SCHILLER, J. F. v., HEINE, H., *and others.* Gems of German literature; ed. with introd. by J. P. Loesberg. The Morse Co. 12°, 40 c.
Containing some of the choicest selections for memorizing from Goethe, Schiller, Heine, Korner, and Lessing.

MATHEWS, W. Nugæ litterariæ; or, brief essays on literary, social, and other themes. Roberts Bros. 12°, $1.50.

MATTHEWS, JA. BRANDER. Aspects of fiction, and other ventures in criticism. Harper. 12°, $1.50.
The titles of these essays are: American literature; Two studies of the south; The penalty of humor; On pleasing the taste of the public; On certain parallelisms between the ancient drama and the modern; Two Scotsmen of letters (Andrew Lang and Robert L. Stevenson); Aspects of fiction treating of the gift of storytelling; Cervantes, Zola, Kipling & Co.; The prose tales of Coppée; The short stories of Halévy; Charles Dudley Warner as a writer of fiction and text-books of fiction.

MOLINEAUX, MARIE ADA. A phrase-book from the poetic and dramatic works of Robert Browning; to which is added an index containing the significant words not elsewhere noted. Houghton, Mifflin & Co. 8°, $3.

STOWE, *Mrs.* HARRIET BEECHER. Writings, with biographical introds. *Riverside ed.* In 16 v. Houghton, Mifflin & Co. 12°, *ea.*, $1.50. *Large-pap. ed., per v.*, $4.

MENTAL AND MORAL.

HIRSCH, W. Genius and degeneration: a psychological study; tr. from the 2d ed. of the German work. Appleton. 8°, $3.50.
Contents: The limits of insanity; The psychology of genius; Genius and insanity; Degeneration; Influence of education upon genius; Secular hysteria; Art and insanity; Richard Wagner and psychopathology. This work was begun before Nordau's "Degeneration" was published, with the purpose of presenting entirely opposite deductions and conclusions. Since that work appeared Dr. Hirsch has extended the scope of his work, which becomes a scientific answer to Dr. Nordau.

STERRETT, J. DOUGLAS. The power of thought: what it is and what it does; with an introd. by J. Mark Baldwin. Scribner. 12°, $1.75.

NATURE AND SCIENCE.

FORD, NELLIE WALTON. Nature's byways: natural science for primary pupils; il. by Gertrude Morse. The Morse Co. 12°, 40 c.

SANTAYANA, G. The sense of beauty: being the outlines of æsthetic theory. Scribner. 12°, $1.50.

THOMPSON, T. E. A nature calendar: a record of the appearance of the flowers and birds. Morse Co. 12°, 35 c.
A long list of birds and flowers, with opposite blanks for filling in observations as to habits, appearance, growth, and development.

POETRY AND DRAMA.

BROWNING, ROB. Saul; with drawings by Frank O. Small. Crowell. 12°, $1.50.
Browning's poem is described in an introductory note by Charlotte Porter and Helen A. Clarke. There are twelve illustrations that picture the various experiments tried by David by means of music to rouse Saul from his lethargy. The book is printed on thick paper, bound in olive-green silk with gold lettering and boxed.

GRISSOM, ARTHUR. Beaux and belles. Putnam. 16°, $1.
A collection of short poems.

MERINGTON, MARGUERITE. Daphne; or, the pipes of Arcadia: three acts of nonsense. Century. il. 16°, $1.25.
A comic opera libretto of the Gilbertian order, by the author of "Captain Letterblair." The scene is laid in Arcadia, the theme is love. The opera won the prize of $500 awarded three years ago by the National Conservatory of Music, the judges being Thomas Bailey Aldrich, Eugene Field, and others. F. T. Richards, of *Life*, has drawn half a dozen droll pictures to accompany the text.

SAWYER, FRANK E. Notes and half notes. [*Poems.*] Putnam. 12°, $1.

THAXTER, *Mrs.* CELIA LEIGHTON. The poems of Celia Thaxter. [*Appledore ed.*] Houghton, Mifflin & Co. 12°, $1.50.
Comprises all of Mrs. Thaxter's poetical works, except her verses for children, published last year, together with some not before printed. Sarah Orne Jewett furnishes a charming preface.

TODD, MABEL LOOMIS, *ed.* A cycle of sonnets. Roberts. 12°, $1.25.
These sonnets, dedicated to "my immortal

love," " bequeathed to me," says the editor,
" by one the tragedy of whose life it has been
mine to know, were written in mature years,
and in the splendor of his first great love for
the fair girl who died during the second year
of their engagement."

POLITICAL AND SOCIAL.

AUBREY, W. HICKMAN SMITH. Stock Exchange
investments: the theory, methods, practice,
and results. Scribner. 8°, $2.

DRAGE, GEOFFREY. The labour problem.
Scribner. 8°, $5.60.

STANWOOD, E. A history of presidential elec-
· tions. *5th ed. rev.* Houghton, Mifflin & Co.
12°, $1.50.
"The story of each presidential election, its
result, and the leading questions at issue in the
several campaigns. Necessarily it involves
the very spirit of the several periods regarding
governmental policy, both domestic and foreign.
It thus makes up in epitome terse, well-digested
political history from the days of Washington
to Cleveland's second term. The facts have
been carefully gathered as to accuracy, as the
documents and party platforms have verified.
It is a good book for the reference library,
edited with much ability and great painstaking,
which the chapters show. The author is simply
the historian, not a partisan. The book is of
like value to all parties."—*Daily Inter-Ocean.*

TOURGÉE, ALBION WINEGAR. The war of the
standards: coin *and* credit *versus* coin *without*
credit. Putnam. 12°, (Questions of the day,
no. 88.) 75 c.; 40 c.
Contents: The currency issue of commanding importance; What is the is-ue?, An old, old
story; The world's verdict; Monetary experiments; " The crime of 1873 "; Depreciation of
silver; A new economic law; The decline of
prices; " Value," " Equivalency," " Money,"
"Credit "; National currency and national credit; Terminal legal tender credit money; The results of free coinage of silver; Currency and
protection; The rich and the poor.

WAGNER, LEOPOLD, *ed.* Modern political ora-
tions. Holt. 12°, $1.
Noted examples of British political oratory of
Victoria's reign. Contains the speech of Lord
Brougham on negro emancipation, Daniel
O'Connell on repeal of the Union, Bulwer on
the Crimean war, Isaac Butt on home rule,
Joseph Cowen on the foreign policy of Eng-
land, Lord Randolph Churchill on the Egyptian
crisis, Charles S. Parnell on the coercion bill,
The Right Honorable John Morley on home
rule, Richard Cobden on the corn laws, etc., etc.

SPORTS AND AMUSEMENTS.

BOARDMAN, EMERY. Winning whist: a harmonious system of combined long-suit and
short-suit play of the game of whist. Scribner. 16°, $1.
While following the lines of Cavendish, and
the now universally accepted system of American leads, the author adds some interesting
variations and developments of his own. The
arrangement of the book and the analyses of the
various hands and plays are notably clear and
simple.

LEWIS, W. H. A primer of college football ;
il. from instantaneous photographs. Harper.
16°, pap., 75 c.

YALE, LEROY MILTON, *M.D.*, CREIGHTON, J. G.
A., [*and others.*] Angling. Scribner. il. 12°,
(The out-of-door lib.) $1.50.
Contents: Getting out the fly books, by Leroy
Milton Yale, M.D.; The land of the Wina-
nishe, by L. M. Yale and J. G. A. Creighton ;
Nepigon River fishing, by A. R. Macdonough ;
Striped-bass fishing, by A. Foster Higgins ; The
haunts of the black sea bass, by C. F. Holder ;
Tarpon fishing in Florida, by Rob. Grant ;
American game fishes, by L. M. Yale ; Izaak
Walton, by Alex. Cargill. These chapters ap-
peared from time to time in *Scribner's Magazine*;
they are now carefully revised.

THEOLOGY, RELIGION, AND SPECULATION.

ABBOTT, LYMAN, *D.D.* Christianity and social
problems. Houghton, Mifflin & Co. 12°,
$1.25.
The book is an endeavor to apply Christ's
teachings on social questions to present conditions. The chapters are entitled: The founder
of Christianity ; Christianity and democracy ; Christianity and communism ; Christianity and socialism ; Christ's law of the family; Christ's law of service ; Christ's standard
of values ; Christ's law for the settlement of
controversies ; Personal international labor ;
The enemies of the social order ; The social
evil ; The brotherhood of man.

BIBLE illustrations: a series of plates illustrating Biblical versions and antiquities; being an
appendix to the " Oxford Bible for teachers."
University of Oxford. 8°, $1.
These illustrations were selected and described by Sir E. Maunde Thompson, principal
librarian of the British Museum, and E. A.
Wallis Budge, keeper of Egyptian and Assyrian
antiquities, British Museum, assisted by A. S.
Murray, keeper of Greek and Roman antiquities.
There are 124 plates accompanied by descriptive letterpress. They are divided into three
groups—1 Illustrations of the languages, writings, and versions of the Scriptures; 2, Illustrations of Old Testament history and religion; and
3, Illustrations of New Testament history.

CHILDREN (THE) OF THE BIBLE. Revell. 4°,
(Good shepherd ser.) 50 c.

MASON, ARTHUR JA., *D.D.* The principles of
ecclesiastical unity: four lectures delivered in
St. Asaph Cathedral on June 16, 17, 18, and
19. Longmans. 12°, $1.

PULLAN, LEIGHTON. Lectures on religion.
Longmans. 12°, $2.

Books for the Young.

ASHLEY, B. FREEMAN. Air Castle Don; or,
from dreamland to hardpan. Laird & L. 12°,
(Young America ser.) $1.

BÉTIS, VICTOR, *and* SWAN, HOWARD. The facts
of life, (*les faits de la vie,*) idiomatically described and systematically arranged, forming
a complete dictionary of the objective language. Pt. 1, Home life, the school, travelling, plants. Scribner. 8°. (Psychological
methods of teaching and studying languages,
French ser., no. 1.) *net,* 80 c.
The first part of a dictionary intended to give
the signification of words not by the usual alphabetical entry with definition or explanation, but

In a collection of those instances in which any given word is rightly employed in the usual language of daily life, thus also bringing in the idiomatic phraseology of each language. This plan will be adopted for the acquiring of the English, German, Latin, and Greek languages. No translations are given. M. Bétis is director of the Normal School of Languages, Boston, Mass., and Howard Swan is director of the Central School of Foreign Tongues, London.

GUERBER, H. A. The story of Greece. American Book Co. il. maps, 12°, (Eclectic school readings.) 60 c.

Elementary history intended for supplementary reading, or as a first history text-book. The plan is to bring out events of Greek history in a series of stories, in which Lycurgus Dædalus, Jason, Philip of Macedon, Demosthenes, and other Grecian heroes are the subjects. The purpose is to make history attractive to children.

In the November Magazines.

THE November *Arena* contains striking papers on the money question from the pens of Prof. Frank Parsons, of the Boston University School of Law; Justice Walter Clarke, of the Supreme Bench of North Carolina; Hon William H. Standish, and B. O. Flower, the editor. It has also an article by Lilian Whiting on Kate Field, who recently died in Honolulu. A picture of whom, never before printed, forms the frontispiece of this number. Other papers are: "Jesus and the Apostles," by Prof. J. R. Buchanan; "The New Charity," by Bolton Hall; "The Simplicity of the Single Tax," by S. Howard Leech; and "Can We Have an Infallible Revelation?" by Rev. T. Ernest Allen.

The Atlantic Monthly opens with "Causes of Agricultural Unrest," by J. Laurence Laughlin. "Cheerful Yesterdays" is the first of a series of exceedingly interesting reminiscences covering the last fifty years of Col. Thomas Wentworth Higginson's life. Another article of reminiscence is that by Charles Warren Stoddard, entitled "Early Recollections of Bret Harte" The fiction of the number is by "Charles Egbert Craddock" and Charles G. D. Roberts. "Out of the Book of Humanity" is a pathetic tale of the tragedies that make up the story of the very poor, from the pen of Jacob A. Riis. A descriptive article by Miriam Coles Harris is called "A Night and a Day in Spain."

"ELECTION Day in New York" is the opening paper of *The Century*, with graphic description by Ernest Ingersoll and pictures by Jay Hambidge. Gen. Horace Porter contributes the first of a series of articles, entitled "Campaigning with Grant," embodying recollections of Grant during the period of his supreme command over the Union army, giving an intimate revelation of his nature and enlivened by abundant anecdote. Two serial novels begin in this number: "Hugh Wynne, Free Quaker," by Dr. S. Weir Mitchell, of Philadelphia, and "A Rose of Yesterday," by F. Marion Crawford. "The Olympic Games of 1896" are the subject of a paper by their founder, Baron Pierre de Coubertin; the artist, Andre Castaigne, was sent to Athens for the express purpose of making the pictures. A timely article is by Duncan Rose, on the topic "Why the Confederacy Failed," the three reasons given being "the excessive use of paper money," "the policy of dispersion," and "the neglect of the cavalry." The short stories are by Chester B. Fernald, Lucy S. Furman, and Harry S. Edwards.

The Fortnightly Review for October includes among its contents "The Russian Ascendancy in Europe," by "Diplomaticus"; "Eastern

Questions, Far and Near":—I. "China, England, and Russia," by Capt. J. W. Gambier.—II. "The Turkish Question in Its Religious Aspect," by Maj. Martin A. S. Hume. Of special interest at this time is "Battle of the Ballots in America," by Francis H. Hardy, and a literary article concerning French fiction in general, and more particularly the works of Paul Hervieu, by Hannah Lynch.

Harper's Magazine for November is marked by the first paper in a new series on South Africa, by Poultney Bigelow, which tells the story of "Jameson's Raid." "The First President of the United States," by Woodrow Wilson, brings to a close his six papers on Washington. It, like its predecessors, is amply illustrated by Howard Pyle and others. Laurence Hutton gives an interesting description of "The Literary Landmarks of Florence," with nine illustrations by Du Mond. "The Nemesis of Perkins" is a humorous sketch by John Kendrick Bangs. The short stories are by Thomas Janvier, E. A. Alexander, and "Octave Thanet."

THE October issue of *The Nineteenth Century* contains "The Cry for Fraudulent Money in America," by George F. Parker; "On the Ethics of Suppression in Biography," by Edmund S. Purcell; "Lord Randolph Churchill as an Official," by Sir Algernon West; "Fra Filippo Lippi," by Sir Jos. Crowe; and "The Massacres in Turkey," by Rev. Dr. J. G. Rogers, the Earl of Meath, and others.

Scribner's contains an article on "Panther-Hunting in India," by Capt. C. J. Melliss, which is full of adventure and of special information about the ways of these beautiful animals. The illustrations are by Van Muyden. M. H. Spielmann has a paper on "The Renaissance of Lithography," illustrated by reproductions from the works of famous artists. In "The Camera and The Comedy" Alexander Black tells how his pictures are made, and of the difficulties which present themselves to the artist. Mary Gay Humphreys, one of the brightest of newspaper writers, tells how many literary and artistic women live in cities, in an article on "Woman Bachelors in New York." Frederick Funston describes the perils of the journey "Over the Chilkoot Pass to the Yukon," to the seeker after fortune or adventure in the new gold fields of Alaska.

The Westminster Review includes among its articles in the October number "Professional Dogmatism," by Maurice Todhunter, a criticism on Prof. George Saintsbury's *History of Nineteenth Century Literature;* also, "Journalism as a Profession," by Fred Wilson, and an article on "Trilby," by Mary G. Husband, which is particularly interesting in view of the recent death of its gifted author.

Freshest News.

LEE & SHEPARD have issued "A Manual for China Painters," by Mrs. Nicola di Rienzi Monachesi, a practical and comprehensive treatise on the art of painting china and glass with mineral colors. The work is divided into two parts entitled Materials and Instruction, both giving directions so clear and definite that amateurs may pursue their work alone. The book contains five plates made in Paris of fac-similes of Lacroix colors, and it bears this artist's endorsement of its teachings.

D. VAN NOSTRAND COMPANY have just issued "Roentgen Rays and Phenomena of the Anode and Cathode," by Edward P. Thompson, author of "Inventing as a Science and an Art," assisted by Louis M. Pignolet, N. D. C. Hodges, and Ludwig Gutmann. A chapter is included on generalization, arguments, theories, kindred radiations, and phenomena, by Professor William A. Anthony, formerly of Cornell University. The book is intended for students, teachers, physicians, photographers, electricians, and general readers. All must be interested in this wonderful discovery by which it is possible through outside garments, flesh and muscles to see even the movements of the human heart.

DODD, MEAD & CO. are the publishers of Ian Maclaren, and now while he is among us it seems a fitting time to call special attention to his delightful books. They have made new and handsomely illustrated editions of "Beside the Bonnie Brier-Bush" and "The Days of Auld Lang Syne," and have just issued "Kate Carnegie," fully illustrated and described elsewhere in this issue. A specially pretty book has been made by taking the wonderful story entitled "A Doctor of the Old School" from "B·side the Bonnie Brier-Bush" and fully illustrating it from drawings made at Drumtochty by Frederick C. Gordon. "The Mind of the Master" and "The Upper Room" show the poetry and helpfulness of the religion Dr. Watson preaches so eloquently.

FREDERICK WARNE & CO. have now a most timely and wonderfully interesting book in their excellent series *Public Men of To-Day*. The biography of Pope Leo XIII., written by Justin McCarthy, treats this most interesting personality from a distinctly living and modern point of view. The N. Y. *Sun* pronounces the book "eminently fair and impartial," and *The Chicago Inter-Ocean* says: "Even those who have the least sympathy with the Roman Church can read the book altogether without offence." A good notice appeared in THE LITERARY NEWS for September, and the very excellent portrait of Leo XIII. included in the book is given in this issue. "Grover Cleveland," by James Lowry White, is now in preparation for this series. Many other books, chiefly of holiday character, will be commented upon next month.

CHARLES SCRIBNER'S SONS have just ready "Sentimental Tommy," James M. Barrie's story, which has had so successful a run in *The Century Magazine*. Mr. Barrie has made Tommy one of the most delightful characters of fiction, and William Hatherell has made

about a dozen telling illustrations of his chequered career. The publishers offer excellent fiction in the "Sprightly Romance of Marsac," by Molly Elliot Seawell ; "The Rogue's March," by E. W. Hornung ; "A Foreign Idyl," by Paul Bourget ; "One of the Visconti," by Eva Wilder; and "Love in Old Cloathes," by Henry C. Bunner. In illustrated works they have "The Edge of the Orient," by Robert Howard Russell, and "In Ole Virginia," by Thomas Nelson Page, illustrated by Frost, Pyle, Smedley, Castaigne, Clinedinst, and the late C. S. Reinhart. Stevenson's and Eugene Field's works are also published by the Scribners.

HENRY HOLT & Co. have published "The Island of Cuba," by Lieut. A. S. Rowan and Professor M. M. Ramsay, a clear, compact, impartial account of the present revolution and the position of the United States in regard to it, with full bibliography, of which *The Philadelphia Times* says: "It conveys just the information needed at this time, more satisfactorily we think than any other recent publication. The authors' opinions on Cuba are of interest and value." A book any publisher may be proud to see bearing his imprint is it. Prof. Kuno Francke's great work on "The Social Forces in German Literature," which, since issued by the Holts, has been approved by those of highest authority in the professional world. It is good to announce the fourteenth edition of Paul L. Ford's "The Honorable Peter Stirling." A great treat is in store for all who have not read this brilliant and truthful novel.

HOUGHTON, MIFFLIN & Co. have just issued an armful of their more important books. The first is an illustrated edition of Mr. Fiske's great work, "The American Revolution," which is enriched with a large number of portraits, maps, plates, and cuts in the text, all of a character to illustrate the historic features of the work. The large-paper edition is brought out with very great care on English hand-made paper. A holiday book of a very different character is an edition of Thoreau's "Cape Cod," in two volumes, beautifully illustrated with 100 water-colors by Miss Amelia M. Watson, of Hartford, the pictures not being printed in the text but in the margin, and the whole promising a very interesting variation in holiday books. At the same time appears Miss Phelps's autobiographical work, "Chapters from a Life," which gives a very interesting story of her experience as a girl, writer, and associate of literary and philanthropic men and women. It promises to be quite as popular as her best stories. Mrs. Wiggin's new story, "Marm Lisa," which is one of her longest and best, appears at the same date ; also, "The Country of the Pointed Firs," a remarkably delightful story, by Miss Sarah Orne Jewett, of a summer on the coast of Maine and adjacent islands. Miss Merriam's book of birds and their nests in Southern California, out at the same time, is entitled "A-Birding on a Bronco," and a new book by Bret Harte, containing eight stories, named from the first, "Barker's Luck," is also just published. The book on football by Mr. Camp and Mr. Deland, who are probably the most competent Americans to write on this subject, is also just ready and ought to have a wide circulation, judging from the almost universal interest in the game.

ROBERTS' RECENT BOOKS

Poems by Johanna Ambrosius.

Translated from the twenty-sixth German edition by MARY J. SAFFORD. Portrait. 16mo, $1.50.

" How she acquired the exquisite literary style she possesses will not be explained this side of the hereafter. . . . Nothing so precious has come from the Fatherland since the hymns of Luther and the writings of Goethe."—*Philadelphia Telegraph.*

" Here is a woman who, by sheer force of genius, has risen in a few months from a common laborer of the fields to be known as one of Germany's most popular modern poets. The striking thing in her poems is their lyrical quality. Whether the thought be sad or hopeful, the singing quality of the verse is ever apparent."—*New York Tribune.*

Mother, Baby, and Nursery.

By Dr. GENEVIEVE TUCKER. Fully illustrated. Small 4to, cloth, $1.50.

The object of the author in presenting this work is to furnish a practical summary of the infant's hygiene and physical development. It purposes to teach and help a mother to understand her child, to feed it properly, to place it in healthful surroundings, and to watch its growth and development with intelligence. The book is not intended in any measure to take the place of a physician.

The Puritan in England and New England.

By EZRA HOYT BYINGTON, D.D., Member of the American Society of Church History. With an introduction by Alexander McKenzie. D.D. Three illustrations. 8vo, cloth, $2.00.

"A noteworthy contribution."— *Philadelphia Bulletin.*

Emily Dickinson's Poems.

Third Series. Edited by MABEL LOOMIS TODD. Uniform with First and Second Series. 16mo, cloth, $1.25 ; white and gold, $1.50.

" The intellectual activity of Emily Dickinson was so great that a large and characteristic choice is still possible among her literary material."—*Introduction.*

Little Daughter of the Sun.

By JULIA P. DABNEY. Illustrated by the author. 16mo, cloth, $1.25.

Armenian Poems.

Rendered into English Verse by ALICE STONE BLACKWELL. 12mo, cloth, $1.25.

Modern French Literature.

By BENJAMIN W. WELLS, Ph.D., author of " Modern German Literature." 12mo, cloth, $1.50.

Public Opinion says of "Modern German Literature": " An interesting and valuab'e contribution to our accounts of German Literature."

Six Modern Women.

Psychological Sketches. By LAURA MARHOLM HANSSON. Translated from the German by Hermione Ramsden. 12mo, cloth, $1.25.

CONTENTS : Sonia Kovalevsky.—George Egerton.—Eleonora Duse.—Amalie Skram.—Marie Bashkirtseff.—A. Ch. Edgren-Leffler.

The Black Dog, and Other Stories.

By A. G. PLYMPTON, author of " Dear Daughter Dorothy," etc. With illustrations by the author. 16mo, cloth, $1.25.

Jerry the Blunderer.

By LILY F. WESSELHOEFT, author of " Sparrow the Tramp," etc. Illustrated from photographs taken from life. 16mo, cloth, $1.25.

A Cape May Diamond.

By EVELYN RAYMOND, author of " The Little Lady of the Horse " and " The Mushroom Cave." Illustrated by Lilian Crawford True. Square 12mo, cloth, $1.50.

AT ALL THE BOOK-STORES.

ROBERTS BROTHERS, Publishers, Boston.

THE LITERARY NEWS

AN ECLECTIC REVIEW OF CURRENT LITERATURE
ILLUSTRATED

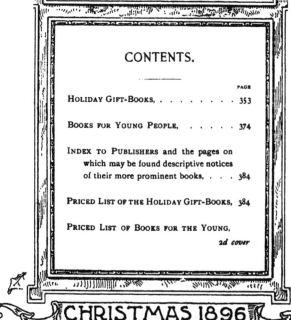

CONTENTS.

CHRISTMAS 1896

PUBLICATION OFFICE
59 DUANE STREET NEW YORK
ENTERED·AT·POST-OFFICE·AT NEW YORK·AS·SECOND-CLASS·MATTER

Books for Young People.

Alden, *Mrs.* G. R. Making fate. Il. $1.50.*Lothrop Pub. Co*

Aspinwall, *Mrs.* Thomas. Short stories for short people. Il. $1.50....................................*Dutton*

Bangs, John Kendrick. The mantel-piece minstrels. Il. by F. Berkeley Smith. 75c.....................

Barnes, James. Midshipman Farragut. Il. by C. T. Chapman. (*Young heroes of the navy ser.*) $1.*Appleton*

Beal, Mary B. Boys of Clovernook. Il. $1.50. *Lothrop Pub. Co*

Beard, Dan C. American boy's book of sport. Il. $2.50.....................................*Scribner*

Blanchard, Amy E. Betty of Wye. Il. $1.25.*Lippincott*

Bolton, Sarah K. Famous givers and their gifts. Il. $1.50.......................................*Crowell*

Brine, Mary D. Little lad Jamie. Il. $1.25...*Dutton*

Brooks, Elbridge S. True story of Abraham Lincoln. Il. $1.50....................................*Lothrop Pub. Co*

Brooks, Elbridge S., *and* Alden, John. The long walls: American boy's adventures in Greece. Il. by Geo. Foster Barnes. $1.50.....................*Putnam*

Brooks, Noah. Our baseball club, and how it won the championship. New rev. ed. Il. $1.50.......*Dutton*

Brundage, *Mrs.* Frances M., *and* Tucker, Elizabeth S. Children of to-day; fac-similes of water-colors. $2. *Stokes*

— Little belles and beaux. Selections from "Children of to-day." $1.25..............................*Stokes*

— Little men and maids. Selections from "Children of to-day." $1.25...............................*Stokes*

Butterworth, Hezekiah. The wampum belt. Il. $1.50...*Appleton*

Chaffey, M. Ella. Youngsters of Murray Home. $1. *Ward & Lock*

Color books for children.......*Dutton; Stokes; Warne*

Couch, Arthur T. Quiller. Fairy-tales far and near. Il. $1.50....................................*Stokes*

Coursen, Frances B. What the dragon-fly told the children. Il. $1.50................*Lothrop Pub. Co*

Crockett, S. R. Sweetheart travellers. Il. by Gordon Browne and W. H. C. Groome. $1.50 ....*Stokes*

Curiosities of nature and art....................*Nelson*

Dabney, Julia P. Little daughter of the sun. Il. $1.50..*Roberts*

Davis, M. E. M. An elephant's track, and other stories. $1.75.......................................*Harper*

Dodge, Mary Mapes. Hans Brinker; or, the silver skates. Il. $1.50.................................*Scribner*

Doudney, Sarah. Katharine's keys. Il. $1.50.*Dutton*

Egyptian Struwwelpeter: a parody. Il. in color. $1.50...*Stokes*

Ellis, Edward S. Uncrowning a king. $1.25. *New Amsterdam Book Co*

Fenn, George Manville. Beneath the sea. Il. $1.50. *Crowell*

— Black Tor. Il. $1.50.....................*Lippincott*

Frith, H:, *and* Rawson, Stephen. Coil and current; wonders of electricity. Il. $1.25........*Ward & Lock*

Frost, W. H. Court of King Arthur. Il. by Burleigh. $1.50..*Scribner*

Gellibrand, Emma. J. Cole. Il. $1.........*Crowell*

Green, E. Everett. The sign of the red cross. Il. $1.25..*Nelson*

Grimm's wonder-book for boys and girls. Il. $1.25. *Crowell*

Harper's round table for 1896. V. 17. 1200 Il. $3.50.*Harper*

Harris, J. C. Story of Aaron, so-named, the son of Ben Ali. Il. by Oliver Herford. $2....*Houghton, M*

Hatton, Bessie. Fairy-tales. Il. $1.50.........*Stokes*

Henty, George A. At Agincourt.—Cochrane the dauntless.— On the Irrawaddy. Il. *Ea.*, $1.50....*Scribner*

Heroes of the nations ser. *Ea.*, $1.50. *New volumes:* Irving's Columbus, abridged; Maxwell's Robert the Bruce.......................................*Putnam*

Hingst, Adolphine, *and* Ruskay, Esther. Rhymes and songs for my little ones. $1....*Lothrop Pub. Co*

Home, Andrew. Romance of industry and invention. $1.50..*Lippincott*

— Through thick and thin. Il. $1.25........*Lippincott*

In far Japan: a story of English children. Il. 60c.*Nelson*

King, Pauline. Christine's career. Il. $1.50.*Appleton*

Kingsley, Henry. Mystery of the island. New ed. Il. $1.25.....................................*Lippincott*

Lee, Albert. Tommy Toddles. Il. by Peter S. Newell. $1.25...*Harper*

Little Frida: tale of the Black Forest. Il. 60c..*Nelson*

Magic lantern Struwwelpeter. Col. il. movable disks. $1..*Warne*

Marshall, Emma. Only Susan. $1.50.........*Dutton*

Mead, Laura T. Catalina. Il. $1.25.......*Lippincott*

Moffat, W: D. Not without honor: a Christmas-book for boys. Il. $1.25................*Arnold & Co*

Molesworth, *Mrs.* Philippa. Il. $1.25...*Lippincott*

Morrison, Sarah E. Chilhowee boys at college. Il. $1.50.......................................*Crowell*

Mother Goose: complete ed. Il. $2.50........*Dutton*

Movable picture-books........*Dutton; Stokes; Warne*

Munroe, Kirk. Rick Dale. Il. $1.25.........*Harper*

— Snow-shoes and sledges. Il. $1.25.........*Harper*

— Through swamp 'and glade. Il. by Victor Pérard. $1.25..*Scribner*

Oxley, J. Macdonald. Boy tramps; or, across Canada. Il. $1.25.......................................*Crowell*

— Romance of commerce. Il. $1.25.............*Crowell*

Ouida. Two little wooden shoes. Il. by Garrett. $1.50. *Lippincott*

Perry, Nora. Three little daughters of the revolution. Il. by Frank T. Merrill. 75c..........*Houghton, M*

Plympton, A. G. Black dog, and other stories. Il. $1.25..*Roberts*

Poulsson, Emilie. Through the farmyard gate. $1.25. *Lothrop Pub. Co*

Pratt, Ella Farman. Happy children. Il. $1.50.*Crowell*

Ray, Anna Chapin. Dick. Il. $1.25.........*Crowell*

— Half a dozen girls. Il. $1.50..............*Crowell*

Raymond, Evelyn. Cape May diamond. Il. $1.50. *Roberts*

Roberts, G. D. Around the camp-fire. Il. $1.50.*Crowell*

Robinson Crusoe. Il. $2.50..................*Dutton*

Round the hearth-stone. $1.50................*Nelson*

Russan, Ashmore, *and* Boyle, Frederick. The orchid-seekers. Il. $1.75........................*Warne*

Russell, Robert Howard. The Delft cat. Il. by F. Berkeley Smith. 75c.......................*Russell*

Sangster, *Mrs.* M. E. Little knights and ladies. Verses for young people. Il. $1.25.........*Harper*

Sidney, Margaret. The gingham bag. Il. $1.25. *Lothrop Pub. Co*

Stables, Gordon. Every inch a sailor.........*Nelson*

— How Jack Mackenzie won his epaulettes. Il. $1.25. *Nelson*

Stockton, Frank R. Captain Chap; or, the rolling stones. Il. by Stephens. $1.50.........*Lippincott*

Stoddard, W. O. The Windfalls. Il. by B. W. Clinedinst. $1.50....................................*Appleton*

Stredder, Eleanor. The hermit princes. Il. $1.*Nelson*

Stuart, Ruth McEnery. Solomon Crow's Christmas pockets. Il. $1.........................*Harper*

Suffling, Ernest R. Fur-traders of the west. Il. $1.50. *Warne*

Swett, Sophie. The Ponkaty branch road. Il. $1. *Lothrop Pub. Co*

Taylor, Fannie J. Adolphe. Il. 50c.........*Revell*

Thomson, E. W. Walter Gibbs, the young boss. Il. $1.25..*Crowell*

Toy-Books...................*Dutton; Stokes; Warne*

Turner, Ethel. Little larrikin. Il. $1..*Ward & Lock*

Underhill, Zoe Dana. The dwarf's tailor. Il. $1.75. *Harper*

Vengeance of Dominique de Gourges. $1.25...*Nelson*

Webster, J. Provand. Oracle of Baal. Il. by Goble. $1.50..*Lippincott*

— Swept out to sea. $1.50...................*Lippincott*

Wesselhoeft, Lily. Jerry the blunderer. Il. from photographs taken from life. $1.25.........*Roberts*

White, Eliza Orne. A little girl of long ago. Il. $1. *Houghton, M*

Whitney, *Mrs.* A. D. T. Friendly letters to girl friends. $1.25...........................*Houghton, M*

Wilson, Calvin Dill, *and* Reeve, James Knapp. Bible boys and girls. Il. $1.25..........*Lothrop Pub. Co*

Wishaw, Fred. Harold the Norseman.........*Nelson*

Woods, Kate Tannatt. Mopsy. Il. $1.25.

Wright, Ernest Vincent. Wonderful fairies of the sun. Il. $1.25.................................*Roberts*

Young pioneers: with La Salle on the Mississippi. $1.75...*Nelson*

THE
LITERARY NEWS
An Eclectic Review of Current Literature.

*Published monthly, and containing the freshest news concerning books and authors; lists of new
publications; reviews and critical comments; characteristic extracts; sketches and
anecdotes of authors; courses of reading; literary topics of the
magazines; and other literary subjects.*

| VOL. XVII. | *CHRISTMAS*, 1896. | NO. 12 |

Copyright, 1896, by R. R. Bowker.

From Wilson's "George Washington."   Copyright, 1896, by Harper & Brothers.

Holiday Gift-Books.

Two Du Maurier Books.—A book about Du
Maurier and a volume of the delightful *Punch*
sketches of the loved artist-novelist are welcome additions indeed to the holiday shelf, and
for these two good works the Messrs. Harper
have earned the graceful appreciation of the
reading public. The first is called " In Bohemia with Du Maurier," and in it Felix Mosche-
les gives a graphic picture of the student days
in the Antwerp Academy, where he first met
Du Maurier. The lively, vivid sketches bring
us into close touch with those gay dwellers in
Bohemia, among whom were Tadema, Mario,
and others since become famous ; and the volume is throughout redolent of the atmosphere
of "Trilby." It is illustrated with sixty-three
original drawings by Du Maurier, and is handsomely printed and bound. The other Du
Maurier volume is entitled " English Society,"
and is a collection of about one hundred of the
best and most characteristic of the *Punch* drawings, prefaced with an introduction by W. D.
Howells. These form, indeed, a bird's-eye
view of the changing fads and fashions of English society for a score of years, and with their
delightful bits of dialogue or conversation, instinct with keen observation and kindly satire,
they show us more of the varying grades of
social strata than the heaviest and most learned
of social treatises. (Harper.)

George Washington.—The revival of popular
interest in American history is one of the
notable incidents in the literary record of the
year. The era of Washington has followed
that of Napoleon, and historical and biographical literature relating to Colonial and Revolutionary days promises to be as abundant and as
notable as that previously evoked by the freshened interest in the Bonapartes. However that
may be, the literature of American biography
is permanently enriched by Prof. Woodrow
Wilson's "George Washington." In this work
the professor of jurisprudence of Princeton
University has given us not only a new biography of Washington, but a new history of
America in Washington's time. He has drawn
with masterly skill and strong simplicity a
picture of the varied elements that made that
memorable period. The culmination of the
Colonial era, the final overthrow of the French
dominion, the Revolutionary War, and the establishment of the Republic upon the firm basis
of constitutional law—all these are phases of
his historic background, and he has made the
whole epoch luminous with the spirit of its
foremost man. In its personal side the work
is specially delightful, and the character of
Washington is revealed to us not only as it
appeared through the storm clouds of war and
statesmanship, but as it was seen in the quiet

WASHINGTON AND BARON VON STEUBEN AT VALLEY FORGE.

parliament. The work is instinct with patriotic spirit and its every chapter is a thrilling story. The chief actors in the stormy scenes—Queen Luise, Stein, Blücher—stand forth as living portraitures, and in describing the events and incidents of the time the author has drawn upon much original material, never before made public. He has also visited personally every battlefield and most of the scenes connected with his subject, and he writes from a fund of careful information and genuine enthusiasm. The work is profusely illustrated by R. Caton Woodville, whose brilliant drawings are as spirited as they are historically accurate, as well as by portraits and maps, and it is handsomely bound in rich covers, emblazoned with the shield of Germany. (Harper. 2 v., $5.)

Naval Actions of the War of 1812.—It is rather difficult to determine why a sea-fight is generally more thrilling and of intenser interest than an engagement on land, but that it is so no one who looks into Mr. James Barnes's account of the actions of the War of 1812 will be apt to deny. Mr. Barnes gives in this important work accounts of every important naval battle that took place between England and the United States during that war, and his own vivid interest in his subject, his graphic descriptions, and his effective style, add to the fascination of a theme that in its barest outline is full of interest. The lives of the greater naval commanders are briefly sketched, the part played by sailors and marines is not forgotten, and there is a lucid exposition of the political condition of the time and of the effects of the war on American commerce. The text is supplemented by many capital full-page colored illustrations by Carlton T. Chapman, which in themselves are notable representations of the men and the times, and the work is a most welcome contribution to the history of a notable epoch. (Harper. $4.50.)

The World Beautiful.—Miss Whiting in this later series of essays dwells at length on the higher possibilities of friendship, and in connection with this theme discusses the determination of social conditions, the art of conversation, the charm of atmosphere, the force of love as a redemptive agency, the virtues of self-control and pleasant speech, and the supreme necessity of an elevated outlook, in adjusting the mind to the experiences of external life. (Roberts. $1; $1.25.)

home retirement of Mount Vernon. A notable feature of the book is the series of beautiful drawings made for it by Howard Pyle, Harry Fenn, and other artists, who make the actors and scenes of those historic days live again in counterfeit presentments. The publishers have spared no pains to make the volume worthy of its contents, and they have attained their aim in letter and in spirit. (Harper. $3.)

History of the German Struggle for Liberty.—The story of the German uprising against the tyranny of Napoleon that culminated with the triumphal entry of the allied monarchs into Paris in March, 1814, is dramatic in itself, and when told with the spirit and enthusiasm with which Mr. Bigelow has invested his narrative, it becomes alive with heroic fire. He aims to show how fully this struggle awakened the desire for German liberty, and how the patriotism then aroused found its fuller expression in the later struggles of 1848 and 1866—struggles that resulted finally in the establishment of the German Empire, manhood suffrage, and a free

History of the Last Quarter Century in the United States.—This work, by President E. Benjamin Andrews, of Brown University, is a work of imposing interest. In preparing the work for book publication the author has enlarged his text one-third, and 100 new illustrations have been added. The original twelve articles, which were received with great favor during their appearance in *Scribner's Magazine,* are expanded into twenty-five chapters, and the rearrangement of material has brought the entire narrative into a direct and natural sequence. An entire chapter is now devoted to Arctic explorations, with much new matter about the De Long and Peary expeditions; our connection with Africa, the Congo Free State, and the Nicaragua and Panama canals occupy another chapter; and a most telling *résumé* of our material and scientific progress, with details of the rise of such organizations as the A. P. A., the Salvation Army, the Woman's Chistian Temperance Union, and the like, is supplemented by an account of the movement for severalty-holding of Indian lands. There also is a whole chapter on the events of 1895, including the Atlanta Exposition, and on the conditions of the South and the negro, as shown by the eleventh census. "Of peculiar interest at the present time," says the *Commercial Advertiser,* "is the detailed account of the United States finances since 1870. The antecedents and rise of the Free Silver party and its strength in previous campaigns are here presented clearly and concisely." The illustrations form a remarkable feature of the book. They are of great number and almost uniform excellence. In the full-page scenes, of which there are thirty-six, appear many familiar faces drawn to the life. The artists are Howard Pyle, W. R. Leight, B. W. Clinedinst, Orson Lowell, and C. K. Linson. Photography has been used to advantage in supporting the realism and historical accuracy of the book. The remaining 400 illustrations are made up of photographic views or drawings after photographs many of them striking "snap-shots," such as the Homestead strike views and those of the convict labor trouble in Tennessee; portraits, of which there are over 200, and plans, maps, and facsimiles, some of the latter having been unearthed after prolonged ransacking of the archives at Washington and the various State capitols. (Scribner. 2 v., $6.)

Illustrated Edition of Fiske's American Revolution.—Houghton, Mifflin & Co.'s leading book is an illustrated edition of *The American Revolution,* by John Fiske, in two large octavo volumes, from new type, and illustrated with twenty-two photogravu es of remarkably fine portraits and paintings, fifteen colored maps and plates, and nearly three hundred cuts and maps in the text. None of these are included merely for the purpose of ornamentation, but all illustrate historic features which are described by Mr. Fiske with such rare charm. The large-paper edition is printed on English hand-made paper, and is in every way an unusually desirable edition for extension. "We remain of the opinion expressed before," says *The Independent,* "that it is the best rational account yet given of the Revolutionary War as a war." "The work in its new dress," says *The Beacon,* "is one of the handsomest examp es of bookmaking ever brought out in this country, and the liberality displayed in the selection of subjects for illustration, the technical excellence with which the pictures have been introduced, and the lavishness shown in making available for the general student some of the choicest treasures of famous historical collections, all combine to give this work an unusual and inexhaustible interest. Professor Fiske in preparing his illustrations has had the oppor-

From " The American Revolution."

PATRICK HENRY MAKING HIS TARQUIN AND CÆSAR SPEECH.

tunity to make free use of the extremely valuable Emmet collection, recently added to the Lenox Library, and from this and other sources he has been able to give engravings of many rare prints. These give a contemporary flavor to the narrative that could not be obtained in any other way, and the series of portraits from old paintings, sketches, and pastels are no less noteworthy. The illustrated holiday edition of Professor Fiske's masterpiece does not exhibit a flaw to the most searching criticism." (Houghton, Mifflin & Co. 2 v., $8; $16.)

The True George Washington.—The humorist who said that he was a greater man than Washington, because Washington couldn't tell a lie and he could and didn't, put in a nutshell the effect of persistent hero-worship on the popular mind. Long continued adulation of George Washington by biographers, who have described him as a being devoid of mortal faults and shortcomings, has made of him a demi-god, admirable but unlovable. Mr. Ford has set himself to show us "the true George Washington"—a man of human character and human limitations —and admirably has he performed the task. In this volume he takes us into the personal circle of Washington's life and family, shows us his family relations, his love-affairs, what he ate and wore, his friends and enemies, his amusements, his illnesses, and his occupations. No one could be better fitted for such a task than Mr. Ford by historical information, patient accuracy, quick humor, and ready sympathy, and when we lay down the volume it is with the feeling that we do at last know the true George Washington, and that our love and reverence for him has been increased by that knowledge. The book is illustrated with many rare portraits, fac-similes, and cuts, it includes much material never before made public, and in historical information and intrinsic interest ranks among the most notable of recent contributions to history or biography. (Lippincott. $2.)

Bill Nye's Posthumous Work.—We can fancy the Muse of History gazing aghast at Bill Nye's "History of England from the Druids to the Reign of King Henry VIII." But after a moment's horror-struck pause the Muse would promptly drop her dignity, put on her spectacles, and for once find her profession a hilarious one. To the majority of mankind, who dearly love a joke, Bill Nye's name alone is a sufficient invitation to fall to and enjoy. To those sober-minded folk who think history too serious a subject for jest, it may be said that a humorous view even of history may instruct as well as amuse, and they should try it for a change; while for all we may quote Dean Hole's comment on Nye's "History of the United States," the precursor of the present volume: "The most invigorating tonic in all the pharmacopœia of comic literature." The "History" has found sympathetic interpreters in W. M. Goodes and A. M. Richards, whose drawings sustain the distinctive humor of the text. (Lippincott. $1.25.)

Chrysanthemums and Violets.—Two beautiful art-books are made of fac-similes of water-color designs, reproduced almost perfectly, one of *Chrysanthemums*, by Paul de Longpré, the other of *Violets*, by Henrietta D. La Praik. The gorgeous chrysanthemums show some of the very best work of one of the most distinguished painters of flowers in this country. They are bound with back and half sides of brown buckram, with the outer half sides in an illuminated design and the title in gold in a white buckram panel. The modest violet, like the primrose on the river's bank, would scarcely know itself in the six water-color drawings of La Praik's, with bindings of green buckram, shown in every style, but chiefly after it has been cultured and grown full and gorgeous like the chrysanthemums. (Stokes. *Ea.*, $2.) These designs are also made into calendars which are of American manufacture and hold their own with the work of the best-known makers. Gorgeous bows hold the leaves together. ($2.)

Edition de Luxe of Thoreau's Cape Cod.—"The *édition de luxe*, in two volumes, of Thoreau's *Cape Cod*," says the *Mail and Express*, "is perhaps the very finest example of artistic book-making this country has ever produced. The paper is excellent, and, needless to state, the typography is up to the high standard of the Riverside Press ; but the amazing feature of the edition lies in the illustrations of Cape Cod scenes. There are quite one hundred of these, scattered through the pages, on the margins, overlapping the text, tucked into corners, and preceding and following chapters; and they include views of the beach, of sand dunes, of fishermen's cottages, of two or three boats, of a large fleet, of windmills, of a bit of village scenery, of wild flowers, etc. And all are done in colors. To make the book the pages had to be run through the presses sixteen times, and so carefully that, as a result, there is not a trace of presswork visible in the illustrations. They appear to be painted by hand, so soft and delicate and finished are they. Taken as a whole, this edition of *Cape Cod* will mark an epoch in bookmaking. We regard the achievement as a triumph of art and mechanics, and a matter of justifiable pride on the part of American book-lovers." (Houghton, Mifflin & Co. 2 v., $5.)

Views from Juliana Horatia Ewing's "Canada Home."—Of that sweet writer, Juliana Horatia Ewing, whose busy pen was not long since laid aside, but whose memory lives with us in the pages of some of the best-loved and brightest stories in the English language, there are a few memories and facts of that portion of her life spent on this side of the Atlantic—a sort of gleaner's sheaf from the rich field of that life already gone over and stored by her sister, Miss H. K. Gatty, who, however in her interesting work has left almost untouched the record of the two years in Canada. This home was in the small provincial city of Fredericton, New Brunswick, where she spent two years of her earnest life, writing many of her sweetest stories; and we find, in following her footsteps and reading her letters, how deeply she loved the quaint old town whither she came, a stranger and a bride with her husband, Major Ewing, when his regiment was ordered there in 1867. Half the book is given up to letters written by Mrs. Ewing to her home friends, interspersed with drawings and water-colors of the things she saw about her. These water-colors are given in fac-simile in this thoroughly bewitching book. (Roberts. $3.)

An Eclipse Party in Africa.—Astronomers and scientists throughout the world had become certain that on the 22d of December, 1889, there would be a total eclipse of the sun. the phases of which could be best studied from Saint Paul de Loanda, Angola, West Africa. Almost every nation had made preparations to send its leading astronomers and scientists to that remote corner of the world to gather facts to add to the scientific knowledge of the age.

Lazy Tours in Spain and Elsewhere.—Judged from the standpoint of people of taste and culture, rather than of fashion, says the Boston Sunday *Herald*, Mrs. Moulton is an ideal traveller. She never wanders at random, that height of Bohemianism lies just beyond; but she stays at each place long enough to see the best of it and get at the heart of it. "The only bit of real estate I ever owned was 'a castle in Spain,'" she says, by way of preface to her

From "An Eclipse Party in Africa."   Copyright, 1896, by Roberts Bros.

STREET SCENE IN FREETOWN, SIERRA LEONE.

The United States placed its investigations under the care of Professor David P. Todd, of Amherst College, and gave him as collaborators Eben J. Loomis, of the United States Nautical Almanac Office, and several other scientific men, each bound to gain information on some specialty. The record of the voyage to Africa as it was taken by the party which started on the United States steamer *Pensacola* has now been published by the Roberts Brothers, and has been illustrated by upwards of 100 photographs taken among the scenes described while chasing summer across the Equator. The book appeals almost wholly to the general reader, for the writer enjoyed the earth as much as the heavens, and kept his eyes upon the beauties of our own planet in a land where the sun sheds its blessings with a lavish hand. The descriptions of St. Helena and other South Pacific islands are vivid, and the author gives some suggestive thoughts upon the career and last days of Napoleon. The portion devoted to diamond-mines and the manner of obtaining and preparing these stones will appeal to the many who delight in these precious stones. Although many scientific details of the expedition are given in the writer's diaries, no one need be deterred by them from becoming acquainted with a wholly delightful book. (Roberts. $4.50.)

story of the "lazy tour" which her party took into that country of rom*a*nce and decay. It is a singular fact, by the way, that she apologizes for having "recorded impressions more often than details"; but in this very fact lies the charm of the book. It is books of the character of "Lazy Tours in Spain and Elsewhere" that we read, and read again, with new ideas and happier thoughts at each perusal. (Roberts. $1.50.)

Literary Reminiscences.—Houghton, Mifflin & Co. have a rich harvest of reminiscences by and about literary people. Miss Phelps's *Chapters from a Life* will undoubtedly command the most interest, being a very attractive and engaging account of one of the most successful of American writers. ($1.50.) In *Authors and Friends,* Mrs. Fields gives delightful chapters devoted to Longfellow, Whittier, Holmes, Mrs. Thaxter, and others. ($1.50.) The first series of *The Letters of Victor Hugo,* a very handsome as well as interesting book, may be mentioned at this point (2 v., $3); and the *Life of Dr. Holmes,* which has not enjoyed the favor of a holiday season, should certainly be included (2 v., $4); and *Whitman: a study,* by John Burroughs, is a book of great interest, both to those who admire Burroughs and those who admire Whitman ($1.25).

Myths and Legends of Our Own Land.—It is an article of faith with many an American that the historic romance of legendary lore must be sought only in old-world lands. To such a one the two charming volumes in which Mr. Charles M. Skinner has gathered this notable array of "Myths and Legends of Our Own Land" will come as a pleasant surprise, while to all who would know and cherish the traditions of their country, they offer a very treasure-house of quaint, curious, and romantic information. Mr. Skinner has for the past fifteen years devoted himself to the pursuit and collection of American local legends and mythical tales; he has retold them in terse, picturesque, and poetic English, and he now gives us this body of American tradition, combining history with myth, strongly invested with the element of the supernatural, and veiling the great figures of our country's history with the shadowy fabric of legend. Here we have legends of the Knickerbocker days in the "Isle of Manhattoes," weird tales of Indian witchcraft, passion, and revenge; stories of the days when Salem's witches walked abroad, and the Maypole was reared on Merrymount; sad or thrilling stories of Revolutionary times, in which Washington is the presiding genius; and an astonishing array of legends of the South and of the North, of myths that cluster about the Rockies, and that relate to storied waters, stones, and cliffs. The volumes are illustrated with photogravures of scenes long haunted by romance; they are beautifully printed, appropriately bound, and in dress and workmanship are well worthy of the novelty, interest, and value of their contents. (Lippincott. 2 v., $3; $6.)

New Works by Charles Morris.—Truly, there is no need for the enforced stay-at-home to mourn his lot! Rather may he rejoice at the prospect of resting comfortably by his own hearth and under the guidance of Mr. Charles Morris wandering at will over America, Europe, Asia, and Africa, through the medium of the company of eminent travellers assembled for his delectation. Mr. Morris has this year contributed to the holiday array a collection of "Half-Hours of Travel at Home and Abroad," consisting of descriptive extracts from the works of notable travellers and explorers and covering the four quarters of the habitable globe. There is a volume devoted to each continent; the work is finely illustrated with numerous photogravures, and it is a striking illustration of the old adage, "Infinite riches in a little room." (Lippincott. 4 v., $6; $10; $13.) To his well-known series of "Historical Tales" he has added two new volumes on "Greece" and "Rome," each containing from twenty-five to thirty stories of history or adventure, and admirably illustrated. (Lippincott. 2 v., ea., $1.25)

Vasari's Lives of the Painters.—This new edition of Vasari's classic work comprises seventy of the most eminent painters, sculptors, and architects, and is edited and annotated in the light of the most recent discoveries by E. H. and E. W. Blashfield and A. A. Hopkins. The work has long called for systematic editing in English. Documents of all kinds have been discovered, new canvases and frescos found, and old ones brought to light. The present editors have for two years been engaged in preparing what must long remain the definitive English edition of this great work. Mr. Blashfield's eminence as a painter and critic, and the familiarity of himself and his collaborators with the Renaissance period, are guarantees of completeness and scholarly accuracy. The edition, limited to 500 numbered sets, is richly illustrated with forty-eight handsome photogravure reproductions of masterpieces of Italian painting and sculpture. (Scribner. 4 v., $15.)

From "Half Hours of Travel" (America).   Copyright, 1896, by J. B. Lippincott Co.

HOMES OF THE CLIFF DWELLERS.

FIELD COLUMBIAN MUSEUM.

The Beginners of a Nation.—The Appletons make another interesting announcement in the *The Beginners of a Nation*, by Edward Eggleston. This is the first volume of "A History of Life in the United States," a new and fruitful subject, and one that the novelist ought to treat with great felicity. To become thoroughly acquainted with his subject, Dr. Eggleston found it necessary not only to prosecute studies in most of the great public libraries of this country, but also to make repeated sojourns in Europe for the purpose of investigations in the British Museum and the State Paper Department of the Record Office and the French National Library. Dr. Eggleston gained access also to papers not before used in private repositories in England and America. To get local color and additional information he has visited all of the original thirteen colonies. In announcing this important work the publishers deem it necessary to call attention to only two facts: one, the modern interest in life and character; the other, that Mr. Eggleston is conspicuously the best-equipped student of the life and character which have gone to the making of American history. It is within bounds to say that the appearance of this work marks an epoch in American historical literature. (Appleton. $1.50.)

Driving for Pleasure.—The bicycle has almost taken the place of the horse as a means of getting about for pleasure. But this is certainly because our people make the best of things and not because they really prefer the selfish, unbeautiful recreation of bicyling, connected with hard work and many chances of accident, to a ride behind high-stepping, finely-groomed horses in a luxurious carriage, of which the roominess and upholstery must certainly be more satisfactory than a hard little about 6 x 4 saddle. Francis T. Underhill, a noted judge of horses and carriages, has prepared a book for the press of D. Appleton & Co., calculated to make even bicyclers pause and wish they had a horse, and one of the many vehicles of every style and of every degree of elegance that are shown in the illustrations to this handsome book. The chapters treat specially of what constitutes "good form" in equipages, general appointments, coaching, four-in-hand, tandem, coaches, men, horses, harnesses, stables, etc., etc. Great pains have been taken in making the pictures which illustrate these details. There are 125 of them, many being made from photographs of the objects described. The book is authoritative, and will be useful in settling many mooted points of custom and fashion. If you have friends who keep horses give them this, or if you cannot give it, put them on the track of getting it. (Appleton. $7.50.)

D. Appleton & Co.'s Important Books.—Science of all kinds is contained in the books of the Appletons. *The Story of Architecture*, by Thomas Mathews, is a compact yet comprehensive history of architecture, and offers a study of the effects of civilization upon architecture as a necessity and an art. Almost all the architectural monuments specially referred to are described from personal knowledge. American architecture receives careful attention, and Asiatic and Oriental architecture, usually neglected in such books, is discussed with an exceptional fulness of information. The work is copiously illustrated. ($3.) *Pioneers of Science in America* is a book of no little educational value, made up of fifty biographical essays on *Pioneers of Science in America*, which originally appeared in the *Popular Science Monthly*, and have been edited and revised for this collection in book form by Dr. W. L. Youmans. The purpose of the work, as defined by the editor, is to indicate briefly and effectively the personal characteristics of the men whose lives are here dealt with, their noteworthy achievements, and the controlling motives that governed the progress of their careers. Portraits are given of all the scientists mentioned. ($4.) *Genius and Degeneration*, a study in psychology, by Dr. ctor William Hirsch, with a preface by Professor E. Mendel, is an imposing work uniform with *Degenera-*

tion, by Dr. Max Nordau, already in its ninth edition ; and *The Warfare of Science with Theology*, by Andrew D. White, formerly president of Cornell University, is "a remarkable book of pre-eminent and eminent value," says the London *Christian World*. "It will stand henceforth among the living books of the world." (Appleton. 2 v., $5.)

A Cycle of Cathay.—" Of the many works relating to the Middle Kingdom which have been published since the recent war in the Far East, none is more trustworthy and valuable than the volume entitled 'A Cycle of Cathay,'" says the New York *Sun*. " Dr. Martin went to China as a missionary forty-six years ago, and was first settled in Ningpo, where he not only acquired the dialect spoken in the province of Che-Kiann, but reduced it to writing in the Roman, so that his converts were able to read and write it. He also learned to read, write, and speak the mandarin, or classical form of the Chinese language, which is spoken by the official and literary class all over the empire. It was this acquisition which caused him to be employed, in conjunction with Dr. Williams, as interpreter to the American Legation in the negotiations for a treaty in 1858–59. The same remarkable qualification led ultimately to his employment by the Chinese Government as the President of the Imperial Tungwen College at Peking, an institution founded for the purpose of training a corps of interpreters to be used in the foreign relations of the Middle Kingdom with European powers. His relatively thorough acquaintance with the languages and with the literature of China, his extensive travels in the Celestial Empire, and his wide and comparatively intimate acquaintance with Chinese statesmen, combine to give uncommon value to his testimony upon all subjects connected with the history of China, and with the actual political and social condition of the country. Nowhere can be found a more luminous sketch of Chinese history, during the last four thousand years, than is here compressed into a few pages ; nowhere are the origin, character, and possibilities of the Taiping Rebellion so intelligently described, and nowhere is there a clearer account of the mandarin system of government." " Probably no other volume,"

THE GARDENER AT WORK.

says *The Critic*, " gives so accurate and trustworthy an account of those great questions, still pending, which have their centre in the Far East, in which Korea is the 'sick man' and the European powers and a few still unconquered Asiatic nations are vitally interested." " Having lived nearly a cycle among the people of China, and coming into direct relations with all classes of them," says *The Interior*, " and possessing a style of limpid clearness and precision, Dr. Martin is able to convey not only a mass of information concerning the country and its interesting people, but to give a better impression and a clearer conception of his subject than is ordinarily conveyed by books of its class. Many books have of late been written on China, but it can unhesitatingly be said that *A Cycle of Cathay* will rank as one of the best that has yet appeared. It is profusely illustrated with engravings taken from the productions of Chinese artists, which adds a flavor of quaintness to a most interesting and instructive volume." (Revell. $2.)

Love-Songs of France.—Baudelaire, Béranger, De Musset, Gautier, Chenier, Lamartine, Hugo, Girardin, Dupont, Sainte-Beuve, Nadaud, and others, whom the French hold in loving remembrance, have voiced every emotion that may come to a lover—highest bliss or deepest despair—in words which are music and painting as well as invisible thought. From their rich treasury of verse the *Love-Songs of France* have been selected with nice discrimination, and have been put into musical English by a translator who withholds his name, although he need not fear to acknowledge his excellent work. The publishers have made an exquisitely pretty book of this fascinating material, have illustrated it with a frontispiece in color and several photogravures in color, and have bound it in white vellum, with slip covers, and protected the delicate work with a substantial box. Two hundred and fifty lovers, and no more, may also obtain an *édition de luxe* of these pretty models for love-making, numbered and signed, bound in white moiré silk, suggestive of the dress for the wedding that should follow such pure wooing, and illustrated with extra photogravures on imperial Japan vellum. A more beautiful gift it would be hard to find for a real old-fashioned sweetheart longing to make a little home the most attractive spot to him who gives it to her. A man whose latest interest centres in a "bicycle girl," "a new woman," or a fashion model, must look elsewhere, for only such as can "be good and let who will be clever" will appreciate all the beauties of the *Love-Songs of France*. (New Amsterdam Book Co. $1.50; $3.75.)

Saul. — Robert Browning's great Hebrew epic, which is, indeed, Hebrew only in its subject, but widely human in its application, has been brought out as one of the leading giftbooks of the holiday season. The wonderful soul-drama, with its vivid Oriental setting and its picturesque actors, offers a fine opportunity for the artist, and Mr. Frank O. Small has made the most of his subject, in a series of twenty drawings, which interpret powerfully and harmoniously the poetic scenes. The book is finely printed, bound in a rich cover of olive, with a conventional design in gold, and neatly boxed. (Crowell. $1.50.)

The Surrey Edition of Bracebridge Hall. — As a suitable companion to the illustrated and decorated editions of "The Alhambra," "The Conquest of Granada," Knickerbocker's "New York," "The Sketch-Book," and "Tales of a Traveller," and in response to numerous requests for a similar edition of Irving's "Bracebridge Hall, or, the humourists," the publishers have prepared the *Surrey edition* of this popular work. That celebrated reviewer, Lord Jeffrey, said of this work: "The great charm and peculiarity of his work consists now, as on former occasions, in the singular sweetness of the composition, and of those soft harmonies of studied speech in which this author is apt to indulge himself; and we have caught ourselves, oftener than we shall confess, neglecting his excellent matter, to lap ourselves in the excellent music of his periods, and letting ourselves float passively down the mellow falls and windings of his soft-flowing sentences, with a delight not inferior to that which we derive from fine versification." Edward Everett pronounced the work "quite equal to anything which the present age of English literature has pro-

From "Constantinople."   (Stamboul ed.)   Copyright, 1896, by G. P. Putnam's Sons.

MELON MERCHANT.

duced in this department. Besides the episodical tales, he has given us admirable sketches of life and manners, highly curious in themselves, and rendered almost important by the good-natured mock gravity, the ironical reverence, and lively wit with which they are described." The two volumes of the *Surrey edition* contain twenty-eight photogravure illustrations from original designs by Arthur Rackham, C. S. Reinhart, C. H. Scholmze, Julian Rix, William Hyde, F. S. Church, Harrison Miller, and Henry Sandham. Each page is surrounded by a decorative border, printed in colors, from designs by Margaret Armstrong. (Putnam. 2 v., $6; $12; $15.)

Rome of To-Day and Yesterday: the Pagan City. — Following the chronological sequence it has been the author's aim to bring together what one absolutely needs for the supreme enjoyment of this famous city : all leading points as to the builders, royal, republican, and imperial ; all important details as to material, construction, and architecture, from the fragments of the tufa wall on the Palatine of the

eighth century before Christ, down to Constantine's beautiful arch of about 315 A.D. Mr. Dennie has long been a resident of Rome, and his book has all the charm of close personal acquaintance with everything described, and of that strong poetic feeling which Rome never fails to inspire in her adopted sons. The volume is handsomely printed; artistically bound, and contains five maps and fifty-eight full-page illustrations of exceptional attractiveness and interest. (Putnam. $4.)

Stamboul Edition of Amicis's Constantinople. — The success of the illustrated editions of Amicis's "Holland" and "Spain," both of which have run through many editions, has induced the publishers to bring out this new impression of one of the author's most picturesque works. Nothing can be more timely than a book on "Constantinople," and the author's well-known descriptive talent is guarantee for great popularity. ($2.25.) The *Vandyke edition* of "Holland," the *Saragossa edition* of "Spain," and the *Stamboul edition* of "Constantinople" are also sold as a set in a box at $6.50. (Putnam.)

STATUE OF DAVID.

An Edition de Luxe of Carmen.—" It would
seem that in the new translation of *Carmen*
American bookmaking had reached its highest mark," says the N. Y. *Commercial Advertiser.*
" Beauty, richness, and many evidences of good
taste all go to make this an entirely praiseworthy
achievement. This translation of Prosper Méri-
mée's masterpiece is by Edmund H. Garrett.
It is prefaced by a memoir of the author from
the appreciative pen of Louise Imogen Guiney.
It is illustrated with five etched plates and seven
etched vignettes from drawings by Mr. Garrett, and a photogravure frontispiece of Calvé
as Carmen. It is a gift-book so handsome that
one would have to be very unselfish to give it
away." (Little, Brown & Co. $2; crushed mo-
rocco, $4.50.)

Little, Brown & Co.'s Important Books.—
Four additional volumes are ready in the beautiful bookish edition of *Captain Marryat's Novels*, edited by R. Brimley Johnson. (22 v., *ea.*,
$1; $3); the two new volumes in the well-pre-
pared edition of George Sand's works are *François the Waif* and *The Devil's Pool*, "both masterpieces of poetic prose," says *Public Opinion*,
"and the translations are very well done"
($1.25); and *In a North Country Village*, by Mrs.
Frances Blundell, is a pleasant volume of descriptive sketches of English rural life and
manners, in the style of Mrs. Gaskell illustrated by Frank Fellows. ($2.) *Mgr. de Sal-
amon's Memoirs During the Revolution, 1790-
1801*, with preface, introduction, notes, and
documents by the Abbé Bridier, of the clergy
of Paris, is an extraordinary story told with a
master's touch and bearing the stamp of truth
and sincerity. The anonymous translator has
done his work remarkably well. ($2.)

*Illustrated Edition of Grimm's Michael An-
gelo.*—It is the unusual space it bestows upon the still existing works of art of this all-
sided genius that gives Hermann Grimm's
biography its standing among artists, connoisseurs, and students. He finished this great
work in 1859, but the English-speaking people
did not for years come into possession of what
is really a history of Italian art in the sixteenth
century. Little, Brown & Co. published this
work in 1872, and they have this year made a
sumptuous holiday edition in two volumes.
These include twenty-three photogravure plates
from the masterpieces of Michael Angelo, together with his steel-engraved portrait. The
remaining seventeen plates embrace works by
Raphael, Titian, Da Vinci, Andrea del Sarto,
Botticelli, Perugino, Donatello, Giotto, Fra
Angelico, Correggio, etc. The publishers have
confined the choice of illustrations entirely to
works of art, and have included reproductions
of Michael Angelo's most famous statues and
paintings. The photogravures have been specially made for this edition. It is an ideal gift-
book and phenomenally cheap. (Little, Brown
& Co. 2 v., $6.)

*George Routledge & Sons' Holiday Publica-
tions.*—Nothing is more wanted in an intelligent, up-to-date family than a good atlas. This
can be had in ideal form in *The Handy Reference
Atlas of the World*, edited by J. G. Bartholomew, complete, compact, accurate, reliable,
with new maps and exhaustively indexed. It
is composed of 160 folio colored plates, containing 262 maps and plans, with complete index
and geographical statistics, strongly bound in
leather. The most recent geographical statistics of the various states of the world have been
added to this fifth edition of a very valuable
and very cheap book. ($3.) The eleventh
edition of *Disc veries and Inventions of the
Nineteenth Century*, by Robert Routledge, has
been revised and partly rewritten, with additions covering the latest discoveries. It contains 450 illustrations, and makes a fine gift-
book of lasting use. ($3.) The Routledges
also have a handsome set of *Captain Marryat's
Novels* in seventeen volumes ($8.50), and
their ever-popular edition of *Shakespeare* in
thirteen volumes. In spite of all the new
"Shakespeares" this little set holds its own
and looks well in all its many costumes, which
range from wood to finest leather. The styles
in which this Shakespeare appears show tasteful originality. ($5-$25.)

Philip Gilbert Hamerton.—About the year
1884 Mr. Hamerton confessed to his wife that
he had begun to write his autobiography, but
that he did not intend it for publication during
his lifetime. He worked upon it at intervals,
as his literary engagements permitted, but upon
his sudden death in 1894 he had only been able
to carry it as far as his twenty-fourth year.
Such a fragment seemed too brief for publication, and his wife earnestly desired to supplement it by a memoir, and thus give to those
who knew and loved his books a more complete understanding of his character and career. The work of Mr. Hamerton covered from
his birth, 1834, to 1858, the year of his marriage. Mrs. Hamerton was therefore able to
relate all the subsequent life from intimate
knowledge, and in the difficulties she expe-

rienced she had the constant help of Mr. Hamerton's intimate friend, John Robert Seeley. As artist and author Mr. Hamerton came in contact with all the men and women who have distinguished themselves in art and letters, and letters from many of these add to the interest of the work. He highly esteemed the great Spanish artist, Vierge, and the portions of the book in which his genius is criticised are specially valuable for art-lovers. (Roberts. $3.)

Rustic Life in France.—"An exceptionally beautiful book," says the Boston *Beacon*, ' has been made of André Theuriet's 'Rustic Life in France,' translated by Helen B. Dole, with reproductions of the illustrations by Léon Lhermitte. André Theuriet is one of the most graceful and refined of the contemporary French poets, and although the tone of the present work is distinctively realistic there is a poetical quality running all through it that gives it an irresistible charm. As for Lhermitte, he is an artist whose paintings of rural scenes and characters have gained for him world-wide fame; his pictures are full of imaginative quality and tenderness of feeling, and they are accepted as genuine revelations of those primitive, picturesque phases of country existence, which in France, as elsewhere, have almost entirely disappeared under the devastating hand of modern progress. It may easily be realized that a writer and an artist like Theuriet and Lhermitte, working together in entire sympathy, could not fail to achieve noteworthy results, and 'Rustic Life in France' is indeed a book having a unique charm. In it all the old time features in French peasant life are depicted, the tasks of farm and vineyard, the gathering and working of the flax, the forest industries, festivals and family life, and the quaint, pathetic customs that make up what might fairly be called the peasant's religion." "The book," says the New York *Commercial Advertiser*, "with its illuminated cover, finely finished paper, and beautiful illustrations, must inevitably attract the attention of those who are seeking gifts for their friends that shall have in them the elements of both surprise and delight." (Crowell. $2.50.)

The Faïence Library.— Three classics have this year been added to the charming volumes of this dainty series. Pierre Loti's beautiful idyl, "An Iceland Fisherman," is given in a sympathetic and graceful translation by Helen B.

Dole, which retains the exquisite sentiment and grace of the original. "The Rubáiyát of Omar Khayyám," in Fitzgerald's translation, comes to us also in the same delightful guise. It includes the same scholaic version of Jámi's "Salámán and Absál," nowhere else obtainable in juxtaposition with the Rubáiyát, and it reproduces the texts of the fifth edition and that of 1859, and includes an excellent sketch of Fitzgerald's life, being, indeed, an apt illustration of the old Latin adage, "Parva sed apta." The trio is completed by the *Faïence edition* of "Fadette," George Sand's ever-fresh and exquisite creation, which has been rendered into graceful English by Mrs. Lancaster, of Washington. None who turn to the Faïence books can go astray in their holiday giving, for with their fine printing, broad margins, dainty title-pages, and simple artistic binding of dull olive and gold, they rank among the most tasteful and attractive of literary gems. (Crowell. *Ea.*, $1.)

Two Books About the Stage.—Mr. C. E. L. Wingate, well known as the historiographer of stageland, has edited, with F. E. McKay, a notable book on "Famous American Actors of To-Day," that will afford interest and

From " Rustic Life in France."

PLOUGHING.

pleasure to the whole wide audience of theatre-goers. "No less than forty-two well-known actors," says the *Philadelphia Inquirer*, "are represented in this handsome volume, each biography and critical estimate being furnished by the author best qualified by opportunity of friendship or study to give a faithful and authentic account. The volume makes a concise encyclopædia of dramatic biography, but the authors have laid themselves out to be entertaining, and it is full of agreeable anecdotes and piquant bits of stage gossip. It will fill a long-felt want. The portraits are carefully reproduced, and add great value to the biographical detail. All lovers of theatrical art will find it a repository of most interesting information." (Crowell. $2.) One of the most important theatrical publications of last year was Mr. Wingate's study of "Shakespeare's Heroines on the Stage." This he has now supplemented with a new work describing "Shakespeare's Heroes on the Stage," which, like its predecessor, abounds with piquant anecdotes and reproductions of rare engravings. It deals with seven of Shakespeare's most famous plays, and describes the different noted actors who have made the parts their own, from the days of Garrick to those of Irving and Richard Mansfield. Biography and anecdote are skilfully combined, and the volume contains a delightful store of little-known histrionic information. (Crowell. $2.)

Society Sketches and Other Works of Art.—There is no charmer like the American girl, and Charles Dana Gibson is her prophet! Of recent years has she not bewitched us all, smiling from the pages of *Life*, or illuminating the sober type of the new magazines? And now in *Pictures of People* we find her, radiant as ever, lending the grace of her presence to the Christmas array, and beguiling even the soberest student of sociology from his solemnity. In the delightful volume bearing this title there are collected eighty-five of Mr. Gibson's latest and choicest drawings, including his well-known studies of English and French society, and showing him at his very best as the graphic delineator and graceful satirist of society. The pictures are printed from new plates on beautiful paper, and the book is richly bound in white vellum and imperial Japan paper, bearing on its cover the likeness of one

of the most charming of Gibson's ever-charming "girls." (Russell. $5.) Mr. Gibson is not alone in his chosen field. Mr. A. B. Wenzell is one of his best-known rivals, and *In Vanity Fair* is a fascinating collection of his spirited and distinctive society pictures. We are indeed "in Vanity Fair" as we turn over these delightful depictions of scenes at the horse show, the opera, the theatres, at balls, afternoon teas, and outdoor gayeties. Like the Gibson volume, this book is a large folio, printed on fine coated paper, and attractively bound. (Russell. $5.) Equally attractive in its way, though strongly contrasted in subject, is the quaintly amusing volume wherein *Kemble's Coons* disport themselves. E. W. Kemble has long been known as *par excellence* the delineator of darky children and Southern scenes, and thirty of his delightfully characteristic drawings are here reproduced in sepia tints. All the sketches here given were drawn from life by Mr. Kemble during a recent trip through the South, and are now presented for the first time. The book is a large quarto, handsomely bound in brown buckram and Japan vellum. (Russell. $2.)

Poster Picturings.—For the admirers of poster art there are two new publications that will gladden their souls. The first is *Posters in Miniature*, a collection of over two hundred and fifty small reproductions of famous posters, exact in coloring and design, with portraits of poster designers, and a descriptive introduction by Edward Penfield (Russell. $1.50); while the second is Penfield's original and striking *Poster Calendar for 1897*, consisting of five effective designs, printed in colors, in the style of the famous Penfield posters. (Russell. 50 c.)

On the Trail of Don Quixote.—The volume is in a sense the outgrowth of a long friendship between the artist, Daniel Vierge, who was born and bred a Spaniard, and the author, Mr. A. F. Jaccaci, who is familiar from boyhood and from recent travel with the province of La Mancha. Mr. Jaccaci is, moreover, himself an artist, and his descriptions have the color and vivacity that come from an eye trained to see what is picturesque and unusual. The book is in no sense an attempt to follow Don Quixote's wanderings in detail, but its plan is to describe Don Quixote's country as it is to-day, with incidental allusions to such scenes as are acknowledged and easily recognizable. The illustrations, of which there are 130, are the best work of the famous artist. (Scribner. $2.50.)

My Village.—E. Boyd Smith, an American artist, has written a description of Valombre, a little place about thirty miles north of Paris, and has illustrated his words with about 150 pictures reproduced by an original process from his spirited drawings. These are the charm and attraction of this pretty portrayal of peasant life. We are shown the lazy men the grasping old women, the young French girls, the primitive fire department, the torch-light processions of *fête* days; we see the aged woman watching by the bedside of her dying husband, her grotesque shadow cast upon the wall. Harvest-time is represented by many illustrations, and the sketches of workers in the quarry are unusually strong and impressive. Sketches are made at all seasons, and no phase of village character is overlooked. (Scribner. $2.)

Sentimental Tommy.—'' Here, at last,'' says the Philadelphia *Evening Telegraph*, '' is 'Sentimental Tommy,' in the full glory of his youth, in the pride of his mendacity, in the tearful tenderness of his heart, which it is his wont to stand off from and admire, like Sterne. We ripple a thumb luxuriously through the 478 pages that chronicle the boyhood of T. Sandys, Esq., and settle ourselves to the delight of those concluding chapters we have not yet read. In 'Sentimental Tommy' Mr. Barrie has written one of the books of the year; as a piece of true art it is unsurpassed. He stands now before the iridescent Ouida, for all the hungry maternal intuition betrayed in her tales of childhood ; he is face-to-face with the Clemens of 'Huckleberry Finn,' which Andrew Lang called 'The Boys' Odyssey'; and even to the lordly Dickens, shrined as he is between Paul Dombey and Little Nell, Barrie can stretch out a hand, saying: 'I claim the tie of kinship.'" (Scribner. $1.50.)

The Edge of the Orient.—Robert Howard Russell has made a handsome record of his trip to the East in "The Edge of the Orient." "To say that the book is illustrated," says *The Commercial Advertiser*, " is to give no idea of its lavish pictorial decorations. Four large pages hardly suffice to give a mere list of the pictures. Mr. Russell's text is soberly descriptive. He writes as one who knows whereof he writes. The ground he covered included Dalmatia, Montenegro—delightful, unfamiliar—Constantinople, Smyrna, Damascus, Cairo, and finally Luxor and Assouan. Mr. Russell is a good traveller and an entertaining writer. His journal of travel is a thoroughly companionable volume."(Scribner. $2.)

Good Cheer for a Year.—The Phillips Brooks Year-Book, selected from the writings of the much-loved Bishop of Massachusetts, is already in its thirty-first year. From the same rich material W. M. L. Jay has this year made a new year-book under the attractive title *Good Cheer for a Year*. The compiler has made the book valuable by references to the volumes of sermons and other writings from which these cheery, stirring, helpful thoughts are taken. For the convenience of those who desire to use the book in other years, selections for the greater movable fasts and feasts of the Christian year are appended to the volume. All the great poets of the ages have been drawn upon to say in rhyme each day of the year what Bishop Brooks voices in prose. These poetical selections have been made with rare taste and not a little skill. The book is uniform with that of last year. (Dutton. $1.25.)

Scribner's Illustrated Fiction.—*In Ole Virginia* contains Mr. Thomas Nelson Page's famous stories of Southern life—"Marse Chan," "Meh Lady," " Polly,", " Unc' Edinburg," "Ole Stracted," and " No Haid Pawn"—with twenty-four beautiful full-page illustrations by A. B. Frost, Howard Pyle, W. T. Smedley, C. S. Reinhart, A. Castaigne, and B. W. Cline-

"THEY SAW THE WINDOW OPEN AND A FIGURE IN A WHITE SHAWL CREEP OUT OF IT."

dinst. The illustrations are as notable for the exquisitely sympathetic manner in which they reflect the spirit of the text, as for their charming artistic qualities. The book is richly made, and in its combination of handsome illustrations, fine paper, and dainty binding forms an ideal holiday gift. ($2.50.) A truly sprightly and vivacious story is *The Sprightly Romance of Marsac*, by Molly Elliot Seawell, the history of two impecunious journalists who live in lodgings in the Latin Quarter of Paris. The story won a prize from the New York *Herald*. The illustrations, by Gustave Verbeek, are numerous and match the story in life and dramatic arrangement. ($1.25.) *Love in Old Cloathes* has a wide variety of theme and only slight diversity of high merit. It will receive special attention, because we all think with love and regret of its genial author, Henry C. Bunner, so lately gone

From "Captive Memories." Copyright, 1896, by James T.
White & Co.

A PAIR OF CUPIDS.

from among us, whom he had charmed so long
with his laughter, which was often akin to
purifying tear-drops. These stories are put
into very effective holiday dress. ($1.50.)
Frank Stockton's *Mrs. Cliff's Yacht*, with many
illustrations, tells the story of a favorite heroine after she became rich but had no tastes or
ideals to gratify. ($1.50.) Mrs. Manning's
classic story of the great plague of London,
called *Cherry and Violet*, has been issued, with
twenty-six illustrations by Herbert Railton and
John Jellicoe. This story by the quaint writer
of "The Household of Sir Thomas More " cannot be too highly recommended. ($2.25.)

Captive Memories.—This is one of the most
beautiful gift-books of the season. It com-
memorates in original and charming verse the
various affection days of life, which are arranged to portray in natural order the awakening, progress, and perfection of love throughout
a lifetime, tracing it through its human phases
to heights of spirituality from which the soul
perceives that love is the all of life and God.
The pages are embellished with California flowers, which are works of art in their harmony of
tone and breadth of style. They are exquisitely drawn, and make an admirable setting for
these beautiful poems, which are as rare as
are the flowers. There are also fifty full-page
cupids—lovable little fellows—who repeat the
story one never tires of hearing. "All the
world loves a lover," and an ideal one will be
found in this beautiful volume, which might appropriately be called "The Memoirs of a Lover."
It is difficult to say whether *Captive Memories*
is most delightful for the delicacy of its verse
or for the beauty of its illustrations. Both are
unusually fine, and the book cannot fail to recall to every one delicious memories which will
be held forever captive between its leaves. The
author plays upon the chords of tenderness
with rare touch, and has made a book which

will be welcomed by all lovers of genuine poetry. It is full of quotable lines which are
applicable to every one's experience, and one
cannot read this lovely book without being
carried back to youth with a delicious tide
of feeling from which he will return to every-day life with a sigh. It is one of the
most beautiful books published in years, and
one which everybody will wish to own, for
it is a lovely gem in an exquisite setting.
To read this book is one of the rare treats of
a lifetime which a man is poorer for having
missed. For a Christmas gift it is particularly
appropriate, having a special Christmas verse
expressing the culmination of love, to which
the rest of the book is a beautiful introduction.
The writer of the pretty verses has shown rare
taste in choosing the quoted verses with which
each memory begins. The book shows at
every page that it was a labor of love which
has occupied its compiler for years. There
was already enough in manuscript some years
ago to obtain the eulogy of a kindred spirit.
John G. Whittier said of it: "The poems are
rarely sweet; the rondeaux are worthy of the
troubadours of Provence." The book is gotten
up in extremely sumptuous style at $3; there
is a wedding edition in white silk at $7.50, and
a superb *édition de luxe* from original plates on
large paper with sixteen hand-painted cupids at
$24. (James T. White & Co.)

F. A. Stokes & Co.'s Fiction.—The novels published by the Frederick A. Stokes Company are
all copyrighted and have all been selected with
the greatest care. Among these are many by
the most popular authors of the day, including
Anthony Hope, John Oliver Hobbes, Sir Walter
Besant, Robert Barr, John Strange Winter,
William Le Queux, and Ouida. Many of these
novels are included in the Frederick A. Stokes
Company's popular series of fiction, but the
following are published in individual and artistic bindings, appropriate to their character :
"The Heart of the Princess Osra," by Anthony Hope, with Princess Osra of Zenda as
the heroine, with sixteen full-page illustrations
by H. C. Edwards ; "Phroso," by the same
author, a novel of adventures with a Greek
heroine ; "The Master Craftsman," by Sir
Walter Besant, a graceful love-story of London and Wapping ; "The City of Refuge," by
the same author, with a plot that deals with the
supernatural, and scenes laid in a community
in the State of New York ; "The Herb-Moon,"
by John Oliver Hobbes, takes its title from an
old term applied to a long engagement, and is
full of rustic wit and common sense ; and "The
C Major of Life," by Havering Bowcher, is a
study of the problems of life in the form of a
well-written novel. ($1–$1.50.) To the *Twentieth Century Series* have been added "I Married
a Wife," by John Strange Winter ; "From
Whose Bourne," a very original detective story
by Robert Barr ; "The Flaw in the Marble," a
powerful novel, with scene laid in Paris studios,
by an anonymous author ; and "Vawder's
Understudy," by James Knapp Reeve, a striking American novel on the theme of platonic
affection. (*Ea.*, 75 c.) In the *Newport Series*
are Robert Barr's "One Day's Courtship,"
Julian Sturgis's "A Master of Fortune," and
"A Full Confession," an anonymous story
about a young English girl who elopes from a
French convent. (*Ea.*, 75 c.)

The World Awheel in Book and Calendar.—
All the world's a stage, and the men and
women players on it seem all to be awheel.
From the most learned philosopher, puzzling
out problems that will always remain "caviar
to the general," to the silliest girl who really
cares for nothing higher than imitation jewelry,
all the world is on wheels, and their whirr becomes more all-pervading day by day. The
enthusiastic man-wheeler seems to throw all
regard for his appearance aside when he takes
to the wheel, but in woman the ruling passion
holds its own even against the wheel, and
girls still study effective costume in preparing
their bicycle suits. Girls ride in Russia, the
Riviera, Holland, Scotland, Switzerland, the
Rhine regions, the Champs Elysées, Pompeii,
and Egypt, as well as on the Riverside Drive
and in Central Park, New York, and their costumes vary according to the fashions of their
different lands. Eugène Grivaz has pictured
the "bicycle girls" of the different nations in
every variety of fanciful "get-up" and painted
them in water-colors, and fac-similes of these
paintings have been combined with prose and
verse born of the bicycle epidemic, compiled
by Volney Streamer with taste and skill from
the tid-bits taken by permission from *The Critic, The American Wheelman, Outing, Truth,
The Detroit Free Press,* etc , for which he
makes courteous acknowledgment to Miss
Harriet Monroe and to Messrs. Charles G. D.
Roberts, Robert Clarkson Tongue, and Eben
E. Rexford, who were the contributors of some
of the most "fetching" contributions. The
preludes to the bicyclers of France and bicyclers of Holland are in the words of Oliver
Goldsmith. Why may not imagination trace
the noble dust of Oliver Goldsmith until we
find it stopping a punctured tire? Bicyclers
say verbatim with the poet we have travestied,
"Report me and my cause aright," and surely this book puts into roseate light the pleasures of the wheel. ($2.50–$3.50.) The same
twelve pictures appear also in "The World
of Cycling Calendar," in which the fair wheel-
ers appear surrounded by numbers that mark
the flight of time. This calendar every girl
may confidently present to her favorite escort,
provided only she be not afraid to provoke
comparison with Russian, French, Egyptian
or other beauty. (Stokes. $2.)

The Quilting Bee, and Other Poems.—One of
the pleasantest surprises of the season thus far
is the appearance of "The Quilting Bee, and
other poems," by John Langdon Heaton.
The verses have a rollicking humor that will
carry them at once into the good favor of the
reader, although the writer can be serious also
when he chooses, as is shown in the spirited
verses printed in the second portion of the book.
The volume opens with about thirty poems
reminiscent of life on the farm and phrased in
the quaint New England dialect which is so
well suited for the expression of pathos and of
a certain quiet grim humor. The preface of
the book is one of the cleverest things between
its covers. It represents a colloquy between
the author and the publisher, and is apparently
devised to give the former an opportunity of
confiding to the reader his own preferences
among his own verse. The binding is very
quaint and attractive, representing an old-
fashioned patchwork quilt in the process of
"quilting." (Stokes. $1–$1.25.)

The Forgotten Isles.—This is a fresh and picturesque travel-book by the well-known French
artist, G. Vuillier, which has been translated by Frederic Breton. It deals with the
islands of Corsica, Sardinia, Majorca, Minorca,
and the surrounding islands. The author-
artist has been equally successful with his text
and his illustrations, of which there are 162,
showing the inhabitants of the beautiful islands
at all their occupations and in all their pleasures. The books of travel grow more and
more interesting as travellers learn more and
more what the reader wants them to see for
him, and the illustrations are scattered through
the well-written pages with more and more lavish hand. *The Forgotten Isles* ranks among
the very best books of travel, and its theme is
new and excellently well treated. (Appleton.
$4.50.)

Under Two Flags. This thrilling and passionate romance is "Ouida's" best-known and
most famous work, and the many who have
fallen under the spell of its vividness and force
will give a cordial welcome to this fine holiday
edition of their long-time favorite. The story
has been put into two handsome volumes,
finely printed, richly yet simply bound, and
neatly boxed. G. Montbard, the well-known
French artist, has made for it eight full-page

From "The Complete Poems of William Cullen Bryant.
Copyright, 1894, by Frederick A. Stokes Co.

"GO WASTE THE CHRISTIAN HAMLETS AND
SWEEP AWAY THEIR FLOCKS."

illustrations that supplement and make still more real the thrilling text; and the publication of this fine edition of her masterpiece is a striking illustration of the place " Ouida " holds in popular favor, as one of the most graphic and eloquent of novelists. (Lippincott. 2 v., $3; $6.)

Bird-Land Echoes.—" Mr. Abbott," says the Chicago *Inter-Ocean*, "is the Audubon of our day, set to music. Like Burroughs and Thompson and Olive Thorne Miller, he is a lover of the fields and woods, and all their wild denizens. But of birds he is especially enamoured. While he loves all wild nature, he says one may grow tired of the trees, and squirrels, and gay butterflies, but never of birds." This new book, uniform in style with its predecessor, " The Birds About Us," is not a scientific treatise, but a series of visits to the homes and haunts of birds, setting forth the ways and customs of bird-land. It is beautifully illustrated by W. E. Cram, who is in bird-art what Dr. Abbott is in bird-lore. (Lippincott. $2.)

Houghton, Mifflin & Co.'s Important Books.— A book of great value to the artist and antiquarian is *The Mycenæan Age*, which has for its basis a book on Mycenæ, by Dr. Chrestos Tsountas, published some three years ago. It has been brought out in excellent English style by Prof. J. Irving Manatt, of Brown University, who has included the results of the excavations and discoveries made within the last three years, in which he has been greatly assisted by Dr. Tsountas. The book contains 150 illustrations of the various objects of inter est found, and is made additionally valuable by an introduction from the pen of Dr. Dörpfeld, the most eminent living archæologist. This book is mechanically and otherwise of much the same value and interest as the works of Schliemann and Lanciani. A book which will appeal especially to autograph lovers and to those interested in facts about literary men and women is *Talks About Autographs*, by Dr George Birkbeck Hill, who gives autographs and talks about some fifty men and women, mostly English and mostly of high degree in the literary and philanthropic world. The book is very handsomely printed and bound. " There are hours of pleasant reading in these *Talks About Autographs*," says the *Mail and Express*, "and a chance for grangerites to extend them into volumes by the addition of extra portraits, views, and other literary bric-à-brac. ($3.50.) To these should be added the *Riverside edition* of *Mrs. Stowe's Works*, in sixteen volumes, from new plates, thoroughly edited, with biographical sketch and notes, and containing portraits and various views of Mrs. Stowe's homes and relatives, the whole forming a very notable memorial of one of the most distinguished women America has produced. "A handsome setting for the brain products of this gifted woman," says the Philadelphia *Press*. " Although Mrs. Stowe's work has been accessible for many years," says *The Examiner*, "there is something peculiarly refreshing about rereading the familiar stories in their present beautiful form." (16 v., *ea.*, $1.50 ; *large pap., per set*, $64.) *A Year in the Fields* is a beautiful volume containing eight essays selected from various books by John Burroughs, describing the aspects of nature throughout the year, and illustrated with twenty pictures

from excellent photographs by Clifton Johnson ($1.50) ; and T. B. Aldrich's poem, *Friar Jerome's Beautiful Book*, has been brought out in attractive holiday form by being printed in black and red and bound in antique leather. ($1.50.) The large-paper edition is a very handsome book printed on Arnold hand-made paper and bound in red parchment and gold. ($5.)

Houghton, Mifflin & Co.'s Poetical Publications.—Four volumes of poetry must be mentioned : " *The Complete Works of James Russell Lowell* in the *Cambridge edition* in uniform style with the *Cambridge editions* of Longfellow, Whittier, Holmes, and Browning ($2–$5 50) ; *Judith and Holofernes*, a long poem by Mr. Aldrich, and one of his strongest and best ($1.25) ; *The Poems of Celia Thaxter* in a handsome *Appledore edition*, containing all of her poems except those included in her volume for children, published last year, and prefaced by a charming introduction by Miss Jewett ($1.50); and *A Quiet Road*, a volume of unusual thoughtfulness and lyric verse, by Lizette Woodworth Reese ($1).

Harper & Brothers' Important Books.—Mark Twain and his illustrator G. Du Mond did almost equally important work in " Personal Recollections of Joan of Arc," which has been characterized as a "great book, a credit to American literature." The London *Speaker* said : " Mark Twain, in the best book he has ever written, has given us a life of Joan of Arc, so amazing in its realism, its vividness, and force, that, like Shakespeare's plays, it compels acceptance." ($2.50.) This work has been given a sumptuous dress. In time it will also take its place in the *Uniform edition* of Mark Twain, which now offers "Huckleberry Finn," " Life on the Mississippi," " A Connecticut Yankee at King Arthur's Court," " The Prince and the Pauper," " Tom Sawyer Abroad," and " The American Claimant." (*Ea.*, $1.75.) No book could give greater pleasure to a middle-aged New Yorker than " Reminiscences of an Octogenarian of the City of New York, 1816–1860," by Charles H. Haswell, profusely illustrated with portraits and old landmarks. ($3.) Other autobiographic works of interest are : "A Few Memories," by Mary Anderson, Countess of Navarro, and " The Memoirs of Barras," indispensable to all who would understand the French Revolution, the Consulate, and the Empire. ($2.50.) To lovers of travel may be recommended "On Snow-Shoes to the Barren Grounds," in which Caspar Whitney describes a journey of 2800 miles after muskoxen and wood-bison, a book profusely illustrated ($3.50), and " Literary Landmarks of Venice," with illustrations by G. Du Mond and Guy Rose ($1). A very pretty series of great literary value is *Contemporary Essayists*, which has opened richly with " Aspects of Fiction " and other ventures in criticism by Brander Matthews ; "Impressions and Experiences," by W. Dean Howells ; and " The Relation of Literature to Life," by Charles Dudley Warner (*ea.*, $1.50). An ideal Christmas gift, if one's purse permits it, is the illustrated edition of Green's " Shorter History of the English People " in four volumes (*ea.*, $5) ; and an equally acceptable work of reference is " Harper's Classical Dictionary," edited by Harry Thurston Peck with about 1500 illustrations ($6).

R. F. Fenno & Co.'s New Fiction.
—Novels by the most popular authors are brought out in most attractive shape by the Fennos. For the holidays Grant Allen has ready *The Desire of the Eyes*, a volume comprising thirteen stories various in character, written in Grant Allen's versatile and always clever manner. The reader who delights in works of fiction in which there is not the faintest suspicion of pessimism, but, on the contrary, has an abiding faith in the goodness of man and his ability to work out his salvation in the old-fashioned, God-fearing way, will give a warm welcome to *The Mist on the Moors*, a wholesome romance just fresh from the hands of Joseph Hocking. *What Cheer ?* and *The Lady Maud*, both thrilling, dramatic stories by William Clark Russell, will delight the admirers and lovers of this breezy sailor story-teller. The former manifests in a poetic and conspicuous manner the love the author has for the sea and for all "who go down to sea in ships"; the latter is a new edition of an old favorite, handsomely illustrated. (*Ea.*, \$1.25.) *The Betrayal of John Fordham*, by B. L. Farjeon, is a story of mystery and passion, love and hate, good and evil, a second edition of which was called for ten days after publication. (\$1.25.) Many will be delighted to hear of the new edition of Besant and Rice's masterpiece, *The Golden Butterfly*, which tells of a lovely heroine brought up by a multi-millionaire father ignorant of reading and writing. It was an epoch-making book full of suggestion on the subject of wild-cat investments; and it is as fresh as ever. (\$1.) *Uncle Scipio*, by Mrs. J. H. Walworth, is a love-story set in the picturesque Mississippi Valley, describing conditions ruli g immediately after the War of the Rebellion. (\$1.25.) *Dust in the Balance*, by George Knight, consists of nineteen sketches of different kinds delicately written. (\$1.25.) *Some Women's Ways*, by Mary A. Dickens, embraces nine literary gems, of which perhaps the most precious is called "Out of Fashion" (\$1.25); and *Eyes that Do Not See*, by Hilton Hill, the brilliant author of *His Egyptian Wife*, shows considerable complexity of plot and entertaining solutions of the same. Mentioned last, as a star-actress, is mentioned last, is *Robe t U quhart*, by Gabriel Setoun, of which this house has the American edition. The Scotch scenery and the remarkable character of the schoolmaster hero are vividly put before the reader. Every word tells and the book is inspiring. (\$1.) All these novels can be had in paper also.

Lamb's History of the City of New York.—To her fine work on "*The History of the City of New York*," first published in two volumes 1877–1881, Mrs. Lamb owed the honor of being made editor of *The Magazine of American History*. It

"WHY, JOYCE ! IS IT YOU, MY BLOSSOM ?"

was at once acknowledged a standard. "The author has spared no labor in research," said *The Nation*, "and from many original sources has gathered a great variety of details and has woven them into a distinct continuous history." A new edition of this history has been prepared for the holidays this year. Mrs. Burton Harrison has edited Mrs. Lamb's celebrated book, and has brought the history down to date by an additional chapter, which forms a third vo ume of "The History of New York," and is also published separately under the title of "The Externals of Modern New York." (Barnes. 3 v., \$15.)

The Externals of Modern New York.—A. S. Barnes & Co. publish for the holidays this year "*The Externals of Modern New York*," by Mrs. Burton Harrison, a beautifully illustrated book on fine paper with embossed cover. In it the author tells the story of the last fifth of a century by "thumb-nail" sketches of the various departments of the city's work, and by a brief

summary of prog-
ress in social de-
velopment. Taking
up Mrs. Lamb's
history in 1880,
when this writer's
chronicle came to
an end, Mrs. Har-
rison describes the
various improve-
ments that have
been made in New
York City during
the eventful sixteen
years that have in-
tervened. The
work specially
dwells upon the ar-
chitectural and ar-
tistic additions to
the great metropo-
lis. The book is
profusely illustrat-
ed, and will delight
any New Yorker
wandering in for-
eign parts, if such a
one is on your list.
(Barnes. $3.)

*Books Suitable for
Holiday Presenta-
tion.*—A. S. Barnes
have Guerber's
"Legends of the
Rhine," an interesting study of folk-lore and
reminiscence of travel abroad, containing forty
full-page illustrations ($2); "Crowns," with
twenty-two original cartoon illustrations by
Blanche McManus, describing promises of future reward for a well-spent life ($1); "Rev.
John Henry," by Percival R. Benson (75 c.), and
"The New Minister," by Kenneth Paul ($1),
both interesting stories of the difficulties and
encouragements of a minister's life; and "Looking Within," by J. W. Roberts, the story of a
scientist who skips over in a trance some of the
years to come, and awakens in the year 2027 to
a much more peaceful condition of things than
seems likely to exist even 132 years from now
($1).

*American-Made Bibles, Prayer-Books, and
Hymnals.*—Thomas Nelson & Sons, recognizing the growing demand for American-made
books, decided to manufacture a complete line
of Bibles, Prayer-Books, and Hymnals. The
result is found in the valuable new series of
books which they now offer for the holidays.
These books are all manufactured in the United
States, printed on the leading presses of the
country, and bound in an elegant and durable
style. It will include "Teachers' Bibles,"
"Reference Bibles," "Text Bibles," "Revised
Bibles," "Testaments," "Psalms," "Prayer-
Books and Hymnals." The "Teachers' Bibles"
contain new "Helps," specially prepared by
leading scholars in America and Great Britain.
The illustrations—in number over 300—form
such a special feature of these Bible "Helps"
that from them they take their name; "The
Illustrated Bible Treasury." A new series of
maps has also been prepared for these Bibles
from the latest surveys. The very complete
line of "Prayer-Books and Hymnals" furnished by the Nelsons has been printed on the
De Vinne Press, a fact which shows in itself
how lavish the publishers have been in procuring for their books every advantage that can
be given them from a manufacturing standpoint. These books are all in every style of
binding, and can be had from the lowest to the
highest price with appointments of binding for
each additional price, that are simply marvellous. "Thomas Nelson & Sons have published
a *Minion Octavo Revised Bible*," says the N. Y.
Observer, "which is entirely an American-made
book, typeset, electrotyped, printed, and bound
in this country. It is a beautiful specimen of
the printer's and binder's arts, and cannot fail
to find favor where seen. The Bible is the
Bible wherever printed, but as Americans we
delight to see so much care and skill bestowed
upon the best of books, and believe that there
is sentiment enough of the kind to make an
American edition reimburse its publishers."
(Nelson.)

Frederick Warne & Co.'s Holiday Books.—
"The Royal Natural History," edited by Prof.
Richard Lydekker, assisted by the leading scientists of the day, is now complete and is published in six volumes, profusely illustrated and
with seventy-two colored plates. This is a
definitive and standard book, and has been
praised by the leading scientists of Europe and
America for its accuracy and great interest of
statement. (6 v., $27–$37.) This very important
work is probably beyond the means of the
many, but any one blessed with enough of this
world's goods to do so should present it to some
library or school this season. This house has
Shakespeare in two editions: *The Bedford
Handy Volume Shakespeare*, in twelve pocket
volumes, and *The Lansdowne Red Line Edition
Shakespeare*, in six pocket volumes, both editions
gotten up in every conceivable style of binding,
ranging in price from $7.50 to $22.50. "Abbeys,
Castles, and Ancient Halls of England and
Wales," by John Timbs and Alexander Gunn,
gives their legendary lore and popular history
in three volumes, embellished with twelve full-
page most interesting photogravures from the
newest and best views procurable of the subject. ($7.50.) "Wood's Dictionary of Quota-
tions" holds its own with all new-comers. Its
alphabetical and subject arrangement is ingenious, and it is a book of marked excellence
for the reference library. ($2.50–$4.50.)

Ward, Lock & Co.'s Holiday Books.—No gift
could be more acceptable than the set of *Henry
Kingsley's Novels*, edited by Clement K. Shorter, which the publishers bring out in twelve
volumes, the last entitled "The Boy in Gray,
and other stories," containing a biography of
the author, who is pronounced by experts a
better story-teller than his brother Charles.
(12 v., *ea.*, $1.25.) The same editor has under-
taken more difficult work in the selecting and
editing of *The Nineteenth Century Classics*, of
which five volumes are now ready, covering
noted books by Thomas Carlyle, Matthew Arnold, De Quincey, and Mrs. Browning. This
nineteenth century has been a specially prolific
one in English literature, and the books published within the first half of it bear in themselves proofs of enduring life. To put such
classics in good shape upon readers' shelves
is an achievement that may lawfully fill a publisher's heart with pride. (*Ea.*, 75 c.)

The Lure of Fame.—Under this title Clive Holland has written a story that deserves highest praise. Eric Probst, coming to Vosse-vangen, a village in the hills of Norway, wearied with the disappointments of his past life, solaces himself with the ways of the primitive peasants, and finally becomes the village schoolmaster. In this rôle he discovers latent genius in two of his pupils. Hans Olsen is a farmer's son, but all his ambition is to be a scholar. Ulrica Brun, his little playmate, has the great gift of song, and Eric, who is a musician, teaches her until an English musician comes into the peaceful neighborhood, and using the lure of fame takes Ulrica to Milan to study singing. The lives of the two Norwegian peasant children grow wider and wider apart. The author makes a fine psychological study of their developing minds, but clothes it in a thoroughly artistic form of fiction. The publishers have made a very handsome book that cannot fail in time to win the place to which it is entitled by its literary and artistic merits. (New Amsterdam Book Co. $1.)

Two Idealistic Works of Fiction. In these days of crude, sometimes even brutal realism in fiction, it is a rest and a profitable recreation to read a book like *Opals from a Mexican Mine,* by George de Valière, a dainty volume in which are confined what purport to be thoughts suggested by the significance of the various colors found in opals. These separate colors appear under the names of The Greatest of the Gods is Quetzalcoatl, the Water Lady, the Mysterious Disappearance of Mrs. T. Tompkins Smith, the Vision of Don Juan on the Piedra de Los Angeles, and Cosmopolitana Mexicana, the title headings of the short stories or rather prose-poems of which the book is composed. (New Amsterdam Book Co. $1.25.) "*Nephelé,* a novel by Francis William Bourdillon, by its very first sentence," says the New York *Sun,* "makes its reader realize that he is breathing a rarer air than usually emanates from the printed page, and at the very last sentence he realizes how he has been kept on the heights. It is a musical novel, dealing with the occult claim of telepathy." "We urge so rare a treat on the attention of our readers," says the *American Bookman.* (New Amsterdam Book Co. $1.)

Old English Customs Extant at the Present Time.—The object of the work is to describe all the old customs which still linger in England and may be witnessed to-day. It contains a spirited account of local observances, festival customs, and many ceremonies yet surviving in Great Britain. The author is specially fitted for his work. He is the Rev. P. H. Ditchfield, rector of Barham, Berkshire, England, and in his beautiful rural surroundings has many opportunities to study the habits and manners of people who have never come in contact with any men and women who have not the same rules of living, the same superstitions as themselves. To any one who has travelled leisurely through the coun-

try districts of England this would be a holiday gift greatly appreciated and enjoyed. (New Amsterdam Book Co. $1.75.)

The Seven Seas.—It has been suggested that the title of Mr. Kipling's new book of verse was taken from these lines of Omar Khayyám:

> " When you and I behind the Veil have passed,
> Oh, but the long, long while the World will last,
> Which of our coming and departure heeds
> As the Seven Seas might heed a pebble cast."

Indeed the spirit that breathes through that stanza permeates most of Kipling's work, but in the present case the title, "The Seven Seas," has a second significance as well. It illustrates the versatility and wide range of this collection of poems and ballads. Their scenes shift from the Indian Ocean to the floes of the Arctic Sea, from the Atlantic to the Pacific, and over each of the seven seas he visits Kipling's art holds empire. Many of the poems here collected have appeared previously in periodicals, but a number are now first published. Admirers of Kipling, who have waited impatiently for a year or more for this volume, will not now wait the critic's verdict; but "The Seven Seas" is final proof—if proof were needed—of his place in the front rank of modern poets. It is a pleasure to note that the publishers have put the book into a dress worthy of its contents, and have spared no pains in perfecting its mechanical details. In matter and in manner it is indeed one of the notable books of the year. (Appleton. $1.50.)

THE BIRTH OF A SOUL.

The Rise and Growth of the English Nation.—This work, by W. H. S. Aubrey, is written in no partisan or sectarian spirit, and is not designed to advocate any particular theory of politics, of philosophy, or of religion; but it claims to be thoroughly patriotic, and is inspired by a love of the freedom that springs out of righteousness and justice. An attempt is made to exhibit the development of the English people, with the varying phases of their daily life, the formation of the national character, the continuity and application of great principles, and the growth of constitutional liberties. It is a history of and for the people, written with special reference to epochs and crises. (Appleton. 3 v., $4.50.)

Year-Books Concerning Children and Friendship.—It is a poor heart that does not love children. True, they are very troublesome at times—they show their humanity at a very early age—but there is so much of innocence, so much of ignorance of etiquette, and such a wealth of gayety, and withal such a readiness to forgive the injustice of their seniors, that they appeal to the sympathies of all who are not self-centred or dyspeptic. Miss Rose Porter's *Concerning Children* is a pretty companion volume to her collections of what men have said about women, and what women have said about men. The three volumes make a pretty set, and each contains many sound bits of philosophy. The book on children, however, will perhaps appeal most strongly to the majority of readers. Miss Eliza Atkins Stone has been equally successful in her pretty book *Concerning Friendship.* (Putnam. *Ea.,* $1.)

Alone in China.—Not long since Julian Ralph journeyed to the Flowery Kingdom, and forthwith set about "takin' notes" of Celestial days and ways. The results of his observations were first given to the world in *Harper's Monthly,* and it is now pleasant to see them given permanent place in book form. In this volume Mr. Ralph gives us a series of charming stories of Chinese life, told with a grace, a sympathetic insight into character, and a wealth of local color that render them unique. The title-story tells of an American girl who married a Chinese diplomat and accompanied him to his home in Shanghai, where henceforth her lot was cast. The illustrations are by C. D. Weldon, who accompanied Mr. Ralph on his Chinese pilgrimage, and the book is appropriately bound in dull yellow, with a panel of white chrysanthemums. (Harper. $2.)

Crowell's Illustrated Standard Sets.—It is a pleasant habit, rapidly increasing, to select for gift-books standard works in reliable editions, and there is certainly no more welcome addition to the home bookshelf than some old friend in new and appropriate attire. Difficult as choice may be among the several standards put forth in new editions by T. Y. Crowell & Co , the decision, whatever it be, cannot fail to be a satisfactory one. Notable among them is the fine five-volume edition of Cooper's *Leather-Stocking Tales,* for which Prof. Brander Matthews, of Columbia University, has furnished an introduction, and Frank T. Merrill has made a series of sympathetic and effective illustrations. The volumes are models of good bookmaking, and no detail of printing or workmanship has been neglected in their preparation. (5 v., *per set,* $7.50 ; $15.)

In two-volume editions of standard works we find *Robert Browning's Poems,* based on the poet's own selection of 1872, with his revisions of 1889 and the addition of some of the more noteworthy later productions, and edited by Charlotte Porter and Helen A. Clarke, editors of *Poet-Lore,* who have supplied careful notes and a scholarly introduction. (2 v., $3.) Similar in general style is John Ormsby's famous translation of *Don Quixote,* of which the Boston *Weekly Transcript* says: " Mr. Ormsby's translation has been pronounced by those competent to judge as coming closer to the original text than any of those which have preceded it." The handsome two-volume edition contains, besides an excellent introduction and biographical sketch, notes and an appendix, together with a portrait and thirty-three etchings from Lalauze. (2 v., $3.) The other works that appeal to all book-lovers in this series of notable editions are Duruy's *History of France,* translated by Mrs. Carey, brought down to date by Prof. Jameson, of Brown University, and illustrated with many valuable portraits and reproductions of old prints. (2 v., $3.) The shorter *Life of Sir Walter Scott,* wherein Lockhart cut down his larger life to more reasonable proportions and brought it into a more artistic and readable whole (2 v., $3) ; Bourrienne's famous *Memoirs of Napoleon,* hitherto obtainable only in four volumes, and retaining all the special features of the original work ; and a new and unexceptionable edition of Pope's *Rape of the Lock,* reprinted with corrections and additions from the *Globe edition,* and containing reprints of the first editions of " The Rape of the Lock " and " The Dunciad,' many illustrations, portraits, and fac-similes of manuscript. (2 v., $3.)

The Ship's Company.—In these pictures of " The Ship's Company and Other Sea People " Lieutenant-Commander J. D. Jerrold Kelley gives us fascinating glimpses of sea-life in times of peace, ranging from the after-deck of the millionaire's steam-yacht to the stoke-hole of the ocean greyhound. He tells of the quaint superstitions of Jack Tar, of his queer pets, his duties and his pleasures; and he tells, too, of the doings of the passengers and pleasure-seeking voyagers. Altogether he has produced a collection of sea-pictures that will awaken pleasant memories in the minds of all familiar with life on the ocean wave, and will be full of fresh interest to landlubbers. (Harper. $2.50.)

Some Books of History.—John Ashton in *When William IV. Was King* has written an entertaining volume of social and political history and personal anecdotes. Mr. Ashton sketches the manners and customs of the time when the first passenger railway was opened and steam navigation began to be general. Like a modern Pepys, although not a contemporary of his characters, he sketches the varied subjects of interest in the reign of the sailor-king. It has forty-seven illustrations. ($3.50.) Two volumes are ready in a new series of *Stories from American History,* in which each State will be made the subject of a separate volume. *New Jersey,* by Frank R. Stockton, and *Georgia,* by Joel Chandler Harris, have been fortunate in their historians. Both the authors have all the art of story-telling, the keenest sense of humor, and the tenderest sympathy and pathos. (Appleton. *Ea.,* $1.50.)

Oxford Bibles ana Prayer-Books and Hymnals.
—"The *Oxford Bible* is an unceasing wonder,"
says the *Bible-Reader*. "About the time one
has concluded that it has reached perfection.
here comes another edition which eclipses all
former efforts. But for this fact we would feel
safe in saying the new edition is as near perfection as modern scholarship and mechanical
skill can make it. It is understood that, in the
preparation of this edition, the 'Helps' were
subjected to a searching examination and
brought up to the existing standard of knowledge. The series of plates illustrating Biblical
versions and antiquities have been greatly enlarged, and is accompanied by full descriptive
letterpress. These plates are by far the finest
we have seen. They are authentic and their
value is permanent." The three characteristics
of the Oxford Bibles which have made them so
popular are the accuracy of the printing, the
general "get-up" of the volumes, and the illustrated letterpress known as "The Oxford
Helps to the Study of the Bible," which goes
to form the famous "Oxford Bible for Teachers." If imitation be the sincerest form of
flattery, what shall be said of the pirated
editions of the Oxford Bible for Teachers, reproduced by photo-lithography? At least a
dozen such editions have been published in
America, which shows that the public appreciate the good points of the Oxford editions of
the sacred writings. The output of the Oxford
Bibles is the largest in the world. It averages
20,000 per week, or upwards of a million a
year. The weekly shipment to the United
States has often exceeded five tons in weight.
There are seventy-one Oxford editions of the
Bible now being circulated, twenty-four of
which have the Apocrypha, while twenty-five
are printed on Oxford India paper. The skins
of upwards of 100,000 animals are used yearly
to cover Oxford Bibles, and 400,000 sheets of
gold are required to letter the backs of the
volumes; the quantity used in gilding the
edges being much larger. These "Bibles" and
"Prayer-Books and Hymnals" are sold from
$1 to $25. In addition to the Bible, Helps, and

Prayer-Books, standard editions of the Poets,
Prayer-Books, and other classic and devotional works published by the Oxford Press,
complete editions of Burns, Byron, and Wordsworth are ready for Christmas, to be known as
the "Oxford Miniature Poets." By use of the
remarkable Oxford India paper the dimensions
have been reduced very much below those of
any book containing the same amount of letterpress matter. (Oxford University Press. *Ea.*,
$4–$12.50.)

Poems of Johanna Ambrosius.—These poems
are in themselves beautiful and of fine lyric
quality. But a special interest attaches to
them owing to the personality of the author.
"Here is a woman," says the *N. Y. Tribune*,
"who, by sheer force of genius, has risen in a
few months from a common laborer of the
fields to be known as one of Germany's most
popular modern poets. The striking thing in
her poems is their lyrical quality. Whether
the thought be sad or hopeful, the singing
quality of the verse is ever apparent." (Roberts. $1.50.)

Poems of Emily Dickinson.—The third series
of poems by this author of curious and wholly
posthumous fame has been selected from an
unexpected deposit. (Roberts. $1.50.) "It is
needless to say," says *The Nation*, "that Miss
Dickinson's poetry achieves its success, in spite
of all its flagrant literary faults, by what Ruskin
describes as 'the perfection and precision of the
instantaneous line.' She is to be tested, not by
her attitude, but by her shot. Does she hit
the mark? As a rule she does. Is it a question
what a book represents to a human being?
This is her answer—only eight lines, but they
tell the story (p. 29):

> ' A BOOK.
>
> ' There is no frigate like a book
>   To take us leagues away,
> Nor any coursers like a page
>   Of prancing poetry.
> This traverse may the poo.est take
>   Without oppress of toll;
> How frugal is the chariot
>   That bears a human soul ! ' "

From " The Oxford Teachers' Bible."   Copyright, 1896, by Henry Frowde. (Oxford University Press.)

ROMAN SOLDIERS CARRYING THE SEVEN-BRANCHED CANDLESTICK, ETC., TAKEN AT THE
CAPTURE OF JERUSALEM, A.D. 70.

Books for Young People.

The Long Walls.—Elbridge S. Brooks has written so many successful books for young people that a new story from his pen will be eagerly welcomed. In writing *The Long Walls* Mr. Brooks and John Alden have given an account of an American boy's adventures in Greece. The book is described as "a story of digging and discovery, temples and treasures," and it is adequately illustrated with 16 full-page illustrations by George Foster Barnes. While recognizing that interest is the first requisite of a story, and keeping this fact in view throughout, the authors have endeavored to throw some light on the life and experiences of archæologists in the field—that little band of enthusiasts of many nations which, in the last half century, has seen as the result of its labors the partial reconstruction of antiquity as it was. (Putnam. $1.50.)

Nimrod Edition of Mayne Reid.—The *Nimrod edition* of Captain Mayne Reid's boys' books comprises three volumes, as follows : " *The Boy Hunters*, or, adventures in search of a White Buffalo"; " *The Bush Boys*, the adventures of a family in South Africa " ; " *The Young Voyageurs*, the boy hunters in the north." The three volumes are handsomely printed in clear type, adequately illustrated, and attractively bound. While the intention of these volumes is primarily to furnish amusement for a boy, they do much more than this, for they inculcate in the mind of the boy who reads them carefully a manliness of thought, an honesty of purpose, and, above all, the habits of close observation and self-reliance which are of so great importance in the formation of character. (Putnam. Ea., $1.25.)

Stories and Legends from Washington Irving.—Washington Irving's skill as a teller of stories has been thrown into the shade by his work as a writer of great historical biographies, which earned him the reputation of the American Addison. Young and old will rejoice this year to find that some of his stirring and dramatic stories have been selected and illustrated in specially attractive style. In this shape a very captivating holiday gift-book is made of " Rip Van Winkle," " Legend of Sleepy Hollow," " The Phantom Island," " Philip of Pokanoket," etc. " We cannot have Irving in too many forms," says the Providence *Sunday Journal.* (Putnam. $1.50.)

Uncrowning a King.—Edward S. Ellis has done a great deal of good work in making history palatable for boys and girls. In this story he presents the period of King Philip's War, the war between the New England colonists and the confederate Indians, 1675–76. King Philip, who was the son of Massasoit, was killed in Rhode Island by a party under command of Captain Benjamin Church. The author introduces all the real characters of this war, in proportion to the population the most disastrous of its kind that ever afflicted our country. Massasoit, the chief of the Wampanoag Indians, who always remained true to the colonists, plays an important part in the story. The book is issued in gray linen covers ornamented with crowns, Indian hatchets, and Indian pipes. (New Amsterdam Book Co. $1.25.)

Books for Boys and Girls.—Thomas Nelson & Sons have several books equally interesting to boys and girls. *Clevely Sahib* is a story of the Kyber Pass, by Herbert Hayens ; Gordon Stables has written *Every Inch a Sailor; The Sign of the Red Cross* is a tale of old London, by E. Everett-Green ; Fred Whishaw has furnished *Harold, the Norseman; Baffling the Blockade* is by J. Macdonald Oxley; *The Hermit Prince* is a story of Japan, by Eleanor Stredder; and *Jack and His Brothers* is a story for wee little ones, by Mrs. Austin Dobson. (Nelson.)

Frederick Warne & Company's Juveniles.—
This house revels in colored toy-books, and
the sweet untearable nursery stories, the help
and comfort of "tired mothers." Under
Warne's Colored Toy-Books they group "The
Dear Old Nursery Rhymes," "The Magic-Lantern Struwwelpeter," "Mother Goose's Nursery Rhymes," and "Aunt Louisa's Jumble
Picture-Book," all brilliant in colored pictures
and covers. "The Little Runaways," by
Harriet M. Capes, and "Very Funny Stories
Told in Rhyme" are additions to the *Red
Nursery Series* and naturally clad in the red
livery of the series. "Playtime Toy-Books,"
"Columbia Toy-Books," are simple little untearable books from which the babies may be
taught their figures and letters and some knowledge of animals. "Stand-Up A B C" speaks
for itself, and easily teaches the alphabet.
(*Ea.,* 50 c. to $1.) The Warnes have their
quota of "twelvemo" story-books, mostly for
boys, the most important of which are "The
Orchid-Seekers," by Ashmore Russan and
Frederick Boyle; "The Fur-Traders of the
West," by E. R. Suffling; "Young Tom Bowling," by J. C. Hutcheson. (*Ea.,* $1.50 ; $1.75.)

*Ward, Lock & Co.'s Juveniles.—*Ethel Turner,
whose successes as a bright, dramatic, and
sympathetic writer of children's stories date from
that charming book,
"Seven Little Australians." has a new story
that will be joyfully received by boys and girls.
It is called "The Little
Larrikin," and, as the
title implies, is set in Australia. The "little larrikin"—*anglicé,* rascal—
is six-year-old Laurence,
or "Lol," Carruthers, the
youngest of a family of
five orphan lads, who
struggle along in an odd,
harum-scarum housekeeping of their own.
"Lol's" astonishing adventures and daredevil
pranks as leader of a bold
band of "larrikins" of
his own years, and the
love-story of his oldest
brother Roger, are the
centre of a succession of
amusing, pathetic, and
dramatic incidents, which
make up a fascinating
story, interesting to the
grown-up as well as to
younger readers. ($1.)
The other notable book
on this firm's juvenile list
is "The Youngsters of
Murray Home," a capital
story of a houseful of
children, who are also little
Australians, whose midsummer Christmas merrymakings, fishing parties,
quarrels, scrapes, and reconciliations are described
with infectious humor and
sympathy by M. Ella Chaffey. (*Ea.,* $1.)

*D. Appleton & Company's Juveniles.—*The
new volume in the very popular *Young Heroes
of Our Navy Series* is "Midshipman Farragut,"
by James Barnes, author of "For King or
Country," etc. Fully possessed with the romance of his story, Mr. Barnes relates in a
vivid, dashing way the story of young Farragut, who became a midshipman when only
ten years old, the youngest officer ever in our
navy. His self-reliance and bravery even at
that early age gave promise of the dashing
deeds of the hero of the *Hartford*—Admiral
Farragut's flagship at the battle of Mobile.
The author sticks closely to history all through,
and introduces many historical persons. The
book is unusually rich in romance and inspiration. The illustrations are by Carleton T.
Chapman. ($1.) Other books for boys are
"The Wampum Belt, or, the fairest page of
history," a tale of William Penn's treaty with
the Indians, written by Hezekiah Butterworth
and illustrated by H. Winthrop Peirce. Mr.
Butterworth has written so much for the young
generations of readers that a book by him has
but to be named to find many eager demands.
"The Wampum Belt" is the sixth volume of
stories of the creators of American liberty, in
which the author has aimed to teach history by
fiction founded on notable incidents in the lives

From "The Wampum Belt."   Copyright, 1896, by D. Appleton & Co.

THE INTRUDER.

of the heroes. This story relates to the wampum belt which was delivered by the Lenape Indians on the Delaware to William Penn, at the great treaty made under the elm-tree at Shackawaxon, in 1682. The pictures are notably bold and striking ($1.50) ; and " The Windfall," by William O. Stoddard, telling of the finding of an immense vein of coal on the farm of poor people living in Pennsylvania ; with the story of this " windfall," which points the way out of many distressing difficulties, are realistic pictures of an explosion in a mine and other scenes from mining and country life, ably illustrated by B. West Clinedinst ($1.50). A story for girls may be looked for under the title of " Christine's Career," by Pauline King; beginning in Paris it follows the life of a little American girl living there with her father, a great artist, who comes to America to decorate one of the buildings in Chicago at the World's Columbian Exposition, the little girl returning with him and going to school in Boston. ($1.50.)

Boy Lives of Shakespeare and Washington.— " The excellent Shakespearian, Dr. William J. Rolfe," says *The Dial,* " has given, in a pretty volume entitled 'Shakespeare the Boy,' an elaborate picture of the Stratford of the dramatist's boyhood, and of the life and manners, especially the local life and manners, of the

" DIS HEAH'S A FUS-CLASS THING TER WORK OFF BAD TEMPERS WID."

period." Little as is known of Shakespeare's life and personality, Dr. Rolfe has contrived to invest his boyhood with a very real element of individuality, and has conjured up a figure that will deeply interest and appeal to the boys and girls of these modern days. (Harper. $1.25.) It is a far cry from the Stratford of Shakespeare's day to the Virginia of the eighteenth century, when George Washington, the hero of "A Virginia Cavalier," by Molly Elliot Seawell, lived his boyhood life as described by this gifted author. Life in the last days of Colonial government in new America under George the Third and life in the last days of Good Queen Bess are brought before the young folks in these two volumes in a way that must make them want to learn and know more about the grown life of these two men, who perhaps more than any other two men have left their impress on the progress of the world.

Harper & Brothers' Important Juveniles.— Kirk Munroe introduces again in "Rick Dale" the enterprising boys who figured in "Snow-Shoes and Sledges" and "The Fur-Seal's Tooth," and with them a new boy, who is the leader throughout this volume. Rick Dale has been so tenderly secluded from the rough and adventurous side of life by too loving parents that he finally rebels and starts off with another boy for a tour of the world, longing for danger and excitement, all of which come to him in abundant measure in his contact with Indians, smugglers, and Northwestern loggers, and make a little man of him. ($1.25.) Zoe Dana Underhill has collected under the title "The Dwarfs' Tailor, and other fairy-tales," favorite and representative tales from France and Germany, sunny Italy and snow-clad Norway, Hungary and Sweden, Denmark and Russia, and other lands. The volume is finely illustrated, and should fill an unoccupied niche in the library of fairy-lore. ($1.75.) Ruth McEnery Stuart, whose tales of Southern life are always delightful, has written "Solomon Crow's Pockets, and other tales," and is at her best among the cheerful people she introduces. ($1.25.) If any one wants unadulterated fun and bewitching pictures, let him take a look at Albert Lee's "Tommy Toddles," perhaps the best of the Harper juveniles for those who can appreciate its rare humor and knowledge of human nature. The Harper juveniles are always satisfactory. (Harper. $1.25.)

Harper's Round Table for 1896 bound in cloth in a single volume is a Christmas present that will bring joy to the whole household. It is a library and a picture gallery in itself, representing the most popular American authors and artists. The volume for 1896 will be found fully up to the high-water mark of previous volumes in every particular. ($3.50.) Some happy boys and girls who have had the *Round Table* during 1896 would perhaps prefer to feel sure of getting their weekly treat in 1897, and so these'a subscription to the periodical for 1897 would be even more satisfactory. For next year the promises include "The Duty of a Young Voter," by Rev. E. E. Hale and Hon. Henry Cabot Lodge, one explaining what a vote means, the other what an election means; "Raising the United States Money and Spending It," by Assistant Secretary of the Treasury Charles S. Hamlin; "The Boyhood of Famous Men," in which Andrew Lang will treat of Alexander Dumas, Austin Dobson of Alexander Pope, and W. E. Henley of Lord Byron; and James Barnes, Kirk Munroe, and Molly Elliot Seawell will furnish the long serials. (Harper. *Subs.*, $2.)

T. Y. Crowell & Co.'s Holiday Juveniles.—"The author of *The Boy Tramps*," says the Providence *Sunday Journal*, "has found a fresh field for boys to explore—the stretch of country through which the Canadian Pacific Railway makes its way—and as it is a region with which he is evidently perfectly familiar, the scenes are vividly described. They are thoroughly manly, likeable boys, and their tramp, both in text and Mr. Sandham's faithful illustrations, is a very fascinating one for boy readers to follow." (Crowell. $1.50.) "A book of sheer adventure and sport is Charles G. D. Roberts's *Around the Camp-Fire*," says the New York *Commercial Advertiser*. "Six cheerful sportsmen start on a canoeing trip in the New Brunswick wilderness, and every evening, as they sit around the camp-fire, each in turn is called upon to spin an enlivening yarn. The illustrations by Charles Copeland are true to the life and add greatly to the charm of the beautiful book. *Around the Camp-Fire* bids fair to be a classic." (Crowell. $1.50.) Mrs. Sarah Knowles Bolton has added to her interesting and useful biographical works a new volume which covers a novel and important field. In *Famous Givers and Their Gifts* she tells of those men who have used their wealth for the benefit of mankind. (Crowell. $1.50.) George Manville Fenn has long held his own in the hearts of boy readers, and his new story will afford them general delight. It is called *Beneath the Sea*, and is a story of the Cornish coast, filled with wild adventure and startling situations. ($1.50.) E. W. Thomson, author of "Old Man Savarin," has a delightful book of short stories, collected from *The Youth's Companion*, and entitled *Walter Gibbs, the Young Boss*, that will appeal to all youthful readers. Miss Sarah Morrison, whose "Chilhowee Boys" have won many friends among young people, continues the adventures of her young heroes in a new volume called *Chilhowee Boys at College*. ($1.50.) The merry company of "Half a Dozen Girls" and "Half a Dozen Boys," with whom we were made acquainted by Miss

From "The Boy Tramps."   Copyright, 1896, by T. Y. Crowell & Co.

ALL THAT AFTERNOON THEY WALKED IN THE SHADOW OF MOUNT STEPHEN.

Anna Chapin Ray a year or so ago, make their appearance, fresher than ever, in new illustrated editions (*ca.*, $1.50); and that bright writer has a new story called *Dick*, in which she describes boy-nature with a freshness, a piquancy, and an infectious humor that are thoroughly delightful. ($1.25.) "A peculiarly attractive book," says the Boston *Beacon*, "has been made of a collection of stories of *Happy Children*, by Ella Farman Pratt, with eight full-page colored plates, and other felicitously designed illustrations. ($1.50.) A book that combines usefulness with interest is *The Romance of Commerce*, by J. MacDonald Oxley, who has collected a store of curious and valuable information on the industrial wonders of our own day ($1.25); while volumes wherein utility is superseded by fancy are the charming new collection of Grimm's *Household Stories*, translated by Lucy Crane, and illustrated in the most charming and sympathetic style by Walter Crane ($1.25), and Hawthorne's famous *Wonder-Book*, issued in the pretty dress of the *Children's Favorite Classics* library ($1.25). James Otis has a capital short sea-story called *A Short Cruise* (50 c.), and the tempting array closes with Emma Gellebrand's pathetic little tale of *J. Cole*, which, despite its pathos, has a "happy ending" ($1).

DRUSILLA FELL ON THE GROUND IN A HEAP.

Houghton, Mifflin & Co.'s Juveniles.—Joel Chandler Harris adds to his *Thimblefinger* books another which he regards as a sequel of these, which he calls *The Story of Aaron*, in which the animals tell stories of themselves and of the families who are brought into the story, and the whole is illustrated by twenty-five admirable pictures by Oliver Herford. The unique central figure of the story, Aaron, who gives to the book its name, is a pure-blooded Arab, whose father, the chief of a marauding band, and mother were captured by slave-traders and conveyed to Virginia before his birth. After many vicissitudes Aaron becomes the property of the grandfather of the two white children of the tale, and his excellent capabilities are made useful as foreman to the laboring negroes upon the plantation. "There can be no question," says *The Beacon*, "that Joel Chandler Harris has chronicled a new and triumphant success in *The Story of Aaron*." ($2.) "No daintier child's book has been issued this season," says the Boston *Gazette*, "than *A Little Girl of Long Ago*, by Eliza Orne White. This writer needs no introduction to the children, who will remember her as the author of that charming story, 'When Molly Was Six.' The delightful child heroine of the book under discussion is Marietta Hamilton, a girl of seventy years ago. The history of her busy little life from the age of three and a half to nine is re-corded, and is so charmingly told that it cannot fail to interest children, to whom the sayings and doings of the Hamilton children will appeal strongly, for these children are so very natural and human." The quaint, old-fashioned illustrations are gems. ($1.) *Three Little Daughters of the Revolution*, by the late Nora Perry, contains three of her best short stories, with illustrations by Mr. Merrill. (75 c.)

Two Charming Children's Books.—John Kendrick Bangs has a new book for children—and that is the same thing as saying that the children have a new delight in store for them. It is called *The Mantelpiece Minstrels*, and is a most attractive little volume, containing four of Mr. Bangs's delightful funny and fanciful conceits, and illustrated by F. Berkeley Smith. Another pretty book is *The Delft Cat, and other stories*, three fascinating tales of queer creatures and their queer doings, by Robert Howard Russell, uniform in size and shape with *The Mantelpiece Minstrels*. (Russell. *Ea.*, 75 c.)

Fleming H. Revell Co.'s Juveniles.—*How the Children Raised the Wind* is a very pretty story of childhood, by Edna Lyall, who always interests her readers from the first word to the last. This story tells of childish plans for earning money and has pretty, unselfish plans for spending it. *Adolph, and How He Found the Beautiful Lady*, is also a well-told story, charmingly illustrated; *The Making of a Hero, and other stories for boys*, contains six lively, stirring stories for boys—real, live, everyday boys; *Probable Sons* is irresistibly pathetic; and *Teddy's Button*, by the same author, is a sweet story full of wisdom and good advice, cleverly hidden and sugar-coated in fiction. All these books are illustrated and bound in handsomely decorated cloth. (*Ea.*, 50 c.)

Primer of College Football.—The author, Mr. W. H. Lewis, who was a member of the Harvard University football team of 1863, intends his book more as a primary work for the great army of beginners than as an addition to the literature of the science and strategy of the game. Nevertheless, he treats the latter subjects very thoroughly, and his points are made clear by carefully designed diagrams, just as his definitions and descriptions of individual work are illustrated by instantaneous photographs taken especially for this purpose. The book covers the entire subject so far as a beginner requires to know it. All the fundamentals are carefully gone into, and there are separate chapters on offensive and defensive play, with a concluding paper on training. Football has come to stay and all the boys want to learn it. (Harper. 75 c.)

Hans Brinker, or, The Silver Skates.—Thirty years have rolled by since Mrs. Dodge wrote this domestic tale of Holland, full of descriptions of Dutch scenery, customs, and general characteristics of the people. The chief incident is a race for a pair of silver skates. In 1879 an illustrated edition appeared, which delighted the souls of the boys and girls who are now fathers and mothers. But what were the illustrations then supplied to those made this year for the new edition? Allan B. Doggett, the artist, took a journey to Holland, and made his sketches of the haunts of Hans and Gretel Brinker on the spot. They accordingly possess the merit of truth in detail and have rare artistic value besides. The artist shows throughout his work that he was in true sympathy with the author's delightful book, which we are heartily glad to see started so auspiciously on a new lease of life. (Scribner. $2.50.)

The American Boy's Book of Sport.—This volume, written and illustrated by Dan C. Beard, contains descriptions of outdoor games for all seasons, made clear by 300 illustrations by the author. It is an entirely new book, and a worthy companion volume to the author's well-known "American Boy's Handy Book," of which over 25,000 copies have been sold, and it will undoubtedly rival that famous book in popularity as it does in interest. (Scribner. $2.50.)

G. A. Henty's New Boys' Books.—The inexhaustible inventiveness and the untiring work of this author have again made ready three books, all imparting historical knowledge and inculcating the principles of true manliness. *Agincourt: a tale of the White Hoods of Paris,* follows the fortunes of an English lad who goes to Paris as page and body-guard to a wealthy Norman lady, and later takes part in the great battle from which the story takes its title. *On the Irrawaddy: a story of the first Burmese war,* has for hero the nephew of an English trader, who on Sir Archibald Campbell's staff performs many daring

exploits. *With Cochrane the Dauntless* tells the experiences of a young midshipman who served in the exploits between Peru and Chili in South American waters. No boy, or girl either, will forego the reading of these stories if they are put in their way, and they can learn much from them. All are illustrated. (Scribner. *Ea.,* $1.50.)

The Brundage and Tucker Books.—Frederick A. Stokes Co. are the publishers of "Royal Little People," "The Children's Book of Cats and Dogs," etc., and no one who has ever seen these gorgeous books of children's pictures will need to, be told what a treat awaits the children and their mothers in *Children of To-Day,* with numerous full-page color plates after paintings in water-colors by Frances Brundage, and decorative borders and other designs as well as new stories and verses by Elizabeth S. Tucker, who has the rare gift of writing for childlike children. The colored plates are all

From "Hans Brinker."

"MAY WE ENTER AND WARM OURSELVES?"

of chubby children who smile upon you from wonderfully pretty and complex bonnets, and all through the borders little men and women are scattered, engaged in every childish pastime a lover of children can imagine, picking flowers, taking tea, etc. A few stray boys have also been painted among the girl cherubs. ($2.50.) Of this material two other smaller volumes have also been made, one called *Little Men and Maids*, the other *Little Beaux and Belles*. The *Children of To-Day* have been equally divided among these two books, and each of them would seem to be almost enough to give a little girl for Christmas. The books are all American-made and are very charming. (*Ea.*, $1.50.) The same pretty children also figure on the *Brundage Calendar*, and the twelve beautiful fac-similes of water-colors seem to look prettiest of all when printed on water-colored paper with roughened edges and tied with handsome ribbons of various shades. ($1.50.)

S. R. Crockett's Sweetheart Travellers.—" The reading public will rejoice and give thanks," says the *Independent*, "that Mr. Crockett did not, after the manner of selfish man, keep to himself the exceeding sweetness of his sweetheart, but, in his delightful fashion, has told us of her charms that we too may worship. His sweetheart (and daughter) is an altogether

adorable little maiden, aged four, who was her father's companion on his wheeling tours through Scotland. The book is a tender study of a child's mind and heart; and Mr. Crockett's sweetheart will bind to her chariot—or rather tricycle—wheels many willing victims." The book appeared in England late in the holiday season and had a phenomenal sale, second barely to that of Du Maurier's " Trilby." " Mr. Crockett has written the prettiest of volumes," says the New York *Times*, " and as the sub-title indicates, it is ' a child's book for children, for women, and for men.' It is a happy father who can unbend, who is overjoyed at being able to enter into his little daughter's mind, who takes her for long trips on his three-wheeled cycle. Mounted on a basket before him, he listens to his little girl's prattling, and he just catches her humor and keeps the record of it. Then, too, there are her brothers. The book is merry with the gladness of laughing children. Mr. Crockett writes as if Sweetheart were present and he had read for her the manuscript, for many are the wise corrections and sage comments she makes." " Sweetheart Travellers " is exquisitely illustrated by Gordon Browne and W. H. C. Groome. (Stokes. $1.50.)

F. A. Stokes's Other Juveniles.—Three new popular books of fairy-tales have been prepared by this house. " The Village of Youth, and other fairy-tales," by Bessie Hatton, are poetically written and illustrated in half-tone after original designs by W. H. Margetson ($1.50); "Fairy-Tales Far and Near" consists of the old, old stories of childhood retold by Arthur T. Quiller-Couch, and has a number of illustrations by H. R. Millar ($1.50) ; and "Turkish Fairy-Tales and F o l k - Tales," collected by Dr. Ignácz Kunos, translated by R. Nisbet Bain, and illustrated by Celia Levetus, is a very instructive and interesting companion to " Cossack Fairy-Tales " published last year ($2). A great novelty for the children is " The Egyptian Struwwelpeter," a very clever parody of the famous story of " Slovenly Peter," with 100 colored illustrations. ($1.50.)

George Routledge & Sons' Holiday Juveniles.—Adventures of Don Quixote, adapted for the young by M. Jones, has 206 illustrations by Sir John Gilbert. ($1.50.) "*Scotland Forever*, or, the adventures of Alec McDonnell," is a new book for boys, by Col. Percy Greeves, with full-page illustrations by Harry Payne. ($2.) Two entirely new books, with all the changes to date, are *Every Boy's Book of Sport and Pastime*, edited by Prof. Hoffmann, and *Every Girl's Book of Sport, Occupation, and Pastime*, edited by Mrs. Mary Whitley. (*Ea*., $3.)

WH(Groome

From ' Sweetheart Travellers."   Copyright, 1896, by Frederick A. Stokes Co.

HUGO WAS PLAYING WITH HIS HORSES.

The *J. B. Lippincott Company's Juveniles.* — A dozen charming story-books, several being for young girls almost out of their "teens," verging, in fact, on the domain of the novel—love and romance forming a large part of the narratives. "Philippa," by Mrs. Molesworth, though encased in a juvenile cover, prettily adorned and colored, is a novel, though a harmless one, and with an excellent, unobtrusive moral. "Philippa" is a charming young English girl, with a rather alarming vein of recklessness and a love of adventure. She indulges in quite an original escapade, which for a time wrecked her happiness completely, but the ending is, after all, perfectly satisfactory. ($1.25.) "Betty of Wye," Amy E. Blanchard's heroine, is an American girl—a daughter of the South. Her home is on the Wye River in Maryland, and is a typical residence of that part of the country in its mixture of refinement and shiftlessness. "Betty" is a saucy, quick-tempered, careless girl, whose whole character is changed by her love for a refined Virginia cousin, who finally woos and wins her. ($1.25.) "Catalina, Art Student," by Laura T. Meade, is for the same class, and is an unusually fresh story of student life with a delightful heroine. ($1.25.) The remainder of the Lippincott "Juveniles" are tales of mystery and adventure, if we except the new edition with Edmund H. Garrett's illustrations of "Ouida's" sweet and natural story of "Two Little Wooden Shoes" ($1.50) and "Prince Little Boy and Other Tales Out of Fairyland," by Dr. S. Weir Mitchell, which claims fresh attention in a new edition ($1.50); "The Oracle of Baal," by J. Provand Webster ($1.50), and "The Black Tor," by George Manville Fenn ($1.50), are as delightfully thrilling as their titles. The first recalls the genius of Jules Verne, being full of strange and curious events, and describing unknown, mysterious countries. The second relates to a feud between two old English houses in the reign of James the First, the "Black Tor" being a lead-mine that has been in the possession of each family and is still a matter of dispute. Each side has a boy of seventeen, and between them in their efforts in the race things are kept pretty lively. "Through Thick and Thin" is a story of a boy's school in England, with an ambitious, persevering hero, by Andrew Home. ($1.25.) "Swept Out to Sea," by David Ker, has its opening scenes on one of the Shetland Islands; wild scenes of adventure in many parts of the world follow. ($1.50.) There is also a new edition, the first American edition, of Henry Kingsley's "The Mystery of the Island," a tale of bush and pampas, wreck and treasure-trove, illustrated by Warne Browne. ($1.25.) "Romance of Industry and Invention," se-

ADAM TUCKING THE OTHER UNDER HIS LEFT ARM.

lected by Robert Cochrane, treats of the romance connected with such subjects as the Krupp and Armstrong works, the Maxim gun, the rise and progress of the cycle industry, and the carrying trade of the world. ($1.25.) Frank Stockton cannot be excelled as a writer for boys and girls, and his "Captain Chap, or, the rolling stones," is fully up to his highest mark. It is captivatingly illustrated by Charles S. Stephens. ($1.50.)

American-Made Calendars and Children's Books. —Frederick A. Stokes Co. are justly proud of the color printing they show in their holiday publications this year. The books have all been made in America, and they are very successful and quite fitted to hold their own among those manufactured in foreign lands. In subjects they are full of interest, and far too good for the children to whom some of the subjects appeal, but who cannot appreciate the beauty and finish of the books. We learn with pleasure that these books have been most successfully distributed, and that everywhere the book-stores are displaying the tempting goods. Ask for them. You can find a gift for every one. (Stokes. 50 c. to $3.50.)

From ' The Boys of Clovernook." Copyright, 1896, by
Lothrop Pub. Co.

LITTLE PETER ON "HIS HORSE."

Juveniles of the Lothrop Publishing Co.—All
healthy, happy children will be interested in
hearing of the fine good times they had upon
the farm of Clovernook after Prof. John Atherton gave up his place at a Western college and
came to live among *The Boys of Clovernook.*
He was deaf, but he was full of fun and he
"knew lots," and the five healthy, happy boys
around him "learned lots" about much that
went on outside of Clovernook from this good,
unselfish father and uncle. ($1.50.) In *What
the Dragon-Fly Told the Children,* through a
little framework of fiction the children are introduced to a number of well-known poets and
some of their familiar verses, especially to those
treating of nature. The dragon-fly sings these
verses to a group of little children as they play
in the fields. Every chapter is devoted to a dif-
erent poet, and is illustrated with his portrait
and other appropriate pictures drawn by the
clever pencil of Amy Brooks. ($1.50.) Boys
and girls cannot hear too much or too often of
Abraham Lincoln, a knowledge of whose great
career should be fostered earnestly among
them. Mr. Brooks knows how to tell a story
for young folks, and his word-painting of the
True Story of Abraham Lincoln has been lavishly illustrated by the publishers. ($1.50.)
The Lothrop Publishing Company have several
books fitted for older young people. If you number such among the dear girls who grow so fast
try *Making Fate,* by "Pansy," containing an
incipient love-story dear to girlish curiosity
and many noble unselfish thoughts about the
duties and pleasures of intelligent, good girls.
($1.50.) Or give them *Mopsy: her tangles and
triumphs,* by Mrs. Kate Tannatt Woods, who
lets a beautiful girl start a mechanics' boarding-
house and do many other noble things to assist
a young man who is trying to improve the

social condition of the poor of Boston. ($1.25.)
The Gingham Bag, by Margaret Sidney, tells
the story of a New England family which had inherited this bag as an heirloom. The young
folks hated it, but in those days the young people did as they were told, and they were obliged
to carry their books to school in the ugly bag.
All at once the dying request of their grandmother is found in the bag and the fortunes of
the family are changed. ($1.25.) *Through the
Farmyard Gate,* by Emilie Poulsson, illustrated
by L. J. Bridgman, is full of rhymes and jingles
for little children, and may also be used in the
kindergarten ($1.25); and another pretty collec-
tion of illustrated things to learn by heart
is *Rhymes and Songs for My Little Ones,* by
Adolphine Charlotte Hingst and Esther J.
Ruskay ($1.50). *Bible Boys and Girls,* by James
Knapp Reeve and Calvin Dill Wilson, tells
how these boys looked, where they lived,
and what they did, and twenty-seven of the
heroes of the Bible are thus brought vividly
before the children, giving definiteness to
the childish imaginations about these far-off
places and characters. Sophie Swett has a
collection of sweet stories called *The Ponkaty
Branch Road.* ($1.)

Jerry the Blunderer.—Lily F. Wesselhoeft
has added to her series of charming fables for
children another bright little story. "Jerry
the Blunderer" has an Irish terrier for its hero.
The story introduces various dumb creatures,
which here are made to talk; also a family of
bright, lovable children, whose sayings and
doings are most amusing. There is a pretty
little motherless baby, for whom the children
want to get a good home, and Jerry the blunderer assists in bringing this about by one of
his impulsive acts. Jerry's portraits, taken
from life, adorn the book. In one he is standing up alone, in another he sits in comical state,
dressed up in an old hat, and with a necktie
tied in a big bow under his chin; in another he
is holding converse with an owl; and yet another shows him harnessed tandem with the
sedate dog, "Business," in a little cart in
which little Rachel is seated, "taking a ride."
The story is simple and yet very entertaining,
and makes a fitting companion to others in Mrs.
Wesselhoeft's remarkably attractive series of
books for the young. (Roberts. $1.25.)

A Cape May Diamond.—This story of life at
the seaside is by Evelyn Raymond, the author
of "The Little Lady and the Horse" and "The
Mushroom Cave." It is illustrated by Lillian
Crawford True and handsomely bound in cloth
and gold. "The book," says the New York *Commercial Advertiser,* "embraces all the incidents of
life at the seashore, heightened by an interesting tale of happiness and family life. The author takes occasion to introduce the thrilling
incidents of a storm at sea, with the surroundings and eventful life of a lifeboat's crew.
The book is one for boys and girls, and is certain to interest those who live by the sea all
their lives as much as those who only occasionally visit it during the summer months." (Roberts. $1.50.)

The Wonderful Fairies of the Sun.—"Children
who have a poetical bent," says *The Beacon,*
"will enjoy *The Wonderful Fairies of the Sun,*
by Ernest Vincent Wright, which is a fairy-tale
on an original plan. The subjects are the Sun

King and the Moon Queen and their flock of servitors—the Raindrop elves, the Snowflakes, the Rainbow fairy, the Cloud, the Wind, the Dream and the Frost fairies, and the Musical sprites. These have their various duties to perform, all told in simple but interesting verse, though the versification is not exactly in conformity to classic models. 'The Wedding of the Man in the Moon' and a bright description of 'Santa Claus's Assistants' finish up the book, which is charmingly illustrated by Cora M. Norman, and handsomely bound and printed." (Roberts. $1.25.)

The Black Dog, and Other Stories.—This is the latest contribution of A. G. Plympton to a juvenile library already known by the production of "Dear Daughter Dorothy," "Robin's Recruit," "Rags and Velvet Gowns," "Little Sister of Wilifred," "Betty a Butterfly," "Penelope Prig," and "Dorothy and Anton." It is profusely illustrated by the author, whose facility with the pencil compares with that of his pen. The little volume contains a number of short anecdotes well told and adapted to the needs of children. "It is entirely modern," says the New York *Commercial Advertiser*, "and more wholesome by far than many of the books of similar character which have held their place by the fireside through the custom and usage of years." (Roberts. $1.50.)

Kitty and Her Kits.—What prettier title could be given to this volume of stories, written by Frances E. Compton, Helen Milman, F. E. Weatherly, Olive Molesworth, Isla Sitwell, etc., and illustrated by Harriet M. Bennett, Eddie J. Andrews, Walter Paget, Ada Dennis, etc.? Bewitching children and comical and sedate animals are scattered through its pages, and several whole pages are devoted to beautiful color printing. Any one who happens to open this book at the sad story of "Marjory and the Mice" and sees the nine little mice of assorted sizes mourning for big fat mouse "Uncle Adam," all sitting in a row, with handkerchiefs to their eyes and crêpe bows on their tails, will not rest until this book is bought for somebody. (Dutton. $1.25.)

E. P. Dutton & Co.'s Juveniles.—Year by year the children's books grow prettier. They are really too pretty for the hands of children, for they are really works of art, and, like other bric-à-brac, should be put out of the way of bread-and-buttery hands, and only shown as a rare treat after faces and hands are clean and they can only come in contact with snowy little night-gowns. *Mother Goose's Nursery Rhymes* is gotten up this year in a style that certainly would lead the dear old lady to make up a new verse if she caught a glimpse of it. But no new verse could go so straight to the active little brains as the dear old lines that are here illustrated with thirty full-page color pictures made in the most artistic style of Nister, the king of color-printers. ($2.50.) *Peeps into Fairyland* is a panorama picture-book of fairy-stories, with an introduction by F. E. Weatherly, illustrated with colored pictures made to move and stand out when the book is open, producing the effect of a deep look into the land of fairies. ($2.50.) Another of Nister's charming movable picture-books is *Sweets from Fairyland*, composed of colored pictures which can be changed each into two pictures to illustrate the lines beneath them. *Only Susan*, by Mrs. Emma Martin Marshall, is told in the first person by a little girl, who was made miserable by the name given her in respect to the wishes of a maiden aunt. Even when she became a celebrated painter of pictures she remained "only Susan" to all her friends. *Katherine's Keys*, by Sarah Doudney, is for older girls, as it introduces the heart history of the daughter of a curate, who did not care to leave London when her father exchanged to a country parish. The gradual overcoming of selfishness in Katherine is the theme of a very pretty story. ($1.50.) *Robinson Crusoe*, with full page colored plates by Nister and deftly designed black and white cuts, is a rare treasure in its artistic dress, made in conformity with all the rules of the modern standard of fine bookmaking. (Dutton. $1.50.)

Short Stories for Short People.—"Little men and little women of to-day will be delighted," says the Boston *Gazette*, "with the imaginative tales told by Alicia Aspinwall, and charmingly illustrated by Marie L. Danforth. The artist has caught the happy, fantastic spirit of the story-teller, and the little ones will be enthusiastic over both text and illustrations. The books read in childhood are the books that are remembered. We may read a thousand novels between childhood and middle age, but the

From "The Black Dog."   Copyright, 1896, by Roberts Bros.

CUPID AND MAY.

Stories of "Jack and the Bean-Stalk," "Little Red Riding Hood," "Mother Goose's Melodies," and "Andersen's Fairy-Tales" are never forgotten, while titles, plots, and characters of other books slip from the mind entirely. "Short Stories for Short People" has a bright yellow cover. The type is large and clear, and the book will be very durable. "The Shadow," "The Lighthouse Lamp," and "The Statue and the Birds" are the most prettily-written stories. The most comical and amusing are "A Quick-Running Squash," "The Toad," "The Runaway Watch," and "The Bold, Bad Bicycle." (Dutton. $1.50.)

E. P. Dutton & Co.'s Calendars and Booklets. —It is impossible to give the titles of all the new calendars and booklets on the list of these publishers; besides, mere titles convey no adequate idea of the wonderful things of beauty which year by year are prepared for the Duttons in the quiet little German city where Nister, the king and emperor of color printers, holds his court. There are booklets of all the hymns and poems dear for sweet memory's sake to "somebodie," and there are calendars of all the poets together and of almost all the poets separately. And these pretty things can be seen in every store in every city. (10c.-$2.50.)

From "Short Stories for Short People."　　　　　Copyright, 1896, by E. P. Dutton & Co.

THE QUICK-RUNNING SQUASH.

☞ *The following names and figures refer to the publishers and to the pages on which may be found descriptive notices of their more prominent books:*

The New Books for the Holiday Season.

Merimee, Prosper. Carmen : translated and Il. by Edmund H. Garrett. $2...................*Little, Brown*

Merriam, Florence A. A-Birding on a Bronco. Il. $1.25.................................*Houghton, M*

Maurice, Paul, *ed.* Letters of Victor Hugo. 2 v. Ea., $3...

Mitchell, J. A. That First Affair, and Other Stories. Il. by C. D. Gibson, A. B. Frost, F. T. Richards, and the author. $1.25...................*Scribner*

Mitchell, Langdon Elwyn. Love in the Backwoods. Il. by A. B. Frost. $1.25...................*Harper*

Molineaux, Marie A., *ed.* Phrase-Book from Robert Browning. $3.............*Houghton, M*

Morley, John. Life of Richard Cobden. *Reduced from* $3 to $1.....................*Roberts*

Morris, Charles. Half-Hours of Travel at Home and Abroad. 4 v. Il. $6; $10; $13.........*Lippincott*

Morris, Charles. Historical Tales : Greece ; Rome. Il. Ea., $1.25. ....*Lippincott*

Morse, John T., *jr.* Life of Dr. Holmes. 2 v. $4. *Houghton, M*

Moulton, Charles Wells. In My Lady's Name. Poems. $1.50.........................*Putnam*

Moulton, Louise Chandler. Lazy Tours in Spain and Elsewhere. $1.50...............*Roberts*

Northfield Year-Book. Il. by Mary A. Lathbury. $1.25......................*Revell*

Nye, Bill (*pseud.*) Comic History of England. Il. $1.25....................*Lippincott*

Ouida. Under Two Flags. *New ed.* 8 il. by Montbard. 2 v. $3-$6.............*Lippincott*

Oxford Miniature Poets : Burns, Byron, Wordsworth. $4-$12 50..................*Oxford Univ*

Page, Thomas Nelson. In Ole Virginia : contains "Marse Chan," "Meh Lady," "Polly," "Unc' Edinburgh," "Ole Stracted," and "No Haid Pawn." 24 full-page il. by Frost, Smedley, Pyle, Reinhart, Castaigne, Clinedinst. $2.50.............*Scribner*

Phelps, Eliz. Stuart. Chapters from a Life. 24 portraits and Il. $1.50............*Houghton, M*

Philips, H. W. Fables for the Times. Il. by T. S. Sullivant. 9½ x 12. $1.25............*Russell*

Phipson, T. L. Famous Violinists and Fine Violins. $1.75..............*Lippincott*

Pope, Alex. Complete Poetical Works. *Globe ed. rev. and enlarged.* 2 v. Il. $3-$6....*Crowell*

Pope, Alex. Rape of the Lock : embroidered with nine drawings by Aubrey Beardsley. *Limited ed.* $3.50. *Lippincott*

Porter, Rose. About Children : What Men and Women Have Said. $1...........*Putnam*

Poster Calendar for 1897. Designed by Edward Penfield. 50c..................*Russell*

Posters in Miniature. With introd. by Edward Penfield. 250 reproductions of posters. $1.50.......*Russell*

Prayer-Books and Hymnals. *Nelson; Oxford Univ. Press; Pott; Young*

Putnam, George Haven. Books and Their Makers During the Middle Ages. 2 v. Ea., $2.50...*Putnam*

Rabelais, François. Works. 4 v. *New ed.*, $4-$10. *Lippincott*

Ralph, Julian. Alone in China, and Other Stories. Il. by C. D. Weldon. $2................*Harper*

Reese, Lizette Woodworth. A Quiet Road. Poems. $1. *Houghton, M*

Regal Series. (Standards.) 61 v. Ea., $1.25.....*Stokes*

Rhodes, James Ford. History of the United States from the Compromise of 1850. 3 v. $2.50....*Harper*

Rothenstein, Will. Oxford Characters. 12 x 18. 24 portraits of well-known Oxford characters. $15...*Russell*

Rousseau, Jean Jacques. Confessions. *New ed.* 3 v. Il. $3..............*Lippincott*

Russell, Robert Howard. Edge of the Orient. 130 il. $2..............*Scribner*

Russell, William Clark. The Lady Maud. *Il. ed.* $1.25..............*Penno*

— What Cheer? *Il. ed.* $1.25................*Penno*

Salomon, Mgr. Memoirs During the Revolution, 1790-1801. $2.............*Little, Brown*

Sand, George. Francis the Waif.—The Devil's Pool. Ea., $1.25............*Little, Brown*

Seawell, Molly Elliot. Sprightly Romance of Marsac. Il. by Verbeck. $1.25................*Scribner*

Shakespeare's Works. 12 v. In a case. $9-$25. *Lippincott*

— *Bedford handy volume ed.* 12 v. $7.50-$35..*Warne*

— *Pocket ed.* 13 v. $5...................*Nelson*

Shelley, Mary Wollstonecraft. Frankenstein. *New ed.* 2 v. $2-$4.50...............*Lippincott*

Shorter, Clement K. Charlotte Brontë and Her Circle. Portraits. $2.50..............*Dodd, Mead*

— *ed.* Nineteenth Century Classics. 7 v. *Ea.*, 75c. *Ward & Lock*

Skinner, Charles M. Myths and Legends of Our Own Land. Il. 2 v. in box. $3; $6........*Lippincott*

Smith, E. Boyd. My Village : Life of the French Peasant. 130 il. by the author. $2..........*Scribner*

Stevenson, Robert Louis. In the South Seas. $1.50. *Scribner*

— Poems and Ballads. $1.50....................*Scribner*

— Weir of Hermiston. $1.50..................*Scribner*

Stockton, F. R. New Jersey. (*Am. hist. serv.*) Il. $1.50.............*Appleton*

Stone, Eliza Atkins. Concerning Friendship: an Every-Day Book. $1.50.............*Appleton*

Story of the Nations Series. *Ea.*, $1.50. *New volumes :* Bohemia, by Maurice; Canada, by Bourinot; The Balkans, by Miller.............*Putnam*

Stowe, *Mrs.* Harriet Beecher. Writings. *New Riverside ed.* In 16 v. Il., *ea.*, $1.50. *Large-pap. ed.* with autograph, 16 v., *per set*, $64.........*Houghton, M*

Streamer, Volney, *ed.* The World A-Wheel. Fac-similes of water colors by Eugene Grivaz. $2.50-$3.50..*Stokes*

Streatfield, R. A. The Opera : with full description of every work in the modern repertory. Introd. by J. Fuller Maitland. $2..............*Lippincott*

Taylor, Henry Osborn. Ancient Ideals. 2 v. $5..*Putnam*

Thaxter, Celia. Poems. *Appledore ed.* $1.50. *Houghton, M*

Theuriet, André. Rustic Life in France. Il. by Leon Lhermitte. $2.............*Crowell*

Thomas, Edith M. A Winter Swallow. Poems. $1.50. *Scribner*

Thoreau, Henry D. Cape Cod. *Holiday ed.* Il. in water-col. by Miss A. M. Watson. 2 v. $5..*Houghton, M*

Tsountas, Chrestos, *and* Manatt, J. Irving. Mycenæan Age. Introd. by Dr. Dörpfeld. 150 il...*Houghton, M*

Tucker, Elizabeth S. Leaves from Ju'liana Horatia Ewing's "Canada Home." Il.; fac-similes of Mrs. Ewing's color sketches. $3.............*Roberts*

Twain, Mark. Joan of Arc. Il. by F. V. Du Mond, and from old paintings and statutes. $2.50.......*Harper*

Underhill, Francis T. Driving for Pleasure., 125 il. $7.50.............*Appleton*

Valiere, George de. Opals from a Mexican mine. $1.25.............*New Amsterdam Book Co*

Van Dyke, Prof. J; C., *ed.* Modern French Masters. 20 biog. and critical reviews by well-known Amer. artists. Superbly Il. $10..............*Century*

Vasari. Lives of the Painters, Sculptors, and Architects. 48 photogravures. 4 v. $15..........*Scribner*

Vignette Series. *Ea.*, $1.25-$4.............*Stokes*

Vuillier, G. The Forgotten Isles : Travels in Corsica, Sardinia, etc. 160 il. $4.50...........*Appleton*

Warner, Charles Dudley. Relation of Literature to Life. $1.50.............*Harper*

Wensell, A. B. In Vanity Fair. 12 x 18 half-tone reproductions of wash-drawings. $5.......*Russell*

White, Andrew D. Warfare of Science with Theology. 2 v. $5.............*Appleton*

White, James T. Captive Memories. Profusely il. $3-$24.............*James T. White*

Whiting, Lilian. The World Beautiful. 2d ser. $1; white and gold, $1.25.............*Roberts*

Whitney, Caspar. On Snow-Shoes to the Barren Grounds. 2800 miles after musk oxen and wood-bison. Il. $3.50.............*Harper*

Wiggin, *Mrs.* Kate Douglas. Marm Lisa. $1. *Houghton, M*

— Nine Love-Songs and a Carol.......*Houghton, M*

Wilson, H. W. Iron-Clads in Action, 1855-1895. Il. 2 v. $8.............*Little, Brown*

Wilson, Woodrow. George Washington. Illustrated by Howard Pyle. $3.............*Harper*

Wingate, Charles E. L. Shakespeare's Heroes on the Stage. Il. with portraits. $2...........*Crowell*

Wolfe, Theodore F. Literary Shrines, and Literary Pilgrimage. *Ed. de luxe.* 2 v. $7.........*Lippincott*

Women of Colonial and Revolutionary Times. 4 v. *Ea.*, $1.50. 4 v. in set, $5.........*Scribner*

Wood's Dictionary of Quotations. $2.50-$4.50..*Warne*

Youmans, W: J., *ed.* Pioneers of Science in America. $4.............*Appleton*